www.aorn.org/psrp

Perioperative Standards and Recommended Practices

D1279437

Association of periOperative Registered Nurses

2009 Edition

2170 South Parker Road
Suite 400
Denver, CO 80231-5711
(800) 755-2676

Perioperative Standards and Recommended Practices
2009 Edition

Copyright © 2009
AORN, Inc.

Clinical Editor
Ramona Conner, RN, MSN, CNOR

Contributing Editors
Joan Blanchard, RN, BSN, MSS, CNOR, CIC
Byron Burlingame, RN, BSN, MS, CNOR
Robin Chard, RN, PhD, CNOR
Bonnie Denholm, RN, BSN, MS, CNOR
Denise Downing, RN, MS, CNOR
Sharon Giarrizzo-Wilson, RN, BSN, MS, CNOR
Sheila Mitchell, RN, BSN, MS, CNOR
Mary Ogg, RN, MSN, CNOR
Carol Peterson, RN, MAOM, CNOR

Jennifer Schmidt
Associate, Kaufman-Wills Group

Editorial Manager: Deb Reno
Cover Design: Cathie Bigam
Production Manager: Terry Isaacs

ISBN 1-888460-66-0

Printed in USA

Table of Contents

Introduction 7
AORN Vision and Mission 8

Section I: Standards of Perioperative Nursing Practice
* Standards of Perioperative Nursing... 11
    Perioperative Nursing Concepts 12
    Standards of Perioperative Clinical Practice... 13
    Standards of Perioperative Professional Practice 15
    Standards of Perioperative Administrative Practice 19
    Exhibit A: Historical Perspectives on the AORN Standards, Competency Statements,
       and Certification 22
    Exhibit B: Perioperative Patient Outcomes... 23
    Exhibit C: Perioperative Explications for the *ANA Code of Nurses* 33
    Exhibit D: Quality and Performance Improvement Standards 65

Section II: AORN Guidelines and Guidance Statements
    Human and Avian Influenza and SARS.. 77
    Bariatric Surgery Guideline 91
    Table 1: Weight category based on body mass index (BMI) 92
    Table 2: History of bariatric surgery... 94
    Figure 1: Biliopancreatic diversion 95
    Figure 2: Proximal gastric bypass.. 96
    Figure 3: Vertical banded gastroplasty 96
    Figure 4: Gastric banding 97
    Figure 5: Roux-en-Y proximal gastric bypass 98
    Figure 6: Distal gastric bypass... 98
    Table 3: Elements to include in a team charter 105
    Latex Guideline.. 111
    Table 1: Types of latex and other glove-associated reactions 112
    Table 2: Known latex allergies.. 114
    Table 3: Anaphylactic reaction assessment criteria 115
    Table 4: Sample latex allergy questionnaire 116
    Table 5: Latex allergy risk groups... 117
    Table 6: Suggested contents for a latex-safe cart 119
    Table 7: Symptoms of latex exposure and possible anaphylaxis.. 121
    Figure 1: Flow chart for planning a latex-safe procedure.. 122
    Malignant Hyperthermia (MH) Guideline 127
    Sidebar: "Awake" MH 127
    Table 1: MH triggering and nontriggering agents 128
    Table 2: MH medication chart.. 130
    Figure 1: Physiology of MH 132
    Figure 2: MH flow chart 134
    Table 3: Example of MH crisis checklist 136
    Table 4: Testing centers and laboratories 139
    Table 5: Suggested contents for an MH cart... 141
    Table 6: Management of an MH crisis 145
    Exhibit A: Outcome management of MH through application of the PNDS 149

* *Indicates items newly revised in 2008 or published here for the first time.*

Table of Contents

Prevention of Venous Stasis 165
  Table 1: Classification of risk levels 176
  Exhibit A: Venous thromboembolism risk factor assessment 181
Do-Not-Use Abbreviations 183
  Table 1: Joint Commission's required list of "do-not-use" abbreviations, acronyms, and symbols.... 183
  Table 2: Potential additional "do-not-use" abbreviations, acronyms, and symbols 184
  Table 3: AORN recommendations 185
Environmental Responsibility 187
Fire Prevention in the Operating Room 195
  Table 1: Fire risk—Ignition 196
  Table 2: Fire risk—Fuel 198
  Table 3: Fire risk—Oxidizers 199
  Sample Form 1: Perioperative services OR code red fire drill evaluation 201
  Sample Form 2: Perioperative services OR code red fire drill record........................... 202
Role of the Health Care Industry Representative in the Perioperative Setting 204
Care of the Perioperative Patient With an Implanted Electronic Device 207
  Exhibit A: Care of the perioperative patient with an IED 224
Mass Casualty, Triage, and Evacuation 229
  Exhibit A: Mass casualty practice scenarios 235
Creating a Patient Safety Culture 237
  Figure 1: Patient-centric safety culture... 238
  Figure 2: Accountability in the face of error... 240
Postoperative Patient Care in the Ambulatory Surgery Setting.. 243
  Table 1: Recommended staffing guidelines... 245
Preoperative Patient Care in the Ambulatory Surgery Setting 251
Reuse of Single-Use Devices 257
  Table 1: Quality system regulation 259
Safe On-Call Practices in Perioperative Practice Settings 264
Safe Medication Practices in Perioperative Practice Settings 267
Sharps Injury Prevention in the Perioperative Setting 275
Perioperative Staffing... 281
  Table 1: Minimum staffing recommendations.. 282
  Table 2: Call relief calculation... 287
Value of Perioperative Clinical Learning Activities in Undergraduate Nursing Curricula.............. 289

Section III: Recommended Practices for Perioperative Nursing
Introduction 295

Recommended Practices for:
Aseptic Practice
Attire, Surgical... 299
Hand Antisepsis, Surgical 307
  Table 1: General hand hygiene and surgical hand antisepsis directives 311
Maintaining a Sterile Field... 317
Traffic Patterns in the Perioperative Practice Setting 327

* Indicates items newly revised in 2008 or published here for the first time.

Table of Contents

Equipment and Product Safety

Electrosurgery.. 331
Endoscopic Minimally Invasive Surgery... 347
   Table 1: Technological advances in endoscopic minimally invasive surgery 354
   Table 2: Procedural advances in endoscopic minimally invasive surgery 355
Gowns and Drapes—Selection and Use 361
Laser Safety in Practice Settings 367
Pneumatic Tourniquet 373
Product Selection in Perioperative Practice Setting 387
Surgical Tissue Banking 391

Patient and Worker Safety

Counts—Sponge, Sharp, and Instrument... 405
Environment of Care... 415
   Sidebar: Recommended HVAC settings... 421
Environmental Cleaning in the Perioperative Setting... 439
   Table 1: Air changes per hour required for contaminant removal 447
Reducing Radiological Exposure in the Perioperative Practice Setting 455
Specimen Care and Handling... 467
   Table 1: Sample policies and procedures for packaging and handling specimens 473
Transmissible Infections, Prevention of.. 475

Patient Care

Documentation of Perioperative Nursing Care 487
Hypothermia, Prevention of 491
Managing the Patient Receiving Local Anesthesia 505
Managing the Patient Receiving Moderate Sedation/Analgesia 513
   Table 1: Physical status classification.. 514
   Table 2: Continuum of depth of sedation.. 519
Positioning the Patient in the Perioperative Practice Setting.................................. 525
   Table 1: Pressure ulcer stages 542
Preoperative Patient Skin Antisepsis 549
   Table 1: Preoperative skin preparation agents... 552

Sterilization and Disinfection

Anesthesia Equipment—Cleaning and Processing... 569
* Disinfection, High-Level... 579
* Flexible Endoscopes—Cleaning and Processing 595
Instruments and Powered Equipment—Cleaning and Care of 611
Packaging Systems—Selection and Use 637
Sterilization in the Perioperative Practice Setting 647
   Table 1: Attire and personal equipment requirements... 648
   Table 2: Parameters for controlled environments during sterilization 649
   Table 3: Typical minimum cycle times for gravity-displacement steam sterilization...... 650
   Table 4: Typical minimum cycle times for dynamic air-removal steam sterilization........ 651
   Table 5: Examples of typical flash steam sterilization parameters............................... 652
   Table 6: Types and applications for use of sterilization monitoring device................... 665
   Table 7: Sterilization process monitoring recommendations 666

* *Indicates items newly revised in 2008 or published here for the first time.*

Table of Contents

Section IV: Additional Resources

* **Appendix A:** Policy and Procedure Template for Use with Recommended Practices 673

    Sample Policy 1: Managing the Patient Receiving Moderate Sedation/Analgesia 676

    Sample Policy 2: Positioning, Transporting, Moving, and Lifting the Patient 681

Appendix B: Glossary of Procedural Times 685

Appendix C: Standards for RN First Assistant Education Programs 692

Index to 2009 Edition 695

Introduction to 2009 Edition

Historically, AORN has demonstrated an ongoing commitment to the surgical patient, the perioperative registered nurse, and the nursing profession as a whole. This publication contains the AORN-approved standards, guidelines, guidance statements, and recommended practices and reflects the perioperative nurse's scope of responsibility.

AORN offers a unified network of interrelated principles that systematically guide activities while allowing for flexibility, individuality, and change. The standards and recommended practices are broad in scope and are attainable, definitive, and relevant for the perioperative setting.

SECTION I: STANDARDS OF PERIOPERATIVE NURSING PRACTICE

The AORN "Standards of perioperative nursing" are consistent with the "Standards of nursing practice" and "Standards of professional performance" published by the American Nurses Association (ANA). They focus on the process of providing nursing care and performing professional role activities; they also provide a mechanism to delineate the responsibilities of the registered nurse engaged in practice in the perioperative setting. These standards serve as the foundation for AORN's recommended practices, competency statements, and core curriculum, as well as the Perioperative Nursing Data Set (PNDS).

This year, the AORN standards of perioperative nursing are presented as a single collection of standards with four exhibits that provide additional information on patient outcomes, ethics, quality improvement, and the evolution of the AORN standards. The exhibits include AORN's "Perioperative explications for the *ANA Code of Ethics*," which relates the the nine provisions of the *ANA Code of Ethics for Nurses with Interpretive Statements* to the practice of perioperative nursing.

The "AORN standards for RN first assistant education programs," formerly included in this section, can be found in the additional resources section of the book. These "education standards" have been separated from the standards collection because they serve a distinctive purpose: they are intended to guide program administrators and faculty in designing and evaluating curricula.

SECTION II: AORN GUIDELINES AND GUIDANCE STATEMENTS

This section includes the AORN guidelines and guidance statements. Guidelines address a specific medical diagnosis or clinical condition and are based on empirical data. Guidelines assist practitioners in clinical decision making and are used to assess and assure the quality of care and guide clinical practice. Guidance statements provide suggested strategies to assist practitioners in developing organization-specific processes related to clinical and administrative issues.

SECTION III: RECOMMENDED PRACTICES FOR PERIOPERATIVE NURSING

AORN's "Recommended practices for perioperative nursing" (RPs) are developed by perioperative nurse specialists in the AORN Center for Nursing Practice, members of the Recommended Practices Committee, and other selected perioperative experts, in collaboration with liaisons from the American Association of Nurse Anesthetists, the American College of Surgeons, the American Society of Anesthesiologists, the American Society for Healthcare Central Service Professionals, the Association for Professionals in Infection Control and Epidemiology, Centers for Disease Control and Prevention, and the International Association of Healthcare Central Service Materiel Management.

SECTION IV: ADDITIONAL RESOURCES

New in this edition, additional resources include a policy and procedure template with sample policies and procedures for moderate sedation/analgesia and patient positioning. These policy examples reflect the recommendations found in the respective recommended practices. Instructions for submitting feedback on the usefulness and format of the template and sample policies also are provided. This information will be used to develop future policies and procedures based on the recommended practices.

Other resources include the "Glossary of times used for scheduling and monitoring of diagnostic and therapeutic procedures"; the "AORN standards for RN first assistant education programs"; and an updated index of important terms and concepts.

AORN and Perioperative Nursing

Understanding that the term *perioperative* may not be well known outside the surgical arena, AORN defines the term *perioperative nursing* as the practice of nursing directed toward patients undergoing operative and other invasive procedures. AORN recognizes the *perioperative nurse* as one who provides, manages, teaches, and/or studies the care of patients undergoing operative or other invasive procedures.

AORN Vision and Mission

Vision statement
The Association of periOperative Registered Nurses (AORN) is the leader in advocating for excellence in perioperative practice and health care.

Mission statement
AORN's mission is to promote safety and optimal outcomes for patients undergoing operative and other invasive procedures by providing practice support and professional development opportunities to perioperative nurses. AORN will collaborate with professional and regulatory organizations, industry leaders, and other health care partners who support the mission.

Strategic Initiatives

1. **Quality.** AORN will promote excellence in the delivery of safe perioperative nursing practice.

2. **Growth.** AORN will develop a diverse approach to membership and organizational growth.

3. **Service.** AORN will develop innovative products and services to support perioperative practice.

4. **People.** AORN will advocate for and represent the interest of perioperative registered nurses in the health care, political, academic and professional arenas.

5. **Finance.** AORN will manage its assets and subsidiaries to meet current and future association needs.

Standards of Perioperative Nursing Practice

Introduction

AORN is dedicated to enhancing the professionalism of perioperative registered nurses, promoting standards of perioperative nursing practice to better serve the needs of society, and providing a forum for interaction and exchange of ideas related to perioperative health care (**Exhibit A**). Standards are authoritative statements that describe the responsibilities for which nursing practitioners are accountable and that reflect the values and priorities of the profession. Clinical and organizational indicators of quality are identified through structure, process, and outcome standards.

As recipients of care, patients are entitled to privacy, confidentiality, personal dignity, and quality health services. The delivery of patient-focused care is guided by ethical, legal, and moral principles. These principles are inherent and serve as a foundation for perioperative nursing practice, and are paramount in achieving optimal patient outcomes.

The AORN standards of perioperative nursing focus on the process of providing nursing care and performing professional role activities. These standards apply to all nurses in the perioperative setting and were developed by AORN using the American Nurses Association's standards of clinical nursing practice as the foundation.

It is the perioperative registered nurse's responsibility to meet these standards, assuming that adequate environmental working conditions and necessary resources are available to support and facilitate the nurse's attainment of these standards. Under certain conditions, nurses may not be able to fully meet the standards. It is important to recognize the link between working conditions and the nurse's ability to deliver care. It is the responsibility of employers or health care facilities to provide an appropriate environment for nursing practice.

Several related themes underlie the "Standards of perioperative nursing." Nursing care must be individualized to meet a particular patient's unique needs and situation. This care should be provided in the context of disease or injury prevention, health promotion, health restoration, health maintenance, or palliative care. The cultural, racial, and ethnic diversity of the patient must always be taken into account in providing nursing services.

The perioperative registered nurse must respect the patient's goals and preferences in developing and implementing a plan of care. One of the nurse's primary responsibilities is patient education; therefore, nurses should provide patients with appropriate information to make informed decisions regarding their care and treatment. It is recognized, however, that some state regulations or institutional policies or procedures may prohibit full disclosure of information to patients.

The perioperative registered nurse's partnership with the patient and other health care providers is recognized in the standards. It is assumed that the nurse works with other health care providers in a coordinated manner throughout the process of caring for a surgical patient. The involvement of the patient, family, or significant others is paramount. The appropriate degree of participation expected of the patient, family, or other health care providers is determined by the clinical environment and the patient's unique situation.

Throughout the standards, terms such as *appropriate, pertinent,* and *realistic* are used. It is beyond the scope of documents such as these to account for all possible scenarios that the professional perioperative nurse may encounter in practice. The nurse will need to exercise judgment, based on education and experience, in determining what is appropriate, pertinent, or realistic. Further direction also may be available from documents such as recommended practices, competency statements, guidelines for care, agency standards, policies, procedures, protocols, and current research findings.

Summary

The "Standards of perioperative nursing" provide a mechanism to delineate the responsibilities of registered nurses providing patient care in the perioperative setting. The standards of perioperative nursing and recommended practices serve as the basis for quality monitoring and evaluation, regulatory systems, nursing service delivery systems and organizational structures, certification activities; job descriptions and performance appraisals, agency policies and procedures, and educational offerings. The "Standards of perioperative nursing" are generic and apply to all registered nurses engaged in perioperative practice, regardless of clinical setting, practice setting, or educational preparation.

I: Perioperative Nursing Concepts

I.A. Perioperative Patient Focused Model

I.A.1. Conceptual Framework
The Perioperative Patient Focused Model (**Figure 1**) is the conceptual framework for the Perioperative Nursing Data Set (PNDS) and the model for perioperative nursing practice. The patient and his or her family, at the core of the Model, provide the focus of perioperative nursing care. Within the Model, concentric circles expand beyond the patient and family representing the perioperative nursing domains and elements. The Model illustrates the relationship between the patient, family, and care provided by the perioperative professional nurse.

I.A.2. Patient Centered
The patient is at the center of the Model, which clearly represents the true focus of perioperative patient care. Regardless of practice setting, geographic location, or nature of the patient population, there is nothing more important to the practicing perioperative nurse than the patient. This Model makes this concept of patient care "visible" in and between all other variables in the surgical setting.

I.A.3. Four Domains
The Model is thus divided into four quadrants, three representing patient-centered domains:
- safety of the patient,
- patient physiologic responses to surgery, and
- patient and family behavioral responses to surgery.

The fourth quadrant represents the health system in which the perioperative care is delivered. The health system domain designates administrative concerns and structure elements (ie, staff, equipment, environmental factors, supplies) essential to successful surgical intervention.

I.A.4. Outcome focused
The Model focuses on outcomes. This is important, as nursing theories and models should embrace and represent all elements of the nursing process, including outcomes. AORN's Model represents the outcomes focus of perioperative nurses by placing outcomes immediately adjacent to the patient care domains. Perioperative nurses have a unique knowledge base that supports high-quality patient outcomes in surgical settings. An individualized

Figure 1

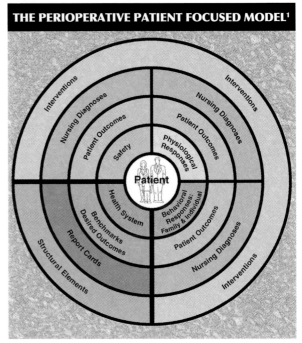

THE PERIOPERATIVE PATIENT FOCUSED MODEL[1]

NOTE
   1. C Petersen, ed, Perioperative Nursing Data Set, revised second ed (Denver: AORN, 2007) 16 and inside front cover.

patient assessment guides the identification of nursing diagnoses and selection of nursing interventions for each patient (**Exhibit B**).

I.B. Goal of Perioperative Nursing Practice
The goal of perioperative nursing practice is to assist patients and their families to achieve a level of wellness equal to or greater than that which they had prior to the procedure.

I.C. Philosophy of Perioperative Nursing Practice

I.C.1. Nursing is a social institution that provides essential and significant health care services to meet evolving societal needs. The perioperative nurse uses knowledge, judgment, and skills based on the principles on physical, biological, physiological, behavioral, social, and nursing sciences.

I.C.2. Nurses must be ethical, responsible, and accountable for quality patient care. The nurse engaged in perioperative nursing practice provides or facilitates care to surgical or other perioperative patients (**Exhibit C**).

I.C.3. Research should be the foundation for perioperative nursing practice.

I.C.4. Learning is a lifelong process, and perioperative nurses must assume responsibility for their ongoing education.

I.C.5. Standards of nursing practice, interdisciplinary collaboration, and appropriate resource utilization enhance perioperative nursing practice.

I.D. Definition of Perioperative Nurse

The perioperative nurse is a registered nurse who, using the nursing process, develops a plan of nursing care and then coordinates and delivers care to patients undergoing operative or other invasive procedures. The perioperative registered nurse has the requisite skills and knowledge to assess, diagnose, plan, intervene, and evaluate the outcomes of interventions. The perioperative registered nurse addresses the physiological, psychological, socio-cultural, and spiritual responses of surgical patients.

II.E. Scope of Perioperative Nursing Practice

I.E.1. Perioperative Nursing Care

The perioperative registered nurse provides care across the surgical continuum, beginning when the patient is first told of the need for an operative or invasive procedure and ending when the patient returns to his or her usual roles and responsibilities. The perioperative registered nurse provides care in a variety of clinical settings including acute care and ambulatory facilities as well as office-based settings and home care. The perioperative registered nurse's focus of concern is the patient and his or her family members, significant others, and friends.

I.E.2. Care Planning

The perioperative registered nurse identifies patients' needs, sets goals with patients, and implements nursing interventions and activities to achieve optimal patient outcomes. Each patient is viewed as a unique individual, and care is planned and provided to meet each patient's specific needs. The perioperative registered nurse is concerned with the patient's safety as well as physiological and behavioral responses throughout the surgical experience.

I.E.3. Role Functions

The perioperative registered nurse may function in one or more roles as a clinical practitioner, manager, educator, and researcher. Perioperative nursing practice is defined both as a caring art and as a science incorporating the critical thinking skills that are derived from knowledge of natural, behavioral, and social sciences and the humanities. Nursing integrates and applies this knowledge through use of the nursing process.

II: Standards of Perioperative Nursing

II.A. Standards of Perioperative Clinical Practice

The "Standards of perioperative clinical practice" are based on the nursing process and provide a basic model by which the quality of perioperative nursing practice can be evaluated (**Exhibit A**).

II.A.1. Assessment

The perioperative nurse collects patient health data.

Interpretive statement:
Assessment is the systematic and ongoing collection of data, guided by the application of knowledge of physiological and psychological principles and experience, and is used to make judgments and predictions about a patient's response to illness or changes in life processes. Assessment is essential to establishing a nursing diagnosis and predicting outcomes. Assessment may occur in a variety of settings.

Criteria:
a. The priority of data collection is determined by the patient's immediate condition or needs, and the relationship to the proposed intervention. Pertinent data include, but are not limited to,
   ◆ current medical diagnoses and therapies;
   ◆ physical status and physiological responses;
   ◆ psychosocial status of the patient;
   ◆ cultural, spiritual, and lifestyle information;
   ◆ the individual's understanding, perceptions, and expectations of the procedure;
   ◆ previous responses to illness, hospitalizations, and surgical, therapeutic, or diagnostic procedures; and
   ◆ results of diagnostic studies.

b. Pertinent data are collected using appropriate assessment techniques.
c. Data collection involves the patient, significant others, and health care providers when appropriate. It may be accomplished through diverse means, such as interview, review of records, assessment, and/or consultation.
d. Data collection is systematic and ongoing.
e. Relevant data are documented in retrievable form.

II.B.2. Diagnosis
The perioperative nurse analyzes the assessment data in determining diagnoses.

Interpretive statement:
The outcome of assessment is the potential for one or more nursing diagnoses. Nursing diagnoses are concise statements about actual, or high risk for, health problems/clinical conditions that are amenable to nursing intervention. Diagnoses result from analysis and interpretation of data about the patient's problems, needs, and health status.

Criteria:
a. Diagnoses are consistent with the assessment data.
b. Diagnoses are validated with the patient, significant others, and health care providers, when possible.
c. Diagnoses are documented in a manner that facilitates the determination of outcomes and plan of care.

III.B.3. Outcome Identification
The perioperative nurse identifies expected outcomes unique to the patient (**Exhibit B**).

Interpretive statement:
Patient outcomes are derived from nursing diagnoses and direct the interventions to correct, alter, or maintain the nursing diagnoses. Areas for the perioperative nurse to consider when formulating outcomes should include, but are not limited to,
  ♦ absence of infection;
  ♦ maintenance of skin integrity;
  ♦ absence of adverse effects through proper use of safety measures related to positioning, extraneous objects, and chemical, physical, and electrical hazards;

  ♦ maintenance of fluid and electrolyte balance;
  ♦ knowledge of the patient and significant others of the physiological and psychological responses to surgical intervention; and
  ♦ participation of the patient and significant others in the rehabilitation process.

Criteria:
a. Outcomes are derived from the diagnoses and are mutually formulated with the patient, significant others, and health care providers, when possible.
b. The patient's present and potential physical capabilities and behavioral patterns are congruent with the expected outcomes.
c. Outcomes are attainable with consideration to human and material resources available to the patient.
d. Outcome statements include measurable criteria for determining expected outcomes as a result of nursing interventions.
e. Outcomes include a time estimate for attainment.
f. Outcomes are prioritized.
g. Outcomes are communicated to appropriate people.
h. Outcomes are documented in a retrievable form.
i. Outcomes provide direction for continuity of care.

II.A.4. Planning
The perioperative nurse develops a plan of care that prescribes interventions to attain expected outcomes.

Interpretive statement:
The outcome statements become the guide for nursing interventions necessary to achieve the desired results. The individualized plan of care reflects the perioperative assessment and a logical sequence to attain outcomes. Priorities for the provision of nursing care are established by the perioperative nurse in collaboration with the patient, significant others, and health care providers. Examples of interventions performed include, but are not limited to,
  ♦ provision of information and supportive perioperative teaching specifically related to the surgical intervention and nursing care,
  ♦ identification of the patient,
  ♦ verification of the surgical site,

- verification of the operative consent and reports of essential diagnostic procedures,
- positioning according to physiological principles,
- adherence to principles of asepsis,
- provision of appropriate and properly functioning equipment and supplies for the patient,
- provision for comfort measures and supportive care to the patient,
- environmental monitoring and safety,
- evaluation of outcomes in relation to the identified interventions, and
- communication of intraoperative information to significant others and the health care team to provide for continuity of care.

Criteria:

a. The plan of care reflects current nursing practice.
b. The plan of care provides for continuity of care.
c. The plan of care specifies nursing diagnoses, interventions necessary to achieve the outcomes, and a logical sequence of interventions.
d. Human and materiel resources are available to implement the plan of care.
e. The plan of care is communicated to appropriate people.
f. Evidence of a plan of care is retrievable through documented intervention and evaluation of progress toward expected outcome.

II.A.5. Implementation

The perioperative nurse implements the interventions identified in the plan of care.

Interpretive statement:
Interventions are consistent with the established plan of care and provide continuity of nursing care in the perioperative period. Interventions are based on expert opinion, scientific principles, and/or consensus. They reflect the rights and desires of the patient and significant others.

Criteria:

a. Interventions are consistent with the established plan of care.
b. Implementation of the plan of care is an ongoing process and is based on the patient's response.
c. Interventions reflect the rights and desires of the patient and significant others.

d. Interventions are implemented with safety, skill, and efficiency and are adjusted according to patient responses.
e. Interventions may be assigned or delegated as appropriate.
f. Interventions are documented and communicated verbally as appropriate to promote continuity of care.

II.A.6. Evaluation

The perioperative nurse evaluates the patient's progress toward attainment of outcomes.

Interpretive statement:
Evaluation is systematic and ongoing. It is based on observations and patient responses to nursing interventions; the effectiveness of interventions is evaluated in relation to the outcomes. Ongoing assessment data are used to revise diagnoses, the plan of care, and/or outcomes as needed. The patient, significant others, and health care providers are involved in the evaluation process.

Criteria:

a. Evaluation of the effectiveness of interventions is systematic and ongoing.
b. The effectiveness of interventions is evaluated in relation to outcomes.
c. Documentation of the patient's progress toward achievable outcomes is retrievable.
d. Ongoing assessment data are used to revise diagnoses, outcomes, and the plan of care, as needed.
e. Revisions in diagnoses, outcomes, and the plan of care are documented.
f. The patient, significant others, and health care providers are involved in the evaluation process when appropriate.

II.B. Standards of Perioperative Professional Practice

The "Standards of perioperative professional practice" describe the activities the nurse is expected to engage in (eg, providing quality care, pursuing education, practicing collegiality). (See **Exhibit A**.)

II.B.1. Quality of Practice

The perioperative nurse systematically evaluates the quality, safety, and appropriateness of nursing practice (**Exhibit D**).

Interpretive statement:
The perioperative nurse engages in the evaluation of care delivery through a systematic quality and performance improvement process. This systematic approach uses specific steps to promote quality and safety in patient care.

Criteria:
a. The perioperative nurse participates in quality of care activities with a focus on nursing practice, safety, continuity of care, and outcomes. These activities are to be appropriate to the individual's position, education, and practice environment. Such activities may include
  ♦ identifying and assigning responsibility for monitoring and evaluation activities,
  ♦ delineating the scope of patient care activities or services,
  ♦ identifying dimensions of performance,
  ♦ developing quality indicators for each identified dimension of performance,
  ♦ establishing thresholds for evaluation of the quality indicators,
  ♦ collecting data related to the dimensions of performance and indicators,
  ♦ evaluating care based on the cumulative data collected,
  ♦ taking actions to improve care or services,
  ♦ assessing the effectiveness of the action(s) taken and documenting the outcomes, and
  ♦ communicating the data organization-wide.
b. Knowledge gained via the quality and performance improvement process is used to initiate change in nursing practice.
c. The perioperative nurse demonstrates that quality by applying that knowledge in a respectful, accountable, and ethical manner.

II.B.2. Practice Evaluation
The perioperative nurse evaluates his or her practice in context with current professional practice standards, rules, and regulations.

Interpretive statement:
Practice evaluation is a process that includes defining and evaluating professional practice behaviors. This process demonstrates the accountability and responsibility for those practice behaviors The perioperative nurse is responsible for self-evaluation as well as receiving constructive feedback.

Criteria:
The perioperative nurse
a. identifies the behaviors that support the level of performance desired within the perioperative setting, role, or situation;
b. provides age-appropriate and culturally sensitive care;
c. assesses perioperative practice behaviors on an ongoing basis, seeking constructive feedback;
d. identifies areas for personal and professional development;
e. develops and initiates an action plan to achieve professional development goals, which may include certification and advanced practice;
f. periodically monitors and evaluates the progress of goal achievement; and
g. participates in peer review.

II.B.3. Education
The perioperative nurse acquires and maintains current knowledge in nursing practice.

Interpretive statement:
The purpose of professional development is to build on varied educational and experiential bases for the enhancement of perioperative nursing practice. The perioperative nurse has primary responsibility for his or her ongoing education and professional development.

Criteria:
The perioperative nurse
a. completes an individualized orientation based on identified learning needs;
b. acquires knowledge and skills appropriate to the specialty area, perioperative setting, role or situation;
c. demonstrates accountability for maintaining competencies within the specific area of practice;
d. participates in ongoing educational activities relevant to professional issues and trends in perioperative nursing; and
e. participates in life-long learning.

II.B.4. Collegiality
The perioperative nurse interacts with and contributes to the professional growth of peers, colleagues, and others.

Interpretive statement:
The perioperative nurse has an obligation to support and advance the specialty and the profession by sharing his or her knowledge and expertise. The perioperative nurse interacts with colleagues to build and maintain the competencies necessary to provide safe, effective care to patients.

Criteria:
a. The perioperative nurse shares knowledge and skills. This is accomplished through a variety of methods, including, but not limited to,
   - providing inservice education, programs, seminars, and workshops;
   - precepting and mentoring;
   - role modeling;
   - publishing;
   - participating in professional organizations;
   - providing consultative services; and
   - participating in performance improvement activities.
b. The perioperative nurse provides peers with constructive feedback regarding their practice. This is facilitated through
   - the peer review process,
   - quality/performance improvement activities,
   - committee participation,
   - interdisciplinary teams, and
   - one-on-one discussions.
c. The perioperative nurse contributes to a supportive and healthy work environment using appropriate communication techniques.
d. The perioperative nurse is a role model for professional behavior.

II.B.5. Collaboration
The perioperative nurse collaborates with the patient, family, health care team, and others in the conduct of professional nursing practice.

Interpretive statement:
Care of the perioperative patient requires cooperative efforts from many internal and external customers in order to achieve optimal outcomes. The perioperative nurse demonstrates accountability, flexibility, and communication skills when collaborating.

Criteria:
a. The perioperative nurse
   - communicates pertinent information relative to care,

   - consults with the health care team and others, and
   - makes referrals, including provisions for continuity of care, as needed.
b. The perioperative nurse has appropriate oversight and supervisory authority over unlicensed assistive personnel.

II.B.5. Ethics
The perioperative nurse's decisions and actions on behalf of patients are determined in an ethical manner.

Interpretive statement:
The basic human rights of individual patients are not forfeited when the patient enters the health care system. Care and services must be delivered without impeding these basic rights. The perioperative nurse is accountable to patients to safeguard these rights while providing appropriate nursing care or services in the perioperative setting. Nursing practice is guided by the *Code of Ethics for Nurses with Interpretive Statements* of the American Nurses Association (**Exhibit C**).

Criteria:
1. The perioperative nurse acts as a patient advocate.
2. Patient confidentiality is maintained.
3. Care is delivered in a nonjudgmental and non-discriminatory manner that is sensitive to cultural, racial, and ethnic diversity.
4. Care is delivered in a manner that preserves and protects the patient's autonomy, dignity, and rights.
5. The perioperative nurse uses available resources to help formulate ethical decisions.

II.B.7. Evidence-Based Practice
The perioperative nurse uses research findings in evidence-based practice.

Interpretive statement:
Perioperative nursing practice is supported by research. The perioperative nurse uses evidence based on research to effect positive changes in patient outcomes. The perioperative nurse, regardless of position, education, or practice environment, participates in various aspects of research activities.

Criteria:
a. The perioperative nurse utilizes the best available evidence, preferably research data, to guide practice decisions.
b. Perioperative nurses participate in research by involvement in one or more of the following activities:
   - identifying clinical problems,
   - participating in data collection,
   - sharing research activities with others,
   - reading and critiquing research for application to practice,
   - participating on a research committee or in a study, and
   - using knowledge gained through research findings to initiate change.

II.B.8. Resource Utilization

The perioperative nurse considers factors related to safety, effectiveness, efficiency, environmental concerns, and cost in planning and delivering patient care.

Interpretive statement:
The perioperative nurse identifies and promotes the most cost-effective and environmentally conscientious method of providing safe and effective patient care in accordance with established standards.

Criteria:
1. The perioperative nurse
   - evaluates factors related to safety, effectiveness, availability, cost, and impact on practice;
   - assigns tasks or delegates care based on the needs of the patient, potential for harm, and the knowledge and skills of the provider selected; and
   - assists the patient and family to become informed economic consumers in identifying appropriate services available to address perioperative patient needs.
2. The perioperative nurse utilizes technical advances in clinical care and information systems.

II.B.9. Leadership

The perioperative nurse provides leadership in the profession and professional practice setting.

Interpretive statement:
The perioperative nurse leader has the responsibility to display professionalism at all times. The perioperative nurse provides leadership in the profession and in the professional practice setting. The perioperative nurse has the responsibility to preserve the integrity and safety of perioperative patient care, and, to maintain competencies by continuing personal and professional growth through leadership development.

Criteria:
a. The perioperative nurse displays leadership by
   - supervising the assigned licensed and unlicensed caregivers,
   - holding self and team accountable for actions taken, and
   - being reliable to the team, the patient, and the organization.
b. The perioperative nurse leader works to create and maintain a healthy environment in local, regional, national, and international communities by
   - embracing life-long learning;
   - being a "systems thinker" and possessing the skills to develop processes;
   - strategizing;
   - planning, both in the short and long term;
   - using analytical skills to make changes; and
   - participating in perioperative research.
c. The perioperative nurse leader directs the coordination of perioperative care across settings and among caregivers.
d. The perioperative nurse leader promotes advancement of perioperative nursing through involvement with professional organizations by
   - taking an active role in the organization,
   - encouraging all team members to be active, and
   - sharing information received through the organizations with team members.
e. The perioperative nurse leader works toward influencing policy-making to improve patient care organization-wide by
   - being prepared to discuss issues that affect the patients in the perioperative setting at all levels of the organization, and
   - participating in various performance improvement activities in the organization.

III. Standards of Perioperative Administrative Practice

The "Standards of perioperative administrative practice" were developed to identify criteria for the creation and maintenance of an environment in which nursing knowledge and skills can be used effectively (**Exhibit A**).

III.A. Adminsitrative Structure
The administrative structure for perioperative services shall be developed and communicated.

Criteria:
a. A philosophy, purpose, and objectives are developed to guide perioperative services.
   i. The philosophy, purpose, and objectives are derived from the mission, vision, and values of the organization.
   ii. Staff members participate in the ongoing development, implementation, and evaluation of the philosophy, purpose, and objectives for perioperative services.
   iii. The philosophy, purpose, and objectives of perioperative services are applied universally throughout the organizational system.
b. An organizational plan for perioperative services is developed, communicated, implemented, and evaluated.
   i. The plan reflects the philosophy, purpose, and objectives of perioperative services.
   ii. The plan defines the lines of formal authority, accountability, and communication for perioperative services.
   iii. The plan describes the relationship of perioperative services to the whole of the organization.
c. A data management system is developed, maintained, and evaluated to support perioperative patient care and resource management.

III.B. Qualifications
A registered nurse qualified by advanced education and management experience shall have administrative accountability for perioperative nursing services.

Criteria:
a. The registered nurse administrator demonstrates management and leadership skills.
b. The registered nurse administrator has experience and expertise in perioperative nursing.
c. The registered nurse administrator maintains competence in management through participation in continuing education or formal education.
d. The registered nurse administrator maintains awareness of local, state, and national legislative and regulatory activities affecting health care.
e. Only a registered nurse directs perioperative nursing care.

III.C. Planning
The registered nurse administrator shall be accountable for planning perioperative nursing services.

Criteria:
a. The registered nurse administrator shares responsibility for the fiscal activities of perioperative nursing services as defined by the organization.
b. The registered nurse administrator allocates resources to meet the needs of the population served.
c. The registered nurse administrator collects data to facilitate planning decisions that address identified patient, family, and community needs and expectations.
d. The registered nurse administrator participates in strategic planning for the organization, integrating perioperative services into the organization as a whole.
e. The registered nurse administrator collaborates with risk management to plan and implement a program for perioperative services.
   i. Legal and regulatory requirements are met.
   ii. Compliance with credentialing regulations is monitored.

III.D. Organizing
The registered nurse administrator shall be accountable for the organization of perioperative nursing services.

Criteria:
a. The registered nurse administrator defines the lines of formal authority and communication.
b. The registered nurse administrator interprets and implements the scope of perioperative nursing practice.
   i. Processes that promote optimal patient outcomes are developed and implemented.

ii. Processes are consistent with nationally recognized professional standards and current nursing research and practice.

iii. Processes are in place to collect key data elements to demonstrate perioperative practice.

c. The registered nurse administrator promotes perioperative nursing research.

 i. Results of nursing research are used to develop perioperative care processes.

 ii. Staff members are encouraged to initiate, promote, and support nursing research projects.

 iii. Research findings and literature review are incorporated into policies and procedures guiding perioperative nursing care.

d. Through development of the performance evaluation tool, the registered nurse administrator implements an effective, ongoing program to monitor, assess, and improve the quality of care delivered to perioperative patients (**Exhibit D**).

 i. Qualifications, competency, and necessary education to promote positive patient outcomes are defined for each staff function.

e. In collaboration with the governing body, management, and medical staff leaders, the registered nurse administrator participates in decision-making structures and processes for the organization.

III.E. Directing

The registered nurse administrator shall be accountable for directing perioperative nursing services.

Criteria:

a. The registered nurse administrator interprets and implements the standards of nursing practice and nursing care.

b. Written policies and procedures guide perioperative services and are developed in collaboration with appropriate departments, are consistent with the mission, and are appropriate to the scope and level of care.

c. The registered nurse administrator ensures that perioperative patient care is consistent with the level of care provided throughout the facility.

III.F. Staffing

The registered nurse administrator shall be accountable for staffing perioperative nursing services.

Criteria:

a. The registered nurse administrator defines the qualifications, competencies, and staffing complement for perioperative nursing services.

 i. A master staffing plan is defined in writing and meets the needs of the population served and scope of services.

 ii. Staff selection is based on facility needs and applicant qualifications.

 iii. Staff assignments are based on patient needs, available resources, and staff competencies.

b. The registered nurse administrator defines the performance expectations for perioperative nursing staff members.

 i. Orientation programs are established and required for all staff members.

 ii. A system for ongoing, periodic competency assessment is in place.

 iii. Education programs are based on competency assessment, performance improvement initiative, and mandatory activities.

 iv. Promotes ongoing development of staff members.

III.G. Controlling

The registered nurse administrator shall be accountable for controlling perioperative nursing services.

Criteria:

a. The registered nurse administrator collaborates with community leaders and multidisciplinary groups in planning and designing a safe, functional, and effective therapeutic environment for patients, health care providers, and other individuals within the community.

b. Performance improvement activities are used to improve patient outcomes; defined in writing; consistent with the organizational mission, vision, and values; designed to meet the needs of key constituents; clinically validated and consistent with sound business practices; and designed to establish a baseline for measurement and assessment activities.

c. The registered nurse administrator ensures perioperative nursing service involvement in safety and infection surveillance programs.

III.H. Ethical Processes

The registered nurse administrator shall be accountable for the identification and utilization of ethical processes to ensure positive patient outcomes.

Criteria:

a. Establishes an environment that promotes the delivery of patient care that is competent, ethical, and legal.
b. Promotes/ensures protection of human rights of all individuals in the perioperative setting.
   i. Maintains privacy and confidentiality.
   ii. Fosters nondiscriminatory climate.
   iii. Maintains sensitivity to sociocultural diversity.

RESOURCES

AACN White Paper, "Hallmarks of the professional nursing practice environment." Washington, DC: American Association of Colleges of Nursing, January 2002.

Bailes, B. "Evidence-based practice guidelines—One way to enhance clinical practice." *AORN Journal* 75 no 6 (June 2002) 1166-1167.

Petersen, C, ed. Perioperative Nursing Data Set, *revised second ed (Denver: AORN, 2007).*

Seifert, P. "Ethics in perioperative practice—Duty to self," *AORN Journal* 76 no 2 (August 2002) 306-313.

PUBLICATION HISTORY
Standards of Perioperative Nursing Practice
   Compiled from previous editions for publication in *Standards, Recommended Practices, and Guidelines* (Denver: AORN, Inc, 2009).

SOURCE DOCUMENTS
Perioperative Patient Focused Model
   Perioperative Nursing Data Set, second ed, S Beyea, ed (Denver: AORN, 2002).

Standards of Perioperative Clinical Practice
   Originally published in *Standards and Recommended Practices for Perioperative Nursing,* 1992 edition (Denver: AORN, 1992).

Standards of Perioperative Professional Practice
   Originally published as "Standards of perioperative professional performance" in the 1992 *Standards and Recommended Practices for Perioperative Nursing.* Revised 2003; approved by the AORN Board of Directors in October 2003.

Standards of Perioperative Administrative Practice
   Originally published June 1976, *AORN Journal,* as "Standards of administrative nursing practice: OR." Revised 1991, 2000; published in *Standards, Recommended Practices, and Guidelines* (Denver: AORN, Inc, 2001).

Perioperative Patient Care Quality
   Originally published in *Standards and Recommended Practices for Perioperative Nursing,* 1990 edition (Denver: AORN, 1990).

Standards of Perioperative Nursing
   Originally published in *Standards and Recommended Practices for Perioperative Nursing,* 1992 edition (Denver: AORN, 1992).

EXHIBIT A:
Historical Perspectives on the AORN Standards, Competency Statements, and Certification

A fundamental precept of AORN is that it is the responsibility of professional registered nurses to ensure safe, high-quality nursing care to patients undergoing operative and other invasive procedures. The Association repeatedly has demonstrated its ongoing commitment to that premise through promulgation of standards of practice, support of perioperative nursing research and certification programs, and development of competency statements, guidelines, guidance statements, recommended practices, and position statements.

The Association's first "Standards of nursing practice: OR" were developed with the American Nurses Association (ANA) Division of Medical Surgical Practice and printed in 1975. Subsequently, AORN provided its membership with a variety of programs and activities to assist nurses in the operating room in becoming aware of and using the standards to evaluate their professional practice. These standards were revised after data was collected from practicing nurses to determine the applicability and usefulness of the standards. The resulting revision, titled "Standards of perioperative nursing practice," was published in 1981. These standards were joined by "Standards of administrative nursing practice: OR" in 1982 and "Patient outcome standards for perioperative nursing" in 1985. In addition to standards of nursing practice, the Association began publishing recommended practices in the technical aspects of perioperative nursing in March 1975.

The "Competency statements in perioperative nursing," first published by AORN in 1986 and revised periodically, provide a means for perioperative nurses to validate and measure the quality of their practice. AORN developed competency statements for the perioperative advanced practice nurse, the perioperative care coordinator, and the RN first assistant in 1994, 1999, and 2002 to define other professional roles of the perioperative nurse. All four sets of competencies were published in a collection titled *Competencies for Perioperative Practice* in 2008. Together with the Perioperative Nursing Data Set (PNDS), recognized by ANA in 1999 and published by AORN in 2000, these resources provide a comprehensive framework for creating job descriptions, performance appraisals, competency checklists, and credentialing documents that affirm and support the contribution of the perioperative registered nurse in providing safe, effective patient care.

Certification in perioperative nursing (CNOR) demonstrates the perioperative nurse's individual commitment to excellence in practice in the clinical setting as well as the Association's ongoing commitment to fostering excellence in the clinical setting. The first perioperative nurse certification program was approved by the AORN House of Delegates in 1978 to "enhance quality patient care" and to "demonstrate accountability to the general public for nursing practice." From this vote, a Certification Council was appointed by the AORN Board of Directors to oversee the development, direction, implementation, and evaluation of the entire certification process. The Council was incorporated in January 1980. Evolution in its organizational mission and structure resulted in name changes in 1985 and 1997. In 2005, the organization became the Competency & Credentialing Institute (CCI). Today, it offers credentialing, nursing competency assessment , education, and consulting on nursing competency issues.

AORN continues to encourage the achievement and maintenance of additional certifications applicable to various arenas of perioperative practice, such as first assisting (CRNFA), administration, nursing informatics, and other subspeciality areas. Resolutions and statements adopted by the House of Delegates consistently reiterate the primacy of the Association's concern for quality and safety in patient care. Striving for excellence in practice, perioperative nurses actively participate in shaping the practice environment and identifying clinical and organizational indicators for quality patient care, patient and workplace safety, and performance improvement.

EXHIBIT B: Perioperative Patient Outcomes

The "Patient outcome standards for perioperative care" were developed by the AORN Nursing Practices Committee and approved by the AORN Board of Directors in November 1983. In November 1991, these standards were renamed "Patient outcomes: Standards of perioperative care." This change was intended to reflect that standards of care describe the desired results that patients can expect to receive during surgical and other diagnostic or therapeutic interventions. In 1995, the Data Elements Coordinating Committee (DECC) charged the DECC outcomes subcommittee with revising the standards. This revision was integral to the committee's work of developing perioperative nursing data elements. The most recent revision of these patient outcomes occurred in 2001 as part of a revision of the first edition of the *Perioperative Nursing Data Set.* Each of these outcome statements can be used in research, teaching, practice, policy development, and information systems.

Patient outcomes are observable, measurable physiologic and psychosocial responses to perioperative nursing interventions. These outcomes, interpretive statements, and accompanying outcome indicators provide a framework for measuring patient responses. Patient outcomes reflect collaborative, interdisciplinary efforts and independent nursing activities. The achievement of patient outcomes is of primary concern for perioperative nurses in assessing, planning, implementing, and evaluating care. Documentation is a means to record and communicate patients' experiences and responses to perioperative plans of care.

The outcome standards focus on high-risk areas for patients undergoing operative or other invasive procedures. They reflect the nurse's scope of responsibility in all phases of the perioperative period. The individual perioperative nurse may use the standards to establish a database to support current nursing practice or as a rationale for practice changes.

As recipients of care, patients are entitled to the assurance of privacy, confidentiality, personal dignity, and quality health services. The delivery of patient-focused care is guided by ethical, legal, and moral principles. These principles are inherent and serve as a foundation for perioperative nursing practice, and are paramount in achieving optimal patient outcomes.

Physiologic responses, behavior responses, and patient safety, each a domain of the "Perioperative patient focused model" described elsewhere in this publication, provide the organizational framework for the outcome statements. Each domain represents specific phenomena of concern to perioperative nurses and the needs of surgical patients and their families. Within the "Perioperative patient focused model," each domain is in continuous interaction with the health system encircling the focus of perioperative nursing practice: the patient. The fourth domain, the health system, is comprised of the structural data elements and focuses on clinical processes and outcomes. The perioperative nurse intervenes to assist the surgical patient to achieve the highest attainable health (ie, physiological, behavioral, and safety) outcomes throughout the perioperative experience.

Editor's note: Each outcome statement is accompanied by a unique identifier for that outcome statement. Please refer to the *Perioperative Nursing Data Set,* second ed, S Beyea, ed (Denver: AORN, 2002), for complete information.

Assumptions

♦ Successful achievement of outcomes may be dependent on the patient's preoperative status.

♦ The perioperative RN is to be actively involved in identifying potential hazards in the practice setting and in implementing appropriate interventions.

♦ The patient has the right to know the risks of operative or other invasive procedures and the right to qualified, competent personnel.

♦ The perioperative nurse uses all phases of the nursing process.

♦ Outcomes are not mutually exclusive of each other and may overlap.

♦ The patient expects to have an operative or other invasive procedure for an intended therapeutic effect without injury.

♦ In this document, the term *signs* refers to objective, observable phenomena, and the term *symptoms* refers to subjective, patient-reported phenomena.

♦ The patient is the primary partner in care. The responsible caregiver, significant other, or family member may perform this role if the patient is unable to do so.

DOMAIN: Perioperative Safety

The patient is free from signs and symptoms of injury caused by extraneous objects. (O2)

Interpretive statement:
Performance of an operative or other invasive procedure requires the use of a variety of equipment (eg, IVs, tracheostomy tubes, pneumatic tourniquet, thermal blanket, and sequential compression devices). Prevention of injury requires application of knowledge regarding each item used during the operative or invasive procedure. Care must be taken to ensure the proper use and coordination of these items so they may serve their intended therapeutic purposes. Factors independent of nursing care can contribute to injury. These include, but are not limited to,
- duration of use of object or contact with object,
- length of procedure, and
- faulty equipment.

Outcome indicators:
- *Skin condition (general):* smooth, intact, and free of ecchymosis, cuts, abrasions, shear injury, rash, or blistering.
- *Skin condition (IV site):* free of discoloration, swelling, or induration.
- *Neuromuscular status:* flexes and extends extremities without assistance; denies numbness or tingling of extremities.
- *Cardiovascular status:* heart rate and blood pressure within expected ranges; peripheral pulses present and equal bilaterally; skin warm to touch.

The patient is free from signs and symptoms of chemical injury. (O3)

Interpretive statement:
Hazards arise from the use of a variety of chemicals in the perioperative environment. Prevention of chemical injury requires application of knowledge of the proper use of each chemical compound. Preexisting patient conditions (eg, open wounds, skin condition, immune status, previous chemical exposure) can influence patient susceptibility to chemical injury. Length of exposure to a chemical may increase the likelihood of injury. These chemicals include, but are not limited to,
- cleaning solutions,
- skin prep solutions,
- pharmaceuticals (eg, irrigation solutions),
- methylmethacrylate, and
- tissue preservatives (eg, formalin).

Outcome indicators:
- *Skin condition (wound):* Skin prepared for surgical incision is free of redness, rash, abrasion, or blistering.
- *Skin condition (general):* smooth, intact, and free of ecchymosis, redness, cuts, abrasions, shear injury, hives, rash, or blistering.
- *Respiratory status:* respirations free of dyspnea, wheezing, or stridor; oxygen saturation (SaO_2) within expected range.
- *Cardiovascular status:* heart rate and blood pressure within expected ranges; peripheral pulses present and equal bilaterally; skin warm to touch.
- *Gastrointestinal status:* free of nausea, vomiting, or diarrhea following exposure to chemical agents.

The patient is free from signs and symptoms of electrical injury. (O4)

Interpretive statement:
Prevention of electrical injury requires application of principles of electrosurgical safety, routine maintenance, and knowledge of potential hazards. Performance of the operative or other invasive procedure relies on many electrical devices, notably the electrosurgical unit (ESU). Electrical equipment must be used according to manufacturers' documented instructions.

Outcome indicators:
- *Skin condition (dispersive electrode and potential alternative ground injury):* smooth, intact, and free of ecchymosis, blisters, or redness.
- *Neuromuscular status:* flexes and extends extremities without assistance; denies numbness or tingling of extremities.
- *Cardiovascular status:* heart rate and blood pressure within expected ranges; peripheral pulses present and equal bilaterally; skin warm to touch.
- *Pain perception:* denies acute pain or discomfort at dispersive electrode ground site.

The patient is free of signs and symptoms of injury related to positioning. (O5)

Interpretive statement:
Prevention of positioning injury requires application of the principles of body mechanics, ongoing assessment throughout the perioperative period, and coordination with the entire health care team. Preexisting conditions (eg, poor nutritional status, extremes of age, vascular insufficiency, diabetes, impaired nerve function) may increase the patient's risk of injury. Other factors, independent of nursing care (eg, type and length of procedure, type of anesthesia), can contribute to the risk of positioning injury.

Outcome indicators:
- *Skin condition (general):* smooth, intact, and free of ecchymosis, cuts, abrasions, shear injury, or blistering.
- *Cardiovascular status:* heart rate and blood pressure within expected ranges; peripheral pulses present and equal bilaterally; skin warm to touch
- *Neuromuscular status:* flexes and extends extremities without assistance; denies numbness or tingling of extremities.

The patient is free from signs and symptoms of laser injury. (O6)

Interpretive statement:
Prevention of laser injury requires application of laser safety principles, coordination with the entire health care team, and knowledge of hazards. Policies that address credentialing of personnel, laser safety, and maintenance must be in accordance with national regulatory standards and manufacturers' documented instructions.

Outcome indicators:
- *Skin condition (general):* smooth, intact, and free of unexplained edema, redness, or tenderness in nontargeted area.
- *Vision:* vision equal to preoperative status (nonopthalmologic patient); vision in nonoperative eye unaffected (opthalmologic patient).
- *Pain perception:* denies corneal pain or discomfort in nontargeted areas.

The patient is free from signs and symptoms of radiation injury. (O7)

Interpretive statement:
Prevention of radiation injury requires the application of principles of physics and radiologic safety standards. Policies addressing education, credentialing, and radiologic safety and maintenance must be in accordance with national regulatory standards and manufacturers' documented instructions. Preexisting patient conditions (eg, length of and/or previous exposure) can influence the patient's susceptibility to radiologic injury.

Outcome indicators:
- *Skin condition (general):* smooth, intact, and free of unexplained edema, redness, blistering, or tenderness in nontargeted areas.
- *Cognition:* responds appropriately to questioning; memory intact.

The patient is free from signs and symptoms of injury related to transfer/transport. (O8)

Interpretive statement:
Prevention of patient injury during transfer/transport requires application of principles of body mechanics, knowledge of transfer/transport techniques and equipment, and coordination of the entire health care team. Appropriate restraints or safety devices are used in accordance with regulatory standards and manufacturers' documented instructions. The condition of the patient will determine the type of health care providers necessary during transfer/transport to ensure safety. Adequate numbers of trained personnel shall attend the patient during transfer/transport activities. The patient may be able to assist in these activities to ensure safety.

Outcome indicators:
- *Skin condition (general):* smooth, intact, and free of ecchymosis, cuts, abrasions, shear injury, or blistering.
- *Musculoskeletal status:* flexes and extends extremities with ease.
- *Pain perception:* reports comfort during and after transfer/transport.

The patient receives appropriate medication(s), safely administered during the perioperative period. (O9)

Interpretive statement:
Medications administered must be within the defined scope of nursing practice. Safe administration of medications during the perioperative period requires knowledge of the intended purpose and side effects of each medication and the patient's condition and current medication usage. Documentation should reflect name, dose, route, time, and effects of all medications administered.

Outcome indicators:
- *Clinical documentation:* name, dose, route, time, and effects of medications administered as ordered and recorded in a manner consistent with the facility's policy.
- *Cognition:* states understanding of purpose, effects, and side effects of medications administered.

DOMAIN: *Physiologic Responses*

The patient is free from signs and symptoms of infection. (O10)

Interpretive statement:
Prevention of infection requires the application of the principles of microbiology and aseptic practice. Measurement of this outcome is based on the stages of wound healing and the Centers for Disease Control and Prevention (CDC) guidelines defining surgical site infections as occurring 30 days postoperative and up to 1 year for transplant surgery. Preexisting patient conditions and other factors independent of nursing care can contribute to the development of infections. These factors include, but are not limited to:
- procedure type;
- organ systems involved;
- tissue trauma;
- wound class (ie, clean, clean contaminated, contaminated, dirty);
- presence of devices (eg, urinary catheters, IVs, invasive monitoring devices, endotracheal tubes);
- procedure length;
- implants;
- administration of prophylactic antibiotics;
- surgical technique; and
- practice setting.

Outcome indicators:
- *Immune status:* afebrile; leukocyte count three to 30 days postoperative within expected range.
- *Skin condition (surgical wound):* incision approximated and free of heat, redness, induration, swelling, or foul odor; drains covered with sterile dressing and/or connected to continuous drainage; wound class identified.
- *Medication regimen:* preoperative antibiotics given according to recommended guidelines; no antibiotic use three to 30 days postoperative.
- *Clinical documentation:* wound class and infection control interventions and measures documented according to facility policy.

The patient has wound/tissue perfusion consistent with or improved from baseline levels established preoperatively. (O11)

Interpretive statement:
Adequate wound/tissue perfusion is necessary to promote optimal healing and maintain cellular function. Preexisting conditions (eg, diabetes, vascular disease) and patient behaviors (eg, smoking) can interfere with the adequate perfusion of both oxygen and nutrients.

Outcome indicators:
- *Skin condition (general):* conjunctiva and/or mucous membranes pink; free of cyanosis or pallor.
- *Skin condition (surgical wound):* incision edges approximated; free of ischemia (pallor, cyanosis, erythema).
- *Vital signs:* temperature, pulse, and respirations within expected ranges.
- *Cardiovascular status:* heart rate and blood pressure within expected ranges; peripheral pulses present and equal bilaterally; skin warm to touch; capillary refill less than 3 sec.

The patient is at or returning to normothermia at the conclusion of the immediate postoperative period. (O12)

Interpretive statement:
The patient must be at or near normal temperature for basal metabolic processes to occur. A core

temperature is preferred to assess thermoregulation. Alterations in temperature, either above or below normothermia, interfere with optimal recovery from anesthesia, thereby increasing the probability of negative postoperative sequelae. Surgical intervention may include intentional alternations in body temperature.

Outcome indicators:

- *Vital signs:* temperature, pulse, and respirations within expected ranges.
- *Cardiovascular status:* heart rate and blood pressure within expected ranges; peripheral pulses present and equal bilaterally; skin warm to touch; capillary refill less than 3 sec.
- *Skin condition (general):* free of shivering (rigor); free of cyanosis or pallor.

The patient's fluid, electrolyte, and acid-base balances are consistent with or improved from baseline levels established preoperatively. (O13)

Interpretive statement:
Continuous monitoring of fluid loss, replacement, and acid-base balance occurs during the perioperative period. Fluid electrolyte and acid-base balances are critical for optimal recovery from anesthesia and surgery.

Outcome indicators:

- *Skin condition (general):* free of new or increasing edema in dependent areas; conjunctiva and/or mucous membranes pink; free of cyanosis or pallor.
- *Vital signs:* temperature, pulse, and respirations within expected ranges.
- *Cardiovascular status:* heart rate and blood pressure within expected ranges; peripheral pulses present and equal bilaterally; skin warm to touch; capillary refill less than 3 sec.
- *Renal status:* output greater than 30 mL/hr; specific gravity 1.010 to 1.030.
- *Laboratory values:* arterial blood gases, serum electrolytes, and hemodynamic monitoring values (if ordered/available) within expected ranges.

The patient's respiratory function is consistent with or improved from baseline levels established preoperatively. (O14)

Interpretive statement:
Adequate pulmonary function is essential to maintain oxygenation and elimination of carbon dioxide. Adequate pulmonary function is critical for optimal recovery and the prevention of hypoventilation, which can lead to cardiac arrest, permanent brain injury, and death.

Outcome indicators:

- *Cognition:* answers questions appropriately; memory intact.
- *Affective response:* awake; cooperative with plan of care.
- *Vital signs:* blood pressure, temperature, and pulse within expected ranges.
- *Respiratory status:* oxygen saturation (SaO_2) within expected range; rate, depth, and symmetry of respirations unchanged or improved from preoperative assessment; breath sounds free of adventitious sounds.
- *Skin condition (general):* conjunctiva and/or mucous membranes pink; free of cyanosis or pallor.

The patient's cardiovascular function is consistent with or improved from baseline levels established preoperatively. (O15)

Interpretive statement:
Adequate cardiac output is essential to maintain perfusion of tissues. Cardiovascular function contributes to tissue perfusion of oxygen and nutrients, removal of cellular waste, and temperature regulation. Cardiac monitoring can be invasive or noninvasive depending on the type of procedure.

Outcome indicators:

- *Cardiovascular status:* heart rate and blood pressure within expected ranges; peripheral pulses present and equal bilaterally; skin warm to touch; capillary refill less than 3 sec.
- *Respiratory status:* oxygen saturation (SaO_2) within expected range; rate, depth, and symmetry of respirations unchanged or improved from preoperative assessment; free of adventitious breath sounds.

♦ *Skin condition (general):* conjunctiva and/or mucous membranes pink; free of cyanosis or pallor.

♦ *Renal status:* output greater than 30 mL/hr; specific gravity 1.010 to 1.030.

The patient demonstrates and/or reports adequate pain control throughout the perioperative period. (O29)

Interpretive statement:
Patient comfort and pain relief is critical to recovery from anesthesia and surgery. Methods to alleviate or reduce pain and/or discomfort may include pharmacologic and/or nonpharmacologic means.

Outcome indicators:
♦ *Pain perception:* patient reports pain controlled based on a recognized pain scale (eg, less than 4 on a 1–10 scale); facial expression relaxed; rests comfortably; denies discomfort in nontargeted areas.

♦ *Cognition:* uses pain scale appropriately to describe level of discomfort.

♦ *Affective response:* cooperative with plan of care; relaxed body position; verbalizes ability to cope.

♦ *Vital signs:* blood pressure, pulse, and respiration within expected ranges.

♦ *Patient satisfaction:* reports satisfaction with level of pain control.

The patient's neurological function is consistent with or improved from baseline levels established preoperatively. (O30)

Interpretive statement:
Adequate neurologic output is essential to maintain affective, cognitive, and neuromuscular function. Neurologic procedures are classified as cranial (brain and accessory structures), spinal (cord and nerves), and peripheral (all other neural tissue). Neurologic status can be measured by noninvasive or invasive methods depending on the type of procedure.

Outcome indicators:
♦ *Cognition:* responds appropriately to questioning; memory intact.

♦ *Affective response:* awake; cooperative with plan of care.

♦ *Psychomotor response:* verbal and motor responses equal to or improved from baseline levels; free of abnormal posturing; follows commands appropriately.

♦ *Neuromuscular status:* flexes and extends extremities; denies numbness or tingling of extremities; pupils equal and reactive to light; swallows without difficulty; reports vision unchanged; tremors decreased from baseline.

♦ *Cardiovascular status:* heart rate and blood pressure within expected ranges; peripheral/intracranial pulses present and equal by Doppler; skin warm to touch; capillary refill less than 3 sec.

♦ *Skin condition (general):* smooth, intact, and free of ecchymosis, cuts, abrasions, shear injury, rash, or blistering.

DOMAIN: Behavioral Responses— Patient and Family

The patient demonstrates knowledge of expected responses to the operative or invasive procedure. (O31)

Interpretive statement:
The patient needs information regarding the expected outcomes, benefits, risks, surgical experience, and recovery process related to the planned operative or other invasive procedure. The information is shared with the patient's family or significant others according to the patient's preference.

Outcome indicators:
♦ *Cognition:* describes sequence of planned procedure; repeats instructions correctly; asks questions based on information provided; participates in plan of care.

♦ *Affective response:* calm; cooperates with plan of care; relaxed facial expression; verbalizes ability to cope.

♦ *Psychomotor skills:* correctly demonstrates deep breathing, coughing, leg exercises, wound care.

♦ *Supportive resources:* family demonstrates willingness to be actively involved in rehabilitation.

♦ *Patient satisfaction:* verbalizes satisfaction with content and process of teaching.

The patient demonstrates knowledge of nutritional requirements related to the operative or other invasive procedure. (O18)

Interpretive statement:
The patient needs information regarding nutritional requirements related to the operative or other invasive procedure. The information is shared with the patient's family or significant others according to the patient's preference.

Outcome indicators:
- *Cognition:* repeats instructions correctly; asks questions based on information provided; verbalizes ability to manage dietary requirements; describes preferred foods/fluids consistent with dietary requirements.
- *Affective response:* verbalizes understanding of the importance of balanced diet to facilitate healing.
- *Supportive resources:* family demonstrates willingness to obtain appropriate food and assist with meal preparation.
- *Patient satisfaction:* verbalizes satisfaction with content and process of teaching.

The patient demonstrates knowledge of medication management. (O19)

Interpretive statement:
The patient needs information regarding administration and management of medication. The information is shared with the patient's family or significant others according to the patient's preference.

Outcome indicators:
- *Cognition:* repeats instructions correctly; asks questions based on information provided; states dose, purpose, frequency, route, side effects, and symptoms to report for each medication.
- *Affective response:* verbalizes acceptance of medication administration responsibility.
- *Psychomotor skills:* demonstrates how to care for surgical wound; prepares and self-administers injectable medication appropriately; demonstrates procedure required prior to medication administration (eg, pulse check).
- *Supportive resources:* family demonstrates willingness to be actively involved in medica-

tion management, including medication acquisition.
- *Patient satisfaction:* verbalizes satisfaction with medication teaching and information provided.

The patient demonstrates knowledge of pain management. (O20)

Interpretive statement:
The patient needs information regarding pain assessment and management plan, realistic outcomes, and pharmacologic and nonpharmacologic methods of pain management. The pain management plan reflects the patient's age, cultural background, and previous experiences with pain and surgery.

Outcome indicators:
- *Cognition:* repeats instructions correctly; asks questions based on information provided; states dose, purpose, frequency, route, and which side effects from pain medication(s) to report; evaluates effect of pain medication using a recognized pain scale; recognizes the importance of timing of administration.
- *Affective response:* verbalizes willingness to accept responsibility for medication administration; agrees to notify health care provider with worsening or uncontrolled pain.
- *Psychomotor skills:* prepares and self-administers injectable medication appropriately; demonstrates ability to use patient controlled analgesic device.
- *Supportive resources:* family demonstrates willingness to be actively involved in pain management plan, including medication acquisition.
- *Patient satisfaction:* verbalizes satisfaction with pain management teaching and information provided.

The patient participates in the rehabilitation process. (O21)

Interpretive statement:
The patient can expect continuity of care. The rehabilitation process begins with the initial patient contact. Appropriate resources are identified and referrals are initiated to support continuity of care throughout the perioperative experience.

Outcome indicators:

- *Cognition:* repeats instructions correctly; asks questions based on information provided; verbalizes expected sequence of events for rehabilitation plan; states activities to avoid/limit during recovery process.
- *Affective response:* cooperates with plan of care; verbalizes willingness to participate in rehabilitation plan and ability to cope.
- *Psychomotor skills:* correctly demonstrates techniques required for postoperative recovery (eg, deep breathing, coughing, leg exercises, wound care).
- *Supportive resources:* family demonstrates willingness to be actively involved in rehabilitation; transportation is available for follow-up visits; states date and time for follow-up appointments.
- *Patient satisfaction:* verbalizes satisfaction with content and process of teaching.

The patient demonstrates knowledge of wound healing. (O22)

Interpretive statement:
The patient needs information regarding wound healing and management. Wound healing is a complex and highly organized physiological response caused by intentional or accidental injury to tissue. The information is shared with the patient's family or significant others according to the patient's preference.

Outcome indicators:

- *Cognition:* repeats instructions correctly; asks questions based on information provided; verbalizes expected sequence for wound healing; describes plan for wound care correctly.
- *Affective response:* cooperates with plan of care; verbalizes ability to manage and cope with wound care.
- *Psychomotor skills:* correctly demonstrates postoperative wound care.
- *Supportive resources:* family demonstrates willingness to be actively involved in wound care.
- *Patient satisfaction:* verbalizes satisfaction with content and process of teaching.

The patient participates in decisions affecting his or her perioperative plan of care. (O23)

Interpretive statement:
Clinical processes support the patient's informed decision-making process in accordance with facility and regulatory standards. The patient receives timely and accurate information regarding diagnosis, surgery, and treatment options, and has his or her questions answered. Care is individualized, and the perioperative plan of care addresses the unique needs of each patient related to

- informed surgical consent,
- informed consent for research/clinical trials, and
- decisions related to self-determination, including resuscitative measures, life-sustaining treatment, and end-of-life decisions.

Outcome indicators:

- *Cognition:* verbalizes understanding of treatment options; describes sequence of planned procedure; repeats provided information correctly; asks questions based on information provided; participates in plan of care.
- *Affective response:* verbalizes concerns about decisions.
- *Clinical documentation:* surgical consent for procedure is signed; Self-Determination Act is implemented according to patient wishes.
- *Supportive resources:* family participates in perioperative plan of care according to patient's preference.
- *Patient satisfaction:* expresses satisfaction with level of involvement in plan of care and decision-making process.

The patient's care is consistent with the perioperative plan of care. (O24)

Interpretive statement:
The patient receives quality health services and continuity of care consistent with the planned intervention. The continuity of care is evident in the plan of care from the preoperative period through rehabilitation.

Outcome indicators:

♦ *Cognition:* describes sequence of planned procedure; repeats instructions correctly; asks questions based on information provided; participates in plan of care.

♦ *Clinical documentation:* plan of care is documented and reflects individual preferences.

♦ *Supportive resources:* family demonstrates willingness to participant in plan of care.

♦ *Patient satisfaction:* expresses satisfaction with delivered care.

The patient's right to privacy is maintained. (O25)

Interpretive statement:
Confidentiality of patient information is an integral component of patient privacy. Caregivers protect patients from undue physical exposure or unwarranted invasions of privacy.

Outcome indicators:

♦ *Affective response:* verbalizes feelings of safety and privacy.

♦ *Skin condition (general):* skin exposure is limited to that required for the operative/ invasive procedure.

♦ *Clinical documentation:* personnel are identified and limited to authorized staff only; personal belongings are identified and secured; only authorized personnel have access to patient records.

♦ *Patient satisfaction:* patient and family verbalize satisfaction with privacy measures.

The patient is the recipient of competent and ethical care within legal standards of practice. (O26)

Interpretive statement:
The perioperative patient is entitled to qualified and skilled care providers. Health care professionals are responsible for maintaining requirements and qualifications for competent practice.

Outcome indicators:

♦ *Administrative policy:* clinicians practice in a manner consistent with credentialing policies; records are maintained and document

professional nursing staff competence licensure and continuing education; perioperative care plans are based on ethical concepts and principles; variances in care are documented and corrective action taken.

♦ *Patient satisfaction:* patients report that care is competent, ethical, and within legal standards.

The patient receives consistent and comparable care regardless of the setting. (O27)

Interpretive statement:
The perioperative patient receives care that fosters a positive self-image and preserves personal dignity. Caregivers respect patients and provide nondiscriminatory and nonprejudicial care.

Outcome indicators:

♦ *Administrative policy:* care is consistent with professional and regulatory standards of care and the facility's human rights policy.

♦ *Performance improvement:* quality improvement indicators demonstrate consistent quality of care across patient populations.

♦ *Patient satisfaction:* patients report high levels of satisfaction with the delivery of care.

The patient's value system, lifestyle, ethnicity, and culture are considered, respected, and incorporated in the perioperative plan of care. (O28)

Interpretive statement:
The implementation of the perioperative plan of care incorporates, but is not limited to, the patient's

♦ cultural and/or ethnic practices,
♦ spiritual or religious beliefs,
♦ psychosocial barriers and/or support systems,
♦ physical and/or cognitive limitations,
♦ language barriers, and
♦ age or developmental stage.

Outcome indicators:

♦ *Cognition:* communicates personal needs related to lifestyle, religion, ethnicity, and culture.

- *Affective response:* verbalizes individual needs and indicates whether they are met.
- *Clinical documentation:* plan of care addresses patient's preferences and needs; cultural/religious practices that influence care are recorded; required interpreter services are facilitated; clinical documents reflect age-specific, functional, physical, or cognitive needs.

- *Patient satisfaction:* states that care is individualized and provided in a nondiscriminatory, nonjudgmental manner.

Revised and updated for the 2002 edition of *Standards, Recommended Practices, and Guidelines* (Denver: AORN, Inc, 2002) 173-182.

EXHIBIT C: Perioperative Explications for the
ANA Code of Ethics for Nurses

Editor's note: *The following is reprinted with permission from American Nurses Association,* Code of Ethics for Nurses with Interpretive Statements, © *2001 American Nurses Publishing, American Nurses Foundation/ American Nurses Association, Washington, DC.*

ANA Code of Ethics for Nurses With Interpretive Statements

Preface

Ethics is an integral part of the foundation of nursing. Nursing has a distinguished history of concern for the welfare of the sick, injured, and vulnerable and for social justice. This concern is embodied in the provision of nursing care to individuals and the community. Nursing encompasses the prevention of illness, the alleviation of suffering, and the protection, promotion, and restoration of health in the care of individuals, families, groups, and communities. Nurses act to change those aspects of social structures that detract from health and well-being. Individuals who become nurses are expected not only to adhere to the ideals and moral norms of the profession but also to embrace them as a part of what it means to be a nurse. The ethical tradition of nursing is self-reflective, enduring, and distinctive. A code of ethics makes explicit the primary goals, values, and obligations of the profession.

The *Code of Ethics for Nurses* serves the following purposes:

- ♦ It is a succinct statement of the ethical obligations and duties of every individual who enters the nursing profession.
- ♦ It is the profession's nonnegotiable ethical standard.
- ♦ It is an expression of nursing's own understanding of its commitment to society.

There are numerous approaches for addressing ethics; these include adopting or subscribing to ethical theories, including humanist, feminist, and social ethics, adhering to ethical principles, and cultivating virtues. The *Code of Ethics for Nurses* reflects all of these approaches. The words "ethical" and "moral" are used throughout the *Code of Ethics.* "Ethical" is used to refer to reasons for decisions about how one ought to act, using the above mentioned approaches. In general, the word "moral" overlaps with "ethical" but is more aligned with personal belief and cultural values. Statements that describe activities and attributes

Preamble

The American Nurses Association (ANA) *Code of Ethics for Nurses with Interpretive Statements* expresses the moral commitment to uphold the goals, values, and distinct ethical obligations of all nurses. As nursing is practiced in a changing social context, the *Code of Ethics for Nurses* becomes a dynamic document. AORN's Ethics Task Force detailed the specific perioperative nursing explications that correspond to the nine provisions from the ANA *Code of Ethics for Nurses with Interpretive Statements* (ANA, 2001). The primary goals and values of a profession are made explicit in a code of ethics.

Together, the ANA code and the explications for perioperative nursing provide the framework within which perioperative nurses can make ethical decisions. The code establishes the profession's nonnegotiable ethical standard. This document demonstrates

---

About This Document

The ANA *Code of Ethics for Nurses with Interpretive Statements,* updated in 2001, is composed of nine provisions, with each provision further subdivided under provision headings. In the following document, the nine ANA provisions are listed in the **left-hand column** and identified by large numerals; the provision headings are identified by numerical subheads (eg, 1.1, 1.2, 1.3, etc). AORN's *Explications* are printed in the **right-hand column** following the same format. Each "Perioperative explication" is illustrated by "Perioperative examples" that pertain to a particular ANA provision heading. The *Explications* read from the top of the right-hand column on one page to the bottom, to the top of the right-hand column on the next page to the bottom, and so on.

The ANA *Code of Ethics for Nurses with Interpretive Statements* can be viewed in its entirety, at no charge, at *http://nursingworld.org/ethics/code/ protected_nwcoe813.htm.* You can purchase a copy online at *http://nursingworld.org/MainMenu Categories/ThePracticeofProfessionalNursing/Ethics Standards/CodeofEthics.aspx.*

EXHIBIT C: Perioperative Explications

of nurses in this *Code of Ethics* are to be understood as normative or prescriptive statements expressing expectations of ethical behavior.

The *Code of Ethics for Nurses* uses the term *patient* to refer to recipients of nursing care. The derivation of this word refers to "one who suffers," reflecting a universal aspect of human existence. Nonetheless, it is recognized that nurses also provide services to those seeking health as well as those responding to illness, to students and to staff, in health care facilities as well as in communities. Similarly, the term *practice* refers to the actions of the nurse in whatever role the nurse fulfills, including direct patient care provider, educator, administrator, researcher, policy developer, or other. Thus, the values and obligations expressed in this *Code of Ethics* apply to nurses in all roles and settings.

The *Code of Ethics for Nurses* is a dynamic document. As nursing and its social context change, changes to the *Code of Ethics* are also necessary. The *Code of Ethics* consists of two components: the provisions and the accompanying interpretive statements. There are nine provisions. The first three describe the most fundamental values and commitments of the nurse, the next three address boundaries of duty and loyalty, and the last three address aspects of duties beyond individual patient encounters. For each provision, there are interpretive statements that provide greater specificity for practice and are responsive to the contemporary context of nursing. Consequently, the interpretive statements are subject to more frequent revision than are the provisions. Additional ethical guidance and detail can be found in ANA or constituent member association position statements that address clinical, research, administrative, educational, or public policy issues.

The *Code of Ethics for Nurses with Interpretive Statements* provides a framework for nurses to use in ethical analysis and decision-making. The *Code of Ethics* establishes the ethical standard for the profession. It is not negotiable in any setting, nor is it subject to revision or amendment except by formal process of the House of Delegates of the ANA. The *Code of Ethics for Nurses* is a reflection of the proud ethical heritage of nursing, a guide for nurses now and in the future.

Code of Ethics for Nurses with Interpretive Statements *reprinted with permission from American Nurses Association, © 2001 Nursesbooks.org, Silver Spring, MD.*

accountability and responsibility to the public, to other members of the health care team, and to the profession. This document helps perioperative nurses relate the ANA *Code of Ethics* to their own areas of practice and provides examples of behaviors that reflect the ethical obligations of perioperative nurses.

Introduction

Ethical decisions for the perioperative nurse are often difficult but necessary during the care of the surgical patient. Additionally, perioperative nurses need to be able to recognize ethical dilemmas and take action. Perioperative nurses are responsible for nursing decisions that are not only clinically and technically sound but also morally appropriate and suitable for the specific problems of the particular patient being treated. The technical or medical aspects of the decision answer the question, "What can be done for this patient?" The moral component involves the patient's wishes and answers the question, "What should be done for this patient?"

The strength of the ethical perspective is its resolute nature. It promotes an action guide for nurses to follow in the realm of patient care. Ethics, as a branch of philosophy, incorporates multiple approaches to take when dealing with or applying actions to real life situations. Thus, each perioperative nurse may experience a situation differently, as well as addressing the situation and identifying the ethical conflict issues, his or her feelings, behaviors, actions, analysis, and resolution of the situation differently.

Health care delivery provided via a team format, such as the surgical team, does not necessarily create ethical conflicts, but it may highlight the conflicts if the values of the team members emphasize different priorities. Additionally, new roles of health care team members may carry expectations about how members should interact with each other and how standards of care should be met.

The perioperative nurse, by virtue of the nurse-patient relationship, has an obligation to provide safe, professional, and ethical patient care. It is important that nurses know how to manage ethical decisions appropriately so that patients' beliefs can be honored without compromising the nurse's own moral conscience. Ethical practice is thus a critical aspect of nursing care, and the development of ethical competency is paramount for present and future nursing practice.

1 : The nurse, in all professional relationships, practices with compassion and respect for the inherent dignity, worth, and uniqueness of every individual, unrestricted by considerations of social or economic status, personal attributes, or the nature of health problems.

1.1 Respect for human dignity

A fundamental principle that underlies all nursing practice is respect for the inherent worth, dignity, and human rights of every individual. Nurses take into account the needs and values of all persons in all professional relationships.

Perioperative Explications

The perioperative nurse is morally obligated to respect the dignity and worth of each individual patient. Perioperative nursing care is provided to each patient undergoing a surgical or other invasive procedure in a manner that preserves and protects patient autonomy, dignity, and human rights.[1] Each nurse has an obligation to be knowledgeable about the moral and legal rights of all patients and to protect and support those rights. As health care does not occur in a vacuum, the perioperative nurse must take into account both the individual rights and the interdependence of individuals in decision-making.

Perioperative examples

- Respects patient's decision for surgery.
- Respects patient's wishes (eg, advance directives, end-of-life choices).
- Implements institutional advance directive policy in the practice setting.
- Restrains patient only when patient poses a direct or potential danger to self or others.

1.2 Relationships to patients

The need for health care is universal, transcending all individual differences. The nurse establishes relationships and delivers nursing services with respect for human needs and values, and without prejudice. An individual's lifestyle, value system, and religious beliefs should be considered in planning health care with and for each patient. Such consideration does not suggest that the nurse necessarily agrees with or condones certain individual choices, but that the nurse respects the patient as a person.

Perioperative Explications

It is the responsibility of the perioperative nurse to provide care for each patient without prejudicial behavior. The care should be planned with consideration for the patient's values, religious beliefs, lifestyle choices, and age. The perioperative nurse respects the worth and dignity of the patient regardless of the diagnosis, disease process, procedure, or projected outcome. When the perioperative nurse is ethically opposed to interventions or procedures in a particular case, the nurse is justified in refusing to participate if the refusal is made known in advance and in time for other appropriate arrangements to be made for the patient's nursing care. When the patient's life is in jeopardy, the perioperative nurse is obliged to provide for the patient's safety, to avoid abandonment, and to withdraw only when assured that alternative sources of nursing care are available to the patient.

Perioperative examples

- ◆ Applies standards of nursing practice consistently to all patients with sensitivity to disability and economic, educational, cultural, religious, racial, age, and sexual differences.[2]
- ◆ Provides nursing care respecting the worth and dignity regardless of diagnosis, disease process, procedure, or projected outcome.[3]
- ◆ Respects the Patient's Bill of Rights.
- ◆ Refrains from derogatory comments about patients, families and significant others, colleagues, and other associates.
- ◆ Seeks guidance for resolving personal belief conflicts with the patient (eg, from supervisor, ethics committee, colleagues with appropriate authority).
- ◆ Uses principles of ethical analysis and moral reasoning to resolve ethical questions.[4]
- ◆ Provides spiritual comfort, arranges for appropriate substitute nursing care if personal beliefs conflict with required care, and respects the patient's decision for surgery.

1.3 The nature of health problems

The nurse respects the worth, dignity, and rights of all human beings irrespective of the nature of the health problem. The worth of the person is not affected by disease, disability, functional status, or proximity to death. This respect extends to all who require the services of the nurse for the promotion of health, the prevention of illness, the restoration of health, the alleviation of suffering, and the provision of supportive care to those who are dying.

The measures nurses take to care for the patient enable the patient to live with as much physical, emotional, social, and spiritual well-being as possible. Nursing care aims to maximize the values that the patient has treasured in life and extends supportive care to the family and significant others. Nursing care is directed toward meeting the comprehensive needs of patients and their families across the continuum of care. This is particularly vital in the care of patients and their families at the end of life to prevent and relieve the cascade of symptoms and suffering that are commonly associated with dying.

Perioperative Explications

Perioperative nurses provide nursing care directed to meet the comprehensive needs of all patients, regardless of diagnosis, taking into consideration aspects of culture, language, perception of pain, significant others, values, and beliefs.[5] Nurses, as individuals, bring to their practice assumptions from their own culture, as well as about the cultures of others. In order to provide care that is culturally relevant to a diverse patient population, it is vital that nurses recognize the importance of each patient's values, beliefs, and health practices. In many instances, nurses provide care across cultures; thus, it becomes an ethical imperative for nurses to develop the skill of culturally competent caring.

To most effectively care for patients of other cultures, the nurse must be a conscientious observer, a perceptive listener, and thorough assessor. Acquiring information about the patient's culture and gaining further personal insight provides the nurse with an increased understanding of culture and values from both perspectives (the patient's and the nurse's) as they relate to providing culturally competent care.

Nurses are leaders and vigilant advocates for the delivery of dignified and humane care. Nurses actively participate in assessing and assuring the responsible and appropriate use of interventions in order to minimize unwarranted or unwanted treatment and patient suffering. The acceptability and importance of carefully considered decisions regarding resuscitation status, withholding and withdrawing life-sustaining therapies, forgoing medically provided nutrition and hydration, aggressive pain and symptom management, and advance directives are increasingly evident. The nurse should provide interventions to relieve pain and other symptoms in the dying patient even when those interventions entail risks of hastening death. However, nurses may not act with the sole intent of ending a patient's life even though such action may be motivated by compassion, respect for patient autonomy, and quality of life considerations. Nurses have invaluable experience, knowledge, and insight into care at the end of life and should be actively involved in related research, education, practice, and policy development.

1.4 The right to self-determination

Respect for human dignity requires the recognition of specific patient rights, particularly, the right of self-determination. Self-determination, also known as autonomy, is the philosophical basis for informed consent in health care. Patients have the moral and legal right to determine what will be done with their own person; to be given accurate, complete, and understandable information in a manner that facilitates an informed judgment; to be assisted with weighing the benefits, burdens, and available options in their treatment, including the choice of no treatment; to accept, refuse, or terminate treatment without deceit, undue influence, duress, coercion, or penalty; and to be given necessary support throughout the decision-making and treatment process. Such support would include the opportunity to make decisions with family and significant others and the provision of advice and support from knowledgeable nurses and other health professionals. Patients should be involved in planning their own health care to the extent they are able and choose to participate.

Code of Ethics for Nurses with Interpretive Statements *reprinted with permission from American Nurses Association, © 2001 Nursesbooks.org, Silver Spring, MD.*

Perioperative examples

- ◆ Provides nursing care respecting the patient's worth and dignity regardless of diagnosis, disease process, procedure, or projected outcome.[6]
- ◆ Overcomes communication barriers to allow patients and their significant others to express preferences for care, providing interpreters when necessary.[7]

Perioperative Explications

Patients have the right to self-determination (ie, the ability to decide for oneself what course of action will be taken in various circumstances). The perioperative nurse provides care to each patient undergoing surgical intervention in a manner that preserves and protects patient autonomy, dignity, and human rights. The patient's autonomy in the decision-making process is acknowledged and supported by the perioperative nurse, who provides accurate, appropriate, and reasonable information to assist the patient in making an informed choice.[8] The perioperative nurse elicits the patient's response regarding perception of the surgical procedure and the implications of decisions. The perioperative nurse ensures that the patient has access to additional and accurate information.[9]

When individual rights must be temporarily overridden to preserve the life of the patient or of another person, the suspension of those rights must be considered a deviation to be tolerated as briefly as possible.

Perioperative examples

- ◆ Provides information and explains the Patient Self-Determination Act (eg, informed consent, living will, power of attorney for health care, do-not-resuscitate order, organ procurement).[10]

Each nurse has an obligation to be knowledgeable about the moral and legal rights of all patients to self-determination. The nurse preserves, protects, and supports those interests by assessing the patient's comprehension of both the information presented and the implications of decisions. In situations in which the patient lacks the capacity to make a decision, a designated surrogate decision-maker should be consulted. The role of the surrogate is to make decisions as the patient would, based upon the patient's previously expressed wishes and known values. In the absence of a designated surrogate decision-maker, decisions should be made in the best interests of the patient, considering the patient's personal values to the extent that they are known. The nurse supports patient self-determination by participating in discussions with surrogates, providing guidance and referral to other resources as necessary, and identifying and addressing problems in the decision-making process. Support of autonomy in the broadest sense also includes recognition that people of some cultures place less weight on individualism and choose to defer to family or community values in decision-making. Respect not just for the specific decision but also for the patient's method of decision-making is consistent with the principle of autonomy.

Individuals are interdependent members of the community. The nurse recognizes that there are situations in which the right to individual self-determination may be outweighed or limited by the rights, health, and welfare of others, particularly in relation to public health considerations. Nonetheless, limitation of individual rights must always be considered a serious deviation from the standard of care, justified only when there are no less restrictive means available to preserve the rights of others and the demands of justice.

1.5 Relationships with colleagues and others

The principle of respect for persons extends to all individuals with whom the nurse interacts. The nurse maintains compassionate and caring relationships with colleagues and others with a commitment to the fair treatment of individuals, to integrity-preserving compromise, and to resolving conflict. Nurses function in many roles, including direct care

Code of Ethics for Nurses with Interpretive Statements *reprinted with permission from American Nurses Association,* © 2001 Nursesbooks.org, Silver Spring, MD.

- Confirms that informed consent has been granted for planned procedure;[11] when possible, obtains surrogate's permission for emergency surgery.
- Explains procedures before initiating action.
- Restrains patient only when patient poses a direct danger to self or others.
- Respects advance directives and end-of-life choices.
- Implements institutional advance directive policy in practice setting.
- Participates in perioperative teaching; answers patient's questions accurately and honestly.
- Allows choices within RN scope of practice (eg, child's preference for transport to the operating room, wagon versus cart).
- Formulates ethical decisions with assistance of available resources (eg, ethics committee, ethicists).

Perioperative Explications
Perioperative nurses must recognize the individuality not only of their patients, but also of their colleagues and others. As health care is not provided in a vacuum, nurses must be able to interact with a variety of other professionals and ancillary providers in the perioperative environment. In working with colleagues, perioperative nurses display the same nondiscriminatory and nonjudgmental behavior as they do with their patients. Treating others with professionalism and respect will enhance the performance of the health care team.

provider, administrator, educator, researcher, and consultant. In each of these roles, the nurse treats colleagues, employees, assistants, and students with respect and compassion. This standard of conduct precludes any and all prejudicial actions, any form of harassment or threatening behavior, or disregard for the effect of one's actions on others. The nurse values the distinctive contribution of individuals or groups, and collaborates to meet the shared goal of providing quality health services.

2: The nurse's primary commitment is to the patient, whether an individual, family, group or community.

2.1 Primacy of the patient's interests

The nurse's primary commitment is to the recipient of nursing and health care services—the patient—whether the recipient is an individual, a family, a group, or a community. Nursing holds a fundamental commitment to the uniqueness of the individual patient; therefore, any plan of care must reflect that uniqueness. The nurse strives to provide patients with opportunities to participate in planning care, assures that patients find the plans acceptable, and supports the implementation of the plan. Addressing patient interests requires recognition of the patient's place in the family or other networks of relationship. When the patient's wishes are in conflict with others, the nurse seeks to help resolve the conflict. Where conflict persists, the nurse's commitment remains to the identified patient.

Code of Ethics for Nurses with Interpretive Statements reprinted with permission from American Nurses Association, © 2001 Nursesbooks.org, Silver Spring, MD.

Perioperative nurses are compelled to treat colleagues and all people in a just and fair manner regardless of disability, economic status, level of education, culture, religion, race, age, and sexuality. Just as nurses have the right not to be abused or harassed in the workplace, so must they treat others in their workplace with respect and compassion. The nurse recognizes the contributions of each member of the health care team and works to collaborate to achieve quality patient care.

Perioperative examples

- ◆ Integrates cultural differences of coworkers.
- ◆ Recognizes and respects the value of all team members, including students and ancillary and support staff members.
- ◆ Provides education and information to coworkers, including ancillary and support staff.
- ◆ Promotes comparable levels of care in all practice settings in which invasive procedures are performed.
- ◆ Uses medical devices in a safe manner and complies with the Safe Medical Devices Act and other laws and regulations.

Perioperative Explications

The perioperative nurse supports both the interdependence and the individual rights of the patient when making decisions. The perioperative nurse collaborates in a manner that preserves and protects the patient's autonomy, dignity, and human rights. When individual rights must be temporarily overridden to preserve the life of the patient or of another person (eg, in the case of violent patients or patients with communicable diseases), the suspension of those rights must be considered a deviation to be tolerated as briefly as possible.

Perioperative examples

- ◆ Collaborates with patient regarding health care whenever possible.
- ◆ Collects patient health data.
- ◆ Analyzes assessment data and utilizes the *Perioperative Nursing Data Set* (PNDS) to formulate a nursing diagnosis and plan nursing care.

- Identifies expected outcomes unique to the patient.[12]
- Considers assessment information, including patient preferences and unique needs, when developing an individualized plan of care to attain designated patient outcomes.[13]
- Includes family/significant others in planning care.[14]
- Provides for spiritual comfort to the patient and significant others (eg, contacts religious counselor).
- Acts as patient advocate.
- Provides interpreters when necessary.
- Respects patient's decision to choose or refuse care or interventions.

2.2   Conflict of interest for nurses

Nurses are frequently put in situations of conflict arising from competing loyalties in the workplace, including situations of conflicting expectations from patients, families, physicians, colleagues, and in many cases, health care organizations and health plans. Nurses must examine the conflicts arising between their own personal and professional values, the values and interests of others who are also responsible for patient care and health care decisions, as well as those of patients. Nurses strive to resolve such conflicts in ways that ensure patient safety, guard the patient's best interests, and preserve the professional integrity of the nurse.

Situations created by changes in health care financing and delivery systems, such as incentive systems to decrease spending, pose new possibilities of conflict between economic self-interest and professional integrity. The use of bonuses, sanctions, and incentives tied to financial targets are examples of features of health care systems that may present such conflict. Conflicts of interest may arise in any domain of nursing activity, including clinical practice, administration, education, or research. Advanced practice nurses who bill directly for services and nursing executives with budgetary responsibilities must be especially cognizant of the potential for conflicts of interest. Nurses should disclose to all relevant parties (eg, patients, employers, colleagues) any perceived or actual conflict of interest and in

Perioperative Explications

Conflicts may arise from financial considerations in the perioperative setting that may contribute to conflicting loyalties between the perioperative nurse and the patient. While the perioperative nurse needs to be fiscally responsible, the perioperative nurse's primary responsibility is to ensure that the patient's safety is maintained.

The perioperative nurse does not give or imply endorsement to advertising, promotion, or sale of commercial products or services in a manner that may be interpreted as reflecting the opinion or judgment of the profession as a whole.

Perioperative examples

- Identifies and resolves conflicts of interest effectively.
- Abstains from influencing purchasing decisions involving companies in which nurses have ownership to make financial gains (eg, stocks, other equity interest).
- The perioperative nurse does not solicit or accept gifts, gratuities, or other items of value that reasonably could be interpreted by others as influencing impartiality.

some situations should withdraw from further participation. Nurses in all roles must seek to ensure that employment arrangements are just and fair and do not create an unreasonable conflict between patient care and direct personal gain.

2.3   Collaboration

Collaboration is not just cooperation, but it is the concerted effort of individuals and groups to attain a shared goal. In health care, that goal is to address the health needs of the patient and the public. The complexity of health care delivery systems requires a multidisciplinary approach to the delivery of services that has the strong support and active participation of all the health professions. Within this context, nursing's unique contribution, scope of practice, and relationship with other health professions needs to be clearly articulated, represented, and preserved. By its very nature, collaboration requires mutual trust, recognition, and respect among the health care team, shared decision-making about patient care, and open dialogue among all parties who have an interest in and a concern for health outcomes. Nurses should work to assure that the relevant parties are involved and have a voice in decision-making about patient care issues. Nurses should see that the questions that need to be addressed are asked and that the information needed for informed decision-making is available and provided. Nurses should actively promote the collaborative multidisciplinary planning required to ensure the availability and accessibility of quality health services to all persons who have needs for health care.

Intraprofessional collaboration within nursing is fundamental to effectively addressing the health needs of patients and the public. Nurses engaged in nonclinical roles, such as administration or research, while not providing direct care, nonetheless are collaborating in the provision of care through their influence and direction of those who do. Effective nursing care is accomplished through the interdependence of nurses in differing roles—those who teach the needed skills, set standards, manage the environment of care, or expand the boundaries of knowledge used by the profession. In this sense, nurses in all roles share a responsibility for the outcomes of nursing care.

Perioperative Explications

The perioperative nurse respects the interdependence of all health care providers in achieving positive outcomes for patients undergoing a surgical or other invasive procedure. As a fundamental member of the surgical team, the perioperative nurse actively participates with other health care professionals when planning and providing patient care. The perioperative nurse, nurse managers, educators, and researchers need to participate in direct and indirect multidisciplinary planning and decision-making regarding patient care protocols and activities.

Perioperative examples

♦ Collaborates with the surgeon and anesthesia care provider to plan care specific to the procedure and the patient's needs.

♦ Collaborates and consults with nursing colleagues in the perioperative setting and practicing in other specialty areas (eg, RN first assistant [RNFA], critical care, psychiatry, pain management, pediatrics, postanesthesia care, home health).

♦ Demonstrates collaborative practice among subspecialties within and outside the perioperative arena.

♦ Collaborates with ancillary and support staff to enhance communication and work patterns that are mutually beneficial for staff and for efficient patient care.

♦ Collaborates with the public, industry, and health care workers regarding environmental and cost-containment issues

♦ Formulates ethical decisions with assistance of available resources (eg, ethics committee, counselors, and ethicists).

2.4 Professional boundaries

When acting within one's role as a professional, the nurse recognizes and maintains boundaries that establish appropriate limits to relationships. While the nature of nursing work has an inherently personal component, nurse-patient relationships and nurse-colleague relationships have, as their foundation, the purpose of preventing illness, alleviating suffering, and protecting, promoting, and restoring the health of patients. In this way, nurse-patient and nurse-colleague relationships differ from those that are purely personal and unstructured, such as friendship. The intimate nature of nursing care, the involvement of nurses in important and sometimes highly stressful life events, and the mutual dependence of colleagues working in close concert all present the potential for blurring of limits to professional relationships. Maintaining authenticity and expressing oneself as an individual, while remaining within the bounds established by the purpose of the relationship, can be especially difficult in prolonged or long-term relationships. In all encounters, nurses are responsible for retaining their professional boundaries. When those professional boundaries are jeopardized, the nurse should seek assistance from peers or supervisors or take appropriate steps to remove her/himself from the situation.

3 : The nurse promotes, advocates for, and strives to protect the health, safety, and rights of the patient.

3.1 Privacy

The nurse safeguards the patient's right to privacy. The need for health care does not justify unwanted intrusion into the patient's life. The nurse advocates for an environment that provides for sufficient physical privacy, including auditory privacy for discussions of a personal nature and policies and practices that protect the confidentiality of information.

Code of Ethics for Nurses with Interpretive Statements *reprinted with permission from American Nurses Association, © 2001 Nursesbooks.org, Silver Spring, MD.*

Perioperative Explications

Perioperative nurses promote and maintain professional relationships with patients, peers, coworkers, and all members of the surgical team. Perioperative nurses are aware of the intimate nature of nursing care, the highly stressful nature of the surgical environment, and the collegial nature of the surgical team. The perioperative nurse respects professional boundaries in the nurse-patient relationship and does not convey undue influence on patient decisions. Perioperative nurses play a critical role in providing information to patients so that decisions affecting that patient will be appropriate and effective.

The nurse should seek the assistance of peers or supervisors, without hesitation, when professional boundaries are unclear or in jeopardy. Perioperative nurses deliver patient care in a nondiscriminatory and nonjudgmental manner according to published, legal, agency, professional, and regulatory standards.[15]

Perioperative examples

- ◆ Plans for appropriate substitute nursing care if personal beliefs conflict with required care.
- ◆ Avoids unprofessional behavior toward patients, coworkers, and other health care professionals.
- ◆ Demonstrates respect toward colleagues and students.
- ◆ Recognizes the professional nature of the nurse-patient relationship and its inherent boundaries.

Perioperative Explications

The perioperative nurse has an obligation to protect patients from undue exposure or unwarranted invasions of privacy. Maintaining the patient's privacy is essential to preserving the trust developed in the nurse-patient relationship. Actions demeaning the dignity of the individual could destroy this relationship and jeopardize the patient's welfare. Maintaining the patient's privacy is reflected by securing mechanisms to protect the patient's physical privacy, all forms of identifiable personal information (ie, verbal, written, electronic), personal belongings, and valuables.

Perioperative examples

- Avoids needless exposure of patient's body.
- Keeps doors to OR or procedure rooms closed except during movement of patients, personnel, supplies, or equipment.[16]
- Restricts access to patient care areas to designated, authorized personnel only.
- Provides cover, warmth, and comfort during transfer from unit to surgical suite as well as during transfer to postoperative unit.
- Provides and maintains respect for deceased.
- Provides protected area for viewing deceased by family/significant others.[17]
- Provides auditory privacy for patient and staff conversations.

Perioperative Explications

In concert with privacy is the professional responsibility to maintain the confidentiality of the patient's personal information. The perioperative nurse has a duty to safeguard the confidentiality of all patient information. Measures must be taken to protect the confidentiality of patient information, including oral, written, and electronic forms. Information pertinent to the patient's treatment and welfare is shared only with members of the health care team directly concerned with the patient's care. While relevant patient information must be shared in an expeditious manner with other members of the health care team in order to provide safe patient care, the patient must have trust and confidence in the nurse that information related to his or her care will be protected. Safeguarding private information about patients is a core belief of nursing; however, new technologies such as electronic records have added a challenge to protecting patient information.

Perioperative examples

- Maintains confidentiality of patient information within scope of practice.
- Closes patient record and logs off whenever leaving the computer unattended to protect patient information.
- Follows facility policies regarding electronic information documentation and storage.
- Is aware of and complies with local, state, and federal privacy and security regulations.
- Limits access to patient's record and information (eg, surgery schedule) to appropriate members of the health care team.

3.2 Confidentiality

Associated with the right to privacy, the nurse has a duty to maintain confidentiality of all patient information. The patient's well-being could be jeopardized and the fundamental trust between patient and nurse destroyed by unnecessary access to data or by the inappropriate disclosure of identifiable patient information. The rights, well-being, and safety of the individual patient should be the primary factors in arriving at any professional judgment concerning the disposition of confidential information received from or about the patient, whether oral, written or electronic. The standard of nursing practice and the nurse's responsibility to provide quality care require that relevant data be shared with those members of the health care team who have a need to know. Only information pertinent to a patient's treatment and welfare is disclosed, and only to those directly involved with the patient's care. Duties of confidentiality, however, are not absolute and may need to be modified in order to protect the patient, other innocent parties, and in circumstances of mandatory disclosure for public health reasons.

Information used for purposes of peer review, third-party payments, and other quality improvement or risk management mechanisms may be disclosed only under defined policies, mandates, or protocols. These written guidelines must assure that the rights, well-being, and safety of the patient are protected. In general, only that information directly relevant to a task or specific responsibility should be disclosed. When using electronic communications, special effort should be made to maintain data security.

- Shares and discusses patient information only with appropriate health care providers and those directly involved in care.
- Protects all forms of confidential patient information (ie, verbal, written, electronic).
- Secures patient's records, belongings, and valuables.
- Maintains patient's record following agency policy, procedure, or protocol.
- Completes record of disposition of belongings and valuables following agency policy, procedure, or protocol.
- Completes operative records accurately and in an objective and nonjudgmental manner.
- Releases patient information only to individuals properly identified and in compliance with established policies, mandates, or protocols.
- Uses information for quality improvement purposes in a manner that protects patient confidentiality.[18]
- Follows regulations regarding disposal of printed records (eg, perioperative schedules, laboratory reports, face sheets).

3.3 Protection of participants in research

Stemming from the right to self-determination, each individual has the right to choose whether or not to participate in research. It is imperative that the patient or legally authorized surrogate receive sufficient information that is material to an informed decision, to comprehend that information, and to know how to discontinue participation in research without penalty. Necessary information to achieve an adequately informed consent includes the nature of participation, potential harms and benefits, and available alternatives to taking part in the research. Additionally, the patient should be informed of how the data will be protected. The patient has the right to refuse to participate in research or to withdraw at any time without fear of adverse consequences or reprisal.

Research should be conducted and directed only by qualified persons. Prior to implementation, all research should be approved by a qualified review board to ensure patient protection and the ethical integrity of the research. Nurses should be

Perioperative Explications

The nurse acts to protect the rights of patients involved in clinical research.[19] These rights include the right of adequately informed consent, the right of freedom from risk of injury, the right of privacy, and the right to the preservation of dignity. The perioperative nurse respects the patient's right to decline or discontinue participation in research. The perioperative nurse should be knowledgeable about the rights of the nurse as well as the patient regarding research studies.

Perioperative nurses have an obligation to (a) ensure that research is conducted by qualified people, (b) obtain information about the intent and nature of the research, and (c) confirm that the study is approved by appropriate review bodies. The researcher should disclose the rights and obligations of the patient and the perioperative nurse. Furthermore, the researcher has an obligation to provide information about the nature of the study to the staff members providing care to the participants. Perioperative nurses should be able to question, report, or refuse to participate in research to which they are morally opposed.

cognizant of the special concerns raised by research involving vulnerable groups, including children, prisoners, students, the elderly, and the poor. The nurse who participates in research in any capacity should be fully informed about both the subject's and the nurse's rights and obligations in the particular research study and in research in general. Nurses have the duty to question and, if necessary, to report and to refuse to participate in research they deem morally objectionable.

3.4 Standards and review mechanisms

Nursing is responsible and accountable for assuring that only those individuals who have demonstrated the knowledge, skill, practice experiences, commitment, and integrity essential to professional practice are allowed to enter into and continue to practice within the profession. Nurse educators have a responsibility to ensure that basic competencies are achieved and to promote a commitment to professional practice prior to entry of an individual into practice. Nurse administrators are responsible for assuring that the knowledge and skills of each nurse in the workplace are assessed prior to the assignment of responsibilities requiring preparation beyond basic academic programs.

The nurse has a responsibility to implement and maintain standards of professional nursing practice. The nurse should participate in planning, establishing, implementing, and evaluating review mechanisms designed to safeguard patients and nurses, such as peer review processes or committees, credentialing processes, quality improvement initiatives, and ethics committees. Nurse administrators must ensure that nurses have access to and

Code of Ethics for Nurses with Interpretive Statements reprinted with permission from American Nurses Association, © 2001 Nursesbooks.org, Silver Spring, MD.

Perioperative examples

- ◆ Confirms informed consent of patient, by physician or responsible researcher, prior to initiation of study and before use of patient information for research.
- ◆ Safeguards patient's rights as a research subject.
- ◆ Submits research proposals to the institutional review board.
- ◆ Follows recommended guidelines and protocols when using investigational devices or when engaging in new procedures.
- ◆ Follows federal guidelines for treatment of human and animal subjects.
- ◆ Provides for patient confidentiality during data collection.
- ◆ Seeks guidance from supervisor to resolve issues regarding any research project that conflict with the nurse's personal beliefs.
- ◆ Plans for appropriate substitute nursing care if personal beliefs conflict with the research project.

Perioperative Explications

The perioperative nurse's primary obligation is to promote the health, welfare, and safety of the patient. The perioperative nurse is responsible for implementing and maintaining standards of perioperative nursing practice. The nurse follows policies, practice guidelines, and laws to safeguard the health and safety of the patient. The nurse participates in the establishment and evaluation of mechanisms to review practice. Competency validation is an essential component to providing safe and effective patient care. Perioperative nurses need to be aware of their own educational and clinical capabilities and seek the assistance of colleagues without hesitation when patient care needs require additional skills. The perioperative nurse uses personal, institutional, professional, and regulatory resources to assist with the resolution of incompetent, unethical, and illegal practices in the work setting.

Perioperative examples

- ◆ Uses institutional ethics committee, practice committee, and peer review.
- ◆ Supports and participates in institutional ethics committee and institutional review boards.
- ◆ Participates in educational programs that enhance patient care (eg, morbidity/mortality conferences, ethics grand rounds, patient care conferences).

inclusion on institutional ethics committees. Nurses must bring forward difficult issues related to patient care and/or institutional constraints upon ethical practice for discussion and review. The nurse acts to promote inclusion of appropriate others in all deliberations related to patient care.

Nurses should also be active participants in the development of policies and review mechanisms designed to promote patient safety, reduce the likelihood of errors, and address both environmental system factors and human factors that present increased risk to patients. In addition, when errors do occur, nurses are expected to follow institutional guidelines in reporting errors committed or observed to the appropriate supervisory personnel and for assuring responsible disclosure of errors to patients. Under no circumstances should the nurse participate in, or condone through silence, either an attempt to hide an error or a punitive response that serves only to fix blame rather than correct the conditions that led to the error.

3.5 Acting on questionable practice

The nurse's primary commitment is to the health, well-being, and safety of the patient across the life span and in all settings in which health care needs are addressed. As an advocate for the patient, the nurse must be alert to and take appropriate action regarding any instances of incompetent, unethical, illegal, or impaired practice by any member of the health care team or the health care system or any action on the part of others that places the rights or best interests of the patient in jeopardy. To function effectively in this role, nurses must be knowledgeable about the *Code of Ethics*, standards of practice of the profession, relevant federal, state and local laws and regulations, and the employing organization's policies and procedures.

When the nurse is aware of inappropriate or questionable practice in the provision or denial of health care, concern should be expressed to the person carrying out the questionable practice. Attention should be called to the possible detrimental affect upon the patient's well-being or best interests as well as the integrity of nursing practice.

- Participates in quality and performance improvement processes.
- Participates in development and revision of professional standards of practice.
- Adheres to professional standards of practice, such as AORN's "Standards of perioperative clinical practice" and "Standards of perioperative professional performance."[20]
- Participates in multidisciplinary review of patient outcomes.
- Complies with institutional policies and procedures regarding competent performance of nursing activities.
- Complies with federal and state regulations such as Occupational Safety and Health Administration regulations, the Americans with Disabilities Act, and state boards of nursing regulations.
- Complies with accrediting agencies such as the Joint Commission and state regulatory agencies.
- Confirms clinicians' practice privileges and credentials (eg, RN first assistants, physicians, physician's assistants).

Perioperative Explications

Care providers in the perioperative environment provide health services within the scope of legitimate and ethical practice and safeguard the health and safety of their patients. The perioperative nurse is responsible for meeting legal, institutional, professional, and regulatory standards. It is the ethical obligation of the perioperative nurse to identify and appropriately report questionable practices by any member of the health care team. There should be an established process for reporting and handling incompetent, unethical, or illegal practice within the employment setting so that such reporting can go through official channels without causing fear of reprisal. The perioperative nurse should be knowledgeable about the process and be prepared to use it if necessary. Written documentation of the observed practices or behaviors must be available to the appropriate authorities.

When incompetent, unethical, or illegal practice on the part of anyone concerned with the patient's care is not corrected within the employment setting and continues to jeopardized the patient's welfare and safety, the problem should be reported to other appropriate authorities, such as practice committees of the pertinent professional organizations or the legally constituted bodies concerned with licensing

When factors in the health care delivery system or health care organization threaten the welfare of the patient, similar action should be directed to the responsible administrator. If indicated, the problem should be reported to an appropriate higher authority within the institution or agency, or to an appropriate external authority.

There should be established processes for reporting and handling incompetent, unethical, illegal, or impaired practice within the employment setting so that such reporting can go through official channels, thereby reducing the risk of reprisal against the reporting nurse. All nurses have a responsibility to assist those who identify potentially questionable practice. State nurses associations should be prepared to provide assistance and support in the development and evaluation of such processes and reporting procedures. When incompetent, unethical, illegal, or impaired practice is not corrected within the employment setting and continues to jeopardize patient well-being and safety, the problem should be reported to other appropriate authorities such as practice committees of the pertinent professional organizations, the legally constituted bodies concerned with licensing of specific categories of health workers and professional practitioners, or the regulatory agencies concerned with evaluating standards or practice. Some situations may warrant the concern and involvement of all such groups. Accurate reporting and factual documentation, and not merely opinion, undergird all such responsible actions. When a nurse chooses to engage in the act of responsible reporting about situations that are perceived as unethical, incompetent, illegal, or impaired, the professional organization has a responsibility to provide the nurse with support and assistance and to protect the practice of those nurses who choose to voice their concerns. Reporting unethical, illegal, incompetent, or impaired practices, even when done appropriately, may present substantial risks to the nurse; nevertheless, such risks do not eliminate the obligation to address serious threats to patient safety.

of specific categories of health workers or professional practitioners. Accurate reporting and documentation undergird all action.

Perioperative examples

♦ Acts as a patient advocate by protecting the patient from incompetent, unethical, or illegal practices.

♦ Questions care that appears inappropriate or substandard.

♦ Expresses concern to person carrying out the questionable practice.

♦ Reports incompetent, unethical, or illegal practice to responsible administrative person.

♦ Consults with colleagues and supervisors to resolve concerns.

♦ Documents observations and occurrences in an objective manner according to institutional policy.

♦ Complies with institutional policies in resolving problems.

♦ Reports verbal, psychological, and physical harassment or abuse.

♦ Intervenes appropriately to protect patient safety.

3.6   Addressing impaired practice

Nurses must be vigilant to protect the patient, the public, and the profession from potential harm when a colleague's practice, in any setting, appears to be impaired. The nurse extends compassion and caring to colleagues who are in recovery from illness or when illness interferes with job performance. In a situation where a nurse suspects another's practice may be impaired, the nurse's duty is to take action designed both to protect patients and to assure that the impaired individual receives assistance in regaining optimal function. Such action should usually begin with consulting supervisory personnel and may also include confronting the individual in a supportive manner and with the assistance of others or helping the individual to access appropriate resources. Nurses are encouraged to follow guidelines outlined by the profession and policies of the employing organization to assist colleagues whose job performance may be adversely affected by mental or physical illness or by personal circumstances. Nurses in all roles should advocate for colleagues whose job performance may be impaired to ensure that they receive appropriate assistance, treatment, and access to fair institutional and legal processes. This includes supporting the return to practice of the individual who has sought assistance and is ready to resume professional duties.

If impaired practice poses a threat or danger to self or others, regardless of whether the individual has sought help, the nurse must take action to report the individual to persons authorized to address the problem. Nurses who advocate for others whose job performance creates a risk for harm should be protected from negative consequences. Advocacy may be a difficult process, and the nurse is advised to follow workplace policies. If workplace policies do not exist or are inappropriate—that is, they deny the nurse in question access to due legal process or demand resignation—the reporting nurse may obtain guidance from the professional association, state peer assistance programs, employee assistance program, or a similar resource.

Perioperative Explications

The perioperative nurse has an ethical responsibility to protect the patient, the public, and the profession from potential harm that could result from a colleague's impairment. It is both caring and compassionate to take action to protect the patient and ensure that the impaired person receives appropriate assistance. Nurse should follow guidelines outlined by the profession and the policies and procedures of the employing agency.

Perioperative examples

- Uses institutional procedural mechanisms to report substance abuse or impairment of colleagues.
- Consults with supervisory personnel.
- Confronts the individual in a supportive, caring manner.
- Use agency resources for helping individual to access treatment and care.
- Acts as patient advocate and takes action to ensure patient safety (eg, makes arrangements to remove unsafe practitioner and replace with appropriate practitioner to continue patient care).

4 : The nurse is responsible and accountable for individual nursing practice and determines the appropriate delegation of tasks consistent with the nurse's obligation to provide optimum patient care.

4.1 Acceptance of accountability and responsibility

Individual registered nurses bear primary responsibility for the nursing care that their patients receive and are individually accountable for their own practice. Nursing practice includes direct care activities, acts of delegation, and other responsibilities such as teaching, research, and administration. In each instance, the nurse retains accountability and responsibility for the quality of practice and for conformity with standards of care.

Nurses are faced with decisions in the context of the increased complexity and changing patterns in the delivery of health care. As the scope of nursing practice changes, the nurse must exercise judgment in accepting responsibilities, seeking consultation, and assigning activities to others who carry out nursing care. For example, some advanced practice nurses have the authority to issue prescription and treatment orders to be carried out by other nurses. These acts are not acts of delegation. Both the advanced practice nurse issuing the order and the nurse accepting the order are responsible for the judgments made and accountable for the actions taken.

4.2 Accountability for nursing judgment and action

Accountability means to be answerable to oneself and others for one's own actions. In order to be accountable, nurses act under a code of ethical conduct that is grounded in the moral principles of fidelity and respect for the dignity, worth, and self-determination of patients. Nurses are accountable for judgments made and actions taken in the course of nursing practice, irrespective of health care organizations' policies or providers' directives.

Perioperative Explications

The individual professional licensee protects the public by ensuring the basic competencies of the professional nurse. Moreover, society grants the nursing profession the right to regulate its own practice. Perioperative nurses bear primary responsibility for perioperative nursing care and are individually accountable for their own practice. The nurse is responsible for nursing decisions made regarding care and is accountable for individual actions. Perioperative nursing practice may include direct patient care, delegation, teaching, research, or administration. Nurses are responsible for judgments they make regarding care and accountable for actions taken.

Perioperative examples
- ◆ Maintains nursing licensure and certification.
- ◆ Accepts responsibility and accountability for perioperative nursing practice, staffing schedules, and on-call assignments.
- ◆ Assumes responsibility for continued education.

Perioperative Explications

Accountability refers to being answerable to one's self, patients, peers, the profession, and society for judgments made and actions taken as a perioperative nurse. Neither physicians' orders nor the employing agency's policies relieve the perioperative nurse of accountability for those actions and judgments. Professional accountability to society is reflected in the ANA *Code of Ethics for Nurses*, standards of practice, educational requirements for practice, certification, and a performance evaluation.

Perioperative examples
- ◆ Provides safe and competent patient care.
- ◆ Accounts for sponges, needles, instruments, and other potential foreign bodies.
- ◆ Practices according to the ANA *Code of Ethics for Nurses;* AORN's *Standards, Recommended Practices, and Guidelines;* and hospital and departmental policies and procedures.

♦ Practices within scope of practice.
♦ Evaluates own performance and solicits peer review.
♦ Alerts surgeon and colleagues to potential risks to patients (eg, positioning, electrical hazards, blood loss, inadvertent laceration of blood vessel).
♦ Questions orders that appear incorrect or inappropriate.

4.3 Responsibility for nursing judgment and action

Responsibility refers to the specific accountability or liability associated with the performance of duties of a particular role. Nurses accept or reject specific role demands based upon their education, knowledge, competence, and extent of experience. Nurses in administration, education, and research also have obligations to the recipients of nursing care. Although nurses in administration, education, and research have relationships with patients that are less direct, in assuming the responsibilities of a particular role, they share responsibility for the care provided by those whom they supervise and instruct. The nurse must not engage in practices prohibited by law or delegate activities to others that are prohibited by the practice acts of other health care providers.

Individual nurses are responsible for assessing their own competence. When the needs of the patient are beyond the qualifications and competencies of the nurse, consultation and collaboration must be sought from qualified nurses, other health professionals, or other appropriate sources. Educational resources should be sought by nurses and provided by institutions to maintain and advance the competence of nurses. Nurse educators act in collaboration with their students to assess the learning needs of the student, the effectiveness of the teaching program, the identification and utilization of appropriate resources, and the support needed for the learning process.

Perioperative Explications

Responsibility refers to carrying out the duties associated with perioperative nursing. Perioperative nurse obligations are reflected in AORN's *Standards, Recommended Practices, and Guidelines.* The acceptance of responsibility for care is determined by an individual's educational preparation, professional competence, and work experience. Nurses in administration, education, and research also are responsible for care through the people they supervise.

Each perioperative nurse is responsible for maintaining competence of professional knowledge and technical skills. It is the nurse's responsibility to assess when care required is beyond an individual's knowledge and to report it to the appropriate support person.

Perioperative examples

♦ Consults other health care providers for assistance when necessary.
♦ Identifies and develops a plan of corrective action related to deficits and limitations in knowledge.
♦ Assumes responsibility for continuous education through personal study; attendance at institutional inservice programs, staff orientation workshops, seminars, AORN chapter and other professional meetings; and reading the *AORN Journal* and other perioperative professional journals.
♦ Remains current on new procedures affecting practice.
♦ Uses the AORN competency statements in perioperative practice.
♦ Provides unit-based orientation.
♦ Provides competency-based orientation.
♦ Practices adult learning theory.
♦ Demonstrates competency in use of new technologies.
♦ Engages in continued professional learning.

4.4 Delegation of nursing activities

Since the nurse is accountable for the quality of nursing care given to patients, nurses are accountable for the assignment of nursing responsibilities to other nurses and the delegation of nursing care activities to other health care workers. While delegation and assignment are used here in a generic moral sense, it is understood that individual states may have a particular legal definition of these terms.

The nurse must make reasonable efforts to assess individual competence when assigning selected components of nursing care to other health care workers. This assessment involves evaluating the knowledge, skills, and experience of the individual to whom the care is assigned, the complexity of the assigned tasks, and the health status of the patient. The nurse is also responsible for monitoring the activities of these individuals and evaluating the quality of the care provided. Nurses may not delegate responsibilities such as assessment and evaluation; they may delegate tasks. The nurse must not knowingly assign or delegate to any member of the nursing team a task for which that person is not prepared or qualified. Employer policies or directives do not relieve the nurse of responsibility for making judgments about the delegation and assignment of nursing care tasks.

Nurses functioning in management or administrative roles have a particular responsibility to provide an environment that supports and facilitates appropriate assignment and delegation. This includes providing appropriate orientation to staff, assisting less experienced nurses in developing necessary skills and competencies, and establishing policies and procedures that protect both the patient and nurse from the inappropriate assignment or delegation of nursing responsibilities, activities, or tasks.

Nurses functioning in educator or preceptor roles may have less direct relationship with patients. However, through assignment of nursing care activities to learners they share responsibility and accountability for the care provided. It is imperative that the knowledge and skills of the learner be sufficient to provide the assigned nursing care and that appropriate supervision be provided to protect both the patient and the learner.

Code of Ethics for Nurses with Interpretive Statements reprinted with permission from American Nurses Association, © 2001 Nursesbooks.org, Silver Spring, MD.

Perioperative Explications

Perioperative nurses are accountable for patient outcomes resulting from nursing care rendered to patients during the perioperative experience. Perioperative nurses are accountable for the assignment of nursing responsibilities to other nurses and for the delegation of nursing care activities to other health care workers. The nurse retains accountability for patient outcomes resulting from delegated nursing tasks. Only the perioperative registered nurse plans and directs the nursing care of every patient undergoing operative and other invasive procedures. The core activities of perioperative nursing are assessment, diagnosis, outcome identification, planning, implementation, and evaluation. The perioperative nurse may delegate certain nursing care tasks, but the nursing activities that cannot be delegated are assessment diagnosis, outcome identification, planning, and evaluation.[21]

The nurse must be aware of specific state legal definitions and guidelines regarding delegation and assignment. The perioperative nurse follows facility policies or directives in delegating functions, but these do not relieve the nurse of accountability for making judgments about the competency of personnel and the appropriateness of delegated activities. Before delegation of patient care tasks, the perioperative nurse uses professional clinical judgment to decide to whom and under what circumstances to delegate appropriate patient care activities.[22] Prior to delegation, consideration also should be given to the patient's condition, the complexity of the procedure, the predictability of the outcome, the level of preparation and competence of the person accepting the delegation, and the amount of supervision needed.[23]

The perioperative work environment supports orientation to less experienced staff. It also provides policies to prevent nurses from accepting inappropriate assignments. This is to protect both the patient and the nurse.

Perioperative examples
- Knows state regulations and definitions regarding delegation and assignment.
- Knows organizational guidelines regarding assignment and delegation.
- Delegates nursing functions to nurses.
- Allows assistive personnel to assist with delegated nursing tasks only when competency has been established and when allowed by state scope of practice.

♦ Bases delegation and assignments on individual competency, patient acuity, complexity of the procedure, predictability of outcomes, amount of supervision required, staffing pattern, and staff availability.[24]

♦ Follows institutional policies for modifying patient care assignments that the nurse or other health care provider does not feel competent in performing.

♦ Participates in perioperative competency-based orientation.

♦ Perioperative nurses define and supervise the training of unlicensed assistive personnel to perform the delegated nursing care tasks.

5 : The nurse owes the same duties to self as to others, including the responsibility to preserve integrity and safety, to maintain competence, and to continue personal and professional growth.

5.1 Moral self-respect

Moral respect accords moral worth and dignity to all human beings irrespective of their personal attributes or life situation. Such respect extends to oneself as well; the same duties that we owe to others we owe to ourselves. Self-regarding duties refer to a realm of duties that primarily concern oneself and include professional growth and maintenance of competence, preservation of wholeness of character, and personal integrity.

Perioperative Explications

Perioperative nurses deliver care in a manner that is respectful not only to patients but also to themselves and their colleagues. Nurses identify areas for personal and professional development and assist others in their development. Nurses participate actively in community education about surgery, invasive procedures, and perioperative nursing, and they correct misinformation and misunderstanding about perioperative patient care.

Perioperative examples

♦ Promotes a positive image of nursing in the media and the community.

♦ Promotes professional autonomy and self-regulation of practice.

♦ Uses nursing titles according to demonstrated professional achievement (eg, CNOR, CRNFA).

♦ Corrects inaccurate portrayals of and misinformation about the profession.

♦ Promotes an environment that does not tolerate harassment and abuse.

♦ Provides an environment that optimizes the occupational health and safety of all employees.

♦ Promotes empowerment and team building.

♦ Supports the nurse's role as a patient advocate.

5.2 Professional growth and maintenance of competence

Though it has consequences for others, maintenance of competence and ongoing professional growth involves the control of one's own conduct in a way that is primarily self-regarding. Competence affects one's self-respect, self-esteem, professional status, and the meaningfulness of work. In all nursing roles, evaluation of one's own performance, coupled with peer review, is a means by which nursing practice can be held to the highest standards. Each nurse is responsible for participating in the development of criteria for evaluation of practice for using those criteria in peer and self-assessment.

Continual professional growth, particularly in knowledge and skill, requires a commitment to lifelong learning. Such learning includes, but is not limited to, continuing education, networking with professional colleagues, self-study, professional reading, certification, and seeking advanced degrees. Nurses are required to have knowledge relevant to the current scope and standards of nursing practice, changing issues, concerns, controversies, and ethics. Where the care required is outside the competencies of the individual nurse, consultation should be sought or the patient should be referred to others for appropriate care.

Perioperative Explications

The perioperative nurse is accountable to society and the profession for appropriate, effective, and efficient nursing practice. Mechanisms are established to demonstrate professional accountability and responsibility for maintaining clinical competence. Knowledge and skill related to technological advances and surgical interventions should be incorporated into the perioperative nurse's practice. The perioperative nurse maintains responsibility for his or her own continuing education.

Perioperative examples

- Incorporates AORN's competency statements in perioperative nursing education.
- Remains current on new procedures related to perioperative clinical practice.
- Participates in certification processes (eg, CNOR, CRNFA, advanced cardiac life support).
- Acquires new knowledge from continuous education through personal study; attendance at institutional inservice programs, staff orientation workshops, seminars, AORN Congress, AORN chapter and other professional meetings; and reading the *AORN Journal, Surgical Services Management,* and other perioperative and professional literature.
- Supports competency-based orientation and annual review process.
- Demonstrates competency in use of new technologies.
- Participates in self-evaluation and peer evaluation of clinical competence, decision-making skills, and professional judgment.
- Seeks consultation as necessary to provide patient care.
- Confirms clinical privileges of all caregivers.
- Promotes individual accountability for maintaining competence.
- Promotes patient safety and other forms of patient advocacy initiatives recommended by professional organizations, legislation, and regulations.

5.3   Wholeness of character

Nurses have both personal and professional identities that are neither entirely separate, nor entirely merged, but are integrated. In the process of becoming a professional, the nurse embraces the values of the profession, integrating them with personal values. Duties to self involve an authentic expression of one's own moral point of view in practice. Sound ethical decision-making requires the respectful and open exchange of views between and among all individuals with relevant interests. In a community of moral discourse, no one person's view should automatically take precedence over that of another. Thus, the nurse has a responsibility to express moral perspectives, even when they differ from those of others, and even when they might not prevail.

This wholeness of character encompasses relationships with patients. In situations where the patient requests a personal opinion from the nurse, the nurse is generally free to express an informed personal opinion as long as this preserves the voluntariness of the patient and maintains appropriate professional and moral boundaries. It is essential to be aware of the potential for undue influence attached to the nurse's professional role. Assisting patients to clarify their own values in reaching informed decisions may be helpful in avoiding unintended persuasion. In situations where nurses' responsibilities include care for those whose personal attributes, condition, lifestyle, or situation is stigmatized by the community and are personally unacceptable, the nurse still renders respectful and skilled care.

5.4   Preservation of integrity

Integrity is an aspect of wholeness of character and is primarily a self-concern of the individual nurse. An economically constrained health care environment presents the nurse with particularly troubling threats to integrity. Threats to integrity may include a request to deceive a patient, to withhold information, or to falsify records, as well as verbal abuse from patients or coworkers. Threats to integrity also may include an expectation that the nurse will act in a way that is inconsistent with the values or ethics of the profession, or more specifically a request that is in direct

Perioperative Explications

The perioperative nurse must be genuine, open, and honest in interactions with patients and other health care providers. Nurses are aware of their powerful influence and offer their opinions based on scientific principles, evidence-based practices, and clinical experiences.

Perioperative examples

- ♦ Assists patients in formulating decisions affecting care as appropriate.
- ♦ Facilitates patient participation in perioperative plan of care.
- ♦ Integrates personal philosophy of nursing into practice setting.
- ♦ Helps peers to be assertive and emotionally healthy.
- ♦ Respects views of others, but clarifies misinformation.
- ♦ Applies standards of nursing practice consistently to all patients regardless of disability, economic status, culture, religion, race, age, lifestyle choices, or sexuality.
- ♦ Plans for appropriate substitute care provider if personal beliefs conflict with required care.

Perioperative Explications

The perioperative registered nurse does not compromise professional or personal integrity. Additionally, the perioperative nurse knows that the use of the title *Registered Nurse (RN),* as granted by state licensure, carries with it the responsibility to act in the public interest. The title *RN* and all other symbols of academic degrees or other earned or honorary professional symbols of recognition may be used in all ways that are legal and appropriate

The pressure to reduce costs, especially in surgical services, reflects the current emphasis on financial well-being. Perioperative nurses can be financially prudent and at the same time discharge their clinical, educational, and administrative duties in a manner that is consistent with ethical principles.

violation of the *Code of Ethics.* Nurses have a duty to remain consistent with both their personal and professional values and to accept compromise only to the degree that it remains an integrity-preserving compromise. An integrity-preserving compromise does not jeopardize the dignity or well-being of the nurse or others. Integrity-preserving compromise can be difficult to achieve, but is more likely to be accomplished in situations where there is an open forum for moral discourse and an atmosphere of mutual respect and regard.

When the perioperative nurse is ethically and morally opposed to interventions or procedures in a particular case, the nurse is justified in refusing to participate if the refusal is made known in advance and in time for other appropriate arrangements to be made for the patient's nursing care. When the patient's life is in jeopardy, the perioperative nurse is obliged to provide for the patient's safety, to avoid abandonment, and to withdraw only when assured that alternative sources of nursing care are available to the patient.

Perioperative examples

- Facilitates a working environment conducive to learning, teaching, and education.
- Makes purchasing decisions equitably and justly to provide cost-effective, quality care.
- Uses and maintains supplies and equipment according to manufacturers' instructions.
- Resterilizes and reprocesses instruments and supplies in a manner consistent with standards and regulations.
- Accepts responsibility and accountability for perioperative nursing practices.
- Is aware of limitations and accepts assignments only when competent to function safely.
- Uses nursing titles (eg, CNOR, CRNFA) according to demonstrated professional achievement.
- Participates in risk management efforts and quality process improvement.
- Plans for appropriate substitute care provider if personal beliefs conflict with required care.

6: The nurse participates in establishing, maintaining, and improving health care environments and conditions of employment conducive to the provision of quality health care and consistent with the values of the profession through individual and collective action.

6.1 Influence of the environment on moral virtues and values

Virtues are habits of character that predispose persons to meet their moral obligations; that is, to do what is right. Excellences are habits of character that predispose a person to do a particular job or task well. Virtues such as wisdom, honesty, and courage

Perioperative Explications

The perioperative nurse is responsible for developing a caring environment that promotes the well-being of patients. This is accomplished by doing what is right and doing it well. The nurse provides a compassionate and therapeutic environment by promoting comfort and preventing unnecessary suffering. The working environment necessary to accomplish these goals supports the growth of virtues and excellences.

are habits or attributes of the morally good person. Excellences such as compassion, patience, and skill are habits of character of the morally good nurse. For the nurse, virtues and excellences are those habits that affirm and promote the values of human dignity, well-being, respect, health, independence, and other values central to nursing. Both virtues and excellences, as aspects of moral character, can be either nurtured by the environment in which the nurse practices or they can be diminished or thwarted. All nurses have a responsibility to create, maintain, and contribute to environments that support the growth of virtues and excellences and enable nurses to fulfill their ethical obligations.

6.2 Influence of the environment on ethical obligations

All nurses, regardless of role, have a responsibility to create, maintain, and contribute to environments of practice that support nurses in fulfilling their ethical obligations. Environments of practice include observable features, such as working conditions, and written policies and procedures setting out expectations for nurses, as well as less tangible characteristics such as informal peer norms. Organizational structures, role descriptions, health and safety initiatives, grievance mechanisms, ethics committees, compensation systems, and disciplinary procedures all contribute to environments that can either present barriers or foster ethical practice and professional fulfillment. Environments in which employees are provided fair hearing of grievances, are supported in practicing according to standards of care, and are justly treated allow for the realization of the values of the profession and are consistent with sound nursing practice.

6.3 Responsibility for the health care environment

The nurse is responsible for contributing to a moral environment that encourages respectful interactions with colleagues, support of peers, and identification of issues that need to be addressed. Nurse administrators have a particular responsibility to assure that employees are treated fairly and that nurses are involved in decisions related to their practice and working conditions. Acquiescing and accepting unsafe or inappropriate practices, even if

Perioperative examples
- Interacts with patients in a compassionate manner.
- Demonstrates empathy, sensitivity, and patience in difficult or stressful situations.
- Uses therapeutic communication.
- Assists families with challenging issues.
- Develops relationships with patients that support mutual involvement in planning care.
- Helps to answer patients' questions related to their care.
- Listens attentively and, when appropriate, refers patient to other resources.

Perioperative Explications

Perioperative nurses create, maintain, and contribute to a work environment that supports individuals in their nursing practice. This environment is safe and has policies, procedures, guidelines, and standards for practice. The nurse is knowledgeable about the various processes and committees to support and promote a professional working environment.

Perioperative examples
- Follows process for addressing unsafe practice.
- Follows process for addressing ethical issues.
- Participates in developing policies, procedures, and standards.
- Maintains knowledge of policies and procedures.
- Promotes a positive work environment.
- Facilitates a working atmosphere conducive to education.

Perioperative Explications

The perioperative nurse treats colleagues and peers respectfully and fairly. The nurse, in all roles, participates in decisions that will affect practice and working conditions. The perioperative nurse identifies and supports conditions of employment that promote practice in accordance with AORN standards and recommended practices. This environment also meets accrediting and other regulatory standards. As a moral agent, if the work environment does not routinely support high quality patient care and safe practice, the nurse should seek employment elsewhere.

Perioperative nurses may need to address concerns about the work environment through appropriate the individual does not participate in the specific practice, is equivalent to condoning unsafe practice. Nurses should not remain employed in facilities that routinely violate patient rights or require nurses to severely and repeatedly compromise standards of practice or personal morality.

7: The nurse participates in the advancement of the profession through contributions to practice, education, administration, and knowledge development.

7.1 Advancing the profession through active involvement in nursing and in health care policy

Nurses should advance their profession by contributing in some way to the leadership, activities, and the viability of their professional organizations. Nurses can also advance the profession by serving in leadership or mentorship roles or on committees within their places of employment. Nurses who are self-employed can advance the profession by serving as role models for professional integrity. Nurses can also advance the profession through participation in civic activities related to health care or through local, state, national, or international initiatives. Nurse educators have a specific responsibility to enhance students' commitment to professional and civic values. Nurse administrators have a responsibility to

Code of Ethics for Nurses with Interpretive Statements *reprinted with permission from American Nurses Association,* © *2001 Nursesbooks.org, Silver Spring, MD.*

channels. Perioperative nurses may need to participate in collective activities (eg, collective bargaining, workplace advocacy) to address concerns about patient care, work environment, or just compensation. These activities should be consistent with AORN standards and recommended practices, accrediting standards, state nurse practice acts, and the ANA *Code of Ethics for Nurses.* In this process, the interests of both nurses and patients must be kept in balance.

Perioperative examples
- ◆ Knows chain of command.
- ◆ Promotes environment that does not tolerate harassment and abuse.
- ◆ Facilitates work environment conducive to learning.
- ◆ Collaborates with all health care team members.
- ◆ Questions unfair employee practices.
- ◆ Identifies and reports unsafe patient practices.
- ◆ Participates in strategic planning and development of departmental and institutional goals.
- ◆ Promotes empowerment.
- ◆ Belongs to state nursing organization.
- ◆ Maintains membership in AORN.

Perioperative Explications
The perioperative nurse has a personal responsibility to contribute to the advancement of the profession by participating in professional organizations. There are various activities within employment agencies and local, state, and national organizations by which one can contribute to the profession. Perioperative educators and managers are additionally responsible for providing an environment conducive to advancing the profession. Nurses can contribute to the advancement of the profession and health care policy by participating in civic activities.

Perioperative examples
- ◆ Maintains membership in AORN.
- ◆ Serves as a committee member at place of employment.
- ◆ Actively participates in AORN local and national initiatives.
- ◆ Volunteers at schools of nursing (eg, teaching, mentoring).

foster an employment environment that facilitates nurses' ethical integrity and professionalism, and nurse researchers are responsible for active contribution to the body of knowledge supporting and advancing nursing practice.

7.2 Advancing the profession by developing, maintaining, and implementing professional standards in clinical, administrative, and educational practice

Standards and guidelines reflect the practice of nursing grounded in ethical commitments and a body of knowledge. Professional standards and guidelines for nurses must be developed by nurses and reflect nursing's responsibility to society. It is the responsibility of nurses to identify their own scope of practice as permitted by professional practice standards and guidelines, by state and federal laws, by relevant societal values, and by the *Code of Ethics.*

The nurse as administrator or manager must establish, maintain, and promote conditions of employment that enable nurses within that organization or community setting to practice in accord with accepted standards of nursing practice and provide a nursing and health care work environment that meets the standards and guidelines of nursing practice. Professional autonomy and self regulation in the control of conditions of practice are necessary for implementing nursing standards and guidelines and assuring quality care for those whom nursing serves.

The nurse educator is responsible for promoting and maintaining optimum standards of both nursing education and of nursing practice in any settings where planned learning activities occur. Nurse educators must also ensure that only those students who possess the knowledge, skills, and competencies that are essential to nursing graduate from their nursing programs.

Code of Ethics for Nurses with Interpretive Statements *reprinted with permission from American Nurses Association, © 2001 Nursesbooks.org, Silver Spring, MD.*

- ♦ Actively seeks opportunity to be involved in activities related to patient care at place of employment (eg, patient care, product selection, safety initiatives, strategic planning, risk management, infection control, and ethics committees).
- ♦ Supports perioperative preceptor programs.
- ♦ Serves as leader or mentor on committees.
- ♦ Maintains awareness of changing health care policy at the local, state, and national levels.
- ♦ Participates in defining and revising scope of practice acts.
- ♦ Consults and collaborates with individuals who shape health care policy.

Perioperative Explications

Perioperative nurses are responsible for monitoring standards of practice pertinent to their role(s) and for fostering optimal standards of practice at the local, regional, state, and national levels of the health care system: "The perioperative nurse systematically evaluates the quality and appropriateness of nursing practice."[25] Perioperative educators and managers are equally responsible to provide an environment conducive to implementing and improving standards and recommended practices.

Perioperative examples

- ♦ Uses standards in nursing practice.
- ♦ Contributes to the work of AORN committees and projects to develop standards.
- ♦ Reviews and critiques practice standards (eg, responds to proposed AORN recommended practices).
- ♦ Participates in development and revision of standards of practice.
- ♦ Participates in quality and process improvement processes.
- ♦ Participates in multidisciplinary review of patient outcomes.
- ♦ Follows investigational device protocol and regulations.

7.3 Advancing the profession through knowledge development, dissemination, and application to practice

The nursing profession should engage in scholarly inquiry to identify, evaluate, refine, and expand the body of knowledge that forms the foundation of its discipline and practice. In addition, nursing knowledge is derived from the sciences and from the humanities. Ongoing scholarly activities are essential to fulfilling a profession's obligations to society. All nurses working alone or in collaboration with others can participate in the advancement of the profession through the development, evaluation, dissemination, and application of knowledge in practice. However, an organizational climate and infrastructure conducive to scholarly inquiry must be valued and implemented for this to occur.

8: The nurse collaborates with other health professionals and the public in promoting community, national, and international efforts to meet health needs.

8.1 Health needs and concerns

The nursing profession is committed to promoting the health, welfare, and safety of all people. The nurse has a responsibility to be aware not only of specific health needs of individual patients but also of broader health concerns such as world hunger, environmental pollution, lack of access to health care, violation of human rights, and inequitable distribution of nursing and health care resources. The availability and accessibility of high quality health services to all people require both interdisciplinary planning and collaborative partnerships among health professionals and others at the community, national, and international levels.

Perioperative Explications

The perioperative nurse has an obligation to the patient and to society to engage in activities that promote scholarly inquiry to identify, verify, and expand the body of perioperative nursing knowledge. Perioperative nursing roles include investigation to further knowledge, participation in research, and application of theoretical and empirical knowledge. Perioperative nurses can support the research process as content experts, data collectors, research subjects, or researchers.

Perioperative examples

♦ Uses research findings to support and improve clinical practice.
♦ Fosters an environment of intellectual curiosity.
♦ Identifies problems amenable to the research process (eg, questions outmoded practices).
♦ Disseminates research findings to colleagues.

Perioperative Explications

Availability of health care involves not only addressing specific health needs, but also factors that affect well-being. These factors include world hunger, environmental pollution, lack of access to care, violation of human rights, and rationing of health care. The perioperative nurse recognizes the interdependence and collaboration of all health care workers to provide quality health care to everyone.

Perioperative examples

♦ Collaborates with members of other professional organizations at international, national, and state levels (eg, joint education offerings, joint patient safety legislative efforts).
♦ Communicates with elected officials about health care needs.
♦ Educates elected officials about health care needs.
♦ Donates to health care-related charities.
♦ Participates in international nursing societies.

8.2 Responsibilities to the public

Nurses, individually and collectively, have a responsibility to be knowledgeable about the health status of the community and existing threats to health and safety. Through support of and participation in community organizations and groups, the nurse assists in efforts to educate the public, facilitates informed choice, identifies conditions and circumstances that contribute to illness, injury, and disease, fosters healthy lifestyles, and participates in institutional and legislative efforts to promote health and meet national health objectives. In addition, the nurse supports initiatives to address barriers to health, such as poverty, homelessness, unsafe living conditions, abuse and violence, and lack of access to health services.

The nurse also recognizes that health care is provided to culturally diverse populations in this country and in all parts of the world. In providing care, the nurse should avoid imposition of the nurse's own cultural values upon others. The nurse should affirm human dignity and show respect for the values and practices associated with different cultures and use approaches to care that reflect awareness and sensitivity.

9 : The profession of nursing, as represented by associations and their members, is responsible for articulating nursing values, for maintaining the integrity of the profession and its practice, and for shaping social policy.

9.1 Assertion of values

It is the responsibility of a professional association to communicate and affirm the values of the profession to its members. It is essential that the professional organization encourages discourse that supports critical self-reflection and evaluation within the profession. The organization also communicates to the public the values that nursing considers central to social change that will enhance health.

Code of Ethics for Nurses with Interpretive Statements *reprinted with permission from American Nurses Association, © 2001 Nursesbooks.org, Silver Spring, MD.*

Perioperative Explications

The perioperative nurse is knowledgeable about the health status of the community and factors that threaten well-being and safety. The nurse participates in educating the public about the various factors influencing health care. The perioperative nurse recognizes cultural differences of various populations and does not allow his or her own beliefs and values to influence the care provided to patients of different beliefs and values. Nursing needs to adequately represent cultural diversity to promote the welfare and safety of all patients.

Perioperative examples

- Volunteers to teach wellness classes.
- Educates members of community about perioperative nursing.
- Collaborates with consumer, service, and support organizations related to health care.
- Fosters collaboration with and education of the public on local, state, and national health care issues.
- Prepares for disasters and threat to community.
- Provides explanations and answers to questions in the patient's primary language.
- Incorporates patient requests regarding religious preferences into practice as much as possible.
- Integrates cultural differences into patient care.
- Incorporates requests for alternative therapies into care, as appropriate.

Perioperative Explications

AORN's mission is to support perioperative registered nurses in achieving optimal outcomes for patients undergoing operative and other invasive procedures. To further its goals, AORN is committed to excellence in support of its mission and values education, representation, and standards that are research based, current, timely, comprehensive, applicable, and achievable.[26]

Perioperative examples

- Participates in educational programs to promote life-long learning.
- Reads professional journals and newsletters.

♦ Incorporates AORN's *Standards, Recommended Practices, and Guidelines* into practice.

♦ Uses the *Perioperative Nursing Data Set* (PNDS) to link perioperative nursing care to positive patient outcomes.

♦ Applies "Patient Safety First" principles to perioperative patient care.

♦ Provides consultative and other services to support perioperative nursing and patient care.

♦ Engages in legislative activities to support perioperative nursing and patient care.

♦ Promotes interaction with regulatory agencies (eg, FDA, CMS) to advance safe, quality patient care.

♦ Maintains membership in AORN.

♦ Participates in AORN chapters, state councils, specialty assemblies, and other organizational units to support AORN and perioperative nursing.

9.2 The profession carries out its collective responsibility through professional associations

The nursing profession continues to develop ways to clarify nursing's accountability to society. The contract between the profession and society is made explicit through such mechanisms as (a) the *Code of Ethics for Nurses,* (b) the standards of nursing practice, (c) the ongoing development of nursing knowledge derived from nursing theory, scholarship, and research in order to guide nursing actions, (d) educational requirements for practice, (e) certification, and (f) mechanisms for evaluating the effectiveness of professional nursing actions.

Perioperative Explications
AORN's purpose is to unite perioperative registered nurses for the purpose of maintaining an association dedicated to the constant endeavor of promoting the highest professional standards of perioperative nursing practice for optimum patient care. AORN cooperates with other professional associations, health care facilities, universities, industries, technical societies, research organizations, and governmental agencies in matters affecting the goals and purposes of AORN.[27]

Perioperative examples

♦ Practices perioperative nursing incorporating AORN's *Standards, Recommended Practices, and Guidelines.*

♦ Participates in nursing research.

♦ Becomes knowledgeable about the ANA *Code of Ethics for Nurses* and the "AORN explications for perioperative nurses."

♦ Collaborates with other organizations (eg, American College of Surgeons, American Association of Nurse Anesthetists, American Society of Anesthesiologists) to foster optimal perioperative patient care.

♦ Collaborates with other nursing organizations (eg, Nursing Organizations Alliance, American Nurses Association) to enhance the nursing profession.

♦ Identifies partnering opportunities with educational, health care, governmental, payer, business, and professional organizations to promote mutually beneficial patient care initiatives.

9.3   Intraprofessional integrity

A professional association is responsible for expressing the values and ethics of the profession and also for encouraging the professional organization and its members to function in accord with those values and ethics. Thus, one of its fundamental responsibilities is to promote awareness of and adherence to the *Code of Ethics* and to critique the activities and ends of the professional association itself. Values and ethics influence the power structures of the association in guiding, correcting, and directing its activities. Legitimate concerns for the self-interest of the association and the profession are balanced by a commitment to the social goods that are sought. Through critical self-reflection and self-evaluation, associations must foster change within themselves, seeking to move the professional community toward its stated ideals.

Perioperative Explications

The ANA *Code of Ethics for Nurses,* together with the "AORN explications for perioperative nursing," expresses the values and ethics of perioperative nursing. Use of the title *RN* carries with it the individual's responsibility to act in public's best interest. The title *RN* and all other academic degrees or other earned or honorary professional symbols of recognition may be used in all ways that are legal and reflect professional achievement.

Perioperative examples

♦ Promotes a positive image of nursing in the media and the community.
♦ Promotes professional autonomy and self-regulation of practice.
♦ Uses nursing titles (eg, CNOR, CRNFA) according to professional achievement.
♦ Identifies and resolves conflicts of interest effectively.
♦ Corrects inaccurate portrayals of and misinformation about the profession.
♦ Incorporates the ANA *Code of Ethics for Nurses* into daily practice.

9.4   Social reform

Nurses can work individually as citizens or collectively through political action to bring about social change. It is the responsibility of a professional nursing association to speak for nurses collectively in shaping and reshaping health care within our nation, specifically in areas of health care policy and legislation that affect accessibility, quality, and the cost of health care. Here, the professional association maintains vigilance and takes action to influence legislators, reimbursement agencies, nursing organizations, and other health professions. In these activities, health is understood as being broader than delivery and reimbursement systems, but extending to health-related sociocultural issues such as violation of human rights, homelessness, hunger, violence, and the stigma of illness.

Code of Ethics for Nurses with Interpretive Statements *reprinted with permission from American Nurses Association,* © *2001 Nursesbooks.org, Silver Spring, MD.*

Perioperative Explications

To promote the welfare and safety of all people, nurses need adequate representation to support effective health care delivery. Individual patients and society as whole benefit from nursing participation in decisions made about health care.

Perioperative examples

♦ Participates in lobbying efforts affecting health care.
♦ Supports political candidates that advance health care issues.
♦ Participates in electoral process at the local, state, and national levels.
♦ Participates in institutional decision-making.
♦ Participates in the electoral process.
♦ Volunteers in community health services.
♦ Supports political candidates, governmental programs, and legislation agenda for improving patient care.

♦ Educates members of the community about perioperative nursing (eg, through health fairs, Perioperative Nurse Week activities, educational programs).

♦ Collaborates with consumer, service, and support organizations (eg, Lions Club, Reach to Recovery, AARP).

♦ Collaborates with the public, industry, and health care workers regarding environmental and cost containment issues.

♦ Fosters collaboration with and education of the public regarding local, state, and national issues (eg, the environment, health care costs).

Conclusion

Perioperative nurses must be familiar with the ethical issues inherent to their practice. To develop familiarity with the issues, one can discuss them with peers and ethics committee members or consult other knowledgeable resources. Nurses may find it beneficial to have a file on ethics available in the department for review. Inservice programs focusing on ethical issues can be implemented for the department by utilizing members of the hospital's nursing ethics and/or medical ethics committees. Other departments and contacts, such as social services, also can be a resource, especially in the area of advance directives. Nurses can use values clarification to identify and understand their moral beliefs and attitudes.

Ethics provides guidelines of action for behavior with others. Such guidelines are both important and necessary when dealing with issues in the context of health care. To effectively deal with ethical situations in practice, nurses must be cognizant of limitations to scope of practice and never jeopardize patient care. Nurses need to realize they have a personal accountability to the care of the patient. As guidelines for practice, nurses can utilize many resources such as the ANA *Code of Ethics for Nurses* and knowledge of patient and individual rights, policies and procedures, standards of care, and community norms. Ultimately, the nurse must provide ethical care for all patients. Utilizing guidelines and recommended practices is a means to an end—safe, competent, and ethical patient care.

REFERENCES

1. S Beyea, ed, *Perioperative Nursing Data Set,* second ed (Denver: AORN, Inc, 2002) 182.

2. *Ibid.*

3. *Ibid.*

4. S Beyea, L Nicoll, "Using ethical analysis when there is no research," *AORN Journal* 69 (June 1999) 1261-1263.

5. S Beyea, ed, *Perioperative Nursing Data Set* (Denver: AORN, Inc, 2000) 150.

6. Beyea, *Perioperative Nursing Data Set,* second ed, 182.

7. *Ibid,* 184.

8. "ANA code for nurses with interpretive statements—Explications for perioperative nursing," in *Standards, Recommended Practices, and Guidelines* (Denver: AORN, Inc, 2002) 54.

9. Beyea, *Perioperative Nursing Data Set,* second ed, 178.

10. *Ibid,* 182.

11. *Ibid,* 183.

12. *Ibid,* 175-176.

13. *Ibid,* 178, 180.

14. *Ibid,* 179, 181.

15. Beyea, *Perioperative Nursing Data Set,* 125.

16. "Recommended practices for traffic patterns," in *Standards, Recommended Practices, and Guidelines* (Denver: AORN, Inc, 2002) 350.

17. Beyea, *Perioperative Nursing Data Set,* second ed, 184.

18. Beyea, *Perioperative Nursing Data Set,* second ed, 183.

19. A Orb, L Eisenhauer, D Wynaden, "Ethics in qualitative research," *Journal of Nursing Scholarship* 33 (2001) 93-96.

20. *Standards, Recommended Practices, and Guidelines* (Denver: AORN, Inc, 2002) 157-162.

21. "AORN official statement on unlicensed assistive personnel," in *Standards, Recommended Practices, and Guidelines* (Denver: AORN, Inc, 2002) 141.

22. *Ibid.*

23. *Ibid.*

24. *Ibid.*

25. "Standards of perioperative professional performance," in *Standards, Recommended Practices, and Guidelines* (Denver: AORN, Inc, 2002) 160.

26. "AORN vision, mission, philosophy, and values," in *Standards, Recommended Practices, and Guidelines* (Denver: AORN, Inc, 2002) 5.

27. "AORN national bylaws," in *Standards, Recommended Practices, and Guidelines* (Denver: AORN, Inc, 2002) 7.

Originally published in the 1994 edition of the AORN *Standards and Recommended Practices.*
Revised; approved by the AORN Board of Directors in November 2002.

EXHIBIT D: Quality and Performance Improvement Standards for Perioperative Nursing

The 2002 AORN Nursing Practices Committee (NPC) was charged with the review and revision of the "Quality improvement standards for perioperative nursing" developed by the 1990 NPC.

Over time, health care has used many different terms to denote the processes used to improve patient care, such as quality assurance (QA), continuous improvement (CI), and continuous quality improvement (CQI). Quality cannot be assured, but it can be measured, assessed, and improved. Perioperative nurses should strive continuously to improve the care provided to patients in the perioperative setting.

Quality improvement (QI) and performance improvement (PI) are the newest terms used in the quest for excellence. They are two different methodologies that are linked together and continuously developing. "QI examines processes in order to improve them. PI addresses human performance within organizations at the individual, process, and organizational levels."[1] The origin of QI is based in industry and has more of a management and process focus; PI focuses more on the people, their motivation, and the tools (eg, work design, technical support, supervision, safety) they use to achieve the goals of the organization.

Government-funded peer review organizations (PROs), Medicare/Medicaid reimbursement regulations, laws generated at the federal and state levels, and private health insurers' standards have refocused the efforts required to assess patient care systematically. The recent focus of regulatory bodies and the Joint Commission on Accreditation of Healthcare Organizations (JCAHO) has placed greater emphasis on patient safety and reducing the errors that have resulted, at times, in patient deaths. The Institute of Medicine's 1999 report, *To Err Is Human: Building a Safer Health System,"* states, "Although there are many kinds of standards in health care, especially those promulgated by licensing agencies and accrediting organizations, few standards focus explicitly on issues of patient safety."[2]

The Joint Commission states, "The goal of the improving organization performance function is to ensure that the organization designs processes well and systematically monitors, analyzes, and improves its performance to improve patient outcomes. Value in health care is the appropriate balance between good outcomes, excellent care and services, and costs. To add value to the care and services provided, organizations need to understand the relationship between perception of care, outcomes, and costs, and how the three issues are affected by processes carried out by the organization. An organization's performance of important functions significantly affects the quality and value of its services."[3] JCAHO bases its evaluation of an institution's QI/PI activities on

- designing processes,
- monitoring performance through data collection,
- analyzing current performance, and
- improving and sustaining improved performance.

An effective quality/performance improvement plan should be consistent with the philosophy, mission, and strategic goals of the organization. Departmental initiatives should be systematic, written, and communicated to leaders, practitioners, and staff. The plan should provide reliable data that is integrated into an organization-wide plan. Implementation of QI/PI standards may provide the basis for selecting mechanisms that measure outcomes and maintain systems to analyze and trend data and corrective actions that result in improved, safer patient care.

Staff participation and a multidisciplinary approach to the program enhance the awareness of personnel providing direct and indirect care and enable challenges to be funneled into opportunities for improvement. Documentation should show that all aspects of care in the department conform to contemporary standards of clinical practice and that data are used to study and improve the quality of care.

AORN's *Standards, Recommended Practices, and Guidelines* should be used as a resource when establishing a QI/PI program. Organizations, depending on their size, resources, and commitment to QI/PI, may have a central department, task force, or steering committee to oversee, expedite, and guide departments in achieving the goals of their QI/PI plan.

Standard I

Assign responsibility for monitoring and evaluation activities.

Interpretive statement 1:
The director and/or the designee (eg, manager or other individual[s] responsible for the department) assume overall responsibility for the monitoring and evaluation processes within the department and in the department's participation in the organization-wide performance improvement plan.

Criteria:
1. The director actively participates in and supports the program.
2. The director may select an individual (ie, designee) to be responsible for the department's overall participation in the QI/PI plan.
3. The director/designee selects the individual/team responsible for each QI/PI project. The team may include, but is not limited to,
   - staff nurses,
   - ancillary staff members,
   - educators,
   - medical director/chief of services,
   - members of the medical staff
   - OR director/supervisor,
   - QI/PI coordinator, and
   - representatives from any departments involved in the process.
4. The director collaborates with other disciplines and departments that share responsibility for QI/PI activities.

Interpretive statement 2:
The director/designee or other responsible individual(s) develops a mechanism for ensuring that departmental initiatives are congruent with the organization-wide QI/PI plan. The departmental initiatives are integrated and communicated throughout the organization.

Criteria:
1. The plan reflects a departmental and organization-wide commitment to patient care excellence.
2. The plan is communicated through organization-wide and unit-based staff development programs.
3. The plan is evaluated and revised at least annually to determine program appropriateness and effectiveness.

4. The plan describes the roles and responsibilities of those involved in quality improvement/performance improvement. This plan may be in the form of a narrative statement, outline, flow chart, or team charter.
5. The plan describes the monitoring and evaluation activities. These may include, but are not limited to,
   - delineating scope of care,
   - identifying important functions and processes,
   - prioritizing areas for improvement,
   - collecting and analyzing data,
   - evaluating patient care,
   - resolving problem areas and/or improving processes that affect patient care,
   - documenting results,
   - communicating findings, and
   - maintaining improvements.
6. The plan identifies collaborating disciplines/departments that share responsibilities and are interdependent in QI/PI. These activities may include, but are not limited to,
   - contracted services,
   - engineering,
   - environmental services,
   - infection control,
   - laboratory,
   - materials management,
   - medical staff,
   - nursing units,
   - pharmacy,
   - radiology,
   - risk management/safety, and
   - special care units.
7. The plan describes the schedule of the quality QI/PI plan. This may include, but is not limited to, schedule of meetings, schedule of times, and locations of monitoring and evaluation activities.
8. The plan reflects the uniqueness of nursing activities performed in the perioperative setting and the outcomes of perioperative patient care.

Standard II

Delineate the scope of patient care activities or services.

Interpretive statement:
The scope of patient care activities or services describes who is served, what services are provided, who provides the services, physical sites, and times that services are provided.

Criteria:

1. The patient population assessment/description may include, but is not limited to,
   ♦ patient acuity,
   ♦ patient socioeconomic status,
   ♦ demographics,
   ♦ support systems, and
   ♦ clinical conditions/diagnoses.
2. Customers are identified, and they are relevant to the type of service provided. Customers may include, but are not limited to,
   ♦ employees,
   ♦ patients,
   ♦ families,
   ♦ practitioners,
   ♦ purchasers, and
   ♦ suppliers.
3. Clinical care activities and nursing services are determined. These may include, but are not limited to,
   ♦ circulating;
   ♦ scrubbing;
   ♦ first assisting;
   ♦ patient education;
   ♦ resource nurses/advanced practitioners (eg, clinical nurse specialists, nurse practitioners); and
   ♦ others identified in AORN's *Standards, Recommended Practices, and Guidelines.*
4. Services provided in the department are inventoried. Services may include, but are not limited to,
   ♦ cardiovascular/thoracic,
   ♦ endoscopy,
   ♦ general surgery,
   ♦ ophthalmology,
   ♦ orthopedics,
   ♦ otolaryngology,
   ♦ obstetrics and gynecology,
   ♦ neurosurgery,
   ♦ pediatrics, and
   ♦ pain management.
5. Departmental practitioners are listed by job title and level of expertise. Individuals who contribute to departmental care and activities may include, but are not limited to,
   ♦ advanced practice nurses,
   ♦ registered nurses,
   ♦ licensed practical/vocational nurses, and
   ♦ unlicensed assistive personnel.
6. Other practitioners/personnel who share patient care responsibilities are listed. These may include, but are not limited to,
   ♦ ancillary departments,
   ♦ contracting agencies,
   ♦ employed caregivers, and
   ♦ physicians.
7. The physical site is described. The description may include, but is not limited to,
   ♦ number and type of suites/rooms,
   ♦ their proximity to each other, and
   ♦ support areas.
8. Dates, days, and hours of operation are described.
9. Suites/rooms are identified by type of service provided.
10. Staffing plans/patterns that support services are identified.[4] A rationale is given for the chosen staffing, and a mechanism is in place to evaluate the effectiveness.

Standard III

Identify processes impacting the quality and safety of patient care.

Interpretive statement:
High-volume, high-risk, and/or problem-prone processes are identified.

Criteria:

1. High-volume types of patient care activities are those performed on a frequent or daily basis to a large volume of patients. High-volume types include, but are not limited to,
   ♦ procedures that occur frequently (eg, cholecystectomy, laparoscopy, cataract extraction);
   ♦ nursing activities frequently performed for patients (eg, placement of electrosurgical dispersive pad, administration of medication, aseptic technique); and
   ♦ nursing care that affects a large number of patients (eg, patient assessments, patient education, discharge planning, intravenous therapy, pain management).
2. High-risk processes are those that carry a greater potential for liability and/or patient injury. High-risk areas may include, but are not limited to,
   ♦ patients at risk of serious consequences (eg, patients with a history of difficult airway management or a high risk assessment for DVT/PE, physiologically compromised patients, elderly patients, children, neonatal patients);

- complex or high-risk procedures that are performed infrequently;
- care delivered that was inconsistent with nursing standards or guidelines (eg, incorrect counts, wrong site/side surgery or failure to verify procedure[s] or patient identity, medication errors, improper positioning, breaks in aseptic technique, lack of appropriate patient education);
- acts of omission/commission;
- patients receiving moderate or deep sedation (refer to JCAHO Standards [TX2]); and
- patients undergoing multiple procedures or recurrent surgeries.
3. Problem-prone processes identify departmental problem areas. Problem-prone areas may include, but are not limited to,
- procedures and/or care that cause patient and/or staff anxiety;
- activities known to generate a number of incident reports;
- activities needing increased efficiency (eg, surgery schedule management, instrument processing);
- equipment known to have a high risk or incidence of user error (eg, new equipment, infrequently used equipment, equipment that has been modified).

Standard IV

Systematic performance measures (ie, indicators) and/or priority areas are identified as opportunities for improvement based on the functions and processes of the perioperative episode.

Interpretive statement:
Performance measures (ie, indicators) should relate to the structure, process, or outcome of care and/or service.

Criteria:
1. Structure measures based on the AORN "Standards of perioperative administrative practice" relate to physical, fiscal, and organizational elements that require
- establishing, controlling, and monitoring a safe perioperative environment (eg, technical and aseptic practice, electrical safety, physical facilities, occupational safety);

- assessing, managing, and monitoring fiscal resources (eg, equipment, supplies, personnel, time); and
- communicating and implementing organizational elements (eg, standards of nursing practice, such as care and professional performance, policies and procedures, staffing patterns, orientation, staff development activities, quality assessment plans).
2. Process measures based on the AORN "Standards of perioperative clinical practice" and "Standards of perioperative professional practice" focus on activities of the nurse or process of nursing that require
- implementation of the nursing process;
- management of complications; and
- adherence to policies and procedures (eg, correct site/side and identity verification, safe medication administration, specimen labeling, counting, positioning).
3. Outcome measures based on the AORN "Perioperative patient outcomes" relate to patient status following delivery of care that requires
- emphasis on adverse events and complications; and
- evaluation of measurable changes in patient health status (eg, free from injury, infection, nerve damage, altered skin integrity).
4. When selecting performance measures (ie, indicators), consideration should be given to the following issues:
- departmental and organizational quality and safety goals;
- accreditation standards and regulatory requirements;
- perioperative clinical and service topics of national or local interest;
- topics of greatest concern to patients and the community; and
- trends of near misses for the purposes of improving processes.

Standard V

Establish performance expectations.

Interpretive statement 1:
The baselines for each of the measures are determined based on the measurement of the current process.

Criteria:
1. Baseline data should be gathered to establish the current level of performance.
2. Baseline data is used as a starting point for measurement.

Interpretive statement 2:
The baseline is evaluated and a determination is made whether there is an opportunity for improvement.

Criteria:
1. Evaluation of the baseline may be accomplished through analysis of collected data, peer review, literature review, etc.
2. A plan for improvement is thoughtfully designed. Tools such as flowcharts and process diagrams may be used to assist in identifying areas of the process with potential for failure.

Standard VI

Collect and organize data for evaluation.

Interpretive statement 1:
Data sources and methods of data collection/organization for each indicator are identified to establish a baseline of performance.

Criteria:
1. Existing sources of data are used. These may include, but are not limited to,
   - surgery schedule log,
   - staffing schedule,
   - incident reports,
   - perioperative documentation,
   - occurrence screens,
   - patient questionnaires,
   - patient records,
   - personnel credentialing/inservice records, and
   - postoperative visit/call log.
2. Other sources for data collection are used. These may include, but are not limited to,
   - direct observation of and inquiries regarding staff and patient care activities, and
   - physical site inspections.
3. Individuals collecting data have appropriate skill levels for the task being monitored and have the information system—or access to an individual who does—for inputting data and formulating meaningful reports.
4. Methods of data collection are concurrent and retrospective. These methods may include, but are not limited to,
   - chart review,
   - departmental reporting forms,
   - focused review,
   - occurrence screening,
   - peer review,
   - interviews, and
   - questionnaires/surveys.
5. Personnel are provided adequate time to participate in data collection and entry.
6. Personnel are encouraged to report incidents, adverse events, and hazardous conditions without fear of punitive action or retribution.

Interpretive statement 2:
The frequency of data collection and the sample size are sufficient to accumulate the necessary data.

Criteria:
1. The frequency of data collection is determined by the type of care or activity being monitored. This may include, but is not limited to,
   - the number of patients affected,
   - the degree of risk involved,
   - the frequency of the event,
   - the significance of the event or activity being monitored, and
   - the extent to which the important aspect of care has been demonstrated to be problem free.
2. Data collection includes all sentinel events (eg, deaths, serious perioperative complications, near misses).
3. Data collection for performance measures is ongoing. A calendar of events is established to determine frequency of data collection for each indicator.
4. Sampling can be used to gather measurement data. Criteria such as volume, risk, and new procedure or provider can be used to determine an adequate sample size.[5]

Interpretive statement 3:
Data are organized, synthesized, and reported to allow for an accurate analysis of performance.

Criteria:
1. The quality of the data is evaluated to determine accuracy. This may be evaluated by answering questions such as the following.
   - Have all cases that were to be included in the study population been identified and reviewed?

- Have all required data fields on the data collection instrument been completed?
- Did the data gatherer(s) follow their explicit data collection instructions?
- If the data were entered into a computerized database, did the edit/validation checks confirm the accuracy of the data?
- If the data were obtained through electronic data transfer, did the edit/validation checks confirm the accuracy of the data?

2. Data collected over a period of time for each measure are aggregated for analysis purposes.
3. Aggregated measurement data are used to identify trends or patterns of performance that might not otherwise be evident in case-by-case review.
4. Statistical analysis techniques and comparative measurement data from outside sources are used to evaluate aggregated measurement data to identify significant undesirable variation from expected performance.

Standard VII

Evaluate care based on data collected.

Interpretive statement 1:
Analysis and evaluation of ongoing, collected data determines the need for action to improve the process(es).

Criteria:
1. Action is taken on adverse trends and patterns. The goal is for the care given to be congruent with perioperative nursing standards.
2. Analysis and evaluation of data collection is timely and provides efficacious opportunities for modifying actions/processes.

Interpretive statement 2:
Measurement data are compared with performance expectations.

Criteria:
1. Performance expectations are compared with actual performance to evaluate compliance with perioperative nursing standards of care and other important aspects of patient care and service.
2. Analysis of measurement data determines the need for more in-depth evaluation and/or initiation of an improvement project.

3. When performance consistently meets or exceeds expectations, the need for continued monitoring of that aspect of care/service is evaluated.
4. Evaluation of performance measurement data is timely.

Interpretive statement 3:
Initiate evaluation of important single events.

Criteria :
1. When an important single event occurs, a root cause analysis will be initiated in accordance with the organization's patient safety policies.
2. People knowledgeable about the systems and processes that affected the occurrence of the event are involved in the evaluation.
3. Evaluation of important single events are coordinated with other involved disciplines or departments.

Standard VIII

Take actions to improve care and services.

Interpretive statement 1:
Action plans/solutions are developed, supported, and approved at the appropriate levels and enacted to solve problems or improve care.

Criteria:
1. Identify the cause(s) of undesirable performance.
2. Corrective action plans are developed based on a thorough understanding of the process problems that are contributing to undesirable performance.
3. Actions are taken to correct defects in systems and/or processes. Actions may include revision of policies and procedures, staffing modifications, judicious use of equipment and supplies, and/or correction of communication or teamwork problems.
4. Relevant knowledge-based information is considered when developing action plans.
5. The plan of corrective action includes who or what is expected to change, individual(s) responsible for implementing the change, what action is needed to bring about the change, and when the change is expected to occur.

6. The action plan/solutions are forwarded to the body that has the authority to act, if the needed action exceeds the authority of the department. This may include, but is not limited to, the
   ♦ administration,
   ♦ board of trustees,
   ♦ chief of service,
   ♦ nursing/medical staff peer review committees,
   ♦ ethics committee, and
   ♦ OR committee.

Interpretive statement 2:
Actions for improvement are appropriate to the cause, scope, and severity of the problem.

Criteria:
1. Active reporting of errors and breaches in patient safety should be embraced without punitive action.
2. Whenever possible, corrective actions should be of a nonpunitive nature. They should be viewed as an opportunity for education and process improvement of the individual(s) involved, the department, and even the institution.
3. Punitive measures can be counterproductive to the goals of QI/PI and should only be used when appropriate (eg, blatant failure to follow policy resulting in injury and/or liability).
4. Actions are taken to correct knowledge deficits. Actions related to insufficient knowledge may require staff development, referral to other resources, and/or recommendations for continuing education.
5. Actions are taken to correct defects in the system. Actions related to systems may require revision of policies and procedures, staffing modifications, judicious use of equipment and supplies, a change in process, and/or correction of communication problems.
6. Actions are taken to correct deficient behavioral performances. Actions related to behavior or performance may require, but are not limited to,
   ♦ education and training;
   ♦ mentoring;
   ♦ counseling;
   ♦ increased supervision;
   ♦ peer review; and
   ♦ transfer, suspension, termination, or other disciplinary action.

Standard IX

Assess the effectiveness of action(s) and document outcomes.

Interpretive statement 1:
Actions are evaluated based on outcomes.

Criteria:
1. Actions delegated to individuals or disciplines for problem solving are monitored.
2. Effectiveness of actions is assessed through continuous monitoring of care. If an opportunity to improve care is identified and improvement does not occur, the action needs to be reevaluated.
3. A time line is established for reevaluation.
4. Further investigation of the cause of the problem and evaluation to identify the less obvious elements that contributed to the failure of the action plan must take place.

Interpretive statement 2:
Document the action plan and the method of communication.

Criteria:
1. A system is established to document the problem-solving process and the effectiveness in improving care or resolving the problem.
2. A system is established to document the results of the action plan, including trends and patterns that affect action.

Standard X

Communicate relevant information to the appropriate individuals, organization-wide, while maintaining confidentiality.

Interpretive statement 1:
The written organization-wide QI/PI plan identifies appropriate channels of communication.

Criteria:
1. Intradepartmental communication channels include, but are not limited to,
   ♦ minutes of departmental meetings,
   ♦ staff meetings, and
   ♦ summary reports.
2 Conclusions, recommendations, actions, and findings are communicated to

- departmental staff,
- appropriate medical staff committees,
- administration,
- interdisciplinary committees,
- organization-wide QI/PI committee,
- governing body, and
- accreditation and/or regulatory agencies as appropriate.

3. Confidentiality of QI/PI data is maintained. Maintenance of QI/PI data and all related communications shall comply with
   - federal Health Insurance Portability and Accountability Act (HIPAA) privacy and confidentiality regulations,
   - pertinent state regulations governing privacy and confidentiality of peer review and quality/ performance data, and
   - organizational privacy and confidentiality policies and procedures.

Interpretive statement 2:
Personnel are informed of the conclusions, recommendations, actions, and findings.

Criteria :
1. Regularly scheduled staff and/or departmental meetings include quality improvement/performance improvement reports and activities.
2. Identified opportunities to improve care are addressed through staff development offerings, deploying changes in process and practice to staff.

Interpretive statement 3:
Results of the organization-wide quality improvement/performance improvement monitoring activities provide the opportunity to improve care and may have applicability in other areas in the organization.

Criteria:
1. Medical staff, administration, and the governing body use outcomes to determine clinical privileges and credentialing decisions.
2. Departmental managers use outcomes to objectively monitor staff performance, develop short- and long-range plans, measure performance, and contain costs
3. Clinical practitioners use the outcomes of the QI/PI activities for self-assessment and peer review activities.

Models and Improvement Processes

The models and processes for performing QI/PI are numerous. More than one model can be used in an effective QI/PI program. No matter which method or model is used, the goal is to "Do the right thing, and do the right thing well."[3] AORN and the NPC are not endorsing any one model or any accrediting body. **Note:** More information is available in the *Notes* and *Resources* listed, or by using the Internet and searching under the terms *quality improvement* and *performance improvement.*

Glossary

Assessment: For purposes of performance improvement, the systematic collection and review of patient-specific data.

"For purposes of patient assessment, the process established by an organization for obtaining appropriate and necessary information about each individual seeking entry into a health care setting or service. The information is used to match an individual's need with the appropriate setting, care level, and intervention."[6]

Baseline: "A set of critical observations or data used for comparison or a control."[7]

Clinical practice guidelines: Systematically developed statements to assist practitioner and patient decisions about appropriate health care for specific clinical circumstances.

Concurrent: An activity that takes place in real time; care in progress.

Failure Mode and Effects Analysis (FMEA): A proactive approach to prevent or lessen the chances of a sentinel event from occurring, or reducing the risk/liability when an event occurs. This differs from root cause analysis, which is done after a sentinel event occurs and is a retrospective review of a process or processes. As with other QI/PI models, FMEA is an analysis technique drawn from non-medical industry. FMEA is an exercise that allows identification of the probabilities for "failure" at any point in the implementation of a process. In utilizing this technique, three questions must be answered:
- What are the steps of the process?
- Where is the process most likely to fail?
- How can we minimize the effects of these failures?

FMEA incorporates many of the same tools that are used in other QI/PI models. In determining the possible effects of potential failures, it is possible to quantify the likelihood, severity, and probability of detecting and preventing each failure. This allows providers to determine how critical each failure will be and give it a priority ranking. It allows one to avoid errors or failures before putting new processes in place.

JCAHO, in its leadership standards, addresses the requirements for the use of FMEA and root cause analysis by organizations seeking accreditation. These requirements are specific to the level of care provided by the organization.

Focused review: A formal review of one particular indicator, procedure, or practitioner over a specified time frame. It can be retrospective or concurrent.

Goal: The result that a department, service, or organization aims to accomplish. Also, a statement of attainment/achievement that is proposed to be accomplished or attained.[8]

Hazard analysis: The process of collecting and evaluating information on the circumstances leading to a higher risk for adverse outcomes. These circumstances or conditions are not related to the disease process or the condition for which the patient is being treated.

High risk: Patients at risk if the aspect of care is not provided correctly and in a timely manner. It may be that the patient themselves are at risk due to physical status, or it may be that the complexity and/or risk of complications related to the procedure puts the patient at risk.

High volume: The procedures or treatments that occur frequently, on a regular basis, or affect a large patient population.

Important aspects of care: Clinical or service-related activities that involve a high volume of patients, entail a high degree of risk for patients, or tend to produce problems for staff or patients. Such activities are deemed most important for purposes of monitoring and evaluation.[8]

Indicator: Well-defined, measurable, objective statement related to the structure, process, or outcomes of care; direct attention to problems or opportunities to improve care.[8]

Methodology: The strategies, models, or steps for gathering and analyzing the data in the quality improvement/performance improvement process.

Near miss: "Any process variation that did not affect the outcome, but for which a recurrence carries a significant chance of a serious adverse outcome. Such a near miss falls within the scope of the definition of a sentinel event, but outside the scope of those sentinel events that are subject to review by the Joint Commission under its Sentinel Event Policy."[6]

Nursing process: A systematic approach to nursing practice utilizing problem-solving techniques, including the components of assessment, planning, implementation, and evaluation.

Occurrence screens: Data that are used to identify individual variations in care, which are reviewed and confirmed by peer review and entered into a database to identify trends and/or patterns.[8]

Outcome identification: The intended, or realistically expected, correction of the patient's problem by a certain point in time.

Peer review: The examination and evaluation by associates of a practitioner's clinical practice. Individuals are evaluated by recognized, established standards. Physicians review physicians, registered nurses review registered nurse, etc.

Performance expectation: The desired condition or target level for each performance measure.

Performance measure: A quantitative tool (eg, rate, ratio, index, percentage) that provides an indication of an organization's performance in relation to a specified process or outcome. (See also *process measure* and *outcome measure.*)[6]

Population: The entire set of individuals sharing some common characteristics (eg, all patients with a particular disease, undergoing the same procedure, or of the same demographics).

Problem-prone: Those processes or steps that commonly generate incidents or barriers for patients and/or staff.

Process: A goal-directed, interrelated series of actions, events, mechanisms, or steps. An interrelated series of events, activities, actions, mechanisms, or steps that transform inputs into outputs.[6]

Retrospective: A review that begins with a current manifestation and links this effect to some occurrence in the past; post-discharge or post-procedure; not concurrent.

Root cause analysis: "A process for identifying the basic or causal factors that underlie variation in performance, including the occurrence or possible occurrence of a sentinel event. A root cause analysis focuses primarily on systems and processes, not individual performance. It progresses from special causes in clinical processes to common causes in organizational processes and identifies potential improvements in processes or systems that would tend to decrease the likelihood of such events in the future, or determines, after analysis that no such improvement opportunities exist."[9]

Sentinel event: "An unexpected occurrence involving death or serious physical or psychological injury, or the risk thereof. Serious injury specifically includes loss of limb or function. The phrase 'or the risk thereof' includes any process variation for which a recurrence would carry a significant chance of a serious adverse outcome. Such events are called 'sentinel' because they signal the need for immediate investigation and response."[9]

Standard: "A statement that defines the performance expectations, structures, or processes that must be substantially in place in an organization to enhance the quality of care."[6]

Structure: Organizational characteristics, fiscal resources, and management qualifications of health professionals; physical facilities and equipment; environment where care takes place.[10]

REFERENCES

1. T Bornstein, "Quality improvement and performance improvement: Different means to the same end?" *QA Brief* 9 (Spring 2001) http://www.qaproject.org/pdf/engv9n1.pdf (accessed 5 March 2003).

2. Institute of Medicine, *To Err is Human: Building a Safer Health System* (Washington, DC: National Academy Press, 2000) 114.

3. Joint Commission on Accreditation of Healthcare Organizations, "Improving organization performance," in *Hospital Accreditation Standards* (Oakbrook Terrace, Ill: Joint Commission on Accreditation of Healthcare Organizations, 2002) 161, 163.

4. Joint Commission on Accreditation of Healthcare Organizations, "Management of human resources," in *Hospital Accreditation Standards* (Oakbrook Terrace, Ill: Joint Commission on Accreditation of Healthcare Organizations, 2002) 234.

5. Joint Commission on Accreditation of Healthcare Organizations, "Management of information," in *Hospital Accreditation Standards* (Oakbrook Terrace, Ill: Joint Commission on Accreditation of Healthcare Organizations, 2002) 254.

6. Joint Commission on Accreditation of Healthcare Organizations, "Glossary," in *Hospital Accreditation Standards* (Oakbrook Terrace, Ill: Joint Commission on Accreditation of Healthcare Organizations, 2002) 331, 346, 351, 354, 360.

7. *Merriam-Webster's Collegiate Dictionary,* 10th ed (Springfield, Mass: Merriam-Webster, Inc., 1993) 95.

8. L A Kepler, E A Stuart, J Kiefel, "Ten-step template," *QRC Advisor* 6 (April 1990) 1-3.

9. Joint Commission on Accreditation of Healthcare Organizations, "Sentinel events," in *Hospital Accreditation Standards* (Oakbrook Terrace, Ill: Joint Commission on Accreditation of Healthcare Organizations, 2002) 51, 52.

10. Joint Commission on Accreditation of Healthcare Organizations, "Official accreditation policies and procedures," in *Hospital Accreditation Standards* (Oakbrook Terrace, Ill: Joint Commission on Accreditation of Healthcare Organizations, 2002) 48-49.

RESOURCES

AORN, Inc. *Standards, Recommended Practices, and Guidelines.* Denver: AORN, Inc. Annual edition.

Joint Commission Resources. *Failure Mode and Effects Analysis in Health Care: Proactive Risk Reduction.* Oakbrook Terrace, Ill: Joint Commission on Accreditation of Healthcare Organizations, 2002.

Joint Commission Resources. *A Guide to Performance Measurement for Hospitals.* Oakbrook Terrace, Ill: Joint Commission on Accreditation of Healthcare Organization, 2000.

Joint Commission Resources. *A Pocket Guide to Using Performance Improvement Tools.* Oakbrook Terrace, Ill: Joint Commission on Accreditation of Healthcare Organization, 1996.

Joint Commission Resources. *Tools for Performance Measurement in Health Care: A Quick Reference Guide.* Oakbrook Terrace, Ill: Joint Commission on Accreditation of Healthcare Organization, 2002.

Organizational Dynamics. *Quality Action Teams: Team Members' Workbook.* Burlington, Mass: Organizational Dynamics, 1987.

Schroeder, P, ed. *Journal of Nursing Care Quality* Published quarterly by Lippincott Williams & Wilkins, Philadelphia.

Shewhart, W A; Deming, W E. *Statistical Method from the Viewpoint of Quality Control.* New York: Dover Publications, 1986.

Spath, P L. *Fundamentals of Health Care Quality Management.* Forest Grove, Ore: Brown-Spath & Associates, 2000.

Originally published as "Quality improvement standards for perioperative nursing" in the 1992 Standards and Recommended Practices for Perioperative Nursing.

Revised; approved by the AORN Board of Directors in June 2003.

AORN Guidelines and Guidance Statements

AORN Guideline: Human and Avian Influenza and Severe Acute Respiratory Syndrome

I. Overview

A. Introduction

Assumptions

The AORN guideline on human and avian influenza and severe acute respiratory syndrome (SARS) is based on research and the experience of health care workers. It is assumed that ongoing research will result in new knowledge, procedures, and medical and nursing interventions for the treatment of patients with human and avian influenza and SARS. This guideline is designed to assist perioperative registered nurses in creating and maintaining an optimal health care environment for patients with human and avian influenza and SARS. The guideline defines the unique physical and psychosocial needs of the influenza and SARS patient populations and presents guidance for establishing a plan of care for these patients.

B. Human and Avian Influenza

During the 20th century, influenza took an enormous toll on human life. More than four pandemics occurred.

- The 1918–1919 pandemic (ie, the "Spanish flu") caused an estimated 20 to 50 million deaths worldwide. In the United States alone, there were 500,000 deaths.
- The "Asian flu" caused 60,000 deaths in the United States in 1957–1958.
- The "Hong Kong flu" pandemic of 1968–1969 caused approximately 40,000 deaths in the United States.
- The pandemic of 1977 (ie, the "Russian flu") had low mortality.[1-3]

During the last decade of the 20th century, while there were no influenza pandemics, influenza-related deaths increased to 36,000 per year in the United States. During periods of epidemics, this number increased to 40,000. Influenza continues to be the sixth leading cause of death in the United States. For those over the age of 65, it is the fifth leading cause of death.[4]

Looking at the first five years of the 21st century, it is clear that the incidence of human influenza is not declining. The emergence of avian influenza as a potential threat to humans has become significant, making the threat of a future pandemic from avian influenza very real.[1]

Definitions

For the purposes of this document, the following definitions apply.

Antigenic drift: Point mutations leading to changes in antigenicity of the major hemagglutinin (HA) and neuraminidase (NA) antigen subtypes of an influenza virus.[5]

Antigenic shift: Change in circulating major antigen (ie, HA, NA) determinants either through exchange and reassortment of genetic material or adaptation to human transmission.[5] Occasionally, the antigenic shift that occurs with the influenza A virus is an abrupt, major change in the virus.[6]

Hemagglutinin: One of the two major surface proteins of the influenza virus. Important for virus attachment to cells of the respiratory epithelium. Subtypes include H1 to H15. The only described determinants involved in sustained human-to-human transmission are H1, H2, and H3.[2]

Influenza epidemic: A seasonal outbreak of influenza viruses that are already in existence among humans.[2]

Influenza pandemic: A global outbreak of disease that occurs when a new influenza A virus emerges in the human population, causes serious illness, and then spreads easily from person to person worldwide. Influenza pandemics are caused by a new subtype or by subtypes that have never circulated among humans or that have not circulated among humans for a long period of time.[2]

Neuraminidase: One of the two major surface proteins of the influenza virus that are less important for attachment but probably are important for propagation and virulence (ie, subtypes N1 to N9).[5]

History

Hippocrates (470 BC to 410 BC) described the first case of influenza-like illness.[1] The first recorded influenza pandemic occurred in 1580 AD and spread from Europe to Asia and Africa. During the 17th century, local epidemics were reported. In the 18th century, three known pandemics occurred, in 1729–1730, 1732–1733, and 1781–1782. In the 19th century, three pandemics occurred, in 1830–1831, 1833–1834, and 1889–1890. The pandemic of 1889–1890, known as the Russian flu, killed approximately one million people. It spread throughout Europe, reaching North America in December 1889 and spreading to Latin America and Asia in 1890.[3]

The most devastating influenza pandemic in recent history (ie, the "Spanish flu") occurred in the 20th century. Worldwide, the death toll was between 20 million and 50 million people, and may have been up to 100 million globally. In the United States, the mortality rate was more than 500,000 people. The Spanish flu was caused by the influenza A (H1N1) strain. It most likely originated in the United States and spread to Europe. The Asian flu of 1957–1958 was caused by the influenza A (H2N2) strain and had a mortality rate of approximately one million people worldwide. The virus was first identified in China. In 1968–1969, the Hong Kong flu, which was caused by the influenza A (H3N2) strain, had an estimated mortality rate in the United States of 40,000. Unlike seasonal influenza, epidemics are particularly hard on people over the age of 65. At least initially, all three of these pandemics were characterized by a shift in age distribution of deaths to the younger population younger than age 65.[3]

The influenza A strain (ie, the Russian flu) appeared in 1977. Isolated in northern China, this virus was similar to the virus that spread before 1957. Consequently, people born before 1957 generally were protected. Children and young adults born after 1957, however, were not protected because they had no prior immunity.[7]

During the 1990s and into the 2000s, avian influenza A strains H5N1 (ie, Hong Kong, China, Thailand, Vietnam), H7N2 (ie, Virginia, New York), H7N3 (ie, Canada), H7N7 (ie, Netherlands), and H9N2 (ie, China, Hong Kong) appeared, causing epidemics in the international poultry industry. With the appearance of these strains came human exposure to avian virus. Of these strains, H5N1 caused 31 deaths and H7N7 caused one death. These outbreaks demonstrated that bird-to-human transmission does occur. In the Netherlands, there were three possible H7N2 transmissions from poultry workers to family members.

Population Affected

Prevalence

In the United States, the influenza season runs from autumn to spring, with peak activity occurring from December to early March.[7] Five percent to 20% of the population contracts influenza every year in the United States. Of the population that contracts influenza, more than 200,000 are hospitalized from influenza complications and of these, approximately 36,000 die from influenza each year.[9] Although any person can contract this disease, some people have a higher risk of contracting influenza. This group includes those age 65 and older, children age six months to 23 months, pregnant women, and persons of any age with certain chronic medical conditions. Persons age 50–64 years also are targeted because they have an elevated prevalence of certain chronic medical conditions. Another high-risk group is those who live with or care for persons at high risk.[10]

The high-risk population described above is always at risk, particularly for the influenza A viruses that currently are circulating. History has shown that there have been influenza pandemics that were devastating to the younger population, as seen with the pandemic of 1918–1919.

Socioeconomic factors

The socioeconomic impact of influenza, whether epidemic or pandemic in nature, can be substantial. Lost productivity as a result of missed work days caused by illness or caring for a sick loved one, the cost of hospitalization, and the impact of deaths related to the disease can be devastating to the community, and indeed to the nation. In one research study, it was estimated that an influenza pandemic in the United could result in an "estimated 89,000 to 207,000 deaths; 314,000 to 734,000 hospitalizations; 18 to 42 million outpatient visits; and 20 to 47 million additional illnesses." The estimated economic impact would be $71.3 to $166.[5] billion, excluding disruptions to commerce and society.[11] Clearly, preventing influenza through vaccination will reduce the incidence of the disease and its potential health effects, as well as reducing mortality, health care costs, and societal economic impact.

Epidemiology

Influenza is caused by a virus that belongs to the family of orthomyxoviridae and is classified as type A, B, or C. The key difference among type A, B, and C influenza viruses is their host range.[1]

Type A influenza viruses are the most predominate and have been isolated from humans, pigs, horses, seals, ferrets, mink, and whales. These viruses can be divided into subtypes based on their surface glycoproteins, HA, and NA.

Subtypes of HA, designated as H1 through H15, are the crucial components of influenza vaccines. "Hemagglutinin facilitates entry of viruses into host cells through its attachment to sialic acid on epithelial cell receptors, promotes membrane fusion, and elicits protective neutralizing antibody response." Hemagglutinin 1 through 3 are found in humans. Hemagglutinin 1 through 15 are found in birds.[1]

Subtypes of NA, designated as N1 through N9, are a target for antiviral agents. "Neuraminidase has enzyme activity, which cleaves sialic acid on virion proteins, facilitating the release of progeny virions from infected cells." Neuraminidase 1 through 2 are found in humans. Neuraminidase 1 through 9 are found in birds. Currently, 15 HA and nine NA glycoproteins have been identified.[1]

Many combinations of HA and NA are possible. Currently, influenza A subtypes H1N1 and H3N2 are circulating worldwide. In 2001, influenza A (H1N2) emerged after genetic reassortment between human A (H1N1) and A (H3N2).[12]

Influenza B viruses usually are found in humans, but have been isolated from seals and pigs.[1] These viruses do not cause pandemics, although they can cause epidemics. The influenza B viruses are not classified according to subtypes. Influenza C viruses cause mild illness in humans and do not cause epidemics or pandemics. Like B viruses, influenza C viruses are not classified according to subtypes.[6]

Another characteristic of influenza B viruses and subtypes of the influenza A virus is their ability to produce new strains. Through the process of antigenic drift, new strains of influenza viruses appear and replace older strains. Antigenic drift is the reason why a person is susceptible to seasonal outbreaks of influenza. "When a new strain of human influenza virus emerges, antibody protection that may have developed after infection or vaccination with an older strain may not provide protection against the strain. Thus, the influenza vaccine is updated on a yearly basis to keep up with the changes in influenza viruses."[6]

Occasionally, the antigenic shift that occurs with the influenza A virus is an abrupt, major change in the virus. When this occurs, the virus has a HA protein or HA and NA protein combination that has not been seen in humans for many years. This leads to a new influenza A subtype for which most people have little or no immunity. If the virus is transmitted human-to-human easily, the result may be a pandemic outbreak of influenza.[6]

Transmission of human influenza (ie, A, B, C) primarily is via virus-laden droplets that are expelled when an infected person coughs or sneezes. When a susceptible person is near by (eg, within three feet) the droplets are deposited onto the mucosal surfaces of the person's upper respiratory tract (ie, close contact). Another mode of transmission may occur from direct or indirect contact with respiratory secretions of an infected person. At this time, studies have not demonstrated transmission of human influenza via contact with environmental surfaces.[13]

Avian influenza, also known as bird flu, is caused by viruses that occur naturally among birds. These viruses, which are seen worldwide, live in the gastrointestinal tract of wild birds. The viruses usually do not cause illness in wild birds, but when transmitted to domestic flocks, particularly poultry (eg, chickens, ducks, turkeys), it can be devastating. All subtypes of the influenza A viruses can be found in birds.[14] Outbreaks of highly pathogenic avian influenza viruses have occurred recently; however, most avian strains are of low pathogenicity.[15] Avian influenza usually does not affect humans. Since 1997, however, several cases of human infection with avian influenza viruses have occurred.[14] Avian viruses cross over to humans by direct contact from infected birds, contaminated surfaces, or through an intermediate host such as a pig.[16]

Adaptation of the avian influenza virus occurs via mutation of the avian virus genome or genetic reassortment, which is the mixing of segments from a virus already adapted to humans.[1] As an example, if a pig is infected simultaneously with a human influenza A virus and an avian influenza virus, the potential for reassortment exists, which could result in a new virus. This virus would have most of the genes from the human virus, and HA protein and/or NA protein from the avian virus, creating a virus with surface glycoproteins not previously seen in humans. The new virus may then infect humans and can spread from person to person.[16]

Human reassortment also is possible. In this case, the human host would be infected with a human influenza strain and an avian influenza strain. If this were to happen, the reassortment would create a virus with HA from the avian virus and genes from the human virus, again resulting in a virus to which humans have little or no immunity. Consequences of this type of reassortment, in theory, could be sustained human-to-human trans-mission leading to an influenza pandemic.[16]

The 1918, 1957, and 1968 pandemics of the 20th century were caused by a novel type of influenza A virus of avian origin. Mutation of the genes of what was originally pure avian virus is the suspected cause of the catastrophic 1918 pandemic. In the 1957 and 1968 pandemics, the viruses involved "had components of previous human viruses as well as avian viruses."[15]

Clinical Signs and Symptoms of Influenza
When exposed, the average incubation period for influenza is two days, but it can range from one to four days. "Adults can be infectious from the day before symptoms begin through approximately five days after illness onset. Children can be infectious for more than 10 days, and young children can shed virus for several days before the onset of their illness. Severely immunocompromised persons can shed virus for weeks or months." Signs and symptoms for an uncomplicated illness include fever, myalgia, headache, malaise, nonproductive cough, sore throat, and rhinitis. Otitis media, nausea, and vomiting are commonly reported in children.[10]

For people with underlying medical conditions, such as pulmonary or cardiac disease, influenza can lead to "secondary bacterial pneumonia or primary viral influenza, or occur as part of a coinfection with other viral or bacteria pathogens." Young children can have initial symptoms mimicking bacterial sepsis with high fevers. More than 20% of children hospitalized with influenza can have febrile seizures. "Influenza ... has also been associated with encephalopathy, transverse myelitis, Reye syndrome, myositis, mycocarditis, and pericarditis."[10]

Clinical signs and symptoms for human influenza are consistently predictable. With the recent outbreak of avian influenza A (H5N1 strain) in Vietnam during 2004 that affected 10 people and the outbreak in Hong Kong during 1997 that affected 18 people, however, differences in patient response became evident. Nine of the people in Vietnam had direct contact with infected chickens. None of these patients had preexisting conditions. Their ages ranged from five to 24, with the median age being 13.7 years. After exposure, the median time of incubation was three days. The range of incubation was two to four days. Similar to human influenza, the patients presented with fever and

cough. They also had diarrhea, pronounced lym-popenia, and radiographic abnormalities. The mortality rate was significant, with eight patients dying after 10 days. These patients experienced liver dysfunction, renal failure, coagulopathy, and pancytopenia. The 1997 Hong Kong outbreak had the same clinical signs and symptoms as the Vietnam outbreak. Additionally, rhabdomyolysis was seen in this patient population. Of the 18 people infected, six died; all were healthy young adults.[1] Although a localized incident, this outbreak nevertheless demonstrates that if human-to-human transmission was efficient, the result could have been a devastating pandemic, particularly for the young, which was also the case for the pandemic of 1918.

Developing a Program
Health care facilities should have a plan for handling influenza epidemics, as well as for future pandemics that many health care planners believe are inevitable.

Operational planning
Impact of influenza on the health care workplace
Unvaccinated health care workers can be a primary cause of influenza outbreaks in health care settings. Throughout the influenza season, health care workers encounter high-risk patients in medical practices, hospitals, home-care sites, long-term care and rehabilitation facilities, and other health care settings.[17] In addition to spreading influenza to patients, health care workers who contract influenza will be unable to provide the necessary care to their patients.

The National Foundation for Infectious Diseases reports that 23% of the staff members in an internal medicine ward became ill with influenza, resulting in 14 person-days of sick leave, postponement of eight scheduled admissions, and suspension of emergency admissions for 11 days. The average additional cost per patient was $3,798. The total cost of the outbreak was $34,179.[17]

When an influenza outbreak occurs in a health care setting, peers often have to work extended shifts. Extended shifts increase overtime costs, and studies show that attention lags after about 12 hours. In many cases, pool or temporary workers must replace health care workers who do not report to work due to illness. Additionally, regular staff members are less prone to patient-care errors than pool or temporary workers such as agency.[17]

Risk to the health care worker
An unvaccinated health care worker is an at-risk health care worker. This, of course, assumes that vaccination effectively protects against the current circulating strain of influenza causing the outbreak. If a strain of influenza rapidly appears in which effective vaccination has not been developed, or health care workers have not developed immunity from previous exposure to the circulating virus, health care workers will be at significant risk because of exposure to patients, family members, and those in the general population who have the disease.

Vaccination

Vaccination is the key to preventing influenza and its severe complications. It reduces "influenza-related respiratory illness and physician visits among all age groups, hospitalization and death among persons at high risk, otitis media among children, and work absenteeism among adults." The Advisory Committee on Immunization Practices of the Centers for Disease Control and Prevention (CDC) recommends annual vaccination for the following groups of people:

- adults 65 years of age and older;
- residents of nursing homes and other chronic-care facilities;
- adults and children with chronic pulmonary or cardiovascular disorders;
- adults and children who have required regular medical follow-up or hospitalization during the preceding year because of chronic metabolic diseases, renal dysfunction, hemoglobinopathies, or immunosuppression;
- adults and children who have conditions that can compromise respiratory function or the handling of respiratory secretions or that can increase the risk for aspiration (eg, cognitive dysfunction, spinal cord injuries, seizure disorders, other neuromuscular disorders);
- pregnant women;
- persons with chronic medical conditions;
- adults aged 50 to 64 years because of elevated prevalence of certain chronic medical conditions;
- children and adolescents aged six months to18 years receiving long-term aspirin therapy who might be at risk for Reye syndrome after influenza infections;

- children aged six to 23 months; and
- persons who live with or care for persons at high risk, to include health care workers.[10]

Vaccination of health care workers is crucial, and all health care workers should be vaccinated against influenza. Mandatory vaccination "will protect health care workers, their patients, and communities, and will improve prevention of influenza-associated disease, patient safety, and will reduce disease burden."[10] According to the National Foundation for Infectious Diseases, 36% of health care workers receive influenza vaccinations each year. The 64% who do not get vaccinated consequently contribute to institutional outbreaks that put high-risk patients at increased risk of contracting influenza and suffering from its potentially major complications.[17]

Although vaccination is crucial in preventing influenza, there are those who should not be vaccinated. This group includes those who have

- a severe allergy to chicken eggs,
- had a severe reaction to an influenza vaccination in the past,
- developed Guillain-Barré syndrome within six weeks of getting an influenza vaccine previously, and
- children less than six months of age.

Vaccination also should be withheld from people who have a moderate or severe illness with fever. The vaccination can be administered when symptoms have lessened.[12]

Personal protective equipment and behaviors

Patients with human influenza
The primary method of transmission of human influenza is via large respiratory droplets. Consequently, standard precautions plus droplet precautions are recommended for the care of patients infected with human influenza.[18] Droplet precautions include patient placement, mask protocol, and patient transport.[19]

A patient infected with human influenza should be placed in a private room. If a private room is not available, the patient should be placed in a room with another patient who is infected with the same microorganism but not with another infection. If this is not possible, spatial separation of a least three feet should be made between infected patients and other patients and visitors.[19]

Staff members and visitors should wear masks according to protocols for droplet precautions.

Additionally, the mask should be worn when anyone is within three feet of the patient. Transporting the patient infected with human influenza should be limited and should be only for essential purposes. If transport becomes necessary, the patient should wear a mask to help minimize dispersal of respiratory droplets.[19]

Patients with avian influenza

Recent outbreaks of avian influenza in humans indicate that the risk of serious disease and increased mortality may be significantly higher than infection by human influenza viruses. Although rare, when a human is infected with avian influenza, viral adaptation can occur, which may result in easier human-to-human transmission. This in turn can possibly lead to the emergence of a pandemic strain.[18]

Avian influenza presents additional challenges to health care workers because of the uncertainty about the exact modes of transmission of avian influenza to and between humans. Additional precautions for health care workers involved in the care of patients with documented or suspected avian influenza should be implemented.[18]

Recommendations for avian influenza

Patients arriving at a health care facility with fever and respiratory symptoms should be managed according to CDC guidelines for respiratory hygiene and cough etiquette. They also should be questioned about their recent travel history. If a patient has traveled within the past 10 days to a country with avian influenza activity and is hospitalized with a severe febrile respiratory illness or is under evaluation for avian influenza, the patient should be managed using the following isolation precautions:

- ◆ standard precautions with careful attention to hand washing before and after patient contact or contact with surfaces potentially contaminated with respiratory secretions;
- ◆ eye protection within three feet of the patient;[20]
- ◆ droplet precautions and contact precautions to include patient placement, and patient transport.[20]

Should there be a suspicion of SARS, manage the patient with airborne precautions (N95 mask protocol (ie, fit tested) as well as contact precautions.[20]

Physical plant considerations

Visual alerts should be posted at facility entrances instructing patients and persons who accompany them to practice respiratory hygiene and cough etiquette (containing respiratory secretions by covering nose/mouth) if they have symptoms of a respiratory infection when they first register at the facility.[20]

During an influenza outbreak, it is best practice to provide infected patients with private rooms. If this is not possible, then semiprivate rooms should be made available. If multiple patients are admitted, and space requirements are limited, then patient care areas should be of sufficient size to maintain a distance of at least three feet between patients.[18]

Integrated services and multidisciplinary participation

Successful containment of the influenza virus requires a multidisciplinary approach. All personnel directly or indirectly involved in patient care must understand protocols for containment. All personnel should implement standard precautions and droplet precautions, and should enforce respiratory hygiene and cough etiquette for infected patients. A coordinated effort must be made to ensure that adequate procedures are in place for the disinfection of environmental surfaces, beds, bedrails, bedside equipment, and other frequently touched surfaces. Linen should be considered infectious and handled in a manner that prevents skin and mucous membrane exposures, as well as contamination of clothing.

Health care provider education and competency

Health care provider education and competency should be mandatory for all facility employees and physicians. Educational activities should include information concerning etiology of human and avian influenza, importance of vaccination, standard precautions, respiratory hygiene and cough etiquette, masking, and droplet precautions. Additionally, health care providers should be able to demonstrate behaviors that are required to successfully implement standard precautions, respiratory hygiene and cough etiquette, masking, droplet precautions, and using fit-tested respirators if SARS is suspected.

C. Severe Acute Respiratory Syndrome

During the 21st century, SARS became a global threat after making its debut in November 2002. By February 2003, the illness had spread to more than 12 countries, including Asia, North America, Europe, and South America. According to the World Health Organization (WHO), a total of 8,098 people worldwide became ill with SARS during the 2003 outbreak. Of the 8,098, 774 died. In the United States, only eight people, all of whom had traveled to global sections of world where SARS had been identified, had laboratory evidence of SARS.[21]

History

Severe acute respiratory syndrome may have originated in Guangdong Province in southern China in November 2002. A Chinese physician carried SARS to a Hong Kong hotel where several hotel guests on the same floor as the physician contracted the disease in February 2003. Airline passengers who had SARS and were traveling from Hong Kong spread the disease to Singapore, Toronto, and Hanoi. In March 2003, a diagnosis of SARS was made on the Chinese physician in Hong Kong.[22] A physician from the Hanoi, Vietnam, office of the WHO was called to investigate a patient with an atypical pneumonia from a Hanoi hospital.[23] Additional WHO officials and the CDC were called in. A global alert was issued for SARS, and infectious disease experts started studying this new infectious respiratory disease.[22]

Population Affected
Prevalence

SARS was recognized as a global threat when it spread to nearly 30 countries in Asia, North America, and Europe.[22] The first pandemic of the 21st century is attributed to SARS.[24] Transmission has occurred most often from person to person via droplet spread when an infected person coughs or sneezes. Most of the SARS outbreaks involved health care workers who were in close contact with infected patients. The 2003 global outbreak was contained, but there is still a possibility of recurrence.

Socioeconomic factors

In 2003, the SARS epidemic resulted in more than 800 deaths and other sequela. Some airports had no passengers, and stock markets lost value.[25] The SARS epidemic spread to more than 30 countries in a short time. The disease created anxiety around the world because of its capacity to spread quickly via international air travel, communicability, novelty, and the fact that a large number of health care workers were becoming infected. Nurses in Canada working with SARS patients were concerned about working conditions, staffing, employee health and safety, and wages.[26]

Epidemiology

The scientific community accepts the coronavirus (CoV) as the cause of SARS.[27,28] To stop the spread of SARS, there must be early diagnosis by virus isolation or serological testing.[29] The coronaviruses are a viral group that, when viewed under a microscope, appear to have a halo or crown-like (ie, corona) structure. These viruses commonly cause mild to moderate upper respiratory illness in humans. In animals, they are linked with respiratory, gastrointestinal, liver, and neurological disease.[30] The SARS-CoV has been found in wild civets and raccoon dogs in southeastern China, where they are considered culinary delicacies; on the other hand, domestic pigs and poultry are not hosts. Asymptomatic humans have a lag time during the incubation period; therefore, because they are still healthy, they are able to travel by air to any destination after being exposed. After the individual becomes symptomatic, SARS is most likely spread through person-to-person transmission. Health care workers are at high risk if there has been no suspicion of SARS but patients are positive for SARS.

Clinical Signs and Symptoms of SARS

Symptoms of SARS include, but are not limited to,

- fever (ie, greater than 100.4° F [38.0° C]);
- cough, shortness of breath, and dyspnea;
- headache;
- general malaise; and/or
- diarrhea (affects only a small percent of patients).[22,30]

Some of the above symptoms, and the patients' chest x-rays, initially led physicians to diagnose the disease as an atypical pneumonia.[30] Patients develop progressive respiratory compromise quickly. Symptoms usually occur in 2 to 7 days; sometimes 10 days after infection. Supportive treatment consists of antibiotics, steroids, and treatment of individual patient symptoms.[22]

Developing a Program

Health care facilities should have a written preparedness and response plan that is flexible and scalable and designed to address the variable nature of a SARS outbreak.

Operational planning

Impact of SARS on the workplace

A SARS coordinator should be appointed to serve as the point person for communicating information both internally and externally.[31] Testing the facility's response via a tabletop exercise is effective.

Staffing needs must be evaluated by health care facilities. Designated teams should be created in advance for the care of SARS patients to provide emergency and routine care. Infection control education also should be provided to these teams in advance to foster preparedness.[31] If there is a more extensive outbreak, nursing staff members may need to be relocated to other areas. Issues may occur that will exceed the scope of the health care facility. These must be addressed at community, regional, and national levels.

Psychology

During a SARS outbreak, it may be exhausting to wear full personal protective equipment (PPE) for lengthy periods of time. The focus required for donning and removing equipment also may be laborious. The health care facility should make arrangements to provide mental health professionals to assist its staff in coping with a SARS outbreak and the related stressors.[31] In 2003, the Toronto nurses and other health care workers were placed under work quarantine and required to wear a mask at all times in the presence of others. They were not allowed any physical contact with their family members. Stress and tension levels were high. Nurses mourned the loss of colleagues and worried about the effect of SARS on their families and what was yet to come.[26] SARS and other emerging infectious diseases may create a new type of workplace.

All health care workers must wear full PPE when caring for patients with SARS or suspected of having SARS. This includes eyewear, gown, gloves, and an N95 mask.

Personnel Protective Behavior: Recommendations for SARS

A comprehensive infection control program should be in place in the health care facility. Primary infection control strategies include the following.

Standard precautions—Health care workers should wear eye protection in addition to using routine standard precautions when caring for patients.[32]

Transmission-based precautions—The second tier of precautions are transmission-based precautions, which include

- ◆ *contact precautions*—health care workers should wear gowns, gloves, and eyewear when caring for patients in their environment;[32,33] and
- ◆ *airborne precautions*—health care workers should wear an N95-filtering disposable respirator during patient care. The facility should have training, fit-testing, and fit-checking in place as part of a complete respiratory program, which is required by the Occupational Safety and Health Administration.[34] Furthermore, the patient should be assigned to an isolation room with negative air pressure.[32]

Physical plant considerations

Key infection control measures for inpatient care areas include the following.

- ◆ Use negative pressure isolation rooms.
- ◆ Use private rooms with separate bathrooms if airborne precautions cannot be fully implemented. Keep doors closed.
- ◆ Assign patients with SARS or suspected of having SARS to the same unit. Keep equipment on that unit dedicated for their care.
- ◆ Use disposable equipment for patient care if available.
- ◆ Organize patient care activities. Keep only essential equipment, items, and supplies in rooms with patients who have SARS.
- ◆ Minimize patient movement or transport.
- ◆ Reduce traffic. Restrict visitors to the health care facility, patient care unit, and patient. Only essential health care workers should have access to patient rooms.[22]

If possible postpone surgery on patients with infectious diseases; if a patient who has SARS is in urgent need of a surgical procedure, the perioperative team must be prepared to follow precautions. Key infection control measures for the OR include the following.

- ◆ Schedule the procedure at the end of the day when other patients are not present and only a minimum number of staff members are present.[32]
- ◆ Place a surgical mask on the patient before transport to the OR.[33]

♦ Ensure that contact precautions are maintained during patient transport.

♦ Handle specimens from patients carefully. Place specimen in a leak-proof container and clean the exterior surface of the container with a chemical germicide when transferred off the surgical field.[34] Ensure that all specimen containers are labeled properly and identified as infectious material. Place the container in a biohazard bag for transport to the laboratory.

♦ Minimize the number of staff members in the OR involved in the care of the patients with SARS. Arrange for additional staff members to assist by stationing them outside the room to get needed supplies and equipment.

♦ Place isolation signage on the doors to the OR indicating that transmission-based precautions should be used.

♦ Remove unnecessary equipment from the OR. Keep supply cabinet doors closed.

♦ Request that the anesthesia care team use a smaller anesthesia cart designated for isolation patients and use single-use items if possible.

♦ Confine and contain contamination during the procedure within the immediate vicinity of the surgical field when possible.[33]

♦ Reestablish a safe and clean environment when a surgical procedure is completed on a patient who has SARS.[35]

♦ Ensure that health care workers wear full PPE as required for contact and airborne precautions to reduce the risk of exposure to bloodborne or infectious microorganisms throughout the surgical procedure, cleaning, and recovery period.

♦ Carefully handle surgical instruments, equipment, furniture, and soiled linen and trash. Clean the patient transport vehicle. Use an Environmental Protection Agency (EPA)-registered hospital disinfectant for cleaning. Discard unused disposable supplies after completion of the surgical intervention.[22]

♦ Environmental services personnel should be trained and supervised in proper cleaning and disinfection methods.

Integrated services and multidisciplinary participation

An optimum level of communication between the facility's infection control team, clinical staff members, and public health authorities should be ongoing.[22]

Nursing staff members in the facility's emergency department and clinics must be prepared to identify patients who are suspected of having SARS and know how to manage an influx of patients.[37] The infection control team should be involved with nursing staff members to provide guidance and direction in coordinating the hospital experience of patients who have SARS.

Health care facility administrators should take a proactive and multidisciplinary approach by conducting a disaster drill involving an influx of patients who have SARS to operationalize their policies and protocols, assess readiness, and evaluate plan effectiveness.[38] A coordinated multidisciplinary response is required to manage a SARS outbreak.[31] Clinical services may include, but are not limited to,

♦ emergency department (eg, entry screening and triage, isolating patients suspected of having SARS as soon as possible);

♦ engineering (eg, air handling system, maintenance of negative pressure isolation rooms);

♦ environmental services.

♦ human resources personnel;

♦ infection control team, which includes infection control practitioners and hospital epidemiologist;

♦ intensive care unit;

♦ laboratory;

♦ materials management (eg, acquisition of PPE and N95 respirators) because supplies may run short during an outbreak;

♦ medical patient care unit;

♦ medical staff members;

♦ nursing leadership;

♦ outpatient clinics;

♦ pharmacy;

♦ public relations department personnel (eg, to communicate with press and public);

♦ radiology;

♦ risk management;

♦ safety department;

♦ security department (eg, access control efforts);

♦ senior management and finance representative; and

♦ staff development and education department.

This multidisciplinary group includes patient care, administration, and support staff. A representative from the local or state health department should be involved to coordinate planning with the community.[31]

Employee education and self-protective behavior

Facility staff members from all disciplines providing care to patients with SARS should participate in a comprehensive education program. The contents of the program should have a basic component for all staff members and a discipline-specific component that is current and appropriate for the specialty. Competency in standard, contact, and airborne precautions and the use of fit-tested respirators is mandatory for the care of patients with SARS.

Staff members must exercise vigilance in their practice by following infection control policies and procedures of the health care facilities where they work. These documents need to be reviewed by the infection control committee and staff development personnel at least annually. Inservice programs should be provided for all staff members so that infection control precautions are understood and followed to prevent SARS transmission; preparation is the key.[36] Practicing self-protective behavior with staff members builds confidence.

During the inservice program, stress the importance of planning and communicating with staff members. In the perioperative arena, communication is vital among the surgical team members throughout the patient's surgical experience. Postoperative disposition of patients with SARS needs to be determined and agreed upon. Nurse managers should take the lead in planning the logistics of patient care in consultation with the infection control practitioner and the hospital epidemiologist. If the facility does not have an isolation cubicle in the postanesthesia care unit, patients with SARS may need to be directly admitted to the intensive care unit isolation room for recovery. The nurse manager must confer with the physicians and OR nurses caring for patients with SARS to implement the plan of care. It is vital to adhere to infection control precautions to limit transmission of SARS to staff members.

Physician education and self-protective behavior

Anesthesia care providers should exercise care during the induction and extubation phases of the procedure to protect members of the surgical team that are in close contact and may be exposed to exhalations from SARS patients. Using PPE, to include full-face shields, is essential, especially if a bronchoscopy is being performed. The patient should be orally suctioned in a gentle manner to prevent aerosolization when intubating. Health care providers must be careful and precise when removing and placing laryngoscope blades, endoscope, or bronchoscopes to prevent splatter and minimize the opportunity of particle aerosolization.[22] The anesthesia care provider is at risk when performing endotracheal intubation.[39] He or she should minimize touching other equipment with gloves used for intubation or extubation.[22]

Employees and physicians should understand the importance of proper hand hygiene after removing PPE. Personnel should wash hands with soap and water or use an alcohol-based waterless hand hygiene product before and after patient contact. The health care facility should require adherence and proficiency in self-protective behavior.

Precautions for Avian Influenza, Human Influenza, and SARS

Human influenza precautions include

- standard precautions (eg, careful attention to hand washing before and after patient contact or contact with surfaces potentially contaminated with respiratory secretions),[22] and
- droplet precautions (eg, surgical mask, patient placement in a private room or shared with another patient with the same epidemiology).[19]

Avian influenza precautions include

- standard precautions (eg, careful attention to hand washing before and after patient contact or contact with surfaces potentially contaminated with respiratory secretions),
- eye protection within three feet of the patient,[22] and
- droplet precautions and contact precautions (eg, patient placement, if SARS is suspected an N95 mask protocol [fit tested], patient transport).[20]

SARS precautions include

- standard precautions with careful attention to hand washing before and after patient contact or contact with surfaces potentially contaminated with respiratory secretions,[32]
- eye protection within three feet of the patient,[22]

♦ contact precautions (eg, gown, gloves, eye-wear),[32,33] and

♦ airborne precautions (eg, patient is placed in a negative air pressure room, health care workers wear fit-tested N95 masks).[32]

II. Nursing Process Application

A. Perioperative Nursing Vocabulary

The perioperative nursing vocabulary is a clinically relevant and empirically validated standardized nursing language. It relates to the delivery of care in the perioperative setting. This standardized language consists of a collection of data elements (ie, the Perioperative Nursing Data Set [PNDS]), and includes perioperative nursing diagnoses, interventions, and outcomes.[40]

Care of the perioperative patient with human and avian influenza SARS, and other types of similar diseases must be individualized to each patient's needs. The perioperative nurse must bear in mind that care must be taken to protect the surgical team, other patients, and their family members because of the contagious nature of these diseases. Documentation should reflect the unique aspects of care provided using the PNDS. The examples listed below may not apply to all types of surgery for patients with human and avian influenza, SARS, and other similar diseases. Each situation must be assessed for appropriate outcomes, nursing diagnoses, and interventions.

B. Nursing Diagnoses

The perioperative nurse analyzes the assessment data to determine nursing diagnoses. Following is a partial list of nursing diagnoses that may be associated with patients who have human or avian influenza or SARS.

X28 (D2)—infection, risk for.

C. Outcome Identification

To develop a plan of care for the patient, the perioperative nurse identifies desired patient outcomes collaboratively with the patient. Following is a partial list of nursing outcomes that may be associated with patients who have human or avian influenza or SARS.

O10 (D2)—The patient is free from signs and symptoms of a surgical site infection.

D. Planning

The perioperative nurse develops a plan of care for patients who have human or avian influenza or SARS that prescribes nursing interventions to attain expected outcomes. Interventions and activities are selected according to individual patient needs and the type of procedure to be performed. Following is a partial list of interventions that may be associated with patients who have human or avian influenza or SARS.

I4	Administers care to wound sites.
I7	Administers prescribed antibiotic therapy.
I21	Assesses susceptibility for surgical site infection.
I83	Manages culture specimen collection.
I86	Monitors body temperature.
I88	Monitors for signs and symptoms of infection.
I98	Protects from cross-contamination.

III. Conclusion

This guideline is intended to be used in the event of an outbreak of human or avian influenza or SARS to promote safe care for those affected patients who may require urgent or emergent surgical intervention or other invasive procedures. Perioperative personnel should use strict infection control measures while caring for these types of infectious patients to limit transmission.

These diseases are extremely complex and require special understanding by perioperative team members to ensure optimal patient outcomes. This document addresses assumptions, definitions, history, prevalence, socioeconomic factors, epidemiology, and clinical signs and symptoms. In addition, it addresses

♦ developing a program;
♦ operational planning;
♦ impact on the workplace;
♦ risks to health care workers;
♦ vaccination;
♦ use of PPE;
♦ personal protective behaviors;
♦ physical plant considerations;
♦ integrated services, which includes a multidisciplinary approach;
♦ employee and physician education and competency; and
♦ the nursing process application regarding this patient population.[40]

This guideline may require modification based on specific patient and facility needs. It is AORN's intent that practitioners will use this document in their facilities to develop policies, procedures, and protocols specific to perioperative care of patients affected by outbreaks of human and avian influenza and SARS for patients who must undergo surgical or other invasive procedures.

REFERENCES

1. A Trampuz, M Rajesh, T Smith, et al, "Avian influenza: A new pandemic threat?" *Mayo Clinical Procedures* 79 (2004) 523-530.

2. "Information about influenza pandemics," Department of Health and Human Services, Centers for Disease Control and Prevention, *http://www.cdc.gov/flu/avian/gen-info/pandemics.htm* (accessed 10 Aug 2005).

3. "Pandemic influenza, academic health center—University of Minnesota," Center for Infectious Disease Research and Policy (CIDRAP), *http://www.cidrap.umn.edu/cidrap/content/ influenza/panflu/biofacts/panflu.htm* (accessed 7 Oct 2005) 3.

4. R K Zimmerman; "Recent changes in influenza epidemiology and vaccination recommendations," *The Journal of Family Practice* 54 (January 2005) S1.

5. Appendix 2, "Glossary of terms, influenza pandemic contingency plan," *Health Protection Agency*, Version 7.0 (February 2005) 47.

6. "Influenza viruses," Department of Health and Human Services, Centers for Disease Control and Prevention, *http://www.cdc.gov/flu/avian/gen-info/flu-viruses.htm* (accessed 10 Aug 2005) 1-2.

7. "Focus on the flu," National Institute of Allergy and Infectious Diseases, National Institutes of Health, *http://www3.niaid.nih.gov/new/focuson/flu/illustrations/timeline/timeline.htm* (accessed 15 Aug 2005).

8. "Information about influenza and its prevention, Influenza Dot Com, *http://www.influenza.com/Index.cfm?FA=HOME* (accessed 17 Aug 2005).

9. "Influenza (flu) fact sheet—Key facts about influenza and influenza vaccine, Centers for Disease Control and Prevention, *http://www.cdc.gov/flu/keyfacts.pdf* (accessed 17 August 2005) 1.

10. S Harper, K Fukuda, T Uyeki, et al, "Prevention and control of influenza—Recommendations of the Advisory Committee on Immunization Practices (ACIP)," *Morbidity and Mortality Weekly Report* 54 no RR-8 (July 29, 2005) 1.

11. M Meltzer, N Cox, K Fukuda, "The economic impact of pandemic influenza in the United States: Priorities for intervention," *Emerging Infectious Diseases* 5 (September–October 1999).

12. "Background on influenza," Department of Health and Human Services, Centers for Disease Control and Prevention, *http://www.cdc.gov/flu/protect/keyfacts.htm* (accessed September 4, 2005) 3.

13. "Updated infection control measures for the prevention and control of influenza in health-care facilities," Department of Health and Human Services, Centers for Disease Control and Prevention, *http://www.cdc.gov/professionals/ infectioncontrol/healthcarefacilities.htm* (accessed 20 Jan 2005).

14. A Monto, "The threat of an avian influenza pandemic," *The New England Journal of Medicine* 352 (January 2005) 323.

15. "Key facts about avian influenza (bird flu) and avian influenza A (H5N1) virus," Department of Health and Human Services, Centers for Disease Control and Prevention, *http://www.cdc.gov/flu/avian/gen-info/facts.htm* (accessed 10 August 2005).

16. "Transmission of influenza A viruses between animals and people," Department of Health and Human Services, Centers for Disease Control and Prevention, *http://www.cdc.gov/avian/gen-info/transmission.htm* (accessed 10 Aug 2005)

17. "Call to action: Influenza immunization among health care workers," National Foundation for Infectious Diseases, *http://www.nfid.org/publications/calltoaction.pdf* (accessed 9 Oct 2005).

18. "Interim recommendations for infection control in health-care facilities caring for patients with known or suspected avian influenza," (May 21, 2004) Department of Health and Human Services, Centers for Disease Control and Prevention, *http://www.cdc.gov/flu/avian/professional /infect-control.htm* (accessed 9 Oct 2005).

19. "Droplet precautions," Department of Health and Human Services, Centers for Disease Control and Prevention, *http://www.cdc.gov/ncidod/hip/ISOLAT/droplet_prec_excerpt_print.htm* (accessed 9 Oct 2005).

20. "Respiratory hygiene/cough etiquette in health-care settings," (Dec 17, 2003) Department of Health and Human Services, Centers for Disease Control and Prevention, *http://www.cdc.gov/flu/professionals /infection-control/resphygiene.htm* (accessed 9 Oct 2005).

21. "Severe acute respiratory syndrome (SARS): What everyone should know about SARS," (May 3, 2005) Department of Health and Human Services, Centers for Disease Control and Prevention, *http://www.cdc.gov/ncidod/sars/basics.htm* (accessed 9 Oct 2005).

22. M Farley, L M Socha, "Severe acute respiratory syndrome and its effects on health care," *SSM* 9 (October 2003) 20-25.

23. B Reilly et al, "SARS and Carlo Urbani," *The New England Journal of Medicine* 348 (May 15, 2003) 1951.

24. J S M Peiris et al," The severe acute respiratory syndrome," *The New England Journal of Medicine* 349 (December 18, 2003) 2431-2441.

25. J M Drazen, "SARS—Looking back over the first 100 days," *The New England Journal of Medicine* 349 (July 24, 2003) 319-320.

26. J Howard-Ruben, "SARS unmasked: Canadian nurses tell of hardship, loss," *Nursing Spectrum* 15 (October 20, 2003) 32-34.

27. J Gerberding, "Faster ... but fast enough? Responding to the epidemic of severe acute respiratory syndrome," *The New England Journal of Medicine* 348 (May15, 2003) 2030-2031.

28. K V Holmes, "SARS-associated coronavirus," *The New England Journal of Medicine* 348 (May 15, 2003) 1948-1951.

29. B Tomlinson, C Cockram, "Experience at Prince of Wales Hospital, Hong Kong," *The Lancet* 361 (May 3, 2003) 1486-1487.

30. D Tilton, "Severe acute respiratory syndrome," *Managing Infection Control* 3 (2003) 14-22.

31. A Srinivasan et al, "Foundations of the severe acute respiratory syndrome preparedness and response plan for healthcare facilities," *Infection Control and Hospital Epidemiology* 25 (2004) 1020-1025.

32. J E Williamson, "SARS Update: CDC finds new coronavirus may cause illness," *OR Today* 3 (2003) 8-9.

33. "Recommended practices for standard and transmission-based precautions in the perioperative practice setting," in *Standards, Recommended Practices, and Guidelines* (Denver: AORN, Inc, 2005) 447-451.

34. K M Pyrek, "Is a global flu pandemic imminent?" *Infection Control Today* 9 (March 2005) 34-42.

35. "Recommended practices for environmental cleaning in the surgical practice setting," in *Standards, Recommended Practices, and Guidelines* (Denver: AORN, Inc, 2005) 361-366.

36. "Canadian warning: ORs should prepare for SARS," *Same-Day Surgery* (March 2004) 30-31.

37. M Fishman et al, "Patient safety tools: SARS, smallpox, monkeypox, and avian flu," *Disaster Management & Response* 3 (July–September 2005) 86-90.

38. "Are you ready for an influx of SARS patients?" *ED Accreditation Update* (November 2004) 1-3.

39. R A Fowler et al, "Transmission of severe acute respiratory syndrome during intubation and mechanical ventilation," *American Journal of Respiratory and Critical Care Medicine* 169 (2004) 1198-1202.

40. Beyea, S, ed, *Perioperative Nursing Data Set: The Perioperative Nursing Vocabulary,* second ed (Denver: AORN, Inc, 2002) 83.

RESOURCES

"AORN guidance statement: Safe on-call practices in perioperative settings," in *Standards, Recommended Practices, and Guidelines* (Denver: AORN, Inc. 2005) 193-195.

Chan, S. "Nurses fighting against severe acute respiratory syndrome (SARS) in Hong Kong," *Journal of Nursing Scholarship* 35 (2003) 209.

Esswein, E J, et al. "Environmental and occupational health response to SARS, Taiwan, 2003," *Emerging Infectious Diseases* 10 (July 2004) 1187-1194.

Fenwick, A. "On the front line of SARS," *American Journal of Nursing* 103 (2003) 118-119.

Maunder, R, et al. "The immediate psychological and occupational impact of the 2003 SARS outbreak in a teaching hospital," *Canadian Medical Association Journal* 168 (May 13, 2003) 1245-1251.

McGillis Hall, L, et al. "Media portrayal of nurses' perspectives and concerns in the SARS crisis in Toronto," *Journal of Nursing Scholarship* 35(2003) 211-215.

Moore, D, et al. "Protecting health care workers from SARS and other respiratory pathogens: Organizational and individual factors that affect adherence to infection control guidelines," *American Journal of Infection Control* 33 (March 2005)

Patrick, D M. "The race to outpace severe acute respiratory syndrome (SARS)," *Canadian Medical Association Journal* 168 (May 13, 2003) 1265-1266.

"Recommended practices for cleaning, handling, and processing anesthesia equipment," in *Standards, Recommended Practices, and Guidelines* (Denver: AORN, Inc, 2005) 289-298.

"Recommended practices for traffic patterns in the perioperative setting," in *Standards, Recommended Practices, and Guidelines* (Denver: AORN, Inc., 2005) 483-485.

Tan, Y M, et al. "Management of inpatients exposed to an outbreak of severe acute respiratory syndrome (SARS)," *Journal of Hospital Infection* 58 (2004) 210-215.

Tsang, K W, et al. "A cluster of cases of severe acute respiratory syndrome in Hong Kong," *The New England Journal of Medicine* 348 (May 15, 2003) 1977-1985.

Approved by the AORN Board of Directors, November 2005. Published in *Standards, Recommended Practices, and Guidelines,* 2006 edition. Reprinted August 2006, *AORN Journal.*

AORN Perioperative Standards and Recommended Practices, 2009 Edition

AORN Bariatric Surgery Guideline

I. Overview

A. Introduction

Assumptions

This document is intended to serve as a guide for perioperative nurses and others currently involved in the care of morbidly obese patients and to assist those working to establish bariatric surgical services in the facilities where they practice. The guideline is designed to assist perioperative practitioners in creating and maintaining an optimal health care environment for bariatric patients. The guideline defines the unique physical and psychosocial needs of the patient population that is morbidly obese and presents guidance for establishing a bariatric surgery program.

The "AORN bariatric surgery guideline" is based on current available research and expert opinion. It is assumed that ongoing research will result in new knowledge, procedures, and medical and nursing interventions for the treatment of morbid obesity. This guideline may require modification based on specific patient and facility needs.

Bariatric surgery is the surgical treatment of morbid obesity. It is a recognized subspecialty in the field of general surgery and is a rapidly growing subspecialty in the United States and throughout the world. The goal of bariatric surgery is to achieve sustained weight loss and reversal of patients' comorbidities. The recent increase in both the popularity of and demand for bariatric surgery can be attributed primarily to two factors: there are no nonsurgical approaches that are effective long term for treating morbid obesity, and the overall success of weight loss surgery has resulted in greater acceptance of surgery as a treatment option.

Definitions

For the purposes of this document, the following definitions apply.

Anastomosis—The surgical connection of two hollow structures (eg, stomach to intestine, intestine to intestine, intestine to colon, bile duct to intestine). The structures can be connected end to end, end to side, or side to end. The connection can be accomplished by use of sutures, surgical staples, or a combination of both.

Band—A constricting device that limits the movement of food from the stomach. The device may be placed around the entire stomach, a portion of the stomach, or a portion of the intestine and may consist of tissue, mesh, silastic tubing, or other material approved for this use.

Bariatric surgery—Any surgical procedure performed for the purpose of producing weight loss.

Biliopancreatic limb—The segment of small bowel connecting the bile duct to the distal end of the Roux limb. This segment follows the Roux limb and is the bile-carrying limb.

Body mass index (BMI)—A mathematical calculation used to determine whether a patient is overweight. It is calculated by dividing a person's body weight in kilograms by his or her height in meters squared (kg/m^2).

Common channel—The segment of small bowel where the biliopancreatic limb and the Roux limb become one and continue to the cecum. Complex proteins, fats, and carbohydrates are digested in the common channel.

Comorbidity—One or more coexisting diseases or conditions in addition to the condition that is the subject of study.

Malabsorption—Incomplete digestion or absorption of food intake.

Morbid obesity—Having a BMI greater than 40 with or without comorbidities.

Pouch—A surgically created portion of the stomach that serves as a reservoir for food immediately after food exits the esophagus.

Restrictive—Decreasing or limiting the amount of food intake.

Roux limb—The segment of small bowel where food exits the stomach and enters the bowel. The Roux limb starts where food enters and ends where the biliopancreatic limb joins it to form the common channel.

Staple line—A row of staples placed in the bowel or stomach by a surgical stapling device. Staples can be used to create an anastomosis, create a partition, or secure the end of the bowel when a side anastomosis is performed.

B. Population Affected

Prevalence

In the twenty-first century, obesity may be the number one US public health problem.[1] The prevalence of obesity is global and ranks high in the United State, as well as in other developed nations.[2] Nearly

Table 1

WEIGHT CATEGORY BASED ON BODY MASS INDEX	
BMI (kg/m²)	**Category**
< 18.5	Underweight
18.5 – 24.99	Normal
25 – 26.99	Overweight
27 – 30	Mild obesity
> 30	Moderate obesity
> 35	Severe obesity
> 40	Morbid obesity
> 50	Super obesity

two-thirds of US adults are overweight, including those who are obese.[3,4] Overweight is defined as having excess body weight compared to preset standards. This excess weight can be composed of muscle, bone, fat, or body water. Obesity refers specifically to having an abnormal proportion of body fat. Although it is possible to be overweight without being obese (eg, heavily muscled athletes, body builders), many people who are overweight also are obese. Of all US adults (ie, people 20 years of age or older), 129.6 million (64.5%) are overweight. This includes 64.5 million women (61.9%) and 65.1 million men (67.2%).[3,4] There also has been a continual increase in the number of children and adolescents who are overweight. Approximately 15.3% of children (ie, ages six to 11) and 15.5% of adolescents (ie, ages 12 to 17) were overweight in 2000, a significant increase from approximately 5% in the 1960s and 1970s.[3,4] Of all US adults, 61.3 million (30.5%) are obese. This includes 34.7 million (33.4%) women and 26.6 million (27.1%) men.[2]

Socioeconomic factors

Health care costs associated with being overweight and obese have escalated. Estimated annual medical spending due to overweight and obesity may have been as high as $78.5 billion in 1998, which is $92.6 billion in 2002 dollars.[5] According to one study, this represents 9.1% of US health care expenditures.[5,6]

Costs are divided into direct health care costs and indirect costs. Direct health care costs refer to diagnostic and treatment services (eg, physician costs, medications, hospital and nursing home care) and preventive services. Indirect costs include the cost of wages lost by people unable to work because of illness or disability, as well as the cost of future lost earnings because of premature

death. Americans spend $33 billion annually on weight-loss products and services, including low-calorie foods, artificially sweetened products, and memberships to commercial weight-loss centers.[6]

C. Pathophysiology

Obesity is a life-threatening, genetically related, costly, life-long, progressive, multifactoral disease of excess fat storage. Body mass index is a mathematical calculation used to determine whether a person is overweight. It is calculated by dividing a person's body weight in kilograms by his or her height in meters squared. A person is considered obese if he or she weighs 20% or more above a predetermined ideal weight, or has a BMI greater than or equal to 30 (**Table 1**).[7]

Morbid obesity, which also is called clinically severe obesity, correlates with a BMI of greater than 40 or with being 100 lbs overweight. Morbid obesity is associated with numerous health problems, which are referred to as comorbidities and is directly related to mortality rates. A 12-year study of 750,000 individuals found that mortality rates for men and women who weighed 50% more than the average weight for their height increased approximately twofold.[8]

Common comorbidities

The most common comorbidities associated with morbid obesity are type II diabetes, hypertension, atherosclerosis, hyperlipidemia, stroke, gallbladder disease, arthritis of weight bearing joints, sleep apnea, alveolar hypoventilation, urinary stress incontinence, gastroesophageal reflux disease, infertility, certain cancers (ie, colorectal, kidney, breast, uterine), and sudden death.[9] To date, long-term medical therapies and regimens have not been effective in treating morbid obesity.

D. History

Bariatric surgery evolved in the 1950s following observation that individuals who had short-bowel syndrome lost weight as a result of inadequate nutrient absorption. Bariatric surgery was introduced by A. J. Kremen, MD, and his associates, who performed and published reports of a jejunoileal bypass procedure.[10] In the procedure, the upper small intestine was anastomosed to the lower small intestine in an attempt to bypass much of the absorptive circuit. At about the same time, a Swedish physician performed a similar procedure, but he excised the redundant portion of the small intestine.

In the 1960s, researchers published reports of 10 jejunalcolic shunt procedures in which the upper small intestine was anastomosed to the colon, with the intent of bypassing even more of the nutrient absorbing gastrointestinal tract.[10] Unfortunately, these patients experienced uncontrollable diarrhea, dehydration, and electrolyte imbalance. Ultimately, the shunts were converted to jejunoileostomies in which the upper portion of the jejunum was anastomosed to the lower portion of the ileum. Nevertheless, patients with jejunoileal bypass continued to experience diarrhea caused by fatty acid irritation of the colon from interference with bile digestion of the ingested fats. This diarrhea resulted in fluid and electrolyte imbalance, which was a major complaint among patients and physicians. Additional complications included mineral and electrolyte imbalances, vitamin depletion, anemia, cholelithiasis, and renal and liver disease. Other procedures were developed, including gastric bypass, because of these complications. The jejunoileal bypass no longer is a recommended bariatric surgical procedure.[10]

In 1966, gastric bypass was developed and introduced by Edward E. Mason, MD, of the University of Iowa. Dr Mason developed the procedure based on the observation that women who had undergone partial gastrectomy for peptic ulcer disease tended to remain underweight after the surgery and that it was difficult to achieve weight gain in this patient population. He applied the principles of partial gastrectomy to women who were obese and found that they lost weight. Using surgical staples, he created a partition across the upper stomach and anastomosed this pouch to the small intestine. Complications of the early gastric bypass procedures led to the further development and refinement of gastroplasty in the late 1960s and early 1970s.

In the mid-1970s, in an effort to simplify gastric restriction, Dr Mason divided the stomach transversely toward the greater curvature where he left a small channel; however, this outlet subsequently enlarged.[11] This led to experimentation with horizontal gastroplasties. Unfortunately, the upper gastric pouch and the outlet tended to enlarge, leading to weight regain.[11] In response, Dr Mason partitioned the stomach vertically (ie, vertical gastroplasty) because the thicker muscle along the lesser curva-

ture was thought to be more resistant to dilatation. In addition, the outlet was banded by a mesh strip or a silastic ring to prevent enlargement.[11]

In the late 1970s, biliopancreatic diversion was developed in Genoa, Italy. The weight loss that occurs after this procedure initially is related to the restriction of food intake from the decreased size of the available gastric pouch, which later enlarges. The weight loss, however, is maintained by a tolerable degree of malabsorption of starches and fats in the common limb. The biliopancreatic diversion provides the greatest loss of excess weight (ie, up to 80% excess weight loss) of any of the bariatric procedures, but it requires surgical expertise and close, long-term follow-up because nutritional deficiencies may develop. In the biliopancreatic diversion, both the Roux limb and the biliopancreatic limb are long with a shortened common channel.

A modification of the biliopancreatic diversion in wide use is the duodenal switch procedure. This is performed by resecting the greater curvature of the stomach, leaving the entire lesser curvature and pylorus in continuity.[10] The biliopancreatic limb is separated from the proximal, food-carrying duodenum and re-anastomosed to the distal portion of the Roux limb to form the common channel. The Roux limb is connected just below the pylorus by means of an end-to-side anastomosis.

In the 1970s and 1980s, gastric banding was developed as another method of limiting food intake.[10] The band is placed near the upper end of the stomach just below the junction of the stomach and the esophagus. Early attempts were unsuccessful because readily available materials, such as arterial grafts, were used for banding. Later, bands were developed specifically for this purpose along with techniques to measure stoma size. Later in the 1980s, the adjustable gastric band—a hollow band with an inflatable balloon as its lining—was developed by Lubomyr I. Kuzmak, MD. The balloon is connected to a small reservoir that is placed under the skin in the upper abdomen. Adjustment of the gastric restriction occurs from injection or withdrawal of saline from the reservoir.[12]

During the past decade, minimally invasive laparoscopic surgery became the technique of choice. These procedures are less invasive, and patients often can return home on the day of surgery. Patients also can return to work and activities of daily living more quickly. Bariatric surgery is a

Table 2

History of Bariatric Surgery	
Decade	**Procedure**
1950s	Jejunoileal bypass
1960s	Jejunocolic bypass
	Gastric bypass
1970s	Gastroplasty
	Biliopancreatic diversion
1980s	Gastric banding
	Adjustable gastric banding
1990s	Laparoscopic procedures

serious undertaking, however, and it should be recommended only for patients who meet carefully defined criteria. **Table 2** provides a summary of bariatric surgery history.

E. Patient Selection Criteria

The option of surgical treatment should be offered to patients who are morbidly obese, well-informed, and motivated and who have acceptable surgical risks. Patients should be able to participate in treatment and long-term follow-up. Patients with manifest psychopathology that would jeopardize informed consent and cooperation with long-term follow-up may not be candidates for bariatric surgery. A decision to select surgical treatment should be determined on an individual basis according to an in-depth assessment of the risks and benefits for each individual. Increased abdominal fat or central obesity (ie, apple shape as opposed to pear shape) is a significant risk factor associated with major complications from obesity. Functional impairments associated with obesity also are important factors for deciding on treatment via surgery. According to the National Institutes Consensus Development Conference statement on the surgical treatment of obesity,

> Patients judged by experienced clinicians to have a low probability of success with non-surgical measures, as demonstrated, for example, by failure in established weight control programs or reluctance by the patient to enter such a program, may be considered for surgical treatment.[13]

Bariatric surgery standards for candidate qualifications are set by the National Institutes of Health (NIH) and the American Society of Bariatric Surgeons (ASBS). To qualify for surgery and possible compensation by the insurer, patients must

- be determined to make lifestyle and eating habit changes,
- be severely obese (ie, BMI greater than 35) with one or more comorbidities,
- have made numerous attempts at medical weight loss, and/or
- be morbidly obese with a BMI greater than 40 with or without comorbidities.

As noted, treatment must be tailored to the individual concerned. The BMI is only one of many criteria for investigating and selecting a surgical option and weight management goal. The following are other factors to consider.

- Medical comorbidities (eg, diabetes, hypertension, sleep apnea, hypercholesterolemia, infertility, urinary stress incontinence, dysmenorrhea).
- Functional factors—is the patient able to perform activities of daily living, dine out, or travel?
- Psychological comorbidities—an evaluation by a licensed psychologist is advised because patients with manifest psychopathology can jeopardize informed consent and cooperation with long-term follow-up.
- Social factors—many morbidly obese patients face harassment and prejudice due to their size. They may have a limited number of friends, and society as a whole regards obesity in the same context as alcoholism and drug addiction. Will the patient have or need a system of support postoperatively?
- Economic factors—people who are obese find it harder to enroll in school or universities or obtain employment. Will the patient's quality of life improve with the selected bariatric procedure?
- Endocrine status—does the patient have an endocrine condition that contributes to or causes the obesity?
- Substance dependency—is the patient alcohol or drug dependent?
- Eating habits—is the patient a grazer (ie, eats small quantities of food continuously), a sweeter (ie, ingests calories mainly from sweets), or a bloater (ie, eats a huge meal at one sitting)? These different eating behaviors should be approached with different surgical options for successful weight loss and weight management outcomes. Often, patients fit more than one category, making selection of the correct procedure more difficult.

F. Surgical Choices in the New Century

There are three categories of bariatric procedures. These include malabsorptive, restrictive, and combined restrictive and malabsorptive procedures.

Malabsorptive procedures

Malabsorptive procedures are associated with incomplete digestion or absorption of food. Jejunoileal bypass is the classic example of a malabsorptive weight loss procedure. Some modern procedures use a lesser degree of malabsorption combined with gastric restriction to induce and maintain weight loss. Any patient undergoing a procedure involving malabsorption must be considered at risk to develop at least some of the malabsorptive complications created by jejunoileal bypass. The multiple complications associated with jejunoileal bypass, although considerably less severe than those associated with jejunocolic anastomosis, were sufficiently distressing both to patients and physicians to result in its being deemed an undesirable procedure.[10]

Biliopancreatic diversion. Biliopancreatic diversion is a malabsorptive procedure used today. In the biliopancreatic diversion, both the Roux limb and the biliopancreatic limb of the small bowel are quite long with a shortened common channel where digestion of proteins, fats, and carbohydrates takes place (**Figure 1**).

Advantages of the biliopancreatic diversion include

- greater weight loss than with other procedures;
- greater long-term success from lifelong malabsorption of food;[14]
- a larger stomach pouch that allows a return to fairly normal eating habits, thus improving quality of diet; and
- an increased chance of improving certain comorbidities, such as diabetes and hypertension.[14]

Disadvantages of biliopancreatic diversion include

- longer surgery time (ie, averaging three to four hours);
- greater risks for both surgical and general complications compared to other procedures;
- greater risks for nutritional and functional deficiencies due to high malabsorption of food—these deficiencies include fat soluble vitamins (eg, A, D, E, K);

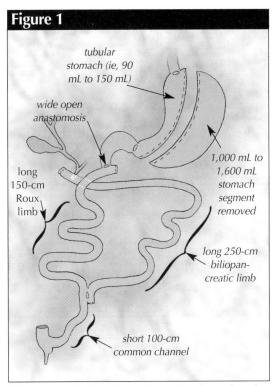

Figure 1

tubular stomach (ie, 90 mL to 150 mL)

wide open anastomosis

long 150-cm Roux limb

1,000 mL to 1,600 mL stomach segment removed

long 250-cm biliopancreatic limb

short 100-cm common channel

Biliopancreatic diversion with duodenal switch and vertical gastroplasty/sleeve gastrectomy.

- risk of liver abnormalities;
- risk of insufficient calcium absorption, resulting in bone disease;
- risk of lactose intolerance;
- risk of severe iron anemia; and
- possible offensive, foul-smelling soft bowel movements and flatus.[14]

Restrictive procedures

Restrictive procedures reduce the size of the stomach to decrease or limit the intake of food so small amounts of food give a feeling of fullness. Examples of restrictive procedures are proximal gastric bypass, vertical banded gastroplasty, and adjustable gastric banding procedures.

Proximal gastric bypass. Proximal gastric bypass primarily is a restrictive procedure, although it does have a minimal absorptive component. Proximal gastric bypass involves creating a small pouch at the top of the stomach. The remainder of the stomach remains intact. The Roux limb of the intestine is attached to the created pouch with a small anastomosis intended to slow emptying of the pouch into the intestine. The Roux limb is relatively

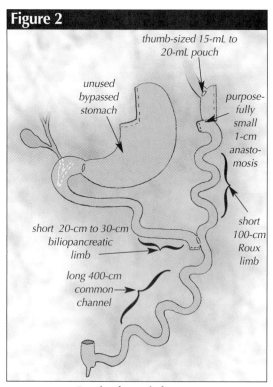

Figure 2

thumb-sized 15-mL to 20-mL pouch

unused bypassed stomach

purpose-fully small 1-cm anasto-mosis

short 20-cm to 30-cm biliopancreatic limb

short 100-cm Roux limb

long 400-cm common channel

Proximal gastric bypass.

Figure 3

Vertical banded gastroplasty creates a tubular stomach that is restrictive.

short before being joined by the short biliopancreatic limb to create a long common channel. The long common channel allows for absorption of nutrients (**Figure 2**).

The proximal bypass works for patients who are sweeters and bloaters, but grazers can successfully overcome the restriction by continuously eating small amounts of food. Patients can achieve 60% to 65% loss of excess body weight, but approximately 25% of patients experience a 20% to 30% weight gain after three years.[7] Advantages of the proximal gastric bypass include

- minimized dumping syndrome, which can be partially controlled by avoiding sugars, and
- absence or minimal occurrence of acid reflux.

Disadvantages of proximal gastric bypass include

- the possibility of an anastomotic stricture and
- the possibility of anastomotic ulceration.[7]

Vertical banded gastroplasty. In vertical banded gastroplasty surgery, the stomach is partitioned vertically along the lesser curvature of the stomach. Unless a duodenal switch is performed to lessen absorption, the pylorus and small intestine remain intact. The procedure (without duodenal switch) is purely restrictive, and weight loss is achieved because of the restricted intake of food. Both polypropylene mesh bands and silastic rings have been used to prevent stretching of the newly created stomach outlet. The bands are placed at the stomal outlet to prevent or limit stomal stretching and subsequent weight gain. The band or ring circumference is somewhat larger than the stoma when it is created, so the limiting effect only occurs after the pouch has stretched to some degree (**Figure 3**).[10]

Vertical banded gastroplasty achieves gastric partitioning, has been widely performed, and generally is associated with satisfactory weight loss. The procedure works well for bloaters, but it often is unsuccessful for sweeters and grazers. Advantages of vertical banded gastroplasty include that

- it has lower perioperative complication rates than other restrictive procedures,
- it technically is easier to perform, and
- it has a low mortality rate.

Disadvantages of vertical banded gastroplasty include

- rare staple line leaks, which can be dangerous if not diagnosed immediately;

- vertical line disruption due to vomiting caused by overeating;
- risk of infection;
- possible incisional hernia; and
- risk of band erosion, usually caused by ulcer formation near the restrictive device.[7]

Adjustable gastric band. Adjustable gastric banding is a restrictive procedure in which the surgeon places an inflatable silicone band completely around the upper portion of the stomach. This band usually is placed endoscopically. The band constricts the stomach, thus producing a small pouch with a narrow opening into the lower stomach. The small pouch size decreases food intake and creates a feeling of fullness. With the adjustable band, there are no anatomical removals or rearrangements. The inflatable band is connected to a small reservoir that is placed under the skin in the upper abdomen. Adjustment of the gastric restriction occurs from injection or withdrawal of saline from the reservoir.[7,10] The adjustable gastric band works best for bloaters. Sweeters and grazers simply must avoid sweets and snacks to achieve success with the adjustable band (**Figure 4**).

Advantages of adjustable banding include
- use of a minimally invasive approach;
- shorter average length of stay (ie, usually 24 hours);
- faster recovery period (ie, usually less than two weeks);
- no staple line to break down;
- that the band can be adjusted;
- that the procedure is reversible with normal stomach restoration; and
- that the band is easily deflated if necessary.

Disadvantages of adjustable banding include
- risk of foreign body reaction,
- that the band position can slip with subsequent tissue erosion,
- the possibility of access port leakage and infection, and
- that some insurance companies will not cover this procedure.

Combined restrictive and malabsorptive procedures
Both restrictive and malabsorptive procedures can result in complications. Combining the two, however, can have less drastic adverse effects on the body's gastrointestinal (GI) function.

Roux-en-Y gastric bypass. Roux-en-Y gastric bypass combines gastric restriction with a small

Figure 4

Gastric banding systems are adjustable and reversible and can be placed laparoscopically.

amount of malabsorption. In this procedure, the stomach is divided into two compartments with the upper part consisting of a small pouch capable of holding 1 oz to 2 oz. The lower compartment, approximately 90% of the original stomach, no longer stores food, but it continues to secrete digestive juices that flow into the duodenum. The jejunum is transected from the duodenum, and the upper jejunum then is connected to the pouch to allow food to pass from the pouch. The lower end of the jejunum is anastomosed to the biliopancreatic limb from which gastric and other digestive juices are delivered to the common channel where absorption takes place. Depending on the length of the Roux limb and the point of anastomosis forming the common channel, more or less absorption will occur. The decrease in absorption occurs because the food is not exposed to the digestive juices until the point of anastomosis.

If the anastomosis point creates a long common channel, the procedure is considered a proximal gastric bypass, and absorption will be greater (**Figure 5**). If the anastomosis creates a short common channel,

Figure 5

Roux-en-Y proximal gastric bypass.

short 20-cm to 30-cm biliopancreatic limb

short 100-cm Roux limb

long 400-cm common channel

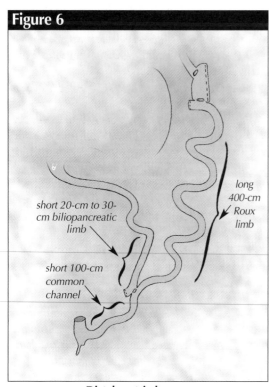

Figure 6

Distal gastric bypass.

short 20-cm to 30-cm biliopancreatic limb

short 100-cm common channel

long 400-cm Roux limb

the procedure is considered a distal gastric bypass, and less absorption will take place (**Figure 6**).

Advantages of the Roux-en-Y gastric bypass include

♦ both food restriction and malabsorption;

♦ optimal long-term weight loss results compared to restrictive only procedures; and

♦ documented improvement in comorbidities, especially type II diabetes.

Disadvantages of the Roux-en-Y gastric bypass include

♦ painful dumping syndrome that occurs with sugar consumption;

♦ longer average length of stay than with a restrictive only procedure;

♦ risk for nutritional complications, such as vitamin (eg, A, B12, D, E) and mineral (eg, calcium, iron, folic acid) deficiencies;

♦ risk for stomal stenosis requiring dilation;

♦ risk for Y-limb obstruction requiring surgical intervention;

♦ risk for anastomosis leakage;

♦ risk for marginal ulceration at the stomach to intestine anastomosis site; and

♦ risk for ventral incisional hernia.

Minimally invasive approach

In the 1990s, use of laparoscopic or minimally invasive surgery gained prominence in bariatric surgery. The development of specialized instruments, which obviate the need for the traditional abdominal incision, has advanced laparoscopic surgery. To perform laparoscopic bariatric procedures, surgeons must be competent and experienced in both open bariatric procedures and in laparoscopic procedures. Every bariatric procedure can be performed laparoscopically.

Laparoscopic surgery involves placing trocars through the skin. These trocars allow for passage of long, fiber-optic telescopes and narrow instruments, such as graspers, scissors, babcocks, and staplers, to perform the surgical procedure. Fiber-optic cameras and videotaping equipment also are used. Most laparoscopic bariatric surgery begins by inflating the patient's abdomen with carbon dioxide to allow the surgeon more visibility and space within the abdomen for greater ease of trocar placement. Advantages of a laparoscopic approach include

♦ enhanced visualization of anatomy;

♦ decreased surgical complications (eg, incisional hernia, infection);

♦ less postoperative pain; and

♦ shorter average length of stay.

Disadvantages of a laparoscopic approach include

♦ increased surgical time compared to an open approach,

♦ increased exposure to anesthetic agents and gases,

♦ added surgical costs because of additional supplies and equipment,

♦ risk of organ perforation, and

♦ possible necessity for conversion to an open approach.

G. Results

Weight loss usually reaches a maximum between 18 and 24 months postoperatively. Mean percent excess weight loss at five years ranges from 48% to 74% after gastric bypass and from 50% to 60% after vertical banded gastroplasty.[8] A study of more than 600 patients who underwent gastric bypass that had a 96% follow-up rate found that mean percent excess weight loss exceeded 50% at 14 years.[15] A 10-year follow-up series from the University of Virginia reported weight loss of 60% of excess weight at five years and more than 50% between years six and 10.[16] Other authors have reported five- and six-year follow-up of their patients with similar weight loss results.[15,17-22]

Weight reduction surgery has been reported to improve several comorbid conditions, including glucose intolerance and diabetes mellitus,[15] sleep apnea, obesity associated hypoventilation,[23,24] hypertension,[25] and serum lipid abnormalities.[23,24] One study demonstrated that type II diabetics treated medically had a mortality rate three times that of a comparable group that underwent gastric bypass surgery.[26] Improved heart function, decreased ventricular wall thickness, and decreased ventricular chamber size have been observed with sustained weight loss. Some patients experience improved mobility and stamina after surgical treatment for morbid obesity. Many patients report a better mood, greater self-esteem, improved interpersonal effectiveness, and enhanced quality of life.[27] They are less self-conscious[28] and are able to explore social and vocational activities formerly unavailable to them. Patients also are less inclined to be disparaging about their body image. If marital satisfaction existed before surgery, that satisfaction is likely to increase after surgery. If the couple experienced marital discord before surgery, the patient's improved self-image may lead to divorce postoperatively.[28]

II. Nursing Process Application

A. Perioperative Nursing Vocabulary

The perioperative nursing vocabulary is a clinically relevant and empirically validated standardized nursing language. It relates to the delivery of care in perioperative settings. This standardized language consists of a collection of data elements (ie, the Perioperative Nursing Data Set [PNDS]), and includes perioperative nursing diagnoses, interventions, and outcomes.[29] In 1999, the PNDS was recognized by the American Nurses Association's Committee on Nursing Practice Information Infrastructure as a data set useful in the practice of nursing. The perioperative patient focused model provides the conceptual framework for the PNDS and the model for perioperative nursing practice. The patient and his or her family members are at the core of the model. The model depicts perioperative nursing in four domains and illustrates the relationship between the patient, his or her family members, and care provided by the perioperative professional nurse. The patient-centered domains are

♦ D1—safety,

♦ D2—physiological responses to surgery,

♦ D3—patient and family member behavioral responses to surgery, and

♦ D4—health system in which perioperative care is provided.

Each data element in the PNDS is represented by a unique identifier. The domains are represented by the letter "D" followed by numbers one to four to indicate the particular domain being addressed. Nursing diagnoses are represented by the letter "X" and a number unique to the diagnosis; interventions are represented by the letter "I" and a unique number; and outcomes are represented by the letter "O" and a unique number. These designations are used in this document as appropriate.

B. Assessment

Perioperative nurses assess, document, and communicate patient status to all members of the health care team. Data collection involves the patient and his or her significant others. Patient assessment begins when the patient initially consults the bariatric physician or surgeon. The anesthesia care provider then should review the patient's medical history and develop a plan of care. Bariatric surgery patients should be assessed for the following risk factors:

- psychopathology—
  - may jeopardize informed consent, and
  - may jeopardize cooperation with long-term follow-up;
- body type—increased abdominal fat (ie, "central tendency");
- potential airway problems—
  - bariatric patients may need an awake intubation,
  - an airway cart should be available, and
  - bariatric patients desaturate quickly;
- circulation problems;
- skin integrity/breakdown; and
- medical comorbidities, including
  - diabetes,
  - hypertension,
  - sleep apnea,
  - hypercholesterolemia, and
  - stress incontinence.

C. Nursing Diagnoses

The perioperative nurse analyzes the assessment data to determine nursing diagnoses. Following is a partial list of nursing diagnoses that may be associated with patients undergoing bariatric surgery.

- X 30 (D3)—knowledge deficit;
- X 1 (D2)—activity intolerance;
- X 34 (D1)—physical mobility, impaired;
- X 4 (D3)—anxiety;
- X 37 (D2)—imbalanced nutrition (ie, more than body requirements);
- X 28 (D1)—infection, risk for;
- X 7 (D2)—breathing pattern, ineffective—related to morbid obesity and/or comorbidities;
- X 20 (D2)—fluid volume, risk for imbalance—related to altered nutritional state;
- X 26 (D2)—hypothermia; and
- X 33 (D3)—therapeutic regime management, ineffective—related to necessary lifestyle changes.

D. Outcome Identification

To develop a plan of care for the patient, the perioperative nurse identifies desired patient outcomes collaboratively with the patient. Following is a partial list of nursing outcomes that may be associated with patients having bariatric surgery.

- O 31 (D3)—The patient demonstrates knowledge of the expected responses to the operative or other invasive procedure.
- O 5 (D1)—The patient is free from signs and symptoms of injury related to positioning.
- O 10 (D2)—The patient is free from signs and symptoms of infection.
- O 13 (D2)—The patient's fluid, electrolyte, and acid-base balances are consistent with or improved from the baseline levels established preoperatively.
- O 18 (D3)—The patient demonstrates knowledge of nutritional requirements related to the operative or other invasive procedure.
- O 20 (D3)—The patient demonstrates knowledge of medication management.

E. Planning

The perioperative nurse develops a plan of care for the patient undergoing bariatric surgery that prescribes nursing interventions to attain expected outcomes. Interventions and activities are selected according to individual patient needs and the type of procedure to be performed. Following is a partial list of interventions that may be associated with patients having bariatric surgery.

- I 30—Develops an individualized plan of care.
- I 32—Elicits perceptions of surgery.
- I 56—Explains expected sequence of events.
- I 124—Verifies consent for planned procedure.
- I 64—Identifies physical alterations that require additional precautions for procedure-specific positioning.
- I 96—Positions the patient.
- I 38—Evaluates for signs and symptoms of injury as a result of positioning.
- I 46—Evaluates postoperative tissue perfusion.
- I 88—Monitors for signs and symptoms of infection.
- I 18—Administers prescribed prophylactic treatments.
- I 107—Provides instruction regarding dietary needs.
- I 108—Provides pain management instruction.
- I 150—Maintains patient's dignity and privacy.

F. Implementation

Interventions can be and usually are composed of many different activities. Implementation refers to the actual performance of the activities comprising the interventions in the individualized plan of care. The following are provided as examples of activities performed when caring for bariatric surgery patients. This is a multidisciplinary team approach (eg, includes members from medical, nursing, laboratory, radiology, nutrition, pharmacy staffs).

Preoperative

During the preadmission process, the nurse ensures that all laboratory work, x-rays, and other tests are performed before the day of admission for surgery. The anesthesia care provider reviews the patient's history and develops an anesthesia care plan. Other preoperative activities include the following.

- Perform a preoperative assessment, noting any circulatory or skin integrity problems and the patient's body type. Body type will affect positioning.
- Assess for comorbidities (eg, diabetes, hypertension, urinary incontinency) and initiate activities to address individual comorbidities.
- Weigh the patient on admission.
  - Scales should be large enough to obtain an accurate weight.
  - Do not use freight scales. This is demoralizing to the patient.
- Use only floor-mounted toilets for these patients. Wall-mounted units can break away when subjected to the patient's weight unless they are reinforced with grab bars.
- Supply larger patient gowns to ensure comfort and protect modesty.
- Perform continuous positive airway pressure procedures according to physician orders.
- Provide a gastric stretcher or gurney for bariatric patients. Other stretchers or gurneys have weight limits and may not be of sufficient dimension to accommodate the patient.
- Ensure that doorways are large enough, especially restroom doorways.

Intraoperative

The following activities should be performed in the OR.

- Place side attachments on the OR bed, if needed, for patients with extra-wide girth.
- Secure the patient to the OR bed.
- Protect skin integrity and circulation.
- Use two straps—one across the patient's thighs and the second across the lower legs.
- Provide emotional support to the patient.

- Assist the anesthesia care provider as necessary.
- Insert a Foley catheter, and attach it to a urimeter.
- Place an electrosurgical grounding pad on the patient's thigh or other appropriate location.
- Apply lower limb sequential compression devices or arterial venous compression boots.
  - Apply to the lower legs only.
  - Avoid devices that will roll and interfere with circulation.
- Position the patient.
  - Place a padded footboard on the foot of the bed to prevent the patient from slipping when the bed is placed in the reverse Trendelenburg position. Ensure that the patient's feet and ankles are in an anatomically neutral position and secure them to the footboard.
  - Place the patient's arms on extended arm boards. Wedges may be used if needed. Some procedures may require the patient's arms to be tucked securely at his or her sides to facilitate the surgeon's positioning (eg, when measuring the small bowel during the duodenal switch procedure).
  - Pay special attention to the breasts of both male and female patients. Secure the patient in a manner to avoid injury.
  - Pad all pressure points.
  - Place padding between the patient and any positioning device attached to the OR bed.
  - Place the patient in reverse Trendelenburg's position to facilitate access to the stomach area according to physician preference.
- Assess extremities for circulatory compromise.
- Place upper and lower temperature-regulating blankets on the patient to maintain his or her body temperature.[30]

Postoperative

The following activities should be performed postoperatively.

- Assess skin integrity, particularly at pressure points.
- Assess extremities for circulatory compromise.
- Move the patient to an appropriately sized bed for transport.
- Continue to perform continuous positive airway pressure procedures according to the physician's orders.

♦ Continue use of sequential compression devices, if ordered.

♦ Check dressings as appropriate for the procedure performed.

G. Evaluation of Outcomes

The perioperative nurse evaluates the patient's progress toward attainment of outcomes. This evaluation should be systematic, ongoing, and documented using the recognized, standardized perioperative nursing vocabulary. Outcome indicators will vary according to the specific desired outcome and may include

♦ physiological indicators (eg, nausea, vomiting, anastomosis leak, stricture, skin condition, deep vein thrombosis);

♦ cognitive indicators (eg, repeats instructions correctly, asks appropriate questions);

♦ affective indicators (eg, verbalizes individual needs and whether they are met, verbalizes and demonstrates willingness to comply with the treatment regimen);

♦ supportive resources (eg, family members participate in care planning and delivery); and

♦ patient satisfaction.

Evaluation of patient progress is based on observations of the patient's responses to nursing interventions and the effectiveness of interventions in moving the patient toward the desired outcome. Desired patient outcomes, nursing interventions, and potentially applicable nursing diagnoses are articulated in the standardized perioperative nursing vocabulary, which provides the basis for documentation of perioperative nursing practice. Ongoing assessment should be used to revise diagnoses, outcomes, and the plan of care as needed. Revisions in diagnoses, outcomes, and the plan of care should be documented. The patient, his or her significant others, and other health care providers should be involved in the evaluation process when appropriate.

III. Developing a Program

A. Financial Implications

When a facility begins a bariatric program, it is a significant financial commitment. It is important that the facility and its physicians understand the impact and begin discussion with payers to determine whether the procedures are covered and, if

so, what number of patients each insurer will cover at what reimbursement rates. If insurance companies do not cover the procedure, a self-pay schedule for these procedures needs to be determined based on total cost per procedure. This information will be used when developing the business plan.

With the increase in the number of bariatric procedures performed, the market has been flooded with new products. It is important for health care providers and administrators to be educated about what is available and to benchmark the facility's program with other programs to be competitive in the marketplace. Many companies help promote programs and surgeons and can help ensure the program is as cost-effective as possible.

Staffing is another significant financial consideration. Additional staffing will be needed to support a bariatric program. Patients who undergo bariatric surgery require more assistance. The surgeon may require additional personnel in the OR. After the patient is on the nursing unit, he or she will need assistance ambulating and with other activities of daily living for a period of time. Staff member availability is a serious consideration.

B. Rationale for a Bariatric Surgery Program

Careful consideration should be given to the driving forces for implementing a bariatric surgery program. Often a decision is made in an effort to differentiate the facility in the marketplace. An absence of such a program in the geographic area represents an opportunity for the facility to distinguish itself in the community. Surgeons with bariatric surgery expertise may be present on the staff of the facility, or it may be necessary to recruit these surgeons from elsewhere. Another driving force for program implementation is the potential return on investment. If bariatric surgeons already are present on staff, implementing a bariatric surgery program can represent new or expanded revenue. Even if the facility must recruit these surgeons, revenue potential exists. In addition, it is likely that a portion of patients having bariatric surgery will be self-pay clients, representing previously untapped revenue. Finally, patient demand may be the primary driving force for developing and implementing a program, provided it can be shown that such a program would be fiscally sound.

C. Elements of a
Financially Successful Program

A successful bariatric surgery program will be multidisciplinary and comprehensive, offering all the necessary services within the program. There must be commitment to the program from the top of the organization down, beginning with the governing body and facility administrators. An accounting system capable of providing information about revenues and actual costs of the program will be essential. Knowledge about payers and reimbursement also will be necessary. As noted, it may be necessary to negotiate with third-party payers to determine exactly what services will be covered and to what extent they will be covered. Based on this knowledge, careful control of case mix will be important to maintain fiscal viability of the program. An appropriate mix of insured, partially insured, and self-pay clients can contribute to a successful program. Program marketing strategies also can play a role in the financial success of a program. This is especially important when there are multiple programs in an area. It will be important for the program to distinguish itself from others.

D. The Business Plan

A business plan should be developed for any new program, a change in an existing program, or for physician recruitment. The planning process will vary according to protocols in the individual facility or system. A bariatric surgery program should be thoroughly planned before procedures are performed. Many departments will be involved in some way in the care of patients having bariatric surgery, so the planning team may be quite large. At a minimum the team should include a

- facility administrator,
- chief financial officer,
- director of business development or marketing,
- director or vice president of clinical program management,
- director or chief of surgery and the sponsoring chief of service,
- director of perioperative services,
- director or vice president of patient care services, including nursing, and
- director of purchasing/contracting.

After completing the business plan and deciding to go forward with the program, others will join in making the plan operational and in actual plan implementation.

The business plan will vary according to the protocols and needs of the individual facility or system. The mission, vision, and strategic plan of the facility should be reviewed to determine that the proposed program fits within those parameters. If it does not, the program may not be appropriate for the facility, or the mission, vision, and strategic plan may require modification for congruency with the proposed program. The business plan should contain a description of the proposed program, including both clinical and educational components. An assessment of the internal environment and external environments will be an important part of the business plan. The internal assessment will consist of identifying strengths, weaknesses, opportunities, and threats (ie, SWOT analysis) of the system as it exists. The external assessment will consider things such as identified need, target market, competition, market share or potential market share, and regulatory or legislative issues.

Finally, the business plan will have a financial component in which projected costs and revenues will be identified. Costs will include the cost of program development and marketing; personnel, including physician recruitment if necessary; and technology and equipment. Space also must be considered, along with that needed for other systems that may be put into place or upgraded. The following list can be used to consider components to be included in the business plan:

- service description with clinical and educational components;
- program objectives;
- program incentives;
- service continuum;
- technology or equipment required for the program;
- timeline (ie, length of time to increase to full incremental volume);
- competition;
- target market and market share, including
  - inpatient surgeries,
  - diagnosis-related groups, and
  - outpatient visits;
- pricing and contracting;
- financial investment (eg, capital and operational costs), including
  - physician full-time equivalents (FTEs);
  - nonphysician FTEs;
  - equipment and supplies;
  - marketing;

- information systems;
- length and volume of OR procedures; and
- effects on the postanesthesia care unit (PACU), intensive care unit, and medical/surgical unit;
♦ regulatory issues; and
♦ barriers and obstacles.

When the business plan has been formulated, top administrative personnel should evaluate the plan and determine whether to proceed. When a decision is made to proceed, the plan should be reviewed with all stakeholders and those who will implement the plan. The plan should be familiar to these participants because their input was sought during creation of the business plan. It is important to include operations personnel during the planning process. The plan can be refined and some detail provided at this point in the process, but substantial changes should not be made without the approval of top administrators.

The plan should be funded from both the operational and capital budgets. After final approval and funding have been secured, staff members can be educated and the program launched. Periodic review and performance measurement will be essential to keep the program on track and viable. Program adjustments can be made based on performance reviews.

E. Operational Planning

After a commitment is made to move forward with a bariatric program, it is helpful to create a multidisciplinary operational planning team. Members of this team should include, but not be limited to,

♦ OR and PACU managers to coordinate program implementation;
♦ nurse educators to provide staff member education;
♦ anesthesia care provider(s) to collaborate on the development of the perioperative care pathway and coordinate education and equipment needs for the anesthesia department;
♦ surgeon(s) to collaborate on the development of the perioperative plan of care;
♦ a nutritionist to provide preoperative and postoperative teaching and support patients' nutritional needs;
♦ a respiratory therapist to promote best possible ventilation;
♦ a physical therapist to provide services, as needed;

♦ a medical/surgical nursing representative to plan for postoperative patient care;
♦ a pharmacist to ensure pharmaceutical needs are met;
♦ radiology and endoscopy representatives to provide for their role in the program, if required;
♦ a clinical psychologist for patient evaluation; and
♦ a materials manager to negotiate contracts and ensure adequate inventory.

The goal of the team is to plan program operation and create timelines and a plan for implementation. The size of the operational planning team and the magnitude of the project makes it useful to develop a team charter as a working document. This charter will provide clarity and a framework for the operational team. The charter should be written and should describe the mission of the team and how the mission will be accomplished. The charter directs the operational planning process, establishes key milestones for the process, and identifies desired outcomes. Elements of the team charter will vary depending on circumstances in the facility. **Table 3** contains an example of elements to be included in a team charter.

F. Impact on the Workplace

To achieve a successful bariatric program, there must be a demonstrated commitment to provide adequate facilities and equipment. There also must be a multifaceted approach throughout the institution.

Physical plant considerations
All support areas of the hospital should have adequate equipment and furnishings to accommodate bariatric patients. The waiting area should contain
♦ appropriate furniture,
♦ love seats or chairs with extra width and side reinforcements,
♦ accessible bathrooms with floor-mounted or reinforced wall-mounted toilets at elevated levels with reinforced grab bars, and
♦ extra large wheelchairs.
The preoperative area should contain
♦ wide stretchers with fully functional hydraulics,
♦ extra large gowns with shoulder snaps,
♦ large and extra large blood pressure cuffs, and
♦ a wheelchair-accessible large scale.

The OR should contain

- an OR bed for bariatric procedures with the capacity to hold up to 1,000 lbs with 600 lbs tilt capacity—attachments to extend the sides of the bed should be included;
- a footboard with holders to attach to the bariatric OR bed;
- a hydraulic lift or appropriate moving device to ensure easy positioning of the patient and easier transfer back to the bed after surgery—this device should be ergonomically safe for staff members and protect them from back injuries;
- sequential compression devices (ie, knee high) or arterial-venous compression boots with appropriate motor units;
- a blanket on the bottom portion of the OR bed to wrap lower extremities to ensure thigh adduction while maintaining physiologic external rotation of the feet;
- foam padding for arms, heels, and feet;
- cotton cast padding to wrap the patient's arms on the arm board because the hook and loop fastener strap normally used alone may not be sufficient;
- a draw-sheet long enough to tuck the patient's arms at his or her sides;
- Hurst or Maloney dilators per the physician's preference (ie, sizes 30 to 60) to ensure adequate size of anastomosis;
- an endoscopy cart with an upper GI endoscope; and
- upper and lower body temperature-regulating blankets to ensure adequate body temperature.

Special instrumentation should include

- esophageal dilators,
- long instruments for open procedures, and
- long instruments for laparoscopic procedures.

Patients must be transported to the PACU in a bed appropriate to the patient's size and weight. The majority of patients will have a nasogastric (NG) tube in place. Within 12 to 24 hours, most patients will be taken to radiology to test the anastomosis for leaks. Some physicians prefer a leak test using methylene blue in sodium chloride via the NG tube.

Integrated services/multidisciplinary participation

A number of departments should be involved in the patient's care. The patient may need psychological, nutritional, and follow-up support.

Table 3

ELEMENTS TO INCLUDE IN A TEAM CHARTER

- Team name (eg, bariatric task force)
- Subject (eg, executing the bariatric business plan), which clarifies the purpose of the team
- Plan/version number—tracks versions as they are developed and accepted by the team
- Team sponsor—the senior leader who supports this effort and will be expected to break down barriers for the team
- Team leader—an individual who will guide the team to a successful outcome and will communicate with senior leadership
- Team facilitator—an optional support person who may be needed to promote effective group dynamics and provide structure and guidance
- Team members and areas of expertise—who will be on the team and why
- Team member time commitments—the team's meeting schedule and allowances for team members' planning
- Problem/opportunity statement—why this effort was initiated and what will be affected by the outcome
- Strategic alignment—how the development of this program aligns with organizational and departmental goals
- Scope—boundaries of the project
- Objectives—specific and measurable objectives
- Available resources—who and what is available to support the team
- Considerations (ie, assumptions, constraints, obstacles, risks)—identifies positive and negative factors and clarifies expectations
- Customers—patient population and customer needs
- Key stakeholders—who will be affected by the team and its work
- Key milestones/dates—specific expectations and deliverables
- Communication/action plan—who, how, and when
- Performance improvement—focus and a way to measure progress

Psychology. Of great concern is the lack of respect that people who are morbidly obese experience. A survey of individuals who were severely obese found that nearly 80% reported being treated disrespectfully by medical professionals.[31] There are widespread negative attitudes that adults who are morbidly obese are weak-willed, ugly, awkward, self-indulgent, and immoral. This intense prejudice cuts across age, gender, religion, race, and socioeconomic status. Numerous studies have documented the stigma people who are obese experience in most areas of social functioning. This can promote psychological distress and increase the risk of developing a psychological disorder. Patients who are morbidly obese are at risk for affective, anxiety, and substance abuse disorders. People who are obese often consider their condition to be a greater handicap than deafness, dyslexia, or blindness.[32,33]

Nutritional implications. Nutrients needed by all patients include water, protein, carbohydrates, fat, and vitamins. Dieticians play a pivotal role preoperatively and postoperatively in bariatric surgery. Preoperatively, the dietitian determines whether patients meet the NIH Consensus Panel's weight criteria calculations.[34] A full nutritional assessment is performed followed by a discussion of postoperative diet. Preoperative diet education classes have proven to be very successful. Postoperatively, the dietitian's role includes monitoring weight loss progress (ie, number of pounds lost; percentage of excess weight loss; percentage of weight loss; adequacy of dietary intake; exercise) and psychological and social support of the multiple changes that can occur in the patient's life.

Follow-up support groups. According to an NIH statement from September 1998, "An integrated program must be in place to provide guidance on diet, physical activity, and behavioral therapy, as well as to provide social support before and after surgery."[34] Patients are encouraged to consider joining a support group. These programs may be offered by the surgeon's office, the hospital, or a third party. Many patients find that a support group helps them deal with the challenges that may occur as a result of life and health changes. In one study, patients who regularly attended group meetings tended to lose more weight, and increased frequency of attendance was associated with greater weight loss.[35] It is critical that a support group leader have a full understanding of and be in compliance with the guidelines set forth by the surgeon. Everything that a support group leader says or does is perceived to be the surgeon's point of view. Great caution should be taken to ensure that support group leaders know and understand what kind of influence they have and are willing to assume the responsibility.

Employee education and competency

Staff members from all disciplines providing perioperative care to bariatric patients should participate in a comprehensive education program. The education plan for different disciplines will vary. For example, the education plan for nursing and specified disciplines should include, but not be limited to,

- an overview of the disease of morbid obesity and its associated comorbidities;
- the procedures performed and the associated complications during each phase of the perioperative period;
- obesity sensitivity training that focuses on the rights of each patient to be treated with dignity and the need to prevent obesity discrimination;
- obesity and bariatric surgery-related nutrition; and
- training and familiarity with all patient education materials, including
  - preoperative preparation materials,
  - nutrition materials,
  - postoperative care, and
  - long-term follow-up care postoperatively.

Nursing staff members who provide patient education should have a clear understanding of the preoperative evaluation process, including the preoperative testing regimen (eg, psychiatric screening, sleep studies, laboratory tests, upper GI series). Perioperative staff members should communicate to other caregivers along the continuum the patient's weight and BMI to individualize patient care needs (ie, gown size, bed selection, OR bed selection, patient transportation needs, other size-related aspects of care).

Intraoperative patient safety concerns, including positioning patients who are morbidly obese, should be reviewed, and competency should be validated. Intraoperative methods for measuring the integrity of the gastrojejunostomy should be the subject of an inservice program, and competency should be validated. Staff members should be knowledgeable about the quality indicators that will be used to monitor bariatric surgery, and results of this monitoring should be made available to staff members as part of a performance improvement process.

Staff members who provide care to bariatric patients would benefit from attending at least one of the classes patients are required to attend, as well as a support group meeting. It is suggested that these classes provide contact hours for hospital staff members who attend.

Physician education and competency

Bariatric surgeons, like those in other subspecialty areas, must be formally educated in bariatric surgery, acquire clinical experience, and demonstrate expertise in performing bariatric surgery before being granted privileges. The ASBS has published guidelines for granting privileges to surgeons who perform bariatric surgery.[36] The ASBS is a recognized educational professional medical society; it is not a credentialing body. Each facility should develop criteria and define acceptable credentials required for general surgeons to be eligible for privileges.

G. Inpatient Outcome Indicators

Each facility should identify and monitor outcome indicators to be reviewed by the hospital-wide process improvement committee. Such criteria should include, but not be limited to,

- average BMI of patients having bariatric surgery;
- postoperative admission to surgical intensive care;
- ambulation on the day of surgery;
- complications (eg, postoperative fever, nausea, vomiting, diarrhea, surgical site infection, deep vein thrombosis, pulmonary embolism, pneumonia);
- need to return to surgery (eg, anastomotic leak, small bowel obstruction, inguinal hernia, stricture);
- average length of stay; and
- readmission within 30 days.

IV. Conclusion

This guideline was developed to promote safe care for morbidly obese patients undergoing bariatric surgery. This surgery is complex and requires a special understanding of the needs of this patient population to ensure optimal outcomes. This document addresses prevalence, history, pathophysiology, program fundamentals, patient considerations, nursing process applications, and impact on the workplace. It is AORN's intent that practitioners will use this document in their facilities to develop policies, procedures, and protocols specific to bariatric surgery and care of patients who are morbidly obese. This guideline may require alteration based on specific patient and facility needs.

REFERENCES

1. "Overweight and obesity threaten US health gains," HHS News, *http://www.surgeongeneral.gov/news/pressreleases/pr_obesity.PDF* (accessed 9 Feb 2004).

2. "Statistics related to overweight and obesity," National Institute of Diabetes and Digestive and Kidney Diseases, Weight Control Information Network, *http://www.niddk.nih.gov/health/nutrit/pubs/statobes.htm* (accessed 9 Feb 2004)

3. C L Ogden et al, "Prevalence and trends in overweight among US children and adolescents, 1999-2000," *JAMA* 288 (Oct 9, 2002) 1728-1732.

4. R P Troiano, K M Flegal, "Overweight children and adolescents: Description, epidemiology, and demographics," *Pediatrics* 101 (March 1998) 497-504.

5. E A Finkelstein, I C Fiebelkorn, G Wang, "National medical spending attributable to overweight and obesity: How much, and who's paying?" *Health Affairs* Web exclusive, *http://content.healthaffairs.org/cgi/reprint/hlthaff.w3.219v1.pdf* (accessed 9 Feb 2004).

6. A M Wolf, G A Colditz, "Current estimates of the economic cost of obesity in the United States," *Obesity Research* 6 (March 1998) 97-106.

7. P Graling, H Elariny, "Perioperative care of the patient with morbid obesity," *AORN Journal* 77 (April 2003) 803.

8. "Rationale for the surgical treatment of morbid obesity," American Society for Bariatric Surgery, *http://www.asbs.org/html/rationale/rationale.html* (accessed 9 Feb 2004).

9. F Pi-Sunyer, "Comorbidities of overweight and obesity: Current evidence and research issue," *Medical Science Sports and Exercise* 31 suppl (November 1999) 602-608.

10. A MacGregory, "The story of surgery for obesity," American Society for Bariatric Surgery, *http://www.asbs.org/html/story/chapter 1.html* (accessed 9 Feb 2004)

11. M Deitel, S A Shikora, "The development of the surgical treatment of morbid obesity," *Journal of the American College of Nutrition* 21 (October 2002) 365-371.

12. L I Kuzmak et al, "Surgery for morbid obesity using an inflatable gastric band," *AORN Journal* 51 (May 1990) 1307-1324.

13. "Gastrointestinal surgery for severe obesity. Proceedings of a National Institutes of Health Consensus Development Conference. March 25-27, 1991, Bethesda, MD," *American Journal of Clinical Nutrition* 55 suppl (February 1992) 487S-619S.

14. B G Woodward, "Bariatric surgery options," *Critical Care Nursing Quarterly* 26 (April-June 2003) 89-100.

15. W J Pories et al, "Who would have thought it? An operation proves to be the most effective therapy for adult-onset diabetes mellitus," *Annals of Surgery* 222 (September 1995) 339-352.

16. H J Sugerman et al, "Gastric bypass for treating severe obesity," *American Journal of Clinical Nutrition* 55 suppl (February 1992) 560S-566S.

17. W C Willett et al, "Weight, weight change, and coronary heart disease in women. Risk within the 'normal' weight range," *JAMA* 273 (Feb 8, 1995) 461-465.

18. J H Linner, R L Drew, "Why the operation we prefer is the Roux-Y gastric bypass," *Obesity Surgery* 1 (September 1991) 305-306.

19. E E Mason, "Gastric surgery for morbid obesity," *Surgery Clinics of North America* 72 (April 1992) 501-513.

20. C E Yale, "Gastric surgery for morbid obesity. Complications and long-term weight control," *Archives of Surgery* 124 (August 1989) 941-946.

21. L D MacLean, B M Rhode, R A Forse, "Late results of vertical banded gastroplasty for morbid and super obesity," *Surgery* 107 (January 1990) 20-27.

22. J C Hall et al, "Gastric surgery for morbid obesity. The Adelaide Study," *Annals of Surgery* 211 (April 1990) 419-427.

23. R E Brolin, "Results of obesity surgery," *Gastroenterology Clinics of North America* 16 (June 1987) 317-338.

24. J J Gleysteen, "Results of surgery: Long-term effects on hyperlipidemia," *American Journal of Clinical Nutrition* 55 suppl (February 1992) 591S-593S.

25. P N Benotti et al, "Heart disease and hypertension in severe obesity: The benefits of weight reduction," *American Journal of Clinical Nutrition* 55 suppl (February 1992) 586S-590S.

26. K G MacDonald, Jr, et al, "The gastric bypass operation reduces the progression and mortality of non-insulin-dependent diabetes mellitus," *Journal of Gastrointestinal Surgery* 1 (May 1997) 213-220.

27. J G Kral, L V Sjostrom, M B Sullivan, "Assessment of quality of life before and after surgery for severe obesity," *American Journal of Clinical Nutrition* 55 suppl (February 1992) 611S-614S.

28. C S Rand, A Macgregor, G Hankins, "Gastric bypass surgery for obesity: Weight loss, psychosocial outcome, and morbidity one and three years later," *Southern Medical Journal* 79 (December 1986) 1511-1514.

29. S Beyea, ed, *Perioperative Nursing Data Set* (Denver: AORN, Inc, 2002).

30. *Health Implications of Obesity* (Rockville, Md: US Department of Health and Human Services, Public Health Service, National Institutes of Health, Office of Medical Applications of Research, 1985).

31. G L Maddox, V Leiderman, "Overweight as a social disability with medical implications," *Journal of Medical Education* 44 (March 1969) 214-220.

32. C S Rand, A M Macgregor, "Morbidly obese patients' perceptions of social discrimination before and after surgery for obesity," *Southern Medical Journal* 83 (December 1990) 1390-1395.

33. C S Rand, A M Macgregor, "Successful weight loss following obesity surgery and the perceived liability of morbid obesity," *International Journal of Obesity* 15 (September 1991) 577-579.

34. National Institutes of Health, "Health Implications of Obesity," NIH Consensus Statement Online, *http://consensus,nih.gov/cons/049/049_statement.htm* (accessed 9 Feb 2004).

35. S E Hildebrandt, "Effects of participation in bariatric support group after Roux-en-Y gastric bypass," *Obesity Surgery* 8 (October 1998) 535-542.

36. "Guidelines for granting privileges in bariatric surgery," American Society for Bariatric Surgery, *http://www.asbs.org/html/story/chapter 4.html* (accessed 7 Feb 2004)

RESOURCES

Bennett, P H, et al. "Epidemiologic studies of diabetes in the Pima Indians," *Recent Progress in Hormone Research* 32 (1976) 333-376.

Benotti, P N, et al. "Gastric restrictive operations for morbid obesity," *American Journal of Surgery* 157 (January 1989) 150-155.

Bierman, E L; Bagdade, J D; Porte, D, Jr. "Obesity and diabetes: The odd couple," *American Journal of Clinical Nutrition* 21 (December 1968) 1434-1437.

Bouchard, C. *The Genetics of Obesity* (Boca Raton, Fla: CRC Press, 1994) 245.

Breaux, C W. "Obesity surgery in children," *Obesity Surgery* 5 (August 1995) 279-284.

Build and Blood Pressure Study (Chicago: Society of Actuaries, 1959).

Calle, E E, et al. "Body mass index and mortality in a prospective cohort of US adults," *The New England Journal of Medicine* 341 (Oct 7, 1999) 1097-1105.

Charuzi, I, et al. "Bariatric surgery in morbidly obese sleep-apnea patients: Short- and long-term follow-up," *American Journal of Clinical Nutrition* 55 suppl (February 1992) 594S-596S.

Colditz, G A, et al. "Weight as a risk factor for clinical diabetes in women," *American Journal of Epidemiology* 132 (September 1990) 501-513.

Dixon, J B; Chapman, L; O'Brien, P. "Marked improvement in asthma after Lap-Band surgery for morbid obesity," *Obesity Surgery* 9 (August 1999) 385-389.

Drenick, E J, et al. "Excessive mortality and causes of death in morbidly obese men," *JAMA* 243 (Feb 1, 1980) 443-445.

Francke, S, et al. "Genetic studies of the leptin receptor gene in morbidly obese French Caucasian families," *Human Genetics* 100 (October 1997) 491-496.

Freidman, J M; Halaas, J L. "Leptin and the regulation of body weight in mammals," *Nature* 395 (Oct 22, 1998) 763-770.

Garfinkel, L. "Overweight and cancer," *Annals of Internal Medicine* 103 (December 1985) 1034-1036.

Hartz, A J, et al. "Relationship of obesity to diabetes: Influences of obesity level and body fat distribution," *Prevention Medicine* 12 (March 1983) 351-357.

"Health implications of obesity. National Institutes of Health Consensus Development Conference statement," *Annals of Internal Medicine* 103 (December 1985) 1073-1077.

Higa, K D; Boone, K B; Ho, T. "Complications of the laparoscopic Roux-en-Y gastric bypass: 1,040 patients—what have we learned?" *Obesity Surgery* 10 (December 2000) 509-513.

Hubert, H B, et al. "Obesity as an independent risk factor for cardiovascular disease: A 26-year follow-up of participants in the Framingham Heart Study," *Circulation* 67 (May 1983) 968-977.

Kalkhoff, R K, et al. "Relationship of body fat distribution to blood pressure, carbohydrate tolerance, and plasma lipids in healthy obese women," *The Journal of Laboratory and Clinical Medicine* 102 (October 1983) 621-627.

Kanders, B S, et al. "Weight loss outcome and health benefits associated with the Optifast program in the treatment of obesity," *International Journal of Obesity* 13 no 2 suppl (1989) 131-134.

Kuczmarski, R J. "Prevalence of overweight and weight gain in the United States," *American Journal of Clinical Nutrition* 55 suppl (February 1992) 495S-502S.

Kuczmarski, R J, et al. "Varying body mass index cutoff points to describe overweight prevalence among US adults: NHANES III (1988 to 1994)," *Obesity Research* 5 (November 1997) 542-548.

Lew, E A; Garfinkel, L. "Variations in mortality by weight among 750,000 men and women," *Journal of Chronic Diseases* 32 no 8 (1979) 563-576.

Linner, J H; Drew, R L. "Reoperative surgery—Indications, efficacy, and long-term follow-up," *American Journal of Clinical Nutrition* 55 suppl (February 1992) 606S-610S.

Macgregor, A M; Greenberg, R A. "Effect of surgically induced weight loss on asthma in the morbidly obese," *Obesity Surgery* 3 (February 1993) 15-21.

Macgregor, A M; Rand, C S. "Gastric surgery in morbid obesity. Outcome in patients aged 55 years and older," *Archives of Surgery* 128 (October 1993) 1153-1157.

Macgregor, A M; Rand, C S. "Revision of staple line failure following Roux-en-Y gastric bypass for obesity: A follow-up of weight loss," *Obesity Surgery* 1 (June 1991) 151-154.

Mason, E E; Renquist, K; Jiang, D. "Predictors of two obesity complications: Diabetes and hypertension," *Obesity Surgery* 2 (August 1992) 231-237.

Murr, M M; Siadati, M R; Sarr, M G. "Results of bariatric surgery for morbid obesity in patients older than 50 years," *Obesity Surgery* 5 (November 1995) 399-402.

Powers, P S, "Conservative treatments for morbid obesity," in *Surgery for the Morbidly Obese Patient*, ed M Deitel (Philadelphia: Lea & Febiger, 1989) 27-37.

Rand, C S; Macgregor, A M. "Adolescents having obesity surgery: A 6-year follow-up," *Southern Medical Journal* 87 (December 1994) 1208-1213.

Rand, C S; Macgregor, A M. "Medical care and pregnancy outcome after gastric bypass surgery for obesity," (letter) *Southern Medical Journal* 82 (October 1989) 1319-1320.

Rand, C S; Macgregor, A M; Hankins, G C. "Eating behavior after gastric bypass surgery for obesity," *Southern Medical Journal* 80 (August 1987) 961-964.

Safer, D J. "Diet, behavior modification, and exercise. A review of obesity treatments from a long-term perspective," *Southern Medical Journal* 84 (December 1991) 1470-1474.

Sjostrom, C D, et al. "Reduction in incidence of diabetes, hypertension and lipid disturbances after intentional weight loss induced by bariatric surgery: The SOS Intervention Study," *Obesity Research* 7 (September 1999) 477-484.

Sjostrom, L, et al. "Swedish obese subjects (SOS). Recruitment for an intervention study and a selected description of the obese state," *International Journal of Obesity and Related Metabolic Disorders* 16 (June 1992) 465-479.

Stevens, J, et al. "The effect of age on the association between body-mass index and mortality," *The New England Journal of Medicine* 338 (Jan 1, 1998) 1-7.

Strauss, R S; Bradley, L J; Brolin, R E. "Gastric bypass surgery in adolescents with morbid obesity," *The Journal of Pediatrics* 138 (April 2001) 499-504.

Stunkard, A J. "An overview of current treatments for obesity," in *Treatment of the Seriously Obese Patient*, ed T A Wadden, T B Van Itallie (New York: Guilford Press, 1992) 34.

Sugerman, H J, et al. "Long-term effects of gastric surgery for treating respiratory insufficiency of obesity," *American Journal of Clinical Nutrition* 55 suppl (February 1992) 597S-601S.

Vallis, M T; Ross, M A. "The role of psychological factors in bariatric surgery for morbid obesity: Identification of psychological predictors of success," *Obesity Surgery* 4 (November 1993) 346-359.

Van Itallie, T B. "Health implications of overweight and obesity in the United States," *Annals of Internal Medicine* 103 (December 1985) 983-988.

"Very low calorie diets. National Task Force on the Prevention and Treatment of Obesity, National Institutes of Health," *JAMA* 270 (Aug 25, 1993) 967-974.

Weintraub, M, et al. "Long-term weight control study. IV (weeks 156-190). The second double-blind phase," *Clinical Pharmacology and Therapeutics* 51 (May 1992) 608-614.

Westlund, K; Nickolaysen, R. "Ten-year mortality and morbidity related to serum cholesterol. A follow-up of 3,751 men aged 40-49," *Scandinavian Journal of Clinical and Laboratory Investigation Supplementum* 127 (1972) 1-24.

Wittgrove, A C; Clark, G W. "Laparoscopic gastric bypass, Roux-en-Y—500 patients: Technique and results, with 3-60 month follow-up," *Obesity Surgery* 10 (June 2000) 233-239.

Wittgrove, A C, et al. "Pregnancy following gastric bypass for morbid obesity," *Obesity Surgery* 8 (August 1998) 461-466.

York, D A. "Peripheral and central mechanisms regulating food intake and macronutrient selection," *Obesity Surgery* 9 (October 1999) 471-479.

Originally published May 2004, *AORN Journal,* and in *Standards, Recommended Practices, and Guidelines,* 2005 edition.

AORN Perioperative Standards and Recommended Practices, 2009 Edition

I. Overview

A. Introduction

Preamble

Natural rubber latex allergy is a significant medical concern because it affects health care workers, as well as the general population. It crosses racial and ethnic boundaries, and it can affect males or females anytime during their lives.

There is no cure at this time, only prevention. Three types of reactions are associated with latex products. In order of frequency of occurrence they are an irritant reaction, a delayed hypersensitivity reaction (ie, type IV), and an immediate hypersensitivity reaction (ie, type I) (**Table 1**). Any individual who experiences any type of latex-associated reaction should be evaluated by a qualified health care practitioner.

Assumptions

Natural rubber latex allergy can be a serious and potentially life-threatening condition. Health care workers and others who experience repeated exposure to latex allergens can develop a latex sensitivity or allergy. Several hundred cases of severe allergic reactions and anaphylaxis and 17 deaths have been reported to the US Food and Drug Administration (FDA).[1,2]

Sensitivity can be described as development of an immunologic memory to the specific latex proteins; however, the affected individual may be asymptomatic. Allergy is the demonstrated outward expression of the sensitivity (eg, hives, rhinitis, conjunctivitis, anaphylaxis). Sensitivity to natural rubber latex is more common than the actual allergy; however, any individual sensitized to natural rubber latex is at risk of a life-threatening reaction and should be treated in the same way as an allergic individual.

Powdered latex gloves are the most common item contributing to the latex load in health care facilities. Recent estimates have shown a 20-fold increase in medical glove use (in billions of pairs) since the introduction of universal precautions in 1987.[3] During the manufacturing process, powder usually is applied to the glove as cornstarch slurry when the glove still is on the mold or former. When the powder slurry is applied to the glove, the extractable, water-soluble proteins leach from the surface of the glove onto the cornstarch particle. When dry, the glove powder then acts as a vector that carries latex proteins from the glove into the environment.

Health care facilities and providers have an ethical responsibility to prevent latex sensitization in patients and employees by creating an environment in which it is safe to be treated and to work. Many facilities in the United States consciously have moved toward a latex-safe environment by switching from powdered latex gloves (eg, examination, surgical) and other latex products to powder-free products with reduced latex protein content. High-protein, powdered latex gloves and other products that create aerosolization can contaminate a facility's environment with latex allergens.

In 1998, Sussman et al reported a 1% annual incidence of sensitization among powdered latex-glove users, whereas users of powder-free, low-protein, latex glove reported a 0% sensitization rate.[4] In 1999, Levy et al studied a group of dental students in both France and England, reporting that students who wore protein-rich (ie, high protein), powdered latex gloves had a 15% and a 5% sensitization rate, respectively, while students who wore powder-free, protein-poor (ie, low protein) gloves had a 0% sensitization rate.[5]

It is unsafe to treat latex-allergic individuals in an environment laden with latex allergens. Individuals who have been clinically diagnosed as either sensitive or allergic to natural rubber latex should be treated or work in an environment that is latex-safe, with additional measures taken for the immediate vicinity (ie, room) in which the individual receives or provides care. If the entire care facility is maintained as a latex-safe environment, few additional precautions will be needed for latex-allergic individuals. If the facility is not maintained as latex-safe, comprehensive latex precautions will be required each time a latex-allergic individual presents for care or services.

This revised "AORN latex guideline" is based on research and expert opinion available at the time of its revision. Ongoing and future research likely will enhance and expand current knowledge about this topic.

Review of this document has been solicited from content experts at the American Association of Nurse Anesthetists (AANA), the American College of Surgeons (ACS), the American Society of Anesthesiologists (ASA), the American Academy of Allergy, Asthma, and Immunology (AAAAI), the American College of Allergy, Asthma, and Immunology (ACAAI), the American Nurses Association (ANA), the Association of Practitioners of Infection Control, Inc (APIC), the Spina Bifida Association, and the

Table 1

TYPES OF REACTIONS TO LATEX[1-4]				
Type of Reaction	**Cause**	**Onset**	**Symptoms**	**Prevention**
Irritant contact dermatitis *(Nonallergic irritation; not a true allergy)*	Frequent hand washing, insufficient rinsing, aggressive scrubbing technique, use of anti-septics, climatic irritation, glove occlusion, glove powder.	Reaction develops gradually over a period of days or weeks.	Scaling, drying, cracking of skin may develop as dermatitis on the backs of the hands. Wearing latex gloves when symptoms are present may increase the risk of developing latex allergy.	Obtain medical diagnosis, dermatology consultation; avoid irritant product; ensure barrier effectiveness of glove material; consider alternative products, cotton glove liners.
Type IV hypersensitivity; T cell-mediated *(Also called delayed cutaneous hypersensitivity; allergic contact dermatitis; chemical allergy)*	Results from exposure to chemicals used in latex harvesting, processing, or manufacturing (eg, thiurams, carbamates, benzothiazoles)	Rash usually begins six to 48 hours after contact and may progress to oozing skin blisters or spread away from the area of skin touched by the latex.	Red, raised, palpable area with bumps, sores, and horizontal cracks may extend up the forearm. May occur after a sensitization period resulting from repeated exposure to latex or irritant chemical.	Obtain medical diagnosis, dermatology consultation; identify irritant chemical; use alternative glove material without chemical; ensure barrier effectiveness of glove material; consider alternative products, cotton glove liners.
Type I hypersensitivity; immunoglobulin-mediated *(Also called immediate reaction hypersensitivity; latex allergy; protein allergy)*	Results from exposure to proteins in latex on glove surface or bound to powder and suspended in the air, settled on objects, or transferred by touch.	Reactions usually begin within minutes of exposure but can occur as much as two hours later. May fade away rapidly after removing the glove.	Mild reactions involve skin redness, hives, or itching on the skin under the glove. The chronic form may mimic irritant and allergic contact dermatitis. More severe reactions may include facial swelling, rhinitis, eye symptoms, generalized urticaria, scratchy throat, respiratory distress, and asthma. In rare cases, anaphylactic shock may occur.	Obtain medical diagnosis, allergy consultation; substitute nonlatex gloves or other nonlatex products; reduce or eliminate exposure to glove powder; clean powder from environment; consider latex-safe environment.

REFERENCES
1. Latex Allergy: Protect Yourself, Protect Your Patients (*Silver Spring, MD: American Nurses Association, 1996*).
2. *"Preventing allergic reactions to natural rubber latex in the workplace," NIOSH publ no 97-135, National Institute of Occupational Safety and Health, http://www.cdc .gov/niosh/latexalt.html (accessed Sept 4, 2008).*
3. *Reddy, S, "Latex allergy," American Academy of Family Physicians, http://www.aafp.org/afp/980101ap/reddy.html (accessed Sept 4, 2008).*
4. *"Potential for sensitization and possible allergic reaction to natural rubber latex gloves and other natural rubber products," Occupational Safety and Health Administration, http://www.osha.gov/dts/shib/shib012808.html (accessed Sept 4, 2008).*

National Institute of Occupational Safety and Health (NIOSH) division of the Centers for Disease Control and Prevention, as well as the AORN Board of Directors and other recognized experts. This guideline may not apply to every individual and may require modification based on specific needs of a given patient, health care provider, or situation.

Definitions
For purposes of this document the following definitions apply.

♦ *Allergen:* A substance that in some individuals can cause an allergic or hypersensitivity reaction but is not normally considered harmful.[6]
♦ *Allergenic:* A substance that can elicit a hypersensitivity reaction in certain individuals.[7]
♦ *Allergy:* An immune reaction to an environmental agent that results in a symptomatic reaction.[6,7]
♦ *Antigen:* Any molecule or substance, more often a protein, that has the ability to bind to an antibody.[6,7] "The name arises from their ability to generate antibodies."[6]

◆ *Irritant contact dermatitis:* A nonallergic, cutaneous response to an irritant. Normally this reaction is primarily localized to the site of exposure. This is not a latex allergy.

◆ *Allergic contact dermatitis (type IV: T-cell mediated/delayed hypersensitivity):* A delayed, T-cell mediated hypersensitivity response attributed to chemicals (ie, antigens) used in the latex and some synthetic manufacturing processes and absorbed through the skin.[6] This reaction generally is localized to the contact area.

◆ *Latex:* Also known as natural rubber latex, this milky cytosol is acquired by tapping the commercial rubber tree, *Hevea brasiliensis.*

◆ *Latex allergy (type immunoglobulin E [IgE]-mediated/immediate hypersensitivity response):* A localized or systemic allergic response to one or more specific proteins (ie, antigens)[6] found in latex to which the individual has been sensitized and has developed antibodies.

◆ *Latex-free environment:* An environment in which all latex-containing products, not simply gloves, have been removed. This state is considered unattainable due to the ubiquitous nature of latex products.

◆ *Latex-safe environment:* An environment in which every reasonable effort has been made to remove high-allergen and airborne latex sources from coming into direct contact with affected individuals. The airborne latex protein load should be less than 0.6 ng per cubic meter.[8]

◆ *Latex precautions:* Interventions to prevent reactions in people (eg, patients, health care workers) allergic to latex proteins.

◆ *Reactions associated with latex:* Irritant contact dermatitis, allergic type IV cell-mediated contact dermatitis, and type I IgE-mediated latex allergy. Only the type I IgE-mediated response constitutes a true latex allergy.

◆ *Sensitization:* The development of immunological memory in response to exposure to an antigen.

◆ *Sensitivity:* A clinical manifestation of symptoms or response that develops after sensitization.

Prevalence

Numerous studies indicate prevalence rates for IgE-mediated latex allergy from 0.8% to 6.5% of the general population.[1,9-13] Latex allergy is believed to be responsible for 70% of anaphylactic reactions occurring in anesthetized children with myelodysplasia

(eg, spina bifida).[12] Further, there is a large population of latex-sensitive individuals. Varying sensitization rates have been reported for both patients with myelodysplasia and health care workers.[14-17] According to Sussman, the prevalence rate of latex sensitization among patients with spina bifida is between 35% and 70%. The sensitization rate for health care workers with significant exposure to latex is reported to be 10% to 17%.[18] Although latex-sensitive individuals do not always present with clinical symptoms, these individuals should be assessed for latex allergy. For those who are latex-sensitive but have yet to manifest frank symptoms, there is no predictor of whether or when they will react; therefore, all individuals presenting with natural rubber latex sensitivity should be treated as if they are allergic.

In 1992, Lagier et al reported a 10.7% latex allergy rate in French perioperative nurses.[19] A study of Canadian perioperative nurses by Mace et al, in 1997, reported a 6.9% latex allergy prevalence.[20] Studies of perioperative personnel demonstrate sensitivity rates between 2.5% and 15.8%. In 1992, Arellano et al reported a 9.9% latex sensitization rate in a study of 101 anesthesiologists, radiologists, and surgeons.[21] In 1996, Grzybowski reported an 8.9% rate for hospital RNs in general, but showed perioperative nurses to be less affected than nurses in other areas. One possible explanation for this disparity was that nurses in the OR who were latex sensitive or allergic may have transferred to other nursing units.[22] In 1997, Konrad et al reported a 15.8% positive skin prick test rate for anesthesiologists.[23] In 1998, Brown et al identified 12.5% of anesthesiologists at a tertiary care hospital as sensitized (ie, IgE antibody positive by skin test or serology) with only 2.5% expressing symptoms.[24]

B. Pathophysiology

The major component of natural rubber latex is the hydrocarbon, cis-1, 4 polyisoprene. Chemicals such as sulfur, ammonia, mercaptobenzothiazole, thiuram, and antioxidants may be added during the manufacturing process. Latex protein content and residual chemical levels differ among producers due to variations in manufacturing processes.

Several natural rubber latex proteins responsible for allergenic reactions have been identified (**Table 2**), and sensitivity appears to differ among risk groups.[25-28] Proteins in natural rubber latex may cause a range of mild to severe or even life-threatening type I allergic reactions. Dipped products made

Table 2

KNOWN LATEX ALLERGENS				
Name	*Description*	*MW (kD)*	*Plant family*	*Cross-food*
Hev b 1	Rubber elongation factor	14.6		Papain
Hev b 2	Beta one=third gluconase	34-36	PR2	
Hev b 3	Prenyltransferase	24-27		
Hev b 4	Microhelix	110/50		
Hev b 5	Acidic protein	16-24		Kiwi
Hev b 6.02	Hevein protein	4.7	PR3	Kiwi, avocado, banana
Hev b 7	Patatin homologue	43-46		Potato
Hev b 8	Hevea profilin	14-14.2	Profilin	Pollens, celery
Hev b 9	Hevea enolase	51		Molds
Hev b 10	Mn superoxide dismutase	22-26		Molds
Hev b 11	Class I chitinase	33	PR3	Banana, avocado
Hev b 12	Lipid transfer protein	9.4	PR-14	Peach, stone fruit
Hev b 13	Esterase	42		

Suggested by Robert Hamilton, PhD, Latex Committee, Chairman, American Academy of Asthma, Allergy, and Immunology.

from liquid natural rubber latex (eg, gloves, balloons, condoms) contain a greater amount of soluble proteins than dry gum rubber or heat molded latex products and, therefore, can release more allergen.[2,9,29]

Several types of synthetic materials also may be referred to as latex (eg, butyl, petroleum-based materials) but these do not contain the proteins that cause allergic reactions. There have been case reports, however, of individuals having a type I natural rubber latex-allergic reaction because synthetic materials may have been mixed with or contaminated with natural rubber latex.[29] Water extractable, residual chemicals found in both latex and synthetic gloves usually are implicated in the development of allergic contact dermatitis in individuals who are presensitized.[30-33]

C. Reactions Associated With Latex and Synthetic Products

Reactions associated with latex and synthetic products include irritant contact dermatitis, allergic contact dermatitis (type IV), and immediate IgE hypersensitivity reactions (type I).[34,35] Only the type I hypersensitivity reaction constitutes a latex allergy. Some individuals may present with a single complaint or a combination of all three reactions listed above. Irritant and allergic contact dermatitis are the most common clinical reactions associated with latex and other additives.[34,35]

Irritant contact dermatitis is the result of damage to the skin, but it is not an allergic reaction. Soaps and cleansers, multiple hand washings, inadequate

hand drying, or mechanical irritation (ie, sweating, rubbing inside powdered gloves) may cause skin irritation. It also can be caused by chemicals added during glove manufacture. An acute localized response is evidenced by redness, swelling, burning, and itching. Chronic exposure to the irritant can lead to dry, thickened, and cracked skin. Health care workers experiencing irritant contact dermatitis or skin breakdown should be referred to an occupational health practitioner, allergist, dermatologist, or immunologist for further diagnostic testing. This type of dermatitis is reduced by removing the irritant source after it is identified. Thoroughly washing and drying hands, using only powder-free gloves, changing gloves more frequently, or changing glove types can reduce skin irritation.[11,36,37]

Other palliative measures include using only water- or silicone-based moisturizing creams, lotions, or topical barrier agents. Avoid using oil- or petroleum-based skin agents with latex products. These agents may cause breakdown of the latex product. Some skin care agents may help reduce glove-related problems and have been clinically formulated not to interfere with the glove's barrier integrity. Always check with the manufacturer of the skin care agent to verify that the chosen agent is latex compatible before putting the product into use.[38]

Allergic contact dermatitis (ie, delayed hypersensitivity) is a type IV immune reaction. It is a T-cell mediated allergic reaction and usually is localized

Table 3

ANAPHYLACTIC REACTION ASSESSMENT CRITERIA

Decreased cardiac output
Assess physical status and document changes. Report:
♦ Vital signs, including, temperature, pulse rate, blood pressure, cardiac rhythm, respiratory rate.
♦ Lung sounds (eg, rales, wheezing, stridor).
♦ Jugular vein distention, pulmonary pressures.
♦ Skin color, rashes, temperature, moisture.
♦ Changes in level of consciousness or mentation.
♦ Changes in patient's level of anxiety.
Defining characteristics: Hypotension, tachycardia, decreased central venous pressure, decreased pulmonary pressures, decreased cardiac output, oliguria.

Ineffective breathing pattern
♦ Monitor respiratory status and observe for changes.
♦ Monitor arterial blood gases and note changes.
♦ Check breath sounds and report changes.
♦ Monitor chest x-ray reports.
Defining characteristics: Dyspnea, wheezing, tachypnea, cyanosis, stridor, tightness of chest.

Impaired skin integrity
♦ Observe for signs of local or generalized flushing.
♦ Watch for development of rashes; note character.
♦ Assess for swelling/edema.
Defining characteristics: Urticaria, pruritus, edema, angioedema, eczema hypersensitivity, dermatitis erythema, swelling, inflammation, vesiculation, blister formation.

Fluid volume deficit
♦ Assess fluid balance (I & O) every hour.
♦ Assess for edema.
Defining characteristics: Decreased urine output, concentrated urine, decreased venous filling, hypotension, thirst, tachycardia.

Altered renal perfusion
♦ Monitor serum and urine electrolytes and osmolarity and document.
♦ Monitor urine output every hour; document changes.
♦ Monitor laboratory data for elevation in BUN (blood urea nitrogen) and creatinine levels, acid-base imbalances, particularly sodium (Na+) and potassium (K+).
Defining characteristics: Decreased urine output, decreased venous filing, hemoconcentration.

Altered level of consciousness
♦ Obtain neurological checks; report and record any changes.
♦ Observe for seizure activity; report and record changes.
♦ Monitor vital signs.
Defining characteristics: Fainting, changes in alertness, changes in orientation.

Gastrointestinal
Defining characteristics: Abdominal cramping, diarrhea, nausea, and vomiting.

Potential anxiety/fear
♦ Recognize patient's level of anxiety and note signs and symptoms.
♦ Assess patient's coping mechanisms.

Knowledge deficit
♦ Assess patient's knowledge of his or her condition and allergens.

to the area of contact. Chemical additives used in the manufacturing processes (eg, accelerators) and not the latex itself causes previously sensitized T-cell lymphocytes to stimulate proliferation of other lymphocytes and mononuclear cells, resulting in tissue inflammation and dermatitis.

The onset of type IV reactions is slow, usually occurring during 18 to 24 hours and peaking at 48 hours after exposure. Reactions may present as pruritis, erythema, swelling, crusty thickened skin, pimples, blisters, and other skin lesions. Symptoms usually resolve within three to four days after exposure.[39,40] Each exposure may lead to increased sensitization and a more severe reaction. Diagnosis is made by a health care provider experienced in chemical allergy testing—patch tests commonly are

used. Treatment involves education; thoroughly drying hands; using water- or silicone-based moisturizing creams, lotions, or topical barrier agents; avoiding oil- or petroleum-based products unless they are latex compatible; and avoiding the identified causative agent.[38,41,42] Continued use of latex products when there are breaks in the wearer's skin is believed to contribute to latex protein sensitization. This is due to absorption of solubilized latex proteins associated with the product.[43,44]

Latex allergy (ie, immediate hypersensitivity) is a systemic type I IgE-mediated response to plant proteins in natural rubber latex. In sensitized individuals, an anti-latex IgE antibody stimulates mast cell proliferation and basophil histamine release, leading to local swelling, redness, edema, itching, and systemic

Table 4

SAMPLE LATEX ALLERGY QUESTIONNAIRE	Yes	No
1. Have you ever had allergies, asthma, hay fever, eczema, or problems with rashes?	❑	❑
2. Have you ever had respiratory distress, rapid heart rate, or swelling?	❑	❑
3. Have you ever had swelling, itching, hives, or other symptoms after contact with a balloon?	❑	❑
4. Have you ever had swelling, itching, hives, or other symptoms after a dental examination or procedure?	❑	❑
5. Have you ever had swelling, itching, hives, or other symptoms following a vaginal or rectal examination or after contact with a diaphragm or condom?	❑	❑
6. Have you ever had swelling, itching, or hives during or within one hour after wearing rubber gloves?	❑	❑
7. Have you ever had a rash on your hands that lasted longer than one week?	❑	❑
8. Have you ever had swelling, itching, hives, runny nose, eye irritation, wheezing, or asthma after contact with any latex or rubber product?	❑	❑
9. Have you ever had swelling, itching, or hives after being examined by someone wearing rubber or latex gloves?	❑	❑
10. Has a physician ever told you that you had rubber or latex allergy?	❑	❑
11. Are you allergic to bananas, papaya, avocados, kiwifruits, other stone fruits, tomatoes, raw potatoes, or chestnuts?	❑	❑
12. Have you ever had an unexplained anaphylactic episode? If so, please describe.	❑	❑

reactions, including anaphylaxis.[39,44] Type I reactions are immediate, with the onset of symptoms usually occurring in minutes.[39] Symptoms include rhinitis, conjunctivitis, urticaria, laryngeal edema, bronchospasm, asthma, angioedema, anaphylaxis, and death.[39,45-48] These responses can occur when materials containing latex come into contact with the skin, mucous membranes, or internal tissues. Aerosolization of very small amounts of natural rubber latex proteins may cause some individuals to react after inhaling traces of powder from latex gloves or balloons.[49,50] The severity of repeat reactions is unpredictable; therefore, individuals who have suffered any type I reaction are considered to be at high risk for anaphylaxis.

Latex allergy is diagnosed by a history of type I reactions to latex products, such as gloves, balloons, or condoms, and a skin prick test—no FDA-approved reagent is yet approved in the United States—or serum test to identify IgE antibodies to latex. Individuals may experience irritant, type IV, and type I reactions simultaneously. If a patient or health care worker experiences any form of reaction to a medical device that may contain latex (eg, medical gloves), the individual should be carefully evaluated by a health care provider experienced in latex allergy diagnosis and management. **Table 3** provides anaphylactic reaction assessment criteria with which health care workers should be familiar.

D. Population Affected/Risk Factors

Children with myelodysplasia or a history of multiple surgeries beginning in infancy and any individual with a past history of type I reaction or positive test results to natural rubber latex are at high risk for developing anaphylaxis. People at risk for developing latex sensitization include individuals occupationally exposed to latex (eg, health care workers, food service workers); atopic individuals with a history of asthma, eczema, and rhinitis; people who react to medications; and individuals with multiple environmental allergies. People with a history of type I allergic

Table 5

LATEX ALLERGY RISK GROUPS

Persons at high risk for systemic reactions
- Children with a history of frequent surgeries or use of instrumentation, particularly if begun in early infancy, as with congenital malformations like myelodysplasia (eg, spina bifida) or genitourinary problems.
- Verifiable history of latex allergic reactions, particularly if intraoperative or asthmatic.
- Positive test results to serum latex antibody test (eg, radioallergosorbent/enzyme-linked immunosorbent assay) or skin prick test.
- History of any immunoglobulin E-mediated symptoms, (eg, urticaria, rhino-conjunctivitis, asthma, bronchospasm) when in contact with natural rubber latex products.

Persons at risk for developing latex allergy
- Occupational exposure to latex products, particularly to powdered products such as gloves, or to aerosolized latex proteins.
- History of latex-fruit syndrome or progressive reactions to foods known to cross-react with NRL—including bananas, kiwifruits, avocados, stone fruits, raw potato, tomato, papaya, or chestnuts—or a history of a latex glove-associated contact dermatitis.

Persons who should be evaluated for latex allergy
- History of any unexplained anaphylaxis—particularly if occurring in a medical or dental setting.
- History of hives or itching after incidental latex exposure, such as dental or gynecological examinations, or on contact with balloons, condoms, or natural rubber latex gloves.
- History of multiple surgical procedures.

Risks suggested by Dr. B. Lauren Charous, Milwaukee Medical Clinic

reactions to certain foods (eg, banana, avocado, chestnut, kiwi) also are at increased risk for latex sensitization. This is because of a cross reactivity that exists between natural rubber latex proteins and certain food allergens.[10,22,24,51] **Table 4** provides a sample questionnaire suitable for assessing patients and others for their risk of latex allergy or sensitization.

The ACAAI recommends that individuals with known latex allergy and those at high risk for allergy be treated in a latex-safe environment. Individuals designated as at risk for developing latex sensitization should be assessed carefully, and health care facility protocol should be followed in determining the need for testing for immediate hypersensitivity to natural rubber latex (**Table 5**).[10,12,52,53]

E. Exposure

Systemic exposure to latex can occur through the following routes: mucous membrane, ingestion, inhalation, or intravascular or cutaneous contact. The majority of severe latex reactions result from latex proteins coming in contact with internal tissues during invasive procedures or after contact with mucous membranes of the mouth, vagina, urethra, or rectum.[45,46] Triggering items include latex gloves, latex glove powder, orthodontic elastic, dental dams, nasogastric tubes, balloons, pacifiers, urinary catheters, enema kits, barium enema catheters, condoms, and balloon catheters. Case reports describe intraoperative anaphylaxis after the peritoneum or other internal tissues are contacted by surgical gloves.[39,45-48]

Inhalation of latex proteins can lead to bronchospasm or laryngeal edema. Aerosolized glove powder is the most common source of latex protein inhalation.[49,50] Latex proteins bind to the glove starch powder during the manufacturing process and are expelled into the air when gloves are opened, donned, or removed.[50] Latex proteins, particularly when bound to starch glove powder and then aerosolized, can and have caused serious health problems for both patients and employees.[3] Use of powdered latex gloves in the same room as a sensitized individual can produce an allergic reaction. Use of powder-free gloves results in only small or negligible amounts of latex in the air.[8,50,54-56]

Cutaneous exposure to latex products can trigger serious systemic reactions in highly sensitized individuals. Examples of products that have triggered reactions include gloves, condoms, anesthesia masks, tourniquets, electrocardiogram electrodes, adhesive tape, elastic bandages, condom catheters, rubber shoes, elastic in clothing, balloons, and racquet handles.

F. Prevention

The goals of prevention are twofold: to prevent reactions in individuals who are latex-sensitized and to prevent initial sensitization of nonsensitized persons. The only effective preventive strategy at this time is latex avoidance. Working in an environment that is free of powdered, high-allergen latex gloves and products will help minimize sensitization of health care workers.[4,5] The NIOSH, AAAAI, ACAAI, and others recommend and encourage the use of low-allergen, powder-free latex gloves as an important factor in developing a latex-safe environment.[8,37,38,41,50,53,55-65] For patients or staff members with a known allergy to natural rubber latex proteins, additional precautions are necessary. The presence of even small amounts of residual aerosolized latex in the air or on surfaces can trigger a life-threatening reaction. Latex-allergic individuals should be treated or work in an environment using strict latex avoidance. Although it is impossible to remove all latex from the environment (eg, wheels on carts), all latex that may potentially contact the individual should be removed.

When establishing a latex-safe environment, pertinent clinical data should be obtained on every latex or latex-containing product used in the facility, with an emphasis placed on the protein and powder content of each product, if powdered gloves or other powdered items are used. Latex products selected for use should be low-allergen and powder-free. The protein content should be less than 50 μg/dm² using the American Society for Testing and Materials (ASTM) D5712 total protein test[66] and less than 10 μg per dm² by the ASTM D6499 antigen test.[67]

AORN's "Recommended practices for product selection in perioperative practice settings" provides guidance to assist practitioners with product evaluation and selection.[68] A master list or directory of products containing latex and appropriate latex-free substitutes for those products should be maintained by the health care facility and be readily accessible to all health care providers. Since September 30, 1998, the FDA has required that all FDA-cleared medical devices containing natural rubber latex carry a warning statement.[69-71] This statement reads "Caution: This product contains natural rubber latex which may cause allergic reactions." This label warning will facilitate alternative product selection for latex-allergic individuals. This ruling does not include pharmaceuticals or products that are not regulated by the FDA.

A latex-free cart may be helpful for consolidating latex-free items in a single place for ease of location and use. Specialty patient care areas, such as the OR, emergency, and labor and delivery departments, should develop a list of items to meet their special care needs. Emergency carts (ie, code carts) also should contain latex-free items (eg, syringes, latex-free gloves, resuscitation equipment). Manufacturer documentation should be obtained to ensure the latex-free status of contents for all carts (eg, code, latex, other specialty carts). It is important that each cart be latex-free as emergency situations can occur without respect for any individual patient considerations. A sample of items to be included in a latex-free cart can be found in **Table 6**.

Pretreating latex-allergic individuals with certain medication regimens (eg diphenhydramine, ranitidine, corticosteroids) may prevent initial allergy symptoms, but it also may give care providers with a false sense of security.[9,34,39,53] This practice remains controversial. Pretreated latex-allergic individuals may present with anaphylaxis as the first sign observed by the health care team.[72]

The use of medication vials with rubber stoppers also is controversial when caring for latex-sensitive or allergic patients. Protein can be leached from the vial stopper. Even when the single-puncture or the pop-the-top-off method is used, individuals already sensitized to natural rubber latex can react.[73] One study reported that the amount of latex found in a medication vial after 40 punctures was below the level of detection using standardized methods.[74] Another study suggested that medication vials should be changed to synthetic vial tops or be clearly labeled as is required for other medical devices.[75] Coring of the stopper also is a concern. Coring may occur from repetitive puncturing of a multi-use vial stopper. This raises a concern about latex-containing particulate matter potentially contaminating the medication. In two studies, the use of sharp needles reportedly caused coring fragments in 73% of solutions in test vials using multi-dose insulin stoppers.[75,76] Whenever possible, medications should be used from a latex-free vial. When this is not possible, arrangements with the pharmacy should be made in advance so medications can be drawn into a latex-free delivery device under aseptic conditions (eg, inside the pharmacy's hood). If neither of these solutions is possible, the stopper should be removed and the medication withdrawn using a latex-free syringe. AORN does not recommend this practice unless all other options have been exhausted.

Reprocessing instruments previously processed in steam and potentially exposed to latex contamination via sterilization tape, container gaskets, or gloves worn in processing is considered unnecessary by most experts because proteins are denatured by heat and steam.[53,77,78] Health care facilities are cautioned not to heat sterilize a known latex product in an attempt to render it safe for use on a latex-allergic individual.

Sterilization of medical products by means other than heat has not been well studied in relation to latex allergy. Each facility should contact the manufacturer of the sterilizing agent or technology to verify its safe use for individuals with a latex allergy.

G. Managing Latex-Allergic Individuals

Patients
Preparing a health care facility to care for latex-allergic patients is a complex process that can be costly and labor intensive. A multidisciplinary task force to address latex issues should be formed and may include representatives from the following areas:

- administration,
- risk management,
- quality management,
- safety management,
- surgical services,
- sterile processing,
- distribution,
- anesthesia services,
- materiel management,
- pharmacy,
- laboratory,
- infection control,
- family medicine,
- department of surgery,
- department of allergy and immunology, and
- various nursing departments (eg, intensive care unit, emergency, medical-surgical, home care, education, occupational health).

Table 6

SUGGESTED CONTENTS FOR A LATEX-SAFE CART

Note: All items must be latex-free.

Safety needles (25 g through 15 g)
Syringes (multiple sizes)
3-way stopcocks
IV tubing
Blood tubing
Tourniquets
Assorted tape (.5", 1", 1.5")
Underpads and small chux
100% silicone or polyvinyl chloride (PVC) urinary catheters
Silicone or PVC external catheters—pediatric and adult
Urinary drainage system
Feeding tubes (5 Fr to 10 Fr)
Feeding pump bag and tubing
Bulb syringe (60 cc)
Blood pressure cuffs and connecting tubing
Stethoscope
Examination gloves
Sterile gloves
Oxygen delivery supplies (eg, cannula, masks)
Anesthesia breathing bag

The role of the task force is to develop a protocol for creating a latex-safe environment for patients who are latex-allergic. Removing devices and supplies with high latex protein content and discontinuing use of powdered latex products should be an integral part of the protocol. The possible increase in purchase costs for nonlatex items must be weighed against the costs of potential anaphylactic episodes or patient death. The protocol also should include a mechanism for patient education about latex allergy and its management.

Patient safety cannot be compromised. If a facility is maintained as latex-safe, additional preparation for latex-allergic patients may not be necessary. If a facility makes the conscious decision not to continuously maintain a latex-safe environment, special preparation and precautions will be required every time a latex-allergic individual presents for care.[64,79-82]

Employees
Latex-allergic individuals should be counseled about the risk of working in environments with

high latex use. They should use only nonlatex gloves and avoid all products containing latex. The ACAAI suggests that these individuals wear an allergic identification bracelet or tag, always carry an epinephrine auto-injector device, and avoid environments where powdered latex gloves are used or balloons are allowed.[52]

For both facility and employee protection, employees new to a facility should be assessed to determine the risk or presence of latex-related problems. This can be done through the employee health service or a similar mechanism during the pre-employment history and physical examination. A simple questionnaire can be used as part of the initial assessment. People at high risk for latex sensitivity should have further evaluation for latex allergy. Individuals considered at high risk

♦ have existing allergies, particularly to fruits (eg, latex-fruit syndrome)[83];
♦ have hand dermatitis or eczema; and
♦ use gloves regularly.

Low-risk employees with a negative clinical history of latex reactions do not need allergy testing, but they should be evaluated if symptoms suggestive of latex sensitivity develop during their employment. For people with contact dermatitis, the causative agent should be identified and avoided if possible. If the dermatitis appears on the hands, the use of glove liners under latex or nonlatex gloves that do not contain the triggering agent has been found to be helpful.[41,52]

All employees should be educated about latex sensitivity and allergy and be able to recognize the symptoms of a latex reaction. Employees should be encouraged to report development of any symptoms to the facility's employee health service or other designated mechanism.

II. Nursing Process Application

A. Perioperative Nursing Vocabulary

The perioperative nursing vocabulary is a clinically relevant and empirically validated standardized nursing language. It relates to the delivery of care in the perioperative setting. This standardized language consists of a collection of data elements (ie, the Perioperative Nursing Data Set [PNDS]) and includes perioperative nursing diagnoses, interventions, and outcomes. In 1999, the PNDS was recognized by the ANA committee on nursing practice information infrastructure as a data set useful in the practice of nursing. The perioperative patient-focused model provides the conceptual framework for the PNDS and the model for perioperative nursing practice.[84] The patient and his or her family members are at the core of the model. The model depicts perioperative nursing in four domains and illustrates the relationship between the patient, family members, and care provided by the perioperative professional nurse. The patient-centered domains are

♦ D1—safety,
♦ D2—physiological responses to surgery,
♦ D3—patient's and family members' behavioral responses to surgery, and
♦ D4—health system in which perioperative care is provided.

Each data element in the PNDS is represented by a unique identifier. The domains are represented by the letter "D" followed by numbers one to four to indicate the particular domain being addressed. Nursing diagnoses are represented by the letter "X" and a number unique to the diagnosis; interventions are represented by the letter "I" and a unique number; and outcomes are represented by the letter "O" and a unique number. These designations are used in this document as appropriate.

B. Assessment

Perioperative nurses assess, document, and communicate patient status to all members of the health care team. Data collection involves the patient and his or her significant others. Assess for the following risk factors:

♦ history of multiple surgeries beginning at an early age (eg, spina bifida, urinary malformations);
♦ food allergies (eg, latex-fruit syndrome);[83]
♦ exposure to latex; and
♦ history of allergic reaction to latex.

Assess for inadvertent latex exposure and impending anaphylaxis. **Table 7** provides a summary of symptoms of latex exposure and possible anaphylaxis for both conscious and anesthetized patients.

C. Nursing Diagnosis

The perioperative nurse analyzes the assessment data when determining nursing diagnoses. Following is a partial list of nursing diagnoses that may be associated with latex-allergic individuals ("X" = nursing diagnosis, "D" = domain).

- X 32 (D2)—latex allergy response (risk for);
- X 30 (D3)—knowledge deficient related to latex hypersensitivity (risk for/actual);
- X 50 (D1)—skin integrity, impaired, related to manifestations of allergic reaction (risk for/actual);
- X 7 (D2)—breathing pattern, ineffective, related to facial angioedema, bronchospasm, and laryngeal edema (risk for/actual);
- X 8 (D2)—cardiac output, decreased, related to severe latex-allergic reaction (risk for/actual);
- X 61 (D2)—tissue perfusion, ineffective, renal, related to hypotension and decreased cardiac output (risk for/actual);
- X 18 (D2)—fluid volume, risk for deficient
- X 11 (D2)—acute confusion related to physiologic condition and decreased circulation;
- X 64 (D3)—verbal communication, impaired, related to hypotension and decreased cardiac output (risk for/actual);
- X 47 (D1)—sensory perception, disturbed, related to hypotension and decreased cardiac output (risk for/actual); and
- X 4 (D1)—anxiety, related to change in physiological status in response to latex.

D. Outcome Identification

The following is a partial list of nursing outcomes that may be associated with the latex-allergic individual ("O" = outcome, "D" = domain).

- O 2 (D1)—The patient is free from signs and symptoms of injury caused by extraneous objects.
- O 3 (D2)—The patient is free from signs and symptoms of chemical injury.
- O 11 (D2)—The patient has wound/tissue perfusion consistent with or improved from baseline levels established preoperatively.
- O 13 (D2)—The patient's fluid, electrolyte, and acid-base balances are consistent with or improved from baseline levels established preoperatively.
- O 14 (D2)—The patient's respiratory status is consistent with or improved from baseline levels established preoperatively.
- O 15 (D2)—The patient's cardiac status is consistent with or improved from baseline levels established preoperatively.
- O 23 (D3)—The patient participates in decision making affecting the perioperative plan of care.

Table 7

SYMPTOMS OF LATEX EXPOSURE AND POSSIBLE ANAPHYLAXIS	
Conscious Patient	**Anesthetized Patient**
Itchy eyes	Facial edema
Generalized pruritis	Urticaria
Shortness of breath	Rash
Sneezing	Skin flushing
Wheezing	Bronchospasm
Nausea	Laryngeal edema
Edema	Edema
Vomiting	Hypotension
Abdominal cramping	Tachycardia
Diarrhea	Cardiac arrest
Faintness	
Feeling of impending doom	

E. Planning

The perioperative nurse develops a plan of care for the latex-allergic patient that prescribes interventions to attain expected outcomes. Interventions and activities are selected according to the procedure to be performed as well as to address the latex allergy. The following is a partial list of interventions that may be associated with the latex-allergic individual ("I" = interventions).

- I 30—Develops individualized plan of care.
- I 139—Implements latex-allergy precautions as needed.
- I 27—Ensures continuity of care.

The natural rubber latex-allergic individual should be identified by the admitting practitioner, and this information should be made available to the entire health care team, thus providing a continuous safe level of care. The latex-allergic individual should be treated in a latex-safe environment with emphasis placed on the removal of all latex-containing devices and products within the immediate care environment. **Figure 1** provides a simple flow chart to assist with planning for a latex-safe procedure.

F. Implementation

Implementation refers to actually performing the activities comprising the interventions identified in the individualized plan of care. This includes taking latex-allergy precautions as appropriate. If the patient is to be cared for in a facility-wide, latex-

Figure 1

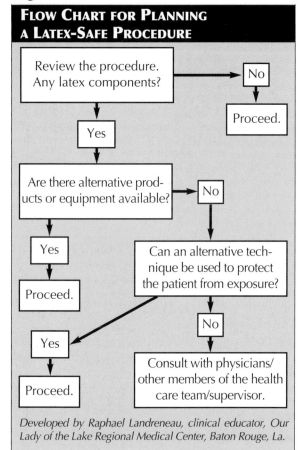

FLOW CHART FOR PLANNING A LATEX-SAFE PROCEDURE

Review the procedure. Any latex components? → No → Proceed.

Yes ↓

Are there alternative products or equipment available? → No

Yes ↓ → Proceed.

Can an alternative technique be used to protect the patient from exposure?

Yes ↓ → Proceed.

No ↓

Consult with physicians/other members of the health care team/supervisor.

Developed by Raphael Landreneau, clinical educator, Our Lady of the Lake Regional Medical Center, Baton Rouge, La.

safe environment, no additional latex precautions should be needed. If latex or latex-containing products remain in the patient's immediate care environment, those products should be removed.

Nursing interventions are composed of many and varied activities. To care for the latex-allergic individual, some or all the following activities will be appropriate, particularly if the patient is not in a facility-wide latex-safe environment.

Preoperative activities
The following activities should take place before the surgical procedure.
- Notify OR of potential or known latex-allergic patient 24 to 48 hours (or as soon as possible) before scheduled procedure.
- Identify the patient's risk factors for latex allergy and communicate same to health care team.
- Schedule procedure as first case of the day if the facility is not latex-safe.

- Notify all other care providers of patient's allergy status.
- Educate patient about latex-safe plan and ensure involvement of all providers.
- Involve patient, family members, and significant others in planning patient's care.
- Plan for a latex-safe environment of care.
- Secure latex-free products for all latex-containing items on surgeon's preference card and those used by anesthesia care provider.
- Notify surgeon if no alternative product is available.
- Notify anesthesia care provider if latex-containing product is to be used, and develop plan for emergency care if needed.
- Remove all latex items from OR unless no nonlatex alternative exists.
  - Remove boxes of latex gloves and replace with nonlatex gloves (eg, sterile, nonsterile).
  - Double-check all supplies and equipment for latex and remove any latex-containing items.

Intraoperative activities
The following activities should be performed during the surgical procedure.
- Continue implementing the perioperative latex-safe plan of care.
- Mark the OR room doors with "Latex precautions" signs.
- Mark the patient's admitting bed and transport vehicles.
- Provide latex-sensitive patients with a "latex allergy" identification band and ensure that the bed and chart also are clearly labeled.
- Remind all health care team members of the necessity for following latex avoidance procedures.
- Restrict traffic flow in the room before and during the procedure.
- Use latex-free IV tubing or replace injection ports with three-way stopcocks. Tape over any remaining ports to prevent inadvertent use.
- Use medication in ampules or latex-free vials when available.
- Use latex-free syringes.
- Use latex-free blood pressure cuffs and connecting tubing. If they are not available, wrap the patient's arm to prevent blood pressure cuff tubing or tourniquet cuff tubing from coming into contact with the patient's skin.

- Do not use latex tourniquets (eg, Penrose drains) to start IV lines or as drains in a wound.
- Use a 100% silicone (ie, not silicone coated) or polyvinyl chloride catheter if a urinary catheter is ordered for a procedure.
- Verify that additional items requested after the case is in progress are latex-free before delivering them to the sterile field.
- Be prepared for the possibility that the procedure may require more than the scheduled equipment (eg, laparoscopy to open).
- Monitor for anaphylactic reactions to latex throughout the procedure as reactions may occur immediately after induction (eg, IV exposure) or up to 40 minutes later.
- Have IV fluids and medications for treatment of allergic reaction available immediately.
- Inform postanesthesia care unit (PACU) staff members in advance of the patient's arrival time.

Postoperative activities
The following activities should be performed after the surgical procedure.

- Continue the perioperative latex-safe plan of care.
- Ensure that latex-free supplies are available to follow the patient to all future locations within the health care facility.
- Provide a latex-free resuscitation bag, oxygen mask, and supplies.
- Transport the patient to a latex-safe area.
- Provide education for patient and his or her family members or significant others.

If the latex-allergic patient is not cared for in a facility-wide, latex-safe environment, he or she is at risk for reaction upon arrival in the PACU. When the patient re-enters the mainstream care environment, he or she is at risk because of the aerosolized powder-containing latex proteins being transferred through the air or shed from scrub attire of individuals working with or near powdered latex products. In a nonlatex-safe facility, it may be necessary to use a positive pressure isolation room if a latex-safe environment of care has not been previously established in preparation for the patient.

G. Evaluation of Outcomes

The perioperative nurse evaluates the patient's progress toward attainment of outcomes. The perioperative nurse's evaluation should be systematic

and ongoing. The patient's progress toward attainment of outcomes should be documented using the recognized, standardized perioperative nursing vocabulary.[84] Outcome indicators will vary according to the specific desired outcome and may include

- physiological indicators (eg, neurological status, cardiovascular status);
- cognitive indicators (eg, repeats instructions correctly, asks appropriate questions);
- affective indicators (eg, verbalizes and demonstrates willingness to comply with treatment regimen); and
- supportive resources (eg family members participate in care planning and delivery).

Patient satisfaction
Evaluation of patient progress is based on observations of the patient's responses to nursing interventions and the effectiveness of interventions in moving the patient toward the desired outcome. Desired patient outcomes, nursing interventions, and potentially applicable nursing diagnoses are articulated in the standardized perioperative nursing vocabulary which provides the basis for documentation of perioperative nursing practice. Ongoing assessment should be used to revise diagnoses, outcomes, and the plan of care as needed. Revisions in diagnoses, outcomes, and the plan of care should be documented. The patient, his or her significant others, and other health care providers should be involved in the evaluation process when appropriate.

III. Conclusion

This guideline has been designed to promote a safe health care environment for latex-sensitive and latex-allergic patients and health care workers. The document addresses prevalence, history, pathophysiology, risk factors, prevention, and nursing process applications. This guideline can be used as a resource by facilities developing latex-safe policies, procedures, and protocols. The guideline may not apply to every individual and may require alteration based on specific needs.

REFERENCES
1. P C A Kam, M S M Lee, J F Thompson, "Latex allergy: An emerging clinical and occupational health problem," *Anaesthesia* 52 (June 1997) 570-575.
2. S Reddy, "Latex allergy," *American Family Physician* 57 (Jan 1, 1998) 93-100.

3. M Swanson, D W Olson, "Latex allergen affinity for starch powders applied to natural rubber gloves and released as an aerosol: From dust to don," *Canadian Journal of Allergy and Clinical Immunology* 5 no 8 (2000) 328-336.

4. G L Sussman et al, "Incidence of latex sensitization among latex glove users," *Journal of Allergy and Clinical Immunology* 101 (February 1998) 171-178.

5. D A Levy et al, "Powder-free protein-poor natural rubber latex gloves and latex sensitization," (Research Letters) *JAMA* 281 (March 17, 1999); also available at http://jama.amaassn.org/issues/v281n11/ffull/jlt0317-5.html (accessed 5 July 2003).

6. C A Janeway et al, "The induction, measurement, and manipulation of the immune response," *Immuno Biology: The Immune System in Health and Disease,* fourth ed (New York: Elsevier Science Ltd/Garland Publishing, 1999) 33-75.

7. *Mosby's Medical and Nursing Dictionary* (St Louis: The C V Mosby Co, 1983)

8. X Bauer, Z Chen, H Allmers, "Can a threshold limit value for natural rubber latex airborne allergens be defined?" *Journal of Clinical Allergy and Immunology* 101 (January 1998) 24-27.

9. *Latex Allergy Protocol* (Park Ridge, Ill: American Association of Nurse Anesthetists, 1993) 1-2.

10. G L Sussman, D H Beezhold, "Latex allergy: A clinical perspective," *Surgical Services Management* 3 (February 1997) 25-28.

11. V J Tomazic, "Adverse reactions to natural rubber latex," *FDA User Facility Report* 19 (Spring 1997) 2.

12. F Porri et al, "Prevalence of latex sensitization in subjects attending health screening: Implications for a perioperative screening," *Clinical and Experimental Allergy* 27 (April 1997) 413-417.

13. R Bernardini et al, "Prevalence and risk factors of latex sensitization in an unselected pediatric population," *Journal of Allergy and Clinical Immunology* 101 (May 1998) 621-625.

14. American College of Allergy and Immunology, "Latex allergy: An emerging healthcare problem," *Annals of Allergy, Asthma, and Immunology* 75 (July 1995) 19-21.

15. P Patterson, "Latex allergy: Managers' actions can aid latex-sensitive employees," *OR Manager* 13 (February 1997) 1-10

16. M Veach, "Latex gloves hand health workers a growing worry," *Latex Allergy News* 4 (December 1997) 1-4.

17. T Kibby, M Akl, "Prevalence of latex sensitization in a hospital employee population," *Annals of Allergy, Asthma, and Immunology* 78 (January 1997) 41-44.

18. G L Sussman, "Latex allergy: An overview," *Canadian Journal of Allergy and Clinical Immunology* 5 (May 2000) 317-322.

19. F Lagier et al "Prevalence of latex allergy in operating room nurses," *Journal of Allergy and Clinical Immunology* 90 (September, 1992) 319-322.

20. S R Mace et al "Latex allergy in operating room nurses," *Annals of Allergy, Asthma, and Immunology* 80 (March 1998) 252-256.

21. R Arellano, J Bradley, G Sussman, "Prevalence of latex sensitization among hospital physicians occupationally exposed to latex gloves," *Anesthesiology* 77 (November 1992) 905-908.

22. M Grzybowski et al "The prevalence of anti-latex IgE antibodies among registered nurses," *Journal of Allergy and Clinical Immunology* 98 (September 1996) 535-544.

23. C Konrad et al, "The prevalence of latex sensitivity among anesthesiology staff," *Anesthesia and Analgesia* 84 (March 1997) 629-633.

24. R H Brown, J A Schauble, R G Hamilton, "Prevalence of latex allergy among anesthesiologists: Identification of sensitized but asymptomatic individuals," *Anesthesiology* 89 (August 1998) 292-299.

25. H Alenius et al, "IgE reactivity to 14-kD and 27-kD natural rubber proteins in latex-allergic children with spina bifida and other congenital anomalies," *International Archives of Allergy & Immunology* 102 no 1 (1993) 61-66.

26. J E Slater, S K Chhabra "Latex antigens," *Journal of Allergy and Clinical Immunology* 89 (March 1992) 673-678.

27. B L Charous, "The puzzle of latex allergy: Some answers, still more questions," *Annals of Allergy* 73 (October 1994) 277-281.

28. H Y Yeang et al, "The 14.6 kd rubber elongation factor (Hev b 1) and 24 kd (Hev b 3) rubber particle proteins are recognized by IgE from patients with spina bifida and latex allergy," *Journal of Allergy and Clinical Immunology* 98 (September 1996) 629-639.

29. J W Yunginger, "Natural rubber latex," *Immunology and Allergy Clinics of North America* 15 (August 1995) 583-595.

30. E M Warshaw, "Continuing medical education: Latex allergy," *Journal of the American Academy of Dermatology* 39 (July 1998) 1-24

31. R M Adams, "Reflecting on developments in occupational dermatitis," *Clinics in Dermatology* 15 (July-August 1997) 473-477

32. S M Wilkinson, M H Beck, "Allergic contact dermatitis from latex rubber," *British Journal of Dermatology* 134 (May 1996) 910-914.

33. M Wyss et al, "Allergic contact dermatitis from natural latex without contact urticaria," *Contact Dermatitis* 28 (March 1993) 154-156.

34. K P Bensky, "Latex allergy: Who, what, when, where, why, and how," *CRNA: The Clinical Forum for Nurse Anesthetists* 6 (November 1995) 177-182.

35. N M Strzyzewski, "Latex allergy: Everyone is at risk," *Plastic Surgical Nursing* 15 (Winter 1995) 204-206.

36. H Zhai, H I Maibach, "Moisturizers in preventing irritant contact dermatitis: An overview," *Contact Dermatitis* 38 (May 1998) 241-244.

37. "Latex allergy: Protect yourself, protect your patients," *Work Place Information Series Brochure,* American Nurses Association, http://www.nursingworld.org/dlwa/osh/wp7.htm (accessed 17 Oct 2003).

38. National Institute for Occupational Safety and Health, *NIOSH Alert: Preventing Allergic Reactions to Natural Rubber Latex in the Workplace.* DHHS Publ 97-135 (Cincinnati: National Institute for Occupational Safety and Health, August 1997).

39. D L Hancock, "Latex allergy: Prevention and treatment," *Anesthesiology Review* 21 (September/October 1994) 153-163.

40. A Heese et al, "Allergic and irritant reactions to rubber gloves in medical health services," *Journal of the American Academy of Dermatology* 25 (November 1991) 831-841.

41. ECRI, "Latex sensitivity: Clinical and legal issues," in *Operating Room Risk Management* (Plymouth Meeting, Pa: ECRI, September 1997) 1-9.

42. W Wigger-Alberti, P Elsner, "Preventive measures in contact dermatitis," *Clinics in Dermatology* 15 (July-August 1997) 661-665.

43. M Evangelisto, "Latex allergy: The downside of standard precautions," *Today's Surgical Nurse* (September/October 1997) 28-33.

44. V M Steelman, "Latex allergy precautions: A research-based protocol," *Nursing Clinics of North America* 30 (September 1995) 475-493.

45. G Sussman, S Tarlo, J Dolovich, "The spectrum of IgE-mediated responses to latex," *JAMA* 265 (June 5, 1991) 2844-2847.

46. J G K Axelsson, S G O Johansson, K Wrangsjo, "IgE-mediated anaphylactoid reactions to rubber," *Allergy* 42 (January 1987) 46-50.

47. T Carrillo et al, "Contact urticaria and rhinitis from latex surgical gloves," *Contact Dermatitis* 15 (August 1986) 69-72.

48. A C Gerber et al, "Severe intraoperative anaphylaxis to surgical gloves: Latex Allergy, an unfamiliar condition," *Anesthesiology* 7 (November 1989) 800-802.

49. K J Kelly, G Sussman, J N Fink, "Stop the sensitization," *Journal of Allergy and Clinical Immunology* 98 (November 1996) 857-858.

50. D K Heilman et al, "A prospective, controlled study showing that rubber gloves are the major contributor to latex aeroallergen levels in the operating room," *Journal of Allergy and Clinical Immunology* 98 (August 1996) 325-330.

51. M Ahlroth et al, "Cross-reacting allergens in natural rubber latex and avocado," *Journal of Allergy and Clinical Immunology* 96 (August 1995) 167-173.

52. G Sussman, M Gold, *Guidelines for the Management of Latex Allergies and Safe Latex Use in Health Care Facilities* (Arlington Heights, Ill: American College of Allergy, Asthma, and Immunology, March 1996) 1-25.

53. K T Kim et al, "Implementation recommendations for making health care facilities latex safe," *AORN Journal* 67 (March 1998) 615-632.

54. O Vandenplas et al, "Prevalence of occupational asthma due to latex among hospital personnel," *American Journal of Respiratory Critical Care Medicine* 151 (January 1995) 54-60.

55. O Vandenplas et al, "Latex gloves with a lower protein content reduce bronchial reactions in subjects with occupational asthma caused by latex," *American Journal of Respiratory and Critical Care Medicine* 151 (March 1995) 887-889.

56. B L Charous, P J Scheunemann, M C Swanson, "Dispersion of latex aeroallergen," (Abstract) *Journal of Allergy and Clinical Immunology* suppl (January 1998) S160-S161.

57. American College of Allergy, Asthma and Immunology, American Academy of Allergy, Asthma and Immunology, "AAAAI and ACAAI joint statement concerning the use of powdered and non-powdered natural rubber latex gloves," *Annals of Allergy, Asthma, and Immunology* 79 (December 1997) 487.

58. *Interim Recommendations to Health Professionals and Organizations Regarding Latex Allergy Precautions* (Arlington Heights, Ill: American College of Allergy and Immunology, March 1992) 1-4.

59. D H Beezhold, G L Sussman, "Determining the allergenic potential of latex gloves," *Surgical Services Management* 3 (February 1997) 35-41.

60. C L Romig, "The powdered latex glove war," (Health Policy Issues) *AORN Journal* 66 (July 1997) 152-153.

61. D M Korniewicz, K J Kelly, "Barrier protection and latex allergy associated with surgical gloves," *AORN Journal* 61 (June 1995) 1037-1044.

62. E F O'Boyle, B Brochard, "Latex allergy: Be prepared," *Surgical Services Management* 4 (March 1998) 34-37.

63. M A Young, "Strategies for a latex-safe environment," *Surgical Services Management* 4 (March 1998) 19-24.

64. V M Steelman, "Is it really necessary to go powder-free?" *Infection Control Today* 2 no 4 29-30.

65. R S Holzman, J D Katzk, "Occupational latex allergy: The end of innocence," *Anesthesiology* 89 (August 1998) 287-289.

66. *Standard Test Method for the Analysis of Aqueous Extractable Protein in Natural Rubber and Its Products Using the Modified Lowry Method,* D 5712 (West Conshohocken, Pa: American Society for Testing and Materials, 1999) 1-7.

67. *Standard Test Method for the Immunological Measurement of Antigenic Protein in Natural Rubber and Its Products,* D 6499 (West Conshohocken, Pa: American Society for Testing and Materials, 2003) 1-6.

68. "Recommended practices for product selection in perioperative practice settings," in *Standards, Recommended Practices, and Guidelines* (Denver: AORN, Inc, 2004) 347-350.

69. "Natural rubber-containing medical devices: User labeling, Final rule," *Federal Register* 62 (Sept 30, 1997) 51021-51030.

70. "Guidance on the content and format of pre-market notification [510(k)] submissions for testing for skin sensitization to chemicals in latex products, draft document" (Rockville, Md: US Department of Health and Human Services Center for Devices and Radiological Health, Feb 13, 1998) 1-14.

71. "Latex allergy position statements, guidelines, and resources," (Trends) *Surgical Services Management* 4 (March 1998) 56.

72. *Natural Rubber Latex Allergy: Considerations for Anesthesiologists* (Park Ridge, Ill: American Society of Anesthesiologists, 1999).

73. S A Vassallo et al, "Allergic reaction to latex from stopper of a medication vial," *Anesthesia & Analgesia* 80 (May 1995) 1057-1058.

74. J W Yunginger et al, "Latex allergen contents of medical and consumer rubber products," *Journal of Allergy Clinical Immunology* 91 (1993) 241.

75. M N Primeau, N F Adkinson, Jr, R G Hamilton, "Natural rubber pharmaceutical vial closures release latex allergens that produce skin reactions," *Journal of Allergy and Clinical Immunology* 107 (June 2001) 958-962.

76. T Asakura, "Occurrence of coring in insulin vials and possibility of rubber piece contamination by self injection," *Journal of the Pharmaceutical Society of Japan* 121 (June 2001) 459-463.

77. S A Sherman, "Precautions reduce risk of latex reactions," *OR Manager* 9 (August 1993) 17-20.

78. B D Zehr, S Gromelski, D Beezhold, "Reduction of antigenic protein levels in latex gloves after gamma irradiation," *Biomedical Instrumentation and Technology* 28 (November/December 1994) 481-483.

79. G Weinert, "Health care latex allergy costs," *Surgical Services Management* 4 (March 1998) 27-30.

80. K Catalano, "Risk management and latex allergies," *Surgical Services Management* 3 (February 1997) 42-46.

81. C Johns, "A call to action: Latex allergy in the workplace," *Surgical Services Management* 4 (March 1998) 41-44.

82. "Natural rubber latex sensitivity: An AAOHN position statement," American Association of Occupational Health Nurses, Inc, http://www.aaohn.org/natrubr.htm#latex (accessed 16 May 1998) 1-3.

83. S Wagner, H Breiteneder, "The latex-fruit syndrome," *Biochemical Society Transactions* 30 (November 2002) 935-940.

84. S Beyea, ed, *Perioperative Nursing Data Set,* second ed (Denver: AORN, Inc, 2002).

RESOURCES

Kim, K, et al. "Implementation recommendations for making health care facilities latex safe," *AORN Journal* 67 (March 1998) 615-632.

Latex Allergy Links, http://latexallergylinks.tripod.com/ (accessed 19 Oct 2003).

"Natural rubber latex allergy: Considerations for anesthesiologists," American Society of Anesthesiologists, http://www.asahq.org/publicationsAndServices/latexallergy.html (accessed 19 Oct 2003).

Phillips, V; Goodrich, M; Sullivan, T. "Health care worker disability due to latex allergy and asthma: A cost analysis," *American Journal of Public Health* 89 (July 1999) 1024-1028.

Steelman, V. "Latex allergy precautions: A research-based protocol," *Nursing Clinics of North America* 30 (September 1995) 475-493.

Sussman, G. "Latex allergy: An overview," *Canadian Journal of Allergy and Clinical Immunology* 5 no 8 (2000) 317-322.

Originally approved by the AORN Board of Directors in November 1998.

Revised; approved by the AORN Board of Directors in November 2003. Published in *Standards, Recommended Practices, and Guidelines,* 2004 edition; reprinted March 2004, *AORN Journal.*

AORN Malignant Hyperthermia Guideline

Part I: Overview

A. Introduction

The "AORN malignant hyperthermia (MH) guideline" was created to provide clarity regarding assessment and treatment of MH and to familiarize perioperative nurses and other health care providers with the resources and tools available for staff development training. This guideline is specific to perioperative care for patients confirmed to have, or who are thought to be susceptible to, MH. This guideline includes the history, pathophysiology, and risk factors of the disease; protocols for treating a patient in MH crisis; considerations for education and counseling for patients and families determined to be at risk for developing MH; evaluation of care after an MH crisis; and a guide for planning staff member education.

This guideline is based on current, available research and incorporates information from the Malignant Hyperthermia Association of the United States (MHAUS) protocol. The MHAUS is a nonprofit organization dedicated to assisting in the diagnosis and treatment of MH. The MHAUS protocol was developed by a panel of experts based on scientific research and is viewed as the national guideline or standard of care for the MH patient.[1] Clinician's may need to tailor this guideline to specific patient needs.

AORN recognizes the numerous types of settings in which perioperative nurses practice. This guideline is intended to be adaptable to various practice settings. These practice settings include traditional ORs, ambulatory surgery units, physicians' offices, cardiac catheterization suites, endoscopy suites, radiology departments, emergency departments, labor and delivery units, and all other areas where operative and other invasive procedures may be performed.

The AORN Board of Directors approved the original guideline in February 1997. This current version of the guideline has been reviewed and updated by the AORN Nursing Practice Committee and approved by the AORN Board of Directors in November 2006. Content experts from various practice disciplines (eg, perioperative nurses, perianesthesia nurses, critical care nurses, nurse anesthetists, anesthesiologists) who have experience in managing MH or specific knowledge about MH were invited to provide feedback for consideration and incorporation into the final guideline.

Definition

Malignant hyperthermia is a rare genetic condition characterized by a severe hypermetabolic state and rigidity of the skeletal muscles. It occurs when affected individuals are exposed to a triggering agent such as inhalation anesthetics and succinylcholine, a depolarizing muscle relaxant.[2,3] The triggering agent causes a series of chain reactions in the body related to an increase in intracellular calcium ion concentration.

"Awake" Malignant Hyperthermia

In 1966 an "awake MH" episode was identified as the Porcine Stress Syndrome when pigs were observed to die rapidly when under stress (eg, fighting). In 1974, studies were done for "human stress syndrome," related to sudden deaths in a MH susceptible family. The deaths were unrelated to surgery and thought to be related to exercise and emotion-induced pyrexia.[1]

Studies have continued since that time focusing on physiological changes resulting from stress-related MH (eg, evidence of pH changes in an MH-susceptible muscle recovering from extreme exercise). In spite of potential correlations between exertional heat stroke and MH, dantrolene sodium is not recommended for routine use when managing heat stroke.[2]

Awake MH triggered by stress is common in MH-susceptible swine, but it is not found to be common in MH-susceptible humans.[3] Humans are not the only species to develop MH crises. Reactions have been described most often in pigs, but there are also reports in horses, dogs, and other animals, which helps facilitate research.

REFERENCES

1. Wingard, D W. Malignant hyperthermia: a human stress syndrome? *The Lancet.* [Letter to the Editor].1974; 2: 1450-1451.

2. Rosenberg, H, Davis, M, James, D. Pollock,N, Stowell, K. Malignant hyperthermia. Orphanet encyclopedia, November 2004. *http://www.orph.net /data/patho/GB/uk-malignant-phyerthermia.pdf.* Accessed September 7, 2006.

3. Gronert, G A, Pessah, I N, Muldoon, S M, Tautz, T J. Malignant hyperthermia. In: Miller, R D, ed. *Miller's Anesthesia.* 6th ed. Philadelphia, Pa: Elsevier, Churchill Livingstone; 2005: 1169-1190.

Table 1

MALIGNANT HYPERTHERMIA TRIGGERING AND NONTRIGGERING AGENTS[1,2]	
Triggering Agents	**Nontriggering Agents**
Halothane	Barbiturates
Isoflurane	Propofol
Enflurane	Local and regional anesthetics
Sevoflurane	Benzodiazepines
Desflurane	Opiods
Succinylcholine	Ketamine
	Nitrous oxide
	Etomidate
	Nondepolarizing muscle relaxants such as:
	◆ Pancuronium
	◆ Cisatracurium
	◆ Vecuronium
	◆ Rocuronium
	◆ Atracurium
	◆ Mivacurium

REFERENCES

1. McCarthy, E J. Malignant hyperthermia: pathophysiology, clinical presentation, and treatment. *AACN.* [Clinical Issues]. 2004; 15: 232-233.
2. Malignant Hyperthermia Association of the United States (MHAUS). MH susceptible patient FAQs. *http://www.mhaus.org/index.cfm/fuseaction/Content.Display/PagePK/SusceptFAQ.cfm.* Accessed November 8, 2006.

B. History

The history of MH as a known and described disorder is relatively short. In 1960, a clinician reported the case of a young man with a compound leg fracture who feared general anesthesia because relatives had died while undergoing ether anesthesia. He was given halothane, a new inhalation anesthetic agent. Intraoperatively, he experienced fever, tachycardia, cyanosis, and hypotension, but survived.[4]

Since that time, extensive progress has been made in the diagnosis and treatment of MH. In 1962 an autosomal dominant mode of inheritance was suggested, leading to the thesis that increased skeletal muscle metabolism, not abnormal central temperature regulation, accounted for the hyperthermia seen in MH. In vitro muscle biopsy testing in the early 1970s showed that freshly cut muscle demonstrated contracture responses to caffeine and halothane.[3,5-7] Biopsy testing still is the current method for the diagnosis of MH susceptibility.[3,8-11]

Dantrolene sodium was introduced in 1979 as the first effective therapy for MH, and to date it remains as the only drug specific to the treatment of MH.[9]

In 1981, MHAUS was formed to provide a central clearinghouse to collect data and to provide education and information to the public on MH. One of the most important features of MHAUS is an emergency hotline, (800) 644-9737 (in US and Canada) or 001-1-315-464-7079 (outside the US), that is available for expert help with the diagnosis and treatment of an ongoing MH episode. The North American Malignant Hyperthermia Registry is a professional subsidiary of MHAUS that collates findings from biopsy centers in the United States and Canada and provides access to specific patient data through their hotline.[1,12,13]

C. Affected Population

All patients undergoing general anesthesia should be screened for a family history of MH. Ethnic groups from all parts of the world are affected. In the United States, Wisconsin, Nebraska, West Virginia, and Michigan have higher reported MH incidences than other states.[14] Males develop reactions more frequently than females. People under 18 years of age have the highest incidence of MH. One study reports that 52% of all reactions occurred in children under the age of 15 years.[15,16] Another study reports patients who are obese or who have muscular physiques have a higher rate of recrudescence.[17]

Incidence and Mortality

Malignant hyperthermia has an autosomal mode of inheritance. Previous uneventful anesthesia does not eliminate the diagnosis of MH, because patients may undergo multiple anesthetics before MH is triggered.[18] Reports vary widely on the incidence of MH. Studies show that in patient populations who have been diagnostically tested there is an incidence of 1:30,000 and 1:37,000.[15] The MHAUS reports that MH occurs as frequently as one in 5,000 patients and may occur as rare as once in 65,000 administrations of general anesthetics with a triggering agent.[14] The MH mortality rate has been reduced from as high as 70% to less than 5%.[19] Four factors are responsible for the significant drop in mortality from MH.

◆ There is better screening for MH susceptibility through careful preoperative interviews and caffeine-halothane contracture testing.

◆ A pharmacologic basis for MH has been established so triggering agents can be avoided when MH is suspected (**Table 1**).

◆ When an unexpected MH crisis occurs, sophisticated monitoring techniques such as capnography and pulse oximetry give an early warning so diagnosis and treatment can be started immediately.

◆ The use of dantrolene sodium, a drug specific for the treatment of MH.[11,20]

Socioeconomic Factors in Malignant Hyperthermia

The social and financial ramifications of an MH episode cannot be overstated. Patients who know they are susceptible to this potentially lethal syndrome are likely to have high levels of preoperative anxiety. They need continual reassurance that everyone is aware of the potential for problems and that an anesthesia treatment plan has been developed to avoid an MH occurrence. Beyond the psychological and emotional factors, there are physical sequelae to an episode of MH, and the treatment is expensive.

Making provisions to deal with MH is costly and time-consuming. A comprehensive MH treatment cart should be available, including a supply of dantrolene sodium (see Section III of this guideline for suggested contents to include on a dedicated MH cart). Despite more than 25 years of research, dantrolene sodium is the only clinically available agent for the treatment of MH, and it is expensive.[21,22] The list price of dantrolene sodium in 2006 was $82 per vial, and the shelf life is three years.[23,24,25]

It is fortunate that an MH occurrence is rare in most settings. Dantrolene sodium may become outdated because it is not used frequently, but the benefit of having an adequate supply of it when a crisis arises will outweigh the cost of not having what is needed during this unexpected emergency.[26] According to the MHAUS, as much as 8 to 10 mg/kg of dantrolene sodium is needed to treat a patient who is having an acute MH crisis.[24,26,27] This means 50 vials must be available to treat a person who weighs 100 to 110 kg (ie, 220 to 250 pounds). (See **Table 2**). Thirty-six vials of dantrolene sodium will allow for initial stabilization and treatment while more vials are being acquired to continue treatment. Strategies can be developed and implemented for the cost-effective inventory management of this expensive medication.

Risk Factors

Malignant hyperthermia is a genetic disorder; therefore, during the preoperative interview the perioperative nurse should ask all patients if they have had a family member who experienced an MH episode or died during surgery. Patients also should be asked if they have had an MH episode themselves during surgery. This information should be given to the anesthesia care provider and surgeon.

Other diseases have been associated with MH. There is a definite association with central core disease (CCD), an inherited neuromuscular disorder. Both CCD and MH are caused by a genetic mutation in the skeletal muscle ryanodine receptor type 1 (RYR1), which causes an association between the two disorders. There are also associations between MH and other neuromuscular disorders, such as

◆ Duchenne muscular dystrophy,
◆ King-Denborough syndrome,
◆ Becker muscular dystrophy,
◆ other myopathies,
◆ periodic paralysis,
◆ myotonia congenita,
◆ Schwartz-Jampel syndrome,
◆ Fukuyama-type congenital muscular dystrophy,
◆ mitochondrial myopathy, and
◆ sarcoplasmic reticulum adenosine triphosphate deficiency.[3,8]

Perioperative nurses also should alert anesthesia care providers about patients who describe a history of nonsurgical related incidences of heat stroke or hyperthermia.[28,29]

Other drugs and physiologic conditions have been known to stimulate a syndrome that closely resembles MH (eg, serotonin syndrome).[30] There remain questions as to whether serotonin has a role in stress-induced episodes of MH.[15] More research is needed to learn if there is a correlation between the relative risk of patients who experienced MH being more susceptible to exertional heat illness, and whether patients who have experienced exertional heat illness may be at risk for MH.[21,28,29] Phenothiazine, haloperidol, and drugs used to treat schizophrenia are some of the medications that may stimulate a condition referred to as neuroleptic malignant syndrome. Physiologic indicators of this MH-like syndrome include muscle rigidity, elevated body temperature, and elevated creatine phosphokinase (CPK). Rhabdomyolysis and myoglobinuria also may occur.[3]

Table 2

MALIGNANT HYPERTHERMIA MEDICATION CHART

This chart is intended to provide a guide for calculating patient weight, medication dosage in relation to weight, and the amount of sterile water needed for reconstitution.

Dantrolene Sodium (Dantrium)

Dosage: 2.5 mg/kg intravenous. **Pediatric dose:** Refer to adult dosing.

Reconstitution: Supplied as a lyophilized powder that contains 20 mg of dantrolene sodium, 3,000 mg of mannitol, and sufficient sodium hydroxide to yield a pH of 9.5 when powder is reconstituted. During an MH crisis, it may take from two to four licensed individuals to reconstitute the required amounts of dantrolene sodium to accomplish rapid administration.

♦ Reconstitute each vial by adding 60 mL of preservative-free sterile water. Do not use bacteriostatic water for injection. Warming the mixing solution will help convert the lyophilized powder into solution.

♦ Shake vigorously until solution is clear.

♦ Do not use glass IV bottles for infusion.

♦ Protect from light.

♦ Use within six hours after reconstitution.[1,2]

Weight	Initial Dose: 2.5 mg/kg (continuous, rapid IV push)		# of vials to have on hand for four doses**	Sterile water necessary for four doses
10 kg	25 mg	(1.25 vials)	5	300 mL
30 kg	75 mg	(3.75 vials)	15	900 mL
40 kg	100 mg	(5 vials)	20	1,200 mL
50 kg	125 mg	(6.25 vials)	25	1,500 mL
60 kg	150 mg	(7.5 vials)	30	1,800 mL
70 kg	175 mg	(8.75 vials)	35	2,100 mL
80 kg	200 mg	(10 vials)	40	2,400 mL
90 kg	225 mg	(11.25 vials)	45	2,700 mL
100 kg	250 mg	(12.5 vials)	50	3,000 mL

**8-10 mg/kg is needed for an MH crisis; repeat 2.5 mg/kg doses up to four doses.[3,4] Risk of phlebitis is decreased if infused through largest possible vein.[5] Note that dantrolene sodium can be administered for spasticity associated with other clinical conditions. Warnings include caution when a patient has impaired cardiac function or impaired pulmonary function. The liver metabolizes dantrolene sodium, and there is a potential for hepatotoxicity. It is contraindicated when there is active hepatic disease.[3,6]

DO NOT USE CALCIUM CHANNEL BLOCKERS.
May lead to life-threatening hyperkalemia and myocardial depression.[7]

REFERENCES

1. Proctor and Gamble Pharmaceuticals. Dantrium IV®: information for health care professionals. [product information]. Cincinnati, OH: Proctor and Gamble; 2006: 1-6.

2. Rosenberg, H. Malignant hyperthermia in the ambulatory setting. *Perioperative Medicine and Pain. [Seminars in Anesthesia]*. 2001; 20: 270-274.

3. Lexi-com. *Drug Information Handbook for Perioperative Nursing*. Adapted from *Anesthesiology and Critical Care Drug Handbook*, 6th ed; and *Drug Information Handbook for Advanced Practice Nursing*, 6th ed. Hudson, Ohio: Lexi-Comp; 2006: 1856, 485-486, 512.

4. Malignant Hyperthermia Association of the United States (MHAUS). Medical professional's FAQs—dantrolene. *http://www.mhaus.org/index.cfm/fuseaction/Content.Display*

/PagePK/MedicalFAQs.cfm. Accessed November 9, 2006.

5. Malignant Hyperthermia Association of the United States (MHAUS). [online brochure]. Drugs, equipment, and dantrolene—managing MH. *http://www.mhaus.org/index.cfm/fuseaction/Content.Display/PagePK/Home.cfm*. Accessed 9 Nov 2006.

6. Krause, T, Gerbershagen, M U, Fiege, M, Weibhorn, R, Wappler, F. Dantrolene—a review of its pharmacology, therapeutic use and new developments. *Anesthesia*. 2004; 59 (11): 1139-1140.

7. Rosenberg, H, Davis, M, James, D, Pollock, N, Stowell, K. Malignant hyperthermia: Orphanet Encyclopedia. November 2004. *http://www.orph.net/data/patho/GB/uk-malignant-hyperthermia.pdf*. Accessed 7 Sept 2006: 8.

Table 2, *continued*

ADDITIONAL MEDICATIONS USED IN THE MANAGEMENT OF AN MH CRISIS

NOTE: Dosage must be calculated for each patient

Weight	Insulin (0.15 units regular insulin/kg)	Glucose (1mL/kg D50W)	Furosemide (Lasix) (0.5–1 mg/kg)	Sodium bicarbonate (NaHCO₃) (1–2 mEq/kg)	Mannitol (Osmitrol) (300 mg/kg IV)
10 kg	1.5 units	10 mL	5 –10 mg	10–20 mEq	When mannitol is used for the prevention or treatment of late renal complications of MH, the 3 g of mannitol needed to dissolve each 20 mg vial of IV dantrolene sodium should be taken into consideration.
20 kg	3.0 units	20 mL	10 –20 mg	20–40 mEq	
30 kg	4.5 units	30 mL	15–30 mg	30–60 mEq	
40 kg	6.0 units	40 mL	20–40 mg	40–80 mEq	
50 kg	7.5 units	50 mL	25–50 mg	50–100 mEq	
60 kg	9.0 units	50 mL	30–60 mg	60–120 mEq	
70 kg	10 units	50 mL	35–70 mg	70–140 mEq	

Insulin /Glucose Drip: Regular insulin (US brand name: Humulin R) is the only type of insulin that can be administered IV. IV administration requires the use of an infusion pump. Combine 0.15 units/kg of regular insulin in 1mL/kg of 50% glucose for the treatment of hyperkalemia or combine 10 units of regular insulin in 50ml of 50% glucose. Infusion rate titrated to results of potassium level.[1]

Calcium chloride (CaCl): 2 to 5 mg/kg or calcium gluconate may be used for treatment for life-threatening hyperkalemia. Gluconate may be less potent, but it is less likely to irritate peripheral veins.[2]

Lidocaine or amiodarone may be used to treat arrhythmias.

REFERENCES

1. Lexi-com. *Drug Information Handbook for Perioperative Nursing.* Adapted from *Anesthesiology and Critical Care Drug Handbook,* 6th ed; and *Drug Information Handbook for Advanced Practice Nursing,* 6th ed. Hudson, Ohio: Lexi-Comp; 2006: 1856, 485-486, 512.

2. Malignant Hyperthermia Association of the United States (MHAUS). Medical professional's FAQs—dantrolene. *http://www.mhaus.org/index.cfm/fuseaction/Content.Display/PagePK/MedicalFAQs.cfm.* Accessed November 9, 2006.

D. Pathophysiology

The primary MH defect resides in the skeletal muscle at the level of calcium release from the sarcoplastic reticulum of the muscle cell. The resultant intracellular hypercalcemia leads to hypermetabolism, which in turn results in increased sympathetic activity, increased carbon dioxide production, increased oxygen consumption, and disruption of the cell membranes.[7,8,31] Muscle tissue is unable to return to a resting state in the susceptible patient, and because of this the primary signs of MH begin to appear. (See **Figure 1.**)

Malignant hyperthermia may present with a variety of signs and symptoms during an acute phase or present in a more subtle fashion and develop over a course of several hours. These changes in physiological state may not present in any particular sequence. Each of the following signs and symptoms has been associated with an MH crisis.[7,8,15,25,32]

Masseter muscle rigidity that is severe, sustained, and may interfere with intubation should be considered a possible sign of an impending MH episode. The muscle contracture may not be relieved with further doses of succinylcholine or a nondepolarizing muscle relaxant. As many as 50% of pediatric patients and 25% of adults who experience succinylcholine-induced masseter rigidity have tested positive for MH by the in vitro contracture test.[25,33]

Unexplained tachycardia is often the first sign of an acute MH episode. This sign may be mistaken for "light anesthesia" with prompt administration of more anesthetic agents. Progression of the syndrome can lead to dysrhythmias such as ventricular fibrillation and sudden cardiac arrest. Inability to maintain blood pressure may also present at this time.

Hypercarbia may occur due to increase in carbon dioxide (CO_2) production that results in

Figure 1

PHYSIOLOGY OF MALIGNANT HYPERTHERMIA		
Physiology of Muscle Contraction/Relaxation in Normal Tissue Versus Malignant Hyperthermia (MH) Crisis[1-4]		
The central regulator of contraction and metabolism in the muscle is calcium. With an MH crisis, biochemical, metabolic, and physiologic conditions are a direct result of sudden and progressive increases in intracellular myoplasmic calcium.		
Normal Muscle Contraction ↓		**Events Triggered by MH** **Note:** *Not every symptom will be observed in every patient*
Tubules of sarcoplasmic reticulum (SR) in skeletalmuscle contain calcium ions. ↓		Tubules of SR in skeletal muscle contain calcium ions. ↓
Calcium is released into myoplasm from SR through calcium release channels ↓		Calcium is released into SR through calcium release channels at an abnormally high rate. ↓
The ryanodine receptor is the calcium release channel within the skeletal muscle cell that mediates calcium release. ↓		Abnormalities associated with the function of the ryanodine receptor and the gene encoding for the receptor may account for MH in certain patients. ↓
Calcium ions lead to activation of actin and myosin filaments. ↓		Imbalance in calcium ions within skeletal muscle cells stimulate metabolism. Sustained hypermetabolic state progresses to: ◆ Excess lactate production ◆ High adenosine triphosphate (ATP) consumption ◆ Elevated oxygen (O_2) consumption ◆ Increased carbon dioxide (CO_2) ◆ Elevated heat production ↓
Calcium ions bind to the troponin-tropomyosin complex, shifting it away from actin filaments ↓		Leads to subsequent loss of cellular integrity due to depletion of ATP ↓
Myoplasmic calcium is reduced via membrane adenosinetriphosphatase (ATPase) pump which breaks ATP down to adenosine diphosphate + phosphate + heat. ↓		Leads to failure of cellular membrane pumps with subsequent leakage of: ◆ Electrolytes (eg, potassium and calcium) ◆ Enzymes (eg, creatinin-phosphokinase) ◆ Myoglobin from the skeletal cell ↓
Calcium returns to the SR. ↓		Sustained hypermetabolic state progresses to: ◆ Tachycardia due to respiratory acidosis and metabolic acidosis. ◆ End-organ damage. ↓
Muscle relaxation.		Death, if unrecognized and untreated.

REFERENCES

1. McCarthy, E J. Malignant Hyperthermia. *AACN.* [Clinical Issue] 2004; 15: 231-237
2. Scanlon, V C, Sanders, T. Essentials of Anatomy and Physiology. 4th ed. Philadelphia, Pa: F A Davis Company; 2003: 135.
3. Thibodeau,G A, Patton, K T. Anatomy & Physiology. 5th ed. St Louis, Mo: Mosby; 2003: 317-319
4. Hopkins, P M. Malignant hyperthermia: advances in clinical management and diagnosis. British Journal of Anaesthesia. 2000; 85(1): 118-28.

elevated end tidal CO_2 and oxygen consumption. Other respiratory system symptoms may include an increase in arterial CO_2, and/or respiratory acidosis. Excess CO_2 can cause the CO_2 absorbent canister associated with the anesthesia machine to become discolored and hot to the touch.

Metabolic acidosis has been observed during MH crises. Associated altered laboratory values may include the following:

♦ Arterial blood gasses (ABGs) may show
  – decreased pH,
  – decreased partial pressure of oxygen in arterial blood (PaO_2),
  – increased partial pressure of carbon dioxide in arterial blood ($PaCO_2$), and
  – increased anion gap.
♦ Coagulation studies may show
  – prolonged prothrombin time (PT),
  – prolonged partial thrombobplastin time (PTT), and
  – decreased platelets.
♦ Electrolyte imbalances may include
  – increased potassium,
  – increased calcium (but can also be decreased as calcium moves into cells),
  – increased magnesium, and
  – decreased sodium.

Core temperature may increase by as much as 1° C (1.8° F) every few minutes. Extreme temperatures of 46° C (114.8° F) have been recorded. Skin temperature may read too high or too low. Body temperature increase is often a late sign of MH, because the site of the temperature elevation is skeletal muscle.

Skin changes may include generalized erythmatous flush or mottling of the skin. Cyanosis may present secondary to generalized vasoconstriction and accelerated oxygen consumption by muscles. Diaphoresis may also be present.

Myoglobinuria may become evident as a result of breakdown of muscle tissue.

Renal function may be altered. Due to leakage of muscle contents and filtering by the kidney, myoglobinuria may occur before elevation in creatine kinase (CK) and may cause renal insufficiency. This condition is treated by alkalizing the urine and maintaining a diuresis. The patient's urine may change color to a dark red or brown and will test positive for blood with the use of a urine test strip. If there are no red blood cells in the

urine, then the presumptive evidence is myoglobin, and urine and/or blood samples should be sent for quantitative myoglobin. This may take time if the facility has to go off-site for the testing. Laboratory studies may include an increased creatinine.

Rhabdomyolysis occurs when muscle is damaged and intracellular contents begin to leak into the bloodstream. Only laboratory tests reveal rhabdomyolysis. Rigidity may or may not be present. Whole-body rigidity in the presence of profound neuromuscular blockade confirms the MH diagnosis. The absence of muscle rigidity does not rule out MH. In rhabdomyolysis, there may be an increased CK. Creatine kinase may be acutely normal and may not peak until approximately 16 hours after the episode.

Serum studies are late findings and should be used for retrospective diagnosis. These may include the following:

♦ increased glucose,
♦ increased lactate,
♦ increased pyruvate,
♦ increased lactic dehydrogenase (LDH), and
♦ increased aldolase.

Part II: Plan of Care

The perioperative nurse develops a plan of care for patients at risk for MH that includes interventions to attain expected outcomes. These outcome statements become a guide for the nursing interventions necessary to achieve the desired results. The individualized plan of care reflects the perioperative assessment and a logical sequence to attain outcomes. Priorities for the provision of nursing care are established by the perioperative nurse in collaboration with other health care providers, the patient, and the patient's significant others. The flow chart in **Figure 2** can be used to assess patients for MH risk in the development of an individualized plan of care for a patient identified as at increased risk for MH.

A. Preoperative Nursing Care

Nursing care begins when the patient is scheduled for any procedure involving general anesthesia. As early as possible in the preoperative phase, the perioperative nurse should ask patients and their families a series of questions to help screen for susceptibility to MH.[25,29,32,34] For example:

Figure 2

MALIGNANT HYPERTHERMIA FLOW CHART

- Has anyone ever told you that you had a "bad" reaction to anesthesia?
- Has anyone ever told you that you or a family member had a problem with anesthesia?
- Have you or a family member experienced a high fever while under anesthesia?
- Has anyone ever told you or a family member they had a difficult time opening your jaw during a general anesthetic?
- Has anyone in your family died unexpectedly in the operating room?

- Have you or anyone in your family experienced sunstroke or heat stroke resulting in hospitalization?
- Have you ever noticed dark "cola-colored" urine after a general anesthetic or after experiencing a heat-related illness?

Opening a discussion using layman's terms may help the patient and family talk about situations that relate to susceptibility for MH. If the perioperative nurse believes a patient is susceptible to MH, the surgeon and anesthesia care provider should be notified. Preoperative education and preparation is crucial for the patient who is identified as susceptible to MH. It is important that the patient and family members understand that answering "yes" to any of the questions above will not mean they will be denied anesthesia during a surgical procedure but that different considerations may be initiated for their anesthesia care. They should participate in decisions about when and where to go for the surgical procedure and understand that counseling is available. Patients who are identified as susceptible to MH can safely undergo surgery in outpatient settings with the use of nontriggering anesthetics and careful monitoring.[24,25,35] More information is provided about this in Section D.

B. Perioperative Nursing Vocabulary

The Perioperative Nursing Data Set (PNDS) is a clinically relevant and empirically validated standardized nursing language. It relates to the delivery of care in perioperative settings. This standardized language consists of a collection of data elements (ie, perioperative nursing diagnoses, interventions, outcomes).[36] In 1999, the PNDS was recognized by the American Nurses Associations' Committee on Nursing Practice Information Infrastructures as a data set useful in the practice of nursing. The perioperative patient focused model provides the conceptual framework for the PNDS and the model for perioperative nursing practice. The patient and his or her family members are at the core of the model. The model depicts perioperative nursing in four domains and illustrates the relationship between the patient, his or her family members, and care provided by the perioperative professional nurse. The patient-centered domains are

- D1—safety
- D2—physiological responses to surgery,
- D3—patient and family member behavioral responses to surgery, and
- D4—health system in which perioperative care is provided.

A unique identifier represents each data element in the PNDS. The domains are represented by the letter "D" and are followed by the numbers one to four to indicate the particular domain being addressed. The letter "X" and a number unique to the diagnosis represent nursing diagnoses; the letter "I" and a unique number represent interventions; and the letter "O" and a unique number represent outcomes. These designations are incorporated into this guideline to help perioperative nurses create a flexible plan of care that can be put into action when circumstances change. The plan of care should be a part of the patient's medical record to increase the perioperative nurse's awareness of the patient's needs during an MH crisis, to provide documentation for third-party payers and accreditation agencies, and to meet legal requirements. **Exhibit A**, at the end of this guideline, provides a sample care plan using PNDS terminology and includes the MH protocol.

C. Post-Crisis Patient Care

After the patient has been stabilized in the OR and before transfer to either the postanesthesia care unit (PACU) or a critical care setting, the team should review the protocol checklist to be sure that all recommended testing and treatments have been completed and appropriately documented (**Table 3**).

During the post-acute crisis phase, the patient should be observed in critical care setting for a minimum of 36 hours after the MH crisis.[31] Arrangements for transfer either directly from the OR to critical care area or from PACU to critical care area should be made according to policy. If an MH crisis occurs at an ambulatory surgical setting or facility without critical care services, arrangements should be made for transfer to a facility providing those services via ambulance. A comprehensive status report from the perioperative registered nurse(s) and anesthesia care provider(s) should be given to the accepting critical care area nurse(s) and physician(s). Any time the perioperative team suspects a patient may have experienced an adverse metabolic reaction to anesthesia (AMRA), the attending anesthesia care provider or designated physician should complete an AMRA form and submit it to the North American Malignant Hyperthermia Registry of MHAUS, preferably within 48 hours of the event.[37] The form can be accessed through *https://www.mhreg.org/Downloads.aspx*.

During the post-crisis phase (eg, 24 to 48 hours) dantrolene sodium 1 mg/kg should be administered IV every four to eight hours.[15,31] Each vial of dantrolene sodium contains 3g of mannitol, which is an osmotic diuretic. When additional mannitol is used for the prevention or treatment of late renal complications of MH, the mannitol that exists in dantrolene sodium should be taken into consideration.

Table 3

EXAMPLE OF MALIGNANT HYPERTHERMIA (MH) CRISIS CHECKLIST[1]

Note: *This checklist is intended to provide a means to quickly summarize what has been done at any point in the MH crisis and what still may need to be done according to the Malignant Hyperthermia Association of the United States (MHAUS) protocol. The actions listed are not necessarily in order, and each action may not be needed for every circumstance. This checklist may be a helpful tool for reporting to personnel in critical care settings.*

Check each item when complete

☐ Discontinue volatile agents and succinylcholine.

☐ Hyperventilate patient with 100% oxygen at flows of 10L/min or more.

☐ Dantrolene sodium 2.5mg/kg IV, given rapidly through large bore needle. Administer repeatedly until resolved.

☐ Change breathing circuits.

☐ Change soda lime canister.

☐ Treat hyperkalemia.
  ■ Regular insulin; dextrose 50%
  ■ For adults, 10mg/kg calcium chloride or 10 to 50mg/kg calcium gluconate

☐ Treat arrhythmias.
  ■ Lidocaine or amiodarone
  ■ Beta blockers
  ■ **DO NOT** use calcium channel blocking agents

☐ Insert arterial line.

☐ Draw arterial blood gasses.
  ■ Watch for:
    – decreased pH,
    – decreased partial pressure of oxygen of arterial blood (PaO$_2$), and
    – increased partial pressure of carbon dioxide of arterial blood (PaCO$_2$).
  ■ Administer sodium bicarbonate if metabolic acidosis (1–2mEq/kg) is present.
  ■ Venous blood gas (eg, femoral vein) may document hypermetabolism better than arterial values.

☐ Monitor renal function
  ■ IV fluids (do not use lactated Ringers because it enhances metabolic acidosis).
  ■ Furosemide, if needed.
  ■ Urine test strip to check for blood.

Check each item when complete

☐ Insert 3-way indwelling urinary catheter.

☐ Insert central line.

☐ Monitor laboratory studies.
Electrolyte studies, watch for:
  ■ increased potassium,
  ■ increased calcium,
  ■ increased magnesium, and
  ■ decreased sodium.

Coagulation studies, watch for:
  ■ prolonged prothrombin time,
  ■ prolonged partial thromboplastin time, and
  ■ decreased platelets.

Serum studies, watch for increased:
  ■ creatine phosphokinase,
  ■ myoglobin,
  ■ creatinine,
  ■ glucose,
  ■ lactate,
  ■ pyruvate,
  ■ lactic dehydrogenase, and
  ■ aldolase.

☐ Decrease temperature.
  ■ Apply cooling blanket.
  ■ Infuse cold saline IV.
  ■ Monitor with esophageal or rectal temperature probe.
  ■ Ice packs to head, axillae, groin, and underneath patient.
  ■ Esophageal lavage.
  ■ Rectal lavage.
  ■ Discontinue cooling measures when body temperature has reached 38° C (100.4° F).

Post Crisis

Complete AMRA form; submit it to the North American Malignant Hyperthermia Registry of MHAUS, preferably within 48 hours of the event. Forms can be accessed at *https://www.mhreg.org /Downloads.aspx* or *https://www.mhreg.org/forms /AMRA_9-1.pdf.*

REFERENCE

1. Malignant Hyperthermia Association of the United States (MHAUS). *Hospital Procedure Manual.* Sherbourne, NY: Malignant Hyperthermia Association of the United States [MHAUS]; 2006.

Urinary output should be monitored using an indwelling urinary catheter. When rhabdomyolysis is present, vigorous diuresis is necessary.[25] The patient's urine output should be greater than 2mL/kg/hour to prevent renal failure. Furosemide may be used to facilitate sufficient output.[31] Creatine Kinase should be measured every six hours until there is a decrease. If the MH crisis was severe, CK may remain elevated for two weeks. When the patient has improved and is considered stable, CK should be measured on a declining time basis until it is normal (eg, every four hours during the acute episode to once a week during convalescence).[9]

Cardiac arrhythmias are usually corrected when the anesthesia care provider disrupts the progression of the MH episode and corrects the hyperkalemia. If cardiac arrhythmias caused by the MH crisis continue into the post-acute crisis phase, standard antiarrhythmic agents may be used. Calcium channel blockers should not be used to treat arrhythmias because they can lead to further hyperkalemia and cardiovascular collapse. Sodium bicarbonate, IV glucose, and insulin are used to treat hyperkalemia.[9,19]

The patient should be monitored for signs of recurrence or complications. This includes assessing the patient closely for muscle rigidity. Vital signs, including core body temperature, should be monitored with an esophageal or rectal probe. Cooling methods should be continued until the temperature is 38° C (100.4° F) and falling; then discontinue to prevent temperature from dropping below 36° C (96.8° F).[15,31] End tidal CO_2 is monitored on the intubated patient. Serum and urine studies are performed until the results return to normal. Serum studies include, but are not limited to, ABGs; serum CK, potassium, calcium, and myoglobin; and clotting values. Urine studies include (but are not limited to) urine output and myoglobin levels.[31]

Patients and family members should be informed of symptoms reported by other patients who have received IV dantrolene sodium. Patients may experience a decrease in grip strength and weakness of their leg muscles. This is especially noticeable when going down stairs. Light-headedness may also be noticed for up to 48 hours, and there may be difficulty swallowing or choking when the patient starts taking food.[21,23,27] There is

---

Expert help is available for diagnosis and treatment of an ongoing MH episode. Call:

MHAUS Emergency Hotline:
800-644-9737
(US and Canada)

001-1-315-464-7079
(outside the US)

---

also a risk of phlebitis if the dantrolene sodium was not infused through a large vein.[24,27]

When patients who are MH susceptible have surgery in ambulatory surgery centers (ASCs) and exhibit a mild masseter spasm or severe masseter rigidity, they should not be discharged without further observation. If there were mild symptoms of jaw tension but no increase in CK, and no signs of myoglobinuria, muscle weakness, muscle soreness, hyperthermia, or abnormal electrolytes, patients should be observed for at least 10 hours. Patients may be discharged after 10 to12 hours with instructions to the family to return to an emergency room at the first sign of elevated temperature.[25]

If there are signs of dark or cola-colored urine, increased temperature or pulse rate, or changes in acid-base balance, patients should be admitted and observed overnight. If the jaw rigidity was severe, overnight observation is necessary to observe for progression of symptoms and the potential for an MH crisis. When MH-susceptible patients undergo uneventful general anesthetics in ASCs, they should be monitored for at least one hour in PACU and at least one and a half hours in the phase II PACU or step-down unit before being discharged.[24,35,38]

Malignant hyperthermia occurs most frequently during administration of anesthesia. Initial symptoms are not generally seen in the PACU, especially more than two hours after discontinuing anesthetic agents.[32] When patients present with symptoms of a fever in PACU, it is generally due to sepsis or iatrogenic heating and is not related to MH. Temperature increases after a patient is discharged are not generally related to MH unless there were signs of MH (eg, myoglobinuria, muscle weakness, muscle rigidity) before discharge.[25]

D. Patient/Family Follow-up Education and Counseling

Patients and relatives should understand the importance of informing the entire surgical team (eg, anesthesia care providers, surgeon, perioperative nurses) about a family history of MH before they undergo any future surgical or invasive procedures requiring general anesthesia. It is critical that patients and their relatives receive counseling and education regarding the pathophysiology and management of MH. It is useful for the patient to have a copy of the anesthesia record, laboratory tests, and the PACU/critical care area notes to show to future care providers.

Patients and their families also should understand that MH is a genetic disease and that it could affect other relatives. An autosomal dominant pattern is inherited when MH is identified in a family member. This translates into the following inheritance patterns:

♦ Children of the MH-susceptible patient have a 50% chance of inheriting the susceptibility.
♦ Grandchildren of the MH susceptible patient have a 25% chance of testing positive for MH susceptibility.
♦ The risk to siblings of the MH susceptible patient depends upon the genetic status of the MHS patient's parent. If a parent of the MHS patient has MH susceptibility, the risk to the siblings is 50%.
♦ More distant relatives have a lesser chance of testing positive for MH susceptability.[3,14,15,39]

Patients are appropriate candidates for muscle biopsy testing if they have a family history of MH or have experienced unexplained hypercarbia and muscle rigidity related to a general anesthetic.[15,40]

The standard diagnostic test for MH is the caffeine-halothane contracture test. This test involves making an incision in the patient's quadriceps muscle, removing a small piece of muscle tissue, and immersing the muscle in a solution of caffeine and/or halothane. Typically, a patient undergoing the diagnostic muscle biopsy will undergo a nerve block or regional anesthetic supplemented with sedation. Occasionally a clinician will supplement the block with a nontriggering general anesthetic. A local anesthetic is contraindicated because it adversely affects the tissue viability when a local anesthetic agent is directly injected into the muscle that is being biopsied. After the biopsy, there may be a period of two to seven days of relative disability.[15,40] This test cannot be performed on children unless they weigh more than 25 kg and are older than 10 years of age.[41] Testing also cannot be done within 6 months of being treated for an MH crisis.[31]

There are three categories of test results:

♦ **MH susceptible.** The muscle biopsy has abnormal contractures to both halothane and caffeine.
♦ **MH negative.** The muscle biopsy has normal contractures, and the patient is not considered susceptible.[3,35]
♦ **Malignant hyperthermia equivocal.** This is a third category is used in Europe and applies when the biopsied muscle responds abnormally to only one agent.

Patients who are identified as equivocal are considered susceptible, however, until proven otherwise. False negatives can occur with the contracture tests.[3] In this case, if the patient had a suspected family history or personal history of possible MH, the patient should be treated as MH susceptible regardless of a contracture test that showed normal contractures when tested.

The muscle biopsy must be analyzed within five hours of the harvest.[3] This usually means it is necessary for patients and their families to travel to a diagnostic center for the testing. Patients who decide to proceed with this type of diagnostic screening are often responsible for their own costs for the test and the associated travel. There are 22 centers in Europe that do MH diagnostic testing, but there are only eight centers in North America where testing is performed (**Table 4**).

Genetic studies have indicated that a defect in the ryanodine type 1 receptor (RYR1) located on chromosome 19 may be linked with MH. The genetic test is less costly and less invasive than the contracture testing, but it is not a clinical screening test at this time. Ongoing genetic research shows promise for patients and relatives affected by MH.[41-43] Until DNA studies are refined, the caffeine-halothane contracture test for the diagnosis of MHS continues to be the "gold standard" for testing.[10,40]

The MHAUS goal is to educate the public and offer support to patients and their relatives about MH. Patients and their families should be given information about MHAUS including the website (mhaus.org), phone number (607-674-7901), and the email address (info@mhaus.org).[1] They can receive medical identification bracelets to wear and identification cards to carry in their wallets from MHAUS to use as a communication tool for emergency surgery and documentation for future elective surgeries.

When assessing patients for blood or organ donations, perioperative nurses should know that susceptibility to MH is not "carried" in the blood or organs, so there is no contraindication to blood or organ donation by a person known to be susceptible to MH. Clinicians who identify themselves as MH-susceptible individuals and are working in the OR may want to avoid close proximity to the anesthesia care provider during a mask induction with a triggering agent, but there are no cases reported of a MH crisis related to waste anesthetic gases while working in the OR.[44]

Part III: Evaluation of Caregiver Response to an MH Crisis

When a patient undergoing an invasive procedure is having a MH crisis, decisions need to be made about potentially postponing subsequent invasive procedures throughout the facility. Emergency surgeries should be diverted until the crisis has been resolved. As responders are handling the MH crisis, a designated team (eg, surgical services director or designee, lead pharmacist, lead anesthesia care provider) should assess the availability of crisis management supplies, including dantrolene sodium throughout the facility. If invasive procedures are to be continued, sufficient quantities of dantrolene sodium must be available to treat the patient who is actively in MH crisis for at least 48 hours and as well as enough to treat a potential second patient in MH crisis.

The designated team should develop a communication action plan if invasive procedures will be delayed or cancelled. In small facilities or ambulatory surgery centers, the nursing supervisor or receptionist may be assigned to participate in the communication plan. This decision should not wait for the current crisis to resolve. Facility administrators should establish a policy that clearly identifies who will be responsible for making the decision about other invasive procedures. Consideration should be given regarding whether the full supply of medication needs to be available in-house before proceeding with other invasive procedures or general

Table 4

TESTING CENTERS AND LABORATORIES

The following medical facilities provide testing in the United States and Canada:
- University of California at Los Angeles, Los Angeles;
- University of Minnesota, Minneapolis;
- University of California Davis, California;
- Thomas Jefferson University, Philadelphia;
- Uniformed Services University of the Health Sciences, Bethesda, Maryland;
- Wake Forest University (Bowman-Gray), Winston-Salem, North Carolina,
- Ottawa Hospital-Civic Campus, Ottawa, Ontario, Canada;
- Toronto General Hospital, Toronto, Ontario, Canada.

SOURCE: Malignant Hyperthermia Association of the United States (MHAUS). MH muscle biopsy centers: directory North American malignant hyperthermia muscle contracture testing centers. *http://www.mhaus.org/index.cfm/fuseaction/Content.Display/PagePK/BiopsyTestCenters.cfm.* Accessed 12 Sept 2006.

For more information about genetic tests for MH, contact the following laboratories:
- Prevention Genetics LLC, Marshfield, Wisconsin, *http://www.preventiongenetics.com.*
- Center for Medical Genetics, University of Pittsburgh Medical Center, *http://path.upmc.edu/divisions/mdx/diagnostics.html.*

anesthetics. The policy should also indicate who might need to help with the communication plan if no one from the perioperative team is available due to the MH crisis.

Performance Improvement

After the patient has been transferred out of the OR and a comprehensive report has been provided to the accepting nurses(s) and physician(s), another assessment should be done to consider the availability for crisis management supplies to complete the remainder of scheduled cases. If it is not safe to proceed with scheduled cases, alternate plans may include transferring patients to another facility or rescheduling cases for a later time or date. Immediate steps should be taken to reorder dantrolene sodium and other crisis management supplies necessary to restock the MH cart. **Table 5** shows suggested contents for a dedicated MH cart.[26]

Contact Information for the Malignant Hyperthermia Association of the United States

Mailing address
11 East State St
PO Box 1069
Sherburne, NY 13460

Web page
http://www.mhaus.org

Phone number
607-674-7901 or 800-986-4287

Email address
info@mhaus.org

All staff members involved in the MH crisis response should hold a debriefing meeting to evaluate their response as soon as possible. This would include ancillary areas and other departments (eg, critical care, pharmacy, central supply, emergency department). This meeting should address areas that the response team may need to improve for future patients in MH crisis. Points to consider include:

- Was the MH cart adequately stocked and immediately available?
- Are there additional supplies that should be added to the cart?
- Were enough staff members available to manage the crisis effectively?
- When staff members responded, were they familiar with tasks expected in an MH crisis?
- How long did it take to get the recommended 36 vials of dantrolene sodium supply replaced?
- How long did it take to get the MH cart restocked with supplies?
- Were scheduled surgeries postponed or cancelled because of inadequate supplies on the cart?
- Was an effective communication plan implemented if scheduled surgeries had to be postponed or cancelled?
- Was an incident report completed and filed?
- Was MHAUS appropriately notified?
- Is a process in place to facilitate patient and family MH education and counseling?

- Do staff members have other ideas about planning care for a future MH crisis?
- Are there plans to have periodic MH crisis drills, including practice sessions to mix dantrolene sodium using outdated vials?
- Do policies need to be created or revised?
- Has a root-cause analysis been done (MH is considered a sentinel event)?

Every facility should include MH training in the orientation plan for new members of the perioperative team and other teams involved in responding to the crisis. Ongoing periodic reviews should be scheduled. The MHAUS recommendations suggest that the perioperative team initiate mock MH drills at least twice a year to improve staff member efficiency in treating a patient during an MH crisis.[45] Because dantrolene sodium is difficult to mix, some institutions reconstitute the outdated medication in staff member education sessions to give hands-on training during the mock drills. For perioperative nurses, it may also be helpful to include a review of electrolyte imbalances and the shifts in ABGs that occur with respiratory and metabolic acidosis during an MH crisis.

Facilities should identify specific tasks assigned to each member of the response team to effectively manage a MH crisis. Procedure manuals are available through MHAUS to assist in assigning specific tasks and to facilitate staff education.[45] Examples of role delineation are provided in **Table 6**.

Part IV: Summary

This guideline outlines the assessment and treatment of MH and presents resources and tools for staff member development training. Perioperative nurses are committed to providing one standard of care to patients regardless of where an invasive procedure is taking place. Nurses should be prepared to monitor the patient and treat an MH crisis if they are working in any type of facility or department where MH triggering agents are used (eg, OR, labor and delivery, interventional radiology, emergency department).[25]

Perioperative nurses and other health care providers should stay up-to-date with new research and treatment recommendations. For more information about MH, contact the MHAUS at 11 East State St, PO Box 1069, Sherburne, NY, 13460; telephone (607) 674-7901 or 1-800-986-4287; Web site, *http://www.mhaus.org*.

Table 5

SUGGESTED CONTENTS FOR A MALIGNANT HYPERTHERMIA (MH) CART				
Medications				
Name	Concentration	Amount	Rationale	Comments
Dantrolene sodium	20 mg vials	36 vials	Skeletal muscle relaxant.	Previously mannitol was included in the list of drugs to be kept on an MH cart. This is no longer necessary because dantrolene sodium has 3 g of mannitol included in each vial.[1]
Preservative-free sterile water (ie, without a bacteriostatic agent)	1,000 mL per bag or bottle	2 bags or bottles	Needed to mix dantrolene sodium.	Contact MHAUS for special supplies for reconstituting dantrolene sodium.
Sodium bicarbonate (NaHCO3) 8.4%	50 mEq	5 syringes	Treats metabolic acidosis.	
Dextrose 50%	50mL vials	2 vials	Treats hyperkalemia.	
Regular insulin (must be refrigerated)	100 units/mL	1 bottle	Treats hyperkalemia.	Regular insulin is the only type of insulin that can be administered IV.[2] IV administration requires the use of an infusion pump.
Furosemide (eg, Lasix)	40mg/ampule	4 ampoules	Increases urine output.	
Calcium chloride 10%	10 mL vial	2 vials	Treats life-threatening hyperkalemia.	Calcium gluconate or calcium chloride can be used. Calcium gluconate may be less potent, but it is less likely to irritate peripheral veins.[1]
Lidocaine hydrochloride 2% for injection	100 mg/5 mL or 100 mg/10 mL in preloaded syringes	3 syringes	Treats cardiac arrhythmias. Requires the use of an infusion pump to administer accurate dose.	Amiodarone is also acceptable. Previously, procainamide had been a recommended stock drug for MH carts. It is no longer necessary because it has been confirmed that lidocaine does not aggravate MH.[1]
Note: Each facility should decide whether to stock more medications for treating cardiac arrhythmias on the MH cart or whether to use an accompanying code cart for advanced cardiac life support (ACLS) for protocols that may be necessary.				

REFERENCES

1. Malignant Hyperthermia Association of the United States (MHAUS). Medical professional's FAQs —dantrolene. April 2006. Available at *http://www.mhaus.org/index.cfm/fuseaction/Content.Display/PagePK/MedicalFAQs.cfm.* Accessed September 8, 2006.

2. Lexi-Comp. *Drug Information Handbook for Perioperative Nursing.* Adapted from *Anesthesiology and Critical Care Drug Handbook,* 6th ed; and *Drug Information Handbook for Advanced Practice Nursing.* 6th ed. Hudson, Ohio: Lexi-Comp; 2006: 933.

Table 5, *continued*

SUGGESTED CONTENTS FOR A MALIGNANT HYPERTHERMIA (MH) CART		
Supplies		
Description of Item	**Amount**	**Comments**
60 mL Luer-lock syringes	5	Used to dilute dantrolene sodium.
60 mL catheter-tip syringes	6	Used for irrigation (eg, nasogastric tube [NG],indwelling urinary catheter).
10 mL Luer-lock syringes	10	
3 mL syringes	10	For blood gas analysis if arterial blood gas (ABG) kits are not available.
Alcohol prep pads	1 box	
Vial spikes	6	
Elastic tourniquets	4	For drawing blood.
Povidone-iodine paint 4 oz	2 bottles	Prepping arterial-line sites.
Sterile gauze 4x4s (boxes of 10)	2	For dressings at IV sites.
Radial artery catheters	2	
Arterial line monitoring kit	1	Sizes appropriate to patient population.
Central venous pressure line kit	1	Sizes appropriate to patient population.
Cassette tubing for IV infusion pumps	4 sets	
Angiocaths: 16 g, 18 g, and 20 g = 2-inch; 22 g = 1-inch; 24 g = 3-inch	6 of each	These supplies need to be readily available on the anesthesia cart or separately stocked on the MH cart.
Tape (various types)	2 rolls of each	
Small and large adhesive IV dressings	6 of each	
Adult IV drip chambers	4	
IV solution sets with drip chambers	4	
IV extension tubing	4	
"T" connectors	4	
Three-way stopcocks	4	
Pediatric arm boards	4	
Adult arm boards	4	
Sharps container	1	

Table 5, *continued*

SUGGESTED CONTENTS FOR A MALIGNANT HYPERTHERMIA (MH) CART		
Anesthesia Equipment		
Description of Item	**Amount**	**Comments**
Soda lime canister	1	
Adult anesthesia breathing circuits	2	
Pediatric anesthesia breathing circuits	2	
NG tubes (various sizes)	3 each	
Esophageal temperature probes	2	Large size esophageal temp probe can be used as a stethoscope.
General purpose temperature probe	2	General-purpose temperature probe cannot be used as a stethoscope.
Heparinized ABG syringes	6	ABG kits may be used. May also be used to assess lactic acid levels.
Pediatric ambu bags	1	
Adult ambu bag	1	
Extra oxygen tank	1	Readily available if not on MH cart.
Infusion pumps	2	Readily available.
Cooling Supplies		
Chilled 0.9% Saline for irrigation	6 bottles each, 1 liter and 3 liter	At the time the cart is requested, add these items from the refrigerator.
Clear, large plastic bags	6	Used for ice.
Clear, small or medium plastic bags	6	Used for ice.
Large containers	2	Used for ice.
Ice		Access to ice machine or bags of ice.
Nursing Equipment		
Large translucent adhesive sterile drape	2	Used for closure of wound.
Closed-system urinary catheter trays	2	
Urinary catheter drainage bags with urimeters	2	
3-way urinary catheters (adult size)	2	
3-way urinary catheters (pediatric sizes)	2	
Rectal tube	1	
Peritoneal lavage trays	2	
Cystoscopy tubing	2	
5-in-1 connectors	2	
Y connectors	2	

Table 5, *continued*

SUGGESTED CONTENTS FOR A MALIGNANT HYPERTHERMIA (MH) CART		
Laboratory Testing Supplies		
Description of Item	**Amount**	**Comments**
Urine specimen containers	2	Myoglobinuria.
Urine test strips	1 bottle	Test for blood in the urine.
Blood specimen tubes appropriate for the following tests: creatin kinase, myoglobin, chemistry screen, lactic hydrogenase, electrolytes, thyroid studies, prothrombin/ partial thromboplastin times, fibrinogen, fibrin split products, complete blood count, platelets.	At least 2 large and 2 small of each tube type	
Forms and Checklists		
Blood gas slips	6	
Hematology forms	2	
Chemistry forms	2	
Coagulation forms	2	
Urinalysis forms	2	
Physician order forms	2	
Blood requisition form	2	
MHAUS label on front of cart listing hotline phone number (ie, 800-644-9737)		
MHAUS MH crisis data management sheet		Can be ordered by calling 800-986-4287; or can be printed from *http://www.mhaus.org.*
Anesthesia records	4	This may not be needed if using MHAUS data sheet.
ICU report form or hand-off transfer report form for ambulance (eg, ambulatory surgery center, office-based setting)	1	
Physician consultation form	1	
Medication labels	At least 10	Consider labeling sterile water for "reconstitution only."
Adverse medical reaction to anesthesia report form from North American MH Registry (NAMHR)		Can be printed online: *https://www.mhreg.org.* Contact NAMHR to receive patient packet with ID cards included.
Guides, checklists, worksheets		Training manual (eg, designed by MHAUS or own facility); worksheets and checklists with assignments for responders.
Other supplies are available through MHAUS (eg, hand-held cards, poster, list of duties)Move this to end of lists.		Can be ordered by calling 800-986-4287; or can be printed from *http://www.mhaus.org.*

Table 6

MANAGEMENT OF A MALIGNANT HYPERTHERMIA (MH) CRISIS

Outline shows examples for delineation of roles)

Anesthesia care provider

- Discontinue volatile agents.
- May hyperventilate patient with 100% oxygen.
- May continue administering nitrous oxide.

Dantrolene sodium
- Administer 2.5mg/kg IV until crisis is resolved.

Treat hyperkalemia (if patient is symptomatic)
- Regular insulin.
- Dextrose 50%.
- 10mg/kg calcium chloride or 10 to 50mg/kg calcium gluconate.

Treat arrhythmias
- Administer lidocaine or amiodarone.
- Administer beta blockers.
- Do not use calcium channel blocking agents, which may cause hyperkalemia or cardiac arrest in the presence of dantrolene sodium.

Arterial line placement
Draw arterial blood gasses (ABGs). Based on ABG results, may need to administer sodium bicarbonate to treat metabolic acidosis.

Decrease temperature (if elevated)
- Apply cooling blanket.
- Infuse cold saline IV.
- Apply ice packs to head, axillae, groin, and underneath patient, if possible.
- Discontinue cooling measures when body temperature has reached 38 ºC (100.4º F).

Monitor renal function
- Administer IV fluids; avoid lactated Ringer's solution as it may contribute to patient's acidosis.
- Administer furosemide as needed.

Surgical Team

- Complete surgical procedure as soon as possible or stop surgical procedure.
- Communicate closely with anesthesia care provider.
- Cold saline irrigation of body cavity, if needed.
- Prepare for/assist with central line placement.
- Insert urinary catheter (3-way).
- If available, help mix dantrolene sodium or with insertion of additional IV lines.

Circulating RN

- Notify anesthesia team leader.
- Notify OR charge nurse.
- Ask for extra personnel (see "Delegation of Duties").
- Assemble ice packs.
- Obtain basins of ice water (may delegate to clinical assistant [CA] as stated below).
- Apply cold face cloths and towels to exposed body surfaces.
- Ensure appropriate documentation forms are available (eg, laboratory order forms, labels); verify correct patient name, medical record number, and correct test/medication is ordered.
- Nurse-to-nurse report to either postanesthesia care unit (PACU) or intensive care unit (ICU).

Delegation of Duties
Circulating nurse assigns arriving staff members to assist in the following roles:
- Nursing personnel or CA to get MH cart.
- Two to four licensed individuals dedicated to reconstitution of dantrolene sodium.
- Medication nurse to
  - obtain other medicationsused for treatment of MH,
  - contact pharmacy department to obtain more dantrolene sodium as needed, and
  - document medications as they are given.
- Nurse recorder: documentation should include, but not be limited to,
  - vital signs,
  - laboratory reports,
  - fluid intake and output,
  - size of urinary catheter,
  - color of urine (brown-colored urine denotes rhabdomyolysis due to muscle breakdown),
  - type of irrigation used and amounts,
  - placement of central venous line, arterial line, and peripheral IV's.
- Lavage nurse to assist with placement of urinary catheter, nasogastric (NG) tube, rectal tube and/or perform lavage of cold saline to irrigate stomach, rectum, and bladder.
- Assign a person to obtain refrigerated IV fluids for infusion. Avoid lactated Ringer's solution as it may contribute to metabolic acidosis.
- If available, assign someone to set up equipment for invasive monitoring.
- If available, assign someone to obtain blood and urine samples for laboratory analysis.

Table 6, *continued*

MANAGEMENT OF A MALIGNANT HYPERTHERMIA (MH) CRISIS

PACU RN

- Responds to OR if available.
- Assigns and prepares bed space in PACU:
  - sets up monitors and ensures that cardiac arrest cart is close,
  - prepares containers for ice,
  - fills containers with ice when patient is on the way, and
  - arranges for ventilator according to orders.

Clinical Assistant

- Obtains basins of ice water.
- Ensures that face cloths and towels are available.
- Runner stays available to retrieve supplies and equipment as needed.
- Stamps laboratory requisition forms, labels and other documentation forms with patient's name and ID.
- Takes worksheet or list of duties to OR front desk to facilitate communication plan.

Anesthesia Technician

- Changes soda lime canister and circuit hoses, if requested by anesthesia care provider.
- Obtains supplies and equipment for placement of arterial line.
- Has two to four infusion pumps available (used to infuse antiarrhythmic medications).
- Obtains chilled bags of IV saline and irrigation bottles of saline from refrigerator.
- Obtains insulin from refrigerator.
- If not already stocked on MH or anesthesia cart, has the following items available:
  - esophageal and rectal temperature probe,
  - various sizes of NG tubes,
  - stopcocks, and
  - phlebotomy supplies and equipment.
- Brings defibrillator into room.
- Stamps laboratory requisition forms and labels with patient's name.
- Changes anesthesia machine, if directed by anesthesia care provider.

OR or Ambulatory Surgery Center Front Desk Personnel

- Receives worksheet or list of duties from OR.
- Initiates communication plan.

Adapted with permission from Malignant Hyperthermia Association of the United States (MHAUS). Malignant Hyperthermia Event OR Response Protocol Flowchart. In: MHAUS Hospital Procedure Manual. Sherbourne, NY: Malignant Hyperthermia Association of the United States (MHAUS); 2006.

REFERENCES

1. Malignant Hyperthermia Association of the United States (MHAUS). What is MHAUS? *http://www .mhaus.org/index.cfm/fuseaction/Content.Display/Page PK/Home.cfm.* Accessed September 10, 2006.

2. *Mosby's Dictionary of Medicine, Nursing & Health Professions.* 7th ed. St Louis, Mo: Mosby Elsevier; 2006: 1144-1145.

3. Rosenberg, H, Dirksen, R T. Malignant hyperthermia susceptibility: GeneReviews. *http://www.genetests.org.* Accessed August 28, 2006.

4. Denborough, M A, Forster, J F A, Lovell, R H R, Maplestone, P A, Villiers, J D. Anaesthetic deaths in a family. *British Journal of Anaesthesia* 1962; 34: 395-396.

5. Hopkins, P M, Halsall, P J, Ellis, F R. Diagnosing malignant hyperthermia susceptibility. [editorial]. *Anaesthesia.* 1994; 49: 373-375.

6. Kalow, W, Britt, B A, Richter, A. The caffeine test of isolated human muscle in relation to malignant hyperthermia. *Journal of the Canadian Anaesthesia Society.* 1977; 24: 678-694.

7. Hopkins, P M, Malignant hyperthermia: advances in clinical management and diagnosis. *British Journal of Anaesthesia.* 2000; 85 (1): 118-128.

8. Miller, J D, Rosenbaum, H, Weiss, L. Malignant hyperthermia: UCLA anesthesiology. *http://www.anes .ucla.edu/dept/mh.html.* Accessed September 22, 2006.

9. Malignant Hyperthermia Association of the United States (MHAUS). Clinical update: managing malignant hyperthermia. *http://www.mhaus.org/index.cfm/fuse action/OnlineBrochures.Display/BrochurePK/3FFCBC12-9479-49.* Accessed September 13, 2006.

10. Rosenberg, H, Antognini, J F, Muldoon, S. Testing for malignant hyperthermia [Clinical Concepts and Commentary] *Anesthesiology.* 2002; 9: 232-237.

11. Carr, A S, Canaliffe, M, McLeod, E E, Britt, B A. Incidence of malignant hyperthermia reactions in 2,214 patients undergoing muscle biopsy. *Canadian Journal of Anaesthesia.* 1995; 42 (4): 281-286.

12. Malignant Hyperthermia Association of the United States (MHAUS). Hotline information. *https://www.mhaus .org/index.crm/fuseaction/Hotline.Home.cfm.* Accessed August 22, 2006.

13. Malignant Hyperthermia Association of the United States (MHAUS). North American malignant hyperthermia registry. *https://www.mhreg.org/Default .aspx.* Accessed September 6, 2006.

14. Malignant Hyperthermia Association of the United States (MHAUS). What is malignant hyperthermia? *http://www.mhaus.org/index.cfm/fuseaction/OnlineBroc hures.Display/BrochurePK .* Accessed August 22, 2006.

15. Rosenberg, H, Davis, M, James, D, Pollock, N, Stowell K. Malignant hyperthermia: Orphanet encyclopedia November 2004. *http://www,orph.net/data /patho/GB/uk-malignant-phyerthermia.pdf.* Accessed September 7, 2006.

16. Strazis, K P, Fox, A W. Malignant hyperthermia: a review of published cases. *Anesthesia and Analgesia.* 1993; 77: 297-304.

17. Malignant Hyperthermia Association of the United States (MHAUS). Burkman, J M, Posner, K L, Domino, D B. Analysis of the clinical variables associated with recrudescence after malignant hyperthermia reactions. *http://www.mhaus.org/index.cfm/fuseaction/Content.Dis play/PagePK/AbstractJMBurkman.* Accessed August 28, 2006. This abstract can also be accessed at *http://www .asaabstracts.com/strands/asaabstracts/abstractList.htm ;jsessionid=FBA057351253B386A3D862B2404C46B4? year=2005&index=12.* Accessed September 20, 2006.

18. Hallsall, P J, Cain, P A, Ellis, F R. Retrospective analysis of anaesthetics received by patients before susceptibility to malignant hyperthermia was recognized. *British Journal of Anaesthesia.* 1979; 51: 949-954.

19. Gronert, G A, Pessah, I N, Muldoon, S M, Tautz T J. Malignant hyperthermia. In: Miller, R D, ed. *Miller's Anesthesia.* 6th ed, vol 1. Philadelphia, Pa: Elsevier, Churchill Livingstone; 2005: 1169-1190.

20. Sheehan, J A. Malignant hyperthermia susceptibility and the trauma patient. *Military Medicine.* 2005; 170: 510-512.

21. Krause, T, Gerbershagen, M U, Fiege, M, Weibhorn, R, Wappler, F. Dantrolene—a review of its pharmacology, therapeutic use, and new developments. *Anaesthesia.* 2004; 59: 364-373, 1139-1140.

22. Podranski, T, Bouillon, T, Schumacher, P M, Taguchi, A, Sessler, D I, Kurz A. Compartmental pharmacokinetics of dantrolene in adults: do malignant hyperthermia association dosing guidelines work? *Anesthesia and Analgesia.* 2005; 101: 1695-1699.

23. Proctor & Gamble Pharmaceuticals. DantriumâIV: information for health care professionals. *http://www.pg pharma.com/healthcareprofessional_dantriumiv.shtml.* Accessed August 23, 2006.

24. Malignant Hyperthermia Association of the United States (MHAUS). Medical professional's FAQ's—dantrolene. *http://www.mhaus.org/index.cfm/fuseaction /Content.Display/PagePK/Medical FAQs.cfm.* Accessed December 5, 2006.

25. Rosenberg, H. Malignant hyperthermia in the ambulatory setting. *Seminars in Anesthesia, Perioperative Medicine and Pain.* 2001; 20: 270-274.

26. Malignant Hyperthermia Association of the United States (MHAUS). Drugs, equipment, and dantrolene—managing malignant hyperthermia: MHAUS online brochure. *http://www.mhaus.org/index.cfm/fuseaction /OnlineBrochures.Display/BrochurePK/B5DBDF12-20C3-453.* Accessed Sept 8, 2006.

27. Lexi-Comp. *Drug Information Handbook for Perioperative Nursing.* Adapted from *Anesthesiology and Critical Care Drug Handbook,* 6th ed; and the *Drug Information Handbook for Advanced Practice Nursing,* 6th ed. Hudson, Ohio: Lexi-Comp; 2006: 1856, 485-486.

28. W Porter, A M. Collapse from exertional heat illness: implications and subsequent decisions. Military Medicine. 2003; 168: 76-81.

29. Wappler, F, Fiege, M, Steinfath, M, et al. Evidence for susceptibility to malignant hyperthermia in patients with exercise-induced rhabdomyolysis. *Anesthesiology.* 2001; 94: 95-100.

30. Rusyniak, D E, Sprague, J E. Toxin-induced hyperthermic syndromes. *The Medical Clinics of North America.* 2005; 89: 1277-1296.

31. McCarthy, E J. Malignant hyperthermia. *AACN.* [Clinical Issues]. 2004; 15: 231-237.

32. Nagelhout, J J, Zaglaniczny, K L. *Nurse Anesthesia.* Second ed. Philadelphia, PA: WB Saunders Company; 2001: 728-732.

33. O'Flynn, R P, Shutack, J G, Rosenberg, H, Fletcher, J E. Masseter muscle rigidity and malignant hyperthermia susceptibility in pediatric patients: an update on management and diagnosis. *Anesthesiology.* 1994; 80: 1228-1233.

34. Halaszynski, T M, Juda, R, Silverman, D G. Optimizing postoperative outcomes with efficient preoperative assessment and management. *Critical Care Medicine.* 2004 April; (Suppl, 32): S76-88.

35. Pollock, N, Langton, E, McDonnell, N, Tiemessen, J, Stowell, K. Malignant hyperthermia and day stay surgery. *Anaesthesia and Intensive Care.* 2006; 34: 40-45.

36. Petersen, C. *Perioperative Nursing Data Set: The Perioperative Nursing Vocabulary.* Revised nd ed. Denver, CO: AORN, Inc; 2007: 17-18, 29.

37. The North American Malignant Hyperthermia Registry of MHAUS, Report of acute adverse metabolic reaction to anesthesia report (AMRA Report) Version 9.1. *https://www.mhreg.org/forms/AMRA_9-1.pdf.* Accessed September 6, 2006.

38. Bryson, G, Chung, F, Cox, R G, et al. Patient selection in ambulatory anesthesia—an evidence-based review: Part II. *Canadian Journal of Anesthesia.* 2004; 51 (8):782-794.

39. Malignant Hyperthermia Association of the United States (MHAUS). MHAUS FAQs—molecular genetic testing for MH. *http://www.mhaus.org/index.crm/fuse action/Content.Display/PagePK/MolecularGeneticsFAQ. cfm.* Accessed September 8, 2006.

40. Malignant Hyperthermia Association of the United States (MHAUS). Molecular Genetic Testing for Malignant Hyperthermia Susceptibility. Sherburne, NY: Malignant Hyperthermia Association of the United States [MHAUS]: 2006; also available at Malignant Hyperthermia Association of the United States (MHAUS). testing for susceptibility to MH; muscle contracture or molecular genetics? *http://www.mhaus.org/index.cfm/fuseaction /OnlineBrochures.Display/BrochurePK/71A5AFFC= 1BC7-4A.* Accessed September 6, 2006.

41. Brandom, B W. The genetics of malignant hyperthermia. *Anesthesiology Clinics of North America.* 2005; 23: 615-619.

42. Sambuughin, N, Holley, H, Muldoon, S, et al. Screening of the entire ryanodine receptor type 1 coding region for sequence variants associated with malignant hyperthermia susceptibility in the North American population. *Anesthesiology.* 2005; 102: 515-521.

43. Rosenberg, H. Malignant hyperthermia syndrome: from barnyard to molecular genetics laboratory. American Society of Anesthesiologists Newsletter. 2005; 69: also available at *http://www.asahq.org/Newsletters /2005/09-05/rosenberg09_05.html.* Accessed May 18, 2006.

44. Malignant Hyperthermia Association of the United States (MHAUS). MH susceptible patients FAQs: drugs and MH susceptibility. *http://www.mhaus.org/index.cfm /fuseaction/Content.Display/PagePK/SusceptFAQ.cfm.* Accessed September 13, 2006.

45. Malignant Hyperthermia Association of the United States (MHAUS). *Hospital Procedure Manual.* Sherbourne, NY: Malignant Hyperthermia Association of the United States [MHAUS]; 2006.

Created by AORN Data Elements Coordinating Committee, 1996. Approved by the AORN Board of Directors, February 1997.

Revised by AORN Nursing Practice Committee, 2006. Approved by the AORN Board of Directors, November 2006. Published in *Standards, Recommended Practices, and Guidelines,* 2007 edition.

EXHIBIT A: Outcome Management of MH Through Application of the PNDS[1]

The Perioperative Nursing Data Set (PNDS) is a clinically relevant and empirically validated standardized nursing language. The tables on the following pages represent a sample care plan for malignant hyperthermia (MH) that uses PNDS terminology to describe the care of patients in the perioperative setting. The diagram below provides more information to assist in reading and understanding the tables.

Nursing assessments for each outcome relate to symptoms covered in the corresponding pathophysiology section incated by the PNDS domain (eg, D2, D3-B). The order of the outcomes is listed in the order the symptoms present as explained in the interpretive statements.

The information in the first column, labeled "Patient who has a personal or familial history of MH," explains the perioperative team's preventive actions to avoid symptoms and crisis.

The second column represents the "Patient who does not have history of MH; unknown risk." This covers basic perioperative competencies and general assessments for all patients. It is included in the care plan as a reminder that any patient could go into an MH crisis, shifting the perioperative nurse's interventions to the third column unexpectedly.

The third column represents the "Patient in crisis; actively having symptoms" and includes the Malignant Hyperthermia Association of the United States (MHAUS) protocol.[2]

Note: Specific clinical interventions are based on the MHAUS protocol, but the protocol may not apply to all patients and should be altered according to specific patient needs.

REFERENCES
1. Beyea, S C, ed. *Perioperative Nursing Data Set: The Perioperative Nursing Vocabulary.* Second ed. Denver, CO: AORN, Inc; 2002: 85, 118, 121, 123, 131, 137, 158, 168, 183.
2. Malignant Hyperthermia Association of the United States (MHAUS). Emergency therapy for malignant hyperthermia. *http://www.mhaus.org/index.cfm /fuseaction/OnlineBrochures.Display/BrochurePK.* Accessed September 13, 2006.

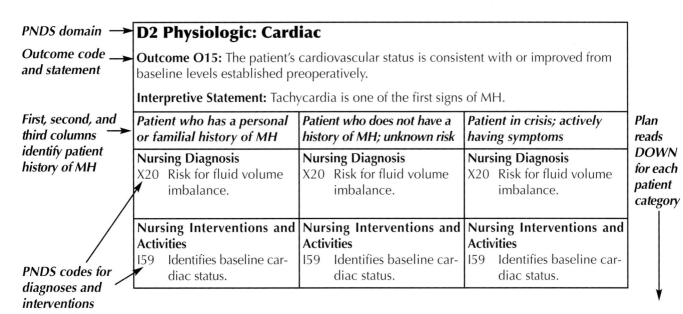

PNDS domain →

D2 Physiologic: Cardiac

Outcome code and statement →

Outcome O15: The patient's cardiovascular status is consistent with or improved from baseline levels established preoperatively.

Interpretive Statement: Tachycardia is one of the first signs of MH.

First, second, and third columns identify patient history of MH →

PNDS codes for diagnoses and interventions →

Plan reads DOWN for each patient category

Patient who has a personal or familial history of MH	Patient who does not have a history of MH; unknown risk	Patient in crisis; actively having symptoms
Nursing Diagnosis X20 Risk for fluid volume imbalance.	**Nursing Diagnosis** X20 Risk for fluid volume imbalance.	**Nursing Diagnosis** X20 Risk for fluid volume imbalance.
Nursing Interventions and Activities I59 Identifies baseline cardiac status.	**Nursing Interventions and Activities** I59 Identifies baseline cardiac status.	**Nursing Interventions and Activities** I59 Identifies baseline cardiac status.

D2 Physiologic: Cardiac

Outcome O15: The patient's cardiovascular status is consistent with or improved from baseline levels established preoperatively.

Interpretive Statement: Tachycardia is one of the first signs of MH.

Patient who has a personal or familial history of MH	Patient who does not have a history of MH; unknown risk	Patient in crisis; actively having symptoms
Nursing Diagnosis X20 Risk for fluid volume imbalance.	**Nursing Diagnosis** X20 Risk for fluid volume imbalance.	**Nursing Diagnosis** X20 Risk for fluid volume imbalance. X8 Decreased cardiac output.
Nursing Interventions and Activities I59 Identifies baseline cardiac status.	**Nursing Interventions and Activities** I59 Identifies baseline cardiac status.	**Nursing Interventions and Activities** I59 Identifies baseline cardiac status. ♦ Monitors physiological parameters. ♦ Assists anesthesia provider as appropriate in monitoring – electrocardiogram (ECG); – vital signs (ie, blood pressure, pulse rate, body temperature); – oximetry; – capnometry; – arterial and venous blood gases for unexplained tachycardia; – core temperature, measured via esophageal, tympanic, axillary, rectal, and bladder probes; – serum potassium; – calcium; – clotting studies; – urine color and output; – diaphoresis; – mottling of skin; and – central venous and arterial pressure.
I120 Uses monitoring equipment to assess cardiac status.	I120 Uses monitoring equipment to assess cardiac status.	I120 Uses monitoring equipment to assess cardiac status. Based on cardiac assessment of arrythmias and indicators of cardiac output, follow MH protocol (see *D1 Safety: Medication* section).

D2 Physiologic: Respiratory

Outcome O14: The patient's respiratory function is consistent with or improved from baseline levels established preoperatively.

Interpretive Statement: Irregular breathing, ineffective breathing pattern, and subsequent impaired gas exchange are early stages of an MH crisis.

Patient who has a personal or familial history of MH	Patient who does not have a history of MH; unknown risk	Patient in crisis; actively having symptoms
Nursing Diagnosis X7 Ineffective breathing pattern (risk for).	**Nursing Diagnosis** X7 Ineffective breathing pattern (risk for).	**Nursing Diagnosis** X7 Ineffective breathing pattern. X21 Impaired gas exchange.
Nursing Interventions and Activities I87 Monitors changes in respiratory status.	**Nursing Interventions and Activities** I87 Monitors changes in respiratory status.	**Nursing Interventions and Activities** I87 Monitors changes in respiratory status.
I121 Uses monitoring equipment to assess respiratory status.	I121 Uses monitoring equipment to assess respiratory status.	I121 Uses monitoring equipment to assess respiratory status.
I45 Evaluates postoperative respiratory status.	I45 Evaluates postoperative respiratory status.	I45 Evaluates postoperative respiratory status.
		I110 Recognizes and reports deviations in arterial blood gas (ABG) studies.

D2 Physiologic: Fluid/electrolyte/acid-base balances

Outcome O13: The patient's fluid, electrolyte, and acid-base balances are consistent with or improved from baseline levels established preoperatively.

Interpretive Statement: Due to cardiac arrhythmias and impaired gas exchanges, acid-base imbalance may be the next progression of symptoms when a patient is in MH crisis.

Patient who has a personal or familial history of MH	Patient who does not have a history of MH; unknown risk	Patient in crisis; actively having symptoms
Nursing Diagnosis X18 Risk for fluid volume deficit.	**Nursing Diagnosis** X18 Risk for fluid volume deficit.	**Nursing Diagnosis** X18 Risk for fluid volume deficit. X17 Fluid volume deficit.
Nursing Interventions and Activities I89 Monitors physiologic parameters.	**Nursing Interventions and Activities** I89 Monitors physiologic parameters.	**Nursing Interventions and Activities** I89 Monitors physiologic parameters.

I23 Collaborates in fluid and electrolyte management.	I23 Collaborates in fluid and electrolyte management.	I23 Collaborates in fluid and electrolyte management.
		♦ Measures urine output
		♦ Observes characteristics of any drainage.
		  – Inserts 3-way indwelling urinary catheter.
		  – Monitors urinary output.
		  – Monitors color, amount, and consistency.

D2 Physiologic: Fluid/electrolyte/acid-base balances (continued)

Patient who has a personal or familial history of MH	Patient who does not have a history of MH; unknown risk	Patient in crisis; actively having symptoms
		Nursing Interventions and Activities I23 Collaborates in fluid and electrolyte management. (continued) ♦ Administers urinary drainage system care. Maintains aseptic technique during insertion. Secures catheter and places it in view of anesthesia care provider. ♦ Administers drainage tube system care. Maintains clean drainage device site, maintain dressings, and secures device properly.
		I84 Laboratory values (specimen collection) ♦ Manages specimen handling and disposition (eg, blood and urine). ♦ Monitors central venous or pulmonary artery (PA) monitoring as needed; records minute ventilation. ♦ Venous blood gas (eg, femoral vein) values may document hypermetabolism better than arterial values. ♦ Follows coagulation profile. Watches for disseminated intravascular coagulation. ♦ Measure creatinine kinase (CK) every six hours until decreased. If event is severe, CK levels may stay elevated for two weeks.

D2 Physiologic: Fluid/electrolyte/acid-base balances (continued)

Patient who has a personal or familial history of MH	Patient who does not have a history of MH; unknown risk	Patient in crisis; actively having symptoms
		Nursing Interventions and Activities (continued) I34 Establishes IV access. ♦ Initiates IV access or helps anesthesia care provider to initiate IV access, if none exists. ♦ Facilitates set-up for central line as needed. ♦ Based on fluid/electrolyte/acid-base assessment, follow MH protocol: – Administers IV fluid therapy. – Administers refrigerated IV normal saline. **Note:** Do not use IV lactated Ringer's solution; it may contribute to the patient's acidosis.
		I9 Administers prescribed medications based on ABG results. Based on fluid/electrolyte/ acid-base assessment, follow MH protocol (see *D1 Safety: Medication"*
		I153 Evaluates response to administration of fluids and electrolytes. ♦ Creatinine kinase and potassium rise persistently, or urine output falls to less than 0.5mL/kg/hr; induce diuresis to at least 2mL/kg/hr to avoid myoglobin-induced renal failure.

D2 Physiologic: Wound/tissue perfusion

Outcome O11: The patient has wound/tissue perfusion consistent with or improved from baseline levels established preoperatively.

Interpretive Statement: When a patient is in an MH crisis, there may not be time to close the wound immediately, acute muscular contraction and changes to tissue profusion may affect the long-term wound healing and the rigorous cooling processes can increase the risk for physical injury to the skin and other tissue being cooled.

Patient who has a personal or familial history of MH	*Patient who does not have a history of MH; unknown risk*	*Patient in crisis; actively having symptoms*
Nursing Diagnosis X51 Risk for impaired skin integrity.	**Nursing Diagnosis** X51 Risk for impaired skin integrity.	**Nursing Diagnosis** X50 Impaired skin integrity.
Nursing Interventions and Activities I60 Identifies baseline tissue perfusion.	**Nursing Interventions and Activities** I60 Identifies baseline tissue perfusion.	**Nursing Interventions and Activities** I15 Assesses factors related to risk for ineffective tissue perfusion. ♦ Assesses for muscle rigidity progressing to cyanosis and mottling. ♦ Administers care to incision sites. ♦ Assists with closure of wound as soon as MH is suspected. ♦ If wound closure is not possible, wound should be packed with saline-soaked towels or laparotomy sponges. ♦ May need to irrigate the wound with cool normal saline solution, not lactated Ringer's solution.
Note: Perioperative nurses assume basic assessment of injury to skin and tissue, but I152 is not specifically included in this column to indicate extra levels of assessment are needed for the patient in crisis.	*Note: Perioperative nurses assume basic assessment of injury to skin and tissue, but I152 is not specifically included in this column to indicate extra levels of assessment are needed for the patient in crisis.*	I152 Evaluates for signs and symptoms of physical injury to skin and tissue.
I46 Evaluates postoperative tissue perfusion.	I46 Evaluates postoperative tissue perfusion.	I46 Evaluates postoperative tissue perfusion.

D2 Physiologic: Normothermia

Outcome O12: The patient is at or returning to normothermia at the conclusion of the immediate postoperative period.

Interpretive Statement: When a patient is in an MH crisis there is hyperthermia related to hypermetabolic crisis and muscular contraction, and hypothermia related to rigorous cooling processes used to treat hyperthermia.

Patient who has a personal or familial history of MH	*Patient who does not have a history of MH; unknown risk*	*Patient in crisis; actively having symptoms*
Nursing Diagnosis X57 Risk for imbalanced body temperature.	**Nursing Diagnosis** X57 Risk for imbalanced body temperature.	**Nursing Diagnosis** X58 Ineffective thermoregulation. X29 Risk for injury.
Nursing Interventions and Activities I131 Assesses risk for inadvertent hypothermia.	**Nursing Interventions and Activities** I131 Assesses risk for inadvertent hypothermia.	**Nursing Interventions and Activities** I131 Assesses risk for inadvertent hypothermia. ♦ Stop cooling if temperature is 38° C (100.4° F) and falling to prevent it from dropping below 36° C (96.8° F).
I86 Monitors body temperature.	I86 Monitors body temperature.	I86 Monitors body temperature.
	♦ Discontinues cooling measures when patient's temperature reaches 38° C (100.4° F). *Note:* Care should be taken to avoid too rigorous cooling, which can result in inadvertent hypothermia.	I78 Implements thermoregulation measures: ♦ Directly lavage peritoneal and/or thoracic cavity with refrigerated normal saline irrigation fluid (ie, if surgical site is open). ♦ Indirectly lavage stomach (eg, connect nasogastric [NG] tube to refrigerated normal saline irrigation, not lactated Ringer's solution, with cystoscopy tubing). ♦ Lavage rectum (eg, connect a 3-way indwelling urinary catheter with 30-mL balloon to refrigerated normal saline irrigation, not lactated Ringer's solution, with cystoscopy tubing). ♦ Surface-cool patient with ice in plastic bags and a hypothermia blanket to neck, axillae, and groin area. ♦ Discontinues cooling measures when patient's temperature reaches 38° C (100.4° F). *Note:* Care should be taken to avoid too rigorous cooling, which can result in inadvertent hypothermia.

D1 Safety: Medication

Outcome O9: The patient receives appropriate medication(s), safely administered during the perioperative period.

Interpretive Statement: When a patient is in an MH crisis, it is important to have a sufficient number of trained responders. The responders should be familiar with their role in the crisis and be able to access the appropriate supplies and prepare or administer medications efficiently.

Patient who has a personal or familial history of MH	*Patient who does not have a history of MH; unknown risk*	*Patient in crisis; actively having symptoms*
Nursing Diagnosis X29 Risk for injury.	**Nursing Diagnosis** X29 Risk for injury.	**Nursing Diagnosis** X29 Risk for injury.
Nursing Interventions and Activities I8 Administers prescribed medications and solutions.	**Nursing Interventions and Activities** I8 Administers prescribed medications and solutions.	**Nursing Interventions and Activities** I8 Administers prescribed medications and solutions. ♦ Anesthesia care provider to discontinue volatile agents and succinylcholine. ♦ Anesthesia care provider hyperventilates patient with 100% oxygen at flows of 10 L/min or more.
		I9 Administers prescribed medications based on ABG results. ♦ Rapidly administers IV dantrolene sodium 2.5 mg/kg given rapidly through large-bore IV for initial bolus. – Dantrolene sodium should be mixed with sterile water for injection USP (without a bacteriostatic agent; 60 mL per 20-mg vial) and shaken vigorously. – Prewarming (not to exceed 38° C) the sterile water will speed dissolving of dantrolene sodium into solution. – Repeat dosages of dantrolene sodium as necessary; titrate to tachycardia, hyperthermia, hypercarbia, and rigidity. – Although the stated upper dosage of 10 mg/kg is suggested, more may be administered as needed. – For at least 24 hours dantrolene sodium should be administered by infusing 1mg/kg every 4 to 6 hours or 0.25mg/kg/hr.

D1 Safety: Medication (continued)

Patient who has a personal or familial history of MH	Patient who does not have a history of MH; unknown risk	Patient in crisis; actively having symptoms

		Nursing Interventions and Activities
		I9 Administers prescribed medications based on ABG results. (continued)
		
		♦ Administer sodium bicarbonate to correct metabolic acidosis as guided by ABG analysis.
		  – If initial ABG results are not available and there are dysrhythmias or cardiac arrest, consider the most likely cause is due to acidosis and/or hyperkalemia.
		  – Administer initial dose of 1 to 2 mEq/kg of sodium bicarbonate IV and repeat as indicated. Thereafter, dose should be based on ABG results.
		♦ Administer IV glucose and insulin.
		  – To treat hyperkalemia in adults use 10 units regular insulin IV and 50 mL 50% glucose.
		  – To treat hyperkalemia in children, use 0.1 units insulin/kg and 1mL/kg 50% glucose.
		♦ Administer calcium chloride to treat life-threatening hyperkalemia.
		  – For adults, 10mg/kg calcium chloride or 10 to 50 mg/kg calcium gluconate for life-threatening hyperkalemia.
		  – Check glucose levels hourly.
		♦ Administer standard anti-arrhythmic agents if dysrhythmias persist following treatment of acidosis and hyperkalemia.

D1 Safety: Medication (continued)

Patient who has a personal or familial history of MH	Patient who does not have a history of MH; unknown risk	Patient in crisis; actively having symptoms

		Nursing Interventions and Activities
		I9 Administers prescribed medications based on ABG results. (continued)
		
		   ♦ Life-threatening dysrhythmias should not be treated with calcium channel blocking agents because they may cause hyperkalemia or cardiac arrest in the presence of dantrolene sodium.
		   ♦ Avoid using solutions containing potassium.

		I78 Implements thermoregulation measures and applies devices to cool the patient as indicated.
		   ♦ Recognizes and reports deviation in diagnostic studies.
		   ♦ Collaborates in maintenance and/or corrective therapy. Requests additional staff members to assist with management of complications.
		   ♦ Monitors physiological parameters. Assists anesthesia provider as appropriate in monitoring
		    – electrocardiogram (cardiac);
		    – vital signs (ie, blood pressure, pulse rate, body temperature; cardiac);
		    – oximetry (respiratory);
		    – capnometry (respiratory);
		    – arterial and venous blood gases for unexplained tachycardia (fluid and electrolytes);
		    – core temperature (esophageal, tympanic, axillary, rectal, bladder);
		    – serum potassium (electrolytes);
		    – calcium (electrolytes);
		    – clotting studies (electrolytes);
		    – urine color and output (electrolytes);
		    – diaphoresis (fluid electrolytes);
		    – mottling of skin (perfusion); and
		    – central venous pressure and arterial pressure (cardiac).

D1 Safety: Freedom from acquired physical injury.

Outcome O2: The patient is free from signs and symptoms of injury caused by extraneous objects.

Interpretive Statement: When a patient goes into an MH crisis, routine count procedures may be disrupted and additional supplies and equipment are used for thermoregulation. The perioperative nurse should reconcile the surgical count (ie, sponge, sharps, instrument) as soon as possible and anticipate prevention of retained surgical items throughout the MH crisis. The perioperative nurse should identify potential hazards associated with controlling patient temperature and establish safe practices.[3,4,5]

Patient who has a personal or familial history of MH	Patient who does not have a history of MH; unknown risk	Patient in crisis; actively having symptoms
Nursing Diagnosis X29 Risk for injury.	**Nursing Diagnosis** X29 Risk for injury.	**Nursing Diagnosis** X29 Risk for injury.
Nursing Interventions and Activities I76 Implements protective measures to prevent skin or tissue injury due to thermal sources.	**Nursing Interventions and Activities** I76 Implements protective measures to prevent skin or tissue injury due to thermal sources.	**Nursing Interventions and Activities** I76 Implements protective measures to prevent skin or tissue injury due to thermal sources. Inspects skin integrity periodically during, when possible, and after using devices (eg, ice packs, temperature-regulating blankets).
I93 Performs required counts.	I93 Performs required counts.	I93 Performs required counts. ♦ Informs the surgeon and perioperative team as soon as a discrepancy in a surgical count (ie, sponge, sharps, instrument) is identified. ♦ Initiates additional measures for prevention of retained surgical items. ♦ Depending on facility policy and procedure, additional measures may include investigation, reconciliation, and documentation.[4]
I122 Uses supplies and equipment within safe parameters. ♦ Use supplies, equipment, and instruments carefully to avoid compromising patient safety.	I122 Uses supplies and equipment within safe parameters. ♦ Uses supplies, equipment, and instruments carefully to avoid compromising patient safety.	I122 Uses supplies and equipment within safe parameters. ♦ Irrigation/infusion solutions should be warmed or cooled to the temperatures appropriate for the surgical need.[5] ♦ Uses supplies, equipment, and instruments carefully to avoid compromising patient safety.

D2 Physiologic: Pain control

Outcome O29: The patient demonstrates and/or reports adequate pain control throughout the perioperative period.

Interpretive statement: Patients who have experienced an MH crisis have potential for pain not only at the surgical wound site, but also as a result of acute muscle contractions and rigorous cooling processes that may have been implemented.

Patient who has a personal or familial history of MH	*Patient who does not have a history of MH; unknown risk*	*Patient in crisis; actively having symptoms*
Nursing Diagnosis X38 (Potential for) Acute pain.	**Nursing Diagnosis** X38 (Potential for) Acute pain.	**Nursing Diagnosis** X38 Acute pain.
Nursing Interventions and Activities I16 Assesses pain control.	**Nursing Interventions and Activities** I16 Assesses pain control.	**Nursing Interventions and Activities** I16 Assesses pain control.
I71 Implements pain guidelines.	I71 Implements pain guidelines.	I71 Implements pain guidelines.
I54 Evaluates response to pain management intervention.	I54 Evaluates response to pain management intervention.	I54 Evaluates response to pain management intervention.
I61 Identifies cultural and value components related to pain.	I61 Identifies cultural and value components related to pain.	I61 Identifies cultural and value components related to pain.
I69 Implements alternative methods of pain control.	I69 Implements alternative methods of pain control.	I69 Implements alternative methods of pain control.
		I118 Transports according to individual needs. ♦ Ensures transfer without tissue injury; altered body temperature; ineffective breathing patterns, altered tissue perfusion; and undue discomfort, pain, or fear. ♦ Gentle handling/movement/positioning.

D3-B Rights/Ethics: Participates in decisions

Outcome O23: The patient participates in decisions affecting his or her perioperative plan of care.

Interpretive Statement: When a patient has a known increased risk for an MH crisis, decisions need to be made about where to have his or her invasive procedure performed, and the patient should be informed about preventive measures.

Patient who has a personal or familial history of MH	*Patient who does not have a history of MH; unknown risk*	*Patient in crisis; actively having symptoms*
Nursing Diagnosis X12 Decisional conflict.	**Nursing Diagnosis** X12 Decisional conflict.	**Nursing Diagnosis** X12 Decisional conflict.
Nursing Interventions and Activities I63 Identifies individual values and wishes concerning care.	**Nursing Interventions and Activities** I63 Identifies individual values and wishes concerning care.	**Nursing Interventions and Activities** I63 Identifies individual values and wishes concerning care.
I79 Includes family members in preoperative teaching.	I79 Includes family members in preoperative teaching.	I79 Includes family members in preoperative teaching.
Discharge planning I80 Includes patient and family members in discharge planning.	**Discharge planning** I80 Includes patient and family members in discharge planning.	**Discharge planning** I80 Includes patient and family members in discharge planning.
I106 Provides instruction based on age and identified needs.	I106 Provides instruction based on age and identified needs.	I106 Provides instruction based on age and identified needs.
I135 Determines knowledge level	I135 Determines knowledge level	I135 Determines knowledge level
I136 Assesses readiness to learn.	I136 Assesses readiness to learn.	I136 Assesses readiness to learn.
I137 Assesses coping mechanisms.	I137 Assesses coping mechanisms.	I137 Assesses coping mechanisms.
I147 Implements measures to provide psychological support.	*Note: Perioperative nurses assume basic role of support, but I147 not specifically included in this column to indicate that extra levels of support are needed for the patient in crisis or susceptible for MH.*	I147 Implements measures to provide psychological support.
I151 Maintains patient confidentiality.	I151 Maintains patient confidentiality.	I151 Maintains patient confidentiality.

D3-B Rights/Ethics: Consistent care

Outcome O27: The patient receives consistent and comparable care regardless of the setting.

Interpretive Statement: Every patient is at risk for a malignant hyperthermia crisis and deserves to have the same level of care regardless of the setting where the procedure is performed.

Patient who has a personal or familial history of MH	*Patient who does not have a history of MH; unknown risk*	*Patient in crisis; actively having symptoms*
Nursing Diagnosis X44 Protection, ineffective (potential for).	**Nursing Diagnosis** X44 Protection, ineffective (potential for).	**Nursing Diagnosis** X44 Protection, ineffective (potential for).
Nursing Interventions and Activities I1 Acts as a patient advocate by protecting the patient from incompetent, unethical, or illegal practices.	**Nursing Interventions and Activities** I1 Acts as a patient advocate by protecting the patient from incompetent, unethical, or illegal practices.	**Nursing Interventions and Activities** I1 Acts as a patient advocate by protecting the patient from incompetent, unethical, or illegal practices.
I97 Preserves and protects the patient's autonomy, dignity, and human rights.	I97 Preserves and protects the patient's autonomy, dignity, and human rights.	I97 Preserves and protects the patient's autonomy, dignity, and human rights.
I99 Provides care in a nondiscriminatory, nonprejudicial manner regardless of the setting in which is given. ♦ Adheres to AORN, JCAHO, and other standards of care. ♦ Provides comparable levels of care regardless of the setting in which care is given (eg, inpatient, outpatient, public, private, home, emergency department).	I99 Provides care in a nondiscriminatory, nonprejudicial manner regardless of the setting in which is given. ♦ Adheres to AORN, JCAHO, and other standards of care. ♦ Provides comparable levels of care regardless of the setting in which care is given (eg, inpatient, outpatient, public, private, home, emergency department).	I99 Provides care in a nondiscriminatory, nonprejudicial manner regardless of the setting in which is given. ♦ Adheres to AORN, JCAHO, and other standards of care. ♦ Provides comparable levels of care regardless of the setting in which care is given (eg, inpatient, outpatient, public, private, home, emergency department).
I27 Ensures continuity of care. ♦ Hand-off communications include extra focus on patient's susceptibility to MH.	***Note:*** *Perioperative nurses assume basic role of continuity and communications, but I27 is not specifically included in this column to indicate that extra levels of communication are needed for the patient in crisis or susceptible for MH.*	I27 Ensures continuity of care. ♦ Transfers to another facility/department ♦ Hand-off communications

D3-B Rights/Ethics: Consistent care

Patient who has a personal or familial history of MH	Patient who does not have a history of MH; unknown risk	Patient in crisis; actively having symptoms
Nursing Interventions and Activities (continued)	**Nursing Interventions and Activities (continued)**	**Nursing Interventions and Activities (continued)**
I92 Obtains consultation from the appropriate health care provider to initiate new treatments or change existing treatments. ◆ Upon suspicion and/or diagnosis of an MH crisis, notify the following personnel as appropriate: – attending anesthesia care provider, – attending physician, – OR charge nurse, – anesthesia technician(s), – postanesthesia care unit/intensive care unit, – OR cardiopulmonary assistant(s), – house supervisor, and – pharmacy supervisor.	I92 Obtains consultation from the appropriate health care provider to initiate new treatments or change existing treatments. ◆ Upon suspicion and/or diagnosis of an MH crisis, notify the following personnel as appropriate: – attending anesthesia care provider, – attending physician, – OR charge nurse, – anesthesia technician(s), – postanesthesia care unit/intensive care unit, – OR cardiopulmonary assistant(s), – house supervisor, and – pharmacy supervisor.	I92 Obtains consultation from the appropriate health care provider to initiate new treatments or change existing treatments. ◆ Upon suspicion and/or diagnosis of an MH crisis, notify the following personnel as appropriate: – attending anesthesia care provider, – attending physician, – OR charge nurse, – anesthesia technician(s), – postanesthesia care unit/intensive care unit, – OR cardiopulmonary assistant(s), – house supervisor, and – pharmacy supervisor. ◆ Counsel the patient and family regarding MH and further precautions; refer them to MHAUS. ◆ Fill out and send the Adverse Metabolic Reaction to Anesthesia (AMRA) form and send a letter to the patient and attending physician. ◆ Refer patient and family to the nearest center for muscle biopsy follow-up.

REFERENCES

1. Peterson, C, ed. *Perioperative Nursing Data Set: The Perioperative Nursing Vocabulary.* Rev 2nd ed. Denver, CO: AORN, Inc; 2007: 85, 118, 121, 123, 131, 137, 158, 168, 183.

2. Malignant Hyperthermia Association of the United States (MHAUS). Emergency therapy for malignant hyperthermia. *http://www.mhaus.org/index.cfm/fuseaction/OnlineBrochures.Display/BrochurePK.* Accessed September13, 2006.

3. Malignant Hyperthermia Association of the United States (MHAUS). Clinical update: Managing malignant hyperthermia. *http://medical.mhaus.org/index.cfm/fuseaction/OnlineBrochures.Display/BrochurePK/3FFCBC12-9479-49C3-8A9E0B304EF08746.cfm.* Accessed January 3, 2008.

4. Recommended practice for sponge, sharp, and instrument counts. In: *Standards, Recommended Practices, and Guidelines.* Denver, CO: AORN, Inc; 2006: 459.

5. "Recommended practices for safe care through identification of potential hazards in the surgical environment. In: *Standards, Recommended Practices, and Guidelines.* Denver, CO: AORN, Inc; 2006: 547.

AORN Perioperative Standards and Recommended Practices, 2009 Edition

AORN Guideline for Prevention of Venous Stasis

Introduction

Deep venous thrombosis (DVT) and pulmonary embolus (PE) are major risk factors for patients undergoing surgical or other invasive procedures, and thromboprophylaxis should be considered for all these patients.[1,2] Prevention of venous thromboembolism (VTE), a combination of DVT and PE, is more effective than treatment and is an important aspect of patient care before, during, and after surgery.[3] Identification of risk factors should be used as a basis to determine if pharmacological and/or mechanical thromboprophylaxis should be initiated.

Deep vein thromboembolisms and PE may be asymptomatic and difficult to detect. Patients with DVT may exhibit symptoms such as local tenderness or impaired drainage of blood vessels distal to the obstruction.[4] In addition to producing localized symptoms, DVT can break off and travel to the lungs, resulting in PE. The incidence of PE is greater when the DVT is close to the heart.[4] Studies indicate as many as 80% of orthopedic surgical patients may develop DVT. Without preventive treatment 4% to 10% of these patients will develop PE.[5] Deep venous thrombosis and subsequent PE remain the most common cause for emergency readmission and death following joint replacement surgery, even when preventive therapies are used.[6]

The National Quality Forum, the Joint Commission on Accreditation of Healthcare Organizations, the Centers for Medicare and Medicaid Services,[7] the American College of Obstetricians and Gynecologists,[8] and many other organizations have created protocols or recommendations on the prevention of venous stasis/DVT/PE. The American College of Chest Physicians recommends that every hospital develop a formal strategy or protocol addressing the prevention of thromboembolic complications.[9] The Surgical Care Improvement Project developed two process measures recommending the presence of orders for venous thromboembolism prophylaxis for surgical patients and that patients receive prophylaxis for DVT within 24 hours before or after surgery.[7]

Use of protocols for prevention of DVT might save the lives of two-thirds of the patients who die from PE. The protocols known to be effective for the management of PE have been severely underused.[10] Estimates indicate that 1% of patients admitted to hospitals die because of PE and at least one-half of these at-risk patients might be saved with effective prophylaxis use.[3] Perioperative nurses should be knowledgeable about venous stasis and should participate in multidisciplinary teams to develop policies, procedures, and protocols to reduce the risk of venous stasis and assist in preventing DVT and PE.

The purpose of this guideline is to provide a framework that perioperative registered nurses and others can use to develop and implement policies, procedures, and protocols for prevention of venous stasis and DVT/PE. This document does not cover the long-term effects of venous stasis, such as venous stasis ulcers or their postoperative treatment.

The "AORN guideline for prevention of venous stasis" is based on current available research and expert opinion. It is assumed that ongoing research will result in new knowledge, procedures, and medical and nursing interventions for prevention of DVT. This guideline may not apply to every individual and may require modification based on the specific needs of a given patient. Review of this document has been solicited from content experts considered knowledgeable in the prevention of venous stasis and included representatives from academia, medicine, perioperative nursing, and clinical nurse specialists.

Definitions

For purposes of this document the following definitions apply.

Anticoagulant: Substance that prevents or delays blood from clotting.[11]

Anticlotting factors: Naturally occurring proteins that, when activated, prevent blood clot formation.[11]

Antiembolism stockings: Elastic stockings that reach from the foot to just below the knee or to the thigh. The stockings are tighter at the ankles than at the knee. The varying tightness of compression stockings helps circulate blood that collects in the calves.[10]

Central access venous catheters: A catheter designed for continuous access to the venous system. Frequently implanted into the internal jugular, antecubital, or subclavian vein.

Clotting factors: Naturally occurring proteins which, when activated, cause blood clot formation.[11]

Deep vein thrombosis: Development of a thrombus (ie, clot) in one of the deep veins of the body, frequently the iliac or femoral veins or major upper-extremity veins. These clots can break off from the vein, travel through the heart, and lodge in the arteries of the lungs, causing a potentially fatal PE.[10]

Intermittent pneumatic compression device (IPC): A mechanical device that uses intermittent pneumatic compression, applied via a cuff that inflates and deflates sequentially or uniformly. The cuff may be applied to the foot, calf, or thigh.[1]

Post-thrombotic syndrome or postphlebitic syndrome: A chronic inflammation of a vein that destroys the valves after an episode of thrombophlebitis or the presence of a thrombus.[12,13]

Pulmonary embolism: A thrombus that breaks free from a vein, travels through the veins, reaches the lungs, and lodges in a pulmonary vessel. A pulmonary embolism is a potentially fatal condition that may cause death within minutes to hours.[10]

Thrombolytic medication: A medication used for dissolving existing blood clots.

Thrombophlebitis: The formation of a venous clot accompanied by inflammation of the vein. This may be the result of trauma to the vessel wall; hypercoagulability of the blood; infection; chemical irritation; intra- or postoperative venous stasis; prolonged sitting, standing, or immobilization; or a long period of IV catheterization.[10]

Venous stasis: A condition that occurs when the normal blood flow though a vein is slowed or halted.[10]

Venous thromboembolism: A condition including DVT and PE.[14]

Venous thrombosis (phlebothrombosis): A condition that occurs when a clot forms within a vein without inflammation.[10]

Virchow's triad: A descriptor listing the three main causative factors in DVT formation—endothelial damage, hypercoagulability, and venous stasis.[15]

Prevalence

The prevalence of thromboembolic events varies by the type of event. The following classifications describe the most common types of thromboembolic phenomenon.

Venous Thromboembolism

This combination of DVT and PE affects more than 1 in 1,000 adults annually in the United States, causing discomfort, suffering, and occasionally death.[16] More than 2.5 million people annually are diagnosed with DVT.[17] Deep vein thrombosis factors into approximately 600,000 hospital admissions annually, and 50,000 to 200,000 of these patients will suffer from PE. In the United States, PE is the third most common

cause of death. Pulmonary embolism occurs most frequently in patients admitted to the hospital for a diagnosis other than PE or DVT.[1,18] A DVT formed in the leg is not life-threatening, but if the clot breaks loose and moves to the lungs, a life-threatening PE can result.[17] Pulmonary embolism is a medical emergency affecting both the cardiovascular and respiratory systems and has mortality rates that may be as high as 25%.[17]

Pulmonary embolism is reported to be the number-one preventable hospital-acquired complication. Autopsies reveal an estimated 10% to 25% of all deaths in hospitals involve a PE.[3] Some studies have shown that in 60% of inpatient deaths the patient had a PE, and as many as 70% of these were not diagnosed.[18]

One study has shown that 8.83 surgical patients with risk factors per 1,000 develop DVT. The study included all surgical patient discharges defined by specific diagnosis-related groups and coded for an operating room procedure according to the *International Classification of Diseases, Ninth Revision, Clinical Modification* (ICD-9-CM) classification system. Patients who were excluded

◆ had ICD-9-CM codes for DVT or PE at time of admission,

◆ were obstetrical patients in Major Diagnostic Category 14,

◆ were patients where a procedure for interruption of the vena cava was the only operating room procedure, or

◆ the procedure performed occurred before or on the same day as the first operating room procedure.

In this study, the day of the operative procedure was not available on some data files, creating a limitation in the study. This may have led to an incidence rate slightly lower than if that information had been available.[19]

Without prophylaxis, the incidence of objectively confirmed, hospital-acquired DVT is approximately 10% to 40% among medical or general surgical patients and 40% to 60% following major orthopedic surgery.[9] In one study, 42% of hospitalized patients with a diagnosis of DVT and PE did not receive prophylaxis.[20,21]

Approximately 300,000 patients are newly diagnosed with DVT yearly in the United States, and possibly three to four times this many may occur without obvious symptoms and thus are not detected.[16] About 80% of DVT are thought to be silent, with no signs or symptoms. There is a direct correlation between asymptomatic DVT and future development of a symptomatic VTE. One study of critical care patients found that patients with asymptomatic DVT had a significantly greater rate of PE development during their index hospitalization compared to those patients with symptomatic DVT (ie, 11.5% vs 0% respectively; $p = 0.01$).[9]

In the United States, published studies estimate that 200,000 to 600,000 patients receive a diagnosis of DVT and PE annually. These two diagnoses are thought to contribute to 60,000 to 200,000 deaths. If simple preventive measures were instituted, many of these deaths could be prevented. Patients need to be warned about DVT risks and assessed for risk factors, and measures need to be used.[22]

Many hospital-acquired VTE are not evident until after discharge, due to the increased number of same-day surgery procedures and the decreased patient length of stay.[9] Lack of VTE prevention often leads to readmission, a rise in anticoagulation therapy complications, an increased risk of long-term morbidity from post-thrombotic syndrome, and a higher rate of future recurrent thrombosis.[9] An estimated $2.9 billion are spent annually in the United States for the treatment of DVT and PE.[9] The most serious outcome resulting from hospital-acquired VTE is death from an undiagnosed PE.

Superficial Venous Thrombophlebitis (SVT)

Generally, thrombophlebitis is used to describe superficial thrombophlebitis that occurs in the veins located near the surface of the body, but the term often is used synonymously with DVT.[23] Superficial thrombophlebitis occurs annually in 400 patients out of 100,000.[24] Cases of SVT occur more frequently in women. The average age of occurrence for women is 58 years. In men, SVT occurs in 35% to 46% of surgical patients. The average age of occurrence for men is 54 years.[24,25] Ninety percent of thrombophlebitis occurs in the leg, with 10% occurring in the arms and other parts of the body. As many as 60% to 80% of the cases of SVT arise in patients with varicose veins. These patients frequently experience the thrombophlebitis after minor trauma such as a bruise to the varicosity.[24,25]

Post-Thrombotic or Postphlebitic Syndrome (PTS)

This is a chronic inflammation of a vein that occurs after an episode of thrombophlebitis or the presence of a thrombus and that destroys the valves. Long-term venous thrombosis is associated with PTS syndrome. The prevalence of PTS has been estimated to be as high as 2% in the general population and occurs in 50% to 67% of subjects who sustain proximal vein thrombosis.[12,17,26]

Pathophysiology

To understand how DVT and PE phenomena can be prevented, practitioners need an understanding of the pathophysiology of the venous system and clotting mechanisms.

Gross Anatomy of the Venous System

The venous system has superficial and deep veins whose function is to return blood to the heart and lungs. Superficial veins are located just under the skin. These superficial veins connect to the deep veins located in the large muscles by the collecting (ie, communicating) veins. Deep veins located in the muscles are largely responsible for returning blood flow to the heart. The venous system is a low-pressure system that acts against gravity; therefore, it acts in a reverse pressure gradient. Valves within the veins prevent backflow in a healthy venous system. The pressure of blood flow against a normal functioning valve is what opens the valve.[17]

Most collecting veins are suprafascial and can dilate to accept large quantities of blood at any one time without interfering with the normal function of the venous system. From the collecting veins, venous blood travels to the deep veins largely located in the lower extremities. The movement of blood from the feet to the right atrium depends on a complex system of muscle pumps. These pumps propel the blood against gravity and are located in the arch of the foot, calf, and thigh. The contraction of the muscle pumps increases the velocity of the blood and forces the blood upward, which in turn increases the pressure against the valve cusps within the vein, causing them to open and push the blood forward. Healthy, functioning muscle pumps and venous one-way valves move the deoxygenated blood toward the right atrium and prevent pooling or backflow in the vascular system.[17]

Deep vein thrombosis develops frequently in the proximal deep veins, with 90% of DVTs occurring in the deep veins of the leg, usually in the femoral vein.[3] In the upper extremities, the increasing use of indwelling venous access catheters is associated with a greater number of DVT cases. Mortality rates for DVT occurring in the legs range from 13% to 21%, and up to 48% in the arms.[15] If the thrombus partially or completely blocks the flow of blood through the vein, blood begins to pool and build up below the site, potentially resulting in chronic swelling and pain. The valves in the blood vessels also may be damaged, leading to venous hypertension.[16]

Clotting Cascade

The clotting cascade is an intricate system of proteins and enzyme actions that must occur in sequence to produce clots, inhibit further clot formation, or cause destruction of an existing clot. Initiation of one of two systems in the clotting cascade (ie, the intrinsic or extrinsic system) begins the actual clot formation process. The following is a simplified explanation of the complex blood clotting progression.[5,27]

Intrinsic Clotting Path

Internal vascular irritation or lesions initiate the intrinsic system with the mobilization of pro-proteins and pro-enzymes to stimulate the transport of kallikrein, Factors XII, XIIa, XI, XIa, IX, and Xa to the site of the irritation.

Extrinsic Clotting Path

If a laceration occurs to the blood vessel the extrinsic system is activated, releasing tissue factor proteins from the damaged cells as well as mobilizing Factors VII and VIIa. The intrinsic system also is stimulated into action if the damage extends to the internal surface of the vein. The two systems unite at IX and IXa and continue the clotting process.

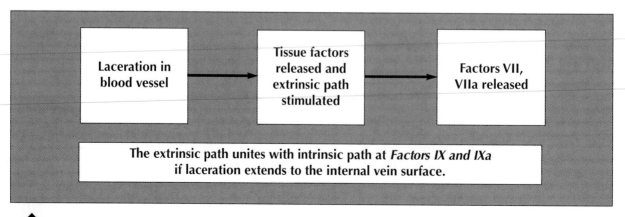

Soft Clot Formation

The next step is soft clot formation, which occurs when Factor X and calcium phospholipids unite with prothrombin, yielding thrombin formation. Thrombin is anchored to the phospholipids, limiting thrombin to the site of the injury or irritation. In the presence of Vitamin K, thrombin and Factor V unite, initiating the development of fibrinogen, which yields fibrin to form a mesh-like structure called a soft clot.

Requires the Presence of Vitamin K

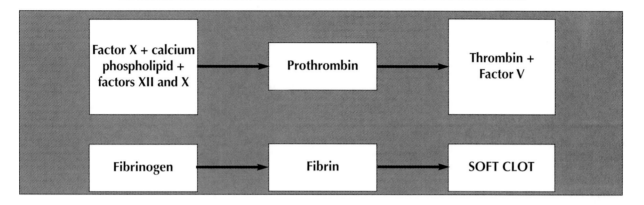

Hard Clot Formation

After soft clot formation, thrombin activates Factor XIII, a fibrin-stabilizing factor. This factor along with the fibrin-soft-clot-matrix, traps platelets, aggregating the platelets at the injury site and resulting in a hard clot.

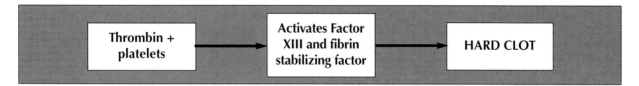

Clotting Termination

At some point, the clotting cascade must terminate, and eventually the clot dissolves. The termination process begins with release of Factors V, VII, VIII, XIII, and Protein C and Protein S. The actual release of Protein C signals the clotting cascade to dismantle. Protein C targets Factors V and VII to slow and eventually stop clot formation.

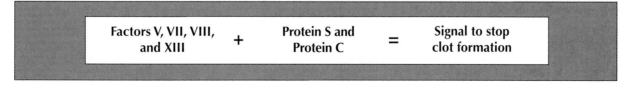

Inhibition of Clotting Process

Antithrombin III is produced to inhibit thrombin. Tissue damage or irritation also stimulates mast cell production. Mast cell production releases heparin and other proteases that function as mild antithrombin-type substances and other antithrombin III enhancers. These actions stop clot formation.

Antithrombin III + Heparin + Other inhibitor = Termination of clotting process

Clot Dissolution (Fibrinolysis)

Fibrinolysis, or clot dissolution, requires plasminogen and tissue plasminogen activator to release plasmin. Plasmin, along with heparin, has a binding affinity to the fibrin, digesting the clot.

Plasminogen +Tissue Plasminogen Activator + Heparin = Clot dissolution

Pathogenesis of Deep Vein Thrombosis and Pulmonary Embolism

Factors that influence venous thrombus formation can be explained by a theory developed by Rudolf Karl Virchow in 1856.[15] This theory, known as Virchow's triad, describes three conditions that contribute to the formation of DVT. Deep vein thrombosis is caused by an abnormality in one or all three of the components of Virchow's triad.[4]

Virchow's Triad

Virchow's triad describes the three main causative factors in DVT formation: endothelial damage, hypercoagulability, and venous stasis.[1,3,5,15,18] The following conditions all can contribute to these causative factors and result in DVT.

Vessel wall injury

Any vessel wall injury that does not include the interior vessel wall initiates the extrinsic pathway of the clotting cascade. When the endothelium (eg, interior) of a vessel is damaged, causing roughening of the vessel wall, the intrinsic pathway of the clotting cascade is initiated, resulting in platelet adhesion and aggregation that promotes blood coagulation at the site of the injury.

Trauma and surgical procedures or interventions cause instantaneous injury to vessel walls, both interior and exterior, and create a risk for thrombosis. Venipunctures, intravenous therapies, venous access catheters, and heart valves cause a constant irritant and also add to the potential for DVT occurrence.

Blood flow alteration

Alterations in blood flow (ie, venous stasis) allow blood to pool within the veins, causing clot production. These clots increase in viscosity and do not get washed away rapidly related to the stasis. They may sit and enlarge and then may be propelled into the remainder of the venous system. Blood flow alteration may be caused by venous stasis, which can occur in sedentary or bedridden patients or pregnant women, especially those with varicosities. Patients with blood dyscrasias that contribute to blood pooling, such as proliferative polycythemia, erythrocytosis, or some malignancies, also can lead to stasis problems.

Blood flow also can be altered due to venous obstruction. A population at risk due to pooling of venous blood includes patients with pelvic tumors, those having long abdominal or pelvic laparoscopic surgical procedures, and patients with congestive heart failure.

Smoking, another cause of blood flow alteration, is a chemical irritant that causes vasoconstriction and thus reduces the oxygen carried in the blood. This alters the blood flow and leads to retention of blood in the vascular system.

Alterations in coagulation

Any increase in the coagulation profile (ie, hypercoagulability) of the blood can result in DVT formation. Factors increasing the risk of blood clot formation can be due to any of the following:

- an increase in the number or amount of clotting factors released (eg, surgery, burns, trauma);
- a decrease or lack of factors that stop the clotting cascade;
- a decrease in the fibrinolysis action of the clotting system caused by medications (eg, estrogen), inflammatory diseases (eg, inflammatory bowel disease), or chronic systemic diseases (eg, lupus erythematosus);
- absence of coagulation modulators that signal clot formation to stop (eg, protein C, protein S, and antithrombin III, and changes in the activity of the fibrolytic system or presence of tissue plasminogen activator, plasmin, or heparin); and
- age. As people age, the presence of additional venous thrombus risk factors within Virchow's triad *(below)* escalate the possibility and occurrence of DVT formation.[22]

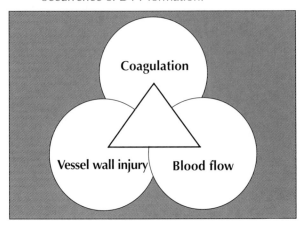

Superficial Venous Thrombophlebitis

Superficial thrombophlebitis occurs when one of the elements of Virchow's triad—ie, vessel wall injury, blood flow, and coagulation—stimulates the clotting process. Superficial thrombophlebitis causes an acute inflammatory reaction that triggers the thrombus to adhere to the vein wall.[25]

Post-Thrombotic or Postphlebitic Syndrome

This syndrome is thought to be caused by venous hypertension resulting from venous valve destruction or persistent obstruction due to thrombosis. The high pressure present renders the perforating veins of the calf incompetent. Blood flow is then directed into the superficial system, leading to edema and, when severe, impaired viability of subcutaneous tissues, leading to venous stasis ulceration.[13,17,26]

Assessing for Risk Factors

It is imperative for perioperative practitioners to identify the risks factors for DVT and/or PE in their nursing assessments.[15,28,29] Assessment of risk factors begins with the initial patient assessment. It continues throughout the patient's surgical/interventional procedure and postoperative recovery until he or she is discharged from care. The process of assessing patients for DVT or PE begins with the identification of risk factors. Risk factors are grouped into three general categories.

Age. Risks for DVT increase in frequency as a person advances in age, beginning at age 40.[3]

Primary admitting medical diagnosis. The primary admitting medical diagnosis (ie, admitting diagnosis, primary diagnosis) is the patient's diagnosis when presenting to the health care facility. The perioperative nurse should develop a plan of care based on increased risk for DVT when this diagnosis includes any of the following:

- trauma;[9]
- orthopedic fractures (eg, hip, major bone, pelvis, knee);[14,22]
- burns;[15,30]
- planned surgery or interventional procedures where
  - patient positioning includes flexion and rotation of a joint that may cause constriction of a vessel leading to vascular damage, or[28,31]
  - surgery may cause an interruption of circulation (eg, tourniquet usage);[28]

◆ use of central venous indwelling catheters;[9,32] and

◆ procedures lasting longer than 30 to 45 minutes.[15]

Past medical history. The patient's past medical history may include or be independent from the current admitting diagnosis. The medical history assessment is based on the patient's past, current, and familial medical history. It should include an assessment of

◆ any recent surgery (especially orthopedic, abdominal, or thoracic);[7]

◆ history or family history of thrombosis, coagulopathy, blood clots, blood-clotting disorders, DVT, or PE;[9]

◆ history of cancer (ie, malignancy with or without treatment);[9]

◆ varicosities or leg swelling;[9]

◆ obesity;[9]

◆ smoking;[9]

◆ chronic obstructive pulmonary disease;[9]

◆ estrogen or hormone therapy;[9]

◆ nephrotic syndrome;[9]

◆ pregnancy or postpartum period of less than one month;[9]

◆ recent myocardial infarction;[9]

◆ congestive heart failure;[9]

◆ history of atrial fibrillation;[9]

◆ inflammatory bowel disease;[9]

◆ sedentary/nonambulatory lifestyle greater than 72 hours;[10]

◆ immobility, including that related to casts, braces, or splints;[9]

◆ stroke;[9]

◆ infection or sepsis;[9]

◆ dehydration or hypovolemia;[15]

◆ recent travel (eg, prolonged air travel or riding in a vehicle);[33] and

◆ ethnicity (ie, greater risk in Caucasians and African Americans).[15]

The presence of any of these in the patient's history indicates a need for increased surveillance for DVT.

Special Considerations for High-Risk Patients

Pediatric Patients

Today more children survive diseases previously considered incurable. Along with this increased survival, the number of children experiencing DVT is increasing (eg, approaching 0.2% in North

America). A second factor for increasing the rate of childhood DVT is the increasing use of central venous access catheters.[9,34]

The epidemiology of DVT in children differs from adults related to the location of the thrombi. Venous thromboembolism in children usually is located in the upper body venous system, primarily because this is the preferred location for central venous access catheter placement.[32] One study found that approximately 40% of thrombi in children occur in the upper venous system, but in adults this occurs only approximately 1% of the time.[35] The greatest risk factor for DVT in children is the placement of central venous access catheters or arterial catheters.[36]

General Surgery

The risk of thromboembolic complications in the general surgery population may be elevated due to more extensive surgical procedures being carried out on older and more critically ill patients, the use of preoperative chemotherapy, and the shorter duration of prophylaxis related to decreased lengths of stay in the hospital. The risk for DVT is decreased by earlier mobilization and increased use of thromboprophylaxis.[9]

Gynecologic Surgery

The rates of VTE after gynecologic surgery are similar to the rates of general surgery patients. Gynecologic patients frequently have a combination of risk factors that make them more susceptible to VTE. Laparoscopic gynecological procedures appear to have a lower risk of VTE compared to open procedures but can result in impaired venous return from the legs and activation of the factors involved in coagulation.[9]

Laparoscopic Surgery

The potential for a longer surgical time for laparoscopic operations leads to a greater risk of VTE. Venous stasis is created in these patients related to both pneumoperitoneum and the use of the reverse Trendelenburg position. The length of stay associated with laparoscopic procedures leads to a decrease in the length of the thromboprophylaxis time, and mobility after discharge is difficult to control.[9]

Urologic Surgery

The rates of VTE in urological patients are decreasing, but VTE remains an important nonsurgical complication. The increased risk factors for patients undergoing major urologic surgery are very similar to those undergoing gynecologic procedures, including the use of the lithotomy position and open procedures resulting in longer operative times.[9]

Orthopedic Surgery

Patients having major orthopedic surgery, including hip and knee arthroplasty and hip fracture repair, are considered to be at high risk of developing VTE. The rates of DVT in patients having surgery for injuries below the femur are poorly studied. Many of these patients have a decreased number of risk factors (eg, younger age, overall healthier status) compared to those having fractured femurs, thus reducing some of their risk factors.[9]

Neurosurgery

Patients undergoing neurosurgery (ie, non-spine) are considered to be in the moderate risk category for the development of postoperative VTE. Some of the risk factors for this population include decreased leg strength and the length of the operative procedure.[9]

Trauma, Spinal Cord Injury, Burns

Trauma patients are at the highest risk (ie, greater than 50%) among hospitalized patients with a risk of having DVT. Pulmonary embolism is the third leading cause of death in those trauma patients who do not receive prophylaxis and who survive the first 24 hours after injury. Trauma patients with spinal cord injury are at greatest risk, with 60% to 100% reported as having DVT.[9]

Serious burns result in a patient with profound systemic hypercoagulabilty. This factor, combined with prolonged bed rest, multiple surgical procedures, femoral venous catheter insertion, and recurrent bouts of sepsis, increases the risk of DVT.[9]

Malignancy

Venous thromboembolism is a common complication seen in patients with cancer, accounting for nearly 20% of all patients with a new VTE diagnosis. Comparing those with and without cancer, those with cancer have a sixfold increased risk of developing VTE. When a cancer patient has a surgical procedure, the risk of postoperative DVT is more than twice that of a noncancer patient, and the risk of a fatal PE is more than three times that of a noncancer patient undergoing a similar procedure.[9]

Critical Care

Patients in a critical care setting have multiple risk factors for VTE (eg, recent surgery, trauma, sepsis, malignancy, immobilization, stroke, advanced age, heart or respiratory failure, previous VTE, and pregnancy), many occurring before the admission. The critical care patient also has additional risk factors such as immobilization, use of pharmacologic agents for paralysis or sedation, central venous access catheters, surgical procedures, sepsis, mechanical ventilation, vasopressor use, heart failure, renal dialysis, and depletion of endogenous anticoagulants during their stay in critical care unit.[9]

Nursing Process Application

Application of the nursing process when caring for patients at risk for DVT or PE includes the use of the Perioperative Nursing Data Set (PNDS). The PNDS vocabulary is a clinically relevant and empirically validated standardized nursing language. It is related to the delivery of care in the perioperative setting. This standardized language consists of a collection of data elements and includes perioperative nursing diagnosis, interventions, and outcomes. In 1999, the American Nurses Association Committee on Nursing Practice recognized the PNDS information infrastructure as a data set useful in the practice of nursing.

The Perioperative Patient Focused Model provides the conceptual framework for the PNDS and the model for perioperative nursing practice.[37] The patient and his or her family members are the core of the PNDS model. The model depicts perioperative nursing in four domains and illustrates the relationship between the patient, family members, and the care provided by the professional perioperative nurse. The patient-centered domains are:

D1 Safety
D2 Physiological Responses
D3-A Behavioral Responses—Patient and Family: Knowledge
D3-B Behavioral Responses—Patient and Family: Ethics
D4 Health System

A unique identifier represents each data element in the PNDS. Domains are represented by the letter "D," followed by numbers one through four to indicate the particular domain being addressed.

Prevention of Venous Stasis

Nursing diagnoses are represented by the letter "X" and a number unique to the diagnosis. Interventions are represented by the letter "I" and a number. These designations are used in this document as appropriate. Desired outcomes are represented by the letter "O."[37]

The following is a partial list of outcomes, nursing diagnoses, and interventions adapted from the PNDS vocabulary that may be associated with the individual with a potential for or having a diagnosis of venous stasis, DVT, or PE. The outcomes, nursing diagnosis, and interventions are grouped by domains.

Domain/Outcome/Nursing Diagnosis/Interventions	Preop	Intraop	Postop
DOMAIN 1: SAFETY			
O5 **The patient is free from signs and symptoms of injury related to positioning.**			
X40 Perioperative positioning injury, risk for impairment of tissue perfusion, or length of surgical procedure.			
X61 Tissue perfusion: Ineffective.			
I77 Implements protective measures to prevent skin/tissue injury due to mechanical sources.	X	X	X
I64 Identifies physical alterations that require additional precautions for procedure-specific positioning.	X		
I96 Positions the patient.		X	
I38 Evaluates for signs and symptoms of injury as a result of positioning.	X	X	X
I152 Evaluates for signs and symptoms of physical injury to skin and tissue.	X	X	X
I138 Implements protective measures prior to operative or invasive procedure.			
I77 Implements protective measures to prevent skin/tissue injury due to mechanical sources.	X	X	X
I15 Assesses factors related to risks for ineffective tissue perfusion.	X	X	X
O9 **The patient receives appropriate medication(s), safely administered during the perioperative period.**			
X29 Injury, risk due to positioning and inadequate mobility.			
I8 Administers prescribed medications and solutions.	X	X	X
I51 Evaluates response to medications.	X	X	X
DOMAIN 2: PHYSIOLOGIC			
O11 **The patient has wound/tissue perfusion consistent with or improved from baseline levels established preoperatively.**			
X18 Fluid volume, risks related to inadequate circulation.			
X28 Infection, risk of circulation or tissue perfusion.			
I60 Identifies baseline tissue perfusion.	X	X	
I15 Assesses factors related to risks for ineffective tissue perfusion.	X	X	
I46 Evaluates postoperative tissue perfusion.		X	X
I3 Administers care to invasive device sites.	X	X	X

174

Domain/Outcome/Nursing Diagnosis/Interventions		Preop	Intraop	Postop
O14	**The patient's respiratory function is consistent with or improved from baseline levels established preoperatively.**			
X7	Breathing pattern: Ineffective due to respiratory compromise.			
X21	Gas exchange: Impaired due to inadequate respiratory exchange.			
X55	Ventilation: Impaired spontaneous.			
	I87 Monitors changes in respiratory status.	X	X	X
	I121 Uses monitoring equipment to assess respiratory status.	X	X	X
	I110 Recognizes and reports deviation in arterial blood gas studies.	X	X	X
	I45 Evaluates postoperative respiratory status.		X	X
O15	**The patient's cardiovascular status is consistent with or improved from baseline levels established preoperatively.**			
X8	Cardiac output: Decreased related to impaired tissue perfusion.			
X41	Peripheral neurovascular dysfunction: Risk for.			
	I59 Identifies baseline cardiac status.			
	I120 Uses monitoring equipment to assess cardiac status.	X	X	X
	I44 Evaluates postoperative cardiac status.	X	X	
O30	**The patient's neurological status is consistent with or improved from baseline levels established preoperatively.**			
X11	Confusion: Acute related to physiological conditions.			
X1	Activity intolerance: Related to multiple conditional factors.			
	I146 Evaluates postoperative neurological status.	X	X	
	I111 Recognizes and reports deviations in diagnostic study results.	X	X	X
DOMAIN 3-A: Behavioral Responses—Patient and Family: Knowledge				
O19	**The patient demonstrates knowledge of medication management.**			
X71	Health maintenance: Ineffective.			
	I104 Provides instruction about prescribed medications.			
O21	**The patient participates in the rehabilitation process.**			
X34	Physical modality: Impaired due to injury or disease process.			
	I106 Provides instructions based on age and identified needs.	X		X
	I50 Evaluates response to instructions.	X		X
DOMAIN 3-B: Behavioral Responses—Patient and Family: Ethics				
O23	**The patient participates in decisions affecting his or her perioperative plan of care.**			
X35	Noncompliance due to knowledge deficit or patients' rights.			
X71	Health maintenance: Ineffective.			
	I80 Includes patient and family members in discharge planning.	X		X
	I79 Includes family members in preoperative teaching.	X		

Prevention of Venous Stasis

Additional interventions should be considered by the perioperative nurse when developing an individualized plan of care for the patient with a potential of venous stasis, DVT, or PE. Interventions should be selected according to the procedure to be performed, and they should address the potential prevention of venous stasis, DVT, or PE. The interventions below are grouped by location of care. Some of the interventions are repeated because this intervention should be carried out in all three areas. An intervention listed in only one area does not mean that it may not be appropriate for other areas depending upon the situation and the setting.

Preoperative

■ Assess all patients to determine risk factors for venous stasis, DVT, or PE. Data collection involves patients and their significant others. A tool such as **Table 1** may be used to classify the patient's risk level. This risk level can be used in determining the appropriate method of prophylaxis.

■ The choice of therapy is a medical decision, but the perioperative registered nurse should collaborate with surgeons, anesthesia care providers, and other health care professionals involved regarding initiating the established protocol orders for DVT or PE prevention.[9]

Table 1

Classification of Risk Levels[1-3]		
Risk Level	**Surgical parameters**	**Prophylactics**
Low	Uncomplicated minor surgery in patients younger than 40 years with no clinical risk factors requiring general anesthesia less than 30 minutes.	■ No specific prophylaxis ■ Early and aggressive ambulation
Moderate	Surgical patients aged 40 to 60 years with no additional risk factors. Major surgery in patients younger than 40 years with no additional risk factors requiring general anesthesia longer than 30 minutes. Minor surgery in patients with risk factors.	■ Low-dose unfractionated heparin every 12 hours ■ Low-molecular-weight heparin (< 3,400 units daily) ■ Graded compression stockings or intermittent pneumatic compression (IPC)
High	Major surgery in patients older than 60 years without additional risk factors. Major surgery in patients aged 40-60 years with additional risk factors. Patients with history of myocardial infarction. Medical patients with risk factors.	■ Low-dose unfractionated heparin; 5,000 units every 8 hours ■ Low-molecular-weight heparin (> 3,400 units daily); elastic stockings or IPC
Highest	Major surgery in patients older than 40 years with multiple risk factors such (eg. prior venous thromboembolism, malignant disease, hypercoagulable state). Patients with elective major lower extremity orthopedic surgery, hip fracture, stroke, multiple trauma, or spinal cord injury.	Low-molecular-weight heparin (> 3,400 units daily); fondaparinux, oral vitamin K antagonists (international normalized ratio [INR] 2–3); low-dose unfractionated heparin or low-molecular-weight heparin; IPC or graded compression stockings.

REFERENCES

1. F A Anderson, A M Audet, "Best practices: Preventing deep vein thrombosis and pulmonary embolism," DVT.org, http://www.outcomes-umassmed.org/dvt/best_practice (accessed 18 June 2006).

2. W H Wilson Tang, "Perioperative DVT prophylaxis," WebMD, http://emedicine.com/med/topic3164.htm (accessed 5 July 2006).

3. J I Arcelus, J C Kudma, J A Caprini, "Venous thromboembolism following major orthopedic surgery: What is the risk after discharge?" Orthopedics 29 (June 2006) 506. Also available at http://www.orthosupersite.com/print.asp?rID=17193 (accessed 30 July 2006).

- If antiembolism stockings are the treatment of choice, the preoperative nurse should measure the patient for proper fit and apply as ordered. If applied incorrectly, stockings may cause DVT, arterial ischemia, gangrene, and necrosis and result in amputation by constricting blood flow. If the stockings roll down, there is the potential that a tourniquet effect will be created.[31]
- Ensure that IPC devices are applied properly, in a timely manner per manufacturer's recommendation, if ordered.[31]
- Ensure that the devices do not hinder ambulation.[9]
- Ensure that prophylactic medications are given as ordered.[9]

Intraoperative

- Confirm that the antiembolism stockings and IPC devices are placed on the patient properly and that medications are given as ordered when performing the preoperative assessment.[9,31]
- After the patient is transferred to the OR bed, the IPC device should be turned on before the beginning of induction of general anesthesia or before regional anesthesia has been administered.[1]
- Instruct the surgical assistant or scrub nurse to avoid extreme degrees of flexion and internal rotation of hip and knee. Preventing endothelial damage due to abnormal leg positioning (eg, during hip surgery when the acetabular head is dislocated and the leg brought across the body, causing kinking of the femoral vein) is an important responsibility shared by the surgery team and the circulating nurse.[28]
- Be aware that unnecessarily high tourniquet pressures and prolonged periods of inflation should be avoided, if possible, when a tourniquet is used.[28]
- Avoid the reverse Trendelenburg position whenever possible because of a potential reduction in blood flow rate to the legs.[28]
- Check antiembolism stockings to ensure that they have not rolled down during movement to the OR bed or during positioning.[31]
- Ensure that the IPC devices work properly during the surgical procedure.[31]
- Continue the established protocol orders for DVT or PE prevention.[9]

Postoperative

- Ensure that the IPC devices do not hinder ambulation.[9]
- Ensure that the device is removed for only a very short period of time.[1]
- Ensure that the IPC device is turned on and working properly and confirm proper functioning and application with the nurse assuming care, if ordered.[1]
- Instruct the patient in the importance of moving and ambulation in preventing postoperative complications per the surgeon's postoperative orders.[1]
- Continue the established protocol orders for DVT or PE prevention.[9]
- Educate patients, caregivers, and health care professionals about prevention of DVT. Education should include common signs and symptoms such as leg pain, swelling, and unexplained shortness of breath.[22]

Treatment and Prevention

A protocol for the prevention of DVT or PE, detailing the primary and secondary prophylactic therapy methods, should be developed by each facility.[22]

Primary Prevention

Perioperative or primary prophylactic therapy in patients with risk factors for DVT or PE involves their prevention, if possible. If preventive measures are unsuccessful, the goal is to reduce the consequences of DVT or PE. The two main strategies are use of nonpharmacologic interventions and pharmacologic interventions. The Seventh American College of Chest Physicians Consensus Conference on Antithrombotic Therapy recommends that patients be classified as low, moderate, high, or very high risk for the development of DVT or PE, and that prophylactic regimens be used according to risk stratification. Examples of the recommended risk stratification are described in **Table 1** and **Exhibit A** at the end of this document.[9] A protocol outlining the preventive measures to be taken for each risk classification should be developed by every health care organization.[22] The pharmacologic and nonpharmacologic interventions can be used together or separately depending upon the patient's risk classification.

Nonpharmacologic interventions

Low-risk patients should receive nonpharmacologic prophylaxis during the perioperative period until ambulation can be initiated.[20] These measures include elastic stockings, IPC devices, and early ambulation, and are especially useful when heparin therapy is contraindicated.

Compression stockings (either thigh-high length or calf-high length) frequently are used after surgery and during airplane rides to promote circulation.[33] Compression stockings may be uncomfortable, but their effect on blood circulation helps to reduce the potential for DVT. Calf-length elastic stockings are effective for patients who undergo low-risk procedures and are relatively free of complications.[1,20]

Intermittent pneumatic compression (IPC) is a nonpharmacologic prophylactic method used to reduce stasis and improve venous return from the lower extremities. Intermittent pneumatic compression is effective in patients with moderately high risk. Devices are available in various designs (eg, foot pumps [arteriovenous impulse system], intermittent uniform pneumatic compression).[1,9]

Caution should be taken in using IPC on patients who have been on bed rest or immobilized for more than 72 hours because of the risk of disrupting newly formed clots.[17,20] Contraindications for IPC include any local leg condition or venous flow compromise that the sleeves would interfere with, such as

- dermatitis,
- gangrene,
- severe arteriosclerosis or other ischemic vascular disease,
- massive leg edema,
- pulmonary edema with congestive heart failure;
- extreme leg deformity,
- preexisting deep vein thrombosis, and
- injuries or surgical sites located in the lower extremities.[26,40]

Early ambulation is the most important and effective nonpharmacologic approach in the prevention of DVT and PE.[3,14,20,38] Vena cava filters can be used in patients who cannot tolerate pharmacologic interventions or in those for whom alternative treatments have been unsuccessful. The primary limitation of these filters is that they become ineffective after one to two years.[5]

Pharmacologic interventions

Pharmacologic interventions are anticoagulant medications that inhibit the blood from clotting. The pharmacologic regimen consists of medications such as coumarin, synthetic pentasacchride (ie, foundaparinux), low molecular weight heparin, and low-dose heparin. The route of administration is dependent on the medication. The platelet active drugs and coumarin are administered orally; heparin and fondaparinux are given by injection.[4,5]

Complications of anticoagulant therapy include bleeding, hematoma formation, compartment syndrome, and heparin-induced thrombocytopenia. The bleeding may be major or minor. Major bleeding can include hemorrhage that alters the patient's treatment or outcome.[5]

Anticoagulant therapy is contraindicated in patients experiencing hemorrhage or with multiple traumas that are in an unstable condition, pregnancy, head trauma, or patients with a spinal catheter in place. Anticoagulants should be given with caution in patients with a history of cerebral or gastrointestinal hemorrhage, thrombocytopenia, or coagulopathy.[5]

Secondary Prevention

Secondary prevention is screening of high-risk postoperative patients. This screening leads to the early detection and therefore timely treatment of subclinical DVT. This is particularly important in those patients in whom primary prophylaxis is either contraindicated or ineffective. Routine ultrasonography screening at discharge or during outpatient follow-up is not affordable or available in many facilities and therefore is not recommended in asymptomatic patients.[3,38]

Evaluation of Outcomes

The perioperative nurse evaluates the patient's progress toward attainment of outcomes. This evaluation should be systematic, ongoing, and documented using the PNDS. Outcome indicators will vary according to specific patient outcomes. These indicators may include

- physiological indicators (eg, cardiovascular status);
- cognitive indicators (eg, asking appropriate questions);

♦ affective indicators (eg, willingness to comply with treatment regimens); and

♦ supportive resources (eg, family member participation in care planning and delivery).

Patient Satisfaction

Evaluation of the patient's progress is based on observation of the patient's response to nursing interventions and the effectiveness of these interventions in moving the patient toward the preferred outcomes. Preferred patient outcomes, nursing interventions, and potentially applicable nursing diagnoses are articulated in the standardized perioperative nursing vocabulary, which provides the basis for documentation of perioperative nursing practice. Ongoing assessments should be used to revise diagnoses, outcomes, and the plan of care as needed. Revisions in diagnoses, outcomes, and the plan of care should be documented. The patient and his or her significant others, working in conjunction with the health care provider, should be involved in the process.

Quality Assessment

Health care organizations that develop a protocol should evaluate the protocol on a periodic basis. The protocol should be evaluated against current research and research-based established guidelines. The effectiveness of the protocol should be evaluated using information supplied by physicians and examination of records of postoperative readmissions for venous stasis or its complications.

Summary

The assessment for patient risk and the prevention of DVT and PE are of prime importance in all patients. Assessment and prevention are especially important in the patient undergoing a surgical intervention. Perioperative nurses can use this document to increase their awareness of and skill at detecting patients at increased risk and to improve their skills in caring for these patients.

REFERENCES

1. S A Van Wicklin, K S Ward, S W Cantrell, "Implementing a research utilization plan for prevention of deep vein thrombosis," *AORN Journal* 83 (June 2006) 1353-1362.

2. T T Horlocker, "New guidelines for antithrombotic therapy: Making blood thinner than water," *ASA Newsletter* 69 (May 2005). Also available at *http://www.asahq.org Newsletters/2005/05-05/horlocker05-05.html* (accessed 3 July 2006).

3. F A Anderson, A M Audet, "Best practices: Preventing deep vein thrombosis and pulmonary embolism," DVT.org, *http://www.outcomes-umassmed.org/dvt/ best_practice* (accessed 18 Dec 2006).

4. M A Quader, L S Stump, B E Sumpio, "Treatment of thrombosis," *Journal of American College of Surgeons* 187 (December 1998) 641-658. Also available at *http//www.facs.org/jacs/articles/sumpioend.html* (accessed 12 July 2006).

5. R S Ennis, "Deep vein thrombosis prophylaxis in orthopedic surgery," WebMD, *http:///emedicine.com /orthoped/topic600.htm* (accessed 23 August 2006).

6. "Deep vein thrombosis," American Academy of Orthopaedic Surgeons, *http://orthoinfo.aaos.org/fact /printer_page.cfm?topcategory=Knee&Thread_ID+264* (accessed 28 July 2006).

7. Joint Commission on Accreditation of Healthcare Organizations, "National data report: VTE measures and consensus standards under development," *Joint Commission Benchmark* 8 no 3 (May/June 2006) 10-11.

8. American College of Obstetricians and Gynecologists, "Clinical management guidelines for obstetricians–gynecologists," *ACOG Practice Bulletin* 21 (October 2000) 1-10. Also available at *http://www.acog.org /acog_districts/dist_notice.cfm?recno=14&bulletin=1955* (accessed 3 July 2006).

9. W H Geerts et al, "Prevention of venous thromboembolism: The seventh ACCP conference on antithrombotic and thrombolytic therapy," *Chest* 126 no 3 suppl (September 2004) 338S-400S. Also available at *http://www.chestjournal.org/cgi/content/full/126/3suppl /338S* (accessed 13 June 2006).

10. *Mosby's Dictionary of Medicine, Nursing & Health Professions,* seventh ed (St. Louis: Mosby, 2006) 115-116, 335, 520, 1454, 1849, 1949.

11. "Deep venous thrombosis (DVT)," Doctors Corner Internet Group, Inc, *http://your-doctor.com/healthinfo center/medical-conditions/cardiovascular/cardiac -conditions/vascular-dz/dvt.html* (accessed 30 June 2006).

12. C Barnes, F Newall, P Mongale, "Post-thrombotic syndrome," *Archives of Diseases in Childhood* 86 no 3 (2002) 221-214. Also available on *http://adc.bmjjournals .com/cgi/reprint/86/3/212* (accessed 03 July 2006).

13. H R Buller et al, "Antithrombotic therapy for venous thromboembolism disease: The seventh ACCP conference on antithrombotic and thrombolytic therapy," *Chest* 126 no 3 suppl (September 2004) 401s-428s.

14. M O'Donnell, J I Weltz, "Thromboprophylaxis in surgical patients," *Canadian Journal of Surgery* 46 (April 2003) 129-135.

15. G J Merli, "Reducing patient risk," *RN* suppl (June 2004) 6-8.

16. S Z Goldhaber, J Fanikos, "Prevention of deep vein thrombosis and pulmonary embolism," *Circulation* 110 no 16 (2004). Also available at *http://circ.aha journals.org/cgi/content/full/110/16/e445* (accessed 13 June 2006).

17. S Sharma, "Pulmonary embolism," WebMD, *http://www.emedicine.com/med/topic1958.htm* (accessed 20 June 2006).

18. M W Day, "Recognizing and managing DVT," *Nursing 2003* 33 (May 2003) 36-41.

19. Agency for Healthcare Research and Quality, "Postoperative pulmonary embolism or deep vein thrombosis: Rate per 1,00 surgical discharges," *AHRQ Quality Indicators: Guide to Patient Safety Indicators* (version 2.1, revision 3; Jan 17, 2005), AHRQ Pub #03-R203. Also available at *http://www.qualitymeasures.ahrq.gov /summary /summary.aspx?ss=1&doc_id=6025* (accessed 18 July 2006).

20. S Z Goldhaber, V F Tapson, "A prospective registry of 5,451 patients with ultrasound-confirmed deep vein thrombosis," *The American Journal of Cardiology* 93 (January 2003) 259-262. Also available at *http://www.science direct.com/science* (accessed 22 August 2006).

21. S Z Goldhaber, K Dunn, R C MacDougall, "New onset of venous thromboembolism among hospitalized patients at Brigham and Women's Hospital is caused more often by prophylaxis failure than by withholding treatment," *Chest* 118 (December 2000) 1680-1684. Also available at *http://www.chestjournal.org/cgi/contnet/full /118/6/1680* (accessed 22 August 2006).

22. American Public Health Association, "Deep vein thrombosis: Advancing awareness to protect patients' lives," *APHA White Paper* (Feb 26, 2003) 1-12.

23. *Medline Plus Medical Encylopedia,* "Thrombophlebitis," Medline, *http://www.nlm.nih.gov/medline plus/ency/article/001108.htm* (accessed 10 July 2006).

24. "Superficial thrombophlebitis," Vascular Unit, *http://www.freevas.demon.co.uk/paper1.htm* (accessed 19 July 2006).

25. E Ascher, A Hingorani, "Superficial venous thrombophlebitis," American Venous Forum, *http//www.venous -info.com/handbook/hbk07a.html* (accessed 10 Feb 2006).

26. M J Oakley, E F Wheelwright, P J James, "Lesson of the week: Pneumatic compression boots for prophylaxis against deep vein thrombosis: Beware occult arterial disease," *British Medical Journal* 316 (February 1998) 454-455. Also available at *http://bmj.bmjjournals.com/cgi /content/full/316/7129/454* (accessed 7 July 2006).

27. "Intrinsic pathway of blood coagulation," General Practice Notebook, *http://www.gpnotebook.co.uk /simplepage.cfm?ID=26869801&linkID=1002&cook=no* (accessed 4 Sept 2004).

28. A Arnold, "DVT prophylaxis in the perioperative setting," *British Journal of Perioperative Nursing* 12 (August 2002) 294-297.

29. K V Leeper, "Detecting and treating pulmonary embolism," *Venous Thromboembolism: An Update, RN* suppl (June 25, 2004) 10-11.

30. W L Wahl et al, "Venous thrombosis incidence in burn patients: Preliminary results of a prospective study," *Journal of Burn Care & Rehabilitation* 23 (March/April 2002) 97-102.

31. A Arnold, "DVT prophylaxis in the perioperative setting," *British Journal of Perioperative Nursing* 12 (Sept 2002) 326-332.

32. C Male et al, "Central venous line-related thrombosis in children: Association with central venous line location and insertion technique," *Blood* 101 (June 1, 2003) 4273-4278. Also available at *http://www.bloodjournal .org/cgi/reprint/101/11/4273* (accessed 03 July 2006).

33. "Deep vein thrombosis," MDtravelhealth.com, *http://www.mdtravelhealth.com/illness/deep_vein_throm bosis.html* (accessed 20 July 2006).

34. M L Levy et al, "Deep vein thrombosis in children and adolescents," *Journal of Neurosurgery: Pediatrics* 101 (August. 2004) 33-37.

35. "Pediatric hemostasis: Decidedly different," McMaster University Medical Center and the Hospital for Sick Children, *http://www.beckman.com/literature /ClinDiag/mcmaster.pdf#search='dvtchildren'* (accessed 30 June 2006).

36. P M Monteleone, "Thromboembolism," WebMD *http://www.emedicine.com/ped/topic2239.htm* (accessed 3 July 2006).

37. S C Beyea, ed, *Perioperative Nursing Data Set: The Perioperative Vocabulary,* second ed (Denver: AORN, Inc, 2002) 81-184.

38. W H Wilson Tang, "Perioperative DVT prophylaxis," WebMD, *http://emedicine.com/med/topic 3164.htm* (accessed 5 July 2006).

39. J I Arcelus, J C Kudma, J A Caprini, "Venous thromboembolism following major orthopedic surgery: What is the risk after discharge?" *Orthopedics* 29 (June 2006) 506. Also available at *http://www.orthosupersite .com/print.asp?rID=17193* (accessed 7 Dec 2006).

40. K I Auguste, A Quinones-Hinojosa, M S Berger, "Efficacy of mechanical prophylaxis for venous thromboembolism in patients with brain tumors," *Neurosurgical Focus* 17 (October 2004) 1-5. Also available at *http://www.aans.org/education/journal/neurosurgical/oct 04/17-4-3.pdf* (accessed 27 Sept 2006).

Approved by the AORN Board of Directors, November 2006. Published in *Standards, Recommended Practices, and Guidelines,* 2007 edition.

EXHIBIT A

Venous Thromboembolism Risk Factor Assessment

Patient's Name:_____ Age: _____ Sex: _____ Wgt: _____ lbs

Choose All That Apply

Choose All That Apply

Each Risk Factor Represents 1 Point

❏ Age 41–60 years
❏ Minor surgery planned
❏ History of prior major surgery
❏ Varicose veins
❏ History of inflammatory bowel disease
❏ Swollen legs (current)
❏ Obesity (BMI > 30)
❏ Acute myocardial infarction (< 1 month)
❏ Congestive heart failure (< 1 month)
❏ Sepsis (< 1 month)
❏ Serious lung disease, including pneumonia (< 1 month)
❏ Abnormal pulmonary function (COPD)
❏ Medical patient currently at bed rest
❏ Leg plaster cast or brace

Each Risk Factor Represents 3 Points

❏ Age over 75 years
❏ Major surgery lasting 2–3 hours
❏ BMI > 50 (venous stasis syndrome)
❏ History of SVT, DVT/PE
❏ Family history of DVT/PE
❏ Present cancer or chemotherapy
❏ Positive Factor V Leiden
❏ Positive Prothrombin 20210A
❏ Elevated serum homocysteine
❏ Positive Lupus anticoagulant
❏ Elevated anticardiolipin antibodies
❏ Heparin-induced thrombocytopenia (HIT)
❏ Other thrombophilia
    Type_____

Each Risk Factor Represents 2 Points

❏ Age 60–74 years
❏ Major surgery (> 60 minutes)
❏ Arthroscopic surgery (> 60 minutes)
❏ Laparoscopic surgery (> 60 minutes)
❏ Previous malignancy
❏ Central venous access
❏ Morbid obesity (BMI > 40)

Each Risk Factor Represents 5 Points

❏ Elective major lower extremity arthroplasty
❏ Hip, pelvis, or leg fracture (< 1 month)
❏ Stroke (< 1 month)
❏ Multiple trauma (< 1 month)
❏ Acute spinal cord injury (paralysis)(< 1 month)
❏ Major surgery lasting over 3 hours

For Women Only (Each Represents 1 Point)

❏ Oral contraceptives or hormone replacement therapy
❏ Pregnancy or postpartum (< 1 month)
❏ History of unexplained stillborn infant, recurrent spontaneous abortion (= 3), premature birth with toxemia or growth-restricted infant

*Total Risk Factor Score*_____

**Please See Following Page for
Prophylaxis Safety Considerations
Revised July 23, 2006**

EXHIBIT A, continued
Venous Thromboembolism Risk Factor Assessment

VTE Risk and Suggested Prophylaxis for Surgical Patients				
Total Risk Factor Score	Incidence of DVT	Risk Level	Prophylaxis Regimen	Legend
0–1	< 10%	Low Risk	No specific measures; early ambulation	**ES** – Elastic Stockings **IPC** – Intermittent Pneumatic Compression **LDUH** – Low Dose Unfractionated Heparin **LMWH** – Low Molecular Weight Heparin **FXaI** – Factor X Inhibitor *Use for major orthopedic surgery*
2	10–20%	Moderate Risk	ES, IPC, LDUH (5000 U BID), or LWMH (< 3400 U)	
3–4	20–40%	High Risk	IPC, LDUH (5000 U TID), or LMWH (> 3400 U)	
5 or more	40–80% 1–5% mortality	Highest Risk	Pharmacological: LDUH, LMWH (> 3400 U)*, Warfarin*, or FXaI* alone or in combination with ES or IPC	

Prophylaxis Safety Considerations: Check Box If Answer Is "YES"
Anticoagulants: Factors Associated With Increased Bleeding
❑ Is patient experiencing any active bleeding?
❑ Does patient have (or has patient had history of) heparin-induced thrombocytopenia?
❑ Is patient's platelet count <100,000/mm^3?
❑ Is patient taking oral anticoagulants, platelet inhibitors (eg, NSAIDS, Clopidogrel, Salicylates)?
❑ Is patient's creatinine clearance abnormal? If yes, please indicate value _____
If any of the above boxes are checked, the patient may not be a candidate for anticoagulant therapy and you should consider alternative prophylactic measures: elastic stockings and/or IPC.
Intermittent Pneumatic Compression (IPC)
❑ Does patient have severe peripheral arterial disease?
❑ Does patient have congestive heart failure?
❑ Does patient have an acute superficial/deep vein thrombosis?
If any of the above boxes are checked, then patient may not be a candidate for intermittent compression therapy and you should consider alternative prophylactic measures.

Examiner _____   Date _____

Based on: Geerts WH et al: Prevention of Venous Thromboembolism. Chest 2004; 126(suppl 3):338S-400S; Nicolaides AN et al: 2001 International Consensus Statement: Prevention of Venous Thromboembolism, Guidelines According to Scientific Evidence; Arcelus JI, Caprini JA, Traverso CI. International perspective on venous thromboembolism prophylaxis in surgery. Semin Thromb Hemost 1991; 17(4):322-325; Borow M, Goldson HJ. Postoperative venous thrombosis. Evaluation of five methods of treatment. Am J Surg 1981;141(2):245-251; Caprini JA, Arcelus I, Traverso CI, et al. Clinical assessment of venous thromboembolic risk in surgical patients. Semin Thromb Hemost 1991; 17(suppl 3):304-312; Caprini JA, Arcelus JI et al: State-of-the-Art Venous Thromboembolism Prophylaxis. Scope 2001; 8:228-240; Caprini JA, Arcelus JI, Reyna JJ. Effective risk stratification of surgical and nonsurgical patients for venous thromboembolic disease. Seminars in Hematology, April 2001; 38(2)Suppl 5:12-19; Caprini, JA. Thrombosis risk assessment as a guide to quality patient care, Dis Mon 2005; 51:70-78; Oger E: Incidence of Venous Thromboembolism: A Community-based Study in Western France. Thromb Haemost 2000; 657-660; Turpie AG, Bauer KA, Eriksson BI, et al. Fondaparinux vs. Enoxaparin for the Prevention of Venous Thromboembolism in Major Orthopedic Surgery: A Meta-analysis of 4 Randomized Double-Blind Studies. Arch Intern Med 2002; 162(16):1833-1840; Ringley et al: Evaluation of intermittent pneumatic compression boots in congestive heart failure. American Surgeon 2002; 68(3):286-289; Morris et al. Effects of supine intermittent compression on arterial inflow to the lower limb. Archives of Surgery 2002; 137(11):1269-1273; Sugarman HJ et al, Ann Surg; 234(1):41-46, 2001.

AORN Guidance Statement: "Do-Not-Use" Abbreviations, Acronyms, Dosage Designations, and Symbols

Preamble

Confusing or easily misinterpreted abbreviations, acronyms, or symbols put caregivers at risk for making errors and compromising patient safety. Unintentional as an error may be, a misplaced decimal point, a "U" interpreted as a "0" (zero), QOD confused for QID, or AS misinterpreted as OS puts patients at risk for medical error with potential catastrophic results (eg, overdose, inadequate dose, omission due to laterality error, wrong medication administered, error in frequency of administration). Improving communication through reducing and standardizing abbreviations, acronyms, and symbols is a significant step toward reducing the occurrence of errors related to the inability to accurately read and interpret written medical orders and transcribed verbal orders.

The purpose of this guidance statement is to heighten the awareness of perioperative registered nurses concerning the dangers associated with the use of abbreviations, acronyms, and symbols, with the goal of eliminating their use in health care documentation. All perioperative settings should address the issue of error-prone abbreviations. These practice settings include, but are not limited to, hospital operating rooms, ambulatory surgery centers, preanesthesia and postanesthesia care units, cardiac catheterization departments, endoscopy suites, radiology departments, and all other areas where operative and other invasive procedures may be performed. Patient safety in the perioperative setting may be improved by focusing on communication among caregivers through the creation of a standardized list of "do-not-use" abbreviations, acronyms, and symbols.

Effective Jan 1, 2004, the Joint Commission (formerly the Joint Commission on Accreditation of Healthcare Organizations [JCAHO]) developed a list of dangerous abbreviations, acronyms, and symbols that are not to be used within accredited health care facilities (**Table 1**). This requirement is intended as a means to improve communication among caregivers (see National Patient Safety Goal #2).[1] The Joint Commission's minimal list of required do-not-use abbreviations, acronyms, and symbols is the beginning of a process to assist organizations with the expansion of their error-prevention programs to improve safety for patients. The Joint Commission recommends that organizations limit the use of abbreviations initially by eliminating nine specific error-prone abbreviations from health care documentation. Seven additional error-prone abbreviations, acronyms, or symbols will be reviewed on an annual basis for inclusion on the

Table 1

THE JOINT COMMISSION'S OFFICIAL "DO-NOT-USE" LIST[1]		
Do Not Use	**Potential Problem**	**Use Instead**
U (for unit)	Mistaken for "0" (zero), the number "4" (four), or "cc."	Write "unit"
IU (for international unit)	Mistaken for IV (intravenous) or the number 10 (ten).	Write "International Unit"
Q.D., QD, q.d., qd (daily) Q.O.D., QOD, q.o.d, qod (every other day)	Mistaken for each other. The period after the Q can be mistaken for "I" and the "O" mistaken for "I."	Write "daily" Write "every other day"
Trailing zero (X.0 mg)* Lack of leading zero (.X mg)	Decimal point is missed.	Write X mg Write 0.X mg
MS MSO_4 and $MgSO_4$	Can mean morphine sulfate or magnesium sulfate; confused for one another.	Write "morphine sulfate" or "magnesium sulfate."

1. *Applies to all orders and all medication-related documentation that is handwritten (including free-text computer entry) or on preprinted forms.*

***Exception:** A "trailing zero" may be used only where required to demonstrate the level of precision of the value being reported, such as for laboratory results, imaging studies that report size of lesions, or catheter/tube sizes. It may not be used in medication orders or other medication-related documentation.*

Reprinted with permission from The Joint Commission, http://www.jointcommission.org/NR/rdonlyres/2329F8F5-6EC5-4E21-B932-54B2B7D53F00/0/dnu_list.pdf (accessed 15 Oct 2008).

Table 2

POTENTIAL ADDITIONAL "DO-NOT-USE" ABBREVIATIONS, ACRONYMS, AND SYMBOLS		
Do Not Use	**Potential Problem**	**Use Instead**
> (greater than) < (less than)	Misinterpreted as the number "7" (seven) or the letter "L." Confused for one another.	Write "greater than" Write "less than"
Abbreviations for drug names	Misinterpreted due to similar abbreviations for multiple drugs	Write drug names in full
Apothecary units	Unfamiliar to many practitioners. Confused with metric units.	Use metric units
@	Mistaken for the number "2" (two).	Write "at"
cc	Mistaken for U (units) when poorly written.	Write "mL" or "milliliters"
μg	Mistaken for mg (milligrams), resulting in one thousand-fold overdose.	Write "mcg" or "micrograms"

Reprinted with permission from The Joint Commission, http://www.jointcommission.org/NR/rdonlyres/2329F8F5-6EC5-4E21-B932-54B2B7D53F00/0/dnu_list.pdf *(accessed 15 Oct 2008).*

official do-not-use list. Implementing this change in practice keeps an organization on a trajectory focused on patient safety as a number-one priority.

Guidance Statement

AORN recommends that all perioperative settings implement the Joint Commission's National Patient Safety Goal #2, adopt the minimum required list of do-not-use abbreviations, educate perioperative registered nurses regarding the removal of these items from all health care documentation, and monitor compliance with this activity. **Table 1** represents the Joint Commission's official list of do-not-use abbreviations, acronyms, and symbols, published Jan 1, 2004.

The minimum required list is the first step in fulfilling the Joint Commission's National Patient Safety Goal #2. With the goal of eliminating all abbreviations from the health care setting, the Joint Commission is encouraging, but not mandating, each organization to voluntarily expand the above list with the addition of the do-not-use abbreviations, acronyms, and symbols identified as possible future inclusions to the "Official 'do not use' abbreviations list." Items in **Table 2** have been identified by the Joint Commission, in concert with the Institute for Safe Medication Practice (ISMP), United States Pharmacopecia (USP), and the National Coordinating Council for Medication Error Report-

ing and Prevention (NCCMERP), to be considered annually as potential error-prone abbreviations to be included on the official do-not-use list.

Furthermore, AORN strongly recommends consideration be given to the selection of problem-prone, high-risk, high-volume abbreviations, acronyms, and symbols unique to the perioperative practice setting when augmenting the minimally required list of do-not-use items. At a minimum, abbreviations related to laterality should be eliminated from all documentation within the perioperative setting (**Table 3**).

Further sources of information to help guide in the selection of do-not-use items may be derived from a review of problem-prone, high-risk, high-volume abbreviations, acronyms, and symbols found within handwritten, preprinted, and electronic forms of perioperative communication, such as

- surgical procedure list,
- surgeon preference or procedure cards,
- perioperative documentation (ie, preoperative, intraoperative, postoperative),
- progress notes,
- specimen labeling,
- consent,
- history and physical,
- surgical schedules,
- staff orientation and competency materials, and
- patient teaching materials.

Table 3

AORN RECOMMENDATIONS		
Error-Prone Abbreviation	**Potential Problem**	**Preferred Term**
L, R, Bil	Illegibility leads to confusion related to correct identification of laterality	Write out "left," "right," and "bilateral"

Another strategy to improve communication among caregivers is a process to ensure that the signatures of the provider initiating the medical order and the caregiver transcribing the verbal order are legible. AORN suggests that all health care providers use block print and sign their names to all written and verbal orders. The extra step of block-printing the name affords the caregiver an opportunity to contact the provider if a question, concern, or issue were to arise related to the written order. If the caregiver is unable to read the written order, confusion or misinterpretation could result and lead to an adverse patient event.

This guidance statement reflects suggested minimal requirements to promote safety in patient care. It is not to be considered an all-inclusive listing of error-prone abbreviations, acronyms, dosage designations, or symbols. It is the responsibility of the health care practitioner, in concert with the patient care organization, to ensure that documentation clearly and unambiguously reflects the individualized treatment of the patient.

REFERENCES

1. "National patient safety goals," The Joint Commission, *http://www.jointcommission.org/PatientSafety /NationalPatientSafetyGoals* (Hospital, 2008–2009) (accessed 15 Oct 2008).

2. "Official 'do not use' list," The Joint Commission, *http://www.jointcommission.org/NR/rdonlyres/2329F8F5 -6EC5-4E21-B932-54B2B7D53F00/0/dnu_list.pdf* (accessed 15 Oct 2008).

RESOURCES

Abbreviations Lists

"New Joint Commission 'do not use' list: Abbreviations, acronyms, and symbols," American Academy of Physical Medicine and Rehabilitation, *http://www.aapmr.org /hpl/pracguide/jcahosymbols.htm* (accessed 7 Sept 2005).

Hicks, R W; Cousins, D D; Williams, R L. *Summary of Information Submitted to MEDMARX in the Year 2002: The Quest for Quality* (Rockville, Md: US Pharmacopecia Center for the Advancement of Patient Safety, 2003) 41-44.

Institute for Safe Medication Practices. "ISMP's list of error-prone abbreviations, symbols, and dose designations," *ISMP Medication Safety Alert* 8 (Nov 27, 2003). Also available at *http://www.ismp.org/PDF/ISMPAbbreviations .pdf* or *http://www.ismp.org/PDF/ErrorProne.pdf* (accessed 8 Sept 2005).

Joint Commission. "Medication errors related to potentially dangerous abbreviations," *Sentinel Event Alert* 23 (September 2001). Available at *http://www.jointcommission .org/SentinelEvents/SentinelEventAlert/sea_23.htm* (accessed 15 Oct 2008).

"Recommendations to enhance accuracy of prescription writing," (adopted Sept 4, 1996, revised June 2, 2005) National Coordinating Council for Medication Error Reporting and Prevention (NCCMERP), *http://www .nccmerp.org/council/council1996-09-04.html* (accessed 8 Sept 2005).

Implementation/Staff Education

Beyea, S C. "Best practices for abbreviation use," *AORN Journal* 79 (March 2004) 641-642.

"Implementation tips for eliminating dangerous abbreviations," The Joint Commission, *http://www.joint commission.org/PatientSafety/NationalPatientSafety Goals/abbr_tips.htm* (accessed 8 Sept 2005).

"Five dangerous medical abbreviations," Ohioans First, *http://www.ohioansfirst.org/abbreviations/abbrev.htm* (accessed 7 Sept 2005).

Regional Medication Safety Program for Hospitals: Health Care Improvement Foundation. *Medication Safety Solutions Kit,* information available from Delaware Valley Healthcare Council, *http://www.dvhc.org/safety/program /details.asp?ID=CQe3RU219Ngec94UQJ3g.* Also available from ECRI, *http://www.ecri.org /products_and _services/products/medication_safety/medsafety brochure.pdf* (accessed 7 Sept 2005).

"Patient safety program," US Department of Defense, *https://patientsafety.satx.disa.mil* (accessed 7 Sept 2005).

"Preventing medical errors: More on dangerous abbreviations," *Patient Safety News,* Show #25, March 2004, US Food and Drug Administration, *http://www.accessdata .fda.gov/scripts/cdrh/cfdocs /psn/transcript.cfm?show=25* (accessed 31 Jan 2006).

"Maximizing patient safety in the medication use process: Practice guidelines and best demonstrated practices," Wisconsin Patient Safety Institute, *http://www.wpsi.org/media/documents/pdf/Max_Pat_ Saft_2002.pdf* (accessed 31 Jan 2006).

Approved by the AORN Board of Directors, November 2005. Published September 2006, *AORN Journal.* (Minor update October 2008.)

AORN Guidance Statement: Environmental Responsibility

Introduction

This document is intended to guide perioperative registered nurses in the development of environmentally responsible practices. This document may be used by health care organizations to provide direction for the creation of environmentally responsible policies and procedures. This guidance document addresses

- infectious and noninfectious waste management,
- recycling practices,
- resource conservation,
- supply conservation and management practices,
- reprocessing, reuse, repair and refurbishing,
- sterilization and disinfection, and
- construction for efficiency and conservation.

It is recognized that not all portions of this document may be usable by all health care organizations because of the varying standards and regulations set forth in various geographic locations. It also is recognized that the perioperative setting is varied and includes hospitals, obstetrical surgical suites, ambulatory facilities, physicians' offices, specialty centers for invasive procedures (eg, cardiac catheterization laboratories, radiology departments, endoscopy suites), and other areas where invasive procedures or interventions are performed

Background

Nurses comprise a large single group of health care providers and are in a position to influence environmental management practices. Nurses have long played a role in the protection of the environment. In the 1800s, Florence Nightingale was one of the first nurses to advocate for a healthy environment.[1] Nurses have an ethical responsibility to actively promote and participate in resource conservation and to protect the environment.

US health care organizations generate in excess of two million tons of waste annually.[2] Approximately 85% of this waste is noninfectious, with a large amount being generated in the operating room.[3] Inpatient facilities spend more than five billion dollars a year on energy consumption. Health care energy consumption is increasing to support new and existing technology.[4] Sterilizing, heating and cooling processes, and hand sanitization contribute to use of water, a limited natural resource.

In addition to waste generation, energy and water consumption has a significant negative impact on the environment.

Guidance Statement

The perioperative registered nurse should serve as a steward of the environment by being knowledgeable about perioperative practices that negatively affect the environment. Perioperative registered nurses should actively promote and participate in resource conservation. Effective resource conservation leads to an improvement of environmental health. The perioperative registered nurse should strive to understand the political, economic, and public health components of environmental responsibility.[5] The following strategies provide a framework on which to build an environmentally responsible practice.

Infectious and Noninfectious Tissue and Waste Management

More than four million tons[2] of general waste are produced annually by US health care facilities.[6] Waste materials can be classified as potentially infectious or noninfectious. Waste management is a major expenditure for health care organizations. Infectious waste management alone can consume as much as 20% of a hospital's annual budget for environmental services.[7]

Waste generated from the operating room includes potentially infectious and noninfectious waste as well as material that requires special disposal (eg, liquid chemicals, hazardous materials). Mercury-based products and dioxin generated by incineration of polyvinylchloride (PVC) are hazardous chemicals. Mercury, a heavy metal and neurotoxin, is a frequent contaminant found in medical waste. Dioxin, a known human carcinogen, has been implicated in cancer of the lung, thyroid, hematopoietic system, and liver as well as soft tissue sarcoma.[8] Polyvinylchloride is found in many medical supplies, packaging, and building materials. The resulting air pollutants from medical waste incineration not only affect the local community, but also can migrate to pollute distant environments and populations.[8] Disposal of mercury and medical waste are subject to regulation by local, state, or federal governmental agencies. Health care organizations must comply with the regulations.[9]

Perioperative nurses can significantly affect waste management practices by encouraging and implementing strategies that promote a safe and healthy environment. These strategies should be cost effective and conserve resources. Strategies that should be considered include, but are not limited to, the following.

♦ Conduct a survey to assess types of waste generated in perioperative practice settings.
♦ Conduct a cost analysis of waste management considering
  – the volume of noninfectious waste, and
  – the weight of potentially infectious waste generated and treatment technology available.[7]
♦ Define potentially infectious waste according to local, state, and federal regulations.
♦ Provide education to all health care workers, to include, but not limited to,
  – the definition of potentially infectious waste,
  – the importance of and process for segregation of potentially infectious waste from noninfectious waste,
  – the costs of waste management,
  – the environmental impact of waste disposal,[10] and
  – state and federal guidelines and regulations for disposal of waste.
♦ Review and update organization-wide waste management policies.
♦ Limit contents of biohazardous waste containers (eg, red bags) to potentially infectious waste.
♦ Explore methods of waste segregation, which may include
  – placing noninfectious waste and biohazard containers side by side in a convenient location, and
  – using a bag-in-bag collection system (ie, clear bag inserted inside red bag for collection of waste used to set up for a procedure; clear bag is removed from bag holder but left in room before start of procedure when infectious waste may be generated).[7] Consider risks to health care workers when using this system.
♦ Eliminate use of mercury-based products—ie, inventory, remove, and replace mercury-containing devices with nonmercury-containing devices (eg, digital thermometers, sphygmomanometers, batteries, bougies, cantor tubes, fluorescent lights).[3]

♦ Work with waste management services to explore alternatives to incineration, including, but not limited to,
  – microwaving,
  – autoclaving,
  – radiowaving, and
  – electrotechnologies.[11]
♦ Explore recycling programs for noninfectious waste (eg, paper, irrigation bottles, sterilization wraps and other plastics).
♦ Evaluate the environmental impact of reusable, reposable, and disposable products.
♦ Develop an ongoing performance improvement program for waste management.
♦ Dispose of chemicals in accordance with state and local regulations, including, but not limited to,
  – dilution,
  – inactivation of solution before release, and
  – consideration of a program of controlled release.[12]
♦ Consider membership in Healthy Hospitals for the Environment (H2E), located online at *http://www.H2E-online.org* (accessed 23 Jan 2006); and Health Care Without Harm (HCWH), located online at *http://www.noharm.org* (accessed 23 Jan 2006).[8]

Recycling Practices

A significant amount of hospital waste is composed of noninfectious material, much of which may be recyclable.[13,14] Recyclable items found in the perioperative environment include, but are not limited to, plastic bottles, sterilization wrap, peel packs, glass, paper, aluminum and metal cans, and corrugated cardboard.[15,16] Only items that are clean and noninfectious, as defined by local, state, and federal regulations, should be recycled.[3] Recycling noninfectious waste materials has environmental and financial benefits that may include[17]

♦ providing materials for remanufacture,
♦ preserving resources for future generations,
♦ decreasing air and water pollution,
♦ conserving energy, and
♦ limiting the expansion of landfills and incinerator use.

Health care facilities should modify purchasing and waste disposal practices to favor recycling.[14,16] Perioperative nurses can significantly affect waste management practices by encouraging and implementing recycling strategies that promote a safe and healthy environment. These strategies should be cost effective and conserve resources. Strategies that should be considered include, but are not limited to, the following.

♦ Perform a waste assessment to identify items appropriate for recycling.

♦ Investigate available community recycling programs to determine feasibility of participation.

♦ Obtain recycling containers from local waste management systems.[18]

♦ Begin with simple items (eg, paper, cardboard, plastics).

♦ Contact manufacturers regarding recycling programs.

♦ Identify waste versus recycling receptacles with distinguishing features:
 – use color-coded receptacles (eg, green for paper, silver for metal, blue for plastic); and
 – use a slotted top for paper, a round top for cans.

♦ Provide receptacles in areas where the waste is generated.

♦ Provide education to all health care workers regarding recycling practices, including separation procedures.[18]

♦ Implement a process improvement program to demonstrate changes and to identify additional recycling opportunities.

♦ Give feedback to healthcare workers related to the results of the waste management efforts to reinforce this behavior.

Resource Conservation

Health care organizations should conserve finite natural resources such as water, electricity, and natural gas. The average water consumption by US hospitals is 139,214 gallons per day.[19] Health care organizations use 62 billion kilowatt hours of electricity annually, with a higher intensity than other commercial buildings (ie, 26.5 kWh per square foot).[20] The average per square foot consumption of electricity in health care organizations is $1.67, compared to $0.99 per square foot in commercial buildings, and inpatient facilities use more electricity than outpatient facilities.[20] Conserving electricity minimizes air pollution caused by electrical generation and reduces costs.[20]

Heath care organizations also consume large quantities of natural gas (252 billion cubic feet annually) and have a much higher natural gas intensity than the average commercial building (143.0 cubic feet per square foot).[21] The average per square foot consumption of natural gas is $0.48 per square foot compared, to $0.24 per square foot in commercial buildings.[21]

Perioperative registered nurses should actively promote and participate in resource conservation measures for water, electricity, and natural gas. Conservation strategies should be incorporated into daily practice, including, but not limited to, the following.

♦ Conduct a resource utilization assessment.

♦ Provide education to health care workers about the importance and benefits of resource conservation.[19,22]

♦ Create resource conservation suggestion boxes and place in prominent areas.[23,24]

♦ Install signs encouraging resource conservation.[23,24]

♦ Develop a team of health care workers (eg, "green team") to evaluate resource conservation opportunities and effectiveness.[16,24]

♦ To conserve electricity,
 – install occupancy sensors in certain areas of the practice setting to control lighting based on the presence or absence of personnel and patients;[25]
 – turn off lights when rooms are not in use;[26]
 – turn off equipment when not in use;[24]
 – install and use energy-efficient electrical equipment, lights, and appliances;
 – reduce flow to surgical vacuum pumps to minimum acceptable level and maintain proper operation;[23,27] and
 – insulate hot water pipes.[28]

♦ To conserve natural gas,
 – insulate hot water pipes,[28] and
 – shut off natural gas to equipment and areas that are not in current use.[28]

♦ To conserve water,
 – ensure the return of sterilizer steam condensate to the boiler tank for reuse;[19,27,28,29]
 – eliminate use of city water for cooling sterilizer condensate, possibly by using holding tanks as an alternative;[23,27,30]
 – establish a preventive maintenance program for the evaluation and replacement of faulty steam traps on sterilizers;[19,23,24,28,31]
 – recirculate noncontact sterilizer cooling water;[30]

- install flow control fixtures on all faucets;[27,28,31]
- install scrub sinks with timers and foot or knee controlled turnoff valves;
- install an on-demand water heater near sinks to avoid running water while waiting for hot water;[31]
- turn off water while scrubbing until needed for wetting or rinsing hands;
- evaluate the use of waterless surgical scrub products;
- evaluate the use of microfiber mops for cleaning;[32]
- install high-pressure, low-volume nozzles on scrub sinks and showers;[29]
- recycle and reduce water use whenever possible;[24]
- operate washers, disinfectors, and steam sterilizers only when full, if possible;[19,23,24,27-29]
- avoid flash sterilization of single items or small loads when possible;[31]
- repair leaks in water lines and faucets;[19,23,31] and
- replace older equipment (eg, sterilizers, ice machines, automated endoscope reprocessors, disinfectors) with water-efficient models.[19,22,29,31]

Supply Conservation and Management Practices

Supply management is essential to ensure that the correct products are available when needed.[33] Cost containment measures that minimize waste production provide economic benefits without compromising quality of care. Effective supply chain management will offer opportunities to minimize process inefficiencies and product waste.

Perioperative nurses can significantly affect supply management practices by encouraging and implementing strategies that promote a safe and healthy environment. The strategies should be cost effective and conserve resources. Strategies that should be considered include, but are not limited to, the following.

- Standardize products, devices, and equipment.[34]
- Collaborate with other health care organizations to purchase partial quantities of infrequently used supplies.
- Preference cards and pick-lists should list the minimum number of items to be routinely opened and specify items to be available but unopened.[33,35]

- Open implantable devices only when the desired specifications are known and confirmed by the surgeon.[35]
- Identify processes or practices that increase efficiency or reduce cost, to include
  - monitoring preference card/pick-list supply utilization and remove items not used;
  - reducing excess supply inventory and returning slow-moving inventory;
  - rotating stock with expiration dates to use oldest inventory first;[36] and
  - evaluating excess supplies from customized packs.
- Evaluate implementation of a value analysis and product standardization program for supply purchase and selection.
- Consider natural resource requirements specific to item (eg, clean water availability).[36,37]
- Consider the impact of the item on the waste stream when purchasing supplies and equipment.[3,16]
- Collaborate with vendors to return unopened, expired items or donate items to charities or nonprofit organizations.[38]
- Purchase items made from recycled products.[39]
- Use double-sided photocopies.[39]
- Use reusable totes and pallets instead of cardboard boxes or wooden pallets for transport of goods.[39]

Reprocessing

Reprocessing single-use devices can potentially reduce the amount of waste entering the waste stream.[39,40,41] A recent estimate shows that facilities with 250 beds or more rely on reprocessing to extend their budgets and reduce waste.[40] In 2004, reprocessing was estimated to have reduced the waste generated by health care organizations by more than 449 tons destined for landfills.[40]

If a health care organization chooses to practice reprocessing of single-use devices as a means of decreasing the amount of waste entering the waste stream, the perioperative registered nurse should investigate and evaluate the environmental impact of reprocessing on the organization's waste stream as well as the total environmental impact. Refer to the AORN guidance statement on the reuse of single-use devices for more tools to use for evaluation of reprocessing[42] and adherence to the US Food and Drug Administration regulations controlling reprocessing of single-use devices.

Reuse, Repair, and Refurbishing

Reuse of medical equipment demonstrates the health care organization's commitment to supply conservation and fiscal responsibility through

- conservation of resources and energy,
- optimization of resources, and
- reduction of the pollution that occurs with waste disposal in the environment.[43] (Pollution is reduced because the final disposal of the item is delayed.[38])

Reuse includes the repair, refurbishing, washing, or recovery of worn or used items.[38] Strategies the perioperative nurse should consider when deciding to purchase reusable items or repair and refurbish an item include, but are not limited to, the following.

- Identify factors affecting the longevity of instruments and equipment, such as
  - adequate inventory to reduce frequency of reprocessing and wear;
  - education of health care workers who use and reprocess instruments;
  - education of health care workers who operate and maintain equipment; and
  - adequate storage facilities to protect the instruments and equipment from damage.[44]
- Implement proactive maintenance, repair, or restoration programs for instruments and equipment to prevent malfunction and maintain integrity.
- Consider purchasing reusable medical equipment, instruments, and supplies.
- Educate health care workers regarding their practice accountability for
  - safe care and handling of instruments and equipment,
  - environmental and workplace practices supporting care and handling of instruments and equipment, and
  - repair and refurbishing initiatives of the health care institution.
- Consider projected life span when purchasing instruments and equipment.
- Consider reuse of clean items internally (eg, corrugated boxes, packaging materials, interoffice envelopes, furniture).

Sterilization and Disinfection

Various sterilization and disinfection technologies that affect the environment are used in health care settings. Sterilization technologies in current use include steam, dry heat, ethylene oxide gas, hydrogen peroxide gas plasma, and ozone.[45] High-level disinfectants commonly used include liquid chemicals such as peracetic acid, glutaraldehyde, and orthophthalaldehyde. Steam and dry heat are not known to generate by-products harmful to the environment, but these methods of sterilization do consume natural resources (ie, water, electricity, or natural gas).[20] Ethylene oxide gas sterilization and liquid chemical disinfectants can result in harm to the environment if used irresponsibly or contrary to existing local, state, and federal regulations.[46] Ethylene oxide gas, for example, is an air pollutant, a known carcinogen, a potential reproductive hazard, an allergic sensitizer, and a potent neurotoxin.[47] When choosing a sterilizing or disinfecting method or product, the effect on the environment should be considered.

Perioperative nurses can significantly affect the environment by encouraging and implementing strategies that are cost effective and/or conserve resources. Strategies that should be considered include, but are not limited to, the following.

- Develop a program for monitoring the environmental effects of sterilization and disinfection products on the environment.
- Ensure that the necessary equipment and supplies are available to deal with spillage of sterilizing or disinfecting chemicals.
- Use, maintain, and monitor sterilizers according to the manufacturers' written instructions.[45]
- Establish, ensure, and maintain proper safety measures for handling hazardous materials (eg, monitoring compliance with emission control regulations for ethylene oxide sterilizers, glutaraldehyde disposal).
- Provide education for health care workers regarding the environmental impact of the sterilant or disinfectant being used and appropriate safety measures.
- Use and dispose of liquid chemicals employed in sterilization or disinfection in accordance with manufacturers' written instructions and local, state, and federal governmental agency requirements.
- When possible, purchase items for which the sterilization or disinfection process has the least potential for harm to the environment.[3]
- Additional glutaraldehyde precautions include
  - using fume cabinets,[48]

- considering cold sterilization alternatives to glutaraldehyde,[45] and
- limiting areas in the facility where glutaraldehyde is used and stored.

Construction for Efficiency and Conservation

Building design, construction, and materials significantly affect the natural environment and health outcomes of patients, staff, and community.[49] Although such a discussion is beyond the scope of this document, perioperative registered nurses involved in the planning, design, and construction of health care facilities should incorporate the principles of "green" building design—ie, designs that are energy efficient and water conserving, among other qualities—wherever possible. Nurses interested in green building codes should refer to Healthy Hospitals for the Environment (H2E), located online at *http://www.H2E-online.org;* Health Care Without Harm (HCWH), located online at *http://www.noharm.org;* or the US Green Building Council, located online at *http://www.usgbc.org* (accessed 23 Jan 2006).[50]

Summary

This document has provided strategies for perioperative registered nurses to use in becoming effective stewards of the environment, addressing

- ♦ infectious and noninfectious waste management;
- ♦ recycling practices;
- ♦ resource conservation;
- ♦ supply conservation and management practices;
- ♦ reprocessing, reuse, repair, and refurbishing,
- ♦ sterilization and disinfection, and
- ♦ construction for efficiency and conservation.

Glossary

Green building codes: Codes used during building design that require the building to be energy efficient and water conserving, have low environmental impact, and have high indoor air quality, among other requirements.[49,50]

Noninfectious waste: Materials with no inherent hazards or infectious potential (eg, packaging materials, paper).[7]

Potentially infectious waste: The definitions of potentially infectious waste vary from state to state, but for the purposes of this document, potentially infectious waste is waste (eg, blood, body fluids, sharps) that is capable of producing infectious diseases.[7]

Reprocessing of single-use devices: Includes all operations necessary to render a contaminated reusable or single-use device patient-ready. Single-use devices to be reprocessed may be either used or unused. Reprocessing steps include disassembling for cleaning, decontamination, inspecting, packaging, relabeling, sterilization, testing, and tracking.[41]

Reuse: The repeated or multiple use of any medical device, whether marketed as reusable or single use. Repeated/multiple use may be on the same patient or on different patients with applicable reprocessing of the device between uses.[41]

Waste: Waste can be classified as potentially infectious and noninfectious materials. In this document, waste refers to the combination of potentially infectious and noninfectious waste.

REFERENCES

1. "Nurses can make a difference: Environmentally responsive health care," The Nightingale Institute for Health and the Environment, *http://www.nihe.org* (accessed 8 Oct 2005).

2. "Medical waste: The issue," Health Care Without Harm, *http://www.noharm.org/us/medicalWaste/issue* (accessed 8 Oct 2005).

3. A Melamed, "Environmental accountability in perioperative settings," *AORN Journal* 77 (June 2003) 1157-1168.

4. B Scrantom, "Health care: New paths to energy savings," *Building Operating Management* (January 2003), *http://www.facilitiesnet.com/bom/article.asp?id=1522* (accessed 8 Oct 2005).

5. B Sattler, "Pioneering the environmental health frontier," Maryland Nurses Association Newsletter, *http://www.oarm.org/details.cfm?type=news&ID=91* (accessed 14 May 2005).

6. B K Lee, M J Ellenbecker, R Moure-Ersaso, "Alternatives for treatment and disposal cost reduction of regulated medical wastes," *Waste Management* 24 no 2 (2004) 143-151.

7. R Garcia, "Effective cost-reduction strategies in the management of regulated medical waste," *American Journal of Infection Control* 27 (April 1999) 165-175.

8. B Sattler, "The greening of health care: Environmental policy and advocacy in the health care industry," *Policy, Politics & Nursing Practice* 4 (Feb 2003) 6-13.

9. J Andrews, "New diet of products can help hospitals watch their 'waste' lines" *Healthcare Purchasing News* (June 2003) 14-19.

10. C Schierhorn, "Haste makes (infectious) waste: Saving money by segregating hospital refuse," *Health Facilities Management* 15 (Sept 2002) 34-37.

11. M Cox, C Rhett, A Gudmundsen, "Environmental protection through waste management: Implications for staff development," *Journal of Nursing Staff Development* 13 (March–April 1997) 67-72.

12. B Jolibois, M Guerbet, S Vassal, "Glutaraldehyde in hospital wastewater," *Archives of Environmental Contamination and Toxicology* 42 (February 2002) 137-144.

13. F D Daschner, M Dettenkofer, "Protecting the patient and the environment—New aspects and challenges in hospital infection control," *Journal of Hospital Infection* 36 (May 1997) 7-15.

14. Walsh Integrated Environmental Systems, "Environmental impact," *http://www.walsh environmental .com/products/ben_environmentalimpact.htm* (accessed 9 Oct 2005).

15. "Recycling fact sheet," Health Care Without Harm, *http://www.noharm.org/details.cfm?type=document &id=599* (accessed 9 Oct 2005).

16. "Waste minimization, segregation, and recycling in hospitals," Health Care Without Harm, *http://www .noharm.org/library/docs/Going_Green_4-1_Waste _Minimization _Segregation.pdf* (accessed 9 Oct 2005).

17. "Reduce, reuse, and recycle," US Environmental Protection Agency, *http://www.epa.gov/epaoswer/non-hw /muncpl/reduce.htm* (accessed 9 Oct 2005).

18. "Hospitals and health care institutions," Recycling Works Tipsheet, Pennsylvania Department of Environmental Protection, *http://www.dep.state.pa.us/dep/deputate /airwaste/wm/recycle/tips/hospitals.htm* (accessed 9 Oct 2005).

19. "Water conservation at work,"Southwest Florida Water Management District, *http://www.swfwmd.state.fl.us /conservation/waterwork/checkhospital.htm* (accessed 9 Oct 2005).

20. "A look at health care buildings—How do they use electricity?" Energy Information Administration, *http://www.eia.doe.gov/emeu/consumptionbriefs/cbecs /pbawebsite/health/health_howuseelec.htm* (accessed 9 Oct 2005).

21. "A look at health care buildings—How do they use natural gas?" Energy Information Administration, *http://www.eia.doe.gov/emeu/consumptionbriefs/cbecs /pbawebsite/health/health_howuseng.htm* (accessed 9 Oct 2005).

22. "Green tips," Ontario Ministry of the Environment, *http://www.ene.gov.on.ca/cons/3781-e.htm* (accessed 9 Oct 2005).

23. "Water conservation checklist: Hospitals/medical facilities—Every drop counts!" North Carolina Department of Environment and Natural Resources, Division of Pollution and Environmental Assistance, *http://64.233.161.104/ search?q=cache:7jnhCXPu4uIJ:www.p2pays.org/ref/23 /22006.pdf+water+use* (accessed 9 Oct 2005).

24. "Water conservation @ hospitals," City of Greeley Water Conservation, *http://www.ci.greeley.co.us/cog /PageX.asp?fkOrgId=44&PageURL=Hospitals* (accessed 9 Oct 2005).

25. US Environmental Protection Agency, *Light Brief* (Washington, DC: US Environmental Protection Agency, June 1992) 7000.

26. R Reeves, "Energy conservation important to MHCP," *Entre Nous* (Winter 2004) 8.

27. "Water efficiency and management for hospitals," North Carolina Department of Environment and Natural Resources, Division of Pollution and Environmental Assistance, *http://www.p2pays.org/ref/14/13679.htm* (accessed 9 Oct 2005).

28. "Water conservation ideas for health care facilities," Pennsylvania Department of Environmental Protection, *http://www.dep.state.pa.us/dep/subject/hotopics/drought /facts/health.htm* (accessed 9 Oct 2005).

29. "Water efficiency practices for health care facilities," New Hampshire Department of Environmental Services, *http://www.des.state.nh.us/factsheets/ws/ws-26-14 .htm* (accessed 9 Oct 2005).

30. "Hospital cost reduction case study: Norwood Hospital," Massachusetts Water Resources Authority, *http://www.mwra.state.ma.us/04water/html/bullet1.htm* (accessed 23 Jan 2006).

31. "Water efficiency in hospitals (small to medium), extended care homes, and laundries," Association of Manitoba Municipalities, *http://www.amm.mb.ca/images /resources/waterefficiency/extcare.pdf* (accessed 26 June 2005).

32. "Using microfiber mops in hospitals," US Environmental Protection Agency, *http://www.epa.gov/region09 /cross_pr/p2/projects/hospital/mops.pdf* (accessed 9 Oct 2005).

33. P Camp, "Controlling costs while maintaining quality care," *Surgical Services Management* 8 (Dec 2002) 24-30.

34. D Karr, "Standardization and cost savings," *Surgical Services Management* 5 (April 1999) 32-38.

35. N Phillips, ed, "Coordinated roles of scrub person and circulator," in *Berry & Kohn's Operating Room Technique,* tenth ed (St Louis: Mosby, 2004).

36. Baker, D; Hale, D. "Potential cost savings opportunities: The supply chain," *SSM* 9 (April 2003) 33-38.

37. "Value analysis helps to tighten surgical products supply chain," *OR Manager* 18 (May 2002) 1, 14-16.

38. *Pollution Prevention Guide for Hospitals,* US Environmental Protection Agency, *http://www.dtsc.ca.gov/Pollution Prevention/p2-hospital-guide.pdf* (accessed 9 Oct 2005).

39. "Green purchasing," Health Care Without Harm, *http://www.noharm.org/greenPurchasing/issue* (accessed 9 Oct 2005).

40. J E Williamson, "Great expectations: Hospitals find FDA regs build stronger case for reprocessing," *Healthcare Purchasing News* (June 2005) 28-32.

41. D Dunn, "Reprocessing single-use devices: The equipment connection," *AORN Journal* 75 (June 2002) 1143.

42. "AORN guidance statement: Reuse of single-use devices," in *Standards, Recommended Practices, and Guidelines* (Denver: AORN, Inc, 2005) 185-191.

43. M Szczepanski, "The nursing process: A tool for healing the environment," *Nursing Management* 24 (Oct 1993) 56-58.

44. "Recommended practices for cleaning and caring for surgical instruments and powered equipment," in *Standards, Recommended Practices, and Guidelines* (Denver: AORN, Inc, 2005) 395-403.

45. "Recommended practices for sterilization in perioperative practice settings," in *Standards, Recommended Practices and Guidelines* (Denver: AORN, Inc, 2005) 459-469.

46. "Ethylene oxide: Hazard summary," US Environmental Protection Agency, *http://www.epa.gov/ttnatw01/hlthef/ethylene.html* (accessed 9 Oct 2005).

47. A D LaMontagne, K T Kelsey, "Evaluating OSHA's ethylene oxide standard: Exposure determinants in Massachusetts hospitals," *American Journal of Public Health* 91 (March 2001) 412-417.

48. M Jim, "Instrument reprocessing in theatres: Drivers for change," *British Journal of Perioperative Nursing* 12 (January 2002) 34-38.

49. G Vittori, *Green and Healthy Buildings for the Health Care Industry* (Austin, Tex: Center for Maximum Potential Building Systems, 2002).

50. "Is green building budding?" in *The Washington Post* (April 16, 2005), USGBC in the News, *http://www.usgbc.org/News/usgbcinthenews_details.asp?ID=1485& CMSPageID=159* (accessed 9 Oct 2005).

RESOURCES

Almuneef, M; Memish, Z A. "Effective medical waste management: It can be done," *American Journal of Infection Control* 31 (May 2003) 188-192

Alt, S. "Think of environment when choosing supplies," *Hospital Materials Management* 26 (Sept 2001) 11.

Association for the Advancement of Medical Instrumentation (AAMI). *AAMI Standards and Recommended Practices: Sterilization, Part 3—Industrial Process Control* (Arlington, Va: AAMI, 1999).

Bultitude, M F, et al. "Prolonging the life of the flexible ureterorenoscope," *International Journal of Clinical Practice* 58 (August 2004) 756-757.

Burdick, J S; Hambrick, D. "Endoscope reprocessing and repair costs," *Gastrointestinal Endoscopy Clinics of North America* 14 (October 2004) 717-724.

"CDC issues new environmental guidelines," *OR Manager* 19 (August 2003) 20, 22.

Cohoon, B D. "Reprocessing single-use medical devices," *AORN Journal* 75 (March 2002) 557-567.

Cys, J. "Speaking of reuse," *Materials Management in Health Care* 12 (June 2003) 26-28.

"FDA wants to know more about reuse of opened-but-unused items," *OR Manager* 18 (September 2002) 1, 7.

"Good manufacturing practices (GMP)/Quality system (QS) regulation," US Food and Drug Administration, *http://www.fda.gov/cdrh/devadvice/32.html* (accessed 9 Oct 2005).

Hensley, S. "More hospitals buy into device recycling," *Modern Healthcare* 29 (February 1999) 88.

"Integrating green purchasing into your environmental management system (EMS), US Environmental Protection Agency, *http://www.epa.gov/epp/ems.htm* (accessed 9 Oct 2005).

International Association of Health Care Central Service Material Management. "IAHCSMM position statement on the reuse of single-use medical devices," presented at the AAMI/FDA Conference on Reuse of Single-Use Devices: Practice, Patient Safety, and Regulation, Washington, DC, May 5, 1999.

Kleinbeck, S V M; English, N L; Hueschen, J H. "Reprocessing and reusing surgical products labeled for single use," *Surgical Services Management* 4 (January 1998) 21-24.

Lewis, C. "Reusing medical devices: Ensuring safety the second time around," *FDA Consumer* 34 (September/October 2000) 8-9.

"New FDA regulations may force hospitals to abandon reprocessing," *Infection Control and Prevention Report* 5 (Sept 2000) 133-136.

Pope, A M; Snyder, M A; Mood, L H. *Nursing, Health, and the Environment: Strengthening the Relationship to Improve the Public's Health* (Washington, DC: National Academy Press, 1995).

"Reuse of single-use devices," (Clinical Issues) *AORN Journal* 73 (May 2001) 957-964.

Schultz, J. *Clinical Study Guide: Minimizing Potential for Endoscope Contamination* (Denver: Healthstream, 2005).

Schultz, J. "Reusing single-use medical devices," *Surgical Services Management* 4 (July 1998) 11-13.

Schroer, P. "Reuse of single-use devices," *Medical Device Technology* 11 (December 2000) 44, 48-53.

Selvey, D. "Medical device reprocessing: Is it good for your organization?" *Infection Control Today*, *http://www.infectioncontroltoday.com/articles/111feat1.html?wts=20051009035349&hc=44&req=Selvey%2c+and+Don* (accessed 9 Oct 2005).

Spry, C; Leiner, D C. "Rigid endoscopes—Ensuring quality before use and after repair," *AORN Journal* 80 (July 2004) 103-109.

"Survey: One-fourth of operating rooms resterilize opened-but-unused medical devices," *OR Manager* 19 (November 2002).

"Survey: ORs are split on reuse of single-use items," *OR Manager* 15 (September 1999) 1, 11, 14-16.

Thomas, L A. "Endoscope precleaning," *Gastroenterology Nursing* 28 (July/Aug 2005) 334-335.

Thomas, L A. "Endoscope staging," *Gastroenterology Nursing* 28 (May/June 2005) 243-245.

Thomas, L A. "Transporting the endoscope," *Gastroenterology Nursing* 29 (March/April 2005) 145-146.

US Food and Drug Administration. "Medical devices; current good manufacturing practice (CGMP) final rule; quality system regulation," *Federal Register* 61 (Oct 7, 1996). Also available at *http://www.fda.gov/OHRMS/DOCKETS/98fr/61FR52654100796.htm* (accessed 9 Oct 2005).

Whelan, C. "Stats: Reprocessing growth," *Materials Management in Health Care* 13 (May 2004) 41-42.

Zafar, A B; Butler, R C. "Effect of a comprehensive program to reduce infectious waste," *American Journal of Infectious Waste* 28 (February 2000) 51-53.

Approved by the AORN Board of Directors, November 2005. Published in *Standards, Recommended Practices, and Guidelines,* 2006 edition. Reprinted October 2006, *AORN Journal.*

AORN Guidance Statement: Fire Prevention in the Operating Room

Introduction

AORN recognizes that fire is an inherent risk in ORs. Fire is an ever-present danger and poses a real hazard to patient and health care worker safety. In 2003, the Joint Commission on Accreditation of Healthcare Organizations (JCAHO) issued a sentinel event alert related to fires that occur during operative and invasive procedures. The bulletin raised the level of awareness about the dangers of surgical fires. The Joint Commission recommends that health care organizations prevent surgical fires by providing education and training for perioperative practitioners.[1] In July 2004, surgical fire prevention was added to the 2005 National Patient Safety Goals for ambulatory and office-based surgical facilities.[2]

The approach to developing policies and procedures to reduce fire risk should be multidisciplinary and involve all professionals who provide patient care. Facilities are encouraged to report surgical fires to JCAHO, ECRI, or the US Food and Drug Administration (FDA). Systematic reporting of fires can help educate care providers about how and why fires occur and can help prevent fires in the future.[1]

Background

Fires involving surgical patients have been reported by hospitals and ambulatory surgical centers; some medical device manufacturers, and other experts, such as ECRI, for many years. There is no centralized database being collected by any agency at present on the total number of surgical fires;[3] however, data from ECRI and the FDA estimate that approximately 100 surgical fires occur each year, resulting in approximately 20 patient injuries that are serious, with one to two deaths per year.[1,4] The overriding consideration with surgical fires is that they are 100% preventable.[1,4]

Fires occur when the elements that support combustion—an ignition source, a fuel source, and an oxidizer—come together. These three elements are referred to as the "fire triangle." All three elements are present in abundance during operative and invasive procedures[4] (**Tables 1–3**). Operating rooms in hospitals and ambulatory surgery suites, physicians' offices, and endoscopy suites are some of the critical areas where fires occur, and they contain all the elements that support combustion.

Ignition sources are anything that produces heat; the two most common sources are the electrosurgical unit (ESU) and the laser. Other equipment that produces heat includes, but may not be limited to, fiber-optic light cables and light source boxes; drills, saws, and burrs; hand-held electrocautery devices; argon beam coagulators; and defibrillators.[4]

Almost everything in the perioperative arena can be a fuel source, especially when an accelerant, such as oxygen, is present. The items used to set up the sterile field and protect the patient (eg, linens, drapes, gowns, supplies, preps, gauzes, clothes) should all be considered fuel sources. The patient's body hair and body gases also can be fuel sources.[5]

The primary oxidizers in the surgical environment are oxygen and nitrous oxide. Fires can occur when the oxygen level in the atmosphere rises above the level of ambient air (ie, 21%). Oxygen can escape into the air when patients are given mask or nasal oxygen. A level above 21% should be treated as an oxygen-enriched environment.[6]

Guideline

Education

Education and training in fire risk reduction strategies for perioperative RNs, surgical technologists, anesthesia care providers, surgeons, and other personnel is essential to promote and maintain a fire-safe perioperative environment. Health care industry representatives and students should be included in fire drill education. Each perioperative team member is responsible for promoting a culture of fire safety. Preparation is the key to ensuring readiness for preventing fires in the OR. Recommendations from ECRI include that

- perioperative team members participate in fire drills;
- team members receive training on the use of fire fighting equipment, rescue methods, and evacuation;
- staff members know where medical gas panels and ventilation and electrical systems are located, which personnel are permitted to shut them off, and when;
- staff members in the perioperative care setting be shown how to initiate a "Code Red" or fire alarm at their facility;
- staff members know specific protocols to contact the local fire department;[4]
- students rotating through the perioperative area are included in fire education and training; and
- health care industry representatives are educated on fire safety hazards in the perioperative area during their credentialing process.

Fire Prevention

Table 1

Fire Risk—Ignition	
Ignition sources	**Strategies to manage**
Electrosurgical unit (ESU)	■ Use the lowest possible power setting. ■ Place the patient return electrode on a large muscle mass close to the surgical site. ■ Large reusable return electrodes should be used according to the manufacturer's instructions. ■ Always use a safety holster. ■ Do not coil active electrode cords. ■ Inspect the active electrode to ensure integrity. ■ Do not use ESU in the presence of flammable solutions. ■ Ensure that electrical cords and plugs are not frayed or broken. ■ Do not place fluids on top of the ESU. ■ Do not use the ESU near oxygen or nitrous oxide. ■ Ensure that the ESU active electrode tip fits securely into the active electrode hand piece. ■ Ensure that any connectors and adaptors used are intended to connect to the ESU and fit securely. ■ Do not bypass ESU safety features. ■ Ensure that the alarm tone is always audible. ■ Remove any contaminated or unused active accessories from the sterile field. ■ Keep the active electrode tip clean. ■ Use wet sponges or towels to help retard fire potential. ■ Never alter a medical device.[1] ■ Do not use rubber catheters or protective covers as insulators on the active electrode tip.[2] ■ Use cut or blend instead of coagulation when possible. ■ Do not open the circuit to activate the ESU. ■ Ensure that the active electrode is not activated in close proximity to another metal object that could conduct heat or cause arcing.[3] ■ After prepping, allow prep to dry and fumes to dissipate. Wet prep and fumes trapped beneath drapes can ignite.[4] ■ Provide multidisciplinary inservice programs on the safe use of ESUs based on the manufacturer's instructions.
Argon beam coagulator	■ Argon beam coagulators combine the ESU spark with argon gas to concentrate and focus the ESU spark. Argon gas is inert and nonflammable, but because it is used with an ESU, the same precautions as with an ESU should be taken. ■ Always use a safety holster. ■ Ensure that the active electrode is not activated in close proximity to another metal object that could conduct heat or cause arcing.[1]
Lasers	■ Use a laser-specific endotracheal tube (ie, a tube that has laser-resistant coating or contains no material that will ignite) if head, neck, lung, or airway surgery is anticipated.[5] ■ Wet sponges around the tube cuffs may provide extra protection to help retard fire potential. Moist towels around the surgical site also may retard fires. ■ Keep towels moist and away from the edge of the surgical site to retard fires. ■ Do not use liquids or ointments that may be combustible. ■ Inflate cuffed tube bladders with tinted saline (eg, methylene blue) so that inadvertent rupture may be detected during chest or upper airway surgery. ■ Do not use uncuffed, standard endotracheal tubes in the presence of a laser or the ESU. ■ If an endotracheal tube fire occurs, oxygen administration should be stopped, and all burning or melted tubes should be removed from the patient immediately.

Table 1, *continued*

Fire Risk—Ignition	
Ignition sources	**Strategies to manage** *(continued)*
	▪ Prevent pooling of skin prep solutions.
	▪ Have water and the correct fire extinguisher type available in case of a laser fire.[6]
	▪ Ensure that the alarm tone is always audible.[6]
Fiber-optic light sources	▪ Ensure that the light source is in good working order.
Fiber-optic light cables	▪ Place the light source in standby, or turn it off when the cable is not connected.
	▪ Place the light source away from items that are flammable.
	▪ Do not place a light cable that is connected to a light source on drapes, sponges, or anything else that is flammable.
	▪ Do not allow cables that are connected to hang over the side of the sterile field if the light source is on.
	▪ Ensure that light cables are in good working order and do not have broken light fibers.[7]
Power tools/drills/burrs	▪ Instruments/equipment that move rapidly during use generate heat. Always ensure that they are in good working order.
	▪ A slow drip of saline on a moving drill/burr helps to reduce heat buildup.
	▪ Do not place drills, burrs, or saws on the patient when they are not in use.
	▪ Remove instruments/equipment from the sterile field when not in use.[8]
Defibrillator paddles	▪ Select paddles that are the correct size for the patient (eg, pediatric paddles on a child).
	▪ Ensure that the gel recommended by the paddle manufacturer is used.
	▪ Adhere to appropriate site selection for paddle placement.
	▪ Contact between the paddles and the patient should be optimal and no gaps should be present before activating the defibrillator.[9]
Electrical equipment	▪ Ensure that all equipment is periodically inspected by biomedical personnel for proper function.
	▪ Check biomedical inspection stickers on the equipment; they should be current.
	▪ Do not use equipment with frayed or damaged cords or plugs.
	▪ Remove any equipment that emits smoke during use.[10]

References

1. "Recommended practices for electrosurgery," in Standards, Recommended Practices, and Guidelines *(Denver: AORN, Inc, 2004) 245-259.*

2. ECRI, *"Surgical fire safety,"* Health Devices *35 no 2 (February 2006) 45-66.*

3. Fire Safety Self Study Guide *(Denver: Health-Stream, 2004).*

4. *"Recommended practices for skin preparation of patients,"* in Standards, Recommended Practices, and Guidelines *(Denver: AORN, Inc, 2004) 357-360.*

5. *K A Ball,* Lasers: The Perioperative Challenge *(Denver: AORN, Inc, 2004) 145.*

6. *"Recommended practices for laser safety in practice settings,"* in Standards, Recommended Practices, and Guidelines *(Denver: AORN, Inc, 2004) 319-324.*

7. *"Recommended practices for endoscopic minimally invasive surgery,"* in Standards, Recommended Practices, and Guidelines *(Denver: AORN, Inc, 2004) 267-271.*

8. ECRI, *"The patient is on fire! A surgical fire primer,"* Medical Device Safety Reports *21 (January 1992) 19-34. Also available at* http://www.mdsr.ecri.org/summary/detail.aspx?doc_id=8197&q=%22The+patient+is+on+fire%22 *(accessed 12 Jan 2005).*

9. ECRI, *"Fires from defibrillation during oxygen administration,"* Health Devices *23 (July 1994) 307-308. Also available at* http://www.mdsr.ecri.org/summary/detail.aspx?doc_id=8128&q=%22Fires+from+Defibrillation%22 *(accessed 12 Jan 2005).*

10. *"Recommended practices for safe care through identification of potential hazards in the surgical environment,"* in Standards, Recommended Practices, and Guidelines *(Denver: AORN, Inc, 2004) 301-307.*

Table 2

Fire Risk—Fuel	
Fuel sources	**Strategies to manage**

Patient and staff linens
  Drapes
  Gowns
  Towels
  Lap pads
  Sponges
  Dressings
  Tapes
  Bed linens
  Caps/hats
  Shoe covers
Collodian
Alcohol-based skin preparations
Wound packings
	■ Assess the flammability of all materials used in, on, or around the patient. Linens and drapes are made of synthetic or natural fibers. They may burn or melt depending on the fiber content.[1]
	■ Do not allow drapes or linens to come in contact with activated ignition sources (eg, laser, electrosurgical unit [ESU], light sources).[2-4]
	■ Do not trap volatile chemicals or chemical fumes beneath drapes.[5]
	■ Moisten drapes, towels, and sponges that will be in close proximity to ignition sources (eg, laser, ESU).[2,3]
	■ Ensure that oxygen does not accumulate beneath drapes.
	■ If drapes or linens ignite, smother out small fires with a wet sponge or towel. Remove burning material from the patient.
	■ Extinguish any burning material with the appropriate fire extinguisher or water, if appropriate.[6]

Prep solutions	■ Use flammable prep solutions with caution. ■ Do not allow prep solutions to pool on, around, or beneath the patient. ■ After prepping, allow prep to dry and fumes to dissipate. Wet prep and fumes trapped beneath drapes can ignite. ■ Do not activate ignition sources in the presence of flammable prep solutions. ■ Do not allow drapes that will remain in contact with the patient to absorb flammable prep solutions.[5]
Skin degreasers, tinctures, aerosols	■ These products may be used before skin prep to degrease or clean the skin or as part of the dressing. These products may contain chemicals that are flammable (eg, ether in collodian). Allow all fumes to dissipate before beginning surgery. The laser or ESU should not be used after the dressing is in place.[3]
Body tissue and patient hair	■ The patient's own body can be a fuel source. Coat any body hair that is in close proximity to an ignition source with a water-based jelly to retard ignition.[4] ■ Ensure that surgical smoke from burning patient tissue is properly evacuated. Surgical smoke can support combustion if allowed to accumulate in a small or enclosed space (eg, the back of the throat).[3]
Intestinal gases	■ Patient intestinal gases are flammable. Electrosurgery or laser should be used with caution whenever intestinal gases are present. Do not open the bowel with the laser or ESU when it appears gas is present. ■ Use suction during rectal surgery to remove any intestinal gases that may be present.[3]

REFERENCES

1. "Recommended practices for product selection in perioperative practice settings," in Standards, Recommended Practices, and Guidelines (Denver: AORN, Inc, 2004) 347-350.

2. "Recommended practices for laser safety in practice settings," in Standards, Recommended Practices, and Guidelines (Denver: AORN, Inc, 2004) 319-324.

3. "Recommended practices for electrosurgery," in Standards, Recommended Practices, and Guidelines (Denver: AORN, Inc, 2004) 245-259.

4. "Recommended practices for endoscopic minimally invasive surgery," in Standards, Recommended Practices, and Guidelines (Denver: AORN, Inc, 2004) 267-271.

5. "Recommended practices for skin preparation of patients," in Standards, Recommended Practices, and Guidelines (Denver: AORN, Inc, 2004) 357-360.

6. ECRI, "Surgical fire safety," Health Devices 35 no 2 (February 2006) 45-66.

Table 3

Fire Risk—Oxidizers	
Oxidizers	**Strategies to manage**
Oxygen (O_2)	■ Oxygen should be used with caution in the presence of ignition sources. Oxygen is an oxidizer and is capable of supporting combustion.[1] ■ Ensure that anesthesia circuits are free of leaks. ■ Pack wet sponges around the back of the throat to help retard oxygen leaks. ■ Inflate cuffed tube bladders with tinted saline (eg, methylene blue) so that inadvertent ruptures can be detected. ■ Use suction to help evacuate any accumulation of O_2 in body cavities, such as the mouth or chest cavity. ■ Do not use the laser or electrosurgical unit (ESU) near where O_2 is flowing. ■ Use a pulse oximeter to determine the patient's oxygenation level and the need for oxygen. ■ Allow O_2 fumes to dissipate before using the laser or ESU. ■ O_2 should not be directed at the surgical site. ■ Ensure that drapes are configured to help prevent oxygen accumulation when mask or nasal O_2 is used.[2-4] ■ With a large fire, turn off the gases; with an airway or tracheal fire, disconnect the breathing circuit and remove the endotracheal tube.[4] ■ Stop supplemental oxygen for one minute before using electrocautery or laser for head, neck, or upper chest procedures.[1]
Nitrous oxide	■ The strategies to manage O_2 also should be used to manage risks associated with nitrous oxide.[2-4]

REFERENCES

1. ECRI, "Surgical fire safety," Health Devices 35 no 2 (February 2006) 45-66.

2. "Recommended practices for electrosurgery," in Standards, Recommended Practices, and Guidelines (Denver: AORN, Inc, 2004) 245-259.

3. "Recommended practices for laser safety in practice settings," in Standards, Recommended Practices, and Guidelines (Denver: AORN, Inc, 2004) 319-324.

4. "Recommended practices for endoscopic minimally invasive surgery," in Standards, Recommended Practices, and Guidelines (Denver: AORN, Inc, 2004) 267-271.

A health care facility's fire plan should be reviewed and actively discussed. This assists the facility in refining the fire plan. The use of fire extinguishers should be demonstrated to provide staff with instruction on the why, when, and how to use extinguishers. Perioperative clinical leaders must take additional action to keep patients and staff members safe. Fire drills should be conducted regularly based on local, state, and JCAHO guidelines.[4] Fire drills should include the following.

♦ Use of National Fire Protection Association (NFPA) standards for classification of the different types of fire extinguishers, including
  – Class A: for use on wood, paper, cloth, and most plastics (eg, combustible materials);
  – Class B: for use on flammable liquids or grease; and
  – Class C: for use on energized electrical equipment.[4]

♦ The acronym **PASS** should be reviewed to operate the fire extinguisher.
  – **P**—Pull the pin.
  – **A**—Aim nozzle at the base of the fire.
  – **S**—Squeeze the handle.
  – **S**—Sweep the stream over the base of the fire.[7]

To enhance user skill and confidence, allow every staff member time to practice handling the fire extinguisher. Teach staff members to use the fire extinguisher with their back toward an escape exit for easier access. Labels on the fire extinguisher should be checked for color, size, and shape of the extinguisher to prevent personnel assisting in extinguishing fires from using the wrong extinguisher (eg, water on an electrical fire). The following information will help staff members become more competent.

- ♦ Staff members should be shown where fire extinguishers are located in the perioperative setting.
- ♦ Operating room doors should be able to open completely without equipment blocking them.
- ♦ Staff members should know the location of all fire exits and ensure that these exits are clear and accessible at all times.
- ♦ Surgical team members should know where the medical gas shutoff valves are and their facility's policy on who should turn them off and when.
- ♦ Review roles of every staff member at the point of the fire's origin and away from the immediate area.
- ♦ Take staff members through evacuation routes, both primary and secondary, to an evacuation location point beyond a firewall.[4]
- ♦ Fire blankets should not be used in the OR; the fire could become trapped on or under the patient.

Depending on the size of the perioperative setting, planning for an initial fire drill may take up to three months.[5] Key points in planning a fire drill include

- ♦ choosing a date and time;
- ♦ developing a well-thought-out scenario(s);
- ♦ obtaining the facility fire drill evaluation form, and modifying it where necessary;
- ♦ completing a fire drill record, and noting all participants and pertinent details;
- ♦ identifying observers and their locations;
- ♦ designating surgical team members who will participate in the event and briefing them on the scenario;
- ♦ reviewing fire safety/drill policy and procedures and their roles with staff members;
- ♦ notifying facility administrators of the upcoming fire drill and posting signs;
- ♦ including the facility safety officer as a resource and advisor;
- ♦ discussing the drill in a debriefing session;
- ♦ evaluating the effectiveness of the staff members and equipment used; and
- ♦ identifying areas for improvement and areas of strength.[8]

Every fire drill should be considered a forum for learning. Perioperative staff member preparedness

will ensure an effective and efficient response to a fire in a smooth and coordinated manner (**Sample Forms 1 and 2**).

Evacuation plan

All perioperative departments should develop and implement a well-rehearsed and well-thought-out fire evacuation plan. Evacuation plans help ensure that all staff members are familiar with the proper evacuation routes and equipment that may be used before or during an evacuation. In the event a fire occurs in the perioperative area, personnel should follow the standard fire emergency response procedure and activate RACE.

Use of the acronym **RACE** as the response component of the fire safety plan:

- – **R**—Rescue the individual that is involved in the fire.
- – **A**—Alarm should be sounded as soon as possible.
- – **C**—Confine the fire.
- – **E**—Extinguish the fire and evacuate if required.[5]

Surgical team duties in a fire evacuation. Each surgical suite should have designated fire responder teams with defined responsibilities to take if a fire occurs in the surgical suite. There should be a chain of command that includes an authority who has jurisdiction to manage the incident. If the operating room must be evacuated, several steps should be taken by personnel responsible for the care of the patient in the OR. First, surgical team members should become oriented in relation to where they are located, the proximity of the nearest exit, and how to safely evacuate to that destination. The roles of the surgical team may be as follows.

- ♦ The surgeon should
  - – remove from the patient materials that may be on fire and help put out the fire;
  - – control bleeding and prepare the patient for evacuation if necessary;
  - – conclude the procedure as soon as possible;
  - – place sterile towels or covers over the surgical site; and
  - – if the patient is not in immediate danger, help move the patient if necessary.
- ♦ The anesthesia care provider should
  - – shut off the flow of oxygen/nitrous oxide to the patient or field and maintain breathing for the patient with a valve mask respirator (ie, ambu bag);

Sample Form 1

PERIOPERATIVE SERVICES OR CODE RED FIRE DRILL EVALUATION FORM			

Fire drill date: _____   Designated observer: _____

Criteria:	Yes	No	Comments
■ Evacuation plan is posted.			
■ Randomly chosen staff member(s)			
■ describes evacuation routes,			
■ knows how to report a fire, and			
■ knows location of extinguisher.			
■ Fire extinguishers			
■ in place, seal intact, charged, properly mounted;			
■ labeled as to type and class of fire;			
■ serviced within past 12 months;			
■ checked monthly; and			
■ staff member describes how to operate fire extinguisher by using PASS method.			
■ Fire exits			
■ free and unobstructed, and			
■ marked with working illuminated signs.			
■ Corridors of egress are free of equipment/obstructions.			
■ Fire/smoke barrier doors closed during activation of pull station.			
■ Staff members activated RACE, the standard fire emergency response procedure.			
■ Staff members use proper body mechanics to transport patients.			
■ Staff members close all doors.			
■ Nursing leader/designee shuts off medical gases.			
■ All patients are accounted for with medical records intact.			
Response evaluated:			
■ Did staff members act in a calm and organized manner?			
■ Did staff members perform as a cohesive team?			

Opportunities for improvement:

_____

_____

_____

Staff member (observer) signature: _____

- collaborate with the circulating nurse on the need to turn off the medical gas shutoff valves;
- disconnect all electrically powered equipment on the anesthesia machine;
- disconnect any leads, lines, or other equipment that may be anchoring the patient to the area;
- maintain the patient's anesthetic state and collect the necessary medications to continue anesthesia during transport; and
- place additional IV fluids on the bed for transport with the patient, if time permits.

♦ The scrub person should
- remove from the patient materials that may be on fire and help put out the fire;
- assist with the conclusion of the procedure if possible;
- obtain sterile towels or covers for the surgical site and instruments;
- gather a minimal number of instruments onto a tray or basin and place them with the patient for transport; and
- assist with patient transfer from the OR table to a stretcher/bed for transport out of the OR.

Fire Prevention

Sample Form 2

PERIOPERATIVE SERVICES OR CODE RED FIRE DRILL RECORD

Fire drill date: _____   Shift: _____

Fire drill start time: _____   Finish time: _____

Designated observers:

_____

_____

_____

List fire drill participants and titles:

Participant	*Title*
_____	_____
_____	_____
_____	_____

Planned scenario: _____

_____

_____

_____

Time and individual who pulled fire alarm: _____

Patient evacuation times: _____

Other remarkable events: _____

_____

_____

_____

Individual completing form: _____

- ◆ The perioperative RN circulating should
  - ensure the patient's safety by remaining with him or her and comforting him or her;
  - activate the fire alarm system and call the fire code to alert all necessary personnel;
  - extinguish small fires or douse them with liquid if appropriate;
  - remove any burning material from the patient or sterile field, and extinguish it on the floor;
  - prevent fire from spreading to shoes or surgical clothing by not stepping on it;
  - provide the scrub person and anesthesia care provider with needed supplies;
  - collaborate with the anesthesia care provider on the need to turn off the medical gas shutoff valves;
  - carefully unplug all equipment if the fire is electrical;
  - be aware of the safest route for escape;
  - obtain a transport stretcher if necessary;
  - remove IV solutions from poles and place them with the patient for transporting out of the OR;
  - help the anesthesia care provider disconnect any leads, lines, or other equipment that may be needed for transporting the patient; and
  - not delay leaving the OR suite.
- ◆ The perioperative registered nurse in charge/ designee should
  - notify the safety officer, telephone operator, or designated person of a fire and its location;
  - document the time the fire started;

- determine how many people are in the department and account for everyone;
- set up a communication point and identify a person to staff it;
- determine the state of ongoing surgery/ procedures in each area;
- consult with the anesthesia care provider in charge on how to handle each patient;
- assign personnel to assist where needed;
- ask visitors to leave if necessary; and
- evacuate patients who may need to be moved immediately.
♦ Ancillary personnel should
  - help clear corridors for evacuation;
  - secure equipment for transporting the patient as directed by the circulating nurse;
  - help prepare a safe area to transfer patients to, if this is needed;
  - follow instructions for evacuating the patient if needed; and
  - assist where directed.

Patients should be evacuated horizontally to a safe area on the same floor. It is very important to maintain an accurate count of all patients and staff members during the evacuation. After evacuation of the room, the last person to leave the room should close the doors and place a wet towel at the base of them. After the fire, everything should be left in place so the safety officer and the fire department can conduct a thorough investigation of the cause of the fire.[9]

Risk reduction strategies

Risk reduction strategies involve educating surgical team members about the components of the fire triangle and developing policies and procedures that will prevent surgical fires. Fuel sources must be managed in a way that will prevent fires, ignition sources must be controlled so that they do not come in contact with fuels, and oxidizers must be contained or properly vented so that they do not come in contact with fuels or ignition sources. Keeping the sides of the fire triangle apart is critical.

REFERENCES

1. "Preventing surgical fires," *Sentinel Event Alert* 29 (June 24, 2003). Also available at *http://www.jcaho.org/about+us/news+letters/sentinel+event+alert/print/sea_29.htm* (accessed 12 Jan 2005).
2. "2005 Ambulatory care National Patient Safety Goals," Joint Commission on Accreditation of Healthcare Organization, *http://jcaho.org/accredited+organizations/patient+safety/05+npsg/05_npsg_amb.htm* (accessed 12 Jan 2005).
3. ECRI, "Surgical fires," *Operating Room Risk Management* 2 (November 2004) 6.
4. ECRI, "Surgical fire safety," *Health Devices* 35 no 2 (February 2006) 45-66.
5. ECRI, "The patient is on fire! A surgical fire primer," *Medical Device Safety Reports* 21 (January 1992) 19-34. Also available at *http://www.mdsr.ecri.org/summary/detail.aspx?doc_id=8197&q=%22The+patient+is+on+fire%22* (accessed 12 Jan 2005).
6. C Smith, "Surgical fires: Learn not to burn," *AORN Journal* 80 (July 2004) 25-26.
7. L Salmon, "Fire in the OR: Prevention and preparedness," *AORN Journal* 80 (July 2004) 42-54.
8. D Stewart, "Fire and life safety for surgical services: What's new and what to review," *SSM* 9 (April 2003) 26-31.
9. P M McCarthy, K A Gaucher, "Fire in the OR: Developing a fire safety plan," *AORN Journal* 79 (March 2004) 588-600.

Originally published in Standards, Recommended Practices, and Guidelines, 2005 edition. Reprinted May 2005, AORN Journal.

AORN Guidance Statement: The Role of the Health Care Industry Representative in the Perioperative Setting

Introduction

The purpose of this statement is to provide general guidelines to assist the individual facility in developing policies relating to the role of the heath care industry representative in the perioperative setting. The term health care industry representative refers to all health care industry employees who provide services in the perioperative setting (eg, clinical consultants, sales representatives, technicians, repair/maintenance personnel). A systematic method of providing education, training, and instruction related to new technology, equipment, techniques, and procedures is essential for perioperative staff to provide safe patient care. The health care industry representative who possesses the requisite education, knowledge, and expertise can play a vital role in providing technical assistance, instruction, and training to perioperative team members.

Background

It may be hazardous to both patients and perioperative team members when clinicians use equipment with which they are unfamiliar. Misuse of complex technology can cause patient injury and even death. Incidents involving new technology and the presence of the health care industry representative in the perioperative setting have been highly publicized, especially when the end result is patient injury or death.[1] Hospitals have been cited and fined for allowing the use of surgical equipment not approved by the hospital; not providing formal training to physicians, nurses, and other perioperative team members on the proper use of the equipment; and permitting an unauthorized person from the medical device company to participate in a procedure.[2]

Tragic incidents have drawn attention to the need for individual facility policies to address formal instruction of physicians, nurses, and other members of the perioperative team on the operation of new medical devices before their use. Policies and procedures should be in place to authorize the introduction of new equipment and the admittance of nonmedical professionals into the room where the surgical or other invasive procedure will be performed. These policies and procedures should delineate acceptable activities and

conduct of the health care industry representative in the perioperative setting. The role of the health care industry representative is to provide essential technical training and assistance related to the device for the safe care of the patient. The health care industry representative should not be considered part of the clinical team and should not be requested to perform tasks outside his or her approved role.[1]

All perioperative team members are responsible for acquiring instruction on new procedures, techniques, technology, and equipment with which they are not familiar, before their use in a surgical procedure. The health care industry representative, who has completed specialized training to provide technical instruction and support to the perioperative surgical team expedites the procedure and facilitates desired safe patient outcomes. Health care industry representatives have a valid, but restricted, role in the perioperative setting.[3]

Guidance Statement

A health care industry representative may be present during a surgical procedure under conditions prescribed by the health care organization, in accordance with accreditation requirements, and in compliance with local, state, and federal regulations. In consideration of patient safety and confidentiality, AORN recommends the following precepts to guide policy development.

Perioperative team members are responsible for acquiring instruction on new procedures, techniques, technology, and equipment before their use in a surgical procedure. This instruction may be provided by a health care industry representative and may take place in a formal inservice program or as one-on-one instruction. The facility should maintain evidence of documented competencies for perioperative team members, especially when introducing new procedures, techniques, technology, and equipment.[4]

As the patient's advocate, the RN responsible for the patient's care during the procedure is accountable for maintaining the patient's safety, privacy, dignity, and confidentiality. The RN should monitor the health care industry representative's activities whenever possible and facilitate the representative's service to the perioperative team during the procedure. The RN should monitor and limit the movement and number of people in the operating room during the procedure to prevent increased airborne contamination.[5] The RN should be informed before the procedure that a health care industry representative will be present during a specific procedure as well as the purpose for being in attendance.

Policies should be developed in collaboration with the facility's risk manager and/or legal counsel to ensure compliance with applicable local, state, and federal laws.[2]

Conditions should be specified under which the health care industry representative may be present during a surgical or other invasive procedure.

Each facility should develop a system that clearly delineates limits on the health care industry representative's activities in the room where the surgical or other invasive procedure is performed based on community standards, accreditation requirements, and local, state, and federal regulations.

The role of the health care industry representative is to provide technical support, as opposed to direct patient care; the representative should never function as a member of the scrubbed team. The health care industry representative with specialized training and facility approval may perform calibration to adjust devices to the surgeon's specification (eg, pacemakers and lasers)

The health care industry representative with previous perioperative experience (eg, RN, surgical technologist) should be held to the same rules and restrictions as all other health care industry representatives.

Each facility should develop a system that addresses informed patient consent regarding the presence and role of the health care industry representative during an operative or other invasive procedure in both routine and emergency situations. This system should include the name of the representative and documentation of consent in the patient's medical record.[5,6]

Each facility should develop a system which documents that the health care industry representative has completed instruction in the principles of asepsis, fire and safety protocols, infection control practices, bloodborne pathogens, and patients' rights. Based on community standards, this may range from maintaining up-to-date documentation supplied by the representative's employing company to providing facility-specific instruction and training.

The health care industry representative must be aware of and follow the regulations of the federal Health Insurance Portability and Accountability Act[7] and the Bloodborne Pathogens Standard.[8]

The health care industry representative's presence and purpose should be authorized by the designated department administrator and the surgeon in accordance the facility policy.

While in the facility, the health care industry representative should wear identification, preferably a photo identification badge, and be appropriately attired, including personal protective equipment as described in the "Recommended practices for surgical attire" and the "Recommended practices for standard and transmission based precautions in the perioperative practice setting" in the AORN *Standards, Recommended Practices and Guidelines.*

Experienced health care industry representatives who are accompanied by persons in training from their own organization for the purposes of orientation should make prior arrangements with the health care organization and comply with accreditation requirements, and local, state, and federal regulations.

The guidelines of the Association for the Advancement of Medical Instrumentation state: "Medical equipment and other complex devices must be reviewed and approved prior to their use by the facility's service provider."[9] The term *service provider* is defined as an entity with the responsibility to provide inspection and/or other maintenance services on a specific piece of equipment. A service provider may be a department within the health care organization or a contracted provider.[9]

A clearly defined mechanism should exist to address departures from established policy.

References

1. E Murphy, "The presence of sales representatives in the OR," *AORN Journal* 73 (April 2001) 822-824.

2. "New York incident underscores need for policy on sales reps in OR," *Operating Room Risk Management* (December 1998).

3. P Lebowitz, M Hart Yeary, "Allowing sales representatives in the OR creates new liability issues," *News & Business* (Nov/Dec 2001).

4. Joint Commission on Accreditation of Healthcare Organizations, *Comprehensive Accreditation Manual for Hospitals: The Official Handbook* (Oakbrook Terrace, Ill: Joint Commission on Accreditation of Healthcare Organizations, 2005).

5. "Recommended practices for traffic patterns in the perioperative practice setting," *Standards, Recommended Practices and Guidelines* (Denver: AORN Inc, 2006) 659-662

6. "Standards for privacy of individually identifiable health information; final rule," 45 CFR Parts 160 and 164, Centers for Medicare and Medicaid Services, *http://www.cms.hhs.gov/hipaa/hipaa2/regulations/privacy/finalrule/PvcFR01.pdf* (accessed 4 Oct 2005).

7. "Administrative simplification in the health care industry," US Department of Health and Human Services, *http://aspe.os.dhhs.gov/admnsimp/index.shtml* (accessed 4 Oct 2005).

8. "Bloodborne pathogens and needlestick prevention," Occupational Safety and Health Administration, *http://www.osha.gov/SLTC/bloodbornepathogens/index.html* (accessed 4 Oct 2005).

9. Association for the Advancement of Medical Instrumentation, "Recommended practice for a medical equipment management program," ANSI/AAMI EQ56:1999/(R)2004 (Arlington, Va: Association for the Advancement of Medical Instrumentation, 1999) 4.1.2.1.

RESOURCES
"AORN OR protocol," Healthstream, *http://www.healthstream.com/Products/STS/RepDirect/orProtocol.htm* (accessed 4 Oct 2005).

Approved by the AORN Board of Directors, November 2005. Published in *Standards, Recommended Practices, and Guidelines,* 2006 edition. Reprinted April 2006, *AORN Journal.*

AORN Guidance Statement: Care of the Perioperative Patient With an Implanted Electronic Device

Introduction

This document is intended to serve as a guide for perioperative nurses involved in the care of surgical patients with implanted electronic devices (IEDs) who are undergoing surgical and other invasive procedures. This document does not address care of patients undergoing surgery for implantation of an electronic device; it covers only issues surrounding the care of patients with existing electronic implants. Because of the rapid advancement of science and medical technology, this document does not presume to address every IED. Manufacturers' written directions for specific devices should be followed. This document is intended to help perioperative nurses provide safe care for patients with IEDs because these patients require extraordinary safety precautions in the surgical environment.

Implanted electronic devices provide a vast number of options in the treatment of many disease processes that cannot be managed with medications alone. Common examples of IEDs include permanent pacemakers, which are used to treat profound bradycardia; implantable cardioverter defibrillators (ICDs), which are used to treat sustained ventricular tachycardia (VT); deep brain stimulators (DBSs), which are used to treat tremors and Parkinson's disease; and spinal cord stimulators (SCSs), which are used to deliver low-voltage stimulation to the spinal cord to block the sensation of pain and to stimulate the sacral nerve for treatment of neurogenic bladder and tremors. Sudden failure of these implanted devices can result in patient injury or sudden cardiac death (SCD).[1] When precautions are implemented, patient risk for injury can be minimized.

The goal of every surgical intervention is to provide optimal patient outcomes while maintaining a safe environment. Some medical equipment devices necessary for performing surgical and other invasive procedures may interfere with the functioning of IEDs. Manufacturers of IEDs recommend precautions for and/or avoiding certain devices that create electromagnetic fields.[2] Because of the potential for interference, patients with IEDs require special safety precautions when undergoing a surgical procedure. The perioperative registered nurse should be knowledgeable about the specific IED and associated precautions that should be implemented to protect the patient from injury.

Implanted electronic devices are widely used in a number of diverse medical applications, ranging from the familiar cardiac pacemaker to the less frequently encountered cochlear implant. The perioperative nurse should be aware that these devices require that special precautions be taken. One predominantly important precaution is managing the sources of inherent electromagnetic interference (EMI) in the perioperative patient care environment. Cardiac patients are particularly at risk because they may be dependent on the proper function of an IED to sustain their lives. Understanding what types of IEDs exist, how they function, and the precautions that must be taken when caring for patients with IEDs is critical for every perioperative nurse because patients with these devices may be encountered in any perioperative environment. The history, application, function, and safety issues of the different types of IEDs will be addressed in this document.

Definitions

For the purposes of this document, the following definitions apply.

Conducted EMI: Occurs when an electromagnetic source comes in direct contact with the body. Can be generated by electrosurgery and defibrillation.[3]

Direct coupling: The contact of an energized metal active electrode tip with another metal instrument or object within the surgical field.

Electromagnetic: Magnetism that is induced by an electric current.[4]

Electromagnetic interference (EMI): Any electromagnetic disturbance that interrupts, obstructs, or otherwise degrades or limits the effective performance of electronics/electrical equipment. *Synonym:* radio frequency interference.[5]

Implanted electronic devices (IEDs): Electronic medical devices that have been implanted in a patient to treat a physiological defect or to replace a sensory function.

Microwave: A short electromagnetic wave between about 1 mm and 1 m in length.

Radiated EMI: Occurs when the body is placed within an electromagnetic field; no contact with the source is necessary. Can be generated by magnetic resonance imaging (MRI), positron emission tomography (PET), and radiation therapy.[3]

Shortwave: A radio wave with a wavelength between 10 m and 100 m.

General Safety Issues and Concerns

Electronic devices implanted in a patient may be affected by other IEDs or medical equipment that a patient may come in contact with in a health care facility. These devices may include

- cardiac pacemakers or ICDs,
- electrosurgical devices,
- ultrasound equipment, or
- MRI equipment.

All of these devices have the potential to adversely affect an IED.[6] Perioperative registered nurses should be aware of potential patient safety hazards associated with specific IEDs and the appropriate patient care interventions required to protect patients from injury. (See **Exhibit A**, at the end of this document, for a summary of potential patient safety hazards.)

Exposure to shortwave and microwave diathermy should be avoided if an implanted device has metallic leads, even if the implanted device is not turned on. The energy from diathermy can cause tissue heating at the site surrounding the implant and has the potential to cause tissue injury. *Note:* As used here, the term "diathermy" does not include electrocautery and electrosurgical devices or ultrasonic imaging devices.[7] Examples of implants with metallic leads include cardiac pacemakers and defibrillators, cochlear implants, bone growth stimulators, deep brain stimulators, spinal cord stimulators, and other nerve stimulators.[7,8]

General Patient Management

Preoperative

- The perioperative registered nurse should routinely assess patients for the presence of any IEDs.[9] Patient education occurring at the time of the implant surgery should include instructions to the patient to always report the presence of the implant to health care providers, especially when a surgical procedure is necessary.[10] A patient who has an IED should have been given a product identification card at the time of implantation; the patient may have the card with him or her, or the medical record may contain a copy of the card.[10]
- The perioperative registered nurse may contact the patient's implanting surgeon to inform him or her that the patient is scheduled for surgery and ask the implanting physician to send the following IED information to the preoperative assessment nurse, the operating surgeon, and the operative suite:[10,11]

- manufacturer and model of IED,
- location of the device,
- when the device was last evaluated,
- if the device can be turned off before or during surgery,
- what settings should be reprogrammed into the device immediately postprocedure,
- whether the implanting physician wishes to be contacted when the patient enters the postanesthesia care unit (PACU), and
- whether the patient needs to schedule an appointment with the implanting physician.[12]
- The information above should be documented on the medical record before surgery.
- Determine whether electrosurgery and/or defibrillation are necessary for the procedure.
- Contact the appropriate health care industry representative and arrange for his or her presence before, during, and after the surgery, if requested by the physician.[13]
- Notify the anesthesia care provider of the presence of the IED.

Intraoperative

- Notify all perioperative team members that the patient has an IED in place, and review potential safety concerns and equipment conflicts.[11,14]
- The programming device and personnel who are qualified to program the IED should be in the OR before the start of the procedure.[3]
- When electrosurgery is necessary, bipolar electrosurgery should be used.[14]
- If the use of monopolar electrosurgery is required, the current pathway should be perpendicular to the IED's lead system. This can be achieved by manipulating the placement of the patient return electrode; however, a perpendicular pathway is not always a realistic possibility. If monopolar electrosurgery must be used, the active electrode and the dispersive electrode should be located as close together as possible.[3] A reusable, capacitive-coupled return electrode may be used if the perpendicular current pathway does not pass through the IED or the IED lead system.[15]
- Place the active electrode and the dispersive electrode as far from the IED generator and wires as possible.[16]
- The current path from the active electrode to the dispersive electrode should not pass through the area containing the IED or the electrodes.[16]

- Avoid placing the dispersive electrode directly over the site of a metal implant.[15] The dispersive electrode should be placed in such a way that the current will flow away from the IED. The distance between the dispersive electrode and the active electrode should be as small as possible.[17]
- To prevent EMI, care should be taken not to arc current between the active electrode and another surgical instrument. The instrument and active electrode should be in direct contact before activation.
- If the IED appears to have been inadvertently reprogrammed by the use of electrosurgery, it is advisable to return the device to the appropriate mode before continuing the procedure.[3]
- The humidity and temperature in the OR should be maintained within recommended ranges to reduce the possibility of creating static electricity in the environment. The OR temperature should be between 20° C and 24° C (68° F and 76° F) and humidity should be between 50% and 60%.[18(p147)]
- For patients who have pacemakers and other IEDs in the chest area and who require defibrillation, anterior-posterior-type paddles should be used. The anterior paddle should be placed as far from the pulse generator as possible. This should allow the current to flow away from the IED. The lowest possible defibrillator current setting should be used. Inability to defibrillate at low current settings will necessitate an increase in power, and damage to the IED may be unavoidable.[3]

Postoperative

- If necessary, notify the implanting physician and/or the health care industry representative that electrosurgery or defibrillation was used during surgery. An evaluation of IED function similar to that performed before surgery should be done early in the postoperative period.[3,16]
- Continue to monitor the patient closely during the postoperative period for signs of complications and IED malfunction.

Cardiac IEDs

Implanted electronic devices provide a vast array of treatments for patients with cardiac dysfunctions. The ability to electrically stimulate the chambers of the heart with an implanted device has helped many

patients who have cardiac dysfunction and limited options for treating their disease with medications. For this reason, IEDs are popular treatment modalities. Pacemakers, ICDs, and ventricular assist devices (VADs) are three examples of IEDs used today to treat cardiac dysfunction. Specifically, pacemakers are used to treat patients with compromised cardiac output caused by profound bradycardia.[1] Implantable cardioverter defibrillators treat patients with a known risk for SCD caused by ventricular fibrillation (VF).[1] Ventricular assist devices are implantable pumps used for circulatory support in patients with congestive heart failure.[3]

History and Current Application

Pacemakers
Cardiac pacemakers first were introduced in 1954.[19] Pacemakers consist of a power source that delivers an electric impulse that travels along leads that have contact with the heart. Early pacemakers fired at a fixed rate and did not have the ability to sense the patient's heartbeat.[1] As technology improved, pacemakers with the ability to sense the patient's heart rate were introduced, helping to eliminate the hazard of the pacemaker competing with the intrinsic heartbeat and potentially creating a ventricular dysrhythmia.[1] The development of the sensing demand pacemaker in the 1960s brought with it the problem of interference.[3] Specifically, sensing pacemakers were able to sense and react to the changing needs of the heart, but they also could sense and react to electromagnetic signals that were not cardiac in origin.[3] Pacemakers have evolved from the limited capability of stimulating only one chamber of the heart to those capable of stimulating both atrial and ventricular chambers, adjusting rates to physiologic demands, providing telemetric information and autoprogramming and reprogramming functions, and providing antitachycardia functions.[20] The transvenous route performed with fluoroscopy is the most common insertion method.[1]

Implanted cardioverter defibrillators
Implanted cardioverter defibrillators are similar to pacemakers in that they have a power source and leads that attach to the heart and sense the patient's heartbeat. Early ICDs consisted of defibrillating patches placed via thoracotomy on the ventricular epicardium and connected to an internal defibrillator that discharged when it sensed VT or VF.[1] Lowe

and Wharton (1955) report that the development of nonthoracotomy lead systems inserted transvenously has made epicardial patch systems rare.[21] The greatest challenge in treating patients with spontaneous VF is that electrical counter shock is the only treatment for patients at risk for SCD caused by VF;[1] therefore, patients may be totally dependent on the ICD to save their lives. Realizing that patients often died of VT or VF because the necessary equipment and personnel to defibrillate patients were unavailable, Mirowski and his associates (1980) conceived of an implantable device that could sense the dysrythmia and deliver a counter shock to terminate the life-threatening disorder.[22] In 1980, the first device of this kind was implanted at Johns Hopkins Hospital in Baltimore.[1]

Ventricular assist devices

A VAD is a type of mechanical heart that is surgically implanted in the patient's chest during open-heart surgery[20] and that is used to treat patients with end-stage heart failure. Blood fills the device through a cannulation site in the ventricle or atrium. Within the device, a diaphragm is actuated pneumatically, electrically, or magnetically, and it pumps blood into the aorta or pulmonary artery.[18] After the pump is implanted, it needs power to operate. The driveline passes through the skin and attaches to the power base unit, which consists of a system controller and batteries. The power source is worn externally in a holster or waist pack.[19] Government-funded research and development work in cardiac support systems began in 1966. Clinical trials of an air-driven left ventricular assist system started in 1986, and an electric system was tested in 1991. The device has been used in patients aged 11 to 78 years, with an average age of 50 years, and in as many as 4,000 patients in the United States and elsewhere.[19]

Ventricular assist devices initially were used as "bridges to transplantation," helping people survive as they waited for a heart transplant. Today, VADs play another role; they allow disease-weakened hearts to recover. In patients not eligible for heart transplantation, VADs offer permanent support, which is called destination therapy.[19] Clinical trials have demonstrated that destination therapy doubles the one-year survival rate of patients with end-stage heart failure as compared to treatment with medication.[20]

Safety Concerns

Pacemakers, ICDs, and VADs are IEDs that rely on sensing capability for proper function of the device and appropriate treatment being delivered to the patient. Electromagnetic interference is the most common safety issue noted when caring for patients with existing cardiac IEDs, mostly because EMI can alter what the device is sensing. This potentially could change the rhythm or, in some cases, render the device incapable of delivering appropriate treatment.

Electromagnetic interference occurs in two forms: conducted and radiated. Conducted EMI occurs when an electromagnetic source comes in direct contact with the body. This type of EMI can be generated by electrosurgery and defibrillation. Radiated EMI occurs when the body is placed within an electromagnetic field; no contact with the source is necessary. This type of EMI can be generated by MRI, PET, and radiation therapy.[3]

The electrosurgical unit (ESU) is a commonly used device that cuts and coagulates tissue with high-voltage, high-frequency (ie, 10,000 Hz) current.[3(p640)] Practically every surgical intervention requires some form of electrosurgery to help facilitate hemostasis. Some surgical procedures would be nearly impossible to perform without electrosurgery. There are two types of electrosurgical current: monopolar and bipolar. Monopolar current begins at the tip of the instrument, travels through the body, and returns to the generator through a dispersing ground pad. When monopolar electrosurgery is used, surgeons may use the active electrode to pass current through other surgical instruments. If the ESU is activated before the active electrode is in contact with the instrument, the current can arc through the air toward the instrument and demodulate the signal to the IED. If allowed to demodulate, the signal can dip well into the frequency range that pacemakers and ICDs are designed to sense. The result is that the IED might interpret the current as cardiac in origin and respond inappropriately or not respond at all.[3]

Ventricular assist devices also are affected by EMI generated by electrosurgery. Theoretically, the timing circuit of one model can be disrupted, but this rarely is reported. Ventricular assist devices that are run by electricity may exhibit an erratic pattern of current output during electrosurgery use. This results in a significant decrease in device output.[3]

Bipolar electrosurgery does not require a patient-return electrode because the current flows between the two tips of a bipolar forceps that is positioned around tissue to create a surgical effect. Current passes from the active electrode of one tip of the forceps through the patient's tissue to the dispersive electrode of the other forceps tip, thus completing the circuit without entering another part of the patient's body. This means that the current flows only through the area of tissue that is in direct contact with the instrument.[17] Using bipolar electrosurgery rather than monopolar electrosurgery may be advantageous when trying to avoid possible arcing that could demodulate; however, bipolar electrosurgery is much less powerful than monopolar electrosurgery and may be inappropriate for many surgical procedures.

Other dangers inherent to monopolar electrosurgery include burns, triggering ventricular or atrial fibrillation, and loss of battery output. A continuous train of electrical impulses conducted down the lead can induce ventricular or atrial fibrillation, cause thermal burns at the lead-tissue interface, and pass from the leads to the pulse generator and cause irreversible loss of battery output.[3]

Some surgeries and emergency situations employ the use of defibrillation as part of the surgical procedure. Patients with existing pacemakers and ICDs may experience permanent damage to the pulse generator, particularly after repeated attempts at defibrillation. In addition, the current shunted away from the pacemaker or ICD can lead to myocardial burns at the lead-tissue interface.[3]

Patient Management

Preoperative

- If the IED was not evaluated within the previous six months, it should be evaluated for programming, telemetry, thresholds, and battery status.
- If the make and model of the IED is unavailable, a chest x-ray may be helpful in identifying the pacemaker or ICD. Each device has a serial number and a unique silhouette that can be used for device identification.[3] Modern pacemakers employ a variety of different pacing modes, so it is important to be familiar with the North American Society of Pacing and Electrophysiology/British Pacing and Electrophysiology Group (NBG) generic pacemaker codes. The first

three letters of the code describe the basic antibradycardia functions, and the last two letters describe the programmability and antitachycardia functions.[3] Similar coding also is found on ICDs. This code, which is located on the device, also can be identified via chest x-ray.

- For a pacemaker-dependent patient, it is advised that the device be reprogrammed to an asynchronous mode if EMI is likely to cause significant malfunction (eg, monopolar electrosurgery for surgical procedures involving the upper abdomen or chest wall).
- For patients with adaptive-rate devices, including ICDs, this feature should be programmed off during surgery because exposure to other EMI might cause a device malfunction.[23] Magnet-activated testing should be programmed off.[20]
- For patients with an ICD, tachycardia sensing should be programmed off.[23]
- Patients with a VAD should be evaluated in a similar manner. Most surgical procedures involving patients with VADs take place at institutions that can provide technical and surgical support for these devices.[3]

Intraoperative

- If monopolar electrosurgery must be used, the current pathway should be perpendicular to the pacemaker's lead system when possible. This is done by manipulating the placement of the dispersive electrode; however, a perpendicular pathway is not always a realistic possibility, especially when the IED has a dual lead system.
- If it is impossible to place the pacemaker in a triggered or asynchronous mode and it becomes apparent that the ESU is adversely affecting the pacemaker, the electrosurgery current should be activated for no more than one second at a time, allowing at least 10 seconds for the device to function properly. This will permit the pacemaker enough time to maintain cardiac output. It is widely assumed that placing a magnet over any pacemaker pulse generator will invariably cause asynchronous pacing as long as the magnet remains in place; however, in some pacemakers, the magnet response may have been programmed off. In others, a variety of magnet responses may have been programmed, some of which do not provide immunity to EMI sensing. In still other pacemakers, the device will continue to pace

asynchronously or pacing will cease after a programmed number of intervals.[24] If possible, one should determine before EMI exposure what type of pulse generator is present and what must be done to provide protection. If this is not possible, one can observe the magnet response during EMI to ascertain whether there is protection from EMI sensing. During electrosurgery, for example, if the active electrode triggers rapid pacing or inhibits pacing stimuli in a pacemaker-dependent patient despite magnet application, then activation of the ESU should be limited to short bursts.[23]

■ The use of electrosurgery also may interfere with the ability of the electrocardiogram (ECG) to monitor the heart, so heart rate and blood pressure should be monitored using an arterial line. When the ESU is not in use, the ECG should be checked for arrhythmias or alterations in pacemaker function.

■ Patients with VADs that require the use of electrosurgery should have the device placed in the fixed rate mode for the duration of the surgery. Adequate pumping is not possible during electrosurgery, so the ESU should be activated for no more than one second at a time, allowing 10 seconds for the VAD to function properly. Cardiac output should be monitored. It may be necessary for an external hand pump to be available in the OR during surgery.[3]

■ Patients with VADs who require defibrillation may need to have the timing circuit disconnected from the external controller before defibrillation. This may require the use of a fixed rate mode, depending on the type of VAD, during the period of defibrillation, but it will eliminate the possibility of damage to the circuit. During this time, a pneumatic or manually run pump will be needed.[3]

■ In patients with pacemakers and ICDs who require defibrillation, anterior-posterior-type paddles should be used. The anterior paddle should be placed as far from the pulse generator as possible. This should allow the current to flow away from the generator. If the anterior type of paddles must be used, the paddles should be placed along a line perpendicular to the lead(s). This may be difficult if the patient has a dual-lead system. The lowest possible defibrillator current setting should be used. Inability to defibrillate at low current settings will necessitate an increase in

power, and damage to the pulse generator may be unavoidable. For these reasons, a temporary pacing system should be available.[3]

Postoperative

■ Inform the cardiologist, cardiothoracic surgeon, and/or the health care industry representative that electrosurgery or defibrillation was used during surgery. An evaluation of pacemaker and ICD function similar to that performed before surgery should be done in the early postoperative period and again 24 to 48 hours later. This is necessary because failure of the device to capture due to damage at the lead-tissue interface may not be apparent until 24 to 48 hours after surgery. If any of the postoperative measurements of the demand or magnet rates vary from those obtained before surgery, one must suspect that the pacemaker has been reprogrammed inadvertently during surgery or has sustained permanent damage.[3]

■ Alteration of the VAD motor current occurs only during exposure to electrosurgery and has no permanent effect on the device. Defibrillation, however, can damage the timing circuit, depending on the model and if the timing circuit is left connected during surgery. The surgeon or cardiologist responsible for the care of the patient should be informed if the circuit is damaged during surgery because repair or replacement should be considered.[3]

Neurostimulators

Deep brain stimulators, SCSs, vagal nerve stimulators (VNSs), and programmable ventricular shunts all are examples of neurological IEDs. Neurological IEDs are devices that help to restore functionality to people who have neurological or sensory impairments. This is accomplished by electrically stimulating the nervous system. Electrodes are placed in specific regions of the nervous system with regard to the patient's pathology. Neurostimulation used to treat movement disorders, such as those caused by Parkinson's disease, involves implanting leads in specific regions of the brain (ie, DBS) that then are connected to a programmable pulse generator. Electrodes may be implanted in the spine (ie, SCS) to control intractable pain, and they also may be used for sacral nerve stimulation to alleviate urinary incontinence and on the left vagus nerve (ie, VNS) to treat intractable seizures.[25]

History and Current Application

In 1964, E. A. Spiegel, MD, and H. T. Wycis, MD, along with their team members at Temple University Hospital, created the first neurological IED.[26] The physicians, however, were reluctant to use a new device, so their first device was never implanted. C. Norman Shealy, MD, is credited with implanting the first neurological IED spinal cord stimulator in 1967.[26] For the past three decades, neurological IEDs have continued to evolve. Thorough patient selection and screening, combined with physician experience, has resulted in a 50% to 60% good long-term results. More than 20,000 DBSs,[27(p76)] 130,000 SCSs,[27(p76)] and 15,000 VNSs have been implanted.[28 (p1,662)]

Deep brain stimulators

The first IED to treat tremors associated with Parkinson's disease was approved by the US Food and Drug Administration (FDA) in August 1997.[29] Deep brain stimulators consist of four electrodes that are placed in the ventricle. These electrodes then are connected to a pulse generator. The pulse generator usually is placed in the subcutaneous tissues in the chest, similar to the cardiac pacemaker.[29] The electrical stimulation blocks the abnormal brain signal that induces tremors. These devices can be turned off and adjusted from high to low frequency settings.

Spinal cord stimulators

The use of electrical stimulation for patient with spinal cord injuries was first attempted in the 1960s.[30] Spinal cord stimulators have been used to stimulate phrenic nerves and the diaphragm to permit a patient freedom from a respirator and to promote easier mobility. Spinal cord stimulators also are used in the treatment of intractable pain. An SCS is used to reduce pain, not eliminate it. Spinal cord stimulator studies have shown a 50% reduction in pain, increased activity levels, and a decreased reliance on narcotic medications.[31(p3)] Spinal cord stimulators have helped patients with chronic pain lead more comfortable and productive lives.

Patients with implanted cardiac pacemakers or defibrillators should not use spinal stimulators. Use of a transcutaneous electrical nerve stimulator unit is acceptable.[32]

Vagal nerve stimulators

In 1985, Zabara[27] developed the concept of vagal stimulation to control seizures; however, it was not until 1997 that the FDA approved the use of VNSs.[27]

Vagal nerve stimulators are composed of implantable (eg, generator, leads) and external (eg, computer, software, programming wands) components. The generator or stimulator, which is the main component, is very similar to a cardiac pacemaker. It is a pulse generator that is programmed by a computer, and it runs on battery power. The pulse generator is implanted on the left side of the upper chest just under the skin. The lead is a flexible tube that is attached to the left vagus nerve on the left side of the neck.[33] The pulse generator has a life span of approximately 16 years. The battery life span ranges from six to 10 years.[33(p4)] Vagal nerve stimulators operate by sending electrical signals through the implanted leads via the left vagus nerve to the brain. This signal stimulates the brain to reduce the frequency and duration of seizures.

Programmable ventricular shunts

Ventricular shunts are used to treat patients with hydrocephalus. Shunts are long tubes that draw cerebrospinal fluid (CSF) away from the brain and into a body cavity, such as the chest or abdomen.[34] One of the major setbacks in ventricular shunts is shunt failure. This leads to repeated surgeries to adjust the shunt to drain the CSF. In September 1999, the FDA approved the first programmable shunt.[34] Programmable shunts allow surgeons to adjust the settings on the shunt from outside the body, thereby decreasing the need for repeated surgeries.

Neurostimulators or neurological IEDs are similar to cardiac pacemakers in design. They deliver electrical stimulation to targeted structures in the appropriate area of the nervous system. After it is programmed, a neurological IED can be turned on and off by a patient or clinician using a magnet or a patient-therapy controller. In the OR, because the neurological IED generates electrical impulses, it may be affected by or have an adverse effect on medical equipment (eg, cardiac pacemakers, cardioverters/defibrillators, external defibrillators, ultrasonic equipment, ESU) or procedures (eg, radiation therapy, some MRI procedures).[25]

Safety Concerns

Neurological IEDs, like implantable cardiac devices, generate electrical impulses and have the potential for interference from other medical devices with electromagnetic forces. Electromagnetic interference is the primary concern. In the perioperative setting, many procedures and devices have the potential to cause interference with IEDs, including electrosurgery, defibrillation, MRI, ultrasonic equipment, and other IEDs.[35]

More than 177,000 neurological IEDs have been implanted,[27(p76)] so perioperative team members must be aware of and understand potential complications before patients with IEDs enter the OR. This knowledge can help team members deal with potential complications and possibly prevent patient injury.[3]

Devices and procedures that may cause damage to or interfere with the function of the neurological IED or harm to the patient include defibrillators, cardioverters, electrosurgery, and MRI. If a patient is in ventricular or atrial fibrillation, patient survival always should be the first consideration. Steps should be taken to minimize the electrical circuit flowing through the neurological IED during defibrillation. These steps include

- positioning paddles as far from the neurological IED as possible,
- positioning paddles perpendicular to the neurological IED,
- using the lowest clinically appropriate output settings, and
- having perioperative team members confirm that the neurological IED is functioning properly after defibrillation.

Use of monopolar electrosurgery may cause the tissue around the leads to be damaged. In addition, the insulation on the leads may be damaged, which could cause device failure or shock the patient.[35] Damage to the neurological IED itself also may occur, and this could cause changes in stimulation settings, changes in parameters, or complete device failure. These are potentially serious risks, so the use of the ultrasonic scalpel is being investigated as an alternative to monopolar electrosurgery. Ultrasonic scalpels do not emit electromagnetic impulses.[3] If electrosurgery is deemed necessary, bipolar electrosurgery is recommended. If bipolar electrosurgery is not a suitable option and monopolar electrosurgery is necessary, the following precautions should be taken.

- The neurological IED should be turned off. If this cannot be accomplished by the patient, a staff member, or the physician, the appropriate health care industry representative may need to be notified.
- Use only a low voltage mode/setting.
- Keep the grounding pad as far from the neurological IED as possible.

- After using the ESU, perioperative team members should confirm that the neurological IED is functioning properly.

With the increasing popularity of intraoperative MRI, perioperative team members should be aware of MRI safety issues. Magnetic resonance imaging is not recommended for patients who have a neurological IED. It may cause heating at the lead site, resulting in tissue damage. Magnetic resonance imaging also may cause damage to the neurological IED itself, resulting in patient injury or device failure.[36]

The following devices used in the perioperative setting are unlikely to cause interference with neurological IEDs; however, special precautions should be taken when using them.[36]

- Keep the external magnetic coils of neurological IEDs a minimum of 18 inches (45 cm) away from bone growth stimulators.
- Turn the neurological IED off when dental drills, ultrasonic probes, diagnostic ultrasound, electrolysis, and lasers are used. Keep the device six inches (15 cm) away from the neurological IED. Keep the laser directed away from the neurological IED.
- For questions about precautions when other IEDs are present, contact the manufacturer of the other IED and notify the physicians involved in both therapies.

Patient Management

Preoperative

■ Vagus nerve stimulators can pose a serious risk to a patient's respiratory status. Patients with VNSs may have increased swallowing difficulties, so the risk of aspiration is increased.[33] The perioperative nurse and anesthesia care provider should be aware of the risk of spontaneous airway obstruction.[28]

Intraoperative

■ The patient, physician, a staff member, or the appropriate representative should turn off the IED.

Implantable Hearing Devices

Four types of implantable electronic hearing devices are used today. These devices are cochlear implants, implanted bone conduction stimulators, implantable and semi-implantable hearing aids, and auditory brainstem implants.

History and Current Application

Cochlear implants

Cochlear implants are used for people with sensorineural hearing loss. The first cochlear implant procedures on humans were done in 1961.[37] Graeme Clark and colleagues in Australia began research into cochlear implants in the late 1960s and implanted a multichannel device into the world's first cochlear implant recipient in 1978.[38] Cochlear implants now are the standard treatment for individuals whose ability to hear, even with hearing aids, is so poor that their ability to effectively communicate through speech is affected.[39] Statistics from 2003 indicate that approximately 60,000 people worldwide have received a cochlear implant since 1983.[39(p1)] Cochlear implants are seen more commonly than the other types of implantable hearing devices described here.

Cochlear implants consist of an implant system and an external component. After being implanted, these components work together to allow a patient with sensorineural hearing loss to hear by converting mechanical sound energy into electrical impulses that are transmitted directly to the acoustic nerve.[37] Cochlear implants consist of internal and external parts. The external parts, which consist of a receiver, speech processor, and transmitting coil, may be removed from the patient at any time. The internal receiver/stimulator is surgically implanted into the patient's inner ear and into the bone behind the ear.[38] The external receiver is worn near the ear and is used to pick up sound.

The external speech processor usually is clipped to the wearer's clothing, or for children, it may be kept in a special backpack. The external transmitting coil is surrounded by the transmitting antenna. This transmitting coil is held in place by two magnets of opposite polarity—one in the transmitting coil and the other implanted within the internal receiver/stimulator. The internal receiver/stimulator is surgically implanted and, in addition to the previously mentioned magnet, contains a multi-channeled electrode. A cochleostomy is made, and the electrode is placed into the cochlea. After all parts are connected, electromagnetic induction will cause stimulation of the cochlear nerve, which allows the patient to perceive sound.[10]

Implantable and semi-implantable hearing aids

Implanted bone conduction stimulators, which also are known as temporal bone stimulators,[40] typically are used for people with a conductive hearing loss.[41] Implantable and semi-implantable hearing aids are implanted in the middle ear[42] or directly stimulate the inner ear.[38] The various designs are categorized by the type of output transducer used. Electromagnetic stimulation of the middle ear was first done in 1957. One of the earliest types used was piezoelectric crystal, which first was used in Japan in about 1978.[40]

The semi-implantable hearing aid allows sound to be produced through direct stimulation of the ossicles.[41] The components of this device include a microphone speech processor, which is connected to a transmitter. This transmitter has an external coil that transcutaneously transmits electrical energy to the internal device. The internal device has an internal receiving coil, which is implanted in the temporal bone. The internal receiving coil is connected to a receiver that provides electrical energy to the mechanical driver. The mechanical driver is attached to the incus. This results in vibration of the ossicles, which allows the patient to hear.[42]

Bone-conduction stimulators

One of the first bone-anchored hearing devices (ie, a temporal bone stimulator) was developed in Sweden in 1977. One brand currently is approved by the FDA.[40] A transcutaneous bone-conduction device was developed in 1986. This device has an external unit and an internal unit. The external unit is composed of a microphone and a sound processor system worn on the user's body and held in place with an implanted magnet assembly behind the user's ear. The internal unit is implanted into the temporal bone.[40] These devices are used in the treatment of severe conductive hearing loss, in patients with mixed hearing loss, and sometimes for patients with sensorineural hearing loss in one ear.[43]

Bone-conduction devices have an external processor, which consists of a microphone, amplifier, and a transducer, a device that connects the bone-anchored implant to the external processor. Both the fixture placed in the mastoid bone and the coupling devices are made of titanium.[42]

Auditory brainstem implants

Auditory brainstem implants are used to restore auditory sensation for patients who are totally deaf. The deafness is due to bilateral eighth cranial nerve lesions or neurofibromatosis Type 2. These patients have undergone surgical removal of a tumor and do not plan to undergo radiation treatment.[44]

One auditory brainstem implant system was approved by the FDA in October 2000.[45] The FDA New Device Approvals notice stated that pre-approval testing involved implantation of this auditory brainstem implant system in 90 patients.[45(p1)] The auditory brainstem implant consists of an implantable receiver/stimulator package, an electrode lead, and an electrode array. The receiver/stimulator comes with a magnet that can be removed via a small incision with local anesthesia if the patient is required to undergo MRI.[43]

Safety Issues and Concerns

Studies have been conducted to determine the compatibility of MRI and cochlear implants.[41] In at least one study, MRI was not an absolute contraindication for these patients. Another study determined that MRI should be done only if there is a strong medical indication for the test.[37] Currently, patients with cochlear implants should avoid undergoing MRI unless it is absolutely necessary because of the possibility that the implant can become inactivated.[46]

Roberts et al studied the effects of EMI on cochlear implants using common dental office equipment. This equipment included a bipolar and monopolar ESU. The ESU was tested using cut level 1 and various coagulation settings.[37] The study concluded that bipolar electrosurgery was safe, but monopolar electrosurgery may present a hazard to the cochlear implant device itself and has the potential to cause tissue damage that would prevent further reimplantation.[37]

Patients with cochlear implants are educated about the importance of avoiding contact with static electricity. A sudden shock from walking across a carpeted room in the wintertime has been known to inactivate an implant.[10] Static electricity can damage the components of an auditory brainstem implant.[47] The speech processor and headset should be removed when the potential for static electricity generation exists.[47]

Patient Management

Preoperative
- The patient should not have an MRI scan because the strong magnetic field can inactivate the implant.
- Computed tomography (CT) scans are acceptable for patients with cochlear implants.[10]

Intraoperative
- External devices can be removed before the beginning of the surgical procedure, so they should be removed after induction of anesthesia, as would be done with other devices that assist with communication, such as hearing aids or eyeglasses.
- The internal receiver/stimulator will be damaged by monopolar electrosurgery. Only bipolar electrosurgery should be used after the internal receiver/stimulator is implanted.[10] The radio frequency current of ESUs can damage the electrodes implanted in the cochlea or the surrounding tissue. Current leakage and direct coupling when an energized metal active electrode tip comes in contact with another metal instrument or object potentially can damage or cause injury to the device or tissues.[15] Monopolar electrosurgery should not be used in the head and neck area of a patient with a cochlear implant.[1,10,45,48]
- Some models of cochlear implants have extracochlear reference electrodes, and some do not. If an implant has extracochlear reference electrodes, bipolar electrosurgical instruments may be used if the electrosurgical device is kept more than 10 cm from the extracochlear electrodes.[35]
- Bipolar electrosurgery may be used on patients with auditory brainstem implants when the following precautions are observed.
  - The electrosurgical electrode must not come in contact with the implant.
  - The electrosurgical electrode should be kept more than 1 cm from the ground electrodes of the auditory brainstem implants.[47]
- An isolated electrosurgical generator should be used. This can significantly decrease the risk of electrosurgical current traveling an alternate pathway to ground.[48]
- Avoid using ionizing radiation therapy directly over the site of the implant. Ionizing radiation can damage the implant.[47]
- Magnetic resonance imaging must be avoided with auditory brainstem implants unless the removable magnet is surgically removed before this test. The external speech processor and headset must be removed before the patient enters the scanner room.[47]

Postoperative
- External devices may be replaced as soon as the surgical procedure has been completed.

■ Testing should be done to be sure the device continues to function.

Implantable Infusion Pumps

There are a number of implantable medication devices available for patients with a variety of therapeutic needs. These needs include chronic pain management, administration of chemotherapeutic medications, and administration of insulin. The devices specifically covered in this document include venous access devices (eg, subcutaneous infusion ports, implantable infusion pumps) and insulin pumps. Some devices are used for intraventricular administration of chemotherapy.[49]

History and Current Application
Intra-arterial medication infusion pumps became widely used in the early 1980s. One common use is hepatic artery medication infusion for the prevention or treatment of metastases from a colon cancer into the liver or for the treatment of hepatocellular carcinoma. This involves inserting a cannula into an artery that provides the blood supply to an area of a tumor. The cannula is connected to a pump device that is placed in the subcutaneous tissue.[49]

Venous access devices include subcutaneous infusion ports and implantable infusion pumps.[50] Subcutaneous infusion ports are implanted in the subcutaneous tissue for administration of medications into a central vein, hepatic artery, the epidural space, or the peritoneal cavity. These usually have a silicone or plastic port with a stainless steel or plastic reservoir. The ports are used for intermittent infusions of medications administered via a special Huber needle to access the port. During the intermittent infusion, the medication is infused and then flushed with a heparinized solution until the next infusion is ordered.[50]

Implantable infusion pumps also are placed into a vein or artery, the spine, a body space, or a ventricle in the brain. These devices can be used to deliver anticoagulants to control thromboembolic disease; insulin to control diabetes; morphine to treat pain from malignancy; or chemotherapy to a localized area for treatment of tumors, such as tumors in the liver or brain.[50] They also can be used to treat locally recurrent ovarian or colon cancer by delivering chemotherapy into the peritoneal space.[49] The implantable infusion pump also may be implanted in an area of subcutaneous tissue as close as is reasonable to the area of the tumor. The pumps usually are made of titanium, stainless steel, and silicone rubber. The pump steadily delivers medication using a bellows device or through radio signals.[50] The prevalence of individuals with an implantable medication delivery system is 0.05 people per 100,000 in Europe, North America, Australia, and Japan.[50(p904)]

One type of insulin pump consists of a pump reservoir connected to a small battery-operated pump via a subcutaneously-implanted infusion set.[51] The infusion set includes a cannula, which is inserted just under the skin and is changed every few days.[52] Other than the need to be aware of the presence of this device and monitor the patient's blood glucose, this type of insulin pump presents no major concern for perioperative nurses because the patient can remove the monitor for the duration of the surgical procedure. This device currently is available in European Union countries and is available only for investigational use in the United States.[53]

Safety Issues and Concerns
Magnetic resonance imaging can affect the function of implantable and programmable medication delivery systems. There has been a report of the pump motor stalling and stopping delivery of the medication when it is exposed to the magnetic field. The pump resumed normal medication delivery after it was removed from the magnetic field. No damage to the mechanical or electrical components of the pump occurred; however, the authors of the report recommend that medication be removed from the pump before MRI tests. Following the procedure, the pump should be refilled and the medication delivery system tested.[51]

If a patient will be undergoing an x-ray, CT scan, MRI scan, or any other type of radiation therapy, patient instructions from an implantable insulin pump manufacturer recommend removing the external pump and remote control from the patient's body and the treatment area. In addition, avoid close exposure to medical imaging equipment. The patient should avoid using the monitor near other strong electromagnetic sources, such as television and radio transmitters and high-voltage power lines.[53]

Patient Management
Refer to General Patient Management.

Sacral Nerve Stimulators

Two treatment modalities currently are available for patients with dysfunction of the lower urinary tract.[54] Used only after more conservative therapies fail to produce positive results, a surgically implanted neurostimulator or sacral nerve stimulator may be a patient's last resort. Patients with spinal cord injuries have been treated successfully with posterior sacral nerve rhizotomies and placement of a nerve stimulator on the anterior sacral nerve roots.[54] Patients with chronic problems, such as urinary urge incontinence, nonobstructive urinary retention, urgency-frequency problems, problems with micturition, and neurogenic bladder, also have benefited from these devices.[54-56]

History and Current Applications

A device called the Finetech-Brindley bladder system was introduced and tested in baboons between 1969 and 1977.[27] This device provided intradural stimulation of the anterior sacral roots, which assisted with emptying the bladder.[54,56] The first human implantation occurred in 1976, but it was not until two years later that additional patients were successfully treated with nerve stimulation.[27]

Sacral nerve stimulation for treatment of overactive bladder conditions initially was developed in the late 1980s by Schmidt and Tanagho. The first of these implants were done in 1981.[27] The model used now was approved by the FDA in 1997.[55]

Currently, two devices are used to treat neurogenic bladder dysfunction.[27] One involves use of "mild electrical stimulation of the sacral nerve that influences the behavior of the bladder, sphincter, and pelvic floor muscles."[57] This device is used to treat urinary retention and to alleviate urinary urge incontinence and urgency-frequency symptoms of overactive bladder.[55] The second device works by initiating a contraction of the detrusor muscle.

Sacral nerve stimulators as therapy for urinary retention and urinary urge incontinence have been placed in about 10,000 patients. Sacral nerve stimulators that facilitate bladder emptying are less frequently implanted, totaling approximately 2,500 systems.[27(p76)]

These systems basically consist of three components. The first component is the pulse generator, which is battery-powered or controlled by an external portable control unit and programmed by a clinician.[56] The second component consists of electrodes placed intradurally or extradurally. The third component consists of the cables used to connect the pulse generator to the electrodes.[27]

Patient Management

Preoperative
- The perioperative nurse should follow the instructions of the neurostimulator's manufacturer. To prevent potential injury to the patient, it is important to determine exactly how the device producing the electrical stimulation works and how it may function during a surgical procedure to determine whether the device should be turned off during that time.[17]

Intraoperative
- Large, reusable, capacitive coupled return electrode systems should not be used.[17]
- The active electrode should be kept at least six inches from the implanted components of the device. This includes any cables, metallic electrodes, or leads, as well as the electrical components.[17]

Osteogenic Stimulators

Osteogenic (ie, bone-growth) stimulators are used to stimulate bone growth in patients with fresh fractures, to assist in healing postosteotomy, to stimulate grafted bone to vertebrae in spinal fusions, and for treatment of delayed fracture healing or nonunion following a fracture.[57] Implanted osteogenic stimulators deliver electrical impulses directly to the site where bone regrowth needs to occur. Types of bone-growth stimulators currently used include electrical, electromagnetic, and ultrasonic. These devices can be used invasively or noninvasively.

History and Current Application

In 1971, successful healing of a nonunion fracture with electrical stimulation was reported. The female patient had a nonhealing fracture of the medial malleolus for more than two years before it was healed successfully with direct current electrical stimulation.[58] Within the next five years, numerous investigators reposted the benefits of various types of electrical energy on bone growth in humans.[58] In 1979, the FDA approved the use of three types of electrical stimulation devices for treatment of long bone nonunion.[58]

The first clinical study on the benefits of electrical stimulation in lumbar spinal fusion was reported in 1974. During the next few years, implantable electrical stimulation devices were used with much success on both anterior and posterior spinal fusions and spinal fractures with nonunion.[58] The FDA approved use of electrical stimulators to be used as an adjunct treatment to spinal fusion in 1987.[59]

Electromagnetic fields typically are used as a noninvasive technique, and direct current electrical stimulation is used when invasive electrical stimulation is indicated.[60] Direct current stimulation involves surgical implantation of electrodes at the desired site for bone growth.[58,61] The negative electrode is placed at the site where bone repair is desired, and the positive electrode is place in nearby soft tissue. A generator is placed in nearby subcutaneous tissue or in an intermuscular plane.

Other techniques of electrical stimulation involve capacitive coupling and inductive coupling pulsed electromagnetic stimulation. These devices either are totally external devices or have a combination of implanted components and external components.[61]

Capacitive coupling for bone growth stimulation is delivered through two charged metal devices attached to a source of voltage that produces an electric field. This form of stimulation is delivered through external electrodes.[58,60]

Inductive coupling involves using single or double coils that deliver an electrical current from an external generator.[60,61] One inductive coupling bone healing system was introduced in 1979, and 300,000 patients have been treated using this system.[62]

Pulsing electromagnetic field therapy involves the use of time-varying current applied to metallic coils. These are applied to the desired treatment area and can be applied externally.[58]

Ultrasonic bone growth stimulators are external devices that apply pulsed ultrasound to the skin over the site of a fracture. This is the newest noninvasive technique and has the advantage that the treatment time may be as short as 20 to 30 minutes per day.

The electrodes and generator of a totally implantable device are made primarily of medical grade titanium containing a lithium battery.[58,63] A portion of one type of a spinal fusion system has a platinum coating.[63] These devices can produce continuous electrical stimulation for about six months.[63] The prevalence of spinal fusion systems is five people per 100,000 in Europe, North America, Australia, and Japan.[64(p904)]

Safety Issues and Concerns

One study measured temperature increases in the area of spinal fusion stimulators when MRI was performed. It was discovered that if a broken lead was present, the temperature was considerably higher than the temperature near an intact lead. This led to the recommendation that before MRI scanning is performed on a patient with a spinal fusion stimulator, it is important to make sure all spinal fusion stimulator leads are intact.[64]

Diathermy used over an area with an implanted bone growth stimulator can cause damage to the tissues surrounding the device or to the electronics of the device itself.[32] The magnetic external coils of a neurological IED should be kept to a minimum of 18 inches (45 cm) from bone growth stimulators.[36]

Patient Management

Preoperative

■ Externally worn spine stimulators should be removed before the surgical procedure.

Intraoperative

■ Electrosurgery should be avoided. Electrosurgical devices can produce radio frequency currents strong enough to cause direct coupling.[32] Direct coupling is the contact of an energized metal active electrode tip with another metal instrument or object within the surgical field.[16] When direct coupling occurs, the active electrode directly touches or comes very close to the implanted device, allowing the implanted device to become energized. This energy will seek a pathway to the return electrode. This could cause injury to the patient or damage to the implanted device.[32]

■ An ultrasonic scalpel is considered safe to use.[14]

■ Specific instructions on the totally implantable bone growth stimulation system specify when electrosurgery is necessary. Following implantation of this device, the electrode (ie, cathodenegative electrode) should remain connected, and the generator should be removed from the tissues and placed outside of the body until the procedure is completed. The generator should be replaced in the subcutaneous tissue at the end of the procedure.[65]

Gastric Electronic Stimulation

Electronic stimulation applied to appropriate areas in the body is beneficial in treating some disease processes that otherwise are difficult or impossible to treat with medication. Gastroparesis is an example of one such disease. Gastroparesis is characterized by delayed gastric emptying of solids without evidence of mechanical obstruction; it presents with nausea and early satiety in mild cases and chronic vomiting, dehydration, and weight loss in severe cases.[66] Gastric motility is controlled by myoelectric activity of the stomach, so abnormalities in gastric myoelectrical activity may result in gastric motility disorders, such as gastroparesis.[67]

Application of pacing techniques to the gastrointestinal tract is an attractive idea because the stomach, like the heart, has a natural pacemaker, and the myoelectric activity it generates may be entrained by electrical pacing.[67] In 1963, Bilgutay proposed the feasibility of using electrical stimulation in the gastrointestinal tract to treat paralytic ileus.[68] Using transluminal electrical stimulation via a nasogastric tube, researchers observed under fluoroscopy augmented gastric contractions and gastric emptying.[68] By the late 1960s and early 1970s, researchers conducted experiments that studied gastrointestinal myoelectric activity and its relationship with contractile activity. The results of these experiments, coupled with new techniques of recording myoelectric activity, gave rise to further research in gastrointestinal pacing.[68] Scientists today study the effects of varying the parameters of electrical stimulation applied to the wall of the stomach by an implanted device.

One IED derived from the research is the gastric electrical stimulation system. This type of therapy is indicated for the treatment of chronic nausea and vomiting associated with gastroparesis when conventional medication therapies are not providing adequate relief of symptoms for diabetic or idiopathic patients.[69] The components of a gastric electrical stimulation system include

- an implanted neurostimulator, usually surgically placed in the upper abdominal region;
- two intramuscular leads with electrodes that are implanted in the muscle wall of the stomach; and
- a programming device that the physician uses to control and adjust the settings of the neurostimulator.[69]

Patient management

Preoperative
■ The perioperative team should be aware of the manufacturer's written warnings and precautions. The system can affect cardiac pacemakers, cardioverters/defibrillators, external defibrillators, MRI, ultrasonic equipment, electrosurgery, and radiation therapy.[69]

Nursing Process Application

The perioperative nursing vocabulary is a clinically relevant and empirically validated standardized nursing language. It relates to the delivery of care in the perioperative setting. This standardized language consists of a collection of data elements (ie, the Perioperative Nursing Data Set [PNDS]) and includes perioperative nursing diagnoses, interventions, and outcomes.[70] In 1999, the PNDS was recognized by the American Nurses Association committee on nursing practice information infrastructure as a data set useful in the practice of nursing. The perioperative patient focused model provides the conceptual framework for the PNDS and the model for perioperative nursing practice. The patient and his or her family members are at the core of the model. The model depicts perioperative nursing in four domains and illustrates the relationship between the patient, family members, and the care provided by the perioperative professional nurse.

Each data element in the PNDS is represented by a unique identifier. The domains are represented by the letter "D," followed by numbers one to four to indicate the particular domain being addressed. Nursing diagnoses are represented by the letter "X" and a number unique to the diagnosis. Interventions are represented by the letter "I" and a unique number, and outcomes are represented by the letter "O" and a unique number. These designations are used in this document as appropriate.

Care of the patient must be individualized and appropriate to the specific device involved. Documentation should reflect the unique aspects of each patient's care. The PNDS provides a common language for perioperative nursing documentation. The examples listed below may not apply to all of the various IEDs. Each patient and device must be assessed for appropriate outcomes, nursing diagnoses, and interventions.

Domains

The following is a list of domains that may be associated with the patient undergoing surgical or other invasive procedures with an IED:

◆ D1—safety,
◆ D2—physiological responses, and
◆ D3-B—behavioral responses—patient and family: rights/ethics.[70]

Outcomes

The following is a partial list of nursing outcomes that may be associated with the patient undergoing surgical or other invasive procedures with an IED.

◆ O2—The patient is free from signs and symptoms of injury caused by extraneous objects.
◆ O4—The patient is free from signs and symptoms of electrical injury.
◆ O14—The patient's respiratory status is consistent with or improved from baseline levels established preoperatively.
◆ O15—The patient's cardiac status is consistent with or improved from baseline levels established preoperatively.
◆ O30—The patient's neurological status is consistent with or improved from baseline levels established preoperatively.
◆ O23—The patient participates in decision making affecting the perioperative plan of care.
◆ O24—The patient's care is consistent with the perioperative plan of care.[70]

Nursing Diagnoses

The following is a partial list of nursing diagnoses that may be associated with the patient undergoing surgical or other invasive procedures with an IED:

◆ X4—Anxiety;
◆ X28—Infection, risk for;
◆ X29—Injury, risk of;
◆ X30—Knowledge, deficient;
◆ X47—Sensory perception, disturbed;
◆ X56—Surgical recovery, delayed;
◆ X62—Urinary elimination, impaired;
◆ X64—Verbal communication, impaired;
◆ X72—Intracranial adaptive capacity, decreased; and
◆ X74—Pain, chronic.[70]

Interventions

The following is a partial list of nursing interventions that may be associated with the patient undergoing surgical or other invasive procedures with an IED.

◆ I3—Administers care to invasive device sites.
◆ I11—Applies safety devices.
◆ I30—Develops individualized plan of care.
◆ I37—Evaluates for signs and symptoms of electrical injury.
◆ I38—Evaluates for signs and symptoms of injury as a result of positioning.
◆ I44—Evaluates postoperative cardiac status.
◆ I45—Evaluates postoperative respiratory status.
◆ I46—Evaluates postoperative tissue perfusion.
◆ I47—Evaluates physiological response to plan of care.
◆ I54—Evaluates response to pain management interventions.
◆ I58—Identifies and reports the presence of implantable cardiac devices.
◆ I72—Implements protective measures to prevent injury due to electrical sources.
◆ I92—Obtains consultation from the appropriate health care providers to initiate new treatments or change existing treatments.
◆ I122—Uses supplies and equipment within safe parameters.
◆ I127—Verifies presence of prosthetics or corrective devices.
◆ I138—Implements protective measures prior to operative or invasive procedure.
◆ I145—Implements protective measures during neurosurgical procedures.
◆ I152—Evaluates for signs and symptoms of physical injury to skin and tissue.[70]

Conclusion

This guideline is intended to promote safe care for patients with IEDs who undergo surgical and other invasive procedures. Perioperative registered nurses should be aware of potential patient safety hazards associated with specific IEDs and the appropriate patient care interventions and resources required to protect patients from injury.

Perioperative registered nurses should be knowledgeable about the types of IEDs that may be encountered in the practice setting, how they function, and the precautions that must be taken when caring for patients with these devices. Competency related to specific devices should be measured and documented according to individual facility policy. It is AORN's intent that perioperative registered nurses use this document to assist in the development and implementation of policies and procedures for caring for patients with IEDs who are undergoing surgical and other invasive procedures.

REFERENCES

1. P Seifert, "Surgical interventions," in *Cardiac Surgery: Perioperative Patient Care* (St Louis: Mosby, Inc, 2002) 508-526.

2. "Sources of electromagnetic interference (EMI) for pacemakers, implantable cardioverter defibrillators (ICDs), and heart failure devices," Guidant, Inc, *http://www.guidant.com/patient/living* (accessed 14 Jan 2005).

3. J D Madigan et al, "Surgical management of the patient with an implanted cardiac device: Implications of electromagnetic interference," *Annals of Surgery* 230 (November 1999) 639-647.

4. *Mosby's Medical, Nursing & Allied Health Dictionary*, fifth ed (St Louis: Mosby-Year Book, Inc, 1998) 545.

5. "Electromagnetic interference (EMI)," Institute for Telecommunication Sciences, *http://www.its.bldrdoc.gov/fs-1037/dir-013/_1935.htm* (accessed 12 Nov 2004).

6. "InterStim therapy for urinary control: Product technical manual must be reviewed prior to use for detailed disclosure," Medtronic, Inc, *http://www.medtronic.com/neuro/interstim/interstim_warning.html* (accessed 12 Nov 2004).

7. "Safety alert (May 16, 2001)," Medtronic, Inc, *http://www.medtronic.com/neuro/diathermy_alert/alert_physicians.html* (accessed 12 Nov 2004).

8. D W Fiegal, Jr, "FDA public health notification: Diathermy interactions with implanted leads and implanted systems with leads," US Food and Drug Administration, *http://www.fda.gov/cdrh/safety/121902.pdf* (accessed 14 Jan 2005).

9. "Competency statements in perioperative nursing," in *Standards, Recommended Practices and Guidelines* (Denver: AORN, Inc, 2004) 19-21.

10. C J Linstrom, "Cochlear implantation: Practical information for the generalist," *Primary Care; Clinics in Office Practice* 25 (September 1998) 583-617.

11. "Perioperative management of implanted medical devices—Draft 2" (Williamsport, Pa: Susquehanna Health System, May 2004).

12. "Preadmission testing pacemaker or ICD letter" (Williamsport, Pa: Susquehanna Health System).

13. "AORN statement on the role of the health care industry representative in the operating room," in *Standards, Recommended Practices, and Guidelines* (Denver: AORN, Inc, 2004) 153-154.

14. "Electrosurgical precautions," in *University of Iowa Hospitals and Clinics Policy and Procedure Manual* (Iowa City: University of Iowa HealthCare, February 2004).

15. "MEGA 2000 and patients with pacemakers" (Draper, Utah: Megadyne Medical Products, Inc, 2004).

16. "Recommended practices for electrosurgery," in *Standards, Recommended Practices, and Guidelines* (Denver: AORN, Inc, 2004) 245-259.

17. C Peterson, "Rectifying counts; neurostimulators; double gloving; reprocessing single-use devices; simultaneous counting," (Clinical Issues) *AORN Journal* 76 (September 2002) 510-512.

18. L Rhyne, B C Ulmer, L Revell, "Monitoring and controlling the environment," in *Patient Care During Operative and Other Invasive Procedures*, ed M L Phippen, M P Wells (Philadelphia: W B Saunders Co, 2000) 147.

19. "HeartMate® destination therapy," Hearthope.com, *http://www.hearthope.com/1.html* (accessed 14 Jan 2005).

20. "Ventricular assist device," HeartCenterOnline for Patients, *http://heartcenteronline.com/myheartdr/common/articles.cfm?ARTID-340* (accessed 30 July 2004).

21. J E Lowe, J M Wharton, "Cardiac pacemakers and implantable cardioverter-defibrillators," in *Surgery of the Chest*, sixth ed, D C Sabiston, Jr, F C Spencer, eds (Philadelphia: W B Saunders Co, 1995).

22. M Mirowski et al, "Termination of malignant ventricular arrhythmias with an implanted automatic defibrillator in human beings," *The New England Journal of Medicine* 303 (Aug 7, 1980) 322-324.

23. J L Atlee, A D Bernstein, "Cardiac rhythm management devices (Part II): Perioperative management," *Anesthesiology* 95 (December 2001) 1492-1506.

24. S P Kutalek et al, "Approach to generator change," in *Clinical Cardiac Pacing and Defibrillation*, second ed, K A Ellenbogen, G N Kay, B L Wilkoff, eds (Philadelphia: W B Saunders Co, 2000) 645-668.

25. C M Bernards, "An unusual cause of airway obstruction during general anesthesia with a laryngeal mask airway," *Anesthesiology* 100 (April 2004) 1017-1018.

26. "History of neurostimulation: Part II: Implanted neuroaugmentive devices," The Burton Report, *http://www.burtonreport.com/InfSpine/NSHistNeurostimPartII_ImpNeuroAugmenDevices.htm* (accessed 12 Nov 2004).

27. N J M Rijkhoff, "Neuroprostheses to treat neurogenic bladder dysfunction: Current status and future perspectives," *Childs Nervous System* 20 no 2 (2004) 75-86.

28. H W Roberts, "The effect of electrical dental equipment on a vagus nerve stimulator's function," *Journal of the American Dental Association* 133 (December 2002) 1657-1664.

29. J Weaver, S J Kim, A Torres, "Cutaneous electrosurgery in a patient with a deep brain stimulator," *Dermatologic Surgery* 25 (May 1999) 415-417.

30. "Electrical stimulation in spinal cord injury," International Functional Electrical Stimulation Society, *http://www.ifess.org/Services/Consumer_Ed/SCI.htm* (accessed 14 Jan 2005).

31. "Introduction to neurostimulation," Medtronic, *http://www.medtronic.com/neuro/paintherapies/pain_treatment_ladder/neurostimulation/neuroneurostimulation.html* (accessed 16 Aug 2004).

32. "Bone growth stimulation: Questions and answers," Spine Universe.com, *http://www.spineuniverse.com/displayaritcle.php/article1555.html* (accessed 13 Aug 2004).

33. *Patient's Manual for Vagus Nerve Stimulation with the VNS Therapy™ System* (Houston: Cyberonics, Inc, 2002).

34. C A Liberante, "New relief for constant condition," York Neurosurgical Associates, *http://www.yna.org/new%20pages/YDRhydro.html* (accessed 12 Nov 2004).

35. E Eisenberg, H Waisbrod, "Spinal cord stimulator activation by an antitheft device: Case report," *Journal of Neurosurgery* 87 (December 1997) 961-962.

36. *Deep Brain Stimulation MRI Guidelines* (Minneapolis: Medtronic, April 2002) 1-14.

37. S Roberts et al, "Impact of dental devices on cochlear implants," *Journal of Endodontics* 28 (January 2002) 40.

38. "Cochlear implants: Wiring for sound," Australian Academy of Science, *http://www.science.org.au/nova/029/029key.htm* (accessed 14 Jan 2005).

39. G A Gates, R T Miyamoto, "Cochlear implants," *The New England Journal of Medicine* 349 (July 31, 2003) 421-423.

40. A J Maniglia, "State of the art on the development of the implantable hearing device for partial hearing loss," *Otolaryngologic Clinics of North America* 29 (April 1996) 225-243.

41. J M Black, J Hokanson-Hawks, A Keene, "Assist hearing in profound deafness," in *Medical-Surgical Nursing*, sixth ed (Philadelphia: W B Saunders Co, 2001) 1840-1841.

42. D R McEwen, "Otologic surgery," in *Alexander's Care of the Patient in Surgery*, 12th ed, J C Rothrock, ed (St Louis: Mosby, 2003) 717-749.

43. "Bone-anchored hearing aid," Hear-it, *http://hear-it.org/printpage.dsp?printable=yes&page=2020* (accessed 14 Jan 2005).

44. M Kalamarides et al, "Hearing restoration with auditory brainstem implants after radiosurgery for neurofibromatosis Type 2," *Journal of Neurosurgery* 95 (December 2001) 1028-1033.

45. "New device approvals—Nucleus 24 auditory brainstem implant system," US Food and Drug Administration, Center for Devices and Radiological Health, *http://www.fda.gov/cdrh/pdf/p000015.html* (accessed 22 Aug 2004).

46. S C Smeltzer, B G Bare, "Sensorineural function," in *Brunner and Suddarth's Textbook of Medical Surgical Nursing* (Philadelphia: Lippincott, Williams and Wilkins, 2004) 1744.

47. "Proposed package insert," US Food and Drug Administration, Center for Devices and Radiological Health, *http://www.fda.gov/cdrh/pdf/p000015.html* (accessed 22 Aug 2004).

48. "Is electrosurgery safe for patients with internal or external electronic devices?" *Clinical Information Hotline News* 6 (December 2001) 1-2. Also available at *http://www.valleylab.com/displaynews.cfm?articlepageid=380&menu* (accessed 12 Nov 2004).

49. M Goodman "Chemotherapy: Principles of administration," in *Cancer Nursing*, fifth ed, C H Yarbro et al, ed (Boston: Jones and Bartlett Publishers, 2000) 407-408.

50. N H Fortunato, ed, *Berry & Kohn's Operating Room Technique*, 10th ed (St. Louis: Mosby, Inc, 2004) 114-116.

51. "The Medtronic Mini-Med 2007 implantable insulin pump system," Medtronic, *http://www.minimed.com/patientfam/pf_products_implantpump_noneu.shtml* (accessed 12 Nov 2004).

52. "How pump therapy works," Medtronic, *http://www.minimed.com/patientfam/pf_ipt_ptov_how therapyworks.shtml* (accessed 12 Nov 2004).

53. "Safety information: Medtronic MiniMed," Medtronic, *http://www.minimed.com/common/safety.html* (accessed 12 Nov 2004).

54. P E V van Kerrebroeck, "The role of electrical stimulation in voiding dysfunction," *European Urology* 34 suppl (1998) 27-30.

55. "InterStim therapy for urinary control: Product technical manual must be reviewed prior to use for detailed disclosure," Medtronic, Inc, *http://www.medtronic.com/neuro/interstim/interstim_warning.html* (accessed 12 Nov 2004).

56. J R Vignes et al, "Dorsal rhizotomy with anterior sacral root stimulation for neurogenic bladder," *Stereotactic and Functional Neurosurgery* 76 no 3-4 (2001) 243-245.

57. "The challenge: Treating selected bladder control problems and improving outcomes," Medtronic, *http://www.medtronic.com/neuro/interstim/solution.html* (accessed 12 Nov 2004).

58. M Oishi, S T Onesti, "Electrical bone graft stimulation for spinal fusion: A review," *Neurosurgery* 47 (November 2000) 1041-1055.

59. J Soyhan et al, "Demography, clinical characteristics, psychological and abuse profiles, treatment, and long-term follow-up of patients with gastroparesis," *Digestive Diseases and Sciences* 43 (November 1998) 2398-2404.

60. J T Ryaby, "Clinical effects of electromagnetic and electric fields on fracture healing," *Clinical Orthopedics and Related Research* 355 suppl (October 1998) S205-S215.

61. R K Aaron, D M Ciombor, B J Simon, "Treatment of nonunions with electric and electromagnetic fields," *Clinical Orthopedics* 419 (February 2004) 21-29.

62. "Frequently asked questions," EBI Medical, *http://www.ebimedical.com/patients/faq.cfm* (accessed 12 Nov 2004).

63. "Products: Spine systems—Spine fusion stimulators," EBI Medical, *http://www.ebimedical.com/products/index.cfm?s=0E* (accessed 12 Nov 2004).

64. W Kainz et al, "Electromagnetic compatibility of electronic implants—Review of the literature," *Wiener Klinische Wochenschrift* 113 (Dec 17, 2001) 903-914.

65. "EBI Bone Healing System," EBI Medical, *http://www.ebimedical.com/products/detail.cfm?p=0C* (accessed 12 Nov 2004).

66. K Hornbuckle, J L Barnett, "The diagnosis and work-up of the patient with gastroparesis," *Journal of Clinical Gastroenterology* 30 (March 2000) 117-124.

67. Z Lin et al, "Treatment of gastroparesis with electrical stimulation," *Digestive Diseases and Sciences* 48 (May 2003) 837-848.

68. A M Bilgutay et al, "Gastro-intestinal pacing: A new concept in the treatment of ileus," *Annals of Surgery* 158 (September 1963) 338-348.

69. "Safety information on Enterra therapy," Medtronic, *http://www.medtronic.com/neuro/gastro/indications use.html#enterra* (14 Jan 2005).

70. S Beyea, ed, *Perioperative Nursing Data Set*, second ed (Denver: AORN, Inc, 2002).

Originally published in *Standards, Recommended Practices, and Guidelines,* 2005 edition. Reprinted July 2005, *AORN Journal.*

Exhibit A: Care of the Patient
With an Implanted Electronic Device

IMPLANTED DEVICE	SAFETY CONCERN	PREOPERATIVE PATIENT MANAGEMENT	INTRAOPERATIVE PATIENT MANAGEMENT	POSTOPERATIVE PATIENT MANAGEMENT
All implanted devices				
	Electrosurgery	Assess patients for the presence of any implanted electronic device (IED). Check for a product identification card if an IED is present. Contact the implanting surgeon to inform him or her that the patient is scheduled for surgery. Obtain and document ♦ manufacturer and model of IED, ♦ location of the device, ♦ when the device was last evaluated, ♦ if the device can be turned off before or during surgery, ♦ settings that should be reprogrammed into the device immediately after the procedure, ♦ if the implanting physician wants to be contacted when the patient enters the postanesthesia care unit, and ♦ if the patient needs to schedule an appointment with the implanting physician. Determine if electrosurgery and/or defibrillation is necessary Contact the appropriate health care industry representative and arrange for his or her presence before, during, and after the surgery if requested by the physician. Notify the anesthesia care provider that an IED is present.	Notify all perioperative team members the patient has an IED in place and review safety concerns and equipment conflicts. Be sure the programming device and qualified programming personnel are in the OR before starting the procedure. Suggest the use of a bipolar electrosurgical unit (ESU). Place the dispersive electrode as far from the IED as possible, maintaining a perpendicular pathway for the current to travel and making sure it is not over an implant and the current does not go through the IED. Do not arc current between the active electrode and another surgical instrument. If the IED has been reprogrammed by electrosurgery, stop the procedure and reprogram the device. Maintain the OR temperature between 20° C and 24° C (68° F and 76° F) and humidity between 50% and 60%.	If necessary, notify the implanting physician and/or the health care industry representative that electrosurgery or defibrillation was used during surgery. Early in the postoperative period, do an evaluation of IED function similar to that performed before surgery. Postoperatively, monitor the patient closely for signs of complications and IED malfunction.
	Defibrillation		For patients with IEDs in the chest area who require defibrillation, use anterior-posterior-type paddles. Place the anterior paddle as far from the pulse generator as possible. Use the lowest defibrillator current setting possible.	

2009 Perioperative Standards and Recommended Practices
Last revised: November 2005. © AORN, Inc. All rights reserved.

IMPLANTED DEVICE	SAFETY CONCERN	PREOPERATIVE PATIENT MANAGEMENT	INTRAOPERATIVE PATIENT MANAGEMENT	POSTOPERATIVE PATIENT MANAGEMENT
Cardiac				
Pacemakers Implantable cardioverter defibrillators (ICDs)	Electrosurgery	1. If the IED has not been evaluated during the previous 6 months, it should be tested for programming, telemetry, thresholds, and battery status. 2. If the make and model of IED is not known, a chest x-ray may be helpful in identifying it. 3. The device should be reprogrammed to an asynchronous mode. 4. Adaptive-rate device features should be programmed off. 5. Magnet-activated testing should be programmed off.	1. The current pathway should be perpendicular to the pacemaker's lead system when possible. 2. The ESU may interfere with electrocardiogram (ECG) monitoring of the heart, so the heart rate and blood pressure (BP) should be monitored through an arterial line. When the ESU is not in use, the ECG should be checked for arrhythmias or alterations in pacemaker function. 3. If it is impossible to place the device in an asynchronous mode, and the ESU is adversely affecting the pacemaker, the ESU current should only be activated for 1 second at a time. Ten seconds should elapse between 1-second activations. 4. Bipolar ESU is recommended. 5. Tachycardia sensing should be programmed off.	1. Inform the patient's cardiologist or cardiothoracic surgeon that ESU or defibrillation was used during surgery. 2. An evaluation of the pacemaker and ICD function should be done in the early postoperative period and again at 24 and 48 hours.
	Defibrillation		1. Position paddles at least 6 inches from the device. 2. Place paddles in the anterior and posterior position. 3. The lowest defibrillator current settings should be used. 4. Have a temporary pacing system available in case of pulse generator damage.	

Care of the Patient With an IED

IMPLANTED DEVICE	SAFETY CONCERN	PREOPERATIVE PATIENT MANAGEMENT	INTRAOPERATIVE PATIENT MANAGEMENT	POSTOPERATIVE PATIENT MANAGEMENT
Cardiac, continued				
Ventricular assist device (VAD)	Electrosurgery	1. If IED has not been evaluated within the previous 6 months, it should be tested for programming, telemetry, thresholds, and battery status. 2. If the make and model of the IED is not known, a chest x-ray may be helpful in identifying it.	1. The ESU may interfere with ECG monitoring of the heart, so the heart rate and BP should be monitored through an arterial line. When the ESU is not in use, the ECG should be checked for arrhythmias or alterations in pacemaker function. 2. The device should be placed in the fixed rate mode for the duration of the surgery. 3. The ESU current should only be activated for 1 second at a time. Ten seconds should elapse between 1-second activations. 4. Cardiac output should be monitored. 5. Have an external hand pump available in the OR.	1. Inform the patient's cardiologist or cardio-thoracic surgeon that ESU or defibrillation was used during surgery. 2. The surgeon or cardiologist responsible for the care of the patient should be informed if the circuit is damaged during surgery. Repair or replacement should be considered.
	Defibrillation		1. Disconnect the timing circuit from the external controller before defibrillation 2. Depending on the type of VAD, a fixed rate mode may be required during defibrillation.	
Neurological				
Deep brain stimulators Programmable ventricular shunts Spinal cord stimulators Vagal nerve stimulators	Electrosurgery	1. Magnetic resonance imaging is not recommended.	1. Bipolar ESU is recommended. 2. The device should be turned off. Notify the appropriate vendor representative. 3. Use only low voltage mode/setting. 4. Keep the grounding pad as far away from the device as possible.	1. Perioperative team members should confirm that the device is functioning properly.
	Defibrillation		1. Position paddles as far away from the IED as possible. 2. Position paddles perpendicular to the IED. 3. Use the lowest output settings.	
	Magnetic resonance imaging (MRI)		1. Magnetic resonance imaging is not recommended.	
	Bone growth stimulator		1. Keep magnetic external coils of a neurological IED a minimum of 18 inches (45 cm) away from bone growth stimulators.	
	Dental drills Ultrasonic probes Diagnostic ultrasound Electrolysis		1. Turn the device off. 2. Keep 6 inches away from device.	

IMPLANTED DEVICE	SAFETY CONCERN	PREOPERATIVE PATIENT MANAGEMENT	INTRAOPERATIVE PATIENT MANAGEMENT	POSTOPERATIVE PATIENT MANAGEMENT
Neurological, continued				
	Lasers		1. Turn the device off. 2. Keep lasers directed away from the device.	
Implantable hearing devices				
Cochlear implants Auditory brainstem implant (ABI) Bone-conduction stimulators	Static electricity	1. Educate patients and staff members that a static electric shock has been known to inactivate cochlear implants.	1. Educate patients and staff members that a static electric shock has been known to inactivate cochlear implants.	1. Perioperative team members should confirm that the device is functioning properly.
	Electrosurgery		1. Bipolar ESU is recommended. 2. Bipolar instruments should be kept more than 10 cm from extracochlear electrodes. 3. Monopolar ESU should not be used in the head and neck area. 4. For patients with ABIs, the bipolar electrode should be kept 1 cm from the ground electrodes of the ABI.	
	MRI	1. Magnetic resonance imaging is not recommended and should only be done if it is a medical necessity.	1. Magnetic resonance imaging is not recommended and should only be done if it is a medical necessity.	
	Miscellaneous		1. Remove external devices after induction of anesthesia. 2. Avoid using ionizing radiation directly over the site of the implant.	
Implantable infusion pumps				
	MRI	1. Magnetic resonance imaging may cause the device to malfunction. 2. Remove the external pump and remote control from the patient's body and the treatment area. 3. Avoid exposure to medical imaging equipment.	1. Remove the external pump and remote control from the patient's body and the treatment area. 2. Avoid exposure to medical imaging equipment.	
	X-ray	1. Remove the external pump and remote control from the patient's body and the treatment area.		

Care of the Patient With an IED

IMPLANTED DEVICE	SAFETY CONCERN	PREOPERATIVE PATIENT MANAGEMENT	INTRAOPERATIVE PATIENT MANAGEMENT	POSTOPERATIVE PATIENT MANAGEMENT
Sacral nerve stimulators				
	Miscellaneous	1. Determine how the device functions and whether it can be turned off.	1. The ESU active electrode should be kept 6 inches from the implanted device.	
Osteogenic (bone-growth) stimulators				
	MRI	1. Before imaging, the stimulator should be tested to make sure all leads are intact.		
	Miscellaneous	1. Externally worn stimulators should be removed before the surgical procedure.		
	Electrocautery		1. Monopolar ESU is not recommended. 2. Ultrasonic scalpel is considered safe. 3. Electrodes should remain connected. 4. The generator should be removed from subcutaneous tissues and placed outside of the body until the procedure is complete.	
Gastric electronic stimulation				
	Miscellaneous	1. Review manufacturers' written warnings and precautions. 2. Devices can affect other IEDs. 3. Device is affected by MRI, ultrasonic equipment, ESU, and radiation therapy.		

AORN Guidance Statement:
Mass Casualty, Triage, and Evacuation

Introduction

This document is intended as a guide for perioperative registered nurses who are developing processes to facilitate a methodical response to disaster situations. This guidance statement may be used by health care organizations in developing policies and procedures related to responding to natural and man-made disasters and correlating hospital-wide disaster plans with specific perioperative challenges. This guidance statement addresses mass casualty, triage, and evacuation as it relates to the perioperative setting.

AORN recognizes that a health care facility's disaster plan, while required by accrediting and state agencies, may not include situational challenges specific to the perioperative setting during a disaster response. AORN also recognizes that the perioperative setting and available resources are varied and dependent on geographic location, ranging from large metropolitan trauma centers, ambulatory surgery centers, and specialty centers for invasive procedures (eg, cardiac catheterization laboratories, endoscopy suites, radiology departments) to small rural health care facilities.

Background

Perioperative registered nurses experience daily schedule changes based on staffing, supplies, and the emergent status of surgical patients and procedures. In recent years, however, these schedule changes have involved more than this. The terrorist attacks of Sept 11, 2001, and the 2005 hurricane disasters in the southeastern United States have challenged perioperative registered nurses to adapt to and overcome difficult new situations.

Perioperative registered nurses must be prepared to handle local and regional casualties from man-made disasters (eg, biological, chemical, nuclear attacks) to natural disasters (eg, hurricanes, tornadoes, earthquakes, fire). Hospitals should have a disaster plan that is accessible to all members of the surgical team. New employees and members of the staff should be familiar with the disaster plan. Updates should be incorporated as new information is acquired and shared with the surgical team.

Traditionally, hospital disaster drills involve a community disaster, such as a mass casualty automobile or airplane accident or hazardous waste spill. Disas-

ter "patients" are triaged and "tagged" for disposition to various hospital departments. Those tagged for "surgery" are shown to the lounge to relax until the disaster scenario is completed. The question now has become: "How do you prepare for the worst, when the 'worst' may be unknown?"

The world in which we live has changed. An approaching disaster can occur at any time, in any place. There may be warnings (eg, hurricanes), or it may come unexpectedly (eg, terrorist attack). Disasters are not selective and can affect any department in the hospital. The Joint Commission on Accreditation of Healthcare Organizations (JCAHO) modified its disaster preparedness standards in 2003 to include requirements for health care facilities to develop disaster plans that include identifying, preparing for, responding to, and recovering from potential disasters.[1] In 2003, the US Department of Health and Human Services (HHS) National Center for Health Statistics conducted a survey that revealed 97.3% of the hospitals that participated were in compliance with disaster plans for responding to natural disasters. The survey also revealed that 75% of the hospitals had plans for chemical, biological, and nuclear incidents, as well as for incidents involving bombs. Hospitals conducting disaster drills involved natural disaster scenarios 69% of the time, while only 27% involved scenarios of weapons of mass destruction. Less than 60% of the hospitals surveyed had contingency plans for obtaining critical supplies, including pharmaceuticals, during a disaster.[2]

It is imperative that a hospital's disaster plan and drills include scenarios that involve the surgery department. Incidents such as flooding, loss of electricity, and fire also need to be part of the planning. Perioperative registered nurses are resourceful and flexible. Their skills, from basic nursing assessment skills to handling advanced surgical technology, can support many aspects of the disaster planning, response, and recovery.

Guidance Statement

Mass Casualty

The US Agency for Healthcare Research and Quality (AHRQ) defines a mass casualty event (MCE) as "an act of bioterrorism or other public health or medical emergency involving thousands, or even tens of thousands, of victims."[3] It is imperative for the perioperative registered nurse to be knowledgeable about his or her health care organization's disaster preparedness plan and ability to provide safe, quality care for patients, family members, and staff members, because disasters and other emergency events can strike with an unexpected and devastating force. Mass casualty templates should be developed and disseminated in all health care settings. They should include, but not be limited to,

- an emergency management task force committee that includes a member from each hospital department;[4,5]
- a plan to coordinate with outside agencies before, during, and after an MCE;[4,6]
- a reliable internal and external communication protocol within the facility;[6,7,8]
- a command center within the facility that can be activated when emergencies occur to provide responses that are organized for the whole facility;[6,3]
- clinical care protocols to include triage, patient care, patient flow, patient tracking, and evacuation plans;
- adequate security protocols;[6,8]
- appropriate staffing to meet emergency needs and to continue to maintain current patient care;[5,8]
- supplies and equipment lists that incorporate possible prolonged demands;[6,8]
- adequate training of all staff members to enable them to respond to MCE emergencies;[6,7]
- MCE drills to be scheduled at least twice a year for hospitals and ambulatory surgery centers with a real emergency or a prearranged drill;[6,7]
- decontamination and containment protocols;[3,6,7] and
- checklists/tool kits for each department.[6,3]

Using the experiences in past MCEs, the Centers for Disease Control and Prevention (CDC) found that there are patterns that involve the use of hospitals. The CDC developed a mass casualty predictor that can be a very useful tool in determining casualty volume and patterns following an MCE. Research by the CDC revealed patterns experienced by hospitals participating in an MCE and demonstrated the following.

- Ninety minutes after an MCE, 50% to 80% of acute casualties that will arrive are at the health care facility nearest the incident. Hospitals farther from that area may receive very few or no casualties.

- Individuals who are not severely injured may leave the scene on their own and go to the closest health care facility. They may not be triaged at the scene by emergency medical services, and these individuals often arrive at the health care facility before the most severely injured patients.
- It may take three to six hours, on average, for casualties to be taken care of in an emergency department.

After an MCE, casualties present quickly; about half of the casualties arrive at the health care facility within one hour of the event. Important points to remember include

- doubling the number of casualties that arrive within the first hour to assist the health care facility in predicting the total number of casualties the facility will receive from the MCE, and
- beginning the one-hour window when the first casualty arrives.[9]

Triage

Triage, as it pertains to the surgical management of casualties from emergencies and disasters, is defined as "the system for prioritization of patients requiring surgical management based on severity of injury, while using available resources for optimal outcome." The word triage originates from the French verb trier, meaning "to sort." Triage was developed during the time of Napoleon to provide rapid evaluation and evacuation of wounded patients who could be treated. The US military adopted a four-tiered system of casualty triage during the Korean War. By the Vietnam War, the mortality rate of wounded soldiers decreased from 4.7% to 1%, primarily "due to the advances in rapid triage and transport."[10]

Today, the goal for triage is to accomplish the greatest good for the greatest number of casualties in emergent situations. Using their assessment and thorough planning skills during realistic drills, perioperative registered nurses can identify available resources required to effectively triage surgical casualties for optimal survival of the majority of patients. All nurses should have basic nursing knowledge and the ability to respond to an MCE. Educational competencies for responding to an MCE should be in place to validate preparedness. Competencies may include

- critical clinical judgment skills (eg, able to make decisions; determine event needs; plan and care for individuals, family, or community);

♦ assessment skills for individuals or a group of individuals who have injuries resulting from chemical, biological, radiological, nuclear, or incendiary incidents;

♦ technical skills to care for an individual or groups of patients;

♦ communication skills appropriate for emergency situations for individuals, families, media, and first responders;

♦ knowledge and the ability to keep in perspective health issues that may be prevalent in the community;

♦ ability to apply knowledge of language and processes used for MCEs;

♦ ability to demonstrate an understanding of the legal, ethical, and regulatory ramifications present during an MCE;

♦ knowledge of containment and decontamination; and

♦ ability to discuss comprehensive community response to an MCE based on cultural, spiritual, and social issues.[11]

There should be an emphasis on the need to establish systems that can render triage treatment and initial stabilization within three hours of an MCE for a specified number of casualties above the daily bed capacity for a health care facility.[6] Unfortunately there remains no clear guidance for initial surgical triage in the field with a coordinated system at an incident command center or for segregation of surgical casualties to different hospitals, based on surgical surge capacity. This preferred system would maximize community resources (ie, available neurosurgical, thoracic, abdominal, orthopedic, or other surgical specialty resources) for optimal survival of the greatest number of casualties requiring immediate surgical intervention.

Development of a comprehensive surgical management plan for casualties is essential for improved outcomes. Prioritizing surgical patients is essential, and a standard system should be used to facilitate effective communication at the incident scene among all caregivers. Health care facilities should establish a system of patient prioritization for triage based on the CDC's color coding or other triage-scoring systems for surgical patients with categories (eg, red = critical or emergent needing immediate surgical care; yellow = semicritical or delayed, needing surgical care within 6 to 8 hours).[10] Developing policies for effective communication of surgical triage is important to meet a facility's immediate surgical capacity (eg, triage tags, tracking

system). Instructing caregivers to complete competencies for surgical triage training is imperative as extensive literature review documents the occurrence of repeated incidents of inexperienced staff members unable to adequately triage casualties during drills.[12]

Creating a surgical plan and involving multidisciplinary caregivers (eg, surgeons; nursing staff members; laboratory, radiology, anesthesia, security, admissions, decontamination team personnel) should include

♦ identifying surgical surge capacity (eg, two neurosurgery red cases, four general abdominal red cases, one open chest red case, two obstetric trauma red cases, two pediatric red cases, four orthopedic red cases, 14 delayed yellow cases) based on available resources;

♦ creating easy-to-follow, laminated trauma case cards as guides for trauma procedures with required equipment and supplies listed;

♦ establishing training modalities, to include both "tabletop" and actual drills, with documentation of competencies that include measurable outcomes. (Two practice scenarios are provided in **Exhibit A**.) Some data exist regarding the ineffectiveness of tabletop drills when compared to actual drills, but more research is warranted to validate this.[12]

Evaluation of resources required for the surgical emergency management plan is vital for the execution of the plan. Numerous disaster drills identifying critical deficiencies in resources for the numbers of presenting casualties have been documented in the literature.[6] Planning needs include

♦ adequate space available to conduct initial assessments and triage for surgical patients;

♦ determining availability of ORs (eg, plan for preoperative, intraoperative, and postoperative placement of casualties);

♦ monetary resources available through annual budget planning and acquisition;

♦ sufficient staffing to meet immediate surgical surge capacity;

♦ required equipment, instrumentation, and supplies;

♦ availability of immediate blood and blood products; and

♦ estimation of maximum output (ie, surgical caseload) before resupply is needed.

The health care facility should use outcome determinations for the triage of surgical patients that have been measured using the historical data of past events and drills, which include categorizing casualties as over-triaged and under-triaged patients.[12] Post-event outcomes should be analyzed and variations to the emergency plan considered for future events. Patients, community members, and staff members all need to be considered when evaluating outcomes.

Nurses should evaluate patients' individual situations for adequate discharge planning to ensure that they have appropriate care and facilities for recuperation upon discharge. There also should be a system to ensure that counseling for posttraumatic stress disorder and other psychiatric issues is available. Community resources also need to be available for support, rebuilding, and recovery. The facilities and agencies involved in providing these services should be accessible to provide feedback to the various emergency agencies.

It is important to have several levels of input from staff members to evaluate the outcome from emergency situations. Debriefing sessions are highly effective and often are used to assist staff members in voicing concerns and identifying positive issues, and for offering closure on stressful situations. Post-incident counseling may be necessary for staff members.

Troubleshooting different areas of concern is necessary to avoid similar concerns in the future. Even if it is not possible to address every situation, care should be taken to focus on the ones that do present and to revise the emergency plan as needed. Resuming routine functions is the main goal of recovery. Rescheduling cancelled elective surgical procedures and restocking supplies are necessary for a return to customary roles and activities.[13]

Evacuation

A facility evacuation plan is an essential component of emergency management. It is imperative that health care facilities be compliant with plans for vertical and horizontal evacuation of patients in the event they cannot sustain safe and appropriate patient care.[14,15] Fires (internal or external), earthquakes, floods, hurricanes, utility outages, human threats, and spilling of hazardous materials (internal or external) are examples of incidents that may necessitate a facility-wide evacuation.[16] Strategies that should be addressed include, but are not limited to the following.

♦ Determine the type of patient population and consider the special resources needed to evacuate to an appropriate receiving facility.[14] The facility chosen may not be the closest, but if possible it should have the available resources for the patient population being evacuated.[17]

♦ Identify patient needs during transfer (eg, basic life support, advanced cardiac life support, trained care providers), mode of transportation (eg, ambulance, helicopter, bus, private car), and evacuation routes.[16]

♦ Provide supervision of health care team members for safe use of supplies and equipment during patient evacuation to areas of safety.[14]

♦ Initiate a multidisciplinary transport team comprising nurses, physicians, and ancillary personnel to move patients safely to awaiting land or air transportation.[17]

♦ Provide properly trained staff members who can respond appropriately to clear and specific directions when evacuation orders are received, including approximate time of departure.[14]

♦ Prepare patients' medical records and medications for the transport process.[14]

♦ Maintain effective communication between affected facility and receiving facility to ensure patient care continuity.[13,14,17]

♦ Initiate a system that has flashlights with functioning batteries available on nursing units and stairway lights and exit signs that also are functioning.

♦ Provide paper documentation reflecting activities pre-, intra-, and post-patient transfer that can be used in an emergent situation.[17]

♦ Ensure that the affected health care facility has a plan in place to provide patient care outside if receiving hospitals become overwhelmed with patient influx or sustain damage in a natural disaster.[18]

♦ Maintain a master log of all patients evacuated; include receiving health care facility, patient name, date of birth, hospital number, physician name, and admission date.[15,17]

♦ Equipment sent with patients must be tracked to ensure return.[17]

Types of evacuation. To facilitate the evacuation process, periodic assessments should be done so there are no obstructions blocking exits, doors, corridors, and stairways.

♦ Horizontal evacuation is used to move patients to the closest safe area on the same floor.[14]

♦ Vertical evacuation is used to move patients to a safe lower level or down a flight(s) of stairs when the horizontal method is thought to pose a danger to the patients.[14]

♦ Total evacuation is used to move patients to receiving health care facilities or areas outside the affected institution.[14]

Order of patient evacuation. Staff members should assemble ambulatory patients together and designate one or more staff members to lead patients to the designated safe area.[14] When evacuating nonambulatory patients (eg, those who are wheelchair-bound or who have mobility deficits or critical care needs), staff members should use appropriate evacuation techniques (eg, sliding patient on bath blanket or mattress, one- or two-person carries, use of back boards or canvas stretchers).[19]

Critical care patients need to be prioritized from least to most critical. Three- to four-member extraction teams, including a nurse and respiratory therapist, may be necessary to evacuate critical care patients.[20] The following items, in addition to others as determined by the facility, should be assessed and available when evacuating critical care patients:

♦ patient assessment (ie, vital signs, IV lines, airways) by health care team member(s);

♦ patient weight;

♦ stability;

♦ minimizing equipment needed (eg, ambu bag rather than a ventilator);[10]

♦ oxygen tanks and portable suction apparatus;[20,21]

♦ transport monitors;

♦ consolidation of medication pumps;[21]

♦ emergency medications;[18] and

♦ ease of movement in stairwells.[20]

Evacuation plans should be in place and scenarios for evacuation should be used to develop staff member consistency and comfort in the evacuation process for each health care facility.

Summary

Disasters are not expected, but they do occur. Perioperative teams must be prepared to implement disaster plans before a disaster occurs. Planning and preparation, including drills and knowledge of the disaster plan, will serve the health care facility and the community well in preventing increased morbidity and mortality. The ability of health care personnel to anticipate and respond to disasters is important in successfully managing emergent events.

REFERENCES

1. "2006 hospital standards for emergency management planning, emergency management drills, infection control, disaster privileges," Joint Commission on Accreditation of Healthcare Organizations, *http://www .jointcommission.org/NR/rdonlyres/F42AF828-7248- 48C0-B4E6-BA18E719A87C/0/06_hap_accred_stds.pdf* (accessed 3 Nov 2006).

2. R W Niska, C W Burt, "Bioterrorism and mass casualty preparedness in hospitals: United States, 2003," Centers for Disease Control and Prevention, National Center for Health Statistics, *http://www.cdc.gov/nchs /data/ad/ad364.pdf* (accessed 3 Nov 2006).

3. "Training of hospital staff to respond to a mass casualty incident: Evidence report/technology assessment, number 95," Agency for Healthcare Research and Quality, *http://www.ahrq.gov/downloads/pub/evidence /pdf/hospmci/hospmci.pdf* (accessed 3 Nov 2006).

4. R W Perry, M K Lindell, "Hospital planning for weapons of mass destruction incidents," (Symposium) *Journal of Postgraduate Medicine* 52 (April/June 2006) 116-120.

5. ECRI, "Disaster planning and response: Guidance for healthcare facilities," *Health Devices* 34 (September 2005) 293-304.

6. Joint Commission on Accreditation of Healthcare Organizations, *Comprehensive Accreditation Manual for Hospitals: The Official Handbook* (Oakbrook Terrace, Ill: Joint Commission on Accreditation of Healthcare Organizations, 2006) EC: 13-16.

7. Joint Commission on Accreditation of Healthcare Organizations, *Comprehensive Accreditation Manual for Ambulatory Care* (Oakbrook Terrace, Ill: Joint Commission on Accreditation of Healthcare Organizations, 2005-2006) EC: 1-14

8. Joint Commission on Accreditation of Healthcare Organizations, *Standing Together: An Emergency Planning Guide for America's Communities* (Oakbrook Terrace, Ill: Joint Commission on Accreditation of Healthcare Organizations, 2005)1-106.

9. "Emergency preparedness and response: Mass casualty predictor," Centers for Disease Control and Prevention, *http://www.bt.cdc.gov/masscasualties/predictor .asp* (accessed 3 Nov 2006).

10. D B Wiseman, R Ellenbogen, C I Shaffrey, "Triage for the neurosurgeon," *Neurosurgery Focus* 12 (March 2002) 1-4.

11. "Educational competencies for registered nurses responding to mass casualty incidents," International Nursing Coalition for Mass Causality Education, July 2003. *http://www.incmce.org/competenciespage.html* (accessed 3 Nov 2006).

12. E B Hsu et al, "Effectiveness of hospital staff mass-casualty incident training methods: A systematic literature review," *Prehospital and Disaster Medicine* 19 (July/September 2004) 191-199.

13. J E Eiland, D Pritchard, D A Stevens, "Emergency preparedness—Is your OR ready?" *AORN Journal* 79 (June 2004) 1276-1283.

14. Joint Commission on Accreditation of Healthcare Organizations, *Guide to Emergency Management Planning in Health Care* (Oakbrook Terrace, Ill: Joint Commission Resources, 2002) 45-52.

15. J Blanchard, ed, *Perioperative Emergency Management Resource Manual,* second ed (Denver: AORN, Inc, 2007).

16. E Sternberg, G C Lee, D Huard, "Counting crises: US hospital evacuations, 1971–1999," *Prehospital and Disaster Medicine* 19 (April/June 2004) 150-157.

17. C S Cocanour et al, "Lessons learned from the evacuation of an urban teaching hospital," *Archives of Surgery* 137 (October 2002) 1141-1145.

18. C H Schultz, K L Koenig, R J Lewis, "Implications of hospital evacuation after the Northridge, California, earthquake," *New England Journal of Medicine* 348 (April 3, 2003) 349-1355.

19. P Manion, I J Golden, "Vertical evacuation drill of an intensive care unit: Design, implementation, and evaluation," *Disaster Management & Response* 2 (January/March 2004) 14-19.

20. J R Gildea, S Etengoff, "Vertical evacuation simulation of critically ill patients in a hospital," *Prehospital and Disaster Medicine* 20 (July/August 2005) 243-248.

21. P Cybulski, "Evacuation of a critical care unit," *Canadian Association of Critical Care Nurses* 14 (Fall 2003) 21-23.

RESOURCES

"Bioterrorism planning template for healthcare facilities." Association for Professionals in Infection Control and Epidemiology, *http://www.apic.org/Content/Navigation Menu/PracticeGuidance/Topics/Bioterrorism/APIC_BT WG_BTRSugg.pdf* (accessed 3 Nov 2006).

Campese, C. "Preparation, experience, and aftermath of Hurricane Floyd," *AORN Journal* 72 (July 2000) 82-93.

Gretenkort, P; et al. "Interface between hospital and fire authorities—A concept for management of incidents in hospitals." *Prehospital and Disaster Medicine* 17 (January/March 2002) 42-47.

"Homeland security emergencies and disasters," National Response Plan, *http://www.dhs.gov/dhspublic /interapp/editorial/editorial_0566.xml* (accessed 3 Nov 2006).

"Mass casualty event preparedness and response." Centers for Disease Control and Prevention, *http://www.bt.cdc.gov/masscasualties/index.asp* (accessed 3 Nov 2006).

"Public health emergency response guide for state, local, and tribal public health directors" Templates 1–5. Centers for Disease Control and Prevention, *http:// www.bt.cdc.gov/planning/pdf/cdcresponseguide.pdf* (accessed 3 Nov 2006)

Romig, L E. "The JumpSTART pediatric MCI triage tool and other pediatric disaster and emergency medicine resources." Team Life Support *http://www.jumpstart triage.com* (accessed 3 Nov 2006).

Szatanjnkrycer, M D; Baez, A A; Luke, N. "FAST, ultrasound as an adjunct to triage using the START Mass Casualty Triage System: A preliminary descriptive study." *Prehospital and Emergency Care* 10 (January/March 2006) 96-102.

Approved by the AORN Board of Directors, November 2006. Published in *Standards, Recommended Practices, and Guidelines,* 2007 edition.

Exhibit A: Mass Casualty Practice Scenarios

Scenario 1: Explosions occurring at the same time in several areas.

Several homemade bombs, which may contain pathogens, have exploded in a train terminal. The trauma hospital nearby also has been a target and is unable to receive casualties. There are approximately 5,000 casualties.

Scenario 2: Release of a biological agent.

A biological agent has been released in a concert hall. The pathogen's identity and incubation period is unknown, and laboratory tests must be performed to determine this. Health care facility staff members receiving the casualties must wear personal protective equipment that includes gowns, masks with eye protection, and gloves. From the first responder's initial report, patient treatment is determined to be isolation and ventilators because of the pathogen's undetermined identity. The treatment regimen's effect is not known.

Triage efforts for both scenarios will include the following:
- saving as many lives as possible,
- determining what resources are available throughout care,
- providing care for current patients in facility,
- using all standards of care that apply,
- maintaining supplies and equipment that may need to be rationed to save lives,
- identifying the number of staff members available who are trained to handle this type of emergency,
- controlling backlog of patients to reduce delays,
- using clinical judgment to make treatment decisions,
- documenting any standards that cannot be met, and
- processing the backlog of fatalities as soon as possible.

Identify how decisions will be made. Questions that need to be asked include the following.
- How do you ensure training of care providers and support staff?
- How are patients triaged by condition, ability to treat, and available resources?
- How are infections controlled and prevented?
- How are supplies and equipment used and reused, if necessary?
- How are supplies that are in short supply and specific to clinical needs allocated?
- How are resources (eg, surgical, laboratory, bed capacity) allocated?
- How are patients with specific conditions identified and cared for?
- How are medications best used?
- How are health care workers and their families safeguarded?
- How are documentation standards adapted to obtain sufficient information to address care given?
- How are a large number of casualty deaths handled?

For further information, consult the following publications and Web sites.

"Educational competencies for registered nurses responding to mass casualty incidents," (2003) International Nursing Coalition for Mass Causality Education, *http://www.incmce.org/competencies page.html* (accessed 6 Dec 2006).

"Bioterrorism and other public health emergencies: Altered standards of care in mass casualty events," Agency for Healthcare Research and Quality, *http://www.ahrq.gov/research/altstand/altstand.pdf* (accessed 6 Dec 2006).

ECRI, "Disaster planning and response: Guidance for healthcare facilities," *Health Devices* 34 no 9 (2005) 293-325.

AORN Perioperative Standards and Recommended Practices, 2009 Edition

AORN Guidance Statement: Creating a Patient Safety Culture

Introduction

The purpose of this guidance statement is to assist managers and clinicians in developing policies and procedures related to creating a patient safety culture.

Since the Institute of Medicine (IOM) report released in 1999, the vast majority of patient safety initiatives have focused on micro issues, such as medication errors and wrong-site surgery, with little emphasis on the macro issue of culture. Edgar Schien, professor of management at the Sloan School of Management, Massachusetts Institute of Technology, defines *culture* as the set of shared, implicit assumptions that a group holds and that determines how it perceives, thinks about, and reacts to its various environments.[1] In broader terms, culture is a mindset centering on shared values, attitudes, or beliefs within an organization. As defined in the health care literature, a safety culture is an environment that encourages reporting,[2] ends blame,[3] involves senior leadership,[4] and focuses on systems.[5]

Lucian Leape, adjunct professor of health policy, Harvard School of Public Health, Harvard University, Boston, has stated the single greatest impediment to error prevention is that "we punish people for making mistakes."[6] Medical errors are grossly unreported across the country; only 2% to 3% of major errors are reported,[6] and when reported, they don't create stories or generate action.[7] Analytical methods such as root cause analysis (RCA) and the failure mode and effects analysis (FMEA) will not work in detecting the causes or errors if health care workers are bound by a "code of silence," fear retribution, or are uncomfortable revealing imperfection in a process for which they are responsible.[8]

To date, most of the work in patient safety has been reactive. As the culture matures with increased information and trust, the emphasis will switch to a more proactive or generative approach.

Background

In review of the literature, few hospitals have assessed their organizations' safety culture, nor have many actually measured the impact of interventions. One study, conducted in April 2001, reported that 15 California hospitals conducted a safety culture survey with two objectives: (1) measure attitudes toward patient safety and organizational culture; and (2) determine how the culture of safety varied among the hospitals and between the various types of health care workers.[9] The majority of the participants in the study responded in ways that indicated a positive safety culture; however, senior leadership gave fewer problematic responses than frontline workers, and clinicians—in particular nurses—were more pessimistic.[10]

Johns Hopkins Hospital conducted a systematic assessment on safety and developed a strategic plan to improve safety.[11] Its study revealed a comparable culture of safety as compared to the airline industry, but identified several areas for improvement. Key messages identified were that senior leaders need to be more visible to frontline caregivers when addressing safety; safety planning must be proactive; physicians are less aware of safety initiatives than nurses; and physicians must actively participate in the education process.[11]

Preamble

The intention of this guidance statement is to provide a framework from which perioperative teams can foster a patient-centric safety culture and assist with the development of policies and procedures that will support that culture. A patient-centric safety culture consists of five major subcultures: reporting, flexible, just, learning,[5] and wary[2] (**Figure 1**).

Reporting Culture

A reporting culture is a culture in which all members of the perioperative team readily report errors and near misses. A reporting culture can be assessed by the types of errors reported by staff. As the safety culture matures, there is increased risk-taking associated with errors reported. In a true reporting culture, individuals report events to allow all staff in the organization to learn from the experience.

Suggested strategies[5-7]
- Focus on both actual events and near misses.
- Use FMEA proactively to anticipate and prevent potential error.
- Discuss close calls, "good catches," and how harm to the patient was avoided or minimized.
- Develop a documentation system that is easy to use.
- Develop a reporting system that focuses on storytelling and knowledge-sharing.

Figure 1

PATIENT-CENTRIC SAFETY CULTURE

© Kate A. O'Toole. Used with permission.

- Focus on individual cases that provide learning opportunities.
- Identify ways to circulate stories and lessons learned throughout the facility.
- Provide feedback to the staff on all issues reported.
- Develop metrics for success (eg, increase number of reports).
- Prioritize improvement initiatives based on themes discovered and potential risks revealed.
- Use a process that emphasizes quality improvement (eg, Plan, Do, Check, Act).

Flexible Culture
A flexible culture is a culture that is nimble enough to keep pace with the rapid changes in health care.

Suggested strategies[7,9-11]
- Identify model for improvement programs that focuses on rapid cycle change.
- Develop processes that ensure shared leadership.
- Shared leadership is a hallmark of the organization.
- An environment of respect, collaboration, and trust exists between all team members and leadership.

Learning Culture
A learning culture is a culture that is capable and ready to gain knowledge from experiences and data, and that is willing to implement major

changes as indicated from safety information systems. A learning culture is informed and learns from incidents and near misses.[8]

Suggested strategies
- Foster learning opportunities through open communication.
- Develop the ability to adapt to the changing health care environment and be receptive to change.
- Frontline staff is engaged to use initiative to problem-solve unique situations.
- Individual performance is linked to team performance.

Wary Culture
A wary culture is a culture in which the all members of the perioperative team are continually aware of the unexpected. Being vigilant is a healthy state that is a combination of being informed and aware that, at any given moment, an untoward event can occur. Healthy reporting, learning, and flexible cultures will facilitate a wary culture.

Suggested strategies[5,7,12,13]
- Go "looking for trouble"; conduct executive walk-arounds in all perioperative areas.
- Become preoccupied with opportunities for improvement.
- Be willing to challenge assumptions.
- How can we "stop the line" and still stay efficient?
- How can we get better when we know we are the best?

Just Culture
A just culture is a culture that provides an environment of trust where all members of the perioperative team are encouraged to provide safety-related data and are acutely aware of the distinction between acceptable and unacceptable behavior. Errors and mistakes must be evaluated in a manner such that contributing factors are reviewed first, and then accountability is determined in relation to actions. A just culture is not a nonpunitive (ie, blame-free) environment, but rather an environment where actions are analyzed to ensure that individual accountability is established and appropriate actions are taken.[12]

Health care organizations must adopt a disciplinary system theory approach in promoting a just culture that freely reports errors. To understand the interrelationship between discipline and patient safety, four behavioral concepts are examined: human error, negligence, intentional rule violations, and reckless conduct.[7]

When evaluating an adverse event, care must be taken to determine whether human error or misconduct has occurred. Historically, most disciplinary actions are based upon the outcome of the mishap; if a patient is harmed, then that health care worker is considered blameworthy. By assigning blame, the health care organization stands to lose an opportunity to learn from the error and the error may reoccur. Disciplinary policies must balance the benefits of a learning culture with the need to retain personal accountability and discipline.[12] Adverse event investigation tools may be created to augment the use of the suggested strategy identified below.

Suggested strategy

James Reason, professor of psychology, University of Manchester, United Kingdom, created a model to assist managers to determine culpability after an untoward event has occurred.[13] (**Figure 2** is an adaptation of the Reason model applied to the perioperative setting.) Perioperative leadership should apply this model when investigating incidences to determine whether disciplinary action is warranted. Six basic steps are used. It is important to focus on the error and not the outcome.

Step 1. The first line of questioning is to establish intent. Was this action or omission deliberate? If there was deliberate intent, the action or omission is culpable.

Step 2. If no intent is established, then determine whether substance use or abuse was involved. If abuse is determined, culpability is established. If the health care worker is taking a medication for medical reasons and is aware that he or she could be impaired, culpability is present; however, it is not as egregious as abuse.

Step 3. If the health care worker is not under the influence of drugs or alcohol, the next determinant is whether he or she knowingly violated safe operating procedures. This aids in determining reckless behavior. The threshold for reckless behavior is met when procedures are available, correct, and workable, but still are violated by the health care worker. If there are no adequate procedures in place, a systems error has occurred. When evaluating the situation, care must be taken to determine whether "normalization of deviance" is taking place—that is, whether there is a policy or procedure in place, but it not widely followed.

Step 4. If a policy or procedure is violated, a substitution test is conducted. Peers are asked how they would behave in a similar situation. If the peers respond the same as in the error in question, a systems-induced error is established. If they respond differently, possible negligence should be considered.

Step 5. The next question is whether the health care worker has a history of unsafe acts. If the questions in steps 1 through 4 are unsubstantiated, and there is no history of unsafe acts, then it is human error with no culpability. If the health care worker does have a history of unsafe acts, this particular incident may not be culpable; however, the organization should review the record for trends and may consider moving the health care worker to a lower-risk environment.

Step 6. The last question and assessment is where the possibility of mitigating circumstances is examined. Possible factors include stressors (eg, anger, fear, personal issues), distractions, and interruptions (eg, pagers, music, environmental temperature, extraneous conversation, overhead paging). Environmental influences include but are not limited to, physical plant and wrong size room for operative and other invasive procedures (eg, overcrowded, not ergonomic).

It is important to note that the accountability model does not evaluate or determine the proof legally required to prove reckless behavior or criminal negligence. This model should not be used for performance rating of surgical team members. It should be utilized by leadership after all the facts have been gathered, but as soon after the event as possible. If more than one person is involved, the model should be applied separately for each person.

Figure 2

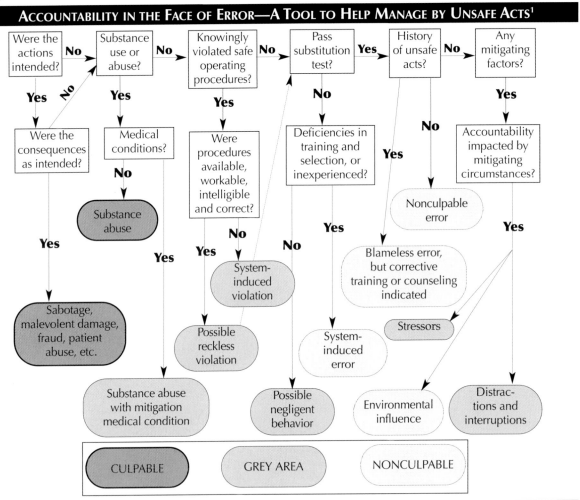

ACCOUNTABILITY IN THE FACE OF ERROR—A TOOL TO HELP MANAGE BY UNSAFE ACTS[1]

Adapted for the perioperative setting from a model developed by J Reason, Engineering a Safety Culture (London: Ashgate Publishing, 1997) 209.

Summary

AORN believes all health care organizations must strive to create a culture of safety. Such a culture will provide an atmosphere where all members of the perioperative team can openly discuss errors, process improvements, or system issues without fear of reprisal. A culture of safety places an emphasis on flexibility and learning as a means of improving safety and reducing errors. Characteristics of a culture of safety include the following:

♦ communication is open and honest;
♦ the emphasis is on the team rather than the individual;
♦ standards and practices are developed in a multidisciplinary framework;
♦ staff members are helpful and supportive of each other;
♦ staff members trust each other;
♦ surgical team members have a friendly, open relationship emphasizing credibility and attentiveness;
♦ the environment is resilient, encourages creativity, and is patient outcomes-driven;
♦ the focus is on work flow and process; and
♦ these attributes are supported by an informed culture that learns from incidents and near misses.

A commitment to safety must be articulated at all levels of the organization. Safety must be valued as the top priority, even at the expense of efficiency. Health care organizations must allocate an appropriate amount of resources and provide the necessary incentives or rewards to promote a robust patient safety culture. AORN recognizes that most patient safety initiatives will fail in the absence of a viable safety culture.

Glossary

Accountable: Responsible for one's actions or conduct.

Adverse event: Experiencing harm from error.

Culture: The shared norms, values, and practices associated with a nation, organization, or profession.[14]

Error: Failure of a planned action to be completed as intended, or the use of a wrong plan to achieve an outcome.

Failure mode and effects analysis (FMEA): A proactive tool used to anticipate and prevent the potential for product or process failure.

Just culture: An environment where actions are analyzed to ensure that individual accountability is established and appropriate actions are taken.[15]

Medical error: An adverse event or near miss that is preventable with the current state of medical knowledge.[16]

Near miss: An event or situation that could have resulted in an accident, injury, or illness, but did not, either by chance or timely intervention.[17]

Negligence: Failure to use such care as a reasonable prudent and careful person would use under similar circumstances.[17]

Root cause analysis (RCA): A process for identifying the basic or causal factor(s) that underlie variation in performance, including the occurrence or possible occurrence of a sentinel event.[18]

Safety: Freedom from accidental injury.

Safety culture: An environment that encourages reporting,[5] ends blame,[9] involves senior leadership,[9] and focuses on systems.[5]

REFERENCES

1. E H Schein, *Organizational Culture and Leadership,* second ed (San Francisco: Jossey-Bass, 1992).

2. P Hudson, "Applying the lessons of high-risk industries to health care," *Quality and Safety in Health Care* 12 Suppl 1 (December 2003) i7-i12.

3. L Larson, "Ending the culture of blame: A look at why medical errors happen-and what needs to change," *Trustee* 53 (February 2000) 6-10.

4. H S Ruchlin et al, "The role of leadership in instilling a culture of safety: Lessons from the literature," *Journal of Healthcare Management* 49 (January/February 2004) 47-59.

5. J M Krumberger, "Building a culture of safety," *RN* 64 (January 2001) 32ac2-32ac3.

6. J Reason, *Human Error* (New York: Cambridge University Press, 1990).

7. D Marx, "Patient safety and the 'Just Culture': A primer for health care executives," Medical Event Reporting System for Transfusion Medicine, *http://www.mers-tm.net/support/Marx_Primer.pdf* (accessed 2 Dec 2005).

8. "The IOM medical errors report: 5 years later, the journey continues," *The Quality Letter for Healthcare Leaders* 17 (January 2005) 2-10.

9. V F Nieva, J Sorra, "Safety culture assessment: A tool for improving patient safety in healthcare organizations," *Quality and Safety in Health Care* 12 suppl 2 (December 2003) ii17-23.

10. S J Singer et al, "The culture of safety: Results of an organization-wide survey in 15 California hospitals," *Quality and Safety in Health Care* 12 (April 2003) 112-118.

11. P J Pronovost et al, "Evaluation of the culture of safety: survey of clinicians and managers in an academic medical center," *Quality and Safety in Health Care* 12 (December 2003) 405-410.

12. "Just culture toolkit," The Risk Management and Patient Safety Institute, *http://www.rmpsi.com/education/liveprograms/JustCultureToolkit.pdf* (accessed 2 Dec 2005).

13. J Reason, *Engineering a Safety Culture* (London: Ashgate Publishing, 1997) 209.

14. R L Helmreich, A C Merritt, *Culture at Work in Aviation and Medicine: National, Organizational, and Professional Influences* (Brookfield, Vt: Ashgate, 1998).

15. R H Kilmann, M J Sexton, R A Serpa, eds, "Five key issues in understanding and changing culture," in *Gaining Control of the Corporate Culture* (San Francisco: Jossey-Bass, 1985), 1-17.

16. "Glossary of terms," in *Doing What Counts for Patient Safety: Federal Actions to Reduce Medical Errors and Their Impact,* Quality Interagency Coordination Task Force, *http://www.quic.gov/report%2Dbackup/mederr8.htm#terms* (accessed 2 Dec 2005).

17. "Sentinel event glossary of terms," Joint Commission on Accreditation of Healthcare Organizations, *http://www.jcaho.org/accredited+organizations/sentinel+event/glossary.htm* (2 Dec 2005).

18. D E Broadbent, *Third Report: Organising for Safety* (London: Health and Safety Commission, 1993).

RESOURCES

Carroll, J S; Quijada, M A. "Redirecting traditional professional values to support safety: Changing organisational culture in health care," *Quality and Safety in Health Care* 13 suppl 2 (December 2004) ii16-21.

Davies, H T; Nutley, S M; Mannion, R. "Organisational culture and quality of health care," *Quality in Health Care* 9 (June 2000) 111-119.

Hofstede, G H; Hofstede, G J. *Cultures and Organizations: Software of the Mind,* second ed (New York: McGraw Hill, 2005).

Kowalczyk, L. "Hospitals study when to apologize to patients," *Boston Globe,* July 24, 2005. Available at *http://www.boston.com/tools/archives* (fee required).

Barach, P; Small, S D. "Reporting and preventing medical mishaps: Lessons from non-medical near miss reporting systems," *BMJ* 320 (March 18, 2000) 759-763.

"Safety climate survey (IHI tool)," Institute for Healthcare Improvement, *http://www.ihi.org/IHI/Topics/Patient Safety/SafetyGeneral/Tools/Safety+Climate+Survey +%28IHI+Tool%29.htm* (accessed 2 Dec 2005).

Schein, E H. "Culture: The missing concept in organization studies," *Administrative Science Quarterly* 41 no 2 (June 1996) 229-240.

Schein, E H. "Three cultures of management: The key to organizational learning," *MIT Sloan Management Review* 38 (Fall 1996) 9-20. Also available at *http://sloanreview.mit.edu/smr/issue/1996/fall/1* (accessed 2 Dec 2005).

Wachter, R M; Shojania, K G. *Internal Bleeding: The Truth Behind America's Terrifying Epidemic of Medical Mistakes,* second ed (New York: Rugged Land, 2005).

Approved by the AORN Board of Directors, November 2005. Published in *Standards, Recommended Practices, and Guidelines,* 2006 edition. Reprinted April 2006, *AORN Journal.*

AORN Guidance Statement: Postoperative Patient Care in the Ambulatory Surgery Setting

Introduction

This guidance statement provides a framework for health care practitioners to use when developing and implementing policies and procedures for postoperative patient care in the ambulatory surgery setting. AORN defines *postoperative* as "the time [that] begins with admission to the postanesthesia care area and ends with a resolution of surgical sequelae."[1(p31)] This includes the postanesthesia phases I, II, and extended observation (formerly phase III) levels of care. These phases are defined by the American Society of PeriAnesthesia Nurses' (ASPAN's) *Standards of Perianesthesia Nursing Practice* as follows.[2]

Phase I focuses on providing a transition from a totally anesthetized state to one requiring less acute interventions. Recovery occurs in the postanesthesia care unit (PACU). The purpose of this phase is for patients to regain physiological homeostasis and receive appropriate nursing intervention as needed.

Phase II focuses on preparing the patient for self-care, care by family members, or care in an extended care environment. The patient is discharged to phase II recovery when intensive nursing care no longer is needed. In the phase II area, sometimes referred to as the step-down or discharge area, the patient becomes more alert and functional.

Extended observation focuses on providing ongoing care for patients who require extended observation or intervention after transfer from phase I or phase II. Interventions are directed toward preparing the patient for self-care or care by family members. Extended observation is designed for patients who are unable to meet the criteria for discharge from phase II and the ambulatory unit. These patients may need alternative care, such as home health care or a stay in an overnight short-stay hospital unit or recovery center.

This guidance statement is directed specifically to ambulatory surgery centers (ASCs). It also may be used in other ambulatory settings that perform surgery or other invasive procedures. The ambulatory surgery setting is defined as an area where outpatient surgery or other invasive procedures are performed, including, but not limited to, freestanding surgery centers, hospital-based ambulatory surgical units, physicians' offices, cardiac catheterization suites, endoscopy units, and radiology departments.

Perioperative nurses have limited contact with patients before surgery, which may lead to an increased risk for adverse patient outcomes. Ambula-tory surgery centers must have consistent approaches to postoperative patient care to ensure patient safety. This guidance statement is intended to promote patient safety in the ambulatory surgery setting.

Guidance Statement

Ambulatory surgery centers should develop written policies and procedures for postoperative patient care. Policies and procedures should include, but not be limited to, the following elements:
- ◆ staffing,
- ◆ supplies and equipment,
- ◆ postanesthesia care,
- ◆ fast tracking of patients,
- ◆ pain management,
- ◆ documentation,
- ◆ discharge criteria,
- ◆ discharge instructions, and
- ◆ monitoring of outcomes.

The criteria in this guidance statement represent the minimum levels of care.

Perioperative Nursing Data Set

The Perioperative Nursing Data Set (PNDS) is a clinically relevant and empirically validated standardized nursing vocabulary describing perioperative nursing. It relates to the delivery of care in all perioperative settings. This standardized language consists of a collection of data elements and includes perioperative nursing diagnoses, interventions, and outcomes. The PNDS should be used to develop ambulatory surgery patient plans of care and to standardize nursing documentation. In addition, PNDS outcomes, as well as outcome indicators, interventions, and nursing diagnoses, can be
- ◆ incorporated into competencies, policies and procedures, job descriptions, pathways, guidelines, and care plans;
- ◆ linked to the electronic health record;
- ◆ used as a tool for teaching new nurses about perioperative nursing; and
- ◆ applied in performance improvement projects and benchmarking.

Each data element in the PNDS corresponds to a unique identifier. The domains are represented by the letter "D" followed by numbers 1 to 3 to indicate the particular domain being addressed. Nursing diagnoses are represented by the letter "X" and a number unique to the diagnosis. Interventions are represented by the letter "I" and a unique number, and outcomes are represented by the letter "O" and a unique number. These designations are identified in this document with unique identifiers noted in parentheses. A list of outcomes, interventions, and nursing diagnoses specific to each domain is printed in an appendix of the PNDS reference book.[3]

The PNDS is conceptualized by the perioperative patient focused model. The patient and his or her family members are at the center of the model's framework. The model depicts perioperative nursing in four domains and illustrates the relationship between the patient, family members, and the care provided by the perioperative RN. The patient-centered domains are

- D1—patient safety;
- D2—physiological responses to surgery; and
- D3—patient and family member behavioral responses to surgery, including
  - behavior responses—knowledge, and
  - behavior responses—rights and ethics.[3]

Nursing Care Policies

Perianesthesia nursing care policies and procedures should be available in the PACU and all areas where other postoperative care (phase I, II, or extended observation) is delivered.[4] At a minimum, each nurse should review the policies and procedures periodically, and the review process should be documented. Specific criteria for postanesthesia care policies and procedures should include

- assessment of data elements;
- supplies and equipment required for each phase of recovery;
- postoperative patient care;
- emergency medications[5] and equipment;
- patient classification;
- infection control (O10);
- pain management (O20), patient knowledge of pain (O29), and pain control;
- documentation of patient care;
- patient transfer; and
- care of patients receiving moderate sedation.[6]

Staffing

A staffing plan should be developed and used to provide an adequate number and mix of personnel to meet patient care needs.[7,8] The staffing plan should include criteria regarding the number of patients, number of ORs and procedure rooms, average patient length of stay, and intensity of care.[6] An operational patient classification system may help in determining and allocating nursing personnel.[9] The ASPAN "Recommended staffing guidelines" should be used as a guide to calculate requirements for postanesthesia staffing needs (**Table 1**).

Staffing for an ASC PACU should conform to national and state guidelines and regulations for safe postanesthesia nursing care.[4] Additional practice standards that apply to postanesthesia care also should be followed and should include personnel competency requirements that meet state licensure guidelines, organizational guidelines, accreditation and professional standards, procedure-specific training, and professional experience.[10,11] Personnel should be trained in the use of emergency equipment and cardiopulmonary resuscitation for both adult and pediatric patients if pediatric care is provided.[12] Advanced cardiac life support and pediatric advanced life support training, if pediatric care is provided, is recommended for all PACU nurses. All staff members should undergo a comprehensive orientation program, and competencies should be documented.

Supplies and Equipment

A checklist of required supplies and equipment for PACU phase I and PACU phase II should be developed.[13] A method should be in place to ensure all equipment is maintained according to manufacturers' specifications.[14] Equipment must be available to

- administer oxygen (I87);
- provide suction (I87);
- maintain IV access (I34); and
- monitor postoperative cardiac status (I44) (I120)
  - blood pressure,
  - heart rhythm and rate, and
  - oxygen saturation.[15]

Emergency equipment, an emergency communication system, and knowledgeable emergency assistive personnel should be readily available.[14,16] Emergency equipment and supplies should include a defibrillator, medications, oxygen, a positive-pressure breathing device, suction equipment, and appropriate nasal and oral airways.[17,18]

Table 1

RECOMMENDED STAFFING GUIDELINES FOR POSTANESTHESIA CARE*

STAFFING IS BASED ON PATIENT ACUITY, CENSUS, PATIENT FLOW PROCESSES, AND PHYSICAL FACILITY. THE PERIANESTHESIA REGISTERED NURSE USES PRUDENT JUDGMENT IN DETERMINING NURSE TO PATIENT RATIOS, PATIENT MIX, AND STAFFING MIX TO REFLECT PATIENT ACUITY AND NURSING INTENSITY.

Phase I level of care
The perianesthesia registered nursing roles during this phase focus on providing postanesthesia nursing care to the patient in the immediate postanesthesia period, and transitioning them to Phase II level of care, the inpatient setting, or to an intensive care setting for continued care. (See "Blended levels of care.")

TWO REGISTERED NURSES, ONE OF WHOM IS AN RN COMPETENT IN PHASE I POSTANESTHESIA NURSING, ARE IN THE SAME ROOM WHERE THE PATIENT IS RECEIVING PHASE I LEVEL OF CARE.

Class 1:2   One nurse to two patients who are:
- One unconscious, stable, without artificial airway, and over the age of 8 years; and one conscious, stable, and free of complications
- Two conscious, stable, and free of complications
- Two conscious, stable, 8 years of age and under, with family or competent support staff present

Class 1:1   One nurse to one patient:
- At the time of admission, until the critical elements** are met
- Unstable airway***
- Any unconscious patient 8 years of age and under
- A second nurse must be available to assist as necessary

Class 2:1   Two nurses to one patient:
- One critically ill, unstable, complicated patient

Phase II level of care
The professional perianesthesia nursing roles during this phase focus on preparing the patient/family/ significant other for care in the home, extended observation level of care, or the extended care environment.

TWO COMPETENT PERSONNEL, ONE OF WHOM IS AN RN COMPETENT IN PHASE II POSTANESTHESIA NURSING, ARE IN THE SAME ROOM WHERE THE PATIENT IS RECEIVING PHASE II LEVEL OF CARE. AN RN MUST BE IN THE PHASE II PACU AT ALL TIMES WHILE A PATIENT IS PRESENT.

Class 1:3   One nurse to three patients:
- Over 8 years of age
- 8 years of age and under with family present

Class 1:2   One nurse to two patients:
- 8 years of age and under without family or support staff present
- Initial admission of patient postprocedure

Class 1:1   One nurse to one patient:
- Unstable patient of any age requiring transfer.

---

* Copyright © 2007. Adapted with permission from the American Society of PeriAnesthesia Nurses.
** Critical elements can be defined as:
  - Report has been received from the anesthesia care provider, questions answered, and the transfer of care has taken place.
  - Patient has a secure airway.
  - Initial assessment is complete.
  - Patient is hemodynamically stable.

***Examples of an unstable airway include, but are not limited to, the following:
  - Requiring active interventions to maintain patency, such as manual jaw lift or chin lift.
  - Evidence of obstruction, active or probable, such as gasping, choking, crowing, wheezing, etc.
  - Symptoms of respiratory distress, including dyspnea, tachypnea, panic, agitation, cyanosis, etc.

Table 1 *(continued)*

RECOMMENDED STAFFING GUIDELINES FOR POSTANESTHESIA CARE

Extended observation level of care

The nursing roles in this phase focus on providing the ongoing care for those patients requiring extended observation/intervention after transfer/discharge from Phase I and Phase II levels of care.

TWO COMPETENT PERSONNEL, ONE OF WHOM IS AN RN POSSESSING COMPETENCE APPROPRIATE TO THE PATIENT POPULATION, ARE IN THE SAME UNIT WHERE THE PATIENT IS RECEIVING EXTENDED OBSERVATION LEVEL OF CARE. THE NEED FOR ADDITIONAL RNS AND SUPPORT STAFF IS DEPENDENT ON THE PATIENT ACUITY, PATIENT CENSUS, AND THE PHYSICAL FACILITY.

Class 1:3/5   One nurse to three to five patients:

♦ Examples of patients that may be cared for in this phase include, but are not limited to,
  - patients awaiting transportation home,
  - patients with no caregiver,
  - patients who have had procedures requiring extended observation/intervention (ie, potential risk for bleeding, pain management, postoperative nausea, vomiting, etc),
  - patients being held for an inpatient bed.

Blended levels of care

Perianesthesia units may provide Phase I, Phase II, and/or Extended Observation levels of care within the same environment. This may require the blending of patients and staffing patterns. The perianesthesia registered nurse uses prudent judgment based on patient acuity, nursing observations, and required interventions to determine staffing needs.

Copyright © 2007. Adapted with permission from the American Society of PeriAnesthesia Nurses.

Postanesthesia Care

A postanesthesia care policy and procedure should be written for transporting, monitoring, and evaluating patients in the PACU.[19] Patients should have a complete systems assessment during the first few minutes of PACU care.[4] This assessment should include, but not be limited to,

♦ vital signs (I59) (I128) (I16);
♦ respiratory adequacy (I45);
♦ postoperative cardiac status (I59);
♦ peripheral circulation (ie, postoperative tissue perfusion) (I46);
♦ postoperative neurological status (I146);
♦ level of consciousness (I144) (I146);
♦ alertness (I144) (I146);
♦ lucidity (I144) (I146);
♦ orientation (I144) (I146);
♦ IV patency (I34);
♦ allergies and sensitivities (I123);
♦ pain management (I16);
♦ motor abilities (I146);

♦ return of sensory and motor control in areas affected by local or regional anesthetics (I146);[4]
♦ skin integrity (I38) (I46);[3,4]
♦ temperature regulation (I78);
♦ positioning (I38);
♦ surgical wound site (I4) (I130);
♦ nausea and vomiting (I128) (I153); and
♦ fluid and electrolyte balance (I132).

The postanesthesia nurse should provide ongoing assessments and reevaluations concurrently with nursing interventions.[4,20]

A nursing care plan should be based on the initial patient assessment and documented appropriately. The perioperative nurse analyzes the assessment data to determine nursing diagnoses. Following is a partial list of nursing diagnoses that may be associated with patients undergoing ambulatory surgery:

♦ X38 (D2)—pain, acute;
♦ X73 (D2)—nausea;
♦ X28 (D2)—infection, risk for;
♦ X26 (D2)—hypothermia; and
♦ X21 (D2)—gas exchange, impaired.[3]

AORN Guidance Statement: Preoperative Patient Care in the Ambulatory Surgery Setting

Introduction

The purpose of this guidance statement is to provide a framework that health care practitioners can use to develop and implement policies and procedures for preoperative patient care in the ambulatory surgery setting. This guidance statement is directed specifically to ambulatory surgery centers (ASCs). It also may be used in other ambulatory settings that perform surgery or other invasive procedures. The ambulatory surgical setting is defined as an area in which outpatient surgery or other invasive procedures are performed, including, but not limited to, freestanding surgery centers, hospital-based ambulatory surgery units, physicians' offices, cardiac catheterization suites, endoscopy units, and radiology departments.

Perioperative nurses have limited contact with patients before surgery, which may lead to an increased risk for adverse patient outcomes. Ambulatory surgery centers must have consistent approaches to preoperative patient care to ensure patient safety. This guidance statement is intended to promote patient safety in the ambulatory surgery setting.

Guidance Statement

Ambulatory surgery centers should develop written policies and procedures for preoperative patient care. Policies and procedures should include, but not be limited to, the following elements:

- staffing,
- preadmission assessment,
- preadmission testing,
- anesthesia evaluation,
- preoperative teaching,
- preoperative nursing assessment,
- documentation of the preoperative nursing assessment,
- fast tracking of patients,
- prevention of postoperative infections, and
- monitoring of outcomes.

The criteria in this guidance statement represent the minimum levels of care.

Perioperative Nursing Data Set

The Perioperative Nursing Data Set (PNDS) is a clinically relevant and empirically validated standardized nursing vocabulary describing periopera-

tive nursing. It relates to the delivery of care in all perioperative settings. This standardized language consists of a collection of data elements and includes perioperative nursing diagnoses, interventions, and outcomes. The PNDS should be used to develop ambulatory surgery patient plans of care and to standardize nursing documentation. In addition, PNDS outcomes, as well as outcome indicators, interventions, and nursing diagnoses, can be

- incorporated into competencies, policies and procedures, job descriptions, pathways, guidelines, and care plans;
- linked to the electronic health record;
- used as a tool for teaching new nurses about perioperative nursing; and
- applied in performance improvement projects and benchmarking.

Each data element in the PNDS corresponds to a unique identifier. The domains are represented by the letter "D," followed by numbers 1 to 3 to indicate the particular domain being addressed. Nursing diagnoses are represented by the letter "X" and a number unique to the diagnosis. Interventions are represented by the letter "I" and a unique number, and outcomes are represented by the letter "O" and a unique number. These designations are identified in this document with unique identifiers noted in parentheses. A list of outcomes, interventions, and nursing diagnoses specific to each domain is printed in an appendix of the PNDS reference book.[1]

The PNDS is conceptualized by the perioperative patient focused model. The patient and his or her family members are at the center of the model's framework. The model depicts perioperative nursing in four domains and illustrates the relationship between the patient, family members, and the care provided by the perioperative RN. The patient-centered domains are

- D1—patient safety;
- D2—physiological responses to surgery; and
- D3—patient and family member behavioral responses to surgery, including
  - behavior responses—knowledge, and
  - behavior responses—rights and ethics.[1]

Nursing Care Policies

Preoperative nursing care policies and procedures should be available in the preoperative care unit.[2] At a minimum, each nurse should review these policies and procedures periodically, and the review process should be documented. Specific criteria for the preoperative care policies and procedures should include

- assessment of data elements;
- preoperative patient care;
- supplies and equipment;
- emergency medications[3] and equipment;
- fast tracking of perioperative patients;
- infection control (O10);
- pain management (O29), patient knowledge of pain, and pain control (O20); and
- documentation of care.

Staffing

A staffing plan should be developed and used to provide an adequate number and mix of personnel to meet patient care needs.[4-6] An adequate number of RNs should be available to provide patient assessments. The staffing plan for the preoperative area should include criteria regarding the number of patients; number of ORs and procedure rooms; types of procedures scheduled; medications to be administered; types of patients (eg, elderly, pediatric); average patient preparation time; preoperative procedures (eg, insertion of invasive lines, radiological studies, regional blocks); patient acuity; and intensity of care.[4,7] Licensed practical nurses (LPNs) and unlicensed assistive personnel (UAP) may be included in preoperative staffing plans. Unlicensed assistive personnel may be assigned to assist with delegated patient care tasks as determined by the RN and according to federal, state, and local regulations.[8] All personnel should be qualified and competent according to state licensure requirements, accreditation and professional standards, procedure-specific training, and experience.[5,9] Personnel should be trained in the use of emergency equipment and cardiopulmonary resuscitation for both adult and pediatric patients if pediatric care is provided.[5] Basic life support training is recommended for all nurses in the preoperative care unit. All staff members should undergo a comprehensive orientation program, and competencies should be documented.

Preadmission Assessment

Specific admission criteria and guidelines should be identified for all perianesthesia care settings, and patients should meet the admission criteria.[10] The perioperative RN should ensure all admissions are identified as appropriate and evaluated based on written guidelines for preadmission.[10-13]

Preadmission telephone calls or face-to-face interviews should be conducted by a professional RN.[13,14] Pre-established admission criteria should be used to identify patients who need a face-to-face interview versus those who can be interviewed by telephone.

Preadmission nursing assessment criteria should determine preoperative status.[13] The assessment should include, but should not be limited to, the following:

- appropriate baseline physical assessment (I59) (I144);
- allergies and sensitivities (I123);
- signs of abuse or neglect (I113);[15]
- cultural, emotional, and socioeconomic assessment (I57) (I68);
- comprehensive pain assessment (I16) (I17);
- medication history, including nonprescription medications, illicit drugs, and herbal medications and supplements (I30);[16,17]
- anesthetic history;[18]
- results of radiological examinations and other preoperative testing (I30) (I111);
- discharge planning (I30) (I80);
- referrals (I63) (I92);
- identification of physical alterations that require additional equipment or supplies (I64);
- preoperative patient teaching (I135) (eg, medications to be taken or held before surgery, preoperative shower, NPO requirements [I107]);[13,19]
- informed consent and/or knowledge of planned procedure (I32);
- advance directive review (I97) (I103);[20]
- development of a care plan (I30); and
- documentation and communication of all information per facility policy (I27) (I92).[6,12]

Preoperative Testing

Policies and procedures that include criteria for preoperative testing should be developed by each ASC and approved by the appropriate medical staff members. The requested preoperative tests should be based on the patient's clinical conditions.[18,21] The criteria also should identify requirements for medical history and physical examination and documentation of such.[16]

A medical history and physical examination should be conducted before a surgical or invasive procedure and documented on the patient's medical record.[6] The history and physical should be reviewed immediately before surgery, and any changes to the patient's condition should be documented. Facility policy should be congruent with regulation and accreditation agency requirements.

Diagnostic testing to determine the patient's health care needs should be performed in a timely manner as defined by the health care organization.[10] Special screening may be needed for high-risk patients with certain conditions (eg, cardiac disease, obesity, sleep apnea).[22] Specific studies may be conducted for special categories of surgical procedures or type of anesthesia. Findings from the history, physical examination, and designated studies must be documented in the patient's medical record before anesthesia is administered or surgery is performed.[22,23]

Anesthesia Evaluation

An appropriate preanesthesia evaluation and assessment should be conducted by an anesthesia care provider before induction of anesthesia and surgery for patients receiving any type or level of anesthesia.[16,18,24] A preanesthesia assessment must be conducted for each patient to determine whether he or she is an appropriate candidate for moderate or deep sedation or anesthesia. A preanesthesia evaluation may not be required when the patient is only receiving local anesthesia. A patient receiving only local anesthesia may require a preanesthesia evaluation if the patient has significant comorbidities (eg, morbid obesity).

The assessment should include past and present medical and medication history, previous anesthesia experiences, evidence of a patient physical status assessment, American Society of Anesthesiologists physical status classification, results of relevant diagnostic studies, and the planned choice of anesthesia.[16] An anesthesia plan should be developed based on this information.[18]

Preoperative Teaching

A preoperative teaching plan should be developed for each patient. The teaching plan should include preoperative instructions[18] and patient preparation. The plan should address acceptable NPO require-

ments before surgery; preoperative showers or medications, when ordered; and physical, emotional, social, and procedural issues.[13,19,25,26] The teaching plan should describe perioperative routine care (I56), as well as the preparation phase; length of time in each phase of the perioperative period; other care providers; use of preoperative medications; management of postoperative pain and nausea; fast tracking, if applicable; discharge criteria; and continuum of care services.[13,27] Preoperative teaching should include the patient's family members or guardian (I79).

Preoperative Nursing Assessment

A perioperative RN should conduct a preoperative nursing assessment on the day of surgery. Perioperative nurses assess, document, and communicate patient status to all members of the health care team. Data collection involves the patient and his or her significant others or guardians. On the day of surgery, the perioperative RN should verify the information obtained during the preadmission assessment. The RN is responsible for ensuring that the preoperative assessment is complete and the patient's emotional needs are met.[13] Assessments for special populations, such as pediatric patients, older adult patients,[27] high-risk patients,[22] and patients with special needs,[13] may require additional preparation.

A preoperative assessment should be completed on admission. Interventions relating to the assessment may include, but are not limited to,

- verification of the patient's identity using two identifiers (I26) (eg, patient's name, date of birth, social security number, an assigned identification number)—neither identifier should be the patient's location or diagnosis.[28]
- review of preadmission assessment;
- appropriate baseline physical assessment (I59) (I144) (I60) (I64) (I66);
- review of preoperative status (I27) (I66);
- review of medications, including nonprescription medications, illicit drugs, and herbal medications and supplements (I30);
- allergies and sensitivities (I123);
- NPO status (I107);[22]
- hypothermia assessment and management (I131);[29]
- pain scale assessment (I16);[30,31]

- relevant preoperative needs of the patient and family members (I57) (I63) (I79);
- advance directives (I103) (I97);
- identification of planned procedure by the patient or his or her significant other or guardian (I32);
- verification of surgical site, side, or level, as applicable (I143);[6,17,32]
- prescribed surgical preparation (eg, preoperative shower, enema, medication) (I30);
- prosthetic devices (eg, dentures, hearing aids, contact lenses, glasses) (I90) (I127);
- implantable electronic devices (eg, pacemakers [I58], brain stimulators, pain pumps);
- availability of safe transportation home and aftercare (I35);
- contact information for the patient's support person (I109);
- understanding of preoperative teaching and discharge planning (I135) (I136) (I137) (I62);[16] and
- documentation of information per facility policy (I27) (I92).

A nursing care plan should be based on the patient assessment and documented appropriately. The perioperative RN analyzes the assessment data to determine nursing diagnoses. Following is a partial list of nursing diagnoses that may be associated with patients undergoing ambulatory surgery.

- X30 (D3)—knowledge deficit;
- X34 (D1)—physical mobility, impaired;
- X4 (D3)—anxiety;
- X28 (D2)—infection, risk for;
- X20 (D2)—fluid volume, risk for imbalance— related to altered nutritional state; and
- X26 (D2)—hypothermia.[1]

Preoperative Patient Outcomes

Nursing interventions are initiated to achieve a desired conclusion and/or to reduce the probability of undesired outcomes.[1,33] Following is a partial list of patient outcomes that may be associated with a patient's perioperative experience:

- (O22)—the patient demonstrates knowledge of wound healing;
- (O25)—the patient's right to privacy is maintained;
- (O20)—the patient demonstrates knowledge of pain management.[1]

Communication of the Preoperative Nursing Assessment

Policies and procedures should be written for communicating to the appropriate surgical team members any changes in the patient's status noted during the preadmission interview and assessment. A process should be developed for reporting and acting on abnormal findings (I27) (I30).

Prevention of Postoperative Infections

Prevention of postoperative infection begins in the preoperative period. Outcome O10 states, "the patient is free from signs and symptoms of infection."[1] Policies and procedures for reducing the risk of postoperative infection should be written and followed.[34,35] Prophylactic antibiotics should be considered and used according to the published guidelines, which include, at a minimum, the following elements (I10):[36]

- surgical procedures for which prophylactic antibiotics are recommended;
- the selection of appropriate medications;
- the timing of administering medications;
- the route of administration; and
- the personnel responsible for procuring, preparing, and administering the medication.[37]

Depending on the type of prophylactic medication used, administration should occur between 30 minutes and one hour before incision.[37,38]

Body temperature should be monitored and maintained as close to normothermia as possible during the preoperative period (I86) (I78) (I55).[39] Hypothermia may delay healing and predispose patients to wound infections.[40]

Documentation

Policies and procedures for documenting preoperative patient information should be established. Nursing documentation should incorporate the PNDS.[1] A preadmission checklist should be implemented to ensure all required patient-specific information is documented properly. Documentation requirements include, but are not limited to,

- a preadmission patient survey;
- a preoperative nursing assessment;
- signed consents for surgery and anesthesia (I124);

- written permission to leave postoperative follow-up telephone messages by voice mail or with a designated individual in keeping with the Health Insurance Portability and Accountability Act privacy guidelines (I151);
- history and physical in the patient's medical record;
- test results;
- preanesthesia assessment;
- pain scale assessment (I16);[30,31]
- identified possible risks, such as the potential for malignant hyperthermia or latex allergy (I123);[13]
- surgical procedure and site verification (I26) (I143);[32]
- advance directives (I103); and
- documentation of education and instructions provided (O31) (I27).

Monitoring of Outcomes

The facility should collect data to monitor its performance.[41] Data collected should include patients' perceptions of care, treatment, and provision of services, including specific individual needs and expectations, how well the facility met those needs, surgical site infections, how the facility can improve patient safety, and the effectiveness of pain management, when applicable.[41]

References

1. *Perioperative Nursing Data Set: The Perioperative Nursing Vocabulary*, second ed, S Beyea, ed (Denver: AORN, Inc, 2002).

2. R Ferrara-Love, "Immediate postanesthesia care," in *Ambulatory Surgical Nursing*, second ed, N Burden, ed (Philadelphia: WB Saunders Co, 2000) 409-476.

3. S Smith, "Progressive postanesthesia care: Phase II recovery," in *Ambulatory Surgical Nursing*, second ed, N Burden, ed (Philadelphia: WB Saunders Co, 2000) 477-503.

4. "Standard III: Staffing and personnel management," in *Standards of Perianesthesia Nursing Practice* (Cherry Hill, NJ: American Society of PeriAnesthesia Nurses, 2004) 14.

5. "Management of human resources," in *2004 Comprehensive Accreditation Manual for Ambulatory Care* (Oakbrook Terrace, Ill: Joint Commission on Accreditation of Healthcare Organizations, 2004) HR1-HR12.

6. "Surgical and related services," in *Accreditation Guidebook for Office Based Surgery* (Wilmette, Ill: Accreditation Association for Ambulatory Health Care, 2004) 47-52.

7. "Resource 3, patient classification/recommended staffing guidelines," in *Standards of Perianesthesia Nursing Practice* (Cherry Hill, NJ: American Society of PeriAnesthesia Nurses, 2004) 25-26.

8. "AORN official statement on unlicensed assistive personnel," in *Standards, Recommended Practices, and Guidelines* (Denver: AORN, Inc, 2004) 167-168.

9. "Quality of care provided," in *Accreditation Guidebook for Office Based Surgery* (Wilmette, Ill: Accreditation Association for Ambulatory Health Care, 2004) 19-21.

10. "Provision of care, treatment, and services," in *2004 Comprehensive Accreditation Manual for Ambulatory Care* (Oakbrook Terrace, Ill: Joint Commission on Accreditation of Healthcare Organizations, 2004) PC1-PC50.

11. "Standard VI: Assessment," in *Standards of Perianesthesia Nursing Practice* (Cherry Hill, NJ: American Society of PeriAnesthesia Nurses, 2002) 17.

12. "Resource 4: Criteria for initial, ongoing, and discharge assessment and management," in *Standards of Perianesthesia Nursing Practice* (Cherry Hill, NJ: American Society for PeriAnesthesia Nurses, 2002) 27-30.

13. G D Williams, "Preoperative preparation of the ambulatory surgery patient," in *Ambulatory Surgical Nursing*, second ed, N Burden, ed (Philadelphia: WB Saunders Co, 2000) 346-362.

14. D Dunn, "Preoperative assessment criteria and patient teaching for ambulatory surgery patients," *Journal of PeriAnesthesia Nursing* 13 (October 1998) 274-291.

15. "Provision of care, treatment, and services" in *2004 Comprehensive Accreditation Manual for Ambulatory Care* (Oakbrook Terrace, Ill: Joint Commission on Accreditation of Healthcare Organizations, 2004) PC.3.10.

16. R E Grundman, "Preoperative patient care," in *Ambulatory Surgery Principles and Practices*, third ed, N J Vinson, ed (Denver: AORN, Inc, 2003) 109-124.

17. "What's being done to make ambulatory surgery safer?" *OR Manager* 19 (March 2003) 30-35.

18. "Guidelines for ambulatory anesthesia and surgery," American Society of Anesthesiology, *http://www.asahq.org/publicationsAndServices/standards/04.pdf* (accessed 29 Sept 2004).

19. P Patterson, "NPO status: Have ASCs changed policies?" *OR Manager* 17 (March 2001) 25-27.

20. "Be proactive on advance directives," *OR Manager* 17 (June 2001) 25-26.

21. J M Mathias, "Assess first, test later, centers say," *OR Manager* 17 (May 2001) 26-28.

22. B A Scales, "Screening high-risk patients for the ambulatory setting," *Journal of Perianesthesia Nursing* 18 (October 2003) 307-316.

23. "Clinical records and health information," in *Accreditation Guidebook for Office Based Surgery* (Wilmette, Ill: Accreditation Association for Ambulatory Health Care, 2004) 29-31.

24. "Anesthesia services," in *Accreditation Guidebook for Office Based Surgery* (Wilmette, Ill: Accreditation Association for Ambulatory Health Care, 2004) 41-45.

25. M J Bernier et al, "Preoperative teaching received and valued in a day surgery setting," *AORN Journal* 77 (March 2003) 563-582.

26. "Practice guidelines for preoperative fasting and the use of pharmacologic agents to reduce the risk of pulmonary aspiration: Application to healthy patients undergoing elective procedures," American Society of

Anesthesiologists, *http://www.asahq.org/publications AndServices/NPO.pdf* (accessed 16 April 2004).

27. R M Tappen, J Muzic, P Kennedy, "Preoperative assessment and discharge planning for older adults undergoing ambulatory surgery," (Elder Care) *AORN Journal* 73 (February 2001) 464-474.

28. "2005 National Patient Safety Goals FAQs," Joint Commission on Accreditation of Healthcare Organizations, *http://www.jcaho.org/accredited+organizations/ patient+safety/05+npsg/05_npsg_faqs.htm* (accessed 1 Jan 2005)

29. M C Karlet, "Malignant hyperthermia: Considerations for ambulatory surgery," *Journal of PeriAnesthesia Nursing* 13 (October 1998) 304-312.

30. K Cunningham, "Pain management," in *Ambulatory Surgery Principles and Practices*, third ed, N J Vinson, ed (Denver: AORN, Inc, 2003) 145-149.

31. D A Krenzischek, L Wilson, "An introduction to the ASPAN pain and comfort clinical guideline," *Journal of PeriAnesthesia Nursing* 18 (August 2003) 228-236.

32. "Correct site surgery toolkit" (Denver: AORN, Inc, 2004).

33. J C Rothrock, *Perioperative Nursing Care Planning* (St Louis: Mosby, 1990) 497.

34. "Surveillance, prevention, and control of infection," in *2004 Comprehensive Accreditation Manual for Ambulatory Care* (Oakbrook Terrace, Ill: Joint Commission on Accreditation of Healthcare Organizations, 2004) IC1-IC24.

35. "Facilities and environment," in *Accreditation Guidebook for Office Based Surgery* (Wilmette, Ill: Accreditation Association for Ambulatory Health Care, 2004) 35-38.

36. "Antimicrobial prophylaxis in surgery," *The Medical Letter on Drugs and Therapeutics* 39 (Oct 24, 1997) 97-101.

37. "ASHP therapeutic guidelines on antimicrobial prophylaxis in surgery," American Society of Health-System Pharmacists, *http://www.medqic.org/cms-service/stream/ asset/TK8_tagged.pdf?asset_id=847853* (accessed 29 Sept 2004).

38. "Suggested recommendations and guidelines for surgical prophylaxis," Medical College of Wisconsin, *http:// www.intmed.mcw.edu/drug/SurgProph.html* (accessed 29 Sept 2004).

39. "Recommended practices for safe care through identification of potential hazards in the surgical environment," in *Standards, Recommended Practices, and Guidelines* (Denver: AORN, Inc, 2004) 301-307.

40. A Kurz, D I Sessler, R Lenhardt, "Perioperative normothermia to reduce the incidence of surgical-wound infection and shorten hospitalization," *The New England Journal of Medicine* 334 (May 9, 1996) 1209-1215.

41. "Improving organizational performance," in *2004 Comprehensive Accreditation Manual for Ambulatory Care* (Oakbrook Terrace, Ill: Joint Commission on Accreditation of Healthcare Organizations, 2004) PI6.

Originally published in *Standards, Recommended Practices, and Guidelines,* 2005 edition. Reprinted April 2005, *AORN Journal.*

AORN Guidance Statement: Reuse of Single-Use Devices

Introduction

Today's economic environment has compelled health care organizations to explore methods to reduce health care costs. One prospective approach to controlling rising costs is to reprocess single-use medical devices. Reprocessing is rigorously regulated by the US Food and Drug Administration (FDA). AORN, the Association of periOperative Registered Nurses, recognizes the need for each health care facility to provide safe, cost-effective, quality care to patients and realizes that many facilities in today's marketplace are reprocessing and reusing devices labeled for single use. These devices are reprocessed either within the facility or by an external third party contracted to provide the reprocessing service.

Background

As surgery evolved and increased in complexity, the number of single-use devices utilized during surgery increased and continues to rise. In response to this trend, the practice of reprocessing and reusing single-use medical devices began during the 1970s.[1] As technology led to a wide variety of materials used in device manufacture and devices became more complex, concern for patient safety, informed consent, and ethical practice intensified. In the late 1990s, the FDA determined that increased regulation of reprocessing was needed to promote safe practice and protect the public's safety. Although original equipment manufacturers have been regulated for many years, the FDA determined that they, along with third-party reprocessors and hospital reprocessors, should be regulated uniformly according to the Food, Drug, and Cosmetic Act. The FDA sought the expertise of manufacturers, reprocessors, hospitals, users, and other interested parties in developing a regulatory document, and in August 2000, it published its rule governing the reprocessing/reusing of devices labeled for single-use only. The document is applicable to both hospitals and third-party reprocessors.

Reprocessing of single-use devices (SUDs) is additionally addressed in the Medical Device User Fee and Modernization Act of 2002 (MDUFMA), which establishes new statutory requirements for SUDs, including labeling to identify the devices as reprocessed, submission of validation data for many reprocessed SUDs, and submission of premarket notification (510[k]) with validation data for some SUDs that previously were exempt from 510(k) submission requirements. Firms and hospitals that are reprocessing are considered by the FDA as manufacturers and therefore must comply with statutory and regulatory requirements.[2] In addition, the FDA has published an approved list of single-use devices that are acceptable for reprocessing and a list of items that may not be reprocessed. In essence, the regulations regard reprocessors in the same way as original equipment manufacturers.[3,4]

Guidance Statement

Reprocessing single-use medical devices is chosen by some health care facilities as a cost containment effort and to reduce the amount of waste generated. It is the role and responsibility of each health care facility to determine whether and to what extent it will engage in such practice. As licensed professionals, perioperative nurses must demonstrate accountability to the nursing profession, to other members of the health care team, and to the public they serve.[5] AORN, the professional organization of and for perioperative nurses, believes certain basic tenets must underpin any reprocessing program. The foremost concern is for the patient's safety. Therefore,

- if a device cannot be cleaned, it cannot be reprocessed and reused;
- if sterility of a post-processed device cannot be demonstrated, the device cannot be reprocessed and reused;
- if the integrity and functionality of a reprocessed SUD cannot be demonstrated and documented as safe for patient care and/or equal to the original device specifications, the device cannot be reprocessed and reused; and
- if anything is opened it needs to be decontaminated before reprocessing.

Per requirements of the MDUFMA regulation, the FDA has published a list of reprocessed SUDs that have 510(k) approval/clearance; whose manufacturers have provided supplemental data on functionality, cleaning, and sterility; and which now are on the published list of devices that are acceptable for reprocessing.[2]

Although some operational savings may be realized by reusing certain devices, any cost-benefit analysis would necessarily include labor costs;

program costs, including quality system requirements such as sterility and post-processing device
testing (see section on quality system requirements); documentation costs; and the potential
cost of device failure. Using the results of a thorough cost-benefit analysis, each provider facility
must make an informed choice as to whether it
wishes to invest the necessary resources to develop
a safe reprocessing system within the facility. Use
of an external reprocessor presents a different, but
related, set of factors for consideration. When a
decision is made in favor of using an external
reprocessing company, it is the user facility's
responsibility to assess the quality of services provided under the contractual arrangement.[6] The user
facility should review the processes used by the
contracted agent and determine whether correct
procedures are being followed.[7] Regardless of
whether an internal reprocessing program is developed or an external reprocessing company is
selected, the user facility should be aware that the
FDA views any reprocessor as a manufacturer and,
as such, subject to federal regulations.[3,8,9]

Federal Regulatory Requirements

In August 2000, the FDA issued guidance on the
practice of reprocessing and reusing medical
devices intended to be used only once. The FDA's
goal in issuing this regulation was to ensure a
reprocessing and reuse regulatory program that is
based on good science and protects the public
health. At the same time, the FDA intended to
ensure equitable regulatory requirements for all
parties engaged in reprocessing. In the guidance
document,[10] the FDA indicates that hospitals and
third parties that reprocess SUDs are subject to the
same regulations as the original equipment manufacturers. The MDUFMA also addressed reprocessing of SUDs by amending the federal Food, Drug
and Cosmetic Act (the Act) and establishing new
statutory requirements applicable to reprocessed
SUDs, including requirements for
- quality system regulations,
- medical device reporting,
- registration and listing,
- labeling,
- premarket approval and premarket notification,
- medical device corrections and removals, and
- medical device tracking.[2]

Quality System Regulation

All manufacturers, including hospital and third-party
reprocessors, are subject to the FDA Good Manufacturing Practices (GMP) requirements. These requirements are presented in the quality system regulation
that governs the methods, facilities, and controls
used for designing, manufacturing, packaging, labeling, storing, installing, and servicing medical
devices.[3] Quality system refers to the organizational
structure, responsibilities, procedures, processes, and
resources for implementing quality management. For
device manufacturers, including reprocessors, this
system is required in addition to any quality improvement program that may be in place as required by
other regulatory bodies. The quality system regulation addresses the areas shown in **Table 1**.[11]

Medical Device Reporting (MDR)

Under MEDWATCH, the FDA's medical device
reporting program resulting from the Safe Medical
Devices Act of 1990 (Public Law 101-629),[12] both
manufacturers and users are required to report deaths
or serious injuries to the FDA if it can be reasonably
determined that a medical device may have caused
or contributed to the incident. Manufacturers also
must report certain device malfunctions.[13] Because
the FDA considers reprocessors to be manufacturers
when they reprocess an SUD,[9] hospital reprocessors
have dual reporting responsibility. They are subject to
manufacturer's reporting requirements (21 CFR, Part
803 Subpart E)[14] as well as those for the device user
facility (21 CFR, Part 803, Subparts A and C).[15,16]
Although user facilities must report only deaths or
serious injury, manufacturers' reporting requirements
are more extensive and require additional supplemental information. Manufacturers (reprocessors)
also must report any event that requires the manufacturer (reprocessor) to take immediate remedial
action. The Jan 26, 2000, issue of the *Federal Register*
contains the most recent MDR requirements. Hospitals that reprocess SUDs are subject to both user
facility reporting and the more comprehensive manufacturer reporting requirements.[17]

Registration and Listing

All persons or entities owning or operating establishments that manufacture, prepare, or process
devices must register with the FDA. The FDA uses

Table 1

QUALITY SYSTEM REGULATION[1]	
Area Addressed	**Code of Federal Regulations**
Management responsibility	21 CFR, Part 820.20, 22, 25
Design controls	21 CFR, Part 820.30
Document controls	21 CFR, Part 820.40
Purchasing controls	21 CFR, Part 820.50
Product identification and traceability	21 CFR, Part 820.60, 65
Production and process validation	21 CFR, Part 820.70, 72, 75
Acceptance activities such as inspections, tests, or other verification activities	21 CFR, Part 820.80, 86
Nonconforming product control	21 CFR, Part 820.90
Corrective and preventive action	21 CFR, Part 820.100
Labeling and packaging controls	21 CFR, Part 820.120, 130
Handling, storage, distribution, and installation controls	21 CFR, Part 820.120, 140, 150, 160
Records including device master record, device history record, quality system record, and complaint files controls	21 CFR, Part 820.180, 181, 184, 186, 198
Servicing controls	21 CFR, Part 820.200
Use of statistical techniques to establish, control, and verify the acceptability of process capability and product characteristics	21 CFR, Part 820.250

1. *"Quality system regulation," CFR 21 Part 820, US Food and Drug Administration,* http://www.accessdata.fda.gov/scripts/cdrh/cfdocs/cfCFR/CFRSearch.cfm?CFRPart=820 *(accessed 3 Oct 2005).*

this information to identify and locate establishments that it is required to inspect. When registering, the following information must be provided:

- name and address,
- business names used,
- business name of owner or operator, and
- establishment type.

When registering for the first time, a specific FDA form is required. An additional registration form must be submitted annually thereafter. In addition to registering with the FDA, each reprocessing entity must provide a list of the devices it intends to reprocess. A separate listing form must be submitted for each device to be reprocessed. Devices are listed by category. The following information is required:

- FDA classification name,
- FDA product code,
- brand name, and
- common or usual name.

Additional information about registration and listing is available in the *Code of Federal Regulations* (21 CFR, Part 807).[18] The necessary forms can be obtained from the Office of Compliance, Center for Devices and Radiologic Health (HFZ-307), US Food and Drug Administration, 2094 Gaither Road, Rockville, MD 20850. The Center for Devices and Radiologic Health (CDRH) offers an additional document, *CDRH Guidance for Industry: Instructions for Completion of Medical Device Registration and Listing Forms FDA 2891, 2891a, and 2892.* This document can be obtained from the

Division of Small Manufacturers Assistance (DSMA) at telephone number 800-638-2041 or 301-638-2041; e-mail DSMA@CDRH.fda.gov.

Labeling

The FDA directions for labeling can be found in 21 CFR, Part 801.[19] The term *labeling* includes package inserts as well as the information printed on the actual label of the package. Labeling requirements include the name and location of the manufacturer (reprocessor) and adequate direction for the device's intended use. If the manufacturer (reprocessor) knows of uses other than the intended use of the device, FDA requires the manufacturer (reprocessor) to provide adequate labeling for alternate uses of the device as are known. In addition, MDUFMA added new labeling requirement for reprocessed SUDs (Section 502[v] of the Act). Beginning after January 26, 2004, reprocessed SUDs that are introduced into interstate commerce must prominently and conspicuously bear the statement "Reprocessed device for single use. Reprocessed by [insert the name of the manufacturer that reprocessed the device]."[2] For additional information about labeling requirements, obtain a copy of the FDA guidance document *Labeling Regulatory Requirements for Medical Devices* from *http://www.fda.gov/cdrh/dsma/470.pdf* or contact the Division of Small Manufacturers Assistance (DSMA) by phone at 800-638-2041 or 301-638-2041; e-mail DSMA@CDRH.fda.gov.

Premarket Approval and Premarket Notification

After registering with the FDA and submitting a list of devices to be manufactured (reprocessed) and distributed for use, the registered entity must meet premarket submission requirements for each listed device. Certain devices may be exempt from the premarket submission requirement. If exempt, the device need only be listed with the FDA. Additional information about exemptions can be found in 21 CFR, Part 807.75.[20] The FDA has defined a phase-in period for premarket submissions to accommodate entities that are presently engaged in reprocessing. Following the phase-in period, a premarket submission must be submitted for any new device to be manufactured (reprocessed) at least 90 days before beginning distribution of the device.

There are two types of premarket submissions: a premarket notification, or 510(k), and a premarket approval (PMA) application. The type of submission required is based on the device classification, as defined in 21 CFR, Part 814.[21] Unless specifically exempted, a premarket notification (510[k]) is required for all Class I and Class II devices. A premarket notification (510[k]) submission must contain enough information for the FDA to determine whether the particular device is "substantially equivalent" to another device that has been previously judged to be safe and effective and has been cleared for marketing/reprocessing. The predicate device selected must have the same intended use as the device for which the 510(k) is submitted. The predicate device may be the original SUD of the original equipment manufacturer (OEM) provided that the 510(k) compares the unique characteristics of the submitted device to those of the predicate device so the FDA can determine equivalency with respect to safety and effectiveness. The following information is required for a premarket notification (510[k]) submission:

- device trade name, proprietary name, usual name, or classification name;
- entity registration number;
- device classification;
- action taken to determine device performance standards;
- proposed labels, labeling, and advertisements to describe the device, its intended use, and the directions for its use, including photos and/or engineering drawings if appropriate;
- appropriate data to show that the registered entity has considered the consequences and effects any changes or modifications in the device might have on the safety and effectiveness of the device;
- 510(k) summary or 510(k) statement as defined in 21 CFR, Part 807.92, 93;[22]
- financial disclosure statement;[9]
- statement certifying truth, accuracy, and completeness of material submitted; and
- any other information requested by the FDA.

For specific guidance on preparing 510(k) submissions, consult *Regulatory Requirements for Medical Devices*, available at *http://ww.fda.gov/cdrh/manual/510kprt1.html*, or contact the Division of Small Manufacturers Assistance. Locate other relevant guidelines at *http://ww.accessdata.fda.gov/scripts/cdrh/cfdocs/cfGGPSearch.CFM*.

All Class III devices require a PMA. A PMA application must include valid scientific evidence demonstrating the safety and effectiveness of the original and/or reprocessed device. Each PMA application should evaluate the unique characteristics of the submitted device. Clinical data (eg, results of clinical trials) may be required. Some clinical trials require FDA approval of an investigational device exemption (IDE) application for the device(s) to be studied. For additional information, consult the following sources:

♦ 21 CFR, Part 814.20;[21]
♦ 21 CFR, Part 812;[22]
♦ *Device Advice: Premarket Approval (PMA)*, available at *http://www.fda.gov/cdrh/devadvice /pma* (accessed 3 Oct 2005);
♦ *Guidance for Institutional Review Boards and Clinical Investigators*, "Significant risk and nonsignificant risk medical device studies," available at *http://www.fda.gov/oc/ohrt /irbs/devices.html* (accessed 3 Oct 2005); and
♦ *Device Advice: Clinical Trials and Investigational Device Exemption (IDE)*, available at *http://www.fda.gov/cdrh/devadvice/ide /application.shtml* (accessed 3 Oct 2005).

The FDA also requires a satisfactory inspection of the manufacturing (reprocessing) facilities before approving a PMA application. The application should include a comprehensive manufacturing (reprocessing) section that clearly identifies all manufacturing (reprocessing) controls. Under MDUFMA, some SUDs that previously were exempt from 510(k) submission requirements under Sections 510(l) or (m) of the Act are no longer exempt and are required under Section 510(o)(2) of the Act to submit 510(k) notifications that include validation data. Validation data also was required for some reprocessed SUDs that already had been cleared under 510(k). Under Section 510(o) of the Act, reprocessors that either did not submit validation data for those reprocessed SUDs within specified time frames or received "not substantially equivalent letters" from the FDA can no longer legally market those reprocessed devices. Finally, under Section 515(c)(2) of the Act, reprocessors of Class III SUDs are required to submit premarket reports instead of premarket approval applications.[2]

Medical Device Corrections and Removals

Device correction and/or removal from the point of use must be promptly reported to the FDA when the correction or removal is initiated by the manufacturer (reprocessor) to reduce a health risk to the user or to correct a violation of the Food, Drug, and Cosmetic Act. For example, if a facility reprocessed an SUD that resulted in a patient's adverse reaction and the hospital chose to remove the remainder of the lot of those reprocessed SUDs from circulation to decrease the possibility of other patients having adverse reactions, that action would be a removal and the facility would be required to report the removal to the FDA. Corrections are defined as

the repair, modification, adjustment, relabeling, destruction, or inspection of a device without its physical removal from its point of use.[23]

Removal is defined as

the physical removal of a device from its point of use to some other location for repair, modification, adjustment, relabeling, destruction, or inspection.[23]

Distributed devices withdrawn from the marketplace due to a minor violation of the Food, Drug, and Cosmetic Act or as a matter of stock rotation need not be reported. Stock recoveries need not be reported, nor should devices removed for routine servicing. The term *stock recoveries* refers to devices that have been prepared for use, but have not left the physical premises and jurisdiction of the manufacturer (reprocessor)—eg, devices that have not left the reprocessing area. However, each correction and/or removal must be documented regardless of whether it is reported to the FDA.

When a report must be filed with the FDA, the report must be filed within 10 days of the correction/removal action. The report should include the following information:

♦ registration number of the entity manufacturing/reprocessing the device;
♦ date of the report;
♦ sequence number of the report from that entity;
♦ name, address, and telephone number of the reporting entity;
♦ name, title, address, and telephone number of individual responsible for the correction/ removal action;
♦ brand name, classification name, and common name of the device and its intended use;
♦ marketing status of the device;
♦ model, catalog, and code number of the device and the manufacturer's (reprocessor's) lot, serial, or other identification number for the device;

◆ description of event leading to correction/removal action;

◆ any injuries resulting from device use;

◆ total number of devices manufactured (reprocessed) subject to the correction/removal action;

◆ date of manufacture/distribution/reprocessing and expected shelf life of the device;

◆ name, address, telephone number of all to whom the device has been distributed and the number of devices distributed to each; and

◆ copies of all communication regarding the correction/removal action and the names and address of all recipients of the communication.

For additional information about correction and removal requirements, consult 21 CFR, Part 806.

Medical Device Tracking

Medical device tracking is intended to ensure that manufacturers (reprocessors) of certain devices can locate those devices should corrective action and/or notification about such devices become necessary. Original equipment manufacturers are subject to the medical device tracking regulation only when the FDA issues a tracking order for a device manufactured by the OEM. Reprocessors are subject to the medical device tracking regulation only when the FDA issues an order for the specific device(s) being reprocessed. For additional information on device tracking, including the types of devices currently subject to tracking orders, consult *Guidance on Medical Device Tracking,* available at *http://www.fda.gov/cerh/modact/tracking/pdf* or from the Center for Devices and Radiologic Health (CDRH) at 301-827-0111. Request document number 169.

Definitions

Class I medical device: A medical device for which general controls provide reasonable assurance of the safety and effectiveness of the device or, if there is insufficient evidence to reasonably ensure safety and effectiveness, the device is not life-supporting or life-sustaining, its use is not substantially important in preventing impairment of human health, and/or its use "does not present a potential unreasonable risk of illness or injury."[23]

Class II medical device: A medical device for which general controls alone do not provide reason-

able assurance of device safety and effectiveness but for which there is sufficient information to establish special controls (eg, performance standards, guidelines, patient registries, postmarket surveillance) to provide that assurance.[23]

Class III medical device: A medical device for which neither general controls nor special controls provide reasonable assurance of device safety and effectiveness and the device is life-supporting or life sustaining or its use "is of substantial importance in preventing impairment of human health" or "presents a potential risk of illness or injury."[23]

Opened-but-unused device: A device whose sterility is compromised before being introduced onto the sterile field and which is not contaminated with blood and/or other potentially infectious materials (OPIM) external to the sterile field.[24]

Reprocessing: Includes all operations to render a contaminated reusable or single-use device patient ready. Single-use devices to be reprocessed may be either used or unused. Reprocessing steps include cleaning, decontamination, and sterilization/disinfection.[9]

Resterilization: The repeated application of a process intended to remove or destroy all viable forms of microbial life, including bacterial spores.[9] Because sterility is not an absolute, the accepted sterility assurance level (SAL) is usually defined as 10^{-6}.

Reuse: The repeated or multiple uses of any medical device whether marketed as reusable or single-use. Repeated/multiple use may be on the same patient or on different patients with applicable reprocessing of the device between uses.[25]

Single-use device (SUD): A device intended by the manufacturer to be used on one patient during one procedure. The device is not intended for reprocessing and/or use on another patient or on the same patient at another time. Device labeling may or may not identify the device as single-use or disposable, but manufacturer instructions for reprocessing are absent.[9]

Third-party reprocessor: A business establishment, separate from the user facility and the device manufacturer, one of whose primary businesses is to reprocess single-use/disposable medical devices.

REFERENCES

1. "Reuse of single-use devices," *AORN Journal* 73 (May 2001) 957-966.

2. "Medical Device User Fee and Modernization Act (MDUFMA) of 2002," PL 107-250, 107th Congress, *http://www.fda.gov/cdrh/mdufma* (accessed 3 Oct 2005).

3. "Guidance for industry and for FDA staff: Enforcement priorities for single-use devices reprocessed by third parties and hospitals," (Aug 14, 2000) US Food and Drug Administration, *http://www.fda.gov/cdrh/reuse/1168.html* (accessed 3 Oct 2005).

4. "Medical devices; reprocessed single-use devices; termination of exemptions from premarket notification; requirement for submission of validation data," US Food and Drug Administration, *http://www.fda.gov/OHRMS/DOCKETS/98fr/03-16109.html* (accessed 3 Oct 2005).

5. "AORN explications for perioperative nursing," in *Standards, Recommended Practices, and Guidelines* (Denver: AORN, Inc, 2005) 86-115.

6. Joint Commission on Accreditation of Healthcare Organizations, "Standard LD.3.50: Services provided by consultation, contractual agreements, or other agreements are provided safely and effectively," in *Comprehensive Accreditation Manual for Hospitals* (Oakbrook Terrace, Ill: Joint Commission on Accreditation of Healthcare Organizations, 2005) LD 13.

7. "Letter re: Reusable medical devices rented or leased from third parties," US Food and Drug Administration, *http://www.fda.gov/cdrh/comp/rentleasethird.html* (accessed 23 Aug 2005).

8. "Quality system regulation, Definitions," CFR 21, Part 820.3, US Food and Drug Administration, *http://www.accessdata.fda.gov/scripts/cdrh/cfdocs/cfCFR/CFRSearch.cfm?fr=820.3* (accessed 3 Oct 2005).

9. "Letter to American College of Healthcare Executives: Reuse of single-use or disposable medical devices," US Food and Drug Administration, *http://www.fda.gov/cdrh/comp/policymayaply.html* (accessed 3 Oct 2005).

10. Center for Devices and Radiological Health, US Food and Drug Administration, US Department of Health and Human Services, *Enforcement Priorities for Single-Use Devices Reprocessed by Third Parties and Hospitals* (Washington, DC: US Government Printing Office, Aug 14, 2000).

11. "Quality system regulation," CFR 21, Part 820, US Food and Drug Administration, *http://www.accessdata.fda.gov/scripts/cdrh/cfdocs/cfCFR/CFRSearch.cfm?CFRPart=820* (accessed 3 Oct 2005).

12. "Safe Medical Devices Act of 1990," Public Law 101-629, *http://thomas.loc.gov/cgi-bin/query/C?c101:./temp/~c101exlXhd* (accessed 23 Aug 2005).

13. "Medical device reporting: General provisions," CFR 21, Part 803.1, US Food and Drug Administration, *http://www.accessdata.fda.gov/scripts/cdrh/cfdocs/cfcfr/CFRSearch.cfm?fr=803.1* (accessed 3 Oct 2005).

14. "Manufacturer reporting requirements," CFR 21, Part 803, Subpart E, US Food and Drug Administration, *http://www.accessdata.fda.gov/scripts/cdrh/cfdocs/cfcfr/CFRSearch.cfm?CFRPart=803* (accessed 23 Aug 2005).

15. "Medical device reporting: General provisions," CFR 21, Part 803, Subpart A, US Food and Drug Administration, *http://www.accessdata.fda.gov/scripts/cdrh/cfdocs/cfcfr/CFRSearch.cfm?CFRPart=803* (accessed 23 Aug 2005).

16. "User facility reporting requirements," CFR 21, Part 803, Subpart C, US Food and Drug Administration, *http://www.accessdata.fda.gov/scripts/cdrh/cfdocs/cfcfr/CFRSearch.cfm?CFRPart=803* (accessed 23 Aug 2005).

17. US Department of Health and Human Services, "Medical device reporting: Manufacturer reporting, importer reporting, user facility reporting, distributor reporting," *Federal Register* 65 (Jan 26, 2000) 4112-4121.

18. "Establishment regulation and device listing for manufacturers and initial importers of devices," CFR 21, Part 807, US Food and Drug Administration, *http://www.accessdata.fda.gov/scripts/cdrh/cfdocs/cfcfr/CFRSearch.cfm?CFRPart=807* (accessed 23 Aug 2005).

19. "Labeling," CFR 21, Part 801, US Food and Drug Administration, *http://www.accessdata.fda.gov/scripts/cdrh/cfdocs/cfcfr/CFRSearch.cfm?CFRPart=801* (accessed 23 Aug 2005).

20. "Exemption from premarket notification," CFR 21, Part 807.65, US Food and Drug Administration, *http://www.accessdata.fda.gov/scripts/cdrh/cfdocs/cfcfr/CFRSearch.cfm?fr=807.65* (accessed 23 Aug 2005).

21. "Premarket approval of medical devices," CFR 21, Part 814, US Food and Drug Administration, *http://www.accessdata.fda.gov/scripts/cdrh/cfdocs/cfcfr/CFRSearch.cfm?CFRPart=814* (accessed 23 Aug 2005).

22. "Investigational device exemptions," CFR 21, Part 812, US Food and Drug Administration, *http://www.accessdata.fda.gov/scripts/cdrh/cfdocs/cfcfr/CFRSearch.cfm?CFRPart=812* (accessed 3 Oct 2005).

23. "Medical devices: Reports of corrections and removals, definitions," CFR 21, Part 806.2, US Food and Drug Administration, *http://www.accessdata.fda.gov/scripts/cdrh/cfdocs/cfcfr/CFRSearch.cfm* (accessed 3 Oct 2005).

24. "Guidance for industry and for FDA staff: Enforcement priorities for single-use devices reprocessed by third parties and hospitals," US Food and Drug Administration, *http://www.fda.gov/cdrh/reuse/1168.html#_Toc492780057* (accessed 2 Feb 2006).

25. Center for Devices and Radiological Health, US Food and Drug Administration, US Department of Health and Human Services, "FDA's proposed strategy on reuse of single-use devices, docket no 99N-4491," *Federal Register* 64 (Nov 3, 1999) 59782-59783.

RESOURCES

Medical Device Quality Systems Manual: A Small Entity Compliance Guidance, US Food and Drug Administration, *http://www.fda.gov/CDRH/DSMA/GMPMAN.HTML* (accessed 3 Oct 2005).

Originally published in *Standards, Recommended Practices, and Guidelines,* 2005 edition. Reprinted November 2006, *AORN Journal.*

AORN Guidance Statement: Safe On-Call Practices in Perioperative Practice Settings

Introduction

The purpose of this guidance statement is to assist managers and clinicians in developing policies and procedures related to safe call practices for perioperative personnel. Providing care for patients requiring urgent or emergent surgery after regular hours of operation is a reality for perioperative nurses. Perioperative personnel are assigned designated times to be available for unplanned, urgent, or emergent procedures or to provide care for patients whose procedures run over the scheduled time. These assignments are referred to as "call."

Many perioperative nurses take call after scheduled hours, on weekends, and on holidays in addition to their daily shift assignments. Call hours vary, but generally are eight to 16 hours on weekdays, 48 to 64 hours on weekends, and 72 hours or more for extended holiday weekends. Actual hours worked during the call period are unpredictable and can range from 30 minutes to the entire length of the call period. Covering call may strain existing resources, create stress for perioperative staff members, affect safe patient care, and increase the potential for occupational injury due to prolonged work hours.

Background

Traditionally, perioperative nurses have worked eight-hour shifts; however, several new trends in perioperative staffing patterns include fewer, but longer, work days in addition to a call schedule. The expansion of work hour flexibility enhances individual nurse satisfaction and accommodates the organization's objectives.[1] Although the call schedule may be assigned on a rotating basis according to patient population, organizational needs, and demographic challenges, perioperative nurses may take extra call to increase compensation (eg, elective overtime). Perioperative nurses also may be mandated to work beyond their scheduled work/call shift to augment staffing requirements, meet unexpected patient needs, or satisfy organizational expectations (eg, mandatory overtime). These new trends in staffing and call hours have converged to create potentially hazardous conditions for patient and employee safety. There is a lack of current research in trending the number of hours worked per day by nurses. Anecdotal reports suggest that perioperative staff nurses are working longer hours with fewer breaks and often have inadequate time for rest between shifts.[2] Twenty-four hour call shifts are becoming more common.[3]

Long hours and prolonged periods of wakefulness are among working conditions that may have a negative effect on human performance.[4-6] It has been reported that 17 hours without sleep can have an adverse affect on performance equivalent to a blood alcohol concentration of 0.05%.[1] At 24 hours without sleep, performance degradation is equivalent to a blood alcohol concentration of 0.10.[7]

Fatigue resulting from working long hours can have a detrimental effect on patient care. Work by Rogers et al demonstrates a link between working long hours and medical errors; the possibility of an error triples after 12.5 hours of work.[3,5] Moreover, this research identified that medication errors, procedural errors, documentation, and transcription errors occur more frequently as work hours increase.[7,8] Studies suggest a correlation between sleep deprivation and negative effects on memory, language/numeric skills, visual attention and concentration.[9-11] In addition to creating a risk to patient safety, research indicates that sleep-deprived and fatigued nurses are at increased risk for personal injury on duty and when driving home after an extended work day.[5,12,13]

The existing nursing shortage is contributing to extended work hours and call shifts for perioperative nurses. It is predicted the number of RNs will fall to 20% below the demand by 2010.[2] More than 126,000 nursing positions currently are estimated to be unfilled.[1] This increases the burden of perioperative nurse fatigue with longer working hours and extended call requirements.

Guidance Statement

Recognizing that long work hours are a growing concern among nursing organizations, regulatory agencies, patient safety organizations, and perioperative nurses, this document offers a framework from which managers and clinicians can develop and implement methodologies to safely establish a call schedule. The call staffing plan retains the perioperative RN as circulator and is consistent with established AORN recommendations for nurse:patient ratios. The call staffing plan should minimize long work hours and allow for adequate recuperation between shifts. This guidance statement may be adapted to any setting in which call schedules are required.

Ultimately, health care organizations are responsible for developing and implementing staffing policies and procedures relevant to individual practice settings. Perioperative nurse leaders should be knowledgeable about emerging research and incorporate new evidence into the development, evaluation, and revision of policies for safe staffing and on-call practices.[6] Health care facilities should develop an organizational culture that promotes and provides safeguards to protect staff members and patients from potential errors and workplace injuries.

Individual facility policy should focus on creating call schedules that consider the effect of working long hours on patient safety as well as on perioperative staff members' well-being.[5,6,14] Safe call practices should be based on the following considerations:

- the type of facility (eg, trauma center, ambulatory surgery center), patient needs, procedure mix, demographics (eg, large metropolitan, rural), and organization structure;
- staff experience, competencies, skill mix; and
- staffing minimums as defined by state regulation, accrediting organization standards, professional organization recommendations, and patient safety requirements.

Suggested Strategies

■ Address staffing limitations in facility-specific policy and procedures based on relevant fatigue-related outcomes studies.

■ Establish a guideline to promote patient and worker safety in relation to the number of hours worked in a 24-hour, seven-day period based on current research. All worked hours should be included. For example, a facility may limit all scheduled and call back hours to 60 hours in a seven-day work week.[6,7]

■ Implement recuperation periods between shifts and establish limits for perioperative call schedules within designated time frames.[5,6]
  - Budget enough full-time equivalents (FTEs) to allow for safe staffing levels.
  - The budget should include adequate replacement staff members to allow rest periods for personnel who have worked long hours.

■ Establish the number of allowed consecutive hours that may be worked. Identify when the next scheduled work shift may begin. Work hour limitations should be determined in accordance with state regulation, accrediting organization standards, professional organization recommendations, and patient safety requirements.

■ Provide education to increase awareness of perioperative staff members' personal responsibility to arrive at work fully rested.[6,7]

■ Consider call requirements for perioperative staff members based on research indicating a correlation between adverse effects of sleep deprivation and aging.[15]

■ Reduce the amount and frequency of unscheduled overtime or last-minute call assignments.

■ Evaluate economic implications of unsafe call practices in relation to workplace injuries and adverse patient outcomes.

■ Develop performance improvement activities to determine if there is a correlation between workplace injuries, errors, adverse patient outcomes, and the number of hours worked during call.

■ Involve perioperative nurses in developing call schedules and work processes.

■ Develop competency-based orientation programs for new perioperative staff members, including skill acquisition to manage urgent and emergent patient care. The orientation time frame should be determined based on the type of procedures performed and experience of perioperative staff members.

■ Establish a staffing plan to recognize and retain staff members with extended tenure.
  - Develop guidelines for self-assignment of call. Management should review the call schedule before posting it to ensure appropriate coverage for patient safety.
  - Explore fiscal and operational benefits of establishing a dedicated call team.
  - Consider providing sleep rooms to allow perioperative staff members the option to stay at the facility during the call shift to alleviate the potential of sleep deprivation and fatigue. A sleep room also would allow for timely response to urgent and emergent cases.

Summary

Call staffing and the associated long work hours can be challenging for both perioperative staff members and the health care organization. A change in culture is needed to recognize exhaustion as an unacceptable risk to patients and perioperative personnel safety. Perioperative health care providers have a personal responsibility to arrive at work fully rested. Health care organizations have a responsibility to create work and call schedules that consider the effect of long work hours on patient safety as well as perioperative staff members' welfare. The development of standardized safe work hours and call practices should reflect current recommendations emerging from authoritative sources, legislation, and empirical data. Prolonged work periods without adequate rest may contribute to diminished performance by perioperative personnel, placing both patients and workers at risk. This guidance statement may assist managers and clinicians in developing policies and procedures for safe call practices.

REFERENCES

1. "Keeping patients safe: Transforming the work environment of nurses," National Academies Press, *http://www.nap.edu/openbook/0309090679/html/1.html* (accessed 13 Dec 2004).
2. A Page, "Appendix C: Work hour regulation in safety-sensitive industries," in *Keeping Patients Safe: Transforming the Work Environment of Nurses* (Washington, DC: National Academies Press, 2004) 384-435.
3. A E Rogers et al, "The working hours of hospital staff nurses and patient safety," *Health Affairs* 23 (July/August 2004) 202-212.
4. "The effect of health care working conditions on patient safety," *Evidence Report: Technology Assessment* 74 (March 2003) 1-3.
5. M R Rosekind et al, "Managing fatigue in operational settings 1: Physiological considerations and countermeasures," *Hospital Topics* 75 (Summer 1997) 23-30.
6. M Rosekind et al, "Managing fatigue in operational settings 2: An integrated approach," *Hospital Topics* 75 (Summer 1997) 31-35.
7. D M Gaba, S K Howard, "Patient safety: Fatigue among clinicians and the safety of patients," *The New England Journal of Medicine* 347 (Oct 17, 2002) 1249-1255.
8. *Long Working Hours for Nurses Lead to Medical Errors* (news release, Bethesda, Md: Health Affairs, July 7, 2004) 1. Also available at *http://www.rwjf.org/news/newsRelease070604.pdf* (accessed 13 Dec 2004).
9. R P Hart et al, "Effect of sleep deprivation on first-year residents' response times, memory, and mood," *Journal of Medical Education* 62 (November 1987) 940-942.
10. R Rubin et al, "Neurobehavioral effects of the on-call experience in housestaff physicians," *Journal of Occupational Medicine* 33 (January 1991) 13-18.
11. J Robbins, F Gottlieb, "Sleep deprivation and cognitive testing in internal medicine house staff," *Western Journal of Medicine* 152 (January 1990) 82-86.
12. A Gurjala et al "Petition to the Occupational Safety and Health Administration requesting that limits be placed on hours worked by medical residents (HRG publication #1570)," (30 April 2001) Public Citizen, *http://www.citizen.org/publications/release.cfm?ID=6771* (accessed 10 Dec 2004).
13. R G Hughes, A E Rogers, "Are you tired?" *American Journal of Nursing* 104 (March 2004) 36-38.
14. M L Parsons, J Stonestreet, "Staff nurse retention: Laying the groundwork by listening," *Nursing Leadership Forum* 8 (Spring 2004) 107-113.
15. K Reid, D Dawson, "Comparing performance on a simulated 12 hour shift rotation in young and older subjects," *Occupational and Environmental Medicine* 58 (January 2001) 58-62.

RESOURCES

Beck, S M; Wood, D S. "Helping OR staff members cope with the anxiety of being on call," *Surgical Services Management* 3 (November 1997) 39-42.

Dexter, F; O'Neal, L. "Weekend operating room on call staffing requirements," *AORN Journal* 74 (November 2001) 664-671.

Lamberg, L. "Impact of long working hours explored," *JAMA* 292 (July 7, 2004) 25-26.

Lucas, C E, et al. "Mathematical modeling to define optimum operating room staffing needs for trauma centers," *JAMA* 192 (May 2001) 559-565.

Tucker, J B, et al. "Using queuing theory to determine operating room staffing needs," *Trauma Injury, Infection, and Critical Care* 46 (January 1999) 71-79.

Tucker, P. "The impact of rest breaks upon accident risk, fatigue and performance: a review," *Work and Stress* 17 (April 2003) 123-137.

Originally published in *Standards, Recommended Practices, and Guidelines,* 2005 edition. Reprinted May 2005, *AORN Journal.*

AORN Guidance Statement: Safe Medication Practices in Perioperative Settings Across the Life Span

Introduction

This guidance statement provides a framework for perioperative registered nurses to develop, implement, and evaluate safe medication management practices specific to the perioperative setting. This evidenced-based framework may be used to facilitate policy development and provide a foundation for the creation of quality improvement (QI)/process improvement (PI) monitors. It is the responsibility of individual health care organizations to develop a culture of medication safety. Proactively reviewing medication errors from the viewpoint of "systems failures" and "systems solutions" will help encourage a culture free from shame and blame.

Perioperative practice settings addressed by this document include traditional operating rooms, ambulatory surgery units, physicians' offices, cardiac catheterization suites, endoscopy suites, radiology departments, and all other areas where operative and invasive procedures may be performed. For the purpose of this document, the term *OR* is inclusive of all perioperative practice environments.

First published in May 2002, the current guidance statement has been reviewed and updated by AORN's Presidential Commission on Patient Safety, in collaboration with the United States Pharmacopeia (USP), to reflect current safe medication practices.

Background

The National Institute of Medicine report *To Err Is Human: Building a Better Health System* increased awareness of medication errors. The report noted that "medication errors account for one out of 131 outpatient deaths and one out of 854 inpatient deaths."[1] Medication errors can originate at any point in the medication use process and affect patients of all ages. Medication error poses a substantial threat to patients. The perioperative setting creates additional challenges for safe medication administration practices. Related factors affecting the medication process in the perioperative environment include

- the aseptic dispensing of medications onto the sterile field,
- an intermediary to receive and transfer dispensed medications to the scrubbed licensed practitioner (eg, surgeon),
- time-sensitive conditions, and
- sensory distractions intrinsic to the environment.

Specific concerns associated with medication errors in the perioperative setting include, but are not limited to,

- inconsistent practices to communicate current and previous medication regimes (ie, medication reconciliation);
- verbal orders delivered through surgical masks may be muffled and contribute to confusion in the medication order (eg, name, strength, and/or dose);
- incomplete, ambiguous, incorrect, or illegibly written or spoken orders;
- inaccurate, illegible, or outdated surgical preference cards;
- removal of the contents from the original manufacturer's packaging to aseptically deliver contents onto the sterile field;
- limited knowledge of medications by scrubbed allied heath professionals receiving medications onto the sterile field;
- inconsistent labeling of medications on and off the sterile field;
- medication dispensed to the sterile field may be handled by multiple individuals before reaching the licensed individual administering the medication;
- high-alert medications available in multiple dose forms and concentrations;
- look-alike and sound-alike medications stored in close proximity;
- patient care complexity requiring rapid perioperative interventions;
- extended work hours leading to health care worker fatigue;
- care provided by multiple health care providers simultaneously; and
- multiple patient handoffs between care providers.

The following guidance is offered to support perioperative registered nurses in the provision of safe perioperative patient care.

Guidance Statement

Health care organizations should identify in policy which people and/or job categories may participate in medication management and administration. Facility policy for safe medication practice should be based on the five "rights" of medication administration:

♦ the right patient,

♦ the right medication,

♦ the right dose,

♦ the right time, and

♦ the right route.

The five rights of safe medication practices should be a final check before the administration of any medication.

Health care organizations should develop standardized procedures for safe medication practices in the OR designed to include, but not be limited to, the following.

♦ Ensure proper patient identification.

♦ Document all patient medications.

♦ Assess for medication contraindications.

♦ Confirm weight-based dosing before administration.

♦ Establish dose limits.

♦ Minimize use of verbal orders to the extent possible.

♦ Manage medications off the sterile field.

♦ Deliver medications to the sterile field.

♦ Manage medications on the sterile field.

♦ Document all intraoperative medications.

♦ Monitor and document patient for effects of medications.

♦ Preserve all original medication/solution containers and delivery devices until the conclusion of the procedure.

♦ Continually evaluate the medication delivery process for patients within the surgical setting.

♦ Define procedures for the questioning of any medication order thought to be unclear or inappropriate.[2]

General Risk Reduction Strategies

The following risk reduction strategies offer guidance for the development of policies, procedures, and associated QI and PI monitoring tools and reporting processes related to safe medication handling in the OR. The goal should be to meet or exceed the expectations for safe medication practice as outlined by published national patient safety initiatives (eg, the National Patient Safety Goals of the Joint Commission on Accreditation of Healthcare Organizations [JCAHO], guidelines of the Institute for Safe Medication Practices [ISMP] and USP).

Patient Identification

Minimize the potential for medication error related to incorrect identification of the patient through the establishment of standardized identification processes. Documentation of these processes may provide the necessary data to monitor outcomes for improvement.

♦ Consider the preoperative checklist as a permanent part of the patient care record.

♦ Perform patient identification using at least two patient identifiers, neither of which are to be the patient's room number.[3]

♦ Verification of patient identification should include information from the patient's identification (ID) band(s) or identification record when an ID band is not appropriate.

♦ Consider using the patient's date of birth as one means of identification (eg, pediatric population).

♦ Ensure that the contents of patient charts are verified for correct patient information.

♦ Imprints of patient information (eg, Addressograph stamp) on documents should be legible.

♦ Standardized forms should have patient identification in the same place on every page; duplexed pages should be identified on both sides in the same place.

♦ Identify in facility policy which people and/or job categories may participate in medication management and administration.

Accurate Medication List

Provider access to patient-specific information facilitates continuity of care and ensures that essential components for patient care decisions related to the medication management process are available. Readily accessible information should aid in the identification of risk related to medication allergy interaction, contraindication, and medication-medication or herbal-medication interaction. Documentation of this activity is an essential component of outcomes management in regard to patient safety.[4]

♦ Develop a consistent multidisciplinary approach for documenting the patient's medications using a standardized reconciliation sheet that is readily available for review before the procedure.[3]

♦ Actively involve the patient or authorized representative in the process of obtaining a complete list of the patient's current medications.[3]

Medication Contraindications

Whenever possible, written medication orders should be reviewed for appropriateness by a pharmacist before dispensing the medication. Concerns and issues related to medication, dose, frequency, route of administration, therapeutic duplication of the medication, its therapeutic class or chemical family, allergies, potential interactions, and contraindications are all elements of the review process.[4,5]

♦ Existing medication allergy information for each patient must be readily available and communicated to all members of the perioperative team.

♦ Allergy information may be obtained from patients, family members, legal guardians, and/or prior medical records.

♦ Health care organizations should provide readily available resources for perioperative personnel to identify medication class, nutrition and herbal supplement interactions (eg, calcium channel blockers and grapefruit) and associated medication class allergies (eg, amoxicillin and keflex).

♦ An organization-wide process should be in place to cross-reference patient drug allergy interactions, contraindication, and medication-medication/herbal-medication interaction potentials.[3]

– Patient medications should be validated and cross-referenced during the medication-ordering phase of the medication delivery process.

– Reference tools such as computer programs or charts should be used.

Accurate Dose Calculation

The patient's weight should be documented in both pounds and kilograms. Both mathematical formats provide a visual cue to eliminate discrepancies and to alert health care personnel to the proper numerical value used in weight calculations. Accurate weight measurement is critical for accurate dose calculation.[4] The medication dose calculation process should include, but is not limited to, the following.

♦ Accurately obtain weights on all patients before surgery.

♦ A facility-approved weight conversion chart (ie, pounds to kilograms) should be available for quick reference.

♦ Redesign patient care forms to clearly reflect weight in both pounds and kilograms.

♦ If there are discrepancies in weight or dose calculations, the patient should be reevaluated and the weight and dose recalculated.

♦ Medications ordered using weight-based dose schedules should be independently calculated and verified by two licensed individuals.

♦ Automate medication dosage calculations whenever possible.

Dose Limits

Health care organizations should identify high-risk and high-alert medications within the organization and develop processes to safeguard against error. Medications with narrow therapeutic ranges are considered at risk for error. Creating conversion charts targeting dose limits for high-risk medications will contribute to their safe use in surgery.[4]

♦ Dosage conversion charts or electronic aids should be used to calculate maximum dose limits, especially for high-alert medications.

♦ Separate weight-based conversion charts for children and adults should be developed for each of the major error-prone medications identified for that population at risk.

Verbal Orders

Verification of critical components of perioperative verbal orders, before the implementation of the order, affords an opportunity to confirm the accuracy of the verbal order.[3] Use of verbal and telephone orders should be limited.[2] When verbal orders are necessary, provide mechanisms to ensure accuracy, such as

♦ record the order in the patient's record according to facility policy as soon as feasible;[2,6]

♦ perform a "read-back" of the written order;[2,6]

♦ verbalize the read-back digit-by-digit (eg, say "one-two," not "twelve");[2,6] and

♦ allow only licensed health care providers to receive verbal orders.

Managing Medications Off the Sterile Field

Medications should be properly stored to ensure a process for safe and efficient delivery to the patient. Several key issues to consider are environmental conditions for storing medications to ensure product stability, look-alike and sound-alike medication storage, modification of the standard alphabetical medication storage system, and the care and handling of medical gases, reagents, and chemicals to eliminate catastrophic mistakes.[4]

- Standardize and limit the variation of strengths and concentrations of medications as much as possible.[3,4]
- Store medications safely with consideration given to separation of look-alikes and sound-alikes. This includes separating by generic name and packaging to the extent possible.[3,4,7]
- Limit the use of multidose vials whenever possible.[4,8,9]
- Include the facility pharmacist in formulating processes to determine when or if unused and unopened medications are allowed to be returned to the pharmacy.[4]
- Do not store medications alphabetically.[4]
- Label storage areas with both the medication's generic and brand names.
- Verify medication labels after medication retrieval and reconfirm with the written medication order.
- Label all medications, medication containers, and other solutions off the sterile field even if only one medication is involved.[3]
- At shift change or upon staff relief, all medications, medication labels, and the amount of medication administered should be verified concurrently by entering and exiting personnel.
- Discard any unlabeled solution or medication found in the OR.
- Treat medical gases, chemicals, and reagents (eg, formalin, normal saline, Lugol's solution, radiopaque dyes, glutaraldehyde) in the OR with the same care and caution as medications.

Delivering Medications to the Sterile Field

Before administering any medication, a verification process should include a review of the product label for the medication name, strength, and expiration date. This review process should be accomplished in conjunction with an examination of the written medication order to confirm that the correct medication is to be administered. A visual inspection should be made for any indication that the medication was compromised during the storage process (eg, particulates, discoloration).[4]

- Confirm all medications listed on the physician's preference list with the surgeon before delivery to the sterile field.

- Orders with abbreviations, symbols, or acronyms should be clarified with the ordering clinician to minimize confusion or misinterpretation.
- Verify medication in its original container for the correct name, strength, dosage, and route with the surgeon's preference card or documented verbal order.
- Actively communicate the medication name, strength, dosage, and expiration date as the medication is passed to the sterile field.[4]
  - Verbally and visually confirm all medications delivered to the sterile field, including medication name, strength, dosage, and expiration date.[4]
  - Medications should be verified concurrently by the circulating registered nurse and scrub person.
  - If there is no designated scrub person, the circulating registered nurse should confirm the medication visually and verbally with the licensed professional performing the surgical procedure.
- Deliver one medication at a time onto the sterile field.
- Do not remove stoppers from vials for the purpose of pouring medications.
- Use commercially available sterile transfer devices when possible (eg, sterile vial spike, filter straw, plastic catheter).
- Reconfirm maximum dose limits.

Managing Medications on the Sterile Field

Communication is a vital key to the success of the medication delivery process.

- Verbally and visually confirm the medication (ie, medication name, strength, dosage, and expiration date) upon receipt from the circulating registered nurse even if only one medication is involved.[4]
- Label the medication container on the sterile field immediately before receipt of the medication. Avoid distractions and interruptions during the labeling process and while dispensing medications onto the sterile field.
- Label all medication containers and delivery devices with a minimum of the medication name, strength, and concentration when needed.[6]
- Verbally and visually confirm the medication name, strength, and dose by reading the

medication label aloud while passing a medication to the licensed professional performing the procedure.[4]

♦ When patient hand-offs (eg, personnel relief) occur, the medication verification process should take place. The medication should be confirmed for accuracy (ie, product label reviewed for the medication name, strength, and expiration date) in conjunction with a review of the written medication order to validate that the correct medication is on the field.[3]

♦ Discard any solution or medication found on or off the sterile field without an identification label.

Documenting All Intraoperative Medications

A complete and accurate accounting of the medications and solutions used during the surgical encounter is essential to address medication-related issues that may arise during all phases of perioperative care.[4]

♦ Ensure that intraoperative documentation reflects all medications (including irrigation solutions, doses, and routes of administration) administered throughout the procedure.

♦ Document medication administration per organizational policy.

♦ Documentation should incorporate the Perioperative Nursing Data Set (PNDS). The expected outcome for safe medication practices is outcome O9, "The patient receives appropriate medication(s), safely administered during the perioperative period." This outcome falls within the domain of Safety (D1). The associated nursing diagnoses may include X29, "Risk for injury." The associated interventions leading to the desired outcome include I123, "Verifies allergies"; I8, "Administers prescribed medications and solutions"; and I51, "Evaluates response to medications."[10(p103-104)]

Monitoring Patients for Effects of Medications

Assessment and documentation of the patient's response to medication administration provides vital clues related to dose effectiveness and the presence of a potential medication-related adverse effect.[4]

♦ Continually assess, monitor, and document the patient's response to medication administered.[4,10(p104)]

♦ Policies and procedures should be developed for reporting and responding to medication errors and other adverse effects.

♦ Error reporting should occur in a nonpunitive culture.[3]

Retaining All Original Medication/Solution Containers and Delivery Devices

The practice of maintaining possession of medication containers and delivery devices until the patient leaves the OR is important in the event of a medication-related error or adverse reaction. A root cause analysis should be performed following any adverse event. Maintaining possession of these containers may facilitate the analysis.

Periodic Evaluation of the Medication Management Process

An essential step in the medication management process includes ongoing review. An established QI/PI program may identify failure points contributing to medication errors and may aid in improvements in patient safety.

♦ The QI/PI program should include a routine review and update of all preprinted order sheets, and facility-approved standing orders, including
 – medication choice;
 – dose; and
 – delivery method.

♦ Eliminate or minimize the use of problem-prone abbreviations, symbols, and acronyms.[11-13]

Additional Strategies for Medication Safety

■ Operationalize a process for the ongoing review of key elements of the medication delivery process known to contribute to medication errors, to include
 ▪ prescribing,
 ▪ order processing,
 ▪ dispensing,
 ▪ administration, and
 ▪ monitoring.[14]

■ Provide OR personnel with appropriate and timely education related to medication safety procedures. Facilities should implement processes for validating perioperative medication competency covering all age-specific populations (eg, periop-erative medication competencies in "AORN's safe medication administration tool kit").[15]

■ Use a competency checklist focused on the med-ication delivery process (eg, perioperative medica-tion performance validation record in "AORN's safe medication administration tool kit").[15]

■ Establish outcomes, standards, and guidelines to monitor and manage institutional improvements in regard to medication safety, to include
  ■ the patient receives appropriate prescribed medication(s) safely administered during the perioperative period;[10(p103)]
  ■ the patient demonstrates knowledge of med-ication management;[10(p179)] and
  ■ the patient demonstrates knowledge of pain management.[10(p179)]

■ Modify work schedule requirements in surgical settings to minimize fatigue-induced errors.

■ Provide adequate lighting in dark environments (eg, endoscopy, minimally invasive procedures, ophthalmic procedures).

■ Initiate constraints and/or forcing functions to minimize risks related to medication manage-ment and administration.
  ■ Constraints are approaches that make a med-ication error difficult. Examples include dose limit protocols, automatic stop orders, triple-checking medications, and labeling all med-ication containers in the OR.
  ■ Forcing functions are approaches that make a medication error impossible. Examples include removing certain medications (eg, cytotoxic agents, concentrations of saline higher than 0.9%) from the OR.[3,16]

■ Adopt guidelines for unapproved abbreviations, acronyms, and symbols outlined in national patient safety initiatives.[11-13]
  ■ Care must be taken to decrease the risk for error and maximize patient safety by avoiding error-prone abbreviations and symbols known to cause confusion or lead to misin-terpretation. Examples:
    – Use of the handwritten letter "U" for "units" can be mistaken for a zero.[11-13]
    – Zeros in combination with decimal points can lead to a 10-fold dosing error when the decimal point is not detected.[16]

■ A supplemental list or poster placed in the workplace outlining common abbreviation mistakes may help to focus attention on high-risk avoidance.[17]
■ Recommendations and guidance provided by the ISMP "List of error-prone abbreviations, symbols, and dose designations"; the USP "Potentially dangerous abbreviations"; and the JCAHO "Official 'do not use' list" should be considered.

■ Ensure that current and reliable medication ref-erence materials with age-specific guidelines are readily available to the perioperative team.

■ Provide pharmacy support for consultation regarding unusual medications and dosages.

■ Standardize institutional forms to aid communi-cation and decrease confusion while enhancing productivity between health care providers.[3]

REFERENCES
1. Institute of Medicine, *To Err Is Human: Building a Safer Health System,* Committee on Quality of Heath Care in America, ed L Kohn, J Corrigan, M Donaldson (Wash-ington, DC: National Academy Press, 2000) 27.
2. "Council recommendations to reduce medication errors associated with verbal medication orders and pre-scriptions," (Feb 20, 2001) National Coordinating Council for Medication Error Reporting and Prevention, *http:// www.nccmerp.org/council/council2001-02-20.html?USP* (accessed 23 Jan 2006).
3. "Facts about 2006 national patient safety goals," Joint Commission on Accreditation of Healthcare Organizations, *http://www.jcaho.org/accredited+organizations/patient +safety/06_npsg/06_facts.htm* (accessed 23 Jan 2006).
4. D S Rich, "New JCAHO medication management standards for 2004," *American Journal of Health-System Pharmacists* 61 (July 2004) 1349-1358.
5. "Therapeutic duplication," Administration on Aging, *http://www.homemeds.org/pdf_files/ProtocolUnnec .Therap_2.pdf* (accessed 23 Jan 2006).
6. "Joint Commission 2006 National Patient Safety Goals: Implementation expectations," Joint Commission on Accreditation of Healthcare Organizations, *http://www.jcaho.org/accredited+organizations/patient +safety/06_npsg_ie.pdf* (accessed 23 Jan 2006).
7. Joint Commission on Accreditation of Healthcare Organizations, "Look-alike, sound-alike drug names," *Sentinel Event Alert* 19 (May 2001). Also available at *http://www.jcaho.org/about+us/news+letters/sentinel +event+alert/sea_19.htm* (accessed 23 Jan 2006).
8. Institute for Safe Medication Practices, "Patient safety movement calls for reexamination of multidose vial use," *ISMP Medication Safety Alert* (June 14, 2000). Also available at *http://www.ismp.org/newsletters/acutecare/articles /20000614.asp* (accessed 23 Jan 2006).

9. Institute for Safe Medication Practices, "New official interpretation of JCAHO standard bars access to pharmacy after hours," *ISMP Medication Safety Alert* (May 30, 2001). Also available at *http://www.ismp.org/newsletters/acutecare articles/20010530.asp* (accessed 23 Jan 2006).

10. S. Beyea, ed, *Perioperative Nursing Data Set: The Perioperative Nursing Vocabulary,* second ed (Denver: AORN, Inc, 2002) 103-104, 179.

11. "The official 'do not use' list," Joint Commission on Accreditation of Healthcare Organizations, *http://www.jcaho.org/accredited+organizations/patient +safety/dnu.htm* (accessed 9 Oct 2005).

12. United States Pharmocopeia, "Abbreviations can lead to medication errors," *USP Quality Review* no 80 (July 2004). Also available at *http://www.usp.org/patient Safety/newsletters/qualityReview/qr802004-07-01.html* (accessed 23 Jan 2006).

13. "ISMP's list of error-prone abbreviations, symbols, and dose designations," Institute for Safe Medication Practices, *http://www.ismp.org/tools/errorproneabbreviations .pdf* (accessed 23 Jan 2006).

14. "Frequently asked questions," Institute for Safe Medication Practices, *http://www.ismp.org/faq.asp#Question_9* (accessed 9 Oct 2005).

15. "AORN's safe medication administration tool kit," AORN Online, *http://www.aorn.org/toolkit/safemed* (accessed 23 Jan 2006).

16. Joint Commission on Accreditation of Healthcare Organizations, "High-alert medications and patient safety," *Sentinel Event Alert* 11 (Nov 19, 1999). Also available at *http://www.jcaho.org/about+us/news+letters/sentinel +event+alert/sea_11.htm* (accessed 23 Jan 2006).

17. "Joint Commission perspectives on patient safety: Maintaining safety/reducing risk," *Joint Commission Resources* 2 (September 2002) 1-11.

RESOURCES

Agency for Healthcare Research and Quality, *http://www.ahrq.gov* (accessed 29 Oct 2003).

Institute for Safe Medication Practices, *http://www.ismp.org* (accessed 29 Oct 2003).

Institute of Medicine, *http://www.iom.edu* (accessed 29 Oct 2003).

The Leapfrog Group, *http://www.leapfroggroup.org* (accessed 29 Oct 2003).

National Patient Safety Foundation, *http://www.npsf.org* (accessed 29 Oct 2003).

The National Quality Forum, *http://www.qualityforum.org* (accessed 29 Oct 2003).

Partnership for Patient Safety, *http://www.p4ps.org* (accessed 29 Oct 2003).

United States Pharmacopeia, *http://www.usp.org* (accessed 29 Aug 2005).

Originally published in *Standards, Recommended Practices, and Guidelines,* 2002 edition. Reprinted May 2002, *AORN Journal.*

Revised November 2003; published in *Standards, Recommended Practices, and Guidelines,* 2003 edition. Reprinted March 2004, *AORN Journal.*

Revised November 2005; published in *Standards, Recommended Practices, and Guidelines,* 2006 edition. Reprinted August 2006, *AORN Journal.*

AORN Perioperative Standards and Recommended Practices, 2009 Edition

AORN Guidance Statement: Sharps Injury Prevention in the Perioperative Setting

Introduction

The purpose of this guidance document is to assist perioperative registered nurses in the development of sharps injury prevention programs using identified best practices to reduce percutaneous injuries. It also suggests strategies to overcome obstacles to compliance with established sharps safety protocols.

The perioperative setting is a high-risk environment, and perioperative RNs are routinely faced with high risk for exposure to bloodborne pathogens from percutaneous injuries. Although the scope of the problem is not completely known, the National Institute for Occupational Safety and Health (NIOSH) estimates that 600,000 to 800,000 percutaneous injuries occur annually among heath care workers.[1] Percutaneous injuries primarily are associated with occupational transmission of the hepatitis B virus (HBV), hepatitis C virus (HCV), and HIV, but they may be implicated in the transmission of more than 20 other pathogens.[2] Understanding the etiology of percutaneous injuries in the perioperative setting is paramount to developing a safe prevention program.

Background

Percutaneous injuries occur throughout all health care facilities, and many occur in the perioperative setting.[3,4] Exposure to bloodborne pathogens occurs during all phases of the perioperative process. Research indicates that injuries from sharp devices or instruments occur in 7% to 15% of all surgical procedures. Procedures identified as posing the highest risk of injury are thoracic, trauma, burn, emergency orthopedic, major vascular, intra-abdominal, and gynecologic surgeries.[5] Risk of a sharps injury increases during more invasive, longer procedures that result in higher blood loss.[6] Fatigue resulting from working extended hours in combination with the fast pace of the perioperative environment also may contribute to increased risk of percutaneous injuries.[7-9]

Nurses comprise the largest segment of health care workers and are reported to sustain the highest number of percutaneous injuries overall.[2] Observational studies have demonstrated that perioperative personnel experience the highest percutaneous injury rates, but 70% to 96% of exposures were underreported.[5] Surgeons and first assistants

have the highest risk of injury and sustain more than half (ie, 59%) of percutaneous injuries in the perioperative setting.[6] Scrub personnel experienced the second highest frequency of percutaneous injury, followed by anesthesia care providers and circulating nurses.[6]

Injuries from hollow bore needles constitute the majority of injuries and pose the highest risk of exposure to bloodborne pathogens.[10] Although the risk of injury from hollow bore needles is prevalent in the perioperative setting, the epidemiology of sharps injuries in the OR is different from that of other locations in health care. Suture needles have been identified as the most frequent mechanism of percutaneous injury in the OR; they are involved in as many as 77% of such injuries.[4,6] Scalpels are the second most frequent mechanism of injury, followed by retractors, skin or bone hooks, and sharp electrosurgical tips.[11,12]

Percutaneous injuries often are self-inflicted. Studies indicate that 6% to 16% of these injuries occur during hand-to-hand passing of sharp instruments, suture needles, and other sharp devices. The most common body part injured is the non-dominant hand. Injuries from suture needles occur most often

- when loading the needle holder or repositioning the needle;
- during hand-to-hand passing of sharp devices between scrub personnel and the surgeon;
- during suturing, particularly muscle and fascia (eg, wound closure) when the needle is being manipulated and guided with fingers;
- when retracting or stretching tissue with hands;
- when the surgeon sews toward his or her own or an assistant's hand;
- when tying suture with the needle attached;
- after the suture has just been used and remains unattended on the operative field—even if suture is unattended on the field for only a short time, the needle holder can fall off the field onto a health care worker's foot, or scrubbed personnel may reach for it in an attempt to prevent it from sliding off the field; and
- when placing the used needle in an over-filled sharps container.[3]

Injuries from scalpels most often occur

- when loading or removing a disposable scalpel blade on a reusable knife handle;

♦ during hand-to-hand passing of the scalpel;

♦ during dissection when the tissue is being retracted or spread with hands;

♦ when cutting toward the surgeon's or an assistant's fingers;

♦ immediately before or after use when the scalpel is left on the operative field unattended—even if this is for only a short time, the scalpel can fall off the field onto a health care worker's foot, or scrubbed personnel may reach for it in an attempt to prevent it from sliding off the field; and

♦ when the scalpel is placed in an over-filled or poorly located sharps container.[3]

Glove barrier failure is a common occurrence in the perioperative setting. Glove failures can be caused by punctures, tears by sharp devices, or spontaneous failures. These failures expose the wearer to bloodborne pathogens. Studies have demonstrated that glove perforations often occur after an average of 40 minutes of use during surgical procedures. When two pairs of gloves are worn (ie, double gloving), in most instances, only the outer glove is perforated when punctured by a sharp device. In addition, research demonstrates that when two pairs of gloves are worn and a puncture occurs, the volume of blood on a solid sharp device (eg, suture needle) is reduced by as much as 95%. There is evidence that double gloving can reduce the risk of exposure to blood and body fluids, if the outer glove is punctured, by as much as 87%.[6]

The Occupational Safety and Health Administration (OSHA) requires health care organizations to protect their workers and have a written exposure control plan. Protection occurs by using universal precautions, engineering controls, work practice controls, organizational controls, and communication. The standard also requires employers to maintain a log of injuries from contaminated sharps.[13]

Guidance Statement

The perioperative environment poses unique challenges for reducing the risk of injuries from sharp devices. Surgery involves precise, regimented actions that require planning, communication, and team work. These same elements can be employed to mitigate the inherent hazards associated with sharp devices encountered in the perioperative setting. Perioperative RNs should actively participate in the development and implementation of strategies to reduce the risk of sharps injuries to health care team members.

Perioperative nursing management should work with the facility risk manager or safety officer to identify the types of sharp devices and how they are used in the perioperative setting. Both perioperative nursing management and the risk manager or safety officer should have a thorough understanding of OSHA's standards.[3]

By law, an effective sharps injury and bloodborne pathogen exposure control program must be written, communicated to all workers in the perioperative setting, and uniformly supported and enforced by perioperative leadership.[2,13] A multidisciplinary team is key to the success of this process. This team, using steps consistent with the continuous quality improvement process, must conduct a baseline assessment and set priorities for developing an action plan.[2,6]

Perioperative-Specific Risk Reduction Strategies

■ Adopt and incorporate safe habits into daily work activities when preparing and using sharp devices.

■ Focus attention on the intent of the action when working with sharp items, and minimize rushing and distractions while applying safety techniques during critical moments.

■ During preparation for operative or other invasive procedures:
  ▪ inspect the surgical field for adequate lighting and space to perform the procedure;
  ▪ organize the work area so that the sharps are always pointed away from staff members;
  ▪ establish a separate area to place a reusable sharp for safe handling during the procedure;
  ▪ use standardized sterile field set-ups; and
  ▪ include identification of the neutral zone in the preoperative briefing.[14]

■ During the operative or other invasive procedure:
  ▪ wear two pairs of gloves (ie, double gloving);
  ▪ monitor gloves for punctures;
  ▪ encourage the use of blunt suture needles;
  ▪ use neutral or hands-free technique for passing sharp items whenever possible or practical, instead of passing hand-to-hand;

- give verbal notification when passing a sharp device;
- keep visual contact with the procedure site and the sharp device;
- take steps to control the location of the sharp device;
- be aware of other staff members in the area when handling a sharp device;
- keep track of and account for all sharp items throughout the procedure;
- contain used sharps on the sterile field in a designated, disposable, puncture-resistant needle container, and replace it as necessary;
- check to be sure the disposable, puncture-resistant needle container is securely closed before handing it off the field;
- load suture needles using the suture packet to assist in mounting the suture needle in the needle holder, and use the appropriate instrument to adjust and unload the needle;
- remove the needle from the suture before tying, or use "control-release" sutures that allow the needle to be removed with a straight pull on the needle holder;
- activate the safety feature of a safety engineered device immediately after use according to manufacturers' instructions;
- keep hands away from the surgical site when sharp items are in use (eg, suturing, cutting);
- use one-handed or blunt instrument-assisted suturing techniques to avoid finger contact with the suture needle or tissue being sutured;
- provide a barrier between the hands and the needle after use; and
- use gloves and an instrument to pick up sharp items (eg, suture needles, hypodermic needles, scalpel blades) that have fallen on the floor.[2,3,6,13-17]

- During postprocedure clean up:
  - inspect the surgical setup used during the procedure for sharps;
  - transport reusable sharps in a closed, secure container to the designated clean-up area;
  - inspect the sharps container for overfilling before discarding disposable sharps in it;
  - make sure the sharps container is large enough to accommodate the entire device;
  - avoid bringing hands close to the opening of a sharps container;
  - do not place hands or fingers into a container to dispose of a device; and
  - keep hands behind the sharp tip when disposing.[3,14,18]

Health care organizations and their employees are responsible for actively participating in strategies to reduce percutaneous injuries. The employing facility should provide an environment that reduces the risk of percutaneous injuries from contaminated sharp devices. A well-developed safety program and support from management sends a clear message to employees about the organization's commitment to preventing injuries and keeping employees safe. Fewer percutaneous injuries are reported in organizations that have a strong culture of safety. Individual health care workers have a responsibility to be educated about the prevalence and mode of transmission of bloodborne pathogens and to use measures to protect themselves.[19]

Individual Perioperative RN's Responsibilities

- Observe local, state, and federal regulations (eg, OSHA regulations).
- Comply with methods to protect yourself from disease transmission (eg, get the hepatitis B vaccination).
- Use devices with safety features that are provided by your employer.
- Prevent hollow bore percutaneous injuries during injections or bodily fluid retrieval by using
  - needleless systems or sharps with engineered sharp injury protection devices whenever possible;
  - retractable, protective sheath or self-resheathing, self-blunting, or hinged re-cap needles to administer local anesthetics and other injectable medications;
  - blunt cannulas to withdraw medications and fluids from vials; and
  - the one-handed recapping technique, only if no other alternatives exist.
- Practice using safety devices to establish familiarity and experience with them before using them in practice.
- Actively participate in the safety conversion process and help others adapt to the change.
- Use personal protective equipment.

- Use sharps receptacles that are
  - identifiable (ie, orange, orange-red), closable, and labeled with the biohazard symbol;
  - appropriately sized with a full line that is readily visible;
  - puncture resistant and leak proof;
  - located close to the point of use;
  - maintained upright when in use; and
  - routinely replaced and not allowed to overfill.
- Participate in education about bloodborne pathogens, and follow recommended infection prevention practices.
- Support and guide perioperative team members to follow these risk reduction strategies.
- Encourage perioperative staff members to proactively report hazards that pose a threat of percutaneous injury.
- Know the location in your department of the exposure control plan.
- Follow exposure control policy if injured (ie, wash site with soap and water, provide immediate care to the exposure site).[9,13]

Employer Responsibilities

- Comply with local, state, and federal regulations regarding percutaneous injury prevention.
- Create a safety-oriented culture.
- Encourage timely reporting of all percutaneous injuries by all perioperative team members.
- Analyze needle-stick and other sharps-related injuries in the perioperative setting to identify hazards and injury trends.
- Establish a communication mechanism to seek input from perioperative team members regarding risks specific to the perioperative setting.
- Provide training for all perioperative personnel that includes risk reduction strategies designed specifically to address the risks encountered in the perioperative setting.
- Evaluate and select safety devices that are acceptable to all members of the perioperative team who use them. The safety device should provide features that work effectively, are reliable, do not compromise patient or worker safety, and are ergonomically designed to the acceptable specifications of the users.
- Provide and have readily available the appropriate sharps safety devices, and provide adequate training on their use.

- Evaluate the effectiveness of established risk reduction strategies and products, provide feedback, and modify them as necessary to reduce the risk of percutaneous injuries.[7]
- Establish staffing patterns that minimize extended work hours and allow for adequate recuperation to decrease the risk of fatigue-related injuries.[20]

Overcoming Obstacles to Compliance

Psychosocial and organizational factors may impede change. An employee's risk-taking personality profile, perception that the organization is not committed to worker safety, and a perceived belief that there is a conflict between providing optimal patient care and protecting oneself from exposure contribute to an employee's resistance to changing to safer practices.[2] For example, although percutaneous injuries continue to occur in the perioperative setting, 71% of respondents in a national survey indicated that they have not evaluated blunt-tip suture needles for use in the OR, and only 2% of respondents have fully implemented blunt-tip suture needles. Only 14% of respondents had implemented safety scalpels into their ORs.[4]

Changes in attitudes about risk of exposure must occur before practice can change to comply with sharps safety protocols. It is difficult to change ingrained habits. People are most likely to change behavior when they perceive a significant personal risk. Education about the risk of contracting a bloodborne disease from a percutaneous injury with a contaminated sharp device should be presented in the early stages of a health care worker's career in order to develop safe practice habits.[5]

Surgery involves precise, regimented actions requiring planning, communication, and team work. These same elements can be employed to overcome obstacles to compliance with measures meant to mitigate the inherent hazards of sharp devices encountered in the perioperative setting. Suggested strategies to overcome obstacles to compliance include the following.

- Use frequent and multiple training methods that include audiovisual aids, articles, hands-on clinical practice, and visual reminders (eg, laminated posters).
- Develop a multidisciplinary sharps injury prevention education plan.

- Incorporate sharps injury prevention instruction into initial nursing education to promote well-established, safe habits.
- Include sharps injury prevention strategies during orientation of new employees.
- Form a multidisciplinary sharps safety committee that includes, but is not limited to, perioperative RNs, surgeons, anesthesia care providers, surgical technologists, and first assistants. This team could be asked to
  - help with the selection and evaluation of acceptable safety devices (eg, scalpels that employ a one-handed technique or are totally disposable) and
  - work with physicians to explore alternative techniques, such as adhesive skin closures; alternatives for securing catheters; use of blunt suture needles, rounded scalpels, or stapling devices, when procedurally appropriate; and use of alternative methods for cutting tissue (eg, harmonic scalpel, rounded scissors, laser devices, electrosurgery active electrodes).
- Network with other facilities to learn about their success stories.
- Collaborate with personnel who use the device, and facilitate change instead of dictating change.
- Inform perioperative team members about current research on disease transmission from percutaneous injuries and relate it to the individual's experience.
- Work with resisters to gain buy-in to the sharps safety program.
- Remove as many conventional sharp items as possible from stock.
- Create a culture of safety in which every team member is empowered to call attention to deficiencies in sharps management.[2,9,12,13]

Selecting and Evaluating New Products

As risk reduction strategies are identified, a multidisciplinary team should evaluate and select the best products to meet the facility's needs. An ongoing review process should be developed to assess, evaluate, and modify the plan as needed. Product evaluation and selection should include the following.

- Assemble a multidisciplinary team to develop, implement, and evaluate a process for selecting

products to reduce sharps injury in the OR. Staff members who work with the product are key components of the team. A strong interdisciplinary commitment to best practices and worker safety is the optimal foundation necessary for change to occur.

- Review the literature for research about the mechanism, frequency, time, and place of injuries, as well as the role and body part of the person sustaining the percutaneous injury to determine priority areas on which to focus.
- Identify the products to be evaluated. Focus on their intended use in the facility and identify any special technique or design factors that will influence safety, efficiency, and user acceptability. Seek data from all sources on the safety and overall performance of the devices.
- Ensure that participants in the evaluation represent all of the end users. To ensure a successful evaluation, users must have adequate training. Use clear, objective, consistent criteria to evaluate safety devices.
- Continue to monitor a safety device after it has been implemented to assess performance and to identify if there is a need for additional training.[2,10]

Summary

Occupational exposure to bloodborne pathogens via percutaneous injuries is one of the most serious dangers perioperative team members face on a daily basis. The risk of sustaining a percutaneous injury can be decreased through employee education, clear communication, device engineering, and focused work practice controls. Risk reduction strategies should include specific practices aimed at reducing the unique risks of percutaneous injuries encountered in the perioperative environment. AORN recognizes the various settings in which perioperative RNs practice, and the suggested risk reduction strategies in this guidance statement are intended to be adaptable to any setting where surgical or other invasive procedures are performed.

REFERENCES
1. "AORN position statement on workplace safety," in *Standards, Recommended Practices, and Guidelines* (Denver: AORN, Inc, 2004) 169-171.
2. "Workbook for designing, implementing, and evaluating a sharps injury prevention program," Centers for Disease Control and Prevention, *http://www.cdc.gov/sharpssafety* (accessed 5 Jan 2005).

3. ECRI, "Sharps injuries in the operating room—A new focus for OSHA," *Operating Room Risk Management* (December 2004) 1-5.

4. J Perry, G Parker, J Jagger, "EPINet report: 2001 percutaneous injury rates," *Advances in Exposure Prevention* 6 no 3 (2003) 32-36.

5. C L Holodnick, V Barkauskas, "Reducing percutaneous injuries in the OR by educational methods," *AORN Journal* 72 (September 2000) 461-476.

6. R Berguer, P J Heller, "Preventing sharps injuries in the operating room" *Journal of the American College of Surgeons* 199 (September 2004) 462-467.

7. K Hanecke et al, "Accident risk as a function of hour at work and time of day as determined from accident data and exposure models for the German working population," *Scandinavian Journal of Work, Environment, and Health* 24 suppl (1998) 43-48.

8. T Roth, T A Roehrs, "Etiologies and sequelae of excessive daytime sleepiness," *Clinical Therapeutics* 18 (July/August 1996) 562-576.

9. Battelle Memorial Institute, JIL Information Systems, "An overview of the scientific literature concerning fatigue, sleep, and the circadian cycle," Air Line Pilots Association, *http://cf.alpa.org/internet/projects/ftdt/backgr/batelle.htm* (accessed 5 Jan 2005).

10. National Institute for Occupational Safety and Health, "Preventing needlestick injuries in health care settings," publ 2000-108 (Washington, DC: US Department of Health and Human Services, November 1999).

11. J Jagger, M Bentley, P Tereskerz, "A study of patterns and prevention of blood exposures in OR personnel," *AORN Journal* 67 (May 1998) 979-987.

12. S Wasek, "10 practical ways to implement safety devices," *Outpatient Surgery Magazine* 4 (December 2003).

13. "Regulations (Standards–29 CFR) Bloodborne pathogens 1910.1030," Occupational Safety and Health Administration, *http://www.osha.gov/pls/oshaweb/owadisp.show_document?p_table=STANDARDS&p_id=10051* (accessed 5 Jan 2005).

14. "Recommended practices for maintaining a sterile field," in *Standards, Recommended Practices, and Guidelines* (Denver: AORN, Inc, 2004) 367.

15. C Twomey, "Does double gloving double the protection?" *Infection Control Today*, *http://www.infectioncontroltoday.com/articles/051feat3.html* (accessed 5 Jan 2005).

16. "Recommended practices for sponge, sharp, and instrument counts," in *Standards, Recommended Practices, and Guidelines* (Denver: AORN, Inc, 2004) 230-231.

17. "Recommended practices for environmental cleaning in the surgical practice setting," in *Standards, Recommended Practices, and Guidelines* (Denver: AORN, Inc, 2004) 273-279.

18. "Recommended practices for standard and transmission-based precautions in the perioperative practice setting," in *Standards, Recommended Practices, and Guidelines* (Denver: AORN, Inc, 2004) 361.

19. "AORN guidance statement: Safe on-call practices in perioperative practice settings" in *Standards, Recommended Practices, and Guidelines* (Denver: AORN, Inc, 2005) 193-195.

20. K Royer, "Primer on prevention of sharps injuries" (Sharps Safety) *Outpatient Surgery Magazine* 5 (September 2004) 50.

Originally published in *Standards, Recommended Practices, and Guidelines,* 2005 edition. Reprinted March 2005, *AORN Journal.*

AORN Guidance Statement: Perioperative Staffing

Introduction

The purpose of this guidance statement is to provide a framework for developing a staffing plan throughout the continuum of perioperative patient care, beginning with scheduling a surgical or invasive procedure through the postoperative phase III/follow-up process. Staffing in the perioperative setting is dynamic in nature and depends on the clinical judgment, critical thinking skills, and administrative skills of nursing management in the perioperative setting. Patients undergoing surgical or invasive procedures require perioperative nursing care provided by a perioperative registered nurse, regardless of the setting. This guidance statement offers suggested staffing strategies to accommodate safe perioperative patient care while promoting a safe work environment.

Background

To provide safe and effective patient care, individual health care organizations should have staffing policies and procedures relevant to individual practice settings. The health care system is affected by increasing demand for health care, continued economic pressures, the looming nursing shortage, and financial ramifications from medico-legal issues. Patient safety is the primary focus of perioperative nurses and other health care providers. Perioperative nursing leaders need to be judicious in meeting the challenge of stretching scarce resources without compromising patient care. Perioperative department nursing leaders have an ethical responsibility to maintain staffing levels that are appropriate for providing safe patient care while they also balance shrinking budgets.

Guidance Statement

Perioperative nurse leaders should identify workforce requirements and the effect of environmental factors on staffing patterns. Surgery is performed in a wide variety of settings with uniquely different needs. Perioperative clinical staffing guidelines should be based on individual patient needs, patient acuity, technological demands, staff member competency, skill mix, practice standards, health care regulations, and accreditation requirements.[1,2] Staffing requirements are relative to department functions and assigned role expectations.

An effective staffing plan is flexible and responsive to short-term and long-term patient and organizational demands. Effective planning involves determining staffing needs, planning for the appropriate staffing mix and number of staff members, budgeting for personnel costs, and scheduling personnel. Perioperative nursing management should determine both direct and indirect patient caregivers for the unit. Additionally, productive and nonproductive time should be considered.[2] The perioperative staffing policy should state the minimum number of nursing personnel that will be provided for various types of surgical procedures. Complexity of the procedure may require more than the minimum number of nursing personnel identified. **Table 1** includes recommended minimum staffing requirements.

Call

The perioperative staffing plan includes provisions for unplanned, urgent, or emergent procedures and how to provide care for patients whose procedures run over scheduled time. Call staffing plans should be based on strategies to minimize long work hours, allow for adequate recuperation, and retain the perioperative RN as circulator. Scheduling requirements for call are subject to facility type, location, nature of services provided, and patient population served. Staffing for call should be provided in accordance with standards of perioperative and perianesthesia nursing practice. Safe call practices should be based on AORN's "Guidance statement: Safe on-call practices in perioperative practice settings."[3-5]

A systematic approach based on the operational needs of the department is required to develop a staffing plan. Identifying the hours of operation defined by the department or facility, in addition to the hours needed to cover off-shift (eg, holidays, nights, weekends) emergent/urgent surgery and the number of operating/procedure rooms is the initial step in determining staffing needs.[6] Review of historical data regarding minutes/hours of service, case volumes, case mix, and technology demands and projections for the coming year are essential for staff scheduling and budgeting. The following formula provides a platform to develop an annual staffing plan and budget. The formula is flexible and can be adapted to meet the specific needs of the perioperative setting. Although the basic formula is based on 100% utilization, it can be modified to coincide with expected volume.

Table 1

MINIMUM STAFFING RECOMMENDATIONS		
Surgical phase	**Minimum requirements**	**Comments**
Scheduling	1 clerical person under the supervision of a perioperative RN	Depending on the size of the facility, this activity may be combined with other business or clerical duties. Additional staff members may be required depending on volume and the hours that the scheduling office is open.
Preplanning	1 RN[1]	Depending on the setting and level of activity, this stage may require additional RNs and ancillary support. This may include preoperative telephone calls/interviews or planning for special supplies and equipment to meet patient needs.
Registration	Clerical person	The number of clerical staff members depends on the setting, level of activity, number of patients scheduled, patient acuity, and types of procedures and may be combined with other tasks.
Day of surgery: Preoperative	1 RN[1]	The number of additional RNs should be based on the number of patients, the number of ORs/procedure rooms, patient acuity, types of procedures, complexity/intensity of patient care requirements, time required to perform tasks, a patient's age-specific needs, and the average time for individual patient preparation. Licensed practical nurses (LPNs) and unlicensed assistive personnel (UAP) may be included in preoperative staffing plans. Unlicensed assistive personnel may be assigned to help with delegated patient care tasks as determined by the RN and according to individual state boards of nursing scope of practice and other local, state, and federal regulations.[2-4]
Intraoperative	1 RN per patient per OR in the role of the circulating nurse.[5] 1 scrub person per patient per room; may be RN, surgical technologist, or LPN. In some circumstances, a scrub person may not be required.	Additional staff members, with appropriate competencies, may be used as appropriate for the following: ◆ moderate sedation—one RN dedicated to monitoring the patient and separate from the dedicated RN circulator; ◆ local anesthesia—depending on patient needs, nursing assessment, and type of procedure, an RN may be needed to monitor the patient in addition to the RN circulator; ◆ complex surgical procedures and patients with compound needs may require an additional RN circulator and scrub person; ◆ technological demands (eg, lasers, robotics, audiovisual equipment, auto transfusion device); ◆ first assist requirements. *Note:* See formula for calculating additional staffing.
Postoperative Phase I level of care[6]	"Two registered nurses, one of whom is a[n] RN competent in Phase I postanesthesia nursing, are in the same unit where the patient is receiving Phase I level of care."[6] Staffing will reflect the American Society of PeriAnesthesia Nurses' (ASPAN's) "Patient classification/ recommended staffing guidelines."	Phase I level of care* Class 1:2—One nurse to two patients who are ◆ One unconscious, stable, without artificial airway, and over the age of 8 years; and one conscious, stable, and free of complications. ◆ Two conscious, stable, and free of complications. ◆ Two conscious, stable, 8 years of age and under, with family or competent support staff member present.[6]

Table 1, *continued*

MINIMUM STAFFING RECOMMENDATIONS		
Surgical phase	Minimum requirements	Comments
		Class 1:1—One nurse to one patient ♦ At the time of admission, until the critical elements** are met. ♦ Unstable airway.*** ♦ Any unconscious patient 8 years of age and under. ♦ A second nurse must be available to assist as necessary.[6] Class 2:1—Two nurses to one patient ♦ One critically ill, unstable, complicated patient.[6] Additional staff members may include support staff. Unlicensed assistive personnel may be assigned to help with delegated patient care tasks according to local, state, and federal regulations.[4]
Phase II level of care[6]	"Two competent personnel, one of whom is a[n] RN competent in Phase II postanesthesia nursing, are in the same room where the patient is receiving Phase II level of care. A[n] RN must be in the Phase II PACU at all times while a patient is present."[6] Staffing will reflect ASPAN's "Patient classification/recommended staffing guidelines."	Phase II level of care* Class 1:3—One nurse to three patients ♦ Over 8 years of age. ♦ 8 years of age and under with family present.[6] Class 1:2—One nurse to two patients ♦ 8 years of age and under without family or support staff member present. ♦ Initial admission of patient postprocedure.[6] Class 1:1—One nurse to one patient ♦ Unstable patient of any age requiring transfer.[6] Additional staff members may include support staff. Unlicensed assistive personnel may be assigned to help with delegated patient care tasks according to local, state, and federal regulations.[4]
Extended observation level of care (formerly Phase III)[6]	"Two competent personnel, one of whom is a[n] RN possessing competence appropriate to the patient population, are in the same unit where the patient is receiving extended observation level of care. The need for additional RNs and support staff is dependent on the patient acuity, patient census, and the physical facility."[6] Staffing will reflect ASPAN's "Patient classification/recommended staffing guidelines."	Extended observation level of care* (formerly Phase III) Class 1:3/5—One nurse to three to five patients ♦ Examples of patients that may be cared for in this phase include, but are not limited to, – patients awaiting transportation home; – patients with no caregiver; – patients who have had procedures requiring extended observation/intervention (ie, potential risk for bleeding, pain management, postoperative nausea, vomiting); and – patients being held for an inpatient bed.[6] Additional staff members may include support staff. Unlicensed assistive personnel may be assigned to help with delegated patient care tasks according to local, state, and federal regulations.[4]

---

* *Phases of postanesthesia care were developed by the American Society of PeriAnesthesia Nurses.*
** *Critical elements can be defined as:*
  – *Report has been received from the anesthesia care provider, questions answered, and the transfer of care has taken place.*
  – *Patient has a secure airway.*
  – *Initial assessment is complete.*
  – *Patient is hemodynamically stable.*

*** *Examples of an unstable airway include, but are not limited to, the following:*
  – *Requiring active interventions to maintain patency, such as manual jaw lift or chin lift.*
  – *Evidence of obstruction, active or probable, such as gasping, choking, crowing, wheezing, etc.*
  – *Symptoms of respiratory distress, including dyspnea, tachypnea, panic, agitation, cyanosis, etc.*

Table 1, *continued*

MINIMUM STAFFING RECOMMENDATIONS		
Surgical phase	**Minimum requirements**	**Comments**
Discharge from service	An RN assesses the discharge readiness of the patient and confirms the order from anesthesiologist/surgeon for discharge according to facility protocol.[7]	"The perianesthesia nurse uses sound judgment in determining the appropriate method of communication and mode of transport to transfer care of the perianesthesia patient."[7] 1. "A policy exists to ensure safe transportation of patients. ♦ The professional nurse determines the mode, number, and competency level of accompanying personnel based on patient need. ♦ The professional nurse ensures the availability of appropriate transportation of the patient from the facility. ♦ An appropriate means of transportation from a freestanding facility to a full-service hospital will be used in emergency situations. 2. A professional nurse should accompany patients who ♦ require continuous cardiac monitoring. ♦ require evaluation and/or treatment during transport (ie, vasopressor infusions or pulse oximetry)."[7]
Postoperative follow-up	An RN completes discharge follow-up.[8]	Ambulatory surgery patients are reassessed postoperatively. The time frames for reassessment are based on patient needs and the care, treatment, and services provided. Individual organizations should develop policies and procedures regarding the mechanism chosen (eg, postoperative telephone calls) based on the patients it serves and the services or care it provides.[9,10]

REFERENCES

1. "Standard III: Staffing and personnel management," in Standards of Perianesthesia Nursing (Cherry Hill, NJ: American Society of PeriAnesthesia Nurses, 2004) 14.

2. "AORN official statement on unlicensed assistive personnel" in Standards, Recommended Practices, and Guidelines (Denver: AORN, Inc, 2004) 167-168.

3. "AORN guidance statement: Preoperative patient care in the ambulatory surgery setting," in Standards, Recommended Practices, and Guidelines (Denver: AORN, Inc, 2007) 319-324.

4 "A position statement on registered nurse utilization of unlicensed assistive personnel," in Standards of Perianesthesia Nursing (Cherry Hill, NJ: American Society of PeriAnesthesia Nurses, 2004) 77.

5. "AORN statement on nurse-to-patient ratios," in Standards, Recommended Practices, and Guidelines (Denver: AORN, Inc, 2004) 157-158.

6. "Resource 3: Patient classification/recommended staffing guidelines," in Standards of Perianesthesia Nursing

(Cherry Hill, NJ: American Society of PeriAnesthesia Nurses, 2006) 61-62.

7. "Resource 11: Safe transfer of care," in Standards of Perianesthesia Nursing (Cherry Hill, NJ: American Society of PeriAnesthesia Nurses, 2004) 49.

8. "Resource 4: Criteria for initial, ongoing, and discharge assessment and management," in Standards of Perianesthesia Nursing (Cherry Hill, NJ: American Society of PeriAnesthesia Nurses, 2004) 27.

9. "Provision of care, treatment, and services," in Comprehensive Accreditation Manual for Ambulatory Care (Oakbrook Terrace, Ill: Joint Commission on Accreditation of Healthcare Organizations, 2005) PC-1, PC-3.

10. "Follow-up phone calls in outpatient surgery," Joint Commission on Accreditation of Healthcare Organizations, http://www.jcaho.org/accredited+organizations/ambulatory +care/standards/faqs/provision+of+care/anesthesia+care /followup+calls.htm (accessed 14 Dec 2004).

Intraoperative Staffing Formula

Direct staff patient care calculation

- **Step 1**—Number of rooms multiplied by number of hours per day multiplied by number of days per week equals total hours to be staffed per week.
- **Step 2**—Total hours to be staffed per week multiplied by number of people per room equals total working hours per week.
- **Step 3**—Total working hours per week divided by 40 hours equals basic full-time equivalents (FTEs).
- **Step 4**—Calculate benefit relief.
- **Step 5**—Basic FTEs multiplied by benefit hours per FTEs per year divided by 2,080 hours equals relief FTEs.
- **Step 6**—Basic FTEs added to relief FTEs equals total minimum direct care staff members.
- **Step 7**—Calculate indirect care staff members.
- **Step 8**—Calculate call replacement relief.

To determine the number of personnel per room:

- Generally, there are at least two staff members for every surgical or other invasive procedure: one RN in the circulator role and one scrub person.
- The scrub position can be filled by an RN or surgical technologist.
- If half the procedures done in the OR require a third person for part or all of the procedure (eg, to monitor patients receiving sedation, operate complex technology, high patient acuity), use a figure of 2.5 people per room in computing staffing needs.
- If more or less than half of the procedures done in the OR require a third person, or if a percentage of procedures require a fourth person, the number of personnel per room will need to be adjusted accordingly.
- In the following example, a figure of 2.5 people per room is used. The following calculation can be used to determine the RN to technologist ratio of 67%:33% (2:1):

Determine the number of RNs per room by multiplying 2.5 x .67 = 1.7 RNs

Determine the number of technologists per room by multiplying 2.5 x .33 = 0.8 technologists

The above calculation can be applied to any number of total people needed per room. If an institution's FTE is greater or less than 2,080 hours per year, this also must be adjusted in the formula.

Indirect staff calculation

For the purposes of this calculation, indirect staff members include, but are not limited to, the budgeted positions of surgical services director, clinical nurse manager, charge nurse, perioperative educator, schedulers, secretaries, aids, orderlies, and housekeeping personnel as appropriate. The number of indirect care staff members will vary according to function, but a traditional compliment is one indirect caregiver to two direct caregivers.

Call hours replacement calculation

The maximum number of call hours is determined by identifying the number of shifts multiplied by the number of hours multiplied by two FTEs. The actual hours on call personnel are called in to work per year divided by 2,080 equals the replacement FTEs for call-time worked.

Relief replacement

- Benefit hours (ie, nonproductive hours) are hours such as vacation time, holiday time, available sick time (whether paid or unpaid), education days, and any other time that personnel policies determine an employee might take off. The number of benefit hours is proportionate to the amount of vacation time and the number of long-term employees. Some organizations use an established percentage to calculate benefit hours.
- In the OR, benefit hours also include breaks and lunches, unless the OR ceases work during those times.
- When determining relief for lunch, it is necessary to add approximately 15 minutes to the allotted time at either end to allow for nurse-to-nurse report about what has transpired during the procedure in progress. It may take less than seven minutes for the circulating nurse to report to the relief nurse, but relief of the scrub person needs to include time needed to scrub, gown, and glove, so 15 minutes is average.
- When computing relief for breaks and lunches, the number of minutes is multiplied by 260 days (ie, 52 weeks multiplied by five days per week).
- Nonproductive time for orienting new staff members also needs to be included.

Example. An OR suite has eight rooms, which are to be staffed and available as follows:
- 8 rooms, 7 AM to 3 PM, Monday through Friday;
- 2 rooms, 3 to 6 PM, Monday through Friday;
- 1 room, 6 PM to 7 AM, seven days per week; and
- 1 room, 7 AM to 6 PM, Saturday and Sunday.

■ **Step 1**—Number of rooms multiplied by number of hours per day multiplied by number of days per week equals total hours to be staffed per week.

8 x 8 x 5 = 320
2 x 3 x 5 = 30
1 x 13 x 7 = 91
1 x 11 x 2 = 22
463 total hours staffed per week

■ **Step 2**—Total hours staffed per week multiplied by number of people per room equals total working hours per week.

463 hours x 2.5 = 1,157.5 total working hours per week

The following calculation can be used to determine the hours for a 67%:33% RN:technologist ratio.

Determine the number of RNs per room by multiplying 2.5 x .67 = 1.7 RN

Determine the number of technologists per room by multiplying 2.5 x .33 = 0.8 technologists

RNs: 1.7 x 463 hours = 787.1 total RN working hours per week

Surgical technologists: 0.8 x 463 = 370.4 total surgical technologist hours per week

Total working hours per week = 1,157.5

■ **Step 3**—Total working hours per week divided by 40 hours worked per week equals basic FTEs.

1,157.5 ÷ 40 = 28.9 basic FTEs

The following calculation can be used to determine the basic RN FTEs and surgical technologist FTEs for a 67%:33% RN:technologist ratio.

RNs: 787.1 hours ÷ 40 = 19.7 basic RN FTEs
Surgical technologists: 370.4 ÷ 40 = 9 basic surgical technologist FTEs

■ **Step 4**—Calculate benefit relief per employee.

Average vacation hours per year = 100
Holiday hours per year = 56
Available sick hours per year = 96
15 minute break x 260 days ÷ 60 minutes
= 65 hours
45 minute lunch x 260 days ÷ 60 minutes
= 195 hours
512 hours of benefit relief

Note: Organizations handle benefit hours differently. Benefits hours may include, but are not limited to the following.
- Vacation hours, holiday hours, and sick hours are grouped together under paid time off (PTO).
- If sick time is not established and included in the PTO, historical average sick time is used to calculate replacement FTEs.
- A percentage is used to calculate benefit hours.

■ **Step 5**—Basic FTEs multiplied by benefit hours per FTE per year divided by 2,080 hours equals relief FTEs.

28.9 x 512 hours ÷ 2,080 = 7.1 relief FTEs

The following calculation determines the RN and surgical technologist relief FTEs for a 67%:33% RN:technologist ratio.

RNs: 19.7 x 512 = 10,086.4 ÷ 2,080
= 4.8 RN relief FTEs
Surgical technologists: 9 x 512 = 4,608 ÷ 2,080 = 2.2 surgical technologist FTEs

Calculating the orientation time for new employees depends on several factors, including, but not limited to, the size and type of OR, anticipated turnover time, and increase in the number of staff due to growth of services and volume. For the purposes of the example, if four people with experience were expected to be hired for a year and each receives 12 weeks of orientation, use the following calculation:

4 staff members x 40 hours per week x 12 weeks = 1,920 hours of orientation ÷ 2,080 = 0.9 FTE for orientation

■ **Step 6**—Basic FTEs added to relief FTEs equals total minimum direct care staff members.

28.9 + 7.1 = 36 FTEs

The following calculation is used for a 67%:33% RN:technologist ratio.

RN: 19.7 basic FTEs + 4.8 benefit relief FTEs = 24.5 RN FTEs

Surgical technologist: 9 basic FTEs + 2.2 benefit relief FTEs = 11.2 surgical technologist FTEs

■ **Step 7**—Calculate indirect care staff members.

1 indirect caregiver per 2 direct caregivers = 1.25 x 463 hours per week = 578.8 ÷ 40 = 14.5 FTEs
512 benefit hours x 14.5 = 7,424 ÷ 2,080 = 3.6 relief FTEs
3.6 + 14.5 = 18.1

■ **Step 8**—Calculate call relief (see **Table 2**).
The total number of FTEs calculated in this example is:

Direct caregivers
RNs: 24.5 FTEs
surgical technologists: 11.2 FTEs
call replacements: 1.5 FTEs
indirect caregivers: 18.1 FTES
orientation FTEs: 0.9 FTE
Total: 56.3 FTEs

This formula is based on 100% utilization.

Post Anesthesia Care Unit (PACU) Staffing Formula

There are no standardized staffing formulas at this time for calculating perianesthesia staffing in the PACU. Neither the American Society of Perianesthesia Nurses nor AORN have a recommended staffing formula at this time. Refer to **Table 1** for PACU staffing recommendations.

Summary

One of the most important responsibilities of a perioperative nursing leader is the development of an effective staffing plan relative to surgical patients' needs. AORN recognizes there are a variety of settings in which perioperative RNs practice.

Table 2

CALL RELIEF CALCULATION				
Call coverage	Maximum possible hours			Historical usage in hours
	Hours	Staff	Total	Total
260 night shifts	8 x	2 =	4,160	3,342
52 weekends	48 x	3 =	7,488	5,256
12 holidays	24 x	3 =	864	689
Total			12,512	9,287*

* The difference between the maximum possible call hours and actual usage of call hours is 3,225 hours worked. The 3,225 call hours worked per year divided by 2,080 hours (ie, one full-time equivalent [FTE]) equals 1.55 FTE replacement for call-time worked.

This guidance statement is intended to serve as a guide for perioperative nursing leaders in developing a staffing plan and is designed to be adaptable to various practice settings.

Glossary

Direct staff members: Personnel directly involved in providing care to patients undergoing surgical or other invasive procedures. These individuals provide direct patient care and include RNs, surgical technologists, nursing assistants, orderlies, RN first assistants, and surgical assistants.[2]

Indirect staff members: Personnel who support nonpatient care activities in the perioperative environment. These positions may include the director, manager, charge nurse, educator, secretaries, environmental services personnel, instrument processing personnel, materials management personnel, and clerical/business personnel. The perioperative director, management team members (eg, team leaders, charge nurse), clinical nurse specialists, and educators may be a combination of direct and indirect personnel.[2]

Productive hours: Actual hours worked; includes direct and indirect hours. Worked hours are those needed to staff the unit.[2]

Nonproductive hours: These are paid hours not worked and considered benefit hours (eg, vacation, sick time, funeral leave, holiday).[2]

Editor's note: *This staffing guidance statement was developed by the Nursing Practice Committee in December 2004. AORN would like to thank the American Society of PeriAnesthesia Nurses for their participation in the development of this statement.*

REFERENCES

1. B Fernsebner, "Key factors affecting staffing," *OR Manager* 16 (December 2000) 10-11.

2. K A Halverson Carpenter, "Staffing and scheduling," *Leadership in Action: A Managers Guide to Success* (Denver: AORN, Inc, 2004) 74.

3. "A position statement on on call/work schedule," in *Standards of Perianesthesia Nursing* (Cherry Hill, NJ: American Society of PeriAnesthesia Nurses, 2004) 79.

4. "Proposed AORN position statement for safe on-call practices," pending ratification by the 2005 House of Delegates.

5. "AORN guidance statement: Safe on-call practices in perioperative practice settings," in *Standards, Recommended Practices and Guidelines* (Denver: AORN, Inc, 2005) 193-195.

6. B Fernsebner, "Building a staffing plan based on OR's needs," (Surgical Staffing) *OR Manager* (1996).

RESOURCES

Perioperative Management Resources: Budgeting (Denver: AORN, Inc, 2004).

Originally published in *Standards, Recommended Practices, and Guidelines,* 2005 edition. Reprinted May 2005, *AORN Journal.*

AORN Guidance Statement: The Value of Clinical Learning Activities in the Perioperative Setting in Undergraduate Nursing Curricula

Introduction

The nature and quality of undergraduate education is key to the future of the profession of nursing. However, nursing faculties face many barriers, existing or potential, when they take on the challenge of designing and implementing innovative curricula. Yet, if they are to prepare graduates who can function effectively in current and future practice arenas, nursing curricula and their component teaching-learning activities and evaluation methods must undergo constant revision, updating, and change.[1]

To facilitate this complex work of faculty, this document has been developed to serve as a guide to help faculties plan clinical learning opportunities in perioperative patient care that develop competencies essential for all undergraduate nursing students. The term *clinical learning activity* or *opportunity* refers to a planned instructional activity designed to facilitate the achievement of a desired learning outcome or competency. *Perioperative patient care* refers to the preoperative, intraoperative, and postoperative care of patients undergoing surgery and other invasive procedures.

In 2006, the AORN House of Delegates ratified a revised position statement on the value of clinical learning activities in the perioperative setting in undergraduate nursing curricula. That position statement reaffirmed that "all clinical settings, including the perioperative setting, have the potential to provide opportunities in which the principles of the art and science of professional nursing can be applied; therefore, these settings should be used during the formal education of nurses. The incorporation of perioperative learning activities into existing undergraduate curricula will assist in meeting end-of-program outcomes."[2] Also in 2006, the National Student Nurses Association (NSNA) House of Delegates passed a resolution submitted by the Florida Nursing Student Association encouraging support for including theoretical and clinical perioperative nursing experiences into nursing curricula.[3]

While the faculty has primary responsibility for curriculum planning and implementation, partnerships with perioperative clinical nurse educators, nurse managers, and staff nurses are essential for successful coordination of these clinical activities. Nursing students also are expected to be active participants in their learning; as such, they have an important role in setting their own individual learning goals. Nursing students can use these guidelines to help design self-directed learning activities in perioperative clinical settings.

Background

Operative or other invasive procedures are a primary treatment for patients admitted to hospitals, accounting for 29% of all admissions.[4] An even greater percentage of surgeries are performed in the ambulatory/outpatient setting. According to the most recent data of the American Hospital Association affiliate Health Forum, 27,401,836 surgeries were performed in the United States in 2004; of these, 37% (10,050,346) were inpatient surgeries, and 63% (17,351,490) were outpatient surgeries.[4] With the forecasted growth of free-standing outpatient surgical settings[5] and other ambulatory care facilities (eg, mobile interventional suites, physicians' offices), an increasingly wide variety of learning sites is available to nursing students.

This rich array of opportunities for planned clinical learning activities throughout the undergraduate nursing curriculum can alleviate some of the problems currently faced by educators:

- increasing enrollments in nursing education programs leading to competition among nursing education programs for the same clinical sites;
- emergence of competition between nursing and other health care professional programs for clinical placements; and
- shortage of nursing faculty members for teaching in clinical settings.

The provision of safe care to these most vulnerable of patients is of paramount importance to health care professionals and the health care agencies in which they receive care. Planned clinical learning activities in ambulatory[6] and other perioperative clinical settings are consistent with many of the knowledge, skills, and values promoted by the American Association of Colleges of Nursing (AACN)[7] and the National League for Nursing (NLN).[1] Perioperative clinical sites can provide opportunities to apply

- critical thinking skills to assess patients' readiness for surgery;[8]
- safety principles to patient care;[8]
- patient and family teaching to enhance expected outcomes;
- aseptic and antiseptic practices to promote wound healing;
- care to diverse patient populations;
- principles of human, technical, and fiscal resource utilization;[8]
- legal and ethical guidelines; and
- concepts of teamwork.[8]

Perioperative clinical learning experiences thus can provide benefit to nursing programs, nursing students, and clients undergoing operative and other invasive procedures.

Guidance Statement

Undergraduate nursing education programs are attempting to produce graduates with a common set of competencies that are necessary for safe, effective nursing practice. However, in the early 1990s the primary national nursing associations involved in establishing standards for nursing education—the NLN, the National League for Nursing Accrediting Commission,[9] the AACN, and the Commission on Collegiate Nursing Education—moved from a prescriptive model that dictated specific content and learning activities to an outcomes model that holds schools accountable for achieving their identified outcomes. The specific outcomes, learning activities, and content of programs are no longer directed by these groups. Nevertheless, they continue work to articulate general expectations for performance of nurses and hence provide guidance to schools as the faculty design curricula. Faculties of nursing education programs are expected to identify the national standards they used when identifying their program outcomes, and they are expected to demonstrate the logic of their curricula and learning activities that are implemented to achieve the national standards they selected. In 1998 the AACN produced guidelines in the form of *The Essentials of Baccalaureate Nursing Education.*[7] The *Essentials* document identified the following graduate characteristics: liberal education, professional values, core competencies, core knowledge, and role development.

The NLN, in its 2006 document *Excellence in Nursing Education,* identified the following knowledge, skills, and values that nurses of today and the future need: "understand the principles that underlie their practice; know how to find, manage, and use information; be comfortable with ambiguity and uncertainty; be leaders and agents for change; think critically and communicate effectively; function effectively in the face of conflict; and manage constant change, including technological developments."[9]

In addition to the standards established by national professional organizations, each prelicensure professional nursing program must prepare students for success on the National Council Licensure Examination-RN (NCLEX-RN). The NCLEX-RN assesses the knowledge, skills, and abilities that are essential for the nurse to meet the needs of clients requiring the promotion, maintenance, or restoration of health. The test plan for the NCLEX-RN provides a summary of the content and scope of this important examination, and nursing faculties also use this test plan as a curriculum planning guide.[10]

Against this background of nonprescriptive and regulatory national expectations, specific program outcomes and the learning experiences designed to achieve the outcomes are determined at the level of the individual schools of nursing. This latitude in program development creates an opportunity for AORN to develop curriculum materials that can be adopted and adapted by individual schools of nursing as they work with their local hospitals and chapters of AORN. Offering meaningful clinical learning activities in perioperative patient care settings can facilitate the achievement of curriculum outcomes while reducing the complexities and problems of clinical site access and learning experience development.

Undergraduate nursing education program are attempting to produce graduates with a common set of competencies that are necessary for safe, effective nursing practice. Benefits of clinical learning activities in perioperative settings that contribute to the development of these competencies include, but are not limited to, the following.

Knowledge

- Applying knowledge of anatomy, physiology, and pathophysiology to understand the patient's surgical procedure, its effects on the patient, and the patient's needs for preoperative and postoperative care.
- Recognizing the ethical and legal responsibilities of the professional nurse and the nurse's accountability to the patient, the profession of nursing, and other members of the health care team.
- Applying nursing research findings to planning and implementing effective care for perioperative patients.

Skills

- Learning and refining aseptic technique so that it can be applied with skill and confidence in other settings.
- Improving patient assessment, communication, organization, coordination, critical thinking, and decision-making skills in an environment where such activities must be performed quickly and accurately.
- Providing opportunities to assess their own interest in and talents for perioperative nursing practice.

Values

- Developing the role of advocate for the surgical patient by identifying the patient's expressed and unexpressed needs.
- Responding appropriately to those needs through the action of facilitating or mediating among all providers involved in the care of the patient.
- Recognizing diverse career opportunities for professional nursing practice in perioperative settings.
- Participating as members of a multidisciplinary health care team that develops and promotes the continuity of patient care in an environment that reinforces an understanding of the professional nurse's independent and interdependent function.

While students can be taught nursing knowledge, skills, and values in didactic and laboratory courses, the ability to apply content to patient care in a clinical environment is often limited by the specific type of unit. In-house and ambulatory surgical settings are an underutilized, and often underestimated, site for learning patient care. Furthermore, practical suggestions for learning opportunities in perioperative sites are numerous within the context of an existing curriculum rather than adding new content or courses. Perioperative clinical learning opportunities can be scheduled for student groups just as they are in other clinical sites in existing courses. The students may practice the most elementary skills, but they may also be required to use more complex critical thinking and sophisticated skills.

For example, the student in a "Fundamentals of Nursing" course could practice sterile technique for insertion of a Foley catheter in both genders and later consider developmental changes that occur with age in patients that may alter the ease of insertion. A more advanced student might be required to consider the patient's health status, length and type of surgery, and lab values to decide whether a simple drainage bag or urometer should be selected. Even more sophisticated critical thinking skills would be needed to establish fluid balance for patients with central and multiple intravenous lines, blood gas analyses, and cardiac output measures being assessed.

Relating nursing interventions to outcomes

Patient outcomes: The patient will maintain fluid output without signs of infection or obstruction throughout the perioperative experience.

Course outcomes: At the end of the course, the student will be able to combine knowledge from the sciences and nursing to provide nursing care to clients.

Program outcomes: By the conclusion of the program, the student will be able to use nursing knowledge, theory, and research findings with knowledge from the humanities and sciences to provide a structure for nursing practice.

Similarly, the beginning student might be learning how to assess vital signs and could be shown that while the patterns displayed in the OR and postanesthesia care unit (PACU) for every patient seem very complex, monitors may be constantly displaying vital signs. This emphasizes how health care professionals in every hospital unit are interested in these assessments of their patients. PACU nurses usually do not announce the placement of equipment as the patient is admitted to their service. However, the beginning student will use critical thinking to assist in the admission of the patient by knowing which arm to use for the blood pressure cuff (ie, the arm without the IV) and which hand to use for the pulse oximeter (ie, the arm where blood flow will not be interrupted by the blood pressure cuff). The student also can see how quickly rhythm patterns of tachycardia, bradycardia, or regularity patterns of heartbeat can be assessed. Patterns displayed for cardiothoracic patients will show differing pressures for each chamber of the heart. If the more advanced student is asked to consider these varying pressures of cardiac chambers, identifying valves opening and closing in relation to the cardiac cycle, the student can see how a pulmonary artery catheter can be floated through the chambers of the heart to reach its destination.

Relating nursing interventions to outcomes

Patient outcomes: The patient's vital signs will remain within normal limits for the duration of the perioperative experience.

Course outcomes: At the end of the course, the student will be able to use critical thinking skills to plan basic nursing care for an individual client.

At the end of the course, the student will be able to demonstrate critical thinking skills in planning, implementing, and evaluating nursing care management across the lifespan of groups of clients who are experiencing health care problems.

Program outcomes: By the end of the program, the student will be able to use critical thinking to solve clinical problems in selected health care delivery systems.

Numerous client needs can be met when the nursing student is assigned to a perioperative practice setting as a primary clinical site in the nursing program. Important elements of providing a safe effective care environment, health promotion and maintenance, psychosocial integrity, and physiological integrity can be learned with perioperative clients in a range of activities such as the following.

- *Shadowing:* Following a perioperative nurse caring for a surgical patient for a designated period of time.
- *Guided observation:* Specific objectives provided by the preceptor or student, or both, for the clinical learning activity, usually with some type of follow-up by the faculty following the guided observation.
- *Follow-through:* One or more patients are accompanied from admission or arrival, through the intraoperative phase, immediate postoperative care in the PACU and postoperative unit, or discharge from the setting.
- *Clinical rotation* in an established course.
- *Elective course.*
- *Capstone course or activity:* A final clinical learning activity in which a student is assigned to the perioperative setting to work with a staff nurse as the student engages in patient care activities and responsibilities similar to those in a postgraduation employment setting.
- *Internship:* Postgraduation employment opportunity directed by the hospital or other health care setting.
- *Externship:* Generally a summer clinical learning opportunity offered as employment to students continuing in an undergraduate nursing program.

Summary

As noted throughout this guidance statement, perioperative patient care environments can be successfully used to apply a variety of learning opportunities for nursing students while caring for perioperative patients. Offering meaningful clinical learning activities in perioperative patient care settings can facilitate the achievement of curriculum outcomes while reducing the above-identified problems faced by nursing faculties as they seek innovative clinical placements.

REFERENCES
1. "Think tank on perioperative learning experiences in the nursing curriculum: Summary report 2004," cosponsored by AORN and the National League for Nursing, *http://www.nln.org/publications/thinktanksummary.pdf* (accessed 6 Nov 2006).
2. "The value of clinical learning activities in the perioperative setting in undergraduate nursing curricula," AORN Position Statement, *http://www.aorn.org/about /positions/pdf/POS-Value%20of%20Clinical%20Learning .pdf* (accessed 6 Nov 2006).
3. "Resolutions 2006," National Student Nurses Association, *http://www.nsna.org/pubs/pdf/Resolution% 202006.pdf* (accessed 6 Nov 2006).
4. American Hospital Association, "Table 3: Total United States utilization, personnel, revenue and expenses, community health indicators 2000–2004," in *AHA Statistics* (Chicago: Health Forum LLC, 2006) 11.
5. K Bragg, N VanBalen, N Cook, "Future trends in minimally invasive surgery," *AORN Journal* 82 (December 2005) 1006-1018.
6. L M Sigsby, J Selzer, T K Wilson, "A successful nursing student practicum in an ambulatory surgery center," *AORN Journal* 84 (August 2006) 219-232.
7. "The essentials of baccalaureate education for professional nursing practice, 1998," American Association of Colleges of Nursing, *http://www.aacn.nche.edu /Education/bacessn.htm* (accessed 6 Nov 2006).
8. P C Seifert, "The operating room as a learning laboratory," *Dean's Notes: A Communication Service to Nursing School Deans, Administrators, and Faculty* 19 (1998) 1-3.
9. "Excellence in nursing education, 2006," National League for Nursing, *http://www.nln.org/about nln/Position Statements/index.htm* (accessed 6 Nov 2006).
10. "NCLEX-RN examination: Test plan for the National Council Licensure Examination for registered nurses, effective April 2007," National Council of State Boards of Nursing, *https://www.ncsbn.org/RN_Test_Plan _2007_Web.pdf* (accessed 6 Nov 2006).

RESOURCES
Girard, N J. "Perioperative education: Perspective from the think tank." *AORN Journal* 80 (November 2004) 827-838.

Approved by the AORN Board of Directors in November 2006. Originally published in *Standards, Recommended Practices, and Guidelines,* 2007 edition.

Introduction to the AORN Recommended Practices

This section contains recommended practices for perioperative nursing practice. They are based on principles of nursing science, microbiology, research, review of the scientific literature, and the opinions of knowledgeable experts. The AORN recommended practices are written by perioperative nurse specialists in the AORN Center for Nursing Practice and selected members of the Association in collaboration with liaisons from the the American Association of Nurse Anesthetists, the American College of Surgeons, the American Society of Anesthesiologists, the American Society for Healthcare Central Service Professionals, the Association for Professionals in Infection Control and Epidemiology, Centers for Disease Control and Prevention, and the International Association of Healthcare Central Service Materiel Management.

These recommended practices represent the Association's official position on questions regarding optimal perioperative nursing practice. The recommended practices appearing in this edition have been approved by the AORN Recommended Practices Committee and the AORN Board of Directors. No attempt has been made to gain consensus among users, manufacturers, and consumers of any material or product. **Compliance with the AORN recommended practices is voluntary.**

AORN's recommended practices are intended as achievable and represent what is believed to be an optimal level of patient care within the surgical and invasive procedure settings. These practice settings include traditional operating rooms, ambulatory surgery centers, physicians' offices, cardiac catheterization laboratories, endoscopy suites, radiology departments, and all other areas where surgery and other invasive procedures may be performed.

Each recommended practice consists of achievable recommendations based on the highest level of evidence available. The recommendations are broad statements intended to be used to guide policy and procedure development in specific work environments. Although they are considered to represent the optimal level of practice, variations in practice settings and clinical situations may limit the degree to which each recommendation can be implemented. The recommended practices are intended to describe best perioperative nursing practices and to promote patient and health care worker safety.

Application in Practice

Application of the recommended practices in individual work settings requires close examination of existing policies and procedures. This review may indicate that revised or new policies and/or procedures are necessary. Individual commitment, professional conscience, and the setting in which perioperative nursing is practiced must guide the nurse in implementing these recommended practices. Variations in practice settings and clinical situations may determine the degree to which the recommended practice can be fulfilled.

As used within the context of the recommended practices, "may" is used to indicate that a course of action is permissible within the limits of the recommended practice; and "can" is used as a statement of possibility and capability. The use of "should" indicates that a certain course of action is recommended. "Must" is used only to describe "unavoidable" situations, including those mandated by government regulation and accreditation organization standards.

Recommended Practices and PNDS

The Perioperative Nursing Data Set (PNDS) is an American Nurses Association (ANA)-recognized structured nursing vocabulary developed by AORN to describe the nursing care for patients undergoing a surgical or other invasive procedure from preadmission to discharge. As a controlled vocabulary, PNDS enables nursing care to be documented in a standardized manner to allow for collection of reliable and valid clinical data on perioperative nurse-sensitive outcomes resulting from nursing interventions during a surgical or invasive procedure.

This standardized language consists of a collection of unique data elements reflecting the nursing process as described in the *Perioperative Standards and Recommended Practices*. The perioperative patient and his or her family members are at the core of the PNDS patient-focused conceptual model. The model depicts perioperative nursing in four domains and illustrates the relationship between the patient, his or her family members, and care provided by the professional perioperative registered nurse. Each data element in the PNDS is represented by a unique identifier. The PNDS structure consists of four domains; within each domain are associated nursing diagnoses, interventions, and outcomes.

The recommended practices were restructured in 2008 to facilitate electronic content management and publication of the documents and to enable electronic mapping of the PNDS interventions and outcomes to the recommendations. An initial attempt to map the PNDS outcomes and interventions to the recommended practices is reflected in some of the recommendations, as noted in parentheses following the purpose and intervention statements. Interventions are represented by the letter "I" and a unique number; outcomes are represented by the letter "O" and a unique number.

AORN is continuing to develop and refine the PNDS. As the PNDS is being restructured to fit into an electronic standardized perioperative record, mapping to the newly developed or revised recommended practices is temporarily suspended. The effort to map the PNDS to the recommended practices will resume at a later date.

Revision Process

AORN began publishing recommended practices in March 1975. A compilation was printed in March 1978 in *AORN Standards of Practice*. The book at hand contains revisions of those previously published recommended practices as well as new ones developed since 1978.

Each recommended practice is reviewed and revised as appropriate at regular periodic intervals. Although only a portion of the recommended practices may be updated for publication in any given year, all 29 recommended practices are under continuous scrutiny by the AORN Recommended Practices Committee, which is charged with keeping them up to date. Two recommended practices have been revised for this 2009 edition:

- Recommended Practices for High-Level Disinfection, and
- Recommended Practices for Cleaning and Processing Flexible Endoscopes and Endoscope Accessories

The important task of developing, reviewing, and updating AORN's recommended practices is ongoing; the work of the Recommended Practices Committee overlaps from one term to the next. Thus, one committee is always building on the efforts of previous committees by revising and updating their work to keep up with changes in nursing practice, nursing and medical research, and surgical technology.

AORN Staff Support

AORN STAFF LIAISONS
Ramona Conner, RN, MSN, CNOR
Manager, Standards and Recommended Practices

Melissa Kovac, MA, MLIS
Research Librarian

Bonnie Kibbe
Administrative Assistant

PERIOPERATIVE NURSING DATA SET
Carol Petersen, RN, BSN, MAOM, CNOR
Manager, PNDS

PERIOPERATIVE NURSING SPECIALISTS
Joan Blanchard, RN, BSN, MSS, CNOR, CIC
Byron Burlingame, RN, MSN, CNOR
Robin Chard, RN, PhD, CNOR
Bonnie Denholm, RN, BSN, MS, CNOR
Denise Downing, RN, MS, CNOR
Sharon Giarrizzo-Wilson, RN, BSN, MS, CNOR
Sheila Mitchell, RN, BSN, MS, CNOR
Mary Ogg, RN, MSN, CNOR

AORN gratefully acknowledges the work of the 2008–2009 Recommended Practices Committee

This section contains the following AORN Recommended Practices:

Aseptic Practice

Attire, Surgical 299
Hand Antisepsis, Surgical 307
Maintaining a Sterile Field 317
Traffic Patterns in the Perioperative Practice Setting 327

Equipment and Product Safety

Electrosurgery 331
Endoscopic Minimally Invasive Surgery 347
Gowns and Drapes—Selection and Use 361
Laser Safety in Practice Settings 367
Pneumatic Tourniquet 373
Product Selection in Perioperative Practice Setting 387
Surgical Tissue Banking 391

Patient and Worker Safety

Counts—Sponge, Sharp, and Instrument 405
Environment of Care 415
Environmental Cleaning in the Perioperative Setting 439
Reducing Radiological Exposure in the Perioperative Practice Setting 455
Specimen Care and Handling 467
Transmissible Infections, Prevention of 475

Patient Care

Documentation of Perioperative Nursing Care 487
Hypothermia, Prevention of 491
Managing the Patient Receiving Local Anesthesia 505
Managing the Patient Receiving Moderate Sedation/Analgesia 513
Positioning the Patient in the Perioperative Practice Setting 525
Preoperative Patient Skin Antisepsis 549

Sterilization and Disinfection

Anesthesia Equipment—Cleaning and Processing 569
* Disinfection, High-Level 579
* Flexible Endoscopes—Cleaning and Processing 595
Instruments and Powered Equipment—Cleaning and Care of 611
Packaging Systems—Selection and Use 637
Sterilization in the Perioperative Practice Setting 647

Indicates items newly revised in 2008 or published here for the first time.

Recommended Practices for Surgical Attire

The following recommended practices were developed by the AORN Recommended Practices Committee and have been approved by the AORN Board of Directors. They were presented as proposed recommended practices for comments by members and others. They are effective January 1, 2005.

These recommended practices are intended as achievable recommendations representing what is believed to be an optimal level of practice. Policies and procedures will reflect variations in practice settings or clinical situations, which will determine the degree to which the recommended practices can be implemented.

AORN recognizes the numerous types of settings in which perioperative nurses practice. These recommended practices are intended as guidelines adaptable to various practice settings. These practice settings include traditional operating rooms, ambulatory surgery units, physicians' offices, cardiac catheterization suites, endoscopy suites, radiology departments, and all other areas where operative and other invasive procedures may be performed.

Purpose

These recommended practices provide guidelines for attire worn within the semirestricted and restricted areas of the surgical environment. The human body is a major source of microbial contamination in this environment; therefore, scrub clothing is worn to promote a high level of cleanliness and hygiene within the surgical environment. These recommended practices are not intended to address sterile attire worn at the surgical field.

Recommendation I

All individuals who enter the semirestricted and restricted areas of the surgical suite should wear freshly laundered surgical attire intended for use only within the surgical suite.

1. Facility approved, clean, and freshly laundered surgical attire should be donned in a designated dressing area of the facility upon entry or re-entry to the facility.[1-3] If scrubs are worn into the institution from outside, they should be changed before entering semirestricted or restricted areas to minimize the potential for contamination (eg, animal hair, cross contamination from other uncontrolled environments).[4]

2. Surgical attire helps contain bacterial shedding and promotes environmental control.[1,5] Surgical attire made of reusable woven fabric or single-use, nonwoven fabric that is low-linting should be worn. Low-linting surgical attire that minimizes bacterial shedding and provides comfort, safety, and a professional appearance should be selected. As personnel move, friction between their bodies and clothing frees bacteria. Research indicates that chafing increases dispersal of body scurf into the environment.[5] If a two-piece pantsuit is worn, the top of the scrub suit should be secured at the waist, tucked into the pants, or fit close to the body. There is little evidence to support a preference for scrub pants over scrub dresses.

3. Surgical attire should be changed daily or whenever it becomes visibly soiled, contaminated, or wet.[2,4,6] Worn surgical attire should be placed in an appropriately designated container for washing or disposal and should not be hung or placed in a locker for wearing at another time. This promotes high-level cleanliness and hygiene within the practice setting. It has been reported that bacterial colony counts are higher when scrub clothing is removed, stored in a locker, and used again.[7-9]

4. Reusable woven or single-use, nonwoven attire should be appropriately placed in designated containers after use.[1,4,5]

5. Visibly soiled, contaminated, or wet surgical attire should be removed as soon as possible and replaced with fresh, clean surgical attire. Changing contaminated, soiled, or wet attire reduces the potential for cross-infection and protects personnel from prolonged exposure to potentially harmful bacteria.[4,5]

6. Surgical attire contaminated with visible blood or body fluids must remain at the facility and be laundered by the hospital or a hospital-contracted commercial laundry.[4-6,10] Controlled laundering of attire contaminated by blood or body fluids reduces the risk of transferring pathogenic microorganisms from the facility to the home or the general public.

7. Home laundering of surgical attire is not recommended.[4,6,10-15] Without clear evidence about the safety for patients, health care workers, and their family members, AORN does not support

the practice of home laundering of surgical attire. Reusable surgical attire, including cover jackets and cloth hats, should be laundered by a designated facility-approved and monitored commercial laundry after daily use.

Commercial laundries are required to follow strict guidelines[4,8,16-19] that incorporate

♦ proper and controlled water temperatures;
♦ use of detergents;
♦ use of oxidizing agents (eg, chlorine bleach) in specified and monitored concentrations;
♦ repeated changes of water; and
♦ dryer or iron and press drying temperatures that typically are not found in home laundry equipment.

Home laundering of surgical attire that is not visibly soiled is controversial, and there is no concrete evidence to either support or refute the practice. Surgical attire becomes soiled or contaminated with microorganisms during wear. Taking worn, soiled, or contaminated surgical attire into the home can result in the spread of contamination to the home environment.

AORN is aware that some provider facilities require personnel to launder scrub attire at home. Although AORN does not support this practice, steps should be taken to minimize contaminants to the home environment; therefore, laundering practices similar to regulations and professional standards for commercial laundries are recommended. When a facility requires home laundering of surgical attire, minimum criteria should be met.[4,8,16-18]

Suggested criteria for home laundering soiled surgical attire should include

♦ using an automatic washer and hot air dryer;
♦ using water temperature of 110° F to 125° F (43.33° C to 51.67° C) to facilitate microbial kill;
♦ using chlorine bleach (ie, sodium hypochlorite);
♦ using detergent according to manufacturer's instructions;
♦ laundering surgical attire in a separate load with no other items;
♦ laundering surgical attire as the last load after all other items have been laundered;
♦ washing hands immediately after placing laundry in the washing machine;
♦ keeping laundry items completely submerged during the entire wash and rinse cycle to facilitate removal of soil and microorganisms;

♦ avoiding placing hands or arms in the laundry or rinse water to keep items submerged;
♦ thoroughly cleaning the door and lid of the washing machine before removing the laundered attire to prevent reintroduction of contaminants on clean attire when removing it from the washing machine and before placing it in the dryer;
♦ using the highest drying setting possible that is safe for the material of attire construction; and
♦ promptly removing attire when dry to avoid desiccation of materials.

8. Laundered surgical attire should be protected from contamination during transfer and storage.[1,20] Freshly laundered surgical attire should be protected during transport to the practice setting.

9. The use of cover apparel should be determined by the individual practice setting. The value of cover apparel within the institution is unsubstantiated.[1,21-23] The use of cover apparel has been found to have little or no effect on reducing contamination, but it is used for practical enforcement and cost considerations. Donning fresh scrubs after each trip to other areas increases costs and is time-consuming. Laboratory coats or the use of cover gowns may provide a professional appearance, but they should be removed before entering a semirestricted or restricted area because they can be a source of contamination.[24] The decision on cover gowns depends on individual state regulatory rulings, the culture in each perioperative suite, and the manager's assessment of priorities.

10. Nonscrubbed personnel should wear long-sleeved jackets that are buttoned or snapped closed during use. Complete closure of the jacket avoids accidental contamination of the sterile field. Long-sleeved attire is advocated to prevent bacterial shedding from bare arms and is included in the Occupational Safety and Health Administration (OSHA) regulation for the use of personal protective equipment (PPE).[1,2]

11. Other garments should be contained completely within or covered by the surgical attire. Clothing that cannot be covered by the surgical attire should not be worn.

Recommendation II

Personnel should cover head and facial hair, including sideburns and necklines, when in the semi-restricted and restricted areas of the surgical suite.

1. A clean, low-lint surgical head cover or hood that confines all hair should be worn. Hair covers eliminate the possibility of hair or dandruff being shed onto surgical attire.[1,2,4,25] A bald or shaved head is covered to prevent shedding of squamous cells (ie, scurf).

2. The head cover or hood should be designed to minimize microbial dispersal. Hair acts as a filter when left uncovered and collects bacteria in proportion to its length, curliness, and oiliness.[1,25] Shedding from hair has been shown to affect surgical wound infection; therefore, complete coverage is necessary. Disposable bouffant and hood-style covers are preferred.[4] Skullcaps that fail to cover the side hair above the ears and hair at the nape of the neck should not be worn in the surgical suite. Net caps should not be used because they do not provide a barrier to dandruff and hair fallout.

3. Single-use headgear should be removed and discarded in a designated receptacle as soon as possible after daily use. Reusable hats or hoods should be laundered in a commercial laundry after each use.[2,4,16]

4. Contaminated headgear must be removed and laundered by the facility.[10]

Recommendation III

All individuals entering restricted areas of the OR suite should wear a mask when open sterile items and equipment are present.

1. A single surgical mask should be worn in surgical environments where open sterile supplies or scrubbed persons are located. A mask should fully cover both mouth and nose and be secured in a manner that prevents venting.[1,2,26] Masks are intended to contain and filter droplets of microorganisms expelled from the mouth and nasopharynx during talking, sneezing, and coughing.[27,28] Use of a double mask creates an impediment to breathing and does not increase filtration; therefore, this is unacceptable.[25,26]

Differences of opinion about whether masks should be worn exist in the literature. AORN recommends further research to determine changes in current practice.[29-31] In addition to possible surgical site contamination, blood exposure occurring on the face and neck of OR personnel is not uncommon; therefore, individual practice settings should develop policies based on OSHA and state-mandated recommendations for wearing masks.[32]

2. Masks should be removed carefully by handling only the ties, and they should be discarded immediately. Masks should not be saved by hanging them around the neck or tucking them into a pocket for future use. The filter portion of a surgical mask harbors bacteria collected from the nasopharyngeal airway. Handling this portion of the mask after use can transfer bacteria to the hands and initiate potential cross contamination.[1,2,33]

Recommendation IV

All personnel entering the semirestricted and restricted areas of the surgical suite should confine or remove all jewelry and watches.[2,34-37]

1. Rings should be removed from hands. These items may harbor organisms that cannot be removed during hand washing. Higher bacterial counts have been noted when jewelry is worn.

2. Other jewelry (eg, watches, earrings, bracelets, necklaces, piercings) should be removed or totally confined within the scrub attire. Although there is no evidence to demonstrate that other jewelry increases bacterial shedding, there is concern that jewelry could fall onto the sterile field or into the wound if not contained. Necklaces could contaminate the front of the sterile gown if not confined.[1]

Recommendation V

Fingernails should be kept short, clean, natural, and healthy.[2,35,38]

1. The subungual region harbors the majority of microorganisms found on the hand. Removing debris from fingernails requires the use of a nail cleaner under running water; additional effort is necessary for longer nails. The risk of

tearing gloves increases if fingernails extend past the fingertips. Long fingernails may cause injury when moving or positioning patients.[38]

Recent studies found no increase in microbial growth related to wearing freshly applied nail polish;[35,37] however, nail polish that is obviously chipped or worn longer than four days is associated with the presence of greater numbers of bacteria and has been associated with infections. Surgical conscience, therefore, must be a foremost behavior in individuals who choose to wear nail polish in the surgical setting.

2. Artificial nails should not be worn.[2,32,38-51] Studies show that artificial (eg, acrylic) nails on healthy hands increase the risk of surgical site infection. Artificial nails harbor organisms and prevent effective hand antisepsis. Higher counts of gram-negative microorganisms have been cultured from the fingertips of personnel wearing artificial nails than from personnel with natural nails, both before and after hand washing. Fungal growth occurs frequently under artificial nails as a result of moisture becoming trapped between the natural and artificial nail.[47-49]

Recommendation VI

Protective barriers must be made available to reduce the risk of exposure to potentially infectious materials.[34,52,53]

1. Gloves should be selected and worn as follows according to the task to be performed.[1]
   ♦ Sterile gloves must be worn when performing sterile procedures.
   ♦ Medical, nonsterile gloves are recommended for nonsterile activities.

2. Gloves should be changed between patient contacts or after contact with contaminated items when a task is complete. Surgical or examination gloves should be changed—not washed—between patient contacts. Hand hygiene should be performed after gloves are removed.[52-54] Gloves are worn to reduce gross contamination of the hands. Changing gloves between patient contacts and after completing a task reduces the risk of microorganism transmission. Disinfecting agents may cause glove deterioration. Research indicates that micro-

organisms are not always removed from gloves despite friction, use of cleansing agents, and drying. In addition, washing the glove may decrease the integrity of the glove.[50]

3. Protective eyewear, masks, or face shields must be worn when splashing or spraying is likely.[1,2,4,6,53,54] Masks should be worn, along with protective eyewear (eg, goggles, glasses with solid side shields, chin-length face shields) whenever eye, nose, or mouth contamination reasonably can be anticipated as a result of splashes, spray, or splatter of blood droplets or other potentially infectious materials.[53,54] Personal protective equipment is considered appropriate only if it prevents blood or other potentially infectious materials from contaminating an employee's work clothes, undergarments, skin, eyes, mouth, or other mucous membranes under normal conditions of use and for the duration of time for which the protective equipment will be used.[52]

4. Protective eyewear or face shields that become contaminated should be discarded or decontaminated promptly according to manufacturers' written instructions.[1,4,6,53] Failure to decontaminate or dispose of these items could result in contamination to the wearer.

5. Additional protective attire (eg, liquid-resistant aprons, gowns, shoe covers) should be worn when exposure to blood or potentially infectious materials is anticipated.[6] Protective barriers are worn to reduce the risk of exposure to blood, body fluids, or other liquids that may contain potentially infectious agents. There is evidence that supports the need for circulating personnel to wear PPE appropriate to the task being performed.[53,55,56]

6. Fluid-resistant shoe covers are considered part of PPE and must be worn when it can be reasonably anticipated that splashes or spills may occur. Foot attire has no proven significance in reducing the incidence of surgical site wound infections; the primary reason for its use is to facilitate sanitation.[1,57] If shoe covers are worn, they should be changed whenever they become torn, wet, or soiled, and they should be removed and discarded in a designated container before leaving the surgical area.[1,4]

7. Shoes worn within the surgical environment should be clean with no visible soiling and should provide protection.[1] Cloth or open-toe shoes do not offer protection against spilled liquids or sharp items that may be dropped or kicked. Shoes should have closed toes and low heels to minimize the risk of injury.[57,58]

Recommendation VII

Policies and procedures for surgical attire should be developed, reviewed periodically, and readily available in the practice setting. These policies and procedures should include, but not be limited to, definition of areas where surgical attire must be worn, appropriate attire within those defined areas, and the choice for the use of cover apparel outside the surgical suite.

1. These recommended practices should be used as guidelines for the development of policies and procedures within the practice setting. Policies and procedures establish authority, responsibility, and accountability and serve as operational guidelines. AORN's "Recommended practices for traffic patterns in the perioperative practice setting"[59] and "Recommended practices for surgical hand antisepsis and hygiene"[54] also should be consulted when developing policies and procedures. An introduction and review of policies and procedures should be included in the orientation and ongoing education of personnel to assist in the development of knowledge, skills, and attitudes that affect patient outcomes. Policies and procedures also assist in the development of quality assessment and improvement activities.

Glossary

Artificial nails: Substances or devices applied or added to the natural nails to augment or enhance the wearer's own nails. They include, but are not limited to, bonding, tips, wrappings, and tapes.

Cleaning: The physical removal of soil or organic material using water or mechanical action with or without detergent; cleaning removes rather than kills microorganisms.

Contaminated: The presence of pathogenic organisms (eg, blood, other potentially infectious material) on or in the material.

Cover gown: A garment, such as a laboratory coat, gown, or jacket, worn over surgical attire to prevent contamination.

Personal protective equipment: Personal protective equipment for standard precautions includes intact gloves, gowns, masks, and eye protection (eg, face shields, goggles, glasses with side shields).

Scrub attire: Additional sterile clothing worn to cover the surgical attire to present sterile boundaries during a sterile invasive procedure.

Scurf: A branlike desquamation of the epidermis.

Soiled: Worn or dirty, especially on the surface. Smirched or stained by body perspiration, body oils, or other substances.

Surgical attire: Nonsterile apparel designated for the OR practice setting that includes two-piece pantsuits, cover jackets, head coverings, shoes, masks, protective eyewear, and other protective barriers.

Restricted area: Includes the OR and procedure room, the clean core, and scrub sink areas. People in this area are required to wear full surgical attire and cover all head and facial hair, including sideburns, beards, and necklines.

Semirestricted area: Includes the peripheral support areas of the surgical suite and has storage areas for sterile and clean supplies, work areas for storage and processing of instruments, and corridors leading to the restricted areas of the surgical suite.

Unrestricted area: Includes a central point that is established to monitor the entrance of patients, personnel, and materials. Street clothes are permitted in this area, and traffic is not limited.

REFERENCES

1. D Fogg, "Infection prevention and control" in *Alexander's Care of the Patient in Surgery*, 12th ed, J C Rothrock, ed (St Louis: Mosby, 2003) 134-147.

2. Centers for Disease Control and Prevention, "Guideline for Prevention of Surgical Site Infection, 1999," *Infection Control and Hospital Epidemiology* 20 (April 1999) 250-278.

3. N L Belkin, "Use of scrubs and related apparel in health care facilities," *American Journal of Infection Control* 25 (October 1997) 401-404.

4. "Safe handling and biological decontamination of reusable medical devices in health care facilities and in nonclinical settings," ANSI/AAMI ST35:2003 (Arlington, Va: Association for the Advancement of Medical Instrumentation, 2003) 11-12; 51-57.

5. B M Anderson, N Solheim, "Occlusive scrub suits in operating theaters during cataract surgery: Effect on airborne contamination," *Infection Control Hospital Epidemiology* 23 (April 2002) 218-220.

6. "Regulations (Standards 29 CFR) Bloodborne pathogens—1910-1030," US Department of Labor, Occupational Safety and Health Administration, *http://www.osha-slc.gov/pls/oshaweb/owadisp.show_document?p_table=STANDARDS&p_id=10051* (accessed 22 May 2004) 15-16.

7. "Report to Congress on workers' home contamination study conducted under the Workers' Family Protection Act (29 USC 671A)" Centers for Disease Control and Prevention, National Institute for Occupational Safety and Health, *http://www.cdc.gov/niosh/contamin.html* (accessed 8 April 2002) 6.

8. A N Neely, M P Maley, "Survival of enterococci and staphylococci on hospital fabrics and plastic," *Journal of Clinical Microbiology* 38 (February 2002) 724-726.

9. I Callaghan, "Bacterial contamination of nurse's uniforms: A study," *Nursing Standard* 13 (Sept 23-29, 1998) 37-42.

10. Centers for Disease Control and Prevention, "Guidelines for environmental infection control in health-care facilities: Recommendations of CDC and the Healthcare Infection Control Practices Advisory Committee (HICPAC)," *Morbidity and Mortality Weekly Report* 52 (June 6, 2003) 27-28.

11. N Hawkes, "Infection Fear Over Nurses Who Wash Uniforms at Home," *The Times*, 30 June 2003, sec 2W.

12. Market and Opinion Research International, "Nurses' uniforms survey for JLA" (June 2003) 1-7.

13. N L Belkin, "Home laundering of soiled surgical scrubs: Surgical site infections and the home environment," *American Journal of Infection Control* 29 (February 2001) 58-64.

14. P Jurkovich, "Home versus hospital-laundered scrubs," *The American Journal of Maternal/Child Nursing* 29 (March/April 2004) 106-110.

15. L Spannraft, "Laundering scrubs at home," (Readers' Responses) *The American Journal of Maternal/Child Nursing* 23 (January/February 1998) 53.

16. D Barrie, "How hospital linen and laundry services are provided," *Journal of Hospital Infection* 27 (March 1994) 219-235.

17. D Fogg, "Body piercings in the OR; tabletop sterilizers; Joint Commission initiative; West Nile virus; home laundering" (Clinical Issues) *AORN Journal* 77 (February, 2003) 428-433.

18. J M Jaska, D L Fredell, "Impact of detergent systems on bacterial survival on laundered fabrics," *Applied and Environmental Microbiology* 39 (April, 1980) 743-748.

19. N L Belkin, "Surgical scrubs—Where we were, where we are going," *Today's Surgical Nurse* 20 (March/April 1998) 28-34.

20. L L McDonald, "Linen services," in *APIC Text of Infection Control and Epidemiology* (Washington, DC: Association for Professionals in Infection Control and Epidemiology, Inc, 2002) 75(1)-75(4).

21. H Kenny, E Lawson "The efficacy of cotton cover gowns in reducing infection in neutropenic patients: An evidence-based study," *International Journal of Nursing Practice* 6 (June 2000) 135-139.

22. J L Thigpen, "Responding to research: Realistic use of scrub clothes and cover gowns," *Neonatal Network* 9 (February 1991) 41-44.

23. C B Mailhot et al, "Cover gowns: Researching their effectiveness," *AORN Journal* 46 (September 1987) 482-490.

24. W Loh, VV Ng, J Holton, "Bacterial flora on the white coats of medical students," *Journal of Hospital Infection* 45 (January 2000) 65-68.

25. B Friberg et al, "Surgical area contamination—Comparable bacterial counts using disposable head and mask and helmet aspirator system, but dramatic increase upon omission of head-gear: An experimental study in horizontal laminar air-flow," *Journal of Hospital Infection* 47 (February 2001) 110-115.

26. N J Mitchell, S Hunt, "Surgical face masks in modern operating rooms—A costly and unnecessary ritual?" *Journal of Hospital Infection* 18 (July 1991) 239-242.

27. M G Romney, "Surgical face masks in the operating theatre: Re-examining the evidence," *Journal of Hospital Infection* 47 (April 2001) 251-256.

28. F McCluskey, "Does wearing a face mask reduce bacterial wound infection? A literature review," *British Journal of Theatre Nursing* 6 (August, 1996) 18-29.

29. N L Belkin "Surgical face masks in the operating theatre: Are they still necessary?" (Letters to the Editor) *Journal of Hospital Infection* 50 (March 2002) 233-235.

30. T G Tunevall, "Postoperative wound infections and surgical face masks: A controlled study," *World Journal of Surgery* 15 (May/June 1991) 383-387.

31. G A J Ayliffe, "Masks in surgery?" (Editorial) *The Journal of Hospital Infection* 18 (July 1991) 165-166.

32. Y Uehara et al, "Bacterial interference among nasal inhabitants: Eradication of *Staphylococcus aureus* from nasal cavities by artificial implantation of *Corynebacterium* sp." *Journal of Hospital Infection* 44 (February 2000) 127-133.

33. L Emsley, "Why wear surgical face masks?" *Nursing Times* 96 (July 2000) 38-39.

34. Centers for Disease Control and Prevention, "Guideline for hand hygiene in health-care settings: Recommendations of the Healthcare Infection Control Practices Advisory Committee and the HICPAC/SHEA/APIC/IDSA Hand Hygiene Task Force," *Morbidity and Mortality Weekly Report* 51, RR-16 (Oct 25, 2002) 29-33.

35. V A Arrowsmith et al, "Removal of nail polish and finger rings to prevent surgical infection," The Cochrane Database of Systematic Reviews 2 (2004) 1-16.

36. W E Trick et al, "Impact of ring wearing on hand contamination and comparison of hand hygiene agents in a hospital," *Clinical Infectious Disease* 36 (June 2003) 1383-1390.

37. E Edel et al, "Impact of a 5-minute scrub on the microbial flora found on artificial, polished, or natural fingernails of operating room personnel," *Nursing Research* 47 (January/February 1998) 54-59.

38. R L Moolenaar et al, "A prolonged outbreak of *Pseudomonas Aeruginosa* in a neonatal intensive care unit: Did staff fingernails play a role in disease transmission?" *Infection Control and Hospital Epidemiology* 21 (February 2000) 80-85.

39. C A Wynd, D E Samstag, A M Lapp, "Bacterial carriage on the fingernails of OR nurses," *AORN Journal* 60 (November 1994) 796-805.

40. R Baran, "Pathogen carriage in health care workers wearing nail cosmetics," *Dermatology Online Journal* 9, no 1 (2003) 17D.

41. C A Baumgardner et al, "Effects of nail polish on microbial growth of fingernails: Dispelling sacred cows," *AORN Journal* 58 (July 1993) 84-88.

42. A Jeanes, J Green, "Nail art: A review of current infection control issues," *Journal of Hospital Infection* 49 (October 2001) 139-142.

43. J Porteous, "Artificial nails: Very real risks," *Canadian Operating Room Nursing Journal* 20 (September 2002) 16-21.

44. L Saiman et al, "Banning artificial nails from health care settings," *American Journal of Infection Control* 30 (June 2002) 252-254.

45. M F Parry et al, "Candida osteomylitis and diskitis after spinal surgery: An outbreak that implicates artificial nail use," *Clinical Infectious Diseases* 32 (February 2001) 352-356.

46. S A Hedderwick et al, "Pathogenic organisms associated with artificial fingernails worn by healthcare workers," *Infection Control and Hospital Epidemiology* 21 (August 2000) 505-509.

47. D J Passaro et al, "Postoperative *Serratia marcescens* wound infections traced to an out-of-hospital source," *Journal of Infectious Diseases* 174 (April 1997) 992-995.

48. E H Winslow, A F Jacobson, "Can a fashion statement harm the patient?" *American Journal of Nursing* 100 (September 2000) 63-65.

49. J Pottinger, S Burns, C Manske, "Bacterial carriage by artificial versus natural nails," *American Journal of Infection Control* 17 (December 1989) 340-344.

50. "Make a 'revolutionary' change in hand hygiene," *Hospital Employee Health* 21 (February 2002) 13-24.

51. "CDC draft guidelines say no artificial nails," *Same-Day Surgery* 25 (August, 2001) 91.

52. B N Doebbeling et al, "Removal of nosocomial pathogens from the contaminated glove," *Annals of Internal Medicine* 109 (September 1988) 394-398.

53. B Goodner, *The OSHA Handbook: Interpretive Guidelines for the Bloodborne Pathogen Standard* (El Paso, Tex: Skidmore-Roth Publishing, Inc, 1993) 61-62.

54. "Recommended practices for surgical hand antisepsis/hand scrubs," in *Standards, Recommended Practices, and Guidelines* (Denver: AORN, Inc, 2004) 291-299.

55. "Occupational exposure to bloodborne pathogens; Final rule," *Federal Register* 56 (Dec 6, 1991) 64177.

56. S Hubbard et al, "Reducing blood contamination and injury in the OR: A study of the effectiveness of protective garments and OR procedures," *AORN Journal* 55 (January 1992) 194-201.

57. M O'Neale, "Used sponge exposure; processing peel packages; flash sterilization; protective arm attire; beverages in the OR" (Clinical Issues) *AORN Journal* 59 (February 1994) 504-506.

58. G Copp et al, "Footwear practices and operating room contamination," *Nursing Research* 36 (November/December 1987) 366-369

59. "Recommended practices for traffic patterns in the perioperative practice setting," in *Standards, Recommended Practices, and Guidelines* (Denver: AORN, Inc, 2004) 397-399.

Originally published March 1975, *AORN Journal,* as AORN "Standards for proper OR wearing apparel." Format revision March 1978, July 1982.

Revised March 1984, March 1990. Published as proposed recommended practices August 1994.

Revised November 1998; published December 1998. *Reformatted July 2000.*

Revised November 2004; published in *Standards, Recommended Practices, and Guidelines,* 2005 edition. Reprinted February 2005, *AORN Journal.*

AORN Perioperative Standards and Recommended Practices, 2009 Edition

Recommended Practices for Surgical Hand Antisepsis/Hand Scrubs

The following recommended practices were developed by the AORN Recommended Practices Committee and have been approved by the AORN Board of Directors. They were presented as proposed recommended practices for comment to members and others. These recommended practices are effective January 1, 2004.

These recommended practices are intended as achievable recommendations representing what is believed to be an optimal level of practice. Policies and procedures will reflect variations in practice settings and/or clinical situations that determine the degree to which the recommended practices can be implemented.

AORN recognizes the numerous types of settings in which perioperative nurses practice. These recommended practices are intended as guidelines adaptable to various practice settings. These practice settings include traditional operating rooms, ambulatory surgery units, physicians' offices, cardiac catheterization suites, endoscopy suites, radiology departments, and all other areas where operative and other invasive procedures may be performed.

Purpose

Microorganism transfer from the hands of health care workers to patients is an important factor in health care-associated (ie, nosocomial) infections and has been recognized since the observations of Semmelweis and others more than 100 years ago.[1] Skin is a major potential source of microbial contamination in the surgical environment. Hand hygiene is a critical step in preventing infections and the spread of infections, is of critical importance for the entire health care team, and remains the most effective and least expensive measure to prevent the transmission of microorganisms and health care-associated infections. It is the single most important step in the prevention of infections.[2] The term *general hand hygiene* refers to decontamination of the hands by one of two methods—hand washing with either an antimicrobial or plain soap and water, or use of an antiseptic hand rub.[3]

The term *surgical hand antisepsis* refers to the antiseptic surgical scrub or antiseptic hand rub performed before donning sterile attire preoperatively. Although scrubbed members of the surgical team wear sterile gloves, the skin of their hands and forearms should be cleaned preoperatively to significantly reduce the number of microorganisms. The moist environment underneath surgical gloves can promote microorganism proliferation on the hands of the wearer. Both surgical and examination gloves can fail during a procedure. Choice of surgical hand antiseptic/scrub agents should be limited to those that are US Food and Drug Administration (FDA) compliant, have a documented ability to kill organisms immediately upon application, provide antimicrobial persistence to reduce regrowth of microorganisms, and have a cumulative effect over time.[3] The purpose of surgical hand antisepsis/hand scrubs is to

- remove debris and transient microorganisms from the nails, hands, and forearms;
- reduce the resident microbial count to a minimum; and
- inhibit rapid rebound growth of microorganisms.

Perioperative nursing vocabulary

The perioperative nursing vocabulary is a clinically relevant and empirically validated standardized language. This standardized language consists of the Perioperative Nursing Data Set and includes perioperative nursing diagnoses, interventions, and outcomes. The expected outcome of primary importance to this recommended practice is outcome 10 (O10), "The patient will be free of signs and symptoms of infection."[4]

Recommendation I

All personnel should practice general hand hygiene.

1. Hand hygiene immediately before and after patient contact remains the most cost-effective and simplest measure for health care workers to prevent cross contamination in the health care setting.[5] General hand hygiene should be performed before and after patient contact, after removing gloves, any time there is a possibility that there has been contact with blood or other potentially infectious materials, before and after eating, and after using a restroom.[3] Wearing gloves is not a substitute for hand hygiene.[6] Hands are a major source of transient flora and, therefore, a major vector of cross contamination in health care. Health care workers should avoid contact with surfaces that are potentially contaminated, such as equipment and other inanimate objects in the patient care setting (see

"Recommended practices for standard and transmission-based precautions").[7]

2. Fingernails should be kept short, clean, and healthy. The subungual region harbors the majority of microorganisms found on hands. Removal of debris underneath fingernails requires the use of a disposable, single-use nail cleaner under running water. Additional effort may be necessary for longer nails. The risk of tearing gloves can increase if fingernails extend past the fingertips. Long fingernails may cause patient injury during the moving or positioning process.[8-12] Ideal nail length has been described as not extending beyond the fingertips.[13] Polish, if used, should not be chipped. Studies have found no increase in microbial growth related to wearing freshly applied nail polish, but chipped nail polish may support the growth of larger numbers of organisms on fingernails.[3,9,12] There is concern, however, that individuals who spend considerable time and money on maintaining their nails may be less inclined to perform a vigorous surgical scrub to protect their nails. If this occurs, there could be a detrimental effect of bacterial growth on the hands, not from the polish itself, but from a change in hygienic practices. Available data indicate that nail polish that has been obviously chipped or worn for more than four days harbors greater numbers of bacteria.[9,12] This time frame may suggest a guide for changing polish so that nails remain well manicured. Individuals who choose to wear nail polish in the surgical setting should be guided by surgical conscience.[8,9,12]

3. Artificial nails should not be worn.[3] The variety and amount of potentially pathogenic bacteria cultured from the fingertips of personnel wearing artificial nails is greater than from the fingertips of personnel with natural nails, both before and after hand washing.[13-16] Numerous state boards of cosmetology report that fungal growth occurs frequently under artificial nails as a result of moisture becoming trapped between the natural and artificial nail.[8,17-19]

4. Cuticles, hands, and forearms should be free of open lesions and breaks in skin integrity. Open lesions and breaks in skin integrity increase the risk of patient and surgical team member infection. Cuts, abrasions, exudative lesions, and hangnails tend to ooze serum, which may contain pathogens. Broken skin permits microorganisms to enter the various layers of skin, providing deeper microbial breeding grounds.[8,17,20]

5. Rings, watches, and bracelets should be removed before performing hand hygiene. During hand hygiene, rings, watches, and bracelets may harbor microorganisms or inhibit their removal. Allergic skin reactions (eg, irritation) have been observed as a result of hand soaps, antimicrobial agents, residual chemicals, or glove powder accumulating under jewelry.[8,21,22] Removal of all jewelry from the hands and forearms permits full skin contact with the chosen surgical hand antimicrobial agent. The risk of infection from transient microorganisms increases exponentially in relation to the number of rings worn. A recent study found that there was no increase in reported microbial counts on the hands of personnel who removed rings before work.[23] Ring wearing has been associated with up to a 10-fold increase in median skin microorganism count (ie, bioload).[23]

6. Lotions, if used, should be chosen based on infection control practices, approved by infection control professionals, and compatible with the hand antimicrobial agent and gloves used. Lotions should be packaged in nonrefillable containers that are discarded when empty.[3] Skin moisturizing products can prevent drying, discomfort, and dermatitis and may help reduce bacterial shedding from the skin.[24,25] The use of moisturizing products in health care facilities should be examined and incorporated in a formalized and standardized manner into policies, procedures, and practices.[26] Petroleum-based products may weaken latex gloves, causing increased permeability.[27] Anionic-based lotions (ie, many over-the-counter products) that commonly are available on the market and used in health care facilities can neutralize the cumulative antimicrobial activity of chlorhexidine gluconate and chloroxylenol, ingredients that are found in many antimicrobial hand antiseptic products.[3,28] Always check with the manufacturer of the skin care product to verify that it is indeed compatible with the chosen hand antiseptic agent.

7. If hands are soiled visibly, wash them as soon as possible with plain or antimicrobial soap and water as follows.
   - Wet hands with warm water.
   - Apply soap to the hands according to the manufacturer's written instructions, if given.
   - Rub hands together vigorously for at least 15 seconds, covering all surfaces of the hands and fingers. Pay particular attention to areas often overlooked (ie, the backs of the hands, fingertips, the thumb and inner web).[29]
   - Rinse hands with warm water and dry thoroughly with a disposable towel.
   - Use towel to turn off the faucet.[3]

   Alcohol-based hand rubs are not appropriate for use when hands are visibly dirty or contaminated with proteinaceous materials (eg, blood, saliva) because these hand rubs do not remove soil or debris.[3]

8. If hands are not soiled visibly, an alcohol-based hand rub may be used for routine decontamination of hands.[3] Degerming with an alcohol-based hand rub is more effective than washing with soap and water and requires much shorter exposure time. Data indicate that the use of an alcohol-based agent may increase overall compliance with hand hygiene.[30-32] When relatively small amounts of proteinaceous material are present (ie, nonvisible soiling), alcohol may reduce viable bacterial counts on hands more rapidly than plain or antimicrobial soap.[3] Follow manufacturers' written directions for product application.[3] Alcohol-impregnated towelettes, if used in the facility, should have the Centers for Disease Control and Prevention's (CDC's) recommended volume and percentage of alcohol (ie, 60% to 95%). Lesser concentrations may be only comparable to soap and water.[3]

9. To improve adherence to general hand-hygiene recommendations among personnel working in busy patient care environments, an appropriate alcohol-based agent should be available in convenient locations (eg, wall, bedside). Individual, disposable, pocket-sized containers may be carried by health care providers.[3,31-34] Specific regulations may limit placement of alcohol-based products because of fire hazard considerations. Consult applicable local, state, and federal regulations for specific direction.

Recommendation II

An FDA-compliant, surgical hand antiseptic agent (ie, surgical hand scrub/rub) approved by the facility's infection control personnel should be used for all surgical hand antisepsis/hand scrubs.

1. The surgical hand antiseptic agent should
   - significantly reduce microorganisms on intact skin;
   - contain a nonirritating, antimicrobial preparation;
   - be broad spectrum;
   - be fast acting; and
   - have a persistent effect.[35]

   An antimicrobial ingredient is intended to kill microorganisms. A characteristic of certain hand antiseptic agents that sets them apart from plain soap is their ability to bind with the stratum corneum of the skin, resulting in persistent chemical activity. Organisms can proliferate in the moist environment underneath gloves. Surgical gloves may become damaged during procedures, placing both the wearer and patient at risk. In appropriate concentrations (ie, 60% to 95%), alcohols provide the most rapid and greatest reduction in microbial counts on skin but have no persistent activity. Persistent antimicrobial activity, measured in hours, helps decrease rebound microbial growth after surgical hand antisepsis.[3] Cumulative effect is a progressive decrease in the number of microorganisms over time, usually measured in days, after repeated applications of product. According to the CDC, alcohol-based preparations containing 0.5% to 1% chlorhexidine gluconate have persistent and cumulative activity that, in certain studies, has equaled or exceeded that of chlorhexidine gluconate-containing detergents.[3,36-39]

2. Product selection for surgical hand antisepsis should follow AORN's recommended practices for product selection.[40] Infection control professionals, managers, and end users should be involved in the trial and selection of surgical hand antiseptic agents. Options should be included for individuals with product sensitivities. If an alcohol-based product is selected, the product should meet FDA requirements as outlined in the Tentative Final Monograph (TFM) for Health-Care Antiseptic Drug Products or be the

subject of a new drug approval (NDA) process or an abbreviated new drug approval process (ANDA).[35] The FDA requires that products for surgical hand scrubs provide a one-log reduction on day one, a two-log reduction on day two, a three-log reduction on day five, and show persistent activity for at least six hours on each of the three test days.[35]

3. Infection control professionals and committees should review the data provided by manufacturers to ensure that the surgical hand antisepsis agents chosen comply with current FDA testing and labeling criteria. Testing should be performed by an independent, FDA-approved testing laboratory employing standard methods as published by ASTM International.

4. Whenever possible, containers of surgical hand antisepsis agents should be placed in areas that facilitate ease of access and use by health care staff members while complying with local, state, and federal guidelines and/or regulations. New products continue to enter the market, and practitioners should consult manufacturers' scientific data when selecting products for use.

5. Surgical hand antisepsis agents should be stored in clean, closed containers. Single-use containers are recommended and should be discarded when empty. Reusable containers, if used, should be washed and dried thoroughly before refilling. Do not top off reusable containers. Refilling before cleaning or topping off dispensers with surgical hand antiseptic agents may cause contamination and could contribute to the spread of potentially harmful microorganisms.[11] Dispensers should function for long periods without becoming occluded or obstructed.[41]

6. Alcohol-based products are flammable and should be stored away from high temperatures, sparking devices, or flames. Reports about alcohol-based hand rubs in Europe, where alcohol-based rubs have been in clinical use for years, indicate few fires.[42] There has been a recent report of one fire associated with an alcohol-based hand rub in the United States.[43] Containers should be designed to minimize spilling, leaking, and evaporation because alcohols are

extremely volatile. The National Fire Protection Agency does not specifically address alcohol-based sanitizers, and the judgment falls to the local authority having jurisdiction. Consideration must be given to location of use, mounting location (eg, near light switches, egress hallways, emergency exits), volume and size of individual dispensing units, bulk storage conditions and location, frequency of use, and the specific medical benefits of the chosen product. Further studies are underway to determine true flammability and improved safety in containers.[33,44-46] The American Society of Healthcare Engineers states that it is permissible to install 1.2-L containers of alcohol-based hand rub in egress corridors.[47] Additional information may be found at http://www.cdc.gov/handhygiene/firesafety/default.htm. Check for individual state regulations.

Recommendation III

Surgical hand antisepsis/hand scrub should be performed before donning sterile gloves for surgical or other invasive procedures. Use of either an FDA-compliant, antimicrobial surgical scrub agent intended for surgical hand antisepsis or an FDA-compliant, alcohol-based antiseptic hand rub with documented persistent and cumulative activity that has been approved for surgical hand antisepsis is acceptable.[3]

1. Rings, watches, and bracelets should be removed before beginning the surgical hand antisepsis/scrub procedure (see recommended practice I, number 5).

2. Hands should be washed with plain or antimicrobial soap and running water immediately before beginning the surgical hand antisepsis/scrub (see recommended practice I, number 7).

3. Each surgical hand antisepsis/scrub procedure should follow a standardized protocol established and approved by the health care facility and the manufacturer's written directions for use, regardless of method. A standardized protocol should be adopted for each method used in the facility. **Table 1** provides a summary of directives for general hand hygiene and surgical hand antisepsis.

Recommendation IV

Surgical hand antisepsis/hand scrub using an FDA-compliant, traditional antimicrobial scrub agent should include a standardized hand scrub procedure that follows the manufacturer's written directions for use and is approved by the health care facility.

1. A traditional, standardized, surgical hand antisepsis scrub procedure should include, but may not be limited to, the following.
   ♦ Wash hands and forearms with soap and running water immediately before beginning the surgical scrub.
   ♦ Clean the subungual areas of both hands under running water using a disposable nail cleaner.
   ♦ Rinse hands and forearms under running water.
   ♦ Dispense the approved antimicrobial scrub agent according to the manufacturer's written directions.
   ♦ Apply the antimicrobial agent to wet hands and forearms. Some manufacturers may recommend using a soft, nonabrasive sponge.
   ♦ Visualize each finger, hand, and arm as having four sides. Wash all four sides effectively. Repeat this process for opposite fingers, hand, and arm.
   ♦ Repeat this process if directed to do so by the manufacturer's written directions for use.
   ♦ Avoid splashing surgical attire.
   ♦ For water conservation, turn water off when it is not directly in use, if possible.
   ♦ Hold hands higher than elbows and away from surgical attire.
   ♦ Discard sponges, if used, in appropriate containers.
   ♦ In the OR, dry hands and arms with a sterile towel before donning a sterile surgical gown and gloves.

   Although the skin never can be rendered sterile, it can be made surgically clean by reducing the number of microorganisms.[17] A short, prescrub wash can loosen surface debris and transient microorganisms.[8] Subungual areas that are cleaned improperly can harbor microorganisms.[3,8,12] The mechanical action associated with hand scrubbing removes

Table 1

GENERAL HAND HYGIENE AND SURGICAL HAND ANTISEPSIS DIRECTIVES

TOPIC	ACTION
General hand hygiene	
Visible soil	Wash hands with plain or antimicrobial soap and water.
No visible soil	Sanitize hands with an alcohol-based hand rub or wash with plain or antimicrobial soap and water.
Surgical hand antisepsis	
Visible soil/no visible soil	Wash hands with soap and water, then use either a US Food and Drug Administration (FDA) compliant, antimicrobial scrub agent or an FDA-compliant, alcohol-based antiseptic hand rub agent that is cleared for surgical hand antisepsis and provides persistent and cumulative activity.

microorganisms. This can be accomplished by rubbing the skin with or without a sponge to produce friction. With the addition of a facility-approved soap, which acts as a surfactant, transient and some resident microorganisms can be lifted and flushed away under running water.[17] Surgical hand antisepsis/hand scrubs are effective only if all surfaces are exposed to the mechanical cleaning and chemical antisepsis processes.[8,17] Hands and forearms should be held higher than the elbows and away from surgical attire to prevent contamination and allow water to run from the clean to the less clean area down the arm.[8,17] Appropriate disposal of sponges, if used, prevents cross contamination of the surgical scrub sink area. A sterile gown cannot be put on over wet or damp surgical attire without resultant potential contamination of the gown by strike-through moisture.[17]

2. A traditional, standardized, anatomical, timed method or a counted stroke method may be used for surgical hand antisepsis/hand scrubs. The degree of microbial reduction necessary

for effective prophylaxis of surgical wound infections has not been characterized fully. The advantages of a shorter scrub time include less skin trauma, greater water conservation, and actual OR time savings. European and Australian studies have evaluated scrub times between two and six minutes, concluding that with specific products, scrub times of three to four minutes are as effective as five-minute scrubs.[3,20] Facilities are encouraged to follow scrub agent manufacturers' written directions for use when establishing policies and procedures for scrub times.[3,20,48-52]

3. The use of a brush for surgical hand antisepsis/hand scrubs is not necessary for adequate reduction of bacterial counts.[3] Skin damage from scrubbing with brushes can lead to an increased number of gram-negative bacteria and *Candida*.[18,53] Scrubbing with a brush is associated with an increase in skin cell shedding.[53-55]

4. General hand hygiene should be performed immediately after surgical gloves are removed and before any further activities are undertaken.

Recommendation V

Surgical hand antisepsis/hand rub with an FDA-compliant, alcohol-based surgical hand rub product should follow a standardized application according to the manufacturer's written directions for use.[3]

1. Alcohol-based solutions reduce bacterial counts on hands more rapidly than do antimicrobial soaps or detergents in the majority of experimental in vivo and in vitro models.[3] Alcohol hand-hygiene products alone kill more organisms than any product on the market but offer no appreciable persistence or cumulative effect. Use of a combination of active ingredients (eg, alcohol and chlorhexidine gluconate) to achieve both rapid reduction of microbial counts and the persistence and cumulative effect needed to prevent microbial regrowth is desirable. Randomized trials demonstrate better compliance with a surgical hand antisepsis protocol using an alcohol-based hand rub agent than with the traditional surgical scrub protocol.[56-59]

2. A standardized protocol for alcohol-based surgical hand rubs should follow manufacturers' written instructions and include, but may not be limited to, the following.
   - Wash hands and forearms with soap and running water immediately before beginning the surgical hand antisepsis procedure.
   - Clean the subungual areas of both hands under running water using a nail cleaner.
   - Rinse hands and forearms under running water.
   - Dry hands and forearms thoroughly with a paper towel.
   - Dispense the manufacturer-recommended amount of the surgical hand rub product.
   - Apply the product to the hands and forearms, following the manufacturer's written directions. Some manufacturers may require the use of water as part of the process.
   - Rub thoroughly until dry.
   - Repeat the product application process if indicated in the manufacturer's written directions.
   - In the OR, don a sterile surgical gown and gloves.

3. General hand hygiene should be performed immediately after surgical gloves are removed and before any further activities are undertaken.

Recommendation VI

Policies and procedures for surgical hand antisepsis should be developed, reviewed periodically, and readily available in the practice setting.

1. Policies and procedures for surgical hand antisepsis should include, but may not be limited to,
   - identifying facility-approved, FDA-compliant, surgical hand antisepsis agents;
   - defining the duration of surgical hand antisepsis procedures; and
   - establishing standardized protocols for each hand antisepsis method used.

   To provide optimal effect, antimicrobial-containing products should be chosen from the FDA's product category defined as surgical hand antisepsis agents.[35] Contact times should follow manufacturers' written directions for optimum efficacy. Policies for general hand hygiene and surgical hand antisepsis should be established in conjunction with infection control practitioners and meet the particular needs of the practice setting. AORN's "Recommended practices for surgical attire" should be consulted when developing guidelines.[60]

2. Education regarding surgical hand antisepsis products and protocols should be ongoing and systematic for all personnel in the perioperative setting.

3. Recommended practices should be used as guidelines for developing policies and procedures in the practice setting. Policies and procedures establish authority, responsibility, and accountability and serve as operational guidelines. Introduction and review of policies and procedures should be included in orientation and ongoing education of personnel to assist in the development of knowledge, skills, and attitudes that affect patient outcomes. Policies and procedures also assist in developing quality assessment and improvement activities.

Glossary

Alcohol-based hand rub: "An alcohol-containing preparation designed for application to the hands for reducing the number of viable microorganisms on the hands. In the United States, such preparations usually contain 60% to 95% alcohol."[3(p3)]

Alcohol-based preparations: Products used for general hand hygiene and/or surgical hand antisepsis. Appropriate products (ie, alcohol-based products) may be used as an alternative to the traditional surgical hand scrub using detergent-based antiseptic agents. These alcohol-based products do not remove soil; therefore, application of these products for surgical hand antisepsis must be preceded by a soap and water wash.

Anatomical timed scrub or counted stroke scrub method: An anatomical scrub method that uses a prescribed number of strokes or specified amount of time for scrubbing each surface of the fingers, hands, and arms.

Antimicrobial soap: Soap containing an FDA-compliant antiseptic agent.

Antiseptic agent: Antimicrobial substance applied to the skin to reduce the log number of microbial flora. Examples include alcohols, chlorhexidine, chlorine, hexachlorophene, iodine, parachloroxylenol, quaternary ammonium compounds, and triclosan.

Artificial nails: Substances or devices applied or added to the natural nails to augment or enhance the wearer's own nails. They include, but are not limited to, bondings, tips, wrappings, and tapes.

Cumulative effect: A progressive decrease over time, usually measured in days, in the number of microorganisms present after repeated applications of a product.

Hand antisepsis: Refers to either hand wash or hand rub using an antiseptic agent.

Hand hygiene: A generic term that applies to hand washing with either a plain or antimicrobial soap or use of an alcohol-based, antiseptic hand rub product.

In vitro: Outside the living body and in an artificial environment.

In vivo: In the living body of a plant or animal.

Persistence: Prolonged or extended antimicrobial activity, usually measured in hours, that prevents or inhibits the regrowth of microorganisms after application of the product.

Resident microorganisms: Microorganisms considered to be permanent residents of the skin and not readily removed by hand washing.

Stratum corneum: The outermost layer of the epidermis. The cells of the stratum corneum are rough and jagged and contain myriad niches in which bacteria dwell.

Subungual: Under the nail (eg, fingernail).

Surgical hand antisepsis: "Antiseptic hand wash or antiseptic hand rub performed preoperatively by surgical personnel to eliminate transient bacteria and reduce resident hand flora. Antiseptic detergent preparations often have persistent antimicrobial activity."[3(p4)] Previously known as surgical hand scrub.

Surgical hand antiseptic agent: An FDA-compliant product that is a broad-spectrum, fast-acting, and nonirritating preparation containing an antimicrobial ingredient designed to significantly reduce the number of microorganisms on intact skin. Surgical hand antiseptic agents demonstrate both persistent and cumulative activity.

Transient microorganisms: Microorganisms isolated from the skin. Such microorganisms are of concern because they can be transmitted readily on hands unless removed by mechanical friction and soap and water hand washing or use of a hand rub agent.

US Food and Drug Administration compliant: Refers to an agent that meets the testing and labeling criteria outlined by the FDA in the TFM for Health-Care Antiseptic Drug Products, a NDA, or an ANDA. The process required depends on the components, concentration, and mixture of ingredients used in the individual product. Both persistence and cumulative effect are critical to providing optimum product effectiveness and patient safety. When following the FDA over-the-counter TFM process, there is no specific clearance or letter of approval from the FDA; however, the FDA requires all studies and product labeling to meet the TFM criteria and remain on file for their review.[35]

Vector: An organism that transmits a pathogen.

Waterless antiseptic agent: "An antiseptic agent that does not require use of exogenous water. After applying such an agent, the hands are rubbed together until the agent has dried."[3(p4)]

REFERENCES

1. L Mody et al, "Introduction of a waterless alcohol-based hand rub in a long-term care facility," *Infection Control and Hospital Epidemiology* 24 (March 2003) 165-171.

2. D Pittet, "Improving adherence to hand hygiene practice: A multidisciplinary approach," *Emerging Infectious Diseases* 7 (March/April 2001) 234-240.

3. Centers for Disease Control and Prevention, "Guidelines for hand hygiene in health-care settings, Recommendations and reports," *Morbidity and Mortality Weekly Report* 51 (RR-16) (Oct 25, 2002).

4. S C Beyea, ed, *Perioperative Nursing Data Set,* second ed (Denver: AORN Inc, 2002).

5. S Hugonnet, D Pittet, "Hand hygiene—beliefs or science?" *Clinical Microbiology and Infection* 6 (July 2000) 350-356.

6. P B Graves, C L Twomey, "The changing face of hand protection," *AORN Journal* 76 (August 2002) 248-258.

7. "Recommended practices for standard and transmission-based precautions in the perioperative practice setting," in *Standards, Recommended Practices, and Guidelines* (Denver: AORN, Inc, 2003) 345-349.

8. N F Phillips, *Berry & Kohn's Operating Room Technique,* tenth ed (St Louis: Mosby, 2004).

9. C A Baumgardner et al, "Effects of nail polish on microbial growth of fingernails," *AORN Journal* 58 (July 1993) 84-88.

10. D Fogg, "OR attire; endoscopic equipment; artificial nails and chewing gum in the OR; monitoring patients," (Clinical Issues) *AORN Journal* 54 (August 1991) 335-339.

11. E L Larson, "APIC guideline for handwashing and hand antisepsis in health care settings," *American Journal of Infection Control* 23 (August 1995) 251-263.

12. C A Wynd, D E Samstag, A M Lapp, "Bacterial carriage on the fingernails of OR nurses," *AORN Journal* 60 (November 1994) 796-805.

13. R L Moolenaar et al, "A prolonged outbreak of *Pseudomonas aeruginosa* in a neonatal intensive care unit: Did staff fingernails play a role in disease transmission?" *Infection Control and Hospital Epidemiology* 21 (February 2000) 80-85.

14. E Edel et al, "Impact of a 5-minute scrub on the microbial flora found on artificial, polished, or natural fingernails of operating room personnel," *Nursing Research* 47 (January/February 1998) 54-59.

15. S A McNeil et al, "Effects of hand cleansing with antimicrobial soap or alcohol-based gel on microbial colonization of artificial fingernails worn by health care workers," *Clinical Infectious Diseases* 32 (February 2001) 367-372.

16. S A Hedderwick et al, "Pathogenic organism associated with artificial fingernails worn by healthcare workers," *Infection Control and Hospital Epidemiology* 21 (August 2000) 505-509.

17. D M Fogg, "Infection prevention and control," in *Alexander's Care of the Patient in Surgery,* 12th ed, J C Rothrock, ed (St Louis: Mosby, 2003) 97-158.

18. J Pottinger, S Burns, C Manske, "Bacterial carriage by artificial versus natural nails," *American Journal of Infection Control* 17 (December 1989) 340-344.

19. A Mangram et al, "Guideline for prevention of surgical site infection, 1999," *Infection Control and Hospital Epidemiology* 20 (April 1999) 250-278.

20. S M Wheelock, S Lookinland, "Effect of surgical hand scrub time on subsequent bacterial growth," *AORN Journal* 65 (June 1997) 1087-1098.

21. M F Fay, "Hand dermatitis: The role of gloves," *AORN Journal* 54 (September 1991) 451-467.

22. D M Salisbury et al, "The effect of rings on microbial load of health care workers' hands," *American Journal of Infection Control* 25 (February 1997) 24-27.

23. W E Trick et al, "Impact of ring wearing on hand contamination and comparison of hand hygiene agents in a hospital," *Clinical Infectious Diseases* 36 (June 2003) 1383-1390.

24. A T Lane, S S Drost, "Effects of repeated application of emollient cream to premature neonates' skin," *Pediatrics* 92 (September 1993) 415-419.

25. G S Hall, C A Mackintosh, P N Hoffman, "The dispersal of bacteria and skin scales from the body after showering and after application of a skin lotion," *Journal of Hygiene* 97 (October 1986) 289-298.

26. E L Larson et al, "Changes in bacterial flora associated with skin damage on hands of health care personnel," *American Journal of Infection Control* 26 (October 1998) 513-521.

27. R D Jones et al, "Moisturizing alcohol hand gels for surgical hand preparation," *AORN Journal* 71 (March 2000) 584-599.

28. C Marino, M Cohen, "Washington state hospital survey 2000: Gloves, handwashing agents, and moisturizers," *American Journal of Infection Control* 29 (December 2001) 422-424.

29. E Pinney, "Hand washing," *British Journal of Perioperative Nursing* 10 (June 2000) 328-331.

30. D Pittet et al, "Effectiveness of a hospital-wide programme to improve compliance with hand hygiene," *The Lancet* 356 (Oct 14, 2000) 1307-1312.

31. S Hugonnet, T V Perneger, D Pittet, "Alcohol-based handrub improves compliance with hand hygiene in intensive care units," *Archives of Internal Medicine* 162 (May 13, 2002) 1037-1043.

32. S Harbarth et al, "Interventional study to evaluate the impact of an alcohol-based hand gel in improving hand hygiene compliance," *Pediatric Infectious Disease Journal* 21 (June 2002) 489-495.

33. F Myers, S Parini, "Hand hygiene: Understanding and implementing the CDC's new guideline," *Nursing Management* 34 (April 2003) 1-14.

34. D Pittet, "Promotion of hand hygiene: Magic, hype, or scientific challenge," *Infection Control and Hospital Epidemiology* 23 (March 2002) 118-119.

35. "Topical antimicrobial drug products for over-the-counter human use; tentative final monograph for health-care antiseptic drug products," in *Code of Federal Regulations* (CFR) 21: Food and Drugs, Parts 333 and 369 (Washington, DC: US Government Printing Office, 1994) 31402-31452.

36. M L Rotter, "Hand washing and hand disinfection," in *Hospital Epidemiology and Infection Control,* second ed, C G Mayhall, ed (Philadelphia: Lippincott Williams & Wilkins, 1999).

37. A Rosenberg, S D Alatary, A F Peterson, "Safety and efficacy of the antiseptic chlorhexidine gluconate," *Surgery, Gynecology & Obstetrics* 143 (November 1976) 789-792.

38. E J Lowbury, H A Lilly, G A Ayliffe, "Preoperative disinfection of surgeons' hands: Use of alcoholic solutions and effects of gloves on skin flora," *British Medical Journal* 4 (Nov 16, 1974) 369-372.

39. G Mulberrry et al, "Evaluation of a waterless, scrubless chlorhexidine gluconate/ethanol surgical scrub for antimicrobial efficacy," *American Journal of Infection Control* 29 (December 2001) 377-382.

40. "Recommended practices for product selection in perioperative practice settings," in *Standards, Recommended Practices, and Guidelines* (Denver: AORN, Inc, 2004) 347-350.

41. C Kohan et al, "The importance of evaluating product dispensers when selecting alcohol-based handrubs," *American Journal of Infection Control* 30 (October 2002) 373-375.

42. A F Widmer, "Replace hand washing with use of a waterless alcohol hand rub?" *Clinical Infectious Diseases* 31 (July 2000) 136-143.

43. K A Bryant, J Pearce, B Stover, "Flash fire associated with the use of alcohol-based antiseptic agent," (Letter) *American Journal of Infection Control* 30 (June 2002) 256-257.

44. G Pugliese, J Bartley, T Lundstrom, "Alcohol-based handwashing agents: A clash with regulators or opportunity for a common-sense approach?" *Infection Control Today* 7 no 2 (2003) 1-4.

45. J M Boyce, M L Pearson, "Low frequency of fires from alcohol-based hand rub dispensers in healthcare facilities," *Infection Control and Hospital Epidemiology* 24 (August 2003) 618-619.

46. W M Wagner, "Double-edged sword: Managing the potential fire hazards posed by alcohol-based hand cleaning products," *Health Facilities Management* 16 (June 2003) 47-50.

47. "Alcohol based hand rubs," HospitalConnect.com, http://www.hospitalconnect.com/ashe/currentevent/abhi.html (accessed 29 Dec 2003).

48. L J Pereira, G M Lee, K J Wade, "An evaluation of five protocols for surgical handwashing in relation to skin condition and microbial counts," *Journal of Hospital Infection* 36 (May 1997) 49-65.

49. M O'Shaughnessy et al, "Optimum duration of surgical scrub-time," *British Journal of Surgery* 78 (June 1991) 685-686.

50. B Rehork, H Ruden, "Investigations into the efficacy of different procedures for surgical hand disinfection between consecutive operations," *Journal of Hospital Infection* 19 (October 1991) 115-127.

51. J R Babb, J G Davies, G A J Ayliffe, "A test procedure for evaluating surgical hand disinfection," *Journal of Hospital Infection* 18 no B suppl (June 1991) 41-49.

52. V Hingst et al, "Evaluation of the efficacy of surgical hand disinfection following a reduced application time of 3 instead of 5 min," *Journal of Hospital Infection* 20 (February 1992) 79-86.

53. K Kikuchi-Numagami et al, "Irritancy of scrubbing up for surgery with or without a brush," *Acta Dermato-Venereologica* 79 (May 1999) 230-232.

54. E L Larson et al, "Alcohol for surgical scrubbing?" *Infection Control and Hospital Epidemiology* 11 (March 1990) 139-143.

55. P D Meers, G A Yeo, "Shedding of bacteria and skin squames after handwashing," *Journal of Hygiene* 81 (August 1978) 99-105.

56. J J Parienti et al, "Hand-rubbing with an aqueous alcoholic solution vs traditional surgical hand-scrubbing and 30-day surgical site infection rates," *JAMA* 288 (Aug 14, 2002) 722-727.

57. E L Larson et al, "Comparison of different regimens for surgical hand preparation," *AORN Journal* 73 (February 2001) 412-432.

58. D Pittet, "Compliance with hand disinfection and its impact on hospital-acquired infections," *Journal of Hospital Infection* 48 no A suppl (August 2001) S40-S46.

59. B J Gruendemann, N B Bjerke, "Is it time for brushless scrubbing with an alcohol-based agent?" *AORN Journal* 74 (December 2001) 859-871.

60. "Recommended practices for surgical attire," in *Standards, Recommended Practices, and Guidelines* (Denver: AORN, Inc, 2003) 215-219.

Originally published May 1976, *AORN Journal,* as "Recommended practices for surgical hand scrubs."

Revised March 1978, July 1982, May 1984, October 1990.

Published as proposed recommended practices August 1994.

Revised November 1998; published April 1999, *AORN Journal.* Reformatted July 2000.

Revised November 2003; published in *Standards, Recommended Practices, and Guidelines,* 2004 edition. Reprinted February 2004, *AORN Journal.*

Recommended Practices for Maintaining a Sterile Field

The following recommended practices were developed by the AORN Recommended Practices Committee and have been approved by the AORN Board of Directors. They were presented as proposed recommended practices for comments by members and others. They are effective January 1, 2006.

These recommended practices are intended as achievable recommendations representing what is believed to be an optimal level of practice. Policies and procedures will reflect variations in practice settings and/or clinical situations that determine the degree to which the recommended practices can be implemented.

AORN recognizes the numerous settings in which perioperative nurses practice. These recommended practices are intended as guidelines adaptable to various practice settings. These practice settings include traditional operating rooms, ambulatory surgery centers, physicians' offices, cardiac catheterization suites, endoscopy suites, radiology departments, and all other areas where operative and other invasive procedures may be performed.

Purpose

These recommended practices provide guidance for establishing and maintaining a sterile field. The creation and maintenance of a sterile field can directly influence patient outcomes. Adherence to aseptic practices by all individuals involved in surgical interventions aids in fulfilling the professional responsibility to protect patients from injury. Aseptic practices are implemented preoperatively, intraoperatively, and postoperatively to minimize wound contamination and reduce patient risks for surgical site infections.

Recommendation I

Scrubbed persons should function within a sterile field.

1. Before donning sterile gowns and gloves, surgical hand antisepsis should be performed according to AORN's "Recommended practices for surgical hand antisepsis/hand scrubs"[1] and the manufacturer's written instructions for the antiseptic. Surgical hand antisepsis decreases the microbial counts on the skin and will reduce the transfer of microorganisms.

2. Personnel within the sterile field should be attired according to both AORN's "Recommended practices for surgical attire"[2] and "Recommended practices for standard and transmission-based precautions."[3] Personnel should wear scrub attire, caps, masks, eye protection, and sterile gowns and gloves to prevent microbial transference to the sterile field, surgical site, and patient during the surgical procedure and to reduce risk of occupational exposure to bloodborne pathogens and other potentially infectious materials.[4-7]

3. Scrubbed personnel should don sterile gowns and gloves from a sterile area away from the main instrument table to prevent contamination of the sterile field.[8-12]

4. Materials for gowns should be selected according to AORN's "Recommended practices for selection and use of surgical gowns and drapes"[13] and according to the required level of barrier protection as outlined in the Association for the Advancement of Medical Instrumentation (AAMI) guideline "Liquid barrier performance and classification of protective apparel and drapes intended for use in health care facilities."[14] Surgical gowns should be of sufficient size to adequately cover the scrubbed person. Surgical gowns should establish a barrier that minimizes the passage of microorganisms between nonsterile and sterile areas.[12,15]

5. The front of a sterile gown is considered sterile from the chest to the level of the sterile field. The sterile area of the gown front extends to the level of the sterile field because most scrubbed personnel work adjacent to a sterile bed and/or table. Gown sleeves are considered sterile from two inches above the elbow to the cuff, circumferentially.

   The neckline, shoulders, underarms, sleeve cuffs, and gown back are areas of friction and, therefore, are not considered effective microbial barriers. The gown back is considered nonsterile because it cannot be constantly monitored.

   Gowns of an adequate size to close completely in the back and a sleeve length adequate to prevent cuff exposure outside the glove should be selected.

6. Sleeve cuffs should be considered contaminated when the scrubbed person's hands pass beyond the cuff.[9,10,12]

   ♦ Cuffs of the gown should remain at or below the natural wrist area.
   ♦ Gown sleeves should not be pulled up, leaving cuffs exposed.
   ♦ Sleeves of the gown should be of sufficient length and should cover the back of the hand to avoid exposing the gown cuff when the gloves slide down.

7. Scrubbed personnel should inspect gloves for integrity after donning them. Intact gloves establish a barrier that minimizes the passage of microorganisms between nonsterile and sterile areas.[4,12,16] AORN's "Recommended practices for standard and transmission-based precautions"[3] should be followed. Policies and procedures in the practice setting should indicate when double-gloving is required to reduce the potential for hand contact with blood and body fluids.

8. Sterile gloves that become contaminated should be changed as soon as possible. The preferred method of changing gloves is assisted gloving, whereby one member of the sterile team assists another member. This technique allows a gowned and gloved team member to touch only the outside of the new glove when applying the glove to a team member's hand. If this method is not possible, the contaminated glove should be changed by the open-glove method. If it is not possible to change the glove at the moment the break in technique is noted, a new glove may be donned over the contaminated/damaged glove until it can be changed.[9,11,12]

Recommendation II

Sterile drapes should be used to establish a sterile field.

1. Surgical drapes should be selected according to AORN's "Recommended practices for selection and use of surgical gowns and drapes"[13] and the AAMI guideline "Liquid barrier performance and classification of protective apparel and drapes intended for use in health care facilities."[14] Surgical drapes should establish an aseptic barrier that minimizes the passage of microorganisms between nonsterile and sterile areas.[15,17,18]

2. To prevent transfer of microorganisms from nonsterile to sterile areas, sterile drapes should be placed on the patient, furniture, and equipment to be included in the sterile field.[19]

3. Sterile drapes should be handled as little as possible. Rapid movement of draping materials creates air currents on which dust, lint, and other particles can migrate.[20,21]

4. Draping material should be held in a compact manner, held higher than the OR bed, and placed from the surgical site to the periphery to minimize contamination of the surgical site. Some procedures may require modified draping techniques (eg, extremities).[9,10,12]

5. During draping, gloved hands should be protected by cuffing the drape material over the gloved hands to reduce the potential for contamination.[9,10,12]

6. The portion of the surgical drape that establishes the sterile field should not be moved after it is positioned. Shifting or moving the sterile drape can compromise the sterility of the field.[9,10,12]

Recommendation III

Items used within the sterile field should be sterile.

1. To ensure that only sterile items are presented to the sterile field, all items should be inspected immediately before presentation to the field for proper packaging, processing, seal, package container integrity, and inclusion of a sterilization indicator. The indicator should be inspected immediately to verify the appropriate color change for the sterilization process selected. If an expiration date is provided, the date should be checked before the package is opened and the contents are delivered to the field. Outdated items should not be used.[12,22]

   An event-related sterility system should be used. Event-related sterility is based on the concept that "sterility is not altered over time, but may be compromised by certain events or environmental conditions."[23] Shelf life refers to the time an item may remain on the shelf and still maintain its sterility. Shelf life is influenced by the type of packaging used, storage conditions (eg, open or closed shelves), humidity, temperature, transport conditions, use of dust covers, and the amount of handling the item receives.[12,22,23]

Spaulding's criteria are used to determine the potential for transmission of infectious agents.[24] Within this classification, items contacting the vascular system, the neurological system, and/or sterile tissues pose the greatest risk of infection and are classified as critical items. Using sterile items when contacting sterile tissues minimizes the risk of infection.[12,25-28]

2. Packaging materials should meet the criteria identified in AORN's "Recommended practices for selection and use of packaging systems."[29]

3. Methods of sterilization, event-related shelf life, and handling of sterile items should be in accordance with AORN's "Recommended practices for sterilization in the perioperative practice setting."[30] Sterilization provides the highest level of assurance that surgical items are free of viable microbes. High-level disinfection reduces the risk of microbial contamination, but it does not ensure the same margin of safety that sterilization provides.[25,26,28,31,32]

Recommendation IV

All items introduced to a sterile field should be opened, dispensed, and transferred by methods that maintain item sterility and integrity.

1. All invasive surgical procedures should be performed using sterile instruments and supplies, and the surgical team should practice aseptic technique for all surgical patients.

The mucous membranes of the mouth, urinary tract, and intestinal tract are effective bacterial barriers when intact. However, ear, nose, and throat procedures, hemorrhoidectomy, and other procedures are invasive and impair the integrity of the mucosal barrier. The normal flora found in these areas is not infectious to the individual in question, but it may be pathogenic when transferred to other tissues by contaminated surgical instruments.

Health care-acquired surgical infections are a leading cause of patient morbidity and mortality in the United States. Rigorous adherence to the principles of asepsis is the foundation of surgical site infection prevention and should never be circumvented to save time or money. A sterile field should be prepared and maintained for every surgical patient.[4,25,26]

2. Unscrubbed individuals should open wrapped sterile supplies by opening the wrapper flap farthest away from them first, to prevent contamination from passing an unsterile arm over a sterile item. Next, they should open each of the side flaps. The nearest wrapper flap should be opened last.[9-11]

3. All wrapper edges should be secured when supplies are presented to the sterile field. Securing the loose wrapper edges prevents them from contaminating the sterile field or a sterile item.[9,10]

4. Sterile items should be presented to the scrubbed person or placed securely on the sterile field. Items tossed onto a sterile field may roll off the edge, create a hole in the sterile drape, or cause other items to be displaced, leading to contamination of the sterile field.[9,10]

   ◆ Sharps and heavy objects should be presented to the scrubbed person or opened on a separate surface. These heavy items may penetrate the sterile barrier if dropped onto the sterile field.[9,10]

   ◆ Peel pouches should be presented to the scrubbed person to prevent contamination of the contents. The edges of the package may curl and the contents may slide over the unsterile edge, contaminating the contents of the package.

   ◆ Rigid container systems should be opened on a separate surface. The external indicator should be verified for appropriate color change. Locks should be inspected for security to verify there has not been a breach of the container seal prior to use. The lid should be lifted toward the person opening the container and away from the container. The filter should be checked and changed according to the manufacturer's written instructions.

5. All items should be delivered to the surgical field in a manner that prevents nonsterile objects or people from extending over the sterile field. Skin is a source of bacteria and scurf shedding; therefore, maintaining distance from

the sterile field can decrease the potential for contamination when items are passed from a nonsterile area to a sterile area.[9,10,19]

6. When solutions are dispensed, the labeled solution receptacle on the sterile field should be placed near the table's edge or held by the scrubbed person. The entire contents of the container should be poured slowly to avoid splashing. Splashing can cause strike-through and splash-back from nonsterile surfaces to the sterile field. Placing the solution receptacle near the edge of the sterile table allows the unscrubbed person to pour fluids without contaminating the sterile field. Any remaining fluids should be discarded. The edge of a container is considered contaminated after the contents have been poured; therefore, the sterility of the contents cannot be ensured if the cap is replaced. Reuse of open containers may contaminate solutions due to drops contacting unsterile areas and then running back over container openings.[9,10]

7. Medications should be delivered to the sterile field in an aseptic manner. Stoppers should not be removed from vials for the purpose of pouring medications. Sterile transfer devices (eg, sterile vial spike, filter straw, plastic catheter) should be used to dispense medications to the sterile field. Medications should be delivered to the sterile field according to AORN's "Recommended practices for safe care through identification of hazards in the surgical environment,"[33] AORN's "Guidance statement: Safe medication practices in perioperative practice settings,"[34] the "AORN latex guideline,"[35] and the policies and procedures of the practice setting.

Recommendation V

A sterile field should be maintained and monitored constantly.

1. The sterile field should be prepared in the location in which it will be used. Moving tables stirs air currents that can contaminate the sterile field.[36]

2. Sterile supplies should be opened for only one patient at a time. Opening several cases in a room at one time increases the risk of cross-infection.

3. One patient at a time should occupy the OR. Concurrent cases performed on two patients in the same room at the same time may expose patients to a variety of hazards and increase the risk of contamination and infection. The transmission of infectious diseases can occur by airborne, contact, and droplet methods. The risk of cross-contamination may be increased significantly when two sterile fields, two surgical teams, and two open surgical wounds are confined to one OR. Operating rooms in the United States are not designed to accommodate the additional personnel and equipment necessary to care for two patients simultaneously. In the United States, general ORs built to the standards of the American Institute of Architects (AIA) are 400 sq ft.[37] Some ORs may be as small as 360 sq ft. This square footage minimum is intended to accommodate the equipment and personnel necessary for one surgical field. To move around the sterile field without contaminating it, nonsterile personnel (eg, the circulating nurse) should maintain a distance of at least 12 inches from the sterile field. When two patients and two sterile fields occupy an area designed to accommodate one patient and one sterile field, contamination of the sterile field is likely.

4. Sterile fields should be prepared as close as possible to the time of use. The potential for contamination increases with time because dust and other particles present in the ambient environment settle on horizontal surfaces over time. Particulate matter can be stirred up by movement of personnel when opening the room and can settle on opened sterile supplies.[4,12,21,36,38,39] The OR environment can be breached by other vectors, such as insects, that potentially could come into contact with open sterile fields, unobserved, unless the sterile field is monitored.

There is no specified amount of designated time that a room can remain open and not used and still be considered sterile. The sterility of an open sterile field is event-related. An open sterile field requires continuous visual observation. Direct observation increases the likelihood of detecting a breach in sterility.[12,39-41]

5. Sterile fields should not be covered. Although there are no research studies to support or

discount the practice, removing a table cover may result in a part of the cover that was below the table level being drawn above the table level or air currents drawing microorganisms from a nonsterile area to the sterile field. It is important to continuously monitor all sterile areas for possible contamination.[12,21]

6. Conversations in the presence of a sterile field should be kept to a minimum to reduce the spread of droplets. Air contains microorganisms on airborne particles, such as respiratory droplets. The primary source of airborne bacteria is health care personnel.[7,12,21,31]

7. Surgical equipment (eg, cables, tubing) should be secured to the sterile field with nonperforating devices. Perforations in a barrier provide portals of entry and exit for microorganisms, blood, and other potentially infectious body fluids.

8. Nonsterile equipment (eg, Mayo stands, microscopes, C-arms) should be covered with sterile barrier material(s) before being introduced to or brought over a sterile field. Only sterile items should touch sterile surfaces. The equipment should be covered with a barrier material on the top, bottom, and all sides. Sterile barrier material also should be applied to the portion of the Mayo stand or other equipment that will be positioned immediately adjacent to the sterile field.[11]

Recommendation VI

All personnel moving within or around a sterile field should do so in a manner that maintains the sterile field.

1. Scrubbed personnel should remain close to the sterile field.[9,10] Walking outside the sterile field's periphery or leaving the OR in sterile attire increases the potential for contamination. Using a closed container system for flash sterilization and transport of items eliminates the need for the scrubbed person to leave the sterile field to retrieve instruments from a sterilizer. Scrubbed personnel should avoid leaving the sterile field when x-rays are taken. Protective devices for reducing radiological exposure should be provided to personnel who cannot leave the room or who cannot stand approximately 6 ft away from the source of radiation.[42]

2. Scrubbed personnel should move from sterile areas to sterile areas to prevent contamination. If they must change position, they should turn back to back or face to face while maintaining safe distances from each other and the sterile field.

3. Unscrubbed personnel should face sterile fields on approach, should not walk between two sterile fields, and should be aware of the need for distance from the sterile field. By establishing patterns of movement around the sterile field and keeping sterile areas in view, accidental contamination can be reduced.

4. Scrubbed personnel should keep their arms and hands above the level of their waists at all times. Hands should remain in front of the body above waist level so the hands remain visible. Contamination may occur when arms and hands are moved below waist level. Arms should not be folded with the hands in the axilla. This area has the potential to become contaminated by perspiration, allowing for strike-through of the gown and, ultimately, contamination of the gloved hands. The gown at the axilla also is an area of friction and, therefore, is not considered an effective microbial barrier.

5. Scrubbed personnel should avoid changing levels and should be seated only when the entire surgical procedure will be performed at that level. When changing levels, exposure of the nonsterile portion of the surgical gown is likely.

6. The number and movement of individuals involved in a surgical procedure should be kept to a minimum per AORN's "Recommended practices for traffic patterns in the perioperative practice setting."[36] Bacterial shedding increases with activity. Air currents can pick up contaminated particles shed from patients, personnel, and drapes and distribute them to sterile areas.[12,21,31,43]

7. When a break in sterile technique occurs, corrective action should be taken immediately unless the patient's safety is at risk. If the patient's safety is at risk, correct the break in technique as soon as it is safe to do so.

8. When a break in sterile technique occurs and cannot be corrected immediately, the organization should determine how it should be reported and recorded, and the wound classification

should be adjusted accordingly and documented on the operative record.

Recommendation VII

Policies and procedures for maintaining a sterile field should be developed, reviewed periodically, revised as necessary, and readily available in the practice setting.

1. Policies and procedures for maintaining a sterile field should be developed by each facility and should include, but not be limited to,
   - aseptic technique, including handling sterile supplies and monitoring a sterile field;
   - surgical hand antisepsis;
   - gowning and gloving with sterile gown and gloves;
   - masks, head coverings, and scrub attire;
   - draping;
   - event-related sterility;
   - traffic patterns; and
   - monitoring of environmental conditions, including OR air exchange rate and pressure, temperature, and humidity.

2. These recommended practices should be used as a guideline for developing policies and procedures in the perioperative practice setting. Policies and procedures serve as operational guidelines and establish authority, responsibility, and accountability within the facility.

3. Personnel and observers should be knowledgeable about the procedures involved in developing and maintaining a sterile field. An introduction and review of policies and procedures for maintaining the sterile field should be included in orientation to the perioperative setting for personnel and observers. Continuing education should be provided when new technologies (eg, sterilization containers, barrier materials) are introduced. Ongoing education of perioperative personnel facilitates the development of knowledge, skills, and attitudes that affect surgical patient outcomes. Policies and procedures also assist in the development of quality assessment and improvement activities.

4. The Perioperative Nursing Data Set (PNDS) should be used in the development of policies and procedures and documentation of nursing

interventions related to maintenance of the sterile field. The expected outcome of primary importance to this recommended practice is outcome O10, "The patient is free from signs and symptoms of infection." This outcome falls within the domain of Physiological Responses (D2). The associated nursing diagnosis is X28, "Risk for infection." The associated interventions that may lead to the desired outcome may be I21, "Assesses susceptibility for infection"; I70, "Implements aseptic technique"; and I98, "Protects from cross-contamination."[44]

Glossary

Asepsis: Process for keeping away disease-producing microorganisms.

Aseptic technique: Methods by which contamination with microorganisms is prevented.

Assisted gloving: Method by which a gowned and gloved person assists another gowned person to don sterile gloves.

Closed gloving method: Used when wearing a sterile gown to prevent exposure of bare skin during gowning and donning of sterile gloves, thereby lessening the chance of contamination.

Critical item: An item that contacts the vascular system or enters sterile tissue, posing the highest risk of transmission of infection.

Event-related sterility: Shelf life of a packaged sterile item depends on the quality of the wrapper material, the storage conditions, the conditions during transport, and the amount of handling.

Noncritical item: An item that comes in contact with intact skin but not with mucous membranes, sterile tissue, or the vascular system.

Open-gloving method: Used when changing a glove during a surgical procedure. A method of donning sterile gloves in which the everted cuff of each glove allows the gowned person to touch the inner side of the glove with ungloved fingers and the outer side of the glove with gloved fingers.

Scurf: A bran-like desquamation of the epidermis.

Semicritical item: An item that comes in contact with mucous membranes or with skin that is not intact.

Sterile: The absence of all living microorganisms.

Sterile field: Area around the site of the incision into tissue or the site of introduction of an instrument into a body orifice that has been prepared for the use of sterile supplies and equipment. This area includes all furniture covered with sterile drapes and all personnel who are in sterile attire.

Sterile technique: Methods by which contamination with microorganisms is prevented to maintain sterility throughout the surgical procedure.

Sterilization: Processes by which all pathogenic and nonpathogenic microorganisms, including spores, are killed.

Strike-through: Contamination of a sterile surface by moisture that has originated from a nonsterile surface and penetrated the protective covering of the sterile item.

Time-related sterility: Expiration dates are established to indicate the maximum duration of time within which a sterile item is considered sterile and safe to use.

REFERENCES

1. "Recommended practices for surgical hand antisepsis/hand scrubs," in *Standards, Recommended Practices, and Guidelines* (Denver: AORN, Inc, 2005) 377-385.

2. "Recommended practices for surgical attire," in *Standards, Recommended Practices, and Guidelines* (Denver: AORN, Inc, 2005) 299-305.

3. "Recommended practices for standard and transmission-based precautions in the perioperative practice setting," in *Standards, Recommended Practices, and Guidelines* (Denver: AORN, Inc, 2005) 447-451.

4. A J Mangram et al, "Guideline for prevention of surgical site infection," *American Journal of Infection Control* 27 (April 1999) 97-134.

5. W A Rutala, D J Weber, "A review of single-use and reusable gowns and drapes in health care," *Infection Control and Hospital Epidemiology* 22 (April 2001) 248-257.

6. H Laufman, N L Belkin, K K Meyer, "A critical review of a century's progress in surgical apparel: How far have we come?" *Journal of the American College of Surgeons* 191 (November 2000) 554-568.

7. Association for Professionals in Infection Control and Epidemiology, *APIC Text of Infection Control and Epidemiology* (Washington, DC: Association for Professionals in Infection Control and Epidemiology, 2002) 27-1 to 27-4.

8. J S Heal et al, "Bacterial contamination of surgical gloves by water droplets spilt after scrubbing," *Journal of Hospital Infection* 53 (February 2003) 136-139.

9. D M Fogg, "Infection prevention and control," in *Alexander's Care of the Patient in Surgery,* 12th ed, J C Rothrock, ed (St Louis: Mosby, 2003) 97-158.

10. N F Phillips, *Berry & Kohn's Operating Room Technique,* 10th ed (St Louis: Mosby, 2004) 247-323.

11. P A Mews, "Establishing and maintaining a sterile field," in *Patient Care During Operative and Invasive Procedures,* second ed, M Phippen, M Wells, eds (Philadelphia: W B Saunders Co, 2000) 61-93.

12. B Gruendemann, S Mangum, *Infection Prevention in Surgical Settings* (Philadelphia: W B Saunders Co, 2001) 47-49, 88-97, 119-219, 250-257, 266-281, 365-371.

13. "Recommended practices for selection and use of surgical gowns and drapes," in *Standards, Recommended Practices, and Guidelines* (Denver: AORN, Inc, 2005) 371-375.

14. Association for the Advancement of Medical Instrumentation, *Liquid Barrier Performance and Classification of Protective Apparel and Drapes Intended for Use in Health Care Facilities,* ANSI/ AAMI PB70 (Arlington, Va: Association for the Advancement of Medical Instrumentation, 2003).

15. Association for the Advancement of Medical Instrumentation, *Selection of Surgical Gowns and Drapes in Health Care Facilities,* AAMI TIR no 11:1994 (Arlington, Va: Association for the Advancement of Medical Instrumentation, 2000.)

16. J Tanner, H Parkinson, "Double gloving to reduce surgical cross-infection," (Cochrane Review) in *The Cochrane Library,* issue 2 (Chichester, UK: John J Wiley & Sons, 2004). Abstract available at *http://www.cochrane.org/cochrane /revabstr/AB003087.htm* (accessed 26 Aug 2005).

17. A Lipp, "An assessment of the clinical effectiveness of surgical drapes," *Nursing Times* 99 (Dec 9, 2003) 28-31.

18. N Belkin, "Selecting surgical gowns and drapes for today's surgery," *SSM* 9 (December 2003) 41-44.

19. J Pournoor, "New scientific tools to expand the understanding of aseptic practices," *Surgical Services Management* 6 (April 2000) 28-32.

20. F Memarzadah, A P Manning "Comparison of operating room ventilation systems in the protection of the surgical site," session 4549, *ASHRAE Transactions,* proceedings of the 2002 annual meeting (Atlanta: American Society of Heating, Refrigerating, and Air-Conditioning Engineers, 2002). Abstract available at *http://resourcecenter.ashrae.org/store/ashrae* (accessed 26 Aug 2005).

21. C Edmiston et al, "Airborne particulates in the OR environment," *AORN Journal* 69 (June 1999) 1169-1183.

22. N Japp, "Packaging: Shelf life," in *Sterilization Technology for the Health Care Facility,* second ed, M Reichert, J Young, eds (Gaithersburg, Md: Aspen Publishers, 1997) 99-103.

23. L O'Connor, "Event-related sterility assurance: An opportunity for continuous quality improvement," *The Surgical Technologist* (January 1994) 8-12.

24. E H Spaulding, "Chemical disinfection of medical and surgical materials," in *Disinfection, Sterilization, and Preservation,* C A Lawrence, S S Block, eds (Philadelphia: Lea & Febiger, 1968) 517-531.

25. W Rutala, D Weber, "Modern advances in disinfection, sterilization, and medical waste management," in *Prevention and Control of Nosocomial Infections,* fourth ed, R P Wenzel, ed (Philadelphia: Lippincott Williams & Wilkins, 2003) 542-574.

26. M C Roy, "Modern approaches to preventing surgical site infections," in *Prevention and Control of Nosocomial Infections,* fourth ed, R P Wenzel, ed (Philadelphia: Lippincott Williams & Wilkins, 2003) 369-384.

27. "Medical devices; semicritical reprocessed single-use devices; termination of exemptions from premarket notification; requirement for submission of validation data," *Federal Register* 69 (April 13, 2004) 19433-19435.

28. W Rutala, "APIC guideline for selection and use of disinfectants," *American Journal of Infection Control* 24 (August 1996) 313-342.

29. "Recommended practices for selection and use of packaging systems," in *Standards, Recommended Practices, and Guidelines* (Denver: AORN, Inc, 2005) 415-420.

30. "Recommended practices for sterilization in perioperative practice settings," in *Standards, Recommended Practices, and Guidelines* (Denver: AORN, Inc, 2005) 459-469.

31. L Sehulster, R Y Chinn, "Guidelines for environmental infection control in health care facilities," *Morbidity and Mortality Weekly Report* 52 RR-10 (June 6, 2003) 1-42.

32. "Recommended practices for high-level disinfection," in *Standards, Recommended Practices, and Guidelines* (Denver: AORN, Inc, 2005) 313-319.

33. "Recommended practices for safe care through identification of potential hazards in the surgical environment," in *Standards, Recommended Practices, and Guidelines* (Denver: AORN, Inc, 2005) 387-393.

34. "Guidance statement: Safe medication practices in perioperative practice settings," in S*tandards, Recommended Practices, and Guidelines* (Denver: AORN, Inc, 2005) 196-198.

35. "AORN latex guideline" in *Standards, Recommended Practices, and Guidelines* (Denver: AORN, Inc, 2005) 117-132.

36. "Recommended practices for traffic patterns in the perioperative practice setting," in *Standards, Recommended Practices, and Guidelines* (Denver: AORN, Inc, 2005) 483-485.

37. American Institute of Architects Academy of Architecture for Health, *Guidelines for Design and Construction of Hospital and Health Care Facilities* (Washington, DC: American Institute of Architects, 2001).

38. A Tammelin et al, "Dispersal of methicillin-resistant *Staphylococcus epidermis* by staff in an operating room suite for thoracic and cardiovascular surgery: Relation to skin carriage and clothing," *Journal of Hospital Infection* 44 (February 2000) 119-126.

39. R Conner, "Washing and restringing instruments; bone debris; preparing setups; patient restraints; Group A *Streptococcus,*" (Clinical Issues) *AORN Journal* 73 (April 2001) 835-838.

40. C Petersen, "Time for unused sterile setups; maintaining instrument count sheets; gowning off back tables; plants in the OR; count discrepancies," (Clinical Issues) *AORN Journal* 80 (August 2004) 321-324.

41. "Surgical site infections," in *APIC Handbook of Infection Control and Epidemiology,* third ed, J Jennings, J Wideman, eds (Washington, DC: Association for Professionals in Infection Control and Epidemiology) 312-321.

42. "Recommended practices for reducing radiological exposure in the practice setting," in *Standards, Recommended Practices, and Guidelines* (Denver: AORN, Inc, 2005) 437-442.

43. F Pryor, P Messmer, "The effect of traffic patterns in the OR on surgical site infections," *AORN Journal* 68 (October 1998) 649-660.

44. S C Beyea, ed, *Perioperative Nursing Data Set: The Perioperative Nursing Vocabulary,* second ed (Denver: AORN, Inc, 2002).

RESOURCES

American Society for Healthcare Central Service Professionals. "Eliminating sterile outdates," (self-study series) *Healthcare Purchasing News* (March 2003) 42-44.

Barrett, R; Stevens, J; Taranter, J. "A shelf-life trial: Examining the efficacy of event related sterility principles and its implications for nursing practice," *Australian Journal of Advanced Nursing* 21 (2003–2004) 8-12.

Belkin, N. "Barrier drapes and their impact on surgical site infections," *Infection Control Today* (May 2002).

Belkin, N. "Barrier materials: Their influence on surgical wound infections," *AORN Journal* 55 (June 1992) 1521-1528.

Bell, M. "Hospital uses team approach to improve processes, reduce costs," *AORN Journal* 68 (July 1998) 68-72.

Donovan, A; Turner, D W; Smith, A. "Successful, documented studies favoring indefinite shelf life," *Journal of Healthcare Materiel Management* 9 (March 1991) 34-40.

Garibaldi, R A, et al. "Comparison of nonwoven and woven gown and drape fabric to prevent intraoperative wound contamination and postoperative infection," *The American Journal of Surgery* 152 (November 1986) 505-509.

Groah, L, ed. "Limiting contamination sources in the operating room," in *Perioperative Nursing,* third ed (Stamford, Conn: Appleton & Lange, 1996) 137-162.

Gruendemann, B; Fernsebner, B. "Asepsis," in *Comprehensive Perioperative Nursing, Volume 1: Principles* (Boston: Jones and Bartlett Publishers, 1995) 180-288.

Hinchliff, S. "Innate defenses," in *Physiology for Nursing Practice,* S Hinchliff, S Montague, eds (London: Baillière Tindall, 1988) 549-578.

Mayworm, D. "Probably sterile," *Infection Control and Sterilization Technology* (March 1995) 7.

Nicolette, L. "Sterilization and disinfection," in *Perioperative Nursing,* third ed, L Groah, ed (Stamford, Conn: Appleton & Lange, 1996) 163-195.

Parker, L. "Rituals versus risks in the contemporary operating theatre environment," *British Journal of Theatre Nursing* 9 (August 1999) 341-345.

Roark, J. "Guidelines for maintaining the sterile field," *Infection Control Today* 7 (August 2003) 14-16.

Saunders, S. "Practical measures to ensure health and safety in theatres," *Nursing Times* 100 (March 16, 2004) 32-35.

Taylor, M; Campbell, C. "The multidisciplinary team in the operating department," *British Journal of Theatre Nursing* 9 (April 1999) 178-183.

Xavier, G. "Asepsis," *Nursing Standard* 13 (May 26, 1999) 49-53.

Originally published March 1978, *AORN Journal,* as "Recommended practices for aseptic technique." Format revision July 1982. Revised March 1987, October 1991.

Revised June 1996; published November 1996, *AORN Journal.* Revised and reformatted; published February 2001, *AORN Journal.*

Revised November 2005; published in *Standards, Recommended Practices, and Guidelines,* 2006 edition. Reprinted February 2006, *AORN Journal.*

AORN Perioperative Standards and Recommended Practices, 2009 Edition

Recommended Practices for Traffic Patterns in the Perioperative Practice Setting

The following recommended practices were developed by the AORN Recommended Practices Committee and have been approved by the AORN Board of Directors. They were presented as proposed recommended practices for comments by members and others. They are effective January 1, 2006.

These recommended practices are intended as achievable recommendations representing what is believed to be an optimal level of practice. Policies and procedures will reflect variations in practice settings and/or clinical situations that determine the degree to which the recommended practices can be implemented.

AORN recognizes the numerous settings in which perioperative nurses practice. These recommended practices are intended as guidelines adaptable to various practice settings. These practice settings include traditional operating rooms, ambulatory surgery centers, physicians' offices, cardiac catheterization suites, endoscopy suites, radiology departments, emergency departments, labor and delivery units that have OR suites, and all other areas where operative and other invasive procedures may be performed.

Purpose

These recommended practices provide guidance for establishing traffic patterns in perioperative practice areas. Traffic control patterns suggest movement into and out of the surgical suite as well as movement within the suite. Clearly defined and enforced traffic control practices protect personnel, patients, supplies, and equipment from potential sources of cross-contamination; safeguard the privacy of patients; and provide security.

The building design of the surgical suite often predetermines traffic patterns. Implementation of all elements of these recommended practices may not be feasible within every facility because of the physical limitations of the setting.

Recommendation I

Traffic patterns should be designed to facilitate movement of patients and personnel into, through, and out of defined areas within the surgical suite. Signs should clearly indicate the appropriate environmental controls and surgical attire required.

1. The surgical suite should be divided into three designated areas that are defined by the physical activities performed in each area. Increasing environmental controls and surgical attire as progression is made from unrestricted to restricted areas decreases the potential for cross-contamination.

   The **unrestricted** area includes a central control point that is established to monitor the entrance of patients, personnel, and materials. Street clothes are permitted in this area, and traffic is not limited. The entrance to the surgical suite should be restricted to authorized personnel based on organizational policies.

   The **semirestricted** area includes the peripheral support areas of the surgical suite. It has storage areas for clean and sterile supplies, work areas for storage and processing of instruments, scrub sink areas, and corridors leading to the restricted areas of the surgical suite. Traffic in this area is limited to authorized personnel and patients. Personnel are required to wear surgical attire and cover all head and facial hair.[1]

   The **restricted** area includes ORs, procedure rooms, and the clean core area. Surgical attire and hair coverings are required. Masks are required where open sterile supplies or scrubbed persons are located. All persons entering the restricted area should follow the AORN "Recommended practices for surgical attire."[1]

   Persons entering the semirestricted or restricted areas of the surgical suite for a brief time for a specific purpose (eg, law enforcement officers, parents, biomedical engineers) should cover all head and facial hair and may don either freshly laundered surgical attire or a single-use coverall suit (eg, jumpsuit) designed to totally cover outside apparel.

2. Movement of personnel from unrestricted areas to either semirestricted or restricted areas should be through a transition zone. A transition zone exists where one can enter the area in street clothing and exit into the semirestricted or restricted zone in surgical attire. Locker rooms serve as transition zones between the outside and inside of a surgical suite and may serve as a security point to monitor people admitted to the suite.

3. Patients entering the surgical suite should wear clean gowns, be covered with clean linens, and have their hair covered. Clean gowns, linens, and hair coverings are worn by patients to minimize particulate shedding during surgical procedures.

Patients are not required to wear masks while in the surgical suite unless they are under airborne precautions (eg, a patient with active pulmonary tuberculosis or other airborne respiratory disease).[2] While in the restricted area, the mask could hinder access to the face and airway and might increase the patient's anxiety.

Personal undergarments may be worn when they will not interfere with the surgical site. Consideration should be given for management of potential incontinence. Many health care organizations now allow specific patients to wear clean personal clothing, including socks and underwear, into the surgical suite to promote the patient's comfort and sense of dignity. The most common surgical procedures that incorporate this new patient care practice are cataract extractions and carpal tunnel releases. Access to patients below the waist usually is not necessary for these surgical procedures. In addition, sterile fields can be maintained easily without the risk of contamination from patient clothing.

Recommendation II

Operating room suites should be secure.

1. The design of perioperative areas and traffic patterns should include the following.
   ♦ Patient privacy must be provided for as required by the Health Insurance Portability and Accountability Act of 1996 (HIPAA).[3]
   ♦ Patient, personnel, and visitor safety should be ensured.
   ♦ Supplies and equipment should be protected from tampering and theft.

2. Identification badges should be worn at all times according to organizational policy.

Recommendation III

Movement of personnel should be kept to a minimum while invasive and noninvasive procedures are in progress.

1. Careful assessment of the patient and planning for patient care needs should reduce the need for excessive movement and activity during the procedure. Air is a potential source of microorganisms that can contaminate surgical wounds. Because microbial shedding increases with activity, greater amounts of airborne contamination can be expected with increased movement of surgical team members.[4]

2. Doors to the operating or procedure rooms should be closed except during movement of patients, personnel, supplies, and equipment. The air pressure within each operating or procedure room should be greater than in the semirestricted area. The air in the OR should be maintained under positive pressure with a minimum of 15 total room air exchanges per hour.[5] When the doors are left open, the heating, ventilation, and air conditioning system is unable to maintain these critical environmental parameters. Leaving the door open can disrupt pressurization and cause turbulent airflow that could increase airborne contamination. Traffic in and out of the OR should be minimized by preplanning so that turbulence from this activity is minimized during the procedure or when sterile supplies are opened.

3. Talking and the number of people present should be minimized during procedures. An increase in airborne microorganisms can occur with an increased number of people present. Movement, talking, and uncovered skin areas can contribute to airborne contamination.[4]

Recommendation IV

The movement of clean and sterile supplies and equipment should be separated from contaminated supplies, equipment, and waste by space, time, or traffic patterns.

1. Surgical supplies prepared for surgical procedures outside the surgical suite (eg, in central processing) should be transported to the surgical suite to maintain cleanliness and sterility and to prevent physical damage. Protecting items from contamination, physical damage, and loss during transportation facilitates their safe use. Use of correct procedures for transporting items preserves the qualities of the sterile and clean environment.[6]

2. Supplies and equipment should be removed from external shipping containers and web-edged or corrugated cardboard boxes in the unrestricted area before transfer into the surgical suite. External shipping containers and web-edged cardboard boxes may collect dust, debris, and insects during shipment and may carry contaminants into the surgical suite.[6]

3. When there is a clean core, the movement of supplies should be from the clean core through the operating or procedure room to the peripheral corridor.

   ♦ Soiled supplies, instruments, and equipment should not reenter the clean core area. They should be contained in closed or covered carts or containers for transport to a designated decontamination area.

   ♦ The decontamination area and soiled linen and trash collection areas should be separated from personnel and patient traffic areas. Separation of clean and sterile supplies and equipment from soiled materials by space, time, and traffic patterns decreases the risk of infection.[6]

Recommendation V

During construction and renovation, specific traffic patterns should be established and maintained in accordance with applicable state regulations.

1. Specific traffic plans for construction personnel and movement of supplies, equipment, and debris should be developed and implemented following applicable guidelines for construction in health care facilities, with infection control personnel monitoring the process.[7,8] Infections have been transmitted through the dissemination of microorganisms from disruptions of environmental reservoirs (eg, drywall, ceiling tiles, flooring, casework).[9]

2. Surgical personnel should be able to move from place to place without contaminating their surgical scrubs. Clean or sterile supplies and equipment must be transported to storage areas by a route that minimizes contamination from the construction site and prevents contact with soiled or contaminated trash and linen. Since traffic patterns may not be easily altered to meet these requirements, the construction

personnel may need to work during off hours. If infection control requirements still cannot be met, some areas may need to be relocated or closed temporarily.[9]

3. A multidisciplinary assessment should be completed to determine the infection control and safety risks involved in a construction, renovation, or maintenance project. A multidisciplinary team performing the assessment should include infection control, safety, and project personnel. An infection control risk assessment (ICRA) matrix may facilitate the process. The ICRA matrix helps the team identify important preventive strategies that may include, but are not limited to,

   ♦ types of barriers necessary,
   ♦ maintenance of barrier integrity,
   ♦ attire for workers,
   ♦ special entrances and exits,
   ♦ negative pressure and high-efficiency particulate air filters, and
   ♦ other infection control prevention and surveillance measures (eg, particulate counts).[9]

   Thorough planning and coordination is necessary to minimize the risk for airborne infection both during projects and after their completion.[10]

4. Compliance with barrier precautions and traffic patterns should be monitored on an ongoing basis throughout and until the completion of the construction, renovation, or repair project. Monitoring provides an opportunity to rapidly correct any barrier or traffic restriction breach.

Recommendation VI

Policies and procedures for traffic patterns for patients, personnel, supplies, and equipment should be developed, reviewed periodically, revised as necessary, and kept readily available in the practice setting.

1. These recommendations should be used as guidelines for developing written policies and procedures in the practice setting. Policies and procedures establish authority, responsibility, and accountability and serve as operational guidelines. Policies and procedures establish guidelines for performance improvement activities to be used when monitoring and evaluating traffic patterns in the surgical practice setting.

2. Information on traffic patterns and methods of handling supplies and equipment should be included in the orientation and continuing education of personnel to assist in the development of knowledge, skills, and attitudes that affect surgical patient outcomes. This education should include ancillary support or delivery personnel whose work activities require them to be within the semirestricted or restricted areas.

3. Policies and procedures should assist in the development of patient safety and quality assessment and improvement activities.

4. The uniform perioperative nursing vocabulary should be used in the development of policies and procedures related to traffic patterns. The perioperative nursing vocabulary is a clinically relevant and empirically validated standardized language. This standardized language consists of the Perioperative Nursing Data Set (PNDS) and includes perioperative nursing diagnoses, interventions, and outcomes. The expected outcome of primary importance to these recommended practices is outcome O10, "The patient is free from signs and symptoms of infection." This outcome falls within the domain of Physiological Responses (D2). The associated nursing diagnosis is X28, "Risk for infection." The associated interventions that may lead to the desired outcome may be I121, "Initiates traffic control"; I109, "Protects from cross-contamination"; I117, "Maintains continuous surveillance"; and I111, "Minimizes the length of invasive procedure by planning care."[11]

Glossary

Corrugated cardboard box: Web-edged box used for the purpose of containing items to be shipped for use in the OR.

Jumpsuit: One-piece suit that completely covers street clothes and can be worn in the semi restricted areas of the OR. *Synonyms:* coveralls, bunnysuit.

REFERENCES

1. "Recommended practices for surgical attire," in *Standards, Recommended Practices, and Guidelines* (Denver: AORN, Inc, 2005) 299-305.
2. J S Garner, Centers for Disease Control and Prevention Hospital Infection Control Practices Advisory Committee, "Guideline for isolation precautions in hospitals," *Infection Control and Hospital Epidemiology* 17 (January 1996) 53-80.
3. "The Health Insurance Portability and Accountability Act of 1996 (HIPAA)," Centers for Medicare and Medicaid Services, http://www.cms.hhs.gov/hipaa (accessed 13 Dec 2005).
4. A J Mangram et al, Centers for Disease Control and Prevention Hospital Infection Control Practices Advisory Committee, "Guideline for prevention of surgical site infection, 1999," *American Journal of Infection Control* 27 (April 1999) 97-134.
5. American Institute of Architects Academy of Architecture for Health, *Guidelines for Design and Construction of Hospital and Health Care Facilities* (Washington, DC: American Institute of Architects Press, 2001).
6. Association for the Advancement of Medical Instrumentation, *Steam Sterilization and Sterility Assurance in Health Care Facilities* (Arlington, Va: Association for the Advancement of Medical Instrumentation, 2002).
7. J M Bartley, "APIC state-of-the-art report: The role of infection control during construction in health care facilities," *American Journal of Infection Control* 28 (April 2000) 156-169.
8. J Bartley, "Construction and renovation," in *APIC Text of Infection Control and Epidemiology,* rev ed, J A Pfeiffer, ed (Washington, DC: Association for Professionals in Infection Control and Epidemiology, 2002) 72-1 to 72-11.
9. S A David, J A Fernandez, L A Herwaldt, "Infection control issues in construction and renovation," in *Practical Handbook for Healthcare Epidemiologists,* second ed, E Lautenbach, K F Woeltje, eds (Thorofare, NJ: Slack, 2004) 337-360.
10. Centers for Disease Control and Prevention, *Guidelines for Environmental Infection Control in Health-Care Facilities* (Atlanta: Centers for Disease Control and Prevention, 2003).
11. S C Beyea, ed, *Perioperative Nursing Data Set: The Perioperative Nursing Vocabulary,* second ed (Denver: AORN, Inc, 2002).

RESOURCE

"Infection control risk assessment matrix of precautions for construction and renovation," US Army Health Facility Planning Agency, http://hfpa.otsg.amedd.army.mil/refs/docs/icra_assessment_form.pdf (accessed 9 Dec 2005).

Originally published March 1982, *AORN Journal.* Format revision July 1982.

Revised November 1988; May 1993; November 1995. Published March 1996, *AORN Journal.*

Revised; published February 2000, *AORN Journal.* Reformatted July 2000.

Revised November 2005; published in *Standards, Recommended Practices, and Guidelines,* 2006 edition. Reprinted March 2006, *AORN Journal.*

Recommended Practices for Electrosurgery

The following recommended practices were developed by the AORN Recommended Practices Committee and have been approved by the AORN Board of Directors. They were presented as proposed recommended practices for comment to members and others. These recommended practices are effective January 1, 2005.

These recommended practices are intended as achievable recommendations representing what is believed to be an optimal level of practice. Policies and procedures will reflect variations in practice settings and/or clinical situations that determine the degree to which the recommended practices can be implemented.

AORN recognizes the various settings in which perioperative nurses practice. These recommended practices are intended as guidelines adaptable to various practice settings. These practice settings include traditional operating rooms, ambulatory surgery units, physician's offices, cardiac catheterization laboratories, endoscopy suites, radiology departments, and all other areas where surgery may be performed.

Purpose

These recommended practices provide guidance to perioperative nurses in the use and care of electrosurgical equipment. Proper care and handling of electrosurgical equipment is essential to patient and personnel safety. Electrosurgery is used routinely to cut, coagulate, dissect, fulgurate, ablate, and shrink body tissue with high frequency (ie, radio frequency) electrical current. Ultrasonic dissectors dissect tissue by vibration. Vessel sealing devices use a combination of pressure and heat to permanently occlude vessels. These recommended practices address all of these technologies and do not endorse any specific product.

Recommendation I

Personnel selecting the electrosurgical unit (ESU) and accessories for purchase or use should make decisions based on safety features to minimize risks to patients and personnel.

1. Equipment selected should include technology to detect stray current that could result in patient injury and to alert the user of this condition. Electrosurgical units are high-risk equipment. Historically, the most frequently reported patient injury has been a skin injury (eg, burn) at the dispersive electrode site.[1] The risk of this type of injury has been minimized through advances in dispersive pad design (eg, nondrying conductive material, dual-contact dispersive electrodes) and the use of return electrode contact quality monitoring.[2] Minimum safety standards for ESU systems have been developed by the Association for the Advancement of Medical Instrumentation and approved by the American National Standards Institute.[3]

2. Equipment should be designed to minimize the risk of alternate site injuries. These injuries can result from use of ground-referenced (ie, spark-gap) ESUs that allow electrical current to seek alternate pathways to complete the circuit.[3,4] The use of isolated (ie, solid-state) ESUs has minimized this risk.

3. Equipment should be designed to minimize the risk of capacitive coupling injuries. During minimally invasive procedures, alternate site injuries have resulted from insulation failure and capacitive coupling.[4,5-11] These injuries are very serious and have increased in number with the increased use of laparoscopic surgery.[12] The use of active electrode monitoring has minimized these risks.[13-17]

4. Equipment should be designed to minimize unintentional activation that could result in patient and personnel injury. Audible activation tones minimize this risk.[3,18,19]

5. Electrosurgical accessories selected should be compatible with the equipment and other accessories. Injuries have resulted when equipment intended for bipolar use is inserted into monopolar connectors and, subsequently, inadvertently activated.[20] Appropriate matching and use of accessories minimizes this risk.

6. Electrosurgical technology continues to evolve, changing the way in which surgical hemostasis is achieved. It is the responsibility of each facility to stay abreast of evolving technology and its impact on patient care and safety.

Recommendation II

Personnel should demonstrate competence in the use of the ESU and accessories.

1. Personnel working with electrosurgery equipment should be knowledgeable about the principles of electrosurgery, risks to patients and personnel, measures to minimize these risks, and corrective actions to employ in the event of a fire or injury. Electrosurgical equipment and accessories have been associated with numerous fires and patient injuries.[1,11,21,22] The National Fire Protection Association has identified ESUs as high-risk equipment, warranting training and retraining of personnel.[23] Personnel should be instructed in the proper operation, care, and handling of the ESU and accessories before use.[23] Initial education on the underlying principles of electrosurgical safety provides direction for personnel in providing a safe environment. Additional, periodic educational programs provide reinforcement of principles of electrosurgery and new information on changes in technology, its application, compatibility of equipment and accessories, and potential hazards.

2. Administrative personnel should assess and document annual competency of personnel in the safe use of the ESU and accessories according to hospital and department policy. Incorrect use can result in serious injury to patients and personnel. A regular competency assessment provides a record that personnel have a basic understanding of electrosurgery, its risks, and appropriate corrective action to take in the event of a fire or injury. This knowledge is essential to minimize the risks of misuse of the equipment and providing a safe environment of care.

Recommendation III

The ESU and accessories should be used according to manufacturers' written instructions.

1. Instructions for ESU use, warranties, and a manual for maintenance and inspections should be obtained from the manufacturer and be readily available to users.[23] Equipment manuals assist in developing operational, safety, and maintenance guidelines, as well as serve as a reference for appropriate use.[23]

2. Each type of ESU has specific manufacturer's written operating instructions to be followed for safe operation of the unit. A brief set of clearly readable operating instructions should be readily accessible with each system.[24] These instructions should be placed on or attached to each ESU for reference.

3. Accessories should be used, handled, cleaned, and processed according to manufacturers' instructions.

Recommendation IV

The ESU system should be used in a manner that minimizes the potential for injuries.

1. The ESU should be securely mounted on a shelf or tip-resistant cart. The ESU electrical cord should be adequate in length and flexibility to reach the electrical outlet without stress or the use of an extension cord.[25] Applying tension on the electrical cord increases the risk that it will become disconnected, frayed, or move the equipment, which may result in injuries to patients and personnel.

2. The ESU should be tested before initial use, inspected periodically, and receive preventive maintenance by a designated individual responsible for equipment maintenance (eg, bioengineering services personnel).[26] Personnel should visually inspect the ESU and test the return electrode contact monitor before each use (eg, attempt to use the device with the dispersive electrode not connected).[25,27,28] The manufacturer's written precautions should be followed for the safety of the patient and personnel involved in the procedure.

3. An ESU that is not working properly or is damaged should be removed from service immediately and reported to the designated individual responsible for equipment maintenance (eg, bioengineering services personnel). Each ESU should be assigned an identification or serial number. This number allows designated personnel to track function problems and document maintenance performed on individual ESUs.[29]

4. Safety/warning alarms should be operational at all times. Lights should be operational and visible. Audible activation indicator(s) and alarms should be present and loud enough to be heard above other sounds in the OR. The volume of the

activation indicator should be maintained at an audible level to immediately alert personnel when the ESU is activated inadvertently.[3,18,19]

5. The ESU should be protected from spills. Fluids should not be placed on top of the ESU. Fluids entering the ESU can cause unintentional activation or device failure. Liquids seeping into the ESU pose an electrical hazard. Personnel should encase the ESU foot pedal in a clean, impervious cover when there is a potential for fluid spills.

6. The operator should confirm the power settings before activation. Settings should be based upon the manufacturer's written instructions and the intended application. The ESU should be operated at the lowest effective power setting to achieve the desired effect. If the operator requests a continual increase in power, personnel should check the entire ESU and accessories circuit, beginning with checking the dispersive electrode. If a single-use electrode is used, it should be replaced, not repositioned.[30] Prolonged current at high power can cause patient injury. The most common cause for ineffective coagulation and cutting is high impedance at the dispersive electrode.[30] Replacing the dispersive electrode provides an opportunity to examine the electrode and the patient's skin condition.

7. After use, personnel should turn off the ESU, clean all reusable parts, and inspect these parts according to the manufacturer's written instructions.

Recommendation V

The electrical cords and plugs of the ESU should be handled in a manner that minimizes the potential for damage and subsequent patient injuries.

1. The ESU should be placed near the sterile field, and the cord should reach the wall or column outlet without stress on the cord and without blocking a traffic path.[25] Stress on the cord may cause damage to the cord, posing an electrical hazard. The cord should be free of kinks, knots, and bends that could damage the cord or cause leakage, current accumulation, and overheating of the cord's insulation.

2. The ESU plug, not the cord, should be held when it is removed from the outlet. Pulling on the cord may cause cord breakage, which poses a fire hazard.

3. The ESU and cord should be kept away from fluids. Fluids dripping into the ESU or connections cause an electrical hazard.

Recommendation VI

The active electrode should be used in a manner that minimizes the potential for injuries.

1. The active electrode should be connected directly into a designated receptacle on the ESU. If an adapter is used, it should be approved by the manufacturers of both the ESU and the accessory and not compromise the ESU's safety features. Incomplete circuitry, unintentional activation, and incompatibility of the active electrode to the ESU may result in patient and personnel injuries.[19,20]

2. The active electrode should be visually inspected at the surgical field, before use, to identify any apparent damage to the cord or hand piece (eg, impaired insulation).[25] Insulation failure allows an alternate pathway for current to leave the electrode. Additional information about use of electrosurgery for endoscopic procedures can be found in the AORN "Recommended practices for endoscopic minimally invasive surgery."[31]

3. If securing the active electrode cord to the drapes, plastic or another nonconductive material should be used. The cord should not be coiled. This minimizes the risk of patient or staff member injury from conduction of stray current.

4. Active electrodes should not be used in the presence of flammable agents, including vapors (eg, antimicrobial skin prep or hand antisepsis agents, tinctures, defatting agents, collodian, petroleum-based lubricants, phenol, aerosol adhesives, uncured methyl methacrylate).[29,32] Opened suture packages containing alcohol should be removed from the sterile field as soon as possible.[19,32] Ignition of flammable substances by active electrodes has

caused fires and patient injuries.[19,32-39] Alcohol-based skin prep agents are particularly hazardous because the surrounding hair or fabric can become saturated. Pooling can occur in body folds and crevices (eg, umbilicus, sternal notch). Vapors can become trapped under an incise drape or surgical drapes. This has led to fires and patient injuries.[37-39] Using nonflammable prep agents eliminates this risk.[19,32,34,38]

5. The active electrode should be placed in a clean, dry, well-insulated safety holster when not in use to minimize the risk of injury from unintentional activation. Injuries have resulted when the active electrode has been left lying on the patient between uses.[18] Electrodes that do not fit in the holster should be placed in a designated location with tips away from flammable material (eg, drapes). When battery-powered, hand-held cautery is used, the protective cap should be reapplied when the cautery is not in use, thus preventing inadvertent pressure on the activation button.[40]

6. The active electrode tips should be securely seated into the hand piece. A loose tip may cause a spark or burn to tissue contacting the exposed, noninsulated section of the tip.[41] Tips should be used according to the manufacturer's instructions and not be altered (eg, bent) unless specified by the manufacturer. If insulation is desired, it should be acquired from a medical device manufacturer. Fires and patient injuries have resulted when insulating sheaths have been made from inappropriate material (eg, rubber catheters).[42,43]

7. The active electrode tip should be cleaned frequently, away from the incision, to remove eschar. Eschar buildup on the active electrode tip impedes the desired current flow, causing the entire unit to function less effectively and serving as a fuel source, which can lead to fires.[42] Debris on the electrode tip can tear tissue and cause rebleeding.[1] Abrasive electrode cleaning pads are commercially available for noncoated electrodes. Electrosurgical tips also are available with a special coating that minimizes eschar buildup.

8. Sponges used close to the active electrode tip should be moist to prevent unintentional ignition. Active electrodes should not be cleaned with a dry sponge. Fires have resulted from ignition of dry sponges near the incision site and when they are used to clean the active electrode.[34,44-46]

9. The active electrode should not be used in the presence of intestinal gases. These gases contain hydrogen and methane, which are highly flammable. Fires and patient injuries have occurred.[47-51]

10. The active electrode should not be used in an oxygen-enriched environment.[22,52] Caution should be exercised during surgery on the head and neck near combustible anesthetic gases. The active electrode should be used as far from the oxygen source as possible. The lowest practical level of oxygen should be administered to the patient. When administering oxygen in an open system (eg, nasal prongs), drapes should be tented or a scavenging system used to prevent buildup of oxygen under the drapes. Fires, including airway fires, have resulted from the active electrode sparking in the presence of concentrated oxygen.[22,52-58]

11. If the active electrode is being used in a fluid-filled cavity, the fluid used should be an electrically inert, near isotonic solution (eg, dextran 10, dextran 70, glycine 1.5%, sorbitol, mannitol) unless the manufacturer of the equipment instructs otherwise.[1,59-63] Using an electrolyte solution instead of a nonconductive medium may render the active electrode less effective. Subsequent increases in the power setting have resulted in burns at the dispersive (ie, return) electrode site.[1,64]

12. If the active electrode becomes contaminated, it should be disconnected from the ESU. This minimizes the risk of unintentional activation and reduces the potential for patient and personnel injuries.

13. When battery-powered, hand-held cautery units are used, the batteries should be removed before disposal of the cautery unit. Inadvertent activation after disposal has caused fires.[40,65] Batteries are hazardous waste.

14. Personnel should be prepared to immediately extinguish flames should they occur. Saline or water should be available on the sterile field. A carbon dioxide (CO_2) fire extinguisher should be readily available.[19,66] This type of fire extinguisher

can extinguish fires involving cloth and paper, and it is safe to use in the presence of electrical current. Fire blankets should not be used in the OR.[19] Using a fire blanket on a patient traps the fire around the patient. Fire blankets should be used only on conscious fire victims who can roll and pinpoint the location of the fire under the blanket so responders can extinguish the fire by vigorously patting the blanket at the identified site. If a fire blanket is present in the OR, staff members may assume it is safe for patient use, thereby placing the patient at further risk. Fire blankets will burn if used in oxygen-enriched atmospheres.

Recommendation VII

When monopolar electrosurgery is used, a dispersive electrode should be used in a manner that minimizes the potential for injuries.

1. The patient's skin condition should be assessed and documented before and after ESU use. The most frequently reported patient injury from electrosurgery has been tissue damage (eg, burn) at the dispersive electrode site.[25] With advances in technology in return electrode monitors and increased use of laparoscopy, this may be changing to other types of injuries (eg, direct coupling, capacitive coupling); however, burns at the site of the dispersive electrode continue to occur. Preoperative and postoperative assessments allow evaluation of the patient's skin condition for possible injuries.

2. Dispersive electrodes should be compatible with the ESU.

3. Single-use dispersive electrodes should be used according to the manufacturer's written instructions for safe operation; in addition to instructions on the electrode package, additional instructions may be located in the box of electrode packages.

   ♦ Electrodes should be an appropriate size for the patient (eg, neonate, infant, pediatric, adult) and not altered (eg, cut, folded). Using the appropriately sized dispersive electrode is important for preventing patient injuries. Using a large dispersive electrode prevents concentration of current and minimizes the potential for electrosurgical injuries.[28,30]

♦ Personnel should verify that the electrode is intact; conductive gel, if present, is moist; and the manufacturer's expiration date has not been reached.[28,30]

♦ The conductive and adhesive surfaces of the electrode should be placed on clean, dry skin, over a large, well-perfused muscle mass on the surgical side, and close to the surgical site. Muscle is a better conductor of electricity than adipose tissue.[28,30]

♦ Electrodes should not be placed over bony prominences, scar tissue, hairy surfaces, or areas distal to tourniquets and pressure points.[28,30] Fatty tissues, tissue over bone, scar tissue, and hair can impede electrosurgical return current flow. High impedance leads to heating of the tissue, arcing to the tissue under the dispersive electrode, and subsequent burns.[67] Burns have resulted when electrodes have been positioned over hairy surfaces.[68] Hair removal may be necessary. Adequate tissue perfusion cannot be assured if the dispersive electrode is placed distal to tourniquets or over scar tissue.

♦ The electrode should not be placed over an implanted metal prosthesis.[1] The tissue over prostheses contains scar tissue, which impedes return of the electric current. Although there has been no reported injury from superheating of the implant causing a tissue burn, this is a theoretical risk; therefore, it is prudent to avoid placing a dispersive electrode on the patient's skin over the site of a metal implant or prosthesis.

♦ Avoid placing the dispersive electrode over a tattoo, many of which contain metallic dyes. Although there have been no reported electrosurgery injuries from dispersive electrodes placed over tattoos, superheating of the tissue has occurred during magnetic resonance imaging;[69,70] therefore, it is prudent to avoid this site when possible.

♦ The single-use dispersive electrode should maintain uniform body contact. Potential problems include tenting, gaping, and moisture, all of which interfere with adhesion to the patient's skin. Injuries have been associated with inadequate adhesion of the dispersive electrode.[71-73]

♦ The single-use dispersive electrode should be placed on the patient after final positioning for the surgical procedure to prevent buckling of the electrode and to maintain good skin contact with the electrode. If any tension is applied to the dispersive electrode cord or if the surgical team repositions the patient, personnel should reassess the integrity of the dispersive electrode, its contact with the patient's skin, and its connection to the ESU. If the patient is repositioned, personnel should verify that the dispersive electrode remains in full contact with the patient's skin to avoid burns resulting from inadequate contact with the dispersive electrode.

♦ The dispersive electrode should be removed carefully. Skin injuries can result when the adhesive border pulls on the skin during electrode removal.[74] Holding the adjacent skin in place and peeling the dispersive electrode back slowly will avoid denuding the surface of the skin.

4. Large, reusable, capacitive-coupled return electrode systems should be used according to manufacturers' written instructions for safe operation in conjunction with a compatible ESU.

♦ These electrodes are inappropriate for patients under 25 lbs. A patient injury has been reported when the electrode was used on a smaller patient.[75]

♦ When using a reusable, capacitive-coupled return electrode, personnel should ensure adequate contact (ie, weight-bearing area) with the patient and use minimal materials between the pad and patient. Thick foam, gel pads, and extra linen increase the distance between the patient and electrode and should not be used. Some complex patient positioning also decreases contact between the skin and the electrode. Distance and barriers between the patient and electrode increase impedance, which can result in an alternate site injury.[76]

♦ Personnel should verify that no small metal material (eg, snaps on gowns) is in contact with the patient's skin. Current can concentrate at the site of metal contact. Snaps on patient gowns have resulted in patient injuries when the capacitive-coupled return electrode was used.[77]

5. Dispersive electrodes should be kept dry and protected from seeping or pooling of fluids

under the dispersive electrode.[30] Liquids may prevent the electrode from adequately contacting the skin. These solutions also can cause skin injury from prolonged skin exposure.

6. There should be no contact between the patient and metal devices that could offer potential alternate return paths for the electrical current (eg, OR beds, stirrups, positioning devices, safety strap buckles). Patient monitoring electrodes (eg, electrocardiogram, oximetry, fetal) should be placed as far away from the surgical site as possible. Alternate pathway burns have been reported at electrocardiogram (ECG) electrode sites and temperature probe entry sites with ground-referenced electrosurgery units.[4]

7. The patient's metal jewelry should be removed if it is within the activation range of the active electrode. Metallic jewelry, including that used in body piercing, presents a potential risk of burn from directed current (ie, active electrode touching it), heat conducted before an electrode cools, and leakage current. Eliminating metal near the activation site minimizes this risk. Although there may be other reasons for removal of all patient jewelry (eg, risk of swelling, theft), the risk of an alternative site injury from stray current is negligible.[78] When using a reusable, capacitive-coupled return electrode, all of the patient's metal jewelry should be removed. Small metal objects touching the return electrode can concentrate current and result in patient injury.[77] Eliminating contact with metal minimizes this risk.

8. If multiple ESUs are used simultaneously during a surgical procedure, the applicable instructions from the manufacturer should be followed. Compatibility of equipment and proper functioning of corresponding electrode monitoring systems should be verified with the manufacturer. Separate dispersive electrodes should be used for each ESU. Personnel should place the dispersive electrodes as close as possible to their respective surgical sites and ensure that single-use dispersive electrodes do not overlap.

9. Two dispersive electrodes should be used in unique situations when high impedance is reasonably anticipated (eg, very obese patients) or

during prolonged application of current at high power settings (eg, ablation).[30,64] Users should refer to the manufacturer's recommendations for these applications.

Recommendation VIII

Personnel should take special precautions when using the ESU during endoscopic procedures.

1. Personnel should understand the risks of electrosurgery during endoscopic procedures. Electrosurgical injuries are caused by direct coupling of current, insulation failure, and capacitive coupling. Direct coupling is caused by the surgeon touching the laparoscopic active electrode to another anatomic structure. This can cause necrosis of underlying tissue. Insulation failure of the laparoscopic electrode can be caused by trauma during use or reprocessing. Current leaves the electrode through this alternate pathway. This can cause serious patient injury, particularly when the injury is internal. Capacitively coupled radio frequency currents can cause undetected burns to nearby tissue and organs outside the endoscope's viewing field. Severe patient injuries have resulted.[7,9,11,79]

2. Endoscopic trocar cannula systems should meet safety criteria established for the practice setting. When an all-metal system is used, capacitive current is safely dispersed through the greater surface area provided by the chest or abdominal wall, thereby reducing current concentration. Metal cannula systems are best for the port of electrosurgical instruments.[6,11,79,80] An all-plastic system is another alternative. Using this system, the capacitor is the patient, which minimizes the concern of concentrated capacitively coupled current;[81] however, a risk of direct coupling injuries remains. Hybrid trocar (ie, combination plastic and metal) systems should not be used.[1,5,11,80] Each trocar and cannula can act as an electrical conductor, thereby inducing an electrical current from one to the other, which could cause capacitive coupling injuries.

3. Personnel should verify that the insufflation gas is nonflammable (ie, carbon dioxide). An intra-abdominal fire has occurred when a carbon dioxide-oxygen mixture was attached inadver-

tently to an insufflator rather than the intended carbon dioxide tank.[82]

4. All electrodes should be examined for impaired insulation before use. Insulation failure of electrodes caused by trauma during use or reprocessing provides an alternate pathway for the electrical current to leave the active electrode. Some insulation failures are not visible. This has resulted in serious patient injuries.[4,6,11,13-15,17,79,80] These injuries may be outside the endoscope's visual field. Use of active electrode shielding and monitoring minimizes the risks of insulation failure and capacitive coupling injuries.[4,6,11,13-15,17,79,80]

5. When active electrode monitoring is not used, additional precautions should be employed to minimize the risks associated with insulation failure and direct and capacitive coupling.
   ♦ The lowest power setting that achieves the desired result should be selected, and
   ♦ the low-voltage cutting waveform setting should be selected whenever clinically feasible.

   Lower power settings for both cut and coagulation reduce the likelihood of insulation failure and capacitive-coupling injuries. Lower power settings also minimize damage from direct coupling when the active electrode is activated while in close proximity to another metal device inserted in an adjacent trocar port.[6]

6. The active electrode should not be activated until it is in close proximity to the tissue; this minimizes the risk of contacting unintended tissue.[6,11] Activating the electrode when it is not in very close proximity to the targeted tissue increases the risk of capacitive coupling. Capacitance is reduced during closed-circuit activation.

7. Patients should be taught to immediately report any signs or symptoms of infection, excessive pain, bleeding, or inability to void. Symptoms of a laparoscopic electrosurgical injury can occur days after discharge from the perioperative setting and may include infection from an injured intestinal tract. Lower gastrointestinal bleeding and inability to void may be early manifestations of a bowel injury.[11] Patients should understand what symptoms to look for and report to ensure prompt treatment that minimizes the adverse outcome.[79]

Recommendation IX

Personnel should take special precautions when using the ESU with patients who have pacemakers, internal cardioverter-defibrillators (ICDs), or other electrical implants.

1. Patients with pacemakers should be continuously monitored (ie, minimally, ECG, peripheral pulse) during electrosurgery use. Electrosurgery can interfere with both the pacemaker's circuitry and function and create ECG artifact.[1,83] Monitoring the peripheral pulse provides a mechanism to evaluate peripheral perfusion in the presence of ECG artifact. Although modern pacemakers are designed to be shielded from radio frequency current, they are subject to interference during electrosurgery use.[1,83,84] For patients with pacemakers, personnel should take additional precautions, which include, but are not limited to,
   - checking with the pacemaker manufacturer or the patient's cardiologist regarding its function during use of electrosurgery and discussing reprogramming the pacemaker to an asynchronous mode during surgery;
   - having a pacemaker programmer unit (or magnet if appropriate for the type of pacemaker) available to place the pacemaker in an asynchronous mode;
   - having a defibrillator immediately available for emergencies during surgery;
   - keeping all electrosurgical cords and cables away from the pacemaker and its leads;
   - using bipolar electrosurgery whenever possible;
   - using the lowest possible power setting on the electrosurgical generator;
   - if monopolar electrosurgery is deemed necessary, ensuring that the distance between the active and dispersive electrodes is as short as possible (place both electrodes as far away from the pacemaker as possible, and ensure that the current path does not pass through the vicinity of the patient's heart or the implanted pacemaker device);[1,83] and
   - having the proper functioning of the pacemaker evaluated by an individual trained in the use of the pacemaker programmer immediately postoperatively.

   The patient's pacemaker may interpret radio frequency from electrosurgery as cardiac activity

and inhibit the pacemaker from initiating a heartbeat. This can result in life-threatening arrhythmia. Reprogramming demand pacemakers to an asynchronous mode protects the patient from this risk. A magnet placed over the pacemaker is effective in temporarily placing some models of pacemaker in asynchronous mode. Other models require the use of a pacemaker programmer unit.[83] Monopolar electrical current seeks a ground through the patient's body. This ground may be through the pacemaker wire, which can result in inadvertent reprogramming of the pacemaker, permanent damage to the pacemaker, or an electrical burn in the heart; therefore, having a programmer and defibrillator readily available is advisable. Short bursts of energy also minimize the risk of injury. Placing as much distance as possible between both the active and dispersive electrode and the pacemaker encourages the energy to return to the ESU through the dispersive electrode, rather than the pacemaker wire. There is a risk of reprogramming or damage to the pacemaker, so evaluation of the pacemaker is warranted.

2. Precautions for a patient with an ICD should include
   - preoperatively obtaining a cardiology consultation to evaluate the correct functioning of the ICD and determine the risks associated with temporarily deactivating the ICD intraoperatively;
   - having a defibrillator immediately available;
   - having the ICD device deactivated by trained personnel before the ESU is activated—using electrosurgery on a patient with an activated ICD may trigger an electrical shock to the patient;[85]
   - having continuous ECG and peripheral pulse monitoring;
   - using bipolar electrosurgery as an alternative whenever possible;
   - if monopolar electrosurgery is deemed necessary, ensuring that the distance between the active and dispersive electrodes is as short as possible (place both electrodes as far away from the ICD as possible, and ensure that the current path from the surgical site to the dispersive electrode does not pass through the vicinity of the patient's heart or the implanted ICD);[83,85] and

- immediately postoperatively, having the correct functioning of the ICD verified by an expert in electrophysiology.

3. Precautions for patients with other electric stimulators (eg, bone growth, cochlear implants) should include the following.

   - Use bipolar electrosurgery as an alternative whenever possible. If monopolar electrosurgery is deemed necessary, ensure that the distance between the active and dispersive electrodes is as short as possible, place both electrodes as far away from the stimulator and wire as possible, and ensure that the current path from the surgical site to the dispersive electrode does not pass through the vicinity of the stimulator or lead wire.
   - In the presence of a cochlear implant, use bipolar electrosurgery at least 1 cm away from the implant.[22]
   - Immediately postoperatively, have the proper functioning of the device verified by a trained individual.

4. Precautions for patients with an implantable mechanical pump (eg, morphine, Baclofen) should include

   - using bipolar electrosurgery as an alternative whenever possible, and
   - immediately postoperatively, having the proper functioning of the pump verified by an individual trained in the programming of the pump.

Recommendation X

Bipolar active electrodes (including vessel occluding devices) should be used according to manufacturers' written instructions.

1. Unlike the monopolar ESU, bipolar technology incorporates an active (ie, efferent) electrode and a return (ie, afferent) electrode into a two-poled instrument, such as forceps or scissors.[5,22,86] Current flows only through the tissue contacted between two poles of instruments; thus, the need for a dispersive grounding pad is eliminated.[86] This also eliminates the chance of stray or alternate pathways for current flow.[86] The bipolar ESU provides precise hemostasis at the surgical site without stimulation or current spread to nearby body structures.[86]

2. Connection of a bipolar active electrode to a monopolar receptacle may activate current, causing a short circuit. Plugs should be differentiated to prevent misconnections of active and inactive electrodes.[20] Molded, fixed-positioned pin placement bipolar cords also are available.

Recommendation XI

Ultrasonic electrosurgical devices function differently from monopolar active electrodes and should be used according to manufacturers' written instructions.

1. When using an ultrasonic electrosurgical device, a dispersive electrode is not necessary. An ultrasonic device has a generator that produces electrical energy that is sent to the hand piece, where it is converted into mechanical energy. This energy is transmitted through a hand piece to a blade or probe that can be used for sharp or blunt dissection, coagulation, or breaking apart of tissue, without damage to adjacent tissues. Some ultrasonic dissectors incorporate an aspirator to remove tissue or fluids from the surgical field. Because no electrical current enters the tissue, current does not need to be returned to the generator by a dispersive electrode.[87]

2. Inhalation of aerosols generated by an ultrasonic electrosurgical hand piece should be minimized by implementing control measures that include, but are not limited to, the use of

   - smoke evacuation systems, and
   - wall suctions with in-line filters, which are only appropriate for a minimal amount of aerosol (aerosols generated using ultrasonic electrosurgery are within the respirable range and include blood, blood by-products, and tissue).[88]

3. Biomedical personnel should routinely inspect ultrasonic electrosurgical equipment to reduce the potential for equipment malfunction.

Recommendation XII

Argon enhanced coagulation (AEC) technology poses unique risks to patient and personnel safety and should be used according to manufacturers' written instructions.

1. All safety measures for monopolar electrosurgery should be used when using AEC technology. The AEC unit uses monopolar alternating current delivered to the tissue through ionized argon gas.[89,90] The risks of monopolar electrosurgery are present. Additional risks are associated with application of argon gas. Precautions should be taken to minimize these risks.

2. Air should be purged from the argon gas line and electrode by activating the system before use after moderate delays between activations and between uses.[89-90] Argon gas pressure exceeds venous pressure in the circulating system, and application to bleeding vessels has resulted in gas emboli in open surgical procedures.[91,92] Activating without adequately purging may present the greatest risk of embolism when operating in an open cavity.[89,90]

3. The coagulation or blended cutting current, which contains coagulation, should be used. The coagulation waveform seals the venous blood vessels, minimizing the risk of gas emboli entering the blood stream. Purging the argon gas line prevents delays in coagulation and reduces the potential for the operator to move the hand piece, thus minimizing the risk of gas embolism.[89,90]

4. The argon gas flow should be limited to the lowest level possible. Argon gas flow is most likely to be directed to tissue without simultaneous coagulation when the initiation of ionization of the argon gas is delayed due to air bubbles in the argon gas line.[89,90]

5. The electrode should not be placed in direct contact with tissue and should be moved away from the patient's tissue after each activation.[89,90] There is a risk of gas emboli when the active electrode is placed in direct contact with tissue.

6. Personnel using the AEC technology should be knowledgeable about signs, symptoms, and treatment of venous emboli.

7. Patient monitoring should include devices that are considered effective for early detection of gas emboli (eg, end-tidal carbon dioxide).[89,90]

Recommendation XIII

When using the AEC unit with endoscopic procedures, personnel should follow the manufacturer's written instructions and recommendations for use.

1. When using the AEC unit during endoscopic procedures, personnel should
   - follow all safety measures identified for AEC technology,
   - flush the patient's intraabdominal cavity with several liters of CO_2 between extended activation periods,[93]
   - use endoscopic CO_2 insufflators equipped with audible and visual overpressurization alarms that cannot be deactivated.[93]

The AEC system acts as a secondary source of pressurized argon gas that can cause the patient's intraabdominal pressure to rise rapidly and exceed venous pressure, possibly creating argon-enriched gas emboli formation. This has resulted in gas emboli.[93] Using the lowest argon gas flow setting, purging the active electrode and argon gas line of air according to the manufacturer's recommendations, and flushing the intraabdominal cavity with several liters of CO_2 between extended periods of deactivation reduces the potential for argon gas emboli formation.[93]

Recommendation XIV

Exposure to smoke plume generated during electrosurgery should be minimized.

1. Inhalation of smoke generated by electrosurgery should be minimized by implementing control measures that include, but are not limited to, the use of
   - smoke evacuation systems and
   - wall suction with in-line filters, which is only appropriate for a minimal amount of plume.

Smoke plume generated from electrosurgery is the same as laser plume. This smoke has been found to contain toxic gases and vapors (eg benzene, hydrogen cyanide, formaldehyde); bioaerosols, including blood fragments; and viruses. In high concentrations, the smoke causes ocular and upper respiratory tract irritation in health care personnel.[94] The smoke generated from electrosurgery contains chemical by-products.[94,95] The National Institutes of Occupational Safety and Health recommends that smoke evacuation systems be used to reduce potential acute and chronic health risks to patients and personnel.[94] The Occupational Safety and Health Administration (OSHA) has no separate standard related to surgical smoke. The OSHA addresses such safety hazards in the General Duty Clause and Bloodborne Pathogen Standard.[95]

2. Smoke evacuation systems and accessories should be used according to manufacturers' written instructions. Health care facilities should consult AORN's "Recommended practices for product selection in perioperative practice settings" to assist in selecting a smoke evacuation system.[96] When a smoke evacuation system is used, the suction wand should be placed as close to the source of the smoke as possible. This will maximize smoke capture and enhance visibility at the surgical site.

Recommendation XV

Health care facilities' policies and procedures for electrosurgery must be in compliance with the Safe Medical Devices Act of 1990.

1. If patient or personnel injuries or equipment failures occur, the ESU and the active and dispersive electrodes should be handled in accordance with the Safe Medical Devices Act of 1990, amended in March 2000.[97] Device identification, maintenance and service information, and adverse event information should be included in the report from the practice setting. Retaining the ESU, the active and dispersive electrodes, and packaging allows for a complete systems check to determine electrosurgical system integrity.

Recommendation XVI

Policies and procedures for electrosurgery should be developed, reviewed periodically, revised as necessary, and readily available in the practice setting.

1. Policies and procedures for electrosurgery should include, but are not limited to,
   ◆ safety features required on ESUs;
   ◆ equipment maintenance programs;
   ◆ supplemental safety monitors required;
   ◆ equipment checks before initial use;
   ◆ reporting and impounding malfunctioning equipment;
   ◆ preoperative, intraoperative, and postoperative patient assessments;
   ◆ precautions during use;
   ◆ reporting of injuries;
   ◆ ESU sanitation; and
   ◆ documentation.

2. Documentation should include, but not be limited to,
   ◆ electrosurgical system identification serial number,
   ◆ range of settings used,
   ◆ dispersive electrode placement and patient's skin condition before and after electrosurgery, and
   ◆ adjunct electrical devices used (eg, ultrasonic scalpel, bipolar forceps).

Documentation of details of the electrosurgical equipment and supplies allows for retrievable information for investigation into an adverse event.

3. These recommended practices should be used as guidelines for the development of policies and procedures in the perioperative practice setting. Policies and procedures establish authority, responsibility, and accountability within the facility. They also serve as operational guidelines.

4. An introduction and review of policies and procedures for electrosurgery should be included in orientation and ongoing education of personnel to assist in the development of knowledge, skills, and attitudes that affect surgical patient outcomes. Policies and procedures also assist in the development of quality assessment and improvement activities.

5. Information about adverse patient outcomes and near misses associated with electrosurgery should be collected, analyzed, and used for performance improvement as part of the institution-wide performance improvement program. To evaluate the quality of patient care and formulate plans for corrective action, it is necessary to maintain a system of evaluation. Quality improvement standards for perioperative nurses that may be used for evaluating electrosurgical safety have been published.[98]

Glossary

Active electrode: The electrosurgical unit (ESU) accessory that directs current flow to the surgical site (eg, pencils, various tips).

Active electrode monitoring: A dynamic process of searching for insulation failures and capacitive coupling during monopolar surgery. If the monitor detects an unsafe level of stray energy, it signals the generator to deactivate.

Argon enhanced coagulation: Radio frequency coagulation from an electrosurgical generator that is capable of delivering monopolar current through a flow of ionized argon gas.

Bioengineering services personnel: Those individuals in an institution who are trained and qualified to check, troubleshoot, and repair medical equipment.

Bipolar electrosurgery: Electrosurgery in which current flows between two tips of a bipolar forceps that is positioned around tissue to create a surgical effect. Current passes from the active electrode of one tip of the forceps through the patient's desired tissue to the dispersive electrode of the other forceps' tip—thus completing the circuit without entering another part of the patient's body. No dispersive electrode is required.

Capacitance: Ability of an electrical circuit to transfer an electrical charge from one conductor to another, even when separatedby an insulator.

Capacitive coupling: Transfer of electrical current from the active electrode through intact insulation to adjacent conductive items (eg, tissue, trocars).

Capacitively coupled return electrode: A large, nonadhesive return electrode placed close to and forming a capacitor with the patient, returning electrical current from the patient back to the ESU.

Current: A movement of electrons analogous to the flow of a stream of water.

Direct coupling: The contact of an energized metal active electrode tip with another metal instrument or object within the surgical field.

Dispersive electrode: The accessory that directs electrical current flow from the patient back to the electrosurgical generator—often called the patient plate, return electrode, inactive electrode, or grounding pad.

Electrosurgery: The cutting and coagulation of body tissue with a high frequency (ie, radio frequency) current.

Electrosurgical accessories: For the purposes of this document, electrosurgical accessories are defined as the active electrode with tip(s), dispersive electrode, adapters, and connectors to attach these devices to the generator.

Electrosurgical unit: For the purposes of this document, the ESU includes the generator that produces the high frequency current waveform that is delivered to tissues, the foot switch with cord (if applicable), the electrical plug, cord, and connections.

Eschar: Charred tissue residue.

Generator: The machine that produces radio frequency waves (eg, ESU, power unit).

Ground-referenced electrosurgical unit: A system in which electrical current is sent to the patient and follows the path of least resistance back to the ground. This technology, which no longer is manufactured, produces high frequency, high voltage current and sometimes is referred to as a "spark gap" unit.

Insulator: A material that does not conduct electricity.

Insulation failure: Damage to the insulation of the active electrode that provides an alternate pathway for the current to leave that electrode as it completes the circuit to the dispersive electrode.

Isolated electrosurgical unit: A system in which electrical current is sent to the patient and selectively returns and is grounded through the generator.

Monopolar electrosurgery: Electrosurgery in which only the active electrode is in the surgical wound, and the electrical current is directed through the patient's body, received by the dispersive pad, and transferred back to the generator, completing the monopolar circuit.

Oxygen-enriched environment: Atmosphere containing more than 23% oxygen, frequently occurring in the oropharynx, trachea, lower respiratory tract, and near the head and neck during administration of oxygen to the patient.

Return electrode contact quality monitoring: A dynamic monitoring circuit measuring impedance of the dispersive return electrode. If the dispersive electrode becomes compromised, the circuit inhibits the ESU's output.

Ultrasonic scalpel: A cutting/coagulation device that converts electrical energy into mechanical energy, providing a rapid ultrasonic motion.

Vessel sealing device: Bipolar technology that fuses collagen and elastin in the vessel walls and permanently obliterates the lumen of the vessel.

REFERENCES

1. "Electrosurgery," (Operating Room Risk Management) *ECRI* (January 1999) 7.

2. "Electrosurgical units," *Health Devices* 27 (March 1998) 93-96.

3. ANSI/AAMI, "Electrosurgical devices," HF18: 2001, 1-26.

4. R C Odell, "Pearls, pitfalls, and advancements in the delivery of electrosurgical energy during laparoscopy," *Problems in General Surgery* 19 no 2 (2002) 5-17.

5. "Laparoscopic electrosurgery risks," (Operating Room Risk Management) *ECRI* (May 1999) 1-11.

6. "Guidance section: Ensuring monopolar electrosurgical safety during laparoscopy," *Health Devices* 24 (January 1995) 20-27.

7. J T Bischoff et al, "Laparoscopic bowel injury: Incidence and clinical presentation," *The Journal of Urology* 161 (March 1999) 888-890.

8. B J Carroll, M Birth, E H Phillips, "Common bile duct injuries during laparoscopic cholecystectomy that result in litigation," *Surgical Endoscopy* 12 (April 1998) 310-314.

9. K A Kern, "Malpractice litigation involving laparoscopic cholecystectomy: Cost, cause, and consequences," *Archives of Surgery* 132 (April 1997) 392-398.

10. R D Tucker, C E Platz, S K Landas, "A laparoscopic complication? A medical legal case analysis. Part I," *Journal of Gynecologic Surgery* 11 no 2 (1995) 113-121.

11. M P Wu et al, "Complications and recommended practices for electrosurgery in laparoscopy," *The American Journal of Surgery* 179 (January 2000) 67-73.

12. *Laparoscopic Injury Study* (Rockville, Md: Physician Insurers Association of America, August 2000) 1-5.

13. "Evaluation of electroscope electroshield system," (Guidance Article) *Health Devices* 24 (January 1995) 11-19.

14. V Dennis, "Implementing active electrode monitoring: A perioperative call," *Surgical Services Management* 7 (April 2001) 32-38.

15. R D Tucker, C R Voyles, S E Silvis, "Capacitive coupled stray currents during laparoscopic and endoscopic electrosurgical procedures," *Biomedical Instrumentation and Technology* 26 (July/August 1992) 303-311.

16. T G Vancaillie, "Active electrode monitoring: How to prevent unintentional thermal injury associated with monopolar electrosurgery at laparoscopy," *Surgical Endoscopy* 12 (August 1998) 1009-1012.

17. C R Voyles, R D Tucker, "Education and engineering solutions for potential problems with laparoscopic monopolar electrosurgery," *The American Journal of Surgery* 164 (July 1992) 56-62.

18. "Burns and fires from electrosurgical active electrodes," (Hazard Update) *Health Devices* 22 (August-September 1993) 421-422.

19. "Fires in the operating room," (Healthcare Hazard Control) *ECRI* (February 2003) 1-10.

20. "Misconnection of bipolar electrosurgical electrodes," (Hazard Report) *Health Devices* 24 (January 1995) 34-35.

21. National Fire Protection Association, *NFPA 99: Standard for Health Care Facilities*, sec D.5.2.1 (Quincy, Mass: NFPA International, 2002) 200.

22. T L Smith, J M Smith, "Electrosurgery in otolaryngology-head and neck surgery: Principles, advances, and complications," *The Laryngoscope* 111 (May 2001) 769-780.

23. National Fire Protection Association, *NFPA 99: Standard for Health Care Facilities*, sec D.5.2.5 (Quincy, Mass: NFPA International, 2002) 200.

24. National Fire Protection Association, *NFPA 99: Standard for Health Care Facilities*, sec D.5.2.3 (Quincy, Mass: NFPA International, 2002) 200.

25. National Fire Protection Association, *NFPA 99: Standard for Health Care Facilities*, sec D.7.3 (Quincy, Mass: NFPA International, 2002) 203.

26. National Fire Protection Association, *NFPA 99: Standard for Health Care Facilities*, sec D.5.3.1 (Quincy, Mass: NFPA International, 2002) 200.

27. National Fire Protection Association, *NFPA 99: Standard for Health Care Facilities*, sec D.5.3.3 (Quincy, Mass: NFPA International, 2002) 200.

28. "Electrosurgery checklist," (Operating Room Risk Management) *ECRI* (January 1999) 1.

29. Joint Commission on Accreditation of Health Care Organizations, *2003 Hospital Accreditation Standards*, section EC.2.10.3 (Oakbrook Terrace, Ill: Joint Commission Resources, 2003) 236.

30. "ESU burns from poor dispersive electrode site preparation," (Hazard Update) *Health Devices* 22 (August-September 1993) 423.

31. "Recommended practices for endoscopic minimally invasive surgery," in *Standards, Recommended Practices and Guidelines* (Denver: AORN, Inc, 2004) 267-271.

32. National Fire Protection Association, *NFPA 99: Standard for Health Care Facilities*, sec C.13.1.3.2.2 (Quincy, Mass: NFPA International, 2002) 182.

33. T D Datta, "Flash fire hazard with eye ointment," (Letters to the Editor) *Anesthesia and Analgesia* 63 (July 1984) 700-701.

34. "The patient is on fire! A surgical fires primer," (Guidance) *Health Devices* 21(January 1992) 19-34.

35. "Medical devices: Reclassification of polymethylmethacrylate (PMMA) bone cement," *Federal Register* 67 (July 17, 2002) 46852-46855.

36. MAUDE database (Feb 2, 2000), 9610726-2000-00003; (Aug 30, 2002), 435173 (Washington, DC: Center for Devices and Radiological Health).

37. S J Barker, J S Polson, "Fire in the operating room: A case report and laboratory study," *Anesthesia and Analgesia* 93 (October 2001) 960-965.

38. "Fire hazard created by the misuse of DuraPrep solution," (Hazard Report) *Health Devices* 27 (November 1998) 400-401.

39. MAUDE database (July 31, 1995), 32071; (Sept 12, 1997) 119838; (March 21 2002), 384493; (April 15, 2002), 1720159-2002-00032 (Washington, DC: Center for Devices and Radiological Health).

40. "Fire caused by improper disposal of electrocautery units," (Hazard Report) *Health Devices* 23 (March 1994) 98.

41. "Alternate-site burns from improperly seated electrosurgical pencil active electrodes," (Hazard Report) *Health Devices* 29 (January 2000) 24-27.

42. "Ignition of debris on active electrosurgical electrodes," (Hazard Report) *Health Devices* 27 (September-October 1998) 367-370.

43. Center for Devices and Radiological Health, MAUDE database (May 7, 2002), 393590.

44. MAUDE database (Aug 23, 2002), 441523 (Washington, DC: Center for Devices and Radiological Health).

45. R A Ortega, "A rare cause of fire in the operating room," *Anesthesiology* 89 (December 1998) 1608.

46. D K Wood, R Hollis, "Thermal cautery causes a gauze pad fire," (Letters) *JAMA* 270 (Nov 17, 1993) 2299-2300.

47. Y Y Bonnet et al, "Explosion of intestinal gas during surgery," *Annales Francaises d'Anesthesie et de Reanimation* 2 no 6 (1983) 431-435.

48. E Gross, O Jurim, M Krausz, "Diathermy-induced gas explosion in the intestinal tract," *Harefuah* 123 no 1-2 (1992) 12-13, 71-72.

49. F S Joyce, T N Rasmussen, "Gas explosion during diathermy gastrotomy," *Gastroenterology* 96 (February 1989) 530-531.

50. E B Soussan et al, "Bowel explosion with colonic perforation during argon plasma coagulation for hemorrhagic radiation-induced proctitis," *Gastrointestinal Endoscopy* 57 (March 2003) 412-413.

51. E Zinsser, et al "Bowel gas explosion during argon beam coagulation," (Unusual Cases and Technical Notes) *Endoscopy* 31 (May 1999) S26.

52. "Electrosurgical airway fires still a hot topic," *Health Devices* 25 (July 1996) 260-261.

53. J A Bennett, M Agree, "Fire in the chest," *Anesthesia and Analgesia* 78 (February 1984) 406.

54. "$40 million sought after electrosurgery burn death," *Biomedical Safety and Standards* 15 (December 1995) 170.

55. W K Chee, J L Benumof, "Airway fire during tracheostomy: Extubation may be contraindicated," *Anesthesiology* 89 (December 1998) 1576-1578.

56. R J Greco et al, "Potential dangers of oxygen supplementation during facial surgery," *Plastic Reconstructive Surgery* 95 (May 1995) 978-984.

57. M J Lucarelli, B N Lemke, "Monopolar electrosurgical flash fire," *Ophthalmic Surgery and Lasers* 29 (March 1998) 249-250.

58. K F Mattucci, C J Militana, "The prevention of fire during oropharyngeal electrosurgery," *Ear, Nose and Throat Journal* 82 (February 2003) 107-109.

59. A M J Michels, S Stott, "Explosion of tracheal tube during tracheostomy," (Correspondence) *Anaesthesia* 49 (December 1994) 1104.

60. R J Reyes et al, "Supplemental oxygen: Ensuring its safe delivery during facial surgery," *Plastic and Reconstructive Surgery* 95 (April 1995) 924-928.

61. J W Thompson et al, "Fire in the operating room during tracheostomy," *Southern Medical Journal* 91 (March 1998) 243-247.

62. E S Wegrzynowicz et al, "Airway fire during jet ventilation for laser excision of vocal cord papillomata," (Case Reports) *Anesthesiology* 76 (March 1992) 468-469.

63. P T J Wilson, U Igbaseimokumo, J Martin, "Ignition of the tracheal tube during tracheostomy," (Correspondence) *Anaesthesia* 49 (August 1994), 734-735.

64. "Skin burns resulting from the use of electrolyte distention/irrigation media during electrosurgery with a rollerblation electrode," (Hazard Report) *Health Devices* 27 (June 1998) 233-235.

65. MAUDE database (Oct 9, 2002), 421908 (Washington, DC: Center for Devices and Radiological Health).

66. National Fire Protection Association, *NFPA 99: Standard for Health Care Facilities*, sec C.13.4.43.4 (Quincy, Mass: NFPA International, 2002) 186.

67. MAUDE database (March 31, 2003) 2110898-2003-00006 (Washington DC: Center for Devices and Radiological Health). Also available at *http://www.accessdata.fda.gov/scripts/cdrh/cfdocs/cfMAUDE/Detail.cfm?MDRFOI__ID=474982* (accessed 24 Sept, 2004).

68. MAUDE database (March 31, 2004) 2110898-2004-00006 (Washington DC: Center for Devices and Radiological Health). Also available at *http://www.accessdata.fda.gov/scripts/cdrh/cfdocs/cfMAUDE/Detail.CFM?MDRFOI__ID=523194* (accessed 24 Sept 2004).

69. M Vahlensieck, "Tattoo-related cutaneous inflammation (burn grade I) in a mid-field MR scanner," (Letters to the Editor) *European Radiology* 10 (January 2000) 197.

70. W A Wagle, M Smith, "Tattoo-induced skin burn during MR imaging," (On the AJR Viewbox) *American Journal of Roentgenology* 174 (June 2000) 1795.

71. MAUDE database (October 15, 2003) 2110898-2003-00016 (Washington DC: Center for Devices and Radiological Health). Also available at *http://www.accessdata.fda.gov/scripts/cdrh/cfdocs/cfMAUDE/Detail.cfm?MDRFOI__ID=495428* (accessed 24 Sept 2004).

72. MAUDE database (November 25, 2003) 1643264-2003-00066 (Washington, DC: Center for Devices and Radiological Health). Also available at *http://www.accessdata.fda.gov/scripts/cdrh/cfdocs/cfMAUDE/Detail.cfm?MDRFOI__ID=499965* (accessed 24 Sept 2004).

73. MAUDE database (February 16, 2004) 2110898-2004-00004 (Washington DC: Center for Devices and Radiological Health). Also available at *http://www.accessdata.fda.gov/scripts/cdrh/cfdocs/cfMAUDE/Detail.cfm?MDRFOI__ID=516905* (accessed 24 Sept 2004).

74. "Skin lesions from aggressive adhesive on electrosurgical return electrode pads," *Health Devices* 24 (April 1995) 159-161.

75. MAUDE database (June 24, 2002), 401617 (Washington, DC: Center for Devices and Radiological Health).

76. "MegaDyne Mega 2000 return electrode," *Health Devices* 29 (December 2000) 445-460.

77. MAUDE database (May 16, 2002), 396295; (July 6, 2002), 286226 (Washington, DC: Center for Devices and Radiological Health).

78. "Allowing patients to wear jewelry during surgical (and electrosurgical) procedures," *Health Devices* 26 (November 1997) 441-443.

79. G J Harrell, D R Kopps, "Minimizing patient risk during laparoscopic electrosurgery," *AORN Journal* 67 (June 1998) 1194-1205.

80. T G Vancaillie, "Electrosurgery at laparoscopy: Guidelines to avoid complications," *Gynaecological Endoscopy* 3 (1994) 143-150.

81. P D Willson et al, "Port site electrosurgical (diathermy) burns during surgical laparoscopy," *Surgical Endoscopy* 11 (June 1997) 653-654.

82. P E Greilich, N B Greilich, E G Froelich, "Intraabdominal fire during laparoscopic cholecystectomy," *Anesthesiology* 83 (October 1995) 871-874.

83. J L Atlee, A D Bernstein, "Cardiac rhythm management devices (Part II): Perioperative management," *Anesthesiology* 95 (December 2001) 1492-1506.

84. M A Rozner, R J Nishman, "Electrocautery-induced pacemaker tachycardia: Why does this error continue?" (Correspondence) *Anesthesiology* 96 (March 2002) 773-774.

85. "Electrosurgery on patients with implantable cardioverter-defibrillators,"(Talk to the Specialist) *Health Devices* 31 (February 2002) 74.

86. National Fire Protection Association, *NFPA 99: Standard for Health Care Facilities*, sec D.6.7.3 (Quincy, Mass: NFPA International, 2002) 202.

87. S D McCarus, "Physiologic mechanisms of the ultrasonically activated scalpel," *The Journal of American Association of Gynecologic Laparoscopists* 3 (August 1996) 601-608.

88. D E Ott, E Moss, K Martinez, "Aerosol exposure from an ultrasonically activated (harmonic) device," *Journal of American Association of Gynecologic Laparoscopists* 5 (February 1998) 29-32.

89. K Matthews, "Argon beam coagulation: New directions in surgery," *AORN Journal* 56 (November 1992) 885-896.

90. "Risk analysis: Argon-enhanced coagulation," (Hospital Risk Control) *ECRI* (January 1991) 1-3.

91. N Stojeba et al, "Possible venous argon gas embolism complicating argon gas enhanced coagulation during liver surgery," *Acta Anaesthesiologica Scandinavica* 43 (September 1999) 866-867.

92. F Veyckemans, I Michel, "Venous gas embolism from an argon coagulator," *Anesthesiology* 85 (August 1996) 443-444.

93. "Fatal gas embolism caused by overpressurization during laparoscopic use of argon enhanced coagulation," (Hazard Report) *Health Devices* 23 (June 1994) 257-259.

94. "Control of smoke from laser/electric surgical procedures," DHHS (NIOSH) publication 96-128 (Atlanta: National Institute for Occupational Safety and Health, September 1996).

95. "Laser/electrosurgery plume," US Department of Labor, Occupational Safety and Health Administration (Feb 13, 2002), *http://www.osha.gov/SLTC/laserelectrosurgeryplume* (accessed 25 April 2003).

96. "Recommended practices for product selection in perioperative practice settings," in *Standards, Recommended Practices, and Guidelines* (Denver: AORN, Inc, 2004) 347-350.

97. "Medical device reporting: Manufacturer reporting, importer reporting, user facility reporting, distributor reporting," *Federal Register* 65 (Jan 26, 2000) 4112-4121.

98. "Quality and performance improvement standards for perioperative nursing," in *Standards, Recommended Practices, and Guidelines* (Denver: AORN, Inc, 2004) 187-196.

Originally published March 1985, *AORN Journal*. Revised April 1991; revised July 1993.

Revised November 1997; published January 1998, *AORN Journal*. Reformatted July 2000.

Revised November 2003; published February 2004, *AORN Journal*.

Revised November 2004; published in *Standards, Recommended Practices, and Guidelines*, 2005 edition. Reprinted March 2005, *AORN Journal*.

AORN Perioperative Standards and Recommended Practices, 2009 Edition

Recommended Practices for Endoscopic Minimally Invasive Surgery

The following recommended practices were developed by the AORN Recommended Practices Committee and have been approved by the AORN Board of Directors. They were presented as proposed recommended practices for comment to members and others. These recommended practices are effective January 1, 2005.

These recommended practices are intended as achievable recommendations representing what is believed to be an optimal level of practice. Policies and procedures will reflect variations in practice settings or clinical situations that determine the degree to which the recommended practices can be implemented.

AORN recognizes the numerous types of settings in which perioperative nurses practice. These recommended practices are intended to provide guidance for various practice settings. These practice settings include traditional operating rooms, ambulatory surgery units, physicians' offices, cardiac catheterization suites, endoscopy suites, radiology departments, and all other areas where operative and other invasive procedures may be performed.

Purpose

Endoscopic minimally invasive surgery (MIS) has evolved from a diagnostic modality to a widespread surgical technique. This evolution occurred in response to the reported benefits of endoscopic surgery compared to the benefits of conventional surgical procedures for patients. These recommended practices provide guidance to help perioperative personnel reduce risks to patients during endoscopic surgery. Benefits to the patient include reduced pain, faster healing, decreased length of hospital stay, and quicker return to normal life. The primary benefit to the hospital is financial, resulting from the decreased length of stay.

The perioperative nursing vocabulary is a clinically relevant and empirically validated standardized language. This standardized language consists of the Perioperative Nursing Data Set (PNDS) and includes perioperative nursing diagnoses, interventions, and outcomes. The expected outcomes of primary import to these recommended practices fall into two categories: freedom from injury during the perioperative period and maintenance/improvement of baseline physiological status. Specifics will be found in the documentation section.

Recommendation I

Potential patient injuries and complications associated with endoscopic MIS should be identified, and practices that reduce the risk of injuries and complications should be established.

1. The perioperative nurse should understand the goals and objectives of endoscopic MIS. Nursing knowledge, technological skills, and a thorough preoperative patient assessment provide the basis for establishing an appropriate plan of care for a patient undergoing endoscopic surgery.[1]

2. Patient monitoring during laparoscopic procedures should include measurement of the patient's
   - electrocardiogram,
   - end tidal carbon dioxide (CO_2),
   - noninvasive blood pressure,
   - oxygen saturation, and
   - temperature.

   Although endoscopic procedures are minimally invasive, using CO_2 for insufflation increases the risk of hypercarbia, subcutaneous emphysema, pulmonary embolism, pneumoscrotum, and hypothermia. End tidal CO_2 is closely monitored to detect the onset of hypercarbia, and the patient is observed for subcutaneous emphysema.[2] Carbon dioxide insufflation is one cause of hypothermia and is one contributing factor to thermal loss, along with irrigation, room temperature, exposed body surface, procedure length, and patient age and medical condition. The higher the flow of the CO_2, the lower the temperature of the gas,[3] but the incidence of hypothermia during endoscopic surgery has been reported to be similar to that of open surgery.[4,5] Additionally, endoscopic surgery presents a risk of limited visibility, which may result in undetected and uncontrolled bleeding.[6]

3. Specific positioning devices should be provided to secure the patient and provide safety in accordance with AORN's "Recommended practices for positioning the patient in the perioperative practice setting."[7] Exaggerated positioning may be used during endoscopic surgery to displace intracavity organs or enhance visibility for the surgical team. Positioning devices should be readily available before the patient is moved onto the OR bed.

---

4. Patients undergoing endoscopic procedures should be prepped and draped for an open procedure when applicable. It may be necessary to convert to an open procedure at any time. Prior preparation reduces anesthesia time and increases OR efficiency.[8] Prior preparation will facilitate conversion to an open procedure should that become necessary.[8] Instruments and supplies for an open procedure should be readily available. When it is necessary to convert to an open procedure, the conversion should be accomplished efficaciously.

5. Instruments that enter sterile body cavities are classified as critical items and should be sterile when used.[9] Endoscopes and endoscopic instruments (eg, biopsy forceps, graspers) used for endoscopic surgery should be processed according to AORN's "Recommended practices for cleaning and processing endoscopes and endoscope accessories."[10] Endoscopes and accessories to be sterilized should be packaged before sterilization or be processed immediately before use.

6. Illuminated endoscopic light cords should not be allowed to remain in contact with drapes, patients' skin, personnel's skin, or any flammable material. The heat from light cords or endoscopes may cause drapes to burn. Turning off light sources when they are not in use and holding cords away from drapes or placing them on a moist towel helps prevent burns and fire.[11] Complete all cable connections before activating the source. Place the source on standby when disconnecting cables. Drape the patient only when all flammable prep solutions have fully dried.[12]

7. In practice settings where technology for sterilization of endoscopes is not available, endoscopes and other heat-sensitive items should receive high-level disinfection immediately before each use. Refer to AORN's "Recommended practices for cleaning and processing endoscopes and endoscope accessories" for appropriate protocols.[10] The availability and use of disinfectants in the health care field is dynamic, and manufacturers' recommendations should be followed. As newer disinfectants become available, selection should be guided by information in the scientific literature.

Recommendation II

Potential patient injuries and complications associated with the distention media used during endoscopic MIS should be identified, and practices that reduce the risk of injuries and complications should be established.

1. The perioperative nurse should demonstrate competence in CO_2 insufflation and management of its risks.
   - Carbon dioxide is the most commonly used insufflation gas because it is readily absorbed by the body and excreted by the lungs, does not support combustion, and is commonly available.[13]
   - Carbon dioxide insufflators should be filtered with a single-use hydrophobic filter that is compatible with the insufflator and impervious to fluids. A hydrophobic filter helps prevent gas cylinder contaminants from flowing through the insufflator into the surgical cavity, prevents backflow of abdominal fluids and particulates that could contaminate the insufflator, and prevents cross contamination. When the filter is compatible with the insufflator, it does not interfere with flow rate. The flow of contaminants occurs more readily when the volume of remaining gas in the cylinder is low. Replacing the primary cylinder before the gas level is low helps prevent contamination of the sterile field by particulate matter.[13] Cylinders with nonferrous internal surfaces and surfaces incapable of creating residual material that could escape during the gaseous phase of delivery may be helpful in preventing the transfer of particulate matter.
   - The cylinder should be checked to verify that the gas is CO_2. Only medical grade CO_2 should be used.
   - The CO_2 cylinder should be replaced as needed. A second CO_2 cylinder should be readily available for each procedure. Methods of monitoring the level of remaining gas in the cylinder include
     - observing the insufflator gas cylinder gauge level,
     - monitoring the refill history, and
     - tracking cylinder use.

- The insufflator should be elevated above the level of the surgical cavity. Insufflator pressures should be monitored throughout the procedure, and the insufflator tubing should be disconnected from the trocar cannula before personnel deactivate the insufflator. When the pressure on the patient side is higher than at the insufflator connecting point, body fluid or gas is allowed to flow up the trocar cannula through the insufflation tubing and into the insufflator. This may result in cross contamination or damage to the insufflating device.[13]

- The insufflator and insufflation tubing should be flushed with gas before personnel connect the tubing to the cannula (eg, Verres needle). Flushing removes residual air from tubing, reducing the risk of air embolism. It also determines whether residues are present inside the insufflator.[13]

2. The perioperative nurse should demonstrate competence in fluid insufflation and management of its risks.

- Resectoscopes have been used for urologic procedures for many years. Since the 1950s, glycine 1.5% has been used as a cavity-distention medium for urologic procedures, primarily transurethral resection of the prostate (TURP), in which the resectoscope is used.[14] A complication sometimes observed with the use of glycine is TURP syndrome, which is caused by excessive absorption of the irrigating solution. Exposed blood vessels from tissue removal and elevated pressure being applied to the distention fluid enables intravasation (ie, distention fluid flows into the vascular system).[14,15] Physiological outcomes that can result from excessive fluid absorption include
  - cardiac overload,
  - cerebral edema,
  - dilutional hyponatremia, and
  - water intoxication.[14,16]

  Comparable symptoms can occur in women undergoing hysteroscopic surgery with distention fluids.

- Some gynecological procedures resect or ablate abnormal tissue using cutting or coagulating monopolar current. Procedures might include
  - endometrial ablation,
  - evaluation of infertility,
  - intrauterine assessment,
  - removal of intrauterine fibroids, and
  - removal of polyps.

  Cavity distention, often with irrigating fluids, provides a broader visual field. Irrigation fluids help clear the field of blood and debris.[17] Only electrically inert (ie, nonconductive), near-isotonic solutions should be used for uterine irrigation when monopolar electrosurgical current is used. Instead of energy being focused on the tissue, conductive solutions diffuse the energy, resulting in decreased tissue effect.

- Perioperative nurses should implement safety measures to minimize fluid-related patient complications during hysteroscopy procedures.

  Selection of distention fluid. When electrosurgical energy is to be used, only non-conductive, salt-free solutions should be used.[11] Media for cavity distention include
  - CO_2 gas;
  - dextran 70;
  - glycine;
  - isotonic electrolytic solution (eg, normal saline, Ringer's lactate);
  - mannitol;
  - sorbitol; and
  - water.

  Fluid deficit monitoring. Fluid deficit is the difference between the volume of fluid infused and the volume recovered.[18] This deficit should be monitored to determine how much fluid is being absorbed by the patient (ie, fluid intravasation). Dilutional hyponatremia is associated with intravasation. Rapid influx of hypotonic fluid increases circulation of free water and reduces the extracellular sodium concentration.[19] As a general rule, serum sodium falls 10 millimoles per L for every liter of hypotonic fluid absorbed.[19] The critical volume of intravasation before symptoms are exhibited is not predictable.[20] The American Association of Gynecological Laparoscopists suggests that 750 mL of fluid absorption implies impending excessive intravasation and completion of the procedure should be planned.[21] Fluid deficit amount should be reported to the anesthesia care provider and surgeon at regular intervals during the procedure.

Fluid pressure monitoring and control. The ideal pressure at which fluid is delivered to the cavity is believed to be at or below the patient's mean arterial pressure.[18] There are four basic types of fluid delivery/monitoring systems.

- Gravity-fed systems deliver fluid at a rate and pressure dependent on the difference between height of the bag and the OR bed, the inner bore of the tubing, how tightly the endoscope sheath fits into the cavity, and the aperture of the outflow valve.[17]
- Automated gravitational systems maintain pressure and outflow control.
- Automated pressure systems deliver fluid at a constant pressure and release return flow when the internal pressure reaches a specified level.
- Automated roller pump systems measure fluid inflow by counting rotations on a pump roller or deliver fluid at a constant, pressure-regulated flow rate maintained by a pressure transducer. Fluid is extracted by a self-contained vacuum system. Fluid deficit is calculated on weight of the fluid infused versus the weight of the fluid returned.[18]

Procedure length. Fluid absorption increases with increased length of the procedure. Safe completion of procedures in an expedient manner (ie, one hour or less) can help limit complications from fluid absorption. Complications from fluid overload are less likely to occur and postoperative recovery time may be decreased with shorter anesthetic and procedure times.[18]

Recommendation III

Potential patient injuries and complications associated with electrosurgery used during endoscopic MIS should be identified, and practices that reduce the risk of injuries and complications should be established.

1. Perioperative team members should continuously monitor the functioning of equipment and the integrity of endoscopic instruments to ensure that hazards are minimized. Electrosurgical injuries are caused by insulation failure, direct coupling of current, and capacitive coupling. Equipment should be used according to manufacturers' written instructions. Perioperative team members should continuously monitor the functioning of equipment and the integrity of endoscopic instruments to ensure that hazards are minimized.

- Insulation failure of the laparoscopic active electrode can be caused by trauma during reprocessing and provides an alternate pathway for the current to leave the electrode. Current leaves the electrode at the point of insulation failure as opposed to the tip of the electrode as intended. This can cause significant tissue damage and serious patient injury, particularly when the injury is internal and not immediately recognized. Routine visual inspection may reveal small cracks or mechanical damage. Use of disposable devices will not guarantee elimination of insulation failure because the quality of the insulation material may be less than that of a reusable item.[22]
- Direct coupling is caused by touching the active electrode to an anatomic structure other than the one intended. Three potential problems arise from direct coupling.
  - Metal-to-metal sparking can cause necrosis of underlying tissue.
  - Metal-to-metal sparking can cause frequency demodulation. The demodulated current results in lower frequency, which can result in neuromuscular stimulation noted by muscular twitching.
  - Metal-to-metal sparking may cause current flow to unintended sites. The density of the current determines the amount of tissue damage. A large point of contact will have low current density, and no tissue damage would be expected. A small point of contact will have high current density, and significant tissue damage is possible.[23]
- Capacitive coupling is caused by stray currents being transferred from one conductor to another with no insulation break. This occurs when magnetic fields are produced around the current-carrying, active electrode. When radio-frequency currents flow through an electrode, the flow may initiate stray currents onto other nearby conductors even though the insulation on the electrode and its wires are intact. Three common equipment arrangements may lead to significant amounts of stray current causing capacitive coupling.

– Active electrodes are placed through metal cannulae.

– Active electrodes are housed through operative laparoscopes.

– Active electrodes are used through metal suction irrigators.[24]

Capacitive-coupled, radio-frequency currents may cause undetected burns to nearby structures outside the endoscope's viewing area. Alternative-site burns can be severe and may damage tissue. These burns are particularly dangerous to hollow organs and may lead to undetected perforation with subsequent infection and possible death.[25] Use of active electrode monitoring devices minimizes the risk of undetected insulation failure, direct coupling, and capacitive coupling.

2. Electrical cords and plugs should be handled in a manner that minimizes the potential for damage and subsequent patient injuries. Equipment should be placed near the sterile field, with cords reaching the wall or column outlet without stress on a cord or blocking a traffic path. Stress on cords may cause damage to the cord, posing an electrical hazard. Cords should be free of kinks, knots, and bends that could damage the cord or cause leakage, current accumulation, and overheating of the cord's insulation. The internal parts of the connectors should be inspected for the appearance of shiny metal. If the presence of char debris is noted, the cord should be removed from use. Cords should be kept away from fluids. Fluids dripping onto the cord or connections cause electrical hazards.

Recommendation IV

Reusable endoscopic instruments should be processed according to AORN's recommended practices using methods that reduce the risk of personnel injury.

1. Perioperative personnel involved with endoscopic procedures should practice according to AORN's "Recommended practices for standard and transmission-based precautions in the perioperative practice setting."[26] Endoscopic surgery is referred to as *minimally invasive*. This terminology may lead to a false sense of security when considering potential hazards. This false

sense of security may result in a less diligent use of standard precautions. Those performing the procedure and those who clean and process instruments and accessory equipment should wear personal protective equipment (PPE).[27]

2. Endoscopic surgery should be performed in a manner that minimizes perioperative personnel's exposure to blood and body fluids, droplets, noxious fumes, gases, or smoke. Smoke and laser plume should be evacuated throughout the procedure with appropriate smoke evacuation equipment. The release of gas, electrosurgical smoke, and laser plume during endoscopic surgery may expose surgical team members to blood products, fluid, and cellular debris. Smoke evacuation systems provide protection and reduce the risk of exposure to potentially infectious or toxic agents. Spontaneous sparking may result if electrosurgical smoke is allowed to accumulate in large amounts. AORN's "Recommended practices for electrosurgery"[28] and "Recommended practices for laser safety in practice settings"[29] should be used when selecting a smoke evacuation system.

3. Cleaning methods should minimize splashing, spraying, splattering, and droplet generation to minimize risk of exposure to blood or body fluids. Using standard precautions (eg, wearing gowns, gloves, goggles or face shields) helps protect employees. Standard precautions should include use of protective barriers or PPE, such as

♦ eye protection (eg, face shields, goggles, glasses with side shields);

♦ gowns; and

♦ intact gloves.

Leg coverings, shoe covers, and other PPE may be used when indicated. Exposure to potentially infectious material is reduced by use of these products.

4. Disposable, reusable, and reposable instruments should be used according to manufacturers' recommendations. To ensure that the device is assembled correctly and will perform as intended after processing and reassembly, manufacturers' recommendations should include clear, understandable instructions for processing that include guidelines for

♦ assembly and disassembly,
♦ cleaning,
♦ routine user testing, and
♦ sterilization.

Products should not be purchased or used unless such information is provided.

Manufacturers are required by the US Food and Drug Administration to supply detailed instructions for processing reusables. Reposable instruments have a reusable component and a single-use or limited-use component. Adhering to AORN's "Recommended practices for cleaning and caring for surgical instruments and powered equipment"[30] and "Recommended practices for cleaning and processing endoscopes and endoscope accessories."[10] will minimize the risk of personnel injury associated with cleaning endoscopes and related equipment.

5. Sharps should be handled, processed, and stored in a manner that reduces the risk of injury to employees. Transporting reusable sharp instruments in containers that allow instrument handles to be immediately accessible to staff members minimizes risk of injury. Disposing of singe-use sharp instruments as regulated medical waste complies with state and federal guidelines.[27]

Recommendation V

Endoscopic instruments and equipment should meet performance and safety criteria established by the practice setting.

1. Written information regarding safety, testing methods, warranties, maintenance, and inspections for all endoscopic equipment should be obtained from the manufacturer. Endoscopic equipment manuals provide guidelines for developing operating, safety, and maintenance practices. Proper inspection, testing, use, and processing of equipment reduces the risk of adverse outcomes or damage to equipment.[27]

2. Each piece of endoscopic equipment (eg, camera system, monitor, insufflator) should be assigned an identification number. Identification numbers allow for inspections and tracking equipment problems.

3. Monitors should be positioned for good visibility for surgical team members and secured to carts or ceiling mounts. Good visibility is essential for patient care. Securing the monitors prevents injury to patients and personnel as well as equipment damage.[11]

4. All endoscopic equipment, including cameras, light sources, and videocassette recorders (VCRs) should be checked before use. Correct control settings should be labeled on equipment and on a quick reference chart attached to the equipment. When practical, equipment should be standardized so that systems are interchangeable.[11] Standardization of equipment allows for interchangeability in the event of equipment malfunction. To promote patient safety without delays during surgical procedures, all equipment should function correctly.

5. Endoscopic trocars should meet safety criteria established for the practice setting. The most frequent catastrophic patient injury involves trocars. Organ and vessel trauma may occur from excessive use of pressure during trocar insertion. When an all-metal system is used, capacitive current is safely dispersed through the metal anchor and the greater surface area provided by the chest or abdominal wall, thereby reducing current concentration. Metal cannula systems are best for the electrosurgical instrument port.[31] An all-plastic system is another alternative. Using this system, the capacitor is the patient, which minimizes the risk of concentrated capacitive-coupled current.[31] A risk of direct coupling injuries, however, remains. Hybrid trocars (ie, metal trocars with plastic anchors) are not recommended due to the unsafe dispersion of electrical energy.[31,32] Each trocar and cannula can act as an electrical conductor, inducing an electrical current from one to the other. This could result in capacitive-coupling injuries.

6. Fiber-optic light cords or cables should be long enough to reach from the surgical field to the equipment without undue stress. The cord should be inspected for broken light bundles before use. Broken light bundles will diminish the transmission of light and decrease visibility. A backup cord should be available. Tension increases the risk that the cords and fiber-optic cables will become disconnected or break, thereby creating a safety hazard for patients and

personnel. Having sterile backup cords readily available decreases surgical delays.[11]

7. Robotic devices may be used to hold and manipulate the laparoscope under the physician's guidance. The movement is voice activated or is managed by hand-held controls or a foot pedal. The robotic arm maintains the laparoscope in proper orientation, maximizing visualization and providing stable images. The laparoscope attaches to the robotic positioning arm with a magnetic coupling device. A sterile drape covers the arm to maintain a sterile field. The control system allows the operator to move the arm for exact positioning of the laparoscope.[33] All robotic equipment should be checked before use. Problematic issues identified with robotics include, but are not limited to,
   ♦ insufficient white balancing, which can cause the robot to misread the marker;
   ♦ limitation of the surgeon's movement due to positioning of the robotic arm; and
   ♦ a potential for conversion to an open procedure or need for a human camera assistant.[33]

Recommendation VI

Personnel should demonstrate competency in the use of endoscopic surgical equipment in the practice setting.

1. Perioperative personnel should demonstrate competence in the use of endoscopic surgical equipment before use. Instruction and return demonstration in proper usage minimizes the risk of injury and extends the life of the equipment.

2. Perioperative practitioners should be knowledgeable about advancing instrumentation, dissection and hemostasis, computer-assisted technologies (eg, voice recognition software, robotics), and camera technologies that simplify endoscopic MIS and expand its application (**Table 1**). Technology is continually evolving. Ongoing advances will need to be monitored and competencies, including skills validation, updated to reflect those advances.

3. Perioperative practitioners should be knowledgeable about procedural advances that simplify endoscopic MIS and that can expand its application (**Table 2**).

Recommendation VII

Perioperative nursing care for patients experiencing endoscopic MIS should be documented in the patient's record.

1. Documentation should be consistent with AORN's "Recommended practices for documentation of perioperative nursing care."[34]

2. The PNDS[35] should be used when documenting perioperative nursing care. Use of standardized nomenclature will facilitate data capture and analysis for safe, quality patient care. Documentation should include safety parameters implemented during MIS. The following PNDS outcomes are expected to be met with this recommended practice.
   ♦ O2—The patient is free from signs and symptoms of injury caused by extraneous objects.[35 (p85-90)]
   ♦ O4—The patient is free from signs and symptoms of electrical injury.[35 (p94-95)]
   ♦ O10—The patient is free from signs and symptoms of infection.[35 (p105-117)]
   ♦ O13—The patient's fluid, electrolyte, and acid-base balances are consistent with or improved from baseline levels established preoperatively.[35 (p123-127)]

   The PNDS should be referred to for identification of specific nursing diagnoses and nursing interventions.[35]

3. Information about adverse patient outcomes related to endoscopic MIS should be collected and analyzed as part of a facility-wide quality management program. To monitor the quality of patient care and formulate recommendations for changes, it is necessary to maintain a system of evaluation. Quality improvement standards for perioperative nurses that can be used for evaluating endoscopic surgery have been published.[36]

Recommendation VIII

Policies and procedures for endoscopic surgery should be developed, reviewed periodically, and readily available in the practice setting.

Table 1

TECHNOLOGICAL ADVANCES IN ENDOSCOPIC MINIMALLY INVASIVE SURGERY

The use of endoscopic surgery has increased exponentially during the past 10 years. Previously lengthy and difficult procedures now are being performed endoscopically. Advances in instrumentation, dissection and hemostasis techniques, and camera technologies have simplified surgical procedures and expanded application of the minimally invasive surgical approach. Following are examples of some of these advances.

Instrumentation advances

- Optical trocars allow for direct visualization when dissecting through layers of the abdominal wall into the peritoneum.[1]
- Blunt-tipped trocars (eg, open Hasson technique) prevent insufflation leakage. An inflatable balloon on the trocar sheath and a compressed sponge collar form an external seal.[1]
- Converterless trocars eliminate the need for adapters or converters when using different diameter instruments.[1]
- Built-in flush ports clean instruments of blood and debris.[1]
- One-handed control rotation wheels rotate instrument shafts.[1]
- Smaller instruments (eg, 2 mm) allow use of miniscopes.[1]

Dissection and hemostasis advances

- Electrosurgical instruments enhance cutting and hemostatic techniques.
- Ultrasonic energy delivered through a vibrating blade creates friction heat that denatures tissue proteins and forms a coagulum.[1]
- High-pressure fluid streams deflect accurately to cleave tissue planes.[1]
- Warming systems avoid potential hypothermia.[1]
- Tripolar cutting forceps have been developed to grasp, coagulate, and transect tissue using bipolar electrosurgery.[1]
- Argon beam coagulators have been adapted for laparoscopic hemostasis.[1]
- Carbon dioxide lasers are being used for ablation of pulmonary bullae.[2]

- Organ entrapment systems have been developed for removal of organs (ie, a plastic and nylon sack can be introduced, opened, and the organ placed inside for retrieval).[3]
- Morcellation techniques (ie, fragmenting tissue into small pieces that then are suctioned out through the barrel of a morcellator).[3]

Equipment advances

- Laparoscopic smoke evacuation has improved visibility.
- Digital documentation recorders allow procedures to be recorded.
- Digital flat panel monitors provide improved images and more flexibility in mounting positions.
- Robotic endoscope holders and positioners provide stability and improved motor control.
- Voice activation is used to control devices.
- Integrated ORs control the environment through touch-screen technologies.

Camera advances

- High resolution cameras using digital-signal processing and minimum illumination provide a distortion-free image.[1]
- Videotape endoscopes have video chips at the tip, thereby placing the camera in the surgical field.[1]
- Three-dimensional endoscopes offer depth perception to facilitate instrument manipulation and accurate internal structure interpretation.[4]

REFERENCES

1. J A Cadeddu et al, "Advances in laparoscopic instrumentation," Contemporary Urology (October 1997) 14-24.
2. M Benner et al, "Thoracoscopic laser ablation of pulmonary bullae," The Journal of Thoracic and Cardiovascular Surgery 107 (July 1993) 883-890.
3. D A Urban et al "Organ entrapment and renal morcellation: Permeability studies," The Journal of Urology 150 (December 1993) 1792-1794.
4. D H Birkett, L G Josephs, J Este-McDonald, "A new 3-D laparoscope in gastrointestinal surgery," Surgical Endoscopy 8 (December 1994) 1448-1451.

1. These policies and procedure should include, but not be limited to,
   - documentation of identification numbers, settings used, and volume of gas;
   - equipment maintenance programs;
   - guidelines for equipment processing; and
   - staff member competency requirements.

2. These recommended practices should be used as guidelines for developing policies and procedures within the practice setting. Policies and procedures establish authority, responsibility, and accountability and serve as operational guidelines. An introduction to reviewing the policies and procedures should be included in

Table 2

PROCEDURAL ADVANCES IN ENDOSCOPIC MINIMALLY INVASIVE SURGERY (MIS)

Like other technologies, procedural advances in MIS are ongoing. Improved technology, enables an ever-growing cadre of MIS procedures within surgical specialty areas. The following represent some of the advances in various surgical specialties.

General surgery
Procedures include mediastinoscopy, an early entry into the MIS field; laparoscopic cholecystectomy; appendectomy; small bowel resection; bariatric procedures; gastrectomy; splenectomy; hernia repair; Nissen fundoplication; thymectomy; various biopsies; node sampling; and others.
- Carbon dioxide insufflation is the standard for providing visualization of abdominal structures and offering safe pneumoperitoneum.[1]
- Gasless laparoscopic procedures are performed to overcome adverse effects of pneumoperitoneum without altering cardiac function.[1]
- Abdominal walls can be elevated by means of a subcutaneous lifting system of curved blades suspended from a mechanical arm attached to a rigid pillar. The arm then is elevated as far as necessary to obtain optimal exposure.[2]
- Hand-assisted laparoscopic surgery has been introduced for use in laparoscopic-assisted splenectomy and colorectal procedures. The hand can be used as a retractor, dissector, and tactile sensor.[3]

Gynecological surgery
Initially, diagnostic procedures were performed, but with time, surgical procedures were performed, including abdominal wall lifting, gasless procedures, and robotics. Combination approaches blend the use of laparoscopy and vaginal approaches for laparoscopy-assisted hysterectomy.[4]
- Endometrial ablation now is performed via hysteroscopy for menorrhagia.
- In the 1980s, methods were developed including neodimium: yttrium-aluminum-garnet (Nd-YAG) laser ablation, transcervical resection of the endometrium, and rollerball electrocoagulation of the endometrium.[5]
- In the 1990s, techniques improved, including balloon heating, intrauterine instillation of heated saline, endometrial laser thermal therapy using a diode laser, global three-dimensional bipolar ablation, punctual vaporization, photodynamic endometrial ablation, microwave endometrial ablation, radio frequency procedures, menostat, and cryotherapy. Discussion of single methods or comparison of two methods can be found in the literature.[5-8]

Orthopedic surgery
Procedures began as diagnostic and were limited primarily to the knee. Procedures now are both diagnostic and surgical. Shoulder, elbow, and ankle arthroscopy now are commonplace. Less commonly performed are hip and wrist arthroscopy.[9]
- Lasers have been used to shrink stretched capsular tissues of the shoulder. When heated to the appropriate temperature, the tissue contracts.[9]
- Articular tissue also can be replaced by various methods, including abrasion arthroplasty; harvesting the patient's own articular cartilage, growing it, and reinjecting it; and mosaicplasty, which consists of taking cores of bone with articular cartilage attached and impacting them into predrilled holes in arthritic areas.[9]

Ear, nose, and throat surgery
Visualization of the larynx was the first reported procedure. Procedural advances now include tumor removal, polyp removal, encephalocele repair, cerebrospinal fluid leak repair, septal reconstruction, pituitary surgery, and others.[10]
- Equipment advances such as the progression from distally lighted endoscopes, to telescopic rod lens systems, to flexible fiber-optic systems have led to enhanced visualization. Brushings, washings, and biopsies can be taken from the upper lobes of the lungs.[11]
- Microscopically controlled laryngoscopy allows for vocal cord procedures.
- Laser surgery allows for precise excision of lesions of the larynx, trachea, and bronchi.[11]
- Endoscopic sinus procedures relieve sinus obstruction.[10]

Urological surgery
Cystoscopy was the first urologic procedure using MIS. Now, this often is performed as an office procedure. Urological MIS procedures now include endoscopic nephrectomy, hand-assisted nephrectomy, and transperitoneal laparoscopic nephrectomy. Additionally, balloon insufflation has been used as a dissection technique in the upper retroperitoneal space allowing for nephrectomy, tumor nephrectomy, nephropexy, renal cyst marsupialization, and renal biopsy.[12]

Cardiovascular/thoracic surgery
Videotape assistance first was used for closed chest internal mammary artery harvests and congenital heart defect procedures.[13] Videotape-assisted thoracic surgery provides for more complete exploration than traditional mediastinotomy and allows better access for biopsies.

Table 2, *continued*

PROCEDURAL ADVANCES IN ENDOSCOPIC MINIMALLY INVASIVE SURGERY (MIS)

■ Mitral valve replacement has advanced to using videotape-directed, voice-activated, robotically-controlled cameras.[13]

■ Computer-enhanced instrumentation allows for endoscopic coronary artery bypass grafting.[14]

■ The first human laparoscopically-assisted aortobifemoral bypass was completed in 1993. With the development of clamps, forceps, and best approaches, the procedure is performed entirely laparoscopically today.[15]

■ Endoscopic subfascial perforator ligation is performed for chronic venous insufficiency with results similar to open procedures and without the concomitant morbidity and mortality.[16]

Plastic surgery

■ Endoscopically-assisted plastic surgery was introduced in the mid 1980s.[17]

■ Procedures evolving during the 1990s include forehead lifts, full facelifts, corrugator muscle resection, breast augmentation, carpal tunnel release, reconstructive breast surgeries, facial fracture reduction, and various muscle harvesting procedures.[17]

Neurosurgery

■ The earliest reported endoscopic neurosurgery was performed in 1910 when two children were treated for hydrocephalus by endoscopic coagulation of the choroids plexus.[18]

■ By 1960, technological advances allowed for additional endoscopic procedures, such as fenestration, biopsy, partial or total removal of cystic lesions; partial or total removal of tumors; evacuation of intracerebral or subdural hematomas; spinal excision of herniated discs; and carpal tunnel release.[18]

■ Endoscopically-assisted procedures include aneurysm excision and repair, acoustic neuroma removal, and transsphenoidal pituitary surgery.[18]

REFERENCES

1. A Vezakis et al, "Randomized comparison between low-pressure laparoscopic cholecystectomy and gasless laparoscopic cholecystectomy," Surgical Endoscopy 13 (September 1999) 890-893.

2. A Alijani, A Cushier, "Abdominal wall lift systems in laparoscopic surgery: Gasless and low pressure systems," Seminars in Laparoscopic Surgery 8 (March 2001) 53-62.

3. Y Miura et al, "Gasless hand-assisted laparoscopic surgery for colorectal cancer," Diseases of the Colon Rectum 44 (June 2001) 896-898.

4. M Canestrelli et al, "The new techniques of gynaecologic laparoscopy: Gasless, open Hasson, optic trocar," Panminerva Medica 41(December 1999) 371-374.

5. O R Kochli "Endometrial ablation in the year 2000—Do we have more methods than indications?" in Contributions to Gynecology and Obstetrics vol 20 (Basel, Switzerland: Karger, 2000) 90-120.

6. O Taskin et al, "Long-term histopathologic and morphologic changes after thermal endometrial ablation," Journal of the American Association of Gynecologic Laparoscopists 9 (May 2002) 186-190.

7. F D Loffer, "Three-year comparison of thermal balloon and rollerball ablation in treatment of menorrhagia," Journal of the American Association of Gynecologic Laparoscopists 8 (February 2001) 48-54.

8. M Pellicano et al, "Hysteroscopic transcervical endometrial resection versus thermal destruction for menorrhagia: A prospective randomized trial on satisfaction rate," American Journal of Obstetrics and Gynecology 187 (September 2002) 545-550.

9. G K Miller "Operative arthroscopy into the next century," Comprehensive Therapy 24 (August 1998) 383-387.

10. D W Kennedy, M Roth, "Functional endoscopic sinus surgery," in Otorhinolaryngology: Head and Neck Surgery, 15th ed, J J Ballenger, J B Snow, eds (Baltimore: Williams & Wilkins, 1996) 173-181.

11. J B Snow, J A Schild, "Introduction to peroral endoscopy," in Otorhinolaryngology: Head and Neck Surgery, 15 ed, J J Ballenger, J B Snow, eds (Baltimore: Williams & Wilkins, 1996) 1189-1199.

12. J J Rassweiler et al, "Retroperitoneal laparoscopic nephrectomy and other procedures in the upper retroperitoneum using a balloon dissection technique," European Urology 25 (1994) 229-236.

13. W R Chitwood, L W Nifong, "Minimally invasive videoscopic mitral valve surgery: The current role of surgical robotics," Journal of Cardiac Surgery 15 (January/February 2000) 61-75.

14. V Falk et al, "Total endoscopic off-pump coronary artery bypass grafting," The Heart Surgery Forum 3 (February 2000) 29-31.

15. Y M Dion, C R Gracia, O Hartung, "Laparoscopic vascular surgery," in Surgical Laparoscopy, second ed, K A Zucker, ed (Baltimore: Lippincott Williams & Wilkins, 2001) 709-719.

16. W Schum, W S Thomas, "Endoscopic technique for subfascial perforating vein interruption," in Surgical Laparoscopy, second ed, K A Zucker, ed (Baltimore: Lippincott Williams & Wilkins, 2001) 720-726.

17. P Giovanoli, M Frey "The history of endoscopy in plastic and reconstructive surgery up to video assisted microsurgery," in Endoscopy and Microsurgery, M Frey, ed (New York: Springer-Verlag Wein, 2001) 1-4.

18. J Caemaert "Endoscopic neurosurgery," in Operative Neurosurgical Techniques: Indications, Methods, and Results, vol 1, fourth ed, H Schmidek, ed (Philadelphia: WB Saunders, 2000) 535-570.

orientation and ongoing educational sessions to help personnel develop the appropriate knowledge, skills, and attitudes that affect patient care. Policies and procedures also assist in developing quality assurance and improvement activities.

3. Policies and procedures for equipment must be in compliance with the Safe Medical Devices Act (SMDA) of 1990, as well as facility-specific policies and procedures.[37] If patient or personnel injuries or equipment failures occur, the laparoscopic equipment and associated attachments must be handled in accordance with the SMDA. Device identification, maintenance and service information, and adverse event information should be included in the report from the practice setting.[38]

4. Policies and procedures must comply with the Standards of Privacy and Security of the Health Insurance Portability and Accountability Act of 1996 for the protection of health information. In addition, these policies and procedures should take into account applicable state laws, as well as applicable national and professional standards. These policies and procedures should cover not only the disclosure of information but also access to and use of databases, including, but not limited to, digital pictures and patient information. Policies and procedures should be revised as needed to account for any changes or amendments to applicable laws, rules, and standards.[39]

Glossary

Capacitive coupling: Transfer of electrical current from the active electrode through intact insulation to adjacent conductive items (eg, tissue, trocars).

Capacitors: Two conductors separated by an insulator (eg, insulated active electrode, trocar cannula); instrument for storing electricity.

Critical item: Instruments or objects that are introduced directly into the human body, either into or in contact with the blood stream or normally sterile areas of the body; an item that enters sterile tissue or the vascular system.

Demodulation: The operation on a previously modulated wave in such a way that it will have substantially the same characteristics as the original modulating wave.

Dilutional hyponatremia: A decrease in the serum sodium level due to intravasation of fluids, which dilute the soluble components of the serum.

Direct coupling: Touching the laparoscopic active electrode to another surgical field.

Endoscopic minimally invasive surgery (MIS): Surgical techniques that use endoscopic approaches rather than dissection.

High-level disinfection: A process that kills all microorganisms with the exception of high numbers of bacterial spores; using an Environmental Protection Agency-registered agent that kills vegetative bacteria, tubercle bacilli, some spores, fungi, and lipid and non-lipid viruses given appropriate concentration, submersion, and contact time. Manufacturers' recommendations may differ.

Hypertonic: Having a greater osmotic pressure (ie, higher solute concentration) than a reference solution. If a cell is surrounded by a hypotonic solution, osmotic pressure tends to force the water out of the cell, and the cell shrinks.

Hyponatremia: An abnormally low concentration of sodium ions in circulating blood.

Hypotonic: Having a lower osmotic pressure (ie, lower solute concentration) than a reference solution. If a cell is in a hypotonic solution, osmotic pressure tends to force the water into the cell, and the cell swells.

Hydrophobic insufflation filter: An in-line filter that retains a high percentage of particulates greater than a specified size. The hydrophobic media protects against fluid backflow into the insufflation gas.

Hysteroscopy: Endoscopic visualization of the uterine cavity and tubal orifices.

Insufflate: To blow into; to fill any cavity or orifice of the body.

Insufflation: The act or instance of insufflating.

Intravasation: The entrance of foreign material into a blood vessel.

Invasive procedures: Surgical entry into tissues, cavities, or organs.

Light cord: A cable of fiber-optic filaments used to transport light to the surgical field.

Morcellation: The process of fragmenting tissue into small pieces.

Osmole: The standard unit of osmotic pressure; the molecular weight of a solute, in grams, divided by the number of ions or particles into which it dissociates in solution.

Osmosis: The passive movement of fluid through a semipermeable membrane from a region of lower solute concentration to a region of higher solute concentration.

Osmotic pressure: The tendency and rate of water to move across a semipermeable membrane toward a region of higher solute concentration.

Reposable: An instrument that has limited use or an instrument with a combination of reusable and disposable components.

Solute: A dissolved substance suspended within a solution.

Solution: A homogeneous mixture of two or more compounds.

REFERENCES

1. "Standards of perioperative clinical practice," in *Standards, Recommended Practices, and Guidelines* (Denver: AORN, Inc, 2004) 181-183.

2. J L Flowers, K A Zucker, R W Bailey, "Complications," in *Laparoscopic Surgery,* ed G H Ballantyne, P F Leahy, I M Modlin (Philadelphia: WB Saunders, Co, 1994) 78-82.

3. K A Ball, "Surgical modalities," in *Alexander's Care of the Patient in Surgery,* 12th ed, J C Rothrock, D A Smith, D R McEwen, eds (St Louis: Mosby, 2003) 41-96.

4. A J Luck et al, "Core temperature changes during open and laparoscopic colorectal surgery," *Surgical Endoscopy* 13 (May 1999) 480-483.

5. E Berber et al, "Intraoperative thermal regulation in patients undergoing laparoscopic vs open surgical procedures," *Surgical Endoscopy* 15 (March 2001) 281-285.

6. R M Colver, "Laparoscopy: Basic technique, instrumentation, and complications," *Surgical Laparoscopy & Endoscopy* 2 (March 1992) 3540.

7. "Recommended practices for positioning the patient in the perioperative setting," in *Standards, Recommended Practices, and Guidelines* (Denver: AORN, Inc, 2004) 341-346.

8. K A Ball "Implementing and evaluation patient care," in *Endoscopic Surgery* (St Louis: Mosby-Year Book, Inc, 1997) 41-49.

9. W A Rutala, 1994-1996 APIC Guidelines Committee "APIC guideline for selection and use of disinfectants," *American Journal of Infection Control* 24 (August 1996) 313-342.

10. "Recommended practices for cleaning and processing endoscopes and endoscope accessories," in *Standards, Recommended Practices, and Guidelines* (Denver: AORN, Inc, 2004) 261-266.

11. K A Ball "Basic endoscopic equipment," in *Endoscopic Surgery* (St Louis: Mosby-Year Book, Inc, 1997) 111-139.

12. "The patient is on fire! A surgical fires primer," *ECRI Health Devices* 12 (January 1992) 21.

13. "Entry of abdominal fluids into laparoscopic insufflator," *ECRI Health Devices* 21(May 1992) 181.

14. O Istre, "Fluid balance during hysteroscopic surgery," *Current Opinions in Obstetrics and Gynecology* 9 (August 1997) 219-225.

15. R H Harrison, J S Boren, J R Robison, "Dilutional hyponatremic shock: Another concept of the transurethral prostatic resection reaction," *Journal of Urology* 75 (January 1956) 95-110.

16. D Gravenstein "Transurethral resection of the prostrate (TURP) syndrome: A review of the pathophysiology and management," *Anesthesia Annals* 84 (February 1997) 438-446.

17. S L Corson "Hysteroscopic fluid management," *The Journal of the American Association Gynecological Laparoscopists* 4 (May 1997) 375-379.

18. K L Bennett, C Ohrmundt, J A Malone, "Preventing intravasation in women undergoing hysteroscopic procedures," *AORN Journal* 64 (November 1996) 792-799.

19. K B Isaacson, "Complications of hysteroscopy," *Obstetrics and Gynecology Clinics of North America* 26 (March 1999) 39-51.

20. D M Morrison, "Management of hysteroscopic surgery complications," *AORN Journal* 69 (January 1999) 194-209.

21. F D Loffer et al, "Hysteroscopic fluid monitoring guidelines," *The Journal of American Association of Gynecological Laparoscopists* 7 (February 2000) 167-168.

22. R C Odell, "Electrosurgery principles and safety issues," *Clinical Obstetrics and Gynecology* 38 (September 1995) 610-621.

23. S Rohlf, "Electrosurgical safety considerations for minimally invasive surgery," *Minimally Invasive Surgical Nursing* 9 (Spring 1995) 26-29.

24. R D Tucker, C R Voyles, "Laparoscopic electrosurgical complications and their precautions," *AORN Journal* 62 (July 1995) 51-71.

25. W Ming-Ping et al, "Complications and recommended practices for electrosurgery in laparoscopy," *American Journal of Surgery* 179 (January 2000) 67-73.

26. "Recommended practices for standard and transmission-based precautions in the perioperative practice setting," in *Standards, Recommended Practices, and Guidelines* (Denver: AORN, Inc, 2004) 361-366.

27. K A Ball, "Care and maintenance of instruments," in *Endoscopic Surgery* (St Louis: Mosby-Year Book, Inc, 1997) 83-110.

28. "Recommended practices for electrosurgery," in *Standards, Recommended Practices, and Guidelines* (Denver: AORN, Inc, 2004) 245-260.

29. "Recommended practices for laser safety in practice settings," in *Standards, Recommended Practices, and Guidelines* (Denver: AORN, Inc, 2004) 319-324.

30. "Recommended practices for cleaning and caring for surgical instruments and powered equipment," in *Standards, Recommended Practices, and Guidelines* (Denver: AORN, Inc, 2004) 309-317.

31. T G Vancaillie, "Electrosurgery at laparoscopy: Guidelines to avoid complications," *Gynaecological Endoscopy* 3 (Spring 1994) 143-150.

32. K A Ball, "Endoscopic instruments," in *Endoscopic Surgery* (St Louis: Mosby-Year Book, Inc, 1997) 51-82.

33. K Omote et al, "Self-guided robotic camera control for laparoscopic surgery compared with human camera control," *The American Journal of Surgery* 177 (April 1999) 321-324.

34. "Recommended practices for documenting perioperative nursing care," in *Standards, Recommended Practices, and Guidelines* (Denver: AORN Inc, 2004) 241-243.

35. S C Beyea, ed, *Perioperative Nursing Data Set: The Perioperative Nursing Vocabulary,* second ed (Denver: AORN, Inc, 2002).

36. "Quality improvement standards for perioperative nursing," in *Standards, Recommended Practices, and Guidelines* (Denver: AORN, Inc, 2004) 187-196.

37. US Food and Drug Administration, "Medical devices; Device tracking: Final rule and request for comments," *Federal Register* 58 (Aug 16, 1993) 43442–43450.

38. M A Heller, *Guide to Medical Device Regulation,* vol 2 (Washington DC: Thompson Publishing, 1998) Appendix 2000; 366.

39. "Standards for privacy of individually identifiable health information; Final rule," *Federal Register* 164 (Aug 14, 2002) 53183-53273.

RESOURCES
Ballantyne, G H. *Atlas of Laparoscopic Surgery* (Philadelphia: WB Saunders, 2000).
Eubanks, S; Swanstrom, L. *Mastery of Endoscopic and Laparoscopic Surgery* (Philadelphia: Lippincott Williams & Wilkins, 2000).
Talamini, M. *Advances in Minimally Invasive Surgery* (Philadelphia: Lippincott Williams & Wilkins, 2001).
Zucker, K. *Surgical Laparoscopy,* second ed, K A Zucker, ed (Baltimore: Lippincott Williams & Wilkins, 2001).

Originally published as proposed recommended practices February 1994, *AORN Journal.*

Revised November 1998; published February 1999, *AORN Journal. Reformatted July 2000.*

Revised November 2004; published in *Standards, Recommended Practices, and Guidelines,* 2005 edition. March 2005, *AORN Journal.*

AORN Perioperative Standards and Recommended Practices, 2009 Edition

Recommended Practices for Selection and Use of Surgical Gowns and Drapes

T he following recommended practices were developed by the AORN Recommended Practices Committee and have been approved by the AORN Board of Directors. They were presented as proposed recommended practices for comments by members and others. They are effective January 1, 2003.

These recommended practices are intended as achievable recommendations representing what is believed to be an optimal level of practice. Policies and procedures will reflect variations in practice settings and/or clinical situations that determine the degree to which the recommended practices can be implemented.

AORN recognizes the numerous types of settings in which perioperative nurses practice. These recommended practices are intended as guidelines adaptable to various practice settings. These practice settings include traditional operating rooms, ambulatory surgery units, physician's offices, cardiac catheterization suites, endoscopy suites, radiology departments, and all other areas where operative and other invasive procedures may be performed.

Purpose

These recommended practices provide guidelines for evaluation, selection, and use of surgical gowns and drapes. These products should provide a safe, effective means of protecting patients and health care personnel during use. Patients are at risk of contamination from both endogenous and exogenous microorganisms. Health care workers are at risk of contamination from a variety of bloodborne pathogens that can be contracted via exposure to patients' blood and body fluids. The barrier quality required of surgical gowns and drapes varies according to the planned use of the product and its anticipated exposure to blood and body fluids.

Recommendation I

Surgical gowns and drapes should be evaluated according to the AORN "Recommended practices for product selection in perioperative practice settings."[1]

1. Materials selected for construction of surgical gowns and drapes should be safe, meet identified needs, and promote patient and personnel safety.

2. Selection of gown and drape products for use in the practice setting should be based on criteria specific to the products' function and use. Surgical gowns and drapes are constructed of either single-use or reusable materials. Each of these has advantages and disadvantages. Further, in each of the two categories, design and performance characteristics vary. This variation stems from trade-offs in cost, comfort, and the amount of barrier protection provided. Both single-use and reusable gowns and drapes often are reinforced to improve their barrier quality. Reinforcements may consist of additional layers of the same material or layers of different material(s).[2]

Recommendation II

Materials used for surgical gowns and drapes should be resistant to penetration by blood and other body fluids as necessitated by their intended use.

1. Perioperative managers and purchasing agents should obtain from manufacturers data verifying that materials used in gowns and drapes are protective barriers against the transfer of microorganisms, particulates, and fluids to minimize strike-through and the potential for personnel contamination. Microorganisms can be transferred through barrier materials by wicking of fluids and/or pressure or leaning on a flooded area of the product. Mechanical action such as pressure can result in both liquid and dry penetration of microbes if the pressure exceeds the maximum level of resistance that the material provides.[3]

2. Surgical gowns should be selected for use according to the barrier quality of the item and the wearers' anticipated exposure to blood and body fluids in accordance with the Occupational Safety and Health Administration guidelines for use of personal protective equipment.[4] Short procedures during which there is little or no anticipated exposure to blood or body fluids can be completed successfully using a surgical gown with minimal barrier protection. As the complexity and length of the planned procedure increases, there may be increased potential for exposure to bloodborne pathogens, and it would be prudent to select a gown with greater barrier capability.

Recommendation III

Surgical gowns and drapes should maintain their integrity and be durable.

1. Surgical gowns and drapes should have an acceptable quality level (ie, be free of holes/defects).

2. Surgical gowns and drapes should be resistant to tears, punctures, and abrasions. The inability to withstand tears, punctures, and abrasions may allow for passage of microorganisms, particulates, and fluids between sterile and non-sterile areas and expose patients to exogenous organisms. Health care workers may be exposed to bloodborne pathogens. Reusable materials should be inspected visually to determine their integrity before use.[5] Reusable textiles should be patched with heat-sealed patches of the same quality material as the item to which they are applied. If the item is of a single-ply material, a patch need only be applied to one side of the item. Patches must allow for penetration and removal of sterilant while maintaining the integrity of the barrier quality of the item. The percentage of exposed surface that can be patched is dependent on the sterilization method and the number of layers of patched textile.[6] Areas covered by heat-sealed patches on woven textiles should be examined carefully before the fabric is used. The patched area should maintain the original barrier properties each time the product is used. Patches of any kind should never be stitched to woven barrier materials as a method of repairing holes. Stitching creates permanent holes that reduce the barrier quality of the item.[7]

3. Surgical gowns and drapes should be low-linting. Barrier materials used for surgical gowns and drapes should be as lint-free as possible. Lint particles are disseminated into the environment where bacteria attach to them. This bacteria-carrying lint may settle in surgical sites and wounds with a resultant increase in postoperative patient complications.[8]

4. Seams of barrier materials should be evaluated to determine their capability to minimize either penetration or passage of potential contaminants. Many surgical gown seams have little or no barrier property. If wicking or pressure on a seam causes liquid transfer between sterile and unsterile surfaces, one or both sides may become contaminated.[9]

Recommendation IV

Materials used for surgical gowns and drapes should be appropriate to the method(s) of sterilization.

1. To achieve a sterile product, the sterilizing agent must contact all surfaces of the item to be sterilized. Common sterilization methodologies include
   - radiation,
   - steam, and
   - ethylene oxide.

   The primary methodologies used in health care facilities are steam and ethylene oxide. Most facilities have neither the capability of nor access to radiation as a means of sterilization.

2. Tightly woven reusable textiles will lose their protective barrier quality after repeated processing. Manufacturers' written instructions for handling, the suggested number of processings, and the useful life of barrier materials should be provided and followed. A system should be established to track the number of processings for each item. This tracking should include, but not be limited to, the number of wash cycles and sterilization processings to which the textile product is subjected. Repeated processing ultimately will diminish the protective barrier ability of reusable textiles; however, items constructed of reusable textiles should continue to meet the original barrier quality level throughout the manufacturer-recommended life cycle (ie, number of processings) for the textile. The user facility should monitor the barrier quality of reusable textiles at intervals while the product is in service. Purchasers of reusable textile gowns and/or drapes should obtain from the manufacturer instructions for testing the material to document the ongoing barrier quality of the item(s) for the entire useful life of the item(s).[10] Products that no longer meet the manufacturer-stated barrier level should be downgraded to a nonprotective category and used accordingly.

3. Unused, single-use surgical gowns and drapes should not be resterilized unless manufacturers provide specific written instructions for reprocessing or the US Food and Drug Administration (FDA) regulations are followed. Surgical gowns and drapes intended for single use may not sterilize adequately, may be damaged during the sterilization process, or may retain toxic residues.[11] If a health care facility chooses to reprocess single-use items, including gowns and drapes, the FDA considers the facility to be the manufacturer of the item(s) and, as such, the facility is subject to the same stringent regulations as the original manufacturer of the item.[12]

Recommendation V

Surgical gowns and drapes should resist combustion.

1. Gowns and drapes selected for use should be consistent with accepted flammability standards that will provide the safest environment for patients and health care workers.[13] Specific standards for surgical materials have not been developed. All materials used in the surgical environment will burn given the right conditions.

2. Barrier materials are made of natural and/or synthetic fibers and may be flammable, needing only a combination of heat, fuel, and oxygen to ignite.[14] Care should be taken when gowns and drapes are exposed to light and heat sources, electrosurgical devices, lasers, and other power equipment. Materials ignite and burn at various rates. Even materials said to be flame-resistant might burn or melt when subjected to intense heat or an oxygen-rich environment.[15] Some materials not only ignite more easily than others but also may burn more rapidly.

Recommendation VI

Surgical gowns and drapes should be comfortable and contribute to maintaining the wearer's desired body temperature.

1. Surgical gowns and drapes should be free of toxic ingredients and allergens. Patients and/or health care workers may experience untoward reactions to toxic ingredients and/or allergens, ranging from mild discomfort to anaphylactic collapse.

2. Surgical drapes should have limited memory and be flexible enough to conform loosely to the patient's contour, allow for placement and unhampered manipulation of surgical instruments, and appropriately drape related equipment.[16] Surgical gowns should have limited memory and be flexible enough to conform loosely to the wearer's body while at the same time protect the wearer from contamination from blood and body fluids.

3. Surgical gowns and drapes should have the ability to maintain an isothermic environment for patients and health care workers. People vary in their ability to tolerate heat and cold. Thermal comfort exists when a balance occurs between the heat the human body loses and the heat the body generates. Care must be taken to avoid hypothermia or hyperthermia in surgical patients. Normothermic or near-normothermic patients may have a more favorable postoperative course.[17]

Recommendation VII

Surgical gowns and drapes selected for use should have a favorable cost-benefit ratio.

1. Surgical gowns and drapes should not be selected on the basis of cost only. Nor should cost be the primary consideration when making a selection. In today's economic environment, however, it is imperative that after providing for patient and provider safety, fiscal factors be considered. Careful selection of the appropriate gowns and drapes for the practice setting will contribute to the fiscal soundness of the provider facility.[18] A lesser-priced product that fails consistently is not cost effective because additional volume will be required to replace the defective or poorly performing item(s).

2. Surgical gowns and drapes are considered medical devices, and failure of these devices is subject to medical device reporting requirements according to the Safe Medical Devices Act of 1990[19] (SMDA) and/or the FDA voluntary Problem Reporting Program. This voluntary program provides users with a mechanism for reporting events that do not meet the strict reporting criteria of the SMDA. Reports should be filed by

telephone at (800) 638-6725. Consistent failure of a surgical gown or drape product should be reported to the manufacturer and the FDA. Any strike-through constitutes a threat of exposure to potentially harmful bloodborne pathogens.

Recommendation VIII

Policies and procedures for selecting and using surgical gowns and drapes should be developed, reviewed regularly, revised as necessary, and readily available in the practice setting.

1. These recommended practices should be used as guidelines when developing policies and procedures. Written policies and procedures establish authority, responsibility, and accountability. They serve as operational guidelines in the practice setting. Other AORN recommended practices addressing packaging systems, sterilization, creating and maintaining a sterile field, and surgical attire also should be consulted when developing policies and procedures for the selection and use of surgical gowns and drapes.

2. Orientation and ongoing education activities for personnel should include an introduction to and/or review of policies and procedures to be applied in the practice setting. Compliance with policies and procedures helps develop and reinforce knowledge, skills, and attitudes that affect patient outcomes. Policies and procedures also may be an integral part of continuous quality assessment and improvement activities.

Glossary

Barrier material: Material that minimizes or retards the penetration of microorganisms, particulates, and fluids.

Heat-sealed patch: A patch of the same textile with an adhesive back applied to reusable textiles containing a hole or tear with high-intensity heat.

Isothermic environment: The surroundings, conditions, or influences that affect maintaining an equal temperature.

Nonwoven material: A manufactured sheet, web, or batt of directionally or randomly oriented fibers or filaments, natural or man-made, excluding paper and paper products, that are woven, knotted, tufted, or stitch bonded and have not been converted into

yarns. Nonwovens are bonded to each other by friction and/or cohesion and/or adhesion. They are designed as single-use materials.

Strike-through: Penetration of microorganisms, particulates, or fluids through a barrier material.

Useful life: The anticipated life of a product, such as a woven material. Useful life is affected by the number of sterilization processing and washing cycles a product can endure and yet maintain an acceptable barrier capability.

Wicking: Absorption of a liquid by capillary action along a thread or through the material.

Woven material: Fabric constructed from yarns made of natural or synthetic fibers or filaments that are woven together to form a web in a repeated interlocking pattern.

REFERENCES

1. "Recommended practices for product selection in perioperative practice settings," in *Standards, Recommended Practices, and Guidelines* (Denver: AORN, Inc, 2004) 347-350.

2. K K Leonas, R S Jinkins, "The relationship of selected fabric characteristics and the barrier effectiveness of surgical gown fabrics," *American Journal of Infection Control* 25 (February 1997) 16-23; *Selection of Surgical Gowns and Drapes in Health Care Facilities* (Arlington, Va: Association for the Advancement of Medical Instrumentation, 2000) 4-12.

3. *Ibid.*

4. "Occupational exposure to bloodborne pathogens; Final rule," *Federal Register* 56 (Dec 6, 1991) 640004-64182; N L Belkin, "A historical review of barrier materials," *AORN Journal* 76 (October 2002) 648-653.

5. *Processing of Reusable Surgical Textiles for Use in Health Care Facilities* (Arlington, Va: Association for the Advancement of Medical Instrumentation, 2000) 23-28.

6. *Ibid,* 27-28; American Society for Healthcare Central Service Professionals of the American Hospital Association, *Training Manual for Central Service Technicians,* third ed (Chicago: American Hospital Association, 1997) 136.

7. *Ibid.*

8. *Processing of Reusable Surgical Textiles for Use in Health Care Facilities,* 24; *Selection of Surgical Gowns and Drapes in Health Care Facilities,* 16-17; C Edmiston et al, "Airborne particulates in the OR environment," *AORN Journal* 69 (June 1999) 1169-1183.

9. J Pournoor, "New scientific tools to expand the understanding of aseptic practices," *Surgical Services Management* 6 (April 2000) 28-32; J W Smith et al, "Determination of surgeon-generated gown pressures during various surgical procedures in the operating room," *American Journal of Infection Control* 23 (August 1995) 238; E A McCullough, "Methods for determining the barrier efficacy of surgical gowns," *American Journal of Infection Control* 21 (December 1993) 368; I D Learmonth, "Prevention of infec-

tion in the 1990s," *Orthopedic Clinics of North America* 24 (October 1993) 736; K W Altman et al, "Transmural surgical gown pressure measurements in the operating theater," *American Journal of Infection Control* 19 (June 1991) 147.

10. *Selection of Surgical Gowns and Drapes in Health Care Facilities,* 17, 18, 23; *Processing of Reusable Surgical Textiles for Use in Health Care Facilities,* 14, 24, 25; D Fogg, "Infection control," in *Alexander's Care of the Patient in Surgery,* 11th ed, M H Meeker, J C Rothrock, eds (St Louis: Mosby, 1999) 145.

11. *Good Hospital Practice: Steam Sterilization and Sterility Assurance* (Arlington, Va: Association for the Advancement of Medical Instrumentation, 1994) 9.

12. *Ibid;* "Reuse of single-use devices," (Clinical Issues) *AORN Journal* 73 (May 2001) 957-966; "AORN guidance statement: Reuse of single-use devices," in *Standards, Recommended Practices, and Guidelines* (Denver: AORN, Inc, 2002) 113-119.

13. *Selection of Surgical Gowns and Drapes in Health Care Facilities,* 15, 16, 18; "Standard for the flammability of clothing textiles," in *Code of Federal Regulations (CFR)* 16: Commercial Practices, Part 1610 (Washington, DC: US Government Printing Office, 2001) 608-616; "Standard for the flammability of vinyl plastic film," in *Code of Federal Regulations (CFR)* 16: Commercial Practices, Part 1611 (Washington, DC: US Government Printing Office, 2001) 622-630.

14. *Ibid;* J R Sommers, "Flammability standards for surgical drapes and gowns: Past, present, and future," *Surgical Services Management* 4 (February 1998) 41-44; *Fire Safety in the Perioperative Setting* (Woodbury, Conn: Ciné-med, 2000) Videotape; "Surgical fires in the OR," ORRM 2 (1992).

15. *Ibid;* "Recommended practices for laser safety in practice settings," in *Standards, Recommended Practices, and Guidelines* (Denver: AORN, Inc, 2002) 277-281.

16. *Selection of Surgical Gowns and Drapes in Health Care Facilities,* 13, 14.

17. *Ibid;* A C Meling et al, "Effects of preoperative warming on the incidence of wound infection after clean surgery: A randomised controlled trial," *The Lancet* 358 (Sept 15, 2001) 876-880; Agency for Healthcare Research and Quality, University of California, San Francisco-Stanford Evidence-Based Practice Center, *Making Healthcare Safer: A Critical Analysis of Patient Safety Practices* (Rockville, Md: Agency for Healthcare Research and Quality, US Department of Health and Human Services, 2001) 231-234; A Kurz, D I Sessler, R Lenhardt, "Perioperative normothermia to reduce the incidence of surgical-wound infection and shorten hospitalization," *The New England Journal of Medicine* 334 (May 9, 1996) 1209-1215.

18. *Selection of Surgical Gowns and Drapes in Health Care Facilities,* 19.

19. *Safe Medical Devices Act of 1990,* sec 519 (21 USC 360); "Medical device reporting," in *Code of Federal Regulations (CFR)* 21: Food and Drugs, Part 803 (Washington, DC: US Government Printing Office, 2002) 38-55; "Medical devices: Reports of corrections and removals," in *Code of Federal Regulations (CFR)* 21: Food and Drugs, Part 806 (Washington, DC: US Government Printing Office, 2002) 55-58.

Originally published February 1988, *AORN Journal.* Revised March 1992.

Revised November 1995; published March 1996, *AORN Journal.* Reformatted July 2000.

Revised; published in *Standards, Recommended Practices, and Guidelines,* 2003 edition. Reprinted January 2003, *AORN Journal.*

AORN Perioperative Standards and Recommended Practices, 2009 Edition

Recommended Practices for Laser Safety in Practice Settings

The following recommended practices were developed by the AORN Recommended Practices Committee and have been approved by the AORN Board of Directors. They were presented as proposed recommended practices for comment by members and others. They are effective January 1, 2004.

These recommended practices are intended as achievable recommendations representing what is believed to be an optimal level of practice. Policies and procedures will reflect variations in practice settings and/or clinical situations that determine the degree to which the recommended practices can be implemented.

AORN recognizes the numerous types of settings in which perioperative nurses practice. These recommended practices are intended as guidelines adaptable to various practice settings. These practice settings include traditional operating rooms, ambulatory surgery units, physicians' offices, cardiac catheterization suites, endoscopy suites, radiology departments, and all other areas where operative and other invasive procedures may be performed.

Purpose

These recommended practices provide guidance to assist practitioners in providing a safe environment for patients and health care workers exposed to a laser environment. This document incorporates activities described in the American National Standards Institute's (ANSI's) *American National Standard for the Safe Use of Lasers in Health Care Facilities,* which specifies standards for the use of class 3 and class 4 laser devices in the health care environment. Health care facilities are encouraged to obtain a copy of the ANSI document and have it readily available for reference in the practice environment.

Recommendation I

A laser safety program should be established for private practitioners and/or health care facilities.

1. According to ANSI, facilities in which laser procedures are performed must develop a laser safety program to include, but not be limited to,
   - delegation of authority and responsibility for supervising laser safety to a laser safety officer;
   - establishment of use criteria and authorized procedures for all health care personnel working in laser nominal hazard zones;
   - identification of laser hazards and appropriate control measures;
   - education of personnel (ie, operators and others) regarding assessment and control of hazards; and
   - management and reporting of accidents or incidents related to laser procedures, including action plans to prevent recurrences.

2. Incidents of safety regulation violation should be reported to the laser safety officer and reviewed by the safety committee.[1]

3. People working in a laser environment should have knowledge of the established laser safety program.

Recommendation II

Personnel working in laser environments should demonstrate competency commensurate with their responsibilities. Education programs should be specific to laser systems used and procedures performed in the facility.

1. Program criteria and content should be in accordance with applicable standards; the facility's policies and procedures; and federal, state, and local regulations.

2. Personnel should be required to demonstrate laser competency periodically and when new laser equipment, accessories, or safety equipment is purchased or brought into the practice environment.

3. The laser safety program should provide participants with a thorough understanding of laser procedures and the technology required for establishing and maintaining a safe environment during laser procedures.

4. Educational activities should be documented and maintained on file in the facility.[1]

Recommendation III

All people should know where lasers are being used, and access to these areas should be controlled.

1. A nominal hazard zone (ie, the space in which the level of direct, reflected, or scattered radiation used during normal laser operation exceeds the applicable maximum permissible exposure) should be identified to prevent unintentional exposure to the laser beam.

- The laser safety officer can determine the nominal hazard zone with reference from ANSI Z136.1 and ANSI Z136.3, as well as the safety information supplied by the laser manufacturer.[1]
- The nominal hazard zone usually is contained within the room but may extend through open doors and/or transparent windows, depending on the type of laser used.
- Personnel in the nominal hazard zone should be aware of all laser safety precautions that are implemented to avoid inadvertent exposure to laser hazards.[1]

2. Regulation laser signs should be placed at all entrances to laser treatment areas when these areas are in service.
- Recognizable warning signs specific to the type of laser being used should be designed according to the information described in *American National Standard for Safe Use of Lasers in Health Care Facilities.*[1]
- Warning signs should be placed conspicuously to alert bystanders of potential hazards.
- Signs should be removed when the laser procedure is completed.[2]

3. Doors in the nominal hazard zone should remain closed, and windows, including door windows, should be covered with a barrier that blocks transmission of a beam as appropriate to the type of laser being used.[2]

Recommendation IV

All people in the laser treatment area should be protected from unintentional laser beam exposure.

1. Procedures should be implemented to prevent accidental activation or misdirection of laser beams.
- Access to laser keys should be restricted to authorized personnel skilled in laser operation.[3]
- Lasers should be placed in standby mode when not in active use.[3]
- The laser foot switch should be placed in a position convenient to the operator, and the activation mechanism should be identified. Attention to proper placement of the foot switch and use of the standby switch can reduce unintended activation of the laser beam and potential injury to the patient, operator,

and/or bystander(s). Removing unneeded foot switches prevents confusion and accidents related to inadvertent activation.[2]
- The laser operator managing the laser equipment should have no competing responsibilities that would require leaving the laser unattended during active use. Note that continual circulating responsibilities may preclude ability to assume the responsibility of laser operation.

2. Anodized, dull, nonreflective, or matte-finished instruments should be used near the laser site. Such instruments decrease the reflectivity of laser beams. Instruments that have been coated (ie, ebonized) should be inspected regularly to ensure the integrity of the coating.[2]

3. Exposed tissues around the surgical site should be protected with saline-saturated or water-saturated materials (eg, towels, sponges) when thermally intensive lasers are being used. These materials should be remoistened periodically to ensure that they do not dry out and become a source for ignition. The solution (eg, saline, water) absorbs or disperses the energy of the laser beam in areas not intended for laser application.[4]

4. Appropriate backstops (eg, titanium rods, quartz rods) or guards should be used during laser surgery to prevent the laser beam from striking normal tissue. Mirrors made of rhodium or stainless steel may be used in hard-to-reach areas. Mirrors made of glass are not used because they will absorb heat from the laser energy and may shatter.[2] Glass rods should not be used because thermal stress from laser beams may cause breakage.[3]

5. When a fiber is used to deliver laser energy through an endoscope, the end of the fiber should extend at least 1 cm past the end of the endoscope and be in view at all times during active use.[2]

When using lasers with flexible endoscopic delivery systems, care should be taken to avoid laser beam exposure within the sheath. Most flexible fiber-optic endoscopic sheaths are damaged easily by heat.[3] Most flexible fiber-optic endoscope sheaths are flammable.[1]
- Backscatter from the laser beam can cause thermal damage, resulting in lens pitting if the fiber is too close to the end of the endoscope.[2]

♦ For rigid endoscopic delivery systems (eg, laryngoscopes, bronchoscopes, laparoscopes), care should be taken to avoid beam heating of the sheath wall. If the metallic tubular system is used improperly, the heat inside the endoscope will cause thermal damage to adjoining tissues.[1]

Recommendation V

All people in the nominal hazard zone should wear appropriate eyewear approved by the laser safety officer.

1. People in the nominal hazard zone should wear protective eyewear of specific wavelength and density. Scattered, diffused, and reflected laser beams, in addition to direct exposure from misdirected and damaged fibers, can cause eye injuries.[1] Appropriate laser safety eyewear filters out the hazardous wavelength of laser radiation to prevent thermal eye injuries.
    ♦ Eyewear must be labeled with the appropriate optical density and wavelength for the laser in use. Laser eyewear is not interchangeable for a variety of lasers.[1]
    ♦ A lens filter of appropriate laser wavelength may be used over the top of an endoscope viewing port to protect the eye from laser backscatter. The other eye, however, would be left unprotected should a break in a light fiber occur. Using an eye lens filter does not reduce or cancel out the need for protective eyewear for other people in the nominal hazard zone.[2]

2. Patients' eyes and eyelids should be protected from the laser beam by a method approved by the laser safety officer.[1]
    ♦ Patients who remain awake during laser procedures should wear goggles or glasses designated for the type of laser being used.
    ♦ Patients undergoing general anesthesia should be provided other appropriate protection, such as wet eye pads or laser-specific eye shields.[2]
    ♦ Patients undergoing laser treatments on or around the eyelids should have their eyes protected by corneal eye shields.[1]

Recommendation VI

Personnel working in the laser environment should avoid exposure to smoke plume generated during laser surgery.

1. To reduce smoke plume inhalation, local exhaust ventilation controls should be implemented. These controls include, but may not be limited to,
    ♦ wall suction units with in-line filters, and
    ♦ smoke evacuator units.

    Laser smoke plume should be removed by use of local exhaust ventilation. The collection device should be placed as near as possible to the point where plume is produced.[1]

2. Personnel should wear high-filtration surgical masks designed for use during laser procedures that generate smoke plume. These specially designed masks help filter particulate matter and may reduce noxious odors.[5] These masks should not be viewed as absolute protection from chemical contaminants.[1]

3. In situations in which minimal plume is generated, a central wall suction system with an in-line filter can be used to evacuate the plume. Central wall suction units are designed to capture liquids, making the use of in-line filters necessary. Low suction rates associated with wall suction units limit their efficacy in evacuating plume, making them suitable for minimal plume only.[6]

4. In circumstances in which large amounts of plume are generated, a mechanical smoke evacuation system with a high-efficiency filter should be used to remove laser smoke plume according to manufacturers' instructions. The evacuator collection apparatus should be placed as close as possible to the laser site. Detectable odor during the use of a laser and smoke evacuation system is a signal that either smoke is not being captured at the site, the airflow through the system is too fast for absorption to occur, or the filter has exceeded its usefulness and should be replaced.[6]

5. Standard precautions should be used when working in the laser environment.[1] Laser gas airborne contaminants produced during laser procedures

have been analyzed and are shown to contain gaseous toxic compounds, bioaerosols, and dead and living cell material. At some level these have been shown to have an unpleasant odor, cause visual problems for physicians, cause ocular and upper respiratory tract irritation, and have demonstrated mutagenic and carcinogenic potential.[1] The potential for bacterial and/or viral contamination of smoke plume remains controversial.

Recommendation VII

All people in the laser treatment area should be protected from electrical hazards associated with laser use.

1. The laser safety officer should approve laser systems and equipment before they are placed in service and after they are evaluated for electrical hazards.[1]

2. Laser service and preventive maintenance should be performed on a regular basis by people who have knowledge of laser systems. Service and maintenance activities should be documented. The laser safety officer should review maintenance documents before allowing any laser to be reentered into service. Documentation of actions taken to ensure the reliability and safe operation of lasers assists the laser safety officer in maintaining a safe laser environment. Recurring problems can be detected and solved with appropriate follow-up.[1]

3. Solutions should not be placed on laser units. Lasers are high-voltage equipment that should be protected against short circuiting associated with spillage or splatter.[3]

Recommendation VIII

All people in the laser treatment area should be protected from flammability hazards associated with laser use.

1. Personnel using lasers should be knowledgeable of the fire hazards associated with laser use. Fire is one of the most significant hazards of laser use. The intense heat of laser beams can ignite combustible/flammable solids, liquids, and gases. Flammable and combustible items in the laser environment include, but may not be limited to,

- flammable liquids or combustible ointments (eg, skin prep solutions, oil-based lubricants);
- gases (eg, oxygen, methane, anesthetic agents, alcohol vapor);
- plastics;
- paper or gauze materials;
- surgical drapes;
- adhesive or plastic tapes; and
- endotracheal tubes.

The presence of increased oxygen concentrations enhances combustion of these products and leads to the rapid spread of flames.[1] Pooled skin prep solutions also can retain laser heat, resulting in patient tissue burns. Pooled solutions should be removed and/or patted dry. Prep solutions can be absorbed into linens and body fibers (eg, hair). These solutions should be allowed enough time to evaporate before drapes are applied. Alcohol-based skin prep vapors can become trapped under drapes and coverings, and the volatility of vapors can increase the risk of surgical drape fires.[2]

2. Laser-appropriate fire extinguishers and water should be immediately available where lasers are used. Immediate action can reduce the magnitude of injury.[1]

3. Special ignition-resistant drapes and/or moistened, reusable fabrics should be used to drape around areas that are close to the laser treatment site to decrease the potential for fire.[7]

4. Protected or specially designed endotracheal tubes should be used to minimize the potential for fire during laser procedures in the patient's airway or aerodigestive tract. Standard endotracheal tubes are combustible and should not be used. Other flammable items associated with endotracheal tube use during laser procedures include
- plastic,
- plastic tape,
- ointment/lubricant, and
- surgical prep solution.

Endotracheal tube cuffs should be inflated with dyed saline so that punctures can be recognized and action taken immediately. Moistened packs around the tube may provide additional protection.[1]

Recommendation IX

Policies and procedures for laser safety should be developed with regard to individual practice settings, applicable standards, and federal and state regulations. Administrative and procedural controls are required according to ANSI Z136.3, section 4, "Control measures." Policies should be reviewed periodically, revised as necessary, and readily available to all personnel.

1. Administrative controls (eg, job description of the laser safety officer, laser committee structure/ function, documentation, education and training, medical surveillance [eg, eye examination], laser service, maintenance) describe instructions or methods that regulate work practices and specify criteria for personnel protection.[1]

2. Procedural controls (eg, assignment of a laser operator, requiring special storage of laser keys to prevent unauthorized use, assuring standby function if the laser is activated during standby periods) are determined by the laser safety officer and used to avoid potential hazards in the use of lasers.[1]

3. Documentation should be consistent with AORN's "Recommended practices for documentation of perioperative nursing care."[8]
   ♦ The Perioperative Nursing Data Set nomenclature should be used when documenting on the patient's record.[9]
   ♦ Documentation regarding the laser procedure should include the type of laser used and safety measures implemented during laser use.[3]

4. A medical surveillance program should be established for health care personnel participating in laser use.
   ♦ Medical surveillance is required for laser users or health care personnel within the nominal hazard zone.
   ♦ All laser accidents require reporting and follow-up.[1]

Glossary

American National Standards Institute (ANSI): Organization that provides guidance for the safe use of lasers for diagnostic and therapeutic uses in health care facilities.

Authorized laser operator: A person educated and trained in laser safety and approved by the facility to operate the laser.

Class 3 laser: Those lasers potentially hazardous for direct exposure to specular (ie, mirror-like) reflection.

Class 4 laser: Those lasers that present significant skin and fire hazards. Most surgical lasers are class 4 lasers.

Combustible: A substance that is capable of catching fire and burning.

Corneal eye shield: A device placed over the eye to protect the cornea from self-induced trauma, such as rubbing, pressure, or excessive use.

Controlled access area: The area where the laser is to be used. Access to this area is restricted to laser team members and/or those given permission to enter the area. Access is granted only to those who have been approved by the laser safety officer.

Fire/flame retardant: A substance that by chemical or physical action reduces flammability of combustibles.

Health care laser system: A system used in health care applications that includes a delivery apparatus to direct the output of the laser, a power supply with control and calibration functions, a mechanical house with interlocks, and associated fluids and gases required for the operation of the laser.

High-efficiency filter or high-efficiency particulate air filter: Filters having a filtration rating of 0.3 microns at 99.7% efficiency.

High filtration masks: Masks having a filtering capacity of particulate matter at 0.3 microns to 0.1 microns in size.

Laser: A device that produces an intense, coherent, directional beam of light by stimulating electronic or molecular transitions to lower energy levels. An acronym for "light amplification by stimulated emission of radiation."

Laser-generated airborne contaminants: Particles, toxins, and steam produced by vaporization of target tissues.

Laser safety officer: Person responsible for effecting the knowledgeable evaluation of laser hazards and authorized and responsible for monitoring and overseeing the control of such laser hazards.

Laser treatment area: Area in which the laser is being operated.

Limiting-exposure duration: The length of time for which tissue can be exposed to the laser beam. This duration is determined by the design and/or intended use of the laser.

Maximum permissible exposure: The level of laser radiation to which a person may be exposed without hazardous effects of adverse biologic changes in his or her eyes or skin.

Nominal hazard zone: The space in which the level of direct, reflected, or scattered radiation used during normal laser operation exceeds the applicable maximum permissible exposure. Exposure levels beyond the boundary of the nominal hazard zone should be below the appropriate maximum permissible exposure level of the laser. Special eye and skin precautions must be enforced in the nominal hazard zone.

Optical density: Ability to absorb a specific laser wavelength.

REFERENCES

1. American National Standards Institute, Laser Institute of America, *American National Standard for Safe Use of Lasers in Health Care Facilities* (Orlando, Fla: The Laser Institute of America, 1996).

2. K A Ball, *Lasers: The Perioperative Challenge,* second ed (St Louis: Mosby, 1995).

3. K A Ball, "Surgical modalities" in *Alexander's Care of the Patient in Surgery,* 12th ed, J C Rothrock, ed (St Louis: Mosby, 2003) 41-96.

4. J A Kneedler, G H Dodge, *Perioperative Patient Care: The Nursing Perspective,* third ed (Boston: Jones and Bartlett Publishers, 1994).

5. C L Romig, P J Smalley, "Regulation of surgical smoke plume," (Health Policy Issues) *AORN Journal* 65 (April 1997) 824-828.

6. "Smoke evacuation systems, surgical," *Healthcare Product Comparison System* (March 2002).

7. *NFPA 115: Recommended Practice on Laser Fire Protection* (Quincy, Mass: National Fire Protection Association, 1999).

8. "Recommended practices for documentation of perioperative nursing care," in *Standards, Recommended Practices, and Guidelines* (Denver: AORN, Inc, 2003) 233-235.

9. S Beyea, ed, *Perioperative Nursing Data Set,* second ed (Denver: AORN, Inc, 2002).

Originally published November 1989, *AORN Journal.* Revised November 1993.

Revised November 1997; published January 1998, *AORN Journal.* Reformatted July 2000.

Revised November 2003; published in *Standards, Recommended Practices, and Guidelines,* 2004 edition. Reprinted April 2004, *AORN Journal.*

Recommended Practices for the Use of the Pneumatic Tourniquet in the Perioperative Practice Setting

The following recommended practices were developed by the AORN Recommended Practices Committee and have been approved by the AORN Board of Directors. They were presented as proposed recommended practices for comments by members and others. They are effective January 1, 2007.

These recommended practices are intended as achievable recommendations representing what is believed to be an optimal level of practice. Policies and procedures will reflect variations in practice settings and/or clinical situations that determine the degree to which the recommended practices can be implemented.

AORN recognizes the numerous settings in which perioperative nurses practice. These recommended practices are intended as guidelines adaptable to various practice settings. These practice settings include traditional operating rooms, ambulatory surgery centers, physicians' offices, radiology departments, and all other areas where operative and other invasive procedures may be performed.

Purpose

These recommended practices provide guidelines for use of pneumatic tourniquets, which are primarily used to occlude blood flow, obtain a near bloodless field for extremity surgery, and to confine a bolus of anesthetic in an extremity for intravenous regional anesthesia (IVRA; ie, Bier block). These recommended practices provide information for testing, applying, and cleaning pneumatic tourniquet equipment, and the patient care associated with the safe use of this equipment. Pneumatic tourniquet equipment consists of a pressure regulator with display, connective tubing, and an inflatable cuff. These recommended practices provide general guidelines for developing policies and procedures for safe use of a pneumatic tourniquet in the practice setting. Due to the variety and complexity of current pneumatic tourniquet equipment, policies and procedures should reflect considerations for the specific pneumatic tourniquet system being used.

Recommendation I

Patient safety should be the primary consideration in evaluation, selection, purchase, and use of the pneumatic tourniquet and accessories.

1. Equipment selected should include technology to determine cuff pressure during use.

2. The pressure regulator should be self-calibrating upon activation.

3. If electric, the regulator should have a backup battery for use during a power failure.

4. The pressure display should be visible whenever the cuff is inflated.

5. An audible activation indicator(s) and alarm(s) should be present and loud enough to be heard above other sounds in the OR to alert personnel to a change in pressure and lapse of a designated duration of inflation time.[1]

6. The pneumatic tourniquet electrical cord should be flexible and adequate in length to reach the electrical outlet without stress or require the use of an extension cord.

7. Tourniquet cuffs and tubing should be compatible with the tourniquet regulator and other accessories. The tourniquet tubing should be incompatible with other tubing (eg, intravenous) or labeled to clearly identify that it is part of the tourniquet system. Although the US Food and Drug Administration (FDA) has not received reports of misconnections involving tourniquet tubing, over 300 cases of misconnections of other types of tubing resulting in injury have been reported.[2] Many of these reports involved luer connections. The Joint Commission for the Accreditation of Healthcare Organizations (JCAHO) has received reports of eight deaths associated with misconnections of tubing.[2]

8. Tourniquet cuffs should be clean. If the cuffs are unable to be adequately cleaned, single-use cuffs should be selected.

9. A variety of sizes and shapes of tourniquet cuffs should be available to meet the needs of the patients treated in the health care organization. Contoured cuffs should be available for use on extremities of patients where there is a significant difference in circumference between the proximal and distal edges of the cuff (eg, those seen in obese patients). Pediatric cuffs should be available for children. Injuries can result from the use of an inappropriate size or shape of cuff.

10. Pneumatic tourniquet technology continues to evolve, changing the way in which limb blood occlusion is achieved. Health care organizations and personnel should stay abreast of evolving technology and its effect on patient care and safety.

Recommendation II

The pneumatic tourniquet and its accessories should be inspected, tested, and maintained according to manufacturers' written instructions.

1. Instructions for pneumatic tourniquet use, warranties, and a manual for maintenance and inspections should be obtained from the manufacturer and be readily available to users. Equipment manuals assist in developing operational, safety, and maintenance guidelines, as well as serve as a reference for appropriate use.

2. A brief set of clearly readable operating instructions should be readily accessible with each tourniquet system. These instructions should be placed on or attached to each pneumatic tourniquet for quick reference.

3. Before initial use, designated personnel within the health care organization should evaluate the pneumatic tourniquet system for safety.

4. Each pneumatic tourniquet should be assigned an identification or serial number. This number facilitates documenting maintenance performed on individual pneumatic tourniquets and tracking of problems that occur.

5. Safety/warning alarms should be operational at all times. Lights should be operational and visible. The volume of the activation indicator should be maintained at an audible level to immediately alert personnel when the pneumatic tourniquet has detected a problem.

6. Before each use, the entire tourniquet system should be checked.
   - If attached to a gas source, the source should be compatible with the equipment design and the connections secure.
   - The cuff, tubing, connectors, gauges, and pressure source should be clean and kept in working order.
   - The tourniquet should be tested for integrity and function. Assuring that the tourniquet functions properly before a procedure minimizes the risk of pressure loss or patient injury. Most electric tourniquets automatically self-test and calibrate upon activation.
   - The cuff and tubing should be inspected for cracks, leaks, and the security of the closure mechanism. Unintentional pressure loss can result from loose tubing connectors, deteriorated tubing, or cuff bladder leaks, and may result in patient injury.[3]

7. The pneumatic tourniquet system should be evaluated for safe use by designated personnel (eg, biomedical engineering personnel) within the health care organization, at intervals consistent with the manufacturer's written instructions and policies of the health care organization. Nerve injuries have been reported when malfunctioning equipment has caused excessive pressure.[4]

8. A pneumatic tourniquet that is not working properly or is damaged should be removed from service immediately, along with all accessories, and reported to the designated individual responsible for equipment maintenance (eg, biomedical engineering personnel).

Recommendation III

The perioperative nurse should assess the patient preoperatively for risks and report potential contraindications to the surgeon.

Note: The operating physician determines use of a tourniquet, based upon the risks and benefits to the patient.

1. The perioperative nurse should assess the patient for considerations related to tourniquet use. This assessment should include, but not be limited to,
   - planned location of the tourniquet;
   - relative contraindications, including, but not limited to
     - extremity infection,[4,5]
     - open fracture,[4,5]
     - tumor distal to the tourniquet,[4,5]
     - sickle cell anemia,[4]

- impaired circulation,[4-6]
- previous revascularization of the extremity,[6]
- extremities with dialysis access (eg, AV shunts, fistulas),
- venous thromboembolism,[6]
- increased intracranial pressure,[4,5] and
- acidosis;[5]
- ◆ size and shape of the extremity.
- ◆ condition of skin under and distal to the cuff site; and
- ◆ peripheral pulses distal to the cuff.

2. Prophylactic antibiotics, when ordered, should be completely infused before tourniquet cuff inflation. Efficacy of the prophylactic antibiotics requires tissue perfusion of the surgical site. Optimum tissue concentrations have been found when antibiotics were administered 20 minutes before tourniquet inflation.[7,8]

Recommendation IV

The pneumatic tourniquet should be connected to the appropriate power/gas source in a manner that minimizes risk of patient injury.

1. The appropriate gas source should be selected according to manufacturers' written instructions. Tourniquet systems use compressed gas to apply a carefully controlled amount of tourniquet pressure. The design of the specific tourniquet system determines whether this gas is nitrogen or air. Gas (either nitrogen or compressed air) may be delivered from a portable canister, tank, or built-in system. Connection of the incorrect gas for inflation creates a fire hazard.[3]

2. Tourniquets should never be inflated with nitrous oxide or oxygen because of risk of fire.[3] Some tourniquets have an internal pump that compresses room air, eliminating the risk of erroneously connecting the system to an oxidizing gas.

Recommendation V

The components of the pneumatic tourniquet should be handled in a manner that minimizes the potential for damage and risk of subsequent patient injuries.

1. The pneumatic tourniquet regulator should be securely mounted on a fixed column or pole with a tip-resistant base. Applying tension on the electrical cord increases the risk that it will become disconnected, frayed, or move the equipment, which may result in injuries to patients and personnel.

2. The pneumatic tourniquet regulator should be placed near the point of use and the electrical cord should reach the wall or column outlet without stress on the cord and without blocking a traffic path. Stress on the cord may cause damage to the cord, posing a hazard. The electrical cord should be free of kinks, knots, and bends that could damage the cord or cause leakage, current accumulation, and overheating of the cord's insulation.

3. The pneumatic tourniquet plug, not the cord, should be held when it is removed from the outlet. Pulling on the cord may cause cord breakage and poses a fire hazard.

4. Tourniquet cuffs should be handled carefully. Care should be taken to avoid puncturing the cuff. Towel clips used near the cuff should be carefully placed to avoid damage to the cuff.

5. Excessive compression of the tourniquet cuff by a limb-positioning device should be avoided.

6. The pneumatic tourniquet and electrical cord should be kept dry. Pooled fluids on the floor and fluids dripping into the pneumatic tourniquet regulator or electrical connections create an electrical hazard.

Recommendation VI

A pneumatic tourniquet cuff should be selected and applied in a manner to minimize the risk of injury to the patient.

Improper tourniquet cuff application may lead to venous congestion, bruising, blistering, pinching, ecchymosis, or necrosis of the skin.

1. The width of the tourniquet cuff should be individualized, with consideration to the size and shape of the patient's limb. The cuff should be wider than half the limb's diameter. Wider cuffs

minimize the risk of injury to underlying tissue by dispersing pressure over a greater surface area. In clinical trials, using a wider cuff has been found consistently to occlude blood flow at a lower pressure in adult patients.[9-14] Similar results were found using wider cuffs in children.[15]

2. Wider, contoured tourniquet cuffs should be used for patient extremities in which there is a tapering of the extremity between the upper and lower edge of the cuff (eg, obese, very muscular). Contoured tourniquet cuffs have been found in clinical trials to occlude arterial flow at lower pressures than straight tourniquet cuffs of equal width.[11,13,14] Contoured tourniquet cuffs minimize the risk of excessive pressure on one edge of the cuff, migration of the cuff, and a shearing injury to underlying tissue.

3. The length of the tourniquet cuff should be individualized, taking into consideration the size and circumference of the patient's limb. The tourniquet cuff should overlap at least three inches but not more than six inches.[4] Too much overlap causes increased pressure and potential rolling or wrinkling of underlying soft tissue. Too small an overlap compromises effective tourniquet inflation and can result in unexpected release or inadequate constriction.

4. The correct surgical site should be verified before application of the tourniquet cuff.

5. A soft padding should be placed around the limb, being careful to stretch the padding so that it is wrinkle-free and does not pinch the skin. In a clinical trial, the overall skin complication rate was lower when padding was used.[16,17] Options include, but are not limited to, limb protection sleeves matched to the specific tourniquet cuff or two layers of stockinette stretched to fit the extremity. Materials that may shed loose fibers (eg, cotton cast padding, sheet padding) should be avoided. Lint from these materials can become embedded in the fasteners and reduce the effectiveness, possibly leading to an unexpected release of the cuff during the procedure.

6. Tourniquet cuffs should be applied to the verified operative extremity in a location with adequate muscle mass to protect nerves and vessels.

♦ Upper arm and thigh tourniquets should be positioned on the limb at the point of maximum circumference proximal to the incision.[18,19]
♦ Forearm tourniquets should be positioned mid-forearm.[18,19]
♦ Calf tourniquets should be placed with the proximal edge on the largest area of calf circumference.[20]
♦ Ankle tourniquets should be placed over the lower third of the lower leg, with the distal edge proximal to the malleoli.[20-23]

There is a potential risk to superficial nerves in unprotected areas during cuff placement. When the tourniquet cuff is inflated, nerves and blood vessels are compressed.

7. To improve tourniquet cuff positioning on an obese patient's extremity, an assistant should manually grasp the adipose tissue of the extremity and gently apply and hold traction distal to the tourniquet site until the padding and cuff are placed. Traction should be maintained until the cuff is secured.[24]

8. The patient's skin under the tourniquet cuff should be protected to prevent fluid accumulation (eg, skin prep solutions, irrigation) under the cuff, which may cause skin injury.

9. The cuff should be applied in its final position. If at any time a cuff position change is necessary, the cuff should be removed and reapplied. Moving a cuff after placement may cause shearing of underlying tissues and subsequent injury.

10. The cuff tubing should be positioned on or near the lateral aspect of the extremity to avoid pressure on nerves and kinking of the tubing.

11. Reusable tourniquet cuffs should be protected from contamination by fluid, blood, and other potentially infectious material during surgery. Tourniquet protectors (eg, U-shaped drapes, adhesive drapes, tourniquet covers) should be used to minimize soiling.

12. The use of a single-use cuff should be considered when adequate protection of the cuff cannot be assured.

Recommendation VII

The extremity should be exsanguinated before inflation of the tourniquet.

1. The extremity should be elevated to allow venous blood to exit the limb.

2. An elastic wrap (eg, Esmarch's bandage) should be available for exsanguination.

   An elastic wrap compresses superficial blood vessels, forcing blood out of the extremity. The surgeon determines use of an elastic wrap with consideration to the risks and benefits to the patient.

   ♦ Use of an elastic bandage for exsanguination enhances the bloodless field and may minimize the pain associated with tourniquet use.

   ♦ Exsanguination using an elastic wrap may not be appropriate following traumatic injury or if the extremity has been in a cast. In these instances, thrombi in blood vessels may become dislodged, resulting in emboli. Fatal pulmonary emboli have been reported following exsanguinations of such extremities.[25-27]

   ♦ In the presence of infection, malignant tumor, or fractures in the extremity, exsanguination should be accomplished by extremity elevation alone. Infection as well as malignant cells can be forced into the torso during aggressive exsanguination. Additional tissue damage can result from compressing of fractures.

3. The anesthesia care provider should be alerted before wrapping the extremity. Notification of the anesthesia care provider facilitates monitoring for potential complications.

Recommendation VIII

Tourniquet inflation pressure should be kept to the minimum effective pressure.[4,11,28,29]

Overpressurization may cause pain at the tourniquet cuff site; muscle weakness; compression injuries to blood vessels, nerve, muscle, or skin; or extremity paralysis. Underpressurization may result in blood in the surgical field, passive congestion of the limb, shock, and hemorrhagic infiltration of a nerve.

1. Pressure settings should be based on limb occlusion pressure (LOP). Research studies have shown that occlusion can be achieved using a lower pressure when using a LOP method in conjunction with a wide tourniquet cuff in adult patients.[12,13,15,28,30,31] The same was found when studying children.[15] Applying lower pressure has been found to result in less postoperative pain.[11,31,32] Some tourniquet systems are designed to determine LOP automatically and add a safety margin to allow for fluctuations in blood pressure intraoperatively. If a standard tourniquet cuff is used, the LOP should be determined using the following steps.

   ♦ Apply the tourniquet cuff over the appropriate limb protection material.

   ♦ Using a Doppler stethoscope, locate an arterial pulse distal to the cuff. Normally, the radial artery is used on the arm and the posterior tibial artery is used on the leg. The dorsalis pedis artery may also be used for the leg.

   ♦ Slowly increase cuff pressure until the arterial pulse stops and remains stopped for several heartbeats.

   ♦ Note the cuff pressure. This is the LOP.

   ♦ Deflate the cuff and confirm that the distal pulse resumes.

   ♦ Before cuff inflation, adjust the cuff pressure setting by adding a safety margin to the LOP as follows:
   - add 40 mm Hg for LOP less than 130 mm Hg,
   - add 60 mm Hg for LOP between 131–190 mm Hg,
   - add 80 mm Hg for LOP greater than 190 mm Hg[33];
   - for pediatric patients, adding 50 mm Hg has been recommended.[34]

2. The LOP measurement should be made when the blood pressure is stabilized to the level expected during surgery. The LOP measurement may be completed before or after induction of anesthesia. Blood pressure at the time of LOP measurement should be documented.

3. The LOP and inflation pressure setting should be confirmed with the surgeon.

4. Inflation of the tourniquet cuff should be under the direction of the surgeon and coordinated with the anesthesia care provider.

5. After limb exsanguination and cuff inflation, there is an increase in blood volume to vital organs and a subsequent increase in systolic blood pressure.[4] Coordination with the anesthesia care provider facilitates management of the patient during this rapid physiologic change.

6. Pneumatic tourniquets should be inflated rapidly. Rapid tourniquet cuff inflation occludes arteries and veins almost simultaneously, preventing filling of superficial veins before occlusion of arterial blood flow.

7. While the tourniquet cuff is inflated, the pressure gauge or digital display should be clearly visible and monitored for excessive fluctuation. Nerve damage may result from excessive tourniquet pressure or uneven padding.[35] Catastrophic neurological complications (eg, permanent nerve palsy) can occur with excessive tourniquet inflation pressures.[36]

Recommendation IX

Pneumatic tourniquet inflation time should be kept to a minimum and deflation managed to minimize risks to the patient.

Excessive inflation time may result in venous engorgement, hyperemia, muscle weakness, ischemic injury, or extremity paralysis. Neurological complications have been found to be associated with longer inflation times.[37]

1. The surgeon should be informed of the duration of the tourniquet time at regular, established intervals. Use of a timer and audible alarm on the tourniquet regulator facilitates this communication. Serious patient injury, including extremity paralysis, may result from prolonged inflation of the tourniquet.[38-40] Safe tourniquet inflation time has not been precisely determined. The time varies with the patient's age, physical status, and the vascular supply to the extremity. There is general agreement that inflation time should not exceed 60 minutes for an upper extremity and 90 minutes for a lower extremity.[33] In pediatric patients, inflation times of less than 75 minutes for lower extremities has been recommended.[41]

2. When prolonged tourniquet time is desired, the tourniquet should be released for reperfusion of the limb every hour. The reperfusion time should be 15 minutes, after which the tourniquet may be reinflated for another full period as above. Reperfusion allows oxygenation and continued viability of the tissue. Fifteen minutes of reperfusion after one hour has been found to minimize the tissue inflammatory response and is recommended.[42-45]

3. Deflation of the tourniquet should be coordinated with the anesthesia care provider. Physiologic changes resulting from deflation of the tourniquet are dependent upon the relative size of the extremity, duration of tourniquet time, and overall physiologic status of the patient. A decrease in blood pressure occurs as blood is shunted to the extremity.[4] A significant decrease in core body temperature occurs upon deflation of a lower extremity cuff.[46,47] Products of anaerobic metabolism enter the circulation upon deflation of the cuff causing a transient hyperemia and a mixed respiratory/metabolic acidosis. This results in a decrease in oxygen saturation and increase in end-tidal carbon dioxide. In a study measuring emboli released upon cuff deflation, the highest number were released within one minute of deflation.[48] Coordination with the anesthesia care provider or perioperative registered nurse monitoring the patient facilitates management of the patient's physiologic status during this rapid change.

4. Pneumatic tourniquets should be deflated as recommended by the manufacturer. The cuff and sleeve/padding should be removed from the extremity upon deflation of the tourniquet. Even the slight impedance of venous return by the padding or deflated cuff may lead to congestion and pooling of blood at the surgical site.[34]

Recommendation X

The patient should be monitored continuously with special consideration to pain and temperature while the tourniquet cuff is inflated.

1. Pain should be assessed and managed. After inflation of the pneumatic tourniquet for 30 to 60 minutes, patients may experience "tourniquet

pain," accompanied by an increase in heart rate and blood pressure.[4,49]

2. The patient's temperature should be continuously monitored during use of a pneumatic tourniquet. In pediatric and adult patients, inflated tourniquets result in an increase in core body temperature.[41,50]

3. Care should be exercised to avoid overheating the patient while the tourniquet cuff is inflated, particularly in pediatric patients.[51,52]

Recommendation XI

The perioperative registered nurse should evaluate the outcome of the patient care at the end of the procedure.

1. The patient should be continuously monitored for 15 minutes after deflation of the pneumatic tourniquet.
   - A decrease in blood pressure occurs as blood is shunted to the extremity.
   - Products of anaerobic metabolism enter the circulation upon deflation of the tourniquet cuff, causing transient hyperemia and a mixed respiratory/metabolic acidosis. This results in a decrease in oxygen saturation.[41,49,53]
   - Increases in end-tidal carbon dioxide occur.[41,49,54-56] The time for clearance of the metabolites depends upon the patient's physiologic status, extremity involved, and duration of tourniquet inflation.
   - A decrease in core body temperature typically occurs upon deflation of a lower extremity tourniquet cuff.[46,47,50]
   - An increase in intracranial pressure can occur.[43,57]
   - An embolism can be released from the extremity upon deflation of the tourniquet cuff.[58-62]

   In a study of patients undergoing total knee arthroplasty, blood pressure dropped immediately upon tourniquet cuff deflation and remained depressed for 15 minutes. Metabolites were reabsorbed within 30 minutes of deflation.[54] The peak number of emboli released occurs within 60 seconds of tourniquet cuff deflation.[56]

2. The immediate postoperative evaluation should include, but not be limited to,
   - vital signs, including oxygen saturation;
   - skin condition under the tourniquet (eg, temperature, color, integrity);
   - pulses distal to the tourniquet cuff; and
   - temperature.

3. Use of the pneumatic tourniquet and patient outcomes should be reported during patient hand-off to other caregivers.[63]

4. Any complications should be reported to the surgeon and anesthesia care provider and discussed during the hand off of care to other caregivers.

5. Potential complications include, but are not limited to,
   - injury to skin, muscle, nerves, and vessels underneath the tourniquet cuff;
   - hematoma;
   - edema;
   - circulatory impairment distal to the tourniquet cuff, venous congestion, or emboli;
   - damage to nerves distal to the tourniquet cuff;[20,37,64]
   - wound effusion;
   - compartment syndrome;[65-68] and
   - pulmonary embolism.[48,69-71]

   Serious injuries due to the use of pneumatic tourniquets are uncommon, but the risk is present. The risk of pulmonary emboli has been found to be associated with duration of tourniquet time.[4,48] Neurological complications have also been found to be associated with longer tourniquet times.[37]

Recommendation XII

Additional care should be taken in procedures involving tourniquet control on two extremities because the risk of complications and the systemic effects of tourniquet use may be increased.

1. The perioperative registered nurse, surgical team, and anesthesia care provider should be familiar with the respective placement of the tourniquets when using tourniquets on more than one extremity. Labeling the tubing to each cuff minimizes the risk of inflating/deflating the wrong cuff.

2. Blood pressure should be closely monitored. Exsanguination and inflating the cuff on both extremities in rapid succession may cause a more pronounced blood pressure rise due to the sudden decrease in effective circulation system volume.

3. Temperature should be monitored and care should be taken not to overheat the patient with warming devices. In studies of children, the rise in core body temperature is significantly greater with bilateral tourniquets compared to a single tourniquet.[34,41]

4. When tourniquets are used on more than one extremity, the first tourniquet cuff inflated should be completely deflated (and the cuff and limb protection removed, if possible) to assure circulation in the first limb has been restored. Problems related to incomplete tourniquet deflation could go unnoticed throughout the second limb procedure.

5. If possible, tourniquet deflations should be staggered 30 to 45 minutes apart to reduce the rapid release of large amounts of metabolic by-products into the vascular system. Tourniquet use causes anaerobic metabolism, which produces lactic acid and other metabolites. Lactic acidosis causes a decrease in vascular resistance and allows an increased blood flow when the tourniquet is deflated. The larger the muscle mass experiencing ischemia from the tourniquet, the greater the production of these metabolic by-products. Sequential deflation lessens the potential for adverse patient reactions to these by-products.[72] In children, when simultaneous deflation of bilateral tourniquets occurred, systolic blood pressure decreased 8–10 mm Hg and a greater decrease in pH was seen.[41]

Recommendation XIII

Potential patient injuries and complications associated with intravenous regional anesthesia (IVRA [ie, Bier block]) should be identified and safe practices should be established.

1. Tourniquet users should be familiar with the inflation-deflation sequence when using a dual-bladder cuff and when using two single-bladder cuffs together for IVRA. Severe injuries

and deaths have occurred when the wrong cuff was deflated.[73]

2. Patient assessment and tourniquet application before IVRA should include, but not be limited to, allergies to local anesthetics.

3. The appropriate tourniquet cuff should be selected.
   ◆ A dual-bladder tourniquet cuff and extra connective tubing are generally required.
   ◆ A wider placement site is needed because of the additional width of the dual-bladder tourniquet cuff.
   ◆ A higher pressure is generally required because each cuff bladder is narrower.

4. The tourniquet user should be fully aware of which cuff is proximal, which cuff is distal, and the inflation/deflation status of each at all times. Labeling or color-coding of the tubings to these cuffs facilitates identification.[2]

5. The tourniquet should be deflated gradually as determined by the physician to minimize the potential for an adverse reaction. As the tourniquet cuff deflates, the anesthetic agent is released into the circulatory system, causing systemic effects.

6. The perioperative registered nurse circulator should be aware of the patient's physiological status. Adverse reactions to local anesthetic agents are potential complications of IVRA. A bolus of local anesthesia entering the general circulation can occur when there is a sudden deflation of the tourniquet, from deflation soon after injection of local anesthetic, or if the bolus is released too rapidly at the end of the procedure. The sudden rush of anesthetic and metabolites into the circulatory system affects the central nervous system (eg, ringing in the ears, tingling, numbness, loss of consciousness, seizures) and the heart.

Recommendation XIV

The pneumatic tourniquet and accessories should be cleaned after each use.

1. After use, personnel should turn off the pneumatic tourniquet, clean all reusable parts, and inspect these parts according to the manufacturer's written instructions.

2. Reusable cuffs and bladders should be cleaned, rinsed, and dried between patients using a US Environmental Protection Agency (EPA) registered, intermediate-level, tuberculocidal disinfectant. The cuff and bladder should be rinsed thoroughly because cleaning solution residue may cause skin irritation, increase the chance of allergic reaction, and decrease the life of the cuff and bladder. If a cuff is unable to be cleaned adequately, it should be discarded in an appropriate receptacle.

3. All tubing should be cleaned, rinsed, and dried between patients and before storage, using an EPA-registered, detergent/intermediate-level disinfectant. Care must be taken to prevent introduction of solutions into the ports. Water in the ports contributes to microbial growth. Subsequent deflation of wet bladders may cause minute droplets of solution to be forced into the tourniquet regulating mechanism, causing damage.

4. Single-use cuffs should be discarded in an appropriate receptacle.

5. Tourniquet components contaminated with blood or other potentially infectious material should be cleaned with an enzymatic solution and an EPA-registered, intermediate-level disinfectant.

Recommendation XV

Patient assessments, the plan of care, interventions implemented, and evaluation of care related to use of a pneumatic tourniquet should be documented.

1. The Perioperative Nursing Data Set (PNDS), the uniform perioperative nursing vocabulary, should be used to document patient care and to develop policies and procedures related to pneumatic tourniquets on the intraoperative patient record. The expected outcomes of primary importance to these Recommended Practices are "The patient is free from signs or symptoms of injury due to equipment, instrumentation, sponges, or sharps" (O2). This outcome falls within the domain of Safety (D1). The associated nursing diagnoses may include "ineffective tissue perfusion" (X61), "risk for

impaired skin integrity" (X51), and "risk for impaired peripheral neurovascular function" (X41). The associated interventions that may lead to the desired outcome may be "Implements protective measures to prevent skin/tissue injury due to mechanical sources" (I77), "Uses supplies and equipment within safe parameters" (I122), "Evaluates for signs and symptoms of physical injury to skin and tissue" (I152), "Identifies baseline tissue perfusion" (I60), "Assesses factors related to risks for ineffective tissue perfusion" (I15), and "Evaluates postoperative tissue perfusion" (I46).[74]

2. Documentation should include, but not be limited to,
   - pneumatic tourniquet system identification serial number (I122),
   - calibrations (I122),
   - cuff pressure (I77),
   - skin protection (I77),
   - location of tourniquet cuff (I143),
   - skin integrity under the cuff before and after use of the pneumatic tourniquet (I77),
   - person placing tourniquet cuff,
   - time of inflation and deflation, and
   - assessment and evaluation of the entire extremity (I77).

3. Documentation of tourniquet testing should reflect the biomedical equipment identification number and/or serial number date of inspection, preventive maintenance, and status of all equipment. Records of equipment failure and preventative maintenance assist in identifying equipment performance problems or hazards and minimize risk of patient injury and equipment failure.

Recommendation XVI

Education, competency assessment, and validation should be conducted before the perioperative registered nurse manages the care of a patient using a pneumatic tourniquet.

1. Education of personnel operating pneumatic tourniquets should include, but is not limited to,
   - indications and contraindications,
   - physiologic changes during and after tourniquet use,
   - risks to patients,

♦ precautions to minimize these risks,
♦ proper operation of the tourniquet regulator,
♦ proper cuff application,
♦ measurement of LOP,
♦ documentation and communication,
♦ corrective actions to employ in the event of a patient injury, and
♦ proper care and handling of the tourniquet and accessories.

Tourniquets and accessories have been associated with patient injuries. Education provides a foundation to guide safe patient care and minimize these risks.

2. Periodic educational programs should be provided as reinforcement of principles and introduction of new technology and procedures. This periodic education should include, but is not limited to,
♦ changes in technology or procedures,
♦ compatibility of equipment and accessories,
♦ potential hazards, and
♦ precautions to be taken.

4. Administrative personnel should ensure that assessment and documentation of initial and annual personnel competency in the safe use of pneumatic tourniquets and accessories is performed. Individual competency assessment should include, but is not limited to,
♦ contraindications,
♦ risks,
♦ assessment of the skin under the cuff before and after use,
♦ assessment of limb perfusion before and after use,
♦ pre-use equipment checks,
♦ appropriate gas source,
♦ appropriate cuff selection,
♦ appropriate cuff pressure,
♦ approved duration and communication of tourniquet times, and
♦ required documentation.

Incorrect pneumatic tourniquet use can result in serious patient injury. Competency assurance verifies that personnel have knowledge of the use of the pneumatic tourniquet and appropriate corrective action taken in the event of a patient injury. This knowledge is essential to minimizing the risks of misuse of the equipment and providing a safe environment of care.

Recommendation XVII

Policies and procedures for pneumatic tourniquets should be developed, reviewed periodically, revised as necessary, and readily available in the practice setting.

1. Policies and procedures for the pneumatic tourniquet should include, but are not limited to,
♦ safety features required on pneumatic tourniquets;
♦ equipment maintenance programs;
♦ supplemental safety monitors required;
♦ equipment checks before initial use;
♦ reporting and impounding malfunctioning equipment;
♦ preoperative, intraoperative, and postoperative patient assessments;
♦ responsibility for cuff application;
♦ precautions during use;
♦ reporting of injuries;
♦ potential adverse events;
♦ care and cleaning of the tourniquet after use; and
♦ documentation.

2. The frequency, method, and criteria for pneumatic tourniquet testing should be established according to manufacturers' written instructions. A pneumatic tourniquet management program assists in identifying equipment problems that may have adverse effects on patient safety.

3. These recommended practices should be used as guidelines for developing policies and procedures in the practice setting. Policies and procedures establish authority, responsibility, and accountability. They also serve as operational guidelines and guide development of performance improvement activities.

Recommendation XVIII

The health care organization's quality management program should include investigation of adverse events and near misses associated with use of a pneumatic tourniquet.

1. Adverse patient outcomes and near misses associated with use of a pneumatic tourniquet should be collected, analyzed, and used for performance improvement as part of the health care organization's system-wide performance improvement program. To evaluate the quality of patient care and formulate plans for corrective action, it is necessary to maintain a system of evaluation.

2. If a patient injury or equipment failure occurs, the pneumatic tourniquet system (eg, regulator, tubing, cuff) must be handled in accordance with the Safe Medical Devices Act of 1990, amended in March 2000.[75] Device identification, maintenance and service information, and adverse event information should be included in the report from the practice setting. Retaining the regulator, tubing, and cuff allows for a complete systems check to determine the tourniquet system integrity.

Glossary

Bier block: A regional anesthetic involving occluding blood flow to and from the extremity and infusing local anesthetic agent intravenously into the extremity.

Contoured cuff: A tourniquet cuff with a distal edge shorter than the proximal edge, creating a funnel-like shape when applied to an extremity.

Compartment syndrome: A pathologic condition caused by the progressive development of arterial compression and consequent reduction of blood supply. Clinical manifestations include swelling, restriction of movement, vascular compromise, and severe pain or lack of sensation.

Exsanguination: The process of forcible expulsion of blood from an extremity before tourniquet use. The term also means massive blood loss.

Limb occlusion pressure (LOP): The unique cuff pressure required to occlude arterial flow in the limb.

Pneumatic: Pertaining to gas or air; filled with compressed gas or air.

Regulator: The mechanical device controlling the inflation, deflation, cuff pressure, and alarms for a tourniquet.

Shearing: A sliding movement of skin and subcutaneous tissue that leaves the underlying muscle stationary.

REFERENCES

1. "2004 National Patient Safety Goals: Practical strategies and helpful solutions for meeting these goals," Joint Commission on Accreditation of Healthcare Organizations, *http://www.jointcommission.org/PatientSafety/NationalPatientSafetyGoals/04_npsgs.htm* (accessed 13 Sept 2006).

2. "Tubing misconnections—A persistent and potentially deadly occurrence," *Sentinel Event Alert* (April 3, 2006) 36.

3. ECRI, "Tourniquets, pneumatic," *Healthcare Product Comparison System* (Plymouth Meeting, Pa: ECRI, 1997) 2.

4. P C Kam, R Kavanagh, F F Yoong, "The arterial tourniquet: Pathophysiological consequences and anaesthetic implications," *Anaesthesia* 56 (June 2001) 534-545.

5. J P Estebe, "Recommandations pour le bon usage du garrot pneumatique en chirurgie," *Annales Francaises d'Anesthesie et de Reanimation* 25 (March 2006) 330-332.

6. T P Kalla et al, "Survey of tourniquet use in podiatric surgery," *Journal of Foot and Ankle Surgery* 42 (March/April 2003) 68-76.

7. E Dounis et al, "Effect of time interval on tissue concentrations of cephalosporins after tourniquet inflation. Highest levels achieved by administration 20 minutes before inflation," *Acta Orthopedica Scandinavica* 66 (April 1995) 158-160.

8. N Papaioannou et al, "Tissue concentrations of third-generation cephalosporins (ceftazidime and ceftriaxone) in lower extremity tissues using a tourniquet," *Archives of Orthopedic Trauma Surgery* 113 (April 1994) 167-169.

9. A G Crenshaw et al, "Wide tourniquet cuffs more effective at lower inflation pressures," *Acta Orthopedica Scandinavica* 59 (August 1988) 447-451.

10. M R Moore, S R Garfin, A R Hargens, "Wide tourniquets eliminate blood flow at low inflation pressures," *American Journal of Hand Surgery* 12 (November 1987) 1006-1011.

11. J P Estebe et al, "Tourniquet pain in a volunteer study: Effect of changes in cuff width and pressure," *Anaesthesia* 55 (January 2000) 21-26.

12. R A Pedowitz et al, "The use of lower tourniquet inflation pressures in extremity surgery facilitated by curved and wide tourniquets and an integrated cuff inflation system," *Clinical Orthopedics and Related Research* 287 (February 1993) 237-244.

13. A S Younger, J A McEwen, K Inkpen, "Wide contoured thigh cuffs and automated limb occlusion measurement allow lower tourniquet pressures," *Clinical Orthopedics and Related Research* 428 (November 2004) 286-293.

14. B Graham et al, "Occlusion of arterial flow in the extremities at subsystolic pressures through the use of wide tourniquet cuffs," *Clinical Orthopedics and Related Research* 286 (January 1993) 257-261.

15. J R Lieberman, L T Staheli, M C Dales, "Tourniquet pressures on pediatric patients: A clinical study," *Orthopedics* 20 (December 1997) 1143-1147.

16. C Olivecrona et al, "Skin protection underneath the pneumatic tourniquet during total knee arthroplasty: A randomized controlled trial of 92 patients," *Acta Orthopedica* 77 (June 2006) 19-523.

17. R Din, T Geddes, "Skin protection beneath the tourniquet a prospective randomized trial," *ANZ Journal of Surgery* 74 (September 2004) 721-722.

18. A C Maury, W S Roy, "A prospective, randomized, controlled trial of forearm versus upper arm tourniquet tolerance," *British Journal of Hand Surgery* 27 (August 2002) 359-360.

19. A Odinsson, V Finsen, "The position of the tourniquet on the upper limb," *British Journal of Bone Joint Surgery* 84 (March 2002) 202-204.

20. V Finsen, AM Kasseth, "Tourniquets in forefoot surgery: Less pain when placed at the ankle," *British Journal of Bone Joint Surgery,*79 (January 1997) 99-101.

21. R Derner, J Buckholz, "Surgical hemostasis by pneumatic ankle tourniquet during 3027 podiatric operations," *Journal of Foot and Ankle Surgery* 34 (May/June 1995) 236-246.

22. N S Lichtenfeld, "The pneumatic ankle tourniquet with ankle block anesthesia for foot surgery," *Foot & Ankle* 13 (July/August 1992) 344-349.

23. A K Rudkin, G E Rudkin, G C Dracopoulos, "Acceptability of ankle tourniquet use in midfoot and forefoot surgery: Audit of 1000 cases," *Foot & Ankle International* 25 (November 2004) 788-794.

24. K A Krackow, "A maneuver for improved positioning of a tourniquet in the obese patient," *Clinical Orthopedics and Related Research* 168 (August 1982) 80-82.

25. R S Cajee, "Fatal thrombo-embolism after limb exsanguination: A case report," *South African Medical Journal* 68 (August 31 1985) 349-350.

26. S Darmanis, A Papanikolaou, D Pavlakis, "Fatal intra-operative pulmonary embolism following application of an Esmarch bandage," *Injury* 33 (November 2002) 761-764.

27. J G Boogaerts, "Fatal pulmonary embolism during limb exsanguination," (Letters to the Editor) *Canadian Journal of Anaesthesia* 45 (October 1998) 1031-1032.

28. J A McEwen et al, "Tourniquet safety in lower leg applications," *Orthopedic Nursing* 21 (September/October 2002) 55-62.

29. B Tuncali et al, "A new method for estimating arterial occlusion pressure in optimizing pneumatic tourniquet inflation pressure," *Anesthesia and Analgesia* 102 (June 2006) 1752-1757.

30. RR Hagenouw et al, "Tourniquet pain: A volunteer study," *Anesthesia and Analgesia* 65 (November 1986) 1175-1180.

31. R J Newman, A Muirhead, "A safe and effective low pressure tourniquet: A prospective evaluation," *British Journal of Bone and Joint Surgery* 68 (August 1986) 625-628.

32. R L Worland et al, "Thigh pain following tourniquet application in simultaneous bilateral total knee replacement arthroplasty," *Journal of Arthroplasty* 12 (December 1997) 848-852.

33. J A McEwen, "Tourniquet use and care," *http://www .interchg.ubc.ca/jamc/use_care.html* (accessed 20 Sept 2006).

34. S J Tredwell et al, "Pediatric tourniquets: Analysis of cuff and limb interface, current practice, and guidelines for use," *Journal of Pediatric Orthopedics* 21 (September/October 2001) 671-676.

35. A J Hodgson, "A proposed etiology for tourniquet-induced neuropathies," *Journal of Biomechanical Engineering* 116 (May 1994) 224-227.

36. M D Jacobson et al, "Muscle functional deficits after tourniquet ischemia," *American Journal of Sports Medicine* 22 (May-June 1994) 372-377.

37. T T Horlocker et al, "Anesthetic, patient, and surgical risk factors for neurologic complications after prolonged total tourniquet time during total knee arthroplasty," *Anesthesia and Analgesia* 102 (March 2006) 950-955.

38. A Y On, O Ozdemir, R Aksit, "Tourniquet paralysis after primary nerve repair," *American Journal of Physical Medicine & Rehabilitation* 79 (May/June 2000) 298-300.

39. ECRI, "Unintended inflation and deflation of Zimmer model ATS 1500 pneumatic tourniquet cuffs," *Health Devices* 26 (September/October 1997) 391-392.

40. K Aho et al, "Pneumatic tourniquet paralysis: Case report," *British Journal of Bone and Joint Surgery* 65 (August 1983) 441-443.

41. A M Lynn et al, "Systemic responses to tourniquet release in children," *Anesthesia and Analgesia* 65 (August 1986) 865-872.

42. P M Sutter et al, "Increased surface expression of CD18 and CD11b in leukocytes after tourniquet ischemia during elective hand surgery," *World Journal of Surgery* 21 (February 1997) 179-184, (Invited Commentary) 185.

43. J P Estebe, Y Malledant, "Le garrot pneumatique d'orthopedie (Pneumatic tourniquets in orthopedics)," *Annales Francaise d'Anesthesie et Reanimation* 15 (February 1996) 162-178.

44. J C Tsui et al, "Altered endothelin-1 levels in acute lower limb ischemia and reperfusion," *Angiology* 55 (September/October 2004) 533-539.

45. A Wakai et al, "Tourniquet-induced systemic inflammatory response in extremity surgery," *Journal of Trauma* 51 (November 2001) 922-926.

46. J P Estebe et al, "Use of a pneumatic tourniquet induces changes in central temperature," *British Journal of Anaesthesia* 77 (December 1996) 786-788.

47. B J Sanders, J G D'Alessio, J R Jernigan, "Intraoperative hypothermia associated with lower extremity tourniquet deflation," *Journal of Clinical Anesthesia* 8 (September 1996) 504-507.

48. K Hirota et al, "The relationship between pneumatic tourniquet time and the amount of pulmonary emboli in patients undergoing knee arthroscopic surgeries," *Anesthesia and Analgesia* 93 (September 2001) 776-780.

49. M Girardis et al, "The hemodynamic and metabolic effects of tourniquet application during knee surgery," *Anesthesia and Analgesia* 91 (September 2000) 727-731.

50. T Akata et al, "Changes in body temperature following deflation of limb pneumatic tourniquet," *Journal of Clinical Anesthesia* 10 (February 1998) 17-22.

51. E C Bloch et al, "Limb tourniquets and central temperature in anesthetized children," *Anesthesia and Analgesia* 74 (April 1992) 486-489.

52. E C Bloch, "Hyperthermia resulting from tourniquet application in children," *Annals of the Royal College of Surgeons of England* 68 (July 1986) 193-194.

53. D L Bourke et al, "Respiratory responses associated with release of intraoperative tourniquets," *Anesthesia and Analgesia* 69 (October 1989) 541-544.

54. H S Townsend et al, "Tourniquet release: Systemic and metabolic effects," *Acta Anaesthesiologica Scandinavica* 40 (November 1996) 1234-1237.

55. H Iwama et al, "Circulatory, respiratory and metabolic changes after thigh tourniquet release in combined epidural-propofol anaesthesia with preservation of spontaneous respiration," *Anaesthesia* 57 (June 2002) 588-592.

56. K Hirota et al, "Quantification and comparison of pulmonary emboli formation after pneumatic tourniquet release in patients undergoing reconstruction of anterior cruciate ligament and total knee arthroplasty," *Anesthesia and Analgesia* 94 (June 2002) 1633-1638.

57. K R Conaty, M S Klemm, "Severe increase of intracranial pressure after deflation of a pneumatic tourniquet," *Anesthesiology* 71 (August 1989) 294-295.

58. B J McGrath et al, "Venous embolization after deflation of lower extremity tourniquets," *Anesthesia and Analgesia* 78 (February 1994) 349-353.

59. J L Parmet et al, "The incidence of large venous emboli during total knee arthroplasty without pneumatic tourniquet use," *Anesthesia and Analgesia* 87 (August 1998) 439-444.

60. J L Parmet et al, "The incidence of venous emboli during extramedullary guided total knee arthroplasty," *Anesthesia and Analgesia* 81 (October 1995) 757-762.

61. J L Parmet et al, "Echogenic emboli upon tourniquet release during total knee arthroplasty: Pulmonary hemodynamic changes and embolic composition," *Anesthesia and Analgesia* 79 (November 1994) 940-945.

62. J L Parmet et al, "Thromboembolism coincident with tourniquet deflation during total knee arthroplasty," *Lancet* 341 (April 24, 1993) 1057-1058.

63. "2006 Critical Access Hospital and Hospital National Patient Safety Goals," Joint Commission on Accreditation of Healthcare Organizations, *http://www.jointcommission.org/PatientSafety/NationalPatientSafetyGoals/06_npsg_cah.htm* (accessed 10 Aug 2006).

64. A S Younger et al, "Survey of tourniquet use in orthopaedic foot and ankle surgery," *Foot & Ankle International* 26 (March 2005) 208-217.

65. D O'Neil, J E Sheppard, "Transient compartment syndrome of the forearm resulting from venous congestion from a tourniquet," *American Journal of Hand Surgery* 14 (September 1989) 894-896.

66. Greene TL, Louis DS. Compartment syndrome of the arm—A complication of the pneumatic tourniquet: A case report," *American Journal of Bone and Joint Surgery* 65 (February 1983) 270-273.

67. F W Blaisdell, "The pathophysiology of skeletal muscle ischemia and the reperfusion syndrome: A review," *Cardiovascular Surgery* 10 (December 2002) 620-630.

68. A Wakai et al, "Pneumatic tourniquets in extremity surgery," *Journal of the American Academy of Orthopedic Surgery* 9 (September/October 2001) 345-351.

69. J D Cohen et al, "Massive pulmonary embolism and tourniquet deflation," *Anesthesia and Analgesia* 79 (September 1994) 583-585.

70. S Araki, M Uchiyama, "Fatal pulmonary embolism following tourniquet inflation: A case report," *Acta Orthopedica Scandinavica* 62 (October 1991) 488.

71. A T Berman et al, "Emboli observed with use of transesophageal echocardiography immediately after tourniquet release during total knee arthroplasty with cement," *American Journal of Bone and Joint Surgery* 80 (March 1998) 389-396.

72. J J Branson, W M Goldstein, "Sequential bilateral total knee arthroplasty," *AORN Journal* 73 (March 2001) 610-635.

73. "Pneumatic tourniquets used for regional anesthesia," *Health Devices* 12 (December 1982) 48-49.

74. S C Beyea, ed, *Perioperative Nursing Data Set: The Perioperative Vocabulary,* second ed, (Denver: AORN, Inc, 2002) 85-87.

75. "Medical device reporting: Manufacturer reporting, importer reporting, user facility reporting, distributor reporting," *Federal Register* 65 (Jan 26, 2000) 4112-4121.

Originally published April 1984, *AORN Journal.* Revised November 1990.

Published as proposed recommended practices March 1994. Revised November 1998; published December 1998. Reformatted July 2000.

Revised November 2001; published February 2002, *AORN Journal.*

Revised 2006; published in *Standards, Recommended Practices, and Guidelines,* 2007 edition.

AORN Perioperative Standards and Recommended Practices, 2009 Edition

Recommended Practices for Product Selection in Perioperative Practice Settings

The following recommended practices were developed by the AORN Recommended Practices Committee and have been approved by the AORN Board of Directors. They were presented as proposed recommended practices for comment to members and others. These recommended practices are effective January 1, 2004.

These recommended practices are intended as achievable recommendations representing what is believed to be an optimal level of practice. Policies and procedures will reflect variations in practice settings or clinical situations that determine the degree to which the recommended practices can be implemented.

AORN recognizes the numerous types of settings in which perioperative nurses practice. These recommended practices are intended as guidelines adaptable to various practice settings. These practice settings include traditional operating rooms, ambulatory surgery units, physicians' offices, cardiac catheterization suites, endoscopy suites, radiology departments, and all other areas where surgical and other invasive procedures may be performed.

Purpose

These recommended practices provide guidelines for selecting medical devices and other products used in perioperative settings. AORN recognizes that many facilities belong to purchasing organizations and may be limited to selecting products from contract vendors. As new medical devices and products are introduced, choices continue to exist, and perioperative nurses continue to have an integral role in evaluating and selecting products that may affect the quality and safety of perioperative patient care.

Patient safety is a primary concern of perioperative nurses, and safety concerns must continue to drive perioperative nurses as they participate in evaluating and selecting medical devices and products for use in practice settings. Patient safety is one of the four domains of perioperative nursing (ie, safety, physiologic responses, behavioral responses, structural data elements) as specified in the Perioperative Nursing Data Set.[1] This nursing vocabulary was defined and published by AORN and is a Health Level Seven registered vocabulary. The National Library of Medicine is considering including the data set in the Unified Medical Language System.

Recommendation I

A mechanism for product and medical device standardization and evaluation should be implemented.

1. Capital equipment and medical device procurement are collaborative processes requiring clinical, business, financial, and legal acumen. Goals of product standardization and value analysis processes are to select functional and reliable products that are safe, cost-effective, and environmentally conscious and that promote quality care and avoid duplication or rapid obsolescence.[2] All departments involved in the selection, purchase, and use of products and medical devices should be represented on a multidisciplinary product evaluation and selection committee.[3,4] These departments may include, but are not limited to,
   - surgical services;
   - nursing services;
   - administration;
   - infection control;
   - surgeons, surgical staff members, OR committee members;
   - central/sterile processing;
   - pharmacy;
   - education;
   - materiel management and purchasing;
   - anesthesia;
   - biomedical engineering;
   - environmental services;
   - risk management;
   - radiology;
   - laboratory; and
   - institutional review board (IRB).

   Committee members other than perioperative personnel should be consulted to obtain input from departments with similar needs to select the most appropriate products and medical devices.[4,5]

2. Additional subcommittees or task forces may be needed because of the size of the facility or because a specialty product may have a limited user group.

3. The role of a perioperative multidisciplinary team may include initiating, coordinating, and participating in clinical evaluation of products and medical devices. Perioperative nurses frequently are involved in direct surgical patient care and in

the use and evaluation of products and medical devices.[4] Manufacturers' representatives should be contacted to serve as resource people for information about new or existing products and medical devices. These individuals have access to information concerning products currently on the market.[4,6] Manufacturers' representatives should be able to provide both clinical and technical data related to product research, new products and medical devices, packaging, sterilization, and environmental conservation.

4. E-commerce business-to-business applications should be used when applicable. Use of e-commerce applications can help with
   - collecting product data,
   - assessing group purchasing organization (GPO) catalogs,
   - soliciting pricing information,
   - comparing prices,
   - exploring online auctions for surplus or refurbished equipment,
   - enhancing buying power,
   - consolidating or reducing inventory, and
   - purchasing items online.[7]

Recommendation II

Product and medical device evaluations should be based on objective criteria specific to an item's function and use.

1. Criteria to evaluate medical devices and other products, including implants, may include, but are not limited to,
   - safety, performance, quality, and improved efficiency;
   - purpose and use;
   - ease of use;
   - compatibility with other products or medical devices;
   - impact on quality patient care and clinical outcomes;
   - efficacy;
   - cost/value analysis;
   - reimbursement potential;
   - compliance with GPOs;
   - sterilization/reprocessing parameters;
   - liability (eg, for investigational devices);
   - regulatory control (eg, from the US Food and Drug Administration);

   - standardization;
   - new technology competitiveness;
   - adaptability to future technology;
   - environmental impact;
   - availability and quality of service after purchase;
   - investment in personnel training; and
   - e-commerce applications (eg, support information, access, operational efficiency, availability).

2. Careful selection of criteria ensures the reliability and validity of trial evaluation results.[3,4,6] Cost considerations should be weighed against patient and personnel safety and user preference. All direct and indirect costs of products and medical devices (eg, waste disposal, processing, training, storage) should be identified and evaluated.[8]

3. Each product or medical device, disposable supply, or capital equipment purchase should be evaluated with criteria pertinent to the item. Specific and unique information may be required. Use a product-specific, written evaluation tool to facilitate objective review and analysis.[3,4,6]

Recommendation III

A clinical evaluation should be initiated based on an identified need or opportunity.

1. Appropriate committee members should screen products and medical devices before clinical evaluations are conducted. Unnecessary expenditure of time and money can be avoided if a viable need, issue, or concern is established first. A review of the literature on products and medical devices being evaluated may prevent clinical evaluations of inappropriate items.[2,3,9]

2. All departments and clinical areas affected by a product or medical device should be represented during the clinical evaluation process. Clinical functioning can best be measured in the practice setting by knowledgeable end users. Including all clinical areas in the evaluation process provides direct feedback from staff members whose practices will be affected by the item.[3-6,9,10] Standardization within the practice setting is increased when all clinical areas are involved.

3. Limits should be placed on the scope and time of the clinical evaluation. These limits should include, but are not limited to,
   - number of users,
   - cost,
   - number of products or medical devices to be evaluated,
   - time span,
   - number of departments and clinical areas involved,
   - desired patient outcomes, and
   - follow-up patient data, if indicated.

   Limits for evaluating products or medical devices increase the usefulness of user feedback. Unlimited time to evaluate products or medical devices may result in decreased evaluator input and enthusiasm.[6]

4. Demonstration of and instruction on use of the product or medical device being evaluated should be conducted before the clinical evaluation begins. Instructing all individuals involved in the clinical evaluation facilitates safe clinical practice and helps establish validity of the product or medical device evaluation.[4-6]

Recommendation IV

Evaluation data should be analyzed to determine product recommendations.

1. When evaluating data, actual clinical performance should be compared to predetermined standards.[4,6] Individuals participating in the clinical evaluation should provide data about the product or medical device to complete the evaluation tool.

2. Data should be analyzed and a summary of findings, conclusions, and recommendations presented. This information facilitates efficient and consistent decisions based on preestablished criteria and an evidence-based product assessment.[2,3]

3. A value analysis may be performed as part of the evaluation and selection process.[2,10] Whenever possible, selected products should have a positive cost-benefit ratio. Products that do not have a positive cost-benefit ratio should have other, more critical redeeming factors that make them an appropriate selection for purchase.

4. Upon completion of the evaluation process, a list of products or medical devices can be compiled as a basis for obtaining competitive bids and making alternative product or medical device purchases.[2-4,6]

5. After a product or medical device has been selected, a comprehensive plan for introduction, use, and further evaluation of the item should be developed and implemented in the facility.[2,4] New product performance and user satisfaction should be evaluated at planned intervals. This evaluation helps ensure that new products are meeting expected performance criteria—including cost-effectiveness performance criteria—and that the preselection evaluation process has met its objectives.

Recommendation V

Policies and procedures for evaluating and selecting products and medical devices should be written, reviewed periodically, and readily available in perioperative practice settings.

1. Policies and procedures establish authority, responsibility, and accountability for product evaluation and selection. They serve as operational guidelines and provide a framework for continuous quality improvement activities related to product evaluation and selection.

2. Written guidelines should be available for all health care personnel involved in the selection and evaluation of commonly used products and medical devices. Orientation and ongoing education activities for personnel should include an introduction to and review of policies and procedures to be applied in the practice setting. Compliance with policies and procedures helps develop and reinforce knowledge, skills, and attitudes that affect patient outcomes.

REFERENCES
1. S Beyea, ed, *Perioperative Nursing Data Set,* second ed (Denver: AORN, Inc, 2002).
2. A M Fernandez et al, "Technology assessment in healthcare: A review and description of a 'best practice' technology assessment process," *Best Practices and Benchmarking in Healthcare* 2 (November/December 1997) 241.
3. R Podabinski, D Monckton, J Thompson, "A new product selection model," (Material Management) *OR Manager* 15 (September 1999) 34-40.

4. M Dickerson, "Product evaluation: A key to controlling costs," *Nursing Economic$* 5 (March/April 1987) 60-64.

5. C Rupert, S Kitzman, "The clinical voice in product selection and implementation," *SSM* 8 (August 2002) 24-26.

6. P Barone-Ameduri, "Equipment trials make sense," *Nursing Management* 17 (June 1986) 43-44.

7. F Doyle C Weisbrod, "Endless possibilities: Using the Internet in the supply chain process," *SSM* 8 (February 2002) 24-28.

8. P S Hunt, "Speaking the language of finance," *AORN Journal* 73 (April 2001) 774-787.

9. E Beaumont, "Technology scorecard: Are you up to date?" *American Journal of Nursing* 96 (December 1996) 23-28.

10. S B Wilen, B M Stone, "Cost versus cost effectiveness: The Achilles' heel for healthcare delivery," (Editorial) *Best Practices and Benchmarking in Healthcare* 2 (May/June 1997) 142-144.

RESOURCES

Baird, M V G. "Product selection in the OR: A decision-making model," *AORN Journal* 48 (September 1988) 512-517.

Weatherly, K S, et al. "Product evaluation process: A systems approach to controlling health care costs," *AORN Journal* 59 (February 1994) 489-494, 496-498.

Wilhelm-Hass, E. "Breaking the time barrier: Learning from a new product evaluation," *AORN Journal* 56 (December 1992) 1074-1081.

Originally published April 1989, *AORN Journal.* Revised August 1993.

Revised November 1997; published January 1998, *AORN Journal.* Reformatted July 2000.

Revised November 2003; published in *Standards, Recommended Practices, and Guidelines,* 2004 edition. Reprinted March 2004, *AORN Journal.*

Recommended Practices
for Surgical Tissue Banking

The following recommended practices were developed by the AORN Recommended Practices Committee and have been approved by the AORN Board of Directors. They were presented as proposed recommended practices for comments by members and others. They are effective January 1, 2006.

These recommended practices are intended as achievable recommendations representing what is believed to be an optimal level of practice. Policies and procedures will reflect variations in practice settings and/or clinical situations that determine the degree to which the recommended practices can be implemented.

AORN recognizes the numerous settings in which perioperative nurses practice. These recommended practices are intended as guidelines adaptable to various practice settings. These practice settings include traditional operating rooms, ambulatory surgery centers, physicians' offices, cardiac catheterization suites, endoscopy suites, radiology departments, and all other areas where operative and other invasive procedures may be performed.

Purpose

Surgical tissue banking encompasses procuring, processing, preserving, and/or storing selected human cells and tissue. Human tissue includes, but is not limited to, bone, cartilage, ligaments, tendons, fascia, dura mater, sclera, corneas, heart valves/conduits, bone marrow, vessels, and skin. It is beyond the scope of these recommended practices to address all areas of tissue banking, solid organ transplantation, or nonhuman tissue. These recommended practices provide guidance for developing organizational policies and procedures that are specific to the needs of surgical patients and address the perioperative practice setting and expertise required of personnel.

A tissue bank should be established only where a need exists. Before the decision is made to establish a tissue bank, consideration should be given to personnel, equipment, and practical operational requirements for providing safe, reliable, and biologically useful products.

In 1997, the US Food and Drug Administration (FDA) announced a program for comprehensive regulatory oversight of tissue banking.[1] In support of this program, the FDA has published proposed guidance documents that were later clarified as final rules.[2-6] The agency intends to propose more regulations in the future in the form of guidance documents. Adherence to these regulations is required during the development and ongoing operation of a human tissue bank. In addition, the standards published by the American Association of Tissue Banks (AATB)[7] should be referred to for additional direction.

Effective July 1, 2005, the Joint Commission on Accreditation of Healthcare Organizations (JCAHO) standards for tissue banking have been updated in the laboratory accreditation program and additionally applied to ambulatory care, critical access hospital and hospital accreditation programs, and office-based surgery practices. The standards apply to organizations that store or issue human, nonhuman, and synthetic tissue, including surgery and outpatient centers.[8]

Recommendation I

Facilities procuring, processing, and/or preserving tissue, and facilities storing tissue for potential transfer to a different facility, must register as tissue banks with the FDA.[4]

1. A list of types of human cells, tissue, and cellular and tissue-based products must be submitted with the application to the FDA.[4] Facilities that recover, screen, test, process, label, package, and/or distribute human cells or tissue for implantation, transplantation, or infusion must register with the FDA. The registration form includes a list of tissues and cells to be used in this process.[4] Facilities must register within five days after beginning operations, notify the FDA within six months of changes in products, and update the registration annually in December. Facilities storing only purchased tissue for use within the same facility, or those who recover autologous skin or skull bone flaps for later reimplantation into the same patient, are not required to register as tissue banks. Additional clarification is available from the FDA.

2. Facilities should verify that tissue and cells acquired from outside sources have been procured, processed, stored, and distributed by tissue banks registered with the FDA and licensed by state agencies.[8] Depending on the type of

tissue being acquired, outside sources of cells or tissues also should be accredited by the AATB, the Eye Bank Association of America (EBAA), or the AABB (formerly known as the American Association of Blood Banks). Accreditation by any of these agencies demonstrates that these sources periodically pass inspections by the accrediting agency and provides minimum assurance of quality control for the recovery, screening, testing, processing, storage, and distribution of the tissue. Some tissue banks purchase tissue procured or processed by other tissue banks and have limited registration or accreditation. All tissue banks involved in handling the tissue must be registered and should be accredited. Copies of current certificates should be requested annually and kept on file.

Recommendation II

Facilities procuring, processing, preserving, storing, or distributing tissue to other facilities should have defined oversight with authority and accountability for all activities performed.[8]

1. A facility performing any tissue-banking activities should appoint an administrator or oversight group accountable for these activities. The administrator of a tissue bank is accountable for all aspects of the tissue bank's activities, including compliance with regulations. This role requires a broad understanding of the processes and responsibilities involved.

2. Administrative personnel should be knowledgeable about
   ♦ all applicable federal, state, and local regulations;
   ♦ applicable standards of the AATB, EBAA, and AABB;
   ♦ accrediting agency requirements;
   ♦ screening and testing criteria;
   ♦ the grieving process;
   ♦ aspects of informed consent;
   ♦ donor and recipient rights;
   ♦ quality control;
   ♦ documentation and record-keeping requirements;
   ♦ confidentiality and release of information;
   ♦ requirements for release of tissue;
   ♦ adverse event reporting; and
   ♦ ethical considerations.

3. A physician or medical advisory committee should be available to provide direction for medical decisions. The AATB recommends that a medical director be appointed.[7]

4. Tissue ordering and receiving, procuring, processing, preserving, storing, and distributing should be coordinated throughout the health care facility.[8] Centralized oversight of all aspects of tissue banking is necessary to ensure that all tissue received and stored is safe for implantation, that processes are validated and monitored on an ongoing basis, and that all tissue can be traced back to the source or easily recalled if necessary.

Recommendation III

Surgical tissue bank personnel must be knowledgeable about the aspects of tissue banking in which they participate.[6]

1. Personnel should be knowledgeable about the importance of the tissue bank products and services. An understanding of the importance of tissue bank activities instills an attitude of attention to detail, and may minimize errors.

2. Personnel soliciting tissue donations must be knowledgeable about
   ♦ federal and state regulations,
   ♦ screening and testing criteria,
   ♦ the grieving process,
   ♦ aspects of informed consent,
   ♦ donor and recipient rights, and
   ♦ ethical considerations.

   Requesting authorization for donation of tissue requires unique interpersonal communication skills to ensure that donations are legally and ethically solicited and accepted.

3. Personnel screening potential donors must be knowledgeable about
   ♦ the grieving process;
   ♦ screening and testing criteria;
   ♦ sources of information for screening (eg, relevant medical records, knowledgeable historian);
   ♦ techniques to obtain accurate and complete information; and
   ♦ resources and options available when screening results are ambiguous or unclear.

Screening requires specific training to learn the best sources of medical history and behavioral risk assessment information. This source may be friends rather than family members. Obtaining the most accurate information requires strategies for interviewing. At times, the results of screening may not be clear. The screening individual needs to know what resources are available to assist with the determination of suitability.

4. Personnel processing and/or packaging tissue must be knowledgeable about
   ◆ environmental conditions required,
   ◆ steps in the processing procedures,
   ◆ labeling requirements,
   ◆ packaging,
   ◆ documentation,
   ◆ appropriate measures to be taken when tissue is compromised, and
   ◆ disposal of unsuitable tissue.

   Understanding the steps of tissue processing is essential to preventing errors that may alter the integrity and/or function of the tissue, contaminate it, or negatively affect the outcomes of transplantation. Disposal of human tissue must be done in compliance with federal and state regulations. Complete and accurate documentation for tracing tissue disposition is required by the FDA.

5. Administrators should ensure that initial and ongoing educational opportunities are provided to meet the needs of personnel who perform tasks within the surgical tissue bank. Regulations and standards affecting tissue bank activities are evolving. Initial education provides a baseline to support a beginning level of job performance. Ongoing education offers personnel an opportunity to enhance skills and learn about changes in regulations and standards. An introduction and review of tissue banking policies and procedures should be included in the orientation and ongoing education of personnel to assist in the development of knowledge, skills, and attitudes that positively affect patient outcomes.

6. Administrators should ensure that the employees performing tasks within the surgical tissue bank are competent to perform these tasks.

Competency assurance is essential because errors may cause breaches in regulations, compromise the integrity or function of the tissue, contaminate it, and/or lead to negative outcomes of transplantation.

Recommendation IV

Potential donors, their families, and recipients of tissue should be treated with respect, dignity, and sensitivity, and their rights should be protected.

1. Personnel approaching living donors or families of potential deceased donors to request consent for donation should be sensitive to the level of distress the situation may cause and respect the individual's rights. Tissue donation is frequently requested at the time of an unexpected death. This event creates distress in the survivors and is emotionally charged. Sensitivity to the needs of the survivors is essential to a successful donation. Perioperative personnel also should recognize that the deceased donor is an individual with the same rights that would be afforded to any other patient. At times, donation is requested of a living relative. This situation also may trigger strong emotions and ethical dilemmas. The person's rights should be honored.

2. Personnel should obtain informed consent from the donor or donor's responsible party before tissue recovery. Permission to retrieve tissue from nonliving donors should be sought from next of kin in order of legal precedence. If the next of kin is unavailable, local, state, and federal regulations should be followed. The Uniform Anatomical Gift Act (UAGA) of 1968, passed in all 50 states, provides guidelines within which consent may be obtained upon death of the donor, including an order of priority for the potential donor's next of kin. Additional guidelines concerning donations appear in the 1987 amendments to the UAGA and were clarified in 2001 by the US Department of Health and Human Services.[9] Individual state laws may vary. Some states expressly honor the donor's documented wishes (eg, donor registry, driver's license, donor card or directive) as legal consent in lieu of obtaining additional authorization from the next of kin.

Key elements of an informed consent include
- identification of tissues to be recovered;
- explanation of the potential uses of the tissue (eg, transplantation, research, education);
- a general description of the recovery process; and
- explanations that the family may limit or restrict the use of the tissue.[9]

3. Personnel should provide the family with written materials disclosing the intended uses of the tissue and the nature of the donation, including
- a copy of the signed consent form,
- instructions on how to follow up with the tissue bank should concerns arise,
- a description of the uses for which donated tissue may be applied, and
- a list and description of other companies and entities with which the tissue bank has relationships for processing and distributing tissue.

The tissue bank is responsible for ensuring that accurate, sensitive, and appropriate information is shared with the person giving consent. Using written materials ensures consistency and allows the person providing consent an opportunity to review the material again.[2]

4. Allograft donations from living donors should be accepted only if the medical, legal, and ethical conditions surrounding the donations meet approved criteria. Questionable conditions include undue medical risk to the donor, coercion, promises of monetary gain, and the diminished capacity of the donor to evaluate the medical or surgical risks.[7]

5. Informed consent should be obtained from patients receiving tissue transplants, following a discussion of the risks, benefits, and alternatives.

Recommendation V

Tissue for transplantation must be recovered only from suitable donors.

1. A responsible individual(s) must determine allograft donor suitability based on results of required screening and testing for risk factors or the presence of relevant communicable disease agents and diseases.[5,7] Individuals making the determination of donor suitability must be knowledgeable about the legal requirements and medical risks involved and must have the formal authority to make this determination. This responsibility may rest with a medical director or a medical advisory committee.

2. A responsible individual should screen donors of allografts for risk factors and clinical evidence of relevant infectious agents and diseases before recovery of tissues. Screening includes documenting the review of relevant medical records, performing a strict physical assessment, and conducting detailed interviews with a knowledgeable historian. Donor screening minimizes the risk of transmission of infectious agents and diseases to the recipient and minimizes the risk of retrieving tissue that is not suitable for transplantation.

3. Allograft donor exclusion criteria include the following:
- active systemic viral, bacterial, or fungal infection;
- disease history of unknown etiology;
- risk associated with human transmissible spongiform encephalopathy (eg, Creutzfeldt-Jakob disease [CJD], a blood relative with noniatrogenic CJD, rapidly progressive dementia, receipt of human pituitary-derived hormones, receipt of human dura mater grafts, travel/residency risks associated with variant CJD);
- certain autoimmune diseases;
- fever associated with a possible infectious etiology; and
- meeting any of the high-risk criteria for relevant communicable disease agents identified by the FDA, including
  - physical evidence for risk of sexually transmitted diseases such as genital ulcerative disease, herpes simplex, syphilis, chancroid;
  - for a male donor, physical evidence of anal intercourse, including perianal condyloma;
  - physical evidence of nonmedical percutaneous drug use, such as needle tracks, (note any tattoos that may be covering needle tracks);
  - physical evidence of recent tattooing, ear piercing, or body piercing;
  - disseminated lymphadenopathy;

- oral thrush;
- blue or purple spots consistent with Kaposi's sarcoma;
- unexplained jaundice, hepatomegaly, or icterus (note that hepatomegaly may not be apparent in a physical assessment unless an autopsy is performed);
- physical evidence of sepsis, such as unexplained generalized rash;
- large scab consistent with recent smallpox immunization;
- eczema vaccinatum;
- generalized vesicular rash (ie, generalized vaccinia);
- severely necrotic lesion consistent with vaccinia necrosum; and/or
- corneal scarring consistent with vaccinial keratitis.[10]

The medical director or medical advisory committee should evaluate potential donors with metabolic or bone disease, malignancy or malignant neoplasm, or disease of unknown etiology on a case-by-case basis. Some diseases have a range of severity that may cause the tissue to be appropriate or inappropriate for donation. A physician with knowledge and oversight responsibilities should evaluate these potential donors and make this determination. Potential donors are screened to minimize the risk of transmission of infection or disease. Recipients of pituitary-derived human growth hormone, human dura mater, or gonadotropin, as well as those who meet the travel/residency parameters associated with an increased exposure risk to the human form of bovine spongiform encephalopathy (BSE), may be at risk of carrying the agent causing CJD or variant CJD and should be excluded from consideration for tissue procurement.[5,10] Xenotransplantation recipients and their intimate contacts should be excluded from potential transplantation because xenotransplants may harbor infectious agents from the donor animal. These infectious agents also may have been transmitted to intimate contacts of the xenotransplant recipient. The FDA considers these individuals not to be suitable donors.[5,10]

Donor screening minimizes the risk of transmitting infectious agents and diseases to tissue recipients through transplantation.[10] Contraindications and exclusion criteria are evolving as new knowledge is gained and infectious disease threats are identified. Tissue bank administrations should remain informed of changes in the recommendations of the Centers for Disease Control and Prevention (CDC), FDA, and AATB and incorporate these changes into screening criteria.

4. Donors of allografts must be tested with FDA-approved, cleared, or licensed tests by laboratories compliant with the Clinical Laboratory Improvement Amendments of 1988 and found negative for relevant infectious agents and diseases, including, but not limited to

- HIV type 1 and type 2 (anti-HIV-1 and anti-HIV-2);
- hepatitis B virus (HBV) surface antigen (HBsAg);
- total antibody to hepatitis B core antigen (antiHBc)—(IgG+IgM);
- hepatitis C virus (HCV) (anti-HCV);
- *Treponema pallidum* (syphilis) confirmatory test;
- human T-lymphotropic virus (Types I and II); and
- cytomegalovirus.[5]

Living donors should be tested for hepatitis HBc core antibody (anti-HBc) and should be retested 180 days after recovery before tissues are released for allogenic use. Testing for these infectious agents minimizes the risk of transmission and is required by the FDA final rule.[3] Donors of dura mater grafts also must be tested for the infectious agent that causes CJD; this includes a recommendation that a qualified pathologist perform an examination of the donor's entire brain.[5]

Recommendation VI

Tissue must be recovered, processed, and transplanted in clean, controlled environments appropriate for sterile surgical procedures.

1. Traffic patterns should be established and maintained in accordance with AORN's "Recommended practices for traffic patterns in the perioperative practice setting."[11] Traffic control in the OR minimizes the potential for contamination of the tissue retrieved. Eyes usually are procured with intact corneas in less controlled

environments; however, the corneas should be removed from the eyes, processed, and transplanted in an OR-type environment.

2. The environment should be cleaned in accordance with AORN's "Recommended practices for environmental cleaning in the surgical practice setting."[12] Cleaning should be performed on a routine basis and as needed to reduce the amount of organic and inorganic debris and microbial load that can potentially contaminate the tissue. The FDA requires that the facility for tissue recovery be controlled to minimize the risk for contamination or cross-contamination through the introduction or transmission of communicable disease.[6(p68683)]

3. Surgical attire should be worn during recovery and transplantation of tissue in accordance with AORN's "Recommended practices for surgical attire."[13] Clean surgical attire minimizes contamination of the tissue.

4. Only powder-free gloves should be used. Glove powder is aerosolized when powdered gloves are used.[14] Powder can contaminate recovered tissue and may lead to adverse reactions or rejections of the tissue by the recipient.[15-23]

5. When it is known that the potential tissue recipient has antibodies to natural rubber proteins, the tissue should be recovered with latex-free supplies in accordance with the "AORN latex guideline."[24] Transplanting tissue with an antigen to which the recipient is allergic can lead to adverse outcomes, including tissue rejection, impaired healing, and allergic reaction.

Recommendation VII

Tissue must be recovered and processed in a manner that minimizes microbial growth, contamination, and cross-contamination.[6(p68681)]

1. Postmortem donors should be placed in refrigeration within 12 hours of asystole, and tissue should be procured within 24 hours of asystole. Refrigeration minimizes cell oxygen consumption and microbial growth. Prolonged times between cell ischemia and tissue recovery provides an opportunity for microbial proliferation. Recommendations for maximum

duration of time between recovery and transplantation have been established by the AATB.[7]

2. A sterile field should be established and maintained in accordance with AORN's "Recommended practices for maintaining a sterile field."[25] Aseptic practices are used to prevent contamination of the tissue and minimize the risk of subsequent infection. Sterile surgical drapes provide a barrier to minimize contamination of the recovered tissue.

3. The donor site and operative site should be prepared in accordance with AORN's "Recommended practices for skin preparation of patients."[26] Adequate skin preparation reduces the microbial count of the skin that can lead to contamination of recovered tissue.

4. The surgical team should perform surgical hand antisepsis and wear sterile gowns and gloves during recovery of tissue, in accordance with AORN's "Recommended practices for surgical hand antisepsis/hand scrubs."[27] Surgical hand antisepsis reduces microbial flora and may reduce the contamination of the tissue. Gowns and gloves provide a barrier to microbial contamination. When corneas are recovered, the sterile field is very small, and gowns may not be necessary.

5. Transplantation of tissue has resulted in transmission of viral, bacterial, and fungal infections. Inadequate tissue processing and quality controls have resulted in postoperative infections and graft failures.[6(p68651)] In 2002, the CDC published an investigation of 26 reported cases of allograft-associated infections.[28] During an investigation of voluntary reports, the FDA identified failure to validate procedures to prevent contamination and cross-contamination during processing in more than half of reported adverse events.[6(p68652)] Proper processing and quality controls minimize the risk of adverse events associated with transplanted tissue.

Recommendation VIII

Tissue must be prepared, processed, and preserved in a manner that minimizes microbial growth and optimizes the condition of the tissue for transplantation.[6(p68681)]

1. Aerobic and anaerobic tissue cultures should be collected when tissue is retrieved. Culture results may identify tissue that is inappropriate for transplantation and also provide a baseline for evaluation of processing and storage.

2. Tissue that will not undergo a sterilization process should be aseptically prepared and transferred to a sterile storage container. Aseptic technique is used to prevent contamination of tissue.

3. The package or container selected should provide an adequate barrier to microbial contamination and should be compatible with the type of sterilization, preservation, and storage conditions. Packages of refrigerated and frozen tissue become wet during storage and form condensation upon removal from storage. Containers should be impervious to moisture.

4. For sterilization of tissue, FDA-approved technology should be used in accordance with the FDA current good tissue practices[6] and AATB standards for guidance. The FDA regulations and recommendations are evolving as new knowledge is gained. The AATB periodically reviews and revises the standards for tissue banking. It is important to review information from these sources to minimize risks of tissue processing.

5. Pooling (ie, commingling) of tissue from two or more donors must not occur.[6(p68684)]

6. When processing dura mater, a validated procedure must be used to minimize the risk of transmitting human transmissible spongiform encephalopathy (eg, prion disease, CJD).[6(p68683)] Transplantation of contaminated tissue has resulted in transmission of viral, bacterial, and fungal infections.[6] Proper processing and quality controls minimize the risk of adverse events associated with transplanted tissue.

Recommendation IX

Tissue must be labeled in a manner that provides direction for preparation and implantation and minimizes the risk of errors.[6,7]

1. Proper labeling of tissue minimizes the risk of errors. The allograft package/storage container should be labeled with the following information:

◆ tissue identification number (this may include a bar code);
◆ description of the tissue;
◆ name, address, and telephone number of the tissue bank responsible for determining donor suitability, processing, storage, and distribution of the allograft;
◆ recovery or distribution center that is responsible for determining donor suitability, processing, and distribution;
◆ recovery date and time;
◆ expiration date, if applicable, including the month and year;
◆ acceptable storage conditions, including recommended storage temperature and acceptable storage temperature range;
◆ the disinfection or sterilization method used, if applicable;
◆ if not sterilized, whether the tissue was procured and prepared under aseptic conditions;
◆ quantity of tissue expressed as volume, weight, dimensions, or a combination of these units of measure, if applicable;
◆ potential residues of processing agents and solutions (eg, antibiotics, ethanol, ethylene oxide, dimethyl sulfoxide); and
◆ package inserts containing instructions for use, indications and contraindications, preparation of tissue for use, expiration dates, and specific tests performed on tissues, warnings and potential adverse reactions, and instructions for opening packages or containers.[6,7]

2. The autograft package/storage container should be labeled with the following information:
◆ name, address, and telephone number of the tissue bank responsible for processing, storing, and distributing the autograft;
◆ the statements "For Autologous Use Only" and "Autologous Donation";[7(p86)]
◆ disinfection/sterilization method, if used;
◆ if not sterilized, whether the tissue was recovered and prepared under aseptic conditions;
◆ the warning "Not Evaluated For Infectious Substances" if infectious disease testing has not been performed;
◆ the warning "Biohazard" if infectious disease tests were performed and found to be positive;
◆ two unique identifiers of the donor/ recipient (eg, name, medical records number), including bar code;

- description of the tissue;
- recovery date and time;
- expiration date, if applicable, including the month and year;
- acceptable storage conditions, including recommended storage temperature and acceptable storage temperature range;
- method of preservation, if applicable; and
- potential residues of processing agents and solutions (eg, antibiotics, ethanol, ethylene oxide, dimethyl sulfoxide).[6,7] This information is necessary for release of the autograft for reimplantation only into the same donor/patient, quality control, and appropriate tissue preparation for implantation.

This documentation is required for certification by the AATB. Some of the information also is required by the FDA. Autografts have not undergone testing for infectious agents and diseases and must be released only to the donor. Release to another recipient may cause serious injury. Using two unique donor/recipient identifiers is consistent with JCAHO's safety goal of patient identification.[29] The application of bar code labeling facilitates matching of tissue to the desired recipient and accurate record keeping. These strategies minimize the potential for errors. The FDA requires that a procedure be maintained to verify the accuracy of labels when labeling human tissue.[6(p68684)]

Recommendation X

Allograft tissue obtained from an outside tissue bank should be handled in a manner consistent with the source facility's or manufacturer's written instructions.

1. Incoming tissue should be recorded, including the unique identifiers of the tissue and expiration date, the identification of the person accepting the tissue, and the date and time of receipt.

2. The packaging and transport conditions of incoming tissue should be examined to verify that the tissue integrity and temperature are acceptable and have been maintained during transport.

3. The tissue should be transferred to storage in manner consistent with the source facility's and manufacturer's written instructions.

Recommendation XI

Tissue is transported and stored in a manner that minimizes the risk of compromise or contamination.[6]

1. Containers for transporting and/or temporarily storing tissue must protect the tissue from contamination and maintain tissue at appropriate temperatures during transport.[6(p68660), 8(PC.17.10.C)]

2. Tissue for transplantation at a later date should be contained and frozen as soon as possible after recovery. Warm tissue is a medium for microbial growth. Tissue contamination may be multifactorial, and no finite time frame has been established. Institutions should determine this time frame with consideration of the type of tissue and recovery conditions.

3. Tissue must be stored in a secure area, with access restricted to authorized personnel, to minimize the risk of mix-ups, contamination, or improper distribution of tissue.[6(p68685)]

4. Temperatures selected for storage should be consistent with the AATB standards.[7]
   - Lyophilized or dehydrated musculoskeletal tissue should be stored at ambient temperature or cooler (but not be frozen).
   - Refrigerated musculoskeletal and osteoarticular tissue should be aseptically recovered, stored in an isotonic solution containing suitable antibiotics, and stored at 33.8° F (1° C) to 50° F (10° C).
   - Refrigerated skin should be stored at 33.8° F (1° C) to 50° F (10° C).
   - Frozen musculoskeletal and osteoarticular tissue should be processed and stored at −40° F (−40° C) or colder for long-term storage; and between −4° F (−20° C) to −40° F (−40° C) for short-term storage (fewer than six months).
   - Frozen or cryopreserved skin should be stored at −40° F (−40° C) or colder.
   - Frozen, cryopreserved cardiovascular tissue should be stored at −148° F (−100° C) or colder.
   - Reproductive cells should be frozen and cryopreserved in a liquid nitrogen freezer. Storage may be in either the liquid or vapor phase.

♦ Refrigeration minimizes oxygen consumption of cells and prolongs their life. Dead cells provide a medium for microbial growth. Refrigeration minimizes microbial growth.

5. Autologous tissue should be segregated from allografts.[7] Autologous tissue usually has not undergone testing for infectious diseases or suitability screening for use for other patients, and its use is restricted to the donor only. Segregation minimizes the risk of error that may result in a negative outcome to a tissue recipient.

6. An expiration date for each tissue must be assigned. This expiration date must be based on tissue type, processing, preservation, storage, and packaging.[6(p68683)] The expiration time of tissue should not exceed the following recommendations of the AATB:[7]
   ♦ refrigerated musculoskeletal tissue: five days;
   ♦ refrigerated skin: 14 days;
   ♦ frozen and cryopreserved cells and tissue (–40° F [–40° C] or colder): five years; and
   ♦ lyophilized or dehydrated tissue: five years.

   Safe duration of storage of autografts may be influenced by processing and packaging methods and should be defined by the facility, not to exceed the recommendations of the AATB listed above. A process should be in place to minimize the number of autografts in storage to those that will be reimplanted. This is facilitated by periodic communication with surgeons or review of medical records to determine whether patients have survived.

7. Refrigerator and freezer units used for storing tissue should
   ♦ be monitored and daily temperature checks recorded,
   ♦ have annual calibration checks, and
   ♦ have an alarm system that is continuously monitored and that sounds when the temperature is not within the acceptable range.

   Restricted access is required to verify the safety and security of tissues. Maintenance of temperatures within the refrigerator or freezer unit ensures tissue integrity. Acceptable temperature range limits for the storage of tissue at each phase of the operation should be set in accordance with established standards and federal and state regulations. Temperature fluc-

tuations outside the recommended temperature range may render tissue unsafe for patient use. The source facility should be consulted if this occurs. The alarm should sound in an area where an individual is present at all times to initiate immediate corrective action.

8. Personnel should have a specific contingency plan for refrigerator or freezer malfunction. Storage freezers and refrigerators should be attached to an emergency power system. In the event of failure of a refrigerator or freezer, the temperature of tissue should be monitored and maintained to prevent compromise of the tissue. All events should be properly documented.

Recommendation XII

Tissue should be quarantined until all steps of the tissue banking process have been reviewed and found acceptable.

1. Allografts should be segregated and not released until all screening, testing, processing, labeling, and storage criteria have been reviewed and determined to be satisfactory. The tissue should remain in an area segregated from available tissue until this review has been completed and the tissue is available for implantation. Segregation minimizes the risk of implanting unsuitable tissue. A checklist of criteria for release provides a standardized method of verifying release criteria and minimizes the potential for errors.

2. Autografts should be segregated and not released until all processing, labeling, and storage criteria have been reviewed and determined to be satisfactory. Segregation minimizes the risk of implanting unsuitable tissue. A checklist of criteria for release provides a standardized method of verifying release criteria and minimizes the potential for errors.

3. Autografts meeting all criteria for release should be released only for reimplantation in the autologous donor. Two unique identifiers (eg, donor name, medical record number) should be used for release of autografts. Autografts usually have not undergone testing for infectious agents and diseases and must be released only for reimplantation in the donor. Release to another recipient may cause serious

injury. Using two unique donor identifiers is in accordance with the Joint Commission's safety goal of patient identification.[29] This strategy minimizes the potential for errors.

4. Tissue not meeting the release criteria should be considered compromised and should be destroyed in accordance with state and federal regulations. Regulations addressing human tissue disposal vary from state to state. Tissue that has not undergone sterilization is considered biohazardous.

5. Before dispensing tissue from the tissue bank, the processes used should be reviewed, and the suitability of the tissue for implantation should be determined. A standardized process should be in place to verify the donor tissue and recipient match, when applicable.

6. Verification of tissue availability should be incorporated into the verification process used to ensure the correct patient, procedure, site, position, and implants.[30]

7. The contents of the package, expiration date, and other pertinent information should be read back and verified before the tissue is dispensed onto the sterile field. Use of bar coding technology facilitates matching tissue to the desired recipient and keeping accurate records.

Recommendation XIII

Each tissue bank must maintain donor, tissue, and recipient records to ensure that pertinent data are retrievable.

1. The surgical tissue bank should have a tissue identification system that allows for tracking of tissues from the donor source to the recipient patient or institution, and vice versa.[6] Quality control issues and infections from implanted tissue have been reported. An identification system provides a means to determine what tissue is affected, rapidly quarantine the tissue, and follow up with affected recipients to ensure timely intervention to minimize morbidity.

2. Surgical tissue banks procuring, processing, distributing, and storing tissues should keep accurate records of the distribution of each tissue according to donor identification number,

tissue type and identifying number, and identifying information for the receiving center, along with the dates of recovery and distribution.[6] This information provides a means to recall tissue that may be compromised.

3. Records should be developed and maintained according to the recommendations of AATB and in compliance with FDA rules. Records should include the following information:
   ♦ FDA registration, if applicable;
   ♦ copies of FDA registration and AATB accreditation of outside vendors from whom tissue is obtained (EBAA for ocular tissue, AABB for stem cells);
   ♦ listing of all tissue products ordered, stored, and used;
   ♦ informed consent documents;
   ♦ donor suitability assessment criteria;
   ♦ recovery;
   ♦ processing;
   ♦ preservation;
   ♦ labeling;
   ♦ storage;
   ♦ quarantining;
   ♦ testing record review;
   ♦ releasing;
   ♦ distribution;
   ♦ ordering and receipt of tissue acquired from other sources:
     – package integrity upon receipt,
     – transport temperature-controlled and acceptable, and
     – source facility and unique identifier of the tissue;
   ♦ instructions/procedures for reconstitution;
   ♦ identity of personnel preparing, accepting, and issuing tissue;
   ♦ dates and times of preparing, accepting, and issuing tissue;
   ♦ documentation in the recipient's health record of the unique identifier of the tissue;
   ♦ quality management records;
   ♦ recall criteria and procedures; and
   ♦ disposal of tissue.

   For tissue obtained from outside tissue banks, copies of pertinent records should be forwarded to the source facility. Documentation assists in clinical evaluation and in tracking recipients if an adverse event is identified.[6]

4. Records must be maintained for 10 years after tissue is dispensed or the tissue expiration date is reached, whichever is longer.[6] Tissue may be used years after recovery. For that reason, the FDA requires that records must be maintained for 10 years.

Recommendation XIV

A quality management program must be in place to evaluate the structure, processes, and outcomes of tissue bank services.[6(68682)]

1. An initial program review should be performed by a multidisciplinary committee, comparing procedures with regulations and standards. Program review should be done annually to ensure ongoing compliance with regulations and ensure safe tissue banking practices.

2. Quality indicators should include, but not be limited to,
   ◆ donor screening and testing;
   ◆ tissue processing procedures;
   ◆ labeling procedures;
   ◆ storage requirements;
   ◆ criteria for release of tissue;
   ◆ the use of two unique donor identifiers for release of autografts; and
   ◆ adverse events (including posttransplantation infections), corrective action, and evaluation.

   Tissue bank services involve significant risks to recipients if errors are made. The FDA requires any facility performing tissue banking to maintain a quality management program intended to prevent the introduction, transmission, or spread of communicable disease for every step of tissue banking performed.[6(p68682)] Ongoing quality management involves verifying that these steps are done in a safe, efficacious manner. These quality indicators address specific issues that may compromise the tissue. Specific quality indicators will depend on the services provided.

3. The FDA final rule for current good tissue practices requires the following aspects of quality management:[6]
   ◆ ensuring that required procedures are established and maintained;
   ◆ ensuring the appropriate analysis and sharing of information that could affect the potential contamination of the product or the potential transmission of communicable disease by the product;
   ◆ ensuring that appropriate corrective actions are taken and documented;
   ◆ ensuring proper training and education of personnel;
   ◆ establishing and maintaining appropriate monitoring systems;
   ◆ establishing and maintaining a system of records;
   ◆ investigating and documenting product deviations and making certain required reports; and
   ◆ conducting evaluations, investigations, audits, and other actions necessary to ensure compliance with the regulations.[6]

   This quality framework is required by the FDA. Administrative personnel should be familiar with this requirement and its application to the components of tissue banking performed.

4. Facilities should report adverse events, including infections for which there is a reasonable possibility that the transplanted tissue caused the event. The tissue bank manufacturing the tissue is required to report adverse events to the FDA.[6] These reports are submitted through MedWatch at *http://www.fda.gov/medwatch/report/instruc.htm*. For events that result from tissue acquired from an outside tissue vendor, the report should be sent to the vendor and also may be submitted to the FDA.

Recommendation XV

Policies and procedures for preserving, storing, and maintaining tissue should be established, reviewed annually, and readily available in the practice setting.

1. Policies establishing authority, responsibility, and accountability for tissue handling and appropriate donor testing within the practice setting must be established and maintained for all steps performed by the facility.[6(p68683)] These policies may include, but are not limited to,
   ◆ authority and accountability for processes;
   ◆ screening and testing criteria;
   ◆ obtaining informed consent from the donor;

- providing information and obtaining informed consent from the allograft recipient;
- evaluating culture and serology tests with appropriate interventions for positive results;
- processing and preserving tissue;
- packaging and labeling tissue;
- sterilizing processes, if applicable;
- monitoring temperature during storage;
- maximum storage duration;
- handling frozen tissue if there is a freezer malfunction or power outage;
- warming or reconstituting preserved tissue;
- rinsing solutions from tissues;
- criteria for return of unused tissue into inventory;
- disposal of tissue;
- documenting implanted and discarded tissue in a retrievable format, and notifying recipients or recalling released tissues;
- responses to adverse events; and
- responses to recalls of tissue from tissue vendors.

2. Before implementation, procedures must be approved by the responsible authority within the health care organization.[6(p68683)] Institutional policies and procedures may seriously affect patient safety and should be reviewed by designated authorities within the facility (eg, infection control committee, pathology department). Tissue may be used years after recovery. For that reason, the FDA final rule for good tissue practices requires that policies and procedures be reviewed periodically, be readily available in the practice setting, and be archived for 10 years after recovery or the expiration date of the tissue, whichever is longer.[6(p68685)] These recommended practices should be used as guidelines, along with the standards of the AATB and regulations and recommendations of the FDA, for the development of policies and procedures for surgical tissue banking in the practice setting. Policies and procedures establish authority, responsibility, and accountability and serve as operational guidelines.

3. The uniform perioperative nursing vocabulary should be used to document perioperative nursing care of the transplant donor and recipient on the intraoperative patient record. The perioperative nursing vocabulary is a clinically relevant and empirically validated standardized nursing language. This standardized language consists of the Perioperative Nursing Data Set (PNDS) and includes perioperative nursing diagnoses, interventions, and outcomes. The expected outcome of primary importance to these recommended practices is outcome O10, "The patient is free from signs and symptoms of infection." This outcome falls within the domain of Safety (D1). Interventions that might lead to the desired outcome include I98, "Protects from cross-contamination"; I121, "Assesses susceptibility for infection"; and I188, "Monitors for signs and symptoms of infection."[31]

Editor's note: The American Association of Tissue Banks can be reached at 1320 Old Chain Bridge Road, Suite 450, McLean, VA 22101; telephone (703) 827-9582.

Glossary

Allografts: Grafts taken from a living or nonliving donor for transplantation to a different individual.

American Association of Tissue Banks (AATB): A nonprofit organization that defines the standards for tissue banking.

Autografts: Tissue derived from an individual for implantation exclusively on or in the same individual.

Donor screening: Review of the donor's relevant medical records and physical assessment for evidence of past or present risk factors for relevant infectious agents or disease.

Donor testing: Laboratory tests on blood specimens collected from a potential donor.

Prion diseases: A classification of infectious diseases, including Creutzfeldt-Jakob disease (CJD), caused by a unique proteinaceous agent.

Tissue bank: A facility that participates in procuring, processing, preserving, and/or storing human cells and tissue for transplantation.

Xenotransplant: Cells or tissue from a nonhuman animal source that are transplanted, implanted, or infused into a human.

Xenotransplantation: Any procedure that involves the transplantation, implantation, or infusion into a human recipient of either (a) live cells, tissues, or organs from a nonhuman animal source (eg, bovine heart valves); or (b) human body fluids, cells, tissues, or organs that have had ex vivo contact with live nonhuman animal cells, tissues, or organs.

REFERENCES

1. US Food and Drug Administration, *Proposed Approach to Regulation of Cellular and Tissue-Based Products* (Rockville, Md: US Food and Drug Administration, Feb 28, 1997) 1-37.

2. US Food and Drug Administration, "Current good tissue practice for manufacturers of human cellular and tissue-based products; inspection and enforcement; proposed rule," *Federal Register* 66 (January 8, 2001) 1507-1559. Also available at *http://www.fda.gov/OHRMS /DOCKETS/98fr/010801c.pdf* (accessed 13 Sept 2005).

3. US Food and Drug Administration, "Suitability determination for donors of human cellular and tissue-based products; proposed rule," *Federal Register* 64 (Sept 30, 1999) 52696-52718. Also available at *http:// www.fda.gov/OHRMS/DOCKETS/98fr/093099a.pdf* (accessed 13 Sept 2005).

4. US Food and Drug Administration, "Human cells, tissues, and cellular and tissue-based products; establishment registration and listing; final rule," *Federal Register* 66 (Jan 19, 2001) 5447-5469. Also available at *http:// www.fda.gov/OHRMS/DOCKETS /98fr/011901a.pdf* (accessed 13 Sept 2005).

5. US Food and Drug Administration, "Eligibility determination for donors of human cells, tissues, and cellular and tissue-based products; final rule and notice," *Federal Register* 69 (May 25, 2004) 29785-29834. Also available at *http://www.fda.gov/OHRMS/DOCKETS /98fr/04-11245.pdf* (accessed 13 Sept 2005).

6. US Food and Drug Administration, "Current good tissue practice for human cell, tissue, and cellular and tissue-based product establishments; inspection and enforcement; final rule," *Federal Register* 69 (Nov 24, 2004) 68612-68688.

7. American Association of Tissue Banks, *Standards for Tissue Banking,* 10th ed (McLean, Va: American Association of Tissue Banks, 2002).

8. Joint Commission on Accreditation of Healthcare Organizations, "Standards approved for transplant and implant tissue storage and issuance," *Joint Commission Perspectives* (February 2005) 8-11.

9. Office of Inspector General, *Informed Consent in Tissue Donation: Expectations and Realities,* publ OEI-01-00-00440 (Boston: US Department of Health and Human Services, January 2001).

10. US Food and Drug Administration, *Guidance for Industry: Eligibility Determination for Donors of Human Cells, Tissues, and Cellular and Tissue-Based Products (HCT/Ps): Draft Guidance* (Rockville, Md: US Food and Drug Administration, May 2004) 1-52.

11. "Recommended practices for traffic patterns in the perioperative practice setting," in *Standards, Recommended Practices, and Guidelines* (Denver: AORN, Inc, 2005) 483-485.

12. "Recommended practices for environmental cleaning in the surgical practice setting," in *Standards, Recommended Practices, and Guidelines* (Denver: AORN, Inc, 2005) 361-366.

13. "Recommended practices for surgical attire," in *Standards, Recommended Practices, and Guidelines* (Denver: AORN, Inc, 2005) 299-305.

14. D Beezhold, D Kostyal, J Wiseman, "The transfer of protein allergens from latex gloves: A study of influencing factors," *AORN Journal* 59 (March 1994) 605-613.

15. D Abeck et al, "Latex allergy and repeated graft rejections," *The Lancet* 339 (June 27, 1992) 1609.

16. D Beezhold, W Beck, "The absorbability and immunology of starch glove powders," *Complications in Surgery* (July/August 1992) 36-40.

17. C Bene, G Kranias, "Possible intraocular lens contamination by surgical glove powder," *Ophthalmic Surgery* 17 (May 1986) 290-291.

18. I Singh, W L Chow, L V Chablani, "Synovial reaction to glove powder," *Clinical Orthopaedics and Related Research* 99 (March/April 1974) 285-292.

19. P H McKee, E F McKeown, "Starch granulomata of the endocardium," *Journal of Pathology* 126 (October 1978) 103-105.

20. S Moriber-Katz et al, "Contamination of perfused donor kidneys by starch from surgical gloves," *American Journal of Clinical Pathology* 90 (July 1988) 81-84.

21. D I Vâge et al, "Elutable factors from latex-containing materials activate complement and inhibit cell proliferation: An in vitro biocompatibility study of medical devices," *Complement Inflammation* 7 (January-February 1990) 63-70.

22. C M Ruhl et al, "A new hazard of cornstarch, an absorbable dusting powder," *The Journal of Emergency Medicine* 12 (January/February 1994)11-14.

23. D A A Verkuyl, "Glove powder introduced in the circulation by autotransfusion and severe cardiac failure," *The Lancet* 340 (Aug 29, 1992) 550.

24. "AORN latex guideline," in *Standards, Recommended Practices, and Guidelines* (Denver: AORN, Inc, 2005) 117-132.

25. "Recommended practices for maintaining a sterile field," in *Standards, Recommended Practices, and Guidelines* (Denver: AORN, Inc, 2005) 453-457.

26. "Recommended practices for skin preparation of patients," in *Standards, Recommended Practices, and Guidelines* (Denver: AORN, Inc, 2005) 443-446.

27. "Recommended practices for surgical hand antisepsis/hand scrubs," in *Standards, Recommended Practices, and Guidelines* (Denver: AORN, Inc, 2005) 377-385.

28. Centers for Disease Control and Prevention, "Update: Allograft-associated bacterial infections—United States," *Morbidity and Mortality Weekly Report* 51 (March 15, 2002) 207-210. Also available at *http://www.cdc.gov /mmwr/preview/mmwrhtml/mm5110a2.htm* (accessed 13 Sept 2005).

29. "2005 Hospitals' National Patient Safety Goals," Joint Commission on Accreditation of Health Care Organizations, *http://www.jcaho.org /accredited+organizations /patient+safety/05+npsg/05_npsg _hap.htm* (accessed 13 Sept 2005).

30. "Universal protocol for preventing wrong site, wrong procedure, wrong person surgery," Joint Commission on Accreditation of Health Care Organizations, *http://www.jcaho.org/accredited+organizations/patient+safety/universal+protocol/universal_protocol.pdf* (accessed 13 Sept 2005).

31. S C Beyea, ed, *Perioperative Nursing Data Set: The Perioperative Nursing Vocabulary,* second ed (Denver: AORN, Inc, 2002).

RESOURCES

Bren, L. "Keeping human tissue transplants safe," *FDA Consumer Magazine* 39 (May/June 2005) 30-36.

Verble, M; Worth, J. "Cultural sensitivity in the donation discussion," *Progress in Transplantation* 13 (March 2003) 33-37.

Verble, M; Worth, J. "Fears and concerns expressed by families in the donation discussion," *Progress in Transplantation* 10 (March 2000) 48-55.

Originally published September 1984, *AORN Journal.* Revised April 1991.

Published as proposed recommended practices, February 1994.

Revised November 1998; published March 1999, *AORN Journal.* Reformatted July 2000.

Revised November 2003; published February 2004, *AORN Journal.*

Revised November 2005; published in *Standards, Recommended Practices, and Guidelines,* 2006 edition. Reprinted February 2006, *AORN Journal.*

Recommended Practices for Sponge, Sharp, and Instrument Counts

The following recommended practices were developed by the AORN Recommended Practices Committee and have been approved by the AORN Board of Directors. They were presented as proposed recommended practices for comments by members and others. They are effective January 1, 2006.

These recommended practices are intended as achievable recommendations representing what is believed to be an optimal level of practice. Policies and procedures will reflect variations in practice settings and/or clinical situations that determine the degree to which the recommended practices can be implemented.

AORN recognizes the numerous settings in which perioperative nurses practice. These recommended practices are intended as guidelines that are adaptable to various practice settings. These practice settings include traditional operating rooms, ambulatory surgery centers, physicians' offices, cardiac catheterization suites, endoscopy suites, radiology departments, and all other areas where operative and other invasive procedures may be performed.

Purpose

These recommended practices provide guidance to perioperative registered nurses in performing sponge, sharp, and instrument counts in their practice settings. Counts are performed to account for all items and to lessen the potential for injury to the patient as a result of a retained foreign body. The expected outcome of primary importance to this recommended practice is outcome O2, "The patient is free from signs and symptoms of injury due to extraneous objects."[1] Complete and accurate counting procedures help promote optimal perioperative patient outcomes and demonstrate the perioperative practitioner's commitment to patient safety.

Legislation does not prescribe how counts should be performed, who should perform them, or even that they need to be performed. The law requires only that foreign bodies not be negligently left in patients.[2] The doctrine of res ipsa loquitur (ie, "the thing speaks for itself") is most applicable in cases involving retained foreign objects, rendering those litigations nearly indefensible.[2,3] Retained objects are considered a preventable occurrence, and careful counting and documentation can sig-

nificantly reduce, if not eliminate, these incidents.[4,5] The "captain of the ship" doctrine is no longer assumed to be true, and members of the entire surgical team can be held liable in litigation for retained foreign bodies.[6-11] All team members should be committed to and involved in establishing meaningful policies and procedures related to surgical counts.[12,13]

Recommendation I

Sponges should be counted on all procedures in which the possibility exists that a sponge could be retained.

1. Sponge counts should be performed
   - before the procedure to establish a baseline,
   - before closure of a cavity within a cavity,
   - before wound closure begins,
   - at skin closure or end of procedure, and
   - at the time of permanent relief of either the scrub person or the circulating nurse (although direct visualization of all items may not be possible).

2. Initial sponge counts should be performed and recorded, establishing a baseline for subsequent counts on all procedures in which the possibility exists that a sponge could be retained. Policies in the health care organization may identify situations in which this possibility does not exist and counts are not required.[14]

3. Accurately accounting for sponges throughout a surgical procedure should be a priority of the surgical team to minimize the risks of a retained sponge.[3,4,15,16] The Institute of Medicine has identified avoiding injuries from the care that is intended to help patients to be one of six aims to a better health care system.[17]

4. Established policies in the health care organization may define when additional counts must be performed or may be omitted (eg, cystoscopy, ophthalmology).[14] Closed claim studies conducted during the past 20 years have demonstrated that roughly two-thirds of reported cases of retained surgical items are attributed to sponges.[5,18-20] Although the majority of retained sponges are found in the abdomen and pelvis, there are reports in the

literature discussing retained sponges in the vagina, thorax, spinal canal, face, brain, and extremities.[5,21-27]

5. Sponges should be separated, counted audibly, and concurrently viewed during the count procedure by two individuals, one of whom should be a registered nurse circulator.[3,17,28] Concurrent verification of counts by two individuals lessens the risk of inaccurate counts. Separating sponges during the baseline count helps to determine whether a sponge has been added to or deleted from a sterilized package.[2,4,17,29] Use of a pocketed bag or other system for separating used sponges may facilitate visualization for counting. Separating sponges after use minimizes errors caused by sponges sticking together.

6. When additional sponges are added to the field, they should be counted at that time and recorded as part of the count documentation to keep the count current and accurate.[4]

7. Perioperative personnel should count all prepackaged sterile sponges for accuracy. Any package containing an incorrect number of sponges should be removed from the field, bagged, labeled, and isolated from the rest of the sponges in the OR. Containing and isolating the entire package helps reduce the potential for error in subsequent counts.[17]

8. Sponge counts should be conducted in the same sequence each time as defined by the facility. The counting sequence should be in a logical progression (eg, from large to small or from proximal to distal). A standardized count procedure, following the same sequence, assists in achieving accuracy, efficiency, and continuity among perioperative team members.[30] Studies in human error have shown that all errors involve some kind of deviation from routine practice.[31(p57)]

9. All sponges used during a surgical procedure should be x-ray-detectable. Radiopaque indicators facilitate locating an item presumed lost or left in the surgical field when a count discrepancy occurs. X-ray-detectable sponges should not be used as dressings. The use of x-ray-detectable sponges as surface dressings may invalidate subsequent counts if the patient

is returned to the OR. X-ray-detectable sponges used as dressings may appear as foreign bodies on postoperative x-ray studies.[29,32-34]

10. Only towels with radiopaque markers should be used in the wound. If towels are used in the open wound, they should be included in the count as miscellaneous items and should be easily distinguishable from other towels.[29,32,33]

11. Sponges should be left in their original configuration and should not be cut. Altering a sponge invalidates subsequent counts and increases the risk of a portion being retained in the wound.[16,22]

12. Nonradiopaque gauze dressing materials should be withheld from the field until the wound is closed or the case is completed. Keeping dressing materials separated from the actual counted sponges will help prevent intermingling with the sponges used in the procedure.[3]

13. All counted sponges should remain within the OR or sterile field during the procedure. Linen and waste containers should not be removed from the room until counts are completed and resolved. Confinement of all counted sponges to the OR helps eliminate the possibility of a count discrepancy.[17]

14. Counted sponges should not be used as postoperative packing. In certain circumstances, such as when counted sponges are intentionally used as packing and the patient leaves the OR with this packing in place, the number and types of sponges retained and the reason for the variation should be documented on the intraoperative record as correct and confirmed by the surgeon.[4,14,35] When the patient returns to surgery and the packed sponges are removed, the number and types should be reconciled with the number and types removed. The number and types removed should be noted in the current patient's record. The sponges removed should be isolated and not included in the counts for the subsequent procedure. The count on the subsequent procedure should be noted as correct after all sponges have been accounted for. If the sponges are removed in an area other than the OR, the number removed should be noted on the patient record.

15. Sponges should be removed from the OR at the end of the procedure. Removing sponges from the OR at the end of the procedure helps prevent potential count discrepancies during subsequent procedures.[17]

16. Contaminated sponges must be handled and disposed of according to the Bloodborne Pathogens Standard of the Occupational Safety and Health Administration (OSHA); AORN's "Recommended practices for environmental cleaning in the surgical practice setting"[36] and "Recommended practices for standard and transmission-based precautions in the perioperative practice setting"[37]; and facility policies and procedures. The use of leak-proof, tear-resistant containers and personal protective equipment (PPE) can help prevent environmental contamination and reduce the risk of personnel exposure to potentially infectious material.[36-38]

Recommendation II

Sharps and other miscellaneous items should be counted on all procedures.

1. Sharps and miscellaneous items (eg, vessel clip bars, vessel loops, umbilical and hernia tapes, vascular inserts, cautery scratch pads, trocar sealing caps) should be counted
   ♦ before the procedure to establish a baseline,
   ♦ before closure of a cavity within a cavity,
   ♦ before wound closure begins,
   ♦ at skin closure or end of procedure, and
   ♦ at the time of permanent relief of the scrub person and/or circulating nurse (although direct visualization of all items may not be possible).

2. Initial sharps counts should be performed and recorded on all procedures. Performing counts constitutes a primary and proactive injury-prevention strategy.[2] Counting sharps and miscellaneous items is not only important in preventing foreign body retention; the continuous accounting for these items can lessen injuries to those scrubbed in the sterile field. As many as 78% of reported needle-stick exposures occur to members of the surgical team.[39,40] Accurately accounting for sharps during a surgical procedure is a primary responsibility of the perioperative nurse and the surgical team members.

3. Sharps and miscellaneous items should be counted audibly and viewed concurrently by two individuals, one of whom should be a registered nurse circulator. Concurrent verification of counts by two individuals lessens the risk for count discrepancies.[2]

4. Additional sharps and miscellaneous items added to the field should be counted when added and recorded as part of the count documentation.

5. Suture needles should be counted and recorded according to the number marked on the outer package and verified by the scrub person when the package is opened.[41] Viewing each needle will help ensure an accurate needle count. Using empty suture packages to rectify a discrepancy in a closing needle count is not recommended.[42] The actual number of needles may not be the same as the number of empty packages.

6. The scrub person should be able to account for all sharps on the sterile field. Sharps remaining unconfined on the sterile field may be unintentionally introduced into the incision or dropped on the floor or may penetrate barriers.

7. Whenever possible, sharps must be handed to and from the surgeon on an exchange basis using a "neutral zone" or "hands-free" technique.[37,42] Passing sharps to the surgeon on an exchange basis will lessen the possibility of a lost sharp item and prevent injury to the surgical team members at the sterile field.[43]

8. Sharps counts should be conducted in the same sequence each time as defined by the facility. The counting sequence should be in a logical progression (eg, from large to small item size or from proximal to distal from the wound). A standardized count procedure, following the same sequence, assists in achieving accuracy, efficiency, and continuity among perioperative team members.[30] Studies in human error have shown that all errors involve some kind of deviation from routine practice.[31(p57)]

9. Members of the surgical team should account for sharps or other miscellaneous items that may have been broken or become separated

within the confines of the surgical site in their entirety. Breakage and/or separation of parts can occur during open as well as minimally invasive surgical procedures. Verification that all broken parts are present or accounted for helps prevent unintentional retention of a foreign body within the patient.[14,44-47]

10. Open sharps on the sterile field should be confined and contained. Used sharps on the sterile field should be kept in a disposable puncture-resistant container. Collecting used needles in a container helps ensure their containment on the sterile field and lessens the risk of injury to personnel at the sterile field.[36,37]

11. All counted sharps should remain within the OR and/or sterile field during the procedure. If a sharp is passed or dropped off the sterile field, the circulating nurse should retrieve it in a safe manner, show it to the scrub person, and isolate it from the field to be included in the final count. Linen or waste containers should not be removed from the OR until all counts are completed and resolved and the patient has been taken from the room. Confinement of all sharps to the OR helps minimize the possibility of a count discrepancy.[17]

12. Sharps must be handled according to the OSHA Bloodborne Pathogens Standard. Proper use, handling, and disposal of contaminated sharps help minimize the risk of exposure to bloodborne pathogens from patient to health care worker and from health care worker to patient.[38] AORN's "Recommended practices for standard and transmission-based precautions in the perioperative practice setting"[37] should be followed. Sharps should be disposed of according to AORN's "Recommended practices for environmental cleaning in the surgical practice setting."[36]

Recommendation III

Instruments should be counted for all procedures in which the likelihood exists that an instrument could be retained.

1. Instrument counts should be performed
   - before the procedure to establish a baseline,
   - before wound closure, and

- when feasible, at the time of permanent relief of the scrub person and/or circulating nurse.

Instrument counts protect the patient by reducing the likelihood that an instrument will be retained in the patient. Instrument counts are a proactive injury-prevention strategy.[2] Retention of surgical instruments accounts for approximately one-third of retained item case reports.[5] Case studies demonstrate that many types and sizes of instruments have been found, ranging from small serrifine clamps to moderately sized hemostats (ie, 6 to 10 inches) to 13-inch-long retractors.[48,49]

2. Instruments should be counted audibly and viewed concurrently by two individuals, one of whom should be a registered nurse circulator. Concurrent verification of counts by two individuals assists in ensuring accurate counts.[2]

3. Instruments should be counted when sets are assembled for sterilization. This assembly count provides a basic reference for the instrument set and is not to be considered the initial count before the surgical procedure. A count performed outside the OR that is considered an initial count increases the number of variables that can contribute to a count discrepancy and unnecessarily extends responsibility to personnel not involved in direct patient care.[32]

4. Initial counts in the OR should be performed to establish a baseline for subsequent counts, including minimally invasive procedures (eg, laparoscopy, thoroscopy). The possibility of any incision being extended to allow for a more extensive procedure than anticipated supports the practice of performing an initial count for all procedures.

5. Individual pieces of assembled instruments (eg, suction tips, wing nuts, blades, sheathes) should be accounted for separately on the count sheet. Removable instrument parts can be purposefully removed or become loose and fall into the wound or onto or off the sterile field.[45]

6. When additional instruments are added to the field, they should be counted when added and recorded as part of the count documentation.

7. Members of the surgical team should account for instruments that may have been broken or become separated within the confines of the surgical site in their entirety. Breakage and/or separation of parts can occur during open as well as minimally invasive surgical procedures. Verification that all broken parts are present or accounted for helps prevent unintentional retention of a foreign body within the patient.[14,44-47]

8. Instrument counts should be conducted in the same sequence each time as defined by the organization. The counting sequence should be in a logical progression (eg, from large to small item size or from proximal to distal from the wound). A standardized count procedure, following the same sequence, assists in achieving accuracy, efficiency, and continuity among perioperative team members.[30] Studies in human error have shown that all errors involve some kind of deviation from routine practice.[31(p57)]

9. The final instrument count should not be considered complete until those instruments used in closing the wound (eg, malleable retractors, needle holders, scissors) are removed from the wound and returned to the scrub person.

10. All counted instruments should remain within the OR during the procedure until all counts are completed and resolved. If a counted instrument is passed or inadvertently dropped off the sterile field, the circulating nurse should retrieve it, show it to the scrub person, and isolate it from the field to be included in the final count.[38] Confinement of all counted instruments to the OR helps eliminate the possibility of a count discrepancy.[40]

11. All instruments should be accounted for and removed from the room during end-of-procedure cleanup. Accounting for all instruments facilitates inventory control and patient safety. Removing all instruments from the room helps avoid potential count discrepancies during subsequent procedures.[13]

12. Instrument sets should be standardized with the minimum variety and number of instruments needed for the procedure. Instruments that are not routinely used on procedures should be deleted from sets. Reducing the number and types of instruments and streamlining standardized sets improves ease and efficiency of counting.[29] Specialty instruments, if needed, can be opened and added to the count at the time of the procedure.[30]

13. Preprinted count sheets that are identical to the standardized sets should be used to record the counted items. Preprinted count sheets provide organization and efficiency, which are key to preventing unnecessary delays.[4] The circulating nurse should record only the number of instruments opened for the procedure. Additional instruments requested by the surgeon should be counted and added to the preprinted count sheet separately.[14]

14. Contaminated instruments must be handled according to the OSHA Bloodborne Pathogens Standard. Proper use and handling of contaminated instruments help minimize the risk of exposure to bloodborne pathogens from patient to health care worker and from health care worker to patient.[38] Contaminated instruments should be handled according to AORN's "Recommended practices for cleaning and caring for surgical instruments and powered equipment"[50] and "Recommended practices for cleaning and processing endoscopes and endoscope accessories,"[51] as well as the institution's policies and procedures.[45] Contaminated instruments may expose personnel to harmful pathogens.[46]

15. Alternative measures should be established to minimize the risk of retained instruments during procedures in which accurately accounting for instruments is not achievable (eg, anterior-posterior spinal procedures). These measures should include the use of an intraoperative x-ray, read by a radiologist, before the patient is discharged from the OR.

16. Organizations should define when instrument counts should be performed for pediatric patients. Instrument counts may be deferred when there is no perceived risk of retained instruments.

Recommendation IV

Additional measures for investigation, reconciliation, documentation, and prevention of retained surgical items should be taken.

1. When a discrepancy in the count(s) is identified, the surgical team is responsible for carrying out steps to locate the missing item.[4,13,45,51] Procedural steps include, but are not limited to,
   - count discrepancy reported to surgeon and surgical team;
   - procedure suspended, if patient's condition permits;
   - manual inspection of the operative site;
   - visual inspection of the area surrounding the surgical field, including floor, kick buckets, and linen and trash receptacles;
   - if the patient's condition permits, intraoperative x-ray taken and read before patient leaves the OR or, if the patient's condition is unstable, an x-ray should be taken as soon as possible;
   - documentation of all measures taken and outcomes on patient's record;
   - reporting of incident following organization policy; and
   - review of incident or near miss for cause, effect, and prevention.

2. The perioperative registered nurse circulator should inform and receive an acknowledgment from the surgeon and team as soon as a discrepancy in a surgical count (ie, sponge, sharps, instrument) is identified.[3,4,14,28,52]

3. The perioperative registered nurse circulator and scrub person should ask the surgeon to conduct a manual search of the wound to locate the missing item(s). The scrub person and perioperative registered nurse circulator should do a manual and visual search, respectively, of the sterile area surrounding the wound and the remainder of the sterile field. The perioperative registered nurse circulator should conduct a search of the nonsterile areas of the room in an attempt to locate the item(s).[3,18,20,45,52]

4. If the item is not recovered, an intraoperative x-ray should be taken before the final closure of the wound. It should be specified that the purpose of the x-ray is to rule out a retained foreign body (eg, needle, sponge, instrument). This x-ray should be read by a radiologist. Studies show greater accuracy when x-rays are read by a radiologist.[4,5,14,20,33] In the case of missing needles, there is no definitive evidence as to how

effective x-rays are in detecting small suture needles. Studies done in recent years have demonstrated that needles 17 mm and smaller may not be consistently visible on an x-ray.[53,54]

5. Following organizational policy, documentation of a count discrepancy should include all the measures taken to recover the missing item and communications made regarding the outcome. Such documentation is considered sound professional practice and demonstrates that all reasonable efforts were made to protect the patient's safety.[2,4,17,34,48]

6. A critical investigation should be conducted of any patient safety incident process.[17(p157)] Error and near-miss reporting are the first steps to addressing error reduction.[55,56] The distraction-prone environment of the OR means that performing routine tasks, such as surgical counts, can be considered at risk for error.[13] Errors can be divided into two categories: those at the human interface in a complex system (ie, active), and those representing failed system design (ie, latent).[57] Elements of the root cause analysis tool should be considered in addressing the contributing causes (eg, human, process, system) and in identifying risks and preventive measures.[58] Multidisciplinary teams should be involved in the process of review and address any changes in policy that can improve patient safety.[17]

7. Additional measures should be established to minimize the risk of retained items in high-risk situations. The following situations have been identified through research to be of higher risk for retained foreign bodies:
   - the emergent nature of a procedure,
   - an unexpected change in the procedure, and
   - patient obesity.[5]

8. Internal data from adverse events and near misses should be reviewed to identify high-risk situations within the organization. Health care organizations should identify conditions or situations that pose an increased risk for retained foreign bodies. Health care organizations should establish measures to be taken, in addition to a count, for identified high-risk situations. These measures should include an intraoperative x-ray for foreign body, read by a staff radiologist, before the patient leaves the OR. In

one study, three of 29 x-rays were read as negative when a retained sponge actually was present.[18] Therefore, x-ray alone may be insufficient to detect a retained item.

Recommendation V

Sponge, sharp, and instrument counts should be documented on the patient's intraoperative record by the registered nurse circulator.

1. The uniform perioperative nursing vocabulary should be used to document counts on the intraoperative patient record. The perioperative nursing vocabulary is a clinically relevant and empirically validated standardized nursing language. This standardized language consists of the Perioperative Nursing Data Set (PNDS) and includes perioperative nursing diagnoses, interventions, and outcomes. The expected outcome of primary importance to this recommended practice is outcome O2, "The patient is free from signs and symptoms of injury due to extraneous objects." This outcome falls within the domain of Safety (D1). The associated nursing diagnosis is X29, "Risk of injury." The associated interventions that may lead to the desired outcome may include (I93) "Performs required counts."[1]

2. Documentation of counts should include, but not be limited to,
   - types of counts (ie, sponges, sharps, instruments, miscellaneous items) and number of counts;
   - names and titles of personnel performing the counts;
   - results of surgical item counts;
   - notification of the surgeon;
   - instruments intentionally remaining with the patient or sponges intentionally retained as packing;
   - actions taken if count discrepancies occur;
   - outcome of actions taken; and
   - rationale if counts are not performed or completed as prescribed by policy.

3. Accurate documentation serves several purposes, including evidence of the patient's treatment, the basis of the plan of care, communication to all caregivers, protection from liability, and a link to reimbursement.[34,59] Documentation

of nursing activities related to the patient's perioperative care provides an accurate picture of the nursing care administered and provides a mechanism for comparing actual versus expected outcomes.[60]

4. Justification for omission of counts in an emergency should be documented. Extreme patient emergencies may necessitate omission of counts to preserve a patient's life or limb. Documenting the omission and reasons for the variation provides a record of the occurrence and an alert to subsequent caregivers that the patient may be at an increased risk for a retained foreign body.[4]

Recommendation VI

Policies and procedures for sponge, sharps, and instrument counts should be developed, reviewed periodically, revised as necessary, and readily available in the practice setting.

1. These policies and procedures should include, but not be limited to,
   - items to be counted,
   - directions for performing counts (eg, sequence, item grouping),
   - procedures in which baseline and/or subsequent counts may be exempt,
   - alternative or additional safety measures for special circumstances,[5]
   - nursing actions and procedures for count discrepancy reconciliation, and
   - competency validation.

   Policies and procedures establish authority, responsibility, and accountability and serve as operational guidelines. Policies and procedures also assist in the development of patient safety, quality assessment, and quality improvement activities.[17] Nurses should collaborate with all members of the health care team to develop policies that address surgical counts.[13,14]

2. Policies and procedures should be written to include organ procurements. Counted items could be at risk for being retained and sent with the donated organ(s), retained in the donor, or left in the OR.

3. Practices, policies, and procedures are subject to change with the advent of new technologies.

4. An introduction and review of policies and procedures should be included in orientation and ongoing education of perioperative personnel to assist them in obtaining knowledge and developing skills and attitudes that affect patient outcomes.

Glossary

Instruments: Surgical tools or devices designed to perform a specific function, such as cutting, dissecting, grasping, holding, retracting, or suturing.

Sharps: Items with edges or points capable of cutting or puncturing through other items. In the context of surgery, items include, but are not limited to, suture needles, scalpel blades, hypodermic needles, electrosurgical needles and blades, and safety pins.

Sponges: Soft goods (eg, gauze pads, cottonoids, peanuts, dissectors, tonsil and laparotomy sponges) used to absorb fluids, protect tissues, or apply pressure or traction.

Minimally invasive surgery: Includes laparoscopy and other procedures that involve small incisions and endoscopic instrumentation performed in the OR.

Miscellaneous items: Includes vessel clip bars, vessel loops, umbilical and hernia tapes, vascular inserts, cautery scratch pads, trocar sealing caps, and any other small items that have the potential for being retained in a surgical wound.

Neutral zone (synonym: hands-free technique): A safe work practice control technique used to ensure that the surgeon and scrub person do not touch the same sharp instrument at the same time. This technique is accomplished by establishing a designated neutral zone on the sterile field and placing sharp items within the zone for transfer of the item between scrubbed personnel.

Near miss: An occurrence that could have resulted in an accident, injury, or illness but did not by chance, skillful management, or timely intervention.

Root cause analysis: A retrospective approach to error analysis that focuses on failures of system design as related to common root causes of adverse events.

REFERENCES

1. S C Beyea, ed, *Perioperative Nursing Data Set: The Perioperative Nursing Vocabulary,* second ed (Denver: AORN, Inc, 2002).

2. E K Murphy, "Operating room records, counts cause concern," (OR Nursing Law) *AORN Journal* 51 (June 1990) 1606-1612.

3. J Zuffoletto, "Nurses' vs surgeons' responsibility for sponge counts," (OR Nursing Law) *AORN Journal* 57 (June 1993) 1457-1458.

4. ECRI, "Sponge and instrument counts," (Risk Analysis, Surgery and Anesthesia 5) *Healthcare Risk Control* 4 (January 1996) 1-9.

5. A A Gwande et al, "Patient safety: Risk factors for retained instruments and sponges after surgery," *The New England Journal of Medicine* 348 (January 2003) 229-235.

6. E K Murphy, "'Captain of the ship' doctrine continues to take on water," (OR Nursing Law) *AORN Journal* 74 (October 2001) 525-528.

7. "Surgical nurses: Sponge count is strictly nurses' responsibility, court rules," *Legal Eagle Eye Newsletter for the Nursing Profession* 8 (September 2000) 2.

8. *Golinski v Hackensack Medical Center, Conley, Irani, Archer, Bruno, and Del Rosario,* 298 NJ Super 650; 690 A2d 147; 1997 NJ Super (New Jersey, 1997).

9. *Stafford v Molinoff and Halfen,* 228 AD2d 662; 645 NYS2d 313; 1996 NY App Div (New York, 1996).

10. *Ravi v Vaughn and Foxworthy v Athens-Limestone Hospital v Coates,* 662 So2d 218; 1995 (Alabama, 1995).

11. L E Rozovsky, F A Rozovsky, "The surgeon and the nurse share the blame: A case of a retained sponge," *Canadian Operating Room Nursing Journal* 9 (September/October 1991) 20-21.

12. A D Tammelleo, ed, "The surgeon's nondelegable responsibility for the sponge count," *The Regan Report on Nursing Law* 38 (July 1997) 2.

13. S C Beyea, "Counting instruments and sponges," (Patient Safety First) *AORN Journal* 78 (August 2003) 290-294.

14. J K Cherry, "Surgery: Foreign object retention," The Doctors Company, *http://www.thedoctors.com/risk /specialty/generalsurgery/J4219.asp* (accessed 8 Sept 2005).

15. E K Murphy, "Nurses' liability for inaccurate counts," (OR Nursing Law) *AORN Journal* 51 (April 1990) 1067-1069.

16. E K Murphy, "Liability for inaccurate counts; assistant circulators," (OR Nursing Law) *AORN Journal* 53 (January 1991) 157-161.

17. Institute of Medicine, *Crossing the Quality Chasm: A New Health System for the 21st Century* (Washington, DC: National Academy Press, 2001).

18. C W Kaiser et al, "The retained surgical sponge," *Annals of Surgery* 224 (July 1996) 79-84.

19. V C Gibbs, "Did we forget something? Retained surgical sponge," AHRQ Web M&M: Case and Commentary, *http://www.webmm.ahrq.gov/case.aspx ?caseID=27&searchStr=%22 retained+surgical+sponge %22+AND+Gibbs* (accessed 8 Sept 2005).

20. P R Lauwers, R H Van Hee, "Intraperitoneal gossypibomas: The need to count sponges," *World Journal of Surgery* 24 (May 2000) 512-527.

21. A P Zbar et al, "Gossypiboma revisited: A case report and review of the literature," *Journal of the Royal*

College of Surgeons of Edinburgh 43 (December 1998) 417-418.

22. B A Hemelt, M A Finan, "Abdominal sacral colpopexy resulting in a retained sponge: A case report," *The Journal of Reproductive Medicine* 44 (November 1999) 983-985.

23. S R Kim, H K Baik, Y W Park, "Retained surgical sponge presenting as a pelvic tumor after 25 years," *International Journal of Gynecology and Obstetrics* 82 (August 2003) 223-225.

24. H Nomori et al, "Retained sponge after thoracotomy that mimicked aspergilloma," *Annals of Thoracic Surgery* 61 (May 1996) 1535-1536.

25. J S Dhillon, A Park, "Transmural migration of a retained laparotomy sponge," *The American Surgeon* 68 (July 2002) 603-605.

26. R J Cruz et al, "Intracolonic obstruction induced by a retained surgical sponge after trauma laparotomy," (Case Reports) *Journal of Trauma* 55 (November 2003) 989-991.

27. R S McLeod, J M Bohnen, "Canadian Association of General Surgeons evidence based reviews in surgery 9: Risk factors for retained foreign bodies after surgery," *Canadian Journal of Surgery* 47 (February 2004) 57-59.

28. T Eskreis-Nelson, "Medical errors and the need for nurses' continuing education," (Nursing Case Law Update) *Journal of Nursing Law* 7 (2000) 49-59.

29. New York State Department of Health, "Retained surgical sponges," New York Patient Occurrence Reporting and Tracking System, *NYPORTS News & Alert* 11 (September 2002). Also available at *http://www.health.state .ny.us/nysdoh/hospital/nyports/annual_report/2000-2001 /news _and_alerts.htm* (accessed 8 Sept 2005).

30. D Fogg, "Retrieving flash sterilized items; occupational exposure to bloodborne pathogens; sponge, needle, and instrument counts," (Clinical Issues) *AORN Journal* 55 (April 1992) 1091-1093.

31. J Reason, "Safety in the operating theater—Part 2: Human error and organisational failure," *Quality and Safety in Health Care* 14 (February 2005) 56-60. Also available at *http://qhc.bmjjournals.com/cgi/search?and orexactfulltext=and&resourcetype=1&disp _type=&sortspec =relevance&author1=reason&fulltext=&volume=14 &firstpage=* (accessed 8 Sept 2005).

32. ECRI, "Retained foreign object: Surgeon admits liability," *Operating Room Risk Management* (March 2003) 15-16.

33. R Gencosmanoglu, R Inceoglu, "An unusual cause of small bowel obstruction: Gossypiboma—Case report," *BMC Surgery* 3 (September 2003) 1-6. Also available at *http://www.biomedcentral.com/1471-2482 /3/6* (accessed 8 Sept 2005).

34. ECRI, "Locating 'lost' neurosurgical sponges, (Risk Analysis, Surgery and Anesthesia 5.1) *Healthcare Risk Control* 4 (January 1996) 1-2.

35. S Henry, "Damage control in 2001: Who, when, and how," *Trauma Quarterly* 15 (2002) 121-137.

36. "Recommended practices for environmental cleaning in the surgical practice setting," in *Standards, Recommended Practices, and Guidelines* (Denver: AORN, Inc, 2005) 361-366.

37. "Recommended practices for standard and transmission-based precautions in the perioperative practice setting," *Standards, Recommended Practices, and Guidelines* (Denver: AORN, Inc, 2005) 447-451.

38. Occupational Health and Safety Administration, "Occupational exposure to bloodborne pathogens; needlestick and other sharps injuries; final rule," *Federal Register* 66 (18 Jan 2001) 5317-5325. Also available at *http://www.osha.gov/pls/oshaweb/owadisp.show _document?p_table=FEDERAL _REGISTER&p_id=16265* (accessed 8 Sept 2005).

39. R Berguer, P J Heller, "Preventing sharps injuries in the operating room," *Journal of the American College of Surgeons* 199 (September 2004) 462-467.

40. J Perry, G Parker, J Jagger, "EPINet Report: 2001 percutaneous injury rates," *Advances in Exposure Prevention* 6 no 3 (2003) 32-36.

41. D Fogg, "Gas sterilizing medication; using wall suction for evacuating laser plumes; counting needles in multipacks," (Clinical Issues) *AORN Journal* 52 (August 1990) 408-412.

42. C Peterson, "Rectifying counts; neurostimulators; double gloving; reprocessing single-use devices; simultaneous counting," (Clinical Issues) *AORN Journal* 76 (September 2002) 510-515.

43. C Peterson, "Deep vein thrombosis; neutral zone; circulating and recovering; environmental controls; wound classifications; sterile field," (Clinical Issues) *AORN Journal* 79 (April 2004) 856-864.

44. L E Mendez, C Medina, "Late complication of laparoscopic salpingoophorectomy: Retained foreign body presenting as an acute abdomen," *Journal of the Society of Laparoendoscopic Surgeons* 1 (January/March 1997) 79-81.

45. ECRI, "Safe use and selection of trocars," (Risk Analysis, Surgery and Anesthesia 25) *Healthcare Risk Control* 4 (July 1999) 1-15.

46. E J Thomas, F A Moore, "The missing suction tip," AHRQ Web M&M: Case and Commentary, *http://www .webmm.ahrq.gov/case.aspx?caseID=37&search Str=%22spotlight+cases%22* (accessed 8 Sept 2005).

47. M Milanokov, S Dragan, N Miljkovic, "Broken blade in the knee: A complication of arthroscopic meniscectomy," *Arthroscopy: The Journal of Arthroscopic and Related Surgery* 18 (January 2002) 1-3.

48. A D Tammelleo, "Were nurses liable for clamp left in cardiac patient?" *The Regan Report on Nursing Law* 40 (July 1999) 1.

49. C Smith, "Surgical tools left in five patients," Seattle Post-Intelligencer, 8 Dec 2001, *http://seattlepi .nwsource.com/local/49883_error08.shtml* (accessed 8 Sept 2005).

50. "Recommended practices for cleaning and caring for surgical instruments and powered equipment," in *Standards, Recommended Practices, and Guidelines* (Denver: AORN, Inc, 2005) 395-403.

51. "Recommended practices for cleaning and processing endoscopes and endoscope accessories," in *Standards, Recommended Practices, and Guidelines* (Denver: AORN, Inc, 2005) 341-346.

52. "Retained foreign bodies: Reducing the risks," Self-Insurance Program: Risk Management and Loss Prevention (revised April 2004), University of Florida, *http://www.riskmanagementeducation.com/brochures/Retained%20Foreign%20Bodies.pdf* (accessed 8 Sept 2005).

53. C J Barrow, "Use of x-ray in the presence of an incorrect needle count," (Clinical Innovations) *AORN Journal* 74 (July 2001) 80-81.

54. M D Macilquham, R G Riley, P Grossberg, "Identifying lost surgical needles using radiologic techniques," *AORN Journal* 78 (July 2003) 73-78.

55. B A Liang, "The adverse event of unaddressed medical error: Identifying and filling holes in the healthcare and legal systems," Symposium: Patient Injury, Medical Errors, Liability and Reform, *The Journal of Law, Medicine and Ethics* 29 no 3–4 (Fall/Winter 2001) 346-368.

56. D Dunn, "Incident reports—Their purpose and scope," (Home Study) *AORN Journal* 74 (July 2003) 45-68.

57. H Wald, K G Shojania, "Root cause analysis," in *Making Health Care Safer: A Critical Analysis of Patient Safety Practices,* Agency for Healthcare Research and Quality (Evidence Report/Technology Assessment, Number 43, AHRQ Pub 01-E058). Also available at *http://www.ahrq.gov/clinic/ptsafety/pdf/ptsafety.pdf* (accessed 8 Sept 2005).

58. "Root cause analysis," VA National Center for Patient Safety, *http://www.patientsafety.gov/tools.html* (accessed 8 Sept 2005).

59. ECRI, "Perioperative documentation," (Risk Analysis, Surgery and Anesthesia 7) *Healthcare Risk Control* 4 (January 1996) 1-4.

60. "Recommended practices for documentation of perioperative nursing care," in *Standards, Recommended Practices, and Guidelines* (Denver: AORN, Inc, 2005) 321-323.

RESOURCES

Gic, J A. "Nursing and the law," in *Legal Medicine,* fifth ed (St Louis: Mosby, 2001) 128-136.

O'Connor, A; Coakley, F; Meng, M. "Imaging of retained surgical objects in the abdomen and pelvis," Department of Radiology, University of California, San Francisco, *http://www.radiology.ucsf.edu/instruction/abdominal/abdominal_ret_objects1.shtml* (accessed 8 Sept 2005).

Patterson, P. "How ORs decide when to count instruments," *OR Manager* 16 (April 2000) 1, 10, 12-14.

Rothrock, J C; Smith, D A. "Patient and environmental safety," in *Alexander's Care of the Patient in Surgery,* 12th ed, J C Rothrock, ed (St Louis: Mosby, 2003) 36-38.

Originally published May 1976, *AORN Journal,* as "Standards for sponge, needle, and instrument procedures." Format revision March 1978, July 1982.

Revised March 1984, March 1990.

Revised November 1995; published October 1996, *AORN Journal.*

Revised; published December 1999, *AORN Journal.* Reformatted July 2000.

Revised November 2005; published in *Standards, Recommended Practices, and Guidelines,* 2006 edition. Reprinted February 2006, *AORN Journal.*

414 *Patient and Worker Safety*   *2009 Perioperative Standards and Recommended Practices*

Recommended Practices for a Safe Environment of Care

The following recommended practices for maintaining a safe environment of care were developed by the AORN Recommended Practices Committee and have been approved by the AORN Board of Directors. They were presented as proposed recommendations for comments by members and others. They are effective January 1, 2008.

These recommended practices are intended as achievable recommendations representing what is believed to be an optimal level of practice. Policies and procedures will reflect variations in practice settings and/or clinical situations that determine the degree to which the recommended practices can be implemented.

AORN recognizes the various settings in which perioperative nurses practice. These recommended practices are intended as guidelines adaptable to various practice settings. These practice settings include traditional operating rooms, ambulatory surgery centers, physician's offices, cardiac catheterization laboratories, endoscopy suites, radiology departments, and all other areas where surgery may be performed.

References to nursing interventions (I) used in the Perioperative Nursing Data Set, second edition, (PNDS) are noted in parentheses when a recommended practice corresponds to a PNDS intervention.[1] The reader is referred to the PNDS for further explanation of nursing diagnoses, interventions, and outcomes.[1]

Purpose

These recommended practices provide guidance for providing a safe environment of care and assist perioperative registered nurses in the identification of potential hazards in the practice setting. They include information on
- security;
- privacy rules;
- workplace ergonomics;
- electrical safety,
- heating, ventilation, air conditioning (HVAC);
- medical equipment;
- clinical alarms;
- blanket- and solution- warming cabinets;
- fire safety;
- medical gases,
- anesthesia gas systems;
- surgical smoke plume;
- chemicals;

- methyl methacrylate bone cement;
- chemotherapeutic agents;
- tubing connections; and
- hazardous upon disposal waste.

They are not intended to cover aspects of perioperative patient care addressed in other recommended practices.

Recommendation I

Potential security risks associated with the perioperative environment should be identified and safe practices should be established.

A security program helps to promote the
- safety of patients,
- safety of staff members,
- safety of visitors,
- prevention of drug diversion,
- theft, and
- protection of patient information.

I.a. A risk assessment should be conducted by an interdisciplinary committee at least annually, to identify potential security issues. The interdisciplinary committee members provide various areas of expertise and the resources necessary to evaluate the entire scope of security issues.

I.a.1. Occurrence reports regarding security-related incidents should be reviewed along with electronic surveillance records and logs to determine the numbers, seriousness, and types of issues.

I.a.2. Potential resolutions should be determined, based upon this risk assessment.[2,3]

I.b An identification process should be in place to identify all persons entering the perioperative suite or the ambulatory surgery center.

Access to the perioperative environment should be limited to those who have authorized access verified by proper identification.[2,4]

I.b.1. Photo identification badges should be
- worn by all authorized personnel,
- worn on the upper body, and
- be visible.[5]

I.b.2. Anyone without an authorized badge should be stopped and questioned to assure the appropriateness of their presence in the facility.[5]

I.b.3. Individuals with limited or temporary access to the perioperative environment (eg, students, health care industry representatives, parents of pediatric patients) should be identified as visitors.

I.b.4. Visitors should wear temporary identification badges.

I.c. Tracking systems should be in place to identify who is present in the perioperative suite, (eg, electronic ID access tracking systems, visitor logs). In case of fire, disaster, evacuation, or other emergency, the identity of those present in the perioperative suite is necessary to assure that everyone has been evacuated and accounted for.

I.d. Door security systems should be used to restrict traffic.

I.e. Video surveillance should be used to monitor access. Video surveillance provides monitoring of entry areas during off-shift hours.

I.f. A written management plan should be created describing security management activities to include:
   – employee and visitor badges;
   – security cameras;
   – alarm systems;
   – emergency alert devices (eg, panic buttons);
   – security illumination;
   – restricted access to the facility during off hours; and
   – restricted access to departments (eg, OR, postanesthesia care unit [PACU], endoscopy suites) or areas (eg, medication storage areas, medical records, sterile supply/equipment storage areas).[2-4]

Recommendation II

The perioperative environment must provide for the privacy of patients and patient information, including their identity and reason for hospitalization.[6,7] (PNDS: I151)

The Health Insurance Portability and Accountability Act of 1996 establishes guidelines for the safe communication of paper, electronic, and oral patient information and must be followed.[6,7]

II.a. Perioperative registered nurses must share only the information necessary to provide safe care (eg, surgery schedules, hand-off report tools), and only if appropriate to their job role.[6-8] (PNDS: I116)
   Information is necessary to enable care to be delivered and continued safely.

II.b. Protected health information should be shared only with individuals (eg, family members, significant others) the patient has identified as being able to receive this information. (PNDS: I116)

II.b.1. Visitors may be assigned a number or pager to ensure that information is shared with the correct person.

II.c. Patient names may be listed on a display board in the restricted area.[7,8] (PNDS: I116)

II.d. Copies of personal health information including, but not limited to,
   – surgery schedules,
   – identification labels,
   – identification/stamp plates,
   – forms with patient identification, and
   – photographs,
   should be shredded. (PNDS: I116)

II.d.1. Paper shredders or secured disposal containers (eg, shredding bins) should be readily available for proper disposal of hard copy or paper copies of personal health information. (PNDS: I151)

Recommendation III

Potential ergonomic hazards associated with the perioperative environment should be identified, and safe practices should be established.

Ergonomic hazards are found throughout the perioperative environment and are created by patient and equipment handling or the physical environment and, if not corrected, can cause injury to staff members.[9,10]

III.a. Perioperative staff members should follow the algorithms outlined in the AORN guidance statement *Safe Patient Handling and Movement in the Perioperative Setting*[10] and their organization's policies and procedures while completing activities including

- lateral transfer from stretcher to OR bed;
- positioning or repositioning the patient on the OR bed;
- lifting and holding extremities and heads for prepping;
- prolonged standing while holding retractors;
- retraction of tissue;
- lifting and carrying supplies or equipment; and
- pushing, pulling, and moving equipment on wheels.[10]

These activities can create ergonomic stressors that, if not recognized, can cause injury to staff members. Ergonomic stressors can be defined as tasks which include, but are not limited to,

- forceful tasks (eg, pushing a stretcher and patient up a ramp);
- repetitive motion (eg, passing instruments, opening suture packets, tying suture);
- static posture (eg, standing for long periods of time in one position);
- moving or lifting patients or equipment;
- carrying heavy instruments or equipment; and
- overexertion (eg, protecting a combative patient emerging from anesthesia).[10]

III.b. The physical environment should be designed to minimize the risk of ergonomic injury (eg, adequate room lighting, adequate storage to eliminate clutter).[9,10]

III.b.1. During the design phase of construction, provisions should be made to minimize hazards (eg, head injuries) to staff members in operating rooms which will contain ceiling-suspended equipment (eg, booms).[10]

III.b.2. Ceiling-, floor-, or wall-mounted booms should be hydraulic or electric and provide for ease of movement.[10]

III.c. Adequate staff members and equipment should be available and used to decrease risks due to ergonomic hazards.[11]

Appropriate mechanical devices should be used to reduce the risk of strain when moving a large or unconscious patient or a patient's large extremities.[11,12]

Recommendation IV

Potential hazards associated with the use of electrical equipment in the practice setting should be identified, and safe practices should be established. (PNDS: I138)

Electrical hazards in the operating room may lead to fires, burns, and electric shocks. These injuries result from electric current flowing through inappropriate pathways.

IV.a. The electrical supply should be reliable and consistent with the needs of the operating room.[13,14] (PNDS: I122)

IV.b. Electrical access panels or circuit breaker panels should be
- located on the same floor they serve,
- easily accessible, and
- not obstructed by equipment or carts.[15]

IV.c. Isolated power systems should be considered for operating rooms, which may be considered wet locations.[16] (PNDS: I138)

Adequate grounding provides protection from electric shock and fire hazards.[16]

IV.d. Line-isolation monitors should be provided for each isolated power system to indicate possible leakage or faulty currents.[16,17]

Line-isolation monitoring systems or ground-fault interrupting systems provide for continuous monitoring of current leakage. Systems that monitor current leakage and ground integrity reduce the hazards of shock, cardiac fibrillation, or burns produced by electrical current flowing through the patient's body to ground.[16,17]

IV.e. General lighting and specialty lighting, such as operating room overhead lights, should be on separate circuits.[15,18]

IV.f. Lighting should be in working order and adequate for illuminating the surgical field, monitoring the patient, and performing perioperative duties. (PNDS: I138)

Adequate lighting is necessary to perform the planned invasive procedure and to evaluate the patient.

IV.f.1. The light over the surgical field should be equipped with an automatic switch to the emergency power source for use if the usual power supply fails.[19] (PNDS: I138)

IV.f.2. Surgical lights should produce a minimum of radiant heat to reduce damage to exposed tissues and discomfort to the surgical team.[18] (PNDS: I138)

IV.f.3. Minimally invasive surgical suites (MIS), gastrointestinal endoscopy suites, and other procedure rooms should provide the low lighting required for optimum surgical visibility while providing adequate lighting for the perioperative team to complete their responsibilities without risk of injury from tripping, slipping, or falling.

Ambient blue or green light enhances the MIS screens and allows adequate visibility for other personnel in the room to work safely.[20]

IV.f.4. Video vendors and the personnel responsible for the organization's lighting should be consulted regarding lighting options and placement.

IV.g. Alternate sources of lighting and electrical power should be available when normal power is interrupted.[15,21]

Battery-powered emergency lights provide immediate lighting in a power failure, which decreases the potential negative effect of a total power interruption.[19]

IV.g.1. Batteries should be labeled with their expiration date and replaced as needed.[19]

IV.h. The emergency/alternate power source should begin operating within 10 seconds and have the capacity to operate equipment for monitoring, anesthesia delivery, and surgical equipment for a minimum of two hours.[14,22]

IV.h.1. Emergency power should be tested per local, state, and federal regulations.[19]

IV.h.2. All emergency electrical outlets should be tested, including those on booms.

IV.h.3. If the testing fails, the organization should implement interim measures, make necessary repairs, and perform a retest.[23]

IV.h.4. Electrical receptacle cover plates should be distinctly colored or marked if supplied by the emergency backup system.[13,15]

IV.i. Life-sustaining medical equipment should have battery backup, and backup supplies should be immediately available.[13]

IV.j. Clinical contingency plans should be developed for periods of loss of emergency power.[21]

Recommendation V

Potential hazards associated with HVAC systems in the practice setting should be identified, and safe practices should be established. (PNDS: I98, I21)

Air in the perioperative environment contains microbial-laden dust, lint, skin squames, and respiratory droplets.[24] The number of microorganisms in the air in an operating room is directly proportional to the number of personnel moving in and around the room. Outbreaks of surgical-site infections have been traced to airborne contamination from colonized health care workers.[24] Heating, ventilation, and air conditioning systems dilute and remove contaminants from the air and control airflow patterns. Key components of an effective HVAC system are proper air quality, air volume changes, and air flow direction. In an operating room or procedural area, proper functioning of these components minimizes the contamination of the sterile field and risk of infection to the patient. A properly functioning HVAC system carries microbial-laden skin squames, dust, and lint away from the sterile field, and removes these contaminants through the exhaust ducts at the periphery.

V.a. The quality of air entering the operating rooms should be carefully controlled. (PNDS: I98)

V.a.1. The air should be sequentially filtered through two filters. The first filter should be rated as 30% efficient and the second should be 90% efficient.[15,22]

V.a.2. A minimum of 20% of the incoming air (ie, three air changes per hour) should be from the outdoors.[15,24]

Filtered outdoor air minimizes the recirculation of indoor contaminants within the perioperative area.

V.b. Relative humidity should be maintained between 30% and 60% within the perioperative suite, including operating rooms, recovery area, cardiac catheterization rooms, endoscopy rooms, instrument processing areas, and sterilizing areas and should be maintained below 70% in sterile storage areas.[14,15] (PNDS: I98)

Low humidity increases the risk of electrostatic charges, which pose a fire hazard in an oxygen-enriched environment or when flammable agents are in use and increases the potential for dust. High humidity increases the risk of microbial growth in areas where sterile supplies are stored or procedures are performed.

V.b.1. Free-standing humidifiers should not be used because they can harbor microorganisms in fluid reservoirs and aerosolize these microorganisms into the clean environment.

V.b.2. Humidity should be monitored and recorded daily using a log format or documentation provided by the HVAC system.[25]

V.c. Temperature should be monitored and recorded daily using a log format or documentation provided by the HVAC system.[25] (PNDS: I128)

V.c.1. Temperature should be maintained between 68° F to 73° F (20° C to 23° C) within the operating room suite and general work areas in sterile processing.[15]

Self-regulating, area-specific chiller units may be required because operating rooms are filled with personnel and heat-emitting equipment; therefore, achieving the low end of this range can be difficult.

V.c.2. The decontamination area temperature should be maintained between 60° F to 65° F (16° C to 18° C).[15]

V.c.3. A temperature of 70° F to 75° F (21° C to 24° C) should be maintained in recovery areas and cardiac catheterization rooms.[15]

V.d. The air-exchange rate in the perioperative area should be carefully controlled. (PNDS: I98, I128)

The number of air changes per hour is based upon the need to remove microbiological or chemical contaminants from the environment.

V.d.1. The minimum rate of total air exchanges per hour should be maintained at a constant level as follows.
- **Operating room:** minimum of 15 air exchanges per hour with a recommended range of 20 to 25 air exchanges.
- **Cardiac catheterization rooms:** 15 air exchanges per hour.
- **Postanesthesia care unit:** six air exchanges per hour.
- **Compressed-gas storage area:** eight air exchanges per hour.
- **Sterile storage area:** four air exchanges per hour.[15]

V.d.2. Air exchanges per hour should be monitored per the organization's policy. (PNDS: I128)

V.e. Air-flow patterns within the perioperative setting should be controlled and uninterrupted. (PNDS: I81, I98, I128)

Air-flow patterns are architecturally designed and engineered to minimize contamination of the sterile field. Disruptions in the air-flow patterns within the operating room can redirect contaminants onto the sterile field, increasing the risk of surgical site infection.

V.e.1. The pressure gradient in the operating room should be positive to outer corridors at all times.[16,25]

V.e.2. Doors to the operating room or invasive procedure room should remain closed except when patients, personnel, and supplies are being actively moved in and out of the room.[26] (PNDS: I81)

V.e.3. Equipment and supplies should be located away from exhaust ducts to allow directed air flow out of the room.

V.e.4. Free-standing fans, humidifiers, or de-humidifiers should not be used in the operating room or sterile processing areas.[22,25,27]

Free-standing fans can disrupt the air-flow patterns, resulting in contamination of the sterile field.

V.f. In the event of a failure of the HVAC system,
- surgeries presently in progress should be completed,
- elective procedures should not be started until the HVAC system is functioning correctly,
- procedures should be redirected to areas of the surgical suite where the HVAC system is functioning or postponed until the problem has been corrected, and
- the event should be reported through the organization event-reporting system.

V.g. Preventive maintenance, including regular inspection, should be performed on HVAC systems, (ie, changing filters on a routinely scheduled basis).

A properly functioning HVAC system minimizes the risk of contamination to the sterile filed and is an essential component to infection prevention. Failure of the system poses an unnecessary risk for the elective surgical patient.

Recommendation VI

Potential hazards associated with the use of medical equipment in the practice setting should be identified, and safe practices should be established.

Hazards associated with medical equipment may be caused by frayed cords, damaged outlets, or extension cords and, if not corrected, may result in injury of patients, staff members, or visitors.

VI.a. Equipment should be inspected periodically by a qualified biomedical technician or engineer.[17,23,28] (PNDS: I138)

VI.a.1. All electrical equipment should be inspected before use. Inspection should include, but not be limited to
- new equipment before it is introduced into the practice setting,[23]

- checking power cords and plugs for fraying or other damage, and
- checking outlets and switch plates for damage.

VI.a.2. Damaged power cords or outlets can result in excessive current being delivered to the patient and/or staff members.

VI.b. Hospital-grade plugs are recommended when available, but plugs with adequate strain relief also may be used.[16,23] (PNDS: I138)

VI.c. Device cord length should be appropriate for the intended use of the equipment. (PNDS: I138)

Cords that do not lie flat create a risk for tripping or accidental unplugging of the equipment.

VI.c.1. Cords should be secured in a safe manner. An electrically safe, cleanable, or disposable device should be used to decrease the potential of tripping by personnel.

VI.c.2. Extension cords should be avoided unless used to decrease the potential for tripping.

Use of extension cords can result in excessive current leakage and/or electrical-system overload.

VI.c.3. Biomedical personnel should change cords of inadequate length to longer cord lengths to eliminate the need for extension cords and decrease the risk of tripping.

VI.d. Equipment found to be in disrepair should be immediately removed from service. (PNDS: I122)

VI.d.1. Organizational policy and procedure should be followed regarding routing of equipment in need of repair.

VI.e. A written plan should be developed describing the processes to be implemented to effectively manage medical equipment including selection, purchase, inspection, and maintenance.

RECOMMENDED HVAC SETTINGS[1,2,3]							
Hospital area/Agency Recommendations	Temperature	Air flow	Humidity	Exchanges per hour	Outdoor air exchanges per hour	Recirculated by room unit (eg, fans)	Exhaust directed outside
Operating room	N/D = Not designated						
American Institute of Architects (AIA)	68°-73° F (20°-23° C)	Positive	30% to 60%	Minimum 15	3	No	N/D
American Association for the Advancement o Medical Instrumentation (AAMI)	N/D	N/D	N/D	N/D	N/D	N/D	N/D
National Fire Protection Association			35%				
Anesthesia gas storage							
AIA	N/D	Negative	N/D	8	N/D	N/D	Yes
AAMI	N/D	N/D	N/D	N/D	N/D	N/D	N/D
Postanesthesia care unit							
AIA	70°-75° F (21°-24° C)	N/D	30% to 60%	6	2	No	N/D
AAMI	N/D	N/D	N/D	N/D	N/D	N/D	N/D
Soiled decontamination							
AIA	68°-73° F (20°-23° C)	Negative	N/D	10	N/D	No	Yes
AAMI	60°-65° F (16°-18° C)	Negative	30% to 60%	10	N/D	N/D	Yes
Sterilizer equipment access							
AIA	N/D	Negative	N/D	10	N/D	N/D	Yes
AAMI	75°-85° F (21°-29° C)	Negative	N/D	10	N/D	N/D	Yes
Sterilizer loading/unloading							
AIA	N/D	N/D	N/D	N/D	N/D	N/D	N/D
AAMI	68°-73° F (20°-23° C)	Positive	30% to 60%	10	N/D	N/D	Yes
Restroom/housekeeping							
AIA	N/D	N/D	N/D	10	N/D	N/D	N/D
AAMI	< 75° F (< 24° C)	Negative	30% to 60%	10	N/D	N/D	Yes
Preparation and packaging							
AIA	75° F (24° C)	Positive	30% to 60%	4	N/D	No	N/D
AAMI	68°-73° F (20°-23° C)	Positive	35% to 50%	10	N/D	N/D	No
Textile packaging room							
AIA	N/D	N/D	N/D	N/D	N/D	N/D	N/D
AAMI	68°-73° F (20°-23° C)	Positive	30% to 60%	10	N/D	N/D	No
Clean/sterile storage							
AIA	75° F (24° C)	Positive	30% to 60%	4	N/D	No	N/D
AAMI	< 75° F (< 24° C)	Positive	<70%	4	N/D	N/D	No

1. *American Institute of Architects.* Guideline for Design and Construction of Hospitals and Health Care Facilities, 2006. *Washington DC: American Institute of Architects Press; 2006:130-131.*

2. *Association for Advancement of Medical Instrumentation.* Comprehensive Guide to Steam Sterilization and Sterility Assurance in Health Care Faciities, 2006. *Arlington, VA: Association for Advancement of Medical Instrumentation; 2006:24.*

3. Bielen RP, ed. *Health Care Facilities Handbook, 2005.* Quincy, MA: National Fire Protection Association, 2005:290.

Recommendation VII

Clinical alarms should be audible and should not be disabled. (PNDS: I122)

A clinical alarm is an alarm that is patient specific and used for the purpose of alerting staff members to a patient emergency.[29]

VII.a. An environmental assessment of every piece of equipment in the clinical setting should be conducted. (PNDS: I122)

VII.a.1. The assessment should
- be developed as a collaborative effort between clinical engineering and nursing; and
- include a list of those devices with alarms, including but not limited to
  - electrosurgery units (ESUs),
  - pneumatic tourniquets,
  - cardiac monitors,
  - carbon dioxide (CO_2) insufflators,
  - anesthesia equipment, and
  - infusion pumps.

VII.b. Alarms should be sufficiently audible to allow them to be heard at reasonable distances and above competing noise. (PNDS: I122)

VII.c. Alarms should be checked
- upon initial setup,
- when connecting or reconnecting a device,
- before transporting a patient, and
- after transporting a patient.[30] (PNDS: I122)

VII.d. Alert alarms (eg, medical gas alarms, code blue alarms) should be tested according to organizational policy and procedure.

Recommendation VIII

Blanket- and solution-warming cabinet temperatures should be controlled.

The danger of thermal burns from heated blankets or solutions is increased in the perioperative setting because patients are unconscious or sedated and cannot feel the increase in temperature or communicate their discomfort. Attention to the temperature of warming cabinets is important. Even when solutions and blankets do not feel warm to staff members, heat continues to build up in these items and can be transferred to the patient.[31]

VIII.a. The warming cabinet temperature should be checked at regular intervals per the organization's policy and documented on a temperature log or recorded on a record provided by an electronic recording system.[31,32,33] (PNDS: I122)

VIII.a.1. The responsibility for setting, maintaining, and monitoring warmers should be assigned to specific personnel (eg, delegated assistive staff members).

VIII.a.2. If solution is stored in the warming cabinet, the cabinet should be labeled with safe temperature range settings as determined by the solution manufacturer.

VIII.a.3. Cabinet temperature above the safe range should be reported to clinical engineering for maintenance.[31,32,33]

VIII.a.4. Dual cabinets should have dual controls for accurate regulation of both cabinets.

VIII.a.5. Blanket-warming cabinet temperatures should not exceed 110° F (43° C).[34]

VIII.a.6. Blankets should be rotated on a first-in, first-out basis.

VIII.b. Solution-warming cabinet temperatures should be limited to the solution manufacturer's specifications for warming.[32] The fluid manufacturer's recommendations should be obtained and followed for the maximum temperature and length of time fluids should remain in the warming cabinet. (PNDS: I122)

Solution stability may vary according to the type of solution and storage container.

VIII.b.1. Fluids kept in fluid warmers should be labeled with the date they should be removed or the date when they were placed in the warmer.

VIII.b.2. Solutions should be rotated on a first-in, first-out basis.

VIII.b.3. IV solutions should only be warmed using technology designed for this purpose.[34]

VIII.c. Intravenous (IV) fluid or irrigation fluid bags should not be used for patient warming devices. (PNDS: I122)

Warmed IV bags used as warming devices have led to patient burns.[35] In a closed claims study of intraoperative patient burns, the most common device causing the burn was either heated IV bags or bottles of irrigation fluids.[33]

VIII.d. Fluids used for intracorporeal irrigation should not exceed 98.6° F (37° C) or approximate normal body temperature.[34,36,37]

VIII.d.1. The temperature of fluid on the sterile field should be measured using a sterile thermometer or a commercially available intraoperative irrigation warming bath to ensure it does not exceed 98.6° F (37° C).[34,37] (PNDS: I76)

VIII.d.2. Solutions warmed to higher temperatures should be cooled to normal body temperature before use inside body cavities.

VIII.e. Surgical skin prep solutions should not be warmed in warming cabinets unless stated as allowable in the manufacturer's directions. (PNDS: I122)

Recommendation IX

Potential hazards associated with fire safety in the practice setting should be identified, and safe practices should be established.

Fire is always a risk to both patients and healthcare workers in the operating room.

IX.a. A written fire prevention and management plan should be developed by a multidisciplinary group and include all categories of perioperative personnel.

IX.a.1. The plan should describe processes to be implemented to safely manage different fire scenarios.[38]

IX.b. Ignition sources should be controlled. (PNDS: I72, I73, I77)

IX.b.1. The active electrode tip of the ESU should be kept clean and in a holster when not in use.

IX.b.2. Electrosurgical units provide an ignition source when not used according to manufacturers' recommendations and when active electrodes are used in the presence of oxidizers, flammable solutions, and volatile or combustible chemicals or liquids.

IX.b.3. Lasers should be used with wet towels placed around the surgical site and after flammable prep solutions have dried.[39]

IX.b.4. The ends of an active fiber-optic light cable should not come in contact with surgical drapes.

Fiber-optic light cables provide an ignition source if they are disconnected from the working element or light source and allowed to contact drapes, sponges, or other fuel sources.

IX.b.5. Light cables should be connected before activating the light source.

IX.b.6. The light source should be placed into a stand-by mode when not in use to prevent ignition.

Backing into the light source or turning the fiber-optic light cable toward the body may cause surgical attire to ignite.[40]

IX.c. Personnel should move any equipment that emits smoke at any time, whether in use or not, to a safe area.[41]

IX.d. Fuel sources should be controlled. (PNDS: I72, I73)

IX.d.1 Waterless, brushless, surgical-scrub solutions should be allowed to dry completely to decrease the potential to produce ignition by static electricity or sparks.

IX.d.2. Local and state fire regulations regarding storage of alcohol-based, surgical-scrub solutions and hand sanitizers should be followed.[14]

IX.d.3. Provide adequate time for the flammable surgical prep solution to dry completely and any fumes to dissipate before applying surgical drapes, using an active electrode or laser, or activating a fiber-optic light cable.[42-44]

IX.d.4. Prevent prep solutions from pooling, or soaking into the table linens or the patient's hair by

- using reusable or disposable sterile towels to absorb drips and excess solutions during the skin prep application,
- removing materials saturated with prep solution before draping the patient,[14] and
- wicking excess solution with a sterile towel to facilitate the surgical prep area drying completely.[14,45,46]

IX.d.5. Drapes should not be applied until prep solutions are dry, to prevent the accumulation of volatile fumes beneath them.

IX.d.6. Surgical skin preparations with clear instructions for use, preferably with unit dosed applicators should be used.[14,45]

IX.d.7. Gowns and drapes should not be exposed to ignition sources.

IX.e. Oxidizers should be controlled. (PNDS: I72, I73)

IX.e.1. Oxygen and nitrous oxide should be used with caution in the presence of any ignition or fuel sources.

IX.e.2. Oxygen-enriched environments are created when the oxygen concentration is greater than 21%. This lowers the temperature and energy at which fuels will ignite.[47,48]

IX.e.3. Anesthesia circuits should be free of leaks.

IX.e.4. Electrosurgical units and lasers should be used with caution where oxygen is flowing.

IX.e.5. Suction should be used to evacuate anesthetic gas accumulation.

IX.e.6. When using a laser, only laser-resistant endotracheal tubes should be used for upper airway procedures or procedures near the trachea.[39,47]

IX.e.7. For surgeries involving the head and neck, water-soluble substances should be used to cover facial hair.[49]

IX.e.8. Oxygen concentration under drapes should be minimized by

- tenting of drapes, and
- using the lowest possible oxygen concentration that provides adequate patient oxygen saturation.[14,39,47,50,51]

Mixing oxygen with nonflammable gases such as medical air reduces the risk of fire.[17,39,49]

IX.e.9. Precautions should be taken when operating in the gastrointestinal tract because hydrogen and methane, which are flammable gases, may be present.[49]

IX.e.10. Nitrous oxide should be considered an oxidizer, and the same precautions that are used with oxygen should be observed.[41]

IX.f. Risk of airway fires should be minimized by

- using radiopaque wet sponges in the back of the throat to prevent or decrease oxygen leaks;
- inflating endotracheal tube cuffs with tinted solutions to improve visibility in the event of a cuff rupture;
- using suction to evacuate oxygen buildup;
- tenting drapes to prevent the accumulation of gases; and
- using pulse oximetry to evaluate the patient's optimal oxygen saturation level.[17,39,49] (PNDS: I73)

IX.g. Processes should be in place to regularly inspect, test, and maintain fire extinguishing equipment and supplies.

IX.h. Fire extinguishers should be selected according to standards established by the National Fire Protection Association (NFPA) and the local authority having jurisdiction, and be immediately available for every operating and procedural room.[14,47,52] (PNDS: I72, I73)

IX.h.1. The NFPA recommends either a water mist or CO_2 extinguisher be used in the operating room.[53]

Water mist extinguishers are rated Class 2A: C.[53]

IX.h.2. The ECRI Institute recommends CO_2 extinguishers because the spray has a cooling effect, does not leave residue, and is not likely to injure patients or personnel.[47,53]

Carbon dioxide extinguishers are rated Class B and C, but may also be used for Class A fires.[53]

IX.i. Fire blankets should not be used in an operating room.[52] (PNDS: I72, I73)

Fire blankets may trap fire next to or under the patient and cause more harm. Fire blankets can burn in an oxygen-enriched environment. Fire blankets are less effective in controlling a fire on a patient than other methods. Usage can lead to wound contamination or spread the fire.

IX.j. Specific evacuation routes should be established for the perioperative environment and developed in collaboration with local authorities and guided by NFPA regulations.[14]

IX.j.1. Personnel and emergency responders should be educated about how to implement the evacuation plan.

IX.j.2. Evacuation routes should be clearly displayed in multiple locations throughout the practice setting.

IX.k. All personnel should recognize medical, gas-control valves and have the ability to shut down medical gases in the event of a fire.[47]

IX.l. All personnel should receive instructions on how to contact the local fire department.[41]

Recommendation X

Potential hazards associated with medical gases in the practice setting should be identified, and safe practices should be established. (PNDS: I122)

The US Food and Drug Administration (FDA) considers compressed medical gases to be prescription drugs that must be dispensed by prescription only. Therefore, these gases should be stored in a secure area with controlled access.[13,54]

X.a. Medical gases should be stored in a secure area, separate from industrial gases. (PNDS: I122)

X.a.1. Full cylinders should be segregated from empty cylinders.[54]

Segregating full cylinders from empty cylinders minimizes the risk of connection to an empty cylinder and a delay in administration of vital gases.

X.b. Medical gas cylinders stored indoors should be in a room with a minimum one-hour fire resistance rating.[14,23]

X.c. Gas cylinders should be stored in a well-ventilated room in a holder or storage rack, away from heat sources.[14]

Securing cylinders with a chain-like device or in racks prevents the cylinders from falling out of the holder or rack.

X.d. Cylinders should not be stored in an egress hallway.[14]

Cylinders and carts directly associated with a currently present patient are considered "in use." Cylinders and carts not directly associated with a specific patient for 30 minutes or more are considered not in use or in storage. These cylinders and carts should be removed from corridors and properly stored.[14]

X.e. Gas-cylinder valves should be closed properly to avoid leakage during storage.

X.f. Gas cylinders should be transported in a carrier designed to prevent tipping, dropping, or damage to the cylinder and not carried by hand. Carrying a cylinder by hand poses a risk of dropping the cylinder and causing sudden release of the compressed gas, which can cause propulsion of the cylinder and subsequent injury.

X.g. Gas cylinders used during patient transport should be secured to the transport cart or bed in holders designed for this purpose and not placed on top of the bed or cart next to the patient.

Holders minimize the risk of the cylinder falling. Transport carts are available with built-in holders.

The maximum amount of oxygen stored inside a health care institution is 566,335 L or 20,000 cubic feet.[14,15] Reserve cylinders provide an emergency backup for use in a medical gas failure.

X.h. Gas cylinders and gas lines must clearly identify the medical gas contained or delivered by the color of the cylinder/line, written labels, and a unique pin-index safety system connector.

The FDA has approved standardized colors for identification of different medical gases (eg, green indicates oxygen).[55,56] The pin-index safety system connector for different medical gases prevents connecting the wrong gas to the delivery system.

Serious injuries and deaths have resulted when an incorrectly identified medical gas has been used. Reliance on the color of the cylinder alone does not differentiate between single gases and combinations of gases that may be contained in a cylinder. In one instance, insufflation of a combination of oxygen and carbon dioxide from a blue cylinder into a patient's abdomen resulted in that patient's death.[54]

X.h.1. Before use, gas cylinders should be checked for
- appropriate label,
- appropriate pin-index safety system connector, and
- appropriate color coding.

X.h.2. When opening a cylinder valve, a small amount of gas should be released before attaching the regulator.[14]

X.h.3. Compressed medical gas tank valves should be opened fully during use to prevent excessive heat buildup through the regulator. Temperatures can increase more quickly if the valve is only partially opened. A flash fire may occur if combustible materials such as dirt or oil are present at the gas outlet.[57]

X.i. Fittings on medical gas cylinders and hoses should not be altered under any circumstances.[58,59] Serious injuries and deaths have resulted when personnel have altered the pin-index safety system, permitting delivery of an incorrect gas into the system.

X.i.1. If the fitting does not easily connect, the label on the gas cylinder or hose should be checked to verify that it is correct.

X.i.2. If the label is correct, the cylinder should be returned to the distributor for examination.[59]

X.i.3. If the label is incorrect; the cylinder should be replaced with a correctly labeled gas cylinder.

X.j. Shut-off valves must be identified with the name of the gas, the location served, and a caution to avoid closing the valve except in emergency situations.[14]

X.j.1. Responsibility and authority for valve shut-off should be defined in the health care organization policy and procedure, but all staff members should be knowledgeable about the procedure.

X.k. Vacuum systems should exhaust outdoors, away from windows, doors, and air intakes.[14]

Exhausting vacuum systems outdoors away from windows, doors, and air intakes will help to prevent contamination of the facility or environment.[14]

X.l. Liquid oxygen tanks must be handled, filled, stored, and transported according to state and federal regulations.[60]

X.l.1. Gloves and personal protective equipment (PPE) must be worn and the tanks held an elbow-length away from the body at filling stations.[60]

X.l.2. Liquid oxygen containers should be stored in a cool, dry place outside of the building or in a separate building.[14]

X.l.3. Liquid oxygen containers should have product identification visible from all sides with a 360-degree label and two-inch high letters.[14]

X.l.4. Liquid oxygen container contents should be verified before use.[14]

X.m. Manufacturer recommendations for attaching regulators to oxygen tanks should be followed.

X.m.1. The sealing gasket specified by the regulator company should be used.

X.m.2. The regulator, gasket, and washers should be inspected before use.

X.m.3. Washers present on oxygen cylinder yokes should be removed before installing the oxygen regulator.

X.m.4. The regulator should be tightened with a T-handle until it is firmly in place.

X.m.5. The valve should be opened slowly to determine if there is a leak, and the valve should be closed quickly if a leak is found.[58,60]

X.m.6. Reusable gaskets on oxygen regulators should be checked regularly and at least with each cylinder change for failure to seal properly.[61]

X.m.7. Reusable gaskets should be discarded if deformed or leaking.[61]

X.m.8. Fluorocarbon, elastomer, and brass gaskets should be used because of their low ignition potential.[61]

X.m.9. An adequate emergency supply of oxygen should be stored at the facility to provide an uninterrupted supply for one day.

Recommendation XI

Potential hazards associated with the use of anesthetic gases in the practice setting should be identified, and safe practices should be established.[13,14]

The level of occupational risk associated with exposure to trace anesthetic gases is unclear. Uncontrolled, retrospective studies conducted in the 1970s found an increase in the incidence of spontaneous abortion and development of congenital abnormalities in offspring among OR personnel.[62-64] Researchers found a relationship between anesthetic gases and chromosome deformities after prolonged exposure.[65] In a prospective study, researchers found no relationship between trace anesthetic gas exposure and adverse health effects.[66] Subjects exposed to sevoflourane concentrations below the National Institute for Occupational Safety and Health (NIOSH) recommended limits showed no kidney damage, in another study.[67,68]

Delivering nitrous oxide through an open system has been found to result in high concentrations of nitrous oxide in the air and is associated with reduced fertility and spontaneous abortion in female dental assistants.[69]

The level of risk from occupational exposure to halogenated anesthetic agents has not been thoroughly studied.[70] Therefore; it remains prudent to limit the amount of waste anesthetic gases in the perioperative environment.

XI.a. The health care organization should establish a waste anesthetic gas management program that minimizes the exposure of health care workers to waste anesthetic gases.

The NIOSH standard for nitrous oxide levels is no more than 25 parts per million (ppm) over an eight-hour period and no more than 2 ppm of any halogenated anesthetic agent over one hour.[67] When scavenging systems are not used, levels can exceed 1000 ppm.[69]

XI.a.1. Air sampling for the most frequently used anesthetic gases should be conducted every six months to evaluate occupational exposures and the effectiveness of control measures.[70]

XI.a.2. Gas monitoring should occur at the organization's defined scheduled intervals for nitrous oxide and other inhalation anesthetics using dosimeters or analyzers.[70]

XI.b. A scavenging system should be used to remove waste anesthetic gases.

XI.b.1. The scavenger system connections should be intact and functioning.[15]

XI.b.2. Scavenging systems should be tested when installed and at three-month intervals for leaks and compliance documentation maintained.[67]

XI.b.3. The scavenger system should be vented directly to the outside of the building.[15]

XI.c. Anesthesia delivery systems should be in proper working order and maintained on a regularly scheduled basis, consistent with the manufacturer's written instructions and the organization's policies.

XI.d. Anesthesia equipment located in areas other than the surgical suite should be included in the safety program.

Recommendation XII

Potential hazards associated with surgical smoke generated in the practice setting should be identified, and safe practices should be established.

Surgical smoke (ie, plume) is generated from use of heat producing instruments such as electrosurgical devices and lasers. This plume has been found to contain toxic gases and vapors (eg benzene, hydrogen cyanide, formaldehyde) that produce an offensive odor; bioaerosols, including blood fragments; and viruses.[71] Experts have noted that there may be more than 600 chemical compounds that exist in surgical smoke.[72] In high concentrations, surgical smoke causes ocular and upper respiratory tract irritation in health care personnel.[73] The smoke generated from electrosurgery and laser contain chemical by-products.[73-76]

The NIOSH recommends that smoke evacuation systems be used to reduce potential acute and chronic health risks to personnel and patients.[73] The Occupational Safety and Health Administration (OSHA) has no separate standard related to surgical smoke. The OSHA addresses such safety hazards in the General Duty Clause and Bloodborne Pathogen Standard.[74]

XII.a. Smoke plume should be removed by use of a smoke evacuation system in both open and laparoscopic procedures.

XII.a.1. The suction wand of the smoke evacuation system should be placed as close to the source of the smoke generation as possible to maximize particulate matter and odor capture and enhance visibility at the surgical site.[77]

XII.a.2. In situations in which minimal plume is generated, a central suction system with an in-line filter may be used to evacuate the plume. The in-line filter is placed between the suction wall/ceiling connection and the suction canister.[77,78]

Central wall suction units are designed to capture liquids, making the use of in-line filters necessary. Low suction rates associated with wall suction units limit their efficacy in evacuating plume, making them suitable for minimal plume evacuation only.[78] A central-

ized system dedicated for smoke evacuation may be available.

XII.a.3. Care should be taken to flush the smoke evacuator lines, according to the manufacturer's instructions, to ensure particulate matter build-up does not occur.

XII.a.4 The risk of patient and caregiver exposure to surgical smoke during laparoscopic procedures should be minimized
- by continuous venting of the smoke from the pneumoperitoneum using a filtering device (eg, an attachment to the cannula), and
- when exhausting the pneumoperitoneum the cannula should be pointed away from all personnel.[75,76]

The continuous venting of the pneumoperitoneum the through filter attachment decreases the amount of particulate matter released, decreases the amount of absorption by the patient, and improves the surgeon's vision during the procedure. Pointing the cannula away from all personnel when exhausting the pneumoperitoneum decreases the amount of particulate matter inhaled by the personnel.

XII.a.5. In circumstances in which large amounts of plume are generated, an individual smoke evacuation unit with an ultra-low penetration air filter should be used to remove smoke plume. Smoke evacuation systems, individual units, and accessories should be used according to manufacturers' written instructions. Filters should be changed as recommended by the manufacturer.[77,78]

XII.a.6. Smoke evacuation systems and accessories should be used according to manufacturers' written instructions.

Detectable odor during the use of a smoke evacuation system is a signal that
- smoke is not being captured at the site where the plume is being generated,
- inefficient air movement through the suction or smoke evacuation wand is occurring, or
- the filter has exceeded its usefulness and should be replaced.[78]

XII.b. Standard precautions should be used when changing smoke evacuation system filters.[77]

Airborne contaminants produced during electrosurgery or laser procedures have been analyzed and are shown to contain gaseous toxic compounds, bioaerosols, and dead and living cell material. At some level, these contaminants have been shown to have an unpleasant odor, cause visual problems for physicians, cause ocular and upper respiratory tract irritation, and have demonstrated mutagenic and carcinogenic potential.[77] The possibility for bacterial and/or viral contamination of smoke plume remains controversial but has been highlighted by different studies.[79,80]

XII.c. Personnel should wear high-filtration surgical masks during procedures that generate surgical smoke.

High-filtration masks are specially designed to filter particulate matter that is 0.1 micron in size and larger and help filter particulate matter found in surgical smoke plume.[81] These masks should not be viewed as absolute protection from chemical or particulate contaminants and should not be used as the first line of protection against surgical smoke inhalation.[77]

Recommendation XIII

Potential hazards associated with the use of chemicals, including methyl methacrylate, in the practice setting should be identified, and safe practices should be established.

Improper handling of chemicals can result in injury to health care workers and patients. Injuries may result from exposure to any portion of the body, including the integumentary or respiratory systems.

XIII.a. Material safety data sheet (MSDS) information for every potentially hazardous chemical must be readily accessible to employees within the practice setting. This information includes identification of hazards, precautions or special handling, signs and symptoms of toxic exposure, and first aid treatments for exposure.[82]

XIII.b. When using chemicals, personnel should read and follow all instructions provided on the container label or found on the MSDS provided by the manufacturer of the chemical. (PNDS: I122)

XIII.b.1. All chemicals should be handled according to their respective MSDS sheets, including, but not limited to,
- disinfectants and sterilants (eg, glutaraldehyde, ortho-phthalaldehyde, ethylene oxide, hydrogen peroxide, peracetic acid);
- tissue preservatives (ie, formalin); and
- antiseptic agents such as hand hygiene products and surgical prep solutions.[83,84]

XIII.c. Chemicals should not be combined unless safe outcomes can be ensured.

Mixing chemicals can result in unsafe substances that are unstable and/or caustic.

XIII.d. Chemicals should be stored according to
- MSDS sheets;
- manufacturer's directions;
- flammability;
- patient and staff safety requirements; and
- local, state, and federal regulations. (PNDS: I122)

XIII.e. Safe practices should be established for the use of methyl methacrylate bone cement. (PNDS: I75)

Methyl methacrylate is a respiratory, eye, and skin irritant. The fumes contain carbon monoxide, hydrogen, and methane, which can cause personnel to experience vertigo, difficulty breathing, and nausea. All of these symptoms are short-term and are relieved once the fumes dissipate.[85] The OSHA permissible exposure limit for methyl methacrylate for general industry is 100 ppm or a time-weighted average of 410 mg/m^3.[85]

XIII.e.1. Methyl methacrylate fumes should be extracted from the environment and the fumes exhausted to the outside air or absorbed through activated charcoal.

XIII.e.2. Vacuum mixers with fume extraction should be used to reduce the fume levels users are exposed to.[84,86]

XIII.e.3. Eye protection should be worn to prevent contact with eyes.[85]

Methyl methacrylate fumes may produce an adverse reaction with soft contact lenses leading to irritation and possible corneal ulceration. There is no documented evidence of problems with hard contact lenses.

XIII.e.4. Manufacturer's recommendations should be followed for mixing and required PPE.[85,87]

XIII.e.5. A second pair of gloves should be worn when handling methyl methacrylate and should be discarded after use.[85] Manufacturer's instructions should be followed regarding the composition of the second pair of gloves.[87]

Methyl methacrylate may be absorbed through the skin and penetrate many plastic and latex compounds, leading to dermatitis.[84] The liquid portion should not come in contact with gloves.[87]

XIII.e.6. A cement gun or mixing system should be used to reduce handling of the product, instead of hand mixing.[84,88] The cement mixture should not be touched until it is the consistency of dough.[87]

XIII.e.7. For spills of methyl methacrylate
- the spill area should be ventilated until odor has dissipated,
- all sources of ignition should be removed,
- appropriate PPE should be worn during clean up,
- the spill area should be isolated,
- the liquid should be covered with an activated charcoal absorbent, and
- the waste product should be disposed of in a hazardous waste container.[89]

XIII.e.8. Methyl methacrylate is hazardous waste and should be disposed of per state, local, and federal requirements.[89]

Recommendation XIV

Hazards associated with chemotherapeutic (eg, cytotoxic) agents used in the practice setting should be identified, and safe practices should be established.

Cytotoxic drugs have the potential to cause serious health risks to health care workers exposed to them. These risks may include carcinogenicity, teratogenicity, reproductive toxicity, organ or tissue damage, and chromosomal damage. Occupational Safety and Health Administration has not determined safe levels of exposure to these drugs and no reliable system is available to monitor exposure levels.[90,91]

XIV.a. Health care organizations should develop a plan for medical surveillance of personnel handling cytotoxic agents.[90]

XIV.b. A current MSDS sheet must be kept on all cytotoxic agents used in the workplace.[91]

XIV.c. Cytotoxic agents should be transported in sealed containers with Luer caps and no needles attached.[92] (PNDS: I122)

XIV.c.1. The transport container should be
- leak proof ,
- resistant to breakage, and
- labeled with warning labels to alert personnel that contents are hazardous.[92]

XIV.d. Personnel handling cytotoxic agents should wear PPE consistent with the type of exposure that can reasonably be anticipated.

XIV.d.1. When administering or handling open containers of chemotherapy drugs, personnel should double-glove and change the outer glove after contact with the cytotoxic agent.[92]

Gloves to be worn for chemotherapy administration should meet the American Society for Testing and Materials D 6978 standards.[93] This information should be received from the glove manufacturers before using the gloves for chemotherapy administration.

XIV.d.2. An impervious or chemotherapy-rated gown should be worn when arms and torso skin contact may occur.[90]

XIV.d.3. Face shields should be worn when the potential for splashing or splattering exists. Face shields protect against mucous membrane and skin exposure. Some cytotoxic agents may cause corneal damage.[92]

XIV.e. Chemotherapy spill kits should be available to contain accidental spills.[92]

XIV.f. Unused chemotherapy agents must be disposed of in accordance with federal, state, and local laws.[88]

Items contaminated with small amounts of chemotherapy agents should be disposed of according to written instructions from the health care organization's waste management vendor.

XIV.g. Manufacturer's recommendations for use of the chemotherapeutic agent should be followed regarding requirements for cleaning and handling of instrumentation exposed to the chemotherapeutic agent.

Some chemotherapeutic agents leave a residue on instruments and require specific PPE and cleaning techniques.

XIV.h. Staff members involved in handling cytotoxic agents should be educated regarding the hazards involved, exposure prevention, and management of spills.[92]

XIV.i. Recommendations from the manufacturer of the chemotherapeutic agent should be followed regarding requirements for disposal of body fluids of patients receiving chemotherapeutic agents (eg, flushing the toilet/hopper twice for disposing of body fluids up to 48 hours after chemotherapeutic agent infusion).

Recommendation XV

Waste that is hazardous upon disposal must be identified and disposed of in manner consistent with federal, state, and local laws.[94]

Waste classified by the Environmental Protection Agency (EPA) as hazardous upon disposal, (eg, hazardous, acutely hazardous, flammable chemicals, acids and bases, heavy metals) is regulated under the Resource Conservation and Recovery Act and must be managed in a way that minimizes environmental effects.[94,95]

XV.a. Chemicals considered hazardous upon disposal must be placed in hazardous waste containers at the point of use to alert handlers to take precautions upon its disposal.[94,96] State and local laws also may apply and may be more stringent.

XV.a.1. Flammable liquids (eg, alcohol, benzoin, collodian, formalin, methyl methacrylate, silver nitrate) must be contained and placed into a hazardous waste receptacle for disposal.[97] These chemicals pose a fire and environmental hazard if discarded in the regular waste stream.

XV.b. The use of mercury-containing devices should be eliminated in the practice setting.[96,98]

Alternative non-mercury products (eg, thermometers, manometers) are available. Mercury poses a serious contamination risk to wildlife and to people, who may eat contaminated fish or game.[99]

Recommendation XVI

Potential hazards associated with misconnections of tubing and lines should be identified and safe practices established. (PNDS: I138)

Multiple cases of tubing which has been incorrectly connected (ie, blood pressure monitors to needleless IV ports; oxygen tubing to needleless IV ports) have led to patient injuries. This has occurred due to Luer connectors that allow different equipment to be connected if a female and male Luer connection are present.[100]

XVI.a. Safe practices should be established when using Luer connectors. (PNDS: I122)

XVI.a.1. When purchasing equipment with Luer connectors, the connector should not be compatible with IV Luer connectors.[101]

XVI.a.2. When connecting two or more lengths of tubing, the tubing should be traced to the point of origin.[102]

XVI.a.3. During the hand-off process, all tubing should be traced to the point of origin.[101]

XVI.a.4. Indirect caregivers, patients, and families should be instructed to obtain help before connecting or disconnecting tubing.[102]

XVI.a.5. Tubing used for high-risk catheters should be labeled and should not have injection ports.[102]

XVI.a.6. Tubing and catheters should be routed to avoid tangling and facilitate easy identification.[100]

XVI.a.7. Standard Luer syringes should not be used for oral medications or enteric feedings.[100]

Recommendation XVII

Competency
Personnel should receive initial education and competency validation and at least annual updates on new regulations, equipment, and procedures.

Ongoing education of perioperative personnel facilitates the development of knowledge, skills, and attitudes that affect patient and worker safety.

XVII.a. An introduction and review of policies and procedures should be included in orientation to the perioperative setting for personnel and observers. Continuing education should be provided when new elements in the environment of care are introduced.

XVII.a.1. Education should include, but not be limited to,
- potential security and other hazards in the environment along with methods of protection;[3,4]
- how to implement the evacuation plan;
- patient privacy policy;[7]
- available ergonomic equipment and safe lifting/moving practices;
- safe use of electrical equipment in the practice setting;
- the location of ventilation and electrical systems and who is permitted to shut them off in the event of an emergency;
- environmental controls, including air exchange rate, temperature, and humidity parameters;
- the safe use of medical equipment in the perioperative environment;
- appropriate responses to clinical alarms;
- the safe use of blanket- and solution-warming cabinets;
- fire prevention education and fire drills, which should be conducted regularly as per the AORN guidance statement, federal, state, local regulations, and accrediting agency standards;
- the safe use and handling of medical and anesthetic gases;
- the location and operation of medical gas shut-off panels;
- the procedures involved in maintaining a safe environment of care; and
- the correct procedures involved to avoid tubing misconnections.[100]

XVII.a.2. Employers must provide training and competency validation of staff members who work with chemicals and other agents in the workplace.[91] Training should include, but is not limited to, the safe handling of
- methyl methacrylate bone cement;
- chemicals (eg, disinfectants, sterilants, formalin);
- cytotoxic agents, the hazards involved, exposure prevention, and management of spills;
- hazardous wastes and their disposal; and
- handling of instruments exposed to chemotherapeutic agents.

Recommendation XVIII

Documentation
Records should be maintained for a time period specified by the health care organization and in compliance with local, state, and federal regulations.

Accurate records are necessary for identifying trends, and demonstrating compliance with regulatory and accrediting agency requirements.

XVIII.a. The following items should be documented per organization policy, including but not limited to
- daily operating room HVAC system function (eg, air exchange rate, temperature, humidity);[25]
- blanket/fluid warming cabinet temperature;
- testing of anesthesia waste gas scavenging systems;[65] and
- employee health records.

Recommendation XIX

Policies and Procedures
Polices and procedures for the provision of a safe environment of care should be developed, reviewed periodically, revised as necessary, and readily available in the practice setting.

Policies and procedures serve as operational guidelines and establish authority, responsibility, and accountability within the organization. Policies and procedures also assist in the development of patient safety, quality assessment, and improvement activities.

XIX.a. The policies and procedures should include, but not be limited to,
- safe patient handling and movement in the perioperative setting;
- description of security management activities, including access control;
- action to be taken during periods of loss of usual and emergency power;[21]
- monitoring of environmental controls including air exchanges per hour, temperature, and humidity;
- describing the processes to be implemented to effectively manage medical equipment, including selection, purchase, inspection, and maintenance processes;
- monitoring and recording the temperature of warming cabinets;
- inspection, testing, and maintenance of fire extinguishing equipment and supplies;
- defining responsibility and authority for gas valve shut-off;
- monitoring of nitrous oxide and other inhalation anesthetics;
- schedule and criteria for maintenance of anesthesia delivery systems;
- medical surveillance of personnel handling cytotoxic agents;
- storage of chemicals according to manufacturer's directions, MSDS sheets, flammability, patient and staff safety requirements and local, state, and federal regulations; and
- other policies as dictated by applicable local, state, and federal regulations.

Recommendation XX

Quality
The health care organization's quality management program should evaluate the environment of care to improve patient safety.

XX.a. Personnel in the perioperative setting should
- identify safety hazards,
- take appropriate corrective actions, and
- report hazards per organizational policy.

XX.b. A quality-management plan should be developed by a team involving representatives from all types of positions within the perioperative area. The quality management plan should include
- critiquing of fire drills by a team that includes members from all perioperative departments and categories of personnel to identify deficiencies and opportunities for improvement;
- collecting and analyzing information about adverse outcomes associated with the environment of care as a part of the institution-wide performance improvement program that addresses adverse events and near misses;[24]
- creation of a patient safety culture, to include policies and procedures supporting that culture;
- the creation of a patient safety culture that will foster reporting of adverse events and near misses;[103]
- monitoring of actual and potential risks in each of the environment of care areas, to be completed on a regular basis (eg, at least monthly environment of care rounds by a team that includes clinicians, administrators, support personnel);[24]
- developing a process to monitor and report incidents of equipment malfunction leading to patient harm as outlined in the Safe Medical Devices Act of 1990;[104]
- developing a plan to monitor compliance with safe handling of chemicals, cytotoxic agents, and hazardous waste in the workplace;
- conducting scheduled "walk-around" safety rounds to test clinical alarms and to observe staff members response to the alarms;
- developing an organization-wide event reporting system for HVAC failures and power interruptions;[29]
- developing processes to regularly inspect, test, and maintain fire extinguishing equipment and supplies; and
- a mechanism for reporting work-related health problems.

Glossary

Clinical alarms: Alarm systems that are patient specific and are used for the purpose of alerting staff members to a patient emergency.

Compressed medical gas (CMG): A liquefied or vaporized gas alone, or in combination with other gases, that is a drug as defined by the FDA (eg, oxygen, nitrogen, nitric oxide, nitrous oxide, carbon dioxide, helium, medical air).

Container: A metal container designed to contain either liquefied or vaporized CMG.

Cylinder: A metal container designed to contain CMG at a high pressure.

Ground-fault circuit interrupter: A device that senses a significant flow of leakage current and interrupts the flow of electricity to prevent electric shock.

Hazardous upon disposal waste: Certain pharmaceutical and chemical products, as determined by the EPA, become hazardous waste when discarded. The residual in the container after use is considered hazardous. Hazardous wastes can be liquids, solids, or contained gases.

Line-isolation monitor: A device used to continuously monitor an ungrounded power system that is isolated from the commercial power supply received from the utility company. Isolated ungrounded power systems may allow leakage currents, also known as hazard currents, to flow from the power system to ground. This leakage current may flow through a person's body and presents a shock hazard to that person. Standards for the maximum allowed leakage current have been established. The line isolation monitor displays the calculated level of leakage current and sounds an alarm if the current exceeds the predetermined level.

Pin-index safety system: A safeguard to eliminate cylinder interchanging and the possibility of accidentally placing the incorrect gas on a yoke designed to accommodate another gas. Two pins on the yoke are arranged so that they project into the cylinder valve. Each gas or combination of gases has a specific pin arrangement.

Teratogenicity: The ability of a substance to cause the development of abnormal structures in an embryo or fetus exposed to that substance during gestation.

Warming device: A device used in the perioperative setting to assist with the control of body temperature and prevent hypothermia.

Wet locations: Patient care areas where procedures are performed that are normally subject to wet conditions, including standing fluids on the floor or drenching of the work area, while patients are present.

REFERENCES

1. Beyea SC, ed. *Perioperative Nursing Data Set.* Rev 2nd ed. Denver CO: AORN, Inc; 2007.

2. Occupational Safety and Health Administration. Guidelines for preventing workplace violence for health care and social service workers. *http://www.osha.gov /Publications/OSHA3148/osha3148.html.* Accessed June 27, 2007.

3. Joint Commission Resources. Protecting your health care workers from violence in the workplace. *The Source.* 2006; 4:1-10

4. Centers for Disease Control and Prevention. Developing and implementing a workplace violence prevention program and policy. *http://www.cdc.gov/niosh/vio lcohnt.html.* Accessed June 27, 2007.

5. Krozek C, Scoggins A. Meeting Environment of Care Standards on the Patient Care Unit: Part I. *http://gateway.ut.ovid.com/gw1/ovidweb.cgi.* Accessed August 22, 2007.

6. Department of Health and Human Services. Rules and regulations, 45 CFR part 162: HIPAA administrative simplification: standard unique health identifier for health care providers; final rule. *Federal Register.* 2004;69:3434–3469

7. Standards for Privacy of Individually Identifiable Health Information. *http://www.hipaadvisory.com/regs /finalprivacy.* Accessed August 22, 2007.

8. Standards of perioperative professional practice. In: *Standards, Recommended Practices, and Guidelines.* Denver, CO: AORN, Inc;2007:433-436.

9. AORN position statement on ergonomically healthy workplace practices. In: *Standards, Recommended Practices, and Guidelines.* Denver, CO: AORN, Inc;2007:382-384.

10. Peterson, C, ed. *Safe Patient Handling and Movement in the Perioperative Setting.* Denver, CO: AORN, Inc;2007.

11. Nelson A, Fragala G, Menzel N. Myths and facts about back injuries in nursing. *American Journal of Nursing.* 2003;103:32-41.

12. AORN position statement: statement on workplace safety. In: *Standards, Recommended Practices, and Guidelines.* Denver, CO: AORN, Inc;2007:416-417.

13. National Fire Protection Association, *National Electrical Code Handbook (NFPA 70).* 10th ed. Quincy, MA; National Fire Protection Association; 2005:408-425.

14. Bielen RP, ed. *Health Care Facilities Handbook, 2005.* Quincy, MA: National Fire Protection Association, 2005:567-568.

15. American Institute of Architects. Ventilation requirements for areas affecting patient care in hospitals and outpatient facilities. In: *Guidelines for Design and Construction of Hospitals and Health Care Facilities,*

2001. Washington, DC: American Institute of Architects Press; 2001:79-80.

16. Electrical safety Q&A: a reference guide for the clinical engineer. *Health Devices.* 2005;34:58-75.

17. McHenry C, Bergue R, Ortega RA, Yowler CJ. Recognition, management, and prevention of specific operating room catastrophes. *Journal American College of Surgeons.* 2004;198:810-821.

18. Illuminating Engineering Society of North America Committee for Health Care Facilities. Recommended practice-29-95. In: *Lighting for Hospitals and Health Care Facilities.* New York, NY; Illuminating Engineering Society of North America;1995:1-75.

19. National Fire Protection Association, *NFPA 110 Standard for Emergency and Standby Power Systems.* 2005 Ed. Quincy, MA; National Fire Protection Association; 2005.

20. American Institute of Architects. The next generation of operating rooms. *http://www.aia.org/nwsltr_print.cfm?pagename=aah_jrnl_20051019_ORs.* The American Institute of Architects. Accessed August 22, 2007.

21. The Joint Commission. Preventing adverse events caused by emergency electrical power system failures. *Sentinel Event Alert:* 2006: 37, *http://www.jointcommission.org/SentinelEvents/SentinelEventAlert/sea_37.htm.* Accessed August 22, 2007.

22. *Standards and Checklist for Accreditation of Ambulatory Surgery Facilities.* Mundelein, IL: American Association for Accreditation of Ambulatory Surgery Facilities, Inc; 2005:4–17.

23. The Joint Commission. Management of the environment of care. In: *Comprehensive Accreditation Manual for Hospitals: The Official Handbook.* Oakbrook Terrace, IL: The Joint Commission; 2006:EC1-EC30.

24. Mangram A, Horan TC, Pearson ML, Silver LC, Jarvis WR. Guideline for prevention of surgical site infection, 1999. Hospital Infection Control Advisory Committee. *Infection Control and Hospital Epidemiology.*1999;20:250-278.

25. Association for Advancement of Medical Instrumentation. *Comprehensive Guide to Steam Sterilization and Sterility Assurance in Health Care Faciities, 2006.* Arlington, VA. Association for Advancement of Medical Instrumentation; 2006:24.

26. Recommended practices for traffic patterns in the perioperative practice setting. In: *Standards, Recommended Practices, and Guidelines.* Denver, CO: AORN, Inc; 2007:703-706.

27. American Society of Heating, Refrigerating and Air-Conditioning Engineers. *HVAC Design Manual for Hospitals and Clinics.* Atlanta, GA: American Society of Heating, Refrigerating and Air-Conditioning Engineers, Inc; 2003:37.

28. Centers for Disease Control and Prevention. Guidelines for Environmental Infection Control in Health-Care Facilities. *http://www.cdc.gov/ncidod/dhqp/pdf/guidelines/Enviro_guide_03.pdf.* Accessed July 24, 2007.

29. Surgical and related services. In: *Accreditation Handbook for Ambulatory Health Care.* Wilmette, IL: Accreditation Association for Ambulatory Health Care; 2006: 48-51.

30. Phillips J, Barnsteiner JH. Clinical alarms: improving efficiency and effectiveness. *Critical Care Nursing Quarterly.* 2005;28:317-323.

31. Williams JS. Meeting the challenge: how hospitals comply with new clinical alarms requirement. *Biomedical Instrumentation and Technology.* 2003;37:319-328.

32. ECRI. *Operating Room Risk Management. http://www.ecri.org/MarketingDocs/0306news.pdf.* Accessed May 25, 2007

33. Kressin KA. Burn injury in the operating room: a closed claims analysis. *ASA Newsletter.* 2004;68:9-11.

34. Limiting temperature settings on blanket and solution warming cabinets can prevent patient burns. [Problem Reports]. *Health Devices.* 2005;34:168 -171.

35. Bonati, et al. *Ex vivo* testing of a temperature- and pressure-controlled amino-irrigator for fetoscopic surgery. *J of Ped Surgery.* 2002;37:18-24.

36. Recommended practices for prevention of unplanned perioperative hypothermia. In: *Standards, Recommended Practices, and Guidelines.* Denver, CO: AORN, Inc; 2008:407-420.

37. Moore SS, Green CR, Wang FL, Pandit SK, Hurd WW. The role of irrigation in the development of hypothermia during laparoscopic surgery. *Am J of Obsterics and Gyn.* 1997;176:598-601.

38. AORN position statement: statement on fire prevention. In: *Standards, Recommended Practices, and Guidelines.* Denver, CO: AORN, Inc; 2007:385-386.

39. American National Standards Institute. Fire and explosive hazards. In: *American National Standard for Safe Use of Lasers in Health Care Facilities; Stamdard Z136.3.* Orlando, FL: American National Standards Institute, Inc; 2005:19-20.

40. A clinician's guide to surgical fires: how they occur, how to prevent them, how to put them out. *Health Devices.* 2003;32:5-24.

41. AORN guidance statement: fire prevention in the operating room. In: *Standards, Recommended Practices, and Guidelines.* Denver, CO: AORN, Inc; 2007:259-267.

42. Recommended practices for skin preparation of patients. In: *Standards, Recommended Practices, and Guidelines.* Denver, CO: AORN, Inc; 2007:653-606.

43. Recommended practices for electrosurgery. In: *Standards, Recommended Practices, and Guidelines.* Denver, CO: AORN, Inc; 2007:515-530.

44. Recommended practices for laser safety in practice settings. In: *Standards, Recommended Practices, and Guidelines.* Denver, CO: AORN, Inc; 2007:593-598.

45. NFPA accepts ASHE's amendment to NFPA 99 on alcohol based surgical prep solutions. American Society for Healthcare Engineering of the American Hospital Association. *http://www.ashe.org/ashe/codes/nfpa/nfpa099_proposeamend_absp.html.* Accessed August 22, 2007.

46. Improper use of alcohol-based skin preps can cause surgical fires. [Hazard Report]. *Health Devices.* 2003;32:441-43.

47. Surgical fires. In: *Operating Room Risk Management.* Plymouth Meeting, PA: ECRI; 2004:2.

48. Guidance article: surgical fire safety. *Health Devices.* 2006;35: 45-66.

49. Podnos Y, Irving CA, Williams R. Fires in the operating room. American College of Surgeons Committee on Perioperative Care available at *http://www.facs.org/about /committees/cpc/oper0897.html.* Accessed June 25, 2007.

50. Rationale and interpretive guidelines for the 2005 National Patient Safety Goals. *Joint Commission Perspectives on Patient Safety.* 2004;I4:3-4.

51. Pollock G. Eliminating surgical fires: a team approach. *AANA Journal.* 2004;72:293–297

52. Medical gas fires: does your staff know how to recognize and extinguish them? [Problem Reports]. *Health Devices.* 2003;32:39–40.

53. National Fire Protection Association, *NFPA 10—Standard for Portable Fire Extinguishers, 2005 Edition.* Quincy, MA: National Fire Protection Association; 2005.8,29-43.

54. Guidance for hospitals, nursing homes, and other health care facilities. FDA public health advisory. US Department of Health and Human Services, Food and Drug Administration, Center for Drug Evaluation and Research. *http://www.fda.gov/cder/guidance/4341fnl.pdf.* Accessed August 22, 2007.

55. US Department of Health and Human Services, Food and Drug Administration, Center for Drug Evaluation and Research. Compressed Medical Gases Guidelines. *http://www.fda.gov/cder/guidance/cmgg89.htm.* Accessed August 22, 2007.

56. Compressed Gas Association. *Standard Color Marking of Compressed Gas Cylinders Intended for Medical Use in the United States.* Arlington, VA: Compressed Gas Association; 1998.

57. Giarrizzo-Wilson S. Postoperative vision loss; cellular telephones; medical gas handling; roller latches**.** [Clinical Issues]. *AORN Journal.* 2006; 84:107-108,111-114.

58. Questions and Answers on the Proposed Rule for Medical Gas Containers. US Department of Health and Human Services, Food and Drug Administration, Center for Drug Evaluation and Research. *http://www.fda.gov/cder /dmpq/MedGas_QA_20060410.htm.* Accessed August 22, 2007.

59. Medical Gas Containers and Closures; Current Good Manufacturing Practice Requirements. US Department of Health and Human Services, Food and Drug Administration. *http://www.fda.gov/OHRMS/DOCKETS /98fr/06-3370.htm.* Accessed August 22, 2007.

60. Regulations (Standards-29CFR) Oxygen—1910.104. US Department of Labor, Occupational Safety and Health Administration. *http://www.osha.gov/pls /oshaweb/owadisp.show_document?p_id=9750&p_table =STANDARDS.* Accessed August 22, 2007.

61. Reusable gaskets on oxygen regulators will wear out. [Hazard Reports]. *Health Devices.* 2003;32:39–40.

62. Askrog V, Harvald B. Teratogenic effects of inhalation anesthetics. [Danish]. *Nord Med.* 1970;83:498-500.

63. Cohen EN, Bellville JW, Brown BW, Jr. Anesthesia, pregnancy, and miscarriage: a study of operating room nurses and anesthetists. *Anesthesiology.* 1971;35:343-347.

64.Knill-Jones RP, Rodrigues LV, Moir DD, Spence AA. Anaesthetic practice and pregnancy: controlled survey of women anaesthetists in the United Kingdom. *Lancet.* 1972;1: 1326-1328.

65. Bilban M, Jakopin CB, Ogrinc D. Cytogenetic tests performed on operating room personnel (the use of anaesthetic gases). *International Archives of Occupational & Environmental Health.* 2005;78:60-64.

66. Spence AA. Environmental pollution by inhalation anaesthetics. *British Journal of Anaesthesiology.* 1987;59:96-103.

67. National Institute for Occupational Safety and Health. *Occupational Exposure to Waste Anesthetic Gases and Vapors: Criteria for a Recommended Standard.* [Publication DHEW (NIOSH)]. Cincinnati, OH: US Dept of Health, Education, and Welfare, Public Health Service, Center for Disease Control, National Institute for Occupational Safety and Health; 1977;77-140.

68. Trevisan A, Venturini MB, Carrieri M, et al. Biological indices of kidney involvement in personnel exposed to sevoflurane in surgical areas. *Am J Ind Med.* 2003;44:474-480.

69. Rowland A.S, Baird DD, Weinberg CR, Shore DL, Shy CM, Wilcox AJ. Reduced fertility among women employed as dental assistants exposed to high levels of nitrous oxide. *N Engl J Med.* 1992;327:993–997.

70. Anesthetic Gases: Guidelines for Workplace Exposures. US Department of Labor, Occupational Safety and Health Administration. *http://www.osha.gov/dts/osta /anestheticgases/index.html.* Accessed August 22, 2007.

71. Ball KA. *Lasers: The Perioperative Challenge.* 3rd ed. Denver, CO: AORN, Inc; 2004.

72. Hoglan M. Potential hazards from electrosurgery plume: recommendations for surgical smoke evacuation. *Canadian Operating Room Nursing Journal.* 1995;13:10-16.

73. NIOSH Hazard Controls. Control of Smoke from Laser/Electric Surgical Procedures-HC11. Available at: *http:// www.cdc.gov/niosh/hc11.html.* Accessed August 22, 2007.

74. US Department of Labor, Occupational Safety, and Health Administration. Safety and Health Topics: Laser/ Electrosurgery Plume. Available at: *http://www.osha.gov /SLTC/laserelectrosurgeryplume/index.html.* Accessed August 22, 2007.

75. Barret W.L, Garber SM. Surgical smoke: a review of the literature: is this just a lot of hot air? *Surgical Endoscopy.* 2003;17:979-987.

76. Alp E, Bijl D, Bleichrodt RP, Hansson B, Voss A. Surgical smoke and infection control. *Journal of Hospital Infection.* 2006; 62:1-5.

77. American National Standards Institute. *American National Standard for Safe Use of Lasers in Health Care Facilities.* Orlando, FL: Laser Institute of America; 2005: 19-20.

78. ECRI Institute. Smoke evacuation systems, surgical, *Healthcare Product Comparison System.* Plymouth Meeting, PA: ECRI Institute; March 2002:1-3.

79. Garden JM, O'Banion MK, Shelnitz LS, et al. Papillomavirus in the vapor of carbon dioxide laser-treated verrucae. *JAMA.* 1988; 259:1199-1202.

80. Hallmo P, Naess O. Laryngeal papillomatosis with human papillomavirus DNA contracted by a laser surgeon. *European Archives of Oto-Rhino-Laryngology.* 1991;248:425-7.

81. Romig Cl, Smalley PJ. Regulation of surgical smoke plume. Health Policy Issues. *AORN Journal.* 1997;65:824-828

82. Hazard Communication OSHA Standards. US Department of Labor, Occupational Safety and Health Administration. *http://osha.gov/SLTC/hazardcommunications/standards.html.* Accessed October 6, 2007.

83. Recommended practices for surgical hand antisepsis/hand scrubs. In: *Standards, Recommended Practices and Guidelines.* Denver, CO: AORN, Inc; 2007:565-574.

84. McHugh E. The principles of mixing and handling to minimise potential hazards of methyl methacrylate bone cement. *British Journal of Theatre Nursing.* 1998;7:9-12.

85. Chemical Sampling Information: Methyl methacrylate. US Department of Labor, Occupational Safety and Health Administration. *http://osha.gov/dts/chemical sampling/data/CH_254400.html.* Accessed July 16, 2007.

86. Eveleigh R. Fume levels during bone cement mixing. *British Journal of Perioperative Nursing.* 2002; 12:145-150.

87. Medical Devices; Reclassification of Polymethyl-methacrylate (PMMA) Bone Cement. Environmental Protection Agency. *http://www.epa.gov/fedrgstr/EPA-IMPACT /2002/July/Day-17/i18036.htm.* Accessed September 26, 2007.

88. Schlegel UJ, Sturm M, Ewerbeck V, Breusch SJ. Efficacy of vacuum bone cement mixing systems in reducing methylmethacrylate fume exposure: comparison of 7 different mixing devices and handmixing. *Acta Orthop Scandinavica.* 2004;75:559-566.

89. Methyl methacrylate MSDS. *http://www.cdc.gov /niosh/ipcsneng/neng0300.html.* Accessed June 25, 2007.

90. Polovich M, White JM, Kelleher LO. Fundamentals of administration. In: *Chemotherapy and Biotherapy Guidelines and Recommendations for Practice.* 2nd ed. Pittsburg, PA: Oncology Nursing Society, 2005:53-62.

91. OSHA Technical Manual. Controlling Occupational Exposure to Hazardous Drugs. *http://www.osha.gov/dts /osta/otm/otm_vi/otm_vi_2.html.* Accessed August 22, 2007.

92. Preventing Occupational Exposure to Antineoplastic and Other Hazardous Drugs in Health Care Settings. NIOSH alert Jan 21, 2005. *http://www.cdc.gov/niosh/docs /2004-165/pdfs/2004-165.pdf.* Accessed August 22, 2007.

93. American Society for Testing and Materials International, ed. *Standard Practice for Assessment of Resistance of Medical Gloves to Permeation by Chemotherapy Drugs, Standard D 6978-05.* West Conshohocken, PA: American Society for Testing and Materials, International; 2005.

94. Laws and Regulations, Chapter 1 – Environmental Protection Agency, Subchapter 1—Solid Wastes, parts 260-270. Environmental Protection Agency. *http://www.epa .gov/docs/epacfr40/chapt-l.info.* Accessed August 22, 2007.

95. AORN guidance statement: environmental responsibility. In: *Standards, Recommended Practices and Guidelines.* Denver, CO: AORN, Inc; 2007:251-258.

96. Environmental Protection Agency. Wastes. *http:// www.epa.gov/epaoswer/osw.* Accessed August 20, 2007.

97. Environmental Protection Agency. Sloan-Kettering fined for failure to properly manage hazardous waste. (January 27, 2004). *http://www.epa.gov/region02/healthcare.* Accessed August 22, 2007, 2007.

98. World Health Organization. Mercury in Health Care. Policy Paper. August, 2005. *http://www.healthcarewaste .org.* Accessed August 22, 2007.

99. Health Care Without Harm. Making Medicine Mercury-free: A Resource Guide for Mercury-free Medicine. Available at: *http://www.noharm.org/library/docs/Going _Green_Making_Medicine_Mercury_Free.pdf.* Accessed August 21, 2007.

100. Joint Commission on the Accreditation of Health Care Organizations. Tubing Misconnections – A Persistent and Potentially Deadly Occurrence. [Sentinel Event Alert]. Issue 36 (April 3, 2006). *http://www.jointcommission .org/SentinelEvents/SentinelEventAlert/sea_36.htm.* Accessed August 22, 2007.

101. Paparella S. Inadvertant attachment of a blood pressure device to a needless "y-site": surprising, fatal connections. *Journal Emergency Nursing.* 2005; 31:180-182.

102. Institute for Safe Medical Practices. Medication Safety Alert. June 17, 2004. *http://www.ismp.org/MSA articles?tubingprint.htm.* Accessed August 21, 2007.

103. AORN guidance statement: creating a patient safety culture. In: *Standards, Recommended Practices and Guidelines.* Denver, CO: AORN, Inc; 2007:305-310.

104. US Department of Health and Human Services, Public Health Service/Food and Drug Administration Center of Devices and Radiological Health. *The Safe Medical Devices Act 1990 and The Medical Device Amendments of 1992* HHS Publication FDA 93-4243.Washington DC: US Department of Health and Human Services, 1992.

Originally published February 1988, *AORN Journal,* as "Recommended practices for safe care through identification of potential hazards in the surgical environment." Revised March 1992.

Revised November 1995; published March 1996, *AORN Journal.* Reformatted July 2000.

Revised; published March 2003, *AORN Journal.*

Revised 2007; published in *Perioperative Standards and Recommended Practices,* 2008 edition, as "Recommended practices for a safe environment of care."

AORN Perioperative Standards and Recommended Practices, 2009 Edition

Recommended Practices for Environmental Cleaning in the Perioperative Setting

The following proposed recommended practices for environmental cleaning in the perioperative setting were developed by the AORN Recommended Practices Committee and have been approved by the AORN Board of Directors. They were presented as proposed recommendations for comments by members and others. They are effective January 1, 2008.

These recommended practices are intended as achievable recommendations representing what is believed to be an optimal level of practice. Policies and procedures will reflect variations in practice settings and/or clinical situations that determine the degree to which the recommended practices can be implemented.

AORN recognizes the numerous types of settings in which perioperative nurses practice. These recommended practices are intended as guidelines adaptable to various practice settings. These practice settings include traditional ORs, ambulatory surgery units, physicians' offices, cardiac catheterization suites, endoscopy suites, radiology departments, and all other areas where operative and other invasive procedures may be performed.

References to nursing interventions (I) used in the Perioperative Nursing Data Set, second edition, (PNDS) are noted in parentheses when a recommended practice corresponds to a PNDS intervention.[1] The reader is referred to the PNDS for further explanation of nursing diagnoses, interventions, and outcomes.

Purpose

These recommended practices provide guidance for environmental cleaning and disinfection in the surgical practice setting. Conscientious application of these recommended practices should result in a clean environment for surgical patients and minimize the exposure risk of health care personnel and patients to potentially infectious microorganisms. Potentially, any patient could be infected with blood-borne or other pathogens; therefore, all surgical procedures should be considered potentially infectious.

Recommendation I

The patient should be provided a clean, safe environment.

Exogenous sources for pathogens that may cause a surgical site infection (SSI) include surgical personnel; the operating room environment (including the air); and all tools, instruments, and supplies brought to the sterile field during the procedure. Exogenous flora are mainly aerobes.[2] Health care-associated infections have been linked to external sources, which can include environmental surfaces.[3] The risk of infection from pathogenic organisms on environmental surfaces is due not only to their presence, but to their ability to survive on and be transferred to many surfaces.[4]

I.a. The perioperative registered nurse should assess the perioperative environment frequently for cleanliness and take action to implement cleaning and disinfection procedures if needed.[5] (PNDS: I98) Cleanliness means the absence of visible dust, debris, soil, or body substances.

Environmental cleaning and disinfection is a team effort involving surgical personnel and environmental services personnel. The responsibility for verifying a clean surgical environment rests with perioperative nurses. (PNDS: I98)

I.a.1. Preparation of the OR should include visual inspection for cleanliness before case carts, supplies, equipment, and instrument sets are brought into the room.

I.b. All horizontal surfaces in the OR (eg, furniture, surgical lights, booms, equipment) should be damp dusted before the first scheduled surgical procedure of the day.[2] Plasma and monitor screens should be cleaned according to manufacturers' instructions.

Dust is known to contain human skin and hair, fabric fibers, pollens, mold, fungi, insect parts, glove powder, and paper fibers among other things.[6-8] Airborne particles range in size from 0.001 microns to several hundred microns. Contamination from particles can come from an external source (eg, ventilation, doors) or an internal source (eg, equipment, personnel activity).[9] (PNDS: I98)

In settings with dry conditions, gram-positive cocci (eg, coagulase negative *Staphylococcus* species) found in dust may persist; in settings with surfaces that are moist and soiled, the growth of gram-negative bacilli may persist.[10] Fungi, which favor moist, fibrous material, also are found in dust. Damp dusting prevents microbial-laden dust from being dispersed throughout the environment.[8] (PNDS: I98)

I.b.1. Equipment from areas outside the restricted area of the OR should be cleaned before being brought into an OR.

I.b.2. A clean, lint-free cloth moistened with an Environmental Protection Agency (EPA)-registered hospital detergent/ disinfectant should be used to damp-dust. (PNDS: 198)

I.b.3. Cleaning and disinfection methods that produce mist, aerosols, or dust (eg, spray bottles containing disinfectant) should not be used.[11]

I.b.4. Gloves used for environmental cleaning and disinfection should be made of natural rubber latex, nitrile, chloroprene blends, or butyl rubber.[12] Vinyl gloves should not be used in environmental cleaning and disinfection. Vinyl glove barrier protection failure rates can be very high.[13]

I.c. Environmental Protection Agency (EPA)-registered disinfectants should be used to clean floors, noncritical equipment, and other surfaces.[8] (PNDS: I98) Material safety data sheets (MSDSs) should be available and reviewed for each disinfectant used in the perioperative setting.

Environmental surfaces that touch intact skin are considered noncritical items requiring low-level disinfection. Environmental surfaces can serve as a means of secondary transmission by providing a reservoir for infectious organisms that can contaminate the hands of health care personnel. This is known as surface-to-hand transfer of bacteria.[3,14-16] Field and laboratory studies have shown the importance of environmental cleaning and disinfection as part of an infection prevention process in reducing microbial bioburden in the environment, thereby interrupting microorganism transmission.[4] One study has shown that vancomycin-resistant enterococci species (VRE) can be transmitted by a contaminated sur-

face.[17] Another study has shown that a persistence of pathogens can survive on fabrics and plastics.[18] (PNDS: I98)

I.c.1. Reusable string and microfiber mops and cleaning cloths should be changed after each use.[8,19] Used cleaning mops or cloths should not be returned to the cleaning solution container.

I.c.2. Single-use disposable mop heads and cloths may be used.[8]

I.c.3. Mops that dispense cleaning disinfectant may be used.

Cleaned and dried mop heads and cleaning cloths decrease the level of contamination.[20] Microfiber mops are an option for mopping floors because

- they can withstand up to 300 launderings;
- the microfiber particles are positively charged and draw negatively charged particles (ie, dirt);
- traditional string mops weigh about 10 pounds while microfiber mops weigh about two pounds; and
- lighter mops may reduce personnel injuries.[19]

Mops that dispense cleaning fluid eliminate the risk of contamination of multi-use containers of cleaning solution and reduce the risk of chemical splashes.

I.d. Measures should be taken to prevent vermin infestation of the perioperative environment.[8,21]

Insects and rodents can carry pathogens that cause disease (eg, flies carrying *Shigella* which can cause diarrhea by contaminating food).[22] Food left out in staff member lounges for long periods of time may be a focus of fly infestation.

I.d.1. To prevent vermin infestations, the following steps should be taken:

- remove food sources and any environment that attracts pests; and
- keep windows and doors closed.[21]

I.d.2. If prevention measures fail, a credentialed pest control specialist should be contacted to eliminate the cause of the infestation.[8,21]

Recommendation II

A safe, clean environment should be reestablished after each surgical procedure.

Routine cleaning and disinfection reduces the amount of dust, organic debris, and microbial load in the environment. Following scientifically based recommendations for cleaning and disinfection practices in health care organizations helps to reduce infections associated with contaminated items. Many studies have documented that failure to comply with scientifically based recommendations has led to infection outbreaks.[14]

II.a.   Operating rooms should be cleaned after each surgical or invasive procedure with a lint-free or microfiber cloth moistened with a detergent/disinfectant and water.[2,8,19]

II.a.1.   When feasible, products that are environmentally friendly should be considered when selecting a disinfectant.[23-25]

II.a.2.   Detergent and EPA-registered disinfectant solutions should be prepared daily or as needed according to manufacturers' instructions.[8]

II.a.3.   Chemicals placed into a secondary container must be labeled with the chemical and the solution's concentration.[26]

II.a.4.   High-level disinfectants or liquid chemical sterilants should not be used for cleaning and disinfection environmental surfaces or noncritical devices.[8]

II.a.5.   Alcohol should not be used to clean large environmental surfaces.[8]

Alcohol is not an EPA-registered disinfectant. Alcohol does not remove soil or debris. Alcohol is a flammable antiseptic which must be used with caution in the surgical setting.[27,28]

II.b.   Mattresses and padded positioning device surfaces (eg, OR beds, arm boards, patient transport carts) should be moisture-resistant and intact.

II.b.1.   Nonporous surfaces such as mattress covers, pneumatic tourniquet cuffs, blood pressure cuffs, and other patient equipment should be cleaned and dis-

infected with an EPA-registered hospital disinfectant between patient use.[8]

II.b.2.   Manufacturers' instructions for cleaning and disinfection specialized beds should be followed.

II.b.3.   Damaged or worn coverings should be replaced.

II.b.4.   Fabric coverings should be changed and laundered after each patient use.

II.b.5.   Penetration of the cover by needles and other sharp items should be avoided.[8,29]

II.c.   Patient transport vehicles including straps and attachments should be cleaned after each patient use.[30]

II.c.1.   Single-use straps should be discarded after one use.

II.d.   All receptacles (eg, bins, kick buckets, pails), work surfaces, and tables should be cleaned and disinfected.[5,8]

II.e.   Contaminated laundry should be handled as little as possible.[8]

Handling contaminated laundry with a minimum of agitation avoids contamination of air, surfaces, and personnel.[5,8]

II.e.1.   Contaminated laundry should be placed in leak-proof containers or bags and labeled appropriately at the location where it was used.[5,8]

II.e.2.   Linen should be laundered in a designated, organization-approved and monitored laundry facility.

II.f.   Laundry chutes in the perioperative setting should be designed to enable cleaning and disinfection and maintenance on a regular basis.[8,31,32]

Laundry bags travel through a laundry chute with a back-and-forth motion that can disperse airborne pathogens throughout a health care facility.[33] Maintaining negative pressure in the chute prevents the spread of pathogens from one floor to the next.[34] (PNDS: I98)

II.g.   Manufacturers' cleaning recommendations should be consulted before cleaning computer keyboards, monitor screens, telephones, and other electronic devices. If appropriate, these items should be cleaned with a detergent- and water-moistened lint-free cloth. If the item cannot be cleaned, it should be covered with a moisture-impervious protective covering that can be cleaned or discarded after each use.[8,35]

Computers and other sensitive electronic devices are likely to become contaminated and may be difficult to clean.[8] Sensitive computer components such as monitor screens may be damaged by cleaning disinfectants.[5]

II.h. Tacky mats should not be used.[8]

Tacky mats have not been shown to reduce the number of organisms on shoes or equipment wheels, nor do they reduce the risk of SSIs. An exception to not using tacky mats would be their use inside the entry of cordoned-off construction areas within the health care facility as a means to contain dust and debris.[8]

II.i. Neonatal patient contact with wet environmental disinfectants should be avoided.[8]

After cleaning and disinfection, all surfaces should be dry before patient contact. Chemical residue may remain on the bassinet or the incubator if not thoroughly dried.[8]

II.i.1. Incubators or bassinets should not be cleaned when the neonate is in the incubator, warming bed, or bassinet. The neonate should be moved to another incubator or bassinet that is clean and dry.[8,36]

II.i.2. An EPA-registered germicide, in the concentration indicated in the manufacturers guideline for nurseries and neonates, should be used.[8,36]

Recommendation III

Contaminated disposable and reusable items should be handled safely according to state and federal regulations.

Disposable and reusable items may be classified as either potentially infectious or noninfectious. Strategies for handling these items help promote a safe and healthy environment.[25]

III.a. Disposable items contaminated with blood and/or tissue that would release blood or other infectious materials in a liquid or semi-liquid state if compressed, or items that are caked with dried blood or other potentially infectious material, must be placed in closable, leak-proof containers or bags that are color coded, labeled, or tagged for easy identification as biohazardous waste.[5]

Leak-proof containers prevent exposure of personnel to blood, tissue, and body fluids and prevent contamination of the environment. Color coding and/or labeling alert personnel and others to the presence of items potentially contaminated with infectious microorganisms, prevent exposure of personnel to infectious waste, and prevent contamination of the environments.[5] (PNDS: I98)

Contaminated disposable items may include gowns; gloves; sponges, procedural drapes; suction tubing, liners, and canisters; and opened or used supplies.

III.a.1. Disposable items that do not release blood and/or other infectious material in a liquid or semi-liquid state if compressed, or that are not caked with dried blood or other potentially infectious materials, are considered noninfectious and should be placed in a separate receptacle designated for noninfectious waste.[5]

III.b. Regulated waste should be stored in an area with a floor drain, cleanable floor and wall surfaces, lighting, and exhaust ventilation and should be safe from weather, insects, animals, and unauthorized entry until transportation for treatment and or disposal.[5]

III.c. Containers or bags containing regulated medical waste should be transported according to state regulations. Containers or bags containing regulated medical waste may be required to be transported in washable and closed or covered carts or vehicles.[5]

III.d. Reusable items contaminated with blood and/or tissue that would release blood or other infectious materials in a liquid or semi-liquid state if compressed, or items that are caked with dried blood or other potentially infectious materials, must be placed in closable, leak-proof containers and labeled as infectious.

Leak-proof containers prevent exposure of personnel to blood, tissue, and body fluids and prevent contamination of the environment. Color coding and/or labeling alert personnel and others to the presence of items potentially contaminated with infectious microorganisms, prevent exposure of personnel to infectious items, and prevent contamination of the environment.[5] (PNDS: I98)

III.e. Personal protective equipment (PPE) must be worn to prevent a splash or splatter when disposing of liquid waste.[37]

III.e.1. Liquid waste may be disposed of according to state regulations including, but not limited to the following methods:
- adding a solidifying powder to the liquid,
- using a medical liquid waste disposal system, or
- pouring the liquid down a sanitary sewer.[37]

Recommendation IV

Surgical and invasive procedure rooms and scrub/utility areas should be terminally cleaned daily.

Terminal cleaning and disinfection of the perioperative environment decreases the number of pathogens, dust, and debris that is created during the day.[2,4]

IV.a. Terminal cleaning and disinfection of operating and invasive procedure rooms should be done
- when the scheduled procedures are completed for the day, and
- each 24-hour period during the regular work week.[2,8]

IV.a.1. Unused rooms should be cleaned once during each 24-hour period during the regularly scheduled work week.[8]
Personnel enter unused rooms and move equipment and supplies in and out of the room.

IV.a.2. Floors should be wet-vacuumed with an EPA-registered disinfectant after scheduled cases are completed.[8]

IV.a.3. Other areas requiring cleaning and disinfection include, but are not limited to,
- all horizontal surfaces (eg, cabinet tops, tops of sterilizers. solution/blanket warmers);
- hallways and floors;
- substerile areas;
- scrub/utility areas; and
- sterile storage areas.

IV.b. Cleaning equipment should be disassembled, cleaned, disinfected with an EPA-registered disinfectant, and dried before reuse and storage.[8]
Equipment is cleaned to prevent the growth of microorganisms during storage and to prevent subsequent contamination of the perioperative area.

IV.c. Refillable liquid hand soap dispensers should not be used.[38,39]
Refillable liquid soap dispensers can become contaminated and serve as reservoirs for microorganisms. Prolonged use of a multi-use container, transferring solutions to secondary containers, and refilling containers such as povidone iodine dispensers has resulted in contamination of the antiseptic with *Pseudomonas aeruginosa*.[40]

Recommendation V

All areas and equipment in the surgical practice setting should be cleaned according to an established schedule.

A clean environment will reduce the numbers of microorganisms present.[2,4]

V.a. A cleaning schedule for areas and equipment that should be cleaned on a daily, weekly, or monthly basis should be established. The schedule should be developed by a multi-disciplinary team to determine appropriate cleaning and disinfection and maintenance frequencies.

V.a.1. Areas and equipment that should be cleaned on a weekly or monthly basis should include, but are not limited to,
- heating and air-conditioning equipment;
- pneumatic tubes and carriers;
- sterilizers and their loading carts/carriages;

- clean and soiled storage areas;
- walls and ceilings;
- unrestricted areas (eg, offices, waiting rooms, lounges, lavatories, and locker rooms).[41]

V.b. Ventilation ducts should be cleaned and filters changed on a regularly scheduled basis.

V.c. All refrigerators and ice machines should be cleaned on a routine basis.

V.c.1. Patient refrigerators should be cleaned weekly and outdated food removed. Cleaning and disinfection should be logged on log sheet.

V.c.2. Ice scoops should not be kept in the ice compartment.

V.c.3. Ice scoops should be cleaned on a weekly basis.[8] Ice machines with a dispenser are preferable to ones that require the use of scoops.

V.d. After cleaning, an EPA-registered disinfectant should be used to disinfect scrub sinks and wash basins following a regular schedule.[8]

An example of a pathogen known to cause health care-associated infection outbreaks is *Pseudomonas aeruginosa,* which thrives in moist and humid environments such as sinks. *Pseudomonas aeruginosa* do not need many nutrients and can grow in large numbers.[33,42] (PNDS: I98)

V.d.1. Aerators on faucets should be cleaned and disinfected weekly by removing the aerator, scrubbing it with a detergent and a brush reserved for this purpose, and immersing it in a disinfectant.[43]

V.e. Eye wash stations should be cleaned and checked weekly to ensure that they are in working order.[5]

Recommendation VI

All personnel should take precautionary measures to limit transmission of microorganisms when performing routine environmental cleaning and disinfection activities.

Federal regulations for bloodborne pathogen standards were first published by the Occupational Safety and Health Administration (OSHA) in 1991 to protect health care workers from exposure to bloodborne infections. The Needlestick Safety and Prevention Act was passed by Congress in 2000 and enacted in 2001 to protect health care workers from contaminated sharps injury.[44]

VI.a. All personnel must comply with OSHA's bloodborne pathogen standards when performing cleaning and disinfection procedures involving contact with blood and other potentially infectious materials.[5]

Following bloodborne pathogen precautions can reduce health risks for personnel who may be exposed to blood and other potentially infectious material. Approximately 8,700 health care personnel are infected with hepatitis B annually, resulting in 200 deaths. Wearing PPE can reduce the risk of becoming infected with HIV/AIDS and hepatitis C as well.[5]

VI.b. Health care personnel must follow standard precautions to prevent contact with blood or other potentially infectious material.[5]

All body fluids (eg, semen, vaginal secretions, cerebrospinal fluid, synovial fluid, pleural fluid, pericardial fluid, peritoneal fluid, amniotic fluid, saliva,) except sweat are potentially infectious.[5] (PNDS: I98)

VI.c. Health care personnel handling contaminated items must wear appropriate PPE to reduce the risk of exposure to bloodborne or other potentially infectious microorganisms and hazardous materials.[4]

VI.c.1. Gloves must be worn when it is reasonably anticipated that personnel may have contact with blood or other potentially infectious materials while handling or touching contaminated items or surfaces.[5,8]

VI.c.2. Masks, eye protection, and face shields must be worn whenever contact with splashes, spray, splatter, or droplets of blood or other potentially infectious material is anticipated.[5,8]

VI.d. Hand hygiene should be performed when gloves are removed and as soon as possible when hands are soiled.[16]

VI.e. When visible soiling by blood or other potentially infectious materials appear on OR surfaces or equipment during or after a surgical procedure, an EPA-registered detergent/disinfectant should be used to clean those areas as soon as possible.[5,8]

VI.f. Spills that contain blood or other potentially infectious material should be removed with an absorbent material as soon as possible, then the area should be disinfected with an EPA-registered disinfectant to confine and contain the spill.[5,8]

VI.f.1. When cleaning spills of blood, other potentially infectious material, or hazardous materials, PPE must be worn. This includes the use of gloves, and may include gown, mask, and eye protection.[5]

VI.f.2. The contaminated absorbent cleaning material used to clean a spill must be disposed of in a designated biohazardous waste receptacle.

VI.g. Items that are in a semi-liquid state when compressed or that are caked with blood must be placed in a biohazardous waste container.[5]

VI.h. Contaminated sharps (eg, needles, blades, sharp disposable instruments) must be immediately discarded in a closable, puncture-resistant, leak-proof (on both sides and bottom) receptacle. The receptacle must be marked with a biohazard label that meets OSHA bloodborne pathogen standards.[5,8]

VI.i. Broken glassware should not be handled directly with unprotected hands.[5]

Recommendation VII

Procedures for environmental cleaning and disinfection and PPE use should be established for circumstances that may require contact or airborne precautions.

In health care organizations, pathogens may be disseminated by person-to-person, direct or indirect contact via a contaminated environmental surfaces or fomites; airborne transmission; fecal-oral transmission; or percutaneous exposure.[45] These pathogens may result in morbidity and mortality for patients and personnel. Standard precautions and disinfection procedures are adequate for most, but not all, of these circumstances.[14] The incidence of multi-drug resistant organisms has risen steadily in hospitals over the past few decades.[46] Both methicillin-resistant *Staphylococcus epidermidis* (MRSE) and VRE have been found to survive for long periods of time on environmental surfaces and fabrics. Methicillin-resistant *Staphylococcus epidermidis* and VRE can survive longer than 90 days on fabrics and plastics.[18] (PNDS: I98)

Prions present unique infection prevention and control challenges. Prions are proteinaceous, infectious agents containing no DNA or RNA and may be transmitted iatrogenically by direct inoculation. Prions cause transmissible spongiform encephalopathies including Creutzfeldt-Jakob disease (CJD). Prions are resistant to traditional chemical and physical decontamination methods.[45,46] (PNDS: I98)

VII.a. Extraordinary cleaning procedures or closure of operating rooms following procedures identified as contaminated or dirty-infected (Class III or IV) is not necessary, with the exception of cases involving patients suspected of having CJD.[8]

VII.b. Appropriate cleaning and disinfection methods should be enforced following care of patients infected or colonized with
– methicillin-resistant *Staphylococcus aureus;*
– VRE;
– any multi-drug-resistant pathogen, including vancomycin-intermediate enteroccocus;
– vancomycin-resistant *Staphylococcus aureus;*
– extended spectrum ß-lactamases;
– multi-drug-resistant gram-negative bacteria; and
– resistant *Streptococcus pneumoniae.* (PNDS: I98)

Although cleaning and disinfection is appropriate for removal of infectious agents, one study found that VRE was recovered from 50% of inadequately cleaned surfaces after inoculation.[47] Conscientious adherence to approved cleaning and disinfection procedures is crucial for the prevention of antibiotic-resistant organism transmission.

VII.b.1. Closure of the room or extraordinary cleaning and disinfection procedures are not required.[8]

VII.b.2. Contact precautions should be instituted when performing environmental cleaning and disinfection of rooms used to care for patients colonized or infected with drug resistant pathogens.[45,46]

VII.b.3. When providing environmental cleaning and disinfection for patients in contact isolation, all health care personnel should wear isolation gowns and gloves. If splash or splatter is anticipated, a mask with a face shield or a mask and goggles must be worn.[5,45]

Personal protective equipment is required by OSHA to protect mucous membranes, airways, skin, and clothing from exposure to potentially infectious material.[5,45]

VII.c. An EPA-registered, hypochlorite-based disinfectant should be used to clean a patient area when the patient is diagnosed or suspected of infection with *Clostridium difficile (C. difficile).*[5,14,48]

Clostridium difficile is transmitted via fecal-oral exposure. In health care settings this primarily occurs when there is hand contact with fecally contaminated surfaces that is then transferred from hands to mouth or by unknowingly inserting fecally contaminated thermometers or other devices into the mouth.

In its spore form, *C. difficile* can survive up to five months in the environment and can be transmitted from person-to-person via fecal-oral transmission as well as by touching surfaces and objects contaminated by feces and placing fingers in the mouth. In the health care setting, *C. difficile* has been cultured in rooms occupied by infected patients up to 40 days after their discharge.[48] (PNDS: I98)

VII.c.1. When performing environmental cleaning and disinfection, all health care personnel should wear isolation gowns and gloves. If splash or splatter is anticipated, a mask with a face shield or a mask and goggles must be worn.[5,45]

Personal protective equipment is required by OSHA to protect mucous membranes, airways, skin, and clothing from exposure to potentially infectious material.[5,45]

VII.d. Personnel performing environmental cleaning and disinfection in the room of a patient who has an airborne disease (ie, rubeola, varicella, tuberculosis [TB]), must use a properly fit-tested N95 mask or powered air purifying respirator until complete air exchange has been achieved.[49]

VII.d.1. Environmental cleaning and disinfection may proceed without respiratory PPE after a complete air exchange has been achieved. The period of time required for the ventilation system to achieve a 99.9% air exchange should be noted (eg, 28 minutes for a 15-air-exchanges-per-hour cycle).[49] Testing of air exchanges should be done according to AORN's "Recommended practices for a safe environment of care[50] (**Table 1**).

VII.d.2. Access to the room should be restricted until the 99.9% air exchange has been completed. Any personnel entering the room before the air exchange has been completed must wear a fit-tested N95 mask or powered air-purifying respirator.

VII.d.3. An EPA-registered germicide disinfectant with a label claim for tuberculocidal activity (ie, intermediate-level disinfectant) may be used for cleaning and disinfection. Floors, walls, or surfaces with minimal hand contact do not need to be cleaned with a tuberculocidal germicide disinfectant. This activity assures that pathogens with less resistance than TB also will be killed.[49]

VII.e. Special cleaning and decontamination procedures should be used after a surgical procedure involving high risk tissue(ie, brain, spinal cord, eye tissue) on a patient who has been diagnosed or is suspected of having CJD.[8]

VII.e.1. Disposable linens should be used when the patient is suspected of having CJD. Before the procedure begins, personnel

Table 1

AIR CHANGES PER HOUR AND TIME REQUIRED FOR AIRBORNE CONTAMINANT REMOVAL EFFICIENCIES OF 99% AND 99.9%[*1]		
Air Changes per Hour (ACH)	Minutes Required for 99% Removal Efficiency[†]	Minutes Required for 99.9% Removal Efficiency[†]
2	138	207
4	69	104
6	46	69
12	23	35
15	18	28
20	7	14
50	3	6
400	<1	1

* This table can be used to estimate the time necessary to clear the air of airborne *Mycobacterium tuberculosis* after the source patient leaves the area or when aerosol-producing procedures are complete.
† Time in minutes to reduce the airborne concentration by 99% or 99.9%.

REFERENCE

1. Jensen PA, Lambert LA, Iademarco MF, Ridzon R. Guidelines for preventing the transmission of Mycobacterium tuberculosis *in health care settings, 2005.* Morbidity & Mortality Weekly Review. *[Recommendations and Reports]. 2005; 54 (RR17): 1-141.*

should cover work surfaces with a disposable, impervious material that can be removed and incinerated after the procedure.

Use of disposable linens minimizes contamination of the room and decreases the need for environmental cleaning and disinfection of these surfaces.

VII.e.2. Reusable linens may be used in cases where the patient is suspected of having CJD. The linen may be laundered as per routine laundering processes if not contaminated with high infectivity tissue (eg, spinal fluid, central nervous system tissue). If such contamination occurs, the contaminated linen should be incinerated.

Chemicals used in hospital laundry are not effective in deactivation of prions. More information on this subject is available in AORN's "Recommended practices for cleaning and care of instruments and powered equipment."[51]

VII.e.3. Environmental surfaces (ie, noncritical surfaces) contaminated with high-risk tissues (ie, brain, spinal cord, eye tissue) should be cleaned and then decontaminated with a solution of sodium hypochlorite (1 part chlorine bleach to 5 parts diluent) or sodium hydroxide (1 Normal or 1 Molar).

• Sodium hypochlorite solution should be prepared daily. Health care facilities without a hood should not mix sodium hydroxide.

• Sodium hydroxide is commercially available in solution. The MSDSs for both sodium hypochlorite and sodium hydroxide should be reviewed. The contact time for both sodium hypochlorite and sodium hydroxide should be 30 to 60 minutes.[8]

No transmissions of prion diseases from environmental surfaces have been reported; however, it remains prudent to eliminate highly infectious material from the operating room surfaces that are contacted during subsequent surgeries.

VII.e.4. Single use disposable gowns, gloves, masks, and eyewear should be worn for environmental cleaning and disinfection.

VII.e.5. Contaminated disposable supplies should be incinerated following the procedure.[52]
Splashing of mucous membranes (eg, eyes, mouth) and accidental ingestion may be considered a risk for incurring prion diseases. The highest potential risk for occupational exposure to high-risk tissue is through needle-stick injuries.[52,53] (PNDS: I98)
Prions have been experimentally transmitted by conjunctival instillation of inoculum.[54] There is a theoretical risk that a mucous membrane splash of prion-contaminated fluid could lead to transmission

VII.e.6. All disposable instruments placed in biohazard sharps boxes should be marked for incineration as well.[52] (PNDS: I98)

VII.e.7. Liquids used in cleaning and disinfection should be solidified and incinerated.

Recommendation VIII

A containment, cleaning and disinfection, and surveillance process should be in place during construction, renovation, remediation, repair, or demolition.

It is important that the environment not serve as a source of pathogens. Fungi such as *Aspergillus* are an example of pathogens that can be released and dispersed as a result of damage to a water pipe in a ceiling or demolition of a wall.[55] (PNDS: I98)

VIII.a. Protective barriers should be maintained to protect patients and personnel from dust and debris. Pathogens may be released into the environment during construction (eg, *Aspergillus*).[55]

VIII.b. Areas within and adjacent to the construction site should be cleaned on an ongoing basis whenever debris or dust is present.[55]

VIII.c. Particle counts should be done adjacent to barriers at seams, joints, and entry/exits into the construction zone to ensure that dust and debris are adequately contained.[56]

VIII.d. Air sampling done in the contaminated room, and adjacent areas may be used to establish whether fungi (ie, *Aspergillus*) are present in the area.[56-58]

VIII.d.1. Air sampling should be done before construction begins, after demolition occurs, and at the end of the project.[56-58]

VIII.d.2. If *Aspergillus* is found in the area, dust and debris first must be cleaned with detergent. The walls and ceilings then should be decontaminated by using copper-8-quinolinolate or other EPA registered fungicide.[55] Personnel trained to do this should wear the appropriate PPE when cleaning and decontaminating the area.

VIII.e. Terminal cleaning and disinfection should be performed before placing equipment and supplies in the area when the construction, renovation, remediation, repair, or demolition is completed.[58]

VIII.f. The health care organization's procedure for preventing risks to patients, health care personnel, and visitors during construction should be documented and shared with employee health, risk management, and plant operations personnel.[55]

Recommendation IX

Competency
Personnel should receive initial education, training, and competency validation on proper environmental cleaning and disinfection methods, agent selection, and safety precautions.

The Occupational Health and Safety Act of 1970 (Public Law 91) mandates employers to provide programs for the education and training of employees in the recognition, avoidance, and prevention of unsafe or unhealthful working conditions.[59]

IX.a. Employees should receive initial education, and competency validation on regulations, equipment, chemicals, and safety procedures.

IX.b. Employees should be provided additional training when procedures or supplies and equipment change.

IX.c. Training materials should be appropriate in content, vocabulary level, literacy, and language of the target personnel.[5]

IX.d. Training content should include, at a minimum,
- an accessible copy of the regulatory text;
- explanation of signs and labels and/or color coding required for contaminated items;
- the employer's exposure control plan and the means for personnel to obtain a copy;
- methods to recognize tasks and other activities that may involve occupational exposure;
- location and use of eye wash stations;
- use and limitations of engineering controls, work practices, and PPE;
- information on the types, proper selection, proper use, location, removal, handling, decontamination, and disposal of PPE;
- information on hepatitis B vaccination; and
- location of MSDSs.

Recommendation X

Policies and Procedures
Policies and procedures for environmental cleaning and disinfection should be written, reviewed annually, and readily available in surgical practice settings.

Policies and procedures establish authority, responsibility, and accountability and serve as operational guidelines. Policies and procedures also assist in the development of patient safety, quality assessment, and improvement activities. Practices and policies and procedures are subject to change with the advent of new technologies.

X.a. Policies and procedures for environmental cleaning and disinfection should include, but not be limited to,
- identification of responsible personnel;
- competency validation;
- standard cleaning and disinfection procedures;
- frequency of cleaning and disinfection;
- chemicals approved for use;
- labeling of secondary containers;
- required PPE; and
- cleaning and disinfection procedures for special cases (ie, transmissible diseases).

X.b. An introduction and review of policies and procedures should be included in orientation and ongoing education of perioperative personnel to assist them in obtaining knowledge and developing skills and attitudes that affect patient outcomes.

Recommendation XI

Quality
A quality management program should be in place to evaluate products, processes, and outcomes of the environmental cleaning and disinfection program.

Quality and performance improvement functions ensure that organizations design processes well and systematically monitor, analyze, and improve their outcomes.[60,61]

XI.a. A multidisciplinary committee involved with the quality management program should include, at a minimum, perioperative, infection control, and environmental services personnel.

XI.b. Quality indicators should include, but not be limited to,
- compliance with regulatory standards;
- review of products and manufacturer directions for use;
- procedures;
- monitoring cleaning and disinfection practices; and
- reporting and investigation of adverse events (ie, outbreaks, product issues, corrective actions, evaluation).

Glossary

Aspergillosis: An opportunistic disease, usually respiratory, that may be life threatening and is caused by *Aspergillus,* a fungi. *Aspergillus* may be aerosolized when building structure, plumbing, and surrounding soil is disturbed.

Clean: The absence of visible dust, soil, debris, blood, or other potentially infectious material.

Cleaning: A process using friction, detergent, and water to remove organic debris; the process by which any type of soil, including organic debris, is removed. Cleaning removes rather than kills microorganisms.

Confine and contain: A principle that recommends prompt cleanup of items contaminated with blood, tissue, or body fluids.

Contaminated: The presence of potentially infectious pathogenic microorganisms (eg, blood, other potentially infectious material) on or in animate or inanimate objects.

Decontamination: Any physical or chemical process that removes or reduces the number of microorganisms or infectious agents and renders reusable medical products or equipment safe for handling or disposal; the process by which contaminants are removed, either by hand cleaning or mechanical means, using specific solutions capable of rendering blood and debris harmless and removing them from the surface of an object or instrument.

Disinfection: A process that kills most forms of microorganisms on inanimate surfaces. Disinfection destroys pathogenic organisms (excluding bacterial spores) or their toxins or vectors by direct exposure to chemical or physical means.

End-of-procedure cleaning: Cleaning that is performed at the end of one surgical procedure and before the start of another surgical procedure in the same room.

Endogenous: A source from the patient (eg, skin).

Environmentally friendly products: Products that contribute to better air quality and are less toxic to patients, visitors, and health care personnel.

EPA-registered agent: A microorganism-killing agent registered with the Environmental Protection Agency (EPA). The EPA classifies germicides as sporicides, general disinfectants, hospital disinfectants, detergents, sanitizers, and others.

Exogenous: From a source other than the patient (eg, personnel, equipment, the environment, instruments, supplies).

Fomites: Inanimate objects which, when contaminated with a viable pathogen (eg, bacterium, virus), can transfer the pathogen to a host.

High-level disinfection: A process that kills all microorganisms with the exception of high numbers of bacterial spores and prions. High-level disinfectants have the capability to inactivate the hepatitis B virus, HIV, and *Mycobacterium tuberculosis,* but do not inactivate the prion that causes Creutzfeld-Jacob disease. Government-registered high-level disinfection agents kill vegetative bacteria, tubercle bacilli, some spores and fungi, and lipid and nonlipid viruses, given appropriate concentration, submersion, and contact time.

Iatrogenic: A response to a medical or surgical treatment which results in a poor outcome.

Intermediate-level disinfection: A process that kills *Mycobacterium tuberculosis,* vegetative bacteria, most viruses, and most fungi but does not necessarily kill bacterial spores.

Low-level disinfection: A process by which most bacteria, some viruses, and some fungi are killed. This process cannot be relied on to kill resistant microorganisms such as *Mycobacterium tuberculosis* or bacterial spores.

Molarity: The number of moles of solute per solution.

Molar solutions: Denoting a concentration of 1 gram molecular weight (1 mol) of solute per liter of solution, the common unit of concentration in chemistry.

Normal solutions: Denotes a solution containing 1 equivalent of replaceable hydrogen ions or hydroxyl per liter (eg, 1 mol/L HCL is 1 N) or a solution containing 1 gram of a substance or its equivalent in hydrogen ions. Normality is a ratio which relates the amount of solute to the total volume of a solution.

Organic debris: Blood, tissue, and body fluids.

Personal protective equipment (PPE): Specialized equipment or clothing for eyes, face, head, body, and extremities; protective clothing; respiratory devices; and protective shields and barriers designed to protect the worker from injury or exposure to a patient's blood, tissue, or body fluids. Used by health care workers and others whenever necessary to protect themselves from the hazards of processes or environments, chemical hazards, or mechanical irritants encountered in a manner capable of causing injury or impairment in the function of any part of the body through absorption, inhalation, or physical contact.

Regulated medical waste: Liquid or semi-liquid blood or other potentially infectious materials; contaminated items that would release blood or other potentially infectious materials in a liquid or semi-liquid state if compressed; items that are caked with dried blood or other potentially infectious materials and are capable of releasing these materials during handling; contaminated sharps; and pathological and microbiological wastes containing blood or other potentially infectious materials.

Reusable: Any product or piece of equipment intended by the manufacturer for multiple uses. As appropriate to each item, the manufacturer is to provide instructions for reprocessing, care, and/or maintenance of the item.

Terminal cleaning: Cleaning that is performed at the completion of surgical practice settings' daily surgery schedules. Terminal cleaning is performed in surgical procedure rooms and scrub/utility areas and includes, but is not limited to, surgical lights and external tracks; fixed and ceiling-mounted equipment; all furniture, including wheels and casters; equipment; handles of cabinets and push plates; ventilation faceplates; horizontal surfaces (eg, tops of counters, sterilizers, fixed shelving); the entire floor; kick buckets; and scrub sinks.

Used items: Items that are opened for a surgical procedure that may or may not have come in contact with a patient's blood, tissue, or body fluids.

REFERENCES

1. Petersen C, ed. *Perioperative Nursing Data Set.* Rev 2nd ed. Denver, CO: AORN, Inc; 2007.

2. Mangram AJ, Horan TC, Pearson ML, Silver LC, Jarvis WR. Guideline for prevention of surgical site infection, 1999. *Infect Control and Hosp Epidemiol.* 1999:20: 250-278.

3. Rutala WA, Weber DJ. Surface disinfection: should we do it? *J Hosp Infect Control.* 2001;48(Suppl A):S64-68.

4. Cozad A, Jones RD. Disinfection and the prevention of infectious disease. *Am J of Infect Control.* 2003;31:243-54.

5. US Department of Labor, Occupational Safety and Health Administration. Final Rule on Occupational Exposure to Bloodborne Pathogens,1910.1030. *http://www.osha.gov /pls/oshaweb/owadisp.show_document?p_table= STANDARDS&p_id=100.* Accessed October 26, 2007.

6. AORN latex guideline. In: *Standards, Recommended Practices, and Guidelines.* Denver, CO: AORN, Inc; 2007:203-218.

7. Bray WJ. What is everyday dust made of? MadSci Network: Environment and Ecology. 2007. *http://www.madsci .org /posts/archives/dec98/912530774.En.r.html.* Accessed October 26, 2007.

8. Sehulster L, Chinn RY. Centers for Disease Control and Prevention, Health care Infection Control Practices Advisory Committee (HIPCPAC). Guidelines for environmental infection control in health-care facilities. 2003. *MMWR Morb Mortal Wkly Rep.* 2003;52[RR-10]:1-44.

9. Air Crafters. Clean Room Concepts: Airborne particulate control. *http://www.air-crafters.com/concepts2.html.* Accessed October 26, 2007.

10. Dancer SJ. Mopping up infection. *J Hosp Infect.* 1999;43:85-100.

11. Centers for Disease Control and Prevention. *Guidelines for Environmental Infection Control in Health-Care Facilities.* Atlanta, GA: Centers for Disease Control and Prevention; 2003:134.

12. Centers for Disease Control and Prevention. Infection Control in Dental Settings. Personal Protective Equipment (Masks, Protective Eyewear, Protective Apparel, Gloves). *http://www.cdc.gov/OralHealth/infectioncontrol/faq /protective_equipment.* Accessed October 29, 2007.

13. Rego A, Roley L. In-use barrier integrity of gloves: latex and nitrile superior to vinyl. *Am J Infect Control.* 1997;27:405-410.

14. Rutala WA, Weber DJ. Cleaning, disinfection and sterilization in health care facilities. In: *APIC Text of Infection Control and Epidemiology.* 2nd ed. Washington, DC: Association for Professionals in Infection Control and Epidemiology; 2005: 21.1-21.12.

15. Association for Professionals in Infection Control and Epidemiology. Disinfection and Sterilization Principles. *http://www.apic.org/AM/AMTemplate.cfm?Section =Brochures&Template=/CM/ContentDisplay.cfm&Content FileID-2558.* Accessed October 26, 2007.

16. Recommended practices for surgical hand antisepsis/ hand scrubs. In: *Standards, Recommended Practices, and Guidelines.* Denver, CO: AORN, Inc; 2007:565-574.

17. Rutala WA, Weber DJ, Gergen MF. Studies on the disinfection of VRE-contaminated surfaces. *Infection Control & Epidemiology.* 2000;21:548.

18. Neely AN, Maley MP. Survival of enterococci and staphylococci on hospital fabrics and plastic. *J of Clin Microbiol.* 2000;38:274-726.

19. Rutala, WA, Weber, DJ. Surface disinfection: new processes and products. In: *Disinfection, Sterilization and Antisepsis Principals, Practices, Current Issues, and New Research.* Rutala WA, ed. Washington, DC: Association for Infection Control Practitioners; 2007:97-106.

20. Scott E, Bloomfield SF. Investigations of the effectiveness of detergent washing, drying, and chemical disinfection on contamination of cleaning cloths. *J Appl Bacteriol.* 1990;68:279-83.

21. Chou T. Environmental services. In: Association for Professionals in Infection Control and Epidemiology, eds. *APIC Text of Infection Control and Epidemiology.* 2nd ed. Washington, DC: Association for Professionals in Infection Control and Epidemiology; 2005:102-1-102-12.

22. Graczyk TK, Knight R, Tamang L, Pandalai SG. Filth, flies, and human diseases. *Recent Res Devel Applied Biotechnol.* 2005;2:21-31.

23. Health Care Without Harm. Cleaning. Chemical Use Hospital Fact Sheet 2004. *http://www.noharm.org/details .cfm?ID=606&type=document.* Accessed October 10, 2007.

24. Cleaning for Health: Products and Practices for a Safer Environment, 2002. *http://www.informinc.org/report pdfs /chp/CleaningForHealth.pdf.* Accessed October 11, 2007.

25. Guidance statement on environmental responsibility. In: *Standards, Recommended Practices, and Guidelines.* Denver, CO: AORN, Inc; 2007:251-258.

26. US Department of Labor, Occupational Safety and Health Administration. [Hazard Communication]. Labels and other forms of warning. In: *29CFR 1910-1200 Toxic and Hazardous Substances.* Washington, DC: US Department of Labor, Occupational Safety and Health Administration; 2007:460-482.

27. Molinari, JA, Harte, JA. Dental services. In: *Association for Infection Control Practitioners Text of Infection Control and Epidemiology.* Washington, DC: Association for Infection Control Practitioners; 2005:51 1-16.

28. ECRI. A team approach to surgical fire prevention. understanding the fire triangle. *Health Devices.* 2006;35:56.

29. Fogg D. Mattress disinfection; hand hygiene; latex safety; abdominal-perineal preps; hand rub characteristics; radiopaque packing. *AORN J.* 2004;79:645-652, 651-652.

30. Friedman C, Petersen KH. Ambulatory surgery. In: *Infection Control in Ambulatory Care.* Boston, MA: Jones and Bartlett Publishers; 2004:64.

31. American National Standards Institute, Association for Advancement of Medical Instrumentation. *Processing of Reusable Surgical Textiles for Use in Health Care Facilities. ANSI/AAMI ST65:2000.* Arlington, VA: Association for the Advancement of Medical Instrumentation; 2005:1-49.

32. Michaelsen GS. Designing linen chutes to reduce spread of infectious organisms. *Hospitals JAHA.* 1965; 39:116-9.

33. Ortolano G, McAlister MB, Angelbeck JA, et al. Hospital water point-of-use filtration: a complementary strategy to reduce the risk of nosocomial infection. *Am J Infect Control.* 2005; 33(Suppl):S1-S19.

34. Whyte W, Baird G, Annand R. Bacterial contamination on the surface of hospital linen chutes. *J Hyg.* [London]. 1969;67:427-35.

35. Public Notification from FDA, CDC, EPA, and OSHA: Avoiding Hazards with Using Cleaners and Disinfectants on Electronic Medical Equipment. US Food and Drug Administration Center for Devices and Radiological Health. October 3, 20007:1-9. *http://www.fda.gov/cdrh/safety.html.* Accessed November 27, 2007.

36. Academy of Pediatrics. The American College of Obstetricians and Gynecologists. Infection control. In: *Guidelines for Perinatal Care.* 5th ed. American Academy of Pediatrics. Washington, DC: The American College of Obstetricians and Gynecologists; 2002:349-350.

37. Ticer J. Choosing and implementing proper storage and disposal for your facility. Medical waste management. In: *Medical Construction and Design.* Scottsdale, AZ: Inform Publications; 2007(3):24-25.

38. Archibald LK, Corl A, Shah B, et al. *Serratia marcescens* outbreak associated with extrinsic contamination of 1% chlorxylenol soap. *Infect Control Hosp Epidemiol.* 1997;18:704-709.

39. Grohskopf LA, Roth VR, Felkins DR, et al. *Serratia liquefaciens* bloodstream infections from contamination of epoetin alfa at a hemodialysis center. *N Engl J Med.* 2001;344:1491-1497.

40. Anderson RI, Vess RW, Panlilio AL, Favero MS. Prolonged survival of *Pseudomonas cepacia* in commercially manufactured povidone–iodine. *Applied Environmental Microbiology.* 1990;56:3598-3600.

41. Lafreniere R, Berguer R, Seifert PC, et al. Preparation of the operating room. In: *American College of Surgeons ACS Surgery: Principles & Practice 2004.* New York, NY: WebMD Professional Publications; 2004:3-16.

42. Trautman M, Lepper PM, Haller M. Ecology of *Pseudomonas aeruginosa* in the intensive care unit and the evolving role of water outlets as a reservoir of the organism. *Am J of Infect Control.* 2005;33(Suppl 1):S41-49.

43. Schraag J. Waterborne pathogens: what's lurking in your facility's pipes? *Infect Control Today.* 2005; 9:14-19.

44. Occupational Safety and Health Administration. 29 CFR Part 1910: Occupational exposure to bloodborne pathogens; needlestick and other sharps injuries. Final rule. *Federal Register.* Jan 18, 2001:5318-5325.

45. Siegel JD, Rhinehart E, Jackson M, Chiarello L, the Health care Infection Control Practices Advisory Committee. CDC. Guideline for Isolation Precautions: Preventing Transmission of Infectious Agents in Healthcare Settings 2007.1-219. *http://www.cdc.gov/ncidod/dhqp/pdf/guidelines/Isolation2007.pdf.* Accessed October 26, 2007.

46. Siegel JD, Rhinehart E, Jackson M, Chiarello L. Management of Multidrug–Resistant Organisms in Healthcare Settings, 2006: CDC and the Health care Infection Control Practices Advisory Committee. Atlanta, GA. *http://www.cdc.gov/ncidod/dhqp/pdf/ar/MDRO Guideline2006.pdf.* Accessed October 29, 2007.

47. Langford MG, Collins S, Youngberg L, Rooney DM, Warren JR, Noskins GA. Assessment of materials commonly utilized in health care: implications for bacterial survival and transmission. *AJIC.* 2006; 34:258-263.

48. *Clostridium difficile:* a sometimes fatal complication of antibiotic use. *Patient Safety Advisory.* 2005;2:1-8.

49. Jensen PA, Lambert LA, Iademarco MF, Ridzon R. Guidelines for preventing the transmission of *Mycobacterium tuberculosis* in health-care settings, 2005. *MMWR Morb Mortal Wkly Rept.* 2005;54:(RR-17):1-102.

50. Recommended practices for a safe environment of care. In: *Standards, Recommended Practices, and Guidelines.* Denver, CO, AORN, Inc: 2008;351-374.

51. Recommended practice for cleaning and care of instruments and powered equipment. In: *Standards, Recommended Practices, and Guidelines.* Denver, CO, AORN, Inc: 2008; 421-445.

52. World Health Organization. WHO Infection Control Guidelines for Transmissible Spongiform Encephalopathies. *http:/whqlibdoc.who.int/hq/2000/WHO_CDS_CSR_APH _2000.3.pdf.* Accessed October 26, 2007.

53. Rutala WA, Weber DJ. Creutzfeldt-Jakob disease: recommendations for disinfection and sterilization. *Clin Dis Inf.* 2001;32:1348-1356.

54. Scott JR, Foster JD, Fraser H. Conjunctival instillation of scrapies in mice can produce disease. *Vet Microbiol.* 1993;934:305-309.

55. Bartley J. Construction and renovation. In: Association for Professionals in Infection Control and Epidemiology, eds. *APIC Text of Infection Control and Epidemiology.* 2nd ed. Washington, DC: Association for Professionals in Infection Control and Epidemiology; 2005:108-1-108-16.

56. Streifel AJ. Design and maintenance of hospital ventilation systems and the prevention of airborne nosocomial infections. In: *Hospital Epidemiology and Infection Control.* 3rd ed. Philadelphia, PA: Lippincott Williams & Wilkins; 2004:1579-1589.

57. Cosgrove SE, Perl TM. Infection control and prevention in hematopoietic stem cell transplant patients. In: *Hospital Epidemiology and Infection Control.* 3rd ed. Philadelphia, PA: Lippincott Williams & Wilkins; 2004: 1019-1023.

58. Bartley J. Prevention of infections related to construction, renovation, and demolition. In: *Hospital Epidemiology and Infection Control.* 3rd ed. Philadelphia, PA: Lippincott Williams & Wilkins; 2004:1549-1575.

59. US Department of Labor, Occupational Safety and Health Administration. OSHA Act of 1970, Pub.L.105.97, Sec 21. *http://www.osha.gov/pls/oshaweb/owadisp.show _document?p_table=STANDARDS&p_id=10051.* Accessed October 26, 2007.

60. AORN quality and performance improvement standards for perioperative nursing. In: *Standards, Recommended Practices, and Guidelines.* Denver, CO: AORN, Inc; 2007:437-446.

61. Joint Commission on Accreditation of Health care Organizations. Improving organization performance. In: *Comprehensive Accreditation Manual for Hospitals.* Oak Brook Terrace, IL: The Joint Commission;2007 PI-1-PI-10.

RESOURCES

Center for Infection Control and Prevention Questions and answers: Creutzfeldt-Jocob Disease Infection Control Practices. *http://www.cdc.gov/ncidod/dvrd/ cjd/infection_control_cjd.htm.* Accessed November 26, 2007.

Originally published June 1975, *AORN Journal,* as "Recommended practices for sanitation in the surgical practice setting."

Format revised March 1978; March 1982; July 1982. Revised April 1984; November 1988; December 1992.

Revised June 1996; published October 1996, *AORN Journal.* Reformatted July 2000.

Revised; published December 2002, *AORN Journal.*

Revised 2007; published in *Perioperative Standards and Recommended Practices,* 2008 edition.

Recommended Practices for Reducing Radiological Exposure in the Perioperative Practice Setting

The following recommended practices were developed by the AORN Recommended Practices Committee and have been approved by the AORN Board of Directors. They were presented as proposed recommended practices for comments by members and others. They are effective January 1, 2007.

These recommended practices are intended as achievable recommendations representing what is believed to be an optimal level of practice. Policies and procedures will reflect variations in practice settings and/or clinical situations that determine the degree to which the recommended practices can be implemented.

AORN recognizes the numerous types of settings in which perioperative nurses practice. These recommended practices are intended as guidelines adaptable to various practice settings. These practice settings include traditional operating rooms, ambulatory surgery centers, physicians' offices, cardiac catheterization suites, endoscopy suites, radiology and interventional radiology departments, and all other areas where operative and other invasive procedures may be performed.

Purpose

Radiological procedures are an invaluable medical diagnostic and treatment tool and, if proper safety procedures are followed, create only minimal risks to both the patient and medical personnel. Ionizing radiation is useful for diagnostic, interventional, and therapeutic procedures. Ionizing radiation can damage living tissues and may produce long-term effects. Patients and personnel should be protected from unsafe levels of radiation that are not medically indicated because of the potential hazardous effects of ionizing radiation exposure on tissue over time. Evidence has demonstrated that ionizing radiation also can harm a developing embryo. The greatest risk is the development of cancer. Health care workers who do not protect themselves from scatter radiation are especially at risk when performing interventional procedures because of significantly increased exposure time and close proximity during the procedure.

Prevention of radiation injury requires the application of principles of physics and radiological safety standards. Policies addressing education, credentialing, and radiological safety and maintenance must be in accordance with national regulatory standards and manufacturers' documented instructions.[1]

The overall goal of a radiation safety program should be to keep the risks from ionizing radiation as low as reasonably achievable.[2] Time, distance, and shielding should be employed to keep radiation exposure within safe levels. The National Council on Radiation Protection and Measurements has established guidelines for total dose radiation limits for radiation workers. In 1995, the Conference of Radiation Control Program Directors, a nonregulatory organization, published recommendations for state regulatory agencies.[3] Each state develops and implements regulations governing safe use of radiation-producing equipment and radioactive materials. Using safety measures of limiting exposure time and using protective shields (eg, thyroid shields, lead aprons, protective eyeglasses) is addressed.[4] Radiology departments use both diagnostic and interventional techniques in a wide variety of invasive applications and are included in this recommended practice. Interventional radiology nurses assist with procedures that include, but are not limited to, intravascular repairs such as

- inserting stents;
- placing shunts;
- performing embolization procedures;
- performing genitourinary procedures (eg, percutaneous nephrostomy tube placement, stone obliteration, balloon dilatation);
- draining abscesses; and
- performing laparoscopic tumor biopsies.

A primary responsibility of the interventional radiology nurse is to protect personnel and patients from high doses of radiation used during these procedures.[4]

Low dose-rate and high dose-rate brachytherapy both use ionizing radiation and are included in this recommended practice. Brachytherapy is the use of radioactive isotopes to treat malignancies and benign conditions. The radioactive source is inserted close to the treatment site or tumor. This therapy is used to treat tumors of the head, neck, breast, cervix, prostate, and endometrium, and to treat obstructive esophageal and bronchial lesions. Delivering high dose-rate brachytherapy, including that which is used during cardiovascular revascularization procedures, requires limiting radiation exposure to the patient and personnel. Personnel should have a thorough understanding of the physical effects of radiation and the regulatory guidelines established to ensure patient and personnel safety.[5]

Lasers, which are recognized to be nonionizing radiation, are not within the scope of these recommended practices. These recommended practices provide guidance for developing institutional policies and procedures that can be used collaboratively by personnel in the radiology and surgical services departments and by the facility radiation safety officer.

The primary nursing diagnosis applicable in this recommended practice is the risk for impaired skin integrity from the effects of gamma radiation. To ensure optimal outcomes, the perioperative nurse should assess the patient at the end of the procedure to ensure that the patient's skin remains smooth, intact, and free from unexpected redness, blistering, or tenderness.[6] Each of the following recommended practices is a nursing intervention intended to protect the patient and staff members and ensure optimal outcomes.

Recommendation I

The patient's exposure to radiation should be minimized.

1. The patient's exposure to radiation should be limited to situations in which it is medically indicated and to the anatomical structures being treated. Fluoroscopy delivers some of the largest doses of radiation to patients.[7] Serious skin injuries to patients undergoing certain fluoroscopic procedures have been reported. The greatest dose of radiation to the patient occurs on the patient's skin, where the beam enters the body. The decision to use fluoroscopy during medical or surgical procedures should be approached with caution, weighing the benefits afforded by the technology against the need to keep radiation exposure limited.[7]

2. The perioperative registered nurse should review the patient record for relevant history involving radiation exposure and record study parameters such as fluoroscopy time and area irradiated. He or she also should advise the treating physician of any pertinent information that would be important in reducing patient risk.

3. The perioperative registered nurse should assess the patient for any previous procedure involving radioactive material (ie, nuclear medicine, radiation oncology). It may be necessary to delay the procedure if there is significant radioactive material remaining in the patient. The physician responsible for the radiation treatment or diagnostic procedure should be consulted to determine exposure levels.

4. All reasonable means of reconciling an incorrect sponge, needle, or instrument count should be attempted before using a radiological examination to locate a sponge, sharp, or instrument that may be missing. Certain procedures, because of the complexity of the number of instruments used, may necessitate a postoperative x-ray as stated in the "Recommended practices for sponge, sharp, and instrument counts."[8] Controlling the amount of total fluoroscopic beam "on" time for these procedures through judicious control of the exposure time may help ensure that radiation exposure is as low as reasonably achievable.[4]

Recommendation II

The patient should be protected from unnecessary radiation exposure.

1. Care should be taken to keep extraneous body parts out of the radiation beam to prevent injury. Reports have shown that arms and breast tissue have been injured as a result of increased unintended radiation.[6] Parts of the patient's body not included in the intended radiation field that are located on the x-ray tube side can accumulate dose rapidly.[4] Implementing protective measures (eg, protective lead shielding) helps to prevent injury from radiation sources.[1] Lead shielding should be placed between the patient and the source of radiation.[9] Shielding placed on the wrong side (ie, away from the source) can actually increase the dose to the patient. Lead shielding should not be in the beam in fluoroscopic procedures (eg, hand surgery).

2. Lead shielding should be used, when possible, to protect the thyroid during x-ray studies of the upper extremities, trunk, and head. Thyroid and lymphoid tissues are shown to be sensitive to radiation exposure.[9]

3. Lead shielding should be used, when possible, to protect the patient's ovaries or testes (ie, gonads) during x-ray studies, including those performed on the hips and upper legs.

4. Female patients of childbearing age should be questioned about the possibility of pregnancy.

♦ If the possibility of pregnancy exists, the surgeon should be notified to determine the advisability of continuing or postponing the procedure.

♦ Lead shielding should be used to protect the fetus when other areas of a pregnant woman's body are x-rayed. The fetus is highly sensitive to ionizing radiation. Scatter radiation may expose the fetus to low-level radiation. Radiation to the abdomen and pelvis in women who are pregnant or may be pregnant poses an increased risk to the fetus and may result in childhood cancers.[10,11] Proper safety measures minimize the actual risk. The perioperative nurse should assess the history of all premenopausal women to ensure that they are aware of radiation exposure risks during pregnancy.[6]

Recommendation III

Occupational exposure to radiation should be minimized.

Guidelines for radiation safety are based on the principles of time, distance, and shielding. When exposed to radiation at a constant rate, the total dose equivalent received depends on the length of time exposed. If the distance from the point source of radiation is doubled, the exposure is quartered.[1] Radiation that scatters as the x-ray beam passes through the patient is the main source of radiation exposure. Passage through materials reduces the amount of radiation. State and government regulations that stipulate the dose limits for occupational exposure are described in the glossary.

1. Warning signs should be posted to alert personnel to potential radiation hazards at entrances to ORs and procedure rooms where radiological equipment is in use, as required by state regulations. State regulations provide requirements for posting warning signs at entrances to rooms where radiation is a potential hazard. These requirements apply equally to all areas where radiological equipment is used. Applicable state regulations should be followed.

2. Personnel should limit the amount of time spent in close proximity to the radiation source when exposure to radiation is possible.[12] Minimizing beam "on" time during fluoroscopic procedures by using the last-image hold feature may decrease the dose of radiation to the patient and personnel.[4,7]

3. The radiation equipment operator should notify personnel present in the treatment room before activating the equipment.[12]

4. During intracoronary brachytherapy, close contact with the patient should be limited to less than five minutes whenever possible. An authorized user, medical physicist, or radiation safety officer should be present before the therapy is initiated to ensure staff member safety. Designated safe areas should be determined before initiating treatment to allow staff members to distance themselves from exposure to increased radiation levels.[13]

5. Personnel should be aware of scatter radiation that is emitted from the patient in all directions in both radiological and fluoroscopic procedures.[13] Scatter radiation is a significant hazard to personnel, especially in fluoroscopic procedures. Variability exists as to the total amount of radiation that is emitted due to the intensity of the radiation primary beam, the size of the beam area, and the patient's dimensions. Larger patients may require greater radiation beam intensity in order to produce greater image quality, which may result in greater radiation scatter.[12]

6. During fluoroscopic procedures, personnel should keep the patient as close as possible to the image intensifier side of the fluoroscopic unit and away from the tube side of the unit. Keeping the patient close to the image intensifier side lowers the dose required to produce an image, decreases the amount of radiation scatter, and decreases the amount of radiation emitted to the personnel assisting with the procedure. Doubling the distance from the source of emitting radiation reduces the intensity of the radiation by a factor of four.[12]

7. To reduce exposure, personnel involved in fluoroscopic procedures should stand on the

RP: Reducing Radiological Exposure

image intensifier side of the fluoroscopic unit whenever possible.[14] Using fluoroscopy in lateral views tends to produce greater radiation scatter from the patient. Personnel standing on the same side as the image intensifier experience a decrease in radiation intensity.[3,12]

8. Personnel assisting with radiological procedures should not hold the patient manually for a study because of the risk of exposure by the direct beam.[12] Slings, traction devices, and sandbags should be used to maintain patient position during radiation exposure. Cassette holders should be used to position films. If manual holding cannot be avoided, the individual should be protected from the primary x-ray beam. A 0.5 mm lead-equivalent shield or apron should be worn.

9. Whenever possible, shielding should be employed to provide attenuation of the radiation being delivered to the personnel potentially exposed.[14] Types of shielding available to personnel may include, but are not limited to,
   ♦ walls, windows, control booths, and doors;
   ♦ mobile rigid shields on wheels for transport to various areas;
   ♦ ceiling-suspended transparent barriers;
   ♦ flexible aprons (eg, wraparound, open backs), vests, skirts, thyroid shields, and gloves; and
   ♦ leaded safety eyeglasses with side shields.

10. Personnel who may have to stand with their backs to the radiation beam should wear wraparound aprons to decrease the risk of exposure. It is important to note, however, that wraparound aprons may not provide the same level of protection to both sides of the staff member because the front of the apron usually is double in thickness.[3] Personnel should turn toward the radiation beam when possible to minimize the dose of radiation during a procedure and maximize safety. Light-weight aprons that meet the thickness requirements should be considered for comfort and user compliance.

11. Shielding of the upper legs of personnel near the radiation beam (eg, oblique imaging with the x-ray tube in close proximity to the lower body of the operator) should be initiated to protect the long bones and bone marrow from increased

doses of radiation. Aprons should be as long and as wide as needed to provide protection.[12]

12. Shielding of the upper chest and neck of personnel nearest the x-ray tube (eg, oblique imaging with the x-ray tube in close proximity to the upper chest of the operator) may reduce radiation risk. Thyroid shields should be worn to protect the thyroid whenever the likelihood of the procedure (eg, orthopedic spinal fixation procedures) places the operator at higher risk because of increased exposure.[15] Females should protect their breasts from radiation exposure and aprons should cover the area completely.[3]

13. Some individuals who will be farther away from the x-ray beam may choose to wear aprons with less protection because they are lighter and cause less muscle strain. If aprons with different levels of protection are stored in the same area, the aprons that have less protection should be easily identified to avoid confusion as to the level of safety afforded to the personnel who are wearing them. State regulations should be followed concerning the minimum thickness required for aprons in the facility.[3]

14. Shielding the lens of the eye by using leaded face shields or leaded eyeglasses with wraparound side shields should be used to reduce scatter radiation to the operator when it is anticipated that increased fluoroscopic time may be necessary. Repeated exposure of the eyes over time can produce ulceration of the cornea and cataracts.[16] Leaded eyewear is recommended for personnel who are likely to receive levels of radiation measured by collar badge readings above 15,000 millirem roentgen equivalent unit (mrem) per year annually. Side eye shields also may be beneficial for personnel who perform procedures during which it is necessary to turn away from the radiation beam.[12]

15. Personnel participating in fluoroscopic procedures during which they are less than 24 inches (ie, 70 cm) away from the x-ray beam may consider routinely wearing a thyroid shield and leaded eyeglasses especially during procedures where increased time/dose to the patient are performed.[17]

16. In general, no part of the operator's body should be in the direct x-ray beam. If the operator's hand will be in the direct beam, radiation attenuation gloves should be considered. These gloves afford some protection and may be of benefit in reducing the amount of radiation exposure during a procedure. Most radiation attenuation gloves provide only 33% to 35% safety attenuation.[15] Outside the direct beam, protective gloves are very cumbersome and the inconvenience may outweigh any protective advantage. Even if protective gloves are worn, hands still should be kept out of the x-ray beam as much as possible. Remote handling devices (eg, forceps) should be used whenever possible to minimize the need for the operator's hand to be exposed to radiation.[12]

17. Occupational exposure should be minimized during sentinel node biopsy. Sentinel node biopsy is useful in demonstrating evidence of micrometastatic disease. A gamma-emitting radiocolloid (ie, technetium-99m) can be injected into the patient's tissue to find the sentinel node.[18] The use of time, distance, and shielding should be employed during these procedures to limit personnel exposure to the radioactive isotope. The risk of radiation exposure in these procedures is minimal. Sentinel nodes demonstrating radioactivity should be labeled as radioactive before transporting the specimens from the OR.

18. Personnel with known or suspected pregnancy should declare this condition to the radiation safety officer or other appropriate facility channels. State regulations vary regarding pregnant personnel and radiation safety. State guidelines are based upon the US Nuclear Regulatory Commission (NRC) guidelines regarding confidentiality in the pregnant worker. Disclosure of the pregnancy, even if it is obvious, is not required. A written, voluntary, official declaration that includes the estimated date of conception may be used to base the total dose limit to the pregnant person.[3] The NRC guidelines include the following.

   ♦ Occupational dose to the embryo or fetus of an occupationally exposed staff member who has declared her pregnancy must not exceed 0.5 rem during the entire gestational period.

   ♦ Dose should be uniform over time and not all at once (ie, at one point in the gestational period).

   ♦ Deep-dose equivalent of the declared pregnant worker must be used as the dose to the embryo or fetus. The dosimeter should be worn at the waist under the apron shield.[3] Radiation must pass through several layers of tissue before reaching the fetus; therefore, this dosimeter reading does not reflect the amount of radiation reaching the fetus. Leaded shielding will attenuate 95% to 98% of the radiation.

19. State regulations regarding the monitoring of radiation in pregnant workers may monitor radiation differently as evidenced by the number of dosimeters worn, the area(s) the dosimeters are placed on the body, and whether the dosimeters are placed under or over shielding during the procedure.[3]

20. Maternity aprons may be worn to decrease the amount of radiation to the embryo or fetus. Although there is double thickness in the area where most pregnant workers need the protection, caution should be used by the pregnant worker when turning away from the x-ray beam. Most aprons do not shield the back of the pregnant worker.[3] These aprons are heavier and may be more difficult to wear, placing extra strain on the shoulders of the pregnant worker. Organizations may decide to purchase these aprons for pregnant workers and should mark the aprons to make the aprons easy to identify and ensure that they will be available for those who choose to wear them.

Recommendation IV

Shielding devices should be handled carefully, visually examined before use, and x-rayed at least annually to detect and prevent damage that could diminish their effectiveness.

1. Newly purchased leaded protective devices should be tested for attenuation and for shielding properties to check for cracks and holes in shipping before use. Subsequently, all leaded protective devices should be checked for defects and wear at least annually and whenever damage is suspected.[3] The frequency of

testing is dependent upon the type of device used and the care that the device receives as it is used because excessive misuse can increase the risk of cracks and damage.[19,20]

2. Leaded aprons and thyroid shields should be stored flat or hung vertically and should not be folded. Leaded aprons and shields are susceptible to cracking, which can reduce the apron's effectiveness as a shielding barrier.

3. Testing documentation of all leaded protective devices should be maintained in the radiology department or in the facility safety office. Areas that purchase new aprons should notify the department where the testing is performed so records are kept up-to-date and accurate. All aprons should be labeled or numbered so that each apron can be tracked if necessary.

4. Protective devices should be cleaned with an EPA-registered hospital disinfectant after every use.

Recommendation V

Individuals should be protected from exposure to patients who have received diagnostic or therapeutic radionuclides that may pose a radiation risk.

1. Facilities that use therapeutic radionuclides should employ a radiation safety officer. This individual should determine specific organizational policies and procedures. The primary function of the radiation safety officer is supervision of the daily operation of the radiation safety program to ensure that individuals are protected from radiation. The radiation safety officer should determine which individuals are in frequent proximity to radiation, which should wear monitoring devices, and how occupational exposure is monitored and recorded.

2. Personnel should use the principles of time, distance, and shielding when caring for patients who have received therapeutic radionuclides. Radionuclide materials are absorbed by the body and safety precautions are required depending on the absorption and excretion of the radionuclide.[3] Patients who have received radionuclides emit radiation

until the nuclide has decayed or has been eliminated.[20] Body fluids and tissue removed from patients who have undergone recent diagnostic nuclear medicine studies should be handled according to radiation safety procedures and standard precautions and should be labeled radioactive. These procedures should be based on government regulations and recommendations.

3. Contamination-control measures should be applied to the use of unsealed radioactive materials.[1] When transferring patients who received therapeutic radionuclides in the OR, perioperative personnel should notify personnel receiving the patients of the radiation source and anatomical location before patient transfer. All radiation precautions should be observed during transfer of the patient from one area or unit to another. The radiation safety officer should establish policies concerning how patients are transferred after receiving therapeutic radionuclides to minimize exposure to staff members. Advance communication allows personnel time to protect themselves, the patient's visitors and family members, and other patients from unnecessary exposure to radiation.[5]

4. Preparation of sealed radionuclides, such as prostatic seeds, may require sterilization before use. Manufacturers' written instructions should be followed for sterilization. Sealed radionuclides requiring sterilization should be packaged and sterilized according to the "Recommended practices for sterilization in perioperative practice settings."[21] Prevacuum sterilization cycles should not be used because the vacuum may displace the seeds and potentially cause a radiation hazard to personnel.[22] Flash sterilization of the seeds should be avoided. Implantable medical devices should not be flash sterilized because of possible patient complications and because it is difficult to ensure aseptic delivery and personnel safety. Varying sterilization times have been cited in the literature. Health care facilities may wish to purchase pre-sterilized seeds or needles to minimize the risk to personnel who have to prepare these devices for use.[23]

5. Manufacturers' written instructions for preparation of eye plaques should be followed. Eye plaques are a form of brachytherapy used for treatment of choroidal melanoma.[24] Radionuclide seeds are placed in silicone tubes and secured to gold discs sutured next to the tumor. Gold is used to decrease the amount of scatter radiation to the adjacent retina, choroid, and optic nerve. The same guidelines should be used as for other types of radioactive seeds. The radiation safety officer or a designee should ensure containment of the seeds.

6. The radiation safety officer or a designee should ensure compliance with NRC regulations when prostatic radionuclides are sterilized and used in the OR. This person should control and maintain strict surveillance of the radionuclides that are in controlled or unrestricted areas and that are not in storage.[25]

7. If radionuclide seeds such as prostate seeds are processed for use in a central processing department, the seeds must remain in constant surveillance during the entire processing period and delivery to the OR.[25] Central processing supervisors should consult the radiation safety officer for questions concerning dose limits and surveillance in central processing. Dosimeter monitoring and specific training may be required to ensure that dose limits fall within the established guidelines. Staff members who sterilize prostatic seeds should receive training from the radiation safety officer that includes techniques for
   ♦ handling radioactive nuclides,
   ♦ minimizing exposure to radiation (ie, as low as reasonably achievable),
   ♦ controlling and providing security for the material (ie, constant surveillance), and
   ♦ emergency response to spills of radioactive material.[23]

Recommendation VI

Radiation monitors or dosimeters should be worn by personnel who are in frequent proximity to radiation as determined by the radiation safety officer.

1. Individuals must comply with state regulations concerning placement of the monitors worn. Personnel who routinely are involved in fluoroscopic procedures should wear at least one radiation monitor approved by the National Voluntary Laboratory Accreditation Program.[26] When single monitoring devices are used, they should be worn on the same area of the body by all health care personnel. Radiation monitoring devices are the principal mechanism for monitoring radiation exposure of the personnel on a day-to-day basis and, therefore, should be used consistently by health care personnel working with radiation.[14]

2. State regulations for radiation monitoring must be followed. When two monitoring devices are used, one usually is worn at the neckline outside the leaded apron and the other inside the leaded apron. The monitor worn under the apron measures whole-body levels, while the one at the neckline measures head, neck, and lens of the eye exposure.[26] The radiation safety officer may require that the monitors be worn at other sites depending on the dose information desired. Personnel monitoring is required for individuals who have a reasonable probability of exceeding 10% of the occupational dose equivalent limit of 0.05 Sievert (Sv) (ie, 5 rem) per year.[27] Practitioners who perform interventional vascular, biliary tract, or genitourinary tract procedures should wear a finger monitor in the same location for every procedure.[26]

3. Radiation monitors or radiation dosimeters should be worn at the waist for all pregnant personnel and read monthly, not quarterly.[1]

4. Radiation monitoring devices or dosimeters should be removed and stored at the facility at the end of every workday. Radiation monitoring devices should not be removed and taken home because the device will collect ionizing radiation from other sources (eg, sun, soil, airport scanners). Documentation of the readings of the dosimeters should be kept in the facility's safety office.

Recommendation VII

Therapeutic radiation sources should be handled minimally to minimize exposure. Protective measures are implemented to prevent injury.[2,6]

1. Radioactive materials always should be used under direct supervision of the radiation safety officer or an authorized user. Radioactive

materials should be kept in a protective container. The container reduces, but does not eliminate, exposure to radiation. Radioactive sources should never be left unattended when not in use.[1] Transport containers should remain under the direct supervision of the radiation safety officer or authorized user, or locked in a safe storage area.[13] Radioactive waste should never be placed in a nonradioactive waste container.

2. Radioactive sealed sources (eg, capsules, seeds, needles) should be handled with forceps, tongs, or tube racks. Forceps are used to increase the distance between the health care worker and the radiation source. Health care workers should never handle a sealed source with hands or fingers. Radiation protective gloves and aprons do not provide adequate shielding of therapeutic radionuclides; their inconvenience precludes their use for therapy. Examination gloves do not provide radiation shielding. They serve to control contamination if the radionuclide is a liquid or an unsealed source.[1]

3. Radioactive spills must be contained and disposed of in accordance with state and federal regulations. The source should be contained and completely removed, and the area cleaned thoroughly to remove any residual contamination. The area should be tested to verify that all radioactive material has been removed. Supplies used for cleanup should be discarded as radioactive waste. Perioperative registered nurses who work in this environment must receive training from the radiation safety officer or designee annually.[1]

4. An appropriate label (ie, radioactive waste label) must be placed on all radioactive waste. Such labels should include at least
   ♦ radioisotope name,
   ♦ activity,
   ♦ date of disposal, and
   ♦ radiation personnel's/authorized user's full name and contact information.[1]

Recommendation VIII

Measures taken to protect patients during the procedure from the risks of direct and indirect radiation exposure should be documented on the perioperative nursing record.

1. Perioperative nursing documentation should include the type of patient protection and the area(s) protected. Documentation of nursing interventions promotes continuity of patient care, improves communication among health care team members, and serves as a medical legal record of patient care.[28] Documentation of the protective measures used is necessary to track outcomes and ensure safety of the patient and staff members.

2. Documentation should include the perioperative nurse's patient skin assessment, including signs and symptoms of injury to the skin and tissue as evidenced by
   ♦ redness,
   ♦ abrasions,
   ♦ bruising,
   ♦ blistering, or
   ♦ edema.[2]

3. The Perioperative Nursing Data Set (PNDS), the uniform perioperative nursing vocabulary, should be used to document patient care and to develop policies and procedures related to radiological safety. The expected outcome of primary importance to this recommended practice is "The patient is free from signs and symptoms of radiation injury" (O7). This outcome falls within the domain of Safety (D1). The associated nursing diagnosis is "Risk of impaired skin integrity" (X51). The associated interventions that may lead to the desired outcome may be "Assesses history of previous radiation exposure" (142); "Verifies operative procedure, surgical site, and laterality" (143); and "Implements protective measures to prevent injury due to radiation sources" (174).[6]

Recommendation IX

Policies and procedures regarding radiation exposure should be written, reviewed periodically, and readily available within the practice setting.

1. Policies and procedures should be developed collaboratively and approved by perioperative personnel, the radiation safety officer, or the director of the radiology department in cooperation with safety committee members or the radiation safety expert in accordance with government regulations. Polices and procedures should be reviewed by a medical radiation

physicist. Collaboration should ensure compliance with current radiation safety policies and contribute to quality patient care.[1]

2. Polices and procedures should include, but are not limited to,
   - ♦ establishing authority, responsibility, and accountability for radiation safety;
   - ♦ identifying measures for protecting patients and personnel from unnecessary exposure to ionizing radiation;
   - ♦ developing procedures for handling and disposing of body fluids and tissue that may be radioactive;
   - ♦ ensuring that appropriate personnel wear radiation monitoring devices; and
   - ♦ scheduling radiographic testing of leaded protective devices.

3. Policies and procedures should be established in conjunction with the radiation safety officer for radiation safety training and competency in special handling techniques for personnel in the central processing department if sterilization of radiation seeds is performed there.

Recommendation X

Personnel should receive initial education, training, and competency validation and at least annual updates on new regulations and procedures.

1. All authorized users and radiation workers should complete initial training to include
   - ♦ radiation safety (eg, risk, hazards, spill containment);
   - ♦ biological effects of radiation;
   - ♦ regulatory requirements; and
   - ♦ environmental workplace techniques and procedures.

2. Documentation of training should include the above components and be maintained by the radiation safety officer.[1] Personnel who have not been involved in radiation procedures during the preceding two-year period should complete a refresher education and training program.

3. The radiation safety officer should provide annual competency validation, to include
   - ♦ a refresher course and testing for radiation safety and
   - ♦ a review of new regulations or procedures.

4. Educational programs should be developed to enhance knowledge that minimizes patient, personnel, and public risk of unnecessary exposure.

Recommendation XI

Only personnel who have received specific state-approved radiological training may be permitted to operate radiographic equipment.[26]

1. State-specific regulations must be followed regarding who may operate radiographic equipment. Legislation has been issued in various states restricting the use of this equipment to specific personnel who have demonstrated successful completion of formal education and training.

2. Operators of miniature mobile fluoroscopy units must adhere to the same state and federal regulations as all other radiological sources. The manufacturer's safety recommendations for the use of the device should be used when writing policies and procedures for the facility.

Glossary

Absorbed dose: The energy imparted to matter by ionizing radiation per unit mass of irradiated material at the place of interest. The special units of absorbed dose are the radiation absorbed dose (rad) (ie, 0.01 joule per kilogram) and gray (gy) (ie, one joule per kilogram), which is equal to 100 rads). The units for biological effective dose are the rem and sievert (sv).

Attenuation: The process by which a beam of radiation is reduced in intensity when passing through some material.

Authorized user: A physician or someone who has received special training or is credentialed to use radioactive materials and understands radiation physics, radiobiology, radiation safety, and radiation management.

Beam: A unidirectional flow of particle or electromagnetic radiation.

Conference of Radiation Control Program Directors (CRCPD): A nonregulatory organization that is a 501(c)(3) nonprofit, nongovernmental, professional organization dedicated to radiation protection.

Deep dose equivalent: The dose equivalent at a tissue depth of 1 cm; applies to the external whole body exposure.

Distance: The physical space between a source of radiation and its target (or the distance away from a source of radiation). The greater the distance an individual or target is from the source of radiation, the less the amount of radiation exposure. The inverse-square law applies—at a 4-ft distance from the source, the exposure received is approximately one quarter of that received at a 2-ft distance. Likewise, at a 6-ft distance the radiation is one ninth that received at a 2-ft distance.

Dosimeter: A device that is used to determine the external radiation dose that a person has received.

Equipment operator: A person with demonstrated qualifications and competency to operate a fluoroscopic system while exposing a patient to radiation. According to the American College of Radiology technical standard, only a physician is qualified to hold this title. Registered and/or licensed radiologic technologists or radiation therapists may perform fluoroscopic procedures if they are monitored by a supervising physician who is readily available.

Exposure: A measure of the total quantity of radiation reaching a specific point measured in the air. The unit of measure is based on the amount of ionization produced in air by a specified amount of x-ray energy. Radiation exposure is controlled in three ways—time, distance, and shielding.

External dose: That portion of the dose equivalent received from radiation sources outside the body.

Fluoroscopy: Observation of the internal features of an object by means of the fluorescence produced on a screen by x-rays transmitted through the object.

Gamma radiation: The emission of electromagnetic energy from the nucleus of an atom.

Gonad: Ovary or testis.

Gonad shield: A leaded device used to reduce x-ray exposure to the reproductive organs.

High radiation area: An area in which radiation levels could result in an individual receiving a dose equivalent in excess of 100 mrem per hour.

Internal dose: That portion of the dose equivalent received from radioactive material taken into the body.

Ionizing radiation: Electromagnetic radiation (eg, x-rays, gamma rays) that yields ions as it passes through an absorbing material (eg, air, tissue). The ions produce chemical reactions that are responsible for the biological expression of radiation (eg, cancer).

Leaded apron: A leaded-rubber material worn to protect personnel from scatter radiation.

US Nuclear Regulatory Commission (NRC): A government group that regulates use of nuclear materials and assists with formulation of regulations that protect workers, the public, and the environment. The NRC also regulates nuclear materials that are used in science, medicine, and industry. The NRC issues licenses to those who operate power plants or use nuclear materials and conducts inspections to make sure these facilities are following established regulations.

Occupational dose: Annual exposure limits that took effect in 1994.[11]

- ♦ Total effective dose equivalent (TEDE) to radiation workers—5 rem.
- ♦ Dose equivalent to the eye—15 rem.
- ♦ Shallow dose equivalent to the skin, extremities—50 rem.
- ♦ TEDE to any other individual organ—50 rem.
- ♦ TEDE to an embryo or fetus of declared pregnant woman—0.5 rem.
- ♦ Minors—10% of worker limit.
- ♦ Members of the public—0.1 rem.

Quantify amount: A millirem is one one-thousandth of a rem.

Rad: Radiation absorbed dose.

Radioactivity: The property, possessed by certain nuclides, of spontaneously emitting particles of gamma radiation or of emitting radiation after orbital electron capture or spontaneous fission.

Radionuclide: A radioactive atom used in nuclear medicine that shows radioactive disintegration and emits alpha and beta particles or gamma rays. Some radionuclides are used for diagnostic studies to trace the function and structure of most organs. Those emitting beta particles are used primarily for treating malignant tumors.

Rem: A special unit of dose equivalent. The dose equivalent in rems is numerically equal to the absorbed dose in rads multiplied by the quality factor, which for most medical radiation is one.

Scatter radiation: Radiation is scattered when an x-ray beam strikes a patient's body, as it passes through the patient's body, and as it strikes surrounding structures (eg, walls, OR furniture).

Shallow dose equivalent: The dose equivalent at a tissue depth of 0.007 cm averaged over an area of 1 cm.[1]

Shielding: Radiation interacts with any type of material, and the amount of radiation is reduced during passage through materials. A thin layer of lead can absorb most scattered diagnostic x-rays. Gamma radiation from medically useful radionuclides is substantially attenuated by 1 to 2 inches of lead.

Time factor: The less time a person is exposed to radiation, the less radiation one absorbs. Remaining close to a source of radiation for 15 minutes, an individual receives one-half the radiation dose received if the exposure time was 30 minutes.

Total effective dose equivalent: The sum of deep-dose equivalent (ie, external exposures) and the committed effective dose equivalent (ie, internal exposures).

Sealed and unsealed sources: Many radioactive pharmaceuticals come in the form of liquids or capsules and are administered orally. These are classified as unsealed sources. Some radioactive materials are sealed in small containment vessels, such as seeds, for implanting into tumors. These are classified as sealed sources.

X-ray intensifier: The radiation detector that produces the image in fluoroscopy.

X-ray tube: The radiation sources for x-ray and fluoroscopic machine.

REFERENCES

1. "Radiation safety manual," (August 1999) Centers for Disease Control and Prevention Radiation Safety Committee, http://www.cdc.gov/od/ohs/manual/radman .htm (accessed 23 May 2004).
2. "Radiation safety guide, chapter 11: Permissible exposure levels (dose limits)," (May 14, 2004) National Institute of Environmental Health Sciences, http://www .niehs.nih.gov/odhsb/radhyg/radguide/sectxi .htm (accessed 12 Dec 2006).
3. L Brateman, "The AAPM/RSNA physics tutorial for residents: Radiation safety considerations for diagnostic radiology personnel," (May 11, 1999) RadioGraphics, http://radiographics.rsnajnls.org/cgi/content/ full/19/4/1037 (accessed 1 Sept 2006).
4. L Strangio, "Interventional uroradiologic procedures," *AORN Journal* 66 (August 1997) 286-294.
5. "ACR practice guideline for the performance of low-dose-rate brachytherapy," (Jan 1, 2001) American College of Radiology, http://www.acr.org/s_acr/bin.asp?CID =0&DID=12243&DOC=FILE.PDF (accessed 30 Aug 2006).
6. S C Beyea, ed, *Perioperative Nursing Data Set: The Perioperative Nursing Vocabulary,* second ed (Denver: AORN, Inc, 2002) 100-101.

7. T G Norris, "Radiation safety in fluoroscopy," *Radiologic Technology* 73 no 6 (July-August, 2002) 511-533.
8. "Recommended practices for sponge, sharp, and instrument counts," in *Standards, Recommended Practices, and Guidelines* (Denver: AORN, Inc. 2006) 459-468.
9. L K Otto, S Davidson, "Radiation exposure of certified registered nurse anesthetists during ureteroscopic procedures using fluoroscopy," *Journal of the American Association of Nurse Anesthetists* 67 (February 1999) 53-58.
10. D Gilmour, "Risks for the new or expectant mother," *British Journal of Perioperative Nursing* 10 (June 2000) 306-310.
11. US Nuclear Regulatory Commission, Office of Nuclear Regulatory Research, *Instruction Concerning Prenatal Radiation Exposure,* Regulatory Guide 8.13, Revision 3 (June 1999) 8.13.11- 8.13.12.
12. S M Fishman et al, "Radiation safety in pain medicine," *Regional Anesthesia and Pain Medicine* 27 (May/June 2002) 296-305.
13. B G Bass, "How to maximize safety and minimize radiation exposure for cath lab personnel," *Cardiovascular Disease Management/COR Healthcare Resources* 7 (March 2001) 5-7.
14. J Newman, "Radiation protection for radiologic technologists," *Radiologic Technology* 71 no 3 (2000) 273-286.
15. Y R Rampersaud, K T Foley, A C Shen, et al "Radiation exposure to the spine surgeon during fluoroscopically assisted pedicle screw insertion," *Spine* 25 no 20 (2000) 2637-2645.
16. E Brailsford, P L Williams, "Evidence based practice: An experimental study to determine how different working practice affects eye radiation dose during cardiac catheterization," *Radiography* 7 no 1 (2000) 21-30.
17. C T Mehlman, T G DiPasquale, "Radiation exposure to the orthopaedic surgical team during fluoroscopy: How far away is far enough?" *Journal of Orthopaedic Trauma* 11 no 6 (1997) 392-398.
18. "Practice guideline for breast conservation therapy in the management of invasive breast carcinoma," (January 1, 2002) American College of Radiology, http://www.acr.org/s_acr/bin.asp?CID=0&DID=12238& DOC=FILE.PDF (accessed 30 Aug 30, 2006).
19. "Testing of lead aprons for QA," Pulse Medical, Inc, http://www.rci-pulsemed.com (accessed 30 Aug 2006).
20. "Recommended guidelines for controlling noninfectious health hazards in hospitals," Standard 5.2.3.6, in *Guidelines for Protecting the Safety and Health of Health Care Workers,* National Institute for Occupational Safety and Health, http://www.cdc.gov/niosh/hcwold5d.html (accessed 30 Aug 2006).
21. "Recommended practices for sterilization in the perioperative practice setting," in *Standards, Recommended Practices, and Guidelines* (Denver: AORN, Inc, 2006) 629-643.
22. Y Yu et al, "Permanent prostate seed implant brachytherapy: Report of the American Association of Physicists in Medicine task group No. 64," *Medical Physics* 26 (October 1999) 2054-2076.

23. T Lembcke, "Sterile loading of radioactive materials into needles," in *Trans-Rectal Ultrasound-Guided Trans-Perineal Implants of the Prostate Using ^{125}I and [103]P and HDR(^{192}Ir)*, Oconee Regional Cancer Center, *http://www.oconeecancercenter.com/prostate/prosbk10.htm* (accessed 30 Aug 2006).

24. J I Hui, T G Murray, "Radioactive plaque therapy," *International Ophthalmology Clinics* 46 no 1 (Winter 2006) 51-68.

25. "What are safe and legal options for radioactive source security during sterilization?" answer to question #212 submitted to "Ask the experts," Health Physics Society, *http://www.hps.org/publicinformation/ate/q212.html* (accessed 30 August 2006).

26. "ACR technical standard for management of the use of radiation in fluoroscopic procedures," (Jan 1, 2003) *Management of Fluoroscopic Procedures,* American College of Radiology, *http://www.acr.org/s_acr/bin.asp?CID=0&DID=12244&DOC=FILE.PDF* (accessed 30 Aug 2006).

27. E C Lipsitz et al, "Does the endovascular repair of aortoiliac aneurysms pose a radiation safety hazard to vascular surgeons?" *Journal of Vascular Surgery* 32 (October 2000) 704-710.

28. "Recommended practices for documentation of perioperative nursing care," in *Standards, Recommended Practices, and Guidelines* (Denver: AORN, Inc, 2006) 477-479.

Originally published October 1989, *AORN Journal.* Published as proposed recommended practices September 1993.

Revised and reformatted; published January 2001, *AORN Journal.*

Revised 2006; published in *Standards, Recommended Practices, and Guidelines,* 2007 edition.

Recommended Practices for the Care and Handling of Specimens in the Perioperative Environment

The following recommended practices were developed by the AORN Recommended Practices Committee and have been approved by the AORN Board of Directors. They were presented as proposed recommended practices for comments by members and others. They are effective January 1, 2006.

These recommended practices are intended as achievable recommendations representing what is believed to be an optimal level of practice. Policies and procedures will reflect variations in practice settings and/or clinical situations that determine the degree to which the recommended practices can be implemented.

AORN recognizes the numerous types of settings in which perioperative nurses practice. These recommended practices are intended as guidelines adaptable to various practice settings. These practice settings include traditional operating rooms, ambulatory surgery centers, physicians' offices, cardiac catheterization suites, endoscopy suites, radiology departments, and all other areas where operative and other invasive procedures may be performed.

Purpose

These recommended practices provide guidance for the implementation of containment, identification, labeling, preservation, transfer, transport, and disposition of surgical specimens. *Specimens* in this document include tissue, blood, body fluids, or foreign bodies (eg, plates, screws) removed from a patient for pathological, microbiological, or gross examination. Specimen identification, collection, and handling are multidisciplinary tasks that require vigilant attention to detail so that each person in the chain of custody understands the patient's needs and is aware of information about the specimen. Mishandling or misidentification of specimens can lead to inaccurate or incomplete diagnosis or the need for additional procedures.[1,2] These recommended practices are not intended to address aspects of perioperative patient care addressed in other recommended practices.

Recommendation I

Assessment of specimen collection and special handling needs should begin when the procedure is scheduled.

1. Specimen handling should be assessed and planned before the procedure. This assessment includes persons and departments to be notified (eg, pathology for frozen section), supplies needed for transfer or transport, availability of personnel, or specific requirements necessary for collection or handling of the specimen (eg, timing of transfer, solution, container). Early patient assessment and preplanning minimizes the time required during the surgical procedure and reduces the potential for mishandling specimens.

2. Containers and collection devices of appropriate size and type, with correct preservatives should be determined and obtained before the procedure. Containers should be large enough to safely secure the specimen and fluids, if used, to prevent leakage and unnecessary exposure of personnel or others handling the container or its contents. The container and collection device also should be of a size appropriate to allow the preservatives or solutions, if used, to contact all surfaces of the specimen. Collection containers may be sterile or clean, depending on collection requirements.

3. The patient's cultural considerations should be assessed to determine appropriate handling and disposal of specimens. Circumstances may require that specimens be handled or disposed of differently than routine requirements. The patient's written permission may be needed in advance for special requests.

Recommendation II

Procedures for correct patient and specimen identification should be implemented, including confirmation of consistent and accurate patient information on labels and forms.

1. Patient identification should be confirmed using two unique identifiers according to health care organization policy at the time the specimen is removed from the patient and when it is placed in the container for transfer and transport. Two unique patient identifiers should be used to minimize the risk of misidentification. Misidentification of a specimen, margins, or other information about a specimen can result in adverse outcomes, delay, error in diagnosis or treatment, or the need for an additional procedure.[2]

2. Specimen identification should begin at the time the specimen is removed from the patient with both verbal and written communica-

tion to confirm information. Communication should include a "read back" verification of the information. Using a "write down, read back" process to confirm the communication minimizes the risk of miscommunication.

3. Identification of the specimen should be confirmed verbally between the surgeon and registered nurse circulator and documented completely on the appropriate form(s). Identification should include, but is not limited to,
   ♦ originating source of specimen (eg, site or side),
   ♦ type of tissue,
   ♦ clinical diagnosis, and
   ♦ pertinent clinical information.

   Specific types of specimens may require additional information (eg, breast masses, which may include tissue markers of various types and suture tags for orientation.)

4. Each specimen removed for examination should be clearly documented on the specimen container, operative record, and pathology documents.

5. Specimens should be protected and secured on the sterile field to maintain the integrity of the specimen. Specimens should be passed off the sterile field as soon as possible. Specimens that must be kept on the surgical field before transfer should be maintained and labeled appropriately to prevent loss, damage, or mishandling.

6. Specimens transferred from the sterile field should be visibly labeled by the scrub person to prevent errors and misidentification, following verbal communication and verification (ie, "write down, read back") of the information. Written communication about the specimen at the time of removal, confirmed with the surgeon, minimizes opportunities for errors during the transfer/transport process.

Recommendation III

Collection and handling of a specimen should be completed in a manner that protects and secures the specimen and prevents contamination of personnel handling the specimen.

1. Specimens secured on the sterile field before transfer should be maintained in a manner to prevent misidentification or mishandling. The method of maintaining the tissue should be consistent with the specimen type; this often requires that tissue remain moistened with sterile saline to prevent drying.

2. The specimen should be contained and labeled immediately to prevent mishandling and errors. Securing specimens at the point of removal (eg, specimen cup) prevents damage and minimizes the risk of mishandling.

   Specimens and containers removed from the surgical field should be handled using standard precautions. The sterility (if indicated) and integrity of the specimen should be maintained during transfer from the sterile field to the container. Clean secondary packaging should be used to prevent contamination of personnel and the environment during transport of specimens.

3. Specimen containers containing a preservative or anticoagulant should be mixed thoroughly before the specimen is placed in the container. The use of preservatives or chemical additives for tissue preservation should be confirmed with the physician. Personnel should practice safety and protective precautions when working with chemical agents.[3]

4. Specimens removed from the procedural area should be secured in an impervious container. The size or type of container is dependent on size of the specimen, timing of the specimen review, preservatives, and containment for transport of the specimen. Containers and collection devices should allow for transfer and transport of biohazardous material without leaking or spilling. Containers should be rigid, leak-proof, sturdy, and nonreactive to fixative solutions such as formalin and alcohol. Lids should fit tightly to prevent spillage.[4]

5. Syringes used for specimen collection and containment should be capped without needles. Needles should not be left on syringes that will be transported. Needles create an unnecessary hazard to those transporting and receiving specimens and may invalidate results due to exposure to air.

6. Caution should be used when handling or dispensing formalin. It can be absorbed through the skin and nasal passages, splashed in the

eyes, and ingested. Exposure can result in irritation, burns, and allergic reactions.[5]

♦ All formalin in the OR should be stored in one location, along with a material safety data sheet. Storage and use of formalin is regulated by the Occupational Safety and Health Administration and other federal and state health regulatory agencies.[6]

♦ Personnel handling formalin should wear appropriate personal protective equipment, which includes face and eye shields, gloves, and other protective garments.[5-7]

♦ Formalin should be dispensed and stored in an area other than the OR. The room should have a ventilation system incorporating negative pressure and an exhaust hood.[7]

♦ Policies and procedures should be established for safe storage and dispensing of formalin in the surgical environment.

♦ Personnel should be educated about the safe handling of formalin, including containment and cleanup of spills, and other measures to minimize risk of exposure.

♦ Formalin should be disposed of according to state and local regulations. Formalin is a U-listed chemical, hazardous upon disposal, and regulated by the US Environmental Protection Agency.[8]

Recommendation IV

Specimen containers should be labeled to communicate patient, specimen, preservative, and biohazard information.

1. Two unique identifiers should be used to identify the patient reference. Information on the label should include, but not be limited to,
   ♦ specimen type and site,
   ♦ health care organization-defined unique identifiers (eg, patient name and hospital number), and
   ♦ current date and time.

   Dark, indelible ink should be used. The label or tag should be secured on the specimen container.

2. Containers should be labeled to indicate that a biohazardous material is being transported to prevent contamination of personnel transporting or receiving the specimen.[4]

3. If chemical preservatives are used, the label should clearly identify these additives.

4. The label should be placed on the container, not the lid. This prevents the loss of appropriate identification after the container is opened for processing.

Recommendation V

Tissue specimens should be designated for routine pathological exam, gross identification only, or disposal according to health care organizational policies.

1. All tissue must be disposed of in a manner consistent with state and federal guidelines, whether or not it needs pathological examination.[2]

2. Health care organizations should develop policies and procedures regarding which tissues require only gross identification or disposal.[9-11]

3. The pathologist has the ultimate responsibility for making decisions about the extent of the examination of the tissue.

Recommendation VI

Health care organizations should establish communication and documentation methods regarding specimen accountability and accurate documentation.

1. Documentation should include, but not be limited to,
   ♦ type of specimen;
   ♦ patient name, age, gender, health care organization, history, and diagnosis;
   ♦ studies required;
   ♦ date and time of collection;
   ♦ information pertinent to the specimen or source;
   ♦ surgeon's name and contact number; and
   ♦ the registered nurse doing the preparation and documentation of the specimen for transport.

2. Documentation via printed tools should be used to minimize errors related to handwriting and inaccuracies. When handwritten documentation is required, it should be accurate and legible. Common reasons for pathology errors are unlabeled containers, insufficient patient

identification, and incomplete or illegible information. Technology applications, such as bar coding, may be used to minimize errors.[12]

3. Specimen identification and requisition forms should accompany the specimen in a manner that protects the form and keeps it secured with the specimen.

4. Documentation should establish the chain of custody from the point of removal until pathological examination. Chain of custody is required for tissue specimens as well as material removed for forensic examination (see Recommendation IX).

5. Methods should be implemented to accurately record critical information such as tissue margins or orientation of the tissue as it relates to the anatomy, special tests requested, or disposition of the specimen. Requests for other than routine handling should be noted (eg, decalcification, x-ray, freezing). Delays or misdiagnosis can occur when the information is not accurately or completely communicated for the examination.[1]

6. Criteria for verbal and written specimen identification should be established to prevent misinformation. Commonly used methods include "write down, read back" verification of verbal communication. Communication should include, but not be limited to,
   ◆ physician to physician,
   ◆ physician to scrub person,
   ◆ scrub person to registered nurse circulator, and
   ◆ physician to registered nurse circulator.

7. Any communication between physicians, such as pathologist and surgeon, should be direct (ie, not through an intermediary) when it relates to diagnosis or specific diagnostic information about the specimen. A record of communication should be documented in the patient's record, such as the direct report of frozen section results to the surgeon. If communication directly between physicians is not possible, it should be written, marked with the date and time, and included in the patient's record.

8. If the patient requests to keep a removed item (eg, implanted medical device), the nurse

should follow procedures for identification and standard precaution guidelines per health care organization policy.

9. Requests for specimens to be returned to the patient should follow health care organization policy after the pathology examination is complete.

10. Disposition of all tissue, devices, and implants removed should be documented on the operative record according to health care organization policy or state guidelines.

Recommendation VII

Explanted defective medical devices must be reported to the manufacturer.[13]

1. Medical devices removed due to apparent failure of the device must be retained by the facility. All portions of the device should be retained together, as well as the packaging, if available.

2. Defective explanted medical devices should be sent for pathology examination for identification purposes.

3. The removed medical device should not be decontaminated or sterilized before it is transported from the surgical suite.

4. A risk management report should be completed regarding the defective device, per health care organization policy, and reported to the manufacturer.

5. Documentation should include the reason for removal, if known.

Recommendation VIII

Transfer and transport methods and processes should be established by the health care organization according to the specimen type and diagnostic requirements.

1. Procedures should be established to prevent mishandling of specimens by verifying patient and specimen information before transfer, and by transport personnel at each point of exchange. Proper documentation allows tracking of the specimen from its source to its final

disposition. A logbook should be used to record specimen, date, time, and the name of each person involved in each transfer process.

2. All specimens must be identified as biohazardous and transported in a manner that prevents contamination by chemical, blood, and other potentially infectious material to personnel and the environment.[3]

3. Containers with chemicals must have proper identifiers and labeling.[3]

4. Accompanying documents should be protected from contamination.

5. Specimens should be transferred and transported in a manner that protects their viability. This may include, but is not limited to, protective packaging, temperature control, adequate fluids, or culture media.

6. Specimens that will not be transported immediately to the laboratory should be temporarily stored to maintain integrity for examination. Appropriate equipment with a biohazard sign should be available for holding specimens at the correct temperature until transport can take place according to the guidelines of the Clinical Laboratory Improvement Act.[14]

7. Specimens should be transported in a manner that ensures confidentiality of personal health information and minimizes visibility of the specimen.[15]

8. Documentation should be completed to establish the chain of custody from the point of removal until examination. Chain of custody is required for tissue specimens as well as materials removed for forensic examination.

Recommendation IX

Forensic specimens should be handled in a manner that preserves the condition of the evidence and verifies that the evidence has been in secure possession at all times.

1. The surgeon should place the evidence directly into a designated envelope or bag. The contents should be listed and described on the appropriate form (eg, "Release of Evidence" or similar form) and attached to the envelope or bag. The evidence envelope or bag should be labeled with the patient's identification, collection date, time, and name of collector.

2. The sealed evidence envelope should be given to the responsible law enforcement officer. If the law enforcement officer is not immediately available, the health care organization's policy for disposition of a sealed evidence envelope and attached documentation should be followed. Documentation in the operative record should include, but not be limited to,
   ◆ description of the removed item,
   ◆ area of the anatomy from which it was removed, and
   ◆ disposition.

3. Bullets should not be handled with metal instruments, if possible, because these may scratch the bullet surface.[16] After the bullet is removed, it should be placed into a nonmetal container and sealed evidence envelope. Bullets should be submitted per local and state law enforcement requirements.

4. In cases involving an ongoing criminal investigation, all of the patient's clothes and belongings should be secured as evidence, regardless of condition. Clothing removed from the patient should be cut along the seams or around bullet or stab wound holes. Items should be placed in a paper bag with the patient's identification, then into a personal belongings bag with the patient's identification. Plastic bags trap moisture and may facilitate growth of mold, which could destroy evidence. After collecting objects in appropriate paper containers, place heavily saturated objects in plastic to avoid leakage of fluids and contamination to evidence collectors.[17] Disposition must be completed per local and state law enforcement requirements.

5. Informational evidence (eg, patient statements, appearance, behavior, bodily marks) should be documented in detail.

6. Documentation should be completed to establish the chain of custody from the point of removal until examination.[18] Chain of custody is required for tissue specimens as well as clothing and other personal items removed for forensic examination.

Recommendation X

Each health care organization should develop written procedures for handling radioactive pathology specimens. These procedures should include, but are not limited to, specimen handling, labeling, transportation, storage, and disposal. The procedures should keep radiation exposure to hospital workers as low as reasonably achievable.[19,20]

1. Procedures should be developed in conjunction with the health care organization's radiation safety officer.

2. Policies should describe how specimen containers are labeled.[21]

3. Specimens containing radioactive materials should be promptly transported from the OR to the pathology department in properly labeled and sealed containers.

4. The health care organization should validate competencies of all personnel handling radioactive specimens.

Recommendation XI

Policies and procedures related to the collection and handling of specimens and establishment of safe practices should be developed, reviewed periodically, revised as necessary, and readily available in the practice setting.

1. Policies and procedures for the collection and handling of specimens should be written and approved by the disciplines responsible for collecting, handling, examining, storing, and transporting specimens and other related activities. Policies and procedures establish authority, responsibility, and accountability and serve as operational guidelines. Policies and procedures also assist in the development of patient and health care worker safety, quality assessment, and improvement activities. Nurses should collaborate with all members of the health care team and related law enforcement agencies to develop policies that address collection and handling of surgical or forensic specimens. Multidisciplinary review of policies and procedures ensures that specimen collection and handling policies are based on current knowledge and legal requirements. Applicable state and federal regulations must be followed.

2. Elements for safe specimen handling should include, but are not limited to,
   ♦ containers, collection devices, and preservatives for each specimen type;
   ♦ specimen, tissue, and patient identification;
   ♦ labeling;
   ♦ transfer and transport;
   ♦ maintenance of the specimen;
   ♦ documentation and communication of test ordered;
   ♦ chain of custody;
   ♦ patient requests or needs;
   ♦ specimen disposition; and
   ♦ communication of test results.

3. Education, competency assessment, and validation should be conducted at the time of employment. This includes, but is not limited to,
   ♦ roles, responsibilities, and methods of communication required when specimens are removed;
   ♦ methods and materials used for various types of specimen collection and handling;
   ♦ regulatory guidelines related to specimen collection and handling; and
   ♦ safety practices that ensure proper collection and handling.

4. Policies and procedures establish authority, responsibility, and accountability and serve as operational guidelines. Introduction and review of policies and procedures should be included in orientation and ongoing education of personnel to assist in the development of knowledge, skills, and attitudes that affect patient care. Policies and procedures also assist in development of performance improvement activities.

5. The uniform perioperative nursing vocabulary should be used to document specimens on the intraoperative patient record. The perioperative nursing vocabulary is a clinically relevant, empirically validated, standardized language describing perioperative nursing care. This standardized language consists of a collection of data elements, the Perioperative Nursing Data Set (PNDS), and includes perioperative nursing diagnoses, interventions, and outcomes.

Table 1

SAMPLE POLICIES AND PROCEDURES FOR PACKAGING AND HANDLING SPECIMENS[1]	
Aerobic culture	Minimize swab exposure to air.
Anaerobic culture	Should be collected via a closed system from deep sites, bypassing normal flora. The best method is an anaerobic tube or sterile container. Do not add fluid. Swabs are the least effective. Tissue or fluid specimens are the best; fluid must be in a capped syringe without air. Tube contains transport medium, and tissue/swab should be imbedded in transport medium. Send to laboratory within 30 minutes. Large specimens may be collected in a closed, sterile container, as they retain anaerobic conditions within the tissue.
Biopsy	Usually sent fresh, no preservative; taken to pathology immediately.
Cultures	Maintain sterility of container when placing specimen.
Cytology	For sputum, bronchial, or peritoneal washings. Saline or heparin may be added to some types.
Frozen section	No fixative, kept moist. Intended for immediate transport to pathology department for a special freezing and slicing process for a tentative diagnostic reading.
Fungal	Examination done on a culture specimen.
Gram stain	Sent with a culture specimen. May request anaerobic or aerobic testing.
Pap smear	A type of cytology in a special pap fixative (99% alcohol).
Routine tissue specimen	Kept moist and placed in a container to protect integrity of tissue. Generally placed in refrigerator for pathology pickup within a few hours or overnight.
Stones	Stones may be placed in a dry specimen container. Tissue specimens that contain stones should be placed in buffered formalin (eg, gallbladder with stones).
Swab	Place in an approved swab transport device.
Urine	Place in a sterile container.

1. "Specimen collection guide," University of Washington Department of Laboratory Medicine, http://depts.washington.edu/labweb/PatientCare/Clinical/Specimen.htm (accessed 12 Jan 2006).

The expected outcomes of primary importance to these recommended practices are outcome 24 (O24), "The patient's care is consistent with the perioperative plan of care," and outcome 28 (O28), "The patient's value system, life-style, ethnicity, and culture are considered, respected, and incorporated in the perioperative plan of care as appropriate." The intervention specific to the domain of Safety is intervention 84 (I84), "Manages specimen handling and disposition."[22]

6. Quality monitoring of specimen collection processes, handling, and transport should be established to identify trends or near misses. A focus on error reduction should be developed. Methods of root cause analysis should be used to examine near misses or specimen handling errors to identify opportunities for improvement.

7. Packaging and handling of specimens should follow policies and procedures developed by the health care organization (**Table 1**).

Glossary

Chain of custody: A legal term that refers to the ability to guarantee the identity and integrity of the specimen from collection through to reporting of the test results. A process used to maintain, secure, and document the chronological history of the evidence.[24]

Cytology: The study of cells, including their formation, origin, structure, function, biochemical activities, and pathologic characteristics.

Forensic evidence: Evidence for use in legal or criminal proceedings.

Frozen section: A method used in preparing a selected portion of tissue for pathologic examination.

The tissue is moistened and, fixed or unfixed, is rapidly frozen and cut by a microtome in a cryostat. This method is very rapid, allowing the pathologist to examine the specimen during a surgical procedure.[23]

Microbiology: The study of microorganisms, including bacteria, fungus, algae, and protozoa.

Specimen: Tissue or body substance removed for study.

REFERENCES

1. R E Nakhleh, G Gephardt, R J Zarbo, "Necessity of clinical information in surgical pathology: A College of American Pathologists Q-probes study of 771,475 surgical pathology cases from 341 institutions," *Archives of Pathology and Laboratory Medicine* 123 (July 1999) 615-619.

2. -L Slavin, M A Best, D C Aron, "Gone but not forgotten: The search for the lost surgical specimens; Application of quality improvement techniques in reducing medical error," *Quality Management in Health Care* 10 no 1 (2001) 45-53.

3. "Occupational exposure to hazardous chemicals in laboratories," 29 CFR 1910.1450, Occupational Safety and Health Administration, *http://www.osha.gov/pls/oshaweb/owadisp.show_document?p_table=STANDARDS&p_id=10106* (accessed 13 Oct 2005).

4. "Guidelines for the safe transport of infectious substances and diagnostic specimens," publ WHO/EMC/97.3 (1997), World Health Organization, *http://www.who.int/csr/emc97_3.pdf* (accessed 29 Nov 2005).

5. "Material safety data sheet: Formalin solution 5%," Science Stuff, Inc, *http://www.sciencestuff.com/msds/C1776.html* (accessed 11 Aug 2005).

6. "Substance technical guidelines for formalin," 29 CFR 1910.1048 App A, Occupational Safety and Health Administration, *http://www.osha.gov/pls/oshaweb/owadisp.show_document?p_table=STANDARDS&p_id=10076* (accessed 13 Oct 2005).

7. "Recommended guidelines for controlling noninfectious health hazards in hospitals (continued)," National Institute for Occupational Safety and Health, *http://www.cdc.gov/niosh/hcwold5a.html* (accessed 29 Nov 2005).

8. "Introduction to hazardous waste identification," 40 CFR Parts 261 (September 2003), US Environmental Protection Agency, *http://www.epa.gov/epaoswer/hotline/training/hwid05.pdf* (accessed 29 Nov 2005).

9. R Zarbo, R Nakhleh, "Surgical pathology specimens for gross examination only and exempt from submission," *Archives of Pathology and Laboratory Medicine* 123 (February 1999) 133-139.

10. P Fitzgibbons, K Cleary, "CAP offers recommendations on selecting surgical specimens for examination," *CAP Today* 10 (July 1996) 40.

11. "College of American Pathologists policy on surgical specimens to be submitted to pathology for examination," (1999) College of American Pathologists, *http://www.cap.org/apps/docs/laboratory_accreditation/surgical_specimens.pdf* (accessed 19 Oct 2005).

12. P N Valenstein, R L Sirota, "Identification errors in pathology and laboratory medicine," *Clinical Laboratory Medicine* 24 (December 2004) 979-996.

13. "Medical device tracking requirements," 21 CFR 821 (April 1, 2005), US Food and Drug Administration, *http://www.accessdata.fda.gov /scripts/cdrh/cfdocs/cfcfr/CFRSearch.cfm?CFRPart=821&showFR=1* (accessed 13 Oct 2005).

14. "CLIA Subpart K—Quality systems for nonwaived testing," Centers for Medicare and Medicaid Services, Clinical Laboratory Improvement Amendments, *http://www.phppo.cdc.gov/clia/regs/subpart_k.aspx#493.1240* (accessed 29 Oct 2005).

15. "Summary of the HIPAA privacy rule," US Department of Health and Human Services, *http://www.hhs.gov/ocr/privacysummary.pdf* (accessed 29 Oct 2005).

16. S L Hanshaw, "Bullet retrieval in the operating room," *Seminars in Perioperative Nursing* 3 (October 1994) 232-236.

17. G A Muro, C R Easter, "Clinical forensics for perioperative nurses," *AORN Journal* 60 (October 1994) 585-593.

18. M M Evans, P A Stagner, "Maintaining the chain of custody: Evidence handling in forensic cases," *AORN Journal* 78 (October 2003) 563-569.

19. P Fitzgibbons, V LiVolsi, et al, "Recommendations for handling radioactive specimens obtained by sentinel lymphadenectomy," *American Journal of Surgical Pathology* 24 (November 2000) 1549-1551.

20. M Cibull, "Handling sentinel lymph node biopsy specimens: A work in progress," *Archives of Pathology and Laboratory Medicine* 123 (July 1999) 620-621.

21. "Exemptions to labeling requirements," 10 CFR 20.1905, Nuclear Regulatory Commission, *http://a257.g.akamaitech.net/7/257/2422/14mar20010800/edocket.access.gpo.gov/cfr_2002/janqtr/10cfr20.1905.htm* (accessed 13 Oct 2005).

22. S C Beyea, ed, *Perioperative Nursing Data Set: The Perioperative Nursing Vocabulary,* second ed (Denver: AORN, Inc, 2002).

23. *Mosby's Medical, Nursing, and Allied Health Dictionary,* sixth ed (St Louis: Mosby, 2002) 710.

24. "Glossary: Chain of custody," Peace-Officers.com, *http://peace-officers.com/content/glossary/def-chain.shtml* (accessed 29 Oct 2005).

Originally approved November 2005, AORN Board of Directors. Published in *Standards, Recommended Practices, and Guidelines,* 2006 edition. Reprinted March 2006, *AORN Journal.*

Recommended Practices for Prevention of Transmissible Infections in the Perioperative Practice Setting

The following recommended practices were developed by the AORN Recommended Practices Committee and have been approved by the AORN Board of Directors. They were presented as proposed recommended practices for comments by members and others. They are effective January 1, 2007.

These recommended practices are intended as achievable recommendations representing what is believed to be an optimal level of practice. Policies and procedures will reflect variations in practice settings and/or clinical situations that determine the degree to which the recommended practices can be implemented.

AORN recognizes the numerous types of settings in which perioperative nurses practice. These recommended practices are intended as guidelines adaptable to various practice settings. These practice settings include traditional operating rooms, ambulatory surgery centers, physicians' offices, cardiac catheterization suites, endoscopy suites, radiology departments, and all other areas where operative and other invasive procedures may be performed.

Purpose

The rapidly changing health care environment presents health care workers with continuing challenges in the form of newly recognized pathogens and well known microorganisms that have become more resistant to today's therapeutic modalities. Protecting patients and safeguarding health care workers from potentially infectious agent transmission continues to be a primary focus of perioperative registered nurses.

Recommendation I

Health care workers should use standard precautions when caring for all patients in the perioperative setting.

1. Standard precautions should be applied across all aspects of health care delivery.[1] Any individual (eg, patient, family member, significant other, visitor, or health care provider) may be transiently or chronically colonized with pathogenic microorganisms and may be asymptomatic, display active infection, or be in the incubation period of the infectious disease.[1]

2. Additional precautions may be needed for specific organisms encountered, but at a minimum, standard precautions should be used for all surgical patients.

   - Standard precautions apply to exposure or the potential for exposure to blood and all body fluids, secretions, and excretions (except perspiration) whether or not they contain visible blood; nonintact skin; and mucous membranes. Standard precautions are designed to protect patients and health care workers from contact with recognized and unrecognized sources of infectious agents.[1]
   - Infectious agents can be transmitted via direct and indirect contact, respiratory droplets, and airborne aerosols.

3. Exposure to potentially infectious agents should be minimized by the use of personal protective equipment (PPE) (eg, gloves, gowns, aprons), work practices, engineering controls, and other measures tailored to the specific work environment.[2]

Recommendation II

Hand hygiene should be performed before and after each patient contact.

1. All personnel should practice general hand hygiene. Prompt and frequent hand antisepsis is the single most important measure to reduce the spread of microorganisms.[1-3] Hand hygiene should be performed
   - at the beginning of a work shift,
   - before and after patient contact,
   - after removing gloves,
   - before and after eating,
   - before and after using the restroom,
   - any time there is a possibility that there has been contact with blood or other potentially infectious materials, and
   - any time when hands may have been soiled or any time the practitioner believes his or her hands may have been soiled.

2. An appropriate alcohol-based hand antiseptic agent should be available in convenient locations (eg, wall, bedside).[3] Frequency of health care providers' hand hygiene can be increased by convenient access to hand wash sinks or hand sanitation stations.[4]

Recommendation III

Protective barriers must be used to reduce the risk of skin and mucous membrane exposure to potentially infectious materials.

Personal protective barriers are required when it can be reasonably anticipated that a health care worker will be exposed to blood and body fluids or other potentially infectious materials.[2]

1. Gloves selected for use should provide an effective barrier against infectious materials (eg, blood, body fluids) and any anticipated chemicals to which the gloves may come in contact. Some chemicals may cause the breakdown of the glove material.

2. Use of polyvinyl chloride (PVC) or vinyl gloves should be limited to brief, low-risk exposures.[5-11] Research has shown that PVC and vinyl gloves have a high failure rate in use.

3. Users should refer to the glove manufacturer's written instructions for use with chemicals (eg, glutaraldehyde, peracetic acid, methyl methacrylate). When handling glutaraldehyde solutions, gloves that are impervious to glutaraldehyde should be worn.[12] Gloves should be changed immediately following direct contact with uncured methyl methacrylate (bone cement). Exposure to uncured methyl methacrylate places the wearer at risk for direct contact with and skin absorption of the methyl methacrylate because it permeates the glove material. Users should contact the specific glove manufacturer and request written reports on specific glove styles and materials for the intrinsic ability of the glove to protect the wearer when exposed to chemotherapeutics, chemical agents, and blood-borne pathogens.

4. Exam gloves should be inspected upon donning, and changed after each patient contact, or when
   ◆ a visible defect is noted,
   ◆ perforation is suspected, and
   ◆ according to organizational policy.

5. Sterile surgical gloves should be inspected immediately upon donning and before contact with sterile supplies and tissue.[13] Sterile gloves should be changed

◆ after each patient contact;
◆ when a visible defect is noted;
◆ when suspected or actual contamination occurs;
◆ when a suspected or actual perforation from a needle, suture, bone, or other event occurs;
◆ immediately following direct contact with uncured methyl methacrylate (ie, bone cement) because the wearer is at risk for direct contact and skin absorption of the methyl methacrylate via penetration of the glove material;[14]
◆ when an unintentional electrical shock from an electrosurgical unit (ESU) is received to the hand(s) of the user;[15]
◆ when gloves begin to swell, expand, and become loose on the wearer's hands, as a result of the material's absorption (hydration) of fluid and fats; and
◆ according to organizational policy.

6. All end users should be familiar with the intended use and the limitations of each glove material.[16] Each surgical glove material has specific characteristics (eg, latex, polyisoprene, chloroprene) that affect the performance and intended use of the glove.

7. Gloves should not be washed between patient contacts or uses. Research has found that pathogens are not effectively removed from gloves by washing.[4] Washing gloves is not a substitute for hand washing.

8. Health care workers must wear masks to protect the mucous membranes of the nose and mouth during procedures and activities that generate splashes, splatters, sprays, or aerosols of blood or other potentially infectious materials.[2]

9. Health care workers must wear protective eye wear when a splatter is anticipated.[2]

10. Health care workers must wear a face shield if a splash is anticipated.[2]

11. Health care workers must wear fluid-resistant attire to protect skin and clothing during activities that generate splashes, splatters, sprays, or aerosols of blood or other potentially infectious materials. Personal protective equipment is required and must be used whenever exposure

to potentially infectious materials is anticipated. The type of PPE required depends upon the type of exposure anticipated. Work garments, such as scrub attire and warm-up jackets, are not considered PPE because they are not impervious to strike-through of hazardous materials.[2]

Recommendation IV

Health care practitioners should double-glove during invasive procedures.

1. Health care practitioners should wear two pairs of gloves, one over the other, during invasive procedures. A systematic review of 18 clinical trials of gloving practices clearly demonstrates that double-gloving minimizes the risk of exposure of health care workers to blood during invasive procedures. Meta-analyses of nine of these studies demonstrate the following.
   - Perforation rates of the glove closest to the skin are significantly less when wearing double gloves compared to single gloves ($P<0.00001$).
   - Perforation rates are no different when wearing single gloves compared to the outer glove when two pairs of gloves are worn ($P=0.3$).
   - More glove perforations are detected when using a colored under-glove indicator system when compared to two pairs of standard latex gloves ($P=0.002$).[17]

   This systematic review also included clinical trials addressing other aspects of gloving practices. These studies found the following.
   - Wearing two pairs of gloves (ie, double-gloving) significantly reduces the number of perforations to the innermost glove, when compared to the outer glove or single gloves.[17]
   - Wearing two pairs of gloves does not increase the likelihood of increased perforations to the outermost glove. [17]
   - Wearing one pair of standard thickness gloves on top of a pair of standard thickness colored gloves facilitates the wearer's rapid recognition of perforations to the outer glove. [17]
   - Wearing a single pair of orthopedic gloves (ie, thicker latex gloves) provides the same protection from perforations as does two pairs of standard latex gloves.[18]
   - Wearing two layers of colored gloves does not assist in recognizing breaches to the glove closest to the wearer's skin.[19-21]
   - Wearing a glove liner between two layers of gloves does reduce perforations to the innermost glove during orthopedic surgical procedures.[22,23]
   - Wearing cloth outer gloves during orthopedic surgical procedures does decrease the number of perforations to the innermost glove when compared to double-glove layers.[24,25]
   - Wearing steel weave outer gloves during orthopedic surgery does not reduce the number of perforations to the innermost gloves when compared to double gloves.[26]

   The Centers for Disease Control and Prevention (CDC), the American College of Surgeons, and the American Academy of Orthopedic Surgeons, support double-gloving during invasive procedures.[27-29]

2. Upon completion of the invasive procedure, both pairs of gloves should be discarded and hand hygiene should be performed.[3]

Recommendation V

Contact precautions should be used when providing care for patients who are known or suspected to be infected or colonized with microorganisms that are transmitted by direct or indirect contact with patients or items and surfaces in patients' environments (eg, herpes simplex, impetigo, infectious diarrhea, smallpox, methicillin-resistant *Staphylococcus aureus* [MRSA], and vancomycin-resistant enterococci [VRE]).

1. Contact precautions include many of the same elements found in the standard precautions requirements. These include
   - wearing gloves when caring for patients or coming in contact with items that may contain high concentrations of microorganisms (eg, fecal material, blood, wound drainage), noting that gloves should be changed after contact with body fluids;
   - wearing gowns when it is anticipated that clothing will have contact with infectious patients or items in the patients' environment (eg, transporting, transferring patient to a bed/cart, positioning);[30]

- wearing a mask when it is anticipated that aerosolized exposure to infectious microorganisms is possible;
- face protection (eg, goggles, face shield) when it is anticipated that splash or sneezing exposure to microorganisms is possible;
- ensuring that precautions are maintained during transport; and
- adequately cleaning and disinfecting patient care equipment and items before use with each patient.

2. When patient transport is necessary, barriers (eg, gown, gloves) should be used to reduce the opportunity for transmission of microorganisms to other patients, personnel, and visitors and to reduce contamination of the environment.[1]

3. Noncritical equipment (eg, equipment that touches intact skin) contaminated with blood, body fluids, secretions, or excretions should be cleaned and disinfected after each use, according to the organization's written policy.[1] The use of dedicated patient equipment may be indicated in some situations (eg, anesthesia, post-anesthesia care unit).

4. Routine cleaning of environmental surfaces (eg, floors and walls) is adequate for inactivation of MRSA, vancomycin intermediate resistant *Staphylococcus aureus* (VISA), and VRE.

5. When additional measures are indicated to prevent the spread of highly transmissible or epidemiologically important infectious organisms, an infection control professional should be consulted for guidance.[1]

Recommendation VI

Droplet precautions should be used when caring for patients who are known or suspected to be infected with microorganisms that can be transmitted by infectious large particle droplets (ie, larger than 5 microns in size) and generally travel short distances of three feet or less (eg, diphtheria, pertussis, influenza, mumps, pneumonic plague).

1. Droplet precautions include
   - wearing a mask when within three feet of infectious patients,
   - positioning patients at a distance of at least three feet from other patients, and

- placing surgical masks on patients during transport.

2. When patient transport is necessary, barriers should be used to reduce the opportunity for transmission of microorganisms to other patients, personnel, and visitors and to reduce contamination of the environment.

3. Noncritical equipment (eg, equipment that touches intact skin) contaminated with blood or other potentially infectious materials should be cleaned and disinfected after use.[1]

4. When additional measures are indicated to prevent the spread of highly transmissible or epidemiologically important infectious organisms, an infection control professional should be consulted for guidance.[1]

5. Droplets are generated from the source person primarily during coughing, sneezing, or talking. Transmission via droplet requires close contact between patients and personnel; droplets do not remain suspended in the air and generally travel short distances (eg, three feet or less).[1]

Recommendation VII

Airborne precautions should be used when caring for patients who are known or suspected to be infected with microorganisms that can be transmitted by the airborne route (eg, rubeola, varicella, tuberculosis [TB], and smallpox).

Microorganisms carried by airborne transmission (eg, droplet nuclei or dust particles) can be dispersed widely by air currents, remain suspended in the air for extended periods, and may become inhaled by a susceptible host within the same room or over a longer distance from the source patient.[1]

1. Airborne precautions should include
   - National Institute of Occupational Safety and Health (NIOSH)–approved N95 mask worn by health care personnel,[1]
   - placing surgical masks on patients during transport,
   - airborne isolation rooms with special air handling, and
   - ventilation for areas outside the surgical suite.

2. Additional perioperative considerations for patients known or suspected to have airborne diseases include the following.
   - Elective surgical procedures on patients requiring airborne isolation precautions, such as TB, should be delayed until the patient is no longer infectious.
   - Attempts should be made to perform procedures on patients requiring airborne isolation precautions at times when other patients are not present in the surgical suite and when a minimum number of personnel are present (eg, at the end of the day).
   - Placing a bacterial filter on endotracheal tubes when operating on patients who have confirmed or suspected TB may help reduce the risk for contaminating anesthesia equipment or discharging tubercle bacilli into the ambient air.[31]
   - Strict traffic control should be enforced.
   - After the patient leaves the room, the room should remain closed and not used until the air in the room has completely changed (eg, 15 air changes per hour requires 28 minutes for a 99.9% removal efficiency).[32]
   - Health care personnel entering the OR suite immediately following a patient on airborne precautions should use an N95 mask and use proper PPE.

3. When surgical procedures are performed on patients who may have infectious TB, respiratory protection worn by personnel protects the sterile field from the respiratory secretions of the health care worker and protects the health care worker from the infectious droplets generated by patients.[32]

Recommendation VIII

Health care workers should be immunized against epidemiologically important agents according to CDC recommendations.

1. All health care workers must receive hepatitis B virus (HBV) immunizations unless medically contraindicated. Immunization against HBV is effective in preventing the disease and should be given before occupational exposure occurs. Information about HBV infection must be provided to employees within 10 days of hire, and informed consent should be given before employees accept HBV immunizations. Health care workers may decline the vaccine but shall do so by signing a declaration statement that declines the vaccine. Vaccination should remain available after this declaration in the event the employee changes his or her mind.[2]

2. Health care workers should be immunized against other communicable and infectious agents.[33,34]

Recommendation IX

Work practices must be designed to minimize risk of exposure to pathogens.

1. Work practice controls must be implemented to reduce the risk of exposure to bloodborne pathogens, based upon input from nonmanagement staff members.[2] Activities involving hand-to-hand, hand-to-skin, hand-to-nose, hand-to-mouth, or hand-to-eye action can contribute to direct or indirect transmission via inanimate surfaces and should be prohibited in the work area.[1] These prohibited activities include, but are not limited to,
   - eating,
   - drinking,
   - smoking,
   - applying cosmetics or lip balm, and
   - handling contact lenses.[2]

   Strict adherence to standard precautions minimizes the risk of cross contamination among health care workers, patients, and their environment.

2. Food and drink should not be stored where the potential for exposure to blood or other potentially infectious materials could occur (eg, refrigerators, shelves, countertops, and cabinets).

3. Food and drink should not be present in the restricted and semirestricted areas of the surgical suite.

4. The environment should be kept in a clean and sanitary condition by cleaning and decontaminating all equipment and environmental surfaces between procedures.[26] Microbes such as HBV and VRE are known to remain viable on environmental surfaces for seven days or longer.[35-38]

Recommendation X

Personnel must take precautions to prevent injuries caused by needles, scalpels, and other sharp instruments.

1. Health care organizations must have a comprehensive exposure control plan that includes engineering and work practice controls.[2,39] Health care organizations must
   - document in the exposure control plan that they have evaluated and implemented safety-engineered sharp devices and needleless systems;
   - review and update changes in the exposure control plan at least annually to reflect changes in sharps safety technology;
   - maintain a sharps injury log with detailed information about percutaneous injuries;
   - solicit and document in the exposure control plan input from nonmanagerial health care workers when identifying, evaluating, and selecting safety engineered sharp devices; and
   - provide engineering controls to include devices with engineered sharps injury protection.[2]

2. Perioperative registered nurses should be familiar with federal, state, and local regulations that mandate the use of needleless systems and sharps safety devices.

3. Sharps with engineering controls must be used when deemed acceptable.
   - Exposure to infectious material and the frequency of sharps injuries can be reduced through the use of safe needle devices and other technologies to minimize contact with sharp instruments.[2]
   - The use of blunt suture needles, when clinically indicated, can reduce the occurrence of glove perforations, needle sticks, and exposures to blood and other potentially infectious materials and are therefore recommended to be used in the perioperative setting as a method for reducing injuries.[29,40-46]
   - The use of a safety scalpel is recommended.[2]

4. Work practice controls must be in place to minimize health care worker exposure when handling sharps.

   - Surgical team members should use a neutral zone or hands-free technique for passing sharp instruments, blades, and needles whenever possible and practical.[16] Studies show that most sharps injuries occur when suture needles or sharps are passed between perioperative team members. Changes in surgical practice to minimize manual manipulation of sharps (ie, neutral zone or no-touch techniques) can have a major effect on these injuries. Creation of a neutral zone (ie, where instruments are put down and picked up, rather than passed hand-to-hand) may decrease injuries from sharp instruments.[2]
   - All sharps must be handled, removed, and disposed of properly. Contaminated sharps should be disposed of in a puncture-resistant, labeled, color-coded, leak-proof container.[2,29] This type of container helps prevent injuries to personnel cleaning the room or equipment after use. Used needles must not be sheared, bent, broken, recapped, or resheathed by hand. If recapping is required, mechanical devices or the one-hand technique must be used.[2] Removable knife blades should be handled using an instrument or device.
   - Reusable sharps must be handled, removed, and sequestered at the end of the procedure in a labeled, puncture-resistant, closed transportation container. Removable, reusable sharps should be handled using an instrument or device.

Recommendation XI

Activities of personnel with infections, exudative lesions, nonintact skin, and/or bloodborne diseases should be restricted when these activities pose a risk of transmission of infection to patients and other health care workers. Identification, evaluation by a physician, and assessment of fitness for work performance in the perioperative setting should be required.

1. Health care workers infected with a bloodborne disease (eg, HIV, HBV, hepatitis C virus [HCV]) should use measures to protect themselves and others. The HIV-infected health care worker who carries out invasive procedures should double-glove during all procedures.[47] Case

reports have demonstrated the nosocomial transmission of HBV, HCV, and other potentially infectious materials from health care professionals to patients during invasive procedures.[48-54]

2. Health care workers who have exudative lesions or weeping dermatitis should refrain from providing direct patient care or handling medical devices used in performing invasive procedures. Restricting personnel who have exudative lesions, nonintact skin, or weeping dermatitis reduces the risk of transmission of bloodborne and other pathogens between workers and patients.[1]

3. Health care workers should follow the organization's written policy regarding reporting potentially infectious conditions.

4. Health care workers should consult with the organization's designated health care provider (ie, employee or occupational health department physician) for assessment, treatment, and limits to perioperative practice, if indicated. The organization's written guidelines should be followed with respect to the worker's ability to perform required job functions in the organization, especially in high-risk environments.

Recommendation XII

Policies and procedures that address responses to threats of intentionally released pathogens (eg, anthrax, botulism) should be written, reviewed periodically, and readily available within the practice setting.

1. Health care workers should follow the organization's emergency preparedness plan as modified from published CDC guidelines for treating patients exposed to a biological agent in the event of an actual or suspected biological agent release (eg, anthrax, botulism, plague, smallpox). The CDC guidelines, available at *http://www.bt.cdc.gov*, outline transmission precautions for each organism and define those recommendations. The current CDC guidelines should be consulted in conjunction with the organization's infection control practitioner.[55]

2. Perioperative registered nurses should actively participate in the organization's emergency

preparedness plan for responding to an intentionally released biological pathogen.

Recommendation XIII

Policies and procedures that address responses to epidemic or pandemic pathogens (eg, severe acute respiratory syndrome [SARS], avian flu, influenza) should be written, reviewed periodically, and readily available within the practice setting.

1. Personnel should follow the organization's infection control plan for epidemics based on published CDC guidelines for treating patients exposed to organisms considered high public health risks. The CDC outlines precautions for each organism on its Web site at *http://www.cdc.gov*.[55] The organization's infection control practitioner should be consulted regarding additional specific precautions in the perioperative arena.

2. Perioperative registered nurses should create and maintain an optimal health environment for patients with human and avian influenza and SARS.[56]

3. Perioperative registered nurses should actively participate in the organization's emergency preparedness plan for responding to an epidemic or pandemic.

Recommendation XIV

Personnel should demonstrate competence in the prevention of transmissible infections.

1. Personnel should be knowledgeable about the principles of infection transmission, risks to patients and personnel, measures to minimize these risks, and actions to be taken in the event of an exposure.

2. Personnel must be instructed in the proper use of PPE and other measures to prevent transmission of infectious agents. Initial education must take place within 90 days of new hire according to the Occupational Safety and Health Administration regulations and updated at least annually.[2]

3. Health care personnel should be educated on the underlying principles of infection control,

which provide direction for personnel in providing direct and indirect patient care. Additional periodic educational programs provide reinforcement of principles of infection control, new evidence on risks and preventive measures, and changes in technology and regulations.

4. Administrative personnel should assess and document initial and annual competency of personnel in the safe use of standard and transmission-based precautions, according to organization and department policy. Incorrect use can result in serious injury to patients and personnel. Competency validation assures that personnel have an understanding of risks and appropriate preventive actions. This knowledge is essential to minimizing the risks of transmission of infectious agents from health care personnel to patients and patients to health care personnel.

Recommendation XV

Policies and procedures should be written, reviewed periodically, and readily available within the practice setting.

1. Personnel should report all exposure incidents (eg, needle sticks, blood exposures), infections, or communicable disease to the health care organization according to organization policy. Prompt reporting enables employers to provide timely and confidential postexposure evaluation, intervention, testing, or appropriate prophylaxis.[2]

2. An introduction and review of policies and procedures for infection prevention, exposure mitigation, and emergency response plans should be included in orientation and ongoing education of personnel to assist in the development of knowledge, skills, and attitudes that affect safety and surgical outcomes. Policies and procedures also assist in the development of quality assessment and improvement activities.

3. The uniform perioperative nursing vocabulary should be used to document patient care related to prevention of transmissible infections on the intraoperative patient record. The perioperative nursing vocabulary is a clinically relevant and empirically validated standardized nursing language. This standardized language consists of the Perioperative Nursing Data Set and includes perioperative nursing diagnoses, interventions, and outcomes. The expected outcome of primary import to this recommended practice document is Outcome 10 (O10), "The patient is free of signs and symptoms of infection." This outcome falls within the domain of Physiologic Responses (D2). The associated nursing diagnosis is (X28): "Risk for infection." The associated interventions that may lead to the desired outcome include (I98) "Protects from cross-contamination."[57]

4. Information about adverse events and near misses should be collected, analyzed, and used for performance improvement as part of the institution-wide performance improvement program. To evaluate the quality of patient care and to formulate plans for corrective action, it is necessary to maintain a system of evaluation.

5. Organizational policies and procedures that address occupational exposure to pathogens must be consistent with federal, state, and local rules and regulations that govern occupational exposure to bloodborne pathogens.

6. These recommendations should be used as guidelines for developing policies and procedures within the practice setting. Policies and procedures establish authority, responsibility, and accountability, and serve as operational guidelines.

Glossary

Airborne precautions: Precautions that reduce the risk of an airborne transmission of infectious airborne droplet nuclei (ie, small particle residue 5 microns or smaller). Airborne transmission refers to contact with infectious airborne droplet nuclei that can remain suspended in the air for extended periods of time or infectious dust particles that can be circulated by air currents.

Anthrax: An acute infectious disease caused by *Bacillus anthracis.* Exposure (ie, skin contact, ingestion, or inhalation) to *Bacillus anthracis* spores from infected animals or animal products can produce infection in humans. Routes of exposure include pulmonary (bioterrorism threat through aerosolization of spores), cutaneous, or gastrointestinal. Person-to-person transmission is not known to occur with inhalation or GI anthrax route of exposure.

Botulism: An acute infectious disease caused by *Clostridium botulinum.* Exposure can occur through contaminated food or aerosolization (ie, inhalation) of *Clostridium botulinum* spores. Person-to-person transmission is not known to occur.

Colonized: The presence of microorganisms that reproduce on tissue without invading tissue or causing disease or infections.

Contact precautions: Precautions designed to reduce the risk of transmission of epidemiologically important microorganisms by direct or indirect contact.

Direct contact: Person-to-person contact resulting in physical transfer of infectious microorganisms between an infected or colonized person and a susceptible host.

Droplet precautions: Precautions that reduce the risk of large particle droplet (ie, 5 microns or larger) transmission of infectious agents.

Droplet transmission: The transfer of infectious microorganisms by contact with conjunctival, nasal, or oral mucosa droplets (eg, coughing, sneezing, talking, suctioning). Viral particles can be acquired from environmental surfaces and transmitted to mucous membranes.

Exam glove: Intended for short duration use, size specific (eg, small, medium, large), can be either nonsterile or can be made sterile by the manufacturer, provided in pairs or singles, made from several materials (eg, latex, PVC, nitrile, chloroprene), but are not intended for invasive surgical procedures because of their lower acceptable quality limit (AQL).

Exposure incident to pathogens: Exposure via specific eye, mouth, or other mucous membranes; nonintact skin; or parenteral contact with blood or other potentially infectious materials that results from the performance of an employee's duties.

Indirect contact: Contact of a susceptible host to a contaminated object (instruments, bed rails, linens, equipment).

Invasive procedures: The surgical entry into tissues, cavities, or organs or repair of major traumatic injuries.

Multi-drug resistant organisms (MDRO): Bacteria that may be resistant to one or more antibiotics (eg, MRSA, VRE).

Neutral zone (synonym: hands-free technique): A safe work practice control technique used to ensure that the surgeon and scrubbed person do not touch the same sharp instrument at the same time. This technique is accomplished by establishing a designated neutral zone on the sterile field and placing sharp items within the zone for transfer of the item between scrubbed personnel.

Personal protective equipment: Protective equipment (eg, masks, gloves, fluid-resistant gowns, goggles, and face shields) for eyes, face, head, and extremities; protective clothing; respiratory devices; and protective shields and barriers designed to protect the wearer from injury. Used wherever it is necessary by reason of hazards of processes or environment, chemical hazards, radiological hazards, or mechanical irritants encountered in a manner capable of causing injury or impairment in the function of any part of the body through absorption, inhalation, or physical contact.

Personnel: Paid or unpaid health care workers, students, volunteers, physicians, and others who may have direct patient contact or opportunity for exposure to patients or devices, supplies, or equipment used for patients.

Plague: An acute, gram-negative, bacterial disease caused by *Yesinia pestis.* Bubonic and septicemic plague transmission is primarily from infected fleas, although pneumonic plague aerosolization of bacteria can result from bioterrorism-related acts. Person-to-person transmission usually occurs through large aerosol droplets of saliva during face-to-face contact (ie, coughing or sneezing).

Potentially infectious material: Blood; all body fluids, secretions, and excretions (except sweat), regardless of whether they contain visible blood; nonintact skin; mucous membranes; and airborne, droplet, and contact-transmitted epidemiologically important pathogens.

Sharps: Sharps include, but are not limited to, suture needles, scalpel blades, hypodermic needles, electrosurgical needles and blades, safety pins, and instruments with sharp edges or points.

Smallpox: An acute, highly contagious viral illness caused by the variola virus. It is transmitted through airborne or droplet exposure (ie, coughing, speaking) and skin contact with skin lesions and secretions. Once exposed, the patient is contagious from the onset of rash until scabs separate (ie, approximately three weeks).

Standard precautions: The primary strategy for successful infection control and reduction of worker exposure. Precautions used for care of all patients regardless of their diagnosis or presumed infectious status.

Surgical glove: Intended for invasive surgical procedures. Size and hand specific (eg, 5½ to 9, right or left). Manufactured to higher AQL for holes than exam gloves.

Transmission-based precautions (enhanced): Second tier of precautions designed to be used with patients known or suspected to be infected or colonized with highly transmissible or epidemiologically important pathogens for which additional precautions are needed to prevent transmission in the practice setting.

REFERENCES

1. Centers for Disease Control and Prevention, "Guideline for isolation precautions in hospitals," *Infection Control and Epidemiology* 17 (January 1996) 53-80.

2. Occupational and Safety and Health Administration, "Bloodborne pathogens" in *Code of Federal Regulations* (CFR) 29: Part 1910.1030.

3. "Recommended practices for surgical hand antisepsis/hand scrubs," in *Standards, Recommended Practices, and Guidelines* (Denver: AORN, Inc, 2006) 537-546.

4. Centers for Disease Control and Prevention, "Guideline for hand hygiene in health-care settings: Recommendations of the healthcare infection control practices advisory committee and the HICPAC/SHEA/APIC/IDSA Hand Hygiene Task Force," *Morbidity and Mortality Weekly Report* 51, No RR-16 (Oct 25, 2002).

5. R C Klein et al, "Bio diagnostics report: Virus penetration of examination gloves," *BioTechniques* 9 no 2 (1990) 196-199.

6. A Douglas et al, "Barrier durability of latex and vinyl medical gloves in clinical settings," *American Industrial Hygiene Association Journal* 58 (September 1997) 672-8.

7. R J Olsen et al, "Examination gloves as barriers to hand contamination in clinical practice," *Journal of the American Medical Association* 270 (July 21, 1993) 350-353.

8. D M Korniewicz et al, "Leakage of latex and vinyl exam gloves in high and low risk clinical settings," *American Industrial Hygiene Association Journal* 54 (January 1993) 22-26.

9. D M Korniewicz et al, "Barrier protection with examination gloves: Double versus single," *American Journal of Infection Control* 22 no 1 (1994) 12-15.

10. A Rego, L Roley, "In-use barrier integrity of gloves: Latex and nitrile superior to vinyl," *American Journal of Infection Control* 27 (October 1999) 405-410.

11. D M Korniewicz et al, "Performance of latex and non-latex medical examination gloves during simulated use," *American Journal of Infection Control* 30 (April 2002) 133-138.

12. "Use of latex surgical exam gloves for protection from glutaraldehyde," Occupational Safety and Health Administration, *http://www.osha.gov* (accessed 24 May 2006).

13. "Recommended practices for maintaining a sterile field," in *Standards, Recommended Practices, and Guidelines* (Denver: AORN, Inc, 2006) 621-628.

14. T H Waegermaekers et al, "Permeability of surgeons' gloves to methyl methacrylate," *Acta Orthopaedica Scandinavia* 54 (December 1983) 790-795.

15. "Recommended practices for electrosurgery," in *Standards, Recommended Practices, and Guidelines* (Denver: AORN, Inc, 2006) 481-496.

16. P Graves "Gloves: How do the pieces of the puzzle fit together?" *Infection Control Today* (September 2001) *http://www.infectioncontroltoday.com/articles/191feat1.htm* (accessed 29 Jan 2005).

17. J Tanner, H Parkinson, "Double gloving to reduce surgical cross-infection," (Cochrane Review) *The Cochrane Library*, Issue 3 (Oxford: John Wilson & Sons, 2003).

18. M Turnquist et al, "Perforation rate using a single pair of orthopedic gloves vs. a double pair of gloves in obstetric cases," *Journal of Maternal-Fetal Medicine* 5 no 6 (November-December 1996) 362-365.

19. C M E Avery, J Taylor, P A Johnson, "Double gloving and a system for identifying glove perforations in maxillofacial trauma surgery," *British Journal of Oral and Maxillofacial Surgery* 4 (August 1999) 316-319.

20. J J Duron et al, "Efficacy of double gloving with a coloured inner pair for immediate detection of operative glove perforations," *European Journal of Surgery* 162 (December 1996) 941-944.

21. P Nicolai, C H Aldam, P W Allen, "Increased awareness of glove perforation in major joint replacement," *Journal of Bone and Joint Surgery,* British Volume 79 (May 1997) 371-373.

22. E J Sebold, L R Jordan, "Intraoperative glove perforation: A comparative analysis," *Clinical Orthopaedics and Related Research* 297 (December 1993) 242-244.

23. P M Sutton, T Greene, F R Howell, "The protective effect of a cut-resistant glove liner," *Journal of Bone and Joint Surgery* 80-B (May 1998) 411-413.

24. R Sanders et al, "Outer gloves in orthopaedic procedures," *Journal of Bone and Joint Surgery* 72 (July 1990) 914-917.

25. M J Underwood et al, "Prevalence and prevention of glove perforation during cardiac operation," (Letters to the Editor) *Journal of Thoracic and Cardiovascular Surgery* 106 (August 1993) 375-377.

26. S S Louis et al, "Outer gloves in orthopaedic procedures: A polyester/stainless steel wire weave glove liner compared with latex," *Journal of Orthopaedic Trauma* 12 (February 1998) 101-105.

27. "Advisory statement: Preventing the transmission of bloodborne pathogens," American Academy of Orthopedic Surgeons, *http://www.aaos.org/wordhtml/papers/advistmt/1018.htm* (accessed 24 May 2006).

28. Centers for Disease Control and Prevention, "Guideline for prevention of surgical site infection, 1999," *Infection Control and Hospital Epidemiology* 20 (April 1999) 247-277.

29. R Berguer, P J Heller, "Preventing sharps injuries in the operating room," *American College of Surgeons* 199 (Sept 2004) 462-467.

30. "Recommended practices for use and selection of barrier materials for surgical gowns and drapes," in *Standards, Recommended Practices, and Guidelines* (Denver: AORN, Inc, 2006) 531-536.

31. "Recommended practices for cleaning, handling, and processing anesthesia equipment," in *Standards, Recommended Practices, and Guidelines* (Denver: AORN, Inc, 2006) 441-450.

32. Centers for Disease Control and Prevention, "Guidelines for preventing the transmission of mycobacterium tuberculosis in health-care settings, 2005," *Morbidity and Mortality Weekly Report* 54 no RR 17 (Dec 30, 2005) 1-141.

33. Centers for Disease Control and Prevention, "Immunization of health-care workers," *Morbidity and Mortality Weekly Report* 46 no RR-18 (Dec 26, 1997) 1-42.

34. Centers for Disease Control and Prevention, "Influenza vaccination of health-care personnel," *Morbidity and Mortality Weekly Report* Early Release 55 (Feb 9, 2006) 1-16.

35. "Recommended practice for environmental cleaning in the surgical practice setting," in *Standards, Recommended Practices, and Guidelines* (Denver: AORN, Inc, 2006) 517-524

36. G A Noskin et al, "Recovery of vancomycin-resistant enterococci on fingertips and environmental surfaces," *Infection Control and Hospital Epidemiology* 16 (October 1995) 577-581.

37. M J Boyce et al, "Controlling vancomycin-resistant enterococci," *Infection Control and Hospital Epidemiology* 16 (November 1995) 634-637.

38. H F Bonilla et al, "Long-term survival of vancomycin-resistant enterococci faecium on a contaminated surface," (Letters to the Editor) *Infection Control and Hospital Epidemiology* 17 (December 1996) 771-772.

39. "Needlestick safety and prevention act," Public Law 106-430, 106th Congress, *http://frwebgate.access.gpo.gov /cgi-bin/getdoc.cgi?dbname=106_cong_public _laws&docid=f:publ430.106* (accessed 24 May 2006).

40. J Jagger, M Bentley, P Tereskerz, "A study of patterns and prevention of blood exposures in OR personnel," *AORN Journal* 67 (1998) 979-984.

41. K U Wright, C G Moran, P J Briggs, "Glove perforation during hip arthroplasty: A randomized prospective study of a new taper point needle," *Journal of Bone and Joint Surgery* 75 B (November 1993) 918-920.

42. A Mingoli et al, "Influence of blunt needles on surgical glove perforation and safety for the surgeon," *American Journal of Surgery* 172 (November 1996) 512-517.

43. J J Rice et al, "Needlestick injury: Reducing the risk," *International Orthopaedics* 20 no 3 (1996) 132-133.

44. J E Hartley et al, "Randomized trial of blunt-tipped versus cutting needle to reduce glove puncture during mass closure of the abdomen," *British Journal of Surgery* 83 (August 1996) 1156-1157.

45. M I Dauleh, A D Irving, N H Townell, "Needle prick injury to the surgeon—Do we need sharp needles?" *Journal of the Royal College of Surgeons of Edinburgh* 39 (October 1994) 310-311.

46. F J Montz et al, "Blunt needles in fascial closure," (The Surgeon At Work) *Surgery, Gynecology, and Obstetrics* 173 (August 1991) 147-148.

47. "Policies and position statements, Guidelines: HIV and AIDS in the workplace," American College of Occupational and Environmental Medicine, *http://www .acoem.org* (accessed 24 May 2006).

48. "Transmission of Hepatitis B to patients from four infected surgeons without hepatitis B e antigen: The incident investigation teams and others," *The New England Journal of Medicine* 336 (Jan 16, 1997) 178-84.

49. B C Gartner et al, "High prevalence of hepatitis G (HGV) infections in dialysis staff," *Nephrology Dialysis Transplantation* 14 no 2 (February 1999) 406-8.

50. J L Esteban et al, "Transmission of hepatitis C virus by a cardiac surgeon," *The New England Journal of Medicine* 334 (Feb 9, 1996) 555-560.

51. R Harpaz et al, "Transmission of hepatitis B virus to multiple patients from a surgeon without evidence of inadequate infection control," *The New England Journal of Medicine* 334 (Feb 29, 1996) 549-554.

52. S A McNeil et al, "Outbreak of sternal surgical site infections due to *Pseudomonas aeruginosa* traced to a scrub nurse with onychomycosis," *Clinical Infectious Disease* 33 (Aug 1, 2001) 317-323.

53. P J van der Broek et al, "Epidemic of prosthetic valve endocarditis caused by *Staphlyococcus epidermis*," *British Medical Journal* 291 (October 5, 1985) 949-950.

54. D L Wooster, R E Louch, S Krajden, "Intraoperative bacterial contamination of vascular grafts: A prospective study," *Canadian Journal of Surgery* 28 (September 1985) 407-409.

55. "Emergency preparedness & response: Bioterrorism agents/diseases," Centers for Disease Control and Prevention, *http://www.bt.cdc.gov/agent/agentlist.asp* (accessed 24 May 2006).

56. "Guidance statement: Human and avian influenza and severe acute respiratory syndrome," in *Standards, Recommended Practices, and Guidelines* (Denver: AORN, Inc, 2006) 225-237.

57. S C Beyea, ed, *Perioperative Nursing Data Set: The Perioperative Nursing Vocabulary,* second ed (Denver: AORN, Inc, 2002).

Originally published February 1993, *AORN Journal,* as "Recommended practices for universal precautions in the perioperative practice setting."

Revised November 1998 as "Recommended practices for standard and transmission-based precautions in the perioperative practice setting"; published February 1999, *AORN Journal.* Reformatted July 2000.

Approved June 2006, AORN Board of Directors, as "Recommended practices for prevention of transmissible infections in perioperative practice settings." Published in *Standards, Recommended Practices, and Guidelines,* 2007 edition.

AORN Perioperative Standards and Recommended Practices, 2009 Edition

Recommended Practices for Documentation of Perioperative Nursing Care

The following recommended practices were developed by the AORN Recommended Practices Committee and have been approved by the AORN Board of Directors. They were presented as proposed recommended practices for comment by members and others. They are effective January 1, 2000.

These recommended practices are intended as achievable recommendations representing what is believed to be an optimal level of practice. Policies and procedures will reflect variations in practice settings and/or clinical situations that determine the degree to which the recommended practices can be implemented.

AORN recognizes the numerous types of settings in which perioperative nurses practice. These recommended practices are intended as guidelines adaptable to various practice settings. These practice settings include traditional operating rooms, ambulatory surgery units, physicians' offices, cardiac catheterization suites, endoscopy suites, radiology departments, and all other areas where operative and other invasive procedures may be performed.

Purpose

These recommended practices provide guidelines to assist perioperative nurses in documenting nursing care in the perioperative practice setting. Documentation using the nursing process should be completed for each surgical and other invasive procedure. The nursing process is a formalized systematic approach to providing and documenting patient care. Perioperative documentation is essential for the continuity of goal-directed care and for comparing achieved patient outcomes to expected patient outcomes.

Recommendation I

The patient's record should reflect the perioperative patient's plan of care, including assessment, diagnosis, outcome identification, planning, implementation, and evaluation.

1. Documentation should include information about the status of the patient, nursing diagnoses and interventions, expected patient outcomes, and evaluation of the patient's response to perioperative nursing care. The nursing process provides the governing framework for documenting perioperative nursing care. When the nursing process is used in perioperative practice settings, it demonstrates the critical-thinking skills practiced by the nurse in caring for the surgical patient.[1]

2. The patient's record should reflect an assessment (ie, physical, psychosocial, cultural, spiritual) performed by the perioperative nurse before surgical or other invasive procedures. A documented assessment forms a baseline for developing nursing diagnoses and planning patient care. Continuing this assessment throughout each subsequent phase of the patient's care (ie, intraoperative, postoperative) contributes to continuity of care.[2]

3. The patient's record should reflect the plan of care. The planning process begins when the perioperative nurse identifies nursing interventions that will address the patient's actual or potential risk for health problems (ie, nursing diagnoses). Documentation facilitates communication among health care team members, promotes continuity of care, and serves as a legal record of care provided.[3] Identifying desired patient outcomes that are individualized, prioritized, measurable, realistic, and obtainable aids in developing the plan of care.[4]

4. The patient's record should specify what nursing interventions were performed and when, where, and by whom during each phase of perioperative care.[5] The implementation process is a result of assessment and planning using nursing judgment and critical thinking skills. The goals of nursing interventions are to prevent potential patient injury or complications and to intervene/treat actual patient problems. Documenting nursing interventions promotes continuity of patient care and improves communication between health care team members.[6]

5. The patient's record should reflect a continuous evaluation of perioperative nursing care and the patient's response to applied nursing interventions. The nursing process directs perioperative nurses to evaluate the effectiveness of nursing interventions toward attaining desired patient outcomes. The evaluation process provides information for continuity of care, performance improvement activities, perioperative nursing research, and risk management. Documentation provides a mechanism for comparing actual versus expected outcomes.[7]

6. Perioperative documentation should include, but not be limited to,
- identification of persons providing perioperative patient care (ie, name, title, signature of person responsible for the care);
- description of patient's overall skin condition on arrival and discharge from the perioperative suite;
- perioperative patient care planning, including baseline physical, emotional, psychosocial, and cultural data;
- presence and/or disposition of sensory aids and prosthetic devices (eg, eyewear, hearing aids, denture, artificial limbs);
- placement of electrosurgical unit (ESU) dispersive pad and identification of the ESU and setting used during the surgical procedure;
- use of temperature-regulating devices, including identification of the unit and documentation of the patient's body temperature before and after discharge from the perioperative suite;
- placement of electrocardiogram electrodes, blood pressure cuff, oximetry and temperature probes, and other invasive and monitoring devices;
- patient positioning and/or repositioning devices and supports, including immobilization devices used during the surgical procedure;
- placement of tourniquet cuffs, including identification of the unit, pressure settings, and inflation and deflation times;
- location of skin prep, including prep solution used;
- use of lasers, including identification of the unit, name of surgeon and support staff members, type of laser used, surgical procedure, the lens used, length of time laser was used, and the wattage;
- use of intraoperative x-rays and fluoroscopy and protective devices used (if any);
- patient specimens and cultures taken during the surgical procedure;
- location and type of drains, catheters, wound packing, casting material, and dressings used;
- placement and location of implants (eg, medical devices, synthetic and biologic grafts, tissue, bone), including the name of the manufacturer or distributor, lot and

serial numbers, type and size of implant, and expiration dates as appropriate, and other information required by the US Food and Drug Administration;
- placement of radioactive implants, including the time, number, location, and type of radioactive material placed in the patient;
- administration of blood or blood products, medications, irrigation solution, and other solutions to the patient during the perioperative period;
- wound classification;
- anesthesia classification and mode of anesthesia provided;
- documentation of sponge, sharp, and instrument count outcomes as appropriate;
- time of patient discharge, patient status at discharge, patient disposition, and method of transfer;
- any significant or unusual occurrences pertinent to perioperative patient outcomes;
- communication with family members or significant others during the surgical procedure; and
- patient/family teaching provided.

Documentation of all nursing activities performed is legally and professionally important for clear communication, collaboration between health care team members, and continuity of patient care.[8]

Recommendation II

Policies and procedures for documenting perioperative nursing care should be written, reviewed periodically, revised as necessary, and be readily available within the practice setting.

1. These recommended practices should be used as guidelines for developing policies and procedures for documentation within the perioperative practice setting. Documentation policies and procedures establish authority, responsibility, and accountability and serve as operational guidelines. An introduction and review of documentation policies and procedures should be included in the orientation and ongoing education of personnel to assist them in obtaining knowledge and developing skills and competencies that will influence perioperative patient outcomes.

2. Every perioperative practice setting uses a formal system of documentation of patient care. Although the method of documenting perioperative nursing care varies among practice settings, documentation forms should include, but not be limited to, the following:

♦ operative record,
♦ preoperative patient checklist,
♦ nurses' notes,
♦ flow sheets,
♦ care plans,
♦ implant records, and
♦ laser logs.

The methods selected for documenting perioperative nursing care will be based on the facility's overall philosophy of documentation and record keeping.

REFERENCES

1. C S Ladden, "Concepts basic to perioperative nursing," in *Alexander's Care of the Patient in Surgery*, 11th ed, M H Meeker, J C Rothrock, eds (St Louis: Mosby, Inc, 1999) 7, 12-13; J Gill et al, "Incorporating nursing diagnosis and King's theory in the OR documentation," *Canadian Operating Room Nursing Journal* (March/April 1995) 10-11; K Blais, "Perioperative nursing process," in *Perioperative Nursing Principles and Practice*, second ed, S S Fairchild, ed (Boston: Little, Brown & Co, 1996) 271-272, 284; L J Atkinson, N H Fortunato, *Berry & Kohn's Operating Room Technique*, eighth ed (St Louis: Mosby-Year Book, Inc, 1996) 23, 53, 437, 447.

2. Ladden, "Concepts basic to perioperative nursing," 12; Gill et al, "Incorporating nursing diagnosis and King's theory in the OR documentation," 10-14; J Palmerini, "Developing a comprehensive perioperative nursing documentation form," *AORN Journal* 63 (January 1996) 239-247; Blais, "Perioperative nursing process," 271-272, 274; L C A Simunek, "Legal and ethical dimensions of perioperative nursing practice," in *Perioperative Nursing Principles and Practice*, second ed, S S Fairchild, ed (Boston: Little, Brown & Co 1996) 390-394; Atkinson, Fortunato, *Berry & Kohn's Operating Room Technique*, 23, 30-31, 53.

3. Atkinson, Fortunato, *Berry & Kohn's Operating Room Technique*, 53-55, 424; Ladden, "Concepts basic to perioperative nursing," 3-19; B J Gruendemann, B Fernsebner, *Comprehensive Perioperative Nursing, Volume I: Principles* (Boston: Jones and Bartlett Publishers, 1995) 95.

4. Ladden, "Concepts basic to perioperative nursing," 8; Blais, "Perioperative nursing process," 271-285; Atkinson, Fortunato, *Berry & Kohn's Operating Room Technique*, 21-31.

5. Gruendemann, Fernsebner, *Comprehensive Perioperative Nursing, Volume I: Principles*, 95, 308; Ladden, "Concepts basic to perioperative nursing," 12; Blais, "Perioperative nursing process," 280; Atkinson, Fortunato, *Berry & Kohn's Operating Room Technique*, 55, 269, 276, 424.

6. Palmerini, "Developing a comprehensive perioperative nursing documentation form," 241; Simunek, "Legal and ethical dimensions of perioperative nursing practice," 391, 394; Atkinson, Fortunato, *Berry & Kohn's Operating Room Technique*, 27-31, 53, 55; S Null, D Richter-Abt, J Kovac, "Development of a perioperative nursing diagnoses flow sheet," *AORN Journal* 61 (March 1995) 57.

7. Gruendemann, Fernsebner, *Comprehensive Perioperative Nursing, Volume I: Principles*, 95; L K Groah, *Perioperative Nursing*, third ed (Stamford, Conn: Appleton & Lange, 1996) 304, 314; Atkinson, Fortunato, *Berry & Kohn's Operating Room Technique*, 24, 30-31, 53, 55, 546; Ladden, "Concepts basic to perioperative nursing," 12, 13; Palmerini, "Developing a comprehensive perioperative nursing documentation form," 241-242; Blais, "Perioperative nursing process," 272, 283.

8. Gruendemann, Fernsebner, *Comprehensive Perioperative Nursing, Volume I: Principles*, 95; Atkinson, Fortunato, *Berry & Kohn's Operating Room Technique*, 55, 424.

Originally published March 1982, *AORN Journal*. Format revision July 1982.

Revised March 1987; revised September 1991; revised November 1995; published June 1996.

Revised; published January 2000, *AORN Journal. Reformatted July 2000.*

AORN Perioperative Standards and Recommended Practices, 2009 Edition

Recommended Practices for the
Prevention of Unplanned Perioperative Hypothermia

The following recommendations for protecting patients from unplanned perioperative hypothermia were developed by the AORN Recommended Practices Committee and have been approved by the AORN Board of Directors. They were presented as proposed recommendations for comments by members and others. They are effective January 1, 2008.

These recommended practices are intended as achievable recommendations representing what is believed to be an optimal level of practice. Policies and procedures will reflect variations in practice settings and/or clinical situations that determine the degree to which the recommended practices can be implemented.

AORN recognizes the various settings in which perioperative registered nurses practice. These recommended practices are intended as guidelines adaptable to various practice settings. Practice settings include traditional operating rooms, ambulatory surgery centers, physicians' offices, cardiac catheterization suites, endoscopy suites, radiology departments, and all other areas where operative and other invasive procedures may be performed.

Purpose

These recommended practices are intended to guide perioperative registered nurses in optimizing patient care practices to maintain normothermia and prevent unplanned hypothermia. Hypothermia, defined as a core body temperature less than 36° C (96.8° F), presents a constant challenge for perioperative registered nurses because many surgical patients are at risk for unplanned hypothermia during surgery. There are three phases of unplanned hypothermia: the redistribution phase, the linear decrease phase, and the thermal plateau phase. These recommended practices focus on the prevention of the redistribution phase of unplanned hypothermia. Planned or therapeutic hypothermia is outside the scope of this document.

In the redistribution phase of unplanned hypothermia, a rapid shift of body heat from the body's core to its periphery occurs, resulting in a core temperature drop of approximately 1.6° C (2.7° F) during the first hour after induction of anesthesia.[1,2] The initial temperature drop of the redistribution phase is followed by a slow linear decrease phase during the second and subsequent hours of anesthesia, in which heat loss exceeds the body's ability to metabolically produce heat. In this second phase, warming the patient can effectively limit further heat loss. After approximately three to five hours of anesthesia, the patient's core temperature often plateaus and is characterized by a core body temperature that remains constant, even during prolonged surgery.[3,4]

Unplanned hypothermia is among the most common complications of surgery. It results from anesthesia-induced thermoregulation impairment and the heat loss inherent to surgery and the surgical environment.[5] The risk of hypothermia is greater in some patients (eg, neonates,[6,7] trauma patients,[8] patients with extensive burns[9]). All patients, however, are at risk of hypothermia as the duration of anesthesia time increases.[1,2,10,11]

Randomized clinical trials have demonstrated that mild hypothermia increases the incidence of serious adverse consequences including surgical site infections[12] and adverse cardiac events including ventricular tachycardia.[13,14] In trauma patients, hypothermia is associated with increased mortality.[15] Mild hypothermia inhibits platelet activation, resulting in increased blood loss.[16,17] A 2° C (3.6° F) drop in temperature increases blood loss by approximately 500 mL.[18] Mild hypothermia also alters medication metabolism and increases the duration of muscle relaxant action.[19,20] Hypothermia extends postanesthesia recovery time[21,22] and prolongs hospitalization.[12,23] The risk of these complications is considered greater for frail, elderly patients undergoing extensive surgery than it is for young, generally healthy patients undergoing comparatively minor procedures.[24]

Recommendation I

The perioperative registered nurse should assess the patient for risk of unplanned perioperative hypothermia.

I.a.   Perioperative registered nurses should evaluate the patient's risk for unplanned hypothermia. Sources of data include chart review, physical assessment and patient interview, and review of the anesthesia planned and proposed surgical procedure.

I.b.   Infancy or neonatal status should be considered. Neonates and infants are more susceptible to hypothermia than adults because they have a high ratio of body surface area to weight, which leads to more heat loss through their skin.[6,7] Studies show that greater temperature decreases occurred in infants and neonates when undergoing major surgery involving an open procedure.[7]

I.c.   The extent and severity of a patient's traumatic injuries should be considered.

Patients with severe traumatic injuries are more likely to be hypothermic upon hospital admission and are at high risk of development of unplanned perioperative hypothermia. Between 21% and 50% of severely injured trauma patients become hypothermic.[8] Predisposing factors include exposure in the field, blood loss and shock, rapid infusions of cool fluids, removal of clothing, and impaired heat production. Hypothermia triggers a cascade of coagulopathy and acidosis. Studies have consistently found that hypothermia increases the risk of death in trauma patients.[15,25,26] In one large study more than half of the hypothermic trauma patients died.[27]

I.d.   The extent and severity of any patient burns should be considered.

Patients with extensive burns lose body heat readily by radiation from burned tissue and convection when tissue is exposed to air currents. Burned patients are at high risk for unplanned hypothermia. The threshold for physiologic response to external temperature is set higher in these patients, triggering a metabolic response to cold at higher ambient temperatures than in unburned patients. The set point is estimated to be 0.03° C higher for each percent of total body surface area burned (eg, 50% burn = 1.5° C higher set point).[9] The natural insulating effect of skin is also impaired. The higher set point, combined with the lack of insulation, places patients with severe burns at high risk for hypothermia.

I.e.   The type and duration of planned anesthesia should be reviewed.

Hypothermia in the operating room results from impaired thermoregulation induced by anesthetic agents and exposure

to the relatively cool environment. General or major regional anesthesia (eg, epidural, spinal) for periods longer than one hour induces hypothermia. General anesthetics inhibit tonic vasoconstriction and cause vasodilatation. This results in a shift of heat from the body's core to its periphery and a drop in core temperature of approximately 1.6° C over the first hour after induction. During the subsequent two hours of anesthesia time, core temperature continues to decrease an additional 1.1° C.[1] Epidural and spinal anesthesia decrease the vasoconstriction and shivering to a slightly lesser degree, depending on the level of the block.[28,29]

I.f.   Perioperative registered nurses should be aware of factors influencing the severity of potential hypothermia in patients under general or major regional anesthesia. These factors include, but are not limited to, the following:

I.f.1.   **Older adults.** In a case control study of adult general surgery patients, increased age was found to be a predictive risk factor for perioperative hypothermia.[30] This has been found in patients receiving either general or epidural anesthesia,[31] or spinal anesthesia.[32] Older patients lose heat more rapidly than younger adults due to decreased fat or muscle mass and changes in vascular tone that inhibit vasoconstriction and decrease heat production.[32] Older patients' thermoregulatory defenses are also impaired more than younger patients by general[11] and neuraxial[33] anesthesia.

I.f.2   **Body weight.** Low body weight has been identified as a risk factor for perioperative hypothermia in general surgery patients.[30] Thin patients have a large body-surface-area-to-weight ratio and limited insulation to prevent heat loss. Obese patients have a high weight-to-body-surface ratio and maintain peripheral tissues at high temperatures due to high body fat and a consistent vasodilated state in the time before induction of anesthesia. These patients generally have low core-to-peripheral temperature gradients and little redistribution hypothermia.[34]

I.f.3. **Metabolic disorders.** Some metabolic disorders inhibit thermoregulation by impeding heat production or physiologic responses to changes in external temperatures. Central nervous system dysfunctions may cause insufficient thermoregulation. Cardiovascular diseases may cause peripheral vasoconstriction. Hypothyroidism and hypopituitarism may inhibit heat production. Patients with diabetic neuropathies have been found to have lower core body temperature after two hours of anesthesia than generally healthy adults undergoing similar surgery.[35]

I.f.4. **Chronic treatment with antipsychotics[36] or antidepressants.[37]** Antipsychotics impair the central thermoregulatory effect of the hypothalamus, resulting in decreased heat production and increased heat loss.[36] The cause of thermoregulation impairment during anesthesia in chronically depressed patients remains unclear.[37]

I.f.5. **Use of a pneumatic tourniquet.** Pneumatic tourniquets help prevent hypothermia while inflated; however, they cause abrupt hypothermia when released. Pneumatic tourniquets reduce hypothermia by preventing blood and heat exchange between the isolated extremity and the remainder of the body. More metabolic heat is thus conserved in the core thermal compartment. Upon release of the tourniquet, a redistribution of heat from the core to the extremity results in a rapid decrease in core temperature.[38-41]

I.f.6. **Cold surgical environment.** Environmental temperature determines the rate at which metabolic heat is lost through radiation and convection from the skin, and by evaporation of skin-preparation solutions.[4,42]

I.f.7. **Open-cavity surgery.** There is substantial heat loss into the relatively cool environment of the operating room from surgical incisions. This decrease in core temperature is more pronounced during large open-cavity procedures than small-cavity procedures.[4,43]

I.f.8. **Infusions of cool fluids, blood, and blood products.** A unit of refrigerated blood or one liter of crystalloid solution administered at ambient temperature decreases mean body temperature approximately 0.25° C in a 70-kg patient.[44]

I.f.9. **Cool irrigation solutions in body cavities.** Irrigation solutions placed into the abdomen, pelvis, or thorax enhance heat transfer from the body core to the solution and increase heat loss.

I.g. Patients' preoperative baseline temperature should be assessed. When preoperative hypothermia is identified, interventions should be undertaken to normalize patients' core temperature before surgery when possible. Preexisting hypothermia is considered one of the most significant contributing factors to intraoperative hypothermia.[6]

Recommendation II

The perioperative registered nurse should develop a plan of care to minimize the risk of unplanned perioperative hypothermia in patients identified at risk.

II.a. The perioperative registered nurse should establish expected outcomes and collaborate with anesthesia care providers in the selection of appropriate temperature monitoring technology and interventions to reduce the risk of unplanned hypothermia.

II.b. The perioperative registered nurse should identify and assure the availability of temperature monitoring technology and patient warming equipment and supplies, as needed, and adjust environmental conditions according to individualized patient needs.[45]

Recommendation III

Equipment to monitor core temperature should be selected based upon reliability and access to the route.

III.a.   The perioperative registered nurse should ensure that equipment to monitor the patient's temperature is readily available. Temperature monitoring devices that provide the most accurate and consistent readings during each phase of perioperative care should be selected. The selection of the best monitoring device should depend upon the accuracy of measuring core body temperature, reliability of the device, accessibility of the monitoring site, patient safety, and ease of use. The ideal thermometer should be accurate within +/– 0.1° C and not sensitive to outside temperature influences.[46] The device should accurately identify temperatures that are above and below normal.

III.a.1.   There are four reliable sites for measurement of core temperature:
- **Tympanic membrane.** The tympanic membrane temperature, measured by a thermocouple, is the preferred method in many preoperative and postoperative areas.[47,48] This method is noninvasive, and the monitoring site receives blood supply from the carotid artery, which supplies the thermoregulatory center of the hypothalamus.
- **Distal esophagus.** The distal esophagus is considered a desirable site to measure temperature, particularly in the operating room, and is less prone to artifact than most others. It is an alternative to the pulmonary artery and is widely used intraoperatively. Placement of the probe in the lower fourth of the esophagus prevents artifactual cooling of the probe by respiratory gases.[48]
- **Nasopharynx.** The nasopharynx is another reliable monitoring site for intraoperative measurement because it approximates core temperature.[48] A thermistor probe is inserted through the nares to the nasopharynx. Measurements may be influenced by the temperature of inspired gases and often are 0.5° C lower than pulmonary artery temperatures.[49,50]

- **Pulmonary artery.** The most accurate measurement of core body temperature is through the pulmonary artery, which is bathed in blood from the core.[48] This invasive form of monitoring, however, is not justified solely for temperature assessment.

III.a.2.   Less reliable sites for estimating core temperature include the following:
- **Axillary.** Temperatures can be measured through a thermocouple or an infrared axillary reading. Axillary temperatures are not accurate.[51-58] Readings have been found to be significantly lower than pulmonary artery measurements.[52] Accuracy of readings in pediatric patients has been shown to decrease as temperature increases.[55]
- **Bladder.** Temperatures can be measured using urinary catheters containing temperature transducers. Bladder temperatures are close to core temperature, but the accuracy of the measurement decreases during cardiopulmonary bypass,[59] when the patient is hypothermic and urinary output is lower,[50] and during lower abdominal surgery. This method is a better approximation of core temperature than rectal or axillary methods.[59]
- **Oral.** A systematic review of research studies comparing oral temperatures taken at the posterior sublingual site found that in the absence of a pulmonary catheter, this method provides a reliable estimate of core temperature, even in intubated patients.[48] This method does not detect malignant hyperthermia, however, and is not recommended for intraoperative use.
- **Rectal.** Temperatures taken by the rectal route are directly related to the area's blood flow, and measurements seriously lag behind core temperatures.[50,60] This method of measurement does not appropriately detect malignant hyperthermia and is not a good alternative for general use.[61,62]

- **Skin.** Skin temperature may be measured using a crystal skin-surface thermometer. Studies have demonstrated that peripheral skin temperature correlates poorly with core temperature.[58,63] A recent study found that redistribution of body heat has little effect on the core-to-forehead temperature difference.[64]

- **Temporal artery.** Temporal artery temperature may be measured noninvasively with a scanner probe attached to the forehead. The temporal artery is a branch of the carotid artery and provides a measurement of core temperature; however, this method has been found to be unreliable.[65-67]

III.b. Equipment selected for measuring temperature should be free of mercury. Mercury is a heavy metal that can cause serious adverse health consequences, including chromosomal abnormalities. Environmental contamination can cause harmful effects on wildlife. Mercury thermometers are identifiable by the liquid mercury bubble used for reading the thermometer. Disposal of mercury is regulated by the Resource Conservation and Recovery Act.[68,69]

III.c. Temperature monitoring devices should be used according to the manufacturers' written instructions. Manufacturers' instructions provide details that may enhance the reliability of measurements.

Recommendation IV

The core temperature of patients at risk for unplanned hypothermia should be monitored preoperatively, intraoperatively, and postoperatively.

Monitoring patient temperature alerts the provider to the need for preventive or corrective action. Changes can be a decrease in core temperature or an increase in temperature associated with application of a heating device or inflation of a pneumatic tourniquet. It is important to measure core temperature because peripheral temperature is often significantly different from core temperature. The perception of cold is an inadequate measure. For example, hypothermia during regional

anesthesia may not trigger a perception of cold by the patient.[62]

IV.a. The patient's temperature should be assessed preoperatively. Assessment of the patient's temperature preoperatively provides a baseline for planning patient care. This assessment alerts care providers of the need to treat preexisting hypothermia or to avoid overheating the patient with an elevated temperature.

IV.b. The patient's core body temperature should be monitored intraoperatively. Intraoperative temperature monitoring is used to provide information to prevent or mitigate hypothermia and to avoid overheating.

IV.c. The temperature of patients should be monitored when undergoing general anesthesia that exceeds 30 minutes and during regional anesthesia when changes are anticipated or suspected.[62]

IV.c.1. The American Society of Anesthesiologists (ASA) recommends that temperature be continually evaluated and monitored "when clinically significant changes in body temperature are intended, anticipated, or suspected."[70]

IV.c.2. The American Association of Nurse Anesthetists recommends monitoring body temperature continuously in pediatric patients receiving general anesthesia and, when indicated, on all patients.[71]

IV.d. The patient's core body temperature should be evaluated postoperatively. The patient's postoperative core temperature provides a basis for evaluation of the effectiveness of intraoperative measures to prevent unplanned hypothermia and provides data to guide the postoperative plan of care.

IV.e. Abnormal patient temperatures should be communicated to the appropriate patient care providers. Managing the patient's temperature requires a coordinated effort among members of the entire perioperative team.

Recommendation V

Interventions should be implemented to prevent unplanned hypothermia.

V.a.   Prewarming the patient for a minimum of 15 minutes immediately prior to induction of anesthesia should be considered for patients at risk of unplanned hypothermia. Warming the patient's skin and peripheral tissues before induction of general or major regional anesthesia prevents redistribution hypothermia. The temperature of the peripheral tissues is increased and vasodilatation triggered. This results in a smaller core to periphery temperature gradient and minimizes the effect of anesthesia-induced vasodilatation.

In a randomized clinical trail of patients undergoing cesarean section, 15 minutes of prewarming and intraoperative forced-air warming resulted in a higher core body temperature in both patients and their infants.[72] In outpatients, 15 minutes of forced-air prewarming resulted in higher core body temperatures upon arrival in the postanesthesia care unit, when compared to prewarming with warm cotton blankets.[73] In a study of volunteers, 30 minutes of forced-air warming resulted in an increase in peripheral temperature determined to be more than the amount typically redistributed from core to periphery under anesthesia.[74]

V.b.   Patients should be kept normothermic intraoperatively. Patients who remain normothermic intraoperatively experience fewer adverse outcomes. Insulating blankets (eg, cotton, reflective) reduce heat loss by 30%,[75,76] but this is usually insufficient to prevent hypothermia in anesthetized patients.[77] Circulating fluid mattresses under the patient are nearly ineffective at minimizing the risk of hypothermia.[62,78-81] The patient's body weight, in combination with the heat of the fluid mattress, increases the risk of pressure ulcer or necrosis.[62]

V.c.   Effective methods of preventing unplanned hypothermia should be used. These methods involve skin surface warming including, but not limited to, the following:

- **Forced-air warming,** which is safe and the most widely used skin surface warming method. The efficacy of forced-air warming in preventing unplanned hypothermia has been proven in many clinical trials.[11,81-86] The method is effective in neonates,[87] pediatric patients,[85] and morbidly obese patients.[88] Forced-air warming has also been found to be effective in rewarming patients after cardiopulmonary bypass.[89-91] Forced-air warming does not increase the risk of wound contamination.[83,92]

- **Circulating-water garments** that circulate warm water through a special, segmented, conductive-heating garment wrapped around the patient. This method has been found to effectively transfer heat to the patient and maintains normothermia in adult[93-97] and pediatric patients.[98] Circulating-water garments maintained normothermia better than a combination of water blanket and fluid warmer in patients undergoing on-pump[96] or off-pump[94,95] cardiopulmonary bypass. Studies have shown that more heat is transferred to the patient by a circulating water garment than forced-air warming.[97] Compared to an upper body forced-air blanket, normothermia was maintained better using the circulating-water garments in patients undergoing abdominal surgery.[99] Circulating-water garments have also been found to effectively rewarm patients after cardiopulmonary bypass[94,100,101] and to rewarm hypothermic patients better than a full-body forced-air blanket.[97]

- **Energy transfer pads** that circulate water through a set of heat-exchange pads that adhere to the patient's skin. Energy transfer pads have been found to be an effective tool to reduce intraoperative hypothermia during off-pump cardiac surgery.[102]

V.d.   Warming intravenous (IV) fluids should be considered only if large volumes (ie, more than 2 liters/hour for adults) are being administered. Warming IV fluids to near 37° C (98.6° F) prevents heat loss from the administration of cold IV fluids and should be considered as an adjunct to skin surface warming. When less than 2 liters of volume is given, fluid warming is of limited value because fluid-induced cooling is minimal.

In studies of patients undergoing major surgery, the combination of forced-air warming and fluid warming decreased the risk of hypothermia more than forced-air warming alone.[103,104] In one study, however, the average temperature in patients in both groups was normothermic.[104] Fluid warming is not a substitute for forced-air warming, which usually transfers far more heat, and warmed fluids alone will not usually keep patients normothermic.[60,104,105] When fluids are being warmed, technology designed for this purpose should be used according to the manufacturers' written instructions.

V.e. Warming irrigation solutions to be used inside the abdomen, pelvis, or thorax should be considered. Warmed irrigation fluid [near 37° C (98.6° F)] should be used as adjunct therapy to decrease heat loss, but it is insufficient alone to prevent hypothermia. In a study of patients undergoing laparoscopy without forced-air warming, patients receiving warmed irrigation solutions maintained higher core body temperatures than those receiving room temperature solutions;[24,106] however, warmed irrigation fluids alone did not prevent hypothermia.[106] No improvement in body temperature was found when using warmed irrigation during arthroscopic surgery.[107] When using warmed irrigation solutions, the temperature of the solution should be measured with a thermometer at the point of use and verified before instillation. Irrigating with hot solutions has resulted in patient injuries.

V.f. Increasing the room temperature should be considered when active skin warming is not feasible, or in addition to active skin warming in cases where active skin warming alone is insufficient. When a large surface area must be exposed for the surgical procedure, forced-air warming may not be sufficient. For these patients, the severity of hypothermia may be reduced by raising the room temperature to more than 23° C (73.4° F).[62,108] In orthopedic procedures, normothermia was successfully maintained without forced-air warming when the room temperature remained above 26° C (78.8° F).[109]

V.g. Equipment to humidify warm anesthetic gases should be available for pediatric patients. Less than 10% of metabolic heat is lost through the respiratory tract, and heating and humidification of the airway have little effect on core temperature.[62] This intervention is more effective in infants and children.[110] This method transfers much less heat than forced air and should not be used in lieu of forced-air warming.

V.h. Skin preparation solutions should be used at a temperature recommended by the solution manufacturer. Heating some skin preparation agents may increase the risk of a chemical or thermal burn. Heating flammable antimicrobial skin preparation agents creates a fire hazard. Manufacturers' written instructions provide guidance for the appropriate storage temperature.

V.i. Additional precautions should be taken to prevent unplanned hypothermia in infants and neonates.

V.i.1. The room should be prewarmed and maintained higher than 26° C (78.8° F).[62] In a study of anesthetized neonates and infants, operating room temperatures less than 23° C (73.4° F) increased the risk of hypothermia by 1.96 times.[7]

V.i.2. Skin exposure should be minimized and limited in time as much as possible.

V.i.3. Equipment should be available to humidify and warm the airway. Active humidification and heating of inspired gases has been found to result in a 0.25° to 0.5° C higher core temperature in infants.[110,111]

V.i.4. Equipment should be available to warm IV fluids.[112]

V.i.5. Irrigation fluids should be warmed to normal body temperature (37° C [98.6° F]) and the fluid temperature verified before use. Instillation of warmed irrigation fluids minimizes heat lost through radiation.

V.i.6. Patient temperature should be monitored continuously intraoperatively. An infant's temperature decreases within 10 minutes after induction of anesthesia.[7] Vigorous warming may cause hyperthermia. Continuous monitoring provides early identification of temperature changes, including hyperthermia caused by overheating.

V.j. Additional precautions should be taken to prevent unplanned hypothermia in patients with severe trauma.

V.j.1. Patients with severe trauma are at risk of hypothermia. In this patient population, hypothermia is associated with increased risk of death.[113] The patient may be hypothermic upon arrival in the perioperative area. Forced-air warming may not be appropriate because of the amount of tissue exposed for the surgical procedure. Extra measures are required to minimize heat loss if forced-air warming is contraindicated and may be necessary in addition to forced-air warming.

V.j.2. The room temperature should be prewarmed higher than 29.4° C (85° F).[45,114]

V.j.3. The room temperature should be maintained higher than 29.4° C (85° F) until active warming devices achieve normothermia.[45,114]

V.j.4. Equipment should be available to warm IV fluids. Large volumes of fluids may be given rapidly to stabilize the patient. Warming these fluids minimizes heat lost through radiation.

V.j.5. Irrigation fluids should be warmed to normal body temperature (ie, 37° C [98.6° F]).

V.j.6. Equipment should be available to humidify and warm the airway.

V.j.7. Patient temperature should be monitored continuously intraoperatively.

V.k. Additional precautions should be taken to prevent unplanned hypothermia in patients with extensive burns.

V.k.1. Forced-air warming should be used when feasible. It may not be feasible for patients with extensive burns, however,

when a large amount of tissue must be exposed for the surgical procedure. Extra measures are required for extensive burns to minimize heat loss.

V.k.2. The room temperature should be prewarmed and maintained higher than 29.4° C (85° F). High ambient temperatures minimize heat loss through radiation and convection.

V.k.3. Body surfaces not involved in the surgical procedure should be covered. Covering these surfaces minimizes heat lost through convection.

V.k.4. Equipment should be available to warm IV fluids.

V.k.5. Irrigation fluids should be warmed to near 37° C (98.6° F).

V.k.6. Equipment should be available to warm and humidify anesthetic gases.

V.k.7. Intraoperative patient temperature should be monitored continuously.

Recommendation VI

Warming devices should be used in a manner that minimizes the potential for patient injuries.

IV.a. Prewarming and continued normothermia management must be provided using only US Food and Drug Administration (FDA)-cleared devices.

IV.b Intravenous fluid bags or irrigation bottles of heated fluid should not be used to warm patients' skin. In 1994, the ASA Closed Claims Project reported that 52% of burn injuries in the operating room were associated with the use of unapproved devices. Sixty-four percent of these injuries resulted from using heated IV fluid bags to warm patients' skin.[115]

IV.c. Warming devices should be used in accordance with manufacturers' written instructions and in a manner that minimizes the potential for injury. Forced-air warming technology should be used only with the appropriate blanket attached to the hose. The hose end has a dangerously high air temperature, and the blanket serves to disperse this heat. Using the air unit without a blanket has resulted in serious burns.[116,117] Intravenous fluid should be warmed only by technology designed for this purpose, at temperatures recommended by the fluid manufacturer.

IV.d.   Ischemic tissue should never be heated. Heat is inadequately distributed in ischemic tissue, and application of heat increases the risk of thermal injury.

Recommendation VII

Competency
Personnel should receive initial education and competency validation and updates on the prevention of unplanned hypothermia and the use of warming equipment.

VII.a. Personnel providing perioperative patient care should be knowledgeable about principles of thermoregulation, risks and consequences of hypothermia, correct use of temperature measurement technology, and measures to minimize the risk of unplanned hypothermia. Personnel should be instructed in the proper operation, care, and handling of warming devices and accessories before use. Initial education of the underlying principles of unplanned hypothermia provides direction for personnel in providing safe care. Additional, periodic educational programs provide reinforcement of these principles and new information on changes in technology, its application, compatibility of equipment and accessories, and potential hazards.

VII.b. Administrative personnel should assess and document annual competency of personnel in prevention of unplanned hypothermia and safe use of warming devices and accessories according to hospital and department policy. Incorrect use of warming devices can result in serious injury to patients. Competency assurance verifies that personnel have a basic understanding of thermoregulation, risks of unplanned hypothermia, and safe use of warming equipment. This knowledge is essential to minimizing the risks of misuse of the equipment and to providing safe care.

Recommendation VIII

Documentation
Patient assessments, the plan of care, interventions implemented, and evaluation of care to prevent unplanned perioperative hypothermia should be documented.

VIII.a. Documentation should include a patient assessment, a plan of care, nursing diagnoses, identification of desired outcomes, interventions, and an evaluation of the patient's response to care provided. The Perioperative Nursing Data Set (PNDS), the uniform perioperative nursing vocabulary, should be used to document patient care and to develop policies and procedures related to prevention of unplanned perioperative hypothermia.

VIII.a.1. Potential diagnoses include:
- Risk for imbalanced body temperature (X57),
- Ineffective thermoregulation (X58), and
- Hypothermia (X26).[45]

VIII.a.2. An expected outcome of primary importance to these recommended practices is "The patient is at or returning to normothermia at the conclusion of the immediate postoperative period." (O12) This outcome falls within the physiologic domain (D2).[45]

VIII.a.3. Interventions that may lead to the desired outcome include the following: assesses risks for unplanned hypothermia (I131); implements thermoregulation measures (I78); monitors body temperature (I86); and evaluates response to thermoregulation measures (I55).[45]

VIII.b. The patient's temperature and the interventions taken to protect him or her from unplanned hypothermia should be documented in the perioperative record. Documentation should include, but not be limited to,
- preoperative assessment with baseline temperature measure;
- plan of care for prevention of hypothermia;
- patient temperature measurements taken throughout perioperative care;

- use of temperature-regulating devices, including identification of the unit and temperature settings used;
- other thermoregulation interventions; and
- postoperative outcome evaluation.

Recommendation IX

Policies and Procedures

Policies and procedures for prevention of unplanned hypothermia should be developed in collaboration with anesthesia care providers, reviewed periodically, revised as necessary, and readily available in the practice setting.

IX.a. These recommended practices should be used as guidelines for the development of policies and procedures in the perioperative practice setting. Policies and procedures establish authority, responsibility, and accountability within the facility. They also serve as operational guidelines.

IX.b. Policies and procedures for prevention of unplanned hypothermia should be developed and include, but not be limited to,
- preoperative, intraoperative, and postoperative patient assessments;
- interventions to be employed;
- documentation of care provided;
- use, care, and cleaning of equipment;
- maintenance of equipment;
- reporting and removal from service of malfunctioning equipment;
- reporting of incidence of hypothermia or injuries; and
- competency verification.

IX.c. Policies and procedures should be reviewed and revised at regularly scheduled intervals and be readily available in the practice setting.

Recommendation X

Quality

A quality improvement/management program should be in place to evaluate the structure, process, and outcomes of interventions used to protect patients from unplanned perioperative hypothermia.

X.a. Unplanned hypothermia should be evaluated as part of the perioperative quality management program. The patient out-comes of preventive measures should be evaluated. Outcomes in high-risk populations should be included (eg, neonates, infants, severe trauma, burn patients). The Surgical Care Improvement Project includes "colorectal surgery patients with immediate postoperative normothermia" as an evidence-based indicator of quality.[118]

X.b. Measures should be implemented as necessary to minimize the incidence of unplanned hypothermia. Corrective measures may include increasing the availability of warming equipment and educational programs, and providing clinicians with feedback about outcomes.

X.c. Adverse events related to warming devices should be reported through the facility's incident reporting system and investigated in compliance with the Safe Medical Devices Act of 1990, amended in March 2000.[119]

X.d. Adverse events should be investigated and analyzed to minimize the risk of recurrence. An injury related to the use of a warming device must be reported to the FDA. Serious injuries and deaths must be reported to the FDA and manufacturer within 10 days. Device identification, maintenance and service information, and adverse event information should be included in the report from the practice setting. Retaining the equipment and accessories allows for a complete evaluation and facilitates determination of the cause of the injury. Semiannual reports must be submitted to the FDA as follow-up to any adverse event report submitted during the previous six-month period.

Glossary

Active skin warming: The application of conductive, convective, or radiative warming to the skin.

Ambient temperature: The temperature of the immediate environment, usually ranging from 20° C to 25° C (68° F to 77° F).

Circulating-fluid garment: A microprocessor-controlled heating and cooling device with temperature sensors; skin thermistor; and a specially designed, segmented garment that wraps around the patient.

Core temperature: The temperature of the thermal compartment of the body containing highly perfused tissues and major organs.

Energy transfer pads: A servo-regulated system circulating temperature-controlled water through energy transfer pads adhered to the patient's skin and used to cool or warm the patient.

Forced-air warming: Convection warming technology dispersing a blanket of warm air over the patient's skin in a controlled manner.

Infant: A child one month after birth to approximately 12 months of age.

Mild hypothermia: A core temperature between 34° C to 36° C (93.2° F to 96.8° F).[24]

Neonate: An infant from birth to 28 days of age.

Neuraxia anesthesia: Spinal or epidural regional nerve blocks.

Normothermia: A core temperature between 36° C to 38° C (96.8° F to 100.4° F).

Passive insulation: Method of containing body heat and insulate the body from heat loss through radiation (eg, blankets, clothing).

Redistribution hypothermia: A decrease in body temperature occurring as heat is exchanged from the body's core compartment to the peripheral tissues.

Thermistor: An electrical resistor using a semiconductor whose resistance varies sharply in a known manner with the temperature.

Thermocouple: A device for measuring temperature in which a pair of wires of dissimilar metals is joined and the free ends connected to an instrument that measures the difference in potential created at the junction of the two metals.

Thermometer: An instrument for measuring temperature.

Thermostat: A device that automatically establishes and mains a desired temperature.

REFERENCES

1. Matsukawa T, Sessler DI, Christensen R, Ozaki M, Schroeder M. Heat flow and distribution during epidural anesthesia. *Anesthesiology.* 1995;83:961-967.

2. Matsukawa T, Sessler DI, Sessler AM, Schroeder M, Ozaki M, Kurz A, Cheng C. Heat flow and distribution during induction of general anesthesia. *Anesthesiology.* 1995;82:662-673.

3. Buggy DJ, Crossley AW. Thermoregulation, mild perioperative hypothermia and postanaesthetic shivering. *Br J Anaesth.* 2000;84:615-628.

4. Sessler DI. Perioperative heat balance. *Anesthesiology.* 2000;92:578-596.

5. Sessler DI. Perioperative thermoregulation and heat balance. *Ann N Y Acad Sci.* 1997;813:757-777.

6. Macario A, Dexter F. What are the most important risk factors for a patient's developing intraoperative hypothermia? *Anesth Analg.* 2002;94:215-220.

7. Tander B, Baris S, Karakaya D, Ariturk E, Rizalar R, Bernay F. Risk factors influencing inadvertent hypothermia in infants and neonates during anesthesia. *Paediatr Anaesth.* 2005;15:574-579.

8. Tisherman S. Hypothermia, cold injury, and drowning. In: Peitzman A, Rhodes M, Schwab C, Yealy D, Fabian T, eds. *The Trauma Manual,* 2nd ed. Philadelphia: Lippincott, Williams, & Wilkins; 2002:404-410.

9. Caldwell FT, Jr., Wallace BH, Cone JB. The effect of wound management on the interaction of burn size, heat production, and rectal temperature. *J Burn Care Rehabil.* 1994;15:121-129.

10. Sessler DI, Moayeri A, Stoen R, Glosten B, Hynson J, McGuire J. Thermoregulatory vasoconstriction decreases cutaneous heat loss. *Anesthesiology.* 1990;73:656-660.

11. Kurz A, Plattner O, Sessler DI, Huemer G, Redl G, Lackner F. The threshold for thermoregulatory vasoconstriction during nitrous oxide/isoflurane anesthesia is lower in elderly than in young patients. *Anesthesiology.* 1993;79:465-469.

12. Kurz A, Sessler DI, Lenhardt R. Perioperative normothermia to reduce the incidence of surgical-wound infection and shorten hospitalization. Study of Wound Infection and Temperature Group. *N Engl J Med.* 1996;334:1209-1215.

13. Flores-Maldonado A, Guzman-Llanez Y, Castaneda-Zarate S, Pech-Colli J, Alvarez-Nemegyei J, Cervera-Saenz M, Canto-Rubio A, Terrazas-Olguin MA. Risk factors for mild intraoperative hypothermia. *Arch Med Res.* 1997;28:587-590.

14. Frank SM, Beattie C, Christopherson R, Norris EJ, Perler BA, Williams GM, Gottlieb SO. Unintentional hypothermia is associated with postoperative myocardial ischemia. The Perioperative Ischemia Randomized Anesthesia Trial Study Group. *Anesthesiology.* 1993;78:468-476.

15. Gentilello LM, Jurkovich GJ, Stark MS, Hassantash SA, O'Keefe GE. Is hypothermia in the victim of major trauma protective or harmful? A randomized, prospective study. *Ann Surg.* 1997;226:439-447; discussion 447-439.

16. Michelson AD, MacGregor H, Barnard MR, Kestin AS, Rohrer MJ, Valeri CR. Reversible inhibition of human platelet activation by hypothermia in vivo and in vitro. *Thromb Haemost.* 1994;71:633-640.

17. Reed RL, 2nd, Johnson TD, Hudson JD, Fischer RP. The disparity between hypothermic coagulopathy and clotting studies. *J Trauma.* 1992;33:465-470.

18. Schmied H, Kurz A, Sessler DI, Kozek S, Reiter A. Mild hypothermia increases blood loss and transfusion requirements during total hip arthroplasty. *Lancet.* 1996;347:289-292.

19. Heier T, Caldwell JE. Impact of hypothermia on the response to neuromuscular blocking drugs. *Anesthesiology.* 2006;104:1070-1080.

20. Leslie K, Sessler DI, Bjorksten AR, Moayeri A. Mild hypothermia alters propofol pharmacokinetics and increases the duration of action of atracurium. *Anesth Analg.* 1995;80:1007-1014.

21. Kurz A, Sessler DI, Narzt E, Bekar A, Lenhardt R, Huemer G, Lackner F. Postoperative hemodynamic and thermoregulatory consequences of intraoperative core hypothermia. *J Clin Anesth.* 1995;7:359-366.

22. Lenhardt R, Marker E, Goll V, Tschernich H, Kurz A, Sessler DI, Narzt E, Lackner F. Mild intraoperative hypothermia prolongs postanesthetic recovery. *Anesthesiology.* 1997;87:1318-1323.

23. Frank SM, Fleisher LA, Breslow MJ, Higgins MS, Olson KF, Kelly S, Beattie C. Perioperative maintenance of normothermia reduces the incidence of morbid cardiac events. A randomized clinical trial. *JAMA.* 9 1997;277:1127-1134.

24. Sessler DI. Complications and treatment of mild hypothermia. *Anesthesiology.* 2001;95:531-543.

25. Jurkovich GJ, Greiser WB, Luterman A, Currerri PW. Hypothermia in trauma victims: an ominous predictor of survival. *J Trauma.* 1987;27:1019-1024.

26. Luna GK, Maier RV, Pavlin EG, Anardi D, Copass MK, Oreskovich MR. Incidence and effect of hypothermia in seriously injured patients. *J Trauma.* 1987;27:1014-1018.

27. Rutherford EJ, Fusco MA, Nunn CR, Bass JG, Eddy VA, Morris JA, Jr. Hypothermia in critically ill trauma patients. *Injury.* 1998;29:605-608.

28. Sessler DI, Moayeri A. Skin-surface warming: heat flux and central temperature. *Anesthesiology.* 1990;73:218-224.

29. Kurz A, Sessler DI, Schroeder M, Kurz M. Thermoregulatory response thresholds during spinal anesthesia. *Anesth Analg.* 1993;77:721-726.

30. Kasai T, Hirose M, Yaegashi K, Matsukawa T, Takamata A, Tanaka Y. Preoperative risk factors of intraoperative hypothermia in major surgery under general anesthesia. *Anesth Analg.* 2002;95:1381-1383.

31. Frank SM, Shir Y, Raja SN, Fleisher LA, Beattie C. Core hypothermia and skin-surface temperature gradients. Epidural versus general anesthesia and the effects of age. *Anesthesiology.* 1994;80:502-508.

32. Frank SM, Raja SN, Bulcao C, Goldstein DS. Age-related thermoregulatory differences during core cooling in humans. *Am J Physiol Regul Integr Comp Physiol.* 2000; 279:R349-354.

33. Vassilieff N, Rosencher N, Sessler DI, Conseiller C. Shivering threshold during spinal anesthesia is reduced in elderly patients. *Anesthesiology.* 1995;83:1162-1166.

34. Kurz A, Sessler DI, Narzt E, Lenhardt R, Lackner F. Morphometric influences on intraoperative core temperature changes. *Anesth Analg.* 1995;80:562-567.

35. Kitamura A, Hoshino T, Kon T, Ogawa R. Patients with diabetic neuropathy are at risk of a greater intraoperative reduction in core temperature. *Anesthesiology.* 2000;92:1311-1318.

36. Kudoh A, Takase H, Takazawa T. Chronic treatment with antipsychotics enhances intraoperative core hypothermia. *Anesth Analg.* 2004;98:111-115.

37. Kudoh A, Takase H, Takazawa T. Chronic treatment with antidepressants decreases intraoperative core hypothermia. *Anesth Analg.* 2003;97:275-279.

38. Estebe JP, Le Naoures A, Malledant Y, Ecoffey C. Use of a pneumatic tourniquet induces changes in central temperature. *Br J Anaesth.* 1996;77:786-788.

39. Sanders BJ, D'Alessio JG, Jernigan JR. Intraoperative hypothermia associated with lower extremity tourniquet deflation. *J Clin Anesth.* 1996;8:504-507.

40. Akata T, Kanna T, Izumi K, Kodama K, Takahashi S. Changes in body temperature following deflation of limb pneumatic tourniquet. *J Clin Anesth.* 1998;10:17-22.

41. Bloch EC, Ginsberg B, Binner RA, Jr., Sessler DI. Limb tourniquets and central temperature in anesthetized children. *Anesth Analg.* 1992;74:486-489.

42. Sessler DI, Sessler AM, Hudson S, Moayeri A. Heat loss during surgical skin preparation. *Anesthesiology.* 1993;78:1055-1064.

43. Roe CF. Effect of bowel exposure on body temperature during surgical operations. *Am J Surg.* 1971; 122:13-15.

44. Sessler DI. Consequences and treatment of perioperative hypothermia. *Anesthesiology Clinics of North America.* 1994;23:425-456.

45. Felciano D. Abdominal vascular injury. In: Moore E, Feliciano D, Mattox K, eds. *Trauma.* 5th ed. New York, NY: McGraw-Hill; 2002:755-880.

46. Moran DS, Mendal L. Core temperature measurement: methods and current insights. *Sports Med.* 2002; 32:879-885.

47. American Society of PeriAnesthesia Nurses. Clinical guideline for the prevention of unplanned perioperative hypothermia. *J Perianesth Nurs.* 2001;16:305-314.

48. Hooper VD, Andrews JO. Accuracy of noninvasive core temperature measurement in acutely ill adults: the state of the science. *Biol Res Nurs.* 2006;8:24-34.

49. Ilsley AH, Rutten AJ, Runciman WB. An evaluation of body temperature measurement. *Anaesth Intensive Care.* 1983;11:31-39.

50. Holtzclaw BJ. Monitoring body temperature. *AACN Clin Issues Crit Care Nurs.* 1993;4:44-55.

51. Bailey J, Rose P. Axillary and tympanic membrane temperature recording in the preterm neonate: a comparative study. *J Adv Nurs.* 2001;34:465-474.

52. Erickson RS, Kirklin SK. Comparison of ear-based, bladder, oral, and axillary methods for core temperature measurement. *Crit Care Med.* 1993;21:1528-1534.

53. Giuffre M, Heidenreich T, Carney-Gersten P, Dorsch JA, Heidenreich E. The relationship between axillary and core body temperature measurements. *Appl Nurs Res.* 1990;3:52-55.

54. Hicks MA. A comparison of the tympanic and axillary temperatures of the preterm and term infant. *J Perinatol.* 1996;16:261-267.

55. Jean-Mary MB, Dicanzio J, Shaw J, Bernstein HH. Limited accuracy and reliability of infrared axillary and aural thermometers in a pediatric outpatient population. *J Pediatr.* 2002;141:671-676.

56. Jensen BN, Jensen FS, Madsen SN, Lossl K. Accuracy of digital tympanic, oral, axillary, and rectal thermometers compared with standard rectal mercury thermometers. *Eur J Surg.* 2000;166:848-851.

57. Weiss ME, Richards MT. Accuracy of electronic axillary temperature measurement in term and preterm neonates. *Neonatal Netw.* 1994;13:35-40.

58. Cork RC, Vaughan RW, Humphrey LS. Precision and accuracy of intraoperative temperature monitoring. *Anesth Analg.* 1983;62:211-214.

59. Lefrant JY, Muller L, de La Coussaye JE, Benbabaali M, Lebris C, Zeitoun N, Mari C, Saissi G, Ripart J, Eledjam JJ. Temperature measurement in intensive care patients: comparison of urinary bladder, oesophageal, rectal, axillary, and inguinal methods versus pulmonary artery core method. *Intensive Care Med.* 2003;29:414-418.

60. Lenhardt R. Monitoring and thermal management. *Best Pract Res Clin Anaesthesiol.* 2003;17:569-581.

61. Iaizzo PA, Kehler CH, Zink RS, Belani KG, Sessler DI. Thermal response in acute porcine malignant hyperthermia. *Anesth Analg.* 1996;82:782-789.

62. Sessler DI. Temperature Monitoring. In: Miller RD, ed. *Miller's Anesthesia.* 6th ed. Philadelphia, PA: Elsevier; 2005:1571-1597.

63. Bissonnette B, Sessler DI, LaFlamme P. Intraoperative temperature monitoring sites in infants and children and the effect of inspired gas warming on esophageal temperature. *Anesth Analg.* 1989;69:192-196.

64. Ikeda T, Sessler DI, Marder D, Xiong J. Influence of thermoregulatory vasomotion and ambient temperature variation on the accuracy of core-temperature estimates by cutaneous liquid-crystal thermometers. *Anesthesiology.* 1997;86:603-612.

65. Hebbar K, Fortenberry JD, Rogers K, Merritt R, Easley K. Comparison of temporal artery thermometer to standard temperature measurements in pediatric intensive care unit patients. *Pediatr Crit Care Med.* 2005;6:557-561.

66. Suleman MI, Doufas AG, Akca O, Ducharme M, Sessler DI. Insufficiency in a new temporal-artery thermometer for adult and pediatric patients. *Anesth Analg.* 2002;95:67-71.

67. Greenes DS, Fleisher GR. Accuracy of a noninvasive temporal artery thermometer for use in infants. *Arch Pediatr Adolesc Med.* 2001;155:376-381.

68. AORN guidance statement: environmental responsibility. In: *Standards, Recommended Practices, and Guidelines.* 2006 ed. Denver: AORN, Inc; 2006:243-250.

69. U.S. Environmental Protection Agency. Mercury. Available at: *http://www.epa.gov/mercury/index.htm.* Accessed August 26, 2006.

70. American Society of Anesthesiologists. Standards for basic anesthetic monitoring. Available at: *http://: www.asahq.org/publicationsAndServices/standards/02 .pdf.* Accessed August 26, 2006.

71. Scope and standards for nurse anesthesia practice. *Professional Practice Manual for the Certified Registered Nurse Anesthetist.* Park Ridge, IL: American Association of Nurse Anesthetists; 1996:1-4.

72. Horn EP, Schroeder F, Gottschalk A, Sessler DI, Hiltmeyer N, Standl T, Schulte am Esch J. Active warming during cesarean delivery. *Anesth Analg.* 2002;94:409-414.

73. Fossum S, Hays J, Henson MM. A comparison study on the effects of prewarming patients in the outpatient surgery setting. *J Perianesth Nurs.* 2001;16:187-194.

74. Sessler DI, Schroeder M, Merrifield B, Matsukawa T, Cheng C. Optimal duration and temperature of prewarming. *Anesthesiology.* 1995;82:674-681.

75. Sessler DI, Schroeder M. Heat loss in humans covered with cotton hospital blankets. *Anesth Analg.* 1993;77:73-77.

76. Sessler DI, McGuire J, Sessler AM. Perioperative thermal insulation. *Anesthesiology.* 1991;74:875-879.

77. Ng SF, Oo CS, Loh KH, Lim PY, Chan YH, Ong BC. A comparative study of three warming interventions to determine the most effective in maintaining perioperative normothermia. *Anesth Analg.* 2003;96:171-176.

78. Matsuzaki Y, Matsukawa T, Ohki K, Yamamoto Y, Nakamura M, Oshibuchi T. Warming by resistive heating maintains perioperative normothermia as well as forced air heating. *Br J Anaesth.* 2003;90:689-691.

79. Morris RH, Kumar A. The effect of warming blankets on maintenance of body temperature of the anesthetized, paralyzed adult patient. *Anesthesiology.* 1972;36:408-411.

80. Negishi C, Hasegawa K, Mukai S, Nakagawa F, Ozaki M, Sessler DI. Resistive-heating and forced-air warming are comparably effective. *Anesth Analg.* 2003;96:1683-1687.

81. Hynson JM, Sessler DI. Intraoperative warming therapies: a comparison of three devices. *J Clin Anesth.* 1992;4:194-199.

82. Borms SF, Engelen SL, Himpe DG, Suy MR, Theunissen WJ. Bair hugger forced-air warming maintains normothermia more effectively than thermo-lite insulation. *J Clin Anesth.* 1994;6:303-307.

83. Huang JK, Shah EF, Vinodkumar N, Hegarty MA, Greatorex RA. The Bair Hugger patient warming system in prolonged vascular surgery: an infection risk? *Crit Care.* 2003;7:R13-16.

84. Lamb FJ, Rogers R. Forced-air warming maintains normothermia during orthotopic liver transplantation. *Anaesthesia.* 1995;50:745.

85. Murat I, Berniere J, Constant I. Evaluation of the efficacy of a forced-air warmer (Bair Hugger) during spinal surgery in children. *J Clin Anesth.* 1994;6:425-429.

86. Russell SH, Freeman JW. Prevention of hypothermia during orthotopic liver transplantation: comparison of three different intraoperative warming methods. *Br J Anaesth.* 1995;74:415-418.

87. Komatsu H, Chujo K, Ogli K. Forced-air warming system for perioperative use in neonates. *Paediatr Anaesth.* 1996;6:427-428.

88. Mason DS, Sapala JA, Wood MH, Sapala MA. Influence of a forced air warming system on morbidly obese patients undergoing Roux-en-Y gastric bypass. *Obes Surg.* 1998;8:453-460.

89. Janke EL, Pilkington SN, Smith DC. Evaluation of two warming systems after cardiopulmonary bypass. *Br J Anaesth.* 1996;77:268-270.

90. Rajek A, Lenhardt R, Sessler DI, Brunner G, Haisjackl M, Kastner J, Laufer G. Efficacy of two methods for reducing postbypass afterdrop. *Anesthesiology.* 2000;92:447-456.

91. Mort TC, Rintel TD, Altman F. The effects of forced-air warming on postbypass central and skin temperatures and shivering activity. *J Clin Anesth.* 1996;8:361-370.

92. Zink RS, Iaizzo PA. Convective warming therapy does not increase the risk of wound contamination in the operating room. *Anesth Analg.* 1993;76:50-53.

93. Hofer CK, Worn M, Tavakoli R, Sander L, Maloigne M, Klaghofer R, Zollinger A. Influence of body core temperature on blood loss and transfusion requirements during off-pump coronary artery bypass grafting: a comparison of 3 warming systems. *J Thorac Cardiovasc Surg.* 2005; 129:838-843.

94. Nesher N, Insler SR, Sheinberg N, Bolotin G, Kramer A, Sharony R, Paz Y, Pevni D, Loberman D, Uretzky G. A new thermoregulation system for maintaining perioperative normothermia and attenuating myocardial injury in off-pump coronary artery bypass surgery. *Heart Surg Forum.* 2002;5:373-380.

95. Nesher N, Uretzky G, Insler S, Nataf P, Frolkis I, Pineau E, Cantoni E, Bolotin G, Vardi M, Pevni D, Lev-Ran O, Sharony R, Weinbroum AA. Thermo-wrap technology preserves normothermia better than routine thermal care in patients undergoing off-pump coronary artery bypass and is associated with lower immune response and lesser myocardial damage. *J Thorac Cardiovasc Surg.* 2005;129:1371-1378.

96. Nesher N, Wolf T, Kushnir I, David M, Bolotin G, Sharony R, Pizov R, Uretzky G. Novel thermoregulation system for enhancing cardiac function and hemodynamics during coronary artery bypass graft surgery. *Ann Thorac Surg.* 2001;72:S1069-1076.

97. Taguchi A, Ratnaraj J, Kabon B, Sharma N, Lenhardt R, Sessler DI, Kurz A. Effects of a circulating-water garment and forced-air warming on body heat content and core temperature. *Anesthesiology.* 2004;100:1058-1064.

98. Nesher N, Wolf T, Uretzky G, Oppenheim-Eden A, Yussim E, Kushnir I, Shoshany G, Rosenberg B, Berant M. A novel thermoregulatory system maintains perioperative normothermia in children undergoing elective surgery. *Paediatr Anaesth.* 2001;11:555-560.

99. Janicki PK, Higgins MS, Janssen J, Johnson RF, Beattie C. Comparison of two different temperature maintenance strategies during open abdominal surgery: upper body forced-air warming versus whole body water garment. *Anesthesiology.* 2001;95:868-874.

100. Motta P, Mossad E, Toscana D, Lozano S, Insler S. Effectiveness of a circulating-water warming garment in rewarming after pediatric cardiac surgery using hypothermic cardiopulmonary bypass. *J Cardiothorac Vasc Anesth.* 2004;18:148-151.

101. Nesher N, Zisman E, Wolf T, Sharony R, Bolotin G, David M, Uretzky G, Pizov R. Strict thermoregulation attenuates myocardial injury during coronary artery bypass graft surgery as reflected by reduced levels of cardiac-specific troponin I. *Anesth Analg.* 2003;96:328-335.

102. Grocott HP, Mathew JP, Carver EH, Phillips-Bute B, Landolfo KP, Newman MF. A randomized controlled trial of the Arctic Sun Temperature Management System versus conventional methods for preventing hypothermia during off-pump cardiac surgery. *Anesth Analg.* 2004;98:298-302.

103. Camus Y, Delva E, Cohen S, Lienhart A. The effects of warming intravenous fluids on intraoperative hypothermia and postoperative shivering during prolonged abdominal surgery. *Acta Anaesthesiol Scand.* 1996;40:779-782.

104. Smith CE, Desai R, Glorioso V, Cooper A, Pinchak AC, Hagen KF. Preventing hypothermia: convective and intravenous fluid warming versus convective warming alone. *J Clin Anesth.* 1998;10:380-385.

105. Sessler DI. Mild perioperative hypothermia. *N Engl J Med.* 12 1997;336:1730-1737.

106. Moore SS, Green CR, Wang FL, Pandit SK, Hurd WW. The role of irrigation in the development of hypothermia during laparoscopic surgery. *Am J Obstet Gynecol.* 1997;176:598-602.

107. Kelly JA, Doughty JK, Hasselbeck AN, Vacchiano CA. The effect of arthroscopic irrigation fluid warming on body temperature. *J Perianesth Nurs.* 2000;15:245-252.

108. Morris RH. Influence of ambient temperature on patient temperature during intraabdominal surgery. *Ann Surg.* 1971;173:230-233.

109. El-Gamal N, El-Kassabany N, Frank SM, Amar R, Khabar HA, El-Rahmany HK, Okasha AS. Age-related thermoregulatory differences in a warm operating room environment (approximately 26° C). *Anesth Analg.* 2000; 90:694-698.

110. Bissonnette B, Sessler DI. Passive or active inspired gas humidification increases thermal steady-state temperatures in anesthetized infants. *Anesth Analg.* 1989;69:783-787.

111. Bissonnette B, Sessler DI, LaFlamme P. Passive and active inspired gas humidification in infants and children. *Anesthesiology.* 1989;71:350-354.

112. Bissonnette B. Temperature monitoring in pediatric anesthesia. *Int Anesthesiol Clin.* Summer 1992;30:63-76.

113. Hildebrand F, Giannoudis PV, van Griensven M, Chawda M, Pape HC. Pathophysiologic changes and effects of hypothermia on outcome in elective surgery and trauma patients. *Am J Surg.* 2004;187:363-371.

114. Rodrick M, Krugh J, Hanson W. Anesthesia for the trauma patient. In: Peitzman A, Rhodes M, Schwab C, Yealy D, Fabian T, eds. *The Trauma Manual.* 2nd ed. Philadelphia, PA: Lippincott, Williams & Wilkins; 2002: 386-395.

115. Cheney FW, Posner KL, Caplan RA, Gild WM. Burns from warming devices in anesthesia. A closed claims analysis. *Anesthesiology.* 1994;80:806-810.

116. Misusing forced-air hyperthemia units can burn patients. *Health Devices.* (17-950).

117. U.S. Food and Drug Administration. Burns from misuse of forced-air warming devices. Available at: *http://www.fda.gov/cdrh/psn/show9.html.* Accessed August 26, 2006.

118. Surgical Care Improvement Project. Available at: *http://www.medqic.org/dcs/ContentServer?cid=1122904 930422&pagename=Medqic%2FContent%2FParent ShellTemplate&parentName=Topic&c=MQParents.* Accessed August 27, 2006.

119. Medical device reporting: Manufacturer reporting, importer reporting, user facility reporting, distributor reporting. *Federal Register.* Jan 26, 2000;65:4112-4121.

Originally published in *Perioperative Standards and Recommended Practices,* 2008 edition.

Recommended Practices for Managing the Patient Receiving Local Anesthesia

The following recommended practices were developed by the AORN Recommended Practices Committee and have been approved by the AORN Board of Directors. They were presented as proposed recommended practices for comments by members and others. They are effective January 1, 2007.

These recommended practices are intended as achievable recommendations representing what is believed to be an optimal level of practice. Policies and procedures will reflect variations in practice settings and/or clinical situations that determine the degree to which the recommended practices can be implemented.

AORN recognizes the numerous types of settings in which perioperative registered nurses practice. These recommended practices are intended as guidelines adaptable to various practice settings. These practice settings include traditional operating rooms, ambulatory surgery centers, physicians' offices, cardiac catheterization suites, endoscopy suites, radiology and interventional radiology departments, and all other areas where operative and other invasive procedures may be performed.

Purpose

These recommended practices provide guidelines for perioperative registered nurses managing patients receiving local infiltration or topical anesthesia, without the use of sedation or regional anesthesia. If any sedation is used, AORN's "Recommended practices for managing the patient receiving moderate sedation/analgesia" should be followed.[1] It is not the intent of these recommended practices to address situations that require the services of anesthesia care providers or to substitute the services of perioperative registered nurses in those situations that require the services of anesthesia care providers, regardless of the complexity of the surgical procedure.

Recommendation I

Patients should be assessed preoperatively by a perioperative registered nurse and an individualized plan of care developed.[2]

1. The criteria for the selection of patients to receive local anesthesia should be established through consensus and collaboration of the perioperative registered nurse, physicians, and other health care professionals within the organization where care is provided.[2-4] Although it has been shown that a variety of patients can be successfully managed with a local anesthetic, local anesthesia is not appropriate for every patient or all types of surgical procedures.[4,5] Highly nervous, apprehensive, or excitable patients, or those who are unable to cooperate because of their mental state or age may not be appropriate candidates for local anesthesia.[6]

2. A perioperative registered nurse should perform a preoperative nursing assessment for all patients undergoing local anesthesia.[3] The perioperative registered nurse should review the patient's history, physical examination findings, laboratory results, and other diagnostic test results as indicated. At a minimum, the perioperative registered nurse should assess the patient for

   ♦ pulse, blood pressure, arterial oxygen percent saturation, skin integrity, level of consciousness, temperature, and respiration;[2]

   ♦ allergies and sensitivities (eg, food, medications, tape, latex, prep solutions);[2]

   ♦ age;

   ♦ current medications and use of alternative/complementary therapies;

   ♦ NPO status (ie, when the patient last consumed solids and/or liquids by mouth);

   ♦ any chronic conditions such as coughs or tremors that may impede the ability of the surgeon to perform the procedure;[5]

   ♦ ability to tolerate the required operative position for the duration of the procedure, as well as draping that may cover the face;[5,6]

   ♦ past or present substance abuse (these conditions may require dosage adjustments for the anesthetics used);[2,7]

   ♦ weight, particularly in children;[8]

   ♦ the need for IV access and/or fluids based upon patient assessment data and plan of care;[9]

   ♦ understanding of the plan of care;

   ♦ ability to understand expectations for participation and ability to cooperate;[6]

   ♦ preoperative pain level and expectation of intraoperative and postoperative pain control; and

   ♦ signs and symptoms of anxiety and fear.[2]

Significant assessment findings allow the surgical team to make adjustments in patient care to provide the safest approach to the procedure and anesthesia.[3]

Each patient has a variety of unique physical characteristics that can influence his or her response to medications. Considerations include, but are not limited to, the patient's weight, age, presence of co-morbidities, medication tolerance.[3,4]

3. The appropriate staffing for the care of the patient should be based on the competency of the staff member and individualized patient assessment. The patient's clinical assessment or behavior may require the presence of a perioperative registered nurse whose sole responsibility is to monitor the patient.

Recommendation II

The perioperative registered nurse should provide information to the patient regarding expected outcomes, benefits, risks, surgical experience, and recovery process related to the operative or invasive procedure.

1. Information should include
   - the expected sequence of events before, during, and immediately after the procedure;
   - performance of pain assessment and administration of pain relief measures during and after the procedure; and
   - postoperative signs and symptoms that should be reported to a designated health care provider.[2]

Recommendation III

The perioperative registered nurse should be knowledgeable about medication administration and be able to recognize both desired responses and adverse reactions to anesthetic medications.

1. Perioperative registered nurses should be familiar with potential adverse medication reactions, especially those associated with local anesthetics. Although rare, local anesthetic agents may cause cardiovascular, respiratory, or central nervous system depression. Adverse reactions stemming from hypersensitivity to the amide

group of local anesthetics, the most common local agents (eg, lidocaine, bupivicaine, mepivicaine), are extremely rare and are usually reactions to the preservatives used. Toxicity may occur if large amounts of local anesthetics are absorbed rapidly.[8-10]

Symptoms of toxicity include, but are not limited to,
- metallic taste,
- tinnitus,
- light-headedness,
- syncope,
- visual disturbances,
- numbness of tongue and lips,
- confusion,
- tremors,
- shivering,
- generalized seizures,
- tachycardia/hypertension (initially),
- bradycardia/hypotension (with increased toxicity),
- ventricular arrhythmias or cardiac arrest, and
- respiratory arrest.[8-11]

2. Emergency medications, a source of supplemental oxygen, suction apparatus, resuscitative equipment, and qualified personnel should be readily available.[9-11] At a minimum, personnel should be competent in basic life support. Serious cardiac or respiratory complications can occur abruptly after the administration of local anesthetic medications. If the medication enters the bloodstream directly, seizures, circulatory and respiratory distress, cardiovascular collapse, or even death can result.[9-11]

3. Techniques should be considered to aid in minimizing the amount of discomfort associated with administration of local anesthetic. These include, but are not limited to:
   - reassurance and distraction (eg, deep breathing, music, conversing with patient),
   - prior application of a topical anesthetic (eg, a cream mixture of lidocaine 2.5% and prilocaine 2.5% in an emulsion base);
   - warming the anesthetic to 37°–42° C;
   - buffering of the local anesthetic agent;
   - use of fine gauge needles (ie, 27–29 gauge);
   - slow, incremental injections; and
   - using smallest volume of solution necessary.[10-13]

Recommendation IV

The perioperative registered nurse managing the nursing care of the patient receiving local anesthesia should monitor and interpret the patient's physiological and psychological responses throughout the procedure.

1. The parameters monitored and the frequency of observation should be individualized to the patient and the surgical procedure.

2. Minimum patient monitoring throughout the procedure should include the patient's
   ◆ heart rate and regularity,
   ◆ respiratory rate,
   ◆ level of consciousness,[9]
   ◆ amount of local anesthetic administered,[13]
   ◆ pain level, and[2]
   ◆ response to medications.[2]

   Additional monitoring parameters may include, but are not limited to,
   ◆ blood pressure,[14]
   ◆ oxygen saturation by pulse oximetry,[14] and
   ◆ skin temperature and color[9,14,]

3. The perioperative registered nurse should monitor the amount of local anesthetic given. Toxic effects are dose-related, especially in children, because the dose-to-weight ratio can easily be overestimated.[8,10] The patient should be monitored not only for physiological changes but for any behavioral changes that may occur due to medications and/or other factors related to the surgical encounter. Monitoring the patient's physiological and psychological status facilitates early detection of potential complications.[10,11,13,14]

4. The perioperative registered nurse should recognize and report to the physician significant changes in the patient's status and should be prepared to initiate appropriate interventions. Immediate intervention at the earliest signs of toxicity can prevent serious complications.[11]

5. The perioperative registered nurse should reassess the patient postprocedure and before discharge to identify any potential latent reactions that may put the patient at risk.[15] If indicated by the postoperative assessment, the patient should be discharged in the company of a responsible adult who is given the appropriate postoperative care instructions.

Recommendation V

Holistic care interventions should be considered and offered to the local anesthetic patient to promote an atmosphere of comfort throughout the procedural experience.

1. Holistic comfort interventions should be considered as they have been shown to positively affect physical and psychological patient outcomes. The use of holistic interventions should be coordinated between the patient and procedural team members. While giving the patient a sense of control, the use of one or more interventions may reduce patient stress and anxiety, decrease pain and narcotic use, decrease side effects, and length of stay.[16-19]

2. Interventions may include, but are not limited to,
   ◆ therapeutic communication,
   ◆ guided imagery,
   ◆ music, and
   ◆ touch.[17-19]

3. Therapeutic communication should begin with the preoperative encounter. The perioperative registered nurse should ask the patient about concerns he or she may have. It is important for the perioperative registered nurse to listen actively to the patient's responses and react with kindness and caring concern for the patient's well-being.

   Additional forms of therapeutic communication, such as guided imagery, may be considered for enhancing patient comfort. Guided imagery is a technique used to divert and focus the patient's thoughts into a state in which the mind is calm, thus leading to relaxation.[16] Patients experience less preoperative and postoperative anxiety, report less pain, and require nearly 50% less narcotic medication when guided imagery is used.[19] Although the actual guided imagery techniques may vary, many organizations supply patients with scripted tapes or CDs to listen to up to several weeks before and, in many cases, during and after their surgery.[16,18,20,21]

4. Music may be used either with guided imagery or alone to enhance relaxation and divert the patient's attention away from frightening or unfamiliar noises. Music can aid in decreasing pain by stimulating the release of endorphins.[16]

Patients also experience a decrease in epinephrine levels resulting in lower respiratory rate, heart rate, blood pressure, and anxiety scores when listening to music.[22]

Research has shown that offering a choice of music to patients or allowing them to bring their own (ie, giving them a sense of situational control) has a particularly beneficial effect.[23-25] Patients wearing headphones report positive experiences because surrounding noises and conversations within the perioperative care areas were filtered out.[17,24,26-29]

5. Touch may be used to convey a sense of reassurance, comfort, and caring. Whether it is simply holding an anxious patient's hand or performing therapeutic touch or massage, the effect conveys compassion and caring on the nurse's part. This promotes a more positive nurse-patient relationship.[17,29]

Recommendation VI

The perioperative nurse should document information to facilitate continuity of care and provide retrievable information for evaluating the care given.

1. Documentation of patient care should reflect the perioperative plan of care which includes assessment, diagnosis, outcome identification, planning, implementation, and evaluation.[30] Documentation of all nursing care is legally and professionally important for clear communication, collaboration among health care providers, and continuity of patient care.

2. Documentation should include, but not be limited to,
   - preoperative assessment;
   - vital signs;
   - level of consciousness;
   - dosage, route, time, and effect of local anesthetics;
   - significant untoward patient reactions and their resolutions; and
   - postoperative evaluation based on preoperative assessment data.`

3. The Perioperative Nursing Data Set, the uniform perioperative nursing vocabulary, should be used to document patient care and to develop

policies and procedures related to managing the patient receiving local anesthesia. The outcomes of primary importance to this recommended practice include the following.
- The patient demonstrates and/or reports adequate pain control throughout the perioperative period (O29).
- The patient receives appropriate medication(s) safely administered during the perioperative period (O9).
- The patient demonstrates knowledge of the expected responses to the operative or invasive procedure (O31).

These outcomes fall within the domains of Safety (D1), Physiologic Responses (D2), and Behavioral Responses (D3). The associated interventions that may lead to the desired outcomes include, but are not limited to, the following.
- Administers prescribed medications (I8).
- Assesses pain control (I16).
- Develops individualized plan of care (I30).
- Elicits perceptions of surgery (I32).
- Evaluates response to medications (I51).
- Evaluates response to pain management interventions (I54).[2]

Recommendation VII

The health care facility's quality management program should include investigation of adverse events and near misses associated with administration of local anesthesia.

1. Adverse patient outcomes and near misses associated with administration of local anesthesia should be collected, analyzed, and used for performance improvement as part of the institution-wide performance improvement program. To evaluate the quality of patient care and formulate plans for corrective action, it is necessary to maintain a system of evaluation. When an adverse event occurs, the surgical team is responsible for reporting the event as soon as possible following the discovery.[31]

2. Following organizational policy, documentation of an event should include what happened, the date and time of incident, its location, and witnesses. Measures taken to reverse the situation and communications made

regarding the outcome should also be included. This is considered a sound professional practice and demonstrates that all reasonable efforts were made to protect the patient's safety.[31]

3. A critical investigation should be conducted of any adverse patient safety process or outcome. Error and near miss reporting are the first steps to addressing error reduction.[32]

4. Elements of the root cause analysis tool should be considered in addressing the contributing causes of an incident or adverse event (eg, human, process, system), identification of risks, and preventive measures.[33,34] Multidisciplinary teams should be involved in the process of review and address any changes in practice that can improve patient safety.

5. Action plans should be developed, approved, and implemented to provide solutions and improve care. Action plans should be based on the understanding of the processes in question, supporting policies/procedures, and relevant knowledge-based information.[35]

6. Action plans should be nonpunitive. Attention should be given to correct knowledge deficits, defects in the system, and deficient behavioral performances.[35]

Recommendation VIII

Education, competency assessment, and validation should be conducted prior to the perioperative registered nurse managing the care of a patient undergoing a procedure with local anesthesia.

1. Perioperative registered nurses should complete initial education and competency validation, to include
   ♦ roles and responsibilities of personnel involved in a procedure with local anesthesia,
   ♦ local anesthetics and safe medication administration,
   ♦ care of the patient receiving local anesthesia,
   ♦ patient safety,
   ♦ guidelines and techniques for holistic comfort interventions,
   ♦ processes for reporting adverse events, and
   ♦ documentation.

2. Continuing education and competency assessment should occur at regular intervals, as designated by the organization's policy and the identified learning needs of the individual.

Recommendation IX

Policies and procedures for managing the patient receiving local anesthesia should be developed, reviewed, and revised at regularly scheduled intervals by a multidisciplinary team and be readily available in the practice setting.

1. These recommended practices should be used as guidelines for developing policies and procedures in the practice setting. Policies and procedures establish authority, responsibility, and accountability. They also serve as operational guidelines and assist in the development of patient safety, quality assessment, and quality improvement activities.[35]

2. Policies and procedures for managing patients receiving local anesthesia should include, but are not limited to,
   ♦ patient selection criteria,
   ♦ type and frequency of monitoring,
   ♦ method and frequency of documentation,
   ♦ medications that may be administered by the perioperative registered nurse and the level of monitoring skills required,
   ♦ interventions that may be implemented based on preapproved protocol and that are within the scope of nursing practice,
   ♦ discharge criteria,[15]
   ♦ staffing requirements based upon the individualized needs of the patient, and
   ♦ management of medical emergencies.

3. Ambulatory surgery facilities should develop policies and procedures for immediately transferring patients that require emergency care beyond the ambulatory surgical center's capability to an acute care facility.[36,37]

4. A review of policies and procedures should be included in orientation and ongoing staff member education.

REFERENCES
1. "Recommended practices for managing the patient receiving moderate sedation/analgesia," in *Standards, Recommended Practices, and Guidelines* (Denver: AORN, Inc, 2006) 433-440.

2. S C Beyea, ed, *Perioperative Nursing Data Set: The Perioperative Nursing Vocabulary*, second ed (Denver: AORN, Inc, 2002).

3. J Cassidy, R A Marley, "Preoperative assessment of the ambulatory patient," (Ambulatory Surgery) *Journal of PeriAnesthesia Nursing* 11 (October 1996) 334-343.

4. E N George et al, "Re-evaluating selection criteria for local anesthesia in day surgery," *The British Journal of Plastic Surgery* 57 (July 2004) 446-449.

5. R MacPherson, "Structured assessment tool to evaluate patient suitability for cataract surgery under local anesthesia," *British Journal of Anesthesia* 93 (August 2004) 521-524.

6. B Hutchisson, C B Nicoladis, "Topical anesthesia—A new approach to cataract surgery," *AORN Journal* 74 (September 2001) 339-360.

7. C F Iocolano, "Perioperative pain management in the chemically dependent patient," *Journal of PeriAnesthesia Nursing* 51 (October 2000) 329-347.

8. M J Donald, S Derbyshire, "Lignocaine toxicity; A complication of local anesthesia administered in the community," *Emergency Medicine Journal* 21 (2004) 249-250. Also available at *http://www.emjonline.com* (accessed 6 Sept 2006).

9. D Fogg, "Expiration dates; alcohol disinfection; OR consents; local anesthesia; marking surgical sites; moderate sedation," (Clinical Issues) *AORN Journal* 78 (August 2003) 295-302.

10. S Achar, S Kundu, "Principles of office anesthesia: Part I. Infiltrative anesthesia," *American Family Physician* 66 (July 2002) 91-94.

11. G L Weinberg, "Current concepts in resuscitation of patients with local anesthesia cardiac toxicity," *Regional Anesthesia and Pain Medicine* 27 (November/December 2002) 568-575.

12. O Quaba et al, "A users guide for reducing pain of local anesthetic," *Emergency Medicine Journal* (Short Report) 22 (2005) 188-189. Also available at *http://www.emjonline.com* (accessed 6 Sept 2006).

13. D W Smith et al, "Local anesthesia: Topical application, local infiltration, and field block," Postgraduate Medicine Online, *http://www.postgradmed.com/issues/1999/08_99/smith.htm* (accessed 6 Sept 2006).

14. R H Stein, "The perioperative nurse's role in anesthesia management," *AORN Journal* 62 (November 1995) 794-804.

15. "Failure to monitor local anesthesia patient before discharge," (Nursing Law Case of the Month) *Nursing Law's Regan Report* 45 (1) 2 (June 2004).

16. D L Tusek, R E Cwynar, "Strategies for implementing a guided imagery program to enhance patient experience," (Clinical Issues Advanced Practice Acute Critical Care) *American Association of Critical-care Nurses* 11 (February 2000) 68-76.

17. C L Norred, "Minimizing preoperative anxiety with alternative caring-healing therapies," *AORN Journal* 72 (November 2000) 840-843.

18. C D Knight, "Alternative medicine calms perioperative patients," (Career Management) *Nursing Spectrum* (21 August 2000). Also available at *http://community.nursingspectrum.com/MagazineArticles/article.cfm?2060* (accessed 6 Sept 2006).

19. D Tusek et al, "Guided imagery as a coping strategy for perioperative patients," *AORN Journal* 66 (October 1997) 644-649.

20. L S Halpin et al, "Guided imagery in cardiac surgery," *Outcomes Management* 6 no 3 (2002) 132-137.

21. "Guided imagery: Its use in heart surgery and other procedures," (2005) Cleveland Clinic Heart and Vascular Institute, *http://www.clevelandclinic.org/heartcenter/pub/guide/prevention/stress/guided_imagery.htm* (accessed 6 Sept 2006).

22. M Brunges, G Avigne, "Music therapy for reducing surgical anxiety," *AORN Journal* 78 (November 2003) 816-818.

23. K Stevens, "Patients' perceptions of music during surgery," *Journal of Advanced Nursing* 15 (September 1990) 1045-1051.

24. E Mok, K Wong, "Effects of music on patient anxiety," *AORN Journal* 77 (February 2003) 396-410.

25. M Reilly, "Incorporating music into the surgical environment," *Plastic Surgical Nursing* 19 no 1 (Spring 1999) 35-38.

26. M F Cunningham et al, "Introducing a music program in the perioperative area," *AORN Journal* 66 (October 1997) 674-682.

27. P Augustin, A Hains, "Effect of music on ambulatory surgery patients' preoperative anxiety," *AORN Journal* 63 (April 1996) 750-758.

28. V Steelman, "Intraoperative music therapy: Effects on anxiety, blood pressure," *AORN Journal* 52 (November 1990) 1026-1034.

29. L D McRee et al, "Using massage and music therapy to improve postoperative outcomes," *AORN Journal* 78 (September 2003) 433-447.

30. "Recommended practices for documentation of perioperative nursing care," in *Standards, Recommended Practices, and Guidelines* (Denver: AORN, Inc, 2006) 477-479.

31. D Dunn, "Incident reports—Their purpose and scope," *AORN Journal* 74 (July 2003) 45-68.

32. B A Liang, "The adverse event of unaddressed medical error: Identifying and filling holes in the healthcare and legal systems," (Symposium: Patient Injury, Medical Errors, Liability and Reform) *The Journal of Law, Medicine & Ethics* 29 (2001) 346-368.

33. H Wald, K G Shojania, "Chapter 5: Root cause analysis," Agency for Healthcare Research and Quality, *http://www.ahrq.gov/clinic/ptsafety/chap5.htm* (accessed 6 Sept 2006).

34. "Root cause analysis", VA National Center for Patient Safety, *http://www.patientsafety.gov/rca.html* (accessed 6 Sept 2006).

35. "Quality and performance improvement standards for perioperative nursing," in *Standards, Recommended Practices, and Guidelines* (Denver: AORN, Inc, 2006) 405-414.

36. Joint Commission on Accreditation of Healthcare Organizations, *Comprehensive Accreditation Manual for Ambulatory Care* (Oakbrook Terrace, Ill: Joint Commission on Accreditation of Healthcare Organizations, 2006) PC-25.

37. Accreditation Association for Ambulatory Health Care, *Accreditation Handbook for Ambulatory Health Care, 2004* (Wilmette, IL: Accreditation Association for Ambulatory Health Care, 2004) 49.

RESOURCES

Stoelting, R K, Miller R D, "Chapter 7: Local anesthetics," in *Basics of Anesthesia*, fourth ed (Philadelphia: Churchill Livingstone, 2000) 80-88.

Guidelines of Care for Local and Regional Anesthesia, American Academy of Dermatology Practice Management, *http://www.aadassociation.org/Guidelines/anesthesia.html* (accessed 6 Sept 2006).

Originally published May 1984, *AORN Journal.* Revised September 1989. Revised August 1993.

Revised November 1997; published February 1998. Reformatted July 2000.

Revised November 2001; published April 2002, *AORN Journal.*

Revised 2006; published in *Standards, Recommended Practices, and Guidelines,* 2007 edition.

AORN Perioperative Standards and Recommended Practices, 2009 Edition

Recommended Practices for Managing the Patient Receiving Moderate Sedation/Analgesia

The following recommended practices for managing the patient receiving moderate sedation/analgesia were developed by the AORN Recommended Practices Committee and have been approved by the AORN Board of Directors. They were presented as proposed recommendations for comments by members and others. They are effective January 1, 2008.

These recommended practices are intended as achievable recommendations representing what is believed to be an optimal level of practice. Policies and procedures will reflect variations in practice settings and/or clinical situations that determine the degree to which the recommended practices can be implemented.

AORN recognizes the various settings in which perioperative nurses practice. These recommended practices are intended as guidelines adaptable to various practice settings. These practice settings include traditional operating rooms, ambulatory surgery centers, physician's offices, cardiac catheterization laboratories, endoscopy suites, radiology departments, and all other areas where surgery may be performed.

References to nursing interventions (I) used in the Perioperative Nursing Data Set, second edition, (PNDS) are noted in parentheses when a recommended practice corresponds to a PNDS intervention.[1] The reader is referred to the PNDS for further explanation of perioperative nursing diagnoses, interventions, and outcomes.

Purpose

Moderate sedation/analgesia is a drug-induced, mild depression of consciousness achieved by the administration of sedatives or the combination of sedatives and analgesic medications, most often administered intravenously, and titrated to achieve a desired effect. The primary goal of moderate sedation/analgesia is to reduce the patient's anxiety and discomfort. Moderate sedation/analgesia also can facilitate cooperation between the patient and caregivers.[2] Moderate sedation/analgesia produces a condition in which the patient exhibits a mildly depressed level of consciousness and an altered perception of pain, but retains the ability to respond appropriately to verbal and/or tactile stimulation. The patient maintains protective reflexes, may experience some degree of amnesia, and has a rapid return to activities of daily living.[3] The

desired effect is a level of sedation with or without analgesia whereby the patient is able to tolerate diagnostic, therapeutic, and invasive procedures through relief of anxiety and pain. The four distinct characteristics of moderate sedation/analgesia are:

- The patient is able to respond purposefully to verbal commands or light tactile stimulation.
- The patient is able to maintain his or her protective reflexes and communicate verbally.
- The patient can maintain adequate, spontaneous ventilation.
- There are minimal variations in vital signs.[2]

Recommendation I

The perioperative registered nurse administering moderate sedation/analgesia must practice within the scope of nursing practice as defined by his or her state and should be compliant with state advisory opinions, declaratory rules, and other regulations that direct the practice of the registered nurse.[4]

The methods of monitoring used with patients who receive moderate sedation/analgesia, the medications selected and administered, and the interventions taken must be within the legal definitions of the scope of practice of the registered nurse.[5]

I.a.   In accordance with state and local laws and regulations, a licensed independent practitioner qualified by education, training, and licensure to administer moderate sedation should supervise the administration of moderate sedation.

I.b.   The perioperative registered nurse should consult with his or her state board of nursing for any changes or revisions to declaratory rulings and other guidelines that relate to the perioperative registered nurse's role as a provider of moderate sedation/analgesia.[5] (PNDS: I1)

The professional obligation of the perioperative registered nurse to safeguard clients is grounded in the ethical obligation to the patient, the profession, society, the American Nurses Association's (ANA) *Standards of Clinical Nursing Practice*, AORN's "Explications for perioperative nursing," and state nurse practice acts.[4,6]

Table 1

PHYSICAL STATUS CLASSIFICATION		
Status	Definition of patient status	Example
P1	A normal healthy patient	No physiologic, psychological, bio-chemical, or organic disturbance.
P2	A patient with mild systemic disease	Cardiovascular disease, asthma, chronic bronchitis, obesity, or diabetes mellitus.
P3	A patient with severe systemic disease	Cardiovascular or pulmonary disease that limits activity; severe diabetes with systemic complications; history of myocardial infarction, angina pectoris, or poorly controlled hypertension.
P4	A patient with severe systemic disease that is a constant threat to life	Severe cardiac, pulmonary, renal, hepatic, or endocrine dysfunction
P5	A moribund patient who is not expected to survive without the operation.	Surgery is done as a last recourse or resuscitative effort; major multi-system or cerebral trauma, ruptured aneurysm, or large pulmonary embolus.
P6	A declared brain-dead patient whose organs are being removed for donor purposes	

Reproduced with permission from the American Society of Anesthesiologists, Park Ridge, IL.

Recommendation II

Patient selection for moderate sedation/analgesia should be based on established criteria developed through interdisciplinary collaboration by health care professionals.

Certain patients may not be candidates for moderate sedation/analgesia administered by perioperative registered nurses. Such patients may require care provided by an anesthesia provider qualified to administer monitored anesthesia care and to rescue the patient from a deeper level of sedation, or qualified to convert to general anesthesia if needed.[5,7,8]

II.a. The perioperative registered nurse should assess the patient to determine the appropriateness of registered nurse-administered sedation/analgesia based on selection criteria defined by the health care organization. (PNDS: I59, I144, I60, I66, I68)

The American Society of Anesthesiologists (ASA) Physical Status Classification (**Table 1**) may be used as a means of determining patient appropriateness for registered nurse-administered sedation/analgesia. Patients classified as P1, P2, and a medically stable P3 are normally considered appropriate for registered nurse-administered moderate sedation/analgesia.[5,6]

II.b. Consultation with an anesthesia provider should be obtained if a patient presents with any one of the following:
  – known history of respiratory or hemodynamic instability;
  – previous difficulties with anesthesia or sedation;[2]
  – severe sleep apnea or other airway related issues;[2]
  – one or more significant co-morbidities;[2] (I58)
  – pregnancy;[2]
  – inability to communicate (eg, aphasic);
  – inability to cooperate (eg, mentally incapacitated);[2]
  – multiple drug allergies;
  – multiple medications with potential for drug interaction with sedative analgesics;[2,3]
  – current substance use (eg, street drugs, herbal supplements, nonprescribed prescription drugs);[5]
  – ASA physical classification of an unstable P3;[3,5] and
  – ASA physical classification of P4 or above.[3,5] (PNDS: I92, I111)

Recommendation III

The perioperative registered nurse should complete a patient assessment before administering moderate sedation/analgesia.

A presedation assessment determines a patient's suitability for registered nurse-administered moderate sedation/analgesia by identifying the potential for adverse events.

III.a. The presedation assessment should include, but is not limited to,[2,5,7]
- verification of consent explaining the risks, benefits, and alternatives to sedation;[2,5] (PNDS: I124)
- review of medical history; (PNDS: I111)
- review of physical examination of the cardiac and pulmonary systems, including vital signs;[1] (PNDS: I66, I58)
- review of height and weight;[3,5] (PNDS: I66)
- verification of pregnancy test results, when applicable; (PNDS: I66)
- review of present medication regimen (eg, prescribed, over-the-counter, herbals, supplements), medication taken within the last 48 hours including any as needed medications, especially opioids or other narcotics;[5] (PNDS: I17)
- review of substance use;[1,2,5] (PNDS: I66, I114)
- review of tobacco and alcohol use;[1,2,5] (PNDS: I66, I114)
- verification of allergies and sensitivities to medications, latex, chemical agents, foods, and adhesives;[1,2,5] (PNDS: I123)
- confirmation of NPO status;[2,5] (PNDS: I56, I66)
- determination of patient's ability to tolerate and maintain the required position for the duration of the planned procedure; and (PNDS: I64, I127)
- verification of a responsible adult caregiver to escort the patient home.[5,9] (PNDS: I80)

The fasting guidelines developed by the ASA may be used.[2]

III.b. The perioperative registered nurse should perform an assessment of the patient's airway before administering moderate sedation/analgesia. (PNDS: I66, I60, I15)

Support of the airway and positive-pressure bag-mask ventilation may be necessary if respirations are compromised by the respiratory depressive effects of moderate sedation medications.[2,5]

III.b.1. The presedation airway assessment should include, but is not limited to, the following risk factors for difficult mask ventilation:
- age > 55 years;[10]
- significant obesity (especially of the face, neck, and tongue);[2]
- missing teeth or edentulous;[10]
- presence of a beard;[10]
- history of snoring or sleep apnea;[10] and
- presence of stridor.[2]

III.c. The perioperative registered nurse should consult with an anesthesia provider if the patient presents with a history of severe obstructive sleep apnea.[2] (PNDS: I92, I64, I15, I111)

Administration of sedatives to the patient with central sleep apnea may inhibit the brain's signal to wake up and breathe.[11]

III.d. Additional precautions should be taken for patients with sleep apnea. (PNDS: I64, I92, I87, I121)

Moderate sedation medications may cause relaxation of the oropharyngeal structures resulting in partial or total airway obstruction.[2,11]

III.d.1. Care of the patient with sleep apnea should include, but is not limited to,
- management by an anesthesia provider if the patient has severe central sleep apnea;[2]
- positioning in the lateral or semi-Fowlers position, if at all possible;
- use of continuous positive airway pressure (CPAP) machines during the procedure and recovery periods for patients who routinely use CPAP machines when they sleep;[11] and
- continuous monitoring and positioning to facilitate an open airway.[11]

III.e. The perioperative registered nurse should collaborate with the licensed independent practitioner in developing and documenting the sedation/analgesia plan.[7]

Recommendation IV

The perioperative registered nurse monitoring the patient receiving moderate sedation/analgesia should have no other responsibilities that would require leaving the patient unattended or would compromise continuous monitoring during the procedure.[12]

Continuous monitoring of the patient's physiological and psychological status by the perioperative registered nurse leads to early detection of potential complications.[12]

IV.a.   A designated perioperative registered nurse should continually monitor the patient during administration of moderate sedation/analgesia.[1,2,7] (PNDS: I30, I27, I128)

IV.b.   An additional perioperative registered nurse should be assigned to the circulating role during the administration of moderate sedation.[7]

IV.c.   When moderate sedation is administered, the supervising licensed independent practitioner should remain immediately available during the procedure and recovery period.

Recommendation V

The perioperative registered nurse should know the recommended dose, recommended dilution, onset, duration, effects, potential adverse reactions, drug compatibility, and contraindications for each medication used during moderate sedation/analgesia.

Safe administration of medications for moderate sedation and analgesia requires knowledge of the intended purpose and potential adverse effects of each medication and continuous monitoring of the patient responses to the medications.[2,5]

V.a.   When medications are administered by the oral, rectal, intramuscular, or transmucosal routes, sufficient time should be allowed for drug absorption and onset before considering additional medication.[2] (PNDS: I8, I51)

The absorption rate of nonintravenous medications is unpredictable.[2]

V.b.   The need for IV access should be assessed and will vary depending on the level of sedation intended; the route of sedative administration (eg, oral); and organizational policy, procedure, and protocol. (PNDS: I34)

– Maintaining IV access throughout the procedure allows for additional sedation as well as resuscitative medications.[2]
– Intravenous administration of both a sedative and an analgesic provides effective moderate sedation/analgesia.[2]

– Sedatives (eg, benzodiazepines) may be prescribed to reduce anxiety.[2,3,5]
– Analgesics (eg, opioid agonists) may be prescribed to manage pain.[2,3,5]

V.c.   Each IV agent should be administered separately in incremental doses and titrated to desired effect (ie, moderate sedation/analgesia that enables the patient to maintain his or her protective reflexes, airway patency, spontaneous ventilation).[2,5] (PNDS: I51, I89)

The incremental administration of agents decreases the risk for overdose and respiratory or circulatory depression because the person administrating the agents may better observe the patient's response to the medications given.[2,3,5]

V.d.   Opioid antagonists (ie, naloxone) and benzodiazepine antagonists (ie, flumazenil) should be readily available whenever opioids and benzodiazepines are administered.[2,3] (PNDS: I51, I89)

V.e.   Only persons trained in administering general anesthesia should administer propofol for moderate sedation/analgesia. (PNDS: I1)

On April 14, 2004, the American Association of Nurse Anesthetists (AANA) and the ASA in a joint statement said:

> *"Because sedation is a continuum, it is not always possible to predict how an individual patient will respond. Due to the potential for rapid, profound changes in sedative/analgesia depth and the lack of antagonistic medications, agents such as propofol require special attention.*
>
> *Whenever propofol is used for sedation/anesthesia, it should be administered only by persons trained in the administration of general anesthesia, who are not simultaneously involved in these surgical or diagnostic procedures. This restriction is concordant with specific language in the propofol insert, and failure to follow these recommendations could put patients at increased risk of significant injury or death.*

Similar concerns apply when other intravenous induction agents are used for sedation, such as thiopental, methohexital or etomidate.[2,7,13]

The AORN Board of Directors endorsed this statement on January 14, 2005.

Recommendation VI

The perioperative registered nurse should continuously monitor the patient throughout the procedure.[1,5,7]

Continuous monitoring throughout the procedure enables the perioperative registered nurse to use clinical data to implement or modify the plan of care.[5]

VI.a.   The perioperative registered nurse, at a minimum, should continuously monitor the patient's heart rate and function via electrocardiogram (ECG); oxygenation using pulse oximetry; respiratory rate and adequacy of ventilation; blood pressure; level of consciousness (LOC); comfort level; and skin condition at regular intervals.[2,7] (PNDS: I89, I87, I59, I128)

VI.b.   The method and the flow rate of administering oxygen should be determined based upon achieving the patient's optimal level of oxygen saturation level as measured with pulse oximetry. (PNDS: I87)

A patient's restlessness resulting from hypercapnia and hypoxia may be misinterpreted as discomfort.

The administration of oxygen does not prevent apnea. Patients manifesting restlessness in the absence of a change in pulse oximetry readings may be overmedicated.[14]

VI.c.   Monitoring end-tidal carbon dioxide by capnography should be considered for those patients whose ventilation cannot be directly observed during the procedure.[2] (PNDS: I87, I89, I128)

VI.d.   Vital signs should be monitored before the start of the procedure, after administration of sedative or analgesic medications, and at least every five minutes during the procedure based on the patient's condition, type and amount of medication administered, and length of procedure.[2] (PNDS: I89, I128)

VI.e.   The patient's LOC and ability to respond to verbal commands should be a routine assessment indicator, except in patients unable to respond (eg, young children, mentally impaired, dental surgery).[2,3] (PNDS: I144, I145, I128)

Assessing the patient's LOC by his or her verbal responses at regular intervals during the procedure can quickly determine if the patient is also breathing well. In addition, verbally reassuring the patient can divert his or her attention and assist in reducing anxiety.[2]

VI.f.   Equipment should be preseent, working properly, and and immediately available in the room where the procedure is performed.[7] (PNDS: I122, I138, I120, I87)

VI.f.1.   The following age- and size-appropriate equipment and supplies should be present:
• suction;
• airway management devices (eg, oral, nasal airways; mask ventilation devices);
• noninvasive blood pressure monitoring device;
• pulse oximetry;
• electrocardiograph; and
• sedative and analgesic antagonists.[2,15]

VI.g.   An emergency resuscitation cart should be immediately available in every location in which moderate sedation/analgesia is administered. (PNDS: I121, I120, I87)

While careful titration of sedation and analgesics to obtain the desired effect can be very safe when using short-acting agents; respiratory depression, hypotension, or impaired cardiovascular function are common sequelae of sedation and analgesia.[2,5]

VI.g.1.   An emergency cart should include
• resuscitation medications;
• intravenous access equipment;
• intravenous fluids; and
• life-support equipment (eg, defibrillator, endotracheal intubation equipment, mechanical positive bag-value mask device).

Recommendation VII

The perioperative registered nurse should monitor the patient who receives moderate sedation/analgesia postoperatively.

Recovery time will depend on the type and amount of sedation/analgesia given, procedure performed, and organizational policy.

VII.a. The same monitoring parameters used during the procedure should be used during the recovery phase. (PNDS: I45, I44, I87, I120, I121)

VII.a.1. Postoperative patient care and monitoring should be consistent for all patients.

VII.a.2. Postoperative monitoring should include, but is not limited to,
- heart rate and rhythm;[5,9]
- LOC;[5,7,9]
- blood pressure;[5,9]
- cardiac monitoring;[5]
- oxygenation monitored by pulse oximetry with an audible pulse rate and alarms;[9] and
- ventilation monitored by direct observation and/or auscultation.[9]

VII.b. All patients should be assessed postoperatively. (PNDS: I4, I3, I16, I130, I153, I54)

VII.b.1. Postoperative patient care assessments should include, but are not limited to:
- wound condition;[5,9]
- dressing condition;[5,9]
- line patency;[5]
- amount of drainage in drains;[5] and
- level of pain.[5,7,9]

Recommendation VIII

The perioperative registered nurse should evaluate the patient for discharge readiness based on specific discharge criteria.[5,7]

Recovery time will depend on the type and amount of sedation/analgesia given, procedure performed, and organizational policy.

VIII.a. Discharge criteria should be developed collaboratively and agreed upon by nursing, surgery, medicine, and anesthesia services. (PNDS: I92)

Establishing discharge criteria may minimize the risk of cardiorespiratory depression after the patient has been released.[16-18]

VIII.b. Patients should remain awake for at least 20 minutes without stimulation before they are considered ready for discharge.[9] (PNDS: I146)

The incorporation of a sedation scale in combination with a modified wakefulness test has been reported as ensuring a more objective criterion as compared to using the caregiver's judgment alone.[9]

VIII.c. Children receiving medication with a long half-life should be monitored post-procedure until able to meet discharge criteria and remain awake for at least 20 minutes without stimulation.[15]

There are numerous reports of deaths of prematurely discharged children that have died in the back seats of cars on the ride home from airway obstruction related to the administration of long-acting agents (eg, chloral hydrate).[9,17]

VIII.d. Discharge criteria should be consistently applied to all patients. (PNDS: I89, I27, I146, I44, I45, I51, I143)

VII.d.1. Criteria for discharge may include, but are not limited to:
- return to preoperative, baseline LOC;
- stability of vital signs;
- sufficient time interval (eg, two hours) since the last administration of an antagonist (eg, naloxone, flumazenil) to prevent resedation of the patient;[2,19]
- use of an objective patient assessment scoring system (eg, Aldrete Recovery Score);[2,20]
- absence of protracted nausea;
- intact protective reflexes;
- adequate pain control; and
- return of motor/sensory control.

VIII.e. Patients and/or their caregivers should receive verbal and written discharge instructions.[5] (PNDS: I50, I80)

Medications used for moderate sedation/analgesia cause retrograde amnesia reducing patient's ability to recall events during the immediate postoperative period.

Table 2

CONTINUUM OF DEPTH OF SEDATION				
Levels of sedation/ analgesia	Minimal sedation (ie, anxiolysis)	Moderate sedation/ analgesia (ie, conscious sedation)	Deep sedation/ analgesia	General anesthesia
Responsiveness	Normal response to verbal stimulation	Purposeful response to verbal or tactile stimulation	Purposeful response following repeated or painful stimulation	Unarousable even with painful stimulation
Airway	Unaffected	No intervention required	Intervention may be required	Intervention often required
Ventilations	Unaffected	Adequate	May be adequate	Frequently inadequate
Cardiovascular function	Unaffected	Usually maintained	Usually maintained	May be impaired

Reproduced with permission from the American Society of Anesthesiologists, Park Ridge, IL.

VIII.e.1. A copy of the written discharge instructions should be given to the patient and a copy should be placed in the patient's medical record.[20]

VIII.e.2. The patient and/or caregiver should be able to verbalize an understanding of the discharge instructions.

Recommendation IX

Competency

The perioperative registered nurse should be clinically competent, possessing the skills necessary to manage the nursing care of the patient receiving moderate sedation/analgesia.

Competency assurance verifies that personnel have an understanding of moderate sedation; the risks of unplanned, deeper sedation; and the safe use of monitoring equipment. This knowledge is essential to minimize the risks of moderate sedation and to provide safe care.[21]

IX.a. The competency of the perioperative registered nurse to administer moderate sedation/analgesia should be assessed, demonstrated, documented, and maintained.[21] (PNDS: I1, I128, I138, I15, I89, I51, I8, I121, I120, I111)

IX.a.1. Competencies related to administration of moderate sedation/analgesia should include, but are not limited to,

- patient selection and assessment criteria;
- selection, function, and proficiency in use of physiological monitoring equipment;[1]
- pharmacology of the medications used;
- airway management;
- CPAP use;
- basic dysrhythmia recognition and management;
- emergency response and management;
- advanced cardiac life support (ACLS) and pediatric advanced life support (PALS) according to patients served;[18]
- recognition of complications associated with sedation/analgesia; and
- knowledge of anatomy and physiology.[12]

IX.b. The perioperative registered nurse administering moderate sedation/analgesia should be able to rescue patients whose level of sedation progresses to deep sedation. (PNDS: I1, I89, I92)

Sedation occurs on a continuum from fully conscious to deep sedation[2,7] (**Table 2**).

XI.c. The perioperative registered nurse should, at a minimum, have the ability to manage a compromised airway and to provide adequate oxygenation and ventilation. (PNDS: I1)

Patients receiving moderate sedation/analgesia may unexpectedly slip to the next level (ie, deep sedation or general anesthesia). A provider with bag-, valve-, mask-ventilation; advance life support; and resuscitation skills should be immediately available (eg, within one to five minutes).[2,7]

IX.d.   Administrators should ensure that initial and ongoing educational opportunities are provided to meet the needs of personnel who perform moderate sedation/analgesia. (PNDS: I1)

Initial education provides a baseline to support a beginning level of competency to assist in the development of knowledge, skills, and attitudes that positively affect patient outcomes. Ongoing education offers personnel an opportunity to enhance skills and learn about changes in practice, regulations, and standards.[21]

IX.d.1.   An introduction and review of moderate sedation/analgesia policies and procedures should be included in the orientation and ongoing education of personnel.

IX.e.   Administrators should ensure that perioperative registered nurses who administer moderate sedation/analgesia for procedures are competent to perform these skills.[21] (PNDS: I1)

IX.f.   Competencies should reflect current regulations, nurse practice acts, standards, recommended practices, and guidelines affecting the administration of moderate sedation/analgesia. (PNDS: I1)

Regulations, nurse practice acts, standards, recommended practices, and guidelines affecting the administration of moderate sedation/analgesia are evolving and may change over time.

IX.g.   The perioperative registered nurse should have the additional knowledge and skills necessary to provide care to the pediatric patient populations they serve.[15]

Recommendation X

Documentation

The perioperative registered nurse should document the care of the patient and their physiological responses throughout the continuum of care.[7]

Documentation of all nursing activities performed is legally and professionally important for clear communication and collaboration between health care team members, and for continuity of patient care.

X.a.   Documentation using the PNDS, should include a patient assessment, a plan of care, nursing diagnoses, identification of desired outcomes, interventions, and an evaluation of the patient's response to the care provided.

X.b.   Documentation should be recorded in a manner consistent with health care organization policies and procedures and should include, but is not limited to,
– name, dose, route, time, and effects of all medications;
– patient's LOC;
– ventilation and oxygenation status;
– vital signs documented at intervals dependent on the type and quantity of medication administered;
– procedure start and end times; and
– condition of the patient.[1]

Recommendation XI

Policies and Procedures

Policies and procedures for managing patients who receive moderate sedation/analgesia should be written, reviewed periodically, and readily available within the practice setting.

Policies and procedures are operational guidelines that are used to minimize patient risk factors, standardize practice, direct staff members, and establish guidelines for continuous performance improvement activities.

XI.a.   Policies and procedures should establish authority, responsibility, and accountability.

XI.b.   Policies and procedures for managing patients receiving moderate sedation/analgesia should include, but are not limited to,

- patient selection criteria;
- personnel requirements;
- staffing requirements;
- monitoring;
- risk assessment and criteria for consultation (eg, anesthesia);
- moderate sedation/analgesia medication administration and dosage guidelines;
- recovery and discharge criteria;
- documentation;
- emergency procedures;[3,7] and
- alternative care arrangements when the patient's acuity and or level of care required is outside the capabilities and scope of practice of the perioperative registered nurse.[22]

Recommendation XII

Quality

A quality assurance/performance improvement process should be in place that measures patient, process, and structural (eg, system) outcome indicators.

A fundamental precept of AORN is that it is the responsibility of professional perioperative registered nurses to ensure safe, high-quality nursing care to patients undergoing operative and invasive procedures.[24]

XII.a. Structure, process, and clinical outcomes performance measures should be identified that can be used to improve patient care and that also monitor compliance with facility policy and procedure, national standards and regulatory requirements.[23,25]

XII.a.1. The measures should have universality across the continuum and relevance to all providers of sedation for procedures.[25]

XII.a.2. Process indicators may include, but are not limited to,
- consent for sedation and procedure;
- NPO status confirmed;
- history and physical completed;
- airway assessment conducted;
- factors requiring anesthesia consultation are noted;
- ASA classification;
- anesthesia intervention required (eg, loss of protective reflexes, bag mask ventilation required);

- reversal agents used;
- providers credentialed for procedure/sedation and practice in compliance with facility policy and procedure; and
- adherence to required physiological monitoring.

XII.b. Adverse events should be reported and investigated through the health care organization's quality review process (eg, root cause analysis).[25]

XII.b.1. Any of the following adverse events should be reviewed, and some may require reporting to the appropriate regulatory agency or accrediting organization:[25]
- death;
- aspiration;
- use of antagonists (eg, reversal agents);
- unplanned transfer to a higher level of care;
- cardiac or respiratory arrest;
- sedation using nonapproved agents (eg, anesthetic agent by nonanesthesia provider); and
- emergency procedure without a licensed, independent practitioner in attendance.

Glossary

Anxiolytic: Pharmacologic agent used to treat anxiety. Synonym for anti-anxiety agent.[21]

Benzodiazepine: Pharmacological agent that has sedative, anxiolytic, amnesic, muscle relaxant, and anticonvulsant properties.[24]

Deep sedation/analgesia: A medication-induced depression of consciousness that allows patients to respond purposefully only after repeated or painful stimulation. The patient cannot be aroused easily, and the ability to independently maintain a patent airway may be impaired with spontaneous ventilation possibly inadequate. Cardiovascular function usually is adequate and maintained.[21]

General anesthesia: Patients cannot be aroused, even by painful stimulation, during this medication-induced loss of consciousness. Patients usually require assistance in airway maintenance and often require positive pressure ventilation due to depressed spontaneous ventilation or depression of neuromuscular function. Cardiovascular function also may be impaired.

Immediately available: Defined by the ASA practice guidelines as having a health care provider trained in ACLS and resuscitation skills available to assist with patient care within one to five minutes.[2]

Licensed independent practitioner: Any individual who is permitted by law and the health care organization to provide care and services, without supervision or direction. The care and services should be within the scope of the individual's license and granted clinical privileges.

Moderate sedation/analgesia: A minimally depressed level of consciousness that allows a surgical patient to retain the ability to independently and continuously maintain a patent airway and respond appropriately to verbal commands and physical stimulation. Often referred to as *conscious sedation.*

Opioid: Pharmacologic agent that produces varying degrees of analgesia and sedation, and relieves pain. Fentanyl, morphine, and hydromorphone are opiod analgesic medications that may be used for moderate sedation/analgesia.[3]

Sedative: Pharmacologic agent that reduces anxiety and may induce some degree of short-term amnesia. Diazapam and midazolam are two benzodiazepines commonly used for sedation.

REFERENCES

1. Beyea SC, ed. *Perioperative Nursing Data Set.* Rev 2nd ed. Denver CO: AORN, Inc; 2007.

2. American Society of Anesthesiologists Task Force on Sedation and Analgesia by Non-Anesthesiologists. Practice guidelines for sedation and analgesia by non-anesthesiologists. *Anesthesiology.* 2002; 96:1004-1017.

3. King CA. *Moderate Sedation/Analgesia Competency Assessment Module.* 2nd ed. Denver CO: Competency & Credentialing Institute; 2005:9, 13-16,19-21,23, 25-26,29,37-38.

4. AORN explications for perioperative nursing. In: *Standards, Recommended Practices, and Guidelines.* Denver CO: AORN, Inc; 2007:171-201.

5. Odom-Forren J, Watson D. *Practical Guide to Moderate Sedation/Analgesia.* St. Louis MO: Elsevier Mosby; 2005:4-5;242-257.

6. American Nurses Association. *Nursing: Scope and Standards of Practice.* Washington DC: Nursebooks.org; American Nurses Association; 2004:36;39;42.

7. Operative and other high-risk procedures and/or the administration of moderate or deep sedation or anesthesia. In: *Comprehensive Accreditation Manual for Hospitals: The Official Handbook.* Oakbrook Terrace IL: Joint Commission on Accreditation of Healthcare Organizations; 2007 PC-41 to PC-43.

8. American Society of Anesthesiologists. Distinguishing monitored anesthesia care ("MAC") from moderate sedation/analgesia (conscious sedation) (Oct 27, 2004). *http://www.asahq.org/publicationsAndServices/standards /35.pdf.* Accessed July 23, 2007.

9. Malviya S, Voepel-Lewis T, Ludomirsky A, Marshall J, Tait AR. Can we improve the assessment of discharge readiness? a comparative study of observational and objective measures of depth of sedation in children. [Comment]. *Anesthesiology.* 2004; 100:218-224.

10. Langeron O, Masso E, Huraux C, et al. Prediction of difficult mask ventilation. *Anesthesiology.* 2000; 92:1229-1236.

11. Gross JB, Bachenberg KL, Benumof JL, et al. Practice guidelines for the perioperative management of patients with obstructive sleep apnea: a report by the American Society of Anesthesiologists task force on perioperative management of patients with obstructive sleep apnea. *Anesthesiology.* 2006; 104:1081-1093.

12. American Nurses Association. The role of the registered nurse (RN) in the management of patients receiving IV conscious sedation for short-term therapeutic, diagnostic, or surgical procedures. In: *Compendium of American Nurses Association Position Statements.* Washington, DC: American Nurses Pub; 1996; 148-150.

13. American Association of Nurse Anesthetists, American Society of Anesthesiologists. *AANA-ASA Joint Statement Regarding Propofol Administration.* Available at: *http://www.asahq.org/news/propofolstatement.htm.* Accessed September13, 2007.

14. Harkness GA, Dincher JR. *Medical-Surgical Nursing: Total Patient Care.* 10th ed. St Louis, MO: Mosby; 1999:502.

15. Committee on Drugs American Academy of Pediatrics. Guidelines for monitoring and management of pediatric patients during and after sedation for diagnostic and therapeutic procedures: addendum. *Pediatrics.* 2002; 110:836-838.

16. Newman DH, Azer MM, Pitetti RD, Singh, S. When is a patient safe for discharge after procedural sedation? the timing of adverse effects events in 1367 pediatric procedural sedations. *Ann Emerg Med.* 2003; 42:627-635.

17. Cote CJ, Karl HW, Notterman DA, Weinberg JA, McCloskey C. Adverse sedation events in pediatrics: analysis of medications used for sedation. *Pediatrics.* 2000; 106:633-644.

18. Cote CJ, Notterman DA, Karl HW, Weinberg JA, McCloskey C. Adverse sedation events in pediatrics: a critical incident analysis of contributing factors. *Pediatrics.* 2000; 105:805-814.

19. *Drug Information Handbook for Perioperative Nursing.* Hudson OH: Lexi-Comp; 2006: 739, 1220.

20. American Society of PeriAnesthesia Nurses. *Standards of Perianesthesia Nursing Practice.* Thorofare NJ: American Society of Perianesthesia Nurses; 2004:63-67.

21. Management of human resources. In: *Comprehensive Accreditation Manual for Hospitals: The Official Handbook.* Oakbrook Terrace IL: Joint Commission on Accreditation of Healthcare Organizations; 2007: HR-2.

22. America Nurses Association. The right to accept or reject an assignment. Available at: *http://nursingworld.org*

/MainMenuCategories/HealthcareandPolicyIssues/ANA
PositionStatements/workplac/wkassign14540.aspx.
Accessed September 18, 2007.

23. AORN. Quality and performance improvement standards for perioperative nursing. In: *Standards, Recommended Practices, and Guidelines.* Denver, CO: AORN, Inc; 2007:437-446.

24. Lee A, Fan LT, Gin T, Karmakar MK, Ngan Kee WD. A systemic review (meta-analysis) of the accuracy of the Mallampati tests to predict the difficult airway. *Anesth & Analg.* 2006;102:1867-1878.

25. Improving organization performance. In: *Comprehensive Accreditation Manual for Hospitals: The Official Handbook.* Oakbrook Terrace IL: Joint Commission on Accreditation of Healthcare Organizations; 2007:PI-8 to PI-9.

Originally published April 1993, *AORN Journal,* as "Recommended practices for monitoring the patient receiving intravenous conscious sedation."

Revised; published in January 1997, *AORN Journal,* as "Recommended practices for managing the patient receiving conscious sedation/analgesia." Reformatted July 2000.

Revised November 2001; published March 2002, *AORN Journal,* as "Recommended practices for managing the patient receiving moderate sedation/ analgesia."

Revised 2007; published in *Perioperative Standards and Recommended Practices,* 2008 edition.

AORN Perioperative Standards and Recommended Practices, 2009 Edition

Recommended Practices for Positioning the Patient in the Perioperative Practice Setting

The following recommended practices for positioning the patient in the perioperative practice setting were developed by the AORN Recommended Practices Committee and have been approved by the AORN Board of Directors. They were presented as proposed recommendations for comments by members and others. They are effective January 1, 2008.

These recommended practices are intended as achievable recommendations representing what is believed to be an optimal level of practice. Policies and procedures will reflect variations in practice settings and/or clinical situations that determine the degree to which the recommended practices can be implemented.

AORN recognizes the various settings in which perioperative registered nurses practice. These recommended practices are intended as guidelines adaptable to various practice settings. These practice settings include traditional operating rooms, ambulatory surgery centers, physicians' offices, cardiac catheterization laboratories, endoscopy suites, radiology departments, and all other areas where surgery may be performed.

References to nursing interventions (I) used in the Perioperative Nursing Data Set (PNDS) are noted in parentheses when a recommended practice corresponds to a PNDS intervention.[1] The reader is referred to the PNDS for further explanation of nursing diagnoses, interventions, and outcomes.

Purpose

These recommended practices provide guidelines for positioning the patient in the perioperative setting. They are not intended to cover aspects of perioperative patient care addressed in other recommended practices. Prevention of positioning injury requires anticipation of the positioning equipment necessary based on the patient's identified needs and the planned operative or invasive procedure, application of the principles of body mechanics and ergonomics, ongoing assessment throughout the perioperative period, and coordination with the entire perioperative team.[1] Attention should be given to patient comfort and safety, as well as to assessing circulatory, respiratory, integumentary, musculoskeletal, and neurological structures. Working as a member of the team, the perioperative registered nurse can minimize the risk of perioperative complications related to positioning.

Recommendation I

Personnel who purchase positioning equipment should make decisions based on the health care organization's patient population, current research findings, and the equipment design safety features required to minimize risks to patients and personnel.

The technology used to create mattresses, padding, and other positioning equipment continues to evolve, and it is important for perioperative registered nurses to be aware of products and current research to support their product selection.

The primary safety feature consideration for positioning equipment is that it redistribute pressure, especially at bony prominences on the patient's body. The National Pressure Ulcer Advisory Panel Support Surface Standards Initiative defines a support surface as "a specialized device for pressure redistribution designed for management of tissue loads, micro-climate, and/or other therapeutic functions (ie, any mattresses, integrated bed system, mattress replacement, overlay, or seat cushion, or seat cushion overlay)."[2]

Although physiologic blood and lymphatic flow rates vary among individuals, capillary pressures may increase to as much as 150 mm Hg during prolonged, unrelieved pressure without position change.[3]

The traditional procedure bed mattress usually is constructed of one to two inches of foam covered with a vinyl or nylon fabric. Research studies have found that foam overlays or replacement pads, which represent most OR and procedure bed mattresses, do not have effective pressure-reduction capabilities.[4] Studies comparing the pressure-reducing abilities of standard foam procedure bed mattresses to gel mattresses (ie, visco-elastic polymer) have found gel mattresses to be more effective.[4,5] One research study reported that polyether mattresses generate a lower capillary interface pressure when the patient was in the supine position than gel mattresses or foam mattresses.[6] Another study found that foam and gel mattresses are effective for preventing skin changes, but visco-elastic overlays are effective for preventing both skin changes and pressure sore formation.[7]

Clinical support surfaces (ie, padding) function differently for persons of different height and weight.[8] A performance improvement study reported that supplemental padding on the procedure bed mattress or the use of other positioning devices may not reduce capillary interface pressure for all body types or for all areas of bony prominences even in patients with the same body type.[9]

Postoperative use of alternating pressure mattresses has been found to minimize the incidence of pressure ulcers. Intraoperative use of this technology may be limited due to concerns about patient movement, electrical safety, and asepsis.[3]

There are studies reporting a reduction in the postoperative incidence of pressure ulcers when pressure-relieving overlays are used on procedure bed mattresses and in the postoperative period; however, use of mattress overlays intraoperatively may not minimize this risk.[10] It is difficult, therefore, to draw firm conclusions about the most effective means of intraoperative pressure relief. Future studies of pressure-relieving surfaces are needed and must address methodological deficiencies associated with many of the available studies. Examples of current study limitations include the following:

- ◆ Trials that do not clearly reflect whether a reduction in risk for skin changes is due to intraoperative or postoperative pressure relief or whether application of the trial is necessary in both settings to achieve a risk reduction.[10]
- ◆ Studies that do not include information gathered on the postoperative skin care of the patient make it difficult to assess the clinical significance of the studies' findings.[10]
- ◆ Cross comparisons of study results often are not effective because of variations of selection criteria. In addition, limited sample sizes, interrater reliability, and contradictory findings further contribute to weak scientific support for recommendations on how to predict and prevent pressure ulcers resulting from intraoperative procedure bed mattresses.[11]
- ◆ Studies that measure only interface pressure (ie, the pressure on different parts of the patient's body that are in contact with the support surface) have serious limitations. The process that leads to the development of a pressure ulcer involves the complex interplay of several factors.[10]

The most frequent predictors of perioperative pressure ulcers have been found to be

- ◆ increasing age of the patient,
- ◆ a patient diagnosed with diabetes or vascular disease, and
- ◆ vascular procedures.[11]

I.a.   Personnel selecting procedure bed mattresses and positioning equipment for purchase and use should make decisions based on criteria that include, but are not limited to,
- – ability to hold the patient in the desired position;
- – available in a variety of sizes and shapes;
- – suitable for the patient population and anticipated position requirements;
- – ability to support maximum weight requirements;
- – durable material and design (eg, maintains resilience under constant use);
- – evidence that it is able to disperse skin interface pressure;
- – resistance to moisture;
- – low risk for moisture retention;
- – radiolucent, if necessary;
- – fire retardant;
- – nonallergenic;
- – promotes air circulation;
- – low risk of harboring bacteria (eg, replacements may be needed when soiled);
- – easy to use and store; and
- – cost effective.[3,4,7,12]

One study found the viscoelastic mattress overlay appears to offer the most benefit for older patient populations; patients who have more serious or chronic health problems, where there is a prevalence of vascular disease; or in situations where surgical procedures extend beyond two-and- one-half hours.[7]

I.a.1.   Positioning equipment for obese patients should include, but is not limited to,
- • lateral transfer devices or patient lifts to move obese patients from stretcher procedure bed to the OR procedure bed;[13] and
- • stretchers and beds in the postanesthesia care unit (PACU) that are able to accommodate at least a 30-degree elevation of the patient's upper body and head to avoid respiratory distress.

Whether or not a facility has a bariatric surgery program, it is necessary to accommodate the unique needs of the obese patient population. Patient demographics, baseline utilization requirements, and peek census requirements may help to determine whether caseloads justify purchasing rather than leasing special bariatric equipment. Upgrading existing equipment with bariatric accessories may be a viable option rather than replacing equipment in its entirety.[14]

I.a.2.   The manufacturer should be consulted for both weight capacity and articulation abilities of the procedure bed.

Many procedure beds are designed to safely support a 500-pound patient, but maximum weight for special functioning capabilities is an important consideration. Heavy-duty procedure beds are available that lift, articulate, and support patients weighing 800 to 1000 lbs.[15]

I.b.   Procedure bed mattresses and positioning equipment should be evaluated according AORN's "Recommended practices for product selection in the perioperative practice setting."[16]

Recommendation II

During the planning phase of patient care, the perioperative registered nurse should anticipate the positioning equipment needed for the specific operative or invasive procedure.

The patient's position should provide optimum exposure for the procedure while providing access to IV lines and monitoring devices. The nurse determines the equipment to be used based on the planned procedure, surgeon's preference, and patient condition. Assessment of surgical case characteristics (eg, procedure length, surgical approach, use of radiological equipment) helps determine positioning equipment and modifications in positioning needed to safely accommodate a patient's physical needs.

II.a.   The perioperative registered nurse should review the surgery schedule before the patient's arrival, preferably before the day of surgery, to identify potential conflicts in availability of positioning equipment. (PNDS: I85, I30, I138)

Compromises in patient safety may result when proper equipment is not available.

II.a.1.   When a procedure is scheduled, the availability of special equipment should be verified.

II.b.   The perioperative registered nurse should confirm that the room is set up appropriately for the planned procedure before the patient arrives. (PNDS: I85, I30, I138)

Compromises in patient safety may result when the room arrangement is not specific to the planned procedure and its laterality.[17]

II.b.1.   The correct patient position and related equipment should be verified during the time out period.[18]

Recommendation III

Positioning and transporting equipment should be periodically inspected and maintained in properly functioning condition.

Properly functioning equipment contributes to patient safety and assists in providing adequate exposure of the surgical site. Patients and health care workers are at risk for injury if equipment is not used according to manufacturers' specifications.

III.a.   Scheduled preventive maintenance and repair should be performed on all equipment used for patient transport. (PNDS: I138)

Preventive maintenance and repair promote proper functioning and decrease the risk for injury to patients and personnel.

III.b.   Surfaces of positioning and transporting equipment should be smooth and intact. (PNDS: I122, I138)

Loss of equipment surface integrity can result in bacterial growth. Surfaces that hold moisture or wrinkle contribute to skin breakdown.

III.c.   Proper working condition of positioning and transporting equipment should be verified before use. (PNDS: I122, I138)

Creating a culture of safety includes designing a work environment that minimizes factors that contribute to errors or injuries.[19]

III.d.   Potential hazards associated with the use of positioning and transporting equipment should be identified, and safe practices should be established in accordance with AORN's "Recommended practices for a safe environment of care."[20] (PNDS: I122, I138)

Recommendation IV

During the preoperative assessment, the perioperative registered nurse should identify unique patient considerations that require additional precautions for procedure-specific positioning.

Assessing patients for pressure ulcer development risk factors serves as a key step to preventing them. Patients who are immobile, as is required during operative procedures, are at increased risk.[3]

Additional precautions may be necessary when positioning special patient populations (eg, neonatal, elderly, malnourished, morbidly obese patients; patients with chronic diseases; patients with existing pressure ulcers) to reduce the risk for integumentary, respiratory, or cardiovascular compromises, and nerve impairment.[12,21] For example:

- ◆ Obesity adversely affects most body systems.[22] Routine skin condition assessments may be difficult because of the patient's size, lack of landmarks, and chronic conditions.[23] Traditional foam positioning products may prove ineffective, due to compression resulting from the patient's weight.[15,23]
- ◆ Patients with vascular disease may have existing tissue ischemia and often have additional risk factors (eg, age, nutritional deficits, obesity, diabetes). Patients with vascular disease who are hypertensive may react unexpectedly to a reduction in blood pressure that is considered normotensive for many patients, but which results in loss of blood flow through stenotic vessels.[24]
- ◆ Patients who smoke often experience vasoconstriction, another mechanism that contributes to pressure ulcer formation.[24]

IV.a. Patient needs should be assessed by a registered nurse before transport to determine the required equipment and the skill level and number of transport personnel needed. (PNDS: I64)

Advance preparation for transport may be required for obese patients or other patients with special needs.[21]

IV.b. The preoperative nursing assessment should include questions to determine patient tolerance to the planned operative position. (PNDS: I15, I60, I64, I66, I127, I144, I148)

IV.b.1. The perioperative registered nurse should take additional precautions to decrease the risk for pressure ulcers in patients who
- are more than 70 years of age;
- require vascular procedures or any procedure lasting longer than four hours;
- are thin, small in stature, or who have poor preoperative nutritional status;
- are diabetic or have vascular disease; and
- have a preoperative Braden Scale score that is less than 20.[11]

Studies report that the duration of a procedure is a significant predictor of pressure ulcer development. One study reported that intraoperative pressure ulcers increased when the procedure time extended beyond three hours. Cardiac, general, thoracic, orthopedic, and vascular procedures were reported to be the most common types of procedures associated with pressure ulcer formation.[25]

IV.b.2. Preoperative assessment should include evaluation of both patient and intraoperative factors.
- Patient assessment should include, but is not limited to,
  - age;
  - height;
  - weight;
  - body mass index (BMI);
  - skin condition;
  - presence of jewelry;
  - nutritional status;
  - allergies (eg, latex);
  - preexisting conditions (eg, vascular, respiratory, circulatory, neurological, immune system suppression);
  - laboratory results;
  - physical or mobility limitation (eg, range of motion);
  - presence of prosthetics or corrective devices;

- presence of implanted devices (eg, pacemakers, orthopedic implants);
- presence of external devices (eg, catheters, drains, orthopedic immobilizers);
- presence of peripheral pulses;
- perception of pain;
- level of consciousness; and
- psychosocial and cultural considerations.[1,12]
  - Intraoperative assessment factors should include, but are not limited to,
    - anesthesia care provider's access to patient;
    - estimated length of procedure; and
    - desired procedural position.

IV.c. Special procedure beds and accessories designed to meet unique patient needs should be used. (PNDS: I30, I64, I122)

When assessing a patient's body weight and condition it is important to assess more than just their BMI. Patients of the same BMI (a relative ratio of height and weight) can have significantly different body composition that affects positioning needs and their risk for pressure ulcer development; therefore, procedure bed and positioning device requirements may be quite different.

The perioperative nursing assessment should include the length and weight capacity of the procedure bed.

IV.d. Perioperative registered nurses should participate in their health care organization's fall-reduction program by including an assessment of the patient's risk for falling. (PNDS: I64)

Patients may be prone to falls before they enter the operating room, during transfer to the procedure bed, and when attempting to sit up or transfer to a recliner in the PACU.[26] Patients may be at a higher risk for falling if the following conditions are present:

- history of a fall during the past three months;
- use of certain medications (eg, psychotropics, antidepressants, benzodiazepines, cardiovascular agents, antihypertensives, diuretics, anticoagulants, antihistamines,

bowel preparation medications, medications related to treating nocturia);[27]
- confusion or depression;
- function or mobility problems (ie, gait),
- age, and
- dizziness.[27,28]

The top three risk factors for predicting falls include a previous fall, medications used, and gait.[27] Age ranks fourth as a risk factor, however, it is not a good predictor of falls because studies show a wide range of age groups experience falls. One study reported a high percentage of injuries due to falls occurring in the 20- to24-year-old age group.[28]

IV.d.1. Regardless of age, patients who have poor vision, postural hypotension, or an altered mental status should be considered to be at a high risk for falling.[27]

Recommendation V

Perioperative personnel should use proper body mechanics when transporting, moving, lifting, or positioning patients.

The incidence of work-related back injuries in nursing is among the highest of any profession worldwide.[29] Manual lifting and other patient-handling tasks are high-risk activities that can result in musculoskeletal disorders.[13] Most injuries are due to overexertion when lifting patients; tasks that require staff members to twist or bend forward; and high-risk tasks performed on a horizontal plane (eg, lateral transfer from bed to stretcher, repositioning patient in bed).[29,30]

Biomechanical studies have demonstrated that health care personnel are at risk for injury, despite the use of proper body mechanics, if patient-handling tasks are beyond reasonable limits and the caregiver's capabilities.[29] The combination of frequency, duration, and the stress of performing high-risk tasks that push the limits of human capabilities (eg, heavy loads; sustained, awkward positions; bending and twisting; reaching fatigue or stress; force; standing for long periods of time) predisposes nurses to musculoskeletal disorders.[13]

V.a. An adequate number of personnel should be available to ensure patient and personnel safety when transporting the patient. (PNDS: I30, I77)

Procedure beds can be very heavy and difficult to move, even without the presence of a patient. When a procedure bed is moved with a patient on it, the risk of injury is increased for both the worker and the patient.[13]

V.b. The perioperative registered nurse should identify high-risk tasks and implement ergonomic solutions to eliminate or reduce occupational risks for injury.

Transferring, lifting, and handling patients have been identified as the most frequent precipitating trigger of back and shoulder problems for nurses.[13] Nurses are often required to use the weaker muscles of the arms and shoulders as the primary lifting muscles, rather than the stronger muscles of the legs, because lifting, turning, or repositioning patients is often performed on a horizontal plane, such as a bed or stretcher.[29]

Experts do not always agree on the safest methods for lifting or assisting dependent patients. One research center recommends the use of a roller or mechanical lifting equipment to reduce the risk of strain when moving a patient who is unable to move independently. The same center studied nurses' behaviors regarding use of lifting equipment and identified the following reasons for continued manual lifting:
- devices were purchased in insufficient quantities,
- lifts were stored in inconvenient locations, and
- equipment was not maintained adequately.[29]

V.c. All perioperative personnel should be educated in the principles of body mechanics and ergonomics.

The majority of musculoskeletal disorders reported by nurses working in the private sector are back injuries that require time away from work. Several studies report that nurses complain of chronic back pain, are unable to do their work because of injuries to shoulder and neck, or are planning to leave the profession because of their concern for personal safety in the health care environment.[13]

Recommendation VI

Potential hazards associated with patient transport and transfer activities should be identified, and safe practices should be established.

Preoperative patient observation and assessment by a perioperative registered nurse allows for identification of potential problems during transport and transfer activities that can be prevented by the implementation of appropriate precautions.

VI.a. When selecting the appropriate transport vehicle, design features to be considered should include, but are not limited to,
- locking devices on wheels;
- protective devices (eg, safety straps, side rails, cribs rails high enough to prevent a standing child from falling out);
- stable, adjustable IV poles or stands;
- holding devices for oxygen tanks;
- positioning capabilities;
- controls that are easy to operate and within reach of the operator;
- maneuverability;
- sufficient size;
- removable head and foot boards;
- mattress-stabilizing devices;
- easily cleanable surfaces; and
- a rack or shelf to hold monitoring equipment. (PNDS: I138)

Equipment safety design features help reduce the risk of injury to patients and personnel during transport.

VI.b. The patient should be attended during transport and transfer by personnel deemed appropriate by the perioperative registered nurse or as determined by the anesthesia care provider or surgeon. (PNDS: I138)

VI.c. Safety measures to be implemented during transport and transfer activities should include, but are not limited to,
- presence of locking wheels on the transport vehicle and the patient's bed during transfer activities;
- side rails that can be elevated;
- use of safety straps;
- hanging and securing IV containers away from the patient's head;

- ensuring that the patient's head, arms, and legs are protected;
- ensuring that one staff member remains at the head of the patient transport vehicle;
- pushing the transport vehicle with the patient's feet first and avoiding rapid movement through hallways or when turning corners;
- maintaining the integrity and function of IV infusions, indwelling catheters, tubes, drainage systems, and monitoring equipment; and
- obtaining appropriately skilled assistance personnel and specific instructions for the patient with special needs. (PNDS: I138)

Locking wheels, raising side rails, and securing safety straps reduce the risk of patient falls. Maintaining proximity to the patient's head provides access to the patient's airway in the event of respiratory distress or vomiting. Rapid movements can cause patient disorientation, nausea and vomiting, and dizziness.

Recommendation VII

Positioning equipment should be used in a safe manner and according to manufacturers' written instructions.

To reduce the risk of injury, it is important to follow manufacturers' written instructions regarding weight limits in flat, articulated, and reverse orientation positions for each type of procedure bed. One researcher reviewed 16 perioperative incident reports and found that 63% involved patients who were above the specified weight limit for the positioning equipment used for back surgery. In all of the reports, it was noted that a staff member notified the surgeon of the problem before the beginning of the surgery, but the equipment was used anyway because alternative equipment was not available.[31]

VII.a. The perioperative registered nurse should verify that the positioning equipment to be used has been designed specifically for surgical procedure positioning. (PNDS: I122)

The goal of using positioning equipment is to use equipment that is designed to redistribute pressure and that decreases the risk for positioning injuries.

The number of pads, blankets, and warming blankets beneath the patient has been implicated as a risk factor for pressure ulcer development.[4,11,26,32,33]
- Foam pads may not be effective as padding devices because they quickly compress under heavy body areas.[33-35] In some situations, however, foam can be an effective pressure-reducing material equal to that of gel or visco-elastic.
- Convoluted foam mattress overlays (eg, egg crate mattresses) may be more effective in redistributing pressure if they are made of thick, dense foam that resists compression. The effectiveness of this type of mattress overlay depends on the weight of the patient and may not provide adequate pressure reduction in obese patients.
- Pillows, blankets, and molded-foam devices may produce only a minimum amount of pressure redistribution and are less effective during long procedures.
- Towels and sheet rolls do not reduce pressure and may contribute to friction injuries.[3]

VII.b. The perioperative registered nurse should select a surface that is able to reduce excessive pressure on the patient's bony prominences. (PNDS: I11, I122)

Pressure against the skin above 32 mm Hg interferes with tissue perfusion.[36,37] Firm, stable devices may help hold the patient in position but may not help redistribute pressure. If care is not taken to minimize pressure points caused by positioning equipment, the positioning equipment may not adequately decrease the potential for injury and may actually increase the potential for pressure injury.

VII.b.1. Rolled sheets and towels should not be used beneath the procedure bed mattress or an overlay. When using positioning equipment such as a uterine displacing wedge or chest rolls, the positioning devices should be placed underneath the patient and not beneath the mattress or overlay.

When rolled towels, sheets, or other positioning equipment are placed beneath the mattress or the overlay, they may negate the pressure-reducing effect of the mattress or overlay.[11]

VII.c. Patients should not be transported in procedure beds unless the manufacturer's written instructions state that the bed is safe to use as a transportation device. (PNDS: I122)

Procedure bed designs vary. Unlocking the bed may make it unstable. Moving an occupied procedure bed is not recommended because the risk of injury increases for both the worker and the patient.[13] There are some procedure beds, however, that are designed for patient transport. It is important to consult the manufacturers' written instructions to determine if unlocking and moving a patient-occupied procedure bed is recommended.

Recommendation VIII

The perioperative registered nurse should actively participate in safely positioning the patient under the direction of and in collaboration with the surgeon and anesthesia provider.

The physiologic effects of anesthesia increase the patient's vulnerability to the effects of pressure. Patients may have preexisting conditions that limit the positions they can assume and may influence the positions they can tolerate.[37]

VIII.a. The perioperative registered nurse should provide for patient dignity and privacy during transport, transfer, and positioning. (PNDS: I100, I102, I150)

Maintaining patient privacy is essential to preserving the trust developed in the nurse-patient relationship. The perioperative registered nurse is responsible for developing a caring environment that promotes the well-being of patients. Perioperative registered nurses should provide care that recognizes the importance of each patient's values, beliefs, and health practices and is culturally relevant to a diverse patient population.[38]

VIII.a.1. The perioperative registered nurse should implement actions that include, but are not limited to, the following:
- Restrict OR patient care area access to designated authorized personnel only.
- Keep doors to patient care areas closed.
- Limit traffic coming into OR procedure rooms.
- Expose only the areas of the patient's body needed to provide care or access to the surgical site during the planned procedure.
- Provide auditory privacy for patient and staff member conversations during transport and transfer.
- Provide care without prejudicial behavior.[38]

VIII.b. Patient jewelry and body piercing accessories should be removed before positioning or transferring to the procedure bed if it will cause potential injury or interfere with the surgical site. (PNDS: I138)

Patients positioned on jewelry may be subject to pressure injuries.[39] Patient jewelry can become entangled in bedding or caught on equipment while moving the patient and cause injuries due to accidental removal.

VIII.c. Movement or positioning of the patient should be coordinated with the surgical team. (PNDS: I96, I77)

Sliding or pulling the patient can result in shearing forces and/or friction on the patient's skin. Shearing can occur when the patient's skin remains stationary and underlying tissues shift or move, as might occur when the patient is pulled or dragged without support to the skeletal system or while using a draw sheet. Friction occurs when skin surfaces rub over a rough stationary surface.[3,40]

VIII.c.1. Specific patient needs should be communicated to the perioperative team before initiating transfer or positioning the patient.

VIII.c.2. Attention should be given to protecting the patient's airway at all times during patient transfer and positioning.

VIII.c.3. Before and during transfer or positioning, perioperative team members should communicate with each other regarding securing tubes, drains, and catheters; take actions to support these devices and prevent dislodging; and confirm that the devices have maintained patency after transfer, positioning, or repositioning.

Indwelling catheters, tubes, or cannulas may be dislodged without proper support.

VIII.c.4. The perioperative registered nurse should actively participate in monitoring the patient's body alignment and confirming that the patient's legs are not crossed during transfer and positioning.

Maintaining the patient's correct body alignment and supporting his or her extremities and joints decreases the potential for injury during transfer and positioning.[12]

VIII.c.5. When on the procedure bed, the patient should be attended by surgical team members at all times.

A lack of clear communication about who should be watching the patient after the safety straps are removed or before the patient is transferred has been reported as a contributing factor for patient falls in the operating room.[28]

VIII.d. The number of personnel and required equipment should be adequate to safely position the patient. (PNDS: I64, I138)

Inadequate numbers of personnel and/or equipment can result in patient or personnel injury.

VIII.e. The perioperative registered nurse should actively participate in monitoring the patient's tissue integrity based on sound physiologic principles. (PNDS: I15, I42, I64, I96, I145)

VIII.f. The perioperative registered nurse should implement general positioning safety measures including, but not limited to, the following:
- Positioning equipment should be used to protect, support, and maintain the patient's position.
- Padding should be used to protect the patient's bony prominences.
- The patient's arms should be positioned to protect them from nerve injury.[37,41]
- The location of the patient's fingers should be confirmed to ensure they are in a position that is clear of procedure bed breaks or other hazards.

- Safety restraints should be applied carefully to avoid nerve compression injury and compromised blood flow.[42]
- The patient's body should be protected from coming in contact with metal portions of the procedure bed.
- The patient's heels should be elevated off the underlying surface when possible.[43]
- The patient's head and upper body should be in alignment with the hips. The patient's legs should be parallel and the ankles uncrossed to reduce pressure to occiput, scapulae, thoracic vertebrae, olecranon processes (ie, elbows), sacrum/coccyx, calcaneae (ie, heel),[12,44] and ischial tuberosities.[9,45]
- The patient's head should be in a neutral position and placed on a headrest.
- A pillow may be placed under the back of the patient's knees to relieve pressure on the lower back.[12]
- If the patient is pregnant, a wedge should be inserted under the patient's right side to displace the uterus to the left and prevent supine hypotensive syndrome, caused by the gravid uterus compressing the aorta and vena cava.[46]
- If patient is attached to a robot, caution should be used before moving either the patient or the robot. (PNDS: I77, I92, I96, I139)

VIII.f.1. Unless necessary for surgical reasons, the patient's arms should not be tucked at his or her sides when in the supine position. If there are surgical reasons to secure the patient's arms at his or her side with the use of a draw sheet, the draw sheet should extend above the elbows and should be tucked between the patient and the procedure bed's mattress.[37,44]

When a patient's arms are tucked tightly at his or her side with sheets, it may add unnecessary pressure on the tucked arms and may lead to tissue injury and ischemia. It may also cause interference with physiologic monitoring (eg, blood pressure monitoring, arterial catheter monitoring) and result in an inability to resuscitate during an emergency due to unrecognized IV infiltration in the tucked arm. There is also an increased risk for the patient to develop compartment syndrome in the upper extremity.[47]

VIII.f.2.   Direct pressure on the eye should be avoided to reduce the risk of central retinal artery occlusion and other ocular damage, including corneal abrasion.

Patients who are at increased risk for development of postoperative visual loss are those that are undergoing procedures that are prolonged (ie, > 6.5 hrs), have substantial blood loss (ie, > 44.7% of estimated blood volume), or who are in a prone position.[48]

- Patients at risk for ocular injury should be positioned so that their heads are level with or higher than their hearts, when possible. In addition, their heads should be maintained in a neutral forward position without significant neck flexion, extension, lateral flexion, or rotation, when possible. The use of a horseshoe headrest may increase the risk of ocular compression.
- The eyes of patients in the prone position should be assessed regularly.
- The surgeon may consider using a series of staged spine procedures for high-risk patients.

VIII.g.   Perioperative team members should implement measures to reduce the risk of nerve injuries when positioning the patient's extremities. (PNDS: I38, I144)

- Patients who undergo general anesthesia are at an increased risk for nerve injury resulting from patient positioning.[42]
- Trauma may result from compression or stretching of nerves, with the most frequent injuries involving the ulnar nerve and brachial plexus. Why some of these injuries occur is unknown.[12,41,42,49,50,51]
- The saphenous, sciatic, and peroneal nerves are vulnerable when the patient is in the lithotomy position. The peroneal nerve is also at risk with the patient in the lateral position.[50]
- Injury to the pudendal nerve may result from inadequate padding or incorrect

placement of the positioning post, when using a fracture table.[37,52,53]

VIII.g.1.   To minimize the risk of nerve injury, safety measures should include, but are not limited to, the following:

- Padded arm boards should be attached to the procedure bed at less than a 90-degree angle for supine patients.[37,41,44,50]
- The patient's palms should be facing up and the fingers should be extended when his or her arms are placed on arm boards.[37,41,50]
- When the patient's arms are placed at the side of the body, they should be in a neutral position (ie, elbows slightly flexed, wrist in neutral position, palms facing inward).[37,41,50]
- Patient shoulder abduction and lateral rotation should kept be to a minimum.[42]
- Patient extremities should be prevented from dropping below procedure bed level.
- The patient's head should be placed in a neutral position, if not contraindicated by the surgical procedure or the patient's physical limitations.[50]
- Adequate padding is required for the saphenous, sciatic, and peroneal nerves, especially when the patient is in a lithotomy or lateral position.[50]
- A well-padded perineal post should be placed against the perineum between the genitalia and the uninjured leg when a patient is positioned on a fracture table.[37,52,53]

VIII.h.   Perioperative team members should implement measures to reduce the risk of injuries when positioning the patient in the supine position. (PNDS: I3, I11, I77, I96, I122)

The supine position may be modified into a sitting or semi-sitting position for access to the shoulder, posterior cervical spine, or posterior or lateral head. While there is better lung excursion and diaphragmatic activity in these positions, there is increased risk for poor venous return from the lower extremities and pooling of blood in the patient's pelvis.[12]

- When using only a draw sheet without a lateral transfer device for a lateral patient transfer in the supine position, the care provider exerts a pull force up to 72.6% of the patient's weight.[54]

- When one care provider (eg, anesthesia care provider) supports the patient's head and neck, the remaining mass of the patient's body equals 91.6% of his or her total body mass.[55] To accommodate this body mass, each caregiver can safely contribute a pull force required to transfer up to 48 lbs.[13]

- When moving the patient into and out of a sitting or modified sitting position, the mass of a patient's body from the waist up, including the head, neck, and upper extremities, equals almost 69% of the patient's total body weight.[55]

VIII.h.1. A lateral transfer device (eg, friction-reducing sheets, slider board, air-assisted transfer device) should be used for supine-to-supine patient transfer. One caregiver and one anesthesia care provider (who is managing the airway, head, and neck) should be assigned to safely transfer a patient who weighs 52 lbs. Two caregivers plus the anesthesia care provider should be assigned to safely transfer a patient up to 104 lbs. Three caregivers plus the anesthesia care provider should be assigned to safely transfer a patient up to 157 lbs. For patients who weigh more than 157 lbs, an appropriate mechanical lifting device (ie, mechanical lift with supine sling, mechanical lateral transfer device, or air-assisted lateral transfer device) should be used and a minimum of three to four caregivers should be assigned.[13]

VIII.h.2. When moving the patient into and out of a sitting or modified sitting position, three caregivers should be assigned to work together to lift up to 67 lbs (30 kg). It is preferable to use mechanical devices and a minimum of three caregivers if the patient weighs more than 68 lbs.[13]

VIII.i. The perioperative team should implement measures to reduce the risk of injuries when positioning the patient in the prone position. (PNDS: I3, I11, I77, I96, I122)

The prone position may be modified into the jackknife position to provide exposure to sacral, rectal, and perineal areas, or modified into the knee-chest position to provide exposure for spinal procedures.[11,36]

Respiratory function may be affected by the ultimate positioning of the patient and is mitigated by many factors, including the angle of incline, external pressure on the rib cage, and whether the diaphragm is free to move.

Respiratory function may be decreased as a result of mechanical restriction of the rib cage and diaphragm when the patient is in a prone position.[12,37]

Ophthalmic complications, including vision loss, have been reported in association with patients undergoing spinal surgery in a prone position.[56] There is an increased risk for direct compression to the orbit and corneal abrasion when the patient is in a prone position. During spinal surgeries, the patient may be turned to a prone position using a frame that causes the head to be lower than the rest of the body. This cerebral-dependent position may lead to a decreased venous return from the head, which can lead to capillary bed stasis and decreased perfusion to the optic nerve and result in blindness.[57]

When transferring a patient from a supine position to a prone position, the most common physiologic changes are related to hypotension.[37]

VIII.i.1. General safety considerations for the prone position should include, but are not limited to, the following.
- The patient's cervical neck alignment should be maintained.
- Protection for the patient's forehead, eyes, and chin should be provided.
- A padded headrest should be used to provide airway access.
- Chest rolls (ie, from clavicle to iliac crest) should be used to allow chest movement and decrease abdominal pressure.

- Breasts and male genitalia should be positioned in a way that frees them from torsion or pressure.
- The patient's toes should be positioned to allow them to hang over the end of the bed or to be elevated off the bed by placing padding under the patient's shins so the shins are high enough to avoid pressure on the tips of the toes.[11]

VIII.i.2. When in the prone position, direct pressure on the patient's eyes and face should be avoided.[58]

Although ocular injuries have been reported with and without the use of a headrest (eg, the head held with pins), the use of a horseshoe headrest may increase the risk of ocular compression and perioperative central retinal artery occlusion.[57]

VIII.i.3. Ideally, the patient's arms should be placed down by his or her sides in the prone position. If this is not possible, each arm should be placed on an arm board with the arms abducted to less than 90 degrees, the elbows flexed, and the palms facing downwards. To safely secure the patient's arms at his or her sides, the palms of the hands should be facing in toward the thighs, the elbows and hands should be protected with padding, and the hands and wrists should be kept in anatomical alignment.[37]

Positioning the arms above the patient's head can cause a stretch injury to the lower trunks of the brachial plexus.[50]

VIII.i.4. Four caregivers should be available for a supine-to-prone patient transfer. One anesthesia care provider should maintain the airway and support the patient's head, while other members of the team are responsible for the patient's trunk and extremities.

Two caregivers, plus the anesthesia care provider, can safely transfer a patient weighing up to 48.5 lbs (22.0 kg) from the supine to the prone position. Three caregivers, plus an anesthesia care provider, can safely transfer a patient weighing up to 72.7 lbs (33.0 kg). If the patient's weight is greater than 73 lbs, it is necessary to use assistive technology and a minimum of three to four caregivers.[13]

VIII.j. The perioperative team should implement measures to reduce the risk of injuries when positioning the patient in the Trendelenburg's and reverse Trendelenburg's positions. (PNDS: I3, I11, I77, I96, I122)

When the patient is in Trendelenburg's position, excessive pressure on the clavicle can compress the brachial plexus as it exits the thorax between the clavicle and the first rib. Morrell closed claims files revealed that brachial plexus injuries were related to the use of shoulder braces and the head-down position.[51]

Positioning a patient with a history of heart failure secondary to increased venous return and increased pulmonary blood flow in a steep, head-down tilt may adversely affect heart function. Trendelenburg's position causes redistribution of the blood supply due to increased venous return from the lower extremities. To ventilate the patient's lungs while in this position, the diaphragm must push against the displaced abdominal contents, which increases the risk for the alveoli to collapse resulting in atelectasis.[12,44]

Circulatory response changes can be rapid and dramatic when moving the patient into or out of Trendelenburg's position. During surgery, there is gravitational flow of blood away from the surgical field, which can mask significant blood loss. The patient may be hypotensive as a result of hypovolemia when returned from Trendelenburg's position to the supine position. Cerebral blood flow may fall as venous and intracranial pressure rises; therefore, patients with known or suspected intracranial pathology should not be placed in Trendelenburg's position if it can be avoided.[12,44] Trendelenburg's position can lead to visual loss related to decreased venous return from the head.[57]

VIII.j.1. Measures should be taken to prevent patient from sliding on the procedure bed.

Risk for shear injuries increase when changing the patient's position from supine to Trendelenburg's or reverse Trendelenburg's.[59]

VIII.j.2. To prevent injury to the shoulders, brachial plexus, or feet in Trendelenberg's or reverse Trendelenberg's positions,[41,42,49,60]
- shoulder braces should be avoided, and
- a padded footboard should be used for reverse Trendelenburg's position.

VIII.k. The perioperative team should implement measures to reduce the risk of injury to patients and caregivers associated with the lithotomy position. (PNDS: I3, I11, I77, I96, I122)
- Some type of leg holder is used in all lithotomy positions. Modifications of the position include low, standard, high, and exaggerated positions depending on how high the legs and pelvis need to be elevated for the procedure.[37,61]
- The length of time that a patient may remain in the lithotomy position without risk of injury is unknown and is related to patient condition.
- In the lithotomy position the patient's heels are at risk for pressure ulcers at the heel support sites, particularly when the legs are supported by the heel in the standard, high, or exaggerated lithotomy position for prolonged procedures.[61]
- Injury to the peroneal nerve on the lateral aspect of the knee is common and results from the fibular neck resting against the vertical post of the stirrup when the patient is in the lithotomy position. This injury can result in foot drop and lateral, lower-extremity paresthesia.[12,37,50,60]
- Compartment syndrome, although infrequent, has been reported as a complication of surgical positioning, especially the lithotomy position.[37,62-64]

There is increased risk for poor venous return from the lower extremities and pooling of blood in the patient's pelvis when the patient is in a lithotomy position. At the end of the procedure, the patient's overall circulating blood volume may be depleted when the patient's legs are lowered to the procedure bed due to the blood returning quickly into the patient's peripheral circulation. Respiratory compromises may occur due to pulmonary congestion. There is increased risk for deep vein thrombus formation due to the increased risk of blood pooling in the calf muscles.[12]

When positioning the patient into and out of the lithotomy position, the maximum load for a two-handed lift is 22.2 lbs (10.1kg). Each complete lower patient extremity (including thigh, calf, and foot) weighs almost 16% of the patient's total body mass.[13]

VIII.k.1. General positioning considerations for patients in the lithotomy position include, but are not limited to, the following:
- Stirrups should be placed at an even height.
- The patient's buttocks should be even with the lower break of the procedure bed and positioned in a manner that securely supports the sacrum on the bed surface. Confirm proper positioning of the patient buttocks before surgery is initiated.[12]
- The patient's legs should be moved slowly and simultaneously into the leg holders to prevent lumbosacral strain.
- The patient's legs should be removed from stirrups slowly and brought together simultaneously before lowering the legs to the bed surface when removing the patient from leg holders, to prevent lumbosacral strain. To maintain the patient's hemodynamic status, his or her legs should be slowly returned to the bed, one at a time if possible.[37]
- The patient's arms should be placed on padded arm boards, extended less than 90 degrees from the long axis of the procedure bed, with the patient's palms up and gently secured.[37,60] The arms should be tucked at the patient's sides only if surgically necessary. When it is necessary to tuck the arms at the patient's side, the elbows should be padded and the palms

should be facing in toward the patient's body. The hands should be enclosed and secured within a foam protector.[37]

- The patient's fingers should be protected from injury when the foot of the procedure bed is repositioned.[37]
- The patient's heels should be placed in the lowest position possible.[61]
- Support should be provided over the largest surface area of the leg possible.[61]
- The patient's legs should not rest against the stirrup posts.[60]
- Scrubbed personnel should not lean against the patient's thighs.[60,62]
- The patient should be in the lithotomy position for the shortest time possible.[61]
- Care should be exercised to avoid shearing when moving the patient to the break in the procedure bed during repositioning.

VIII.k.2. In prolonged procedures (ie, longer than four hours), the perioperative team should consider repositioning the patient in the lithotomy position as a strategy to reduce the risk of pressure injury (eg, skin damage, nerve injury, compartment syndrome).[60,62]

One research review suggests that perioperative team members remove the patient's legs from support structures every two hours, if the procedure is anticipated to last four hours or more.[63] Research does not identify how long the patient's legs should be out of the stirrups before repositioning.

VIII.k.3. The perioperative registered nurse should monitor the patient at all times, especially when the safety strap is removed.

Proper placement of the safety strap is difficult in the lithotomy position. The perioperative registered nurse may not be able to place the safety strap low across the patient's pelvis without restricting access to the surgical site. Use of a safety strap that is placed high or too tight across the abdomen increases the

risk of restricting respiration or causing pressure injuries. The patient's legs may seem to be secure in leg holders with his or her arms tucked at the side. It is important to remember that there is still a risk for the patient to shift on the procedure bed, especially when moving into or out of Trendelenburg's position, which is often used in conjunction with the lithotomy position.

VIII.k.4. When positioning the patient into and out of the lithotomy position, a minimum of two caregivers is needed to lift the legs. Mechanical devices such as support slings can be used to lift the legs to and from the lithotomy position.[13]

VIII.l. The perioperative team should implement measures to reduce the risk of injury to patient and caregivers associated with the lateral position. (PNDS: I3, I11, I77, I96, I122)

The patient in the lateral position is at risk of injury due to spinal misalignment and vulnerable pressure points on the dependent side, specifically the ear, acromion process, iliac crest, greater trochanter, lateral knee, and malleolus.[9]

In a lateral position, the patient is positioned on the nonoperative side. This dependent side is the reference point for documentation. For example, when documenting a right lateral position, the patient is lying on his or her right side. This position provides exposure for a left-sided procedure (eg, upper chest or kidney procedure). When documenting the left lateral position, the patient is lying on the left side. The left lateral position provides exposure for a surgical or invasive procedure on the patient's right side.

One research study on interface pressures found that the highest pressures occurred in the lateral position and that there was an increased risk for the procedure bed mattress to become fully compressed under the weight of the patient's body and cause a "bottoming out" effect.[6] Another study found an increased risk for ulceration when a solid object or positioning device (eg, "bean bag" product) is used to maintain patients in a specific position. The firm pressure of the positioning device may compromise the circulatory system due to the tight restraint and because of the overall effect of gravity on the horizontal body posture.[25]

The lateral position increases the risk of damage to the common peroneal nerve if there is not padding to protect the nerve on the dependent leg from being compressed between the fibula and the procedure bed.[50]

VIII.l.1. Safety considerations for the lateral position should include, but are not limited to, the following:
- The patient's spinal alignment should be maintained during turning.
- The patient's dependent leg should be flexed for support.[37]
- The patient's straight upper leg should be padded and supported with pillows between the legs.
- Padding should be used under the patient's dependent knee, ankle, and foot.
- A headrest or pillow should be placed under the patient's head to keep the cervical and thoracic vertebrae aligned.
- The patient's dependent ear should assessed to ensure that it is not folded, and the ear should be well padded.[37]
- The patient's arm should be secured to prevent movement during the procedure.

VIII.l.2. To safely position a patient weighing up to 76 lb (ie, 34.5 kg) into and out of the lateral position, three caregivers should be assigned; one caregiver (eg, the anesthesia care provider) should be assigned specifically to support the patient's head and neck and maintain the patient's airway during the lateral transfer.

When positioning or repositioning the anesthetized patient into and out of the lateral position, pushing and pulling forces can occur rather than lifting forces. Three caregivers plus an anesthesia care provider can safely position a patient weighing up to 115 lbs (ie, 52.2 kg). If the patient's weight exceeds 115

lbs (ie, 52.2 kg), it is important to use lateral positioning devices.[13]

VIII.m. The perioperative team members should implement measures to reduce the risk of injury to patient and caregivers associated with the morbidly obese patient. (PNDS: I3, III, I64, I77, I96, I122)

Morbid obesity is associated with patients who have a BMI of greater than 40 or who weigh 100 lbs or more over their recommended weight. Patients who are morbidly obese tend to have other health conditions, such as type II diabetes, hypertension, atherosclerosis, arthritis of weight bearing joints, sleep apnea, alveolar hypoventilation, urinary stress incontinence, and gastroesophageal reflux disease. Morbidly obese patients are at increased risk for stroke and sudden death.[65]

It is essential for perioperative team members to understand the pathophysiology of obesity and the effects that various positions have on the obese patient's cardiopulmonary function.[66]
- Respiratory issues include
  - airway compromise due to a patient's short, thick neck;
  - risk of difficult intubation;
  - increased risk for hypoxia;
  - increased risk for intra-abdominal pressure on diaphragm; and
  - increased risk of aspiration.
- Circulatory issues include
  - increased cardiac output,
  - increased pulmonary artery pressure, and
  - risk of inferior vena cava compression.

VIII.m.1. Safety considerations for positioning the morbidly obese patient should include, but are not limited to, the following:
- The procedure bed should be capable of articulating and supporting patients weighing 800 to 1000 lbs (363.2 kg to 454 kg.[15] Specialized hydraulics should be capable of lifting patients weighing 800 to 1000 lbs (363.2 kg to 454 kg).[67]
- Mattresses should provide sufficient support and padding and should not "bottom out."[23]

- The width of the patient's legs determines whether the lower legs will remain on the procedure bed or must be supported by stirrups. Side attachments may be available on more recent procedure bed models.
- The patient's size may cause difficulty in determining if arms are positioned at less than a 90-degree angle. Padded sleds/toboggans may be used to contain the patient's arms at the side of the body if necessary, provided they can be used without causing excessive pressure on the arms.
- An extra wide, extra long safety strap should be used for patients who exceed the length limits for a regular size safety strap. Sheets should not be substituted for inadequately-sized safety straps. Two separate safety straps may be necessary to decrease the risk for the patient falling off the procedure bed due to instability and weight load shifts. One safety strap should be placed across the patient's thighs and one over the patient's lower legs.[22]
- When in the supine position, a roll or wedge should be placed under the patient's right flank to relieve compression of vena cava.
- Patients may not be able to tolerate the supine position due to respiratory or circulatory compromises; it may be necessary to reposition the patient into a sitting or lateral position.[66]
- When in the prone position, the patient's upper chest and pelvis should be adequately supported to free the abdominal viscera to reduce pressure on the diaphragm and inferior vena cava.[66]
- Trendelenburg's position should be avoided because the added weight of the abdominal contents press against the diaphragm causing respiratory compromise, and the increased blood flowing from the lower extremities into central and pulmonary circulation causes vascular congestion.

- In reverse Trendelenburg's position, care should be taken when placing the patient's feet against a padded footboard to ensure that his or her feet are aligned and flat against the board. This prevents rotation and increased pressure on the ankle.
- The lithotomy position should be avoided, if possible, due to the weight of the patient's thighs pressing on his or her abdomen and raising intra-abdominal pressure, thus increasing the risk of circulatory complications.
- If the patient is placed in the lithotomy position, heavy-duty stirrups should be used, and the perioperative nurse should be aware of and institute measures to reduce risks for respiratory, circulatory, and neurological complications.
- The lateral position may be preferred over the prone position as the bulk of the patient's panniculus can be displaced off the abdomen. The perioperative nurse should be aware, however, that a shift of the patient's panniculus may increase the risk of falling or other injury due to unintentional change in position.[15]

Recommendation IX

After positioning the patient, the perioperative registered nurse should assess the patient's body alignment, tissue perfusion, and skin integrity.

Respiratory function may be compromised after positioning the surgical patient depending on individual factors and patient position.[12,37]

Circulatory function is influenced by anesthetic agents and surgical techniques that may result in vasodilatation, hypertension, decreased cardiac output, and inhibition of normal compensatory mechanisms.[37]

Intraoperative skin injury occurs because of a combination of events:
- ◆ unrelieved pressure,
- ◆ duration of the pressure, and
- ◆ the individual patient's ability to withstand the insult.

Several studies indicate that procedures over two-and-one-half to three hours significantly increase the patient's risk for pressure ulcer formation.[37,68] External skin pressure exceeding normal capillary interface pressure (ie, 23 to 32 mm Hg) can cause capillary occlusion that will restrict or block blood flow. The resulting tissue ischemia leads to tissue breakdown. Both high pressure for a short duration and low pressure for extended duration are pressure injury risk factors. Other extrinsic factors for skin injury include shear forces and friction.[3,4,7,34,64,68]

IX.a.   After the desired patient position is attained, the perioperative registered nurse should reassess the patient to include, but not be limited to, the following systems:
    – respiratory,
    – circulatory,
    – neurological, and
    – musculoskeletal/integumentary.[1,11] (PNDS: I38, I87, I96, I128)

    Positions such as lithotomy and Trendelenburg's can cause redistribution and congestion of the patient's blood supply.[12,43]

    Circulatory responses to certain positions or position changes can be rapid and dramatic.[12,43]

IX.b.   The perioperative registered nurse should monitor the patient for external pressure from surgical team members leaning against the patient's body. (PNDS: I77, I128)

    Retractors, equipment, or instruments resting on the patient and members of the perioperative team resting or leaning on the patient add to the risk of pressure injuries that cause nerve or tissue damage.[37,60]

IX.b.1.   The perioperative registered nurse should communicate with the surgical team about the position of surgical instruments, retractor frames, Mayo stands, or other items placed on or over the patient throughout the procedure.[12,60]

IX.c.   The perioperative registered nurse should reassess the patient's body alignment, placement of the safety strap, and the placement of all padding after repositioning or any movement of the patient, procedure bed, or any equipment that attaches to the procedure bed.[12] (PNDS: I11; I128)

Changing the patient's position may expose or damage otherwise protected body tissue. The safety strap may shift and apply increased pressure when repositioning the patient or adding extra padding.

Patient repositioning may increase the risk of pressure ulcer development due to shearing of tissue.[24,40]

An injury may result from adding or deleting positioning equipment, adjusting the procedure bed, or moving the patient on the procedure bed.[12]

In nonsurgical settings, patients who are identified as being at risk for developing pressure injuries are turned or repositioned at least once every two hours. If a patient is chair-bound preoperatively, it is optimal to reposition the patient once every hour.[3] When patients receive anesthesia, they are even more vulnerable to the effects of pressure due to physiological changes.[67] One study found that the incidence of occipital alopecia was significantly reduced when the patient's head was repositioned at regular intervals during prolonged procedures (ie, longer than four hours).[69]

When a prolonged surgical procedure is expected, a patient who is in the lithotomy position may need to be repositioned every two hours to reduce the risk of pressure injury and compartment syndrome.[60,62,63]

Patients who have a radial intra-arterial catheter in place throughout the procedure may have their wrists in a hyperextended position for the duration of the surgical procedure. One study suggests that patients' wrists should be returned to the neutral position following arterial catheter placement as a strategy to decrease the risk of injury to the median nerve.[70]

Literature searches demonstrate that it is difficult to determine the effect of patient repositioning during a surgical procedure because, while position changes are documented, these changes are not normally identified as a strategy to prevent pressure injuries.[71,72]

IX.c.1.   The perioperative registered nurse should communicate with anesthesia personnel and the surgeon when assessing the need for repositioning the patient every two hours for prolonged procedures.

Table 1

PRESSURE ULCER STAGES	
Suspected deep tissue injury Purple or maroon localized area of discolored intact skin or blood-filled blister due to damage of underlying soft tissue from pressure and/or shear. The area may be preceded by tissue that is painful, firm, mushy, boggy, warmer, or cooler as compared to adjacent tissue. ***Further description:*** Deep tissue injury may be difficult to detect in individuals with dark skin tones. Evolution of the injury may include a thin blister over a dark wound bed. The wound may further evolve and become covered by thin eschar. Evolution may be rapid, exposing additional layers of tissue even with optimal treatment. **Stage I** Intact skin with nonblanchable redness of a localized area usually over a bony prominence. Darkly pigmented skin may not have a visible blanching; its color may differ from the surrounding area. ***Further description:*** The area may be painful, firm, or soft, and warmer or cooler than adjacent tissue. Stage I may be difficult to detect in individuals with dark skin tones. **Stage II** Partial-thickness loss of dermis presenting as a shallow, open ulcer with a red-pink wound bed, without slough. May also present as an intact or open/ruptured serum-filled blister. ***Further description:*** Presents as a shiny or dry shallow ulcer without slough or bruising.* This stage should not be used to describe skin tears, tape burns, perineal dermatitis, maceration, or excoriation. *Bruising indicates suspected deep tissue injury.* *Adapted with permission from* The National Pressure Ulcer Advisory Panel, *Washington, DC.*	**Stage III** Full-thickness tissue loss. Subcutaneous fat may be visible, but bone, tendon, or muscles are not exposed. Slough may be present but does not obscure the depth of tissue loss. May include undermining and tunneling. ***Further description:*** The depth of a stage III pressure ulcer varies by anatomical location. The bridge of the nose, ear, occiput, and malleolus do not have subcutaneous tissue,and stage III ulcers can be shallow. In contrast, areas of significant adiposity can develop extremely deep stage III pressure ulcers. Bone/tendon is not visible or directly palpable. **Stage IV** Full-thickness tissue loss with exposed bone, tendon, or muscle. Slough or eschar may be present on some parts of the wound bed. Often include undermining and tunneling. ***Further description:*** The depth of a stage IV pressure ulcer varies by anatomical location. The bridge of the nose, ear, occiput, and malleolus do not have subcutaneous tissue, and these ulcers can be shallow. Stage IV ulcers can extend into muscle and/or supporting structures (eg, fascia, tendon, joint capsule), making osteomyelitis possible. Exposed bone/tendons are visible or directly palpable. **Unstageable** Full-thickness tissue loss in which the base of the ulcer is covered by a yellow, tan, gray, green, or brown slough and/or tan, brown, or black eschar in the wound bed. ***Further description:*** Until enough slough and/or eschar are removed to expose the base of the wound, the true depth, and therefore stage, cannot be determined. Stable wounds are dry, adherent, and intact without erythema or fluctuance. Eschar on the heels serves as "the body's natural (ie, biological) cover" and should not be removed.

IX.c.2. The perioperative registered nurse should place his or her hand between the safety strap and the patient to ensure the strap is not applying excessive pressure to the patient's tissue.[12]

IX.c.3. The perioperative registered nurse should assess the patient for adequate padding by positioning a hand, palm up, below the part of the body at risk to be sure there is more than an inch of support material between the body part and any hard surface.[3]

IX.c.4. The perioperative registered nurse should confirm that prep solutions have not pooled beneath the patient and check for excessive moisture (eg, urine from incontinence) between the patient and positioning devices before the start of the surgical procedure.

A patient's skin may be more susceptible to pressure and friction due to prep solutions that change the pH of the skin and remove protective oils. When prep solutions pool beneath a patient, there is increased risk for skin maceration.[4,24]

Recommendation X

The perioperative registered nurse should collaborate with the postoperative patient caregiver to identify patient injury due to intraoperative positioning.

The incidence of pressure ulcers occurring as a result of surgery may be as high as 66%. Pressure ulcers that originate in surgery may be assessed and documented as burns and may not appear until one to four days postoperatively. Operating room-acquired pressure injuries have a unique purple appearance initially. They tend to progress outwardly with origination at the muscle overlying bony prominences, which explains why they may not be detected when the initial skin assessment is done in the operating room. Pressure injuries in nonsurgical patients progress inward, getting deeper as the tissue injury advances[3] (**Table 1**).

Epithelialization may be delayed in patients who are obese, which may cause poor postoperative wound healing and increased risk of infection.[21]

X.a. Perioperative registered nurses should evaluate the patient for signs and symptoms of physical injury related to intraoperative positioning. (PNDS: I44, I45, I46, I146; I152)

Pressure ulcers are staged according to the degree of tissue damage.[4,73,74] Refer to **Table 1** for assessment descriptors.

X.a.1. Perioperative registered nurses should identify patients who are high risk for postoperative injuries due to positioning and communicate areas of concern with postoperative care provider. (PNDS: I64)

X.a.2. When the patient has been in the lateral position for an extended amount of time in the OR, the perioperative nurse should alert the nurses caring for the patient postoperatively to carefully inspect the areas that are at high risk for pressure injuries. It is important to change the patient's positions postoperatively to avoid recurring pressure on those high risk areas.[6]

X.a.3. Patients who have been identified to be at-risk for development of postoperative vision loss should be assessed when the patient becomes alert postoperatively.

The patient who has anemia preoperatively, who undergoes a prolonged procedure, and who experiences substantial blood loss is identified as a high-risk patient for perioperative vision loss. Patient assessment, position modification, and staged procedures are strategies identified to minimize the risk of this rare complication.[56,58]

The incidence of postoperative eye injury in nonocular surgery is relatively uncommon, but the risk may be greater in patients whose surgery involves the face, head, or neck, and in patients whose surgery requires use of the lateral position. The patient's age and length of procedure are also factors for ocular injury.[75]

X.b. Perioperative registered nurses should establish open communications with postoperative care providers to obtain feedback about postoperative injuries due to positioning. (PNDS: I38, I42)

X.b.1. When patients are discharged the same day as the surgery, perioperative registered nurses should include an evaluation for signs and symptoms of injury due to positioning in the postoperative phone call.

Recommendation XI

Competency
Perioperative personnel should receive initial education, competency validation, and updated information on patient positioning, new positioning equipment and procedures, and ergonomic safety.

Competency verification serves as an indicator that personnel have a basic understanding of patient positioning, the risks of injury to patient and to staff members, and understand what may be implemented as appropriate corrective action when a process failure occurs.

XI.a. The perioperative registered nurse should be educated in, and demonstrate knowledge about, the physiologic effects and implications of positioning in relation to the patient's assessed status and limitations.[3,12]

Knowledge of anatomy and physiology enhances the perioperative registered nurse's appreciation of injury mechanisms associated with common intraoperative patient positions.[12]

XI.b. Perioperative personnel should be familiar with the proper function and use of positioning equipment.

Ongoing education of perioperative personnel will assist them in developing skills that will decrease the risk of patient injury due to positioning.

XI.c. Perioperative personnel should receive education and competency validation in new positioning equipment as they are introduced into the perioperative setting.

XI.d. Members of the perioperative team who transport patients should demonstrate competency in operating transport equipment.

XI.e. Administrative personnel should periodically assess and document the competency of personnel in safe patient positioning and use of positioning equipment according to facility and department policy. (PNDS: I1)

Recommendation XII

Documentation

Patient care and use of positioning devices should be documented on the intraoperative record by the registered nurse circulator.

Documenting nursing activities provides a description of the perioperative nursing care administered, status of patient outcomes upon transfer, and provides information for continuity of patient care.[76]

XII.a. Documentation should include, but not be limited to,
- preoperative assessment including a description of the patient's overall skin condition on arrival and discharge from the perioperative suite;
- type and location of positioning equipment;
- name and titles of persons participating in positioning the patient;
- patient position and new position, if repositioning becomes necessary; and
- postoperative assessment for injury related to position.[1,76]

XII.b. Photography used to document injuries due to positioning should be consistent with health care organization's policies regarding medical photography and videotaping.

Although the American Medical Directors Association's guidelines for pressure-ulcer prevention and treatment suggest photographs as a means to monitor the progress of wound care, risk management experts and health care attorneys may advise against photographs being included in the patient's chart. If photography is used, high-definition grid film may be recommended for accuracy. Digital images can be modified, resulting in questions about the accuracy and integrity of the image.[3]

Recommendation XIII

Policies and Procedures

Policies and procedures related to positioning should be developed, reviewed annually, revised as necessary, and readily available in the practice setting.

Policies and procedures establish authority, responsibility, and accountability. Policies also assist in the development of performance improvement activities. These recommended practices should be used to guide the development of policies and procedures within the individual perioperative practice setting.

XIII.a. Policies and procedures for positioning should include, but not be limited to,
- assessment and evaluation criteria,
- required documentation,
- safety interventions,
- positioning equipment care and maintenance, and
- ergonomic safety.

XIII.b. Perioperative policies on positioning should be consistent with the health care organization's risk-control plan for pressure ulcer prevention and management

Recommendation XIV

Quality

A quality management program should be in place to evaluate the outcomes of patient positioning practices and to improve patient safety.

To evaluate the quality of patient care and formulate plans for corrective action, it is necessary to maintain a system of evaluation.[77,78]

XIV.a. Perioperative administration members should participate in developing and monitoring an organization-wide risk control plan for pressure ulcer prevention and management.

XIV.a.1. Pressure ulcer prevention and management risk-control plans should include, but not be limited to, the following:
- a method for identifying patients at risk for pressure ulcers;
- a documentation system to follow the progress of a wound;
- prevention protocols that protect the patient's skin integrity; and
- education programs for caregivers, patients, and family members.[3,79]

XIV.b. Information about adverse patient outcomes and "near-miss incidents" associated with positioning should be collected, analyzed, and used for performance improvement as part of the institution-wide performance improvement program.

To demonstrate that all reasonable efforts were made to protect the patient's safety, it is considered a sound professional practice to document information according to organizational policy when an event occurs.[80]

XIV.b.1. Following organizational policy, documentation of an event related to positioning should include, but not be limited to,
- a description of what happened,
- the date and time of the incident,
- location of the incident,
- witnesses,
- corrective action to be implemented, and
- communications made regarding the outcome.

XIV.b.2. Data on health care personnel injuries related to positioning activities should be collected, analyzed, and used for performance improvement.

Glossary

Body mass index (BMI): The measure of a person's body fat based on height and weight that applies to both adult men and women.

Braden scale: A widely used assessment tool for predicting the development of pressure sores.

Capillary interface pressure: The amount of pressure placed on the skin's resting surface over a bony prominence.

Compartment syndrome: A pathologic condition caused by the progressive development of arterial compression and consequent reduction of blood supply. Clinical manifestations include swelling, restriction of movement, vascular compromise, and severe pain or lack of sensation.

Ergonomics: The science of fitting the demands of work to the anatomical, physiological, and psychological capabilities of the worker to enhance efficiency and well-being.

Friction: The act of rubbing one object (or tissue surface) against another.

Morbid obesity: A person whose body mass index (BMI) is more than 40.

Procedure bed: A type of bed used in ORs or procedure rooms that allow the surgical team access to the patient and the ability to position the patient for a surgical procedure through the use of the bed, its positions, and its attachments.

Positioning equipment/devices: Any device or piece of equipment used for positioning the patient and/or providing maximum anatomic exposure. Devices include, but are not limited to,
- support devices for head, arms, chest, iliac crests, and lumbar areas;
- pads in a variety of sizes and shapes for pressure points (eg, head, elbows, knees, ankles, heels, sacral areas);
- securing devices (eg, safety belts, tapes, kidney rests, vacuum-pack positioning devices);
- procedure beds equipment (eg, headrest/holders, overhead arm supports, stirrups, footboard); and
- specialty surgical beds (eg, fracture table, ophthalmology carts/stretchers, chairs).[16]

Shearing: A sliding movement of skin and subcutaneous tissue that leaves the underlying muscle stationary.

REFERENCES

1. Petersen C, ed. *Perioperative Nursing Data Set.* Rev 2nd ed. Denver, CO: AORN, Inc; 2007:43-44, 64-66.

2. National Pressure Ulcer Advisory Panel Support Surface Standards Initiative. Terms and definitions related to support surfaces. Ver. 01/29/07. *http://invisible caregiver.com/docs/NPUAP_Standards.pdf.* Accessed December 7, 2007.

3. ECRI. Pressure ulcers. *HRC Risk Analysis.* 2006;3(Nursing 4):1-37.

4. Armstrong D, Bortz P. An integrative review of pressure relief in surgical patients. *AORN J.* 2001;73:645, 647-648, 650-653.

5. Nixon J, McElvenny D, Mason S, Brown J, Bond S. A sequential randomised controlled trial comparing a dry visco-elastic polymer pad and standard operating procedure bed mattress in the prevention of postoperative pressure sores. *Int J Nurs Stud.* 1998;35:193-203.

6. Defloor T, De Schuijmer JD. Preventing pressure ulcers: an evaluation of four operating-table bed mattresses. *Applied Nursing Research.* 2000;13:134-141.

7. Hoshowsky VM, Schramm CA. Intraoperative pressure sore prevention: an analysis of bedding materials. *Res Nurs Health.* 1994;17:333-339.

8. Shelton F, Lott JW. Conducting and interpreting interface pressure evaluations of clinical support surfaces. *Geriatr Nurs.* 2003;24:222-227.

9. King CA. Comparison of pressure relief properties of operating room surfaces. *Perioperative Nursing Clinics.* 2006;1:261-265.

10. Cullum N, McInnes E, BellSyer SEM, Legood R. Support surfaces for pressure ulcer prevention. *Cochrane Database Syst Rev.* 2007;(1):ID10300075320-1000 00000-01074.

11. Schultz A. Predicting and preventing pressure ulcers in surgical patients. *AORN J.* 2005;81:986-1006.

12. McEwen DR. Intraoperative positioning of surgical patients. *AORN J.* 1996;63:1058-1063, 1066-1075, 1077-1082.

13. Petersen C, ed. *AORN Guidance Statement: Safe Patient Handling and Movement in the Perioperative Setting.* Denver, CO: AORN, Inc; 2007:1-32.

14. Facility design, equipment, and supplies. In: *Bariatric Services: Safety, Quality, and Technology Guide.* Plymouth Meeting, PA: ECRI; 2004:77-110.

15. Dybec RB. Intraoperative positioning and care of the obese patient. *Plastic Surgical Nursing.* 2004;24:118-122.

16. Recommended practices for product selection in perioperative practice settings. In: *Standards, Recommended Practices, and Guidelines.* Denver, CO: AORN, Inc; 2007:637-640.

17. AORN position statement on correct site surgery. In: *Standards, Recommended Practices, and Guidelines.* Denver, CO: AORN, Inc; 2007:371-374.

18. Joint Commission. Implementation expectations for the universal protocol for preventing wrong site, wrong procedure, and wrong person surgery, 2003. *http://www.jointcommission.org/NR/rdonlyres/DEC4A816-ED52-4C04-AF8C-FEBA74A732EA/0/up_guidelines.pdf.* Accessed May 3, 2007.

19. AORN guidance statement: creating a patient safety culture. In: *Standards, Recommended Practices, and Guidelines.* Denver, CO: AORN, Inc; 2007:305-310.

20. Recommended practices for a safe environment of care. In: *Standards, Recommended Practices, and Guidelines.* Denver, CO: AORN, Inc; 2008:351-373.

21. Keller C. The obese patient as a surgical risk. *Semin Perioper Nurs.* 1999;8:109-117.

22. Graling P, Elariny, H. Perioperative care of the patient with morbid obesity. *AORN J.* 2003;77:801-819.

23. Bushard S. Trauma in patients who are morbidly obese. *AORN J.* 2002;76:585-589.

24. Sieggreen M. OR-acquired pressure ulcers in vascular surgery patients. *Adv Wound Care.* 1998;11:12.

25. Aronovitch SA. Intraoperatively acquired pressure ulcer prevalence: a national study. *Journal of WOCN.* 1999/5;26:130-136.

26. Catalano, K. Update on the national patient safety goals—changes for 2005. *AORN J.* 2005;81:336-341.

27. Robey-Williams C, Rush KL, Bendyk H, Patton LM, Chamberlain D, Sparks T. Spartanburg Fall Risk Assessment Tool: a simple three-step process. *Applied Nursing Research.* 2007;20:86-93.

28. Beyea S. Preventing patient falls in perioperative settings. [Patient Safety First]. *AORN J.* 2005; 81:393-395.

29. Nelson A, Fragala G, Menzel N. Myths and facts about back injuries in nursing. *Am J Nurs.* 2003;103:32-40.

30. Stetler CB, Burns M, Sander-Buscemi K, Morsi D, Grunwald E. Use of evidence for prevention of work-related musculoskeletal injuries. *Orthop Nurs.* 2003; 22:32-41.

31. Chappy, S. Perioperative patient safety: a multisite qualitative analysis. *AORN J.* 2006; 83:871-897.

32. Sewchuk D, Padula C, Osborne E. Prevention and early detection of pressure ulcers in patients undergoing cardiac surgery. *AORN J.* 2006; 84:75-96.

33. Feuchtinger J, de Bie R, Dassen T, Halfens R. A 4-cm thermoactive viscoelastic foam pad on the operating room procedure bed to prevent pressure ulcer during cardiac surgery. *J Clin Nurs.* 2006;15:162-167.

34. Ramsay J. Pressure ulcer risk factors in the operating room. *Advances in Wound Care.* 1998;11:5-6.

35. Reddy M, Gill SS, Rochon PA. Preventing pressure ulcers: a systematic review. *JAMA.* 2006; 296: 974-984.

36. Landis EM. Micro-injection studies of capillary blood pressure in human skin. *Heart.* 1930;15:209-228.

37. O'Connell MP. Positioning impact on the surgical patient. *Nurs Clin North Am.* 2006;41:173-192.

38. AORN explications for perioperative nursing. In: *Standards, Recommended Practices, and Guidelines.* Denver, CO: AORN, Inc; 2007;171-201.

39. Larkin BG. The ins and outs of body piercing. *AORN J.* 2004;79:333-342.

40. Aronovitch SA, Wilber M, Slezak S, Martin T, Utter D. A comparative study of an alternating air mattress for the prevention of pressure ulcers in surgical patients. *Ostomy Wound Management.* 1999;45:34-40.

41. Practice advisory for the prevention of perioperative peripheral neuropathies: a report by the American Society of Anesthesiologists Task Force on Prevention of Perioperative Peripheral Neuropathies. *Anesthesiology.* 2000;92:1168-1182.

42. Fritzlen T, Kremer M, Biddle C. The AANA Foundation Closed Malpractice Claims Study on nerve injuries during anesthesia care. *AANA J.* 2003;71:347-352.

43. Ayello EA. Preventing pressure ulcers and skin tears. In: Mezey M, Fulmer T, Abraham I, Zwicker DA, eds. *Geriatric Nursing Protocols for Best Practice.* 2nd. ed. New York, NY: Springer Publishing Company, Inc; 2003:165-184.

44. Walsh J. *AANA Journal* course: update for nurse anesthetists—patient positioning. *AANA J.* 1994;62:289-298.

45. Lindgren M, Unosson M, Krantz AM, Ek AC. Pressure ulcer risk factors in patients undergoing surgery. *J Adv Nurs.* 2005;50:605-612.

46. Birnbach DJ, Browne IM. Anesthesia for obstetrics. In: *Miller's Anesthesia, Volume Two.* Miller RD, ed. 6th ed. Philadelphia, PA: Elsevier; 2006: 2309.

47. Liau, DW. Injuries and liability related to peripheral catheters: a closed claims analysis. *ASA Newsletter.* June 2006. *http://www.asahq.org/newsletter/2006 /06/liau06_06.html.* Accessed December 12, 2007.

48. Faust RJ, Cucchiara RF, Bechtel PS. Patient positioning. In: *Miller's Anesthesia, Volume One.* Miller RD, ed. 6th ed. Philadelphia, PA: Elsevier; 2006:1155-1158.

49. Coppieters MW, Van de Velde M, Stappaerts KH. Positioning in anesthesiology: toward a better understanding of stretch-induced perioperative neuropathies. [Comment]. *Anesthesiology.* 2002;97:75-81.

50. Sawyer RJ, Richmond MN, Hickey JD, Jarrratt JA. Peripheral nerve injuries associated with anaesthesia. [Comment]. *Anaesthesia.* 2000;55:980-991.

51. Cheney FW, Domino KB, Caplan RA, Posner KL. Nerve injury associated with anesthesia: a closed claims analysis. *Anesthesiology.* 1999;90:1062-1069.

52. France MP, Aurori BF. Pudendal nerve palsy following fracture procedure bed traction. *Clinical Orthopaedics & Related Research.* 1992;276:272-276.

53. Toolan BC, Koval KJ, Kummer FJ, Goldsmith ME, Zuckerman JD. Effects of supine positioning and fracture post placement on the perineal countertraction force in awake volunteers. *J Orthop Trauma.* 1995;9:164-170.

54. Lloyd JD, Baptiste A. Friction-reducing devices for lateral patient transfers: a biomechanical evaluation. *American Association of Occupational Health Nurses.* 2006;54:113-119.

55. Chaffin DB, Andersson G, Martin BJ. *Occupational Biomechanics.* 3rd ed. New York: J Wiley & Sons; 1999:73.

56. American Society of Anesthesiologists Task Force on Perioperative Blindness. Practice advisory for perioperative visual loss associated with spine surgery: a report by the American Society of Anesthesiologists Task Force on Perioperative Blindness. *Anesthesiology.* 2006; 104:1319-1328.

57. Rupp-Montpetit K, Moody, ML. Visual loss as a complication of non-ophthalmologic surgery: a review of the literature. *AANA Journal.* 2004;72:285-292.

58. Giarrizzo-Wilson S. Postoperative vision loss; cellular telephones; medical gas handling; roller latches. [Clinical Issues]. *AORN J.* 2006;84:107-108, 111-114.

59. Biddle C, Cannaday MJ. Surgical positions. their effects on cardiovascular, respiratory systems. *AORN J.* 1990;52:350-359.

60. Irvin W, Andersen W, Taylor P, Rice L. Minimizing the risk of neurologic injury in gynecologic surgery. *Obstet Gynecol.* 2004;103:374-382.

61. Roeder RA, Geddes LA, Corson N, Pell C, Otlewski M, Kemeny A. Heel and calf capillary-support: pressure in lithotomy positions. *AORN J.* 2005;81:821-830.

62. Wilde S. Compartment syndrome. the silent danger related to patient positioning and surgery. *Br J Perioper Nurs.* 2004;14:546-550.

63. Raza A, Byrne D, Townell N. Lower limb (well leg) compartment syndrome after urological pelvic surgery. *J Urol.* 2004;171:5-11.

64. Pfeffer SD, Halliwill JR, Warner MA. Effects of lithotomy position and external compression on lower leg muscle compartment pressure. [Comment]. *Anesthesiology.* 2001;95:632-636.

65. Recommendations for facilities performing bariatric surgery. *Bull Am Coll Surg.* 2000;85:20-23.

66 Brodsky JB. Positioning the morbidly obese patient for anesthesia. *Obesity Surg.* 2002;12:751-758.

67. ECRI. Bariatric surgery. *Operating Room Risk Management.* May 2005:14-17.

68. Schouchoff B. Pressure ulcer development in the operating room. *Crit Care Nurs Q.* 2002;25:76-82.

69. Lawson N, Mills NL, Oschner JL. Occipital alopecia following cardiopulmonary bypass. *J Thorac Cardiovasc Surg.* 1976;71:342-347.

70. Chowet AL, Lopez JR, Brock-Utne JG, Jaffe RA. Wrist hyperextension leads to median nerve conduction block: Implications for intra-arterial catheter placement. *Anesthesiology.* 2004;100:287-291.

71. Stotts, NA. Risk assessment of pressure ulcer development in surgical patients. *Adv Skin Wound Care.* 1998;11(suppl 3):7.

72. Price MC, Whitney JD, King CA. Wound care. development of a risk assessment tool for intraoperative pressure ulcers. *J WOCN.* 2005;32:19-32.

73. Schoonhoven L, Defloor T, Grypdonck MH. Incidence of pressure ulcers due to surgery. *J Clin Nurs.* 2002;11:479-487.

74. National Pressure Ulcer Advisory Panel. Pressure ulcer definition and stages. February 2007. *http://www. npuap.org/pr2.htm.* Accessed November 6, 2007.

75. Roth S, Thisted RA, Erickson JP, Black S, Schreider BD. Eye injuries after nonocular surgery. a study of 60,965 anesthetics from 1988 to 1992. *Anesthesiology.* 1996;85:1020-1027.

76. Recommended practices for documentation of perioperative nursing care. In: *Standards, Recommended Practices, and Guidelines.* Denver, CO: AORN, Inc; 2007:511-514.

77. Dunn D. Incident reports: their purpose and scope. First in a two-part series. [Home Study Program]. *AORN J.* 2003;78:45-46, 49-61, 65-70.

78. Quality and performance improvement standards for perioperative nursing. In: *Standards, Recommended Practices, and Guidelines.* Denver, CO: AORN, Inc; 2007:437-446.

79. Agency for Healthcare Research and Quality. *Pressure Ulcers in Adults: Prediction and Prevention. Clinical Practice Guideline Number 3.* Pub No 92-0047 (May 1992). *http://www.ncbi.nlm.nih.gov/books/bv.fcgi?rid=hstat2.chapter.4409.* Accessed November 6, 2007.

80. Liang BA. The adverse event of unaddressed medical error: Identifying and filling the holes in the health-care and legal systems. *J Law Med Ethics.* 2001;29:346-368.

Originally published November 1990, *AORN Journal.* Revised November 1995; published August 1996, *AORN Journal.*

Revised and reformatted; published January 2001, *AORN Journal.*

Revised 2007; published in *Perioperative Standards and Recommended Practices,* 2008 edition.

From the Editor

The AORN guidance document titled *Safe Patient Handling and Movement in the Perioperative Setting* is referenced extensively in these recommended practices. It can be ordered online from AORN's Perioperative Bookstore, *http://www.aornbookstore.org,* by searching for MAN-167 as the ISBN product code. To go directly to the product page to place an order, type the following URL into your browser:

http://www.aornbookstore.org/product/product.asp?sku=MAN167

For assistance, call AORN Customer Service, 800-755-2676 ext. 1, and mention MAN-167.

Recommended Practices for Preoperative Patient Skin Antisepsis

The following recommended practices for preoperative patient skin antisepsis were developed by the AORN Recommended Practices Committee and have been approved by the AORN Board of Directors. They were presented as proposed recommendations for comments by members and others. They are effective January 1, 2008.

These recommended practices are intended as achievable recommendations representing what is believed to be an optimal level of practice. Policies and procedures will reflect variations in practice settings and/or clinical situations that determine the degree to which the recommended practices can be implemented.

AORN recognizes the various settings in which perioperative nurses practice. These recommended practices are intended as guidelines adaptable to various practice settings. These practice settings include traditional operating rooms, ambulatory surgery centers, physician's offices, cardiac catheterization laboratories, endoscopy suites, radiology departments, and all other areas where surgery may be performed.

References to nursing interventions (I) used in the Perioperative Nursing Data Set, second edition, (PNDS) are noted in parentheses when a recommended practice corresponds to a PNDS intervention.[1] The reader is referred to the PNDS for further explanation of perioperative nursing diagnoses, interventions, and outcomes.

Purpose

These recommended practices provide a guideline for achieving skin preparation of the surgical site. The goal of preoperative preparation of the patient's skin is to reduce the risk of postoperative surgical site infection by removing soil and transient microorganisms from the skin; reduce the resident microbial count to subpathogenic levels in a short period of time and with the least amount of tissue irritation; and inhibit rapid, rebound growth of microorganisms. The following recommended practices are considered established guidelines for perioperative practice.

Recommendation I

Patients undergoing open Class I surgical procedures below the chin should have two preoperative showers with chlorhexidine gluconate (CHG) before surgery, when appropriate.[2]

The act of washing and rinsing removes microorganisms from the skin. Some organisms may be difficult or impossible to kill with the application of CHG alone.

Staphylococcus aureus is the most common organism causing surgical site infections.[2,3] In 2003, 64.4% of health care-associated *Staphylococcus aureus* infections were from methicillin-resistant *Staphylococcus aureus* (MRSA).[4,5] Many surgical site infections result from colonization of the surgical site with the patient's own flora; and colonization with *Staphylococcus aureus* is a known risk factor for surgical site infection.[2,6,7] Clinical trials support the use of preoperative antiseptic showers to reduce the number of microorganisms on the skin, including *Staphylococcus aureus*.[8-11] In 1999, the Centers for Disease Control and Prevention recommend requiring patients to "shower or bathe with an antiseptic agent at least the night before the operative day" (Category IB).[2]

I.a.   Unless contraindicated, patients should be instructed or assisted to perform two preoperative baths or showers with CHG before surgery to reduce the number of microorganisms on the skin and reduce the risk of subsequent contamination of the surgical wound. (PNDS: I48, I123, I104, I50, I36, I106)

I.a.1.   Four percent CHG is more effective than povidone-iodine or soap, and more than one shower is necessary to achieve maximum antiseptic effectiveness.[8,9] One preoperative shower with 4% CHG was found to be twice as effective in reducing skin bacterial flora as showering with nonmedicated soap.[3] Two showers with 4% CHG were found to result in lower microbial counts than showers with bar soap, medicated soap, or povidone-iodine.[8,9] This greater reduction in microbial counts persisted for more than 11 hours.[8] One randomized clinical trial found two consecutive showers or baths with 4% CHG resulted in lower surgical site infection rates than bar soap (ie, 9% versus 12.8%).[9] Showering three times with 4% CHG was found to reduce skin flora 20-fold preoperatively and to lower bacterial counts of the incision taken at the end of the procedure.[10]

Researchers studied the effects of preoperative showering with 4% CHG and povidone-iodine on skin microbial counts of patients colonized with *Staphylococcus aureus*. Two consecutive showers with 4% CHG the evening before surgery reduced microbial counts in the subclavian and groin areas; however, povidone-iodine had little effect on colonization of the groin. Showering both the evening before and the morning of surgery with 4% CHG reduced the bacterial count further at both sites; povidone-iodine provided inconsistent results; and showering with lotion soap increased the colony counts in both the subclavian site and groin.[11]

A sequential process of two applications of CHG with a minimum of two minutes contact time for intraoperative skin preps is suggested by manufacturers' recommendations and supported by one efficacy study for surgical scrub agents.[12-15]

I.a.2. The reduction of the patient's own flora is more important with regard to surgical wounds that are classified as clean or surgical wound Class I.[2] For wounds that are partially or heavily contaminated, other organisms are more likely to contribute to surgical site infection, and showering with CHG may not be as advantageous. Research has not addressed the value of decolonizing patients before surgery on the eyes, ears, face, or before laparoscopic procedures.

I.a.3. Although there is sufficient evidence of the effectiveness of two CHG showers to reduce microbial counts, there is insufficient research to definitively link this decrease in microbial count to a reduction in surgical site infection rates.

I.a.4. Following each preoperative shower, the skin should be
- thoroughly rinsed;
- dried with a fresh, clean, dry towel; and
- the patient should don clean clothing.

Rinsing the skin removes residual CHG that may cause skin irritation.

After use, towels contain microorganisms that can grow in the presence of moisture. Using a fresh towel after each shower and donning clean clothing minimizes the risk of reintroducing microorganisms to clean skin.

I.b. Chlorhexidine gluconate preparation products used for preoperative showers should be US Food and Drug Administration (FDA)-approved or cleared for use as a general cleansing agent. (PNDS: I22, I75)

The FDA determines the appropriate uses for all approved or cleared products.[16,17]

I.c. Patients undergoing surgery on the head should be instructed or assisted to perform two preoperative shampoos with 4% CHG before surgery to reduce the number of microorganisms and subsequent contamination of the surgical site. (PNDS: I48, I123, I104, I51, I36, I106, I50)

Two shampoos with 4% CHG reduce the emergence of resident skin flora and contamination of the surgical wound.[18] Researchers found that patients receiving two 4% CHG-shampoos and an intraoperative skin prep with 4% CHG had fewer bacteria on the scalp, both preoperatively and postoperatively, and had significantly fewer positive postoperative scalp cultures than patients receiving either shampoos with povidone-iodine or no shampoos.[18]

Conditioners and other hair care products should not be used after performing preoperative shampoos because a chemical reaction between CHG and the hair care product may impede the antiseptic effectiveness of the CHG.[19]

I.c.1. Hair spray and other alcohol-based hair products should not be used during head and neck surgery.

Alcohol-based hair products are flammable and should not be left on the hair during head and neck surgery because they pose a fire hazard.[19,20]

I.d. Caution should be exercised to avoid CHG contact with the eyes, the inside of the ears, the meninges, or other mucous membranes. (PNDS: I75, I104, I36, I51)

CHG

Chlorhexidine gluconate is irritating to the eye and can cause corneal damage.[19] Exposure of CHG to the inner ear can result in permanent deafness.[13,19,22]

I.d.1. If CHG solution gets into the eye, immediately rinse the area with copious amounts of running water for at least 15 minutes and seek medical attention.[23]

I.d.2. Chlorhexidine gluconate should not be used on the head if the patient's tympanic membrane is not intact.

I.e. Chlorhexidine gluconate should not be used on patients for whom it is contraindicated, including patients with a known hypersensitivity to CHG or any other ingredient in the product.[19,22](PNDS: I123, I75)

Isolated incidents of hypersensitivity to CHG have been reported. Relatively minor symptoms upon exposure have preceded more serious reactions in some patients.[19]

Recommendation II

Preoperative skin antiseptic agents that have been FDA-approved or -cleared and approved by the health care organization's infection control personnel should be used for all preoperative skin preparation. (PNDS: I122)

The FDA determines the appropriate uses for products which the agency has approved or cleared.[16]

II.a. Current research, recommendations from the Association for Professionals in Infection Control and Epidemiology, FDA information, manufacturers' literature, and material safety data sheets (MSDSs) should be consulted when selecting antiseptic agents for skin preparation within health care organizations. (PNDS: I122, I75)

Decisions about which skin antiseptics should be used in the practice setting are complex. A variety of products may be necessary to meet the needs of various patient populations. Input from an infection control professional knowledgeable about antiseptics is helpful when reviewing the current research and documentation provided by manufacturers.

II.b. The preoperative skin antiseptic agent should:
- significantly reduce microorganisms on intact skin,
- contain a nonirritating antimicrobial preparation,
- be broad spectrum,
- be fast acting, and
- have a persistent effect.[17]

An antimicrobial ingredient is intended to kill microorganisms. A characteristic of certain antiseptic agents that sets them apart from plain soap is their ability to bind with the stratum corneum of the skin, resulting in persistent chemical activity. Alcohols provide the most rapid and greatest reduction in initial microbial counts on skin, but have no persistent activity.[8]

Persistent antimicrobial activity (ie, measured in hours) helps decrease rebound microbial growth after skin preparation. **Table 1** provides a summary of the characteristics of commonly used skin antiseptic agents.

II.c. Products selected for preoperative skin preparation should meet FDA requirements, as outlined in the Tentative Final Monograph (TFM) for Health-Care Antiseptic Drug Products, or be the subject of a "New Drug Approval" or an "Abbreviated New Drug Approval" process.[16,17,24] (PNDS: I75, I122)

The FDA requires products for preoperative skin preparation to be
- fast acting (ie, a two-log bacterial reduction on the abdomen and three-log reduction on the groin within 10 minutes), and
- persistent (ie, no return to baseline flora count at six hours post application).[16]

II.c.1. Persistence of the antimicrobial effect suppresses the regrowth of residual skin flora not removed by preoperative prepping, as well as suppressing transient microorganisms contacting the prepped site.

II.c.2. Infection control professionals and committees should review the data provided by manufacturers to ensure that surgical antisepsis agents comply with current FDA testing and labeling criteria. The testing should be performed at an independent testing laboratory complying with current FDA requirements and subject to FDA inspection.

Table 1

ACTIVITY AND CONSIDERATIONS FOR PREOPERATIVE SKIN PREPARATION ANTISEPTICS						
Antiseptic agent	Mechanism of action	Gram + bacteria	Gram − bacteria	Viruses	Rapidity of action	(continues on next page)
Alcohol	Denatures proteins.[1]	Excellent[1]	Excellent[1]	Good[1]	Excellent[1]	
Chlorhexidine gluconate	Disrupts cell membrane.[1]	Excellent[1]	Good[1]	Good[1]	Moderate[1]	
Povidone-iodine	Oxidation/substitution with free iodine.[1]	Excellent[1]	Good[1]	Good[1]	Moderate[1]	
Chlorhexidine gluconate with alcohol	Disrupts cell membrane and denatures proteins.[1,2]	Excellent	Excellent	Good	Excellent	
Iodine-based with alcohol	Oxidation/substitution by free iodine denatures proteins.[1,3,4]	Excellent[1,3,4]	Excellent	Good	Excellent	
Parachoroxylenol (PCMX)	Disrupts cell membrane.[1]	Good[1]	Fair[1]	Fair[1]	Moderate[1]	

REFERENCES

1. Mangram AJ, Horan TC, Pearson ML, Silver LC, Jarvis WR. Guideline for prevention of surgical site infection, 1999. *Infect Control Hosp Epidemiol.* 1999;20:250-278.

2. Denton GW. Chlorhexidine. In: *Disinfection, Sterilization and Preservation.* 5th ed. Block SS, ed. Philadelphia, PA: Lippincott Williams & Wilkins; 2001: 321-36

3. Bryant WP, Zimmerman D. Iodine-induced hyperthyroidism in a newborn. *Pediatrics.* 1995;95:434-436.

4. Smerdely P, Lim A, Boyages SC, et al. Topical iodine-containing antiseptics and neonatal hypothyroidism in very-low-birthweight infants. *Lancet.* 1989;2:661-664.

5. EnviroSystems, Incorporated. Technical Overview, Biocides. *http://www.envirosi.com/TechInfo/technical overview.html.* Accessed November 6, 2007.

(continued on following page)

Table 1 *(continued)*

ACTIVITY AND CONSIDERATIONS FOR PREOPERATIVE SKIN PREPARATION ANTISEPTICS					
Antiseptic agent	Persistent/ residual activity	Use on eye or ear	Use on mucous membranes	Contraindi-cations	Cautions
Alcohol	None[1]	No. Can cause corneal damage or nerve damage.[1]	No		Flammable. Does not penetrate organic material. Optimum concentration is 60% to 90%.[1]
Chlorhexidine gluconate	Excellent[1]	No. Can cause corneal damage. Can cause deafness if in contact with inner ear.[1]	Use with caution.[2]	Known hypersensitivity to drug or any ingredient.[2] Lumbar puncture and use on meninges.[2]	Prolonged skin contact may cause irritation in sensitive individuals. Rare severe hypersensitivity reactions have been reported.[2] Use with caution on mucous membranes.
Povidone-iodine	Minimal[1]	Yes. Moderate ocular irritant.	Yes	Sensitivity to povidone-iodine. (Shellfish allergies are not a contra-indication).[6]	Prolonged skin contact may cause irritation. May cause iodism in susceptible individuals; avoid use in neonates.[3,4] Inactivated by blood.[7,8]
Chlorhexidine gluconate with alcohol	Excellent	No. Can cause corneal damage. Can cause deafness if in contact with inner ear.	No	Known hypersensitivity to drug or any ingredient. Lumbar puncture and use on meninges.	Flammable.
Iodine-based with alcohol	Moderate	No. Can cause corneal damage or nerve damage.	No	Sensitivity to povidone-iodine. (Shellfish allergies are not a contra-indication.)	Flammable.
Parachoroxylenol (PCMX)	Moderate[1]	Yes[5]	Yes[5]	Known hypersensitivity to PCMX or any ingredient.[5]	Minimally effective in the presence of organic matter. The FDA has classified PCMX as a Category III (data are insufficient to classify it as safe and effective). The FDA continues to evaluate PCMX.[5]

(continued from previous page)
6. American Academy of Allergy Asthma and Immunology. Academy Position Statement: *The Risk of Severe Allergic Reactions from the Use of Potassium Iodide for Radiation Emergencies.* http://www.aaaai.org/media/resources/academy_statements/position_statements/potassium_iodide.asp. Accessed August 28, 2007.

7. Zamora JL, Price MF, Chuang P, Gentry LO. Inhibition of povidone iodine's bactericidal activity by common organic substances: an experimental study. *Surgery.* 1985;98:25-9.
8. Gottardi W. Iodine and iodine compounds. In: *Disinfection, Sterilization and Preservation.* 5th ed. Block SS, ed. Philadelphia, PA: Lippincott Williams & Wilkins; 2001:159-83.

The laboratory should employ either ASTM International (formerly known as the American Society for Testing and Materials) standard methods, or methods specifically approved by the FDA for use in conjunction with a particular New Drug Application subject product.

II.c.3. Consult scientific data when selecting new products for use.[25]

Recommendation III

The antiseptic agent used should be selected based on the patient assessment. (PNDS: I94)

The patient should be assessed for considerations affecting skin preparation.

III.a. The patient should be assessed for allergy or sensitivity to skin preparation agents. (PNDS: I123)

II.a.1. Povidone-iodine can cause contact dermatitis or irritant reactions and does not indicate an allergy to iodine. Anaphylaxis to povidone-iodine is extremely rare and has not been proven to be from the iodine.[26] There is no correlation between reactions to povidone-iodine and allergy to seafood or contrast media.[27,28]

II.a.2. Chlorhexidine gluconate has triggered allergic reactions in sensitized individuals ranging from mild local symptoms to severe anaphylaxis. Mild symptoms may precede severe attacks.[29]

III.b. The patient should be assessed for contraindications to specific skin preparation agents. (PNDS: I75, I122)
- Alcohol can cause tissue trauma (ie, necrosis, burns) in neonates with underdeveloped stratum corneum.[30-32]
- Transcutaneous absorption of iodine in neonates can result in iodism.[33-36]
- Safe use of CHG on neonates with underdeveloped stratum corneum has not been established.
- Chlorhexidine gluconate is neurotoxic and can cause permanent injury if the inner ear is exposed to CHG through a nonintact tympanic membrane. Chlorhexidine gluconate can cause corneal irritation if allowed to contact the eye.[19]
- Use of any agent is contraindicated if the patient has a known sensitivity.

III.b.1. The manufacturer's written instructions should be reviewed for additional information about their product's use.

III.c. The surgical site should be identified before skin preparation. (PNDS: I143, I124, I26)
The surgical site should be confirmed before initiating the skin prep. This verification minimizes the risk of prepping the wrong area, which could contribute to wrong-site surgery.

III.c.1. Verification should be done in advance of the "time out" period, which occurs immediately before the surgeon makes the incision.

III.d. The marker used to make the surgical site mark should
- not facilitate microbial growth, and
- provide a mark that remains visible after the surgical prep.[25,37] (PNDS: I138, I122, I98, I77, I75)
Marking the skin with an alcohol-based surgical site marker before skin preparation does not increase the amount of microorganisms on the skin.[38] Water-based skin markers may wash off during skin preparation and have been found to transmit MRSA in laboratory tests.[39]

III.d.1. Ballpoint pens should not be used for surgical skin marking because they may cause trauma to the skin during use.

III.e. The patient's skin condition should be assessed for the presence of lesions or other tissue conditions at the surgical site before skin preparation begins. (PNDS: I94, I77, I15, I21)
Unintentional removal of lesions (eg, nevi) traumatizes the skin at the surgical site and provides an opportunity for wound colonization by microorganisms.

III.e.1. The presence of excessive hair that may interfere with the surgical procedure should be identified.

III.f. The antiseptic product used for an individual patient should be selected based on
- patient allergies;
- a patient's report of significant skin irritation from specific antiseptic agents;
- contraindications to specific antiseptic agents;
- the surgical site to be prepped;
- the presence of organic matter, including blood;
- neonatal status;
- large, open wounds;
- a review of written manufacturer's information; and
- surgeon preference. (PNDS: I123, I94, I21, I75, I85)

Antiseptic agents used on the skin of patients with known hypersensitivity reactions (ie, allergies) may cause adverse outcomes (eg, blisters, rashes). Some antiseptic agents are affected by organic matter and/or saline and are rendered less effective (see **Table 1**). Some antiseptic agents may be absorbed by the skin or mucous membranes and become neurotoxic or ototoxic. Certain antiseptic agents are believed to be potentially harmful to neonates. Products made specifically for use on mucous membranes should be used following manufacturers' recommendations.

Recommendation IV

Hair at the surgical site should be left in place (ie, not removed) whenever possible. (PNDS: I94)

Research studies have found that preoperative shaving of the surgical site increases the risk of surgical site infection[40-42] and results in higher surgical site infection rates than using a depilatory cream or clipping.[42] Hair has successfully been left in place for neurosurgery without increasing the risk of surgical site infection.[43,44]

IV.a. The patient should be instructed not to shave or use a depilatory on the surgical site before surgery. (PNDS: I136, I77, I106)

Removing hair at the surgical site abrades the skin surface and enhances microbial growth. Shaving has been found to increase the risk of surgical site infection.[40-42] Depilatory creams may cause skin reactions in some individuals, which could result in cancellation of surgery.[42]

IV.b. Hair at the surgical site should not be removed with a razor. (PNDS: I77, I94)

Shaving increases the risk of surgical site infection.[39-41]

IV.b.1. Alternatives to hair removal for head and neck surgery include:
- braiding hair instead of shaving; and
- using a nonflammable gel to keep the hair away from the incision.[44]

IV.b.2. If the presence of hair will interfere with the surgical procedure and removal is in the best interest of the patient, the following precautions should be taken:
- Hair removal should be performed the day of surgery, in a location outside of the operating or procedure room.
- Only hair interfering with the surgical procedure should be removed.
- Hair should be clipped using a single-use electric or battery-operated clipper, or a clipper with a reusable head that can be disinfected between patients.

Clipping hair the morning of surgery has resulted in fewer surgical site infections than shaving or clipping the day before surgery.[45] Limiting the amount of clipping minimizes the risk of microscopic nicks. Clipping the hair outside of the operating room minimizes the dispersal of loose hair and the potential for contamination of the sterile field and surgical wound. During use, the clipper handle is contaminated with the patient's skin flora. The clipper head may become contaminated with microscopic blood or body fluids; therefore, decontamination for bloodborne pathogens is necessary to prevent transmission.

IV.b.3. Depilatories may be used for hair removal if skin testing has been performed without tissue irritation.

Depilatories may be used when hair is to be removed from the operative site. The use of depilatories, however, does increase the risk of hypersensitivity reactions. The written manufacturers' instructions regarding skin testing and the use of chemical depilatories should be followed.

Recommendation V

The skin around the surgical site should be free of soil, debris, exudates, and transient microorganisms to minimize contamination of the surgical wound before application of the antiseptic skin preparation. (PNDS: I94)

The efficacy of antiseptic agents is dependent on the cleanliness of the skin. Removal of superficial soil, debris, and transient microbes before applying antiseptic agents reduces the risk of wound contamination by decreasing the organic debris on the skin.

- No skin antiseptic alone is effective in killing spores (eg, clostridium).
- Some anatomic areas contain more debris than others (eg, umbilicus, under fingernails, under foreskin). Cleaning these areas separately from the surgical prep prevents distribution of microorganisms from these areas to the surgical site.
- Cleaning the foot before antiseptic skin preparation for surgery was found more effective in reducing bacterial counts between the toes than application of the antiseptic alone.[46]

V.a. If preoperative showers have not been performed, perioperative personnel should wash the surgical site either in the preoperative area or immediately before applying the antiseptic agent in the practice setting. (PNDS: I94, I85)

Preoperative washing removes gross contaminants and oils that may block penetration of the antiseptic agent and removes spores and other organisms that are not killed by the antiseptic agent.

V.b. Cosmetics should be removed before the preoperative skin prep. (PNDS: I94, I85)

Cosmetics may contribute to increased soil and contamination and impede the effectiveness of the antiseptic agent. The removal of facial cosmetics also may be indicated to prevent debris from irritating the eyes, to facilitate securing the endotracheal tube, or for other reasons identified by the surgical team.

V.b.1. To remove facial cosmetics, the face should be gently cleansed with a non-irritating agent.

Initial cleansing of the eyes, before application of the antiseptic agent, is not necessary because tears naturally rinse most contaminants from the eye.

V.c. For abdominal surgery, the umbilicus should be cleaned before the antiseptic skin preparation. (PNDS: I94, I98)

The organic and inorganic material in the umbilicus is a contaminant and cannot be adequately disinfected.

V.c.1. To soften umbilical detritus, antiseptic solution may be instilled into the umbilicus before cleaning.

V.c.2. Cotton applicators may be used to remove the detritus.

V.d. Jewelry (eg, body piercing ornaments) at the surgical site should be removed before cleansing the skin. (PNDS: I94, I98, I102, I77, I72, I75, I57)

Jewelry harbors microorganisms and traps these organisms in adjacent skin. Wearing of rings has been associated with up to a 10-fold increase in median skin microorganism count (ie, bioload).[47] Removal of jewelry before skin cleansing provides an opportunity to more effectively remove these microorganisms from the area that will be prepped.

V.d.1. Jewelry should be removed to reduce the risk of injury related to
- positioning,[48] and
- proximity to the incision site or active electrosurgical unit (ESU) electrode.[49]

V.e. An intestinal or urinary stoma within the surgical field should be cleansed gently and separately from the rest of the prepped area. (PNDS: I94, I98, I85)
- Some antiseptics are ineffective in the presence of organic material.
- Cleansing of the stoma removes mucin and organic material that impedes the effectiveness of the antiseptic agent.

V.f. Surgical fields that include the penis require the foreskin (ie, prepuce), if present, to be retracted before the glans is gently cleansed. (PNDS: I94, I98, I85, I75, I150, I152)

Organic material (ie, smegma) and microorganisms accumulate under the foreskin.

V.f.1. After cleaning, the foreskin should be pulled back over the glans to prevent circulatory compromise.

V.g. For surgery on the hand or wrist, the patient's nails should be short and natural without artificial nail surfaces (eg, extensions, overlays, acrylic, silk wraps, enhancements) in the prepped area. (PNDS: I94, I98, I85, I138)

The subungual region harbors the majority of microorganisms found on the hand. The variety and amount of potentially pathogenic bacteria cultured from fingertips of persons wearing artificial nails is greater than from those with natural nails, both before and after handwashing.[50-52]

There is insufficient evidence to determine whether fresh or chipped nail polish in the surgical field increases the risk of surgical site infection.[53] There is, however, a theoretical risk of chipped nail polish fragments entering the wound.

V.h. Cleansing traumatic orthopedic injuries with exposed bone may be facilitated by pulse lavage, high-pressure parallel water-jet, or brush-suction irrigation. (PNDS: I94, I98, I85, I138, I152, I122, I77, I128, I38)

In a randomized clinical trial, low-pressure pulse lavage decreased wound contamination by 86.9% and high-pressure parallel water-jet decreased contamination by 90.8%.[54] In a laboratory study, high-pressure lavage removed less inorganic contaminants and caused more tissue damage than a brush-suction method.[55]

When irrigating traumatic wounds:
- sterile 0.9% saline solution should be used for the irrigation;
- caution should be exercised to avoid aerosolization of wound contaminants onto the sterile field during irrigation; and
- the use of a pulse lavage protective shield may be beneficial.

Recommendation VI

Protective measures should be implemented to prevent skin and tissue injury due to prolonged contact with skin prep agents. (PNDS: I94, I98, I85, I138, I75, I70)

Chemical burns and skin irritations are more likely when antiseptic solutions are not allowed to dry and remain in contact with the skin for prolonged periods of time.[22,31,56]

The iodine in povidone-iodine prep solutions remains free until it has dried and can chemically irritate the skin. When the skin is occluded, the solution is unable to dry, the chemical contact is sustained, and the skin is macerated. The use of forced-air warming under the surgical drapes adds heat to antiseptic solutions, which may increase the likelihood of a chemical or thermal injury. In a series of povidone-iodine burns, authors reported burns resulting from
- soaked linen,
- soaked adhesive tape,
- drips on padding under tourniquet cuffs,
- solution running off surgical sites and onto the patients' backs, and
- a povidone-iodine-soaked gauze being used to cover an epidural site during surgery.[56]

VI.a. Sheets, padding, positioning equipment, and adhesive tape should be protected from the dripping or pooling of prep agents beneath and around the patient. (PNDS: I94, I75, I138)

If antiseptic solutions drip onto fabrics and positioning equipment, the surgical drapes may prevent the solution from evaporating, thus prolonging skin contact with the wet solution.

VI.a.1. Special attention should be paid when the patient is in lithotomy position because antiseptic solution running down the gluteal cleft may not be apparent.

VI.a.2. For vaginal procedures, using a fluid-resistant towel or drape with an adhesive strip below the patient's buttocks may be beneficial.

VI.b. Electrodes, including the ESU dispersive electrode, should be protected from dripping or pooling of antiseptic agents. (PNDS: I122, I75, I72)

Antiseptic solutions contacting these electrical devices may cause chemical or thermal burns. The adhesive material holds the solution next to the skin, and the solution is unable to dry. Solution between the skin and the electrode increases impedance and increases the risk of a pad-site injury or equipment malfunction.

VI.b.1. If antiseptic solution contacts the ESU dispersive electrode,
- the dispersive electrode should be removed,
- the antiseptic solution cleaned from the patient's skin, and
- a new dispersive electrode applied.

VI.c. If a tourniquet is used, the cuff, padding, and skin under the cuff should be protected from contact with prep solutions. (PNDS: I75, I77, I122)

Antiseptic solutions contacting tourniquet cuffs are compressed against and occlude the skin, increasing the likelihood of a chemical burn.

VI.c.1. Use of an impervious tourniquet cuff protector or towelette drape with an adhesive strip may prevent prep solution contact with the skin under the tourniquet.

VI.c.2. If contact occurs, the cuff and/or padding should be replaced before draping.

Recommendation VII

The antiseptic agent should be applied to the skin over the surgical site and surrounding area in a manner to minimize contamination, preserve skin integrity, and prevent tissue damage. (PNDS: I10, I77, I75, I94, I98, I122, I152, I150)

VII.a. Nonscrubbed personnel should apply the skin antiseptic. (PNDS: I10, I94, I98)

The risk of contamination to sterile gown and gloves is high, in most circumstances, when scrubbed personnel perform the prep.

VII.b. Hand hygiene should be performed before initiating the surgical prep.[57,58] (PNDS: I98, I138, I122) Hand hygiene prevents contamination of the prepped area in the event of a glove failure.

VII.c. Antiseptic agents used for skin preparation should be applied using sterile supplies. (PNDS: I70, I94)

There is insufficient evidence to determine if using only clean supplies is a safe practice. In one study, using a combination povidone-iodine scrub and paint, researchers found that using clean prep kits with reusable sponge sticks for the paint, assembled in a central sterilizing area, did not result in higher microbial counts on the skin than when similar trays were sterilized first.[59]

VII.c.1. Sterile gloves should be worn unless the antiseptic prep applicator is of sufficient length to prevent the antiseptic and patient's skin from contact with the nonsterile glove.

VII.c.2. Any supplies touching the prepped area after the prep has been completed should be sterile to prevent introduction of microorganisms.

VII.d. When not part of the surgical procedure, a highly contaminated site (eg, anus, colostomy) should be isolated from the area to be prepped. (PNDS: I21, I94, I98)

Isolating the contaminated area confines and contains microorganisms away from the surgical site.

VII.d.1. An adhesive, fluid-resistant or plastic drape may be beneficial in sealing the contaminated area.[60,61]

VII.e. Application of the skin antiseptic should progress from the incision site to the periphery of the surgical site. (PNDS: I94, I98)

In most surgical procedures, the incision site is in close proximity to anatomic areas with high microbial counts (eg, laparotomy incision/umbilicus/groin; neck/mouth/nares; ankle/toes; shoulder/axilla; hand/fingernails). Progressing from the incision site to the periphery prevents reintroducing microorganisms from these areas into the incision site.

VII.e.1. The prep sponge or applicator should be used for a single application and discarded.

VII.e.2. Subsequent applications should be applied with a fresh sponge or applicator to prevent contamination of the incision site.

VII.e.3. When using a commercially available applicator, refer to the manufacturer's instructions to ensure uniform distribution of the antiseptic.

VII.f. Special consideration on skin prep implementation is necessary when the incision site is more highly contaminated than the surrounding skin. (PNDS: I21, I94, I98, I150)

VII.f.1. If a highly contaminated area is part of the procedure, the area with a lower bacterial count is prepped first, followed by the area of higher contamination, as opposed to working from the incision site toward the periphery.

VII.f.2. When prepping the anus or vagina or a stoma, sinus, ulcer, or open wound, the sponge should be applied once to that area and then discarded.

VII.f.3. An antiseptic-soaked sponge may be applied to the contaminated area during prepping of the surrounding skin.

VII.f.4. Vaginal preps for procedures that include the abdomen should be performed in a manner to prevent splashing of antiseptic agent expelled from the vagina onto the prepped abdomen.

VII.f.5. Urinary catheter insertion should be performed using sterile supplies and aseptic technique. Using sterile supplies for the urinary catheter insertion prevents the risk of cross-contamination of the genitourinary tract.

VII.g. Special precautions and consideration for skin prep implementation is necessary for burns, open wounds, and fragile skin. (PNDS: I21, I94, I98, I36, I75, I77, I152, I131, I138, I122, I128, I51)

VII.g.1. When prepping fragile tissues, gentle friction should be used to prevent tissue damage.

VII.h. The prepared area of skin should extend to an area large enough to accommodate potential shifting of the drape fenestration, extension of the incision, the potential for additional incisions, and all potential drain sites. (PNDS: I21, I94, I98, I138)

An unprepared area may be exposed when enlarging the drape fenestration or if shifting of the drapes occurs, resulting in contamination of the surgical site.

VII.h.1. Consideration of the potential need to convert a minimally invasive procedure to an open procedure will determine the extent of the area to be included in the prep.

VII.i. The antiseptic agent should remain in place for the full time suggested by the manufacturer's written recommendations. (PNDS: I94, I122)

Testing of antiseptic agents has demonstrated effectiveness under specific conditions and contact times. Complying with recommended exposure times facilitates the occurrence of the best antiseptic conditions. For example, povidone-iodine reaches maximum effectiveness only after it has dried.

VII.i.1. To prevent surgical fires, flammable prep agents must have thoroughly dried and vapors dissipated before applying drapes.[62-64]

VII.j. Adhesive incision drapes may be used to minimize the gaping and shifting of surgical drapes and to contain residual microorganisms on the skin. (PNDS: I70, I98)

Adhesive incision drapes may be advantageous in sealing the surgical field; however, the utility of the iodine-impregnation of these drapes has not been demonstrated.[65] One randomized clinical trial investigating the utility of these drapes after povidone-iodine prep reported no reduction in surgical site infection risk when using iodine-impregnated incision drapes.[66]

Recommendation VIII

If a flammable prep agent is used, additional precautions should be taken to minimize the risk of a surgical fire and patient burn injury. (PNDS: I76, I75, I122)

Using flammable skin prep agents in the operating room or procedural area poses a serious risk of fire because of the common use of ignition and heat sources (eg, electrosurgery, lasers, drills, fiberoptic cables). Special precautions have been developed by the National Fire Protection Association (NFPA), and have been incorporated in the National Patient Safety Goals by the Joint Commission.[63,67]

VIII.a. Perioperative personnel should be familiar with the flammability characteristics of all prep agents stored or used in the patient care area. (PNDS: I122)

Fires have resulted when personnel did not know or remember that a prep agent was flammable and used a heat source during the procedure.[68]

VIII.b. When flammable prep agents are used, they should be packaged in small quantities appropriate for a single application or be prepackaged in a unit dose.[63,67] (PNDS: I122)

Packaging in small quantities may minimize the risk of soaking materials adjacent to the prepped area and limits the amount left over for disposal.

VIII.c. The prep agent should not contact fabric or be allowed to pool on or under body parts (eg, umbilicus, groin). (PNDS: I75, I76, I122)

Solution in contact with fabric may not dry adequately. Pooled prep agents require longer periods of time for evaporation.

VIII.d. If pooling occurs, the excess solution should be wicked away. Any solution-soaked materials should be removed from the procedure room before draping or using electrosurgery, laser, or other heat source.[63,64,67] (PNDS: I75, I76, I122)

Wicking solution away from pooled areas allows the remaining solution to dry adequately. Solution-soaked materials are easily ignitable, and removal from the operating room minimizes the risk of fire.

VIII.e. The prep agent should be allowed to dry and vapors to dissipate before application of an incise drape or surgical drape, or use of electrosurgery, laser, or other heat source.[62-64] (PNDS: I75, I76, I122)

The prep agent remains flammable until completely dry. Vapors occurring during evaporation are also flammable. Trapping of solution or vapors under drapes increases the risk of fire or burn injury.

VIII.f. The use of a flammable prep agent should be discussed during the "time out" period used to verify the surgical procedure and site. (PNDS: I75, I76, I122)

Active communication about the use of flammable prep agents alerts all personnel to the inherent risks and verifies that appropriate precautions have been taken. At times, the person operating the heat (ie, ignition) source may be unaware that a flammable prep agent was used. Active communication prevents this misunderstanding.

VIII.f.1. Active communication between the surgical team members should include that
- a flammable prep agent was used;
- the application site was dry before draping;
- pooling of the prep solution did not occur or has been corrected; and
- any materials soaked with the prepping agent have been removed from the procedure room.[63,67]

VIII.g. Disposal of unused flammable prep agents must be handled in a manner to decrease the risk of fire and in accordance with federal, state, and local regulations. (PNDS: I138, I122)

Disposal of residual flammable prep agents is regulated by the Environmental Protection Agency.[69] Fires can occur when these agents are discarded in nonhazardous trash. Incineration or autoclaving of biohazardous waste can rapidly ignite flammable prep agents.

VIII.g.1. Residual flammable prep agents may be safely discarded in a chemical hazardous waste receptacle outside of the operating or procedure room or immersed in water in a soiled utility room to render the agents nonhazardous.

VIII.h. Flammable skin preparation agents should not be heated. (PNDS: I122)

Heating flammable preparation agents poses a serious risk of fire. When the temperature of these agents increases, they become more unstable and may ignite easily.

Recommendation IX

Manufacturers' written recommendations and MSDSs for handling, storing, and heating of all skin preparation agents should be readily available, reviewed, and followed. (PNDS: I122)

Testing antimicrobial agents is a complex process and not practical in the patient care setting. Data from current research, manufacturers' literature, and the FDA provides direction for storage, safe use, and product efficacy.

IX.a. Skin antiseptic agents should be stored in their original containers; these containers should not be refilled. (PNDS: I138, I122)

Prolonged use of a multi-use container, transferring solutions to secondary containers, and refilling containers of povidone-iodine has resulted in contamination of the antiseptic with *Pseudomonas aeruginosa*.[70-74] These microorganisms can survive more than one year in povidone-iodine;[71] and contaminated povidone-iodine has resulted in transmission of the contaminating organism and subsequent infections.[71,72,74-76] Use of single-dose containers eliminates this risk.

IX.b. If the skin preparation solution is poured into a secondary container, it should be labeled and the label verified before use of the prep agent. (PNDS: I138)

A label placed on the secondary container communicates to anyone using the agent the contents of the container. A patient death resulted when a skin preparation agent was erroneously mistaken for another drug and injected.[77] Health care accreditation agencies require labeling to identify the skin preparation name and strength.[78-80]

IX.c. Heating of nonflammable skin preparation solutions should only be performed in accordance with the manufacturer's written instructions. (PNDS: I122)

Heating these solutions may cause thermal or chemical burns. Heating may alter the chemical composition of the prepping agent and may alter the effectiveness of the antiseptic. Heating povidone-iodine alters the equilibrium of the iodine content.[81] Manufacturers may have a time limit that an antiseptic agent may be warmed slightly, after which it should be discarded.

IX.d. Skin preparation agents should never be warmed in a microwave oven or autoclave. (PNDS: I122)

The temperature of the skin preparation agent is uncontrolled when heated in a microwave or autoclave, and temperature extremes may result in a patient injury.

IX.e. Material safety data sheets for all antiseptic agents and other chemicals used must be available in the practice area.[82] (PNDS: I122, I138)

Material safety data sheets provide information about the flammability of skin antiseptic agents and the maximum safe storage temperature. The Occupational Safety and Health Administration (OSHA) requires that MSDSs be available for all chemicals used in the practice setting. These documents outline the hazards related to the chemicals and appropriate action to be taken in the event of an exposure (eg, splash to the eyes).[82]

IX.f. Storage of flammable preparation agents must be in compliance with local, state, and federal regulations. (PNDS: I138, I122)

Alcohol-based antiseptics are flammable and should be stored away from high temperatures, sparking devices, or flames.[62-64,67]

IX.f.1. Alcohols are extremely volatile, and their containers should be sealed to prevent spilling, leaking, and evaporation.

IX.f.2. Flammable antiseptic agents should not be stored in egress hallways.

IX.f.3. Large quantities of flammable preparation agents should not be stored in an operating room or procedure area.

The NFPA recommends solutions are to be stored in a flammable solutions cabinet designed to minimize the risk of ignition when the amount of alcohol stored in one location is 10 gallons or more.[83]

IX.f.4. Perioperative personnel should refer to their facility's policies and procedures and individual state regulations for additional information.

Recommendation X

At the end of the surgical procedure, the skin preparation agent should be thoroughly removed from the skin unless otherwise indicated by the manufacturer's written instructions. (PNDS: I75, I122, I51, I36)

Active and inactive ingredients in the solution may cause skin irritation and contact dermatitis in sensitive individuals.[19,22,56]

X.a.   Residual antiseptic agent should be removed before application of an occlusive dressing or tape.

Removing the solution as soon possible after completion of the procedure minimizes the risk of ongoing irritation. Trapping antiseptic solutions under occlusive dressings has resulted in chemical burns.

X.a.1.   All visible antiseptic agent should be removed from the skin.

Residual antiseptics can cause irritation.[22,56] Some manufacturers recommend that specific preparation agents be left on the skin and allowed to wear off naturally.

X.a.2.   As soon as feasible, the patient should be rolled to the side and posterior skin surfaces examined to identify any residual antiseptic that should be removed.

A thorough evaluation of the patient's skin may need to be postponed until after the patient is transferred to the postoperative area.

Recommendation XI

Competency
Personnel should receive initial education, training, and competency validation on skin preparation agent selection, application procedures, and patient assessments.

Initial competency validation, in addition to the annual review and evaluation of individual competency skills, should be performed to maintain proficiency in application of knowledge and use of critical thinking concerning performance of skin preparation.

XI.a.   Personnel who could be potentially exposed to antiseptic preparation agents must be made aware of the exposure risk associated with these chemicals.[82]

Workers have the right to know about workplace hazards and OSHA requires employers to provide this information. Information about chemical hazards should be offered during initial orientation.[82]

XI.b.   Personnel should receive education and training on selection of skin preparation agents.

Personnel should be knowledgeable about skin preparation agents, indications, contraindications, and special precautions to be used when handling flammable antiseptic agents.

XI.c.   Personnel providing preoperative patient instructions should receive education on the evidence base for preoperative patient showers.

Patient compliance is enhanced by appropriate education about the importance of preoperative showers, strategies for facilitating the shower, and preventing recontamination of the skin.

XI.d.   Personnel removing hair should receive instruction on the risks associated with shaving, shaving alternatives, and proper hair-removal techniques.

Understanding risks and alternatives to hair removal reinforces discernment to avoid hair removal. Appropriate hair-removal techniques minimize the risk of skin injury and surgical site infection.

XI.e.   Personnel should receive education and guidance on skin preparation for the types of procedures performed and precautions to be taken.

Skin preparation techniques vary by surgical procedure and patient condition. Educating personnel about these variations and providing didactic instruction enhances required skills.

XI.f.   Administrative personnel should validate the competence of personnel participating in skin preparation activities. (PNDS: I1)

Validation of competence provides an indication that personnel are able to appropriately perform skin preparation.

Recommendation XII

Documentation
Patient skin preparation should be documented in the medical record. (PNDS: I27;I30;I116)

Documentation provides communication among all care providers involved in planning and implementing the patient's care. Documentation of surgical skin preparation may assist in the investigation of infections or adverse reactions and identify opportunities for performance improvement. Accountability is established by recording names of personnel who perform procedures. Predetermined documentation fields or indicators also may prompt compliance with policies and procedures.

XII.a. Documentation should include, but not be limited to,
- preoperative instructions;
- patient report of compliance with preoperative showering instructions;
- removal and disposition of any jewelry;
- condition of the skin at the surgical site (eg, presence of rashes, skin eruptions, abrasions, redness, irritation, burns);
- hair removal, if performed, including method, time of removal, and area;
- antiseptic agent used;
- area prepped;
- name(s) of person(s) performing skin preparation;
- precautions taken when flammable agents are used (eg, agent allowed to completely dry);
- removal of prepping agent; and
- postoperative skin condition, including any skin irritation or hypersensitivity (allergic) response to preparation solutions.

Recommendation XIII

Policies and Procedures
Policies and procedures on the skin preparation of patients should be written, reviewed annually, and readily available within the practice setting.

Policies and procedures assist in the development of patient safety, and quality assessment and improvement activities. Policies and procedures establish authority, responsibility, and accountability and serve as operational guidelines. Policies and procedures establish guidelines for performance improvement activities to be used when monitoring and evaluating skin preparation in the operating room.

XIII.a. Policies about preoperative skin preparation should be developed in collaboration with surgeons and an infection control professional.

XIII.a.1. Policies should include, but not be limited to,

- patient education or assistance in performing two CHG-showers;
- appropriate restrictions on and alternatives to hair removal;
- removal of jewelry at the surgical site;
- assessments to be performed before skin preparation;
- approved skin antiseptic agents;
- if flammable skin preparation agents are permitted or not;
- precautions to be taken if flammable skin preparation agents are used;
- removal of preparation agents and evaluation of the skin condition at the end of the procedure;
- documentation;
- storage of flammable skin preparation agents;
- maintenance of MSDS sheets; and
- reporting adverse events.

XIII.b. An introduction and review of policies and procedures should be included in the initial orientation and ongoing education of health care personnel.

Review of policies and procedures assist health care professionals in the development of knowledge, skills, and attitudes that affect patient outcomes.

Recommendation XIV

Quality
A quality management program should be in place to evaluate skin preparation procedures and identify and respond to opportunities for improvement.

A fundamental precept of AORN is that it is the responsibility of professional perioperative registered nurses to ensure safe, high-quality nursing care to patients undergoing operative and invasive procedures.

XIV.a. A quality management program should be in place to evaluate skin preparation procedures and to identify and respond to opportunities for improvement.

"Surgery patients with appropriate hair removal" is a Surgical Care Improvement Project and National Hospital Quality Measures evidence-based practice indicator used by the Centers for Medicare and Medicaid

Services and the Joint Commission.[84-86] The abstraction criterion indicating compliance is: "Surgical patients with surgical site hair removal by clippers or depilatory or no surgical site hair removal."[84] Public reporting of the percent of compliance with this indicator is required for Medicare or Medicaid reimbursement.[86,87]

XIV.b. Adverse reactions to skin antiseptic agents should be reported in the health care organization's adverse event reporting system and reviewed for potential opportunities for improvement. (PNDS: I92)

XIV.b.1. Surgical fires resulting from skin preparation agents should be reported and investigated as serious adverse events through a root cause analysis and corrective action taken to prevent recurrence.

XIV.b.2. Near misses should be investigated and corrective action taken to prevent serious adverse events.

Glossary

Antisepsis: The prevention of sepsis by preventing or inhibiting the growth of resident and transient microbes.

Antiseptic: A product with antimicrobial activity that formerly may have been referred to as an *antimicrobial agent.*

Antiseptic agent: Antimicrobial substance applied to the skin to reduce the log number of microbial flora. Examples include alcohols, chlorhexidine gluconate, chlorine, hexachlorophene, iodine, parachloroxylenol, quaternary ammonium compounds, and triclosan.

Denature: To alter the chemical structure of a protein so that biological activity is diminished or eliminated. Made unnatural or changed from the normal in any of a substance's characteristics.

Detritus: Accumulated debris resulting from the wearing away or deterioration of tissue or other deposited material. Any broken-down material.

Flammable: Capable of being easily ignited and burning rapidly.

Gluteal cleft: Cleft of the buttocks.

Iodism: Poisoning by iodine, manifested by severe rhinitis, frontal headache, emaciation, weakness, and skin eruptions. Caused by the administration of iodine or one of the iodides.

Log reduction: The logarithmic death progression of microorganisms after exposure to a sterilant or antiseptic agent. The reduction difference between average surviving microbes for control and test carriers used as an efficacy parameter.

Neurotoxic: Poisonous or destructive to nerves, nerve tissue, or nervous system.

Ototoxic: Having a toxic or injurious effect on the ear, especially the nerve supply, affecting hearing and balance.

Oxidation: The combination of a substance with oxygen, altering cell biologic activity.

Subungual: Under the nail (eg, fingernail).

Toxicity: The degree to which a substance can harm humans or animals.

REFERENCES

1. Peterson, C, ed. *Perioperative Nursing Data Set.* Rev 2nd ed. Denver, CO: AORN, Inc; 2007.

2. Mangram AJ, Horan TC, Pearson ML, Silver LC, Jarvis WR. Guideline for prevention of surgical site infection, 1999. *Infect Control Hosp Epidemiol.* 1999;20:250-278.

3. Centers for Disease Control and Prevention. Management of multidrug-resistant organisms in healthcare settings, 2006. *Clin Infect Dis.* 2006; 42, 389-391.2. Also available at *http://www.cdc.gov/ncidod/dhqp /pdf/ar/mdroGuideline2006.pdf.* Accessed October 5, 2007.

4. Centers for Disease Control and Prevention. MRSA in Healthcare Settings, 2007. *http://www.cdc.gov/ncidod/ dhqp/ar_MRSA_spotlight_2006.html.* Accessed November 5, 2007.

5. Klevens RM, Edwards JR, Tenover FC, McDonald LC, Horan T, Gaynes R. Changes in the epidemiology of methicillin-resistant *Staphylococcus aureus* in intensive care units in US hospitals, 2992-2003. *Clin Infect Dis.* 2006;42:389-91.

6. Kluytmans JA, Mouton JW, Ijzerman EP, et al. Nasal carriage of *Staphylococcus aureus* as a major risk factor for wound infections after cardiac surgery. *J Infectious Disease.* 1995;171:216-219.

7. Leigh DA, Stronge JL, Marriner J, Sedgwick J. Total body bathing with 'hibiscrub' (chlorhexidine) in surgical patients: a controlled trial. *J Hosp Infect.* 1983;4:229-235.

8. Garibaldi RA. Prevention of intraoperative wound contamination with chlorhexidine shower and scrub. *J Hosp Infect.* 1988;11(Suppl B):5-9.

9. Hayek L, Emerson JM, Gardner AMN. A placebo-controlled trial of the effect of two preoperative baths or showers with chlorhexidine detergent on postoperative wound infection rates. *J Hosp Infect.* 1987;10:165-72.

10. Byrne DJ, Napier A, Phillips G, Cuschieri A. Effects of whole body disinfection on skin flora in patients undergoing elective surgery. *J Hosp Infect.* 1991;17:217-222.

11. Kaiser AB, Kernodle DS, Barg NL, Petracek MR. Influence of preoperative showers on staphylococcal skin colonization: a comparative trial of antiseptic skin cleansers. *Am J Infect Control.* 1988;45:35-38.

12. Aly R, Maibach HI. Comparative antibacterial efficacy of a 2-minute surgical scrub with chlorhexidine gluconate, povidone-iodine, and chloroxylenol sponge-brushes. *Am J Infect Control.* 1988;16:173-177.

13. Molnycke Health Care. Product information Hibiclens® Antiseptic/Antimicrobial Skin Cleanser. *http://www.molnlycke.com/item.asp?id=23793&lang=2&si=182.* Accessed September 10, 2007.

14. Steris Corporation. Product information Bactosheild CHG 2% and 4% (Chlorhexadine Gluconate) Handwash/preoperative/surgical scrub technical data. Mentor, IL: Steris Corporation; 1999.

15. Cardinal Health. Exidene® CHG (Chlorhexidene Gluconate) Directions for Use. McGaw Park, IL: Cardinal Health; 2003.

16. US Department of Health and Human Services, Food and Drug Administration. Tentative final monograph for health care antiseptic drug products proposed rule. CFR.21.333, CFR.21.369. *Federal Register.* June 17, 1994: 31402-31452.

17. US Department of Health and Human Services, Food and Drug Administration, Food and Drug Administration Center. Tentative final monograph for health-care antiseptic drug products; proposed rule. 21 CFR Parts 33 and 369. *Federal Register.* June 17, 1994.

18. Leclair JM, Winston KR, Sullivan BF, O'Connell JM, Harrington SM, Goldmann DA. Effect of preoperative shampoos on resident scalp flora. *Today's OR Nurse.* 1988;10:15-21.

19. Denton GW. Chlorhexidine. In: *Disinfection, Sterilization and Preservation.* 5th ed. Block SS, ed. Philadelphia, PA: Lippincott Williams & Wilkins; 2001: 321-36.

20. National Fire Protection Association. Germicide. In: NFPA 99, *Standard for Health Care Facilities.* Quincy, MA: National Fire Protection Association; 2005:99-109.

21. ECRI. Surgical fire safety. In: *Health Devices.* Plymouth Meeting, PA: ECRI; 2006:45-66.

22. LexiComp, AORN. *Drug Information Handbook for Perioperative Nursing.* Hudson, OH: Lexi-Comp, Inc; 2006:373-375.

23. Chlorhexadine gulconate solution materials safety data sheet. ScienceLab.com. *http://www.sciencelab.com/xMSDS-Chlorhexidine_Gluconate_Solution-9923401.* Accessed August 28, 2007.

24. US Department of Health and Human Services, Food and Drug Administration Center for Drug Evaluation and Research (CDER). Guidance for Insustry: Changes to an Approved NDA or ANDA. *http://www.fda.gov/cder/guidance/2766fnl.htm.* Accessed July 25, 2007.

25. Recommended practices for product section in perioperative practice settings. In: *Standards, Recommended Practices, and Guidelines.* Denver, CO: AORN, Inc; 2007:637-40.

26. Adachi A, Fukunaga A, Hayashi K, Kunisada M, Horikawa T. Anaphylaxis to polyvinalpyrrolidone after vaginal application of povidone iodine. *Contact Dermatitis.* 2003;48;133-36.

27. American Academy of Allergy Asthma and Immunology. Academy Position Statement: The Risk of Severe Allergic Reactions from the Use of Potassium Iodide for Radiation Emergencies. *http://www.aaaai.org/media/resources/academy_statements/position_statements/potassium_iodide.asp.* Accessed August 28, 2007.

28. Sampson AH. Food allergy. *J Allergy Clin Immunol.* 2003; 111[2 Suppl]:S540-547.

29. Aalto-Korte K, Makinen-Kiljunen S. Symptoms of immediate chlorhexidine hypersensitivity in patients with a positive prick test. *Contact Dermatitis.* 2006;55:173-177.

30. Harpin V, Rutter N. Percutaneous alcohol absorption and skin necrosis in a preterm infant. *Arch Dis Child.* 1982;57:477-479.

31. Reynolds PR, Banerjee S, Meek JH. Alcohol burns in extremely low birthweight infants: still occurring. *Arch Dis Child Fetal Neonatal Ed.* 2005;90:F10.

32. Schick JB, Milstein JM. Burn hazard of isopropyl alcohol in the neonate. *Pediatrics.* 1981;68:587-588.

33. Bryant WP, Zimmerman D. Iodine-induced hyperthyroidism in a newborn. *Pediatrics.* 1995;95:434-436.

34. Pyati SP, Ramamurthy RS, Krauss MT, Pildes RS. Absorption of iodine in the neonate following topical use of povidone iodine. *J Pediatr.* 1977;91:825-828.

35. Smerdely P, Lim A, Boyages SC, et al. Topical iodine-containing antiseptics and neonatal hypothyroidism in very-low-birthweight infants. *Lancet.* 1989;2:661-664.

36. Linder N, Davidovic N, Reichman B, et al. Topical iodine-containing antiseptics and subclinical hypothyroidism in preterm infants. *J Pediatr* 1997;131:434-39.

37. Joint Commission. Frequently Asked Questions about the Universal Protocol for Preventing Wrong Site, Wrong Procedure, Wrong Person Surgery. *http://www.jointcommission.org/PatientSafety/UniversalProtocol/up_faqs.htm.* Accessed August 28, 2007.

38. Cronen G, Ringus V, Sigle G, Ryu J. Sterility of surgical site marking. *J Bone Joint Surg Am.* 2005;87:2193-2195.

39. Wilson J, Tate D. Can preoperative skin marking transfer methicillin-resistant *Staphylococcus aureus* between patients? a laboratory experiment. *J Bone Joint Surg Br.* 2006;88:541-542.

40. Mishriki SF, Law DJ, Jeffery PJ. Factors affecting the incidence of postoperative wound infection. *J Hosp Infect.* 1990;16:223-230.

41. Moro ML, Carrieri MP, Tozzi AE, Lana S, Greco D. Risk factors for surgical wound infections in clean surgery: a multicenter study. Italian PRINOS study group. *Ann Ital Chir.* 1996;67:13-19.

42. Tanner J, Moncaster K, Woodings D. Preoperative hair removal: a systematic review. *J Perioper Pract.* 2007;17:118-21, 124-32.

43. Bekar A, Korfali E, Dogan S, Yilmazlar S, Baskan Z, Aksoy K. The effect of hair on infection after cranial surgery. *Acta Neurochir* (Wien). 2001;143:533-6; [discussion] 537.

44. Kretschmer T, Braun V, Richter HP. Neurosurgery without shaving: indications and results. *Br J Neurosurg.* 2000;14:341-344.

45. Alexander JW, Fischer JE, Boyajian M, Palmquist J, Morris MJ. The influence of hair-removal methods on wound infections. *Arch Surg.* 1983;118:347-352.

46. Brooks RA, Hollinghurst D, Ribbans WJ, Severn M. Bacterial recolonization during foot surgery: a prospective randomized study of toe preparation techniques. *Foot Ankle Int.* 2001;22:347-350.

47. Trick WE, Vernon MO, Hayes RA, et al. Impact of ring wearing on hand contamination and comparison of hand hygiene agents in a hospital. *Clin Infect Dis.* 2003;36:1383-1390.

48. Recommended practices for positioning the patient in the perioperative practice setting. In: *Standards, Recommended Practices, and Guidelines.* Denver, CO: AORN, Inc; 2007:631-36.

49. Recommended practices for electrosurgery. In: *Standards, Recommended Practices, and Guidelines.* Denver, CO: AORN, Inc; 2007:515-29.

50. Hedderwick SA, McNeil SA, Lyons MJ, Kauffman CA. Pathogenic organisms associated with artificial fingernails worn by health care workers. *Infect Control Hosp Epidemiol.* 2000;21:505-509.

51. McNeil SA, Foster CL, Hedderwick SA, Kauffman CA. Effect of hand cleansing with antimicrobial soap or alcohol-based gel on microbial colonization of artificial fingernails worn by health care workers. *Clin Infect Dis.* 2001;32:367-372.

52. Moolenaar RL, Crutcher JM, San Joaquin VH, et al. A prolonged outbreak of *Pseudomonas aeruginosa* in a neonatal intensive care unit: did staff fingernails play a role in disease transmission? *Infect Control Hosp Epidemiol.* 2000;21:80-85.

53. Arrowsmith VA, Maunder JA, Sargent RJ, Taylor R. Removal of nail polish and finger rings to prevent surgical infection. Cochrane Database Syst Rev. 2007; (2): CD003325.

54. Granick MS, Tenenhaus M, Knox KR, Ulm JP. Comparison of wound irrigation and tangential hydrodissection in bacterial clearance of contaminated wounds: results of a randomized controlled clinical study. *Ostomy Wound Manage.* 2007;53:64-6, 68-70, 72.

55. Draeger RW, Dahners LE. Traumatic wound debridement: a comparison of irrigation methods. *J Orthop Trauma.* 2006;20:83-88.

56. Lowe DO, Knowles SR, Weber EA, Railton CJ, Shear NH. Povidone iodine-induced burn: case report and review of the literature. *Pharmacotherapy.* 2006;26:1641-1645.

57. Boyce JM, Pittet D, Health care Infection Control Practices Advisory Committee. Society for Health Care Epidemiology of America. Association for Professionals in Infection Control. Infectious Diseases Society of America. Hand Hygiene Task Force. Guideline for hand hygiene in health-care settings: recommendations of the health care infection control practices advisory committee and the HICPAC/SHEA/APIC/IDSA hand hygiene task force. *Infect Control Hosp Epidemiol.* 2002;23[12 suppl]:S3-40.

58. Recommended practices for surgical hand antisepsis/hand scrubs. In: *Standards, Recommended Practices, and Guidelines.* Denver, CO: AORN, Inc; 2007:565-73.

59. Pearce BA, Miller LH, Martin MA, Roush DL. Efficacy of clean vs sterile surgical prep kits. *AORN J.* 1997;66:464-470.

60. Association for the Advancement of Medical Instrumentation. Selection and use of protective apparel and surgical drapes in health care facilities. In: *Technical Information Report:TIR11:2005.* Arlington, VA: Association for the Advancement of Medical Instrumentation, 2005.

61. Recommended practices for selection and use of surgical gowns and drapes. In: *Standards, Recommended Practices, and Guidelines.* Denver, CO: AORN, Inc; 2007:559-564.

62. ECRI. A clinician's guide to surgical fires: How they occur, how to prevent them, how to put them out. *Health Devices.* January 2003;32:5–24.

63. National Fire Protection Association. Tentative interim amendment. In: NFPA 99 *Standard for Healthcare Facilities.* Quincy, MA: NFPA; 2005:13.4.1.2.2-A-13.4.1.2.2.3.

64. AORN guidance statement: Fire prevention in the operating room. In: *Standards, Recommended Practices, and Guidelines.* Denver, CO: AORN Inc; 2007:259-267.

65. Pottinger JM, Starks SE, Steelman VM. Skin preparation. *Periop Nurs Clin.* 2006;1:203-210.

66. Dewan PA, Van Rij AM, Robinson RG, Skeggs GB, Fergus M. The use of an iodophor-impregnated plastic incise drape in abdominal surgery—a controlled clinical trial. *Aust N Z J Surg.* 1987;57:859-863.

67. Joint Commission. FAQs for the Joint Commission's 2007 National Patient Safety Goals Questions about Goal 11 (Reduce surgical fires). *http://www.jointcommission .org/NR/rdonlyres/61AEFEC2-3970-4856-B518-C9CCDB7B5779/0/07_NPSG_FAQs_11.pdf.* Accessed August 28,

68. Best practices for fire prevention in perioperative settings. *AORN Journal.* 2006;84 [Suppl 1]:S37-S44. 2007.

69. Environmental Protection Agency. RCRA Online. *http://www.epa.gov/rcraonline.* Accessed August 28, 2007.

70. Anderson RL, Vess RW, Panlilio AL, Favero MS. Prolonged survival of Pseudomonas cepacia in commercially manufactured povidone iodine. *Appl Environ Microbiol.* 1990;56:3598-3600.

71. Berkelman RL, Lewin S, Allen JR, et al. Pseudobacteremia attributed to contamination of povidone iodine with *Pseudomonas cepacia.* Ann Intern Med. 1981;95:32-36.

72. Craven DE, Moody B, Connolly MG, Kollisch NR, Stottmeier KD, McCabe WR. Pseudobacteremia caused by povidone iodine solution contaminated with *Pseudomonas cepacia.* N Engl J Med. 1981;305:621-623.

73. Oie S, Kamiya A. Microbial contamination of antiseptics and disinfectants. *Am J Infect Control.* 1996; 24:389-395.

74. Parrott PL, Terry PM, Whitworth EN, et al. *Pseudomonas aeruginosa* peritonitis associated with contaminated poloxamer-iodine solution. Lancet. 1982;2:683-685.

75. O'Rourke E, Runyan D, O'Leary J, Stern J. Contaminated iodophor in the operating room. *Am J Infect Control.* 2003;31:255-256.

76. Panlilio AL, Beck-Sague CM, Siegel JD, et al. Infections and pseudoinfections due to povidone iodine solution contaminated with *Pseudomonas cepacia.* Clin Infect Dis. 1992;14:1078-1083.

77. Institute for Safe Medication Practices. Loud wake-up call: unlabeled containers lead to patient's death. *http://www.ismp.org/Newsletters/acutecare/articles/20041202.asp.* Accessed August 28, 2007.

78. Joint Commission. National Patient Safety Goals: Goal 3 (Improve the Safety of Using Medications). *http://www.jointcommission.org/PatientSafety/National PatientSafetyGoals.* Accessed August 28, 2007.

79. Accreditation Association for Ambulatory Health Care. *Accreditation Handbook for Ambulatory Health Care: 2006.* Wilmette, IL: Accreditation Association for Ambulatory Health Care, Inc; 2006:63.

80. Accreditation Association for Ambulatory Health Care. *Accreditation Guidebook for Office Based Surgery: 2006.* Wilmette, IL: Accreditation Association for Ambulatory Health Care, Inc; 2006:63.

81. Gottardi WJ. The influence of the chemical behaviour of iodine on the germicidal action of disinfectant solutions containing iodine. *Hosp Infection.* 1985; 6 [suppl]:1-11.

82. Occupational Safety and Health Administration. Hazard Communication Standard. *http://osha.gov/SLTC/hazardcommunications/standards.html.* Accessed August 28, 2007.

83. National Fire Protection Association. NFPA 30: Flammable and Combustible Liquids Code. Quincy MA: National Fire Protection Association; 2003.

84. Joint Commission. National Hospital Quality Measures/The Joint Commission Core Measures. *http://www.jointcommission.org/NR/rdonlyres/A929F4B9-4F77-4983-9D9A-8661FDE01F1B/0/oryx_hap_cm_list.pdf.* Accessed October 10, 2007.

85. Centers for Medicare and Medicaid Services. SCIP Process and Outcome Measures. *http://www.medqic.org/dcs/BlobServer?blobcol=urldata&blobheader=multipart%2Foctet-stream&blobheadername1=Content-Disposition&blobheadervalue1=attachment%3Bfilename%3DNumbered+Measures+for+SCIP+21006.pdf&blobkey=id&blobtable=MungoBlobs&blobwhere=114297 4279114.* Accessed October 10, 2007.

86. CMS plans changes in guidelines for consent, alcohol-based preps. *OR Manager.* 2007;23:1, 7.

87. Centers for Medicare and Medicaid Services. Details for: FY 2008 Inpatient prospective payment system proposed rule improving the quality of hospital cares. *http://www.cms.hhs.gov/apps/media/press/factsheet.asp?Counter=2119&intNumPerPage=10&checkDate=&checkKey=&srchType=1&numDays=3500&srchOpt=0&srchData=&keywordType=All&chkNewsType=6&intPage=&showAll=&pYear=&year=&desc=&cboOrder=date.* Accessed August 28, 2007.

RESOURCES

AORN guidance statement: Fire prevention in the operating room In: *Standards, Recommended Practices, and Guidelines.* Denver, CO: AORN, Inc; 2007:259-267.

Association for Professionals in Infection Control and Epidemiology. *http://www.apic.org.* Accessed August 28, 2001.

Centers for Disease Control and Prevention. *http://www.cdc.gov/ncidod/dhqp/index.html.* Accessed August 28, 2007.

Environmental Protection Agency. Treatment, storage, and disposal of hazardous waste. *http://www.epa.gov/epaoswer/osw/tsds.htm#dispose.* Accessed August 28, 2007.

US Food and Drug Administration. *http://www.fda.gov.* Accessed August 28, 2007.

Originally published May 1976, *AORN Journal,* as "Standards for preoperative skin preparation of patients." Format revision March 1978, July 1982.

Revised February 1983, November 1988, November 1992, June 1996. Published November 1996, *AORN Journal;* reformatted July 2000.

Revised November 2001; published January 2002, *AORN Journal.*

Revised 2007; published as "Recommended practices for preoperative patient skin antisepsis" in *Perioperative Standards and Recommended Practices,* 2008 edition.

AORN Perioperative Standards and Recommended Practices, 2009 Edition

Recommended Practices for Cleaning, Handling, and Processing Anesthesia Equipment

The following recommended practices were developed by the AORN Recommended Practices Committee and have been approved by the AORN Board of Directors. They were presented as proposed recommended practices for comment to members and others. These recommended practices are effective January 1, 2005.

These recommended practices are intended as achievable recommendations representing what is believed to be an optimal level of practice. Policies and procedures will reflect variations in practice settings or clinical situations that determine the degree to which the recommended practices can be implemented.

AORN recognizes the numerous types of settings in which perioperative nurses practice. These recommended practices are intended as guidelines adaptable to various practice settings. These practice settings include traditional operating rooms, ambulatory surgery units, physicians' offices, cardiac catheterization suites, endoscopy suites, radiology departments, and all other areas where operative and other invasive procedures may be performed.

Purpose

Anesthesia equipment is a potential vector in the transmission of microorganisms. Proper handling and processing of medications, supplies, and equipment can reduce the risk of infection to the patient. These recommended practices provide guidelines for the handling, cleaning, disposal, and reprocessing of anesthesia equipment and instrumentation.

Recommendation I

Anesthesia equipment that comes in contact with the vascular system or sterile body tissue should be sterile at the time of use.

1. Items such as IV catheters, tubing, and stopcocks; syringes and needles; and medication vials and ampules are considered critical items. The Centers for Disease Control and Prevention (CDC) uses Spaulding's criteria to determine the potential for transmission of infectious agents. In this classification, items contacting the vascular system or sterile tissues pose the greatest risk of infection and are classified as critical.[1] Using sterile items when contacting the vascular system or sterile tissues minimizes the risk of infection.

2. Aseptic technique should be used when preparing medications. Breaks in aseptic technique have contaminated IV anesthetic agents and medications, resulting in clusters of infections.[2-9] Good practices include
   - performing hand hygiene before preparing medications,
   - cleaning vial stoppers before puncturing them,
   - using multiple needles to withdraw medication into multiple syringes,
   - not transferring syringes of unused medication between patients, and
   - not storing syringes of propofol at room temperature for the day.

   Medications should be stored in a clean area. Personnel should perform basic hand hygiene according to the CDC's "Guideline for hand hygiene in health-care settings,"[10] before preparing medication. Vial stoppers should be cleaned with alcohol before they are punctured. Single-dose vials should be used for only one patient. Syringes of unused medication should be discarded at the end of the procedure. Propofol should be withdrawn immediately before administration.

3. Aseptic technique should be used when administering medications. Bacteria from hands can contaminate syringes and their contents.[11-16] Multidose vials have been found to be contaminated.[17] Syringe contents have been found to contain blood or bloodborne pathogens after one injection or entry into IV tubing.[13,18-23] Using a common syringe in the IV tubing ports of more than one patient has transmitted infectious diseases.[9,24] Syringes and needles should be used for only one application (eg, one syringe and one needle per entry into a multidose vial). Intravenous tubing ports should be cleaned with alcohol before they are punctured with a needle.

Recommendation II

Anesthesia equipment that comes in contact with mucous membranes should be sterilized or undergo high-level disinfection before use.

1. Reusable items (eg, airways, breathing circuits, connectors, fiberoptic endoscopes, forceps, laryngoscope blades, masks, self-inflating bags,

some laryngeal mask airways [LMAs], transducer tubing, transesophageal probes) are considered semicritical. The CDC has determined that their potential for transmitting infectious agents is significant and has classified these items as semicritical.[1]

2. Reusable semicritical items should be cleaned as the first step in reprocessing. Removal of organic material provides optimal conditions for proper exposure of equipment to disinfectants and sterilants.[1,25,26] Rigid laryngoscopes should be disassembled and all components cleaned, including handles. Some automated pasteurization equipment has a cleaning step within the pasteurizing cycle.

3. Clean, semicritical reusable items should be processed by high-level disinfection, pasteurization, or sterilization with a US Food and Drug Administration (FDA)-approved agent, according to AORN's "Recommended practices for high-level disinfection" or "Recommended practices for sterilization in the practice setting."[27,28] Written instructions from the manufacturers of reprocessing equipment, chemicals, and instruments should be followed. High-level disinfection kills vegetative bacteria, tubercle bacilli, some spores, fungi, and viruses.[1] The CDC recommends that reusable semicritical items be high-level disinfected, pasteurized, or sterilized to minimize the risk of transmission of infectious agents.[1] This recommendation is supported by professional organizations, including the Association for Professionals in Infection Control and Epidemiology, Inc (APIC), the American Society of Anesthesiologists (ASA), and the American Association of Nurse Anesthetists (AANA).[1,29,30] Inadequately disinfected laryngoscope blades have been implicated in clusters of infections.[31-33] Laryngoscopes should be disassembled and all parts thoroughly cleaned and the blades high-level disinfected before they are reassembled. Some LMAs are designed for limited reuse. Manufacturers' instructions should be followed.

4. Flexible endoscopes should be processed according to AORN's "Recommended practices for cleaning and processing endoscopes and endoscope accessories,"[34] and the manufac-

turer's written instructions. Infections have been transmitted when flexible endoscopes have been reprocessed in an automated endoscope reprocessor with the biopsy port caps off or adapters that were incompatible with the equipment.[35,36] Users of this equipment should verify compatibility of the reprocessor with the endoscope and that adapters are approved by the manufacturer of the reprocessing equipment for use with the particular endoscope being processed. Manufacturers' written instructions should be followed.

5. Residual chemicals should be removed and the reprocessed item thoroughly dried before storage or use on a patient. Residual chemicals on items have led to allergic reactions and tissue burns.[37] Chemical stains have occurred when orthophthalaldehyde was not rinsed off adequately before use.[38] Users of chemical disinfectants should verify the appropriateness of the chemical's use on items being disinfected and thoroughly rinse the items according to the manufacturer's written instructions. These recommendations may include a triple rinse. Disinfected items should be dried thoroughly and stored in manner that prevents recontamination or damage. Use of contaminated tap water to rinse semicritical items has resulted in transmission of *Pseudomonas aeruginosa*.[39-43] This agent proliferates in the channels of endoscopes.[39,40,43] Items should be rinsed with sterile water after the chemical disinfection process. If sterile water is not used, the item should be rinsed first with water and then with 70% alcohol, and it should be thoroughly dried, along with its lumens and channels.[43]

6. Disinfected semicritical items should be stored in a clean location in a manner that prevents recontamination or damage. Storing semicritical items in a clean location minimizes the risk of contamination with pathogens before use. Endoscopes should be stored vertically with control valves, caps, and hoods removed.[43]

7. Personnel should be trained in the reprocessing procedures and equipment. Training personnel regarding the complexities of the equipment, chemicals, and processes used minimizes the risk of human error.

8. Quality control of reprocessing procedures should be performed and documentation maintained in accordance with

   ♦ AORN's "Recommended practices for high-level disinfection,"[27]
   ♦ AORN's "Recommended practices for sterilization in the practice setting,"[28] and
   ♦ manufacturers' written instructions.

   Quality control measures provide assurance that mechanical and chemical conditions are optimal for high-level disinfection. Documentation provides a mechanism for process improvement and investigation of adverse events.

Recommendation III

Anesthesia equipment contacting intact skin should be clean at the time of use.

1. Items such as blood pressure cuffs, electrocardiogram (ECG) leads, and oximeter probes that contact only intact skin are considered noncritical. The CDC

   ♦ has determined that the potential for transmission of infectious agents is lower when items contact only intact skin,
   ♦ has classified these items as noncritical, and
   ♦ recommends low-level disinfection.[1]

2. Reusable items and surfaces contacting intact skin (eg, blood pressure cuffs, ECG leads, skin temperature probes) should be cleaned between use on patients. Cleaning removes organic and inorganic material, which allows the disinfectant to contact all surfaces.[1,25,26]

3. Reusable laryngoscope handles should be cleaned and low-level disinfected between patients. Laryngoscope handles become contaminated during airway management. In studies, 40% to 50% of handles tested positive for blood.[44,45] Cleaning and disinfecting these handles minimizes the risk of transmission of bloodborne pathogens. The disinfectant selected should be registered with the Environmental Protection Agency (EPA) for use as a hospital disinfectant and used according to the manufacturer's written instructions.[46]

4. Reusable noncritical items should be low-level disinfected between patients. Low-level disinfection with an EPA-registered hospital disin-fectant kills most bacteria and some viruses and fungi but may not kill tubercle bacilli or bacterial spores.[1] After subjection to low-level disinfection, the device is considered safe to come in contact with intact skin.

5. Surfaces of anesthesia equipment that are touched by personnel while they are providing patient care or handling contaminated items should be cleaned and low-level disinfected between use on patients, according to manufacturers' written instructions. Surfaces of anesthesia equipment become contaminated with oral secretions and blood during surgical procedures.[47-50] Researchers have found occult or visible blood on 29.5% to 35.5% of anesthesia machines, carts, and monitors.[47,48] Blood also has been found on ventilator controls, flow meter knobs, vapor controls, ECG leads, oximeter probes, and blood pressure cuffs (ie, 25% to 64.3%).[48] Surfaces of anesthesia carts, drawer handles, touch screens, flow meter knobs, ventilator controls, ECG leads, oximeter probes, and blood pressure cuffs should be cleaned and disinfected between use on patients. Other surfaces known to have been touched during patient care also should be cleaned and disinfected between patients.

6. Exterior surfaces of anesthesia equipment (eg, anesthesia cart, machine, monitors) that are not knowingly contaminated during patient care should be terminally low-level disinfected at the end of the day according to manufacturers' written instructions. Contact with blood and body fluids is routinely associated with tasks performed by anesthesia care providers.[50] These surfaces may become contaminated during use, without the knowledge of the provider.[51] Low-level disinfection with an EPA-registered hospital disinfectant renders the surfaces safe to contact intact skin.[1] Manufacturers recommend specific agents to clean complex electronic equipment. These instructions should be followed.

Recommendation IV

Single-use items (eg, breathing circuits, endotracheal tubes, filters, needles, some LMAs, stylets, suction catheters, syringes) should be used once and discarded in accordance with local, state, and federal regulations.

1. Single-use items should be used for a single patient and not reused on subsequent patients. Patient care equipment and supplies are potential vectors of microorganisms and can transmit infectious agents. Safe cleaning and reuse of single-use items has not been established. These items should be discarded after use on a single patient.

2. Single-use items should not be reprocessed unless requirements for validation testing can be met. Reuse of items designed for single use creates the potential for injury related to mechanical failure, residual bioburden, and chemical residue from the reprocessing agent. For these reasons, reprocessing of items designed for single use is regulated by the FDA. Under the Federal Food, Drug, and Cosmetic Act, facilities reprocessing single-use devices must meet all regulatory requirements of a device manufacturer, including
   ◆ facility registration and device listing,
   ◆ premarket clearance or approval,
   ◆ labeling,
   ◆ corrections and removals,
   ◆ medical device tracking,
   ◆ medical device reporting, and
   ◆ quality system regulation.[52]

   These requirements exceed the capabilities of most perioperative settings.

Recommendation V

Anesthesia equipment should meet performance and safety criteria established by the practice setting and that is consistent with the manufacturer's written instructions.

1. Written information regarding safety and testing methods, warranties, and a manual for maintenance and inspections should be obtained from the manufacturer for all anesthesia equipment. These manuals help in developing operational, safety, and maintenance guidelines. Recommendations vary by manufacturer and equipment model. Manuals should be maintained for each.

2. Anesthesia equipment should be assigned an identification number. Identification numbers allow for documentation of inspections, safety checks, preventive maintenance, repairs, and tracking in the event of a patient or equipment problem.

3. Before placing anesthesia equipment into service, the safety features of the equipment should be tested by qualified, trained personnel, according to manufacturers' written instructions. These tests should be specific to the type and model of equipment involved and include, but not be limited to, calibrations and alarms. Testing the equipment before initial use minimizes the risk of patient injury resulting from faulty equipment.

4. Before use, anesthesia equipment should be tested according to manufacturers' written instructions and the safety standards of the facility. This check provides assurance that basic safety features of the equipment are operational. The FDA's "Anesthesia apparatus checkout recommendations" can be adapted for this purpose.[53]

5. Routine maintenance of anesthesia machines should be conducted on a regular schedule by qualified, trained personnel, according to manufacturers' written instructions. Regular preventive maintenance minimizes the risk of mechanical failure of anesthesia equipment.

6. Any equipment not meeting safety standards should be removed from service. Equipment failing safety checks poses a risk to patients and/or personnel. Removal of the equipment minimizes these risks. The ASA has published guidelines for determining when anesthesia machines should be considered obsolete.[54] Obsolete machines and equipment should be replaced.

7. Before use on a patient susceptible to malignant hyperthermia (MH), the anesthesia machine should be prepared in a manner that minimizes trace anesthetic agents. Halogenated anesthetic agents may trigger MH in susceptible patients.[55] Removing traces of these agents minimizes this risk. The Malignant Hyperthermia Association of the United States recommends changing the soda lime and breathing circuit, draining and inactivating vaporizers, and flushing the machine with 10 L of air or oxygen for 10 minutes before using the machine for an MH-susceptible patient.[56]

8. Equipment containing mercury should be replaced with alternatives that are mercury-free. Mercury poses a risk to patients and personnel as well as the environment. Removing mercury from the health care environment minimizes these risks.[57]

Recommendation VI

Internal components of the anesthesia machine breathing circuit should be cleaned regularly.

1. Reusable absorbers and valves should be cleaned on a regular basis according to manufacturers' written instructions. Particular attention should be given to the valves. An appropriate and cost-effective schedule for reprocessing has not been established.[58] Single-use absorbers are available and should be used for only one patient. Routine sterilization or high-level disinfection of the internal components of anesthesia machines is unnecessary.[29,30,58]

2. Anesthesia ventilator bellows should be cleaned regularly according to manufacturers' written instructions.

3. Soda lime should be changed according to the manufacturer's written instructions. Soda lime canisters do not filter bacteria adequately.[59-61] In one study, 40% of bacteria passed through the soda lime.[61] The bactericidal activity of soda lime also is unreliable.[61,62] *Mycobacterium tuberculosis* has been found to survive three hours in soda lime.[61] Soda lime, therefore, should not be used as the only method of filtration. Canisters and contents should be replaced according to the manufacturer's written instructions.

4. Routine use of single-use breathing circuits with bacterial filters should be considered. Bacteria circulate through the anesthesia circuit and proliferate inside the absorber and accessories.[63-65] Filters prevent microorganisms from contaminating the ventilator and escaping into the OR through the positive pressure relief valve of the waste gas scavenging system.[62,66-73] Research findings indicate that the absence of bacterial filters does not lead to an increased rate of nosocomial pneumonias.[58,74] In one investigation, however, contamination of the anesthetic circuit was identified as the likely cause of transmission of hepatitis C virus.[75] Currently, there is no consensus about the routine use of bacterial filters.[29,30,58,76,77] For patients with known or suspected tuberculosis, the CDC, ASA, and AANA recommend using a bacterial filter between the patient and breathing circuit.[29,30,58] The Canadian Society of Anesthesiologists also recommends use of bacterial filters for patients with severe acute respiratory syndrome (SARS).[78] With the increased prevalence of tuberculosis, increased numbers of immunocompromised patients, and the advent of SARS, it is prudent to consider the routine use of bacterial filters on the inspiratory and expiratory limbs of the anesthesia circuit. Some single-use circuits have a heat and moisture exchanger equipped with these filters. Reusable circuits should be cleaned and undergo high-level disinfection, pasteurization, or sterilization between use on patients.

5. Humidifiers should be used and cleaned according to manufacturers' written instructions. The water in humidifiers is heated to temperatures that reduce or eliminate microbial growth.[79] Tap water may contain stationary-phase forms of *Legionella pneumophila,* which are heat resistant.[66] Sterile water should be used in humidifiers.[58,79-81] Reusable humidifying chambers should undergo sterilization or high-level disinfection between patient uses.[58,79] Single-use chambers should be discarded after use on one patient.

Recommendation VII

Waste must be disposed of in a manner consistent with local, state, and federal regulations.

1. Biohazardous waste should be placed in a biohazardous waste bag. Some anesthetic waste poses a risk of transmission of bloodborne pathogens. Placing it in designated biohazardous containers alerts handlers to this risk. Management of biohazardous waste within the health care facility is regulated by the Occupational Safety and Health Administration (OSHA).[82] State and local laws also apply. Perioperative professionals should be aware of and act in accordance with these laws.

2. Sharps should be handled in a manner that minimizes the risk of percutaneous injury. To minimize the risk of injury from contaminated sharps, OSHA requires that puncture-resistant sharps containers be located at the point of use.[82] Placing the container next to or on the anesthesia equipment meets this expectation. Sharps should be placed directly into the container.

3. Waste that is hazardous upon disposal must be managed in a way that minimizes environmental impact. Some waste poses a risk to the environment (eg, alcohol, bezoin, epinephrine, mercury). This waste is classified by the EPA as hazardous upon disposal and is regulated under the Resource Conservation and Recovery Act.[83] The EPA requires that this waste be placed in hazardous waste containers at the point of use to alert handlers to the need to take precautions upon its disposal.[84] State and local laws also may apply.

Recommendation VIII

Potential hazards to perioperative personnel that are associated with handling and processing clean and contaminated anesthesia equipment (eg, exposure to infectious organisms, chemicals) should be identified, and practices should be established to reduce the risk of injury.

1. Contaminated sharps must be discarded in a puncture-resistant container at the point of use. Immediate disposal of sharps prevents injuries to people unaware of the location of the sharp and is required by OSHA.[82]

2. All personnel involved with cleaning and processing anesthesia equipment should practice according to AORN's "Recommended practices for standard and transmission-based precautions."[85] These precautions define general measures for infection control.

3. Anesthesia equipment should be processed using methods that reduce the risk of exposure to pathogens and injury. Manual cleaning methods that minimize splashing, spraying, spattering, and generation of droplets protect personnel from exposure to blood, body fluids, and cleaning agents.

4. Personnel must be apprised of the hazards in the workplace, including chemicals used for reprocessing anesthesia equipment. Knowledge of the hazards in the workplace, preventive measures, and exposure management minimize the risk of injury to employees and are required by OSHA.[86]

5. Personal protective equipment (PPE) must be provided to minimize the risk of exposure to bloodborne pathogens and chemicals used in the workplace. Use of barrier protection minimizes the risk of exposure to bloodborne pathogens by personnel performing tasks likely to generate contact with blood. According to OSHA regulations, employers are required to provide PPE (eg, gloves, gown, mask, protective eyewear, face shield) for their employees.[82]

6. Personnel should actively participate in the evaluation of engineering devices and work practice controls to minimize the risk of exposure to bloodborne pathogens. Active participation in the selection of PPE and practices provides the best opportunity for designing a safer workplace. According to OSHA regulations, employers are required to solicit nonmanagerial employee input during evaluation of engineering devices and work practice controls to minimize exposures to bloodborne pathogens.[87]

Recommendation IX

Anesthesia equipment should be handled, cleaned, processed, or discarded in the same manner in all areas of the practice setting.

1. Guidelines should be developed and approved by appropriate mechanisms and governing bodies in the practice setting. Equipment may be located in satellite areas (eg, labor and delivery). Guidelines should be consistent throughout the practice setting because all patients are entitled to the same standard of care.[88]

Recommendation X

Policies and procedures on cleaning and processing anesthesia equipment should be developed, reviewed periodically, and readily available in the practice setting.

1. These recommended practices should be used as guidelines for developing policies and procedures in the practice setting. Policies and procedures establish authority, responsibility, and accountability for cleaning, handling, and processing anesthesia equipment and serve as operational guidelines. Policies and procedures also help in developing performance improvement activities.

2. Policies and procedures for cleaning and processing anesthesia equipment should include, but not be limited to,
   ◆ disposal of single-use items,
   ◆ equipment maintenance programs,
   ◆ equipment quality checks,
   ◆ personal protection,
   ◆ personnel education,
   ◆ processing reusable equipment, and
   ◆ waste disposal.

Glossary

Anesthesia equipment: Equipment used to provide anesthesia and/or monitor the patient under sedation or anesthesia.

Cleaning: A process using friction, detergent, and water to remove organic debris.

Critical item: An item that contacts the vascular system or enters sterile tissue, posing the highest risk of transmission of infection.

High-level disinfection: A process that uses a government-registered agent that kills vegetative bacteria, tubercle bacilli, some spores, fungi, and lipid and nonlipid viruses, given appropriate concentration, submersion, and contact time.

Low-level disinfection: A process by which most bacteria, some viruses, and some fungi are killed. This process may not kill resistant organisms, such as mycobacterium tubercle or bacterial spores.

Noncritical item: An item that comes in contact with intact skin but not with mucous membranes, sterile tissue, or the vascular system.

Pasteurization: A process that employs time and hot water (ie, 160° to 170° F [21.7° C to 25° C] for 30 minutes) for high-level disinfection. The intensity of heat and duration of exposure must be determined by the manufacturer of the pasteurization unit and the manufacturer of the product or device to be cleaned.

Semicritical item: An item that comes in contact with mucous membranes or with skin that is not intact.

REFERENCES
1. W A Rutala, APIC Guidelines Committee, "APIC guideline for selection and use of disinfectants," *American Journal of Infection Control* 24 (August 1996) 313-342.
2. Centers for Disease Control and Prevention, "Postsurgical infections associated with an extrinsically contaminated intravenous anesthetic agent—California, Illinois, Maine, and Michigan, 1990," *Morbidity and Mortality Weekly Report* 39 (June 29, 1990) 426-427, 433.
3. M J Daily, J B Dickey, K H Packo, "Endogenous Candida endophthalmitis after intravenous anesthesia with propofol," *Archives of Ophthalmology* 109 (August 1991) 1081-1084.
4. M E Villarino et al, "Postsurgical infectious associated with an extrinsically contaminated intravenous anesthetic agent," program and abstracts of the 31st Interscience Conference on Antimicrobial Agents and Chemotherapy, Chicago, 29 Sept-2 Oct 1991.
5. B Veber et al, "Severe sepsis after intravenous injection of contaminated Propofol," *Anesthesiology* 80 (March 1994) 712-713.
6. K Kidd-Ljunggren et al, "Nosocomial transmission of hepatitis B virus infection through multiple-dose vials," *Journal of Hospital Infection* 43 (September 1999) 57-62.
7. M J Kuehnert et al, "*Staphylococcus aureus* bloodstream infections among patients undergoing electroconvulsive therapy traced to breaks in infection control and possible extrinsic contamination by Propofol," *Anesthesia and Analgesia* 85 (August 1997) 420-425.
8. M Massari et al, "Transmission of hepatitis C virus in a gynecological surgery setting," *Journal of Clinical Microbiology* 39 (August 2001) 2860-2863.
9. Centers for Disease Control and Prevention, "Transmission of hepatitis B and C viruses in outpatient settings—New York, Oklahoma, and Nebraska, 2000-2002," *Morbidity and Mortality Weekly Report* 52 (Sept 26, 2003) 901-906.
10. J M Boyce, D Pittet, "Guideline for hand hygiene in health-care settings: Recommendations of the Healthcare Infection Control Practices Advisory Committee and the HICPAC/SHEA/APIC/ISAD Hand Hygiene Taskforce," *Morbidity and Mortality Weekly Report* 51 (Oct 25, 2002) (RR16) 1-44.
11. C E Blogg, M A Ramsey, J D Jarvis, "Infection hazard from syringes," *British Journal of Anaesthesia* 46 (April 1974) 260-262.
12. M R Lessard et al, "A microbiological study of the contamination of the syringes used in anaesthesia practice," *Canadian Journal of Anaesthesia* 35 (November 1988) 567-569.
13. C T Lutz et al, "Allergy testing of multiple patients should no longer be performed with a common syringe," *The New England Journal of Medicine* 310 (May 17, 1984) 1335-1337.

14. J W Koepke, J C Selner, "Allergy testing of multiple patients with a common syringe," *The New England Journal Medicine* 311 (Nov 1, 1984) 1188-1189.

15. D J Shulan et al, "Contamination of intradermal skin test syringes," *Journal of Allergy and Clinical Immunology* 76 (August 1985) 226-227.

16. J W Koepke et al, "Viral contamination of intradermal skin test syringes," *Annals of Allergy* 55 (December 1985) 776-778.

17. A Carbonne et al, "Patient to patient transmission of hepatitis C in surgery clinic through multi-dose vials," abstract presented at the 13th annual meeting of the Society for Healthcare Epidemiology of America, Arlington Va, 5-8 April 2003.

18. A Fleming, A C Ogilvie, "Syringe needles and mass inoculation technique," *British Medical Journal* 1 (March 17, 1951) 543-546.

19. R R Hughes, "Post-penicillin jaundice," *British Medical Journal* 2 (Nov 9, 1946) 685-688.

20. R Uren, C Commens, R Howman-Giles, "Intradermal injections: A potential health hazard?" *Medical Journal of Australia* 161 (August 994) 226.

21. H A Hein et al, "Recapping needles in anesthesia—Is it safe?" *Anesthesiology* 67 (September 1987) A161.

22. C A Trepanier et al, "Risk of cross-infection related to the multiple use of disposable syringes," *Canadian Journal of Anaesthesia* 37 (March 1990) 156-159.

23. J L Parlow, "Blood contamination of drug syringes used in anaesthesia," *Canadian Journal of Anaesthesia* 36 suppl (1989) S61-S62.

24. B Meier, "Reuse of needle at hospital infects 50 with hepatitis C," *New York Times,* Oct 10, 2002.

25. Association for the Advancement of Medical Instrumentation, "Safe handling and biological decontamination of reusable medical devices in health care facilities and in nonclinical settings; ANSI/AAMI ST35" (Arlington, Va: Association of the Advancement of Medical Instrumentation, 2003) 16.

26. "Sterilization or disinfection of medical devices: General principles," Centers for Disease Control and Prevention, *http://www.cdc.gov/ncidod/hip/sterile/sterilgp.htm* (accessed 24 Sept 2004).

27. "Recommended practices for high-level disinfection," in *Standards, Recommended Practices, and Guidelines* (Denver: AORN, Inc, 2004) 235-240.

28. "Recommended practices for sterilization in the practice setting," in *Standards, Recommended Practices, and Guidelines* (Denver: AORN, Inc, 2004) 373-384.

29. American Society of Anesthesiologists Committee on Occupational Health of Operating Room Personnel, *Recommendations for Infection Control for the Practice of Anesthesiology,* second ed (American Society of Anesthesiologists: Park Ridge, Ill, 1998). Also available at *http://www.asahq.org/publicationsAndServices/infectioncontrol.pdf* (accessed 24 May 2004).

30. American Association of Nurse Anesthetists, *Infection Control Guide* (Park Ridge, Ill: American Association of Nurse Anesthetists, 1997) 13-23.

31. J E Foweraker, "The laryngoscope as a potential source of cross-infection," *Journal of Hospital Infections* 29 (April 1995) 315-316.

32. T J Neal et al, "The neonatal laryngoscope as a potential source of cross-infection," *Journal of Hospital Infections* 30 (August 1995) 315-317.

33. K E Nelson et al, "Transmission of neonatal listerosis in a delivery room," *American Journal of Diseases of Children* 139 (September 1985) 903-905.

34. "Recommended practices for cleaning and processing endoscopes and endoscope accessories," in *Standards, Recommended Practices, and Guidelines* (Denver: AORN, Inc, 2004) 261-266.

35. Centers for Disease Control and Prevention, "Bronchoscopy-related infections and pseudoinfections—New York, 1996 and 1998," *Morbidity and Mortality Weekly Report* 48 (July 9, 1999) 557-560.

36. US Department of Health and Human Services, "Infections from inadequately processed endoscopes," *User Facility Reporting* 28 (Fall 1999) 1-5.

37. "Manufacturer and User Facility Device Experience Database. Report Numbers 2084725-2002-00033; 2084725-2003-00084; 2084725-2004-00010; 2084725-2004-00003; 2084725-2004-00011; 2084725-2004-00012; 3003723454-2004-0001," US Food and Drug Administration, *http://www.accessdata.fda.gov/scripts/cdrh/cfdocs/cfMAUDE/Search.cfm* (accessed 30 Sept 2004).

38. "Manufacturer and User Facility Device Experience Database. Report Numbers 2084725-2003-00008; 3003723454-2004-0001," US Food and Drug Administration, *http://www.accessdata.fda.gov/scripts/cdrh/cfdocs/cfMAUDE/Search.cfm* (accessed 30 Sept 2004).

39. H J O'Conner, J R Babb, G A Ayliffe, "*Pseudomonas aeruginosa* infection in endoscopy," *Gastroenterology* 93 (December 1987) 1451.

40. J I Allen et al, "*Pseudomonas* infection of the biliary system resulting from use of contaminated endoscope," *Gastroenterology* 92 (March 1987) 759-763.

41. D E Low et al, "Infectious complications of endoscopic retrograde cholangio-pancreatography. A prospective assessment," *Archives of Internal Medicine* 140 (August 1980) 1076-1077.

42. M J Arfa, D L Sitter, "In-hospital evaluation of contamination of duodenoscopes: A quantitative assessment of the effect of drying," *Journal of Hospital Infections* 19 (October 1991) 89-98.

43. C J Alvarado, M Reichelderfer, "APIC guideline for infection prevention and control in flexible endoscopy," *American Journal of Infection Control* 18 (April 2000) 138-155.

44. R C Morell et al, "A survey of laryngoscope contamination at a university and a community hospital," *Anesthesiology* 80 (April 1994) 960.

45. R A Phillips, W P Monaghan, "Incidence of visible and occult blood on laryngoscope blades and handles," *AANA Journal* 65 (June 1997) 241-246.

46. Centers for Disease Control and Prevention, "Guidelines for environmental infection control in health-care facilities: Recommendations of CDC and the Healthcare Infection Control Practices Advisory Committee (HICPAC)," *Morbidity and Mortality Weekly Report* 52 (June 6, 2003) No RR-10 22.

47. J R Hall, "Blood contamination of anesthesia equipment and monitoring equipment," *Anesthesia and Analgesia* 78 (June 1994) 1136-1139.

48. S M Perry, W P Monghan, "The prevalence of visible and/or occult blood on anesthesia and monitoring equipment," *Journal of the American Association of Nurse Anesthetists* 69 (February 2001) 44-48.

49. H Arkoff, R A Ortega, "Touchscreen technology: Potential source of cross-infections," *Anesthesia and Analgesia* 75 (December 1992) 1073.

50. M S Kristensen, E Sloth, T K Jensen, "Relationship between anesthetic procedure and contact of anesthesia personnel with patient body fluids," *Anesthesiology* 73 (October 1990) 619-624.

51. L A Herwaldt, J M Pottinger, S A Coffin, "Nosocomial infections associated with anesthesia," in *Hospital Epidemiology and Infection Control,* third ed, C G Mayhall ed (Philadelphia: Lippincott Williams & Wilkins, 2004).

52. US Food and Drug Administration, "Important enforcement date for reprocessing single-use devices," *User Facility Reporting* 39 (Summer 2002). Also available at *http://www.fda.gov/cdrh/fusenews/ufb39.html#1* (accessed 24 Sept 2004).

53. "Anesthesia apparatus checkout recommendations, 1993," US Food and Drug Administration, *http://www.fda.gov/cdrh/humfac/anesckot.html* (accessed 24 Sept 2004).

54. "Guidelines for determining anesthesia machine obsolescence," American Society of Anesthesiologists, *http://www.asahq.org/PublicationsAndServices/machineobsolescense.pdf* (accessed 24 Sept 2004).

55. B Abraham et al, "Malignant hyperthermia susceptibility: Anaesthetic implications and risk stratification," *Quarterly Journal of Medicine* 90 (January 997) 13-18.

56. "Medical FAQs," Malignant Hyperthermia Association of the United States, *http://www.mhaus.org/index.cfm/fuseaction/Content.Display/PagePK/MedicalFAQs.cfm* (accessed 24 Sept 2004).

57. "Reducing mercury use in healthcare: Promoting a healthier environment: A how-to manual," US Environmental Protection Agency, *http://www.epa.gov/glnpo/bnsdocs/merchealth* (accessed 24 Sept 2004).

58. Centers for Disease Control and Prevention, "Guidelines for prevention of nosocomial pneumonia, 2003," *Morbidity and Mortality Weekly Report* 53 (March 26, 2004) (RR03) 1-36.

59. G E Dryden, "Risk of contamination from the anesthesia circle absorber: An evaluation," *Anesthesia and Analgesia* 48 (November/December 1969) 939-943.

60. J R Jenkins, W M Edgar, "Sterilization of anaesthetic equipment," *Anaesthesia* 19 (April 1964) 177-190.

61. P M Murphy, R B Fitzgeorge, F Barrett, "Viability and distribution of bacteria after passage through a circle anaesthetic system," *British Journal of Anaesthesia* 66 (March 1991) 300-304.

62. D T Leijten, V S Rejger, R P Mouton, "Bacterial contamination and the effect of filters in anaesthetic circuits in a simulated patient model," *Journal of Hospital Infections* 21 (May 1992) 51-60.

63. G E Dryden, "Uncleaned anesthesia equipment," *JAMA* 233 (September 1975) 1297-1298.

64. B C Stratford, R R Clark, S Dixson, "The disinfection of anaesthetic apparatus," *British Journal of Anaesthesia* 36 (August 1964) 471-476.

65. "Bacterial contamination of anesthesia machines revealed," *Excerpta Medica* (Lawrenceville, NJ: Convention Reporter, 1991) 12-14.

66. H Aranha-Creado et al, "Removal of *Mycobacterium* species by breathing circuit filters," *Infection Control and Hospital Epidemiology* 18 (April 1997) 252-254.

67. A J Berry, F S Nolte, "An alternative strategy for infection control of anesthesia breathing circuits: A laboratory assessment of the Pall HME filter," *Anesthesia and Analgesia* 72 (May 1991) 651-655.

68. I Hogbarth, "Anaesthetic machine and breathing system contamination and the efficacy of bacterial/viral filters," *Anaesthesia and Intensive Care* 25 (April 1996) 154-163.

69. G Lloyd et al, "Barriers to hepatitis C transmission within breathing systems: Efficacy of a pleated hydrophobic filter," *Anaesthesia and Intensive Care* 25 (June 1997) 235-238.

70. H H Luttropp, L Berntman, "Bacterial filters protect anaesthetic equipment in a low-flow system," *Anaesthesia* 48 (June 1993) 520-523.

71. J Rathgeber et al, "Prevention of patient bacterial contamination of anaesthesia-circle-systems: A clinical study of the contamination risk and performance of different heat and moisture exchanges with electret filter (HMEF)," *European Journal of Anaesthesia* 14 (July 1997) 368-373.

72. G M Shiotani et al, "Prevention of contamination of the circle system and ventilators with a new disposable filter," *Anesthesia and Analgesia* 50 (September/October 1971) 844-845.

73. C Smith et al, "An evaluation of one and two airflow filters preventing the movement of bacterial through the anesthesia circle system," *Journal of the American Association of Nurse Anesthetists* 64 (April 1996) 153-156.

74. S Van Hassel et al, "Bacterial filters in anesthesia: Results of nine years of surveillance," *Infection Control and Hospital Epidemiology* 20 (January 1999) 58-60.

75. K Chant et al, "Investigation of possible patient-to-patient transmission of hepatitis C in a hospital," *New South Wales Public Health Bulletin* 5 (May 1994) 47-51.

76. Association of Anaesthetists of Great Britain and Ireland, *Infection Control in Anaesthesia* (London: The Association of Anaesthetists of Great Britain and Ireland, 2002) 4.

77. "Policy on infection control in anaesthesia, 1995," Australian and New Zealand College of Anaesthetists, *http://www.medeserv.com.au/anzca/pdfdocs/P28_1995.PDF* (accessed 25 Sept 2004).

78. "Anesthetic management of a SARS-Infected patient," Canadian Society of Anesthesiologists, *http://www.asahq.org/clinical/pracadvsars.htm* (accessed 25 Sept 2004).

79. Centers for Disease Control and Prevention, "Guidelines for prevention of nosocomial pneumonia," *Morbidity and Mortality Weekly Report* 46 (Jan 3, 1997) (RR-1) 1-77.

80. P M Anrow et al, "Nosocomial Legionnaire's disease caused by aerosolized tap water from respiratory devices," *Journal of Infectious Diseases* 146 (October 1982) 460-467.

81. D E Craven, T A Goularte, B J Make, "Contaminated condensate in mechanical ventilator circuits: A risk factor for nosocomial pneumonia?" *American Review of Respiratory Disease* 129 (April 1984) 625-628.

82. "Bloodborne pathogens—1910.1030," US Department of Labor Occupational Safety and Health Administration, *http://www.oshaslc.gov/pls/oshaweb/owadisp.show_document?p_table=STANDARDS&p_id=10051* (accessed 25 Sept 2004).

83. "RCA online," US Environmental Protection Agency, *http://www.epa.gov/rcraonline* (accessed 25 Sept 2004).

84. "Identification and listing of hazardous waste," in *Electronic Code of Federal Regulations (e-CFR)* 40: Protection of Environment, Part 261, *http://www.epa.gov/epahome/cfr40.htm* (accessed 25 Sept 2004).

85. "Recommended practices for standard and transmission-based precautions," in *Standards, Recommended Practices, and Guidelines* (Denver: AORN, Inc, 2004) 361-366.

86. "Hazard communication in the 21st century workplace," US Department of Labor, Occupational Safety and Health Administration, *http://www.osha.gov/dsg/hazcom/finalmsdsreport.html* (accessed 25 Sept 2004).

87. "Bloodborne pathogens and needlestick prevention," US Occupational Safety and Health Administration, *http://www.osha.gov/SLTC/bloodbornepathogens/index.html* (accessed 25 Sept 2004).

88. Joint Commission on Accreditation of Healthcare Organizations, "Crosswalk of 2003 standards for hospitals to 2004 leadership standards for hospitals," in *2004 Comprehensive Accreditation Manual for Hospitals: The Official Handbook* (Oakbrook Terrace, Ill: Joint Commission on Accreditation of Healthcare Organizations, 2003) LD.3.20.

Originally published June 1977, *AORN Journal, as* AORN "Recommended practices for cleaning and processing anesthesia equipment."

Revised March 1978; July 1982; March 1991. Published as proposed recommended practices September 1994.

Revised; published November 1999, *AORN Journal.* Reformatted July 2000.

Revised November 2004; published in *Standards, Recommended Practices, and Guidelines,* 2005 edition. Reprinted April 2005, *AORN Journal.*

Recommended Practices for High-Level Disinfection

The following recommended practices were developed by the AORN Recommended Practices Committee and have been approved by the AORN Board of Directors. They were presented as proposed recommendations for comments by members and others. They are effective January 1, 2009.

These recommended practices are intended as achievable recommendations representing what is believed to be an optimal level of practice. Policies and procedures will reflect variations in practice settings and/or clinical situations that determine the degree to which the recommended practices can be implemented. AORN recognizes the various settings in which perioperative nurses practice. These recommended practices are intended as guidelines adaptable to various practice settings. These practice settings include traditional operating rooms, ambulatory surgery centers, physician's offices, cardiac catheterization laboratories, endoscopy suites, radiology departments, and all other areas where surgery may be performed.

Purpose

These recommended practices provide guidance for achieving safe and effective high-level disinfection (HLD) of reusable instruments and equipment. Care and cleaning of flexible endoscopes is outside the scope of these recommended practices. Refer to the AORN "Recommended practices for cleaning and processing endoscopes and endoscope accessories."

Recommendation I

Items to be reprocessed should be categorized as critical, semicritical, and noncritical.

The Spaulding classification system, developed by Earle Spaulding in 1968, has withstood the passage of time and continues to be used today by infection preventionists and others to determine the correct processing methods for preparing instruments and other items for patient use. According to the Spaulding system, the level of processing required is based on the nature of the item requiring processing and the manner in which it is to be used (**Table 1**).[1-5]

I.a.   Items that enter sterile tissue or the vascular system are categorized as critical and should be sterile when used. Sterility may be achieved by physical or chemical processes.[1,5,6,7,8,9]

When critical items are contaminated with microorganisms, including bacterial spores, the risk of infection is substantial.[2,10-12] Examples of critical items include, but are not limited to,
- surgical instruments;
- cutting endoscopic accessories that break the mucosal barrier;
- endoscopes used in sterile body cavities;
- cardiac, vascular, and urinary catheters;
- implants;
- needles; and
- ultrasound probes used in sterile body cavities.

I.b.   Items that come in contact with nonintact skin or mucous membranes are considered semicritical and should receive a minimum of high-level disinfection.[1,5-9,13]

Intact mucous membranes generally provide a barrier to common bacterial spores but not to organisms such as tubercle bacilli and viruses.[2,11] Examples of semicritical items include, but are not limited to,
- vaginal and rectal probes, even when sheaths are used;
- respiratory therapy equipment;
- anesthesia equipment;
- bronchoscopes; and
- gastrointestinal endoscopes and accessories.

I.b.1.   Semicritical devices contaminated or potentially contaminated with hepatitis B virus (HBV), hepatitis C virus (HCV), HIV, multi-drug resistant bacteria, or *Mycobacterium tuberculosis* (TB) should receive a minimum of high-level disinfection.[2]

Literature has supported and research has demonstrated that high-level disinfectants inactivate these and other pathogens that may contaminate semicritical devices.[3,6,10,14-22] The practice of using HLD is consistent with standard precautions, which presume that all patients potentially are infected.[2]

Table 1

SPAULDING CLASSIFICATION SYSTEM[1-7]			
Device category/ Classification	**Level of Disinfection**	**Effectiveness of Method**	**Examples**
Critical Items that come in contact with the blood-stream or sterile body tissues	**Sterilization** *Examples:* saturated steam, ethylene oxide, dry heat, ozone, low-temperature hydrogen peroxide gas plasma, glutaraldehyde-based formulations, peracetic acid, stabilized hydrogen peroxide 6%. **Chemical sterilants** *Examples:* glutaraldehyde-based formulations, peracetic acid, stabilized hydrogen peroxide 6%, wet pasteurization, sodium hypochlorite	Sterilization kills all microbial life, includ-ing pathogenic and nonpathogenic micro-organisms and spores.	• surgical instruments • acupuncture needles • foot care instruments • implants • cardiac and urinary catheters • endoscope acces-sories that penetrate the mucosal barrier
Semicritical Items that come in contact with mucous membranes or non-intact skin	**High-level disinfection** Use when sterilization is not possible. *Examples:* glutaraldehyde-based formulations, peracetic acid, stabilized hydrogen peroxide 6%, wet pasteurization, sodium hypochlorite	High-level disinfection kills all microorgan-isms but not necessar-ily a large number of bacterial spores.	• scopes (eg, broncho-scopes, colono-scopes, and similar scopes) • laryngoscope han-dles and blades, • reusable peak flow meters • vaginal and rectal probes • cryosurgical instru-ments • thermometers
Noncritical Items that come in con-tact with intact skin and those exposed to blood or other potentially infectious material	**Intermediate-level disinfection** Use an EPA-registered hospital disinfectant with label claim for tuberculocidal activity. *Examples:* chlorine-based products, phenolics	Intermediate-level dis-infection kills viruses, mycobacteria, fungi, and vegetative bacteria but not bacterial spores.	• skin probes • blood pressure cuffs • pneumatic tourni-quet cuffs • hydrotherapy tanks • examination tables
Items that do not come in contact with the patient's skin and have not been exposed to blood or other poten-tially infectious material	**Low-level disinfection** Use an EPA-registered hospital disinfectant with-out label claim for tuberculocidal activity. *Examples:* chlorine-based products, phenolics, quaternary ammonium compounds, hydrogen peroxide (approximately 3%), iodophors, 70% to 90% alcohol	Low-level disinfection kills vegetative forms of bacteria, some fungi, and lipid viruses but cannot be relied on to destroy mycobacteria, bacterial endospores, or nonlipid viruses.	• stethoscopes • dishes • scales • furniture • bed pans

REFERENCES

1. Spaulding EH. Clinical disinfection and antisepsis in the hospital. *J Hosp Res* 1972; 95.

2. Appendix B: Decontamination and disinfection. In: *Biosafety in Microbiological and Biomedical Laboratories (BMBL)*. 5th ed. Centers for Disease Control and Prevention; National Institutes of Health, eds. Washington, DC: US Government Printing Office; 2007:328-336. Available at http://www.cdc.gov/od/ohs/biosfty/bmbl5/bmbl5toc.htm. Accessed December 5, 2008.

3. Alvarado CJ, Reichelderfer M. APIC guideline for infection prevention and control in flexible endoscopy. Association for Professionals in Infection Control. *Am J Infect Control* 2000;28(2):138.

4. *AAMI TIR12:2004—Designing, Testing and Labeling Reusable Medical Devices for Reprocessing in Health Care Facilities: A Guide for Medical Device Manufacturers*. Arlington, VA: Association for the Advancement of Medical Instrumentation; 2005.

5. Rutala WA, Weber DJ. How to assess risk of disease transmission to patients when there is a failure to follow recom-mended disinfection and sterilization guidelines. *Infect Control Hosp Epidemiol* 2007; 28(2):146.

6. Multi-society guideline for reprocessing flexible gastrointestinal endoscopes. *Am J Infect Control* 2003; 31(5):309.

7. Rutala WA, Weber DJ. Cleaning, disinfection, and sterilization in healthcare facilities. In: *APIC Text of Infection Control and Epidemiology*. Washington, DC: Association for Professionals in Infection Control and Epidemiology; 2005:21-31.

I.c. Items that contact only intact skin are categorized as noncritical items and should receive intermediate-level disinfection, low-level disinfection, or cleaning.[1,5-9]

Intact skin acts as an effective barrier to most organisms.[2] Examples of noncritical items include, but are not limited to,

- tourniquets and blood pressure cuffs,
- linens,
- Mayo stands, and
- other OR furnishings.

Recommendation II

Items should be thoroughly cleaned and decontaminated before high-level disinfection.[10]

Cleaning and decontamination are the initial and most critical steps in breaking the chain of disease transmission. Debris, blood, mucous, fat, tissue, and organic matter will interfere with the action of the disinfectant. Microbial biofilms (ie, collections of bacteria and fungi existing in a multicellular matrix) adhere to each other or to medical devices, particularly those with lumens, where they affect tissues adjacent to virtually any medical device. Biofilms are difficult to remove and may serve as sources of bacterial toxin that can affect remote locations in the body. Friction and oxidizing chemicals must be used to remove biofilms. Initiating cleaning immediately after use reduces or eliminates the growth of biofilm-forming microorganisms.[10,24-43]

II.a. Appropriate personal protective equipment (PPE) should be worn during cleaning and decontamination.[6,22,44]

Personal protective equipment protects the worker from hazardous chemicals and exposure to blood and other potentially infectious materials.

II.a.1. Personnel should wear PPE that may include, but is not limited to,
- 100% nitrile rubber or 100% butyl rubber gloves when handling glutaraldehyde (polyvinyl chloride [PVC] gloves are not recommended because they absorb glutaraldehyde);[18]
- less than 100% nitrile or butyl rubber gloves for handling all other HLD solutions except glutaraldehyde;

- protective eyewear (eg, goggles, face shields);
- masks (ie, to prevent contact with skin and not inhalation of fumes); and
- moisture-repellent or splash-proof skin protection (eg, gowns, jumpsuits, aprons).[45]

Chemical disinfectants can irritate or stain skin and mucous membranes.[46,47] Use of protective apparel decreases the potential for exposure to the chemical agent.[48]

II.b. Soiled instruments and devices should be handled using PPE and transported in a contained, covered, and secure manner to the point of decontamination and processing.[22]

These practices prevent environmental contamination and protect employees from bloodborne pathogen exposure.

II.c. Meticulous cleaning and decontamination should precede high-level disinfection.

Adherence to a written cleaning protocol results in consistency of practice and facilitates the disinfection process.[6,12,22,44,49,50] According to the US Food and Drug Administration (FDA), manufacturers are obliged to provide users with adequate instructions for the safe and effective use of an instrument or device, including methods to clean and disinfect or sterilize the item if it is marked as reusable.[51,52]

II.c.1. Particular attention should be given to complex medical devices with multiple pieces (eg, endoscopes, robotic devices) that have crevices, joints, lumens, ports, and channels because they are difficult to clean.[12]

II.d. Instruments to be disinfected should be cleaned according to AORN's "Recommended practices for cleaning and care of surgical instruments and powered equipment"[49] and "Recommended practices for cleaning and processing flexible endoscopes and endoscope accessories."[53]

Adherence to a written cleaning protocol results in consistency of practice and facilitates the disinfection process.[12,22,49]

II.e. High-level disinfection should not be used for items exposed to prions. Refer to the AORN

"Recommended practices for sterilization in the perioperative practice setting."[15,49,53-55]

Prions present unique infection prevention and control challenges. Prions are proteinaceous, infectious agents containing no DNA or RNA and may be transmitted iatrogenically by direct inoculation. Prions cause transmissible spongiform encephalopathies (TSE), including Creutzfeldt-Jakob disease (CJD) and variant Creutzfeldt-Jakob disease (vCJD). Prions are resistant to traditional chemical and physical decontamination methods. High-level disinfection does not inactivate prions. Critical and semicritical items or surfaces contaminated with the CJD agent require unique decontamination procedures because of an extremely resistant subpopulation of prions.[36,49] Although some discrepancies exist between studies, all studies show that these prions resist normal inactivation methods.[33,54,56]

II.e.1.   Critical and semicritical devices that come into contact with internal tissues of patients with known or suspected TSE should be processed using the highest level and method of decontamination that can be tolerated by the instrument.[54]

Many complex and expensive instruments such as intracardiac monitoring devices, fiber-optic endoscopes, and microscopes cannot be decontaminated by the harsh procedures recommended for the decontamination of critical items exposed to high-infectivity tissue.

II.e.2.   Extended steam sterilization cycles are the preferred method of inactivating resistant prions on critical and semicritical devices. Effective exposure inactivation parameters for gravity displacement is 30 minutes at 131° C (268° F) and 18 minutes at 134° C to 138° C (273° F to 280° F) for dynamic-air removal.[2] Critical and noncritical items used in low-infectivity tissue (eg, intestines) do not have to be incinerated.[54]

II.e.3.   Disposable endoscopic accessories should be used whenever possible when there is a patient with known or suspected TSE infectivity.

Prions are highly resistant to chemical and physical processes that normally inactivate microorganisms. The risk of transferring prion protein is greatest in cases that manipulate high-risk tissue (ie, brain, dura matter, cornea). Few reports have revealed transmission of spongiform encephalopathy from endoscopic procedures; however, iatrogenic transmission of the disease has catastrophic consequences that warrants conservative treatment of accessories.[39,57]

II.e.4.   Disposable cover sheets should be used whenever possible to avoid environmental contamination of noncritical items.[54]

Transmissible spongiform encephalopathy infectivity persists for long periods on work surfaces, although they have not been implicated in iatrogenic transmission.

II.e.5.   Noncritical patient care items and surfaces should be disinfected with double-strength sodium hydroxide solution (2N NaOH) or undiluted sodium hypochlorite for one hour and rinsed with water. Sodium hypochlorite may be corrosive to some surfaces.[57]

Noncritical patient care items and surfaces have not been implicated in disease transmission.[2]

Recommendation III

Pasteurization may be used to achieve thermal high-level disinfection.

Pasteurization is a heat-automated high-level disinfection process that employs time and heat (ie, 160° F to 170° F [21.7° C to 25° C] for 30 minutes) for HLD of heat-sensitive semicritical patient care items. Pasteurization destroys all microorganisms except high numbers of bacterial spores.[15] The process originally developed by Louis Pasteur consists of heating milk, wine, or other liquids to between 140° F and 212° F (60° C to 100° C) for approximately 30 minutes to kill or significantly reduce the number of pathogenic and spoilage organisms.

III.a. Items to be high-level disinfected using pasteurization should be placed inside the washer/pasteurizer chamber according to the manufacturer's written instructions.

Medical washer/pasteurizers have wash, rinse, and pasteurization cycles. The wash cycle is accomplished either through a horizontal agitation method or a vertical rotational method, depending on the manufacturer's specifications, using warm water and detergent cleaning solution. The length of this cycle is determined by the manufacturer's written instructions. At the conclusion of the wash and rinse cycles, the tank automatically drains in preparation for the pasteurization cycle. Pasteurization is achieved by immersing all devices in a hot water bath heated to 140° F to 212° F (60° C to 100° C) and held for 30 minutes.[58] Medical washer/pasteurizers may offer quality assurance data recorders that document the temperature of the pasteurizing bath and cycle time.

Recommendation IV

An FDA-cleared agent should be used to achieve chemical high-level disinfection of medical devices.

The FDA has primary responsibility for premarket review of safety and efficacy requirements for liquid chemical germicides intended for use on critical and semicritical devices.[59] A list of products that have been cleared for marketing by the FDA can be found on the web site of the FDA Center for Devices and Radiological Health (CDRH).[17]

IV.a. Products selected for chemical disinfection should be efficacious and compatible with the materials or items to be disinfected. Many disinfectants are used in the practice setting (eg, glutaraldehyde, stabilized hydrogen peroxide, peracetic acid, orthophthalaldehyde [OPA]). These agents are not interchangeable.[48]

Devices may be damaged by these chemicals. The use of incompatible chemicals can damage the surfaces of the instrument, causing corrosion, scratches, and other surface irregularities. This damage can create a challenge for cleaning and high-level disinfection, interfere with the proper function, and reduce the life and cosmetic appearance of the device.

IV.a.1. Factors that influence the efficacy of a chemical agent include, but may not be limited to,
  • organic load present on the items to be disinfected;
  • type and level of microbial contamination;
  • precleaning, rinsing, and drying of the items;
  • active ingredients of the chemical agent;
  • concentration of the chemical agent;
  • exposure time to the chemical agent;
  • physical configuration of the item;
  • temperature and pH of the chemical agent;
  • inorganic matter present;
  • water hardness; and
  • presence of surfactants.

IV.a.2. An ideal high-level disinfectant should
  • possess a broad spectrum of antimicrobial effectiveness,
  • demonstrate rapid activity,
  • possess material compatibility,
  • be nontoxic,
  • be odorless,
  • have no disposal restrictions,
  • possess prolonged reuse and shelf life,
  • be easy to use,
  • demonstrate resistance to organic material,
  • be able to be monitored for concentration, and
  • be cost effective.[17]

Emerging pathogens such as *Cryptosporidium parvum,* human papilloma virus, rotavirus, Norwalk virus, *Helicobacter pylori, Escherichia coli 0157:H7,* multidrug-resistant bacteria, nontuberculous mycobacteria *(M chelonae),* and prions are a growing concern for members of the public and infection preventionists. The susceptibility of each of these pathogens has been studied, and

Table 2

USE OF FDA-APPROVED CHEMICAL AGENTS FOR HIGH-LEVEL DISINFECTION (HDL)[1-5]				
NOTE: This is not intended to be a comprehensive list of all HLD products. Manufacturers' directions for use should be followed.				
HLD chemical	Advantages	Disadvantages	Concentration	Contact time/Conditions
Peracetic acid (PA) and hydrogen peroxide solutions	No activation required. Odor or irritation not significant.	Concerns regarding compatibility with materials (eg, lead, brass, copper, zinc) and both cosmetic and functional damage. Limited clinical use. Potential for eye and skin damage.	0.08% PA and 1.0% hydrogen peroxide 0.23% PA and 7.35% hydrogen peroxide	25 min contact time at 20° C (68° F); 14 days maximum reuse 15 min contact time at 20° C (68° F); 14 days maximum reuse
Glutaraldehyde solutions	Numerous published studies of use. Relatively inexpensive. Excellent compatibility with materials.	Respiratory irritation from glutaraldehyde vapor. Pungent and irritating odor. Relatively slow mycobactericidal activity. Coagulates blood and fixes tissue to surfaces. Allergic contact dermatitis.	2.5% glutaraldehyde automated endoscopic reprocessor (AER) 1.12% glutaraldehyde and 1.93% phenol	5.0 min at 35° C (95° F); 28 days maximum reuse 20 min contact time at 25° C (77° F); 14 days maximum reuse
Hydrogen peroxide	No activation required. May enhance removal of organic material and organisms. No disposal issues. No odor or irritation issues. Does not coagulate blood or fix tissues to surfaces. Inactivates *Cryptosporidium*. Published studies of use.	Concerns regarding compatibility with materials (eg, brass, zinc, copper, nickel/silver plating) and both cosmetic and functional damage. Serious eye damage with contact.	7.5% hydrogen peroxide	30 min contact time at 20° C (68° F); 21 days maximum reuse
Ortho-phthalaldehyde	Fast-acting high-level disinfectant. No activation required. Odor not significant. Claim of excellent compatibility with materials. Claim of not coagulating blood or fixing tissues to surfaces.	Stains protein gray (eg, skin, mucous membranes, clothing, environmental surfaces). More expensive than glutaraldehyde. Eye irritation with contact. Slow sporicidal activity. Repeated exposure may result in hypersensitivity in some patients with bladder cancer.	5.75% orthophthalaldehyde 0.55% orthophthalaldehyde manual processing AER	5 min at 50° C (122° F); single use 12 min at 20° C (68° F); 14 days maximum reuse 5 min at 25° C (77° F); 14 days maximum reuse
Peracetic acid *Indication for sterilization only*	Environmentally friendly by-products (ie, acetic acid, oxygen, and water). Fully automated. Single-use system eliminates need for concentration testing. Standardized cycle. May enhance removal of organic material and endotoxins. No adverse health effects to operators under normal operating conditions.	Potential incompatibility with materials (eg, aluminum anodized coating becomes dull). Used for immersible instruments only. Biological indicator may not be suitable for routine monitoring. Only one endoscope or a small number of instruments can be processed in a cycle. More expensive (eg, endoscope repairs, operating costs, purchase costs) than high-level disinfection. Serious eye and skin damage after contact with concentrated solution. Point-of-use system; cannot save sterilized items for later use or storage.	0.2% peracetic acid	rapid sterilization cycle time (30–45 min) low-temperature (50°–55°C/122°–131° F) liquid-immersion sterilization; single use

REFERENCES

1. Appendix B: Decontamination and disinfection. In: *Biosafety in Microbiological and Biomedical Laboratories (BMBL)*. 5th ed. Centers for Disease Control and Prevention; National Institutes of Health, eds. Washington, DC: US Government Printing Office; 2007:328-336. Available at http://www.cdc.gov/od/ohs/biosfty/bmbl5/bmbl5toc.htm. Accessed December 5, 2008.

2. Alvarado C J, Reichelderfer M. APIC guideline for infection prevention and control in flexible endoscopy. Association for Professionals in Infection Control. *Am J Infect Control* 2000;28(2):138.

3. Favaro MS, Bond WW. Chemical disinfection of medical and surgical materials. In: Block SS, ed. *Disinfection, Sterilization, and Preservation*. 5th ed. Philadelphia, PA: Lippincott Williams & Wilkins; 2001:881.

4. FDA-cleared sterilants and high-level disinfectants with general claims for processing reusable medical and dental devices; September 28, 2006. US Food and Drug Administration. http://www.fda.gov/cdrh/ode/germlab .html. Accessed December 5, 2008.

5. Association for the Advancement of Medical Instrumentation. *ANSI/AAMI ST58:2005—Chemical Sterilization and High-Level Disinfection in Health Care Facilities*. Arlington, VA: Association for the Advancement of Medical Instrumentation; 2005.

with the exception of *C parvum* and prions, all are susceptible to available chemical disinfectants and chemical sterilants.[21,46] Glutaraldehyde-resistant strains of *M chelonae* have been isolated in some automated endoscope reprocessors but have been found to be sensitive to other high-level disinfectants such as ortho-phthalaldehyde.[38,47]

IV.a.3.   FDA-approved high-level disinfectant liquid chemical agents should be used according to workload requirements, instrumentation characteristics, and workplace design (**Table 2**). *Note:* A full and comprehensive list of high-level disinfectant solutions and contact conditions is available from the FDA.

IV.a.4.   High-level disinfection should occur at appropriate temperature, contact time, and length of use following solution activation. **Table 2** provides FDA-approved chemicals for HLD with recommended conditions for use.[2,16,17,27,46,51,56,60,61]

Improper use of cleaners and disinfectants can cause contamination and lead to outbreaks.[62]

IV.b.   Chemical high-level disinfection should be achieved by immersing an item for specified contact conditions (ie, period of time, temperature, concentration) in a chemical agent (also called a chemical germicide) that has been cleared by the FDA as a high-level disinfectant.

Disease transmission can result from improper selection and/or use of disinfecting agents.

IV.c.   Manufacturers' written instructions should be followed when preparing disinfectant solutions, calculating expiration dates, and labeling solution soaking containers.

The appropriate conditions for use are provided on solution container labels. Labels indicate clearly the appropriate time for discarding solutions that may no longer be effective. Most chemical disinfectants are effective for only a specific period of time. [36]

IV.c.1.   Manufacturers' written instructions about the type of container used should be followed.

The correct container ensures that no interaction occurs between the container and the active ingredients of the disinfectant.[36]

IV.c.2.   A test strip or other FDA-cleared testing device specific for the disinfectant and minimum effective concentration of the active ingredient should be used for monitoring solution potency prior to each use.[36,51]

The test strip expiration date should be checked before use.

IV.c.3.   If a solution falls below its minimum effective concentration, it should be discarded, even if the designated expiration date has not been reached.

High-level disinfection solution potency cannot be guaranteed when the solution falls below the minimum effective concentration.

IV.d.   Items to be chemically disinfected should be cleaned and completely immersed in the disinfectant solution according to device and HLD solution manufacturers' written instructions and consistent with established infection control practice.

Total immersion permits contact of all surfaces. Perfusion of the disinfectant into all channels eliminates air pockets and ensures contact with internal channels.

IV.e.   Lumens and ports should be flushed and filled with the disinfectant and the entire item completely immersed for the designated exposure time.

Disinfection of all surfaces can be achieved only if all surfaces of the items are clean and in constant contact with the disinfecting solution. Flushing lumens and ports eliminates air pockets and facilitates contact of the disinfectant with internal channels.[2,12,21]

IV.f.   The automated endoscopic reprocessor (AER) manufacturer's written instructions should be congruent with the endoscope manufacturer's written instructions when an AER is used for high-level disinfection, or the endoscope should not be processed in the AER.

Device-specific instructions ensure adequate function of the reprocessing equipment and prevent damage to the scope.[6]

IV.g. After being exposed to the disinfectant solution for the required exposure time, critical and semicritical items should be thoroughly rinsed with water according to the manufacturer's written instructions.

Rinsing removes toxic and irritating residues that can result in tissue damage or staining.[7,63] Rinsing critical and semicritical items with sterile water prevents potential recontamination that could result from tap water.[2,6,9,15,25]

Recommendation V

HLD items should be protected from contamination until the item is delivered to the point of use.

Use of aseptic technique will protect the items from being contaminated before patient use.[2,6,36,59]

V.a. High-level disinfected items should be transported to the point of use using a technique that does not result in recontamination of the instrument (eg, aseptic technique).

Performance of hand hygiene, donning gloves to handle HLD items, and transferring immediately to point of use following processing are examples of practices that minimize recontamination.

V.b. High-level disinfected items should be processed immediately before use. Flexible endoscopes should be cleaned, high-level disinfected, and stored according to the "Recommended practices for cleaning and processing flexible endoscopes and endoscope accessories.[36,53]

HLD devices that cannot be placed in appropriate barrier materials are prone to recontamination when stored.

Recommendation VI

Health care organizations should provide a safe environment for personnel who are using chemical disinfectants.

Health care organizations are responsible for providing a safe work and patient care environment. Patients, visitors, and health care workers should be protected from injuries and illnesses caused by hazardous chemicals used in the facility.

VI.a. When handling chemical disinfectants, personnel should wear protective apparel that may include, but is not limited to,
- 100% nitrile rubber or 100% butyl rubber gloves when handling glutaraldehyde (polyvinyl chloride [PVC] gloves are not recommended because they absorb glutaraldehyde);[18]
- less than 100% nitrile or butyl rubber gloves for handling all other HLD solutions except glutaraldehyde;
- protective eyewear (eg, goggles, face shields);
- masks (ie, to prevent contact with skin and not inhalation of fumes); and
- moisture-repellent or splash-proof skin protection (eg, gowns, jumpsuits, aprons).[45]

Chemical disinfectants can irritate or stain skin and mucous membranes, cause allergic reactions, and may pose other health risks.[46,47] Use of protective apparel decreases the potential for exposure to the chemical agent.[36]

VI.b. Chemical disinfectants should be contained and used in well-ventilated areas.

Vapor generated from glutaraldehyde can be irritating to the respiratory tract and may aggravate preexisting respiratory conditions. Glutaraldehyde should be used in well-ventilated areas or in freestanding or vented chemical fume hoods. The American Conference of Governmental Industrial Hygienists (ACGIH) recommends a ceiling limit of 0.05 parts per million (ppm) for occupational exposure to glutaraldehyde vapors. The Occupational Safety and Health Administration (OSHA) has established occupational exposure limits for several agents. No exposure limits have been established by OSHA for glutaraldehyde; however, OSHA can regulate exposure to glutaraldehyde and has recommended that the ACGIH limits be followed.[22]

VI.b.1. Chemical disinfectants should be kept in covered containers with tight-fitting lids and clearly labeled with contents and expiration date.

VI.b.2. Methods (eg, transfer pumps) should be used to limit worker exposure during loading of chemical disinfectants into automated endoscopic reprocessors.

VI.b.3. Chemical disinfectants should be used according to manufacturers' written instructions and federal, state, and local regulations.

Recommendation VII

Chemical disinfectants should be disposed of according to federal, state, and local regulations.[64,65]

The most stringent regulations should be followed. State and local regulations may be more stringent than those imposed at the federal level.[36,66]

VII.a. Personnel should know their obligations under state laws and local ordinances and use appropriate PPE when disposing of high-level disinfectants.

Recommendation VIII

Personnel should receive initial education and competency validation on procedures, chemicals used, and personal protection and should receive additional training when new equipment, instruments, supplies, or procedures are introduced.

Ongoing education and competency validation of perioperative personnel facilitates the development of knowledge, skills, and attitudes that affect patient and worker safety.[8,67]

VIII.a. Personnel should receive initial education on
   – decontamination methods;
   – preparation of instruments and equipment for high-level disinfection;
   – selection of cleaning agents and methods;
   – proper use of cleaning agents, including an understanding of specific applications, appropriate dilution, and special precautions;
   – decontamination of specific instruments and equipment used within the practice setting;
   – procedures for decontamination of instruments contaminated with prions and the effectiveness of various methods of deactivation;

   – personal protection required during instrument processing; and
   – exposure risk associated with chemical cleaning agents.[22]
   Workers have the right to know the about the safe use of disinfectants and about the hazards in the workplace. The OSHA requires that employers provide hazardous material safety information to employees.[22]

VIII.b. Personnel should receive education on new instruments and equipment, new cleaning agents and methods, and new procedures.[9,67-69]

VIII.c. Personnel responsible for HLD should maintain the technical skills needed to establish and maintain a safe practice environment for patients and other staff members.
   Adverse effects resulting from the exposure to HLD is well documented in patients and health care workers.[70-74] Adverse effects include, but are not limited to,
   – OPA-related anaphylaxis in patients with carcinoma of the urinary bladder,[32,56]
   – OPA-related bronchial asthma in health care workers,[75]
   – glutaraldehyde-related asthma and contact dermatitis,[76]
   – glutaraldehyde-induced bowel injury after laparoscopy,[77] and,
   – toxic anterior segment syndrome with glutaraldehyde.[78]

VIII.d. Administrative personnel should ensure competency validation of personnel participating in decontamination and high-level disinfection of invasive instruments.[67,79]
   Competency validation is an essential component to providing safe and effective patient care.

VIII.e. The validation of competencies should include all types of instruments that the individual is authorized to reprocess.
   Validation of competency supports demonstration of mastery level knowledge and skill required to correctly perform decontamination procedures.

VIII.f. Employers must provide employees with the information and training needed to protect themselves from chemical hazards in the workplace according to federal standards.[22]

Employers must provide a written hazard communication program, hazard evaluation, hazardous materials inventory, materials safety data sheets (MSDS), labels on all containers of hazardous chemicals, and employee training.

VIII.f.1.   Employee training includes an explanation of the standard, identification of hazards and health effects, location of the written hazard communication program and MSDS, procedures to detect and measure contaminants, safe work practices, appropriate PPE, an explanation of labeling, and locations of spill kits and eyewash stations in accordance with employees' right to know about hazards in the workplace.[6,22]

VIII.f.2.   The latest version of the MSDS must be maintained on site and be readily accessible to personnel when they are in their work areas. Material may be available in hard copy and/or electronic format.[22]

The MSDS provides users with valuable information about toxicity, reactivity, required protective equipment and apparel, storage, and disposal of the material.[36]

Recommendation IX

Documentation should be completed to enable the identification of trends and demonstrate compliance with regulatory and accrediting agency requirements.

Documentation policies and procedures establish authority, responsibility, and accountability and serve as operational guidelines.[80]

IX.a.   HLD processing records should be kept and include, but not be limited to,
- the patient identifier, when applicable;
- the procedure and physician;
- load contents (item description, serial number if applicable);
- name of the individual performing cleaning, disinfection, rinsing, and transport;
- method of cleaning;
- number or identifier of the mechanical decontaminator;
- date and time disinfection was performed;
- type of disinfectant used and lot number;
- test results before each load indicating the solution used was at the proper concentration (ie, MEC) and within the expiration date;
- temperature of the disinfectant;
- submersion time;
- verification of rinsing of the disinfected item;
- use of device-specific biological and chemical indicators (BI, CI) for automated peracetic acid processors;
- testing results of insulated electrical instruments, and;
- disposition of defective equipment.[2,36,81]

Some washer decontaminators have digital readouts or printers that facilitate recordkeeping. Records of washer testing provide a source of evidence for review when investigating clinical issues, including surgical site infections.

IX.b.   Records should be maintained for a time period specified by the health care organization and in compliance with local, state, and federal regulations.[22]

Employers are required to maintain hazardous communication training to ensure that employees are aware and knowledgeable of hazardous chemical exposure and exposure consequences.[22]

Recommendation X

Policies and procedures for high-level disinfection should be developed using the validated instructions provided by the medical device manufacturers, reviewed at regular intervals, revised as necessary, and readily available in the practice setting.

Policies and procedures establish authority, responsibility, and accountability and serve as operational guidelines. Policies and procedures also assist in the development of patient safety, quality assessment, and improvement activities. Policies and procedures are subject to change with the advent of new technologies.

X.a.   Policies regarding high-level disinfection should be developed by a multidisciplinary team to include perioperative nurses, sterile processing personnel, surgeons, and infection preventionists.

Using a multidisciplinary team provides varied input and improved ownership of policies and procedures. Involving surgeons in review of policies educates them on the expectations for high-level disinfection and facilitates planning for instrument use. The expertise of infection preventionists facilitates establishment of minimum standards of infection control.

X.b.   Policies should include, but not be limited to
  – review of validated manufacturers' written instructions before purchase or consignment,
  – cleaning of instruments before initial use,
  – precautions to be taken when handling contaminated items,
  – precautions to be taken when handling chemical agents,
  – frequency of AER checks,
  – frequency and method of evaluation of manual cleaning,
  – criteria for identification and precautions taken for instruments used on patients with known or suspected prion disease,
  – documentation of high-level disinfection,
  – initial education and annual competency,
  – maintenance of material safety data sheets,
  – reporting exposures to bloodborne pathogens, and
  – reporting adverse events.

X.c.   Introduction to and review of policies and procedures should be included in the orientation and ongoing education of personnel to help develop knowledge, skills, and attitudes that affect patient care and occupational safety.

Policies and procedures may guide performance improvement activities.

X.d.   Written policies and procedures should be in place to designate how critical and semicritical items are transported from the area where disinfection takes place to the point of use in patient areas.[44,48,82]

Recommendation XI

A quality-control program should be established for the health care organization in all areas where high-level disinfection is used.

The health care organization's quality management program should evaluate high-level disinfection to improve patient and worker safety.[52,67,79,83-85]

XI.a.   Quality-control programs should be documented and should include, but not be limited to,
  – orientation programs;
  – competency assurance;
  – continuing education;
  – quality-control checks;
  – investigation of adverse events, including outbreaks and exposures; and
  – monitoring of solution replacement intervals.
  Quality and performance improvement functions ensure that organizations design processes well and systematically monitor, analyze, and improve their outcomes.

XI.a.1.   The HLD solution should be tested prior to each use.[9,86]

XI.a.2.   The solution should be discarded even if it is within its use life if the test strip indicates the solution is below the minimum effective concentration.[36]

The test strip is the only indicator that the solution is effective.

XI.a.3.   In the event of test strip failure, items processed with HLD solution below the minimum effective concentration should be considered inadequately processed and should not be used until reprocessed in an acceptable minimum effective concentration of high-level disinfection solution.[36]

XI.b.   A comprehensive quality management program should include ongoing monitoring including scheduled testing of mechanical cleaning and AER equipment with supportive documentation.

Adequate cleaning and processing of endoscopes is essential to remove or destroy microorganisms and eliminate endotoxins.

XI.b.1. Mechanical instrument washers and AERs should be tested for proper functioning according to AORN "Recommended practices for cleaning and processing flexible endoscopes and endoscope accessories."[53]

Testing washer decontaminators and AERs on a regular basis verifies that the equipment is functioning properly or identifies an opportunity for corrective action. Washer-testing products are commercially available.

XI.b.2. Manual cleaning processes and skills should be evaluated when new types of instruments are reprocessed and periodically, at intervals determined by the health care organization.

Periodic testing provides an opportunity to evaluate the health care worker's understanding of principles and validate performance. Manual cleaning is a learned skill and subject to human error. New instruments can pose unique challenges when cleaning.

XI.b.3. Personnel should identify and respond to opportunities for improvement.

XI.c. Reporting mechanisms for adverse events and near misses related to HLD should be in place.

Systematic performance measures (ie, indicators) and/or priority areas are identified as opportunities for improvement based on the functions and processes of the perioperative episode.[87]

XI.c.1. Adverse events should be reported in the adverse event reporting system and reviewed for potential opportunities for improvement.[36]

Continuous quality improvement opportunities arise from documented and structured quality processes and measures that can define and resolve problems.

XI.c.2. Near misses should be investigated and corrective action taken to prevent serious adverse events.

XI.d. When investigating surgical infections, documentation of the decontamination and HLD processes should be reviewed.[6,8,9,32,39]

Pathogen transmission from endoscopy has been associated with failure to follow cleaning and disinfection protocols.[6,9,15]

Glossary

Automated endoscope reprocessor: A unit for mechanical cleaning, disinfecting, and rinsing of flexible endoscopes.

Bioburden: The degree of microbial load; the number of viable organisms contaminating an object.

Biofilms: "A thin coating containing biologically active organisms, that have the ability to grow in water, water solutions, or in vivo, which coat the surface of structures (eg, teeth, inner surfaces of catheters, tubes, implanted or indwelling devices, instruments, other medical devices). Biofilms contain viable and nonviable microorganisms that adhere to surfaces and become trapped within a matrix of organic matter (eg, proteins, glycoproteins, carbohydrates), which prevents antimicrobial agents from reaching the cells." (**SOURCE**: Favero MS, Bond WW. *Chemical disinfection of medical and surgical materials. In:* Disinfection, Sterilization, and Preservation. *5th ed. Block SS, ed. Philadelphia, PA: Lippincott Williams & Wilkins; 2001:910-911.*)

Cavitation: "A process by which high-frequency sound wave energy is produced in an ultrasonic cleaner causing microscopic bubbles to form, become unstable, and implode, thus creating minute vacuum areas that draw particles of debris off of instrument surfaces and from crevices in instruments." (**SOURCE**: *Topical antimicrobial drug products for over-the-counter human use; tentative final monograph for health-care antiseptic drug products. In:* Code of Federal Regulations (CFR) 21: Food and Drugs, Parts 333 and 369. *Washington, DC: US Government Printing Office; 1994:31402-31453.*)

Chemical disinfectant/germicide: A generic term for a government-registered agent that destroys microorganisms. Germicides are classified as sporicides, general disinfectants, sanitizers, and others.

Critical item: An item that has contact with the vascular system or enters sterile tissue, or body cavities and thus poses the highest risk of transmission of infection.

Decontamination: A process that removes contaminating infectious agents and renders reusable medical products safe for handling.

Disinfection: A process that kills most forms of microorganisms on inanimate surfaces. Disinfection destroys pathogenic organisms (excluding bacterial spores) or their toxins or vectors by direct exposure to chemical or physical means.

Free-rinsing: Ability to be removed without leaving residue.

High-level disinfection: A process that kills all microorganisms with the exception of high numbers of bacterial spores and prions. High-level disinfectants have the capability to inactivate the hepatitis B and C viruses, HIV, and *Mycobacterium tuberculosis,* but do not inactivate the virus-like prion that causes Creutzfeld-Jakob disease. Government-registered high-level disinfection agents kill vegetative bacteria, tubercle bacilli, some spores and fungi, and lipid and nonlipid viruses, given appropriate concentration, submersion, and contact time.

Hospital disinfectant: A chemical germicide with label claims for effectiveness against *Salmonella, Staphylococcus,* and *Pseudomonas.* Hospital disinfectants may be low-, intermediate-, or high-level disinfectants.

Iatrogenic: A response to a medical or surgical treatment, usually denoting an unfavorable response.

In vitro: Outside the living body and in an artificial environment.

Intermediate-level disinfection: A process that kills *Mycobacterium tuberculosis,* vegetative bacteria, most viruses, and most fungi, but does not necessarily kill bacterial spores.

Low-level disinfection: A process by which most bacteria, some viruses, and some fungi are killed. This process cannot be relied on to kill resistant microorganisms such as *Mycobacterium tuberculosis* or bacterial spores.

Minimum effective concentration: The minimum concentration of a liquid chemical germicide that achieves the claimed microbicidal activity as determined by dose-response testing.

Nidus; (pl) nidi: A focus of infection; or the coalescence of small particles that is the beginning of a solid deposit.

Pasteurization: "A process originally developed by Louis Pasteur of heating milk, wine, or other liquids to between 140° F and 212° F (60° C to 100° C)

for approximately 30 minutes to kill or significantly reduce the number of pathogenic and spoilage organisms" (**Source:** *Block SS. Definition of terms. In:* Disinfection, Sterilization, and Preservation. *5th ed. Block SS, ed. Philadelphia, PA: Lippincott Williams & Wilkins; 2001:19-28.)* A process that employs time and heat (ie, 160° F to 170° F [21.7° C to 25° C] for 30 minutes) for high-level disinfection. The intensity of heat and duration of exposure must be determined by the manufacturer of the pasteurization unit and the manufacturer of the product or device to be cleaned.

Personal protective equipment (PPE): Specialized equipment or clothing for eyes, face, head, body, and extremities; protective clothing; respiratory devices; and protective shields and barriers designed to protect the worker from injury or exposure to a patient's blood, tissue, or body fluids. Used by health care workers and others whenever necessary to protect themselves from the hazards of processes or environments, chemical hazards, or mechanical irritants encountered in a manner capable of causing injury or impairment in the function of any part of the body through absorption, inhalation, or physical contact.

Sterilization: Processes by which all microbial life, including pathogenic and nonpathogenic microorganisms, and spores, are killed.

References

1. Spaulding EH. Clinical disinfection and antisepsis in the hospital. *J Hosp Res* 1972;95.

2. Rutala WA. APIC guideline for selection and use of disinfectants. 1994, 1995, and 1996 APIC Guidelines Committee. Association for Professionals in Infection Control and Epidemiology, Inc. *Am J Infect Control* 1996; 24(4):313.

3. Tablan OC, Anderson LJ, Besser R, Bridges C, Hajjeh R, et al. Guidelines for preventing health care-associated pneumonia, 2003: Recommendations of CDC and the Healthcare Infection Control Practices Advisory Committee. *MMWR Recomm Rep* 2004;53(RR-3):1.

4. Class II special controls guidance document: Medical washers and medical washer-disinfectors; guidance for the medical device industry and FDA review staff. US Food and Drug Administration. http://www.fda.gov/cdrh/ode/guidance/1252.html. Accessed December 5, 2008

5. Appendix B: Decontamination and disinfection. In: *Biosafety in Microbiological and Biomedical Laboratories (BMBL).* 5th ed. Centers for Disease Control and Prevention; National Institutes of Health, eds. Washington, DC: US Government Printing Office; 2007:328-336. Available at http://www.cdc.gov/od/ohs/biosfty/bmbl5/bmbl5toc.htm. Accessed December 5, 2008.

6. Alvarado C J, Reichelderfer M. APIC guideline for infection prevention and control in flexible endoscopy. Association for Professionals in Infection Control. *Am J Infect Control* 2000;28(2):138.

7. *AAMI TIR12:2004—Designing, Testing and Labeling Reusable Medical Devices for Reprocessing in Health Care Facilities: A Guide for Medical Device Manufacturers.* Arlington, VA: Association for the Advancement of Medical Instrumentation; 2005.

8. Rutala W A, Weber D J. How to assess risk of disease transmission to patients when there is a failure to follow recommended disinfection and sterilization guidelines. *Infect Control Hosp Epidemiol* 2007;28(2):146.

9. Multi-society guideline for reprocessing flexible gastrointestinal endoscopes. *Am J Infect Control* 2003;31(5):309.

10. Rutala W A, Gergen M F, Weber D J. Disinfection of a probe used in ultrasound-guided prostate biopsy. *Infect Control Hosp Epidemiol* 2007;28(8):916.

11. Perkins John J. *Principles and methods of sterilization in health sciences.* 2nd ed. Springfield, Ill.: Thomas; 1969.

12. Favaro MS, Bond WW. Chemical disinfection of medical and surgical materials. In: Block SS, ed. *Disinfection, Sterilization, and Preservation.* 5th ed. Philadelphia, PA: Lippincott Williams & Wilkins; 2001:881.

13. Thomas L A. Essentials for endoscopic equipment. High-level disinfection. *Gastroenterol Nurs* 2006;29(2):179.

14. Camp S, Dawson C. Best practice forum: Standard high-level disinfection protocol development. *ORL Head Neck Nurs* 2003; 21(2):18-21.

17. FDA-cleared sterilants and high-level disinfectants with general claims for processing reusable medical and dental devices; September 28, 2006. US Food and Drug Administration. http://www.fda.gov/cdrh/ode/germlab .html. Accessed December 5, 2008.

18. Society of Gastroenterology Nurses and Associates Inc. Guidelines for the use of high-level disinfectants and sterilants for reprocessing of flexible gastrointestinal endoscopes. *Gastroenterol Nurs* 2004;27(4):198.

19. Lee J H, Rhee P L, Kim J H, Kim J J, Paik S W, Rhee J C, Song J H, Yeom J S, Lee N Y. Efficacy of electrolyzed acid water in reprocessing patient-used flexible upper endoscopes: Comparison with 2% alkaline glutaraldehyde. *J Gastroenterol Hepatol* 2004;19(8):897-903.

20. Bhattacharyya N, Kepnes L J. The effectiveness of immersion disinfection for flexible fiberoptic laryngoscopes. *Otolaryngol Head Neck Surg* 2004;130(6):681.

21. Rutala W A, Weber D J. Disinfection of endoscopes: Review of new chemical sterilants used for high-level disinfection. *Infect Control Hosp Epidemiol* 1999; 20(1):69.

22. *Hazard Communication.* (29 CFR §1910.) Occupational Safety and Health Administration. Washington, DC: US Government Printing Office; 2007. Available at http://www.osha.gov/SLTC/hazardcommunications/ standards.html. Accessed December 5, 2008.

23. Rutala WA, Weber DJ. Cleaning, disinfection, and sterilization in healthcare facilities. In: *APIC Text of Infection Control and Epidemiology.* Washington, DC: Association for Professionals in Infection Control and Epidemiology; 2005:21-31.

24. Cantrell S. High-level disinfection vs sterilization: Six of one, half dozen of the other? *Healthc Purchasing News* 2005;29(4):38, 40, 42.

25. Rutala WA, Weber DJ. Reprocessing endoscopes: United States perspective. In: Proceedings of the 7th International BODE Hygiene Days, May 2003. *J Hosp Infect* 2004 (April); 56 Supplement 2:S27-S39.

26. Alfa MJ. Can biofilm prevent high-level disinfection? *J Genca* 2006;16(1):23.

27. Raffo P, Salliez AC, Collignon C, Clementi M. Antimicrobial activity of a formulation for the low temperature disinfection of critical and semicritical medical equipment and surfaces. *New Microbiol* 2007;30(4):463.

28. Marion K, Freney J, James G, Bergeron E, Renaud F N, Costerton J W. Using an efficient biofilm detaching agent: An essential step for the improvement of endoscope reprocessing protocols. *J Hosp Infect* 2006;64(2):136.

29. Murdoch H, Taylor D, Dickinson J, Walker J T, Perrett D, Raven N D, Sutton J M. Surface decontamination of surgical instruments: An ongoing dilemma. *J Hosp Infect* 2006;63(4):432.

30. Rerknimitr R, Eakthunyasakul S, Nunthapisud P, Kongkam P. Results of gastroscope bacterial decontamination by enzymatic detergent compared to chlorhexidine. *World J Gastroenterol* 2006;12(26):4199.

31. Thomas LA. Manual cleaning. *Gastroenterol Nurs* 2005;28(6):512.

32. Dettenkofer M, Block C. Hospital disinfection: Efficacy and safety issues. *Curr Opin Infect Dis* 2005; 18(4):320.

33. Kampf G, Bloss R, Martiny H. Surface fixation of dried blood by glutaraldehyde and peracetic acid. *J Hosp Infect* 2004;57(2):139.

34. Vickery K, Pajkos A, Cossart Y. Removal of biofilm from endoscopes: Evaluation of detergent efficiency. *Am J Infect Control* 2004;32(3):170.

35. Cowen A E. The clinical risks of infection associated with endoscopy. *Can J Gastroenterol* 2001;15(5):321.

36. Association for the Advancement of Medical Instrumentation. *ANSI/AAMI ST58:2005—Chemical Sterilization and High-Level Disinfection in Health Care Facilities.* Arlington, VA: Association for the Advancement of Medical Instrumentation; 2005.

37. Morck DW, Olson ME, Ceri H. Microbial biofilms: Prevention, control, and removal. In: Block SS, ed. *Disinfection, Sterilization, and Preservation.* 5th ed. Philadelphia, PA: Lippincott Williams & Wilkins; 2001:675.

38. McDonnell G, Pretzer D. New and developing antimicrobials. In: Block SS, ed. *Disinfection, Sterilization, and Preservation.* 5th ed. Philadelphia, PA: Lippincott Williams & Wilkins; 2001:431.

39. Cowen A, Jones D, Wardle E. *Guidelines: Infection Control in Endoscopy.* 2nd ed. Sydney, Australia: Gastroenterological Society of Australia; 2003.

40. Spach D H, Silverstein F E, Stamm W E. Transmission of infection by gastrointestinal endoscopy and bronchoscopy. *Ann Intern Med* 1993;118(2):117.

41. Weber DJ, Rutala WA, DiMarino AJ. The prevention of infection following gastrointestinal endoscopy: The importance of prophylaxis and reprocessing. In: DiMarino

AJ, Benjamin SB, eds. *Gastrointestinal Disease: An Endoscopic Approach.* Thorofare, NJ: Slack; 2002:87.

42. Miner N, Harris V, Ebron T, Cao T. Sporicidal activity of disinfectants as one possible cause for bacteria in patient-ready endoscopes. *Gastroenterol Nurs* 2007; 30(4):285.

43. Cheetham NWH. Comparative efficacy of medical instrument cleaning products in digesting some blood proteins [corrected]. *Aust Infect Control* 2005;10(3):103; erratum *Aust Infect Control* 2005;10(4):142.

44. Nelson DB, Jarvis WR, Rutala WA, et al; Society for Healthcare Epidemiology of America. Multi-society guideline for reprocessing flexible gastrointestinal endoscopes. *Infect Control Hosp Epidemiol* 2003;24(7):532.

45. Hospital eTool: Healthcare-wide hazards module—Glutaraldehyde. Occupational Safety and Health Administration. http://www.osha.gov/SLTC/etools/hospital/hazards/glutaraldehyde/glut.html. Accessed December 5, 2008.

46. Fraud S, Maillard J Y, Russell AD. Comparison of the mycobactericidal activity of ortho-phthalaldehyde,, glutaraldehyde, and other dialdehydes by a quantitative suspension test. *J Hosp Infect* 2001;48(3):214.

47. Rutala W A, Weber D J. New disinfection and sterilization methods. *Emerg Infect Dis* 2001;7(2):348.

48. *ANSI/AAMI ST58:2005—Chemical Sterilization and High-Level Disinfection in Health Care Facilities.* Arlington, VA: Association for the Advancement of Medical Instrumentation; 2005.

49. Recommended practices for cleaning and care of surgical instruments and powered equipment. In: *Perioperative Standards and Recommended Practices.* Denver, CO: AORN; 2008:421-446.

50. Banerjee S, Nelson DB, Dominitz JA, et al. Reprocessing failure. *Gastrointest Endosc* 2007; 66(5):869.

51. Lin CS, Fuller J, Mayhall ES. Federal regulation of liquid chemical germicides by the US Food and Drug Administration. In: Block SS, ed. *Disinfection, Sterilization, and Preservation.* 5th ed. Philadelphia, PA: Lippincott Williams & Wilkins; 2001:1293.

52. Procedures for performance standards development. (21 CFR §861.) US Food and Drug Administration. Washington, DC: US Government Printing Office; 2008. Available at http://www.accessdata.fda.gov/scripts/cdrh/cfdocs/cfcfr/CFRSearch.cfm?CFRPart=861. Accessed December 5, 2008.

53. Recommended practices for cleaning and processing flexible endoscopes and endoscope accessories. In: *Perioperative Standards and Recommended Practices.* Denver, CO: AORN; 2009:595-610.

54. WHO infection control guidelines for transmissible spongiform encephalopathies. Report of a WHO consultation, Geneva, Switzerland, 23-26 March 1999. World Health Organization. http://www.who.int/csr/resources/publications/bse/WHO_CDS_CSR_APH_2000_3/en. Accessed December 5, 2008.

55. Rutala W A, Weber D J. Creutzfeldt-Jakob disease: Recommendations for disinfection and sterilization. *Clin Infect Dis* 2001;32(9):1348.

56. Gray J. How safe is your endoscope disinfectant? *Br J Perioper Nurs* 2005;15(3):134.

57. NINDS Creutzfeldt-Jakob disease information page. National Institute of Neurological Disorders and Stroke. http://www.ninds.nih.gov/disorders/cjd/cjd.htm. Accessed December 5, 2008.

58. Definition of terms. In: Block SS, ed. *Disinfection, Sterilization, and Preservation.* 5th ed. Philadelphia, PA: Lippincott Williams & Wilkins; 2001:19.

59. Nelson DB, Jarvis WR, Rutala WA, et al. Multi-society guideline for reprocessing flexible gastrointestinal endoscopes. *Dis Colon Rectum* 2004;47(4):413.

60. Acosta-Gío AE, Rueda-Patiño JL, Sánchez-Pérez L. Sporicidal activity in liquid chemical products to sterilize or high-level disinfect medical and dental instruments. *Am J Infect Control* 2005;33(5):307-309.

61. Omidbakhsh N. A new peroxide-based flexible endoscope-compatible high-level disinfectant. *Am J Infect Control* 2006;34(9):571.

62. Weber DJ, Rutala WA, Sickbert-Bennett EE. Outbreaks associated with contaminated antiseptics and disinfectants. *Antimicrob Agents Chemother* 2007;51(12):4217.

63. *AAMI TIR34:2007—Water for the Reprocessing of Medical Devices.* Arlington, VA: Association for the Advancement of Medical Instrumentation; 2007.

64. Guidelines for protecting the safety and health of health care workers, chapter 6: Hazardous waste disposal. National Institute for Occupational Safety and Health. http://www.cdc.gov/niosh/hcwold6.html. Accessed December 5, 2008.

65. *Code of Federal Regulations.* Title 40: Protection of Environment. http://ecfr.gpoaccess.gov/cgi/t/text/text-idx?c=ecfr;sid=4990e762d7b81851bef18f82dc851826;rgn=div5;view=text;node=40:25.0.1.1.2;idno=40;cc=ecfr#40:25.0.1.1.2.3.1.4. Accessed December 5, 2008.

66. Public health notification from FDA, CDC, EPA and OSHA: Avoiding hazards with using cleaners and disinfectants on electronic medical equipment. US Food and Drug Administration. http://www.fda.gov/cdrh/safety/103107-cleaners.html. Accessed December 5, 2008.

67. AORN explications for perioperative nursing. In: *Perioperative Standards and Recommended Practices.* Denver, CO: AORN; 2008:633-660.

68. Newsome C. Education in product safety: Glutaraldehyde in high-level disinfection applications. *Occup Health Rev* 2005;((118)):18.

69. Rideout K, Teschke K, DimichWard H, Kennedy S M. Considering risks to healthcare workers from glutaraldehyde alternatives in high-level disinfection. *J Hosp Infect* 2005;59(1):4-11.

70. Suzukawa M, Yamaguchi M, Komiya A, Kimura M, Nito T, Yamamoto K. Ortho-phthalaldehyde-induced anaphylaxis after laryngoscopy. *J Allergy Clin Immunol* 2006; 117(6):1500.

71. Cohen NL, Patton CM. Worker safety and glutaraldehyde in the gastrointestinal lab environment. *Gastroenterol Nurs* 2006;29(2):100.

72. Ghasemkhani M, Jahanpeyma F, Azam K. Formaldehyde exposure in some educational hospitals of Tehran. *Ind Health* 2005;43(4):703.

73. Cogliano V, Grosse Y, Baan R, Straif K, Secretan B, El Ghissassi F; WHO International Agency for Research on Cancer. Advice on formaldehyde and glycol ethers. *Lancet Oncol* 2004; 5(9):528.

74. Sokol WN. Nine episodes of anaphylaxis following cystoscopy caused by Cidex OPA (ortho-phthalaldehyde) high-level disinfectant in 4 patients after cytoscopy. *J Allergy Clin Immunol* 2004; 114(2):392.

75. Fujita H, Ogawa M, Endo Y. A case of occupational bronchial asthma and contact dermatitis caused by ortho-phthalaldehyde exposure in a medical worker. *J Occup Health* 2006; 48(6):413.

76. Best practices for the safe use of glutaraldehyde in health care. OSHA document number 3258-08N-2006. Occupational Safety and Health Administration. http://www.osha.gov/Publications/3258-08N-2006-English .html. Accessed December 5, 2008.

77. Karpelowsky J S, Maske C P, Sinclair-Smith C, Rode H. Glutaraldehyde-induced bowel injury after laparoscopy. *J Pediatr Surg* 2006; 41(6):e23.

78. Unal M, Yücel I, Akar Y, Oner A, Altin M. Outbreak of toxic anterior segment syndrome associated with glutaraldehyde after cataract surgery. *J Cataract Refract Surg* 2006 Oct;32(10):1696-1701.

79. Standards of perioperative administrative practice. In: *Perioperative Standards and Recommended Practices.* Denver, CO: AORN; 2008:15.

80. Recommended practices for documentation of perioperative nursing care. In: *Perioperative Standards and Recommended Practices.* Denver, CO: AORN; 2008: 311-314.

81. American Society for Healthcare Central Service Professionals. *Training Manual for Health Care Central Service Technicians.* 5th ed. San Francisco, CA: Jossey-Bass; 2006.

82. Thomas L A. Essentials for endoscopic equipment. Recommended care and handling of flexible endoscopes: Endoscope storage. *Gastroenterol Nurs* 2005; 28(1):45.

83. Perioperative patient care quality. In: *Perioperative Standards and Recommended Practices.* Denver, CO: AORN; 2008:11-12.

84. Standards of perioperative professional practice. In: *Perioperative Standards and Recommended Practices.* Denver, CO: AORN; 2008:23-26.

85. Sciortino CV Jr, Xia EL, Mozee A. Assessment of a novel approach to evaluate the outcome of endoscope reprocessing. *Infect Control Hosp Epidemiol* 2004; 25(4):284.

86. Standards of infection control in reprocessing of flexible gastrointestinal endoscopes. Society of Gastroenterology Nurses and Associates. http://www.sgna.org/Resources /standards.cfm. Accessed December 5, 2008.

87. Quality and performance improvement standards for perioperative nursing. In: *Perioperative Standards and Recommended Practices.* Denver, CO: AORN; 2008:27-36.

Acknowledgments

LEAD AUTHORS

Sheila Mitchell, RN, BSN, MS, CNOR
Perioperative Nursing Specialist
AORN Center for Nursing Practice
Denver, Colorado

Judith Goldberg, RN, MSN, CNOR
Clinical Director
Backus Hospital
Norwich, Connecticut

CONTRIBUTING AUTHOR

Ardene Nichols, RN, MSN, CNS, CNOR, PAHM
Health Care Consultant
Conroe, Texas

Originally published August 1980, *AORN Journal,* as AORN "Recommended practices for sterilization and disinfection."

Format revision July 1982; revised February 1987.

Revised October 1992 as "Recommended practices for disinfection"; published as proposed recommended practices September 1994 as "Recommended practices for chemical disinfection."

Revised November 1998 as "Recommended practices for high-level disinfection"; published March 1999, *AORN Journal.*

Revised November 2004; published in *Standards, Recommended Practices, and Guidelines,* 2005 edition. Reprinted February 2005, *AORN Journal.*

Revised November 2008; published in *Perioperative Standards and Recommended Practices,* 2009 edition.

Recommended Practices for Cleaning and Processing Flexible Endoscopes and Endoscope Accessories

The following recommended practices were developed by the AORN Recommended Practices Committee and have been approved by the AORN Board of Directors. They were presented as proposed recommendations for comments by members and others. They are effective January 1, 2009.

These recommended practices are intended as achievable recommendations representing what is believed to be an optimal level of practice. Policies and procedures will reflect variations in practice settings and/or clinical situations that determine the degree to which the recommended practices can be implemented. AORN recognizes the various settings in which perioperative nurses practice. These recommended practices are intended as guidelines adaptable to various practice settings. These practice settings include traditional operating rooms, ambulatory surgery centers, physician's offices, cardiac catheterization laboratories, endoscopy suites, radiology departments, and all other areas where surgery may be performed.

Purpose

These recommended practices provide guidelines to assist personnel in the care, cleaning, decontamination, maintenance, handling, storage, sterilization, and/or disinfection of flexible endoscopes and related accessories. Use of these recommended practices will assist personnel in providing a safe environment for patients and health care workers.

These recommended practices are based on the most current evidence available at the time of development. They should be used to develop policies and procedures for care of flexible endoscopes and accessories in the practice setting. As new information becomes available, perioperative nurses should consult with infection preventionists and epidemiologists to review and revise procedures as appropriate. These recommended practices pertain only to flexible endoscopes and are divided into the following sections:

- following manufacturer's instructions,
- precleaning,
- transport to decontamination,
- leak testing,
- cleaning,
- high-level disinfection
- alcohol treatment,

- drying,
- storage,
- handling damaged flexible endoscopes,
- care of accessories, and
- personal protective equipment (PPE).

Competencies, documentation, policies and procedures, and quality management suggestions also are discussed. For more information on the care and cleaning of rigid endoscopes and related equipment, refer to the AORN "Recommended practices for care and cleaning of instruments and powered surgical equipment."[1]

Recommendation I

Flexible endoscopes should be cleaned and stored in accordance with the manufacturer's written instructions.

Failure to follow the manufacturer's written instructions could result in ineffective cleaning that interferes with high-level disinfection or sterilization, creating a risk of infection for the patient. The manufacturer's warranty may be void if the written instructions for care and use of the device are not followed.

I.a.   The manufacturer's written instructions for flexible endoscopes and all accessories should be followed regarding
  – cleaning processes,
  – selection of cleaning product,
  – selection of disinfectant/sterilization products,
  – use of alcohol, and
  – compatibility with automatic endoscope reprocessors.
    Flexible endoscopes manufactured by different companies require different cleaning processes as described in the manufacturer's written instructions. The flexible endoscope manufacturer is required to demonstrate to the US Food and Drug Administration in the premarket clearance application that the cleaning/disinfecting instructions are adequate and that the results are reproducible.[2] All flexible endoscopes and accessories cannot be processed successfully in all automatic endoscopic reprocessors.[3]

I.b. High-level disinfectant and chemical cleaner manufacturers' written instructions should be followed regarding
- compatibility with the flexible endoscope and accessories,
- water quality,
- dilution,
- temperature of solution,
- testing for minimum effective concentration,
- time of exposure, and
- rinsing.[4]

Following the manufacturer's written instructions will deliver the recommended concentration of cleaning solution, disinfectant, or sterilant required for adequate cleaning and to create effective high-level disinfection or sterilization.[5,6] Improper dilution may result in ineffective high-level disinfection or sterilization if the solution is too weak. If the solution is too strong, it may become abrasive or corrosive, possibly contributing to corrosion and degradation of the surfaces of the flexible endoscope.[7] The high-level disinfectant and chemical cleaner may remain on the scope if the manufacturer's written instructions for rinsing are not followed. For more information on high-level disinfection, refer to the AORN "Recommended practices for high-level disinfection."[8]

I.c. New, repaired, or refurbished flexible endoscopes and accessories should be leak tested, cleaned, and high-level disinfected or sterilized before use in a health care organization.

Cleaning and high-level disinfection of newly acquired or repaired flexible endoscopes removes any soil related to manufacturing, repairing, refurbishing, or shipping. Leak tests determine if perforations in either the outer covering or the lining of the internal channels may have occurred during manufacturing, shipping, repairing, or refurbishing.[9]

Recommendation II

Precleaning of flexible endoscopes and accessories should occur at the point of use, before organic material has dried on the surface or in the channels of the endoscope, and before transport to the decontamination area.

Flexible endoscopes, by virtue of the body cavities in which they are used, acquire high levels of microbial contamination during each use. Failure to completely follow the defined cleaning process, beginning with precleaning, has been shown to cause inadequate decontamination leading to patients being exposed to infectious agents.[10] Precleaning of endoscopes and related equipment at the point of use before transport to the decontamination area helps prevent drying of the organic material on the flexible endoscope surfaces.

The presence of dried organic material makes decontamination/disinfection more difficult. Organic materials (eg, blood and body fluids) that have dried on the flexible endoscope surfaces are difficult to remove and can inhibit sterilization and high-level disinfection.[11] Precleaning reduces the likelihood of the formation of biofilms, which contain viable and nonviable microorganisms that become trapped within a matrix of organic matter (eg, proteins, glycoproteins, carbohydrates) and adhere to the surfaces of flexible endoscopes. Biofilms are difficult to remove, and it is difficult for sterilizing/disinfecting agents to penetrate and kill the microorganisms within the biofilms. The biofilm formation process can begin within minutes after completion of a procedure.[7,12]

II.a. Precleaning measures include the following:
(1) External surfaces of the flexible endoscope insertion tube should be washed with an enzymatic detergent solution using a soft cloth or sponge.
(2) Internal suction/biopsy channels should be cleaned by suctioning copious amounts of enzymatic solution (ie, enzymatic detergent mixed with tap water) and air.
(3) Air and water channels should be flushed with an enzymatic solution, then flushed using low-pressure compressed air (ie, pressure should not exceed maximum channel pressure specified by manufacturer), if available. If low-pressure compressed air is not available, a syringe may be used for flushing with air.
(4) Additional complex design components or channels (eg, forward water jet channel, exposed elevator wire channels, balloon channels) should be flushed or purged with water and/or enzymatic

detergent solution as described in the manufacturer's written instructions.

(5) The tip of the endoscope should be visually inspected for damage to any surface and any working part and for cleanliness.

(6) The video protective cap, if available, should be attached after removing the flexible endoscope from the light source and suction.

(7) All detachable parts (eg, hoods, valves, water bottle) should be removed and immersed in an enzymatic detergent solution until transport to the decontamination room. When flexible endoscopes and accessories are used on a sterile field,

- the external surfaces should be wiped with a lint-free cloth saturated with sterile water;
- sterile water and air should be alternately suctioned through the channels; and
- the endoscope and accessories should be handed to the circulator as soon as possible, enabling steps 1–7 to be accomplished.

(8) The enzymatic detergent solution should be discarded after a single use.

Washing the external surfaces of the endoscope and flushing the internal channels with enzymatic solution helps to soften, moisten, dilute, and remove organic soils (eg, blood, feces, respiratory secretions).[13]

Alternating cleaning solution with air may help to soften, moisten, dilute, and remove organic soils (eg, blood, feces, respiratory secretions). It is more effective to alternate the use of air and water when cleaning rather than prolonged use of either.[13]

Flushing with low-pressure compressed air helps to dry the channel. Low-pressure compressed air should be used because it is possible to damage the channel linings with uncontrolled or high-flow air.[7]

Depending upon design and intended use, endoscopes vary in complexity. Certain flexible endoscopes may have more channels than the standard air, water, and suction. Therefore, whenever scopes have additional channels or complex components, each should also be flushed or purged by following the original scope manufacturer's recommendations.

A visual inspection after precleaning should be done to verify that no obvious organic debris remains.

The video protective cap protects video connections from moisture during decontamination and disinfection.[13]

Soaking the detachable parts of the endoscope in enzymatic detergent solution assists in degrading and preventing biofilms.[7] Wiping the flexible endoscope and accessories with lint-free cloth saturated with sterile water and alternately suctioning sterile water and air while the endoscope remains on the sterile field will prevent drying of proteins on the endoscope surfaces until the cleaning process may be accomplished.

The enzymatic detergent cleaning solution should be discarded after each use because it does not possess bactericidal activity and may support growth of organisms if stored. There are no tests to verify the strength of the solution prior to use.

Recommendation III

After precleaning, contaminated flexible endoscopes and accessories should be transported to the decontamination area before remaining organic material dries on the surface or in the channels of the endoscope.

Transport to the decontamination area before remaining organic material is able to dry on the surface or in the channels of the flexible endoscope facilitates cleaning which helps to reduce the formation of biofilms.[7,12]

III.a. During transport to the decontamination area, soiled flexible endoscopes must be contained (eg, enclosed by a plastic bag, container with a lid) in a manner to prevent exposure of environmental surfaces, patients, and personnel to bloodborne pathogens and other potentially infectious organisms. If the decontamination area is adjacent to the procedure room, the contaminated items may be transported in an open container by personnel wearing appropriate PPE.[14]

Contaminated flexible endoscopes and accessories present a risk of contaminating the environment and can expose healthcare workers to blood and other potentially infectious materials during transport to the decontamination area.[14]

III.b.   The transport container must be labeled to indicate biohazardous contents. The types of label may include, but are not limited to, magnetic signs, stickers, or plastic placards.[14]

Labeling the transport container communicates to others that the items are potentially infectious.[14]

Recommendation IV

In the decontamination area and before cleaning, pressure (ie, leak) tests should be performed on flexible endoscopes with leak testing capabilities.[9]

Leak tests determine if there are any openings in the external surfaces and internal channels that would permit fluid to enter the internal body of the endoscope.[9]

IV.a.   During leak testing, the flexible endoscope control knobs should be manipulated in all directions.

Manipulating the flexible endoscope control knobs in all directions exposes the surfaces to the maximum extension, thereby revealing small perforations if present.[9]

IV.b.   When using a leak test system requiring water, the leak test system should be attached to the flexible endoscope, followed by submersion of the entire endoscope in water that does not contain cleaning agents, to check for the presence of bubbling.[9]

Leakage in either the covering or one or more of the internal channels can be determined by the presence of air bubbles when air pressure is applied to the inside of the insertion tube. Discoloration and foam caused by the detergent agent may prevent small bubbles from being visible.[9]

IV.b.1.   When a leak is detected, the leak testing device should remain attached to the flexible endoscope and under pressure until the endoscope is removed from the water.[9]

Continuous air pressure helps to prevent water from entering the internal (ie, working) portions of the flexible endoscope which may cause more extensive damage to the internal parts.[15]

IV.c.   When using a leak test system that does not require water, the leak test should be completed before submersion in water or cleaning solution.[9]

Leaks in either the covering or one or more of the inside channels can be determined by a drop in pressure after inflation or by the inability to inflate the inside of the insertion tube.[9]

Recommendation V

Following leak testing and before high-level disinfection using a manual process or an automatic endoscope reprocessor, flexible endoscopes and their accessories should be manually cleaned before any remaining organic material dries on the surface or in the channels of the endoscope.[16]

Immediate cleaning reduces the amount of microbial contamination and the formation of biofilms. For the high-level disinfectant to be effective, the solution must reach all surfaces of the flexible endoscope. If the microbial contamination and biofilm are not removed, the surface under the bioburden will not be disinfected.[7]

V.a.   When manually cleaning flexible endoscopes:
(1) The flexible endoscope should be submerged in an enzymatic detergent solution.
(2) The insertion tube of the flexible endoscope should be washed using a soft, lint-free cloth or sponge.[17]
(3) All internal channels should be flushed thoroughly with an enzymatic detergent using manufacturer-provided channel cleaning adapters.
(4) All endoscope components (eg, shroud, valves) should be flushed thoroughly with an enzymatic detergent.
(5) Brushes should be inspected prior to insertion to confirm that they are sized appropriately to the channel(s), not kinked, not missing bristles, and that a protective tip is present to prevent damage to the channel.[17]

(6) The brush should be inserted through the channel with the entire endoscope submerged to prevent aerosolization. The bristles should be wiped to remove excess moisture prior to retracting the brush back through the channel.[17] All channels should be flushed thoroughly and all exterior surfaces of the flexible endoscope and accessories rinsed with potable tap water.[4]

(7) The flexible endoscope should be dried using low-pressure forced air through the internal channels and the exterior surfaces wiped with a soft cloth before placing the endoscope in high-level disinfecting solution or an automatic endoscope reprocessor.

Submersion of the flexible endoscope in enzymatic detergent solution helps ensure contact between the solution and all surfaces of the endoscope and decreases the potential for the cleaning solution to splash.[17]

Washing the exterior of the insertion tube with an enzymatic detergent and a soft cloth removes organic material remaining after precleaning.

Flushing all internal channels with detergent solution exposes these surfaces to the enzymatic detergent solution. Using the manufacturer-provided channel cleaning adapters facilitates opening of the ports.

Brushing accessible channels removes particulate matter. Using the appropriate size brush will maximize the amount of soil removed without damaging the inside of the channel. Using a brush that is kinked or missing bristles or without its protective tip may cause damage to the flexible endoscope.[12,17]

The tip of the flexible endoscope and the lens may be abraded by vigorous brushing and wiping. Brushing and wiping the tip of the flexible endoscope removes any debris or tissue that might be lodged around the air-water outlet.[17] Thorough flushing of the channels and rinsing of the flexible endoscope and accessories with potable tap water removes residual debris and cleaning agents. Potable tap water may be used at this point if it does not cause corrosion or tarnishing or leave salt deposits on the flexible endoscope or its accessories. If corrosion, tarnishing, or salt deposits are found on the flexible endoscope, the water filtration process should be examined.[4]

Moisture remaining on the surface and in the flexible endoscope's lumens may dilute the high-level disinfecting solution, potentially reducing its effectiveness.

Recommendation VI

After cleaning, flexible endoscopes and accessories should be high-level disinfected or sterilized.[8,18]

Flexible endoscopes and accessories contact mucous membranes and/or nonintact skin during use and require a minimum of high-level disinfection. Some flexible endoscopes are heat-labile and cannot be steam sterilized. Sterilization is only required if the flexible endoscope is to be used on a sterile field.[11]

VI.a. When using a manual process for high-level disinfection:
(1) The flexible endoscope and its accessories should be manually cleaned, as described in Recommendation V, before beginning the manual high-level disinfection process.
(2) The flexible endoscope and its accessories should be completely immersed in the disinfecting solution.
(3) All channels should be flushed with disinfecting solution after immersion.[19]

For the high-level disinfectant to be effective, the solution must reach all surfaces of the item. If the microbial contamination and biofilm are not removed, the surface under the bioburden will not be disinfected.[7,16] Complete immersion is required to ensure complete coverage of all surfaces of the flexible endoscope.[20] Flushing helps to ensure that the high-level disinfectant has contact with all surfaces, including internal channels, which is necessary for complete disinfection.[19,20]

VI.b. When using an automatic endoscope reprocessor for high-level disinfection:
(1) Manual cleaning should be accomplished as described in Recommendation V.

(2) The flexible endoscope and components should be inserted into the automatic endoscope reprocessor.

(3) All the flexible endoscope channels should be attached to the unit using compatible connectors.[19]

For the high-level disinfectant to be effective, the solution must reach all surfaces of the flexible endoscope. If the microbial contamination and biofilm are not removed, the surface under the bioburden will not be disinfected.[7,16] Failure to use approved connectors may result in disinfection failure because the disinfectant/sterilant may not reach all surfaces of the flexible endoscope. The use of incompatible connectors have lead to the transmission of infections.[7,21]

VI.b.1.   When the compatible connectors of the automatic endoscope reprocessor cannot be connected to a specific channel (ie, the wire elevator channel of a duodenoscope), the steps for manual high-level disinfection should be followed for this channel or for the entire flexible endoscope.[7,22]

Manual high-level disinfection is the only method by which the high-level disinfectant will reach the entire inner surface of the channel.[3,7,21,22]

Recommendation VII

After high-level disinfection, flexible endoscopes should be rinsed and the internal channels flushed with water (eg, sterile water, filtered or unfiltered tap water) followed by a 70% to 90% ethyl or isopropyl alcohol rinse and flush, unless contraindicated by the manufacturer's written instructions.[4,19]

The water rinse and flush removes the residual disinfecting solution. Use of filtered tap water or sterile water reduces the potential for recontamination by waterborne microorganisms. Filtered tap water is created at the point of use, using a filter with 0.2 or 0.1 micron pores.[4,7,19] Rinsing with alcohol assists with removing the water because the alcohol binds with the water remaining in the channel, facilitating the drying process and killing any microorganisms contained in the water.[7,19,23]

VII.a.   After rinsing with 70% to 90% ethyl or isopropyl alcohol, the channels should be dried using low-pressure forced air.

Using forced air assists with removal of moisture remaining in the channels. Dry air channels do not support microbial growth.[7]

Recommendation VIII

Flexible endoscopes, accessories, and associated equipment should be inspected for integrity, function, and cleanliness:
- before use,
- during the procedure,
- after the procedure,
- immediately after decontamination, and
- before disinfection or sterilization.[24]

Visual inspection helps to identify structural damage, when and where the damage occurred, what caused the damage, and how to prevent further damage. Loss of function and gross soil that may affect further processing and patient outcomes can also be identified during visual inspection.[16]

VIII.a.   Damaged flexible endoscopes and accessories should be removed from use, and the manufacturer should be consulted for directions regarding actions to be taken prior to shipping for repair, such as reprocessing or not reprocessing the damaged flexible endoscope.

Immediate removal from use will prevent further damage to the internal mechanisms of the flexible endoscope that may be caused by water entering the mechanism and will prevent the damaged endoscope from being inadvertently used. The manufacturer will determine the correct method of shipping and whether the endoscope should be cleaned before shipping based on the nature of the damage.[9]

VIII.a.1.   Unless otherwise specified in the manufacturer's instructions, a damaged flexible endoscope should not be submerged.[9]

Submersion may lead to additional damage related to water entering the interior of the flexible endoscope.[9]

VIII.a.2.   Before shipping a contaminated flexible endoscope or its accessories, the item must be packaged in impervious material in compliance with Department of Transportation shipping regulations.[14]

Flexible endoscopes and accessories returned to the manufacturer for repair are considered a biohazard and precautions must be taken to protect anyone who may come in contact with the device.[14]

VIII.a.3. Flexible endoscopes and accessories returned to the manufacturer for repair must be labeled with a biohazardous label visible during shipping.

Contaminated flexible endoscopes and accessories returned to the manufacturer for repair are considered a biohazard. The biohazard label will act as a warning of potentially infectious material for anyone who handles the package.[14]

Recommendation IX

Flexible endoscopes should be stored in a manner that protects the device from damage and minimizes microbial contamination.

IX.a. Flexible endoscopes should be stored
- in a closed cabinet with
  - venting that allows air circulation around the flexible endoscopes,
  - internal surfaces composed of cleanable materials,
  - adequate height to allow flexible endoscopes to hang without touching the bottom of the cabinet, and
  - sufficient space for storage of multiple endoscopes without touching;
- hanging in a secure vertical position;
- with all removable endoscope components (eg, valve mechanisms, biopsy valve covers, irrigation tubes) detached;
- with all accessories removed; and
- with scope protectors applied if the protector does not interfere with the flexible endoscope hanging straight or restrict the air movement around channel openings.[25-28]

When flexible endoscopes are hung in the vertical position, coiling or kinking is prevented, allowing any remaining moisture to drain out of the endoscope and decreasing

the potential development of an environment conducive to microbial growth in the endoscope. Proper storage facilitates drying and decreases potential for contamination. Opening all valves and removing all accessories facilitates drying. The scope protector may create an environment favorable for microbial growth if the flexible endoscope is not dry and cannot hang straight.[28-30]

IX.a.1. Flexible endoscopes should not be stored in the original shipment cases.

The cases are difficult to clean, may be contaminated, and are designed for shipping only.

IX.b. Flexible endoscopes should be reprocessed before use if unused for more than five days.[25-27,31]

In research studies, flexible endoscopes cleaned and processed as recommended and stored by hanging in closed cabinets have been shown to grow organisms after five days of no use. In a prospective observational study, flexible endoscopes in active service during the three-week study period were microbiologically sampled prior to reprocessing before the first case of the day. The contamination rate was 15.5%, with a pathogenic contamination rate of 0.5%. Mean shelf life (ie, time between the last reprocessing one day and reprocessing before the first case on the following day) was 37.62 hours (SD 36.47). Median shelf life was 18.8 hours (range 5.27 to 165.35 hours). The most frequently identified organism was coagulase-negative *Staphylococcus*, an environmental nonpathogenic organism.[31]

One study evaluated the contamination of high-level disinfection of upper endoscopes, duodenoscopes, and colonoscopes endoscopes stored in a dust-proof cabinet for five days. After completion of the endoscopic procedure, the endoscopes were subjected to an initial decontamination, followed by manual cleaning with the endoscope immersed in detergent. The endoscopes then were placed in an automatic reprocessor that provides high-level disinfection. They then were stored by hanging in a dust-proof cabinet. Bacteriologic samples were obtained from the surface of the endoscopes, the openings for the piston valves, and the accessory channels daily for five days and by flush-through (combined with brushing) from the accessory channels after five days of storage. Samples were cultured for all types of aerobic and anaerobic bacteria, including bacterial spores, and for *Candida* species. For all assays, all endoscopes were bacteria-free immediately after high-level disinfection. Only four assays (of 135) were positive (for skin bacteria cultured from endoscope surfaces) during the subsequent five-day assessment. All flush-through samples were sterile. The study concluded that when endoscope reprocessing guidelines are strictly observed and endoscopes are stored in appropriate cabinets for up to five days, reprocessing before use may not be necessary.[25]

In a multiphase study, four endoscopic retrograde cholangiopancreatography (ERCP) scopes and three colonoscopes were evaluated. In phase 1, endoscopes were assayed after initial high-level disinfection and daily for a period of two weeks. In phase 2, this procedure was repeated to confirm phase 1 results. In phase 3, endoscopes were assayed after high-level disinfection and again following a seven-day storage period. In phase 1, 6 of 70 (8.6 %) assays were positive. This involved two colonoscopes and two ERCP scopes out of the seven total scopes (57 %) and was limited to the first five days of the study. No cultures were positive in phase 2. In phase 3, one endoscope had a positive culture. Positive cultures grew only *Staphylococcus epidermidis,* a low-virulence skin organism.[27]

One study conducted in the clinical environment to determine shelf life for flexible colonoscopes, which were processed using peracetic acid, suggests that colonoscopes with all channels thoroughly reprocessed and dried may be stored for up to one week before needing to be reprocessed. This study was limited by the small sample size, completion at a single site with a single processing method, and artificial contamination of a single colonoscope without a control measure to measure the level of contamination following inoculation.[26]

IX.c. Flexible endoscopes should be reprocessed before use if evidence of improper drying exists (eg, evidence of discoloration, wet spots, or stains, or soil in the storage cabinet) when the scope is removed from storage.[25-27,31]

Evidence of improper drying may include wet spots or stains on the bottom of the cabinet where the flexible endoscopes have been hanging. Improper drying creates an environment conducive to growth of microorganisms.[31]

IX.d. Storage cabinets should be cleaned and disinfected with an Environmental Protection Agency (EPA)-registered disinfectant when visibly soiled and on a weekly or monthly schedule.[32]

Cleaning and disinfecting storage cabinets periodically will decrease dust and soil build up.[32]

Recommendation X

Flexible endoscope accessories (eg, water bottle, cap, water tubing, biopsy forceps, cytology brushes, cleaning brushes) should be decontaminated after use and inspected for damage.

Flexible endoscope accessories have been found to be a source of contamination.[30,33]

X.a. Endoscopic accessories (eg, biopsy forceps, cytology brushes) that enter sterile tissue or the vascular system should be cleaned and sterilized between use as described in the AORN "Recommended practices for care and cleaning of surgical instruments and powered equipment" and the AORN "Recommended practices for sterilization in the perioperative practice setting."[1]

These devices enter sterile tissue and, if contaminated, increase the risk of patient infection.[11]

X.b.1. All surfaces of accessories should be brushed using brushes of the appropriate size and style.

Brushing all surfaces of accessories, some of which may be irregular, assists with removing all organic debris.[17]

X.b.2. Insulated electrosurgical instruments should be handled as described in the

AORN "Recommended practices for care and cleaning of surgical instruments and powered equipment" and the AORN "Recommended practices for electrosurgery."[1,34]

X.b.3. Reusable cleaning brushes should be thoroughly cleaned using an ultrasonic cleaner, inspected for integrity, and sterilized or high-level disinfected after each use.[17]

Damaged reusable brushes can cause perforations in any flexible endoscope surface. Reusable brushes may be a cause for cross contamination. Ultrasonic cleaning of reusable endoscopic accessories removes soil and organic material from hard to clean places. Disposable cleaning brushes are available commercially and may be safer, more efficient, and more economic to use.[17]

Recommendation XI

Flexible endoscopes should be decontaminated in an area physically separated from locations where clean items are handled and patient care activities are performed.[35]

Physical separation of decontamination areas from areas where clean items are handled minimizes the risk of cross-contamination. Cross-contamination can result when soiled items are placed in close proximity to clean items or placed on surfaces upon which clean items are later placed. Aerosols created during cleaning can also cause cross-contamination.[7]

XI.a. The decontamination area should be physically separated from clean patient care areas and include a door.[35] This area should contain, but not be limited to,
- sinks to manually clean flexible endoscopes,
- hand-washing facilities,[14]
- eyewash station,[36]
- automated equipment consistent with the types of flexible endoscopes to be decontaminated,
- adapters and accessories to connect the flexible endoscopes with cleaning equipment and utilities,

- leak testing equipment,
- low-pressure air,
- closed storage facilities, and
- proper ventilation.

The design of the decontamination area facilitates the safe and effective decontamination of flexible endoscopes and accessories. Appropriate equipment and utilities facilitate desired infection control practices. Keeping the door closed supports the functioning of the building ventilation system which is designed to vent potentially contaminated room air out of the building, minimizing contamination of adjacent areas.

Sinks are required to manually clean or remove gross bioburden from flexible endoscopes before high-level disinfection via manual or automatic endoscope reprocessor methods.

Hand washing facilities are required to decontaminate hands after removal of PPE.[14]

An eyewash station is required to flush eyes when cleaning and disinfecting chemicals are accidentally splashed into the healthcare worker's face.[37]

Automated cleaning and decontamination of flexible endoscopes and accessories provides a high level of cleaning that is difficult to consistently replicate using manual methods.

Compressed air is needed to dry lumens after cleaning.[7]

Closed storage facilities help to prevent contamination of stored supplies.[1]

Adequate ventilation is required to protect personnel from the high-level disinfecting fumes.[35]

XI.b. The decontamination area should be supplied at a minimum with
- enzymatic detergent,
- soft-bristle brushes,
- cleaning cloths,
- alcohol, and
- personal protective equipment (PPE).

Enzymatic cleaner is used for manual and automated cleaning of flexible endoscopes. Soft-bristle brushes, designed for flexible endoscope cleaning, can effectively clean scopes and accessories without damaging surfaces. Cleaning cloths are used for external surfaces. Alcohol is used to irrigate after the final rinse to assist with drying. When cleaning flexible endoscopes with water, it can be reasonably anticipated that there is a potential for exposure to chemicals and bloodborne pathogens.[14]

XI.c. Flexible endoscopes and accessories should not be decontaminated in scrub or hand sinks.

Cleaning soiled instruments in a scrub or hand sink can contaminate the sink and faucet, which also may be used for clean activities (eg, hand washing, surgical hand antisepsis).

Recommendation XII

Personnel handling contaminated endoscopic equipment must wear appropriate PPE.[14]

Personal protective equipment (PPE) helps to protect the employee from exposure to bloodborne pathogens and other potentially infectious materials.

XII.a. Personal protective equipment consistent with the anticipated exposure must be worn.[14,37] The appropriate PPE for these types of exposures include, but is not limited to,
- a fluid-resistant gown,
- disposable chemical resistant glove,
- a mask, and
- face protection.

Splashes, splatters, and skin contact can be reasonably anticipated when handling contaminated flexible endoscopes. Glutaraldehyde may be absorbed through neoprene and PVC gloves; use gloves made of butyl rubber, nitrile, and Viton®. Latex surgical exam or polyethylene gloves may be used for short-term, or incidental contact only.[8,38]

XII.a.1. Hands must be washed after removing PPE.[14]

Perforations can occur in gloves, and hands can become contaminated when removing PPE.[14]

XII.a.2. Reusable protective attire must be decontaminated and the integrity of the attire confirmed between uses.[14]

Reusable gloves, gowns, aprons, and face shields become contaminated and their integrity can be compromised during use. Decontamination and confirmation of integrity helps to protect the wearer from exposure.[37]

Recommendation XIII

Personnel should demonstrate competency in the use, care, and processing of flexible endoscopes and related equipment periodically and before new endoscopic equipment and/or accessories are introduced into the practice setting.[11]

Ongoing competency validation and education of personnel facilitates the development of knowledge, skills, and attitudes that affect patient and health care worker safety.

XIII.a. Personnel working with flexible endoscopes and accessories should demonstrate competency commensurate with their responsibilities, including but not limited to,
- cleaning/decontamination methods;
- preparation of flexible endoscopes and related accessories for sterilization/high-level disinfection;
- selection of cleaning agents and methods;
- proper use of cleaning agents, including an understanding of specific applications, appropriate dilution, and special precautions;
- decontamination of specialized flexible endoscopes and related accessories used within the practice setting;
- personal protection required during instrument processing;
- exposure risk associated with chemical cleaning agents; and
- location of material safety data sheets.[11,37]

Workers have the right to know the hazards that exist in the workplace.[37] An understanding of procedures involved in cleaning each type of flexible endoscope is necessary to provide the foundation for compliance with procedures. Failure to follow decontamination practices has been shown to be the leading cause of flexible endoscope contamination.[10] Knowing the location of the material safety data sheets assists in obtaining information in the event of an emergency.

XIII.a.1. Education programs should be specific to the type and design of flexible endoscopes used and the procedures performed in the facility.[11]

XIII.a.2. Orientation and ongoing education activities for personnel should include an introduction to and/or review of policies and procedures to be applied in the practice setting.

XIII.b. Personnel should receive education before new flexible endoscopes, accessories, cleaning agents, cleaning methods, and procedures are introduced.

XIII.c. Designated administrative personnel should validate the competencies of personnel participating in decontamination of flexible endoscopes and accessories. The validation of competencies should include all types of flexible endoscopes and accessories the individual is authorized to reprocess.

Validation of competencies provides an indication that personnel are able to appropriately perform inspection, decontamination, cleaning, and sterilization or high-level disinfection procedures.

Recommendation XIV

Cleaning and processing of flexible endoscopes, accessories, and related equipment should be documented to enable the identification of trends and demonstrate compliance with regulatory and accrediting agency requirements.

Documentation provides a source of data to review processes and evaluate corrective actions.

XIV.a. Records of flexible endoscope cleaning and processing should include, but not be limited to,
  – date,
  – time,
  – flexible endoscope identification,
  – method of cleaning,
  – number or identifier of automatic endoscope reprocessor,
  – name of person performing the cleaning,
  – dilution testing results on high-level disinfectants if used multiple times,
  – routine and unscheduled maintenance or repairs, and
  – disposition of defective equipment.
    Most high-level disinfection and sterilization failures result from inadequate cleaning. Some automatic endoscope reprocessors have digital readouts or printers that facilitate recordkeeping. Records of testing of the dilution of the high-level disinfectant provide a source of evidence for review when investigating clinical issues.[7]

XIV.b. High-level disinfection and sterilization records should be maintained for a time period specified by the health care organization and in compliance with local, state, and federal regulations.

Recommendation XV

Policies and procedures for cleaning and processing flexible endoscopes, accessories, and related equipment should be developed, reviewed regularly, revised as necessary, and readily available in the practice setting.

Policies and procedures serve as operational guidelines to develop/reinforce knowledge, skills, and attitudes and establish authority, responsibility, and accountability within the organization. Policies and procedures also assist in the development of patient safety guidelines and quality assessment and improvement activities.

XV.a. Policies and procedures should establish authority, responsibility, and accountability for flexible endoscope care, cleaning, and processing; should be developed by a multidisciplinary team; and should be based on current literature and manufacturer's written instructions.

Multidisciplinary team participation in policy and procedure development and review provides varied input and improves compliance. Involving surgeons, infection preventionists, and health care workers in review of policies educates them on the requirements of flexible endoscope reprocessing and facilitates safe patient care.

XV.b. Policies should include, but not be limited to,
- review of manufacturers' written instructions before purchase,
- cleaning of flexible endoscopes and accessories before initial use,
- precautions to be taken when handling contaminated items,
- precautions to be taken when handling chemical agents,
- frequency and method of evaluation of mechanical washers,
- frequency and method of evaluation of manual cleaning,
- frequency of checking insulated electrosurgery instruments for leakage current,
- documentation of cleaning,
- initial education and annual competency,
- maintenance of material safety data sheets,
- reporting exposures to bloodborne pathogens, and
- reporting adverse events.

XV.c. A procedure should be developed in the event of a potential disinfection or sterilization failure and should include, but not be limited to,
- assessment to confirm failure;
- assessment of patient risk;
- removal of all improperly disinfected equipment;
- removal of defective cleaning equipment from use;
- notification of departments and physicians involved;
- root cause analysis;
- corrective action plan;
- identification of potentially involved patients;
- determination if patients require notification;
- identification of regulatory, accrediting, and governing agencies requiring notification;
- notification of all medical device manufacturers potentially related to the disinfection or sterilization failure, and
- development of an action plan for disinfection/sterilization failure prevention.[11]

A procedure provides an outline of the steps to follow after a potential disinfection or sterilization failure has occurred.

Recommendation XVI

The health care organization's quality management program should evaluate the cleaning and processing of flexible endoscopes and accessories.

Evaluation of cleaning and processing of flexible endoscopes and accessories improves patient safety.

XVI.a. A quality management program should be in place to test mechanical and manual cleaning processes when new types of flexible endoscopes and accessories are purchased and at intervals determined by the health care organization.[39]

Testing of mechanical cleaners assures proper functioning to the equipment because malfunctioning automatic endoscope reprocessors have been shown to cause contamination of flexible endoscopes.[10] Periodic testing of cleaning methods provides an opportunity to evaluate the performance of personnel and equipment. Manual cleaning is a learned skill and subject to human error.[23,39] New instruments can pose unique challenges when cleaning.

XVI.a.1. Automatic endoscope reprocessors should be tested for proper functioning before initial use, annually during service, and after major repair.[40]

Testing automatic endoscope reprocessors on a regular basis verifies that the equipment is functioning properly or identifies an opportunity for corrective action. Washer testing products (eg, protein indicators) are commercially available to assist with this evaluation.[39]

XVI.a.2. Adverse events and near misses related to flexible endoscope and accessory cleaning should be reported in the healthcare organization's adverse event reporting system and reviewed for potential opportunities for improvement.

Reporting mechanisms assist in the discovery of opportunities for improvement and prevention of repeat adverse events.

XVI.b. Water quality should be tested periodically for bacterial contamination and purity (eg, hardness, mineral content, pH).[4]

Contaminated water has been shown to cause contamination of flexible endoscopes after the decontamination process has been completed.[4,10]

XVI.c. Perioperative nurses should collaborate with infection preventionists to monitor and validate flexible endoscope cleaning, disinfection, and storage processes.

XVI.d. A program should be developed to monitor appropriate storage conditions, including but not limited to,
   – length of storage time, and
   – lack of evidence of the presence of moisture in or on the flexible endoscope after hanging.
   Improper storage conditions may cause bacterial growth.

XVI.d.1. The length of storage time after high-level disinfection and before next use should be measured and monitored using a system to determine the date for removal of the flexible endoscope from use for reprocessing (eg, expiration date label on endoscope, log of serial numbers and the date of processing).
   Recording the date the flexible endoscope was last processed will reduce the risk of a flexible endoscope being used more than five days after processing.

Glossary

Automated endoscope reprocessor: A unit for mechanical cleaning, disinfecting, and rinsing of flexible endoscopes.

Bioburden: The degree of microbial load; the number of viable organisms contaminating an object.

Biofilms: "A thin coating containing biologically active organisms, that have the ability to grow in water, water solutions, or in vivo, which coat the surface of structures (eg, teeth, inner surfaces of catheters, tubes, implanted or indwelling devices, instruments, other medical devices). Biofilms contain viable and nonviable microorganisms that adhere to surfaces and become trapped within a matrix of organic matter (eg, proteins, glycoproteins, carbohydrates), which prevents antimicrobial agents from reaching the cells." (*SOURCE: Favero MS, Bond WW. Chemical disinfection of medical and surgical mate-*

rials. In: Disinfection, Sterilization, and Preservation. 5th ed. Block SS, ed. Philadelphia, PA: Lippincott Williams & Wilkins; 2001:910-911.)

Chemical disinfectant/germicide: A generic term for a government-registered agent that destroys microorganisms. Germicides are classified as sporicides, general disinfectants, sanitizers, and others.

Cleaning: A process using friction, detergent, and water to remove organic debris; the process by which any type of soil, including organic debris, is removed. Cleaning removes rather than kills microorganisms.

Contaminated: The presence of potentially infectious, pathogenic organisms (eg, blood, other potentially infectious material) on or in animate or inanimate objects.

Critical item: An item that has contact with the vascular system or enters sterile tissue, or body cavities and thus poses the highest risk of transmission of infection.

Decontamination: A process that removes contaminating infectious agents and renders reusable medical products safe for handling.

Disinfection: A process that kills most forms of microorganisms on inanimate surfaces. Disinfection destroys pathogenic organisms (excluding bacterial spores) or their toxins or vectors by direct exposure to chemical or physical means.

Electrosurgical accessories: Electrosurgical accessories are defined as the active electrode with tip(s), dispersive electrode, adapters, and connectors to attach these devices to the generator.

Enzymatic cleaner: A cleaner that uses enzymes to remove protein from surgical instruments.

High-level disinfection: A process that kills all microorganisms with the exception of high numbers of bacterial spores and prions. High-level disinfectants have the capability to inactivate the hepatitis B and C viruses, HIV, and *Mycobacterium tuberculosis,* but do not inactivate the virus-like prion that causes Creutzfeld-Jakob disease. Government-registered high-level disinfection agents kill vegetative bacteria, tubercle bacilli, some spores and fungi, and lipid and nonlipid viruses, given appropriate concentration, submersion, and contact time.

Minimum effective concentration: The minimum concentration of a liquid chemical germicide that achieves the claimed microbicidal activity as determined by dose-response testing.

Personal protective equipment (PPE): Specialized equipment or clothing for eyes, face, head, body, and extremities; protective clothing; respiratory devices; and protective shields and barriers designed to protect the worker from injury or exposure to a patient's blood, tissue, or body fluids. Used by health care workers and others whenever necessary to protect themselves from the hazards of processes or environments, chemical hazards, or mechanical irritants encountered in a manner capable of causing injury or impairment in the function of any part of the body through absorption, inhalation, or physical contact.

Potable water: Water that is of sufficient quality to be considered appropriate for drinking.

Semicritical item: An item that comes in contact with mucous membranes or with skin that is not intact.

Sterile: The absence of all living microorganisms.

Sterilization: Processes by which all microbial life, including pathogenic and nonpathogenic microorganisms, and spores, are killed.

Tap water: High-quality potable water that meets federal clean water standards at the point of use.

REFERENCES:

1. Recommended practices for cleaning and care of surgical instruments and powered equipment. In: *Perioperative Standards and Recommended Practices.* Denver, CO: AORN; 2008:421-446.

2. *ANSI/AAMI ST81:2004—Sterilization of Medical Devices: Information to Be Provided by the Manufacturer for the Processing of Resterilizable Medical Devices.* Arlington, VA: Association for the Advancement of Medical Instrumentation; 2004.

3. The Steris Reliance EPS endoscope processing system: A new automated endoscope reprocessing technology. *Health Devices* 2007;36(1):22.

4. *AAMI TIR34:2007—Water for the Reprocessing of Medical Devices.* Arlington, VA: Association for the Advancement of Medical Instrumentation; 2007.

5. Zuhlsdorf B, Emmrich M, Floss H, Martiny H. Cleaning efficacy of nine different cleaners in a washer-disinfector designed for flexible endoscopes. *J Hosp Infect* 2002;52(3):206.

6. Zuhlsdorf B, Winkler A, Dietze B, Floss H, Martiny H. Gastroscope processing in washer-disinfectors at three different temperatures. *J Hosp Infect* 2003;55(4):276.

7. Rutala WA, Weber DJ. Reprocessing endoscopes: United States perspective. In: Proceedings of the 7th International BODE Hygiene Days, May 2003. *J Hosp Infect* 2004 (April); 56 Supplement 2:S27-S39.

8. Recommended practices for high-level disinfection. In: *Perioperative Standards and Recommended Practices.* Denver, CO: AORN; 2008:303-310.

9. Thomas L A. Essentials for endoscopic equipment: Leak testing. *Gastroenterol Nurs* 2005;28(5):430.

10. Seoane-Vazquez E, Rodriguez-Monguio R, Visaria J, Carlson A. Endoscopy-related infections and toxic reactions: An international comparison. *Endoscopy* 2007;39(8):742.

11. Rutala WA, Weber DJ. How to assess risk of disease transmission to patients when there is a failure to follow recommended disinfection and sterilization guidelines. *Infect Control Hosp Epidemiol* 2007;28(2):146.

12. Martiny H, Floss H, Zuhlsdorf B. The importance of cleaning for the overall results of processing endoscopes. In: Proceedings of the 7th International BODE Hygiene Days, May 2003. *J Hosp Infect* 2004 (April); 56 Supplement 2:S16.

13. Standards of infection control in reprocessing of flexible gastrointestinal endoscopes. *Gastroenterol Nurs* 2006;29(2):142.

14. *Bloodborne Pathogens.* (29 CFR §1910.1030.) Occupational Safety and Health Administration. http://www.osha.gov/pls/oshaweb/owadisp.show_document?p_table=STANDARDS&p_id=10051. Accessed December 15, 2008.

15. Thomas LA. Essentials for endoscopic equipment: Endoscope staging. *Gastroenterol Nurs* 2005;28(3):243.

16. Garces E. Endoscope repair prevention: It takes a team. *Healthc Purchasing News* 2006;30(11):50, 55.

17. Thomas L A. Essentials for endoscopic equipment: Manual cleaning. *Gastroenterol Nurs* 2005;28(6):512.

18. Recommended practices for sterilization in the perioperative practice setting. In: *Perioperative Standards and Recommended Practices.* Denver, CO: AORN; 2008:575.

19. Pang J, Perry P, Ross A, Forbes GM. Bacteria-free rinse water for endoscope disinfection. *Gastrointest Endosc* 2002;56(3):402.

20. *ANSI/AAMI ST58:2005—Chemical Sterilization and High-Level Disinfection in Health Care Facilities.* Arlington, VA: Association for the Advancement of Medical Instrumentation; 2005.

21. Thomas LA. Essentials for endoscopic equipment: Care of the specialty scope. *Gastroenterol Nurs* 2006;29(1):68.

22. Nelson DB, Jarvis WR, Rutala WA, et al; Society for Healthcare Epidemiology of America. Multi-society guideline for reprocessing flexible gastrointestinal endoscopes. *Infect Control Hosp Epidemiol* 2003;24(7):532.

23. Alfa MJ, Olson N, Degagne P, Jackson M. A survey of reprocessing methods, residual viable bioburden, and soil levels in patient-ready endoscopic retrograde choliangiopancreatography duodenoscopes used in Canadian centers. *Infect Control Hosp Epidemiol* 2002;23(4):198.

24. Fisher C. The blame game: Don't play it. *Surg Technol* 2007;39(3):121.

25. Rejchrt S, Cermak P, Pavlatova L, McKova E, Bures J. Bacteriologic testing of endoscopes after high-level disinfection. *Gastrointest Endosc* 2004;60(1):76.

26. Riley R, Beanland C, Bos H. Establishing the shelf life of flexible colonoscopes. *Gastroenterol Nurs* 2002;25(3):114.

27. Vergis AS, Thomson D, Pieroni P, Dhalla S. Reprocessing flexible gastrointestinal endoscopes after a period of disuse: Is it necessary? *Endoscopy* 2007; 39(8):737.

28. Thomas L A. Essentials for endoscopic equipment. Recommended care and handling of flexible endoscopes: Endoscope storage. *Gastroenterol Nurs* 2005; 28(1):45.

29. Goldstine S. Endoscopy storage: Preventing distal tip protector contamination. *Gastroenterol Nurs* 28(1), 45-46.

30. Bisset L, Cossart YE, Selby W, West R, Catterson D, O'Hara K, Vickery K. A prospective study of the efficacy of routine decontamination for gastrointestinal endoscopes and the risk factors for failure. *Am J Infect Control* 2006; 34(5):274.

31. Osborne S, Reynolds S, George N, Lindemayer F, Gill A, Chalmers M. Challenging endoscopy reprocessing guidelines: a prospective study investigating the safe shelf life of flexible endoscopes in a tertiary gastroenterology unit. *Endoscopy* 2007; 39(9):825.

32. Recommended practices for environmental cleaning in the perioperative setting. In: *Perioperative Standards and Recommended Practices.* Denver, CO: AORN; 2008:375-382.

33. Reprocessing of endoscopic accessories and valves. *Gastroenterol Nurs* 2006; 29(5):394.

34. Recommended practices for electrosurgery. In: *Perioperative Standards and Recommended Practices.* Denver, CO: AORN; 2008:315-330.

35. AIA Health Facilities Guidelines Institute. *Guidelines for Design and Construction of Health Care Facilities.* Washington, DC: American Institute of Architects; 2006.

36. *OSH Act of 1970.* Public Law 91-596 84; STAT. 1590; 91st Congress, S.2193 (December 29, 1970). http://www.osha.gov/pls/oshaweb/owadisp.show_document?p_id=2743&p_table=OSHACT. Accessed December 15, 2008.

37. *Hazard Communication.* (29 CFR §1910.) Occupational Safety and Health Administration. Washington, DC: US Government Printing Office; 2007. Available at http://www.osha.gov/SLTC/hazardcommunications/standards.html. Accessed December 5, 2008.

38. Hospital eTool: Healthcare wide hazards module—Glutaraldehyde. Occupational Safety and Health Administration. http://www.osha.gov/SLTC/etools/hospital/hazards/glutaraldehyde/glut.html. Accessed December 5, 2008.

39. *ANSI/AAMI ST79:2006—Comprehensive Guide to Steam Sterilization and Sterility Assurance in Health Care Facilities.* Arlington, VA: Association for the Advancement of Medical Instrumentation; 2008.

40. Gillespie EE, Kotsanas D, Stuart RL. Microbiological monitoring of endoscopes: 5-year review. *J Gastroenterol Hepatol* 2008 (July); 23(7 Pt 1):1069-1074.

Acknowledgments

Lead Authors

Byron Burlingame, RN, BSN, MS, CNOR
Perioperative Nursing Specialist
AORN Center for Nursing Practice
Denver, Colorado

Maria Arcilla, RN, BSN, CNOR
Perioperative Coordinator
Texas Childrens Hospital
Houston, Texas

Contributing Author

Carla McDermott, RN, CNOR
Educator, Staff Development
South Florida Baptist Hospital
Plant City, Florida

Originally published February 1993, *AORN Journal.* Revised November 1997; published January 1998. Reformatted July 2000.

Revised November 2002; published in *Standards, Recommended Practices, and Guidelines,* 2003 edition. Reprinted February 2003, *AORN Journal.*

Revised November 2008; published in *Perioperative Standards and Recommended Practices,* 2009 edition.

AORN Perioperative Standards and Recommended Practices, 2009 Edition

Recommended Practices for Cleaning and Care of Surgical Instruments and Powered Equipment

The following recommended practices for the cleaning and care of surgical instruments and powered equipment were developed by the AORN Recommended Practices Committee and have been approved by the AORN Board of Directors. They were presented as proposed recommendations for comments by members and others. They are effective January 1, 2008.

These recommended practices are intended as achievable recommendations representing what is believed to be an optimal level of practice. Policies and procedures will reflect variations in practice settings and/or clinical situations that determine the degree to which the recommended practices can be implemented.

AORN recognizes the various settings in which perioperative nurses practice. These recommended practices are intended as guidelines adaptable to various practice settings. These practice settings include traditional operating rooms, ambulatory surgery centers, physicians' offices, cardiac catheterization laboratories, endoscopy suites, radiology departments, and all other areas where surgery may be performed.

References to nursing interventions (I) used in the Perioperative Nursing Data Set, second edition, (PNDS) are noted in parentheses when a recommended practice corresponds to a PNDS intervention.[1] The reader is referred to the PNDS for further explanation of nursing diagnoses, interventions, and outcomes.

Purpose

These recommended practices provide guidelines to assist perioperative nurses in decontaminating and preparing surgical instruments and powered equipment for terminal sterilization and disinfection. These recommended practices are general recommendations, as it is impossible to make a separate recommendation for every instrument used. These recommended practices complement AORN's "Recommended practices for sterilization in perioperative practice settings"[2] and "Recommended practices for high-level disinfection in perioperative practice settings."[3]

Perioperative nurses should consult these documents to assist them in providing a safe environment for the patient. Perioperative nurses are advised to review the Association for the Advancement of Medical Instrumentation (AAMI) standards for additional practice details. Information about flexible endo-scope cleaning can be found in the AORN "Recommended practices for cleaning and processing endoscopes and endoscopic accessories."[4]

Recommendation I

The manufacturer's written, validated instructions for handling and reprocessing should be obtained and evaluated to determine the ability to adequately clean and reprocess the equipment within the health care facility before purchasing surgical instruments and powered equipment. (PNDS: I122)

Cleaning and handling instructions recommended by the device manufacturer vary widely. Specific types of equipment, pneumatically powered instruments, and specialty instruments can require special cleaning and maintenance procedures.[5]

I.a. The manufacturer's written instructions should be used to determine how to replicate the validated cleaning and processing methods.[6] (PNDS: I122)

I.a.1. The manufacturer's written instructions should identify requirements related to
- utilities (eg, type of water, compressed air);
- cleaning equipment;
- accessories (eg, adaptors) for creating a proper connection between the instruments and equipment, utilities, and cleaning equipment;
- accessories for cleaning lumens, ports, and internal parts;
- cleaning agents;[6]
- lubricants; and
- processing methods.

I.b. The accessories necessary to reprocess the instrument according to the manufacturer's validated instructions should be obtained at the time of purchase. (PNDS: I122)

Using the proper accessories that fit the instruments and equipment and that were used during testing provides the best opportunity to replicate validated cleaning methods.

Recommendation II

New, repaired, and refurbished instruments should be examined, cleaned, and sterilized according to manufacturers' written instructions before use in a health care organization.

II.a.	When new, repaired, or refurbished instruments are received into a facility all moving parts, tips, box locks, ratchets, screws, and cutting edges should be examined for defects and to ensure proper working order. (PNDS: I98, I138)

Inspecting the instrument verifies that the instrument has no obvious defects and has not sustained damage during shipping.

II.b.	When indicated, new instruments should be pretreated according to the instrument manufacturer's written instructions. (PNDS: I122)

Some manufacturers recommend a series of treatments in a steam sterilizer to harden the coating on the instruments before initial cleaning. When this is indicated, details are provided in the manufacturer's written instructions.

II.c.	New, repaired, or refurbished instruments should be decontaminated according to the manufacturer's written instruction before use. (PNDS: I70, I122, I138)

Decontamination of newly acquired or repaired instruments removes any soil related to manufacturing, repair, refurbishing, or shipping.

Recommendation III

Borrowed or consigned (ie, loaner) instruments should be examined, cleaned, and sterilized by the receiving health care organization before use, according to manufacturers' written instructions. (PNDS: I38, I70, I85, I98, I122)

Parameters of in-house sterilization can be verified. If an instrument has been sterilized by another health care organization, the user will have no record of the sterilization process in the event of a recall. There is a high probability of an event occurring during transport that could compromise sterility.

III.a.	Before receiving loaner instruments, the instrument manufacturer's instructions for handling and reprocessing should be obtained and evaluated to determine the ability to adequately clean and reprocess the equipment. (PNDS: I122, I138)

When instructions are received in advance, proper conditions can be created for cleaning and sterilization before the arrival of the instruments. This can prevent a potential delay in the scheduled case and help ensure adequate sterilization. Requests that cleaning instructions arrive before receiving the instrument tray improves the efficiency of reprocessing.[7]

III.b.	The accessories necessary to reprocess loaner instruments according to the manufacturer's validated instructions should be received at the same time as the instruments. (PNDS: I85, I122, I138)

The best opportunity to replicate valid cleaning methods is to use the proper accessories that fit the instruments and equipment and that have been used during testing.

III.c.	When a loaner instrument is received, all moving parts, tips, box locks, ratchets, screws, and cutting edges should be examined for defects and to ensure proper working order. (PNDS: I85, I128, I138)

Inspecting the instrument verifies the absence of obvious defects and damage during shipping.

III.d.	Loaner instruments should be decontaminated and sterilized in the borrowing facility according to the manufacturer's written instructions before use. (PNDS: I70, I98, I122)

Instruments consigned or borrowed from other facilities may not have been adequately decontaminated. Conditions during storage and transport are not known. The quality of any previous processing has not been verified, and sterile storage conditions have not been maintained during transport.[7]

III.e.	Loaner instruments should be requested when the surgery is scheduled and delivered to the health care organization with sufficient time available before the surgical procedure to allow inspection and inventory of the instruments and to perform reprocessing in the same manner as a facility-owned instrument. (PNDS: I85)

Managing loaner instruments requires planning. Requesting the instruments when the surgery is scheduled allows the vendor to deliver the instruments far enough in advance for proper cleaning, decontamination, inspection, and sterilization to occur. Vendor collaboration is more likely when delivery and other expectations are communicated in advance.

III.f.   Loaner instruments should be logged in and inventoried within the receiving facility before use.

Keeping logs and inventory lists of instruments helps to provide verification that the instrument set is complete and available for the intended surgical procedure upon their arrival. Requesting that an inventory list accompany the instrument tray improves the efficiency of reprocessing.[7] Digital images may be used for documentation.

III.g.   Loaner instruments should be disassembled and decontaminated after use. (PNDS: I98)

III.g.1.   Loaner instruments should be inventoried and documentation created regarding the disposition of the items after completion of decontamination.

Recommendation IV

Instruments should be kept free of gross soil during surgical procedures. (PNDS: I70, I98)

Blood and body fluids can cause pitting of instruments and, if left to dry, can be difficult to remove. If blood and body fluids are not removed, they can prevent adequate sterilization, which could be an avenue for transmission of other potentially infectious materials.

IV.a.   Instruments should be wiped as needed with sterile surgical sponges moistened with sterile water during the procedure to remove gross soil. (PNDS: I70, I98)

Blood and body fluids, as well as saline, are highly corrosive. Corrosion, rusting, and pitting occur when saline, blood, and debris are allowed to dry in or on surgical instruments. Dried blood and debris can be difficult, if not impossible, to remove from all surfaces during the decontamination process; therefore, subsequent disinfection or sterilization may not be achieved.

IV.b.   Instruments with lumens should be irrigated with sterile water as needed throughout the surgical procedure. (PNDS: I70, I98)

Cannulated instruments or instruments with lumens can become obstructed with organic material. Irrigating these instruments with sterile water helps remove residue. Instruments should be rinsed with water because of the corrosive nature of saline.

IV.c.   Electrosurgical unit (ESU) active electrode tips should be cleaned frequently, away from the surgical site, to remove eschar. (PNDS: I72)

Eschar on the ESU electrode tip impedes the current flow, causing the equipment to work less efficiently. Eschar also serves as a fuel source that can lead to surgical fires.[8] Debris on the tip can cause tissues to tear and lead to bleeding.[9]

Recommendation V

Cleaning and decontamination should occur as soon as possible after instruments and equipment are used. (PNDS: I70, I98)

Cleaning and decontamination should occur as soon as possible after instruments and equipment are used to prevent the formation of biofilm. Cleaning and decontamination must be thoroughly accomplished or disinfection and sterilization may not be effective.

V.a.   Preparation for decontamination of instruments should begin at the point of use. (PNDS: I70, I98)

Removing gross soil and moistening soil at the point of use improves the efficiency and effectiveness of decontamination.

V.b.   All instruments opened in the operating or procedure room should be decontaminated whether or not they have been used. (PNDS: I70, I98)

All instruments opened during a surgical procedure are considered contaminated. Scrubbed persons may touch instruments without being aware of it. Used instruments also may come in contact with other instruments.

V.c.   Sharp instruments should be segregated from other instruments.

Segregation of sharp instruments minimizes the risk of injury to personnel handling the instruments during decontamination. The Occupational Safety and Health

Administration (OSHA) prohibits processes that require employees to place their hands into basins of sharp instruments submerged in water because of the risk of a percutaneous exposure to bloodborne pathogens.[10]

V.c.1. Disposable sharps (eg, scalpel blades, suture needles) should be removed and discarded into the proper receptacles.

V.c.2. Reusable sharp instruments, including scissors, should be placed in a separate receptacle.

V.c.3. Reusable scalpel handles should be considered sharp and placed in a receptacle designated for sharp instruments.

Considering a reusable scalpel handle to be sharp minimizes the risk of injury if a blade has been left on the handle.

V.c.4. Reusable sharps must be placed in a puncture-proof container for transport.[10]

V.d. When instruments are composed of more than one piece, they should be opened, disassembled, and arranged in an orderly fashion within the original set configuration. (PNDS: I70, I98)

Disassembling and opening of instruments followed by their placement into original set configuration minimizes the risk of instrument displacement and improves the efficiency of reprocessing.

V.d.1. Instruments should be placed in a perforated or mesh-bottom instrument tray before mechanical decontamination.

Using perforated trays allows all surfaces to be exposed when processed in an automated cleaner.

V.d.2. Instrument box locks should be fully open and the instrument secured to prevent closing by using stringers, racks, or instrument pegs designed to contain instruments.

V.e. Delicate instruments should be protected from damage.

Instruments shift may during transport. The weight of heavy instruments can easily damage delicate instruments, unless preventive measures are taken.

V.e.1. Lightweight instruments should be placed on top of heavier instruments or segregated into separate containers.

V.e.2. Microsurgical instruments should be segregated into separate containers.

V.e.3. Heavy instruments should be placed on the bottom of storage containers or in a separate tray.

V.f. Instruments should be treated with an instrument cleaner according to the instrument or device manufacturer's recommendation before transport. (PNDS: I70, I98)

When decontamination will not occur immediately, or the decontamination area is remote from the surgical suite, treating instruments with an instrument cleaner at the point of use can facilitate the efficiency and effectiveness of cleaning. Corrosion, rusting, and pitting occur when blood and debris are allowed to dry in or on surgical instruments. Cannulas or lumens can become obstructed with organic material.

V.f.1. If items are soaked in water or an instrument cleaning solution at the point of use, the liquid should be contained or discarded before transport.

Disposal of cleaning solution before transport of instruments minimizes the risk of a spill and limits the weight of the container, which makes transportation easier and less likely to result in injury to personnel. When disposal at the point of use is not feasible, containing the solution will prevent spills and subsequent exposures.

V.f.2. A towel soaked with water, not saline, may be used to cover instruments to keep them moist.

Recommendation VI

Contaminated instruments must be contained during transport and should be transported in a timely manner to a location designed for decontamination.[10]

Proper containment of instruments decreases the potential for injury to personnel or their exposure to infectious organisms and prevents damage to the instruments during transport.

VI.a. During transport to a decontamination area, soiled instruments must be contained in a manner to prevent exposure of patients or personnel to bloodborne pathogens and other potentially infectious organisms.[10] (PNDS: I98)

The OSHA requires that contaminated instruments be contained in a leak-proof container to minimize the risk of exposing personnel to contaminants during transport.[10]

VI.a.1. Hand-carried items must be contained (eg, enclosed by a plastic bag, container with a lid).[10]

VI.a.2. Large quantities of items may be contained within a larger transport container (eg, transport cart with doors or plastic cover).

VI.a.3. Items placed on top of a transport cart must be contained (eg, plastic bag).[10]

VI.a.4. Items with sharp or pointed edges must be contained in a puncture-resistant container.[10]

VI.a.5. Liquids must be contained in a spill-proof container.[10]

VI.a.6. Transport carts should be designed to prevent items from falling over or off the cart during transport to the decontamination area.

VI.b. The transport container must be labeled to indicate biohazardous contents.[10] The type of label may include, but is not limited to, magnetic signs, stickers, or plastic placards.

Labeling the transport container communicates to others that the items are potentially infectious. This labeling is required by OSHA.[10]

VI.c. Care should be taken to avoid contaminating the outside of the transport containment method. If the outside container has been contaminated, it must be either cleaned at the point of use or enclosed during transport.[10]

Contact with contaminated surfaces can transmit infectious agents during transport.

VI.d. Transport of soiled instruments should be separated from the delivery of clean and sterile supplies to the operating or procedure room.[11] (PNDS: I98)

Separation of soiled instruments from clean supplies minimizes the risk of cross-contamination.[11]

VI.e. Contaminated surgical instruments should be transported to the decontamination area as soon as possible after completion of the surgical procedure.

Removal of organic material from instruments becomes more difficult after the debris has dried. Blood and body fluids that have dried on the instruments are hard to remove, can cause continuing surface corrosion damage (ie, pitting) over time, and can inhibit sterilization.

Recommendation VII

Instruments should be decontaminated in an area separated from locations where clean activities are performed.[12] (PNDS: I70, I98)

Physical separation of decontamination areas from areas where clean items are handled minimizes the risk of cross-contamination. Cross-contamination can result when soiled items are placed in close proximity to clean items or placed on surfaces upon which clean items are later placed. Aerosols created during cleaning can also cause cross-contamination.

VII.a. Instruments should not be decontaminated in scrub or hand sinks. (PNDS: I98)

Cleaning soiled instruments in a scrub or hand sink can contaminate the sink and faucet, which also may be used for clean activities (eg, hand washing, surgical hand antisepsis).

VII.b. The decontamination area should be physically separate from clean areas and include a door.[12] This area should contain, but not be limited to, the following equipment:
- sinks to manually clean instruments,
- hand-washing facilities,[10]
- eye wash station,[13]
- automated equipment consistent with the types of instruments to be decontaminated,
- adaptors and accessories to connect instruments with cleaning equipment and utilities, and
- a compressed air supply. (PNDS: I70, I98)

The design of the decontamination area facilitates the appropriate decontamination of instruments. Having equipment and utilities in place facilitates desired infection control practices. Keeping the door closed exhausts aerosols out of the building, minimizing contamination of adjacent rooms.

Sinks are required to provide a place to manually clean or remove gross bioburden from instruments before using a washer decontaminator and are required for single instruments.

Hand-washing facilities are required by OSHA for use after removal of personal protective equipment (PPE).[10]

An eye wash station is required by OSHA when chemicals such as those used to clean instruments are used.[13]

Automated cleaning and decontamination of equipment is recommended because it provides a high level of cleaning that is difficult to consistently replicate using manual methods. Compressed air is needed to clear lumens after cleaning.

VII.c. The decontamination area heating, ventilation, and air conditioning (HVAC) system should be controlled and monitored according to local requirements. (PNDS: I98)

Proper HVAC controls facilitate desired infection control practices. Local requirements vary depending upon the location.

VII.c.1. At a minimum, the following HVAC settings should be maintained in the decontamination area:
- negative air pressure,[12]
- at least six air exchanges per hour,[12]
- temperature of 68° F to 73° F (20° to 23° C),[12] and
- 30% to 60% humidity.[5]

VII.c.2. Doors to the decontamination area should be kept closed, except when moving personnel and equipment.

Keeping the door closed exhausts aerosols out of the building, minimizing contamination of adjacent areas. Negative pressure within the decontamination room cannot be maintained, if the door is held open.

VII.d. The decontamination area should be stocked, at a minimum, with the following supplies:
- soft-bristle brushes,
- cleaning cloths,
- alcohol, and
- appropriate PPE.

Enzymatic cleaner is used for manual and automated cleaning of instruments. Soft-bristle brushes, designed for surgical instrument cleaning can effectively clean instruments without damaging surfaces. Cleaning cloths are used for external surfaces. Alcohol is used to render instruments safe to handle after cleaning, if not rendered safe by another means. When cleaning instruments with water, it can be reasonably anticipated that there will be some splatter or splash of potentially infectious material. In these situations OSHA requires that personnel wear skin and mucous membrane protection (ie, fluid-resistant or impervious gown, gloves, face protection).[10]

Recommendation VIII

The type of water available for cleaning should be consistent with the manufacturer's written instructions and intended use of the equipment and cleaning agent. (PNDS: I122)

Water quality is affected by conductivity; the presence of dissolved mineral solids, chlorides, and other impurities; and its acidity or alkalinity. Water quality also fluctuates over time. The optimum combination of chemicals used in a washer decontaminator is based on the hardness of the available water.

VIII.a. Potable water should be used for manual or mechanical (ie, automated) decontamination methods unless contraindicated by instrument manufacturers' instructions.[5]

VIII.b. Softened or deionized water should be used for the final rinse.

Softened or deionized water removes soil and detergent residues more efficiently. Water with a high chloride or chlorine content can damage surgical instruments and equipment. Water softeners remove the calcium and magnesium ions that cause spots on instruments.

Deionizing water removes ionized salts and particles that could harm instruments.[5]

VIII.c. A water quality assessment should be performed periodically and after major maintenance to the water source.

Water quality varies seasonally and after water source maintenance. Periodic testing can indicate if the chemical combination used to condition the cleaning and decontamination water should be adjusted. Water quality checks determine the hardness of the water and if any impurities are present.

Impurities present in the water also can be a reflection of insufficient filtration. Repairs or modifications in the filtration system should be made based upon this testing.

Recommendation IX

Surgical instrument, medical device, and equipment manufacturers' validated instructions should be followed regarding the types of cleaning agents (eg, enzyme preparations, detergents) to be used for decontamination. (PNDS: I122)

Following manufacturers' instructions decreases the possibility of selecting cleaning agents that can be harmful to instruments (eg, abrasives can damage the protective surfaces of instruments, contribute to corrosion, impede sterilization). Use of inappropriate cleaning agents can result in damage to surgical instruments and equipment, and possibly limit their warranties.

IX.a. Manufacturers' written instructions and AORN's "Recommended practices for product selection in perioperative practice settings" should be followed for cleaning agent selection and proper use.[14] (PNDS: I122, I138)

IX.a.1. Neutral detergents with a pH of seven that are low-foaming and free-rinsing should be used for manual or mechanical cleaning of surgical instruments and equipment unless contraindicated by instrument or equipment manufacturers' instructions.

Neutral pH detergents work well when enzymatic solutions are used as a part of the cleaning regimen. Low-foaming detergents are more easily removed during rinsing and are generally recommended for use by mechanical washer manufacturers.

IX.b. Highly acidic or highly alkaline pH detergents should be handled carefully and used only if recommended by instrument or equipment manufacturers.

Highly acidic or highly alkaline detergents can cause injuries to the skin or mucous membranes. Careful handling minimizes the risk of exposure.

IX.c. Cleaning agent manufacturers' written instructions should be followed
 – during dilution,
 – when selecting water temperature, and
 – during use. (PNDS: I75, I122)

IX.c.1. A titration unit may be used to efficiently dilute chemicals at a consistent ratio.

IX.d. Abrasive cleaning devices and agents (eg, metal scouring pads, metal brushes, cleaning agents containing chlorides, abrasive cleaners, scouring powders) should not be used.

Abrasive cleaning devices and agents can cause permanent damage to the instruments and equipment.

Recommendation X

All surgical instrument and medical device or equipment manufacturers' validated instructions should be followed regarding the types of cleaning methods (eg, manual, automated) to be used for decontamination. (PNDS: I70, I75, I98, I122)

Use of inappropriate cleaning methods could result in damage and can limit the warranty of the surgical instruments or equipment.

X.a. Before beginning the cleaning process, instruments received into the decontamination area should be rinsed with cold running water.

A rinse with cold running water will remove gross debris and help prevent coagulation of the blood present on instruments.[5]

X.b. When manually cleaning, instruments should be washed in a manner that provides proper decontamination.[5] (PNDS: I70, I98)

Although automated methods are preferred, some delicate instruments (eg, microsurgery, eye), powered equipment, and other instruments that cannot be submerged can require manual cleaning.

X.b.1. Manual cleaning should be accomplished by submerging the instrument in warm water with an appropriate detergent followed by complete submersion of the instrument in rinse solution to minimize aerosolization of contaminants.[5]

Aerosolization of contaminants, splashing of infectious material, and injury from sharp objects are possible when manual cleaning is performed under a stream of running tap water.

X.c. Mechanical cleaning of surgical instruments should be accomplished by ultrasonic cleaners, washer decontaminators/disinfectors, or washer sterilizers.[5]

Mechanical cleaning is preferred because it removes soil efficiently and provides consistent washing and rinsing parameters during the process. Mechanical equipment specifically designed to decontaminate (ie, clean, disinfect) special types of medical devices also is available.

X.c.1. Ultrasonic cleaners should be used according to the manufacturer's operating instructions.

Ultrasonic cleaners use a process called *cavitation* that facilitates removal of small particles and debris from instrument joints, crevices, and hard to reach places (eg, lumens).[5] Ultrasonic energy is passed through a water bath, creating bubbles that implode. This process of implosion creates a suction action that pulls debris away from instrument surfaces.[15]

X.c.2. Ultrasonic cleaners should be used only after gross soil has been removed.

X.c.3. Manufacturers' instructions should be followed regarding detergent selection for use in ultrasonic cleaning devices.

Low-foaming detergents are commonly used in ultrasonic cleaning devices.

X.c.4. Ultrasonic cleaning device manufacturers' written instructions should be followed regarding "degassing" the cleaning solution before processing instruments.

Degassing conditions the solution by removing some air to improve cavitation and soil removal.

X.c.5. Only instruments made of similar metals should be combined in the ultrasonic cleaner unless specified otherwise in the instrument manufacturer's written instructions.[15]

Placing only instruments made of similar metals in the ultrasonic cleaner will prevent instrument etching and pitting from occurring because of the transfer of ions from one instrument surface to another.

X.c.6. Some instruments should not be placed in an ultrasonic cleaner; these include
- chrome-plated instruments;
- power instruments;
- rubber, silicone, or plastic instruments; and
- endoscopic lenses.

The mechanical vibrations of the ultrasonic cleaner can cause chrome plating to flake.[15]

Power instruments can be damaged by fluid contacting internal parts. Rubber materials, plastics, and endoscopic lenses can be damaged by the vibration.[6]

X.c.7. Instruments with lumens should be fully submerged and filled with cleaning solution to remove air from within the channel.

The presence of air prevents the solution from contacting the inner lumen of instruments and affects the cavitation process.[5]

X.c.8. Instruments should be thoroughly rinsed after ultrasonic cleaning.[5]

X.c.9. A lid should be in place when the ultrasonic cleaner is in use.

The presence of the lid prevents aerosolization of contaminants.[5]

X.c.10. Cleaning solution should be checked between cycles and changed if visibly soiled.

The presence of gross soil in the water impedes the effectiveness of cavitation on the instruments surface.[5]

X.c.11. Ultrasonic cleaners should be emptied, cleaned, rinsed with sterile water, and the chamber wiped with alcohol or other disinfectant, as recommended by the equipment manufacturer, when visibly soiled and at least daily.

The fluid in the ultrasonic cleaner can harbor gram-negative bacteria. Growth of these bacteria results in the production of endotoxins, which are heat-resistant, can survive steam sterilization, and can have serious patient consequences. Endotoxins from contaminated eye instruments have been shown to cause toxic anterior segment syndrome (TASS), an acute inflammation of the anterior segment of the eye.[16] Alcohol disinfects the ultrasonic cleaner and prevents microbial growth.

X.c.12. Automated washer decontaminators or disinfectors and washer sterilizers should be used according to the manufacturer's written instructions.

Washer decontaminator cycles are intended to process instruments and equipment to a level that renders them safe to handle by persons who will inspect and prepare them for terminal sterilization. This type of decontamination equipment can use a single chamber for rinsing, cleaning, and drying or can use multiple chambers and is usually referred to as a *tunnel washer* (ie, one chamber for each phase of the cycle). These phases can include

- an initial cool-water rinse to remove protein debris,
- an enzymatic rinse,
- a detergent wash,
- an ultrasonic cleaning,
- a sustained hot-water rinse,
- a deionized water final rinse,
- a lubrication rinse,

- a liquid chemical germicide rinse, and
- a drying cycle.[15]

The sequencing and number of stages can vary among manufacturers.

Washer decontaminators or disinfectors can accomplish the microbicidal part of the process by thermal or chemical means, once the items have been thoroughly cleaned and rinsed.

The washer sterilizer first cleans instruments through several phases of a cycle that can include a cold water pre-rinse, a high-temperature wash with final rinse, and then sterilization. This process can be accomplished in a small or large chamber.

X.c.13. The instrument manufacturer's instructions should be used to determine the amount of time necessary to efficiently clean and rinse the instruments.

X.c.14. The operator should ensure that the proper cycle is being used.

Many mechanical washers have pre-programmed cycles, and the wash and rinse phases of the cycles are often adjustable. The manufacturer of the mechanical washer should be consulted to determine

- what level of decontamination is achieved with the washer decontaminator (ie, low-level, intermediate-, high level- disinfection); and
- how the user can verify that a cycle was sufficient to render the processed items safe to handle.

Recommendation XI

Surgical instruments should be inspected for cleanliness and proper working order after decontamination. (PNDS: I70, I98, I138)

Inspecting instruments for sterilization before assembly of trays provides an opportunity to identify those instruments that require additional cleaning or repair before use.

XI.a. Instruments should be inspected for
- cleanliness;
- alignment;

- corrosion, pitting, burrs, nicks, and cracks;
- sharpness of cutting edges;
- loose set pins;
- wear and chipping of inserts and plated surfaces;
- missing parts;
- any other defects;
- removal of moisture; and
- proper functioning. (PNDS: I70, I98)

Instruments can become damaged during use or decontamination. Sterilization may not occur in the presence of soil or water.

XI.b.   Instruments should be thoroughly dried. (PNDS: I70, I98)

Elimination of moisture helps prevent rust formation during instrument storage. The presence of moisture can impede the sterilization process.

Moisture on instrument surfaces alters the moisture content of steam and can pose a challenge for effective heating of the instrument.

Ethylene oxide (EO) combines with water and creates ethylene glycol (ie, antifreeze), which is toxic and is not removed during aeration.

Excess moisture inhibits the hydrogen peroxide plasma sterilization process and can result in an aborted cycle.[2]

XI.c.   The instrument manufacturer's written instructions should be followed for selection and appropriate use of lubricants. (PNDS: I122)

Lubricants decrease friction between working surfaces. Some instruments do not require lubrication. Cleaning, particularly ultrasonic cleaning, removes lubricants from instruments.

XI.c.1.   Instruments should be clean before lubricant is applied.

Applying lubricants to soiled instruments can compound the problem of stiff joints and inhibit smooth movement.

XI.c.2.   Lubricants should be compatible with the method of sterilization to be used.

Water soluble lubricants allow steam penetration during sterilization; oil-based products, however, cannot be penetrated and prevent the sterilant from contacting the instrument's surface.

XI.d.   Instruments in disrepair should be tagged or labeled and removed from service until repaired. (PNDS: I70, I77, I138)

Identification of defective instruments facilitates segregation of these instruments from those to be used when assembling sets and prevents defective instruments from being used on patients.

XI.e.   Instruments to be sterilized should be packaged according to AORN's "Recommended practices for selection and use of packaging systems for sterilization."[17] (PNDS: I70, I98)

XI.f.   The AORN "Recommended practices for sterilization in the perioperative practice setting"[2] should be referred to for recommendations regarding instrument sterilization.(PNDS: I70, I98)

Recommendation XII

Cleaned surgical instruments should be organized for packaging in a manner to allow the sterilant to contact all exposed surfaces. (PNDS: I70)

Proper organization will facilitate sterilant contact on all surfaces and adequate drying.

XII.a.   Instruments should be placed in a container tray or basket that is large enough to evenly distribute the metal mass in a single layer. (PNDS: I70)

Instruments should be contained within the tray or basket in a manner that protects the instruments from damage and prevents puncturing of the sterilization wraps. Overloading trays can cause wet packs because an increase in metal mass in the tray results in more condensate, which requires additional drying at the end of the cycle.

XII.b.   Broad-surfaced instruments and those with concave surfaces (eg, malleable retractors, hip skids) should be placed on edge. (PNDS: I70)

Instruments placed on edge facilitate drying because in this position, steam condensate will drain off the instrument rather than pool on it.

XII.c.   Instruments with hinges should be opened and those with removable parts should be disassembled when placed in trays designed for sterilization, unless the manufacturer has provided validated instructions to the contrary. (PNDS: I70)

Sterilization occurs only on surfaces that have direct contact with the sterilant. Disassembly of multiple-part instruments and those with sliding parts (eg, retractors) enables the sterilant to contact all surfaces.

XII.c.1.   Instruments should be kept in the open and unlocked position using instrument stringers, racks, or instrument pegs designed to contain instruments.

XII.d.   Delicate and sharp instruments should be protected using a device such as a tip protector. The tip protector should be used according to the manufacturer's instructions. (PNDS: I70)

Damage to delicate and sharp instruments can render them ineffective.

XII.d.1.   Tip protectors should be
- used for sharp or delicate instruments,
- validated for use with the chosen method of sterilization,
- used according to manufacturers' instructions, and
- loose-fitting so that the sterilant can contact the surface to be sterilized.

XII.d.2.   Heavy instruments should be positioned on the bottom of trays.

Positioning heavy instruments on the bottom of trays helps prevent damage to delicate items that may be present.

XII.e.   Only validated containment devices should be used to organize or segregate instruments within sets. (PNDS: I70)

Many devices used to organize or segregate instruments within sets have not been validated as safe and effective by container or wrap/pouch manufacturers. The presence of these devices inside of a packaged instrument set can prohibit
- air removal,
- sterilant contact with instruments in close proximity to the containment device,
- sterilant evacuation, and
- condensate drainage and drying.

XII.e.1.   Rubber bands should not be used to keep several instruments together.

Sterilant cannot contact surfaces beneath rubber bands and instruments may not be sterilized.

XII.e.2.   Paper-plastic peel pouches should not be used to organize or segregate instruments within sets unless their use is validated by the containment device manufacturer.

XII.e.3.   Small accessory baskets or boxes with lids or covers to contain instruments, parts, or accessories should not be incorporated into sets unless their use is validated by the containment device manufacturer.

XII.e.4.   Nonabsorbent, nonwoven disposable wrap material (eg, polyolefin spunbound) should not be used as a tray liner or to organize or segregate a small group of instruments to be placed into the instrument set.

This type of material is not intended for use within an instrument set that is to be steam-sterilized because it does not absorb moisture. Moisture can pool on this material, causing a wet pack.

XII.f.   Suction lumens and other devices with similar channels should be flushed with distilled, demineralized, or sterile water before steam sterilization.[5] (PNDS: I70)

When the moisture within the lumen is heated it will produce steam, which moves air out of the lumen resulting in lumen sterilization. The steam in the compartment does not move into the lumen because the lumen acts as a diffusion restrictor. Tap water might contain pyrogens.

XII.g.   Stylets should be removed from lumens.

Removal of stylets enables sterilant contact with the inside of lumens.

XII.h.   The instrument tray or basket should be lined with an absorbent, lint-free surgical towel if indicated.

The towel will absorb and disperse moisture to assist in drying the set.[5]

XII.i.   Nonabsorbent plastic or silicone fingered mats should be used according to the mat manufacturer's validated instructions for the various sterilization cycles in which they will be used. (PNDS: I122)

Improper use of nonabsorbent plastic or silicone mats may cause condensate to pool and inhibit drying.

XII.j. Information provided by the container manufacturer describing how instruments should be placed within the container or tray should be followed for each sterilization method used. (PNDS: I70, I122)

Recommendation XIII

Powered surgical instruments and all attachments should be decontaminated, lubricated, assembled, sterilized, and tested before use according to the manufacturer's written instructions. (PNDS: I122, I138)

Proper care and handling of powered surgical instruments minimizes the risk of injury to patients and personnel. Manufacturers' instructions are validated for specific instruments only and are not transferable to other devices because the design of powered surgical instruments and equipment varies.

XIII.a. Powered equipment and attachments should be cleaned and maintained according to manufacturers' written instructions. (PNDS: I70, I122)

Improper care and cleaning of powered equipment lead to patient and personnel exposure to pathogens and potential injury.

XIII.b. Attachments should be properly affixed to the units and tested before use. (PNDS: I77, I138)

Improperly seated attachments can be ejected from the equipment with great force and cause injury to patients and personnel. Testing the equipment or device before use can decrease the risk of injury.

XIII.b.1. Trigger handles should be placed in the safety position when changing attachments.

Accidental activation of powered equipment can cause injury.

XIII.c. Medical-grade compressed air or compressed dry nitrogen (ie, 99% pure) should be used to operate air-powered equipment according to the manufacturer's written instructions.

Use of contaminated gases to run powered equipment can result in equipment damage and injury to patients or personnel.

XIII.d. Manufacturers' written instructions should be used to determine the correct pressure settings required to operate equipment. The setting should be measured with the equipment operating. (PNDS: I77, I122)

Using excessive pressure can damage equipment and exert great stress on air hoses. Unless pressure is set with the equipment operating, incorrect pressures can result. Pneumatic equipment may not perform in the designated manner, if the pressure is set above or below recommended limits.

XIII.d.1. When an extension hose is used, the manufacturer should be consulted for appropriate pressure setting.

Pressure at the hand piece decreases when an extension hose is used.

XIII.e. Only grounded outlets should be used for electrical powered equipment.

XIII.f. Powered equipment should be cleaned and decontaminated thoroughly after use, following manufacturers' written, validated cleaning instructions. (PNDS: I98, I122)

Organic debris left on powered equipment hinders the sterilization process and can interfere with proper functioning. Powered instruments contain complex lumens, movable parts, and intricate internal components and may not be immersible in cleaning solutions. Permanent damage can result if fluid enters the internal mechanisms of powered equipment. Special attention is required to ensure that blood and contaminated tissue are adequately removed from the instrument before sterilization. Following manufacturers' instructions reduces the possibility of damaging or inadequately cleaning the instrument.

XIII.f.1. Blades and drill bits should be removed from powered equipment in the OR by the scrub person after the procedure has ended.

XIII.f.2. Instrument manufacturers' written recommendations for detergent or germicide use should be followed.

Abrasive detergents can damage protective surfaces, contribute to corrosion, and impede sterilization.

XIII.f.3. Powered equipment should not be immersed or placed under running water, in ultrasonic cleaners, washer disinfectors, or washer sterilizers, unless indicated in the equipment manufacturers' instructions.

XIII.f.4. When pneumatic hand pieces are cleaned, air hoses should be attached.

Attaching the air hose to the pneumatic hand piece during cleaning facilitates keeping the internal parts of the hand piece dry.

XIII.f.5. All traces of detergent or germicide and excess fluids should be wiped from the equipment and attachments.

XIII.f.6. The outer surfaces of the powered equipment and attachments should be dried with lint-free towels.

XIII.f.7. Powered equipment, batteries, attachments, and power cords should be inspected for damage or wear after decontamination and before use.

XIII.g. Air hoses should not be immersed or placed in ultrasonic cleaners, washer disinfectors, or washer sterilizers, unless indicated in the air hose manufacturer's instructions. (PNDS: I122)

Ultrasonic cleaners, washer sterilizers, and washer decontaminators force fluids into internal parts. Fluid in air hoses is not evacuated during these cycles, possibly leading to evacuation of this contaminated fluid during the surgical procedure.

XIII.g.1. Air hoses should be inspected for damage or wear before and after decontamination and before use.

XIII.g.2. Air hoses should be wiped with a clean, damp cloth using detergent or germicidal solution.

XIII.g.3. All traces of detergent or germicide and excess fluids should be wiped from the surface of the air hose.

XIII.h. Powered equipment and attachments should be lubricated with a product specifically recommended by the manufacturer and applied according to manufacturers' instructions. (PNDS: I122)

Lubricants decrease friction between working surfaces, which is essential for optimal functioning of the instrument and helps to prolong equipment life. Some instruments are sealed and do not require lubrication. Manufacturers may recommend oil-based or non-oil based lubricant for powered equipment.

XIII.i. Manufacturers' written instructions for packaging powered equipment and attachments should be followed. Packaging instructions should include methods to
– disassemble powered equipment before sterilization,
– protect delicate parts of the equipment, and
– loosely coil air hoses when packaged for sterilization. (PNDS: I70, I122)

Manufacturers' validated sterilization parameters should be followed for powered equipment, batteries, and attachments.

Recommendation XIV

Special precautions should be taken for reprocessing ophthalmic surgical instruments.[18] (PNDS: I70, I98)

Toxic anterior segment syndrome (TASS) can result from contaminants introduced into the eye during ophthalmic surgery.[16,19,20,21] An incidence of TASS can cause serious damage to a patient's intraocular tissue and result in vision loss.[16] More than 300 cases of TASS associated with balanced salt solution contaminated with endotoxins were reported to the US Food and Drug Administration (FDA), leading to the contaminated product being recalled by the FDA.[22] Other potential etiologies of TASS include

♦ antiseptics,[23,24]
♦ antibiotic ointment,[19]
♦ medications,[25] and
♦ powder from surgical gloves.[26,27]

Most cases of TASS appear to result from inadequate instrument cleaning and sterilization.[16] Other reported TASS cases were associated with gluteraldehyde and detergent residue on instruments,[28,29] endotoxins from gram-negative bacteria in ultrasonic

RP: Care of Instruments

cleaners,[30,31] impurities in steam from improperly maintained sterilizers,[20] and degradation of brass surgical instruments sterilized by hydrogen peroxide gas plasma.[32] Prevention of TASS requires thorough cleaning and rinsing of surgical instruments.[18]

XIV.a. Instruments should be wiped clean with sterile water and a lint-free sponge during the surgical procedure. (PNDS: I70, I75, I98)

Viscoelastic solution can harden on instruments within minutes.

XIV.b. Instruments should be immersed in sterile water immediately at the end of the procedure. (PNDS: I70, I98)

Biofilm adheres to the surfaces of instruments and is very difficult to remove. Keeping the organic material moist prevents the formation of biofilm.

XIV.c. Single-use cannulae should be used whenever possible. If reusable cannulae are used, the lumens should be flushed with sterile water immediately at the end of the procedure. (PNDS: I70, I75, I98)

Lumens are difficult to clean and can harbor contaminants.

XIV.d. Manufacturers' written instructions for cleaning each instrument should be reviewed and followed. (PNDS: I122)

The method of cleaning and the compatibilities of cleaning agents are unique to each instrument. Instructions for cannulated instruments indicate the type and volume of solution to be used for rinsing and cleaning, the frequency of flushing, and the number of times the cannula should be flushed.

XIV.e. The irrigation and aspiration ports of phacoemulsification hand pieces, tips, and tubing should be flushed before disconnecting the handpiece from the unit. (PNDS: I70, I98)

Several centers have reported occluded tips as a potential cause of TASS.[16] Flushing the hand piece prevents build-up of material inside the hand piece, which is difficult to remove during cleaning.

XIV.f. Intraocular lens injectors/inserters should be carefully cleaned. (PNDS: I70, I98)

Residue in the injector can be inserted into the eye chamber and cause TASS.[16]

XIV.g. Single-use items must be used only once and discarded or reprocessed using validated methods in accordance with FDA regulations.[33]

XIV.h. Detergents and enzymatic detergents should be used and diluted according to cleaning agent manufacturers' written instructions. (PNDS: I70, I75, I122)

Some cleaning agent manufacturers' instructions require the use of deionized or distilled water for diluting the detergent.

XIV.i. Enzymatic detergents should be used only if recommended by the surgical instrument manufacturer. (PNDS: I75, I122)

Following instrument manufacturers' instructions assures compatibility of the detergent with the instrument.

XIV.j. After cleaning or decontamination, instruments should be thoroughly rinsed with distilled or deionized sterile water and dried. (PNDS: I70, I75)

Residual enzymes and detergents not rinsed from the instruments can cause TASS.[16,18]

XIV.k. After cleaning, lumens should be thoroughly flushed with sterile water (expelling the liquid into a drain not the rinse water) and dried with filtered, oil-free compressed air. (PNDS: I70, I75)

Sterile water removes detergent residue. Expelling the lumen rinse into a drain prevents recontamination of the instrument with lumen contents. Compressed air forced through the lumen eliminates moisture that can serve as a medium for microbial growth.

XIV.l. Syringes and brushes used to clean ophthalmic instruments and cleaning solutions should be discarded after each use (if designed for single use) or sterilized following all recommended precautions.

Cleaning tools can harbor contaminants that can be reintroduced during cleaning of the next instrument.

XIV.m. After manual or ultrasonic cleaning, instruments should be wiped with alcohol before preparation for sterilization.

Wiping with alcohol disinfects the instruments and renders them safe to handle.

XIV.n. After cleaning and disinfection, instruments contacting viscoelastic material should be inspected for residue under magnification.

Viscoelastic material is difficult to remove during cleaning, and inspection with magnification can enhance detection of residual material.

XIV.o. Records should be maintained of all cleaning methods, detergent solutions used, and lot numbers of cleaning solutions.

These records can be used to facilitate investigation of any suspected or confirmed cases of TASS.

XIV.p. An adequate inventory of instruments should be provided to allow for thorough instrument cleaning and sterilization.

An adequate inventory of instruments facilitates compliance with proper decontamination and sterilization processes.

XIV.q. Adequate time should be provided for thorough instrument cleaning and sterilization.

Time constraints may create a disincentive for personnel to adhere to decontamination procedures and may result in non-compliance.

Recommendation XV

Insulated electrosurgery instruments should be decontaminated after use according to manufacturers' validated, written instructions and inspected for damage. (PNDS: I70, I98, I122)

Breaks in the insulation of electrosurgery instruments can occur during use and handling. These insulation failures can result in current leakage and subsequent burns. Inspection of the instruments provides a screening mechanism to identify visible insulation breaks.[34] Additional information about electrosurgery can be found in AORN's "Recommended practices for electrosurgery."[9]

XV.a. Insulated electrosurgical instruments should be inspected for small breaks in the insulation before initial use. (PNDS: I72)

Breaks in insulation can occur during manufacturing and transportation.

XV.b. Insulated instruments should be handled in a manner to prevent sharp instruments from contacting the insulation, and they should be segregated from sharp objects during use, transport, and decontamination.

Sharp objects and rough handling can damage the insulation during use, transport, and decontamination.

XV.c. Electrosurgical instruments should be decontaminated according to manufacturers' written instructions using care to avoid damaging the insulation on the device. (PNDS: I72, I122) Abrasive cleaning may damage insulation.

XV.d. The insulation on electrosurgical instruments should be inspected for impairment using a magnifying lens after decontamination. (PNDS: I72)

Visual inspection identifies obvious breaks in insulation, but will not identify all insulation failures. Using a magnifying lens can assist with identifying small imperfections.[34]

XV.e. Technology should be used to conduct stray current leakage tests at the end of each decontamination cycle.

Current can leak through insulation, even when breaks are not clearly visible. Performing a visual inspection and performing any recommended technological evaluation before preparation for sterilization minimizes the risk of using defective instruments that could lead to patient injury. Detecting insulation failures well in advance of a surgical procedure provides time for equipment replacement.

XV.f. Equipment found to have insulation damage should be immediately removed from service and repaired or replaced.

Instruments with impaired insulation are unsafe for use.

XV.g. Manufacturers' written recommendations limiting the use of insulated instruments to a specific time frame or number of reprocessings should be followed. (PNDS: I122)

Manufacturers validate the life span of the equipment insulation, and use after that period of time can result in injury to the patient. If injury occurs in this situation, the health care organization may have to assume the liability.

Recommendation XVI

Special precautions should be taken when cleaning robotic instruments.(PNDS: I70)

Robotic instruments and equipment have lumens with complex, difficult to clean internal and external components that require special attention to adequately decontaminate the instruments.

XVI.a. Gross soil should be removed from the external surfaces using a soft-bristled brush. (PNDS: I70, I98)

Robotic "wrists" and electrosurgical tips can become soiled during use.

XVI.b. The ports of robotic instruments and equipment should be flushed
- with a water line,
- in the sequence and for the duration identified by the manufacturer's written instructions,
- while moving the robotic wrist through a full range of motion, and
- until the fluid exiting the ports is clear.

Moving the robotic wrist through a full range of motion exposes all of its surfaces to the cleaning solution.

XVI.b.1. The fluid expelled from the ports during flushing should be directed into a drain and not allowed to run into the receptacle of clean solution.

XVI.c. Ports should be primed with clean enzymatic cleaner and the device cleaned in an ultrasonic cleaner according the manufacturer's written instructions. (PNDS: I70, I122)

Ultrasonic cleaning facilitates removal of debris that has adhered to components.

XVI.c.1. After ultrasonic cleaning, ports should be flushed
- with deionized water, under pressure; and
- in the sequence and for the duration identified by the manufacturer's written instructions.

Flushing of ports removes residual cleaning solution.

XVI.d. Ports should be cleared with compressed air in the sequence and duration identified by the manufacturer's written instructions. (PNDS: I70, I98, I122)

Clearing lumens and internal components with compressed air removes residual water that can serve as a medium for microbial growth.

XVI.e. Movable parts of the robotic instruments and equipment should be lubricated according to the manufacturer's written instructions. (PNDS: I122)

Lubrication facilitates the functioning of the hinges and joints of robotic instruments and equipment which coordinate fine dissection and manipulation of tissue.

XVI.f. The outside of the instruments should be wiped with alcohol or an instrument disinfectant, before preparation for steam sterilization. (PNDS: I70, I98)

Wiping with alcohol or another disinfectant renders the instrument safe to handle.

Recommendation XVII

Special precautions should be taken to minimize the risk of transmission of prion diseases. (PNDS: I98, I145)

Prions are a unique classification of infectious agents with a genetic component that are thought to be transmitted through direct inoculation, rather than the traditional routes (ie, bloodborne, skin contact, droplet, airborne). The resulting human prion diseases (ie, Creutzfeldt-Jakob disease [CJD], variant CJD, fatal familial insomnia, Gertsmann-Straussler syndrome) are fatal, degenerative neurological disorders.[35]

Prions have been transmitted experimentally through direct inoculation (eg, oral ingestion, inoculation of scratched skin, injection, implantation) and have been transmitted iatrogenically through transplanted contaminated tissue (eg, cornea, dura mater) and injections of human pituitary hormones (eg, growth hormone, gonadotropin).[36] Six cases of transmission via neurosurgical instruments occurred before 1980 in Europe.[36] No other cases have been reported resulting from transmission via instruments in other types of surgery or since that time.

Prions are resistant to chemical disinfection (eg, alcohol, gluteraldehyde) and routine sterilization (ie, steam, ethylene oxide, gas plasma, peracetic acid).[37] These agents remain infective for years, and special precautions are required to eliminate their infectivity.[38]

XVII.a. An interdisciplinary team should develop processes to minimize the risk of prion disease transmission. These processes should be based upon the probability or possibility of
  – a patient having a prion disease,
  – the level of infectivity of the tissue involved, and
  – the characteristics of the surgical instruments involved. (PNDS: I98, I145)

Use of a defined protocol helps protect patients and health care workers from pathogen transmission. Including personnel with different types of expertise (eg, anesthesia providers, central sterilizing employees, housekeeping personnel, infection control team members, neurosurgeons, perioperative services personnel) in the protocol development maximizes the likelihood of developing effective strategies and enhances compliance with the procedures that are developed.

Diagnostic criteria for CJD have been developed by the World Health Organization (WHO). Diagnosis can be confirmed, but cannot be ruled out, by brain biopsy.[35] Prion diseases can be genetically acquired or acquired through contact with infectious material; however, all prion diseases are infectious regardless of mode of acquisition.

Patients at high risk of having or developing prion diseases include
  – patients with rapidly progressive dementia consistent with CJD in whom a diagnosis has not been confirmed or ruled out;
  – members of families in which prion disease has occurred (eg, two or more family members with a confirmed diagnosis); and
  – recipients of cadaveric dura mater grafts or human pituitary gland hormones (eg, growth hormone, gonadotropin).

Cadaveric dura mater has been replaced with fascia grafts, and synthetic pituitary hormones have replaced those derived from human pituitary glands to reduce the risk of prion transmission.[36]

While all prion diseases are infectious, infectivity is based primarily on laboratory studies of different prion diseases in humans and animals.[36,39] Central nervous system tissue (eg, brain, spinal cord, dura mater, pituitary) has been shown to be highly infectious as has tissue from the posterior eye (eg, optic nerve, retina). Other tissues and fluids that have shown to have a lower level of infectivity include
  – corneal tissue;
  – lymphoid tissue, the spleen, thymus, appendix, tonsils, and lymph nodes;
  – the kidneys, liver, lungs, and placenta;
  – skeletal muscle;
  – olfactory cilia and pathways;
  – cerebral spinal fluid; and
  – blood.

Other areas of the body demonstrate no infectivity, such as
  – the heart muscle, intestine, peripheral nerves, prostate, testis, thyroid;
  – adipose tissue, bone marrow, skin; and
  – feces, milk, nasal mucus, saliva, semen, serous fluid, sweat, tears, urine, and vaginal secretions.

XVII.a.1. Considerations regarding instruments used on patients suspected of having prion disease should include, but not be limited to,
  • the use of single-use versus reusable instruments if possible;
  • the ability of the instrument to tolerate heat;
  • the complexity of cleaning required (eg, lumens); and
  • the intended use of the instrument (eg, in internal tissues).

XVII.b. Patients should be screened for the risk of prion disease and any information discovered should be conveyed to the OR during scheduling of the surgical procedure. (PNDS: I98, I145)

Screening patients provides a mechanism to identify which patients are at high risk of having a prion disease. Conveying this information during scheduling provides adequate time to plan instrument use and decontamination and to discuss alternatives to the use of complex instruments and implant sets requiring reprocessing.

XVII.c. When treating patients at high risk for a prion diseases, instruments used on highly infective tissue should be minimized, limited to those that are easily cleaned, and replaced with single-use devices, when possible. (PNDS: I98, I145)

Minimizing the number of instruments limits the number of items that need to be decontaminated and reduces the risk of an error that can result in exposure of subsequent patients or personnel.

XVII.c.1. Single-use brain biopsy sets should be used. Creutzfeld-Jacob disease is often definitively diagnosed by brain biopsy. Single-use brain biopsy sets are commercially available or can be assembled using older instruments.

XVII.c.2. Instruments with lumens (eg, suction tips, needles) should be single use when possible.

Lumens are difficult to effectively decontaminate.

XVII.c.3. Flexible neuroendoscopes should be replaced with rigid alternatives.

Flexible endoscopes are difficult to clean and will be damaged during the cleaning and sterilization methods known to deactivate prions infectivity.

XVII.c.4. Power drills should not be used.

Power drills may splatter potentially infective material and are difficult to clean, and the cleaning and sterilization methods known to eliminate prion infectivity damage these instruments.

XVII.c.5. Surgical drapes, gowns, and single-use supplies should be used whenever possible and incinerated after use.

Drapes and gowns are in contact with highly infectious tissue during these procedures. Routine hospital laundry does not deactivate prions.

XVII.c.6. Work surfaces should be covered with disposable, impervious material that can be removed and incinerated after the procedure.

Minimizing contamination of the room minimizes the need for special precautions during environmental cleaning.

XVII.c.7. Trays of implants (eg, burr hole covers, screws) should be limited to those implants essential for the specific patient. Implants opened and handled by scrubbed personnel after the surgery has started should be discarded and not reprocessed for subsequent patient use.

The determination of the need for and size of implant rests with the surgeon. Collaboration between the perioperative nurse and surgeon can result in elimination of implants that the surgeon determines are nonessential. If implants normally delivered to the sterile field in sets (eg, plates and screws) are required, removing implants that are not needed for the patient before sterilizing the tray decreases the amount of implant inventory needing to be discarded.

XVII.d. Single-use instruments that have come in contact with tissue considered to be highly infective from patients at high risk for a prion disease should be incinerated.

XVII.e. Work surfaces contaminated with prions should be cleaned with sodium hydroxide (NaOH) or sodium hypochlorite (ie, bleach).[40]

No transmissions of prion diseases from environmental surfaces have been reported; however, it remains prudent to eliminate highly infectious material from operating room surfaces that patients and personnel will be in contact with during subsequent surgeries.

For more information on cleaning of contaminated work surfaces consult AORN's "Recommended practice for environmental cleaning in the surgical practice setting."[41]

XVII.f. Reusable instruments that have come in contact with highly infective tissue of patients at high risk for a prion disease should be treated to reduce infectivity using the following steps listed below. (PNDS: I70)

When a potentially contaminated device can be cleaned and prion or tissue load decreased or physically removed, the probability of infection transmission is reduced significantly. There is currently no consensus on the best method of managing instruments that are likely contaminated with prions. Peracetic acid is ineffective and hydrogen peroxide gas plasma alone is only partially effective against prions.[42]

XVII.f.1. Instruments that cannot be adequately cleaned or require low-temperature sterilization (ie, ethylene oxide, hydrogen peroxide gas plasma) should be discarded.

XVII.f.2. Instruments should be kept moist until they are cleaned and decontaminated.

Drying renders prions more resistant to steam sterilization. Keeping instruments moist and cleaning them immediately after use minimizes drying.

XVII.f.3. Personnel should wear impervious gowns, heavy-duty gloves, and face shields while decontaminating instruments.

XVII.f.4. Instruments should be cleaned with an instrument cleaner as soon as possible after use.

Instrument cleaners reduce the amount of contamination and challenge to subsequent sterilization.[43] If allowed to dry, prion-contaminated material adheres to the surface of instruments, which can make subsequent terminal sterilization ineffective.[44]

XVII.f.5. After thorough cleaning, one of the following methods should be used to steam sterilize the instruments.

- Eighteen minutes in a prevacuum sterilizer with a cycle temperature of 134° C (272° F).
- Sixty minutes in a gravity-displacement sterilizer with a cycle temperature of 132° C (272° F).
- Immersion of instruments in 1N sodium hydroxide (NaOH) (ie, 1 Normal or 1 Molar concentration of NaOH) for one hour, followed by removal and a water rinse, followed by a steam sterilization cycle as noted above.

The WHO has recommended instruments exposed to prions be immersed in 1N sodium hydroxide for one hour followed by steam sterilization of the immersed instruments in the container at 121° C (250° F) for 30 minutes. Sterilizing instruments in a bath of sodium hydroxide creates dangerous vapors that can injure the airway and eyes of health care workers and can cause burns.[45] This practice also damages sterilizers, invalidates the sterilizer warranty, and corrodes some surgical instruments.[46,47] Using a polypropylene containment pan with a lid when sterilizing the instruments in the 1N sodium hydroxide bath has been found to contain the vapors within the pan.[45]

XVII.f.6. After initial cleaning, instruments should be processed in a washer decontaminator and sterilized in the usual fashion.

XVII.f.7. Solidify and incinerate any liquids used for cleaning.

XVII.g. Devices that have been contaminated with medium-, low-, or no-infectivity tissue can be cleaned and disinfected or sterilized using conventional protocols of heat, chemical sterilization, or high-level disinfection.

When a device is contaminated with tissue or body fluids that are not deemed to be of high-infectivity and the device can be cleaned effectively, the probability of infection transmission appears to be so low that it would not be measurable. During surgery on patients at high risk for prion disease, most surfaces in the operating room are not contaminated with highly infectious material and routine cleaning will limit contamination to what is considered a safe level.[40]

XVII.h. If a patient is identified postoperatively as having had a prion disease at the time of surgery, special precautions should be taken. Devices determined to be potentially contaminated with highly infectious tissue of this patient should be pulled from service and decontaminated as described above after the device has been reprocessed.

Prions can survive for years.[38] Inadequately decontaminated instruments pose a risk to subsequent patients who have had contact with the instruments.

XVII.i. Perioperative nurses should review current research on methods of detecting prion infectivity and decontamination methods.

Knowledge about detection of prion contamination on instruments and the effectiveness of various methods of deactivation is evolving as new research is published.

Recommendation XVIII

Personnel handling contaminated instruments and equipment must wear appropriate personal protective equipment (PPE)[10] and should be vaccinated against the hepatitis B virus.

Personal protective equipment helps to protect the employee from exposure to bloodborne pathogens and other potentially infectious materials.

XVIII.a. Personal protective equipment consistent with the anticipated exposure must be worn.[10,48]

Splashes, splatters, and skin contact can be reasonably anticipated when handling contaminated instruments.

XVIII.a.1. The appropriate PPE for these types of exposures include, but are not limited to,
- a fluid-resistant gown,
- heavy-duty gloves,
- a mask, and
- face protection.

XVIII.b. Hands must be washed after removing PPE.[10]

Perforations can occur in gloves, and hands can become contaminated when removing PPE. The OSHA requires hand washing after removal of PPE.[10]

XVIII.c. Reusable protective attire must be decontaminated and the integrity of the attire confirmed between uses.[10]

Reusable gloves, gowns, aprons, and face shields become contaminated and their integrity can be compromised during use. Decontamination and confirmation of integrity helps to protect the wearer from exposure.[48]

XVIII.d. Two pairs of gloves should be worn when cleaning instruments and equipment, if there is a risk for perforation of the outer glove.

XVIII.e. Personnel working with contaminated instruments should be vaccinated against hepatitis B virus.

Hepatitis B vaccination provides protection against one of the most common bloodborne pathogens. The OSHA requires the vaccination be offered to employees at risk of exposure at no charge.[10]

XVIII.f. Exposures to bloodborne pathogens should be reported immediately through the approved health care organization channels.

Antiviral medication is most effective if given as soon as possible after an exposure.

Recommendation XIX

Competency
Personnel should receive initial education and competency validation on procedures, chemicals used, and personal protection and should receive additional training when new equipment, instruments, supplies, or procedures are introduced.

Ongoing education and competency validation of perioperative personnel facilitates the development of knowledge, skills, and attitudes that affect patient and worker safety.

XIX.a. Personnel should receive initial education on
- decontamination methods;
- preparation of instruments and equipment for sterilization;
- selection of cleaning agents and methods;
- proper use of cleaning agents, including an understanding of specific applications, appropriate dilution, and special precautions;
- decontamination of specific instruments and equipment used within the practice setting;
- procedures for decontamination of instruments contaminated with prions and the effectiveness of various methods of deactivation;
- personal protection required during instrument processing; and
- exposure risk associated with chemical cleaning agents.[48]

Workers have the right to know the hazards that exist in the workplace and OSHA requires that employers provide this information.[48] An understanding of procedures involved in cleaning each type of instrument is necessary to provide the foundation for compliance with procedures.

XIX.b. Personnel should receive education on
- new instruments and equipment,
- new cleaning agents and methods, and
- new procedures.

XIX.c. Administrative personnel should validate the competencies of personnel participating in decontamination of surgical instruments. The validation of competencies should include all types of instruments that the individual is authorized to reprocess.

Validation of competencies provides an indication that personnel are able to appropriately perform decontamination procedures.

Recommendation XX

Documentation

Documentation should be completed to enable the identification of trends and demonstrate compliance with regulatory and accrediting agency requirements.

Documentation provides a source of data to review processes and evaluate corrective actions.

XX.a. Documentation should include maintaining records of the cleaning of instruments including, but not limited to,
- date,
- time,
- instruments,
- method of cleaning,
- number or identifier of mechanical decontaminator,
- name of person performing the cleaning,
- lot numbers of chemicals used,
- testing results on mechanical instrument washers,
- testing results on insulated electrical instruments, and
- disposition of defective equipment.

Most sterilization failures result from inadequate cleaning of the instruments before sterilization. Toxic anterior segment syndrome has been associated with inadequate cleaning processes. Some washer decontaminators have digital readouts or printers that facilitate recordkeeping. Bar code scanning technology also is available making this process more efficient. Records of washer testing provide a source of evidence for review when investigating clinical issues including surgical site infections.

XX.b. Records should be maintained for a time period specified by the health care organization and in compliance with local, state, and federal regulations.

Recommendation XXI

Policies and Procedures

Policies and procedures regarding the care and cleaning of surgical instruments and powered equipment should be developed using the validated instructions provided by the medical device manufacturers, reviewed at regular intervals, revised as necessary, and be readily available in the practice setting.

Policies and procedures serve as operational guidelines and establish authority, responsibility, and accountability within the organization. Policies and procedures also assist in the development of patient safety guidelines and quality assessment and improvement activities.

XXI.a. Policies regarding instrument cleaning should be developed by a multidisciplinary team to include perioperative nurses, sterile processing personnel, surgeons, and an infection control professional.

Using a multidisciplinary team provides varied input and improved ownership of policies and procedures. Involving surgeons in review of policies educates them on the expectations for instrument cleaning and facilitates planning for instrument use. The expertise of infection control professionals facilitates establishment of minimum standards of infection control.

XXI.b. Policies should include, but not be limited to,
- review of validated manufacturers' written instructions before purchase or consignment;
- cleaning of instruments before initial use;
- management of loaner instruments, to include advanced notification of vendors, required time frame for advance delivery, a

process for cleaning and sterilization before use, and a process for cleaning and return after use;
– precautions to be taken when handling contaminated items;
– precautions to be taken when handling chemical agents;
– reprocessing powered surgical equipment;
– reprocessing ophthalmic surgical instruments;
– reprocessing robotic instruments and equipment;
– frequency of mechanical washer checks;
– frequency and method of evaluation of manual cleaning;
– frequency of checking insulated electrosurgery instruments for leakage current;
– criteria for identification and precautions taken for instruments used on patients with known or suspected prion disease;
– documentation of cleaning;
– initial education and annual competency;
– maintenance of material safety data sheets;
– reporting exposures to bloodborne pathogens; and
– reporting adverse events.

Recommendation XXII

Quality
The health care organization's quality management program should evaluate the care of instruments to improve patient safety.

XXII.a. A quality management program should be in place to test mechanical cleaning equipment.
– Mechanical instrument washers should be tested for proper functioning before initial use, weekly during service, and after major maintenance.
– Manual cleaning should be evaluated when new types of instruments are reprocessed and periodically, at intervals determined by the health care organization.
– Insulated electrical instruments should be tested for leakage current before initial use and after decontamination. Testing after decontamination allows a defective device to be replaced before sterilization.

– Personnel should identify and respond to opportunities for improvement.
– Reporting mechanisms for adverse events and near misses related to instrument cleaning should be in place.

XXII.a.1. Adequate cleaning of surgical instruments is essential to remove or destroy microorganisms and eliminate endotoxins. Testing washer decontaminators on a regular basis verifies that the equipment is functioning properly or identifies an opportunity for corrective action. Washer testing products are commercially available.

XXII.a.2. Periodic testing provides an opportunity to evaluate the performance of personnel. Manual cleaning is a learned skill and subject to human error. New instruments can pose unique challenges when cleaning. Protein indicators are commercially available to assist with this evaluation.

XXII.a.3. Visual inspection of insulation on electrosurgery instruments provides a screening mechanism to identify obvious breaks. Electrical testing can identify very small insulation failures that may not be apparent visually. Doing this testing after decontamination provides an opportunity to take corrective action well in advance of the surgical procedure.

XXII.a.4. Adverse events should be reported in the adverse event reporting system and reviewed for potential opportunities for improvement. When investigating surgical infections, documentation of the cleaning process of instruments should be reviewed. Near misses should be investigated and corrective action taken to prevent serious adverse events.

Glossary

Biofilm: A thin coating containing biologically active organisms that have the ability to grow in water, water solutions, or in vivo and which coat the surface of structures (eg, teeth, inner surfaces of catheters, tubes, implanted or indwelling devices, instruments and other medical devices). Biofilms contain viable and nonviable microorganisms that adhere to the surface and are trapped within a matrix of organic matter (eg, proteins, glycoprotein's, carbohydrates), which prevents antimicrobial agents from reaching the cells.

Decontamination: Any physical or chemical process that removes or reduces the number of microorganisms or infectious agents and renders reusable medical products or equipment safe for handling or disposal; the process by which contaminants are removed, either by hand cleaning or mechanical means, using specific solutions capable of rendering blood and debris harmless and removing them from the surface of an object or instrument.

Endotoxin: A toxin produced by certain bacteria and released upon destruction of the bacterial cell.

Enzymatic cleaner: A cleaner that uses enzymes to remove protein from surgical instruments.

Eschar: Charred tissue residue.

Ethylene oxide: An alkylating agent that, under the right conditions of time, temperature, concentration, and humidity, can result in microbial death.

Free-rinsing: Ability to be removed without leaving residue.

Iatrogenic: A response to medical or surgical treatment, usually denoting an unfavorable response.

Normal: Denotes a solution containing 1 equivalent of replaceable hydrogen ion per liter or a solution containing 1 gram of a substance or its equivalent in hydrogen ions.

Personal protective equipment (PPE): Specialized equipment or clothing for eyes, face, head, body, and extremities; protective clothing; respiratory devices; and protective shields and barriers designed to protect the worker from injury or exposure to a patient's blood, tissue, or body fluids. Used by health care workers and others whenever necessary to protect themselves from the hazards of processes or environments, chemical hazards, or mechanical irritants encountered in a manner capable of causing injury or impairment in the function of any part of the body through absorption, inhalation, or physical contact.

Potable water: Water that is of sufficient quality to be considered appropriate for drinking.

Prion: A proteinaceous and infectious agent containing no DNA or RNA.

Robotic surgical instruments: A remote-controlled surgical instrument system, including scalpels,

scissors, forceps, and needle holders, used to perform minimally invasive surgery.

Toxic anterior segment syndrome (TASS): A complication of ophthalmic surgery involving a severe, noninfectious inflammation of the anterior segment of the eye, caused by various contaminants in solutions, medications, steam, and residue on surgical instruments and supplies.

Ultrasonic cleaner: A processing unit that transmits ultrasonic waves through the cleaning solution in a mechanical process known as cavitation. Ultrasonic cleaning is particularly effective in removing soil deposits from hard-to-reach areas.

Viscoelastic: A gel injected into the anterior chamber during ophthalmic surgery to maintain the depth of the chamber, protect the corneal endothelium, and stabilize the vitreous.

Washer/decontaminator: A processing unit that cleans by a spray-force action known as impingement. This machine combines a vigorous agitation bath with jet-stream air to create underwater turbulence. A sterilization cycle follows the washing cycle.

REFERENCES
1. Peterson C, ed. *Perioperative Nursing Data Set:* Rev 2nd ed. Denver, CO: AORN, Inc; 2007.
2. Recommended practices for sterilization in the perioperative practice setting. In: *Standards, Recommended Practices, and Guidelines.* Denver, CO: AORN, Inc; 2007:673-688.
3. Recommended practices for high-level disinfection. In: *Standards, Recommended Practices, and Guidelines.* Denver, CO: AORN, Inc; 2007:503-510.
4. Recommended practices for cleaning and processing endoscopes and endoscope accessories. In: *Standards, Recommended Practices, and Guidelines.* Denver, CO: AORN, Inc; 2007:531-536.
5. Association for the Advancement of Medical Instrumentation. *ANSI/AAMI ST79: 2006 Comprehensive Guide to Steam Sterilization and Sterility Assurance in Health Care Facilities.* Arlington, VA: Association for the Advancement of Medical Instrumentation, 2006.
6. Association for the Advancement of Medical Instrumentation. *ANSI/AAMI ST81: 2004 Sterilization of Medical Devices: Information to Be Provided by the Manufacturer for the Processing of Resterilizable Medical Devices.* Arlington, VA: Association for the Advancement of Medical Instrumentation; 2004.
7. American Society of Healthcare Central Service Professionals, International Association of Healthcare Central Service Materiel Management. ASHCSP/IAHCSMM position paper on loaner instrumentation. http://www.iahcsmm .org/current_issues_Joint_paper_loaner_instrumentation.htm. Accessed October 27, 2007.
8. Ignition of debris on active electrosurgical electrodes. *Health Devices.* 1998;27:367-370.

9. Recommended practices for electrosurgery. In: *Standards, Recommended Practices, and Guidelines.* Denver, CO: AORN, Inc; 2007:515-530.

10. Occupational Safety and Health Administration. Bloodborne pathogens. 29CFR 1910.1030. *http://www.osha.gov/pls/oshaweb/owadisp.show_document?p_table=STANDARDS&p_id=10051.* Accessed October 27, 2007.

11. Recommended practices for traffic patterns in the perioperative practice setting. In: *Standards, Recommended Practices, and Guidelines.* Denver, CO: AORN, Inc; 2007:703-706.

12. American Institute of Architects Academy of Architecture for Health. Facilities Guidelines Institute. *Guidelines for Design and Construction of Health Care Facilities.* Washington, DC: American Institute of Architects; 2006.

13. Occupational Safety and Health Administration. OSHA Act of 1970. *http://www.osha.gov/pls/oshaweb/owasrch.search_form?p_doc_type=OSHACT&p_toc_level=0&p_keyvalue=&p_status=CURRENT.* Accessed October 27, 2007.

14. Recommended practices for product selection in the perioperative practice setting. In: *Standards, Recommended Practices, and Guidelines.* Denver, CO: AORN, Inc; 2007:637-640.

15. American Society for Healthcare Central Service Professionals. *Training Manual for Health Care Central Service Technicians.* San Francisco, CA: Jossey-Bass ; Health Forum; 2006.

16. Mamalis N, Edelhauser HF, Dawson DG, Chew J, LeBoyer RM, Werner L. Toxic anterior segment syndrome. *Journal of Cataract & Refractive Surgery.* 2006;32:324-333.

17. AORN. Recommended practices for selection and use of packaging systems for sterilization. In: *Standards, Recommended Practices, and Guidelines.* Denver, CO: AORN, Inc; 2007:607-616.

18. American Society of Cataract and Refractive Surgery, American Society of Ophthalmic Registered Nurses. Recommended practices for cleaning and sterilizing intraocular surgical instruments. *J Cataract Refract Surg.* 2007;33:1095-1100.

19. Werner L, Sher JH, Taylor JR, et al. Toxic anterior segment syndrome and possible association with ointment in the anterior chamber following cataract surgery. *Journal of Cataract & Refractive Surgery.* 2006;32:227-235.

20. Hellinger WC, Hasan SA, Bacalis LP, et al. Outbreak of toxic anterior segment syndrome following cataract surgery associated with impurities in autoclave steam moisture. *Infection Control & Hospital Epidemiology.* 2006;27:294-298.

21. American Society of Cataract and Refractive Surgery. Final TASS Report. *http://www.ascrs.org/press_releases/Final-TASS-Report.cfm.* Accessed October 27, 2007.

22. US Food and Drug Administration. FDA-Requested Recall:Cytosol Laboratories, Inc. Product Contains Dangerous Levels of Endotoxin. *http://www.fda.gov/bbs/topics /news/2006/NEW01315.html.* Accessed October 27, 2007.

23. Mac Rae SM, Brown B, Edelhauser HF. The corneal toxicity of presurgical skin antiseptics. *Am J Ophthalmol.* 1984;97:221-232.

24. Phinney RB, Mondino BJ, Hofbauer JD, et al. Corneal edema related to accidental Hibiclens exposure. *Am J Ophthalmol.* 1988;106:210-215.

25. Anderson NJ, Nath R, Anderson CJ, Edelhauser HF. Comparison of preservative-free bupivacaine vs. lidocaine for intracameral anesthesia: a randomized clinical trial and *in vitro* analysis. *Am J Ophthalmol.* 1999;127:393-402.

26. Cox MJ, Woods JA, Newman S, Edlich RF. Toxic effects of surgical glove powders on the eye. *J Long Term Eff Med Implants.* 1996;6:219-226.

27. Bene C, Kranias G. Possible intraocular lens contamination by surgical glove powder. *Ophthalmic Surg.* 1986;17:290-291.

28. Unal M, Yucel I, Akar Y, Oner A, Altin M. Outbreak of toxic anterior segment syndrome associated with glutaraldehyde after cataract surgery. *Journal of Cataract & Refractive Surgery.* 2006;32:1696-1701.

29. Breebaart AC, Nuyts RM, Pels E, Edelhauser HF, Verbraak FD. Toxic endothelial cell destruction of the cornea after routine extracapsular cataract surgery. *Arch Ophthalmol.* 1990;108:1121-1125.

30. Kreisler KR, Martin SS, Young CW, Anderson CW, Mamalis N. Postoperative inflammation following cataract extraction caused by bacterial contamination of the cleaning bath detergent. *J Cataract Refract Surg.* 1992;18:106-110.

31. Richburg FA, Reidy JJ, Apple DJ, Olson RJ. Sterile hypopyon secondary to ultrasonic cleaning solution. *J Cataract Refract Surg.* 1986;12:248-251.

32. Duffy RE, Brown SE, Caldwell KL, et al. An epidemic of corneal destruction caused by plasma gas sterilization. the toxic cell destruction syndrome investigative team. *Arch Ophthalmol.* 2000;118:1167-1176.

33. US Food and Drug Administration. Medical devices; reprocessed single-use devices; requirement for submission of validation data. *Fed Reg.* 2006;71:55729-55737.

34. ECRI Institute. Safety technologies for laparoscopic monopolar electrosurgery: devices for managing burn risks. *Health Devices.* 2005;34:259-271.

35. Blattler T. Implications of prion diseases for neurosurgery. *Neurosurg Rev.* 2002;25:195-203.

36. Pana A, Jung M. Prion diseases and iatrogenic infections I. a review. *Ig Sanita Pubbl.* 2005;61:325-377.

37. Jung M, Pistolesi D, Pana A. Prion diseases and iatrogenic infections II. decontamination. *Ig Sanita Pubbl.* 2005;61:379-410.

38. Brown P. Survival of scrapie after 3 years' inteament. *Lancet* [- 8736]. 1991;337:269-270.

39. Peden AH, Ritchie DL, Head MW, Ironside JW. Detection and localization of PrPSc in the skeletal muscle of patients with variant, iatrogenic, and sporadic forms of Creutzfeldt-Jakob disease. *Am J Pathol.* 2006;168:927-935.

40. Rutala W.A, Weber DJ. Creutzfeldt-Jakob disease: Recommendations for disinfection and sterilization. *Clin Dis Inf.* 2001;32:1348-1356.

41. Recommended practices for environmental cleaning in the surgical practice setting. In: *Standards, Recommended Practices, and Guidelines.* Denver, CO: AORN, Inc; 2008:*475-482.*

42. Fichet G, Comoy E, Duval C, et al. Novel methods for disinfection of prion-contaminated medical devices. *Lancet.* 2004;364:521-526.

43. Yan ZX, Stitz L, Heeg P, Pfaff E, Roth K. Infectivity of prion protein bound to stainless steel wires: A model for testing decontamination procedures for transmissible spongiform encephalopathies. *Infect Control Hosp Epidemiol.* 2004;25:280-283.

44. Lipscomb IP, Pinchin H, Collin R, Keevil CW. Effect of drying time, ambient temperature and pre-soaks on prion-infected tissue contamination levels on surgical stainless steel: Concerns over prolonged transportation of instruments from theatre to central sterile service departments. *J Hosp Infect.* 2007;65:72-77.

45. Brown SA, Merritt K. Use of containment pans and lids for autoclaving caustic solutions. *Am J Infect Control.* 2003;31:257-260.

46. STERIS. Overview of current CJD decontamination and sterilization methods and possible effects on product warranty. Document M236OEN. *http://www.steris.com /search/search2.cfm#.* Accessed December 24, 2007.

47. Brown SA, Merritt K, Woods TO, Busick DN. Effects on instruments of the World Health Organization recommended protocols for decontamination after possible exposure to transmissible spongiform encephalopathy-contaminated tissue. *Journal of Biomedical Materials Research. Part B, Applied Biomaterials.* 2005;72:186-190.

48. Occupational Safety and Health Administration. Hazard Communication: OSHA Standards. *http://osha.gov /SLTC/hazardcommunications/standards.html.* Accessed October 27, 2007.

Originally published February 1988, *AORN Journal.* Revised March1992.

Revised November 1996; published January 1997, *AORN Journal.* Reformatted July 2000.

Revised November 2001; published March 2002, *AORN Journal.*

Revised 2007; published in *Perioperative Standards and Recommended Practices,* 2008 edition.

AORN Perioperative Standards and Recommended Practices, 2009 Edition

Recommended Practices for Selection and Use of Packaging Systems for Sterilization

The following recommended practices were developed by the AORN Recommended Practices Committee and have been approved by the AORN Board of Directors. They were presented as proposed recommended practices for comments by members and others. They are effective January 1, 2007.

These recommended practices are intended as achievable recommendations representing what is believed to be an optimal level of practice. Policies and procedures will reflect variations in practice settings and/or clinical situations that determine the degree to which the recommended practices can be implemented.

AORN recognizes the numerous settings in which perioperative nurses practice. These recommended practices are intended as guidelines adaptable to various practice settings. These practice settings include traditional operating rooms, ambulatory surgery centers, physicians' offices, cardiac catheterization suites, endoscopy suites, radiology departments, and all other areas where operative and other invasive procedures may be performed.

Purpose

These recommended practices provide guidelines for the evaluation, selection, and use of packaging systems for items to be sterilized. Packaging systems should ensure the integrity of the sterilized contents until opened for use and should permit aseptic delivery of the contents to the sterile field. These packaging systems include woven fabrics, nonwoven materials, paper-plastic pouches, plastic-plastic pouches, and containment devices (eg, rigid sterilization containers, instrument cases and cassettes, and organizing trays). These recommended practices do not include recommendations for loading the sterilizer or sterilization processes.

Recommendation I

Packaging systems should be evaluated before purchase and use to ensure that items to be packaged can be sterilized by the specific sterilizers and or sterilization methods to be used.[1]

1. Packaging systems should be appropriate for items being sterilized. The package system should

- provide an adequate barrier to microorganisms, particulates, and fluids;
- maintain sterility of package contents until opened;
- allow sterilant penetration and direct contact with the item and surfaces, and removal of the sterilant;
- be free of toxic ingredients and nonfast dyes;
- permit aseptic delivery of contents to the sterile field (eg, minimal wrap memory, removal of lids from containers);
- permit complete and secure enclosure of item(s);
- protect package contents from physical damage (eg, compression, stacking);
- provide adequate seal integrity;
- resist tears, punctures, abrasions, and prevent the transfer of microorganisms;
- be tamper-proof and able to seal only once;
- permit adequate air removal;
- be low-linting;
- permit identification of contents;
- be large enough to evenly distribute the mass;[2]
- allow ease of use by personnel preparing and/or opening the package or container;
- have a favorable cost/benefit ratio; and
- include manufacturer's instructions for use.

2. Packaging systems should be appropriate to the method of sterilization. The packaging system should be compatible with, and designed and approved for use with, the specific technology employed, and able to withstand physical conditions of the sterilization process. Purchasers should request, review, and be familiar with the manufacturer's written sterilization validation studies.[2]

3. Purchasers should evaluate and test the performance of each packaging system before selection and use this information to determine that conditions for sterilization, shelf life, transport, storage, and handling can be met. The packaging system compatibility with the intended sterilization process(es) and equipment should be verified before purchase. If the packaging represents a major change in product type (eg, change from woven textiles to

nonwoven materials, increased weight of trays) product testing should be performed. Product testing should include

- placing biological indicators (BIs) inside a variety of items to be processed (eg, basin sets, instrument sets). The BI should be located in the most challenging location inside the package (eg, geometric center of the pack, in between folds of gowns in linen packs, between nested basins in basin sets);
- packages containing the test BIs should be placed in the most challenging locations inside the sterilizer (eg, over the drain) in a full chamber;
- sterilization of the test packages and removal and incubation of the BIs. Test package contents should be reprocessed before use; and
- documentation of the test results should be maintained with the sterilization records.[2]

4. The total weight of instrument containment devices should not exceed 25 pounds including the contents and containment method (eg, wrappers, rigid container systems, cassettes, organizing trays).[2] Excessively heavy instrument sets may compromise sterilization and drying. The focus should be on the set configuration (ie, how the instruments are distributed in the set) and the overall weight of the set. Lifting and moving heavy instrument sets may cause health care worker injury.[2]

Recommendation II

Packaging systems should be compatible with the specific sterilization process for which it is designed.

1. Packaging systems for steam sterilization should permit adequate drying.[2]

    The efficacy of steam sterilization can be affected by humidity; altitude; packaging material; package contents; load; position of items within the sterilizer; size, weight, and density the pack or container; and the parameters of the sterilization cycle. Practice settings should follow manufacturers' written instructions for each packaging system for steam sterilization.[2]

2. Packaging systems for ethylene oxide (EO) should

- be permeable to EO, moisture, and air;
- permit aeration;
- be constructed of a material recommended by the sterilizer and sterilant manufacturer; and
- maintain material compatibility (ie, nondegradable) with the sterilization process.[3]

    Woven, nonwoven, peel-pouch packages, and some rigid container materials are permeable to EO and do not impede rapid aeration of contents. Woven materials, however, may absorb a large amount of the relative humidity that is needed for EO sterilization. This may prevent adequate hydration of microorganisms for penetration of EO gas to all surfaces of the package contents.[3]

3. Packaging systems for low-temperature gas plasma sterilization should

- allow sterilizing plasmas to penetrate packaging materials;
- be compatible (ie, nondegradable, nonabsorbable) with the sterilization process;
- be constructed of a material recommended by the sterilizer manufacturer; and
- be used according to the packaging manufacturer's written instructions.

    Low-temperature gas plasma sterilization is affected by absorbable packaging materials (eg, cellulose-based packaging material, textile wrappers, paper-plastic pouches, or porous wrap); both the packaging and sterilizer manufacturer's written instructions should be followed.[4] The absorption of the plasma sterilant (ie, hydrogen peroxide) by paper-plastic pouches or porous wrap could have an adverse affect on the effectiveness of the sterilization process. Pouches used in low-temperature gas plasma sterilizers should be made of all plastic (eg, polypropylene).[4,5] Not all containment systems are compatible with low-temperature gas plasma; the user should obtain the manufacturer's technical data verifying the containment device has been validated for use in low-temperature gas plasma. If the containment device requires a filter, the filter should be made of noncellulose material.

4. Packaging systems for ozone sterilization should comply with the sterilizer manufacturer's written recommendations. Packaging not intended for

use in ozone sterilizers may compromise the sterilization process. Packaging materials suitable for ozone sterilization include uncoated nonwoven material, polyethylene pouches and commercially available anodized aluminum containers using noncellulose disposable filters.[5]

Recommendation III

Packaging materials should be stored and processed to maintain the qualities required for sterilization.

1. Reusable woven textile materials should be laundered between every use for rehydration. Resterilization without relaundering may lead to superheating and could be a deterrent to achieving sterilization.[2] Over-drying, heat-pressing, and storage in areas of low humidity also may lead to superheating and sterilization failure. When woven textiles are not rehydrated after sterilization, and/or if repeated sterilization is attempted, the textiles may absorb the available moisture present in the steam, thereby creating a dry or superheated steam effect.[2]

2. Packaging materials should be stored at 20° C to 23° C (68° F to 73° F) and at a relative humidity of 30% to 60% for least two hours before use. Maintaining room temperature and moisture content of packaging materials facilitates steam penetration and prevents superheating during the sterilization process. Room temperature and humidity levels in the packaging area should be monitored.[2]

3. Single-use packaging material should be used for one sterilization cycle. Disposable packaging material should be discarded after opening.

Recommendation IV

Package contents should be assembled, handled, and wrapped in a manner that provides for an aseptic presentation of package contents.

1. The appropriate size wrapping material should be selected to achieve adequate coverage of the item being packaged. The item should be wrapped securely to prevent gapping, billowing, or air pockets from forming, which may lead to compromised sterilization.

2. The method of packaging should be performed in a manner that facilitates the aseptic presentation of the contents.

   Sequential wrapping using two barrier-type wrappers provides a tortuous pathway to impede microbial migration and permits ease of presentation to the sterile field without compromising sterility. A fused or bonded, double-layer, disposable, nonwoven wrapper used according to manufacturers' written recommendations may provide a bacterial barrier comparable to the sequential double wrap, allowing safe and easy presentation to the sterile field. Correct use of a single disposable, nonwoven, double-bonded wrapper may eliminate the need to double-wrap sequentially.[6]

3. Count sheets should not be placed inside wrapped sets or rigid containers. Although there are no known reports of adverse events related to sterilized count sheets, there is no available research regarding the safety of toners and/or various papers subjected to any sterilization method. Chemicals used in the manufacture of paper and toner ink pose a theoretical risk of reaction in some sensitized individuals.[7]

Recommendation V

Paper-plastic pouch packages should be used according to manufacturers' written instructions.

1. Paper-plastic pouch packages should be used only for small, lightweight, low-profile items (eg, one or two clamps, scissors). Heavy metal instruments (eg, drills, retractors, weighted vaginal speculums) should not be sterilized in peel pouches because problems (eg, wet packages following sterilization) and sterility maintenance problems (eg, package seal break) may occur.[2]

2. Paper-plastic pouch packages should have as much air removed as possible before sealing. Air acts as a barrier to heat and moisture. Expansion of air may cause rupturing of packages during the sterilization process.[8]

3. Paper-plastic pouch packages should provide a seal of proven integrity and not allow resealing. A break in the seal may allow microorganisms to enter and contaminate package contents.[8]

4. Paper-plastic pouch packages should be sealed airtight. Air-tight sealing can be accomplished by applying heat to the open end of the peel pouch or pressure to the mating surfaces of self-sealing pouches to cure and make permanent the seal.[5]

5. Paper-plastic pouch packages should be inspected for intact seals and barrier integrity before and after sterilization and before use.

6. Double paper-plastic pouch packaging is not routinely required for sterilization; however, double packaging may be used to facilitate containment of multiple small items to be sterilized and facilitate aseptic presentation to the sterile field.[5]

   ♦ Double paper-plastic pouch packages should be used in such a manner as to avoid folding the inner package to fit into the outer package. Folding edges of inner peel packages may entrap air and inhibit the sterilization process. [2,5]

   ♦ During sterilization of double paper-plastic pouch packages, the paper portions should be placed together to ensure penetration and removal of the sterilant, air, and moisture. Sterilizing agents penetrate paper portions of peel-pouch packages; plastic portions allow items to be viewed.[2]

7. Paper-plastic pouches should not be used within wrapped sets or containment devices because the pouches cannot be positioned to ensure adequate air removal, sterilant contact, and drying. The practice of confining instruments in paper-plastic pouches and then including them in wrapped or containerized sets has not been validated as appropriate and efficacious by packaging and container manufacturers.[2]

8. Paper-plastic pouch packages should open without tearing, linting, shredding, or delaminating. Contamination of sterile contents can occur due to functional failure of plastic-paper pouch packages.[9]

Recommendation VI

Design, material, and construction of the containment device (eg, rigid containers, instrument cases/cassettes, organizing trays) should be considered before selection, purchase, and use.

1. Purchasers should verify that the containment device has been tested and validated for the sterilization method and cycles to be used. Purchasers should request, review, and be familiar with the manufacturer's sterilization validation studies.[2]

2. Pre-purchase evaluation and biological testing of the containment device should be performed.[2]

   ♦ Pre-purchase evaluation should determine
      - whether the facility can verify the manufacturer's test results;
      - if the container device has been cleared by the US Food and Drug Administration (FDA) for use in a sterilization process;
      - if the container device is compatible with the design of the sterilizer(s) in which it will be used;
      - if the container device will allow complete air removal, adequate sterilant penetration, and drying; and
      - requirements for disassembly and cleaning.[2]

   ♦ Pre-purchase biological testing should be performed according to Association for the Advancement of Medical Instrumentation standards. Each size container should be tested under the sterilization methods and cycles to be used.[2]

   ♦ Sealed flash sterilization containers should be biologically tested during the pre-purchase evaluation and routinely thereafter. The container manufacturer should provide technical data regarding the best method for biologically testing the container.[2]

3. The recommended sterilization method and cycle exposure times for each rigid container system should be provided in the manufacturers' data and instructions. Construction materials and container design may affect compatibility with the sterilization process (eg, penetration of sterilant [gas plasma], release of moisture or sterilant [EO]). Recommendations related to the type of sterilization method vary by the container manufacturer. Prevacuum sterilizers may be preferred because air removal is difficult in gravity displacement sterilizers.[2]

4. Rigid containers with single use or reusable filters and valve systems should be secured and in proper working order before sterilization.

♦ Filter plates should be examined for integrity both before installation and after the sterilization process. If the filter is damp; dislodged; or has holes, tears, or punctures, the contents should be considered unsterile.[2]

♦ Only components of the rigid container system specified by the manufacturer and compatible with the system should be used.

♦ The integrity of the rigid container should be inspected and damaged items repaired or replaced after each use. Inspection should ensure that
  – sealing and mating surfaces and edges of the container and lid are free of dents or chips;
  – filter retention mechanisms and fasteners (eg, screws, rivets) are secure and not distorted or burred;
  – securing mechanisms are functioning;
  – integrity of the filter media is not compromised;
  – gaskets are pliable, securely fastened, and without breaks or cuts; and
  – valves work freely.[2]

Loosened rivets, improperly maintained valves, worn gaskets, dents, or other damage compromises the integrity of the container and will compromise the sterilization process.[2]

5. Rigid container systems should be cleaned after each use. All components (eg, filter retention plates) should be disassembled for proper cleaning.[2]

6. The manufacturer's written instructions for cleaning, inspection, repair, and preventive maintenance should be followed.[2]

7. The manufacturer's written instructions for loading rigid containers should be followed. Instructions should include instrument set configuration requirements.[2]

8. The manufacturer's instructions for recommended filter material, security locks, and external chemical indicators should be followed.[2]

9. Additional materials placed inside rigid containers (eg, silicone mats, surgical towels) should not be used unless the container manufacturer has provided validation for their use.

10. The manufacturer's technical data for types of devices validated for use inside the container (eg, power equipment, items with lumens) should be obtained and special instructions for sterilization followed.

Recommendation VII

Packages to be sterilized should be labeled.

1. Packaging systems should be labeled before sterilization. The label information should include, but not be limited to,
   ♦ a description of the package contents,
   ♦ a method to identify the package assembler, and
   ♦ lot control number.

2. Package labels should be visible and remain securely fixed to the package throughout processing, storage, and distribution to the point of use. If tape or a computer-generated label is used, it may be placed on either side of the peel-pouch package.

3. Label information should be written on indicator tape and not on the packing material. Markers used to label packages should be indelible, nonbleeding, and nontoxic. If a marking pen is used to label peel-pouch packages, the information should be written only on the plastic side of the pouch. If a marking pen is used to label wrapped packages, the information should be written on the indicator tape or affixed labels.[2]

Recommendation VIII

Sterilized packages should be considered sterile until an event occurs to compromise the package barrier integrity.[2]

1. Health care organizations should determine the best methods and materials for packaging sterile items, based upon the anticipated storage, handling, and environmental events that may be encountered. Loss of sterility of a packaged sterile item is event related. An event must occur to compromise package content sterility. Events that may affect the sterility of a package include, but are not limited to,

- ◆ multiple handling that leads to seal breakage or loss of package integrity;
- ◆ compression during storage;
- ◆ moisture penetration;
- ◆ exposure to airborne and other environmental contaminants;
- ◆ storage conditions (eg, type of shelving, cleanliness, temperature, humidity, traffic control);
- ◆ type and configuration of packaging materials used; and
- ◆ use of sterility maintenance covers and method of sealing.

2. Sterile packages should be stored under environmentally controlled conditions. Sterile storage area temperature should be controlled and should not exceed 75° F (24° C). The humidity should not exceed 70%. There should be a minimum of four air exchanges per hour, and the air flow should be under positive pressure in relation to adjacent areas.[2]

3. The end user should visually inspect the package or container before opening for package integrity (eg, free of holes in fabric/paper, effective seal in containers).

Recommendation IX

A chemical indicator/integrator should be placed inside each package and an external chemical indicator affixed outside each package to be processed.[2]

1. External chemical indicators, classified as Class I chemical indicators, should be specific to the sterilization process selected.

2. Internal chemical indicators should be specific to the sterilization process. Class III (single parameter indicators), Class IV (multi-parameter indicators), or Class V (chemical integrators) may be used.

3. End users should obtain and follow the chemical indicator manufacturer's instructions for storage, use, and expiration.

4. The internal chemical indicator/integrator should be placed in the geometric center of the package, not on top, to verify that air has been removed and that the sterilant has penetrated

into the center of the pack or set. The indicator should be visible to the user when the package is opened so the user can see that the indicator has changed before touching the contents.

5. Two chemical indicators/integrators should be placed inside rigid containers, one in each of two opposite corners of the inside basket.[2]

   Multi-level containers should have a chemical indicator/integrator placed in two opposite corners (eg, one in each of two corners) of each level.

6. A chemical indicator/integrator should be placed on each level of multi-level wrapped sets.[2]

Recommendation X

The health care organization's quality management program should include sterile packaging selection and use.

1. Product testing should be performed whenever there is a major change in packaging systems, materials, tray configuration, or content density[2] Two types of testing should be performed.
   - ◆ ***Biological testing.*** The biological indicator should be placed inside the tray, set, or pack being tested, usually in each corner and in the center of the set.
   - ◆ ***Verification of the ability to dry the set under user conditions.*** The set should be observed for any condensate on the instruments or package contents, wet or moist towels or silicone mats, or visible water inside the container. Evidence of retained moisture will require additional steps to determine the necessary cycle parameters and sterilizer load configuration required to ensure adequate drying.

2. Wet packs should be investigated and resolved.[10] Internal or external moisture has the potential to provide a pathway for microorganisms to enter and contaminate a sterilized item.[2]
   - ◆ Measures to resolve wet packs should include, but are not limited to,
     - – determine the set/tray configuration and weight,
     - – evaluate the packaging materials and methods used,
     - – evaluate the pan/tray used to contain the set,

– determine the placement (ie, location) of the tray/set on the sterilizer cart,

– determine the entire contents of the sterilizer load in question (eg, the number and various types of items) including placement on the sterilizer cart,

– determine if the chamber drain line basket is clogged,

– investigate the steam quality with the engineering department, and

– determine if the steam sterilizer is functioning properly (eg, insufficient vacuum during the drying cycle).[2]

♦ One method that may be used to minimize wet pack issues is to "precondition" the load. Instruments should be placed inside the steam sterilizer before starting the cycle for 10 to 15 minutes with the door closed. The heat in the chamber, from steam stored in the jacket, will heat the instruments. The heating of the instruments before injection of steam may resolve wet pack issues that are not associated with steam quality or packaging/loading errors.[2]

3. A quality control program should be developed and implemented when woven textile packaging is used.

♦ All woven textiles should be de-linted after washing and before packaging. Textiles should be inspected on a light table for defects (eg, holes, tears) each time they are processed. Any defects should be repaired using a vulcanized patch applied with a heat patch machine. Vulcanized patches do not permit penetration of most sterilants; therefore, the quantity as well as the location of the patches should be evaluated. The defect should be patched on both sides. If there are multiple patches in the same general area, the item should be removed from service even if the overall quality of the material is acceptable.

♦ Tears should not be sewn. Sewing increases the number of holes in the textile where microbes can enter. Cross stitching of textiles is not recommended due to the number of holes created in the woven material.

♦ A system of inspection for the overall integrity of the material should be developed, implemented, and monitored for quality. If the material appears very thin, even though there are no patches on the item, the item should be removed from use.

♦ Reusable textiles should maintain a protective barrier throughout the life of the product. Multiple processing will eventually diminish the protective barrier of the material. Manufacturers' instructions should be followed for the suggested number of reprocessings.[11] A method should be established to monitor, control, and determine useful life when reprocessing woven materials. This should include, but not be limited to, the number of sterilization processes and washing cycles that may occur while maintaining the acceptable barrier quality of the material.[11] If a printed area (eg, grid system) for marking the number of uses is available on the woven textile, the printed area should be marked each time the item is processed. When the grid is full, the item should be removed from service.[11]

4. Evaluation and biological testing of rigid containers should be performed periodically in each specific sterilizer and with each cycle type used.[2] Various sterilizers having the same sterilization cycles may have different air-removal efficiencies.

Recommendation XI

Personnel should demonstrate competence in the use of sterilization packaging systems and accessories.

1. Personnel selecting and using packaging systems should be knowledgeable about the principles of sterilization, manufacturers' instructions, risks, measures to minimize these risks, and corrective actions to employ in the event of a failure of the packaging system.

2. Personnel should be competent in the proper selection and use of packaging systems before use. Education should be provided during the orientation period. Additional periodic educational programs should be provided to reinforce safe use; new information on changes in technology, its application, and compatibility of sterilization equipment and processes; and potential hazards.

3. Administrative personnel should periodically assess and document the competency of personnel in the use of packaging systems, according to hospital and department policy. Incorrect use can result in serious injury to patients. Competency assurance verifies that personnel have a basic understanding of packaging systems, risks, and appropriate corrective action to take in the event of a product or process failure. This knowledge is essential to minimizing the risks of misuse and providing a safe environment of care.

4. An introduction to related policies and procedures should be included in the orientation and ongoing education of personnel to assist in the development of knowledge, skills, and behaviors that affect patient outcomes.

Recommendation XII

Policies and procedures for the selection and use of packaging systems should be written, reviewed periodically, and readily available within the practice setting.

1. These recommended practices should be used as guidelines for the development of policies and procedures for packaging. The AORN recommended practices that deal with sterilization and protective barrier materials also should be consulted when developing policies and procedures. Policies and procedures establish authority, responsibility, and accountability for the selection and use of packaging systems within the practice setting.

2. Maximum weight and tray configurations should be identified in the policy.

3. Policies and procedures establish guidelines for performance improvement activities to be used in monitoring packaging system efficacy.

4. The Perioperative Nursing Data Set, the uniform perioperative nursing vocabulary, should be used to develop policies and procedures related to sterilization and sterile packaging. The expected outcome of primary import to this recommended practice is, "The patient is free from signs and symptoms of infection" (O10). This outcome falls within the domain of Physiologic Responses (D2). The associated

nursing diagnosis is "Risk for infection" (X28). The associated interventions that may lead to the desired outcome may include "Protects from cross-contamination" (I98).[12]

Glossary

Chemical indicators: Devices used to monitor exposure to one or more sterilization parameters.

Class I: Process indicator that demonstrates that the package has been exposed to the sterilization process to distinguish between processed and unprocessed packages.

Class II: Process indicators that are used for a specific purpose such as the dynamic air removal test (formerly called the Bowie-Dick test).

Class III: A single-parameter indicator that reacts to one of the critical parameters of sterilization.

Class IV: A multi-parameter indicator that reacts to two or more of the critical parameters of sterilization.

Class V *(integrating indicator):* An indicator that reacts to all critical parameters of sterilization.

Containment device: Reusable rigid sterilization container, instrument case, cassette, or organizing tray intended for the purpose of containing reusable medical devices for sterilization.

Flash sterilization container: A container specifically designed for steam flash sterilization. The container is used to contain a device before, during, and after the sterilization process. It is sealed and may require special extended sterilization exposure times.

Instrument case/cassette: A device with a lid and a base to sterilize devices that permits air removal and sterilant penetration/removal. These devices require wrapping in packaging material if sterility of the contents is to be maintained.

Low-temperature gas plasma sterilization: This type of sterilization process involves an ionizing hydrogen peroxide gas or cloud or low-temperature plasma produced by exciting a strong electrical field over a contained precursor vapor that serves as a sterilizing agent.

Nonwoven materials: A fabric made by bonding fibers together as opposed to weaving threads.

Organizing tray: A reusable metal or plastic tray that permits organization of the contents and provides protection for the contents. Some organizing trays have diagrams of the respective instruments etched onto the surface of the tray to facilitate their location inside. These trays must be wrapped with an approved packaging material.

Package integrity: Unimpaired physical condition of a final package.

Packaging material: Any material used in the fabrication or sealing of a packaging system or primary package.

Packaging systems: One or more packaging materials assembled into a single unit intended as part or all of a primary package.

Paper-plastic pouch: A type of packaging suitable for steam and EO sterilization usually made of Mylar® (a polyester film manufactured by DuPont) and paper. The plastic (Mylar®) side is clear, permitting viewing of the contents. Paper-plastic pouches are available in various size pouches or on rolls and can be self-sealed or heat-sealed. They should not be confused with all-plastic (eg, Tyvek®, a polyethylene material manufactured by DuPont) pouches, which are not compatible with steam sterilization.

Rigid sterilization container system: Specifically designed heat-resistant, metal, plastic, or anodized aluminum receptacles used to package items, usually surgical instruments, for sterilization. The lids and/or bottom surfaces contain steam- or gas-permeable, high-efficiency microbial filters.

Sequential wrapping: A double-wrapping procedure that creates a package within a package.

Sterilization validation studies: Tests performed by the device manufacturer that demonstrate that a sterilization process will consistently yield sterile container contents under defined parameters.

Superheating: A condition in which dehydrated textiles are subjected to steam sterilization. The superheated package or product becomes too dry, which causes destructive effects on the strength of the cloth fibers. When woven textiles are not rehydrated after sterilization, and/or if repeated sterilization is attempted, the textiles could absorb the available moisture present in the steam, thereby creating a dry or superheated steam effect and adversely affecting the steam sterilization process.[2]

Useful life: Length of time, as determined by the manufacturer, for which a product maintains acceptable safety and performance characteristics. The manufacturer should provide data to support useful life of the material.

Shelf life: When this term is used in conjunction with a sterile device, shelf life is considered the length of time a device is considered safe to use.

Sterility maintenance cover (synonym: dust cover): A plastic bag, usually 2 to 3 thousandths of an inch (ie, mils) in thickness, applied to a cooled, sterilized item to provide extra protection from dust, moisture, and other environmental contaminates. These covers can be heat-sealed or self-sealed closed.

Wet packs: Packs are considered wet when there is moisture in the form of dampness, droplets, or puddles of water found on or within a textile pack, instrument, basin set, rigid container or containment device after a completed sterilization cycle and at least one hour after cooling. Wet packs generally are associated with steam sterilization; however, they also can occur with EO sterilization.

Woven textile: A reusable fabric constructed from yarns made of natural and/or synthetic fibers or filaments that are woven or knitted together to form a web in a repeated interlocking pattern.

REFERENCES

1. "Recommended practices for product selection in perioperative practice settings," in *Standards, Recommended Practices, and Guidelines* (Denver: AORN, Inc, 2006) 593-596.

2. Association for the Advancement of Medical Instrumentation, "Comprehensive guide to steam sterilization and sterility assurance in health care facilities," ANSI/AAMI ST79:2006 (Arlington, Va: Association for the Advancement of Medical Instrumentation, 2006) 54-111.

3. Association for the Advancement of Medical Instrumentation, "Ethylene oxide sterilization in health care facilities: Safety and effectiveness," ANSI/AAMI ST41-1999 (Arlington, Va: Association for the Advancement of Medical Instrumentation, 1990) Section 6.7.1.

4. Association for the Advancement of Medical Instrumentation, "Chemical sterilization and high level disinfection in health care facilities," ANSI/AAMI ST-58 (Arlington, Va: Association for the Advancement of Medical Instrumentation, 2005) Annex "H", H.3.

5. American Society for Healthcare Central Service Professionals, *Training Manual for Central Service Technicians,* fifth ed (San Francisco: Jossey-Bass, 2006) 175.

6. N Gorman-Annis, "Non-wovens," in *Sterilization Technology for the Health Care Facility,* second ed, M Reichert, J H Young, eds (Gaithersburg, Md: Aspen Publishers, Inc, 1997) 60.

7. N Chobin, personal communication with Consumer Response Center, Georgia Pacific Paper and J Kerns, Xerox Corporation, November 17, 2005.

8. D Alexander, "Packaging: Pouches," in *Sterilization Technology for the Health Care Facility,* second ed,

M. Reichert, J H Young, eds (Gaithersburg, Md: Aspen Publishers, Inc, 1997) 69.

9. L Nicolette, "Sterilization and disinfection," in *Perioperative Nursing,* third ed, L K Groah, ed (Stamford, Conn: Appleton & Lang, 1996) 169.

10. D Karle, "Solving wet pack problems," *Journal of Hospital Supply, Processing & Distribution* 2 (January/ February 1984) 22-27.

11. Association for the Advancement of Medical Instrumentation, "Processing of reusable surgical textiles for use in health care facilities," ANSI/AAMI ST65:2000 (Arlington, Va: Association for the Advancement of Medical Instrumentation, 2000) Section 7.1.

12. S C Beyea, ed, *Perioperative Nursing Data Set: The Perioperative Nursing Vocabulary,* second ed (Denver: AORN, Inc, 2002).

Originally published February 1983, *AORN Journal.* Revised November 1988, February 1992.

Revised November 1995; published May 1996, *AORN Journal.*

Revised and reformatted; published December 2000, *AORN Journal.*

Revised 2006; published in *Standards, Recommended Practices, and Guidelines,* 2007 edition.

Recommended Practices for Sterilization in the Perioperative Practice Setting

The following recommended practices for sterilization were developed by the AORN Recommended Practices Committee and have been approved by the AORN Board of Directors. They were presented as proposed recommended practices for comments by members and others. They are effective January 1, 2008.

These recommended practices are intended as achievable recommendations representing what is believed to be an optimal level of practice. Policies and procedures will reflect variations in practice settings and/or clinical situations that determine the degree to which the recommended practices can be implemented.

AORN recognizes the various settings in which perioperative nurses practice. These recommended practices are intended as guidelines adaptable to various practice settings. These practice settings include traditional operating rooms, ambulatory surgery centers, physician's offices, cardiac catheterization laboratories, endoscopy suites, radiology departments, and all other areas where surgery may be performed.

References to nursing interventions (I) used in the Perioperative Nursing Data Set, second edition, (PNDS) are noted in parentheses when a recommended practice corresponds to a PNDS intervention.[1] The reader is referred to the PNDS for further explanation of nursing diagnoses, interventions, and outcomes.

Purpose

These recommended practices provide guidance for sterilizing items to be used in the surgical environment. The creation and maintenance of an aseptic environment has a direct influence on patient outcomes. A major responsibility of the perioperative registered nurse is to minimize patient risk for surgical site infection. One of the measures for preventing surgical site infections is to provide surgical items that are free of contamination at the time of use. This can be accomplished by subjecting them to cleaning and decontamination, followed by a sterilization process.[2] Steam, ethylene oxide (EO), low-temperature hydrogen peroxide gas plasma, peracetic acid, ozone, and dry heat are sterilization methods that are used in the health care environment. Sterilization provides the highest level of assurance that surgical items are free of viable microbes.

Recommendation I

Items to be sterilized should be cleaned, decontaminated, sterilized, and stored in a controlled environment and in accordance with AORN's "Recommended practices for cleaning and caring of instruments and powered equipment"[2] and the device manufacturer's written instructions.

Effective sterilization cannot take place without effective cleaning. The process of sterilization is negatively affected by the amount of bioburden and the number, type, and inherent resistance of microorganisms, including biofilms, on the items to be sterilized. Soils, oils, and other materials may shield microorganisms on items from contact with the sterilant or combine with, and inactivate, the sterilant.[3,4]

I.a. Functional workflow patterns should be established to create and maintain physical separation between the decontamination and sterilization areas. (PNDS: I81, I98)

Physical separation aids in environmental and microbial control. During manual cleaning of instruments, particulates, aerosolized matter, dust, and microbial counts are elevated. Physical separation and vented airflow to the outside minimizes contamination of processed items.

I.a.1. Attire, use of personal protective equipment (PPE), and limitations in personnel access and movement should be based on expected contamination levels (**Table 1**).

I.a.2. Functional workflow patterns should be established in the following order from potentially high contamination areas to
- clean areas:
- decontamination,
- preparation and packaging,
- sterilization processing,
- sterile storage, and
- clean distribution.

I.a.3. Traffic patterns should be established that define access restrictions, movement of personnel, and appropriate attire according to AORN's "Recommended practices for traffic patterns in

Table 1

ATTIRE AND PERSONAL PROTECTIVE EQUIPMENT REQUIREMENTS[1]						
Work area	Scrubs	Head cover	Gloves*	Gown or apron#	Eye Protection+	Masks or face shields±
Decontamination	X	X	X	X	X	X
Preparation and packaging	X	X				
Sterilization processing	X	X				
Sterile storage	X	X				

*Gloves should be waterproof, general-purpose utility, or heavy duty.
#Gowns must be liquid-resistant with sleeves. Aprons may be liquid-resistant but do not need to have sleeves.
+Eye protection includes goggles/eye glasses with side shields or chin-length face shields.
± Masks should be fluid-resistant.

REFERENCE
   1. US Department of Labor, Occupational Safety and Health Administration. 29 CFR Bloodborne pathogens—1910.1030, Occupational safety and standards, Appendix A. Federal Register. 1991;56:64004.

the perioperative practice setting" to protect personnel, equipment, supplies, and instrumentation from sources of potential contamination.[5]

I.b.   Room temperature, humidity, and ventilation should be controlled in accordance with local, state, and federal policy and regulation. **Table 2** provides parameters for the controlled environment.[3] (PNDS: I81, I98)

Bacteria and fungi thrive at warm temperatures; cooler temperatures may impede bacterial and fungal growth in the decontamination area. Regulated environmental controls in work areas are essential for the comfort of personnel wearing appropriate attire and PPE.[3]

I.c.   Room temperature, humidity, and ventilation for each work area should be monitored and recorded daily.[3] (PNDS: I98)

I.c.1.   Organizations should monitor and record environmental controls in each area to ensure that, at minimum, recommended parameters are met and maintained.

I.d.   Health care personnel should refer to the "Recommended practices for cleaning and care of surgical instruments and powered equipment" and must use standard precautions when performing decontamination activities.[2] (PNDS: I70, I98)

Standard precautions are designed to protect patients and health care workers from contact with recognized and unrecognized sources of infectious diseases.

Recommendation II

Items to be sterilized should be packaged in accordance with AORN's "Recommended practices for selection and use of packaging systems for sterilization."[6]

Appropriate packaging ensures that sterility can be achieved and maintained to the point of use.

II.a.   Manufacturers of packaging systems should be consulted for package preparation, configuration, and sterilization.[6,7] (PNDS: I70: I98)

II.b.   The total weight of an instrument set should not exceed 25 lbs. (PNDS: I122)

Table 2

PARAMETERS FOR CONTROLLED ENVIRONMENTS DURING STERILIZATION[1]					
Functional area	Airflow	Minimum number of air exchanges per hour	All air exhausted directly to the outdoors	Temperature	Relative humidity
Soiled/ decontaminated	Negative (in)	10	Yes	60° F to 65° F (16° C to 18° C)	30% to 60%
Sterilizer equipment access	Negative (in)	10	Yes	75° F to 85° F (24° C to 29° C)	30% to 60%
Sterilizer loading/ unloading	Positive (out)	10	Yes	68° F to 73° F (20° C to 23° C)	30% to 60%
Restrooms/ housekeeping	Negative (in)	10	Yes	≤ 75° F (≤ 24° C)	30% to 60%
Preparation and packaging	Positive (out)	10 (downdraft type)	No	68° F to 73° F (20° C to 23° C)	30% to 60%
Textile packaging room	Positive (out)	10 (downdraft type)	No	68° C to 73° F (20° C to 23° C)	30% to 60%
Clean/sterile storage	Positive (out)	4 (downdraft type)	No	≤ 75° F (≤ 24° C)	≤ 70%

REFERENCE

1. *Association for the Advancement of Medical Instrumentation.* ANSI/AAMI ST79: 2006 Comprehensive Guide to Steam Sterilization and Sterility Assurance in Health Care Facilities. *Arlington, VA: Association for the Advancement of Medical Instrumentation; 2006:24-25. Adapted with permission.*

Instrument sets weighing more than 25 lbs are known to be difficult to dry without lengthy drying times and present an increased risk of ergonomic injury.[3,8]

II.c. Combination paper/plastic peel pouches should not be placed in a container or wrapped set.[3,6] (PNDS: I70, I122)

It may not be possible to position pouches to ensure adequate air removal, steam contact, or drying. The practice of using wraps or pouches inside container systems has not been validated by pouch or container manufacturers. Medical-grade, all-paper pouches may be used for this purpose.[3]

Recommendation III

Saturated steam under pressure should be used to sterilize heat- and moisture-stable items unless otherwise indicated by the device manufacturer.

Saturated steam under pressure is the preferred sterilization method. It is an effective, inexpensive, and relatively rapid sterilization method for most porous and nonporous materials.[9]

III.a. Manufacturers' written instructions for operating steam sterilizers should be followed. (PNDS: I98, I122).

Steam sterilizers vary in design and performance characteristics. A variety of steam sterilization cycles are used in health care organizations. Some examples are gravity-displacement cycles, dynamic air-removal (ie, prevacuum), steam-flush pressure-pulse cycles, flash cycles, and express cycles (ie, abbreviated steam sterilization cycles used for flash sterilization).[2] In addition, some sterilizers may be designed to permit only one type of cycle. For example, some sterilizers are identified as gravity-displacement sterilizers because that is the only type of cycle this type of sterilizer permits.

Table 3

TYPICAL MINIMUM CYCLE TIMES FOR GRAVITY-DISPLACEMENT STEAM STERILIZATION[1]						
Item	Exposure time at 250° F (121° C)	Minimum drying time	Exposure time at 270° F (132° C)	Minimum drying time	Exposure time at 275° F (135° C)	Minimum drying time
Wrapped instruments	30 min	15 to 30 min	15 min	15 to 30 min	10 min	30 min
Textile packs	30 min	15 min	25 min	15 min	10 min	30 min
Wrapped utensils	30 min	15 to 30 min	15 min	15 to 30 min	10 min	30 min

1. Association for the Advancement of Medical Instrumentation. ANSI/AAMI ST79:2006 Comprehensive Guide to Steam Sterilization and Sterility Assuring in Health Care Facilities. Arlington, VA: Association for the Advancement of Medical Instrumentation; 2006. Reprinted with permission.

Table 3 and **Table 4** provide typical minimum sterilization times for gravity-displacement and dynamic air-removal steam sterilization cycles.[3]

III.b. Cycle parameters recommended by the device manufacturer should be reconciled with the sterilizer manufacturer's written instructions for the specific sterilization cycle and load configuration.[3,10] Certain types of equipment and implants (eg, some pneumatically powered instruments; specialty orthopedic, neurosurgery, trauma instruments) may require prolonged exposure times or drying times.[3,10] (PNDS: I98, I122)

III.c. Following steam sterilization, the contents of the sterilizer should be removed from the chamber and left untouched for a period of 30 minutes to two hours depending on the load contents.[3] (PNDS: I70, I98, I122)

The potential for the formation of condensation is decreased by allowing the contents of the sterilizer to remain untouched until the equalization of the temperature differential between the chamber and outside environment has occurred.[3]

III.c.1. Steam sterilizer doors should not be left ajar to cool loads following a cycle.[11]

Removing the sterilizer load from the sterilizer as soon as possible after steam sterilization allows the cooling process to begin earlier.

Cracking the sterilizer door may hinder the drying process.

Wet packs may be a result of excessively wet steam, poor loading techniques, or a true sterilizer malfunction.

III.d. Warm or hot items should not be placed on cool or cold surfaces. (PNDS: I70, I98, I122)

When hot and cold surfaces are brought together, moisture condenses from both inside and outside the package. At the end of the steam sterilization cycle and after an appropriate drying time, items still may contain some steam vapor. Touching packages at this vulnerable stage could compromise the barrier properties of the packaging material by causing moisture and/or contaminants to wick through the package. Droplets inside or outside of the container can form because rigid container materials are nonabsorbent. Condensate can drip onto surrounding containers, compromising the sterility of other packages.[3]

III.e. Sterilized packages or containers that have formed condensate should be considered unsterile and none of the contents used.[3] (PNDS: I70, I98, I122)

Moisture can compromise the integrity of barrier material and the sterility of the contents. Moisture may indicate problems with the packaging and sterilization process.[3]

Recommendation IV

Use of flash sterilization should be kept to a minimum. Flash sterilization should be used only in selected clinical situations and in a controlled manner.

Table 4

TYPICAL MINIMUM CYCLE TIMES FOR DYNAMIC AIR-REMOVAL STEAM STERILIZATION[1]				
Item	Exposure time at 270° F (132° C)	Minimum drying time	Exposure time at 275° F (135° C)	Minimum drying time
Wrapped instruments	4 min	20 to 30 min	3 min	16 min
Textile packs	4 min	5 to 20 min	3 min	3 min
Wrapped utensils	4 min	20 min	3 min	16 min

1. *Association for the Advancement of Medical Instrumentation.* ANSI/AAMI ST79:2006 Comprehensive Guide to Steam Sterilization and Sterility Assurance in Health Care Facilities. *Arlington, VA: Association for the Advancement of Medical Instrumentation; 2006. Reprinted with permission.*

Flash sterilization may be associated with increased risk of infection to patients because of pressure on personnel to eliminate one or more steps in the cleaning and sterilization process.

IV.a Flash sterilization should be used only when there is insufficient time to process by the preferred wrapped or container method. Flash sterilization should not be used as a substitute for sufficient instrument inventory.[12] (PNDS: I70, I98)

Proper decontamination is essential in removing bioburden and preparing an item for sterilization by any method. Failures in instrument cleaning have resulted in transmission of infectious agents.[3]

IV.a.1. Items to be flash sterilized should be subjected to the same decontamination processes as described in AORN's "Recommended practices for cleaning and care of surgical instruments and powered equipment."[2]

IV.a.2. Flash sterilization should be performed only if all of the following conditions are met:
- The device manufacturer's written instructions on cycle type, exposure times, temperature settings, and drying times (if recommended) are available and followed.
- Items are disassembled and thoroughly cleaned with detergent and water to remove soil, blood, body fats, and other substances.
- Lumens are brushed and flushed under water with a cleaning solution and rinsed thoroughly.
- Items are placed in a closed sterilization container or tray, validated for flash sterilization, in a manner that allows steam to contact all instrument surfaces.
- Measures are taken to prevent contamination during transfer to the sterile field.

Flash-sterilized items are to be used immediately and not stored for later use.[3]

Table 5 provides examples of typical flash sterilization parameters.

IV.b. Packaging and wrapping (eg, textiles, paper/plastic pouches, nonwoven wrappers) should not be used in flash sterilization cycles unless the sterilizer is specifically designed and labeled for this use. (PNDS: I70, I98)

Cycle parameters vary according to sterilizer design.

IV.b.1. Sterilizer manufacturers' written directions should be followed and reconciled with the packaging manufacturer's instructions for sterilization.[3]

IV.c. Process challenge devices (PCDs) should be used with routine process monitoring devices (ie, chemical indicators, biological indicators, physical monitoring devices).[3] (PNDS: I70, I98)

Process challenge and process monitoring devices provide information to demonstrate that conditions for sterilization have been met.

Table 5

EXAMPLES OF TYPICAL FLASH STEAM STERILIZATION PARAMETERS[1]				
Type of sterilizer	Load configuration	Time	Exposure Temperature	Drying Times
Gravity displacement	Metal or nonporous items only (ie, no lumens)	3 minutes	270° F–275° F (132° C–135° C)	0 to 1 minutes
	Metal items with lumens and porous items (eg, rubber, plastic) sterilized together. Complex devices (eg, powered instruments requiring extended exposure times). Manufacturer instructions should be consulted.	10 minutes	270° F–275° F (132° C–135° C)	0 to 1 minute
Dynamic air-removal (prevacuum)	Metal or nonporous items only (ie, no lumens)	3 minutes	270° F–275° F (132° C–135° C)	N/A
	Metal items with lumens and porous items sterilized together	4 minutes 3 minutes	270° F (132° C) 275° F (135° C)	N/A N/A

- The sterilizer manufacturer's instructions for use of express cycles should be followed. One sterilizer manufacturer provides an express flash cycle that permits flash sterilization with a single-ply wrapper to help contain the device to the point of use. This cycle is not recommended for devices with lumens. Express cycles should only be used if the sterilizer is designed with this feature.
- Steam-flush pressure-pulse: See manufacturers' written instructions for time and temperature.
- This table does not include specific instructions for rigid flash sterilization containers. The container manufacturer's instructions should be followed.

REFERENCE

1. *Association for the Advancement of Medical Instrumentation.* ANSI/AAMI ST79:2006 Comprehensive Guide to Steam Sterilization and Sterility Assurance in Health Care Facilities. *Arlington, VA: Association for the Advancement of Medical Instrumentation; 2006:60-72. Adapted with permission.*

IV.c.1. Each sterilization cycle should be monitored to verify that parameters required for sterilization have been met.[3]

IV.c.2. The sterilizer operator should use physical monitoring devices to verify cycle parameters for each load.[3]

Physical monitoring devices (eg, printouts, graphs, gauges) can indicate immediate sterilizer failure. Physical monitors record cycle parameters (ie, time, temperature) for each cycle.

IV.c.3. Biological (BI) and chemical indicators should be used to monitor sterilizer efficacy and assess compliance of monitoring standards established for gravity-displacement and dynamic air-removal sterilizers. Class 5 chemical integrating indicators should be used within each sterilizer container or tray.[3]

IV.d. Users should adhere to aseptic technique for flash-sterilized items during transport to the point of use. It is important that sterilization processing be carried out in a clean environment and that flash-sterilized devices are transferred to the point of use in a manner that prevents contamination.

IV.e. Rigid sterilization containers designed and intended for flash-sterilization cycles should be used. (PNDS: I70, I98)

Rigid flash-sterilization containers

- reduce the risk of contamination during transport to the point of use,
- facilitate ease of presentation to the sterile field, and
- protect sterilized items during transport.[3]

X.b. Personnel should coordinate requests for loaner instrumentation in sufficient time for loaner items to be processed by conventional sterilization methods. (PNDS: I138)

Advance delivery of loaner items to the receiving health care organization ensures sufficient time to permit in-house disassembly, cleaning, packaging, quality assurance testing, and sterilization of the instruments before scheduled procedures.

X.b.1. Personnel requesting loaner items should specify quantities, estimated time of use and return, and restocking requirements to circumvent the need for flash sterilization.

X.b.2. Flash sterilization should not be used as a substitute for sufficient instrument inventory resulting from late delivery of loaner instrumentation.

X.c. Loaner instrumentation sterility assurance should begin on receipt at the point where the health care organization personnel assume responsibility for the items.[3]

Failures in instrument cleaning have resulted in transmission of infectious agents

X.c.1. All loaner instruments should be considered contaminated and delivered directly to the decontamination area for processing. Instruments should be thoroughly cleaned and dried in a manner consistent with AORN's "Recommended practices for cleaning and care of surgical instruments and powered equipment"[2] and the standards of the Association for the Advancement of Medical Instrumentation before sterilization.[3,15] (PNDS: I70, I98, I122, I138)

X.c.2. Newly manufactured loaner items should be properly decontaminated before sterilization to remove bioburden and substances (eg, oils, greases) remaining on the item during the manufacturing process.[3]

X.c.3. Clean or sterile items transported to sterile processing should be removed from external shipping containers.[3]

External shipping containers may have potentially high microbial contamination due to environmental exposures during transport.

X.c.4. Rigid sterilization containers should be thoroughly inspected on receipt and cleaned and decontaminated according to manufacturers' instructions.

Containers should be inspected for integrity and function.

X.c.5. Loaner items, type, and quantity should be inventoried and documented.

X.c.6. Implants and instruments should be visually inspected for damage.

X.c.7. Manufacturers' instructions on processing and sterilizing loaner items should be followed.

X.c.8. Loaner items should be decontaminated and handled in accordance with organizational policy following the procedure.

X.c.9. Implantable devices should be sterilized with a BI and a Class 5 integrating indicator and documented in accordance with FDA regulations and AORN recommended practices.

Recommendation XI

Sterilized materials should be packaged, labeled, and stored in a manner to ensure sterility, and each item should be marked with the sterilization date.[3,34]

Limiting exposure to moisture, dust, excessive light or handling, and temperature and humidity extremes decreases potential contamination of sterilized items.[3]

XI.a. The shelf life of a packaged sterile item should be considered event-related. (PNDS: I70, I98, I122)

An event must occur to compromise package content sterility. Events that may compromise the sterility of a package include, but are not limited to,
- multiple handling that leads to seal breakage or loss of package integrity,
- moisture penetration, and
- exposure to airborne contaminants.[3,15,32]

NOTE: Ambulatory surgery centers should refer to the *Centers for Medicare and Medicaid Services State Operations Manual for Ambulatory Services* that states, "Sterilized materials should be packaged, labeled, and stored in a manner to ensure sterility and that each item is marked with the expiration date."[35]

XI.b. Sterile packages should be stored under environmentally controlled conditions.[2] (PNDS: I70, I98, I122)

Controlled conditions reduce the risk of contamination.

XI.b.1 The temperature in the sterile storage areas should not exceed 24° C (75° F).

XI.b.2. The storage area should have at least four air exchanges per hour.

XI.b.3. Relative humidity should be controlled, not to exceed 70%.

XI.b.4. Traffic should be controlled to limit access to those trained in handling sterile supplies. (PNDS: I81)

XI.b.5. Supplies should be stored in a manner that allows adequate air circulation, ease of cleaning, and compliance with local fire codes. (PNDS: I98)

XI.b.6. Sterile items should be stored at least eight to 10 inches above the floor, at least 18 inches below sprinkler heads, and at least two inches from outside walls.

XI.b.7. Outside shipping containers should not be allowed in the sterile storage area because they serve as generators of, and reservoirs for, dust. (PNDS: I98)

XI.c. Storage conditions should be evaluated before policies and procedures on event-related sterility are written for perioperative practice settings. (PNDS: I70, I98, I122, I138)

The shelf life of packaged sterile items is event-related and dependent on packaging material, storage conditions, transport and handling. Adequacy and quality of storage space are factors to be considered when writing policies and procedures.[3]

XI.c.1. All storage items should be rotated according to the principle of "first in, first out."

Recommendation XII

Transportation of sterile items should be controlled.

Sterility is event-related and depends on the amount of handling, conditions during transportation and storage, and the quality of the packaging material.

XII.a. Sterile items should be transported in covered or enclosed carts with solid-bottom shelves. (PNDS: I70, I81, I98, I122)

Covered or enclosed carts will protect sterile items from exposure to environmental contaminants during transportation.

XII.a.1. Carts and reusable covers should be cleaned after each use because contaminants are picked up from the environment during transport.[3]

XII.b. Written policies and procedures should address prevention of physical damage and maintenance of package sterility during transport.

Procedures for transporting sterile items can help preserve the quality of sterile packages and maintain the integrity of processed items until the time of use.[3,15]

XII.b.1. Transportation conditions should be evaluated before policies and procedures for the transportation of sterile items are written for perioperative practice settings.[3,15,32] (PNDS: I70, I81, I98, I122, I138)

Recommendation XIII

Competency
An introduction and review of policies and procedures should be included in personnel orientation to sterile processing of surgical instruments in the perioperative setting. Continuing education should be provided for employees when new equipment, instruments, and processes are introduced. (PNDS: I1)

Operator and processing errors are minimized with regularly scheduled education, training, and competency demonstration.[3,15]

XIII.a. Sterilization-specific education and competency assessment of personnel should encompass all sterilization methodologies in use in the organization, to include

- operation and maintenance of sterilization equipment;
- selection and monitoring of sterilization cycles;
- use of chemical, biological, and physical monitoring measures; and
- documentation requirements.

XIII.b. Education should address, but not be limited to,
- orientation programs to equipment and work area;
- infection control policy and procedure, including exposure plans;
- potential hazards in the environment and methods of hazard protection;
- safe ergonomic practices; and
- use and location of MSDS.

Recommendation XIV

Documentation
Sterilization records should be maintained for a time specified by the health care organization's policies and in compliance with local, state, and federal regulations.[3,15,32]

Accurate and complete records are required for process verification and used in sterilizer malfunction analyses. Documentation establishes accountability.

XIV.a. Every sterilization cycle and modality, including steam (eg, wrapped, unwrapped), EO, hydrogen peroxide gas plasma, liquid peracetic acid, ozone, and dry heat should be documented. Documentation should include
- the assigned lot number;
- contents of each load; and
- results of physical, chemical, and biological monitors.

Recommendation XV

Policies and Procedures
Policies and procedures for sterilization processes should be developed, reviewed periodically, and readily available in the practice setting. (PNDS: I1)

Policies and procedures establish authority, responsibility, and accountability and serve as operational guidelines. Policies and procedures

also assist in the development of continuous quality improvement activities.

XV.a. Policies and procedures for routine cleaning of sterilizer chambers, carts, and exterior surfaces should be developed and implemented. (PNDS: I122)

XV.b. These recommended practices for sterilization should be used to guide the development of policies and procedures within individual perioperative practice settings.

XV.c. The sterilizer manufacturer's written instructions for cleaning should be reviewed and followed.

XV.d. An introduction and review of policies and procedures should be included in the orientation and ongoing education of health care personnel to assist in the development of knowledge, skills, and attitudes that affect patient outcomes.

XV.e. User manuals for all sterilization equipment should be readily available to the sterilizer operators. (PNDS: I122)

As new technologies are introduced for use in perioperative practice settings, it is imperative that health care personnel strictly follow manufacturers' written instructions for the operation and maintenance of sterilization equipment and are aware of the occupational hazards that different sterilants may pose to patients, health care personnel, and the environment. Compliance with the Safe Medical Device Act of 1990, which was amended in 2000, is required and will contribute to patient safety.[36]

XV.e.1. Equipment manuals should be retained for the life of the sterilizer.

XV.f. When selecting a new sterilization technology, perioperative nurses and nurse managers should follow AORN's "Recommended practices for product selection in perioperative practice settings."[37]

Capital equipment and medical device procurement are collaborative processes requiring clinical, business, financial, and legal acumen. Goals of product standardization and value analysis processes are to select functional and reliable products that are safe, cost-effective, and environmentally conscious and that promote quality care and avoid duplication or rapid obsolescence.

Recommendation XVI

Quality
A quality control program should be established and maintained. (PNDS: I1)

Quality control programs that enhance personnel performance and monitor sterilization efficacy are established to promote patient and employee safety.

XVI.a. The health care organization should establish quality control and improvement programs to monitor the work place environment and practices associated with cleaning, disinfection, and sterilization of surgical instruments.

Monitoring the sterilization process allows results to be compared to a predetermined level of quality. Reviewing the findings provide a method of identifying problems and trends to change and improve practice.

XVI.b. All sterilizer failures and corrective actions should be documented and reported to the infection control professional and/or quality assurance committee, and to administration.

XVI.c. All BI test results, including results from controls, should be interpreted by qualified personnel in the time frame specified by the BI manufacturer and should be included in the sterilization records. (PNDS: I70, I98, I122, I138)

Accurate interpretation and reporting of positive results promotes safe patient care.[3]

XVI.c.1. Positive BI test results should be reported immediately so that appropriate action can be taken.
- The sterilizer printout should first be checked to determine if the cycle parameters were met.
- If retrievable, items processed in the suspect sterilizer (ie, back to the last known negative BI test) should be recalled and reprocessed before use.[3]

- The positive BI vial should be sent to the laboratory for subculturing for bacilli (the recall should not be delayed during this testing).
- All actions taken in response to a positive BI test should be documented.
- A positive control should be placed in each incubator each day a test vial is run and incubated.

XVI.c.2. All control vials should be from the same lot number as the BI test vial for the test to be considered valid.[3]

XVI.d. Processed items should be labeled with lot control numbers to identify the sterilizer used, the cycle or load number, and the date of sterilization. (PNDS: I122)

Lot control numbers allow items to be identified or retrieved in the event of a sterilizer failure or malfunction.[3,15,32]

XVI.d.1. Information should be recorded from each sterilization cycle and should include, but not be limited to,
- identification of sterilizer (eg, "sterilizer #1");
- type of sterilizer and cycle used;
- lot control number; load contents (eg, major set, Kelly clamps);[3]
- critical parameters for the specific sterilization methodology (eg, exposure time, temperature for steam sterilization);
- operator's name; and
- results of sterilization process monitoring (ie, biological, chemical, physical).

XVI.e. Physical monitors should be used to verify time, temperature, and pressure recordings for steam sterilization cycles. (PNDS: I70, I98, I122)

Physical monitoring provides real-time assessment of cycle conditions while providing historical records by means of graphs, printouts, or charts. Reviewing data from physical monitoring can readily identify sterilizer malfunctions to expedite corrective actions.[3]

XVI.e.1. Recordings of physical data should be used, when available, for all sterilization methodologies to ascertain that sterilization systems function within manufacturers' specifications.[3,15]

XVI.e.2. The printout should be reviewed at the end of each cycle and signed by the sterilizer operator verifying that all sterilization parameters were met.

XVI.f. A sterilization chemical indicator should be used inside and outside each package and load sterilized. (PNDS: I122)

The purpose of the external chemical indicator is to differentiate between processed and unprocessed items.

Internal chemical indicators do not establish whether the item is sterile, but they do demonstrate that the contents were exposed to the sterilant.

XVI.f.1. Although external chemical indicators do not verify sterility, they help detect procedural errors and equipment malfunctions; therefore, the color change should be verified before opening.

XVI.f.2. An external chemical indicator should be used on the outside of each package unless the internal chemical indicator is visible.

XVI.f.3. Chemical indicators should be reviewed for a proper endpoint response (eg. color, migration or other change).

XVI.f.4. If the interpretation of the external or internal process monitors suggests inadequate processing, the item should not be used.[3,15,38] (PNDS: I70, I98, I122, I138)

XVI.f.5. The internal chemical indicator should be reviewed for a proper end point response (eg, color, migration, other change) before placing the items or tray on the sterile field.

XVI.g. Quality assurance testing of rigid containers should be performed before initial use, and periodically, according to manufacturers written instructions.[3] (PNDS: I122, I138)

Rigid sterilization container systems vary widely in design, mechanics, and construction. These variables can affect the performance of characteristics and suitability of containers with sterilization methods.

XVI.g.1. The following measures should be evaluated when conducting periodic product quality assurance testing of sterilization containers for each sterilizer type used:
- sterilization efficacy, and
- drying effectiveness.

Health care organizations are responsible for obtaining and maintaining manufacturers' documentation of methodology and performance testing of the container system.

Health care personnel are responsible for ensuring that container systems are suitable for proposed sterilization uses and are compatible with existing sterilizers.

XVI.g.2. Personnel should perform product testing to verify and collaborate with the sterilizer manufacturer for resolution of technological concerns.

XVI.h. Sterilization conditions such as exposure time should be evaluated with physical, biological, and chemical monitoring by strategically placing monitors alongside each other at locations that present the greatest challenge to air evacuation and sterilant penetration. (PNDS: I70, I122, I138)

Table 6 indicates types and applications of sterilization monitoring devices.

XVI.h.1. Monitors should be used for routine load release, routine sterilizer efficacy monitoring, sterilizer qualification testing (eg. after installation, relocation, malfunctions, major repairs, sterilization process failures) and periodic product quality assurance testing for all sterilization processes. Table 7 provides recommendations for sterilizer testing process monitoring.[3,15,32,33,39]

XVI.h.2. **Steam sterilizers:** *Geobacillus stearothermophilus* biological indicators should be used for routine load release, routine sterilizer efficacy monitoring, sterilizer qualification testing, and periodic product quality assurance testing.

Routine sterilizer efficacy monitoring should be done weekly, preferably daily, as follows:

- each load containing an implantable device should be monitored with a BI and quarantined until the results of the BI testing are available, and
- one BI PCD should be run in three consecutive empty cycles for sterilizer qualification testing.

    If a steam sterilizer is intended to be used for multiple types of cycles (eg, gravity-displacement, dynamic air-removal, flash), each sterilization mode should be tested.[3]

XVI.h.3. **Ethylene oxide sterilizers:** *Bacillus atropheus* (formerly *Bacillus subtilis*) spore testing should be performed with every load.

XVI.h.4. **Low temperature hydrogen peroxide gas plasma sterilizers:** *Geobacillus stearothermophilus* biological indicators are used for routine load release, routine sterilizer efficacy monitoring, sterilizer qualification testing and periodic product quality assurance testing.[28]

    Routine sterilizer efficacy monitoring should be done daily, preferably with each load, as follows:
- each load containing an implantable device should be monitored with a BI and quarantined until the results of the BI testing are available,
- one BI PCD should be run in three consecutive empty cycles for sterilizer qualification testing, and
- the sterilizer manufacturer should be consulted for the specific monitoring product(s) to use and the appropriate placement of the product within the sterilizer.

XVI.h.5. **Ozone sterilizers:** *Geobacillus stearothermophilus* biological indicators are used for routine load release, routine sterilizer efficacy monitoring, sterilizer qualification testing and periodic product quality assurance testing.[28]

    Routine sterilizer efficacy monitoring should be done daily, preferably with each load, as follows:

- each load containing an implantable device should be monitored with a BI and quarantined until the results of the BI testing are available,
- one BI PCD should be run in three consecutive empty cycles for sterilizer qualification testing, and
- the sterilizer manufacturer should be consulted for the specific monitoring product(s) to use and the appropriate placement of the product within the sterilizer.

XVI.h.6. **Liquid peracetic acid sterilizers:** *Geobacillus stearothermophilus* biological indicators should be performed daily for routine sterilizer efficacy monitoring.
- The test product used should be designed specifically for use with liquid peracetic acid processes.
- The sterilizer manufacturer's written instructions for use should be followed.

XVI.h.7. **Dry-heat sterilizers:** *Bacillus atropheus* biological indicators should be used for routine load release, routine sterilizer efficacy monitoring, sterilizer qualification testing and periodic product quality assurance testing.

    Routine sterilizer efficacy monitoring should be done weekly, preferably daily, as follows:
- each load containing an implantable device should be monitored with a BI and quarantined until the results of the BI testing are available;
- sterilizer qualification testing one BI PCD should be run in three consecutive empty cycles;
- mechanical convection (ie, forced air) dry-heat sterilizers should be monitored according to the manufacturer's recommendations, additional monitoring of three consecutive sterilization cycles should be performed after installation, major repair, redesign, or relocation of sterilizers; and
- this testing is performed in an otherwise empty sterilizer.

Table 6

TYPES AND APPLICATIONS FOR USE OF STERILIZATION MONITORING DEVICES[1,2]		
Monitor	**Frequency of Use**	**Application** *(release of sterilizer, package, load)*
Physical Monitors Time, temperature, and pressure recorder displays; digital printouts; and gauges	Should be used for every load of every sterilizer.	Part of load release criteria.
Chemical Indicators (CIs)		
External CIs Class I (process indicators)	Should be used on outside of every package.	Part of load and package release criteria.
Bowie-Dick-type indicators Class 2 (Bowie-Dick)	For routine sterilizer testing (dynamic air-removal sterilizers only): Should be run within a test pack each day in an empty sterilizer before the first processed load.	Test of sterilizer efficacy of air removal and steam penetration; part of release criteria for using sterilizer for the day.
	For sterilizer qualification testing (dynamic-air-removal sterilizers only): Should be run within a test pack after sterilizer installation, relocation, malfunction; after major repairs; and after sterilization process failures. Test should be run three times consecutively in an empty chamber after biological indicator (BI) tests.	Part of release criteria for placing sterilizer into service after qualification testing.
Internal CIs	Should be used inside each package.	Part of package release criteria at use site.
	Should be used in periodic product quality assurance testing.	Part of release criteria for changes made to routinely sterilized items, load configuration, and/or packaging. Release criteria should include BI results.
Class 3 (single-variable indicator) Class 4 (multi-variable indicator)[2]	May be used to meet internal CI recommendation.	Part of package release criteria at use site; NOT to be used for release of loads.
Class 5 (integrating indicator) Enzyme-only indicator	• May be used to meet internal CI recommendation. • Within a process challenge device (PCD), may be used to monitor nonimplant sterilizer loads . • Within a PCD, should be used to monitor each sterilizer load containing implants. The PCD should also contain a BI.	• Part of package release criteria at use site. • Part of load release criteria for nonimplant loads. • Part of release criteria for loads containing implants. Except in emergencies, implants should be quarantined until BI results are known.
Biological Indicators	• Within a PCD, may be used to monitor nonimplant loads. • Within a PCD should be used in every load containing implants. The PCD should also contain a Class 5 integrating indicator or an enzyme-only indicator. • Within a PCD, should be used for weekly, preferably daily (ie, each day the sterilizer is used), routine sterilizer efficacy testing, (The PCD may also contain a CI). Should be run in a full load for wrapped items; for table-top sterilization, should be run in a fully loaded chamber; for flash sterilization, should be run in an empty chamber. • Within a PCD should be used for sterilizer qualification testing (after sterilizer installation, relocation, malfunction, major repairs, sterilization process failures). The PCD may also contain a CI. • Test should be run three times consecutively in an empty chamber except for table-top sterilizers, where the test should be run three times consecutively in a full load. • Should be used for periodic product quality assurance testing.	• Part of load release criteria. • Part of release criteria for loads containing implants. Except in emergencies, implants should be quarantined until Bi results are known. • Part of sterilizer/load release and recall criteria. • Part of release criteria for placing sterilizer into service after qualification testing. • Part of release criteria for changes made to routinely sterilized items, load configuration, and/or packaging.

Adapted with permission from Association for the Advancement of Medical Instrumentation.

1. Association for the Advancement of Medical Instrumentation. ANSI/AAMI ST79:2006—Comprehensive Guide to Steam Sterilization and Sterility Assurance in Health Care Facilities. *Arlington, VA: Association for the Advancement of Medical Instrumentation; 2006.*

2. Association for the Advancement of Medical Instrumentation. ANSI/AAMI/ISO 11140-1: Sterilization of health care products—Chemical indicators, Part 1: General requirements. *Arlington, VA: Association for the Advancement of Medical Instrumentation; 2005.*

Table 7

STERILIZATION PROCESS MONITORING RECOMMENDATIONS[1]				
Routine load release		Routine sterilizer efficacy monitoring	Sterilizer qualification testing *(after installation, relocation, malfunctions, major repairs, sterilization process failures)*	Periodic product quality assurance testing
Nonimplants	Implants			
Physical monitoring of cycle. External and internal chemical indicator monitoring of packages. Optional monitoring of the load with a process challenge device (PCD) containing one of the following: • a biological indicator (BI), • a BI and a Class 5 integrating indicator, • a BI and an enzyme-only indicator • a Class 5 integrating indicator, • an enzyme-only indicator.	Physical monitoring of cycle. External and internal chemical indicator monitoring of packages. Monitoring of every load with a PCD containing a BI and a Class 5 integrating indicator or a PCD containing a BI and an enzyme-only indicator.	Physical monitoring of cycle. External and internal chemical indicator monitoring of packages. Weekly, preferably daily (or each day the sterilizer is used), monitoring of a full load with a PCD containing a BI (The PCD may also contain a chemical indicator [CI]). In flash sterilization cycles, monitoring is done in an empty chamber. For dynamic air-removal sterilizers, daily Bowie-Dick testing in an empty chamber	Physical monitoring of cycle. External and internal chemical indicator monitoring of packages. For sterilizers larger than 2 cubic feet and for flash sterilization cycles, monitoring of three consecutive cycles in an empty chamber with a PCD containing a BI. (The PCD may also contain a CI.) For table-top sterilizers, monitoring of three consecutive cycles in a fully loaded chamber with a PCD containing a BI. (The PCD may also contain a CI.) For dynamic air-removal sterilizers, monitoring of three consecutive cycles in a empty chamber with a Bowie-Dick test pack.	Physical monitoring of cycle. Placement of BIs and CIs within product test samples.

REFERENCE

1. Association for the Advancement of Medical Instrumentation. ANSI/AAMI ST79:2006—Comprehensive Guide to Steam Sterilization and Sterility Assurance in Health Care Facilities. *Arlington, VA: Association for the Advancement of Medical Instrumentation; 2006. Adapted with permission.*

XVI.h.8. **Dynamic air-removal steam sterilizers:** A Bowie-Dick air removal test should routinely be performed daily in an empty chamber.

- The air-removal test is designed to detect residual air in the sterilizer chamber.
- The test should be run in accordance with the test manufacturer's instructions before the routine biological indicator testing.

  Whenever a dynamic air-removal sterilizer is installed, relocated, malfunctions, undergoes a major repair, or has a sterilization process failure, three consecutive cycles in an empty chamber should be tested with a BI PCD followed by three consecutive cycles in an empty chamber with a Bowie-Dick test.

XVI.i. Preventive maintenance on sterilizers should be performed by qualified personnel on a scheduled basis. (PNDS I122)

Periodic inspections, maintenance, and replacement of components subject to wear (eg, recording devices, steam traps, filters, valves, drain pipes, gaskets) help maintain proper functioning of sterilizers.

XVI.i.1. Inspection and cleaning should be performed as outlined in the manufacturer's written instructions.[3,10,15]

Proper inspection and cleaning minimizes sterilizer downtime and helps prevent sterilizer malfunctions.

XVI.i.2. Preventive maintenance and repairs should be performed by qualified personnel as specified in the manufacturer's written instructions.

XVI.i.3. Maintenance records should be kept for each sterilizer. Accurate and complete records are required for sterilization process verification. Information should include, but not be limited to,

- date of service;
- sterilizer model and serial number;
- sterilizer location;
- description of malfunctions;
- name of person and company performing maintenance;

- description of service and parts replaced;
- results of biological indicator testing, if performed;
- results of Bowie-Dick testing, if performed;
- where appropriate, the name of the person requesting the service; and
- the signature and title of the person acknowledging the completed work.

Glossary

Aeration: Method by which absorbed ethylene oxide (EO) is removed from EO-sterilized items by circulating warm air in an enclosed cabinet specifically designed for this purpose.

Anhydrous: Items that are free of water.

Bioburden: The degree of microbial load; the number of viable organisms contaminating an object.

Biofilm: A thin coating containing biologically active organisms that have the ability to grow in water, water solutions, or in vivo and that coat the surface of structures (eg, teeth, inner surfaces of catheters, tubes, implanted or indwelling devices, instruments, other medical devices). Biofilms contain viable and nonviable microorganisms that adhere to the surface and are trapped within a matrix of organic matter (eg, proteins, glycoproteins, carbohydrates), which prevents antimicrobial agents from reaching the cells.

Biological indicator: A sterilization process-monitoring device commercially prepared with a known population of highly resistant spores that tests the effectiveness of the method of sterilization being used. The indicator is used to demonstrate that conditions necessary to achieve sterilization were met during the sterilizer cycle being monitored.

Chemical indicator: A sterilization-monitoring device used to monitor the attainment of one or more critical parameters required for sterilization. A characteristic color or other visual change indicates a defined level of exposure based on the classification of the chemical indicator used.

Class 5 chemical integrating indicator: A chemical indicator designed to react to all critical parameters over a specified range of sterilization cycles and whose performance has been correlated to the performance of the stated test organism under the labeled conditions of use.

Decontamination: Any physical or chemical process that removes or reduces the number of microorganisms or infectious agents and renders reusable medical products safe for handling or disposal; the process by which contaminants are removed, either by hand cleaning or mechanical means, using specific solutions capable of rendering blood and debris harmless and removing them from the surface of an object or instrument.

Downtime: A period of time when an item or device is not operational.

Dynamic air-removal: Mechanically assisted air removal from the sterilization chamber. Includes prevacuum and steam-flush pressure-pulse steam sterilizers.

Dynamic air-removal test (ie, Bowie-Dick test): A diagnostic test to determine the adequacy of air removal from the chamber of a dynamic-air-removal steam sterilizer. The air-removal test is not a test for sterilization.

Emergency spill plan: A plan of action for any unanticipated release of ethylene oxide or other hazardous chemicals into the workplace.

Flash sterilization: A process designed for the steam sterilization of patient care items for immediate use.

Gravity-displacement sterilizer: Type of sterilization cycle in which incoming air displaces residual air through a port or drain near the bottom of the sterilizer chamber.

Physical monitor: Automated devices (eg, graphs, gauges, printouts) that monitor sterilization parameters for the sterilization method in use.

Process challenge device: A predetermined item/package (ie, test pack) designed to simulate the product to be sterilized and that is used to assess the efficacy of the sterilization process.

Prevacuum steam sterilizer: A steam sterilization cycle in which air is removed from the chamber and load via a series of pressure and vacuum excursions.

Shelf life: The length of time an item is considered sterile and safe to use.

Short-term exposure limits: Durations of exposure to a potentially toxic or harmful substance lasting for less than 15 minutes that cannot be repeated more than four times per day.

Steam-flush pressure-pulse (SPPP): A steam sterilization cycle in which air is removed from the chamber and load via a series of steam flushes and pressure pulses.

Sterilization process monitoring device: A device used to monitor sterilization processes. Sterilization monitoring devices can be biological, chemical, or physical.

REFERENCES

1. Petersen, C, ed. *Perioperative Nursing Data Set.* Rev 2nd ed. Denver, CO: AORN, Inc: 2007.

2. Recommended practices for cleaning and care of surgical instruments and powered equipment. In: *Standards, Recommended Practices, and Guidelines.* Denver, CO: AORN, Inc; 2008:421-446.

3. Association for the Advancement of Medical Instrumentation. *ANSI/AAMI ST79: 2006—Comprehensive Guide to Steam Sterilization and Sterility Assurance in Health Care Facilities.* Arlington, VA: Association for the Advancement of Medical Instrumentation, 2006:4,24-25,36-37,39,54,60,62-74,77-80,83,87,90,110.

4. Alvarado CJ, Reichelderfer M. 1997-1999 APIC Guidelines Committee: APIC guideline for infection prevention and control in flexible endoscopy. *American Journal of Infection Control.* 2000;28:138-155.

5. Recommended practice for traffic patterns in the perioperative practice setting. In: *Standards, Recommended Practices, and Guidelines.* Denver, CO: AORN, Inc; 2007:703-706.

6. Recommended practices for selection and use of packaging systems. In: *Standards, Recommended Practices, and Guidelines.* Denver, CO: AORN, Inc; 2007:607-616.

7. Association for the Advancement of Medical Instrumentation. *ANSI/AAMI/ISO 11607—Packaging for Terminally Sterilized Medical Devices.* Arlington, VA: Association for the Advancement of Medical Instrumentation, 2000.

8. Position statement on ergonomically healthy workplace practices. In: *Standards, Recommended Practices, and Guidelines.* Denver, CO: AORN, Inc; 2007:382.

9. Joslyn LJ. Sterilization by heat. In: *Disinfection, Sterilization, and Preservation.* 5th ed. Block SS, ed. Philadelphia, PA: Lippincott Williams & Wilkins; 2001: 695-728.

10. Association for the Advancement of Medical Instrumentation. *ANSI/AAMI ST8—Hospital steam sterilizers.* Arlington, VA: Association for the Advancement of Medical Instrumentation; 2001.

11. Clement L, Bliley J. Cracking the steam sterilizer door: Dispelling the myth. *Healthcare Purchasing News.* May 2007:40-42.

12. Mangram AJ, Horan TC, Pearson ML, Silver LC, Jarvis WR. Guideline for prevention of surgical site infection, 1999. [Special Report]. *Infection Control and Hospital Epidemiology.* 1999; 20:250-278. Available at *http://www.cdc.gov/ncidod/dhqp/pdf/guidelines/SSI.pdf.* October 26, 2007.

13. Conviser S. The Future of Ethylene Oxide Sterilization. *Infection Control Today.* June 2000. Available at *http://www.infectioncontroltoday.com/articles/061feat4.html.* Accessed October 26, 2007.

14. US Environmental Protection Agency. Code of Federal Regulations Title 40: Protection of Environment, Part 261Identification and Listing of Hazardous Waste. Available at *http://www.epa.gov/epahome/cfr40.htm*. Accessed October 26, 2007.

15. Association for the Advancement of Medical Instrumentation. *ANSI/AAMI ST41—Ethylene Oxide Sterilization in Health Care Facilities: Safety and Effectiveness*. Arlington, VA: Association for the Advancement of Medical Instrumentation; 2000.

16. Joslyn LJ. Gaseous chemical sterilization. In: *Disinfection, Sterilization, and Preservation*. 5th ed. Block SS, ed. Philadelphia, PA: Lippincott Williams & Wilkins; 2001:337-359.

17. Crane T, Preziotti R. Hospital sterilization after the CFC phase out. [Viewpoint]. *Surgical Services Management*. 1996;2:10-11.

18. US Department of Labor, Occupational Safety and Health Administration. 29 CFR 1910.1047, Ethylene oxide. Available at *http://www.osha.gov/pls/oshaweb/owadisp.show_document?p_table=STANDARDS&p_id=10070*. Accessed October 26, 2007.

19. Material Safety Data Sheet: Ethylene Oxide Sterilant, April 23, 2007. St. Louis, MO: STERIS Corporation: 2007:1-2.

20. US Department of Labor, Occupational Safety and Health Administration. Hazard communication in the 21st century workplace; March 2004. Available at *http://www.osha.gov/dsg/hazcom/finalmsdsreport.html*. Accessed October 26, 2007.

21. Schneider PM. Ethylene oxide sterilization: employee monitoring. In: *Sterilization Technology for the Heath Care Facility*. 2nd ed. Reichert M, Young JH, eds. Gaithersburg, MD: Aspen Publishers; 1997:220-227.

22. National Institute for Occupational Safety and Health. Appendix I Guidelines For Minimizing Worker Exposure To Ethylene Oxide. Current Intelligence Bulletin 35. Available at *http://www.cdc.gov/niosh/81130_35.html #Recommendations*. Accessed October 26, 2007.

23. US Department of Labor, Occupational Safety and Health Administration. 29 CFR 1910.1020, Access to employee exposure and medical records. Available at *http://www.osha.gov/pls/oshaweb/owadisp.show_document?p_table=STANDARDS &p_id=10027*. Accessed October 26, 2007.

24. *Material Safety Data Sheet 09461-0-001: Hydrogen Peroxide Solution, August 7, 2003*. Irvine, CA: Advanced Sterilization Products; 2003:1-8.

25. Rutala WA, Gergen MF, Weber DJ. Comparative evaluation of the sporicidal activity of new low-temperature sterilization technologies: ethylene oxide, 2 plasma sterilization systems, and liquid peracetic acid. *American Journal of Infection Control*. 1998;26:393-398.

26. Jacobs PT, Lin SM. Sterilization processes utilizing low-temperature plasma. In: *Disinfection, Sterilization, and Preservation*. 5th ed. Block SS, ed. Philadelphia, PA: Lippincott Williams & Wilkins; 2001:747-763.

27. Malchesky PS. Medical applications of peracetic acid. In: *Disinfection, Sterilization, and Preservation*. 5th ed. Block SS, ed. Philadelphia, PA: Lippincott Williams & Wilkins; 2001:979-996.

28. Association for the Advancement of Medical Instrumentation. *AAMI ST58 Chemical Sterilization and High Level Disinfection in Health Care Facilities*. Arlington, VA: Association for the Advancement of Medical Instrumentation; 2005.

29. Smith DF. STERRAD 200 Sterilization System. Advanced Sterilization Products: 2000: 1-22. Available at: *http://sterrad.com/SI/Products_&_Services/STERRAD/STERRAD_200_GMP/Literature/200_white_paper.pdf*. Accessed October 26, 2007.

30. Recommended practices for cleaning and processing endoscopes and endoscope accessories. In: *Standards, Recommended Practices, and Guidelines*. Denver, CO: AORN, Inc;2007:531-536.

31. Weavers LK, Wickramanayake GB. Disinfection and sterilization using ozone. In: *Disinfection, Sterilization, and Preservation*. 5th ed. Block SS, ed. Philadelphia, PA: Lippincott Williams, & Wilkins; 2001:205-214.

32. Association for the Advancement of Medical Instrumentation. *ANSI/AAMI ST40—Table-top Dry Heat (Heated Air) Sterilization and Sterility Assurance in Health Care Facilities*. Arlington, VA: Association for the Advancement of Medical Instrumentation; 2004.

33. *ASHCSP/IAHCSMM Position Paper on Loaner Instrumentation*. *http://www.iahcsmm.org/current_issues_Joint_paper_loaner_instrumentation.htm*. Accessed October 26, 2007.

34. US Department of Health and Human Services; Centers for Medicaid and Medicare Services (CMS) State Operations Manual Appendix L, §416.42 Condition for Coverage: Surgical Services, *http://www.cms.hhs.gov/manuals/downloads/som107ap_l_ambulatory.pdf*. Accessed October 26, 2007.

35. US Department of Health and Human Services; Centers for Medicaid and Medicare Services (CMS) State Operations Manual Appendix A§482.51 Condition of Participation: Surgical Services, *http://www.cms.hhs.gov/manuals/downloads/som107ap_a_hospitals.pdf*. Accessed October 26, 2007.

36. Medical device reporting: manufacturer reporting, importer reporting user facility reporting, distributor reporting; final rule. *Federal Register*. 2000;65 no 17:4112-4121. Also available at *http://www.fda.gov/OHRMS/DOCKETS/98fr/012600c.pdf*. Accessed October 26, 2007..

37. Recommended practices for product selection in perioperative practice settings. In: *Standards, Recommended Practices, and Guidelines*. Denver, CO: AORN, Inc; 2007:637-640.

38. Association for the Advancement of Medical Instrumentation. *ANSI/AAMI/ISO 15882 Sterilization of Health Care Products-Chemical Indicators-Guidance for the Selection, Use, and Interpretation of Results*. Arlington, VA: Association for the Advancement of Medical Instrumentation; 2003.

39. Recommended practices for sterilization in the perioperative setting. In: *Standards, Recommended Practices, and Guidelines*. Denver, CO: AORN, Inc; 2007:673-687.

RESOURCES

Bailey A. Updating sterilization technology. *Infection Control and Sterilization Technology.* 1995;2:31-33.

Bastedo G. Ethylene oxide sterilization. [Viewpoint]. *Surgical Services Management.* 1995;1:14-15.

Bronowicki JP, Venard V, Botte C, et al. Patient-to-patient transmission of hepatitis C virus during colonoscopy. [Brief Report]. *New England Journal of Medicine.* 1997;337:237-240.

Centers for Disease Control and Prevention. Bronchoscopy-related infections and pseudoinfections—New York, 1996 and 1998. *Morbidity and Mortality Weekly Report.* 1999;48:557-576. Available at *http://www.cdc.gov/mmwr/preview/mmwrhtml/mm4826a1.htm.* Accessed August 3, 2007.

Chobin N. Cost analysis of three low-temperature sterilization systems at Saint Barnabas Medical Center. *Journal of Healthcare Materiel Management.* 1994;12:29-32.

DesCoteaux JG, Poulin EC, Julien M, Guidon R. Residual organic debris on processed surgical instruments. *AORN Journal.* 1995;62:23-30.

Gross D. Ethylene oxide sterilization and alternative methods. [Viewpoint]. *Surgical Services Management.* 1995;1:16-18.

Lagergren E. Gas plasma sterilization. [Viewpoint]. *Surgical Services Management.* 1995;1:26-28.

Spry C. Sterilization regulations—who's in charge here? [Focus on Quality]. *Surgical Services Management.* 1995;1:56-59.

Tablan OC, Anderson LJ, Besser R, et al. Guidelines for preventing health care-associated pneumonia, 2003. Recommendations of the Centers for Disease Control and Prevention and the Healthcare Infection Control Practices Advisory Committee. *Morbidity and Mortality Weekly Report.* 2004;53 no RR03:1-36. Available at *http://www.cdc.gov/mmwr/preview/mmwrhtml/rr5303a1.htm.* Accessed August 3, 2007.

Ward SF. Today's new sterilization technology presents new decision variables. [Editorial]. *Surgical Services Management.* 1995;1:4-5.

Originally published August 1980, *AORN Journal.* Format revision July 1982.

Revised February 1987, October 1992. Published as proposed recommended practices in July 1994.

Revised; published August 1999, *AORN Journal.* Reformatted July 2000.

Revised November 2005; published March 2006, *AORN Journal.*

Revised 2007; published in *Perioperative Standards and Recommended Practices,* 2008 edition.

Additional

Resources

Section IV

Policies and Procedures

```
┌─────────────────────────────┐
│   Insert facility name here  │
│   or use a header or footer  │
└─────────────────────────────┘
```

Policy Template

INSERT POLICY TITLE AND ANY FACILITY-SPECIFIC INFORMATION HERE

Purpose:

> Insert brief purpose statement here.

The purpose statement is the intention of the policy. It is a concise summary with brief highlights. The purpose statement may be based on the Perioperative Nursing Data Set (PNDS) outcome statements or on the purpose statement of the recommended practice related to the policy and procedure.

Policy:

> It is the policy of *[name of facility]* that:

The policy is a statement describing activities that must be completed, including requirements from regulatory and accrediting agencies. Recommendations or intervention statements from the recommended practice may be used as policy statements. The recommendations are signified by a Roman numeral (eg, I, II, III) in **bold** font. The intervention statements are signified by a Roman numeral followed by an alpha character (eg, I.a., I.b., I.c.). The "should" statements in the recommended practice may be changed to *must* or *will,* and several recommendations may be grouped into one policy statement.

Procedure Interventions:

> Insert the specific sequence of steps required to achieve the purpose and the policy.

The procedure consists of statements describing the sequence of steps necessary to accomplish the purpose of the policy. Intervention statements or activity statements from the recommended practice may be used as steps in the procedure. The intervention statements are signified by a Roman numeral followed by an alpha character (eg, I.a., I.b., I.c.). The activity statements are signified by a Roman numeral followed by an alpha character followed by an Arabic numeral (eg, I.a.1., I.a.2., I.a.3.). The "should" statements in the recommended practice may be changed to *must* or *will* or may be converted into action statements. If the intervention cannot be delegated, the procedure statements may include a reference to the title of the person required to complete the intervention (eg, "The perioperative registered nurse assesses the patient"). If the task may be delegated, the procedure may be described in an action statement (eg, "Remove all contaminated supplies from the operating room").

Documentation:

> Insert here the information your facility requires to be documented, the area on the chart where this information is to be documented and who is responsible for the documentation.

The documentation section of the recommended practice may be used to assist in determining the facility's baseline for documentation.

Competency:

> INSERT HERE a statement of the knowledge, skills, and abilities your facility deems necessary for the person to successfully perform the steps in this policy and procedure.

The competency section of the recommended practice may be used to assist in determining the facility's baseline competencies.

Definitions:

> INSERT HERE the definitions of any words or phrases used that have a new or unfamiliar use in this policy and procedure.

The glossary section of the recommended practice may be used as a guideline for determining the definitions used in the policy and procedure.

References:

> INSERT HERE a list of the references used to compile the policy and procedure, using the format chosen by your facility.

Suggested references may include the most current edition of the AORN *Perioperative Standards and Recommended Practices.*

Administrative Approval:

> INSERT HERE the publication history of the document and the signatures of the person or persons in a leadership role who are responsible for the policy and procedure (eg, educator, manager, director, vice president of nursing; also may include the responsible physician) in accordance with organizational policy.

Date of original approval, review, or revision.

Created: _____

Reviewed:_____

Revised: _____

Approval signature(s) with position title and date of signature:

_____	_____	_____
Signature	*Title*	*Date*
_____	_____	_____
Signature	*Title*	*Date*
_____	_____	_____
Signature	*Title*	*Date*

Policies and Procedures

Policy & Procedure

MANAGING THE ADULT PATIENT RECEIVING MODERATE SEDATION/ANALGESIA

Purpose:

To provide direction to nonanesthesia providers, procedurists, and prescribers in the care and management of the patient receiving moderate sedation/analgesia.

This policy is intended to apply to the following settings:
- traditional operating rooms,
- ambulatory surgery centers,
- physicians' offices,
- cardiac catheterization laboratories,
- endoscopy suites,
- radiology departments, and
- other areas where surgery and invasive procedures may be performed.

The PNDS outcome is O9: **The patient will receive appropriate medication(s), safely administered during the perioperative period.**

Policy:

It is the policy of *[insert name of facility]* that:
- The registered nurse administering moderate sedation/analgesia must practice within the scope of nursing practice for his or her state. *[Script the policy statements to reflect your facility's medical staff bylaws and your individual state's advisory opinions, declaratory rules, or other regulatory rulings specific to the administration of moderate sedation/analgesia by the RN nonanesthesia provider. Spell out any continuing education that would be required.]*
- Patient selection for moderate sedation/ analgesia is based on established criteria developed through interdisciplinary collaboration of health care professionals.
- The registered nurse completes a patient assessment before administering moderate sedation/analgesia.
- The registered nurse monitoring the patient has no other responsibilities that require leaving the patient unattended or that would compromise continuous monitoring during the procedure.
- An additional registered nurse is assigned to the circulating role during the administration of moderate sedation.
- The registered nurse collaborates with the licensed independent practitioner in developing and documenting the sedation/analgesia plan of care.
- Prior to the procedure, the registered nurse calculates the recommended dose and dilution and knows the onset, duration, effects, potential adverse reactions, drug compatibility, and contraindications for each medication used during moderate sedation/analgesia.
- The registered nurse continuously monitors the patient throughout the procedure.
- The registered nurse monitors the patient receiving moderate sedation/analgesia postoperatively until discharge from the postanesthesia care unit.
- The registered nurse evaluates the patient for discharge readiness based on specific criteria.
- The registered nurse is clinically competent, possessing the skills necessary to manage the nursing care of the patient receiving moderate sedation/analgesia.
- A licensed independent practitioner, qualified by education, training, and licensure to administer moderate sedation, supervises the administration of moderate sedation.
- The supervising licensed independent practitioner remains immediately available during the administration and recovery period.

Procedure Interventions:

The registered nurse assesses the patient to determine the appropriateness of nurse-administered sedation/analgesia using the American Society of Anesthesiologists (ASA) Physical Status Classification. Patients who are classified as P1, P2, and medically sable P3 are considered appropriate for registered nurse-administered moderate sedation/analgesia.

The registered nurse should consult an anesthesia provider if the patient presents with any of the following:
- known history of respiratory or hemodynamic instability;
- previous difficulties with anesthesia or sedation;
- severe sleep apnea or other airway-related issues;
- one or more significant comorbidities;
- pregnancy;
- inability to communicate (eg, aphasic);
- inability to cooperate (eg, mentally incapacitated);
- multiple drug allergies;
- multiple medications with potential for drug interaction with sedative analgesics;
- current substance use (eg, street drugs, herbal supplements, nonprescribed prescription drugs);
- ASA physical classification of unstable P3;and
- ASA physical classification of P4 or above.

The presedation assessment includes the following:
- verification of consent explaining risks, benefits, and alternatives to sedation;
- review of medical history;
- review of physical examination of the cardiac and pulmonary systems including vital signs;
- review of height and weight;
- verification of pregnancy test results, when applicable;
- review of present medication regimen (eg, prescribed, over-the-counter, herbals, supplements), medication taken within the last 48 hours including any as needed medications, especially opioids or other narcotics;
- review of substance use;
- review of tobacco and alcohol use;
- verification of allergies and sensitivities to medications, latex, chemical agents, foods, and adhesives;
- confirmation of NPO status using the ASA fasting guidelines;
- determination of patient's ability to tolerate and maintain the required position for the duration of the planned procedure; and
- verification that a responsible adult caregiver is available to escort the patient home.

The registered nurse performs an assessment of the patient's airway before administering sedation. The assessment includes the following risk factors:
- age > 55 years;
- significant obesity (especially of the face, neck, and tongue);
- missing teeth or edentulous;
- presence of a beard;
- history of snoring or sleep apnea; and
- presence of stridor.

Procedure Interventions, continued

Evaluate the need for IV access depending on the route of sedation and the level of sedation intended.

Administer each IV agent separately in incremental doses and titrated to desired effect (sedation, analgesia, maintenance of protective reflexes, airway patency, and spontaneous ventilation).

Opioid antagonists (ie, naloxone) and benzodiazepines antagonists (ie, flumazenil) are readily available whenever opioids and benzodiazepines are administered.

Monitor vital signs before the start of the procedure, after administration of a sedative or analgesic, and at five minute intervals during the procedure based on the patient's condition, type and amount of medication, and length of procedure. The following parameters are monitored:
- heart rate and function via continuous electrocardiogram (ECG);
- oxygenation using pulse oximetry;
- respiratory rate and adequacy of ventilation;
- blood pressure;
- level of consciousness (LOC);
- comfort level; and
- skin condition.

Ensure that equipment is present, working properly, and immediately available where the procedure is performed. Age- and size-appropriate equipment should include the following:
- suction;
- airway management devices (eg, oral and nasal airways, mask ventilation devices);
- noninvasive blood pressure monitoring device;
- pulse oximetry;
- electrocardiograph.

Ensure that an emergency resuscitation cart is immediately available in every location where moderate sedation/analgesia is administered. An emergency cart includes:
- resuscitation medications;
- intravenous access equipment;
- intravenous fluids; and
- life-support equipment (eg, defibrillator, endotracheal intubation equipment, mechanical positive bag-valve mask device).

The registered nurse monitors the patient who receives moderate sedation/analgesia postoperatively using the same parameters used during the procedure. Postoperative monitoring includes:
- heart rate and rhythm;
- LOC;
- blood pressure;
- cardiac monitoring;
- oxygenation; and
- ventilation.

The registered nurse assesses the patient postoperatively. The assessment includes
- wound condition;
- dressing condition;
- line patency;
- amount of drainage in drains; and
- level of pain.

Procedure Interventions, continued

Interdisciplinary developed discharge criteria are applied consistently to all patients. Discharge criteria include:

- return to preoperative, baseline LOC;
- stability of vital signs;
- sufficient time interval (eg, two hours)since the last administration of an antagonist (eg, naloxone, flumazenil) to prevent resedation of the patient;
- use of an objective patient assessment scoring system (eg, Aldrete Recovery Score);
- absence of protracted nausea;
- intact protective reflexes;
- adequate pain control; and
- return of motor/sensory control.

The patient and the caregiver receive verbal and written discharge instructions.

The patient or caregiver should be able to verbalize understanding of the discharge instructions.

A copy of the written discharge instructions is given to the patient.

A copy of the written discharge instructions is placed in the patient's medical record.

Documentation:

The perioperative register nurse documents the care of the patient receiving moderate sedation/analgesia and the physiological responses throughout the continuum of care. The following elements must be documented:

- patient assessment;
- plan of care;
- nursing diagnosis;
- identification of desired outcomes;
- interventions;
- medications—name, dose, route, time, and effects;
- patient's level of consciousness (LOC);
- ventilation and oxygen status;
- vital signs at intervals dependent on the type and quantity of medication administered;
- procedure start and stop times;
- time out;
- condition of patient; and
- evaluation of patient response to the care provided.

Competency:

The competency of the perioperative registered nurse to administer moderate sedation/ analgesia is assessed, demonstrated, documented, and maintained. The competencies include:

- patient selection and assessment criteria;
- selection, function, and proficiency in use of physiological monitoring equipment;
- pharmacology of the medications used;
- airway management;
- CPAP use;
- basic dysrhythmia recognition and management;
- emergency response and management;
- advanced cardiac life support (ACLS) and pediatric advanced life support (PALS) according to patients served;
- recognition of complications associated with sedation/analgesia; and
- knowledge of anatomy and physiology.

Competency, continued

The perioperative registered nurse administering moderate sedation/analgesia is able to rescue patients whose level progresses to deep sedation.

The perioperative registered nurse at a minimum has the ability to manage a compromised airway and provide adequate oxygenation and ventilation.

Definitions:

Moderate sedation/analgesia: A drug-induced, mild depression of conscious during which the patient is able to independently and continuously maintain a patent airway and respond purposely to verbal commands and/or little tactical simulation.

Immediately available: Defined by the ASA practice guidelines as having a health care provider trained in ACLS and resuscitation skills available to a to assist with patient care within one to five minutes.

Licensed independent practitioner: Any individual who is permitted by law and the health care organization to provide care and services, without supervision or direction. The care and services should be within the scope of the individual's license and granted clinical privileges.

References:

ASA Physical Status Classification System. American Society of Anesthesiologists. http://www.asahq.org /clinical/physicalstatus.htm. Accessed December 16, 2008.

Petersen, C, ed. *Perioperative Nursing Data Set.* Revised 2nd ed. Denver, CO: AORN; 2007:49-50.

Practice guidelines for sedation and analgesia by non-anesthesiologists. *Anesthesiology* 2002 (April); 96(4):1004–1017.

Recommended practices for managing the patient receiving moderate sedation/analgesia. In: *Perioperative Standards and Recommended Practices.* Denver, CO: AORN; 2008:461-472.

[Cite additional references as needed.]

Administrative Approval:

Date of original approval, review, or revision:

Created: _____

Last Revised:_____

Last Reviewed: _____

Next Review: _____

Approval signature(s) with position title and date of signature:

Signature	*Title*	*Date*
Signature	*Title*	*Date*
Signature	*Title*	*Date*

<table>
<tr><td>Insert facility name here
or use a header or footer</td></tr>
</table>

Policy & Procedure

POSITIONING, TRANSPORTING, MOVING, AND LIFTING THE PATIENT IN PERIOPERATIVE PRACTICE SETTINGS

Purpose:

To establish the authority, responsibility, and accountability for positioning, transporting, moving, and lifting the patient in perioperative practice settings.

The patient should be free from signs and symptoms of injury related to positioning, transporting, moving, or lifting.

Health care providers should be free from signs and symptoms of injury related to positioning, transporting, moving, and lifting patients in perioperative settings.

These policies are not intended to cover detailed aspects of purchasing, surgical scheduling, equipment maintenance, or perioperative patient care addressed in other *[name of facility]* policy statements (eg, pressure ulcer prevention, prevention of DVT). These policies are intended to apply to the following settings:

- traditional operating rooms,
- ambulatory surgery centers,
- physicians' offices,
- cardiac catheterization laboratories,
- endoscopy suites,
- radiology departments, and
- all other areas where surgery and invasive procedures may be performed.

Policy:

It is the policy of *[name of facility]* that:

- All members of the perioperative team will use proper body mechanics when positioning, transporting, moving, lifting or patients.
- The patient's position will be included in the Time-out process.
- When on the procedure bed, the patient will be attended by one or more of the perioperative team members at all times.
- The perioperative registered nurse (RN) will actively participate in safely positioning the patient under the direction of and in collaboration with the surgeon and anesthesia provider.
- The perioperative RN will continuously assess the patient's position throughout the procedure and communicate with the surgeon and anesthesia provider in a timely manner when there are concerns.
- The Association of periOperative Registered Nurses (AORN) recommended practices for positioning the patient in the perioperative practice setting will be a primary source of information for establishing competency statements for positioning the patient in perioperative settings.
- Patient positioning will be included in the overall organizational or department plan for annual competency validation or education plan for perioperative team members.

Procedure Interventions:

1. The perioperative RN will confirm that appropriate positioning equipment is available and in working order before the patient arrives.
   a. Confirms the patient position with the operative surgeon.
   b. Anticipates positioning equipment needed for specific operative procedure.

Policies and Procedures

Procedure Interventions, continued

2. Perioperative personnel will initiate action when necessary to ensure that an adequate number of personnel will be used to safely transport, move, lift, and position patients during all phases of care.

   a. **Supine transfer**
      - A lateral transfer device (eg, friction reducing sheets, slider board, air assisted transfer device) should be used for supine-to-supine patient transfer.
      - One caregiver and one anesthesia care provider (who is managing the airway, head, and neck) should be assigned to safely transfer a patient who weighs 52 lbs.
      - Two caregivers plus the anesthesia care provider should be assigned to safely transfer a patient up to 104 lbs.
      - Three caregivers plus the anesthesia care provider should be assigned to safely transfer a patient up to 157 lbs.
      - For patients who weigh more than 157 lbs, an appropriate mechanical lifting device (ie, mechanical lift with supine sling, mechanical lateral transfer device, or air-assisted lateral transfer device) should be used and a minimum of three to four caregivers should be assigned.

   b. **Transferring into and out of sitting or modified sitting position**
      - Three caregivers should be assigned to work together to lift up to 67 lbs (30 kg).
      - Mechanical devices and a minimum of three caregivers should be used if the patient weighs more than 68 lbs.

   c. **Supine to prone transfer**
      - Four caregivers should be available for a supine-to-prone patient transfer. One anesthesia care provider should maintain the airway and support the patient's head, while other members of the team are responsible for the patient's trunk and extremities.
      - Two caregivers, plus the anesthesia care provider, can safely transfer a patient weighing up to 48.5 lbs (22.0 kg) from the supine to the prone position.
      - Three caregivers, plus an anesthesia care provider, can safely transfer a patient weighing up to 72.7 lbs (33.0 kg).
      - If the patient's weight is greater than 73 lbs, it is necessary to use assistive technology and a minimum of three to four caregivers.

   d. **Transferring into and out of the lithotomy position**
      - A minimum of two caregivers is needed to lift the legs.
      - Mechanical devices such as support slings can be used to lift the legs to and from the lithotomy position.

   e. **Transferring into and out of the lateral position**
      - For a patient weighing up to 76 lb (ie, 34.5 kg), three caregivers should be assigned; one caregiver (eg, the anesthesia care provider) should be assigned specifically to support the patient's head and neck and maintain the patient's airway during the lateral transfer.
      - Three caregivers plus an anesthesia care provider can safely position a patient weighing up to 115 lbs (ie, 52.2 kg).
      - If the patient's weight exceeds 115 lbs (ie, 52.2 kg), it is important to use lateral positioning devices.

   f. **Positioning the patient who is morbidly obese**
      - Assistive technology and a minimum of three to four caregivers patients is required for patients who have a BMI of greater than 40 or who weigh 100 lbs or more over their recommended weight.

Procedure Interventions, *continued*

3. The perioperative RN will identify physical alterations that require additional precautions for procedure-specific positioning.
   a. Reviews chart for information on patient's weight, preexisting medical conditions, and laboratory results.
   b. Assesses patient skin condition, level of consciousness, perception of pain, presence of peripheral pulses, mobility, and preexisting conditions (eg, poor nutritional status, extremes of age, vascular insufficiency, diabetes, impaired nerve function) that may increase the patient's risk of injury due to positioning.
   c. Identifies factors independent of nursing care (eg, type and length of procedure or type of anesthesia) that may increase the patient's risk injury due to positioning.
   d. Initiates additional precautions based on identified risk factors to reduce the risk of positioning injury.

4. The perioperative RN will verify the presence of prosthetics or corrective devices.
   a. Notifies appropriate members of health care team when patient is known to have a metal or synthetic prostheses or implants, pacemaker, automated implanted cardioverter defibrillator (ACID), hearing aid, intraocular lens, or plastic/fluid implant (e.g., penile implants, testicular implants, breast implants).
   b. Adjusts positioning methods to accommodate individual patient needs as identified.

5. Perioperative personnel will maintain patient dignity and privacy for the patient during transport, transfer and positioning.

6. The perioperative RN will ensure that patient jewelry and body piercing accessories are removed before transferring onto or positioning the patient on the procedure bed.

7. The perioperative RN will actively participate in positioning the patient under the direction of the surgeon and in collaboration with the anesthesia provider.
   a. Selects positioning devices based on patient's identified needs and the planned operative or invasive procedure.
   b. Uses positioning devices to protect, support, and maintain patient position.
   c. Confirms that positioning devices are available, clean, free of sharp edges, padded as appropriate, and in working order before patient is transferred to the procedure bed.
   d. Modifies procedure bed as necessary before attaching positioning devices.
   e. Applies safety belt loosely as to not constrict blood flow or compress nerves.
   f. Confirms the patient position with the perioperative team during the Time-out process.
   g. Ensures patient's correct anatomical position is maintained while providing surgical exposure.
   h. Prevents limbs from dropping below bed level to prevent compression of peripheral nerves.
   i. Maintains proper body alignment with legs uncrossed.
   j. Prevents body parts from coming in contact with metal portions of procedure bed.
   k. Ensures the patient's fingers are free of any moveable parts (eg, breaks in the procedure bed).
   l. Elevates patient's heels off of the support surface when possible.
   m. Reassesses patient throughout case for proper body alignment and tissue integrity.
   n. Supervises placement of equipment and/or surgical instruments placed on patient.
   o. Monitors patient for external pressures from members of health care team.
   p. Assists in repositioning by removing devices as appropriate in preparation for transfer.
   q. Removes positioning devices from patient and procedure bed while maintaining patient's body alignment.

Policies and Procedures

Procedure Interventions, continued

8. Perioperative personnel will cross reference the "AORN recommended practices for positioning the patient in the perioperative practice setting" for positioning considerations specific to supine, prone, Trendelenburg's, lithotomy, and lateral positions and morbidly obese patients.

9. The perioperative RN will evaluate for signs and symptoms of injury as a result of positioning using the following patient indicators for outcome achievement at the time of transfer.
   a. Skin condition: smooth, intact and free from ecchymosis, cuts, abrasions, shear injury or blistering
   b. Cardiovascular status: heart rate and blood pressure within expected ranges; peripheral pulses present and equal bilaterally; capillary refill less than three seconds; skin warm to touch.
   c. Neuromuscular status: flexes and extends extremities equal to or better than noted during preoperative assessment; denies numbness or tingling of extremities.

Documentation:

Patient care and use of positioning devices will be documented on the intraoperative record by the perioperative RN in accordance with the *[insert name of facility]* policy on intraoperative documentation. Documentation should include, but not be limited to,
- preoperative assessment including a description of the patient's overall skin
- condition on arrival and discharge from the perioperative suite;
- type and location of positioning equipment;
- name and titles of persons participating in positioning the patient;
- patient position and new position, if repositioning becomes necessary; and
- postoperative assessment for injury related to position.

When it is necessary to document injuries due to positioning, photography may be used in accordance with the *[insert name of facility]* policy regarding medical photography and videotaping.

References:

Recommended practices for positioning the patient in the perioperative practice setting. In: *Perioperative Standards and Recommended Practices*. Denver, CO: AORN; 2008:497-520.

Petersen C, ed. AORN guidance statement: Safe patient handling and movement in the perioperative setting. Denver, CO: AORN; 2007.

[Cite additional references as needed]

Administrative Approval:

Date of origin: _____

Last date revised or reviewed:_____

Date of next scheduled review: _____

Approval signature(s) with position title and date of signature:

_____	_____	_____
Signature	*Title*	*Date*
_____	_____	_____
Signature	*Title*	*Date*
_____	_____	_____
Signature	*Title*	*Date*

Glossary of Times Used for Scheduling and Monitoring of Diagnostic and Therapeutic Procedures

The following glossary was developed by the Association of Anesthesia Clinical Directors (AACD) and was approved by their board of directors in October 1995. It has been endorsed by AORN, Inc, and the Society for Technology in Anesthesia and has been accepted without revision by the American Society of Anesthesiologists Committee on Quality Improvement and Practice Management. It is reprinted here with permission of the AACD.

Background

Elevated concerns regarding the economics of health care are dramatically intensifying the pressure for health care providers to establish critical pathways and/or total quality management programs. In addition, negotiating fiscally sound managed care contracts with health maintenance organizations and health insurance carriers, as well as meeting state and federal government documentation requirements, requires justification for each aspect of patient care as well as improved techniques in cost factor analysis and accounting. Few hospital administrators would deny that operating rooms/procedure rooms (OR/PR) are expensive to run, and all would concur that economic analyses of running OR/PRs are not readily available.

During the planning for multicenter studies of OR/PR scheduling, utilization, and efficiency, members of the Association of Anesthesia Clinical Directors (AACD) felt semantics were introducing a major impediment to data comparison and economic analysis. To provide a universal lexicon for the acquisition of data, the AACD has developed a glossary which inclusively, yet restrictively, defines the procedural times that permit comprehensive analyses of OR/PR scheduling, utilization, and efficiency. The AACD proposes adopting this lexicon as a standardized "Glossary of Times Used for Scheduling and Monitoring of Diagnostic and Therapeutic Procedures."

The glossary is divided into four sections: 1) Procedural Times, 2) Procedural and Scheduling Definitions and Time Periods, 3) Utilization and Efficiency Indices, and 4) Patient Categories. The terms defined under Procedural Times are listed in what is the usual chronological order, while terms defined in the other sections are presented in alphabetical order.

1. Procedural Times

(For purposes of analyzing efficiency, each of the times defined below may be further classified by the subscripts S and A, for "Scheduled" and "Actual," respectively.)

1.1 Patient in Facility (PIF) = Time patient arrives at health care facility (applicable to outpatient or same day admission patients).

1.2 Patient Ready for Transport (PRT) = Time when all preparations required prior to transport (eg, labs, consent, gowning) have been completed.

1.3 Patient Sent-for (PS) = Time when transporting service is notified to deliver patient to the OR/PR.

1.4 Patient Available (PA) = Time the patient arrives in the OR/PR preprocedure area.

1.5 Room Set-up Start (RSS) = Time when personnel begin setting up, in the OR/PR, the supplies and equipment for the next case.

1.6 Anesthesia Start (AS) = Time when a member of the anesthesia team begins preparing the patient for an anesthetic.

1.7 Room Ready (RR) = Time when room is cleaned and supplies and equipment necessary for beginning of next case are present (see Discussion).

1.8 Patient In Room (PIR) = Time when patient enters the OR/PR.

1.9 Anesthesiologist, First Available (AFA) = Time of arrival in OR/PR of first anesthesiologist who is qualified to induce anesthesia in patient (see Discussion).

1.10 Procedure Physician, First Available (PPFA) = Time of arrival in OR/PR of first physician/surgeon qualified to position and prep the patient (see Discussion).

1.11 Anesthesiologist of Record In (ARI) = Time of arrival in OR/PR of anesthesiologist of record (see Discussion).

1.12 Anesthesia Induction (AI) = Time when the anesthesiologist begins the administration of agents intended to provide the level of anesthesia required for the scheduled procedure.

1.13 Anesthesia Ready (AR) = Time at which the patient has a sufficient level of anesthesia established to begin surgical preparation of the patient, and remaining anesthetic chores do not preclude positioning and prepping the patient (see Discussion).

1.14 Position/Prep Start (PS) = Time at which the nursing or surgical team begins positioning or prepping the patient for the procedure.

1.15 Prep-Completed (PC) = Time at which prepping and draping have been completed and patient is ready for the procedure or surgery to start.

1.16 Procedure Physician of Record In (PPRI) = Arrival time of physician/surgeon of record (see Discussion).

1.17 Procedure/Surgery Start Time (PST) = Time the procedure is begun (eg, incision for a surgical procedure, insertion of scope for a diagnostic procedure, beginning of exam under anesthesia [EUA], shooting of x-ray for radiological procedure).

1.18 Procedure/Surgery Conclusion Begun (PCB) = Time when diagnostic or therapeutic maneuvers are completed and attempts are made by the physician or surgical team to end any noxious stimuli (eg, beginning of wound closure, removal of bronchoscope).

1.19 Procedure Physician of Record Out (PPRO) = Time when physician/surgeon of record leaves the OR/PR (see Discussion).

1.20 Procedure/Surgery Finish (PF) = Time when all instrument and sponge counts are completed and verified as correct; all postoperative radiological studies to be done in the OR/PR are completed; all dressings and drains are secured; and the physician/surgeons have completed all procedure-related activities on the patient.

1.21 Patient Out of Room (POR) = Time at which patient leaves OR/PR.

1.22 Room Clean-up Start (RCS) = Time housekeeping or room personnel begin clean-up of OR/PR.

1.23 Arrival in PACU/ICU (APACU) = Time of patient arrival in PACU or ICU.

1.24 Anesthesia Finish (AF) = Time at which anesthesiologist turns over care of the patient to a postanesthesia care team (either PACU or ICU).

1.25 Room Clean-up Finish (RCF) = Time OR/PR is clean and ready for set-up of supplies and equipment for the next case.

1.26 Ready-for-Discharge from Postanesthesia Care Unit (RDPACU) = Time that patient is assessed to be ready for discharge from the PACU.

1.27 Discharge from Postanesthesia Care Unit (DPACU) = Time patient is transported out of PACU.

1.28 Arrival in Same Day Surgery Recovery Unit = Time of patient arrival in same day surgery recovery unit.

1.29 Ready-for-Discharge from Same Day Surgery Recovery Unit (RDSDSR) = Time that patient is assessed to be ready for discharge from the same day surgery recovery unit.

1.30 Discharge from Same Day Surgery Recovery Unit (DSDSR) = Time patient leaves SDSR unit (either to home or other facility).

2. Procedural and Scheduling Definitions and Time Periods

(For purposes of analyzing efficiency, each of the time periods defined below may be further classified by the subscripts E and A for "Estimated" and "Actual," respectively.)

2.1 Anesthesia Preparation Time (APT) = Time from Anesthesia Start to Anesthesia Ready Time.

2.2 Average Case Length (ACL) = Total hours divided by total number of cases performed within those hours.

2.3 Block Time (BT) = Hours of OR/PR time reserved for a given service or physician/surgeon. Within a defined cutoff period (eg, 72 hours prior to day of surgery), this is time into which only the given service may schedule. (NB: In some institutions, this is known as available or allocated time.)

2.4 Case Time (CT) = Time from Room Set-up Start to Room Clean-up Finished (see Discussion).

2.5 Early Start Hours (ESH) = Hours of Case Time performed prior to the normal day's start time when it is not expected that the Patient Out of Room Time will be before the normal start time for that day.

2.6 Evening/Weekend/Holiday Hours (EWHH) = Hours of Case Time performed outside of Resource Hours.

2.7 In-own Block Hours (IBH) = Hours of Case Time performed during a service's own Block Time. (NB: For a case to be counted in IBH, it must begin during that given service's Block Time.)

2.8 Open Time (OT) = Hours of OR/PR time not reserved for any particular service, into which any service or physician/surgeon may schedule according to the rules established by the given institution. (NB: In some institutions, this is known as discretionary time).

2.9 Outside-own Block Hours (OBH) = Hours of Case Time performed during Resource Hours but outside of the service's Block Time.

2.10 Overrun Hours (OVRH) = Hours of Case Time completed after the scheduled closure time of the OR/PR (ie, after the end of that day's Resource Hours).

2.11 Released Time (RT) = Hours of OR/PR time that are released from a service's Block Time and converted to Open Time (typically done when a service anticipates that it will be unable to use the Block Time due to meetings or vacation).

2.12 Resource Hours (RH) = Total number of hours scheduled to be available for performance of procedures (ie, the sum of all available Block Time and Open Time). This is typically provided for on a weekly recurring basis, but may be analyzed on a daily, weekly, monthly, or annual basis (see Discussion).

2.13 Room Clean-up Time (RCT) = Time from Patient Out of Room to Room Clean-up Finished.

2.14 Room Close (RC) = Time at which the room should be empty and the assigned personnel free to be discharged.

2.15 Room Open (RO) = Time when appropriate staff are scheduled to be present and are expected to have the OR/PR available for patient occupancy.

2.16 Room Set-up Time (RST) = Time from Room Set-up Start to Room Ready.

2.17 Service = A group of physicians or surgeons that together perform a circumscribed set of operative or diagnostic procedures (eg, cardiothoracic surgery, interventional radiology). Generally, any member of a service may schedule into that service's block time. Similarly, OR/PR time used by a given physician or surgeon is credited to his/her service's Total Hours.

2.18 Surgical Preparation Time (SPT) = Time from Position/Prep Start to Procedure/Surgery Start Time.

2.19 Start Time (ST) = Patient In Room Time (see Discussion).

2.20 Total Cases (TC) = Cumulative total of all cases done in a given time period. May be subdivided by service or physician/surgeon.

2.21 Total Hours (TH) = Sum of all Case Times for a given period of time. TH = IBH + OBH + EWHH. May be subdivided by service or individual physician/surgeon.

2.22 Turnover Time (TOT) = Time from prior Patient Out of Room to succeeding Patient In Room Time for sequentially scheduled cases (see Discussion).

3. Utilization and Efficiency Indices

3.1 Adjusted-Percent Service Utilization (ASU) = (IBH + OBH) x 100 ÷ BT. This measures the percentage of time a service utilizes their Block Time during Resource Hours. It is adjusted, compared to Raw Utilization, in that it gives a service "credit" for the time necessary to set up and clean up a room, during which time a patient cannot be in the room. It may exceed 100% because of the inclusion of cases performed during Resource Hours that are Outside-own Block Hours (see Discussion).

3.2 Adjusted-Percent Utilized Resource Hours (AURH) = (Total Hours-Evening/Weekend/Holiday Hours) ÷ Resource Hours x 100. This calculation provides the percentage of time that the OR/PRs are being prepared for a patient, are occupied by a patient, or are being cleaned after taking care of a patient during Resource Hours. It is adjusted, compared to Raw Utilization, in that it includes the time necessary to set up and clean up a room, during which time a patient cannot be in the room (see Discussion).

3.3 Delays may be due to:

    3.3.1 Patient issues
        Insurance problems
        Patient arrived late
        Patient ate/drank
        Abnormal lab values
        Surgery issues
        Complications arose

    3.3.2 System issues
        Test results unavailable
        Blood unavailable
        Patient not ready on floor
        Transport delay
        Elevator delay
        Previous case ran late
        Case bumped for emergency case
        Equipment unavailable
        Equipment malfunction
        X-rays unavailable
        X-ray technician unavailable
        Delay in receiving floor bed
        Insufficient post procedure care beds
        ICU delay
        Instrument problem

    3.3.3 Practitioner issues
        Needs more workup (eg, labs, consults)
        No consent
        Physician/surgeon arrived late
        Anesthesiologist arrived late
        Physician/surgeon unavailable
        Anesthesiologist unavailable
        Inaccurate posting
        Prolonged set-up time

3.4 Early Start = When Patient In Room, Actual, is prior to Patient In Room, Scheduled.

3.4.1 With overlap—When a case starts early but prior to the Room Clean-up Finished, Actual, of the case originally scheduled to precede it (this occurs when either the preceding or following case is moved to a different OR/PR than originally scheduled).

3.4.2 Without overlap—When a case starts early but after the Room Clean-up Finished, Actual, of the case originally scheduled to precede it (this may occur because there is no preceding case or because the preceding case finishes earlier than scheduled).

3.5 Late Start = When Patient In Room, Actual, is after Patient In Room, Scheduled.

3.5.1 With no interference—when the Room Clean-up Finished, Actual, of the preceding case occurs before the Room Set-up Start, Scheduled, of the following case (ie, the OR/PR is available prior to or at the time that preparation for the next case is supposed to begin).

3.5.2 With interference—When Room Clean-up Finished, Actual, of the preceding case occurs after the Room Set-up Start, Scheduled, of the following case (ie, the OR/PR is not available at the time that preparation for the next case is supposed to begin, either because it is still occupied or because it has not been cleaned).

3.6 Overrun = When Room Clean-up Finished, Actual, for the last scheduled case of the day is later than Room Close. This may be caused by a late start; a Case Time, Actual, greater than Case Time, Scheduled; or a combination of late start and longer than scheduled Case Time.

3.7 Productivity Index (PI) = Percent of time per hour that a patient is in the OR/PR during the prime shift time (eg, first 8 hours).

3.8 Raw Utilization (RU) = For the system as a whole, this is the percent of time that patients are in the room during Resource Hours (see Adjusted-Percent Utilized Resource Hours). For an individual service, this is the percent of its Block Time during which a service has a patient in the OR/PR (see Adjusted-Percent Service Utilization).

3.9 Room Gap = Time OR/PRs are vacant during Resource Hours.

3.9.1 Empty Room (or Late Start) Gap (LSG)
Planned—When Patient In Room, Scheduled, is later than Room Open.

Unplanned—When Patient In Room, Actual, is later than Room Open.

3.9.2 Between Case Gaps (BCG)
Planned—When Patient In Room, Scheduled, is later than the Room Clean-up Finished, Actual, of the preceding case.
Unplanned—When Patient In Room, Actual, is later than the Room Clean-up Finished, Actual, of the preceding case.

3.9.3 End of Schedule Gaps (ESG)
Planned—When Room Clean-up Finished, Scheduled, occurs before Room Close.
Unplanned—When Room Clean-up Finished, Actual, occurs before Room Close.

3.9.4 Total Gap Hours (TGH) = LSG + BCG + ESG.

4. Patient Categories

4.1 In-house (IH) = Patient admitted to and residing in the hospital prior to scheduled surgery/procedure.

4.2 Outpatient (OP) = Patient who is coming in on the day of surgery/procedure and is expected to return home following the procedure.

4.3 Same Day Admit (SDA) = Patient who is coming in on the day of surgery/procedure and will be admitted to the hospital following the procedure.

4.4 Overnight-Recovery (ONR) = Patient who comes in on the day of surgery/procedure but requires overnight recovery prior to returning home. These patients are never admitted to the hospital as inpatients, but may remain in the recovery facility for 12 to 23 hours post surgery/procedure.

Discussion

The foregoing list of the procedural times was intentionally made exhaustive in order to be all inclusive. This by no means suggests that all of the data points defined need to be collected by all institutions. Where problems with OR/PR efficiency exist, whether they are real or perceptual, collecting the appropriate times listed above, and calculating the pertinent time periods, will permit objective evaluation of where the real problems lie. Use of common definitions across the country will also permit inter-institutional comparisons that have been previously impossible.

Several terms listed in the "Procedural Times Glossary" have not had heretofore universally accepted definitions. For several of these, the authors, the board of directors of the Association of Anesthesia Clinical Directors, and the Society for Technology in Anesthesia National Database Committee felt that there existed significant controversy over which definition should be chosen. Although for each of these a consensus was generated which led to the definition chosen, general acceptance of these choices may be improved if the logic behind the decision is known. For those terms which created serious debate, the following discussion of terms is provided.

Adjusted-Percent Service Utilization (ASU) = (IBH + OBH) x 100 ÷ BT. This measures the percentage of time a service utilizes its Block Time during Resource Hours. It is adjusted, compared to raw utilization, in that it gives a service "credit" for the time necessary to set up and clean up a room, during which time a patient cannot be in the room. It may exceed 100% because of the inclusion of cases performed during Resource Hours that are Outside-own Block Hours.

Adjusted-Percent Utilized Resource Hours (AURH) = (Total Hours-Evening/Weekend/Holiday Hours) ÷ Resource Hours x 100. This calculation provides the percentage of time that the OR/PRs are being prepared for a patient, are occupied by a patient, or are being cleaned after taking care of a patient during Resource Hours. It is adjusted, compared to raw utilization, in that it includes the time necessary to set up and clean up a room, during which time a patient cannot be in the room.

Raw Utilization (RU) = For the system as a whole, this is the percent of time that patients are in the room during Resource Hours (see Adjusted Percent Utilization Resource Hours). For an individual service, this is the percent of its Block Time during which a service has a patient in the OR/PR (see Adjusted-Percent Utilization).

Frequently, institutions attempt to assess the extent to which a service uses its allotted Block Time by calculating a utilization percentage. Such a calculation should be performed for the system as a whole to measure the extent to which the "normal" hours of operation are actually used for patient care. If one considers only the time that a patient is in the OR/PR (raw utilization), then the percent of time that a service uses its Block Time is

artificially lowered because the time necessary to set up and clean up a room, during which time a patient cannot be in the room, is not accounted for. Similarly, the calculation of percentage utilization of Resource Hours is artificially reduced if only Patient In Room time is used. The larger the number of procedures done in a given room during Resource Hours, the greater the error.

Cost-effective utilization requires highly effective scheduling and optimum utilization of the Resource Hours, with minimal overtime and/or uses of more highly paid on-call personnel. For proper assessment of the extent to which a service or system utilizes its Block or Resource Hours, respectively, the utilization calculations should be adjusted as defined above. For the individual service, this provides a fairer determination of how much of its Block Time is truly used. For the system as a whole, it provides the actual percentage of time that the OR/PRs are being used for patient care. Perhaps as important, it provides an accurate percentage of time that is not used and therefore available for efficiency improvements.

Anesthesiologist, First Available (AFA) = Time of arrival in OR/PR of first anesthesiologist who is qualified to induce anesthesia in patient.

Procedure Physician, First Available (PPFA) = Time of arrival in OR/PR of first physician/surgeon qualified to position and prep the patient.

If delays in starting cases are thought to be due to the late arrival of either a qualified anesthesiologist or surgeon, recording of these times will allow documentation of the extent of that cause of delay.

Anesthesia Ready (AR) = Time at which the patient has a sufficient level of anesthesia established to begin surgical preparation of the patient, and remaining anesthetic chores do not preclude positioning and prepping the patient.

To maximize efficiency, surgical preparation of the patient should begin as soon as an adequate level of anesthesia has been obtained. In some instances however, the anesthesiologist may need to continue anesthetic preparation of the patient (eg, insertion of Swan-Ganz catheter) that precludes moving or prepping the patient. Anesthesia Ready is thus defined as that time when the anesthesiologist may allow surgical preparation to begin.

Anesthesiologist of Record In (ARI) = Time of arrival in OR/PR of anesthesiologist of record.

Procedure Physician of Record In (PPRI) = Arrival time of physician/surgeon of record.

In academic settings, delays may be due to the late arrival of either the attending anesthesiologist or surgeon. Recording of these times will allow one to determine if tardiness of either attending contributes to delays. Further, in the future, accrediting bodies and insurance carriers may require documentation of the time of presence of the physicians of record.

Case Time (CT) = Time from Room Set-up Start to Room Clean-up Finished.

This definition includes all of the time for which a given procedure requires an OR/PR. It allows for the different duration of Room Set-up and Room Clean-up Times that occur because of the varying supply and equipment needs for a particular procedure. For purposes of scheduling and efficiency analysis, this definition is ideal because it includes all of the time that an OR/PR must be reserved for a given procedure.

Procedure Physician of Record Out (PPRO) = Time when physician/surgeon of record leaves the OR/PR.

Because perceptual differences of turnover times abound, it is important to note when the physician of record leaves the OR/PR, as this may be significantly earlier than when the patient leaves the OR/PR. In those situations when an anesthesiologist is supervising another anesthesia care provider (resident or CRNA), the anesthesiologist of record may be in and out of the OR/PR multiple times, and thus no analogous definition has been provided for.

Resource Hours = Total number of hours scheduled to be available for performance of procedures (ie, the sum of all available Block Time and Open Time). This is typically provided for on a weekly recurring basis, but may be analyzed on a daily, weekly, monthly, or annual basis.

For a given institution, this is the time during which an optimum number of appropriate personnel are available to do cases. This may include more than one shift of personnel, or personnel working extended shifts (ie, greater than 8 hours), in order to gain vertical expansion of OR/PR hours. It may also include electively scheduled time on weekends to gain horizontal expansion of OR/PR hours. Resource hours do not include time gained through overtime or use of on-call personnel, even though this time may be routinely accrued at a given institution.

Room Ready (RR) = Time when room is cleaned and supplies and equipment necessary for beginning of next case are present. To maximize efficiency, the patient should be brought into the OR/PR as early as possible. Although some wish to have all the supplies and equipment necessary for the entire case present and open before the patient is brought in, institutions that have minimized turnover times move patients into the OR/PR as soon as it is clean and only the minimum supplies and equipment (ie, those needed to start the case) are present, but not necessarily open. In those institutions, room preparation continues as anesthesia in induced, allowing an overlap of processes (anesthesia induction and room preparation) that saves time.

Start Time (ST) = Patient in Room Time. Significant debate, indeed, even argument, exists over the proper definition of Start Time. Operating and procedural room nurses generally feel that they have properly accomplished their preparatory tasks if the room is ready at the scheduled start time (Room Ready = Start Time, Estimated), regardless of where the patient is at that time. Anesthesiologists often feel that they are "on time" if anesthesia induction has been completed by the scheduled start time (Anesthesia Ready = Start Time, Estimated). Surgeons generally believe start time should be the time at which the procedure is begun (Procedure/Surgery Start Time = Start Time, Estimated). Since Room Set-up Time is procedure specific and therefore generally known at the time of scheduling, one can reasonably predict Room Ready Time. Anesthesia Preparation Time, however, depends on both the procedure and patient needs. It is thus more variable and not known at the time a procedure is scheduled, making accurate prediction of Anesthesia Ready Time impossible.

This variability in Anesthesia Preparation Time also makes prediction of Procedure/Surgery Start Time inaccurate. Variability in Case Times, due to varying length of surgery, makes prediction of Start Times after the first scheduled case of the day even more inaccurate.

Much of the concern over Start Time is for the first case of the day, particularly when a service or surgeon follows herself/himself in the same OR/PR throughout the day. Prediction, then, of accurate Start Times for the first case of the day appears to be most critical. Once the procedure is known, it is almost always possible to have the Room Ready at any time that is desired for the start of the day. It should also be possible, and desirable for maximizing efficiency, to have the patient in the room for the first case of the day as soon as the room is ready. For maximizing scheduling accuracy and attempting to encourage the most efficient patient flow, the authors have elected to define Start Time as Patient In Room Time.

Turnover Time (TOT) = Time from prior Patient Out of Room to succeeding Patient In Room Time. Strong perceptual differences exist over the definition of Turnover Time. Anesthesiologists and OR/PR nurses usually consider turnover time to be the time between cases when the room is not occupied by a patient. Surgeons consider any time when they are unable to operate as "down time," and thus more often consider turnover time to be the time between the end of surgery on one case and the beginning of surgery on the next case. The latter may appear to be particularly long to an academic surgeon who leaves an OR before the wound is closed (allowing the residents to close and dress the incision) and does not re-enter the OR until the next patient is ready for incision.

As with Start Time, the variability of Anesthesia Preparation Time (APT) makes prediction of turnover times inaccurate if APT were to be included. Thus, to maximize scheduling accuracy and to encourage distinction of time spent preparing the OR/PR from time spent preparing the patient, the authors have elected to define Turnover Time as time from prior Patient Out of Room to succeeding Patient In Room Time for sequentially scheduled cases. As this definition attempts to include the time spent cleaning and preparing the OR/PR for the next case, it should only be calculated if a subsequent case is scheduled to immediately follow. With non-sequential cases, idle time between Room Clean-up Finished for the prior case to Room Set-up Start for the subsequent case should be identified and recorded under the appropriate room-gap category.

Editor's note: The Association of Anesthesia Clinical Directors changed its name to the American Association of Clinical Directors in 2004. The purpose of the society is to provide a forum for anesthesiologists whose primary responsibility is operating room management. *("About us," American Association of Clinical Directors,* http://aacdhq.org *[accessed 28 Dec 2006].)*

AORN Standards for RN First Assistant Education Programs

egistered nurse first assistant (RNFA) education programs are designed to provide RNs with the educational preparation necessary to assume the role of the first assistant in operative and other invasive procedures.

The "Standards for RN first assistant education programs" serve as the foundation upon which RNFA programs are developed and implemented. These standards are intended to guide program administrators and faculty in designing and evaluating curricula. These standards are broad in scope, definitive, relevant, and attainable, and they provide the framework for RNFA education.

Standard I

Requirements for RNFA education programs shall include the following:

Programs shall

A. be equivalent to one academic year of formal, post-basic nursing study.
B. award college credits and degrees or certificates of RNFA status upon satisfactory completion of all requirements.
C. be associated with schools of nursing at universities or colleges that are accredited for higher education by an accrediting agency that is nationally recognized by the Secretary of the US Department of Education.

    The registered nursing program shall be approved by a state licensing jurisdiction for nursing programs at the university, college, or community college level or by another national or regional agency that is nationally recognized by the Secretary of the US Department of Education as a specialized accrediting agency for nursing programs.
D. recognize AORN's "Official statement on RN first assistants."[1]
E. address all of the modules in the *Core Curriculum for the RN First Assistant*.[2]

Standard II

Preadmission requirements for RNFA education programs shall include the following:

A. General admission requirements as determined by each educational institution.
B. Proof of licensure to practice as an RN in the state in which the clinical internship will be undertaken.

C. Verification of certification as one of the following:
1. CNOR or CNOR eligible or
2. board certified or board eligible as an advanced practice nurse (APN).

    APNs without competence in intraoperative patient care must undergo an assessment regarding clinical skills and knowledge. If it is determined that skills and knowledge are deficient, faculty in the educational institution shall develop a plan to remediate identified deficiencies.
3. Certification must be submitted before program completion.
D. Cardiopulmonary resuscitation (CPR) or basic cardiac life support certification (BCLS) is required; advanced cardiac life support (ACLS) is preferred.
E. Letters of recommendation attesting to the years of experience as an RN and knowledge, judgment, and skills specific to surgical patient care.

Standard III

The didactic component of the curriculum for RNFA education programs shall be designed and evaluated based on a course description that identifies course content, faculty, length of the course, instructional and evaluation methodologies, and instructional resources.

A. Course content shall emphasize the expanded functions unique to the RNFA during operative and other invasive procedures, including, but not limited to,
1. preoperative patient management in collaboration with other health care providers, including, but not limited to,
   - performing a preoperative evaluation/focused nursing assessment,
   - communicating or collaborating with other health care providers regarding the patient's plan of care, and
   - writing preoperative orders according to established protocols;
2. intraoperative surgical first-assisting, including, but not limited to,
   - using instruments and medical devices,
   - providing exposure,
   - handling and cutting tissue,
   - providing hemostasis, and
   - suturing;

3. postoperative patient management in collaboration with other health care providers in the immediate postoperative period and beyond, including, but not limited to,
   - writing postoperative orders and operative notes according to established protocols,
   - participating in postoperative rounds, and
   - assisting with discharge planning and identifying appropriate community resources as needed.[1]

B. A multidisciplinary faculty shall include a minimum of
   1. a perioperative nurse with a master of science in nursing degree,
   2. a CRNFA, and
   3. a board-certified surgeon.

C. The course shall be a minimum of one academic semester of study, including student assignments, classroom instruction, and laboratory practicums.

D. Instructional methodologies shall include, but not be limited to, lecture, interactive discussion, independent study, instructional media, demonstration/ return demonstration, and laboratory practicums.

E. Evaluation methodologies shall include, but not be limited to, written examinations, laboratory practicums, and independent critical thinking assignments.

F. Instructional resources shall include
   1. *Core Curriculum for the RN First Assistant*[2] and
   2. texts or other instructional media that include anatomy and physiology, operative and other invasive procedures, and preoperative and postoperative patient assessment and management.

Standard IV

Specific requirements for matriculation in the clinical component shall include:

A. Successful completion of all requirements of the didactic component and

B. Evidence of current personal professional liability insurance for student/intern RNFA practice.

Standard V

The clinical component of the curriculum for RNFA education programs shall be designed and evaluated based on a course description that identifies course content, faculty, length of the course, instructional and evaluation methodologies, and instructional resources.

A. Course content emphasizes the expanded functions unique to the RNFA intern during operative and other invasive procedures, including, but not limited to,
   1. preoperative patient management in collaboration with other health care providers, including, but not limited to,
      - performing and documenting preoperative evaluation/focused nursing assessment,
      - communicating and collaborating with other health care providers regarding the patient plan of care, and
      - writing preoperative orders according to established protocols;
   2. validated documentation of intraoperative surgical first-assisting clinical experience, including, but not limited to,
      - using instruments and medical devices,
      - providing exposure,
      - handling and cutting tissue,
      - providing hemostasis, and
      - suturing;
   3. postoperative patient management in collaboration with other health care providers in the immediate postoperative period and beyond, including, but not limited to,
      - writing postoperative orders and operative notes according to established protocols,
      - participating in postoperative rounds, and
      - assisting with discharge planning and identifying appropriate community resources as needed.[1]

B. A multidisciplinary faculty shall include
   1. a board-certified surgeon in the RNFA intern's primary area of practice,
   2. an RNFA program faculty member, and
   3. an RNFA/CRNFA mentor, if available and/or desired by the student.

C. The clinical course shall be a minimum of one academic semester and shall include, but not be limited to, intern assignments as assistant at surgery and patient care management.

D. Instructional methodologies shall include, but not be limited to, physician-supervised clinical activities, assigned independent learning activities, a self-evaluative learning diary, a clinical case study project, and a surgical intervention participation log.

E. Evaluation methodologies shall include, but not be limited to, completion of assigned independent learning activities, a self-evaluative learning diary, a clinical case study project, preceptor evaluations, a surgical intervention participation log, and mentor evaluations when applicable. Students must satisfactorily complete all requirements. The RNFA program faculty reviews all documentation. The surgeon preceptor provides a summative evaluation of achievement of competence and a letter of recommendation based on all required learning activities, as does the RNFA/CRNFA mentor when applicable.

F. Instructional resources shall include
   1. *Core Curriculum for the RN First Assistant*,[2]
   2. texts or other instructional media, and
   3. consultation and collaboration with other health care providers.

Glossary

Faculty: A person who is appointed by the educational institution to design, teach, or evaluate a course of instruction.

Advanced practice nurse (APN): Advanced practice nurse is a term used to refer to an RN prepared at the graduate level who has met advanced educational and clinical practice requirements for a particular and unique clinical practice focus. There are four principle types of APNs, including nurse practitioner (NP), clinical nurse specialist (CNS), certified nurse midwife (CNM), and certified RN anesthetist (CRNA).

CNOR: The documented validation of the professional achievement of identified standards of practice by an individual registered nurse providing care for patients before, during, and after surgery.

CRNFA: The documented validation of the professional achievement of identified standards of practice by an individual registered nurse first assistant providing care for patients before, during, and after surgery.

Preceptor: One who teaches, counsels, inspires, serves as a role model, and supports the growth and development of the novice for a fixed and limited period.

Mentor: One who provides encouragement and acts as a guide and facilitator while modeling professional nursing behaviors.

REFERENCES
1. AORN official statement on RN first assistants. In: *Standards, Recommended Practices, and Guidelines.* Denver, CO: AORN, Inc, 2007:404-406.
2. Vaiden RE, ed. *Core Curriculum for the RN First Assistant.* 4th ed. Denver, CO: AORN, Inc, 2005.

Originally published March 1995, *AORN Journal,* as "AORN recommended education standards for RN first assistant programs."

Revised December 2004; approved by the AORN Board of Directors in February 2005.

Revised June 2007; approved by the AORN Board of Directors July 2007. Published in *RN First Assistant Guide to Practice,* third edition, 2007.

A

AABB (formerly known as the American Association of Blood Banks) 392

Adhesive incision drapes 559

Administrative practice standards 19-21

Advanced practice nurse 692, 694

Aeration, definition 667

Air exchanges 419, 421

Air flow patterns 419

Air hoses 623

Air pressure, OR 328, 419

Airborne precautions 478-479, 482

Airway fire, prevention 370, 424

Allografts 402

Ambulatory surgery guidelines
  postoperative patient care 243-250
  preoperative patient care 251-256

American Association of Clinical Directors (AACD) 685-691; *See also* Glossary of procedural times

American Association of Colleges of Nursing (AACN) 289, 570

American Association of Nurse Anesthetists (AANA) 495

American Association of Tissue Banks (AATB) 402

American Conference of Governmental Industrial Hygienists (ACGIH) 586 *(gutaraldehyde recommendations)*

American Society of Anesthesiologists (ASA)
  continuum of depth of sedation 519
  physical status classification 514
  recommendations for sterilization of semicritical items 570
  temperture monitoring recommendations 495

American Society of Bariatric Surgeons (ASBS) 94

American Society of Healthcare Engineers 310

American Society of PeriAnesthesia Nurses (ASPAN) 243, 245-246, 282-283

ANA Code of Ethics, perioperative explications for 33-64; *See also* Explications for perioperative nursing

Analgesia and moderate sedation 513-524; *See also* Moderate sedation/analgesia

Anesthesia equipment, cleaning, handling, and processing 569-578
  aseptic technique in 569
  bacterial filters, use of 573
  CDC recommendations for 569-571
  competency of personnel 570

critical items 569
  exterior surfaces, cleaning 571
  guidelines for processing 574
  hazards, potential 574
  humidifiers, use of 573
  internal components, cleaning 573
  malignant hyperthermia (MH) risk 572
  medication administration 569
  noncritical items 571
  performance and safety criteria 572
  personal protective equipment (PPE) for 574
  policies and procedures for 575
  reprocessing single-use devices 572
  reusable equipment 571
  semicritical items 570
  sharps handling 574
  single-use items 571-572
  storage of items 570
  waste disposal 573

Anhydrous, definition 667

Anthrax 482

Antiembolism stockings 165

Antimicrobial agent, definition 564

Antisepsis, definition 564

Antisepsis, surgical hand scrub 307-316; *See also* Hand antisepsis, surgical

Antiseptic agent, skin prep 551, 558, 564; *See also* Skin antisepsis, preoperative patient

Anxiolytic, definition 521

Argon-enhanced coagulation 339-340

Artificial nails 302, 308

Aseptic practices 317-326; *See also* Sterile field, maintaining

Aspergillosis, Aspergillus 448, 449

Association for Professionals in Infection Control and Epidemiology (APIC)
  recommendations for sterilization of semicritical items 570

Association for the Advancement of Medical Instrumentation (AAMI)
  barrier protection recommendations 317
  service provider, definition 205

Association of Anesthesia Clinical Directors; *See* American Association of Clinical Directors

Attire, surgical 299-306
  cover apparel, use of 300
  disposal of 299
  fabric selection 299
  gloves, selection and use 302

hair, head and facial 301
head covers, use of 301
home laundering of 299-300
in restricted and semirestricted areas 299-300
jewelry 301
laundering 299-300
masks, when to wear 301, 302
nonscrubbed personnel 300
personal protective equipment (PPE) 300
policies and procedures for 303
protective attire 302
protective barriers 302-303
protective eyewear 302
purpose of 299
shoe covers 302
shoes 303
transporting 300
Avian influenza 77-90; *See also* Human and avian influenza
    precautions for 86
    recommendations for 82
"Awake" malignant hyperthermia 127
Autografts 402
Automated endoscope reprocessor (AER) 598-600
    definition 590
    for disinfection 585
    testing 606

B

Bariatric surgery guideline 91-110
    biliopancreatic diversion 93-94, 95
    body mass index 91, 92
    business planning for program 103-107
    combined procedures 97
    comorbidities 92
    definitions 91
    duodenal switch procedure 93
    elements of successful program 103-107
    financial implications for facility 102
    gastric banding 93, 96, 97
    gastric bypass 93, 95-96, 98
    Roux-en-Y 97, 98
    history of 92-94
    impact on the workplace 104-107
    equipment and furnishings 104
    surgical staff 105-107
    implementation of interventions 100-102
    jejunoileal bypass procedure 92
    malabsorptive procedures 95

maximum weight loss in 99
minimally invasive approach 98
negative attitudes toward patients 105
nursing diagnoses in 100
operational planning 104
outcome evaluation 102
outcome identification in 100
outcome indicators 107
pathophysiology 92
patient assessment for 99-100
patient positioning 101
patient selection criteria 94
plan of care 100
population affected 91-92
prevalence of 91-92
program development 102-107
rationale for program 102
restrictive procedures 95
support services 106
SWOT analysis for 103-107
Barrier materials for surgical gowns and drapes 361-366; *See also* Gowns and drapes, surgical
Benzodiazepine, definition 521
Bier block 373; *See also* Intravenous regional anesthesia (IVRA)
Bioburden, definition 590
Biofilm, definition 590
Biological agent release 481
Bird flu 77-90; *See also* Human and avian influenza
Body mass index (BMI) 91, 92, 545
Body mechanics 529
Body piercing 336, 532, 556
Botulism 483
Bowie-Dick test 667, 668
Brachytherapy 455
    eye plaques in 461
Braden scale, definition 545
Bunnysuit, definition 330
Burn prevention, chemical/thermal 557

C

Call staffing 264-266, 281-288
Canadian Society of Anesthesiologists 573
Capillary interface pressure, definition 545
Cavitation, definition 590
Chemical disinfectant/germicide 583, 590
Chemical disinfection; *See* High-level disinfection
Chemical indicator/integrator 642, 644, 663, 665
Circulating fluid garment 496, 500

implantable hearing devices 214-217, 227
implantable infusion pumps 217, 227
neurological IEDs 212-214, 226
osteogenic stimulators 218-219, 228
sacral nerve stimulators 218, 228
Peel pouches 621, 639-640, 649
labeling 641
presentation to sterile field 319
Peracetic acid sterilization 656-657
sterilizer efficacy monitoring 664
Perioperative nurse, definition 8, 13
Perioperative nursing standards 11-21
administrative practice standards 19-21
clinical practice standards 13-15
professional practice standards 15-18
Perioperative Patient Focused Model 12
Perioperative patient outcomes 23-32
Personal protective equipment (PPE) 483, 630
definition 450, 591
for high-level disinfection 581
prevention of transmissible infection 476-477
Phlebothrombosis, definition 166
Physical monitoring device, sterilization 652, 668
Pin-index safety system 434
Plague 478, 483
Pneumatic tourniquet, use of 373-386
cleaning equipment 380-381
compartment syndrome in 383
compatibility of accessories 373
competency of personnel 381-382
contraindications 374-375
cuff placement 376
documentation 381
evaluation of outcomes 379
exsanguination 377, 383
FDA reports 373
gas sources for 375
handling equipment 375
in children 380
inflation pressure 377
inflation time 378
inspection of equipment 374
Joint Commission reports 373
length of cuff 376
limb occlusion pressure (LOP) 377, 383
obese patients 376
operating instructions for 374
padding 376, 378
patient hand-off 379
patient monitoring 378-379

policies and procedures for 382
potential complications 379, 380
preoperative patient assessment for 374
prophylactic antibiotics 375
quality management 382-383
risk of patient injury 375-376
risk of pulmonary embolism 379
safety/warning alarms 374
selection of equipment 373
shearing injury 376, 383
tourniquet deflation 378, 380
tourniquet inflation 377-378
tourniquet use on two extremities 379-380
types of cuffs 373
width of cuff 375
Policies and procedures template 673-674
Positioning equipment/devices
for obese patients 526-527
inspection and maintenance 527
safe use 531
Positioning the patient 525-548
body alignment 533, 540
body mass index (BMI) 529, 545
competency of personnel 543-544
documentation 544, 684
interventions 681-683
intraoperative assessment 529
lateral position 538-539
lithotomy position 537-538
modified sitting position 535
morbidly obese patient 526, 539-540
older adult patient 526
policies and procedures 544, 681-684
preoperative assessment 528-529
preprocedure planning 527
prone position 535-536
quality management 544-545
reassessment of patient position 540-541
reverse Trendelenburg's position 536-537
risk for nerve injury 534
risk for ocular injury 534, 536, 543
sample policy 681-684
shearing injury 532, 545
sitting position 535
supine position 533, 534-535
support surface, definition 525
Trendelenburg's position 536-537
worker injury 529-530
Post-thrombotic syndrome 166, 167, 171
Postanesthesia phases I, II, and III 243, 245

Postoperative patient care in ambulatory surgery 243-250
  discharge 247-248
  documentation 247
  fast tracking of patients 247
  nursing care plan for 246
  nursing care policies 244
  pain management 247
  patient outcomes 247, 248
  patient transfer 248
  postanesthesia care 246
  staffing requirements 244
  supplies and equipment 244
Postphlebitic syndrome 166, 167, 171
Potable water 616, 633
Potentially infectious material 483
Powered instruments, care and cleaning 622-623; *See also* Surgical instruments and powered equipment
Preceptor, definition 694
Preoperative patient care in ambulatory surgery 251-256
  anesthesia evaluation 253
  documentation 254-255
  infection prevention 254
  nursing care plan 254
  patient outcomes 254, 255
  preadmission assessment 252
  preoperative nursing assessment 253
  preoperative teaching plan 253
  preoperative testing 252-253
  staffing requirements 252
Pressure ulcers 542-543
  patient assessment 528
  predictors of 526
  stages of 542
Prevention of transmissible infections 475-486
Prion diseases 402, 445-446, 626-630
Procedural times glossary 685-691
Procedure bed; *See also* Positioning the patient
  selection 526
  transport in 532
  types of 525
Process challenge devices (PCDs) 665, 668
Product selection 387-390
Pulmonary embolism 166

Q

Quality and performance improvement standards 65-74

R

RACE (acronym) 200
Radiation attenuating gloves 459
Radiation safety; *See* Reducing radiological exposure
Radioactive pathology specimens, handling 472
Radioactive spill cleanup 462
Radionuclides, radiation risk of 460-461
  definition 464
  sealed and unsealed sources, defined 465
Recommended Practices Committee 297
Reconciling incorrect counts 409-410, 456
Recycling 188-189
Reducing radiological exposure 455-466
  aprons, use of 458
  brachytherapy 455, 457
  competency of personnel 461, 463
  deep dose equivalent, defined 463
  documentation 462
  dosimeter use 461, 464
  during pregnancy 457, 459
  during sentinel node biopsy 459
  eye plaques 461
  eye protection 458
  fluoroscopy, defined 464
  glossary of terms 463-465
  handling radiation sources 461-462
  lead shielding, use of 456-457
  maternity aprons, use of 459
  occupational dose limits 461, 464
  occupational exposure to radiation 457-459
  patient positioning 458
  policies and procedures for 462-463
  preparation of sealed radionuclides 460
  principles of 455, 457, 460
  protecting the fetus 457, 459
  protecting the patient 456
  radiation monitoring 461
  reconciling incorrect counts 456
  regulation 455, 459
  role of interventional radiology nurse 455
  scatter radiation 455, 457, 464
  signs and symptoms of injury 462
  sterilization of prostatic seeds 460
  storage of shielding devices 460
  testing of shielding devices 459
  thyroid shield 458
  types of shielding 458, 459-460
  warning signs 457
Regulated medical waste 442, 450

Reprocessing instruments 611
Reprocessing single-use devices 190, 192, 257-263
Resource conservation 189-190
Restricted area 327
Reusable, definition 450
Reuse of single-use devices 257-263
    Class I, II, III devices 260-261, 262
    medical device corrections and removals 261
    federal regulatory requirements 258
    labeling requirements 260
    medical device reporting 258
    opened-but-unused device 262
    premarket approval and notification 260
    quality system regulation 258, 259
    registration and listing 258
    resterilization 262
    third-party reprocessor 257, 262
Rigid sterilization container systems 640-641, 645, 652, 659, 663
RN first assistant 692-694
Robotic surgical instruments 626, 633
Role of the health care industry representative 204-206
Roux-en-Y 97-98

S

Safe environment of care 415-438
    air exchanges 419
    anesthetic gas hazards 427
    chemical hazards 429-430
    chemotherapeutic agents 430-431
    competency of personnel 432
    documentation 432
    electrical equipment hazards 417
    ergonomic hazards 416-417
    fluid warmers 422-423
    fire hazards 423
    hazardous waste 431
    HVAC hazards 418-419
    medical equipment hazards 420
    medical gas hazards 425-427
    lighting hazards 417-418
    patient privacy rules 416
    policies and procedures 432-433
    pressure gradient 419
    quality management 433
    relative humidity 419
    room temperature 419
    security risks 415-416
    surgical smoke 428-429
    tubing misconnection 431
Safe Medical Devices Act 258
Safe medication practices 267-274
    accurate dose calculation 269
    accurate patient medication list 268
    age-specific guidelines 272
    competency of personnel 272
    constraints vs forcing functions 272
    documentation 271
    dose limits 269
    error-prone abbreviations 272; See also "Do-Not-Use" abbreviations, acronyms, dosage designations, and symbols
    five rights of medication safety 268
    high-risk medications 269
    key elements of medication delivery 271
    managing medications on and off the sterile field 269-270
    medication contraindications 269
    medication storage 270
    patient identification in 268
    patient monitoring 271
    retaining containers 271
    review and evaluation 271
    risk reduction strategies 268
    specific concerns 267
    standardized institutional forms 272
    standardized procedures for 268
    verifying verbal orders 269
Safe on-call practices 264-266
    change in culture 266
    competency-based orientation in 265
    considerations for 265
    economic implications 265
    nurse:patient ratios 264
    patient risk 266
    recuperation periods 265
    strategies for 265
Scatter radiation 455, 457, 464
Sedative, definition 522
Semirestricted area 327, 479
Serotonin syndrome 129
Service provider, AAMI definition 205
Severe acute respiratory syndrome (SARS) 83-90, 481, 573
    clinical signs and symptoms 83
    epidemiology 83
    infection control measures 84
    precautions for 82, 84, 86

Sharps counts 407-408
Sharps injury prevention 275-280, 480
   causes of injury 275
   communication of program 276
   culture of safety for 279
   employer responsibility for 278
   individual responsibility for 277-278
   NIOSH estimates 275
   obstacles to compliance 278
   rate of percutaneous injury 275
   risk reduction strategies 276-277
   selecting new products for 279
Shearing injury 532, 545
Shelf life 319, 641-642, 659-660, 668
Shipping containers 329
Shoes, shoe covers 302-303
Single-use devices, reuse of 257-263
Skin antisepsis, preoperative patient 549-568
   antiseptic agents for 551-554
   burns and open wounds 559
   cleansing, preoperative 556
   competency of personnel 562
   definition 564
   documentation of care 562-563
   FDA requirements for 551
   flammability of 559-560
   hair removal 555, 562
   handling and storage 560-561
   injury prevention 557
   method 558-559
   of contaminated body areas 556, 559
   patient assessment 554
   policies and procedures 563
   preoperative shampoo 550
   preoperative shower 549-550
   product selection 551, 552, 555
   quality management 563-564
   removal of agents 561-562
   surgical site marking 554
Smallpox 483
Spaulding classification system 319, 569
Specimens, care and handling 467-474
   assessment of 467
   collection guide 473
   competency assessment 472
   containers/collection devices 467, 468-469
   cytology 473
   designation of 469
   disposal of 469
   documentation 468-469

   explanted defective medical devices 470
   forensic specimens 471
   formalin 468-469
   frozen section 473
   glossary of terms 473
   labeling 468-469
   patient identification 467, 469
   patient request for specimen return 470
   patient's cultural considerations 467
   planning for 467
   policies and procedures for 467-468, 472-473
   preventing contamination 468
   radioactive specimens 472
   secondary packaging of 468
   specimen identification 468
   specimen, definition 474
   syringes/needles 468
   transfer/transport 470-471
   use of preservatives 468
Sponge counts 405-407
Staffing patterns, perioperative 281-288
   call hours replacement calculation 285
   call staffing 281, 287
   direct staff patient care calculation 285
   discharge 284
   indirect staff calculation 285
   intraoperative staffing 285-287
   minimum staffing recommendations 282-284
   number of personnel per room 285
   PACU staffing 287
   postanesthesia 282-283
   relief replacement 285
Standard precautions 475-486; *See also* Transmissible infections, prevention of
Steam-flush pressure-pulse (SFPP) 668
Steam sterilization
   gravity displacement sterilizers 650
   packaging materials for 649
   prevacuum sterilizers 650
   sterilizer efficacy testing 663-664
Sterile field, maintaining 317-326
   asepsis, definition 322
   aseptic technique, definition 322
   assisted gloving, definition 322
   break in technique 321
   closed gloving method 322
   concurrent cases 320
   covering the sterile field 320
   critical items 319
   dispensing medications 320

dispensing solutions 320
drapes, sterile 318
event-related sterility 319, 320
glossary of terms 322-323
gloves, sterile 317, 318
gowns, sterile 317, 318
inspection of sterile items 318
methods of sterilization 319
monitoring 320
movement of arms and hands 321
movement of draping material 318
movement of scrubbed personnel 321
movement of unscrubbed personnel 320, 321
nonsterile equipment 321
open-gloving method, definition 322
opening cases 321
packaging materials 319
policies and procedures for 322
preparation of 320
presenting items to sterile field 319
shelf life 319
sleeve cuffs 318
sterile area of gown 317
sterile field, definition 322
sterile items, handling 319
sterile technique, definition 323
surgical attire 317
Sterilization 647-670; *See also* Sterilizers
    competency of personnel 660-661
    controlled environment for 649
    documentation 661
    dynamic air-removal steam sterilization 651
    environmental controls for 660
    ethylene oxide sterilization 620, 653-655
    flash sterilization 652
    gas plasma sterilization 655-656
    gravity-displacement steam sterilization 650
    minimum cycle times 650-651
    policies and procedures 661
    preferred method 649
    quality management 662
    storage of sterile items 659-660
    table-top sterilizer 665
    transportation of sterile items 660
    use of loaner equipment 658-659
    weight recommendations 648-649
Sterilization of tissue 397
Sterilization packaging 637-646
Sterilization process monitoring devices 665-666
Sterilizer efficacy monitoring 663-667

Sterilizers; *See also* Sterilization
    dry-heat 657-658
    dynamic air-removal 651, 668
    ethylene oxide 653-655
    gravity displacement 649-650, 668
    low-temperature hydrogen peroxide gas plasma 655-656
    ozone 657
    peracetic acid 656-657
    prevacuum 649, 668
    steam-flush pressure-pulse (SFPP) 649, 668
    steam sterilizers, types of 649
Storage of sterilized items 659-660
    controlled conditions for 660
    in ambulatory surgery centers 660
Strike-through 323, 477
Surface-to-hand transfer of bacteria 440
Surgical attire 299-306; *See also* Attire, surgical
Surgical gowns and drapes 361-366; *See also* Gowns and drapes, surgical
Surgical hand scrubs 307-316; *See also* Hand antisepsis, surgical
Superheating, definition 645
Superficial venous thrombophlebitis (SVT) 167
Surgical instruments and powered equipment, care and cleaning 611-636
    cleaning and decontamination 613-614
    cleaning methods 617-618
    competency of personnel 630-631
    containment devices 614-615
    decontamination of 615
    disposable sharps 614
    documentation 631
    drying 620
    handling and maintenance 611
    inspection of 619-620
    lubricating 620
    manual cleaning 618
    mechanical cleaning 618
    point-of-use pretreatment 614
    policies and procedures 632
    preparation for decontamination 613-614
    pretreatment of new instruments 612
    quality management 633
    repaired and refurbished instruments 611-612
    reporting adverse events 632
    reusable sharps 614
    transport 615
    treatment of gross soiling 613
Surgical smoke 428-429

T

Table-top sterilizer 665
Tacky mats 442
Temperature monitoring
    ambient (room) temperature 419, 500
    malignant hyperthermia 133, 494
    patient core temperature 494-495, 501
Teratigenicity, definition 434
Terminal cleaning 451
Therapeutic touch 507-508
Third-party reprocessor 257, 262
Thrombophlebitis 166
Time-related sterility 323
Tip protectors 621
Tissue banking 391-404
    allografts, definition 398, 402
    autografts, definition 399, 402
    autologous tissue, segregation of 399
    competency of personnel 392
    cornea recovery 395-396
    disclosure of intended uses 394
    documentation for 397-398, 400
    donor exclusion criteria 394
    donor screening 394-395
    donor site prep 396
    donor testing 395
    dura mater grafts 395, 397
    expiration dates 399, 400, 401
    glossary of terms 402
    informed consent 392-393
    Joint Commission standards for 391
    labeling 397
    latex allergy in 396
    living donors 394, 395
    monitoring of refrigeration units 399
    operative site prep 396
    oversight of 392
    packaging 397-398
    policies and procedures 401
    pooling/commingling of tissue 397
    postmortem donor, refrigeration of 396
    processing tissue 396-397
    quality management for 401
    quarantine of tissue 399-400
    record keeping 400-401
    recovery of tissue 396
    registration/accreditation 392
    reporting adverse events 401
    rights of donor/family 393-394
    soliciting tissue donations 392
    sterilization of tissue 397
    storage of tissue 398
    temperatures for storage 398
    tissue bank, definition 391, 402
    tissue recipients 394
    tracking system for 400
    transmission of infection in 396
    transportation of tissue 398
    xenotransplant, xenotransplantation 402
Tourniquet, See Pneumatic tourniquet
Toxic anterior segment syndrome (TASS) 587, 619, 633
Toxicity, definition 564
Traffic patterns 327-330
    air exchanges per hour 328
    clean core area 329
    during construction and renovation 329
    movement of patients and personnel 327, 328
    movement of supplies and equipment 328
    policies and procedures 329
    designated areas, defined 327
Transmissible infections, prevention of 475-486
    air exchanges in 479
    airborne precautions 478-479, 482
    competency of personnel 481-482
    contact precautions 477-478, 483
    double-gloving 477
    droplet precautions 478, 483
    during patient transport 478
    exposure incidents 482, 483
    fluid-resistant attire 476-477
    hand hygiene 475
    hands-free technique 480, 483
    HBV immunization 479
    HIV, HBV infected personnel 480-481
    injury prevention 480
    neutral zone 480, 483
    one-hand technique 480
    personal protective equipment 483
    personnel with lesions or dermatitis 481
    policies and procedures for 481-482
    prohibited activities 479
    protective barriers 476
    restriction of personnel 480-481
    standard precautions 475
    steel weave outer gloves 477
    surface contamination 479
    surgical gloves 476, 484
    tuberculosis 478-479
    washing gloves 476

Transmissible spongiform encephalopathies 582; *See also* Creutzfeldt-Jakob disease (CJD)
Transmission-based precautions 484
Trendelenburg's position 536-537
Triage of casualties 230-232
Tunnel washer 619

U

Ultrasonic cleaner 618-619, 633
Ultrasonic electrosurgical devices 339
Ultrasonic scalpel 342
Undergraduate nursing curricula, value of perioperative learning in 289-292
Uniform Anatomical Gift Act (UAGA) 393
Unrestricted area 327
US Food and Drug Administration (FDA) requirements for skin prep products 551
US Nuclear Regulatory Commission (NRC) 464
Used items, definition 451

V

Vancomycin-resistant enterococci (VRE) 440
Variant Creutzfeldt-Jakob disease (vCJD) 582
Venous stasis, prevention 165-182
    anatomy of 167
    anticlotting factors 165
    anticoagulant 165
    clotting factors 165
    considerations for high-risk patients 172-173
    definition 166
    nonpharmacologic interventions 178
    nursing process application in 173-175
    pathophysiology of 167
    pharmacologic interventions 178
    phlebothrombosis 166
    prevalence of 166
    risk considerations by specialty 172-173
    risk factors for 171-172
    risk stratification in 177-178
    secondary prevention, definition 178
    thrombolytic medication 166
    thrombophlebitis 166
    treatment of 177-178
Venous thromboembolism 166
Vessel-sealing device 342
Virchow's triad 166, 170-171
Viscoelastic, definition 633, 625
Vulcanized patch 643

W

Warming cabinets 422
Warming device, definition 434
Washer decontaminator 619, 633
Washer disinfector 619
Washer sterilizer 619
Waste management 187-188, 192
Wet locations 434
Wet pack 642-643, 645, 650
Wicking, definition 364
Workflow patterns 647
Work-related back injuries 529-530
Woven textile sterilization packaging 639
    definition 645
    quality control 643

X

Xenotransplantation 402
X-ray-detectable sponges, use of 406
X-ray intensifier, definition 465
X-ray protection; *See* Reducing radiological exposure
X-ray tube, definition 465